Copyright © 1997

by
PANEL PUBLISHERS
A division of Aspen Publishers, Inc.
A Wolters Kluwer Company

1185 Avenue of the Americas
New York, NY 10036
(212) 597-0200

ISBN 1-56706-361-6

Printed in the United States of America

The Pel
Answer Bc

1997 Edi

Revised by: Stephen J. Krass
Krass & Lund, P.C.
New York City

(Original Edition by Krass and Keschner)

Stephen J. Krass, Esq.

THE PANEL ANSWER BOOK SERIES

A PANEL PUBLICATION
ASPEN PUBLISHERS, INC.

About Panel Publishers

Panel Publishers derives its name from a panel of business professionals who organized in 1964 to publish authoritative and timely books, information services, and journals written by specialists to assist business professionals in the areas of compensation and benefits management, pension planning and compliance, and human resources, as well as owners of small to medium-sized businesses and their legal and financial advisors. Our mission is to provide practical, solution-based "how-to" information to business professionals.

Also available from Panel Publishers:

The Pension Answer Book: Forms & Worksheets
Pension Distribution Answer Book*
401(k) Answer Book*
Pension Investment Handbook
Individual Retirement Account Answer Book*
Nonqualified Deferred Compensation Answer Book*
Estate and Retirement Planning Answer Book
ERISA Fiduciary Answer Book
Pension Plan Administrator
Journal of Pension Planning & Compliance
Journal of Pension Benefits
Panel Pension Library on CD-ROM

Companion volume of Forms and Worksheets also available.

PANEL PUBLISHERS
A division of Aspen Publishers, Inc.
Practical Solutions for Business Professionals

SUBSCRIPTION NOTICE

This Panel product is updated on a periodic basis with supplements to reflect important changes in the subject matter. If you purchased this product directly from Panel Publishers, we have already recorded your subscription for this update service.

If, however, you purchased this product from a bookstore and wish to receive future updates and revised or related volumes billed separately with a 30-day examination review, please contact our Customer Service Department at 1-800-901-9074, or send your name, company name (if applicable), address, and the title of the product to:

PANEL PUBLISHERS
A division of Aspen Publishers, Inc.

7201 McKinney Circle
Frederick, MD 21701

For Sallie

About the Authors

STEPHEN J. KRASS, ESQ., is a member of the law firm of Krass & Lund, P.C. in New York City. Mr. Krass received his B.S. (Accounting) from The Ohio State University and LL.B. and LL.M. (Taxation) from New York University School of Law. Mr. Krass is a member of the American Bar Association Sections on Taxation, and Real Property, Probate and Trust Law (Member, Committee on Employee Benefits) and the New York State Bar Association Sections on Trusts and Estates, and Taxation (Member, Committees on Qualified Plans and Estates and Trusts). He has served on the Board of Directors of the Estate Planning Council of New York City and currently serves as its Secretary. Mr. Krass is a member of the Advisory Boards of the N.Y.U. Institute on Federal Taxation, *CCH Financial and Estate Planning Reporter, Journal of Pension Planning & Compliance,* and *Pension Benefits,* and serves as a member of the New York Regional Planned Giving Committee of the Anti-Defamation League. Mr. Krass has been a panelist on AICPA and New York State Bar Association programs and The C.P.A. Report. He has spoken at the N.Y.U. Institute on Federal Taxation; The Ohio State University College of Law; Fordham Law School; New York Law School; Baruch College; Columbus (Ohio) Tax Conference; Purdue University Insurance Marketing Institute; UJA-Federation Annual Tax and Estate Planning Conference; The American College-CCH National Conference on Financial Planning; Institute of Certified Financial Planners Annual Conference; International Association for Financial Planning; American Academy of Matrimonial Lawyers; Hofstra University-Center for Business Studies; C. W. Post Tax Institute; Iona College Tax Institute; and New York State Society of Certified Public Accountants. Mr. Krass has been an instructor in the Long Island University Paralegal Program. He has contributed articles to *The Journal of Taxation of Estates and Trusts; Estate Planning; Taxes—The Tax Magazine; Journal of the Institute of Certified Financial Planners; The Pension Actuary; The Practical Accountant; CLU Journal; CCH Financial and Estate Planning Reporter; The Journal of Financial Planning; Journal of*

Pension Planning & Compliance; Taxation for Accountants; and *Taxation for Lawyers.* Mr. Krass is a frequent lecturer on employee benefit plans, estate planning, and taxation.

STEVEN SCHMUTTER, ESQ., is a member of the law firm of Krass & Lund, P.C. Mr. Schmutter received his B.S. (magna cum laude) from the State University of New York at Binghamton, his J.D. from St. John's University School of Law, and his LL.M. (Taxation) from New York University School of Law. He has written on employee benefit plan topics.

RICHARD L. KESCHNER, ESQ. (1945–1989), was a sole practitioner in New York City. Mr. Keschner received his B.S. from Brooklyn College, his M.B.A. from Baruch College, and his J.D. from Brooklyn Law School.

Acknowledgments

As with previous editions of *The Pension Answer Book,* the *1997 Edition* incorporates the efforts of many people. Again, I express my appreciation to my partner, Steven Schmutter, and our associate, Floyd Bookbinder, for their invaluable assistance; and I also thank my partner, Daniel P. Lund, for his contribution.

I express my gratitude to our secretaries, Stella Chin, Terry Joe, and Susan Esterman, for their efforts.

Thanks again to my editor, Ellen Ros, and to all the people at Panel Publishers, without whose efforts the *1997 Edition* would not be possible.

S J K

Preface

The accuracy, clarity, and comprehensiveness of *The Pension Answer Book* have made it the largest-selling and most respected single-volume reference work in the United States for pension professionals. Prepared with exacting attention to detail, its 30 chapters use clear, jargon-free language to cover the full spectrum of pension topics—from funding requirements to taxation of distributions, from fiduciary responsibilities to employee stock ownership plans.

The *1997 Edition* of *The Pension Answer Book* is fully updated to incorporate the extensive changes brought about by the Small Business Job Protection Act of 1996 (SBA '96). In particular, SBA '96:

- Repeals five-year income averaging for lump-sum distributions
- Repeals the $5,000 employee death benefit exclusion
- Simplifies the method for taxing installment distributions
- Repeals salary reduction simplified employee pensions and replaces them with SIMPLE plans
- Extends 401(k) plans to nongovernmental tax-exempt employers
- Eases nondiscrimination testing for 401(k) plans
- Simplifies the definition of highly compensated employee
- Repeals the family aggregation rule
- Limits the minimum participation requirement to defined benefit plans
- Repeals for certain participants the required distribution of benefits after a participant reaches age 70½ if the participant does not retire
- Suspends the imposition of the excess distributions tax for three years
- Eliminates the 1.0 rule

- Increases the penalty tax on prohibited transactions
- Eliminates the special vesting rule for multiemployer plans
- Repeals the 50 percent interest exclusion for certain ESOP loans
- Increases the spousal IRA limitation from $250 to $2,000

The *1997 Edition* discusses these provisions and their effect on pension practice. In addition, it updates subscribers on the most current and pertinent Internal Revenue Code and ERISA sections, Treasury and Department of Labor Regulations, Revenue Rulings and Procedures, Letter Rulings, Notices and Announcements, and case law. It also contains a newly expanded index, designed to make your search for the information you need even easier and faster.

Replete with examples that illustrate the complex issues presented, *The Pension Answer Book, 1997 Edition* brings insight and practical expertise to all areas of pension practice.

How to Use This Book

The *1997 Edition* of *The Pension Answer Book* integrates the most recent changes in pension practice into a single-volume reference. It is designed for professionals who need quick and authoritative answers to help them decide whether to institute or continue pension and other retirement plans, how to choose the plans most suited to their needs, and how to comply with the morass of federal requirements. This book uses simple, straightforward language and avoids technical jargon when possible. Citations of authority are provided as research aids for those who need to pursue particular items in greater detail.

The question-and-answer format, with its breadth of coverage and its plain-language explanations (plus numerous illustrative examples), offers a clear and useful guide to understanding the complex but extremely important area of qualified pension and profit sharing plans.

Numbering System: The questions are numbered consecutively within each chapter (e.g., 2:1, 2:2, 2:3).

Detailed List of Questions: The detailed List of Questions that follows the Table of Contents in the front of this book helps the reader locate areas of immediate interest. This list is like a detailed table of contents that provides both the question number and the page on which it appears.

Glossary: Because the pension area is replete with technical terms that have specific legal meanings, a special glossary of terms is provided following the question-and-answer portion of this book. Expressions not defined elsewhere, and abbreviations used throughout the book, are defined in the glossary, which is arranged in alphabetical order.

Tables: In order to facilitate easy access to a particular section of the Internal Revenue Code, Treasury Regulations, ERISA, Department of Labor Regulations, Revenue Rulings, Revenue Procedures, Letter Rulings, Notices and Announcements, and to pertinent legal cases, tables of all of the sections and cases referenced in the text and their appropriate question number have been included.

Index: An index is provided as a further aid to locating specific information. Key words included in the glossary are used in the index as well. All references in the index are to question numbers rather than page numbers.

Use of Abbreviations: Because of the breadth of subject area, a number of terms and statutory references are abbreviated throughout *The Pension Answer Book*. Among the most common of these shorthand references are:

- Code—The Internal Revenue Code of 1986.
- ERISA—The Employee Retirement Income Security Act of 1974, as amended.
- IRS—The Internal Revenue Service.
- DOL—The U.S. Department of Labor.
- COBRA—The Consolidated Omnibus Budget Reconciliation Act of 1985.
- PBGC—Pension Benefit Guaranty Corporation.
- TRA '86—The Tax Reform Act of 1986.
- TAMRA—The Technical and Miscellaneous Revenue Act of 1988.
- SBA—The Small Business Job Protection Act of 1996.

For explanations of other abbreviations, consult the Glossary.

Contents

Table of Contents

List of Questions

Chapter 2   Types and Choices of Plans

Chapter 3   Highly Compensated Employees

Chapter 4   Requirements for Qualification

Chapter 5 Eligibility and Participation

Chapter 6   Contribution and Benefit Limitations

Chapter 7 Permitted Disparity

Chapter 8   Funding Requirements

Chapter 9   Vesting

Chapter 10 General Distribution Requirements

Chapter 11   Minimum Distribution Requirements

Chapter 12 Tax Deduction Rules

Chapter 13   Taxation of Distributions

Chapter 14 Life Insurance and Death Benefits

Chapter 15 Determination Letters

Chapter 16   Operating the Plan

Chapter 17 Reporting to Government Agencies

Chapter 18 Summary Plan Descriptions

Chapter 19 Fiduciary Responsibilities

l

Chapter 20 Prohibited Transactions

Chapter 21   Termination of the Plan

Chapter 22   Top-Heavy Plans

Chapter 23   401(k) Plans

Chapter 24 Employee Stock Ownership Plans

Chapter 25 Multiemployer Plans

Chapter 26 Individual Retirement Plans

Chapter 28   Rollovers

Chapter 29   Tax-Sheltered Annuities

Chapter 30   Qualified Domestic Relations Orders

Chapter 1

Overview

There is no better way for a company to accumulate a substantial nest egg for its loyal employees—and the working owner—than to establish a tax-favored retirement plan. This chapter examines qualified retirement plans—what they are, their tax advantages, the types of costs involved, and the kinds of benefits that can be provided.

Q 1:1 Why should a company adopt a qualified retirement plan?

A qualified retirement plan is one of the best tax shelters available. The company is allowed a current deduction for its contributions to the plan; the employee pays no tax on money contributed for the employee's benefit until a distribution is made; earnings from investments made with funds in the plan accumulate tax-free; and distributions from the plan may be afforded favorable income tax treatment.

A qualified retirement plan is especially attractive to working owners of closely held corporations and to self-employed individuals. Their long-term service with their companies gives them the best opportunity to accumulate large sums of money through the tax-free build-up of capital. Although benefits must be provided for other employees as well, the owner usually receives a much larger benefit than the other employees.

The nontax reasons for adopting a qualified retirement plan include the following: (1) attracting employees; (2) reducing employee turnover; (3) increasing employee incentive; and (4) accumulating funds for retirement.

Q 1:2 How do the working owners of a closely held corporation benefit from a qualified retirement plan?

There are two basic ways for a working owner to get money out of a closely held corporation: compensation and dividends.

If a working owner earns a salary or bonus from a closely held corporation, the corporation will get a deduction for the amounts paid to the owner.
In turn, the owner is taxed on compensation at ordinary income tax rates.
A dividend paid to the working owner is treated differently: it is not
deductible by the corporation. The dividend is also taxable to the working
owner at ordinary income tax rates. Payments of dividends, therefore, are
subject to double taxation.

Adoption of a qualified retirement plan provides the corporation with a
deduction for the amount it contributes to the plan. The working owner, as
a participant in the plan, is not currently taxed on the amounts contributed
for the owner's benefit. Further, earnings from investments made by the
plan build up tax-free. When the owner eventually receives the plan benefits, the distribution may be eligible for special tax treatment if it is made in
a lump sum. [IRC § 402(d)]

Therefore, adoption of a qualified retirement plan provides the corporation with the same tax benefits as does the payment of current compensation; but the working owner of a closely held corporation is able to defer
payment of taxes until benefits are received, and these benefits may be
eligible for special tax treatment.

Q 1:3 How can the adoption of a qualified retirement plan increase the wealth of the owner of a closely held corporation?

Dramatic results can be achieved by a qualified retirement plan.

Example. Neal, the owner of a closely held corporation, earns a $50,000
annual salary, and the corporation is able to pay a 15 percent bonus
($7,500) each year. From the additional $7,500 each year, Neal will keep
about $5,400 after taxes (assuming a 28 percent bracket). If that $5,400
is invested at 8 percent per year, Neal will earn about 6 percent net after
taxes. Over a 25-year period, he will be able to build up about $314,000
after taxes.

If the corporation has a qualified profit sharing plan and, instead of giving
Neal a $7,500 bonus, contributes that $7,500 to the plan each year on
his behalf, the corporation gets the same $7,500 deduction that it would
have received had it paid the bonus.

If the profit sharing trust earns the same 8 percent that Neal would have
earned individually, then, because the profit sharing trust pays no income
taxes, the total build-up of these annual investments in the trust on Neal's
behalf, over the 25-year period, will come to $592,000. (Remember, the

full $7,500 per year—not $5,400 after taxes—is accumulating in the trust. Furthermore, it is accumulating at the full 8 percent interest rate.)

If this $592,000 build-up in funds is paid out to Neal in one year upon his retirement, he may be eligible to elect special tax treatment.

The above example is oversimplified, especially in the case of a small or medium-size corporation. To give this type of dramatic build-up to the business owner, other employees must also be covered. This, of course, boosts costs, but there are methods that can be used to reduce costs. These methods (e.g., permitted disparity) may be incorporated into the plan.

Q 1:4 How does the adoption of a qualified retirement plan reduce a corporation's tax liability?

To illustrate how a qualified retirement plan reduces a corporation's tax liability, assume the corporation had taxable income of $45,000 in 1996 and no qualified plan. Its income tax liability would be $6,750. If, however, the owners decided to adopt a qualified retirement plan and make a tax-deductible contribution of $21,000 to the plan, the corporation's taxable income would now be $24,000 ($45,000 minus $21,000). Its income tax liability would be reduced to $3,600. By adopting the plan and making the contribution, this corporation would cut its tax liability by almost 50 percent. [IRC § 11(b)]

Q 1:5 What is a qualified retirement plan?

There are two distinct elements embodied in the term "qualified retirement plan." The main element is the term "retirement plan." A retirement plan means any plan or program maintained by an employer or an employee organization (or both) that (1) provides retirement income to employees or (2) results in a deferral of income by employees for periods extending generally to the end of employment or beyond, regardless of how plan contributions or benefits are calculated or how benefits are distributed. [ERISA § 3(2)]

The other element is the term "qualified," which means that the retirement plan is afforded special tax treatment for meeting a host of requirements of the Internal Revenue Code (the Code). Qualified retirement plans fall into two basic categories: defined contribution plans and defined benefit plans. A defined contribution plan provides benefits based on the amount contributed to an employee's individual account, plus any earnings and forfeitures of other employees that are allocated to the account. A defined benefit plan provides a definitely determinable annual benefit; that is, the benefits are determined on the basis of a formula contained in the plan.

When the term "qualified retirement plan" is used in this book, it refers to both defined contribution and defined benefit plans.

Q 1:6 What are the basic tax advantages of a qualified retirement plan?

A qualified retirement plan is afforded special tax treatment. These tax advantages include the following:

1. The sponsoring company is allowed an immediate tax deduction for the amount contributed to the plan for a particular year. [IRC § 404]

2. Participants pay no current income tax on amounts contributed by the company on their behalf. [IRC §§ 402, 403]

3. Earnings of the plan are tax-exempt—permitting the tax-free accumulation of income and gains on investments. [IRC §§ 401, 501]

4. Reduced tax rates may apply to lump-sum distributions to certain participants. [IRC § 402(d)]

5. Income taxes on certain types of distributions may be deferred by rolling over the distribution to an individual retirement account (IRA) or to another qualified retirement plan. [IRC §§ 401(a)(31), 402(c), 403(a)(4), 403(a)(5)]

6. Income taxes on certain types of distributions to a deceased participant's spouse may be deferred by rolling over the distribution to an IRA. [IRC § 402(c)(9)]

7. Installment or annuity payments are taxed only when they are received. [IRC §§ 72, 402(a), 403(a)]

Q 1:7 Must a company incorporate to have a qualified retirement plan?

No. The benefits of a qualified retirement plan are available to incorporated and unincorporated businesses alike. Sole proprietorships and partnerships can have retirement plans that are comparable to corporate retirement plans.

A plan covering a self-employed individual (see Q 6:33) must, however, satisfy certain requirements in addition to the normal corporate retirement plan qualification requirements. [IRC §§ 401(c), 401(d)] A self-employed individual is an individual who has income from self-employment for the taxable year.

Q 1:8 What tax advantage does a self-employed individual gain by adopting a qualified retirement plan?

The basic tax advantages of adopting a qualified retirement plan, which are similar to those received by the owner of a closely held corporation, are:

1. The self-employed individual receives a federal income tax deduction, subject to the applicable limitations of the Code, for contributions made to the qualified retirement plan.

2. To the extent the contribution the self-employed individual makes to a qualified retirement plan is tax-deductible, the tax on this income is deferred (it will be taxable when it is ultimately received from the plan).

3. Income earned on contributions to the plan (whether or not tax-deductible when made) will escape tax while in the plan, thereby permitting a greater total compounding of earnings than would otherwise be possible.

4. Reduced tax rates may apply to lump-sum distributions to the self-employed individual or the individual's beneficiary.

Q 1:9 Is it worthwhile for a self-employed individual to incorporate?

Although there generally is parity between qualified corporate retirement plans and qualified retirement plans for the self-employed, the incorporated business owner will still have advantages that will be unavailable to the unincorporated business owner. Among the advantages are the following:

1. The incorporated business owner may be permitted to borrow from the plan. [IRC §§ 72(p), 401(a)(13), 4975(d)]

2. Plan contributions for the incorporated business owner allocable to life, accident, health, or other insurance are deductible. [IRC § 404(e)]

3. The incorporated business owner can terminate employment for lump-sum distribution purposes. [IRC § 402(d)(4)(A)]

4. Plan contributions on behalf of an incorporated business owner can create or increase a net operating loss. [IRC § 172(d)(4)(D)]

5. The incorporated business owner may receive tax-free group term life insurance benefits. [IRC § 79]

6. The incorporated business owner may receive tax-free benefits under a medical expense reimbursement plan. [IRC §§ 105(b), 105(g)]

Note: An individual who incorporates principally to obtain tax deductions not otherwise available to a self-employed individual should review those circumstances in which IRS may allocate income and deductions of a personal service corporation to an employee-owner.

Q 1:10 How should an existing qualified retirement plan be handled if a self-employed individual incorporates the business?

The simplest and most practical arrangement may be to have the corporation adopt the qualified retirement plan. If the corporation establishes a new qualified retirement plan, the assets of the prior plan can be merged into the new plan or transferred directly to the trustees of the new plan.

If the qualified retirement plan that covered the self-employed individual (see Q 6:33) is being terminated, IRS should be notified (see Q 21:67).

Another alternative is to freeze the plan. Since the individual is no longer self-employed, the individual can make no further contributions to the plan. However, amounts in the plan will continue to accumulate on a tax-free basis. Distributions can later be made from the plan in accordance with its provisions. However, if a qualified retirement plan covering a self-employed individual is frozen, the plan must still comply with the requirements of the Code. [Rev Rul 89-87, 1989-2 CB 81; IRC § 401(a); Treas Reg § 1.401(a)(26)-2(b)]

Q 1:11 How does the deductibility of employer contributions differ between qualified and nonqualified plans?

Qualified retirement plans are given favorable tax treatment for meeting special requirements of the Code. There is no special tax treatment for nonqualified retirement plans. The basic difference between a qualified plan and a nonqualified plan is that contributions by the company to the nonqualified plan are not deductible until they are includible in the participant's income. This means the company does not get a current deduction for contributions made to a nonqualified plan. In contrast, contributions to a qualified plan are immediately deductible. [IRC §§ 83, 162, 404]

Q 1:12 How do qualified and nonqualified plans differ with regard to the taxation of employer contributions?

A participant in a qualified plan is not taxed until the benefits are distributed to the participant. This is also true in a nonqualified, unfunded plan. If the nonqualified plan is funded, however, the participant generally is taxed in the first year that the participant's rights are transferable or are not subject to a substantial risk of forfeiture. [IRC §§ 83, 402(b)]

Q 1:13 How do qualified and nonqualified plans differ with regard to coverage of employees and benefit or contribution limitations?

The nonqualified plan is designed primarily to provide retirement income for essential employees. Such a plan does not have to cover a broad spectrum of employees, as the qualified plan does. Furthermore, there are no limits on benefits or contributions, nor are there any reporting or bookkeeping requirements in connection with the nonqualified plan so long as it is not funded. [IRC § 401(a)]

Q 1:14 How is the employee affected by the employer's choice of a qualified or nonqualified plan?

From the employee's standpoint, benefits paid under a nonqualified plan will usually be taxed at and after retirement, when, presumably, the employee will be in a lower tax bracket. This same income tax advantage is available to those who participate in a qualified plan, but there are some additional tax benefits in that case. If the benefits are paid in a lump sum, for example, the distribution might qualify for forward averaging tax treatment, which is a special method of tax computation that is unavailable for distributions from IRAs, simplified employee pensions (SEPs), tax-sheltered annuities (TSAs), and nonqualified plans. [IRC § 402(d)]

Q 1:15 What is the Employee Retirement Income Security Act?

The Employee Retirement Income Security Act of 1974 (ERISA) became law on September 2, 1974. ERISA completely overhauled the federal pension law after Congress found that:

1. Employees with long years of service were losing anticipated retirement benefits due to the lack of plan provisions relating to the vesting of benefits;

2. Many plans lacked adequate funds to pay employees promised retirement benefits; and

3. Plans were being terminated before enough funds had been accumulated to pay employees and their beneficiaries promised retirement benefits.

To protect the interests of retirement plan participants and their beneficiaries, ERISA (1) established a new set of rules for participation in retirement plans, (2) added mandatory schedules for the vesting of benefits, (3) fixed minimum funding standards, (4) set standards of conduct for administering the plan and handling plan assets, (5) required disclosure of plan information, and (6) established a system for insuring the payment of pension benefits.

Q 1:16   What other Acts have affected retirement plans?

The following Acts have affected retirement plans:

- The Multiemployer Pension Plan Amendments Act of 1980 (MPPAA)
- The Economic Recovery Tax Act of 1981 (ERTA)
- The Tax Equity and Fiscal Responsibility Act of 1982 (TEFRA)
- The Tax Reform Act of 1984 (TRA '84)
- The Retirement Equity Act of 1984 (REA)
- The Single-Employer Pension Plan Amendments Act of 1986 (SEPPAA)
- The Tax Reform Act of 1986 (TRA '86)
- The Omnibus Budget Reconciliation Act of 1986 (OBRA '86)
- The Pension Protection Act (PPA), attached to the Omnibus Budget Reconciliation Act of 1987 (OBRA '87)
- The Technical and Miscellaneous Revenue Act of 1988 (TAMRA)
- The Revenue Reconciliation Act (RRA), Title VII of the Omnibus Budget Reconciliation Act of 1989 (OBRA '89)
- The Omnibus Budget Reconciliation Act of 1990 (OBRA '90)
- The Unemployment Compensation Amendments of 1992 (UC '92)
- The Revenue Reconciliation Act of 1993 (RRA '93)
- The Uniformed Services Employment and Re-employment Rights Act of 1994 (USERRA)
- The Pension Annuitants Protection Act (PPA '94)
- The Retirement Protection Act of 1994 (RPA '94)
- The State Taxation of Pension Income Tax Act of 1995
- The Small Business Job Protection Act of 1996 (SBA '96)
- The Health Insurance Portability and Accountability Act of 1996 (HIPA '96)

Q 1:17 What is the Uniformed Services Employment and Re-employment Rights Act of 1994?

This Act (USERRA) was signed into law by President Clinton on October 13, 1994. USERRA prohibits discrimination against employees because of membership in the uniformed services. USERRA generally became effective for reemployment initiated more than 60 days after the law was enacted. However, qualified retirement plans have two years, or until October 12, 1996, to comply.

USERRA provides that an individual who is reemployed following protected military service must be treated as not having incurred a break in service (see Q 5:10). Furthermore, upon reemployment, the plan must grant vesting and benefit credit (see Qs 9:1, 9:2) for the period of time the employee was absent for military service. Defined contribution plans (see Q 2:2) must credit the employee with any allocations of employer contributions, but not earnings or forfeitures, to which the employee would have been entitled had there been no interruption in employment. For this purpose, the employee's compensation is assumed to be at the rate the employee would have received had there been no interruption in employment.

USERRA further provides that any qualified retirement plan benefit or contribution that is contingent upon the making of contributions or deferrals by the employee is due the reemployed person only if the employee makes up the missed contributions or deferrals. A make-up of employee contributions or deferrals may be contributed by the employee over a period of time equal to three times the period of absence due to military service, but not to exceed five years. For example, if a participant in a 401(k) plan (see Q 23:1) that provides employer matching contributions is called to 12 months' active military duty, the employee would have 36 months after returning to employment to make up the missed deferrals. As the deferrals are made up, the corresponding employer matching contributions would be credited to the participant's account under the plan. However, USERRA contains no amendments to the Code to address coordination of these catch-up contributions, deferrals, and matching contributions with various limitations (see Qs 6:1, 23:26). In addition, nondiscrimination testing for qualification purposes is not addressed (see Qs 23:8, 23:48).

SBA '96 (see Q 1:21) incorporated the provisions of USERRA into the Code and also clarified a number of plan qualification issues that had not been addressed by USERRA.

The requirements of USERRA posed potential problems for employers because the annual limits on contributions and benefits under various provisions of the Code did not authorize exceptions for make-up contributions by or for reemployed veterans. In addition, the nondiscrimination, minimum coverage, minimum participation, and top-heavy rules (see chapters 4, 5, 6, 22) did not make an exception for contributions for reemployed veterans.

Under SBA '96, make-up contributions by an employer or employee to a defined contribution plan (including a tax-sheltered annuity, simplified employee pension, or qualified salary reduction arrangement) or contributions by an employee to a defined benefit plan (see Q 2:3) that provides for employee contributions, on behalf of reemployed veterans that are required by USERRA, are not subject to the generally applicable plan contribution limits or the limits on deductible contributions with respect to the year in which the contributions are made. Moreover, the make-up contributions will not be considered in applying the limits to any other contributions made during the year. However, the make-up contributions (including elective deferrals) may not exceed the aggregate amount of contributions that would have been permitted under the applicable limits for the year for which the contributions are made if the individual had continued to be employed by the employer during the period of military service.

A make-up contribution may not exceed the contribution that would have been allowed under the limits that applied in the year to which the contribution relates. Because the limits are subject to cost-of-living adjustments, the amount of a make-up contribution may vary. For example, a reemployed veteran may make an elective deferral under a 401(k) plan of $9,500 for the 1996 plan year. However, the make-up contribution would be limited to $9,240 if the contribution related to the 1995 plan year.

Make-up contributions made on behalf of reemployed veterans also will not cause a plan to violate the nondiscrimination, minimum coverage, minimum participation, and top-heavy rules applicable to qualified retirement plans. In applying these qualification rules, the contributions will not be considered for the year in which they are made *or* the year to which they relate.

Generally, loans from a qualified retirement plan to a plan participant must be repaid within five years. However, a plan may suspend an employee's obligation to repay a plan loan during the period of the employee's military service without risking disqualification or engaging in a prohibited transaction (see Qs 13:44–13:52, 20:9).

The above rules are effective as of December 12, 1994. [IRC § 414(u), as added by SBA '96 § 1704(n)]

Q 1:18   What is the Pension Annuitants Protection Act?

The Pension Annuitants Protection Act (PPA '94) was signed into law by President Clinton on October 22, 1994. Under this Act, a qualified retirement plan participant, beneficiary, or fiduciary can bring an action for appropriate relief if the purchase of an insurance contract or annuity in connection with the termination of a person's status as a plan participant would violate fiduciary standards.

Effective for legal proceedings pending, or brought after May 31, 1993, the Act requires the posting of security, if necessary, to assure that beneficiaries receive the amounts provided by the annuities. Although interest can also be awarded, the Act does not authorize awards of punitive, extracontractual, or consequential damages.

Q 1:19   What is the Retirement Protection Act of 1994?

On December 8, 1994, President Clinton signed into law the Uruguay Round Agreements Act, implementing agreements related to the General Agreement on Tariffs and Trade (GATT). Included in the Act was the Retirement Protection Act of 1994 (RPA '94), the main purpose of which was to strengthen the Pension Benefit Guaranty Corporation (PBGC; see Q 21:10). RPA '94:

1. Strengthened funding in underfunded plans;
2. Removed impediments to funding certain plans;
3. Eliminated the quarterly contribution requirement for fully funded plans;
4. Waived excise taxes on certain nondeductible contributions;
5. Phased out the PBGC variable-rate premium cap;
6. Prohibited benefit increases during bankruptcy proceedings;
7. Required that annual plain-language explanations of a plan's funding status and the limits of other PBGC guarantees be given to participants;
8. Changed the interest rate and mortality assumptions that may be used to calculate distributions;
9. Rounded cost-of-living adjustments down to the next lowest multiple of a specified dollar amount;
10. Extended the IRS user fee program; and
11. Extended the use of excess pension assets for retiree health benefits.

Q 1:20   What is the State Income Taxation of Pension Income Act of 1995?

On January 16, 1996, President Clinton signed the State Income Taxation of Pension Income Act of 1995 (H.R. 394). This Act prohibits states from taxing the retirement income payments of their former residents, effective for retirement income payments received after December 31, 1995.

The Act exempts all retirement income received from certain plans from taxation by states other than the state of the recipient's residence. Retirement income means any income received from, among others, a qualified retirement plan, a simplified employee pension (see Q 27:1), a tax-sheltered annuity (see Q 29:1), and an individual retirement plan (see Q 26:1). Nonqualified plan benefits (see Q 1:14) are protected under the Act if (1) the distribution is made from an excess benefit plan and payments are received after termination of employment, or (2) the distribution is made from any other type of nonqualified plan and the retirement income is part of a series of substantially equal periodic payments (not less frequently than annually) made for the life or life expectancy of the recipient (or the joint lives or joint life expectancies of the recipient and a designated beneficiary) or for a period of not less than ten years.

Q 1:21   What is the Small Business Job Protection Act of 1996?

The Small Business Job Protection Act of 1996 (SBA '96) was enacted into law on August 20, 1996. SBA '96 adopted many of the pension simplification proposals that were contained in RRB '95 and RRB '96 (see Q 1:22A). SBA '96:

1. Repeals five-year income averaging for lump-sum distributions;
2. Repeals the $5,000 employee death benefit exclusion;
3. Simplifies the method for taxing installment distributions;
4. Repeals salary reduction simplified employee pensions and replaces them with SIMPLE plans;
5. Extends 401(k) plans to nongovernmental tax-exempt employers;
6. Eases nondiscrimination testing for 401(k) plans;
7. Simplifies the definition of highly compensated employee;
8. Repeals the family aggregation rule;
9. Limits the minimum participation requirement to defined benefit plans;
10. Repeals for certain participants the required distribution of benefits after a participant reaches age 70½ if the participant does not retire;

11. Suspends the imposition of the excess distributions tax for three years;

12. Eliminates the 1.0 rule;

13. Increases the penalty tax on prohibited transactions;

14. Eliminates the special vesting rule for multiemployer plans;

15. Repeals the 50 percent interest exclusion for certain ESOP loans; and

16. Increases the spousal IRA limitation from $250 to $2,000.

Q 1:22   What is the Health Insurance Portability and Accountability Act of 1996?

This Act (HIPA '96), enacted into law on August 21, 1996, provides that distributions from individual retirement plans (IRAs) made after 1996 will not be subject to the 10 percent penalty tax on early withdrawals if the amounts are used to pay medical expenses in excess of $7\frac{1}{2}$ percent of adjusted gross income. In addition, the 10 percent penalty tax will not apply to IRA distributions that are used by certain unemployed, formerly unemployed, or self-employed individuals to pay health insurance premiums.

Q 1:22A   What are the Revenue Reconciliation Bill of 1995 and the Revenue Reconciliation Bill of 1996?

The Revenue Reconciliation Bill of 1995 (RRB '95) was passed by the House and Senate late in 1995 but was vetoed by President Clinton. RRB '95 contained many of the pension simplification provisions that were incorporated in SBA '96 (see Q 1:21). However, RRB '95 contained a number of provisions affecting IRAs that were not adopted as part of SBA '96. RRB '95 would:

1. Increase the income limits at which the IRA deduction would be phased out for active participants in qualified retirement plans;

2. Index the $2,000 IRA deduction limit for inflation in $500 increments;

3. Create an American Dream IRA (AD IRA) to which increased nondeductible contributions could be made and from which qualified distributions would be tax-free if made after five years from the year the AD IRA was established;

4. Exempt from the 10 percent penalty tax on early withdrawals qualified distributions from AD IRAs and regular IRAs; and

5. Establish special rollover rules.

The Revenue Reconciliation Bill of 1996 (RRB '96) was part of President Clinton's 1997 balanced budget proposal. RRB '96 also contained many of the same pension simplification provisions as RRB '95. However, RRB '96 would have replaced simplified employee pensions with national employee savings trusts (NESTs) for employees of small employers and would have replaced ages 59½ and 70½ with ages 59 and 70 for purposes of the 10 percent penalty tax on early withdrawals and required minimum distributions. RRB '96 also contained provisions affecting IRAs that were not adopted as part of SBA '96. RRB '96 would:

1. Increase the income limits at which the IRA deduction would be phased out for active participants in qualified retirement plans;

2. Index the $2,000 IRA deduction limit for inflation in $500 increments;

3. Coordinate the IRA deduction limit with the limit on elective deferrals applicable to 401(k) plans, salary reduction SEPs, and tax-sheltered annuities;

4. Create a Special IRA for nondeductible contributions from which distributions of earnings would be tax-free if attributable to contributions that had been in the Special IRA for at least five years;

5. Exempt from the 10 percent penalty tax on early withdrawals certain qualifying distributions from IRAs and Special IRAs;

6. Impose the 10 percent penalty tax on certain withdrawals from IRAs even if the individual has attained age 59½; and

7. Establish special rollover rules.

Q 1:23   Does the adoption of a qualified retirement plan by an employer constitute a contractual obligation to maintain the plan?

No. Although a qualified retirement plan must be a permanent plan (see Qs 1:26, 21:1), continuance of the plan is voluntary. It is not a contractual obligation of the company, except in the case of certain collectively bargained plans.

A carefully drafted plan will specifically limit the company's obligation to maintain and fund the plan. In addition, the company should expressly retain the right to reduce, suspend, or discontinue contributions and the right to terminate the plan (see Q 21:2).

Q 1:24 What costs will the company incur in adopting a qualified retirement plan?

Professional fees vary, depending on the type of plan adopted by the company. However, the following types of services are generally required:

1. Legal services for drafting the plan and trust, and for submitting those and other required documents to IRS to obtain tax qualification;

2. Accounting services; and

3. Actuarial services to provide cost and benefit computations if a defined benefit plan is adopted.

It is also possible to adopt a master or prototype plan (see Q 2:25) designed by an insurance company, a bank, or other investment-oriented company (a mutual fund, for example). These institutions generally charge less for their services because they expect to profit from the products (e.g., life insurance policies) that the adopting company may be required to purchase.

Q 1:25 Is there any type of tax-favored qualified retirement plan for the business owner that is easy to adopt and inexpensive to operate?

Yes, a simplified employee pension (SEP) requires only a minimal amount of paperwork and expense to adopt and administer. Effective in 1997, an employer may adopt a savings incentive match plan for employees (SIMPLE) that is also expected to require minimal paperwork and expense. For details on SEPs and SIMPLE plans, see chapter 27.

Q 1:26 Must the company contribute to the plan each year once it adopts a qualified retirement plan?

It depends on the type of plan adopted. IRS says that the adoption of a qualified retirement plan commits the company to maintaining the plan on a permanent basis. For this purpose, permanent means that, from the plan's inception, the company must intend to support the plan over a number of years. [Treas Reg § 1.401-1(b)(2)]

Annual contributions to a pension plan are required. Although there are exceptions to this rule, a company considering the adoption of a pension plan must recognize that it is undertaking a commitment to maintain and fund the plan. For details on funding requirements, see chapter 8.

Annual contributions to a profit sharing plan are not usually required. Further, a company that has not done well in a particular year may decide to make either a minimal contribution or no contribution at all for that year (unless the plan itself mandates a contribution each year). Nevertheless, a profit sharing plan is not permanent unless contributions are "recurring and substantial." [Treas Reg § 1.401-1(b)(2)]

Q 1:27   Must a qualified retirement plan include all employees?

No. A company is permitted to exclude certain categories of employees from participation in its qualified retirement plan. These exclusions are optional and apply only if they are specified in the plan. [IRC § 410]

Q 1:28   What are the most common eligibility requirements for participation in a qualified retirement plan?

The most common eligibility requirements are those relating to minimum age and length of service with the company.

A plan may exclude any employee who has not yet reached age 21. Plans of certain educational institutions may exclude employees who are under age 26, provided that the service requirement does not exceed one year and the plan provides full and immediate vesting of benefits after one year of service. [IRC §§ 170(b)(1)(A)(ii), 410(a)(1)(A)(i), 410(a)(1)(B)(ii)]

In most instances, the plan requires an employee to complete a certain period of service before being eligible to participate. This service requirement usually does not exceed one year; otherwise, the plan must provide full and immediate vesting of benefits. Under no circumstances may the service requirement exceed two years. The service requirement for 401(k) plans cannot exceed one year. [IRC §§ 401(k)(2)(D), 410(a)(1)(A)(ii), 410(a)(1)(B)(i)]

Q 1:29   What statutory exclusions from participation in a qualified retirement plan are permitted?

The two most common statutory exclusions from plan participation are minimum age and length of service requirements (see Q 1:28).

Other than these exclusions, the most common statutory exclusion applies to union employees on whose behalf negotiations for retirement benefits have been conducted with the company. The company may exclude union employees from coverage, whether or not they are covered under a separate retirement plan, as long as retirement benefits were the subject of good-faith bargaining. Statutory exclusions for air pilots and nonresident aliens are also available. [IRC § 410(b)(3)]

Q 1:30   What other exclusions from participation in a qualified retirement plan are permitted?

Other exclusions—so-called plan exclusions—usually fall into the following categories: (1) classification by job description, (2) classification by geographic location of employment or by specific division of the company, and (3) classification by method of compensation (e.g., hourly as opposed to salaried). Bear in mind, however, that regardless of the plan's eligibility provisions, coverage of a sufficient number of employees not excluded by statute (see Q 1:29) is needed to satisfy the minimum coverage requirements of the Code. The minimum coverage requirements have become stricter, and a minimum participation requirement is also applicable (see Qs 5:15, 5:25). [IRC §§ 401(a)(26), 410(b)]

Q 1:31   Can a company establish two qualified retirement plans?

Yes. The Code permits a company to maintain as many qualified retirement plans as it chooses, provided that all the plans meet the Code's requirements, including limitations on benefits and contributions.

Quite often, large companies establish separate plans for individual subsidiaries or divisions. These plans need not be comparable in all cases. Indeed, as explained in chapter 5, not all divisions or subsidiaries of the same company or members of a controlled group must adopt a plan in order for another division, subsidiary, or member to maintain a plan for its employees.

The minimum participation requirements (see Q 5:25) may curtail an employer's ability to maintain separate plans for individual subsidiaries or divisions. [IRC § 401(a)(26)]

Q 1:32   What kinds of benefits may be provided under a qualified retirement plan?

Qualified retirement plans are primarily intended to provide retirement benefits. Nevertheless, qualified retirement plans also frequently provide benefits upon death, disability, early retirement, or some other termination of employment. These benefits are usually funded by a trust fund, insurance contracts, or a combination of the two.

A profit sharing plan need not be limited to retirement benefits; it may also provide for hardship distributions, for example. In addition, a profit sharing plan may permit distribution of all or part of a participant's vested interest that has remained in the plan for at least two years prior to the distribution. It may also permit a participant with at least five years of participation in the plan to withdraw all or part of the participant's vested interest, including any amount contributed within the last two years. [Rev Rul 68-24, 1968-1 CB 150; Rev Rul 71-224, 1971-1 CB 124; Rev Rul 71-295, 1971-2 CB 184; Rev Rul 73-553, 1973-2 CB 130] If a money purchase plan (see Q 2:4) is merged into, or its assets are transferred to, a profit sharing plan, the merged or transferred assets do not take on the character of the profit sharing plan. Thus, the assets attributable to the money purchase plan cannot be subject to the profit sharing plan's early withdrawal provisions. [Rev Rul 94-76, 1994-2 CB 46]

A 10 percent excise tax applies to most premature distributions from qualified retirement plans and IRAs. Consequently, a profit sharing plan can provide for in-service distributions of plan benefits after the passage of at least two years or because of hardship, but the distribution may be subject to the 10 percent excise tax, in addition to ordinary income tax. [IRC § 72(t)]

Q 1:33 Is a voluntary contribution feature attractive to the business owner?

A business owner can make voluntary nondeductible contributions to a qualified retirement plan, but such contributions are now subject to limitations and nondiscrimination tests. These nondiscrimination requirements reduce the attractiveness of allowing voluntary employee contributions. For details regarding the limitations on voluntary contributions, see Qs 6:20 and 23:48 through 23:55.

Q 1:34 May a qualified retirement plan provide life insurance benefits for participants?

Yes. However, different limits may apply to life insurance policies acquired under defined contribution plans and those acquired under defined benefit plans (see Q 14:4). The following general rules also apply:

1. The policies can be ordinary life, term life, universal life, retirement income, or endowment;

2. The insurance must be incidental to the primary purpose of the plan (i.e., to provide benefits at retirement); and

3. The participant pays tax on the cost of the current life insurance protection that is received each year.

By including life insurance in the plan, the corporate business owner is able to shift a personal expense (not tax-deductible) to the corporation. Just as the corporation's plan contributions are deductible, contributions (within limits) to pay for the life insurance are deductible. The corporate business owner will, however, have to include in gross income the cost of the current life insurance protection received under the plan (see Q 2:23).

There is a different rule for self-employed individuals (see Q 6:33). Plan contributions made on behalf of a self-employed individual that are allocable to the purchase of pure life insurance (the term element, not the entire premium) are not deductible (see Q 14:3). [IRC §§ 404(a)(8)(C), 404(e); Treas Reg § 1.404(e)-1A(g)] For further details, see chapter 14.

Q 1:35   May a qualified retirement plan provide health insurance?

Yes, although the rules governing how much health insurance can be acquired and for whom vary, depending on whether the plan is a pension plan or a profit sharing plan.

A pension plan may provide health insurance, but only for retired employees and their families. [IRC § 401(h); Treas Reg § 1.401-14]

A contribution allocated to an individual medical account under a pension plan is treated as part of the annual addition (see Q 6:1) to a defined contribution plan. [IRC § 415(l)]

A profit sharing plan may provide health insurance benefits for all plan participants and their families. If this insurance is purchased with funds that have been in the plan for more than two years, there is no limit on how much the plan may pay for insurance coverage. If the plan uses other funds to buy the insurance, the amount of the premiums must be incidental; that is, the premiums may not exceed 25 percent of the funds allocated to the participant's account that have not been in the plan for at least two years. [Treas Reg § 1.401-1(b)(1)(ii); Rev Rul 61-164, 1961-2 CB 99]

A profit sharing plan that allowed a participant to have elective contributions (see Q 23:13) allocated to a separate retiree medical subaccount under the plan also permitted the participant either to receive distributions from the subaccount or to use the subaccount to pay health care premiums. IRS ruled that amounts used to pay premiums would be includible in the participant's gross income in the taxable year so used. [Ltr Rul 9405021]

Q 1:36 Is a contribution to a qualified retirement plan adopted on the last day of the taxable year fully deductible?

Yes, if the plan and trust are executed by the end of the year and other procedural requirements established by IRS are met, then contributions made by the due date for filing the company's income tax return for that year (including extensions) are fully deductible. [IRC § 404(a)(6); Rev Rul 81-114, 1981-1 CB 207]

Example. Sallie Corp., a calendar-year corporation, adopts a pension plan to become effective December 31, 1996. If the documents are executed by December 31, 1996, and the contribution is made by March 17, 1997 (or as late as September 15, 1997, if the company has received an extension until that time for filing its tax return), a full deduction will be allowed for 1996.

Q 1:37 May excess contributions made to a qualified retirement plan be returned to the company?

If the company makes an excess contribution to its qualified retirement plan, that excess may be returned to the company only in the following circumstances:

1. An actuarial error caused the excess funds to remain in the trust after the plan's termination and after the payment of all benefits to participants or their beneficiaries. [Treas Reg § 1.401-2]

2. The contribution was conditioned on the initial qualification of the plan, the plan did not qualify, and the plan was submitted to IRS for a determination letter (see Q 15:1) within the remedial amendment period. [ERISA § 403(c)(2)(B); IRC § 401(b)]

3. The contribution was conditioned on its deductibility, and the deduction was denied. [ERISA § 403(c)(2)(C)]

4. The excess contribution was made due to a mistake of fact. [ERISA § 403(c)(2)(A)]

In any event, the plan itself must permit the return of the excess contribution; and, in either of the last two situations, earnings attributable to the excess contribution may not be returned to the company. Losses attributable to the excess contribution will reduce the amount to be returned. Further, returns to the employer must be made within one year of the mistaken contribution, denial of qualification, or denial of the deduction. [Rev Rul 91-4, 1991-1 CB 57; Rev Rul 77-200, 1977-1 CB 98; Rev Proc 90-49, 1990-2 CB 620; Ltr Ruls 9624037, 9436045]

A 10 percent excise tax is now imposed on nondeductible contributions to a qualified retirement plan (see Q 12:8). [IRC § 4972]

Special rules apply to excess contributions made to a 401(k) plan. See chapter 23.

Q 1:38   May the company borrow from its qualified retirement plan to acquire assets needed in its business?

Generally, no. A penalty tax (see below) is imposed on any prohibited transaction (see Q 20:1), which includes the lending of money between a plan and the company. Thus, a company may not borrow from its plan for any purpose. [ERISA § 406; IRC § 4975(c)(1)(B)]

DOL, however, may grant an exemption from the loan restrictions. Generally, an exemption is granted only if it is (1) administratively feasible; (2) in the interests of the plan, its participants, and beneficiaries; and (3) protective of the rights of participants and beneficiaries of the plan. [ERISA § 408; IRC § 4975(c)(2)]

Exemptions for loans from a qualified retirement plan to the company to buy business assets have been approved by DOL. The company must have a good credit rating, the interest rate must be comparable to what a bank would charge, and adequate security must be provided. For examples of when an exemption will be allowed, see Q 20:16.

The penalty tax on a prohibited transaction is imposed at the rate of 5 percent of the amount involved in the transaction for every year (or part of a year). If the 5 percent tax is imposed and the prohibited transaction is not corrected within the taxable period, an additional tax equal to 100 percent of the amount involved in the transaction is imposed.

Both the initial and additional taxes are payable by the individual who participated in the prohibited transaction. The taxable period begins when the prohibited transaction occurs; it ends, if it is not corrected, on the earlier of the date the notice of deficiency with respect to the 5 percent tax is mailed or the date the 5 percent tax is assessed. [IRC §§ 4975(a), 4975(b), 4975(f)]

Q 1:39   May a business owner borrow from the qualified retirement plan?

Yes, if the owner is a participant in the corporation's qualified retirement plan and the plan contains a provision authorizing loans to participants. However, a shareholder-employee (i.e., a more-than-5-percent shareholder) of an S corporation, and certain related individuals, may not borrow from the corporation's qualified retirement plan. [IRC §§ 401(a)(13), 4975(d)]

The general rules for loans apply to self-employed individuals (see Q 6:33) other than owner-employees (see Q 5:34). However, the law prohibits a qualified retirement plan from lending to an owner-employee or to the owner-employee's spouse and certain other relatives. [IRC §§ 401(a)(13), 4975(d)]

See Qs 13:44 through 13:52 and Q 20:9 for further discussion.

Chapter 2

Types and Choices of Plans

The range of retirement plan alternatives is extensive. There are defined contribution plans and defined benefit plans; there are pension plans and profit sharing plans. Before the employer can evaluate the relative merits of the various types of plans and choose the most appropriate plan, the employer must know what each type of plan offers. This chapter describes the categories of retirement plans, examines the basic choices available to a company, and offers guidelines for choosing the appropriate plan.

Q 2:1   What are the basic choices among qualified retirement plans?

Qualified retirement plans generally fit into one of two categories: defined contribution plans (see Q 2:2) and defined benefit plans (see Q 2:3).

Q 2:2   What is a defined contribution plan?

A defined contribution plan is a retirement plan that "provides for an individual account for each participant and for benefits based solely upon the amount contributed to the participant's account, and any income, expenses, gains and losses, and any forfeitures of accounts of other participants which may be allocated to such participant's account." [ERISA § 3(34); IRC § 414(i)]

Defined contribution plans include the following:

- Money purchase pension plans (see Q 2:4)

- Target benefit plans (see Q 2:5)
- Profit sharing plans (see Qs 2:6, 2:7)
- Thrift or savings plans (see Q 2:11)
- 401(k) plans (see Q 2:12)
- Stock bonus plans (see Q 2:13)
- Employee stock ownership plans (ESOPs) (see Q 2:14)
- Simplified employee pensions (SEPs) (see Q 2:15)
- Savings incentive match plans for employees (SIMPLE plans) (see Q 2:15A)

Three major consequences result when a retirement plan is classified as a defined contribution plan: (1) plan contributions are determined by formula and not by actuarial requirements (except for target benefit plans); (2) plan earnings and losses are allocated to each participant's account and do not affect the company's retirement plan costs; and (3) plan benefits are not insured by the Pension Benefit Guaranty Corporation (PBGC).

Q 2:3 What is a defined benefit plan?

A defined benefit plan is a retirement plan "other than an individual account plan." In other words, a plan that is not a defined contribution plan is classified as a defined benefit plan. Under a defined benefit plan, retirement benefits must be definitely determinable. For example, a plan that entitles a participant to a monthly pension for life equal to 30 percent of monthly compensation is a defined benefit plan. [ERISA § 3(35); IRC § 414(j)] The most common types of defined benefit plans are flat benefit plans (see Q 2:16) and unit benefit plans (see Q 2:17).

If a plan is categorized as a defined benefit plan: (1) plan formulas are geared to retirement benefits and not to contributions (except for cash balance plans—see Q 2:22); (2) the annual contribution is usually actuarially determined; (3) certain benefits may be insured by PBGC; (4) early termination of the plan is subject to special rules; and (5) forfeitures reduce the company's cost of providing retirement benefits.

Q 2:4 What is a money purchase pension plan?

A money purchase pension plan is a defined contribution plan in which the company's contributions are mandatory and are usually based solely on each participant's compensation.

The obligation to fund the plan makes a money purchase pension plan different from most profit sharing plans. In most profit sharing plans, there are generally no unfavorable consequences for the company if it fails to make a contribution. However, if the company maintains a money purchase pension plan, its failure to make a contribution can result in the imposition of a penalty tax (see Q 8:18). Contributions must be made to a money purchase pension plan even if the company has no profits.

Forfeitures that occur because of employee turnover may reduce future contributions of the company or may be used to increase the benefits of remaining participants.

Retirement benefits are based on the amount in the participant's account at the time of retirement; that is, whatever pension the money can purchase.

The following is an example of a money purchase pension plan formula:

> The company shall contribute each plan year during which the plan is in effect on behalf of each participant an amount equal to 10 percent of compensation.

Under the formula, an equal percentage of compensation is allocated to each participant's account. The age and length of service of the participant are irrelevant for both contribution and allocation purposes, although length of service could be considered. [IRC § 411(b)(2); Treas Reg § 1.401-1(b)(1)(i)]

This concept is illustrated in the following example. The allocation in column (d) reflects a contribution formula that does not include permitted disparity. When permitted disparity is considered, differences in compensation become more relevant. See chapter 7 for more details.

L & Y Corporation
Schedule of Contributions to
Money Purchase Pension Plan
for
Plan Year Ended December 31, 1996

(a)	*(b)*	*(c)*	*(d)*
			Allocation of Company
Participant	*Age*	*Compensation*	*Contributions*
Leonard	45	$150,000	$15,000
Yvette	30	50,000	5,000
Total		$200,000	$20,000

The mere fact that a money purchase pension plan has a zero percent-of-compensation contribution formula does not prevent the plan from being a qualified retirement plan (see Qs 1:5, 1:6). An example of a "zero percent" money purchase pension plan is a plan established solely for the purpose of receiving rollover contributions or transfers from another qualified retirement plan (see Qs 28:7, 28:8). [Internal IRS Memorandum from Chief, Employee Plans Technical Branch 2 to District Director, Los Angeles Key District, Aug 10, 1995]

The requirements of a zero percent plan are:

1. Zero percent contributions by the employer;
2. A tax-exempt trust (see Q 1:6);
3. Definitely determinable benefits; and
4. Satisfaction of the nondiscrimination requirements (see Q 4:9).

These requirements are satisfied by:

1. Providing that no contribution other than employee, rollover, or transfer contributions from another qualified retirement plan will be accepted;
2. Establishing a trust consisting of transferred or rolled over contributions;
3. Maintaining separate participant rollover accounts that will provide definitely determinable benefits based upon the account balances at retirement or separation from service; and
4. Drafting a plan document that contains the form language needed to satisfy the nondiscrimination requirements and language that permits the acceptance of contributions from all employees, rather than only the highly compensated employees (see Q 3:2).

Q 2:5   What is a target benefit plan?

A target benefit plan is a hybrid or cross between a defined benefit plan (see Q 2:3) and a money purchase pension plan (see Q 2:4). It is like a defined benefit plan in that the annual contribution is determined by the amount needed each year to accumulate (at an assumed rate of interest) a fund sufficient to pay a projected retirement benefit (the target benefit) to each participant on reaching retirement age. Thus, if a target benefit plan contains a target formula, such as 40 percent of compensation, that is identical to the benefit formula in a defined benefit plan and is based on identical actuarial assumptions (e.g., interest rates, mortality, employee turnover), the employer's initial contribution for the same group of employees will be the same.

However, this is where the similarity ends. In a defined benefit plan, if the actual experience of the plan differs from the actuarial assumptions used (for example, if the interest earned is higher or lower than the assumptions), then the employer either increases or decreases its future contributions to the extent necessary to provide the promised benefits. In a target benefit plan, however, the contribution, once made, is allocated to separate accounts maintained for each participant. Thus, if the earnings of the fund differ from those assumed, this does not result in any increase or decrease in employer contributions; instead, it increases or decreases the benefits payable to the participant.

In this regard, the target benefit plan operates like a money purchase pension plan. In fact, the only difference between a money purchase pension plan and a target benefit plan is that, in a money purchase pension plan, contributions are generally determined and allocated as a percentage of current compensation; in a target benefit plan, contributions are determined as if the plan were to provide a fixed benefit. In a money purchase pension plan, contributions for identically compensated employees are the same even though their ages differ; in a target benefit plan, age is one of the factors that determines the size of the contributions. Because older employees have less time in which to have their benefits funded, employer contributions on their behalf are greater, as a percentage of compensation, than for younger employees. Consequently, target benefit plans appeal to employers that desire to benefit older employees.

Since target benefit plans are defined contribution plans, they are subject to the limit on annual additions to a participant's account (see Q 6:1).

Q 2:6 What is a profit sharing plan?

A profit sharing plan is a defined contribution plan to which the company agrees to make "substantial and recurring," though generally discretionary, contributions (see Q 1:26). Amounts contributed to the plan are invested and accumulate (tax-free) for eventual distribution to participants or their beneficiaries either at retirement, after a fixed number of years, or upon the occurrence of some specified event (e.g., disability, death, or termination of employment) (see Q 1:32).

Unlike contributions to a pension plan, contributions to a profit sharing plan are usually keyed to the existence of profits. However, neither current nor accumulated profits are required for a company to contribute to a profit sharing plan. [IRC § 401(a)(27)]

Even if the company has profits, it can generally forgo or limit its contribution for a particular year if the plan contains a discretionary formula. The following is an example of such a formula:

The company shall contribute each plan year during which the plan is in effect out of its earnings for its taxable year, or out of its accumulated earnings, an amount decided upon by the Board of Directors [or owner, partners, etc., as appropriate]. The contribution shall be allocated among the participants in the proportion that the compensation of each participant bears to the aggregate compensation of all the participants.

Under the allocation formula (the second sentence in the example), each participant receives the same percentage of the contribution as the participant's compensation bears to total compensation. The participant's length of service is irrelevant, although this factor can be considered in the allocation formula if prohibited discrimination does not result. However, note that, in a discretionary profit sharing plan, the actual amount to be allocated to each participant cannot be determined until the company decides upon its contribution for the year. [Treas Reg § 1.401-1(b)(1)(ii)]

Although many profit sharing plans adopt a discretionary contribution formula, others adopt a fixed formula. For example, a company may obligate itself to contribute to its profit sharing plan a specified percentage of each participant's compensation if profits exceed a specified level.

As with other defined contribution plans, retirement benefits in profit sharing plans are based on the amount in the participant's account at retirement. Unlike defined benefit plans, forfeitures in profit sharing plans arising from employee turnover may be reallocated among the remaining participants.

Q 2:7   What is an age-based profit sharing plan?

An age-based profit sharing plan is a profit sharing plan (see Q 2:6) that uses both age and compensation as a basis for allocating employer contributions among plan participants. This concept is similar to a target benefit plan (see Q 2:5), where age and compensation are factors used to determine the amount of the employer contribution.

All of the basic requirements that apply to regular profit sharing plans also apply to an age-based profit sharing plan. An age-based profit sharing plan can have a discretionary contribution formula and provide the employer with flexibility over the amount of the contribution to be made each year. Because age is a factor, this type of plan favors older employees who have fewer years than younger employees to accumulate sufficient funds for retirement (see Q 2:8). [Treas Reg § 1.401(a)(4)-8] For purposes of satisfying the nondiscrimination requirements, an age-based profit sharing plan is tested under the cross-testing rules (see Qs 4:10, 4:20).

Q 2:8 How does an age-based profit sharing plan benefit older employees?

The basis for allocating employer contributions under an age-based profit sharing plan is determined by calculating the present value of a straight (i.e., single) life annuity beginning at the testing age (see Q 2:9). A standard interest rate, which may not be less than 7.5 percent nor more than 8.5 percent, compounded annually, and a straight life annuity factor that is based on the same or a different standard interest rate and on a standard mortality table, must be used. [Treas Reg §§ 1.401(a)(4)-8(b)(2), 1.401(a)(4)-12]

The following is an example of an allocation formula under an age-based profit sharing plan:

The contribution shall be allocated among the participants in the proportion that the allocation factor of each participant bears to the aggregate allocation factors of all the participants. The allocation factor of a participant for the plan year shall be the product of (a) the participant's compensation for the plan year, multiplied by (b) the present value of $1.00, discounted with interest at 8.5 percent from the testing age to the participant's age as of the last day of the plan year.

The following scenario provides a practical application of this allocation formula:

Example. For 1996, Ess-UU-Kay Corporation adopts an age-based profit sharing plan with a calendar year plan year. The following six employees are eligible to participate in the plan:

Participant	Age	Compensation
A (owner)	50	$100,000
B	40	50,000
C	35	50,000
D	35	40,000
E	30	35,000
F	25	25,000
Total		$300,000

Ess-UU-Kay contributes $39,000 to the plan. The plan uses a testing age of 65. The contribution is allocated among the participants based upon each participant's allocation factor, as follows:

Participant	Present Value (PV) of $1.00	Allocation Factor (PV × Compensation)	Contribution
A	.294	29,400	$24,547
B	.130	6,500	5,427
C	.087	4,350	3,632
D	.087	3,480	2,906
E	.058	2,030	1,695
F	.038	950	793
Total		46,710	$39,000

If the contribution is allocated among the participants in proportion to compensation, A's allocation would be only $13,000 ($100,000/$300,000 × $39,000). If the allocation formula takes permitted disparity into consideration, A will receive $14,417 (see chapter 7 for details). Because A is the oldest participant, A benefits most under the age-based profit sharing plan.

In the above example, the contribution, as a percentage of compensation, is the same for C and D because their ages are the same; but A and B, who are older, receive a greater percentage, and E and F, who are younger, receive a lesser percentage. The plan can be designed to have B through F all receive the same contribution as a percentage of compensation, with A receiving a much greater percentage. See Q 4:20 for a discussion of cross-testing.

Q 2:9 What is the testing age for an age-based profit sharing plan?

The testing age is the age from which present value is calculated. If the testing age is 65, the present value of $1.00 at age 65 will be $1.00 and the present value of $1.00 at any lesser age will be a lesser amount. The standard interest rate currently used must not be less than 7.5 percent nor more than 8.5 percent, compounded annually. [Treas Reg §§ 1.401(a)(4)-8(b)(2), 1.401(a)(4)-12]

An example of a present value table is set forth below:

Present Value Table
8.5% Interest
Testing Age of 65

Age	Present Value	Age	Present Value
65	1.000	44	.180
64	.922	43	.166
63	.849	42	.153
62	.783	41	.141
61	.722	40	.130
60	.665	39	.120
59	.613	38	.111
58	.565	37	.102
57	.521	36	.094
56	.480	35	.087
55	.442	34	.080
54	.408	33	.073
53	.376	32	.068
52	.346	31	.062
51	.319	30	.058
50	.294	29	.053
49	.271	28	.049
48	.250	27	.045
47	.230	26	.042
46	.212	25	.038
45	.196		

If the testing age is 65, the factor for a 50-year-old participant is .294. The testing age is the participant's normal retirement age (see Q 10:53) under the plan if the plan provides the same uniform normal retirement age for all participants, or is age 65 if the plan does not provide a uniform normal retirement age—even if the participant is beyond the testing age. For example, if the uniform normal retirement age under the plan is 65 and Bernard is age 70, the factor used for Bernard is 1.000. [Treas Reg §§ 1.401(a)(4)-8(b)(1), 1.401(a)(4)-12]

Q 2:10 What is a new comparability plan?

A new comparability plan is generally a profit sharing plan (see Q 2:6) or a money purchase pension plan (see Q 2:4) in which the contribution percentage formula for one category of participants is greater than the contribution percentage formula for other categories of participants. As with an age-based profit sharing plan (see Q 2:7), to satisfy the nondiscrimination requirements, a new comparability plan is tested under the cross-testing rules (see Qs 4:10, 4:20).

Q 2:11 What is a thrift or savings plan?

A thrift or savings plan is a defined contribution plan in which employees are directly involved in contributing toward the ultimate benefits that will be provided. The plan can be in the form of a money purchase pension plan (see Q 2:4) or a profit sharing plan (see Q 2:6).

These plans are contributory in the sense that employer contributions on behalf of a particular employee are geared to mandatory contributions by the employee. Employees can participate in the plan only if they contribute a part of their compensation to the plan.

Employer contributions are made on a matching basis—for example, 50 percent of the contribution made by the employee. The plan may permit the employer, at its discretion, to make additional contributions and may also permit employees to make voluntary contributions.

A contributory plan must satisfy a nondiscrimination test that compares the relative contribution percentages of highly compensated employees with those of non-highly compensated employees (see Q 6:19).

Q 2:12 What is a 401(k) plan?

A 401(k) plan is a qualified profit sharing or stock bonus plan (see Qs 2:6, 2:13) that offers participants an election to receive company contributions in cash or to have these amounts contributed to the plan. A participant in a 401(k) plan does not have to include in income any company contributions to the plan merely because an election could have been made to receive cash instead. [IRC §§ 401(k)(2), 402(a)(8)]

A 401(k) plan may also be in the form of a salary reduction agreement. Under this type of arrangement, each eligible employee may elect to reduce current compensation or elect to forgo a salary increase and have these amounts contributed to the plan. [Treas Reg § 1.401(k)-1(a)(3)(i)]

Benefits attributable to employer contributions to a 401 (k) plan generally may not be distributed without penalty until the employee retires, becomes disabled, dies, or reaches age 59½. Contributions made by the employer to the plan at the employee's election are nonforfeitable (i.e., 100 percent vesting is required at all times). For a complete discussion of 401(k) plans, see chapter 23.

Q 2:13 What is a stock bonus plan?

A stock bonus plan is similar to a profit sharing plan (see Q 2:6), except that benefit payments must be made in shares of stock of the company. However, a stock bonus plan may distribute cash to a participant, subject to the participant's right to demand a distribution of employer securities. Further, if the plan permits cash distributions and the employer securities are not readily tradable on an established market, participants must be given the right to require the company to repurchase the shares of stock it distributes to them under a fair valuation formula. [IRC § 401(a)(23); Treas Reg §§ 1.401-1(a)(2)(iii), 1.401-1(b)(1)(iii)]

Q 2:14 What is an employee stock ownership plan?

An ESOP is a special type of defined contribution plan (usually profit sharing or stock bonus) that can qualify for favorable tax treatment. For a discussion on ESOPs, see chapter 24.

Q 2:15 What is a simplified employee pension?

A SEP is a defined contribution plan that takes the form of an individual retirement account (IRA) but is subject to special rules. A SEP may be adopted by both incorporated and unincorporated businesses. For a discussion on SEPs, see chapter 27.

Q 2:15A What is a savings incentive match plan for employees (SIMPLE)?

A SIMPLE plan may be adopted by small employers who do not maintain another employer-sponsored retirement plan. A SIMPLE plan may be either in the form of an IRA for each employee or part of a 401(k) plan (see Q 2:12). If established in an IRA form, a SIMPLE plan will not be subject to the nondiscrimination rules generally applicable to qualified retirement plans (including top-heavy rules), and simplified reporting requirements will apply. A SIMPLE plan may be adopted by both incorporated and unincorporated businesses. For a discussion of SIMPLE plans, see chapter 27.

Q 2:16 What is a flat benefit plan?

Under this type of defined benefit plan, the benefit for each participant depends solely on compensation. The following is a typical formula used in a flat benefit plan:

> Each participant shall be entitled to a monthly pension, commencing at normal retirement age and thereafter payable for life, of an amount equal to 30 percent of monthly compensation.

Under this formula, a participant whose monthly compensation is $2,000 would receive a monthly pension of $600; a participant whose monthly compensation is $4,000 would receive a monthly pension of twice as much (i.e., $1,200).

Q 2:17 What is a unit benefit plan?

This type of defined benefit plan recognizes service with the company by providing greater benefits for a long-service employee than for a short-term employee with the same average compensation. The following formula represents a type of unit benefit plan:

> Each participant shall be entitled to a monthly pension, commencing at normal retirement age and thereafter payable for life, of an amount equal to 1 percent of monthly compensation multiplied by the number of years of service with the company.

Under this formula, a participant with a monthly compensation of $2,000 and 30 years of employment at retirement would receive a monthly pension of $600, while a participant with the same monthly compensation but only ten years of employment would receive a monthly pension of $200.

These examples and those in Q 2:16 reflect plan formulas that do not take into consideration permitted disparity. When permitted disparity is considered, differences in compensation become more relevant. See chapter 7 for more details on this issue.

Q 2:18 How is the cost of providing benefits under a defined benefit plan determined?

The cost of funding the plan (other than a fully insured plan; see Q 2:23) is determined actuarially. An actuary (generally one enrolled under the auspices of the Joint Board for the Enrollment of Actuaries) may take into consideration many factors in determining each year's plan contribution needed to fund the benefits the plan is to provide. [IRC § 412(c)] Among the most common actuarial assumptions are the following:

- Interest
- Mortality
- Employee turnover
- Salary scale

Each individual actuarial assumption is required to be reasonable or, if not, the assumptions, in the aggregate, must result in a total contribution equivalent to that which would be determined if each assumption were reasonable. Also, the actuarial assumptions must, in combination, offer the actuary's best estimate of anticipated experience under the plan (see Q 2:3). [IRC § 412(c)(3); Citrus Valley Estates, Inc v Comm'r, 49 F 3d 1410 (9th Cir 1995); Wachtell, Lipton, Rosen & Katz v Comm'r, 26 F 3d 291 (2d Cir 1994); Vinson & Elkins v Comm'r, 7 F 3d 1235 (5th Cir 1993); Rhoades, McKee & Boer v United States, 1:91-CV-540 (WD Mich 1995); Jerome Mirza & Assocs Ltd v United States, 882 F 2d 229 (7th Cir 1989); IR 95-43 (June 7, 1995)]

Q 2:19   Must the actuarial assumptions be set forth in the plan?

The actuarial assumptions used to determine the cost of funding a defined benefit plan need not be set forth in the plan. However, the actuarial assumptions used to determine the value of a benefit (e.g., postretirement interest and mortality) must be set forth in the plan in a manner that precludes employer discretion. In other words, the lump-sum value of a participant's benefit and the present value of the monthly benefit must be the same (i.e., actuarially equivalent). If the postretirement actuarial assumptions are not specified, the benefits under the defined benefit plan are not considered to be definitely determinable (see Q 2:3). [IRC § 401(a)(25)]

Q 2:20   What is a Keogh plan?

A Keogh, or H.R. 10, plan is a qualified retirement plan maintained by a self-employed individual (see Q 6:33), either a sole proprietor or a partner. The self-employed individual may take a tax deduction for annual contributions to the plan made on behalf of the individual and on behalf of any eligible employees. A Keogh plan may be either a defined contribution plan (see Q 2:2) or a defined benefit plan (see Q 2:3).

For more details, see Qs 6:32 through 6:36.

Q 2:21 What is a floor-offset plan?

A floor-offset plan is a hybrid arrangement in which the employer maintains a defined benefit plan (see Q 2:3) and a defined contribution plan (see Q 2:2), and the benefits provided under the defined benefit plan will be reduced by the value of the participant's account in the defined contribution plan. In essence, the defined benefit plan provides a guaranteed floor benefit, but the amount is offset by the benefit provided under the defined contribution plan. [ERISA § 407(d)(9); Treas Reg § 1.401(a)(4)-8(d); Rev Rul 76-259, 1976-2 CB 111]

If the value of the participant's account in the defined contribution plan declines, the participant will be insulated from the risk of investment loss because the full amount of pension benefits will be received under the defined benefit plan. Alternatively, if the value of the participant's account exceeds the amount of the benefit under the defined benefit plan, the participant will receive benefits exclusively from the defined contribution plan. In other words, the participant has the best of both worlds: the participant is protected against any risk of adverse investment experience under the defined benefit plan and receives the favorable investment experience under the defined contribution plan.

The defined contribution plan component of this type of arrangement may be subject to certain restrictions that are not imposed on a defined contribution plan that is not part of a floor-offset arrangement (see Q 19:54).

Q 2:22 What is a cash balance plan?

A cash balance plan is a defined benefit plan (see Q 2:3), but it exhibits features of both defined benefit and defined contribution plans (see Q 2:2). The most recognizable feature of the cash balance plan is its use of a separate account for each participant. A cash balance account is established for each employee upon the employee's becoming a member of the plan. [Treas Reg § 1.401(a)(4)-8(c)(3)]

If the plan is replacing an existing defined benefit plan, employees are credited with an opening balance, typically the actuarial present value of their accrued prior plan benefits. Thereafter, the employee's cash balance account receives additional credits. These are likely to be computed as a flat percentage of the employee's pay, such as 4 percent or 5 percent. In addition, employees' balances grow based on interest credits. The rate varies from year to year and is communicated to employees before the start of the year. As an example, it might be the yield on one-year Treasury bills. The interest rate is not tied to the actual investment performance of the plan's assets and is determined independently, based on specific provisions in the plan document. The plan may also set forth a minimum and/or maximum rate; but the minimum cannot be more than the lowest standard interest rate, and the maximum cannot be less than the highest standard interest rate. [Treas Reg § 1.401(a)(4)-8(c)(3)(iv)(C), 1.401(a)(4)-12]

The amounts an employer contributes to the plan are determined actuarially to ensure sufficient funds to provide for the benefits promised by the plan. The minimum funding standards (see Q 8:1) apply to cash balance plans, as is the case with other types of defined benefit plans. [IRC § 412]

From the employee's perspective, one of the cash balance plan's advantages is that investment risks are borne by the employer as in any other defined benefit plan. This differs from a defined contribution plan.

Cash balance plans provide higher benefits for younger employees and lower benefits for older employees, in contrast to traditional defined benefit plans. However, the costs of providing these benefits are also correspondingly higher for younger employees and lower for older employees, as compared with traditional defined benefit plans.

Q 2:23 What is an insured qualified retirement plan?

An insured plan is a qualified retirement plan that is funded in whole or in part through the purchase of life insurance policies. The plan can be either split-funded or fully insured.

In a split-funded plan, there is partial funding of retirement benefits through insurance policies, with the balance of the retirement benefit coming from an investment fund. The portion of the plan's assets accumulated in the investment fund can be invested as the trustee determines.

In a fully insured plan, all company contributions are directed toward the purchase of insurance, normally in the form of retirement income policies or annuity contracts. One advantage of a fully insured plan is that the plan may qualify for an exemption from the minimum funding requirements (see Qs 8:4, 8:5).

Qualified retirement plans can be attractive vehicles for acquiring life insurance. Premiums indirectly paid by the company in the form of plan contributions are deductible. Each insured participant reports taxable income, as determined under IRS tables, representing the cost of current life insurance protection. For further details, see chapter 14.

Q 2:24 What is a custom-designed retirement plan?

A custom-designed (or individually designed) retirement plan is a plan tailored to meet the needs of the client. The custom-designed plan reflects the company's desires and needs more fully than a master or prototype (see Q 2:25) because the client has a greater variety of available options.

Q 2:25   What are master and prototype retirement plans?

A master plan is a form of retirement plan in which the funding organization (trust, custodial account, or insurer) is specified in the sponsor's application. A prototype plan is a form of retirement plan in which the funding organization is specified in the adoption agreement.

Insurance companies, mutual funds, banks, brokerage firms, and other investment management firms have created IRS-approved master and prototype plans. The client adopts the plans by executing an adoption agreement and electing certain available options. Any change in the preapproved plan provisions causes the plan to lose its master or prototype status. [Rev Proc 93-39, 1993-2 CB 513; Rev Proc 93-10, 1993-1 CB 476; Rev Proc 89-9, 1989-1 CB 780]

Q 2:26   How does a company's cash position affect its choice of a qualified retirement plan?

Because adoption of a pension plan entails a commitment to fund the plan even if the company has no profits, a company experiencing a weak cash position would be ill-advised to establish that type of plan. Generally, it does not make good sense for a company to borrow funds to meet its pension obligations. In this situation, a profit sharing plan (see Qs 2:6, 2:27) would be more appropriate.

Q 2:27   What type of retirement plan should a company adopt if profits fluctuate from year to year?

A profit sharing plan (see Qs 2:6, 2:26) is the only type of plan that can afford a company significant flexibility with respect to the contributions it makes from year to year. The typical profit sharing plan—probably most profit sharing plans maintained by small companies—specifies that the company's contribution will be determined annually by its board of directors (or owners, partners, etc., as appropriate). The amount contributed in any year may vary from zero to 15 percent of the total compensation of all plan participants.

Q 2:28   Are profit sharing plans best for small companies?

There is no general answer to this question. The decision about the type of retirement plan best suited for a small company must be made on the basis of all the facts and circumstances, including the owner's goals.

Profit sharing plans (see Q 2:6) are usually recommended for recently formed companies because no profit pattern exists (see Q 2:27). Often, both a discretionary profit sharing plan and a 10 percent money purchase pension plan (see Q 2:4) are recommended for the company. This combination permits a total contribution of 25 percent of compensation (as opposed to the 15 percent limitation for a profit sharing plan alone), but entails only a 10 percent of compensation commitment by the company, allowing some flexibility. [IRC §§ 404(a)(3)(A), 404(a)(7)]

Remember, however, that a company's size is not always a factor in choosing the best plan. In many cases, a small company may decide to maximize its tax-deductible contributions. For example, a company with an older work force that adopts a defined benefit plan increases the amount of the contribution that must be made each year to fund retirement benefits, which in turn increases the company's tax deduction (see Q 2:29).

Q 2:29   What type of qualified retirement plan is best for a company whose essential employees have reached an advanced age?

For a company whose essential employees have reached an advanced age, a defined benefit plan (see Q 2:3) is a better choice than a defined contribution plan (see Q 2:2) for the following reasons:

1. A defined contribution plan limits the company's tax-deductible contributions on behalf of each employee regardless of age. Except for a target benefit plan (see Q 2:5), an age-based profit sharing plan (see Q 2:7), and a cross-tested defined contribution plan (see Q 4:20), age is not a factor in determining the company's contribution or the allocation of the company's contribution to plan participants. Contributions on behalf of older employees are based on the same percentage of compensation as those made on behalf of younger employees. Since contributions are limited, there may not be sufficient time left before retirement to accumulate a desired amount for older employees.

2. A defined benefit plan allows a company with older essential employees to make larger contributions to accumulate sufficient funds for retirement. The limit on contributions under a defined benefit plan is the amount necessary to fund the annual pension, and this may

far exceed the allowable contribution to a defined contribution plan. [IRC §§ 404(a)(1), 415(b), 415(c)]

Q 2:30 Can the bulk of qualified retirement plan contributions and benefits be set aside for the business owner and other essential employees under the terms of the plan?

Generally, no. A qualified retirement plan may not discriminate in favor of employees who are considered highly compensated. Discrimination in favor of highly compensated employees (see Q 3:2) must be avoided in coverage, contributions, and benefits. [IRC §§ 401(a)(4), 410(b)]

An example of discrimination could be a money purchase pension plan (see Q 2:4) that provides for a contribution equal to 25 percent of compensation for highly compensated employees, but only 10 percent of compensation on behalf of all other employees. Such a plan will not qualify for tax-favored status unless it satisfies cross-testing (see Q 4:20). An important exception applies if the plan takes permitted disparity into account (see Qs 2:38, 7:1).

For details on minimum contribution and benefit requirements that may apply to the plan, see chapter 22.

Q 2:31 May a qualified retirement plan lose its tax-favored status if only the business owner and other essential employees will receive benefits?

Even if the plan is not discriminatory as it is written (see Q 4:1), the operation of the plan can result in discrimination, and the plan may lose its tax-favored status.

Example. A plan covers all employees and provides a schedule for the vesting of benefits that meets the requirements of the Code (see Q 9:3). If the only employees attaining vested benefits are the business's highly compensated employees (because rank-and-file workers leave before they have enough years of service to earn vested benefits, for example), the plan—in actual operation—may discriminate in favor of the highly compensated employees and may lose its tax-favored status (see Q 2:37). [Rev Rul 66-251, 1966-2 CB 121]

In one case, IRS denied tax-favored status to a profit sharing plan because the rapid rate of turnover among lower-paid employees caused the bulk of the benefits to go to the business owner and the essential employees. However, IRS was rebuffed by the court. The court found that, if there was any discrimination in the operation of the plan, it was in favor of permanent employees and against transient employees, not in favor of the highly compensated employees and against rank-and-file employees. This type of discrimination is not prohibited. [Lansons, Inc, 69 TC 773 (1978), *aff'd*, 622 F 2d 774 (5th Cir 1980)]

On the other hand, if discrimination in benefits results from a pattern of abuse by the business owner—for example, if rank-and-file employees are fired before their benefits become nonforfeitable—the plan is likely to lose its tax-favored status. [IRC § 411(d)(1)(A)]

Q 2:32 How much can a business owner contribute to the qualified retirement plan?

It depends on the type of retirement plan the business owner adopts. If either a single defined contribution plan (see Q 2:2) or a combination of defined contribution plans is adopted, the annual addition (see Q 6:1) to the business owner's account during any year may not exceed the lesser of (1) $30,000 (with adjustments for inflation) or (2) 25 percent of compensation. [IRC § 415(c)]

The maximum annual benefit that may be provided to a participating business owner under a defined benefit plan (see Q 2:3) is the lesser of (1) $90,000 (with adjustments for inflation) or (2) 100 percent of the business owner's average compensation for the highest three consecutive years. [IRC § 415(b)]

Bear in mind that, under a defined benefit plan, the limitation is placed on the annual benefit payable, not the annual contribution necessary to fund the benefit. The annual contribution is determined actuarially, based on the business owner's age and anticipated annual benefit, the plan's normal retirement age, the form of benefit payable, and the actuarial assumptions used (see Qs 2:18, 2:36).

For a discussion of the limitations on contributions and benefits, see chapter 6.

Q 2:33 Is there any limit on tax-deductible contributions to a qualified retirement plan by a corporation?

Yes. Compensation paid to any employee is tax-deductible by the corporation only if the amount paid is reasonable. In determining reasonableness, all forms of compensation are considered, including contributions to the corporation's qualified retirement plan. Whether a particular business owner's compensation is reasonable is a question of fact in each case (see Q 12:1). [IRC §§ 162, 404; Treas Reg § 1.404(a)-1(b)]

For a discussion on the limits of tax-deductible contributions, see chapter 12.

Q 2:34   What type of qualified retirement plan should the business owner install?

From a business viewpoint, it depends initially on the business owner's objectives. The plan may be used to achieve one or more of the following:

1. Building a tax-sheltered retirement fund for the business owner and essential employees;

2. Recruiting essential employees from competitors;

3. Reducing employee turnover; and

4. Establishing a market for the corporate business owner's shares of stock in a closely held corporation.

Another consideration is the ability of the business to support the retirement plan. In choosing a plan, the business owner must decide what contributions the business can afford to make.

From a personal viewpoint, the business owner's objectives must be ascertained. These may include one or more of the following:

- Maximizing retirement benefits
- Maximizing contributions made on the owner's behalf
- Having flexibility with regard to annual contributions

If the business owner wants to maximize retirement benefits (the amount available at retirement), the owner's age may be the key factor in determining what type of plan to adopt. A younger business owner may accumulate the most dollars for retirement using a defined contribution plan (see Q 2:2); older business owners may do better using a defined benefit plan (see Q 2:3).

Similarly, if maximizing contributions is the goal, the older business owner can accomplish that by using a defined benefit plan; the younger business owner might do better using a defined contribution plan, although a defined benefit plan could also accomplish the objective.

If flexibility is the goal, a profit sharing plan (see Qs 2:6, 2:27) should be considered. This type of defined contribution plan gives the business owner control over the amount of annual contributions. Although a profit sharing plan generally reduces the maximum amount that may be contributed on behalf of the business owner, it can be combined with a money purchase pension plan to afford the business owner the opportunity to make larger contributions.

Other factors, however, may influence the business owner's decision. For example, how much will it cost to cover the employees? This will depend on how many of them must be covered, their compensation, and their ages. If the business owner's goals would be achieved using a defined benefit plan, but the cost of funding benefits for employees who are older than the business owner is substantial, it may be necessary to modify the objectives and use a defined contribution plan. But, if the employees are younger than the business owner, a defined benefit plan may be better than a defined contribution plan. In either situation, taking permitted disparity into consideration in designing the plan (see Qs 2:38, 7:1) may cut the cost of covering the business owner's employees and enable the objectives to be accomplished.

The older business owner may both maximize contributions and retain flexibility over the amount of annual contributions by adopting an age-based profit sharing plan (see Q 2:7).

Q 2:35 What type of qualified retirement plan (or plans) should a business owner use to maximize retirement benefits?

There is no one answer. The age of the business owner and the expected rate of return on the plan's investments, however, are the key factors in determining what type of qualified retirement plan will provide the most at retirement.

In a defined benefit plan (see Q 2:3), the actuary first determines the amount needed at retirement to pay the business owner's annual benefit as set by a formula in the plan. The actuary then determines the amount that must be contributed to the plan each year to reach the amount needed at retirement. The actuary uses various factors to compute the annual contribution, including an interest factor (the rate of return on plan investments). This interest factor is usually conservative, even when market rates are greater (see Qs 2:18, 8:8).

Investment gains and losses affect the amount of each year's contribution. Thus, if the interest assumption is 6 percent and the investment return is 9 percent, the investment gain reduces the business owner's future contributions. If the investment return is only 4 percent, the investment loss increases the subsequent contributions. Whether or not the interest assumption holds true, the annual adjustment in required contributions does not affect the final result—the amount in the plan at retirement. If the business owner's compensation remained constant over the period of participation, the amount available at the end would be known at the beginning.

In a defined contribution plan, generally, no actuarial calculations are made and no interest factor is assumed (see Q 2:2). The annual contribution is generally determined by multiplying the business owner's compensation for the year by the contribution percentage established in the plan. Gains from the investment of plan assets inure to the business owner's benefit, and losses are absorbed to the owner's detriment. Thus, if compensation stays constant, under a money purchase pension plan (see Q 2:4), the business owner will know the annual contribution, but not how much will be available at retirement. That will depend on the investment performance.

> **Example.** Matthew, a business owner aged 45, will retire at age 65 and has $30,000 a year to contribute to the qualified retirement plan. Under a defined contribution plan that provides for a $30,000 annual contribution, Matthew will have at retirement $600,000 plus the actual earnings or minus the actual losses on the plan's investments. Thus, if Matthew thinks the plan can realize a return on its investments greater than the interest assumption, the defined contribution plan may be preferable to the defined benefit plan.

In this example, the business owner's age had no bearing on the final result. If, under the defined contribution plan, the maximum contribution is $30,000 and, under the defined benefit plan, the amount that could be contributed is $50,000, the business owner would have more available at retirement under the defined benefit plan (unless the defined contribution plan's investment return was very high). If the business owner is age 35 at the time the plan is adopted, the extra ten years of compounded earnings—assuming a better-than-average return—may make the defined contribution plan a better choice.

Q 2:36 How can the use of a normal retirement age earlier than 65 benefit the business owner?

In a defined benefit plan, using a retirement age earlier than 65 may substantially increase the amount of contributions that must be made each year to fund the retirement benefits, which, in turn, increases the business owner's tax deduction. This is because there are fewer years in which to fund the retirement benefits.

There are several obstacles that must be overcome to take advantage of this planning opportunity. First, IRS says that a retirement age earlier than 65 can be used as a basis for computing required contributions only if the lower age approximates the age at which company employees customarily retire. [Rev Rul 78-331, 1978-2 CB 158; Rev Rul 78-120, 1978-1 CB 117; Ltr Ruls 8610002, 8552001]

Second, because the defined benefit plan will require larger contributions, the company will have to produce a higher cash flow to fund the plan. If it cannot meet the increased funding required, it may be subject to a penalty tax (see Q 8:18).

Finally, the business owner must be able to show that the total compensation package, salary plus retirement plan contributions made on the business owner's behalf, is reasonable (see Qs 2:33, 12:1).

The IRS position regarding the use of a normal retirement age earlier than 65 is that an actuarial assumption that employees retire at a normal retirement age that ignores the actual incidence of retirement in the work force could cause the assumptions to be unreasonable and the contributions not to be currently deductible. Assumptions should be monitored and adjusted accordingly to reflect current experience. The analysis for funding purposes is based on an assumption of the age at which retirement is most likely to take place, a determination of probability that is derived from the average retirement age of the group. [Ltr Rul 8808005; Rev Rul 78-331, 1978-2 CB 158; also see Jerome Mirza & Assocs, Ltd v United States, 882 F 2d 229 (7th Cir 1989)]

In more recent years, however, courts have concluded that, since the assumptions used were not "substantially unreasonable" and represented the actuary's best estimate of anticipated experience under the plans based on actuarial assumptions used by similar plans, IRS was precluded from requiring a retroactive change of assumptions. [Citrus Valley Estates, Inc v Comm'r, 49 F 3d 1410 (9th Cir 1995); Wachtell, Lipton, Rosen & Katz v Comm'r, 26 F 3d 291 (2d Cir 1994); Vinson & Elkins v Comm'r, 7 F 3d 1235 (5th Cir 1993); IR 95-43 (June 7, 1995); but see Rhoades, McKee & Boer v United States, 1:91-CV-540 (WD Mich 1995)] For a discussion of these cases, see Q 8:8.

Q 2:37 How can an ESOP or a stock bonus plan benefit a corporation and its shareholders?

An ESOP (see Q 2:14) or a stock bonus plan (see Q 2:13), like all other qualified retirement plans, must be organized and operated for the exclusive benefit of the employees or their beneficiaries. This does not mean that the company and its shareholders cannot also derive a benefit from the plan. In fact, an ESOP or a stock bonus plan can benefit the company and its shareholders by:

1. Providing a market for the owner's closely held shares of stock as a tax-favored alternative to a stock redemption;
2. Giving the company tax deductions without affecting its cash flow; and
3. Keeping company stock in what is generally considered friendly hands in the event of a hostile takeover of the company.

See chapter 24 for more details.

Q 2:38 Can the company take Social Security wage tax payments or benefits into consideration in its qualified retirement plan?

Yes. The company can combine (integrate) its qualified retirement plan with Social Security and thereby reduce the cost of maintaining its plan. This is referred to as permitted disparity.

Taking permitted disparity into consideration can help business owners reach what may be their primary goal in setting up a retirement plan: rewarding themselves and their essential employees. By designing the retirement plan with permitted disparity, the business owners can give proportionately greater benefits or make proportionately greater contributions to the plan on their behalf than they do for rank-and-file workers. A qualified retirement plan that covers self-employed individuals (see Q 6:33) may consider permitted disparity in the same way that a corporate qualified retirement plan may.

For details on how permitted disparity works, see chapter 7.

Q 2:39 After an employer has chosen a type of qualified retirement plan, what options are available?

After the employer has determined the most suitable qualified retirement plan, consideration must be given to the actual plan provisions. Among the employer's choices are the following:

1. Eligibility requirements (see chapter 5), including:
   a. Length of service (Q 5:2)
   b. Minimum age (Q 5:2)
   c. Exclusion of union employees (Q 5:5)
   d. Other classification exclusions (Q 5:18)
2. Contributions or benefits, including:

   a. Defined contribution plan formula
   b. Defined benefit plan formula
   c. Permitted disparity (i.e., integration with Social Security) (Q 7:1)
   d. Voluntary contributions (Q 6:20)
   e. Mandatory contributions (Q 6:19)
   f. Minimum benefits or contributions (Qs 22:37, 22:43)
   g. 401(k) features (Q 23:1)
3. Vesting (see chapter 9), including:
   a. Cliff vesting
   b. Graded vesting
   c. Full and immediate vesting
   d. Top-heavy vesting (Q 22:32)
4. Investment provisions (see chapter 19), including:
   a. Participant-directed accounts
   b. Insurance benefits (Q 14:2)
5. Methods of payment of benefits (see chapters 10 and 13), including:
   a. Lump-sum distributions
   b. Annuities
   c. Installment distributions
   d. Hardship distributions (Qs 1:32, 23:34)
6. Miscellaneous provisions, including:
   a. Designation of plan administrator (Q 16:1)
   b. Definition of compensation (Q 6:37)
   c. Choice of plan year
   d. Normal retirement age (Q 10:53)
   e. Rollover provision (Q 28:6)
   f. Death benefits
   g. Loan provisions (Qs 13:44–13:52)

Chapter 3

Highly Compensated Employees

One of the most important terms in the Code is highly compensated employee. The definition of this term is incorporated in many of the nondiscrimination requirements applicable to qualified retirement plans, and is also incorporated in other Code provisions relating to the qualified retirement plan area. The definition of highly compensated employee has been simplified for years beginning after 1996. This chapter analyzes which employees are considered highly compensated.

Q 3:1 To what qualified retirement plan provisions does the definition of highly compensated employee apply?

The term "highly compensated employee" is relevant in determining if a plan satisfies the general nondiscrimination requirements that apply to all qualified retirement plans (see Q 4:9), the actual deferral percentage test applicable to 401(k) plans (see Q 23:8), the actual contribution percentage test applicable to employer matching contributions and employee contributions (see Q 23:48), certain requirements applicable to SEPs (see Q 27:3), the minimum coverage requirements (see Qs 5:16, 5:17), and the minimum vesting standards (see Q 9:5). The definition also applies in determining if an organization is a member of an affiliated service group (see Q 5:37) and if a loan is exempt from the tax on prohibited transactions (see Q 13:48). [IRC §§ 401(a)(4), 401(a)(5), 401(k)(3), 401(m), 408(k), 410(b)(1), 411(d)(1), 414(m), 414(q), 4975(d); Temp Reg § 1.414(q)-1T, Q&A 1(b)(1)]

The definition of highly compensated employee is applicable *only* to those qualified retirement plan provisions that incorporate the definition by reference, and the definition does *not* apply to provisions that do not incorporate it. For example, the definition of highly compensated employee generally has no application to the limitation on plan contributions and benefits (see chapter 6). [IRC § 415; Temp Reg § 1.414(q)-1T, Q&A 1(a) and (b)(2)]

Q 3:2   Who is a highly compensated employee?

Highly compensated employees are divided into two groups: highly compensated active employees (see Q 3:3) and highly compensated former employees (see Q 3:12). In certain circumstances, highly compensated active employees and highly compensated former employees are considered separately in applying the provisions for which the definition of highly compensated employee is applicable (see Q 4:19). [IRC § 414(q); Temp Reg § 1.414(q)-1(T), Q&A 2]

Q 3:3   Who is a highly compensated active employee?

For years beginning before 1997, to determine if an employee is a highly compensated active employee for the determination year, two calculations are required: the look-back year calculation and the determination year calculation (see Q 3:11).

For the *look-back* year calculation, a highly compensated active employee is an employee who performs services for the employer (see Q 3:10) during the determination year, and who during the look-back year:

1. Was a 5 percent owner of the employer (see Q 3:4);
2. Received compensation from the employer of more than $75,000 (see Qs 3:8, 3:9);
3. Received compensation from the employer of more than $50,000 (see Qs 3:8, 3:9) and was a member of the top-paid group (see Q 3:5) of employees; or
4. Was an officer (see Q 3:6) of the employer who received compensation of more than $45,000 (one-half of the defined benefit plan maximum dollar amount; see Qs 3:8, 3:9, 6:8).

For the *determination* year calculation, an employee is a highly compensated active employee only if, during the determination year, the employee is either (a) a 5 percent owner, or (b) both described in paragraph 2, 3, or 4 above (substituting determination year for look-back year) *and* one of the 100 employees paid the most compensation.

[IRC §§ 414(q)(1), 414(q)(2), prior to amendment by SBA '96 § 1431; Temp Reg § 1.414(q)-1T, Q&A 3(a)]

Example 1. During the years specified below, Jack, who commenced employment with the employer in 1992, was not a 5 percent owner, an officer, or one of the top 100 paid employees; but, during each year, Jack was a member of the top-paid group. For the purpose of this example, the dollar amounts in paragraphs 2, 3, and 4 above are not increased for inflation. For each of the following years, Jack is included in, or excluded from, the highly compensated group as specified below:

Year	Compensation	Status
1992	$45,000	Excluded
1993	80,000	Excluded
1994	80,000	Included
1995	45,000	Included
1996	45,000	Excluded

For 1992, Jack was excluded because he was not in any of the applicable categories (i.e., paragraphs 1 through 4 above) during the look-back year (1991); for 1993, Jack was excluded because he was not within any of the applicable categories for the look-back year (1992); for 1994, Jack was included because he was described in paragraphs 2 and 3 for the look-back year (1993); for 1995, Jack was included again because he was described in paragraphs 2 and 3 for the look-back year (1994); but, for 1996, Jack again became excluded because he was not in any of the applicable categories for the look-back year (1995).

Example 2. The facts are the same as in Example 1, except that Jack was one of the top 100 paid employees in 1993 and 1996. For 1993, Jack is included because he was described in paragraphs 2 and 3 for the determination year (1993) and was one of the top 100 paid employees that year. In 1996, even though Jack was in the top 100 that year, he would still be excluded because he was not described in paragraph 2, 3, or 4 for the look-back year (1995) or the determination year (1996).

[Temp Reg § 1.414(q)-1T, Q&A 3(e)]

An employer may substantiate compliance with the nondiscrimination requirements (see Q 4:9) on the basis of snapshot testing, that is, on the basis of the employer's work force on a single day during the plan year (the "snapshot day"), provided that day is reasonably representative of the employer's work force and the plan's coverage throughout the year. The snapshot day selected generally must be consistent from year to year. IRS has established a simplified method of determining highly compensated employees for purposes of testing for compliance with the nondiscrimination requirements. An employer that uses this simplified method may choose also to apply the method on the basis of the employer's work force as of a snapshot day and use reasonably approximated or projected compensation as part of the simplified method of determining highly compensated employees. [Rev Proc 93-42, 1993-2 CB 540]

IRS has provided model language to enable plan sponsors to use the simplified method. The model language contains two options for sponsors electing to use the simplified method of determining highly compensated employees. Option 1 provides model language for sponsors that choose to apply this simplified method on the basis of the employer's work force as of a snapshot day. If option 1 is selected, the particular snapshot day must be specified and be reasonably representative of the employer's work force and the plan's coverage throughout the plan year. Option 2 may be used by sponsors that are not applying this simplified method on the basis of a snapshot day. Neither option permits the use of reasonably approximated or projected compensation as part of the simplified method of determining highly compensated employees. [Rev Proc 95-34, 1995-29 IRB 7]

For years beginning after 1996, to determine if an employee is a highly compensated active employee for the determination year, two calculations are still required: the look-back year calculation and the determination year calculation.

For the *look-back* year calculation, a highly compensated active employee is an employee who performs services for the employer during the determination year, and who during the look-back year:

1. Was a 5 percent owner of the employer; or
2. Received compensation from the employer of more than $80,000 and, if the employer elects, was a member of the top-paid group of employees.

For the *determination* year calculation, an employee is a highly compensated active employee only if, during the determination year, the employee is a 5 percent owner.

[IRC § 414(q)(1), as amended by SBA '96 § 1431]

Depending on employee demographics, an employer's election to use membership in the top-paid group may allow an employer to include fewer employees in the highly compensated employee group. As a result, employees who earn more than $80,000 may be in the non-highly compensated employee group, increasing the plan's chances of passing the nondiscrimination test. For example, if 30 percent of the employees, including 5 percent owners, earn more than $80,000, this election will limit the highly compensated employee group to 20 percent of the employer's employees. For the purpose of determining whether an employee is a highly compensated employee in *1997*, the amendments are treated as having been in effect in *1996*. [SBA '96, Act § 1431(d)(1)]

Q 3:4   Who is a 5 percent owner?

An employee is a 5 percent owner of the employer for the determination or look-back year (see Q 3:11) if, at any time during the year, the employee is a 5 percent owner for top-heavy plan purposes (see Q 22:28). [IRC §§ 414(q)(2), as amended by SBA '96 § 1431, 416(i)(1)(B)(i)]

If the employer is not a corporation, the ownership test is applied to the person's capital or profits interest in the employer. In determining ownership percentages, each employer, whether related or unrelated (see Q 5:31), is treated as a separate entity. For example, an individual who is a 5 percent owner of a subsidiary corporation that is part of a controlled group of corporations (see Q 5:33) is treated as a 5 percent owner for purposes of determining which employees are highly compensated employees (see Q 3:2). [Temp Reg § 1.414(q)-1T, Q&A 8]

Q 3:5   What is the top-paid group?

For years beginning before 1997, an employee is in the top-paid group of employees for the determination or look-back year (see Q 3:11) if the employee is in the group consisting of the top 20 percent of the employer's employees when ranked on the basis of compensation (see Q 3:8) received from the employer (see Q 3:10) during the year. The identification of the employees who are in the top-paid group for a year involves a two-step procedure:

1. The determination of the number of employees that corresponds to 20 percent of the employer's employees; and

2. The identification of the employees who are among the number of employees who receive the most compensation during the year.

Employees who perform no services for the employer during the year are not included in making either of these determinations. [IRC § 414(q)(4), prior to amendment by SBA '96 § 1431; Temp Reg § 1.414(q)-1T, Q&A 9(a)]

For years beginning after 1996, the same two-step procedure is used, but is applied only for the look-back year; the determination year is no longer relevant for this calculation. In addition, use of the top-paid group determination is elective by the employer (see Q 3:4). [IRC §§ 414(q)(1), 414(q)(3), as amended by SBA '96 § 1431]

For purposes of determining the number of employees in the top-paid group for a year, the following employees are excluded:

1. Employees who have not completed six months of service by the end of the year;

2. Employees who normally work less than $17\frac{1}{2}$ hours per week during the year;

3. Employees who normally work six months or less during any year;

4. Employees who are not age 21 by the end of the year; and

5. Certain nonresident aliens.

Union employees (see Qs 1:28, 4:5) are excluded only if they constitute 90 percent of the employer's work force and the retirement plan covers only nonunion employees. Including union employees has the effect of expanding the number of employees in the top-paid group. [IRC §§ 414(q)(5), 414(q)(8), as amended by SBA '96 § 1431]; Temp Reg § 1.414(q)-1T, Q&A 9(b)(1)]

The employer may elect to reduce the period of service or lower the age specified above, including a zero service or age requirement, provided the election applies to all plans of the employer. [IRC § 414(q)(5), as amended by SBA '96 § 1431; Temp Reg. § 1.414(q)-1T, Q&A 9(b)(2)]

Q 3:6   Who is an officer?

For years beginning after 1996, the determination as to who is an officer of the employer is not relevant because an officer is no longer, *per se,* a highly compensated employee (see Q 3:3). Furthermore, for determining who is a highly compensated employee in 1997, the fact that an employee was an officer in 1996 is not relevant because, for the purposes of determining whether an employee is a highly compensated employee in 1997, the amendments are treated as having been in effect in 1996. [IRC § 414 (q)(1), as amended by SBA '96 § 1431; SBA '96, Act § 1431(d)(1)]

For years beginning before 1997, if necessary, to determine if an employee is an officer of the employer for highly compensated employee purposes, the same general test used in determining who is an officer for top-heavy plan purposes is applied (see Q 22:25). [IRC § 414(q)(1)(D), prior to amendment by SBA '96 § 1431; Temp Reg § 1.414(q)-1T, Q&A 10(a)]

For an officer to be a member of the group of highly compensated employees, the officer must receive compensation (see Q 3:8) during the determination year or look-back year (see Q 3:11) that is more than one-half of the defined benefit plan maximum dollar amount (see Qs 3:9, 6:8). If no officer satisfies the compensation requirement, the highest paid officer for the year is treated as a highly compensated employee by reason of being an officer without regard to the amount of compensation. This is true whether or not the employee is also a highly compensated employee on any other basis. For example, if no officer of the employer meets the compensation requirement and an employee is both the highest paid officer and a 5 percent owner (see Qs 3:3, 3:4), the employee is treated as an includible officer for this minimum inclusion rule. [IRC § 414(q)(5)(B), prior to amendment by SBA '96 § 1431; Temp Reg § 1.414(q)-1T, Q&A 10(a) and (c)]

The number of employees that can be considered officers is equal to 10 percent of all employees, or three, whichever is greater. In no case, however, can the total number of officers exceed 50. Thus, if the employer has fewer than 30 employees, no more than three can be considered officers. [IRC § 414(q)(5)(A), prior to amendment by SBA '96 § 1431; Temp Reg § 1.414(q)-1T, Q&A 10(b)]

Q 3:7   Can an employee be described in more than one highly compensated employee category?

Yes. An individual who is a highly compensated active employee (see Q 3:3) for a determination year (see Q 3:11) by reason of being described in one category, during either the look-back year or the determination year (see Q 3:11), is not disregarded in determining whether another individual is a highly compensated active employee by reason of being described in another category. An individual who is a highly compensated active employee for a determination year by reason of being a 5 percent owner (see Q 3:4) during that year, and who receives compensation in excess of $50,000 (see Qs 3:8, 3:9) during both the look-back year and the determination year, is taken into account in determining the group of employees who are highly compensated active employees for the determination year by reason of (1) receiving more than $50,000 and (2) being in the top-paid group (see Q 3:5) during either or both the look-back year or the determination year. [Temp Reg § 1.414(q)-1T, Q&A 3(d)]

> **Example.** Elaine is the sole shareholder and officer of The Pearlmans of Wisdom, Inc. and, in 1996, earns $150,000. There are nine other employees, and the two next highly compensated are Fred ($95,000) and Tami ($70,000). Even though Elaine is a highly compensated active employee by reason of being a 5 percent owner, she is not disregarded for purposes of determining the top-paid group. Consequently, Tami is not a highly compensated active employee even though she earns more than $50,000 (adjusted for inflation) because she is not in the top-paid group.

This same rule should continue to apply for years beginning after 1996; however, the determination need be made only for the look-back year.

Q 3:8 How is compensation defined for purposes of determining who is a highly compensated employee?

The definition of compensation is the same as is used for purposes of the annual addition limitation applicable to defined contribution plans (see Q 6:3). However, in addition, elective or salary reduction contributions to a 401(k) plan (see Q 23:13), a cafeteria plan, a simplified employee pension (SEP; see Q 27:1), or a tax-sheltered annuity (see Q 29:1) are included. Only compensation received by an employee during the determination year or during the look-back year (see Q 3:11) is considered in determining whether the employee is a highly compensated employee under either the look-back year calculation or the determination year calculation (see Q 3:3). Compensation is not annualized for purposes of determining an employee's compensation in the determination year or the look-back year. [IRC § 414(q)(7), prior to amendment by SBA '96 § 1431; Temp Reg § 1.414(q)-1T, Q&A 13]

Example. Janeth earns $6,000 a month and is employed for five months during 1996. Janeth's compensation for 1996 is $30,000 and not $72,000 ($6,000 × 12).

For years beginning after 1997, the calculation of compensation is relevant only for the look-back year (see Q 3:3).

Q 3:9 Are the highly compensated employee dollar thresholds adjusted for inflation?

Yes. *For years beginning before 1997*, the dollar amounts in paragraphs 2, 3, and 4 of Q 3:3 are adjusted for inflation. The first adjustment occurred in 1988, and the adjusted amounts for the last five years are:

Year	Paragraph 2 Amount	Paragraph 3 Amount	Paragraph 4 Amount
1996	$100,000	$66,000	$60,000
1995	100,000	66,000	60,000
1994	99,000	66,000	59,400
1993	96,368	64,245	57,821
1992	93,518	62,345	56,111

[Notice 95-55, 1995-45 IRB 11; IRC § 414(q)(1), prior to amendment by SBA '96 § 1431; Temp Reg § 1.414(q)-1T, Q&A 3(c)(1)]

The applicable dollar amount for a determination year or look-back year (see Q 3:11) is the dollar amount for the calendar year in which the determination year or look-back year begins. The dollar amount for purposes of determining the highly compensated active employees (see Q 3:3) for a particular look-back year is based on the calendar year in which this look-back year begins, not the calendar year in which the look-back year ends or in which the determination year with respect to that look-back year begins. [Temp Reg § 1.414(q)-1T, Q&A 3(c)(2)]

The paragraph 2 and paragraph 3 dollar amounts are adjusted for inflation at the same time and in the same manner as under Section 415(d) (see Qs 6:2, 6:8). However, an adjustment is made only if it is $5,000 or greater and then is made in multiples of $5,000 (i.e., rounded down to the next lowest multiple of $5,000). For example, an increase in the cost-of-living of $4,999 will result in no adjustment, and an increase of $9,999 will create an upward adjustment of $5,000. Therefore, for the paragraph 2 dollar amount to increase, the cost-of-living must increase by 5 percent before the first adjustment to that amount will occur (5% × $100,000 = $5,000). For the paragraph 3 dollar amount to increase, the cost-of-living must increase by almost 7.6 percent (7.6% × $66,000 = $5,016). The paragraph 4 dollar amount is equal to one-half of the defined benefit plan maximum dollar amount (see Qs 3:3, 3:9, 6:8), which is also subject to the new $5,000 adjustment rule. Consequently, the paragraph 4 dollar amount will increase in multiples of $2,500. The effect of these new rules retarding upward adjustments will be to increase the number of employees falling within the highly compensated category. Although an increase in the dollar limit can be abrogated (see Q 6:25), the dollar limit cannot be reduced below the 1994 amounts. [IRC § 415(d); RPA '94, Act § 732(e)(2)]

For years beginning after 1997, the $80,000 compensation amount (see Q 3:3) will be adjusted for inflation in the same manner, and the first adjustment may occur in 1998 if the adjustment is at least $5,000. [IRC § 414(q)(1), as amended by SBA '96 § 1431]

Q 3:10 Who is the employer for purposes of determining highly compensated employees?

The employer is the entity employing the employees and includes all other entities aggregated with the employing entity under the aggregation rules. The following entities must be treated as a single employer for purposes of determining the employees who are highly compensated employees (see Q 3:2):

1. All corporations that are members of a controlled group of corporations that includes the employing entity (see Q 5:33). [IRC § 414(b)]

2. All trades or businesses (whether or not incorporated) that are under common control that includes the employing entity (see Q 5:31). [IRC § 414(c)]

3. All organizations (whether or not incorporated) that are members of an affiliated service group that includes the employing entity (see Q 5:37). [IRC § 414(m)]

4. Any other entities required to be aggregated with the employing entity pursuant to Section 414(o). [IRC § 414(q)(7), as amended by SBA '96 § 1431; Temp Reg § 1.414(q)-1T, Q&A 6(a)]

The separate lines of business rules (see Q 5:46) do not apply in determining the group of highly compensated employees; an employer with separate lines of business is still treated as a single employer. [IRC § 414(r); Temp Reg § 1.414(q)-1T, Q&A 6(c)]

Q 3:11   What are the determination year and the look-back year?

The determination year is generally the plan year, and the look-back year is the 12-month period immediately preceding the determination year. [Temp Reg § 1.414(q)-1T, Q&A 14]

Example. The Rube Corporation has two qualified retirement plans, Plan R and Plan J. If Plan R has a calendar year plan year and Plan J has a July 1 to June 30 plan year, the determination year calculation and the look-back year calculation for Plan R are made on the basis of the calendar year, and the determination year calculation and the look-back year calculation for Plan J are made on the basis of the July 1 to June 30 year.

Q 3:12   Who is a highly compensated former employee?

A highly compensated former employee for a determination year (see Q 3:11) is a former employee who had a separation year prior to the determination year and was a highly compensated active employee (see Q 3:3) for either (1) the employee's separation year or (2) any determination year ending on or after the employee's 55th birthday. The separation year generally is the determination year during which the employee separates from service with the employer. For example, an employee who is a highly compensated active employee for the employee's separation year is a highly compensated former employee for determination years after the separation year. Under an alternative rule, the employer may elect to include as a highly compensated former employee any former employee who separated from service prior to 1987 and was either a 5 percent owner (see Q 3:4) or received compensation (see Q 3:8) in excess of $50,000 in the year of separation or any determination year ending on or after the employee attained age 55. [IRC § 414(q)(6), as amended by SBA '96 § 1431; Temp Reg §§ 1.414(q)-1T, Q&A 4(a), Q&A 4(d), and Q&A 5]

The term "highly compensated former employee" is relevant only if a provision of the Code makes a specific reference to the term (see Q 4:19). [Temp Reg § 1.414(q)-1T, Q&A 4(e)(1)]

Q 3:13   Who is a non-highly compensated employee?

A non-highly compensated employee is any employee who is not a highly compensated employee (see Q 3:2). Therefore, a non-highly compensated active employee is an employee who is not a highly compensated active employee (see Q 3:3), and a non-highly compensated former employee is an employee who is not a highly compensated former employee (see Q 3:12).

Q 3:14   Does a family aggregation rule apply?

Yes, *but only for the years beginning before 1997.* If an individual, during the determination year or look-back year (see Q 3:11), is a member of the family of either (1) a 5 percent owner (see Q 3:4) who is an active or former employee, or (2) a highly compensated employee (see Q 3:2) who is one of the ten most highly compensated employees, the individual is not considered a separate employee and any compensation paid to such individual (and any plan contribution or benefit of such individual) is treated as if it were paid to the 5 percent owner or highly compensated employee. [IRC §§ 414(q)(6)(A), 414(q)(6)(C), prior to repeal by SBA '96 § 1431; Temp Reg § 1.414(q)-1T, Q&A 11(a)]

The determinations of which employees are highly compensated employees, which highly compensated employees are among the ten most highly compensated employees, the number and identity of employees in the top-paid group (see Q 3:5), and the identity of individuals in the top 100 (see Q 3:3) employees are made prior to the application of the family aggregation rule. [Temp Reg § 1.414(q)-1T, Q&A 11(c)]

Individuals who are family members include the employee's spouse and lineal ascendants or descendants and the spouses of such lineal ascendants and descendants. If an individual is a family member on any day during the year, the individual is treated as a family member for the entire year so that, if an individual is a family member on the first day of a year, the individual continues to be a family member throughout the year even if the relationship changes as a result of death or divorce. [IRC § 414(q)(6)(B), prior to repeal by SBA '96 § 1431; Temp Reg § 1.414(q)-1T, Q&A 12]

Example. Irv is the sole shareholder and an employee of Le Group Singer, Inc. Among its other employees are his wife, Iris, and his children, Adam, Jonathan, and Jennifer. Irv and his four family members are treated as a single employee.

For years beginning after 1996, the family aggregation rule is repealed. [SBA '96, Act § 1431(b)(1)]

Chapter 4

Requirements for Qualification

A company's retirement plan will receive favorable tax treatment only if the plan is qualified. The Code sets out a host of requirements that a retirement plan must meet in order to qualify. This chapter analyzes those requirements.

Q 4:1 What basic requirements must all retirement plans meet to qualify for favorable tax treatment?

The four fundamental requirements for a qualified retirement plan are the following:

1. The plan must be a definite written program.
2. The plan must be communicated to the employees.
3. The plan must be permanent.
4. The plan must prohibit the use or diversion of funds for purposes other than the exclusive benefit of employees or their beneficiaries.

[IRC §§ 401(a)(1), 401(a)(2); Treas Reg §§ 1.401-1, 1.401-2]

When a retirement plan made 22 unsecured loans, representing 75 percent of plan assets, to the sole shareholder of the employer and the sole trustee of the plan over a two-year period, IRS ruled that the loans violated the exclusive benefit rule. [Ltr Rul 9145006] The exclusive benefit rule was also violated when the plan functioned as a bank for the sole shareholder. [Ada Orthopedic, Inc, 68 TCM 1392 (1994)] IRS has also ruled that an ESOP (see Q 24:1) that permits a trustee to consider *nonfinancial* employment-related factors, such as continuing job security and employment opportunities, before acting upon tender offers violates the exclusive benefit rule. [GCM 39870] However, IRS ruled that the exclusive benefit rule was not violated when a terminated defined benefit plan (see Q 2:3) made a loan to the employer from excess funds that would revert to the employer after the satisfaction of all plan liabilities (see Q 21:53). The loan, however, was a prohibited transaction (see Q 20:1). [Ltr Rul 9430002]

IRS has established a special procedure under which employers may make restorative payments to defined contribution plans (see Q 2:2) that have invested in guaranteed investment contracts (GICs) or guaranteed annuity contracts (GACs) of insurance companies that have become insolvent. Under the procedure, a plan that enters into a closing agreement with IRS that requires (1) the employer to make restorative payments to the plan due to such an insolvency and (2) the plan to repay the employer once the insurance company resumes payments under the GIC or GAC will not be considered as violating the exclusive benefit rule or the requirement that plans not discriminate in favor of highly compensated employees (see Q 4:9). [Rev Proc 95-52, 1995-51 IRB 14]

An individual rolled over (see Q 28:8) a distribution from a terminated qualified retirement plan into an IRA (see Q 26:1) that had previously been established with contributions from other sources. Subsequently, the individual transferred the rollover funds to a new retirement plan. Because the IRA was not a conduit IRA (see Q 28:40), the new plan was disqualified (see Qs 1:5, 1:6, 4:23). [Ltr Rul 9604028]

The following requirements must also be met before a retirement plan qualifies for favorable tax treatment:

1. The plan must satisfy minimum coverage and minimum participation requirements. For details, see chapter 5. [IRC §§ 401(a)(3), 401(a)(26)]

2. Contributions or benefits under the plan may not discriminate in favor of highly compensated employees (see Q 3:2). For details, see Qs 4:9 through 4:23. [IRC § 401(a)(4)]

3. The plan must meet requirements for the vesting of benefits. For details, see chapter 9. [IRC § 401(a)(7)]

4. The plan must provide for required minimum distribution of benefits. For details, see chapter 11. [IRC § 401(a)(9)]

5. Additional requirements apply to top-heavy plans. These additional requirements include minimum vesting rules and, for employees who are not key employees, minimum benefits and/or minimum contributions. A retirement plan can qualify only if it contains provisions satisfying the top-heavy plan requirements that automatically take effect if the plan becomes top-heavy. For details, see chapter 22. [IRC § 401(a)(10)(B)]

6. With few exceptions, plans must provide for the payment of benefits in the form of a joint and survivor lifetime annuity and for death benefits in the form of a preretirement survivor annuity. For details, see chapter 10. [IRC § 401(a)(11)]

7. The plan must provide that benefits may not be assigned or alienated. For details, see Qs 4:24 through 4:27. [IRC § 401(a)(13)]

8. The plan must comply with rules regarding the commencement of benefit payments. For details, see Q 10:51. [IRC § 401(a)(14)]

9. The plan must limit the contributions that can be made to the plan on behalf of an employee (in the case of a defined contribution plan), or it must limit the benefits that can be paid to an employee (in the case of a defined benefit plan). For details, see chapter 6. [IRC § 401(a)(16)]

10. The plan must impose a $150,000 cap (subject to cost-of-living adjustments) on the amount of compensation that can be taken into account (see Q 6:23). [IRC § 401(a)(17)]

11. A defined benefit plan must specify the actuarial assumptions that are used to determine the value of a benefit (see Q 2:19). [IRC § 401(a)(25)]

12. The plan must permit certain types of distributions to be made by a direct trustee-to-trustee transfer to another eligible retirement plan. For details, see Qs 28:8 through 28:32. [IRC § 401(a)(31)]

13. A defined benefit plan subject to PBGC coverage (see Qs 21:10, 21:12) cannot be amended to increase plan liabilities while the employer is in bankruptcy (see Q 21:24). [IRC § 401(a)(33)]

Q 4:2   Does a 401(k) plan qualify for favorable tax treatment?

Yes, provided certain special requirements are met in addition to the regular retirement plan qualification requirements. For details, see chapter 23.

Q 4:3   Can an oral trust created in a state that recognizes its validity be used for a qualified retirement plan?

No. Since a qualified retirement plan must be a definite written program (see Q 4:1), an oral trust, which may be valid under local law, will not meet the Code requirements for favorable tax treatment. [Rev Rul 69-231, 1969-1 CB 118; Fazi, 102 TC 695 (1994); Attardo, 62 TCM 313 (1991)]

Q 4:4 Can a trust that is not valid under local law be part of a qualified retirement plan?

No. Contributions to a qualified retirement plan's trust must be made to a trust that is valid under local law. [Rev Rul 69-231, 1969-1 CB 118; Rev Rul 81-114, 1981-1 CB 207]

Q 4:5 Must all qualified retirement plans have trustees?

No. The most common type of qualified retirement plan that has no trustee is an annuity plan funded solely through contracts issued by an insurance company (see Q 2:23).

Q 4:6 Does a retirement plan have to be submitted to IRS for approval?

A retirement plan may qualify for tax-favored status without first being submitted to IRS. Nevertheless, it is prudent to submit the retirement plan for IRS approval since this is the most important step that can be taken to preserve a retirement plan's qualified status. If, upon review of the application for a determination letter, IRS finds defects in the retirement plan, the timely filing of the application allows the plan to be corrected retroactively (see Q 4:7). The procedure for submitting a retirement plan to IRS is discussed in chapter 15. [IRC § 401(b); Treas Reg § 1.401(b)-1]

There is another reason for applying for a determination letter from IRS with regard to the initial qualification of a retirement plan. If IRS does not approve the retirement plan, the employer may recover its contribution only if the employer made a timely request for the determination (see Q 1:37). In that case, the return of the employer's contribution must be made within one year after receipt of the adverse determination. [ERISA § 403(c)(2)(B); Rev Rul 60-276, 1960-2 CB 150]

Q 4:7 Even if a retirement plan is not submitted to IRS for approval, must it nevertheless be amended periodically?

Yes. A retirement plan must be amended to comply with changes in laws, regulations, and rulings that affect retirement plans in general, or the specific type of retirement plan in particular, even if it is not submitted to IRS for approval. A retirement plan's qualification can be revoked if the employer fails to make required plan amendments timely to comply with changes in law, even if such changes would not affect the operation of the plan. [Ronald R Pawluk, PC, 69 TCM 1603 (1995); Fazi, 102 TC 695 (1994);

Mills, Mitchell & Turner, 65 TCM 2127 (1993); Hamlin Development Co, 65 TCM 2071 (1993); Kollipara Rajsheker, MD, Inc, 64 TCM 1153 (1992); Attardo, 62 TCM 313 (1991); Stark Truss Co, Inc, 62 TCM 169 (1991); Basch Eng'g, Inc, 59 TCM 482 (1990); Halligan, 51 TCM 1203 (1986); Bolinger, 77 TC 1353 (1981); Tionesta Sand & Gravel, Inc, 73 TC 758 (1980)] (See also Qs 13:23, 28:41.)

The Voluntary Compliance Resolution Program (VCRP) applies to a plan only if it has received a favorable determination letter for TRA '86 (see Qs 1:16, 15:17).

Q 4:8   May an employee's benefits be reduced after retirement to reflect Social Security benefit increases?

No. A qualified retirement plan must provide that benefits cannot be reduced because of increases in Social Security benefits or wage base levels after (1) benefit payments commence to a participant or beneficiary or (2) a participant who has vested benefits under the plan separates from service. [IRC § 401(a)(15)]

Q 4:9   What is the general nondiscrimination rule that applies to every qualified retirement plan?

A retirement plan is a qualified plan only if the contributions or the benefits provided under the plan do not discriminate in favor of highly compensated employees (see Q 3:2). A plan will satisfy this nondiscrimination rule only if it complies *both* in form and in operation with the requirements promulgated by IRS. [IRC § 401(a)(4); Treas Reg § 1.401(a)(4)-1(a)]

There are three requirements a plan must meet to satisfy the nondiscrimination rule. The first requirement is that either the contributions or the benefits provided in the plan must be nondiscriminatory in amount (see Q 4:10). A plan generally is permitted to satisfy this requirement on the basis of either contributions or benefits, regardless of whether the plan is a defined contribution plan (see Q 2:2) or a defined benefit plan (see Q 2:3). Thus, a plan is *not* required to establish nondiscrimination in amount with respect to both the contributions and the benefits provided. [Treas Reg § 1.401(a)(4)-1(b)(2)(i)]

The second requirement is that the benefits, rights, and features provided under the plan must be available to participants in a nondiscriminatory manner (see Q 4:18). The benefits, rights, and features subject to this requirement are the optional forms of benefit (e.g., retirement annuities and single-sum payments), ancillary benefits (e.g., disability benefits), and other rights and features (e.g., loans and investment options) available to participants. [Treas Reg § 1.401(a)(4)-1(b)(3)]

The third requirement is that the effect of plan amendments, including grants of past service credit, and of plan terminations must be nondiscriminatory (see Q 4:19). [Treas Reg § 1.401(a)(4)-1(b)(4)]

Q 4:10   What does nondiscrimination in amount of contributions or benefits mean?

The first requirement a retirement plan must satisfy is that either the contributions (see Q 4:11) or the benefits (see Q 4:13) provided under the plan must be nondiscriminatory in amount. [Treas Reg §§ 1.401(a)(4)-2, 1.401(a)(4)-3]

A defined contribution plan (see Q 2:2) generally will satisfy the nondiscriminatory amount requirement by showing that the *contributions* provided under the plan are nondiscriminatory in amount. However, a defined contribution plan also is permitted to satisfy the nondiscriminatory amount requirement by showing that the *equivalent benefits* provided under the plan are nondiscriminatory in amount (see Q 4:20). 401(k) plans are deemed to satisfy this requirement because such plans must contain a qualified cash-or-deferred arrangement that incorporates a nondiscriminatory amount requirement; however, plans providing for employee or matching contributions must satisfy special rules (see chapter 23). [Treas Reg § 1.401(a)(4)-1(b)(2)(ii)(B)]

A defined benefit plan (see Q 2:3) generally will satisfy the nondiscriminatory amount requirement by showing that the employer-provided *benefits* under the plan are nondiscriminatory in amount. However, a defined benefit plan also is permitted to satisfy the nondiscriminatory amount requirement by showing that the *equivalent contributions* provided under the plan are nondiscriminatory in amount (see Q 4:20).

Plans may use certain alternative methods to demonstrate that contributions or benefits are nondiscriminatory in amount.

Q 4:11   How is the nondiscrimination in amount of contributions requirement satisfied?

To determine whether the contributions provided under a defined contribution plan (see Q 2:2) are nondiscriminatory in amount (see Q 4:10), two safe harbor tests are permitted. [Treas Reg § 1.401(a)(4)-2(b)(1)]

The first safe harbor is design based. A defined contribution plan complies with this safe harbor if the plan allocates all employer contributions and forfeitures (see Q 9:17) for the plan year under a single uniform formula that allocates to each participant the same percentage of compensation, the same dollar amount, or the same dollar amount for each uniform unit of service (not to exceed one week) performed by the participant. Differences in allocations attributable to permitted disparity (see chapter 7) do not cause the plan to fail to satisfy this safe harbor. The following is an example of a defined contribution plan formula that satisfies this safe harbor:

> The company shall contribute each plan year during which the plan is in effect on behalf of each participant an amount equal to 10 percent of compensation.

[Treas Reg § 1.401(a)(4)-2(b)(2)]

The second safe harbor permits a defined contribution plan to have a uniform allocation formula weighted for age or service if the average rate of allocations for highly compensated employees (see Q 3:2) under the plan does not exceed the average rate of allocations for non-highly compensated employees (see Q 3:13) under the plan. A single uniform formula weighted for age or service is one that would allocate to each participant the same percentage of compensation or the same dollar amount if every participant was the same age and had the same number of years of service or plan participation. A uniform allocation formula need not grant points for both age and service, but must grant points for at least one of them. If points are granted for years of service, the number of years taken into account may be limited to a maximum number. Plans using this second safe harbor need not grant points for units of compensation; but, if the allocation formula takes compensation into account, the plan must provide the same number of points for each unit of compensation, and each unit of compensation must not exceed $200. This type of plan is known as a uniform points plan.

> **Example.** Adam & William Corporation adopts a profit sharing plan that allocates its plan contribution among the participants based on points awarded to each participant. Each participant is awarded one point for each $200 of compensation earned during the plan year and ten points for each year of service with Adam & William. The contributions allocated to highly compensated employees average 8 percent of compensation, and the allocations to the non-highly compensated employees average 10 percent of compensation. The second safe harbor is satisfied.

[Treas Reg § 1.401(a)(4)-2(b)(3)]

The safe harbors are available even though the plan contains, in addition to other permitted provisions, the following provisions:

1. The plan limits allocations to employees in accordance with Section 415 (see chapter 6).

2. The plan limits allocations otherwise provided under the formula to a maximum dollar amount or a maximum percentage of compensation, or limits the dollar amount of compensation or the number of years of service or plan participation taken into account in determining the amount of allocations.

3. The plan provides that an allocation to an employee for the plan year is conditioned on the employee's employment on the last day of the plan year or on the employee's completion of a minimum number of hours of service during the plan year (not to exceed 1,000). (See Qs 5:20, 5:21.)

[Treas Reg § 1.401(a)(4)-2(b)(4)]

Plans that do not satisfy either of the safe harbors must satisfy the general test for nondiscrimination in the amount of contributions (see Q 4:12).

Q 4:12 Is there a general test for the nondiscrimination in amount of contributions requirement?

Plans that do not satisfy either of the safe harbors (see Q 4:11) generally comply with this nondiscrimination requirement only if each rate group under the plan satisfies the minimum coverage requirements (see Q 5:15). Each rate group consists of a highly compensated employee (see Q 3:2) participating in the plan and all other participants (both highly and non-highly compensated) who have an allocation rate greater than or equal to that highly compensated employee's allocation rate. In determining allocation rates, permitted disparity may be taken into account. [Treas Reg § 1.401(a)(4)-2(c)(1)]

The allocation rate for an employee equals the sum of the allocations to the employee's account for the plan year expressed either as a percentage of compensation or as a dollar amount. The amounts taken into account in determining allocation rates include all employer contributions and forfeitures that are allocated to the employee's account for the plan year, but exclude allocations of income, expenses, gains, and losses. [Treas Reg § 1.401(a)(4)-2(c)(2)]

For purposes of determining whether a rate group satisfies the minimum coverage requirements, the rate group is treated as if it were a separate plan that benefits only the employees included in the rate group for the plan year. Generally, the rules that apply in determining whether a rate group satisfies the minimum coverage requirements are the same as apply in determining whether a plan satisfies those requirements. For example, if the rate group does not satisfy the ratio percentage test (see Q 5:16), the rate group must satisfy the average benefit test (see Q 5:17). [Treas Reg §§ 1.401(a)(4)-2(c)(3), 1.401(a)(4)-2(c)(4)]

Example 1. (a) A & L Fleischer Ltd. has only six nonexcludible employees, all of whom benefit under Plan D. The highly compensated employees are H1 and H2, and the non-highly compensated employees are N1 through N4. For the 1997 plan year, H1 and N1 through N4 have an allocation rate of 5 percent of plan year compensation. For the same plan year, H2 has an allocation rate of 7.5 percent of plan year compensation.

(b) There are two rate groups under Plan D. Rate group 1 consists of H1 and all those employees who have an allocation rate greater than or equal to H1's allocation rate (5 percent). Thus, rate group 1 consists of H1, H2, and N1 through N4. Rate group 2 consists only of H2 because no other employee has an allocation rate greater than or equal to H2's allocation rate (7.5 percent).

(c) The ratio percentage for rate group 2 is zero percent; i.e., zero percent (the percentage of all non-highly compensated nonexcludible employees who are in the rate group) divided by 50 percent (the percentage of all highly compensated nonexcludible employees who are in the rate group). Therefore, rate group 2 does not satisfy the ratio percentage test. Rate group 2 also does not satisfy the nondiscriminatory classification test and, therefore, does not satisfy the minimum coverage requirements. As a result, Plan D does not satisfy the general test even though the ratio percentage for rate group 1 is 100 percent.

Example 2. (a) The facts are the same as in Example 1, except that N4 has an allocation rate of 8 percent.

(b) There are two rate groups in Plan D. Rate group 1 consists of H1 and all those employees who have an allocation rate greater than or equal to H1's allocation rate (5 percent). Thus rate group 1 consists of H1, H2, and N1 through N4. Rate group 2 consists of H2 and all those employees who have an allocation rate greater than or equal to H2's allocation rate (7.5 percent). Thus, rate group 2 consists of H2 and N4.

(c) Rate group 1 satisfies the ratio percentage test because the ratio percentage of the rate group is 100 percent; i.e., 100 percent (the percentage of all non-highly compensated nonexcludible employees who are in the rate group) divided by 100 percent (the percentage of all highly compensated nonexcludible employees who are in the rate group).

(d) Rate group 2 does not satisfy the ratio percentage test because the ratio percentage of the rate group is 50 percent; i.e., 25 percent (the percentage of all non-highly compensated nonexcludible employees who are in the rate group) divided by 50 percent (the percentage of all highly compensated nonexcludible employees who are in the rate group).

(e) However, rate group 2 does satisfy the nondiscriminatory classification test because the ratio percentage of the rate group (50 percent) is greater than the safe harbor percentage applicable to the plan (45.5 percent).

(f) If rate group 2 satisfies the average benefit percentage test, then rate group 2 satisfies the minimum coverage requirements. In that case, Plan D satisfies the general test because each rate group under the plan satisfies the minimum coverage requirements.

Q 4:13   How is the nondiscrimination in amount of benefits requirement satisfied?

The basic rules for determining whether a plan is nondiscriminatory with respect to the amount of benefits generally apply to defined benefit plans (see Q 2:3). They may, however, also be applied to defined contribution plans (see Q 2:2) in testing nondiscrimination on the basis of equivalent benefits (see Qs 4:10, 4:20). [Treas Reg § 1.401(a)(4)-3(a)]

There are five safe harbors under which a plan is considered nondiscriminatory with respect to the amount of benefits (see Qs 4:14–4:16). Four of the safe harbors are design based and require no determination or comparison of actual benefits under the plan. All of the safe harbors require that the plan have a uniform benefit formula, that each subsidized optional form of benefit (see Q 10:42) be provided on similar terms to substantially all participants, that the plan not require employee contributions, that the plan have a uniform normal retirement age for all employees, and that each employee's benefit be accrued over the same years of service that are taken into account in applying the plan's benefit formula to that employee. Uniform normal retirement age means a single normal retirement age under the plan that does not exceed the maximum age and that is the same for all of the employees in a given group. The maximum age is generally 65. However, if all employees have the same Social Security retirement age (SSRA; see Q 6:14), the maximum age is the employees' SSRA. Thus, for example, a plan has a uniform normal retirement age of 67 if it defines normal retirement age as SSRA and all employees in the plan have a Social Security retirement age of 67. The definition of uniform normal retirement age has been expanded to provide generally that a plan's normal retirement provisions will not fail to be uniform merely because benefits commence on different dates for different employees, provided that each employee's normal retirement date does not differ by more than six months from a uniform normal retirement age. [Treas Reg §§ 1.401(a)(4)-3(b)(2), 1.401(a)(4)-12]

Plans that do not satisfy any of the five safe harbors must satisfy the general test for nondiscrimination in the amount of benefits (see Q 4:17).

The safe harbors are available even though the plan contains, in addition to other permitted provisions, the following:

1. The plan provides for benefits that were previously accrued under a formula that does not satisfy any of the safe harbors.

2. The plan limits accruals in accordance with Section 415 (see chapter 6) or provides for increases in accrued benefits based solely on adjustments to the dollar limitation.

3. The plan limits accruals to a maximum dollar amount or a maximum percentage of compensation or limits the dollar amount of compensation or the number of years of service or participation taken into account in determining the amount of accruals.

4. The plan takes permitted disparity into account (see chapter 7).

[Treas Reg § 1.401(a)(4)-3(b)(6)]

Q 4:14   What safe harbors apply to unit credit plans for the requirement of nondiscrimination in amount of benefits?

The first two safe harbors enable *unit credit plans* (see Q 2:17) to satisfy the nondiscrimination requirement with respect to the amount of benefits on the basis of plan design. A unit credit plan is a defined benefit plan (see Q 2:3) that contains a formula under which all employees accrue a fixed benefit (either as a percentage of compensation or as a dollar amount) for each year of service, and all employees with the same number of years accrue the same benefit. For example, a plan constitutes a unit credit plan for this purpose if it provides a benefit of (1) 1 percent of average compensation times years of service up to 20, and (2) 1.25 percent of average compensation times years of service in excess of 20 but not in excess of 30.

The first safe harbor applies to unit credit plans that accrue benefits under the 133⅓ percent rule (i.e., the benefit accrued in a plan year does not exceed by more than 133⅓ percent the benefit accrued in any prior plan year). [IRC § 411(b)(1)(B); Treas Reg § 1.401(a)(4)-3(b)(3)(i)]

> **Example.** Plan A provides a specific annual accrual for each employee in the plan payable at normal retirement age. For each of the first five years of service, the annual accrual is 1.5 percent of compensation. For the next five years of service, the annual accrual is 1.75 percent; and, for each additional year of service, the annual accrual is 2 percent. Plan A

satisfies this safe harbor because the benefit accrued in a later year (2 percent) does not exceed the lowest benefit accrual in a prior year (1.5 percent) by more than 133⅓ percent (2% ÷ 1.5% = 133⅓%).

The second safe harbor applies to unit credit plans that accrue benefits under the fractional rule; that is, the employee's accrued benefit (see Q 9:2) as of a given year equals the benefit projected as of normal retirement age (see Q 10:53) multiplied by the ratio of the employee's years of service as of the year to the employee's projected years of service as of normal retirement age. [IRC § 411(b)(1)(C)]

A plan under which benefits are calculated under a unit credit formula but accrue under the fractional accrual rule may also satisfy the unit credit safe harbor even though all employees with the same number of years of service may not accrue the same benefit. Such a plan satisfies the safe harbor only if the benefit (expressed as a percentage of compensation or a dollar amount) that any employee may accrue in any year is not more than one-third larger than the benefit that any other employee can accrue (disregarding employees with more than 33 years of projected service under the plan). [Treas Reg § 1.401(a)(4)-3(b)(4)(i)(C)(1)]

Example. Plan B provides for a benefit equal to 1.6 percent of compensation times each year of service up to 25. Plan B further provides that the plan benefits accrue under the fractional rule. The greatest benefit that an employee can earn in any one year is 1.6 percent of compensation (this is the case for any employee in the plan who will have 25 or fewer years of projected service at normal retirement age). The lowest benefit that will accrue for an employee in the plan with no more than 33 projected years of service is 1.212 percent (this is the case for any employee in the plan with 33 years of projected service under the formula: 1.6% × 25 ÷ 33). Since 1.6 percent is not more than one-third larger than 1.212 percent, Plan B satisfies this safe harbor.

Q 4:15 What safe harbors apply to flat benefit plans for the requirement of nondiscrimination in amount of benefits?

The third safe harbor is a design-based safe harbor for *flat benefit plans* (see Q 2:16) that satisfy the fractional accrual rule (for example, a defined benefit plan (see Q 2:3) that provides a benefit of 50 percent of compensation, accrued ratably over all years of service). Such a plan satisfies the safe harbor only if the plan provides that the maximum flat benefit will be accrued over a period of at least 25 years. The 25-year rule reduces the potential differences in the rates at which benefits accrue between those employees who enter the plan at younger ages and those who enter at older ages. In this way, this safe harbor applies nondiscrimination rules to flat benefit plans in a manner that takes into account the rate of benefit accrual.

The 25-year rule does not mean, however, that an employee must participate in a plan for 25 years to accrue the maximum annual retirement benefit (see Q 6:8). Rather, the maximum annual retirement benefit can be accrued in less than 25 years if the plan formula would produce a maximum calculated benefit in 25 years that is higher than the maximum annual retirement benefit permitted. The plan must still limit actual benefits to the maximum amount. For example, assume an employee is age 55, earns $150,000 (see Q 6:23), and the maximum annual retirement benefit permitted is $120,000 (80 percent of the employee's compensation). To satisfy the safe harbor while permitting this employee to accrue the maximum annual retirement benefit in ten years, the employer could establish a plan that provides a benefit of 200 percent of compensation at normal retirement age, accrued ratably over all years of service (thereby satisfying the fractional accrual rule). The benefit would be proportionately reduced for years of service less than 25, and the accrued benefit at any time would be limited to the maximum annual retirement benefit. Under this plan, at age 65, the employee would have ten years of service and would therefore accrue a benefit of 10/25 of 200 percent of compensation, or 80 percent of compensation. [Treas Reg § 1.401(a)(4)-3(b)(4)(i)(C)(2)]

The fourth safe harbor, also for flat benefit plans, requires that the average accrual rate of non-highly compensated employees (see Q 3:13) as a group be at least 70 percent of the average accrual rate of highly compensated employees (see Q 3:2) as a group. This safe harbor is applied by taking into account all nonexcludible employees of the employer whether they are covered under the plan or not. [Treas Reg § 1.401(a)(4)-3(b)(4)(i)(C)(3)]

Q 4:16 What safe harbor applies to insurance contract plans for the requirement of nondiscrimination in amount of benefits?

The fifth and final safe harbor is for *insurance contract plans* (see Q 8:5). Because these plans are subject to special accrual rules and deliver benefits in the form of insurance contract cash values, they are not designed in a way that accords with any of the four safe harbors discussed above (see Qs 4:14, 4:15). An insurance contract plan generally satisfies this safe harbor if it satisfies a special accrual rule and certain funding requirements, and if the stated benefit formula under the plan would satisfy either the unit credit fractional accrual safe harbor (see Q 4:14) or the flat benefit fractional accrual safe harbor (see Q 4:15) if the stated normal retirement benefit were accrued ratably over each employee's period of plan participation through normal retirement age (see Q 10:53). [Treas Reg § 1.401(a)(4)-3(b)(5)]

Q 4:17   Is there a general test for the nondiscrimination in amount of benefits requirement?

Those plans that do not satisfy any of the five safe harbors (see Qs 4:14–4:16) must satisfy the general test for nondiscrimination with respect to the amount of benefits. Under this test, the employer must identify, for each highly compensated employee (see Q 3:2) benefiting under the plan, the group of employees consisting of that highly compensated employee and all other employees (both highly compensated and non-highly compensated) with equal or greater normal and most valuable accrual rates (a rate group). Thus, depending on their accrual rates, employees may be included in more than one rate group. A rate group must be determined for each highly compensated employee benefiting under the plan. Each rate group so identified must satisfy the minimum coverage requirements (see Q 5:15) as though it were a separate plan. Generally, the rules that apply in determining whether a rate group satisfies the minimum coverage requirements are the same as apply in determining whether a plan satisfies those requirements. For example, if the rate group does not satisfy the ratio percentage test (see Q 5:16), the rate group must satisfy the average benefit test (see Q 5:17). [Treas Reg §§ 1.401(a)(4)-3(c)(1), 1.401(a)(4)-3(c)(2), 1.401(a)(4)-3(c)(4)]

Example 1. (a) BeeAndEll Bernstein, Inc. has 1,100 nonexcludible employees: N1 through N1000 are non-highly compensated employees, and H1 through H100 are highly compensated employees. BeeAndEll maintains Plan A, a defined benefit plan that benefits all 1,100 nonexcludible employees. The normal and most valuable accrual rates (determined as a percentage of average annual compensation) for the employees in Plan A for the 1997 plan year are listed in the following table:

Employee	Normal Accrual Rate	Most Valuable Accrual Rate
N1–N100	1.0	1.4
N101–N500	1.5	3.0
N501–N750	2.0	2.65
N751–N1000	2.3	2.8
H1–H50	1.5	2.0
H51–H100	2.0	2.65

(b) There are 100 rate groups in Plan A because there are 100 highly compensated employees in Plan A.

(c) Rate group 1 consists of H1 and all those employees who have a normal accrual rate greater than or equal to H1's normal accrual rate (1.5 percent) and who also have a most valuable accrual rate greater than or equal to H1's most valuable accrual rate (2.0 percent). Thus, rate group 1 consists of H1 through H100 and N101 through N1000.

(d) Rate group 1 satisfies the ratio percentage test because the ratio percentage of the rate group is 90 percent; i.e., 90 percent (the percentage of all non-highly compensated nonexcludible employees who are in the rate group) divided by 100 percent (the percentage of all highly compensated nonexcludible employees who are in the rate group).

(e) Because H1 through H50 have the same normal accrual rates and the same most valuable accrual rates, the rate group with respect to each of them is identical. Thus, because rate group 1 satisfies the minimum coverage requirements, rate groups 2 through 50 also satisfy the minimum coverage requirements.

(f) Rate group 51 consists of H51 and all those employees who have a normal accrual rate greater than or equal to H51's normal accrual rate (2.0 percent) and who also have a most valuable accrual rate greater than or equal to H51's most valuable accrual rate (2.65 percent). Thus, rate group 51 consists of H51 through H100 and N501 through N1000. (Even though N101 through N500 have a most valuable accrual rate [3.0 percent] greater than H51's most valuable accrual rate [2.65 percent], they are not included in this rate group because their normal accrual rate [1.5 percent] is less than H51's normal accrual rate [2.0 percent].)

(g) Rate group 51 satisfies the ratio percentage test because the ratio percentage of the rate group is 100 percent; i.e., 50 percent (the percentage of all non-highly compensated nonexcludible employees who are in the rate group) divided by 50 percent (the percentage of all highly compensated nonexcludible employees who are in the rate group).

(h) Because H51 through H100 have the same normal accrual rates and the same most valuable accrual rates, the rate group with respect to each of them is identical. Thus, because rate group 51 satisfies the minimum coverage requirements, rate groups 52 through 100 also satisfy the minimum coverage requirements.

(i) The benefits under Plan A are nondiscriminatory in amount because each rate group under the plan satisfies the minimum coverage requirements.

A plan that fails the general test discussed above may demonstrate that, on the basis of all relevant facts and circumstances, the plan is not discriminatory. This demonstration is available only to a plan that fails the general test with respect to 5 percent or less of the highly compensated employees (i.e., the plan could pass the test were it allowed to disregard the participation of not more than 5 percent of the highly compensated employees). For this purpose, 5 percent of the number of highly compensated employees may be determined by rounding to the nearest whole number (e.g., 1.4 rounds to 1 and 1.5 rounds to 2). Among the relevant factors that will be considered in determining nondiscrimination are:

1. The extent to which the plan fails the general test;

2. The extent to which the failure is for reasons other than the design of the plan;

3. Whether the highly compensated employees causing the failure are 5 percent owners (see Q 3:4) or are among the highest paid nonexcludible employees;

4. Whether the failure is attributable to a nonrecurring event (e.g., a plant closing); and

5. The extent to which the failure is attributable to benefits accrued under a prior benefit structure or when a participant was not a highly compensated employee.

[Treas Reg §§ 1.401(a)(4)-3(c)(3), 1.401(a)(4)-3(c)(4)]

Example 2. The facts are the same as in Example 1, except that H96 has a most valuable accrual rate of 3.5. Each of the rate groups is the same as in Example 1, except that rate group 96 consists solely of H96 because no other employee has a most valuable accrual rate greater than 3.5. Because the plan would satisfy the general test by disregarding H96 (who constitutes less than 5 percent of the highly compensated employees in the plan), IRS may determine that, on the basis of all of the relevant facts and circumstances, the plan does not discriminate with respect to the amount of benefits.

The normal accrual rate for a plan year is the increase in the employee's accrued benefit (see Q 9:2) during the measurement period (current plan year, current plan year and all prior years, or current plan year and all prior and future years), divided by the employee's testing service (the employee's years of service as defined in the plan for purposes of applying the benefit formula under the plan) during the measurement period, and expressed either as a dollar amount or as a percentage of the employee's average annual compensation. [Treas Reg § 1.401(a)(4)-3(d)]

The most valuable accrual rate for a plan year is the increase in the employee's most valuable optional form of payment of the accrued benefit during the measurement period, divided by the employee's testing service during the measurement period, and expressed either as a dollar amount or as a percentage of the employee's average annual compensation. It reflects the value of all benefits accrued or treated as accrued that are payable in any form and at any time under the plan, including early retirement benefits, retirement-type subsidies, early retirement window benefits, and so forth. Alternatively, an employee's most valuable accrual rate for the current plan year may be determined as the employee's highest most valuable accrual rate determined for any prior plan year. This option may be used only if the employee's normal accrual rate has not changed significantly from the normal accrual rate for such prior plan year and there has been no plan amendment in the interim period that affects the determination of the most valuable accrual rate. [Treas Reg §§ 1.401(a)(4)-3(d)(1)(ii), 1.401(a)(4)-3(d)(1)(iii), 1.401(a)(4)-3(d)(1)(iv)]

Q 4:18 What is the nondiscriminatory availability requirement?

The second nondiscrimination requirement a qualified retirement plan must satisfy is that the benefits, rights, and features provided under the plan must be made both currently and effectively available to the participants in a nondiscriminatory manner. The benefits, rights, and features that must satisfy this requirement are the optional forms of benefits, ancillary benefits, and other rights and features provided under the plan. Each optional form of benefit, each ancillary benefit, and each other right or feature provided under a plan must separately satisfy the nondiscrimination requirements with respect to its availability. Two or more benefits, rights, and features may be permissively aggregated if one of the benefits, rights, or features is inherently of equal or greater value than the other, and if the more valuable benefit, right, or feature, standing alone, satisfies the current and effective availability requirements. [Treas Reg §§ 1.401(a)(4)-4(a), 1.401(a)(4)-4(b), 1.401(a)(4)-4(c), 1.401(a)(4)-4(d)(4)]

The term "optional form of benefit" (see Q 10:42) means a distribution alternative that is available under a qualified retirement plan. Different optional forms of benefit exist if the distribution alternative is not payable on substantially the same terms. The relevant terms include all terms affecting the value of the optional form, such as the actuarial assumptions used to determine the amount distributed or the method of benefit calculation (see Q 2:19). Different optional forms of benefit may result from differences in payment schedule, timing, commencement, medium of distribution (e.g., in cash or in kind), election rights, eligibility requirements, or the portion of the benefit to which the distribution alternative applies. [Treas Reg § 1.401(a)(4)-4(e)(1)]

> **Example.** Peterelke Greenberg Corporation adopts a defined benefit plan that benefits all employees of Divisions S and T. The plan offers a qualified joint and survivor annuity at normal retirement age, calculated by multiplying an employee's single life annuity payment by a factor. For an employee of Division S whose benefit commences at age 65, the plan provides a factor of 0.90; but, for a similarly situated employee of Division T, the plan provides for a factor of 0.85. The qualified joint and survivor annuity is not available to employees of Divisions S and T on substantially the same terms and constitutes two separate optional forms of benefit.

The term "ancillary benefit" includes the following:

- Social Security supplements described in Section 411(a)(9)
- Disability benefits not in excess of a qualified disability benefit described in Section 411(a)(9)
- Ancillary life insurance and health insurance benefits
- Death benefits under a defined contribution plan (see Q 2:2)
- Preretirement death benefits under a defined benefit plan (see Q 2:3)
- Other similar benefits

Different ancillary benefits exist if an ancillary benefit is not available on substantially the same terms as another ancillary benefit. [Treas Reg § 1.401(a)(4)-4(e)(2)]

The term "other right or feature" means any right or feature applicable to participants, other than a right or feature taken into account as part of an optional form of benefit or ancillary benefit provided under the plan, and other than a right or feature that cannot reasonably be expected to be of meaningful value to an employee (e.g., administrative details). Different rights or features exist if the right or feature is not available on substantially the same terms as another right or feature. Other rights and features include, but are not limited to, the following:

- Plan loan provisions
- The right to direct investments [Ltr Rul 9137001]
- The right to a particular form of investment, including, for example, a particular class or type of employer securities (taking into account any difference in conversion, dividend, voting, liquidation preference, or other rights conferred under the security)
- The right to make rollover contributions and transfers to and from the plan

[Treas Reg § 1.401(a)(4)-4(e)(3)]

A plan must satisfy the nondiscriminatory availability requirement not only with respect to employees who are currently benefiting under the plan but also with respect to employees with accrued benefits (see Q 9:2) who are not currently benefiting under the plan (i.e., frozen participants). A plan satisfies the availability requirement with respect to this latter group of employees if any of the following requirements is met:

1. The benefit, right, or feature must be one that would satisfy the current and effective availability requirements if it were not available to any employee currently benefiting under the plan.

2. The benefit, right, or feature must be one that would satisfy the current and effective availability requirements if all frozen participants were treated as employees currently benefiting under the plan.

3. No change in the availability of the benefit, right, or feature may have been made that is first effective in the current plan year with respect to a frozen participant.

4. Any change in the availability of the benefit, right, or feature that is first effective in the current plan year with respect to a frozen participant must be made in a nondiscriminatory manner. Thus, any expansion in the availability of the benefit, right, or feature to any highly compensated frozen participant must be applied on a consistent basis to all non-highly compensated frozen participants. Similarly, any contraction in the availability of the benefit, right, or feature that affects any non-highly compensated frozen participant must be applied on a consistent basis to all highly compensated frozen participants.

[Treas Reg § 1.401(a)(4)-4(d)(2)]

Certain corrective amendments to the availability of benefits, rights, and features are permitted. Because it is difficult or impossible, in many cases, to make a benefit, right, or feature meaningfully available on a retroactive basis, a corrective amendment increasing availability is required only on a prospective basis. However, in order to take the correction into account for a plan year, the group of employees to whom the benefit, right, or feature is available (after taking the amendment into account) generally must satisfy a nondiscriminatory requirement. In addition, the amendment must remain in effect until the end of the plan year following the year in which the amendment is effective, and must not be part of a pattern of amendments used to correct repeated failures of the same benefit, right, or feature. Other rules relating to retroactive correction also apply (e.g., the requirement that the correction be made no later than the 15th day of the tenth month after the close of a plan year).

As an alternative to increasing availability, an employer may make a corrective amendment by the last day of the plan year eliminating the benefit, right, or feature (to the extent permitted under Section 411(d)(6)). In that case, the amendment will be treated as if it were in effect throughout the plan year for purposes of nondiscrimination testing. [Treas Reg § 1.401(a)(4)-11(g)]

Q 4:19　What is the nondiscriminatory requirement for plan amendments?

The third nondiscrimination requirement a qualified retirement plan must satisfy is that the effect or timing of plan amendments must be nondiscriminatory. Under this requirement, plan amendments must not have the effect of discriminating significantly in favor of highly compensated active employees (see Q 3:3) or highly compensated former employees (see Q 3:12). A plan amendment includes the establishment or termination of the plan and any change in the benefits, rights, or features, benefit formulas, or allocation formulas under the plan. Whether a plan meets this requirement depends on the relevant facts and circumstances. [Treas Reg § 1.401(a)(4)-5(a)(1)]

A plan does not satisfy this requirement if the timing of a plan amendment or series of amendments (including amendments terminating the plan) discriminates significantly in favor of highly compensated active or former employees at the time the amendment first becomes effective. Relevant facts and circumstances include the relative numbers of highly and non-highly compensated active and former employees affected by the plan amendment, the relative accrued benefits (see Q 9:2) of the highly and non-highly compensated active and former employees before and after the effective date of the plan amendment, the relative length of service of the highly and non-highly compensated active and former employees, the length of time the plan or plan provisions have been in effect, and the turnover of employees prior to the plan amendment. [Treas Reg §§ 1.401(a)(4)-5(a)(2), 1.401(a)(4)-5(a)(4)]

> **Example.** The Glener Corporation adopted a defined benefit plan many years ago that has covered both highly compensated and non-highly compensated employees for most of its existence. The Glener Corporation decides to wind up the business. Shortly thereafter, at a time when the plan covers only highly compensated employees, the plan is amended to increase benefits and thereafter is terminated. The plan does not satisfy this requirement because the timing of the amendment increasing benefits discriminates significantly in favor of highly compensated employees.

A plan does not satisfy this requirement if plan provisions that provide past service credit have the effect of discriminating significantly in favor of highly compensated active and former employees. Past service credit includes benefit accruals for an employee's service prior to the time a plan is established, increases in existing accrued benefits resulting from an employee's service prior to the effective date of a plan amendment, and benefit accruals for service with another employer. Relevant facts and circumstances include the amount of benefits that former employees would have received had the plan or benefit increase been in effect throughout the period to which the past service credit applies. In addition, those facts and circumstances that are generally relevant to other plan amendments are taken into account. A safe harbor is provided under which a grant of up to five years of past service credit is deemed to be nondiscriminatory. The existence of this safe harbor does not mean that a grant of past service credit for a longer period violates the nondiscrimination rules. [Treas Reg §§ 1.401(a)(4)-5(a)(2), 1.401(a)(4)-5(a)(3), 1.401(a)(4)-5(a)(4), 1.401(a)(4)-11(d)(3)]

Example 1. Lyla-Howard Ltd. currently has six employees, two of whom, A and B, are highly compensated employees, and the remaining four of whom, C, D, E, and F, are non-highly compensated employees. The ratio of highly compensated employees to highly compensated former employees is significantly higher than the ratio of non-highly compensated employees to non-highly compensated former employees. Lyla-Howard Ltd. establishes a defined benefit plan providing a 2 percent benefit for each year of service with the employer, including service rendered before the plan is established. A and B have 15 years of prior service each, C has nine years of past service, D has five years, E has three years, and F has one year. The plan violates the special effect requirement because the grant of past service discriminates significantly in favor of highly compensated employees.

Example 2. Assume the same facts as in Example 1, except that the plan limits the past service credit to five years. The grant of past service credit does not discriminate significantly in favor of highly compensated employees and is within the safe harbor.

The requirement that a plan must be nondiscriminatory also covers plan terminations. Existing rules (see Q 21:8) that restrict distributions to highly compensated active and former employees upon termination of a defined benefit plan have been liberalized. These restrictions are inapplicable if the payment is less than 1 percent of plan assets or, after the payment of the benefit, the value of plan assets is at least 110 percent of the plan's current liabilities (see Q 8:2). [Treas Reg § 1.401(a)(4)-5(b)]

Q 4:20 What does cross-testing mean?

A qualified retirement plan may not discriminate in favor of highly compensated employees (see Q 3:2) with respect to the amount of contributions or benefits. Whether a defined contribution plan (see Q 2:2) satisfies this requirement is generally determined with respect to the amount of contributions (see Q 4:11). As an alternative, however, a defined contribution plan (other than an ESOP (see Q 24:1)) may be tested with respect to the equivalent amount of benefits. Similarly, whether a defined benefit plan (see Q 2:3) satisfies this requirement is generally determined with respect to the amount of benefits (see Q 4:13). As an alternative, however, a defined benefit plan may be tested with respect to the equivalent amount of contributions. [Treas Reg § 1.401(a)(4)-8]

Example. For 1997, The Sal-Lee Ocean Club Corporation adopts a profit sharing plan with a calendar year plan year. The following six employees are eligible to participate in the plan:

Participant	Age	Compensation
A (owner)	55	$150,000
B	45	85,000
C	40	50,000
D	35	35,000
E	30	25,000
F	25	20,000
Total		$365,000

Sal-Lee contributes $40,750 to the plan. The contribution is allocated among the participants on a cross-tested basis with each participant receiving an allocation of no less than 5 percent of compensation. The contribution allocation is as follows:

Participant	Contribution	Percentage of Compensation	Accrual Rate
A	$30,000	20%	4.50%
B	4,250	5	2.77
C	2,500	5	4.07
D	1,750	5	5.68
E	1,250	5	8.04
F	1,000	5	11.51
Total	$40,750		

The accrual rate for A, the sole highly compensated employee, is 4.50 percent, and the average accrual rate for the non-highly compensated employees (see Q 3:13) is 6.41 percent. Since the accrual rate for the non-highly compensated employees is 70 percent or more of A's accrual rate, the plan does not discriminate in favor of the highly compensated employee with regard to the equivalent amount of benefits (see Q 4:12).

In the above example, cross-testing enables A to receive the maximum allocation (see Q 6:1) without providing all other employees with an allocation equal to 20 percent of compensation (see Q 6:26). An age-based profit sharing plan (see Qs 2:7–2:9) could also provide A with the $30,000 maximum but would provide differing percentages for all of the other employees.

A defined contribution plan that is cross-tested by using the current plan year as the measurement period under the general test (see Q 4:12) may disregard income, expenses, gains, and losses allocated during the current plan year that are attributable to the allocation for the current plan year. Thus, only contributions and forfeitures allocated during the current plan year are taken into account. [Treas Reg §§ 1.401(a)(4)-8(b)(2)(i), 1.401(a)(4)-8(b)(2)(ii)]

Q 4:21 Do special rules apply to target benefit plans?

A target benefit plan (see Q 2:5) is generally subject to the alternative cross-testing method applicable to defined contribution plans (see Q 4:20). However, a target benefit plan will be deemed to satisfy the nondiscrimination requirement with respect to the amount of equivalent benefits if each of the following requirements is satisfied:

1. Each employee's stated benefit is determined as the straight life annuity commencing at the employee's normal retirement age (see Q 10:53);

2. The same benefit formula applies to all employees, and the benefit formula provides all employees with an annual benefit payable in the same form commencing at the same uniform normal retirement age (see Q 4:13);

3. The stated benefit under the plan complies with one of the defined benefit plan safe harbors that uses the fractional accrual rule (see Qs 4:14, 4:15);

4. Contributions necessary to fund the stated benefit for an employee are determined under the individual level premium funding method and are based on the employee's theoretical reserve. An employee's theoretical reserve generally consists of prior contributions with

interest accumulated at the plan's assumed interest rate used for funding purposes for prior years;

5. Generally, an employee's stated benefit may not take into account service prior to the first plan year that the employee benefited under the plan;

6. Forfeitures under the plan are applied to reduce contributions;

7. Employee contributions are not used to fund the stated benefit; and

8. Stated benefits and contributions after normal retirement age satisfy certain additional requirements.

[Treas Reg §§ 1.401(a)(4)-8(a), 1.401(a)(4)-8(b), 1.401(a)(4)-12]

Q 4:22   When are the new nondiscrimination requirements effective?

The new nondiscrimination requirements (see Q 4:9) are generally effective for plan years beginning on or after January 1, 1994. For plan years beginning before 1994, a retirement plan must be operated in accordance with a reasonable, good-faith interpretation of the new requirements. [Treas Reg § 1.401(a)(4)-13(a); Rev Proc 95-34, 1995-29 IRB 7; Rev Proc 93-42, 1993-2 CB 540; Ann 93-130, 1993-31 IRB 46; Notice 92-36, 1992-2 CB 364; Ann 92-81, 1992-22 IRB 56; Ann 92-29, 1992-9 IRB 37; IRS Field Office Directive on Good-Faith Compliance (June 12, 1992)]

Q 4:23   What happens if a retirement plan fails to satisfy the new nondiscrimination requirements?

If a retirement plan fails to satisfy any of the qualification requirements of Section 401(a) (see Q 4:1), including the nondiscrimination requirements (see Q 4:9), the tax-exempt status of plan earnings is revoked, employer deductions for contributions may be deferred or eliminated, and all employees must include the value of their vested plan contributions in income. [IRC § 402(b)(1); Ltr Rul 9502030]

However, if the plan fails to satisfy the minimum coverage requirements (see Q 5:15), each highly compensated employee (see Q 3:2) must include in income an amount equal to the employee's entire vested accrued benefit (see Q 9:2) not previously included in income, not just current vested plan contributions. If, however, the plan is not qualified solely because it fails to satisfy the minimum coverage requirements, no adverse tax consequences are imposed on non-highly compensated employees (see Q 3:13). [IRC § 402(b)(4); Ltr Rul 9502030]

IRS has opined that, with the integrated approach underlying the new nondiscrimination requirements and the minimum coverage requirements, any failure to satisfy the nondiscrimination requirements can be viewed as failure to satisfy the minimum coverage requirements. Consequently, failure to meet the nondiscrimination requirements will subject highly compensated employees to the special sanctions. [Preamble to final regulations (Sept 19, 1991)]

Q 4:24   May a participant assign his or her vested interest in a qualified retirement plan?

As a general rule, benefits provided under a qualified retirement plan may not be assigned or alienated. There are, however, exceptions to this rule.

A participant or beneficiary whose benefits are in pay status may assign or alienate the right to future benefit payments provided the following conditions are satisfied: (1) the assignment or alienation is voluntary and revocable; (2) the amount does not exceed 10 percent of any benefit payment; and (3) there is no direct or indirect defraying of plan administration costs. [ERISA § 206(d); IRC § 401(a)(13)(A); Treas Reg § 1.401(a)-13(d)(1)]

A loan made to a participant or beneficiary is generally not treated as an assignment or alienation if the loan is secured by the participant's vested interest and is not a prohibited transaction (see Qs 1:39, 13:44–13:52, 20:9). [IRC §§ 401(a)(13)(A), 4975(d)(1); Treas Reg § 1.401(a)-13(d)(2)] Even though a loan may be secured by the participant's vested interest, the secured loan could not be accorded priority status in a bankruptcy proceeding concluded one court. [In re Scott, No. 91-34119 (Bankr ED Va 1992)] Similarly, payroll deductions to repay a plan loan cannot be excluded from the participant's bankruptcy estate. Although the participant's interest in the plan is exempt from claims of creditors (see Q 4:25), the exemption does not apply to amounts owed to repay the loan. [In re Harshbarger, 1995 US App Lexis 26335 (6th Cir 1995)]

If a participant designates a beneficiary to receive benefits under a qualified retirement plan upon the participant's death, a disclaimer of the death benefits by the designated beneficiary does not constitute a prohibited assignment or alienation of benefits. [GCM 39858]

If a qualified domestic relations order (QDRO; see Q 30:1) requires the distribution of all or part of a participant's benefits to another individual, even though the participant is still employed, the distribution is not considered an assignment or alienation. [IRC §§ 401(a)(13)(B), 414(p); Treas Reg

§ 1.401(a)-13(g)] Because a postnuptial agreement requiring that a portion of the husband's benefits in a qualified retirement plan be segregated in a separate plan account for the wife was not a QDRO, the segregation violated the anti-assignment rule. [Merchant v Kelly, Haglund, Garnsey & Kahn, 874 F Supp 300 (DC Col 1995)]

A participant's waiver assigning his defined benefit plan (see Q 2:3) benefits to the employer constituted a prohibited assignment or alienation and resulted in his receipt of a taxable distribution (see Q 13:1). The court ruled that the waived benefits did not represent excess assets reverting to the employer (see Q 21:48). [Gallade, 106 TC No. 20 (1996)]

Where a union official embezzled funds from the union, the United States Supreme Court ruled that the official's union pension plan benefits could not be used to satisfy the union's judgment against him because such use would violate the prohibition on assignment or alienation of pension benefits. [Guidry v Sheet Metal Workers Nat'l Pension Fund, 493 US 365 (1990)] A different result was reached when a union official embezzled from the union pension plan, when a trustee made unauthorized withdrawals from the plan (see Q 19:27), and also when a company owner stole funds from the plan. [United States v Gaudet, No. 91-3647 (5th Cir 1992); Friedlander v Doherty, No. 91-CV-0832 (ND NY 1994); Parker v Bain, No. 94-55123 (9th Cir 1995)] However, one court ruled that a participant's plan benefits could not be offset for an alleged breach of fiduciary duty because the participant was not a fiduciary. [Cottrill v Sparrow, Johnson & Ursillo, Inc, Nos. 95-1363 and 95-1434 (1st Cir 1996)]

One court ruled that improper plan contributions made by an employer would not be excluded from the employer's bankruptcy estate because the anti-alienation rule did not apply. [Bell & Beckwith v Society Bank and Trust, 1993 US App Lexis 23740 (6th Cir 1993)]

Q 4:25   Are qualified retirement plan benefits exempt from participants' creditors?

In 1992, the United States Supreme Court held that a participant's interest in a qualified retirement plan is exempt from the claims of creditors in a bankruptcy proceeding, which, hopefully, resolved the conflict among the courts of appeals. [Patterson v Shumate, 112 S Ct 2242 (1992)]

ERISA and the Code require every qualified retirement plan to prohibit the assignment or alienation of benefits under the plan (see Q 4:24). [ERISA § 206(d)(1); IRC § 401(a)(13)] Federal Bankruptcy Code Section 541(c)(2) excludes from the bankruptcy estate property of the debtor that is subject to a restriction on transfer enforceable under applicable nonbankruptcy law.

The Supreme Court ruled that the anti-alienation provision contained in a qualified retirement plan constitutes a restriction on transfer enforceable under applicable nonbankruptcy law; and, accordingly, a debtor may exclude his interest in such a plan from the property of the bankruptcy estate. [In re Winkler, No. 94-1475 (4th Cir 1995); In re Schlein, 1993 US App Lexis 31333 (11th Cir 1993); Arkison v UPS Thrift Plan, No. 91-36347 (9th Cir 1993)] One court ruled that the exception extends to voluntary contributions (see Q 1:33). [In re Conner, No. 94-16001 (9th Cir 1996)]

The Supreme Court referred to an "ERISA qualified" plan, which, one court opined, could have one of three interpretations:

1. A plan subject to ERISA;

2. A plan subject to ERISA that contains an anti-alienation clause; or

3. A plan that is tax-qualified under the Code, is subject to ERISA, and has an anti-alienation provision as required by ERISA.

[In re Kaplan, 1993 Bankr Lexis 1534 (Bankr ED Pa 1993)]

Courts have concluded that only the second interpretation was relevant. [SEC v Johnson, 1996 US Dist Lexis 5074 (ED Mi 1996); In re Hanes, 1994 Bankr Lexis 33 (Bankr ED Va 1994)] In either case, the common thread is "subject to ERISA." For purposes of Title I of ERISA, the term "employee benefit plan" does not include any plan under which no employees are participants covered under the plan. For example, a plan under which only a sole proprietor or only partners are participants is not covered under Title I. However, a plan under which one or more common-law employees, in addition to the self-employed individuals (see Q 6:33), are participants is covered under Title I. Furthermore, an individual and the individual's spouse are not deemed to be employees with respect to a trade or business, whether incorporated or unincorporated, that is wholly owned by the individual or by the individual and the spouse; and in a partnership, a partner and the partner's spouse are not deemed to be employees with respect to the partnership. [DOL Reg § 2510.3-3]

When the debtor was the sole shareholder and employee of his corporation and the sole participant in the qualified retirement plan, the creditors successfully challenged the exclusion of the shareholder's interest in the plan on the basis that, as the sole shareholder, he was not an employee and, as such, the plan was not an employee benefit plan under ERISA. [In re Branch, 1994 US App Lexis 2870 (7th Cir 1994); In re Witwer, 148 BR 930 (Bankr CD Cal 1992)] In other cases, because the plan covered only the sole shareholder and his wife and, as such, was a plan without employees, courts concluded that the plan was not subject to ERISA and that the bankruptcy exemption is contingent upon qualification under both ERISA and the Code. [In re Blais, 1994 Bankr Lexis 1427 (Bankr SD Fla 1994); In re Hall, 151 BR 412 (Bankr WD Mich 1993)]

After the Supreme Court decision, bankruptcy trustees developed a new strategy. Since ERISA may protect only qualified retirement plan benefits, bankruptcy trustees are bringing into question the qualified status of the plan. What was once the domain of IRS (see Q 15:1) may now become a territorial dispute with the bankruptcy courts.

Although a qualified retirement plan was not an ERISA qualified plan because the only participants were owners of the employer, the plan assets could still be exempted from bankruptcy under a state statute *provided* the IRS did not disqualify the plan. Courts have also concluded that they need not step into the shoes of IRS to determine if the plan was still qualified, nor were they required to perform a rigorous analysis of the plan to see whether it remained qualified in order to grant a bankruptcy exemption. [Youngblood v FDIC, 29 F 3d 225 (5th Cir 1994); In re Feldman, 1994 Bankr Lexis 1377 (Bankr ED NY 1994); In re Kaplan, 1993 Bankr Lexis 1534 (Bankr ED Pa 1993)]

In another case, the debtor, a self-employed dentist, sought to exclude from the bankruptcy estate his benefits in two plans. Although there were common-law employees who had satisfied the eligibility requirements, and although the plans were top-heavy (see chapter 22), the debtor had made no contributions to either plan on behalf of the employees. The court determined that the plans were not qualified plans and, therefore, were includible within the bankruptcy estate. [Bernstein v Greenpoint Savings Bank, 149 BR 760 (Bankr ED NY 1993); see also In re Harris, 1995 Bankr Lexis 1534 (Bankr MD Fla 1995); Stochastic Decisions, Inc v Wagner, 1994 US App Lexis 24110 (2d Cir 1994); Pitrat v Garlikov, 1993 US App Lexis 10361 (9th Cir 1993); In re Lane, Jr, No. 91-17010-260 (Bankr ED NY 1993)]

Q 4:26 Can IRS levy against a participant's qualified retirement plan benefits?

Although one court has ruled that IRS could not levy against the participant's benefits because they were exempt under ERISA [ERISA § 206(d); In re Lewis, No. 90-B-02776 D (Bankr D Col 1990)], most courts have held that the prohibition against the assignment or alienation of retirement plan benefits does not preclude the enforcement of a federal tax levy or the collection by IRS on a judgment resulting from an unpaid tax assessment. [IRC §§ 6331, 6334; Treas Reg §§ 1.401(a)-13(b)(2), 301.6334-1–301.6334-4; TD 8568; United States v Sawaf, 1996 US App Lexis 1050 (6th Cir 1996); In re Wesche, 95-1224-BKC-3F3 (Bankr MD Fla 1996); Travelers Ins Co v Rattermann, C-1-94-466 (SD Ohio 1996); IBEW Local Union No. 640 v

Forman, CIV 94-2431 (D Ariz 1995); Ameritrust Co, NA v Derakhshan, No. 1:92CV0931 (D ND Ohio 1993); Hyde v United States, No. 90-1258 (D Ariz 1993); In re Raihl, No. 91-2200 RMJ (9th Cir US Bankr App Panel 1993); In re Anderson, 1992 Bankr Lexis 2197 (9th Cir US Bankr App Panel 1992); In re Jacobs, Sr, No. 91-00748E (Bankr WD Pa 1992); United States v Weintraub, No. C-1-76-0032 (SD Ohio 1990)] One court permitted IRS to levy on plan benefits that were payable under the PBGC insurance program (see Q 21:20). [Shanbaum v United States, 32 F 3d 180 (5th Cir 1994)] However, another court ruled that, since a tax lien was not equivalent to a levy or judgment, the IRS lien did not attach to the participant's account. [In re Taylor, 1991 Bankr Lexis 711 (Bankr D Md 1991)]

Even though the United States Supreme Court has held that a participant's interest in a qualified retirement plan is exempt from the claims of creditors in a bankruptcy proceeding (see Q 4:25), the enforcement of a federal tax levy against, or the collection by IRS of an unpaid tax assessment from, plan benefits appears to be permitted. It remains the position of IRS that such levies are permissible. IRS agents have been instructed to levy qualified retirement plan benefits only in flagrant and aggravated cases; and, generally, IRS will not levy benefits if the annual benefits are $6,000 or less. [IRM 536(14).5 and .22]

One court ruled that, under the doctrine of sovereign immunity, a qualified retirement plan was precluded from suing IRS for a refund of a tax levy on a participant's benefit that the plan claimed was improper. [Operating Engineers Pension Trust v United States, No. CV-92-2730-RSWL (CD Cal 1992)]

With regard to state taxes, one court has held that a state statute that allows tax levies against pension benefits to collect delinquent state income taxes was preempted by ERISA as a violation of the anti-alienation rule and the benefits were protected from attachment. [Retirement Fund Trust of the Plumbing, Heating and Piping Industry of S California v Franchise Tax Bd, Nos. 99-6355 and 88-6415 (9th Cir 1990)]

Q 4:27 May a participant's qualified retirement plan benefits be attached or garnished?

According to IRS, an attachment, garnishment, levy, execution, or other legal or equitable process of or against a participant's qualified retirement plan benefits is not a voluntary assignment or alienation (see Q 4:24) and, therefore, violates the anti-alienation rule. IRS has also held that a transfer of a participant's plan benefits, which violates the anti-alienation rule, results in the disqualification of the plan. [Treas Reg § 1.401(a)-13(d)(1); Ltr Ruls 9011037, 8829009]

However, if benefits have been distributed to the participant, the attachment or assignment of the distributed plan benefits will not violate the anti-alienation provisions. [Guidry v Sheet Metal Workers Nat'l Pension Fund, 1994 US App Lexis 30640 (10th Cir 1994); Trucking Employees of North Jersey Welfare Fund, Inc v Colville, 16 F 3d 52 (3d Cir 1994); Guidry v Sheet Metal Workers Int'l Assn, Local No. 9, 10 F 3d 700 (10th Cir 1993); In re Collin, 1995 Bankr Lexis 781 (Bankr ND Ohio 1995); Brosamer v Mark, No. 27S02-9011-CV-700 (S Ct Ind 1990)] To the contrary, one court has held that monthly benefit payments, even after receipt by the retired participant, are protected by ERISA. [United States v Smith, 1995 US App Lexis 4151 (4th Cir 1995)]

A former participant's argument that his pension plan benefits should not be attachable by creditors for a period of 60 days after receipt, because he could elect to roll over his benefits during that period (see Q 28:37), was rejected. [NationsBank of North Carolina v Shumate, No. 93-2092 (4th Cir 1994)]

Chapter 5

Eligibility and Participation

A company's retirement plan does not qualify for tax-favored status unless certain minimum standards for coverage of, and participation by, employees are met. This chapter examines those standards, describes the problems regarding related companies, and discusses important terms.

Q 5:1 Must a company's qualified retirement plan cover all of its employees?

No. However, certain minimum coverage and participation requirements, in terms of a percentage or a number of the company's workforce (see Qs 5:15, 5:25), must be satisfied. A retirement plan that meets the minimum coverage and participation requirements may qualify for favorable tax treatment even though some employees are excluded.

It is important to recognize that the coverage and participation requirements are minimum standards that must be satisfied by a qualified retirement plan. A company may use more liberal standards than those discussed in this chapter. [IRC §§ 401(a)(26), 410(b)]

In the first instance, a determination must be made as to whether or not an individual is an employee. ERISA Section 3(6) defines an employee as any individual employed by an employer. Concluding that the ERISA definition is completely circular and explains nothing, the United States Supreme Court adopted a common-law test for determining employee status. Under the test, the following should be considered:

- The right of the hiring party to control the manner and means by which the product is accomplished
- The skill required

- The source of the instrumentalities and tools
- The work location
- The duration of the parties' relationship
- Whether the hiring party has the right to assign more projects to the hired party
- The extent to which the hired party may decide when and how long to work
- The payment method
- The role of the hired party in hiring and paying assistants
- Whether the work is part of the hiring party's regular business
- Whether the hiring party is in business
- The provision of employee benefits
- The tax treatment of the hired party

All incidents of the relationship must be taken into account, and no single factor will be decisive. [Nationwide Mutual Ins Co v Darden, 112 S Ct 1344 (1992); Roth v Amer Hosp Supply Corp, 965 F 2d 862 (10th Cir 1992); Keleher v Dominion Insulation, Inc, 1992 US App Lexis 25561 (4th Cir 1992); Community for Creative Non-Violence v Reid, 490 US 730 (S Ct 1989); Herr v McCormick Grain-The Heiman Co, Inc, 1993 US Dist Lexis 15622 (DC Kansas 1993)]

A plan was disqualified for failure to satisfy the minimum coverage and minimum participation requirements because the employer improperly characterized employees as independent contractors and did not include them as participants in the plan. [Kenney, 70 TCM 614 (1995)] A similar problem could arise if independent contractors are improperly characterized as employees and then participate in the plan. IRS has ruled that the participation of an independent contractor in a company's plan did not disqualify the plan where the contractor had been treated as an employee up until a court decision that he was actually an independent contractor. To prevent plan disqualification, the contractor's participation was cancelled retroactively, and the contractor's elective contributions and the earnings thereon were distributed to him. [Ltr Rul 9546018]

For a further discussion of the employer-employee relationship, see Q 29:5.

Q 5:2 What minimum age and service requirements may be set by a qualified retirement plan?

A qualified retirement plan may require an employee to reach age 21 before becoming eligible to participate in the plan. A plan may also require an employee to complete one year of service (see Qs 5:5, 5:8) with the company before becoming eligible to participate. [IRC § 410(a)(1)(a)]

For qualified retirement plans that provide full and immediate vesting (see Q 9:12), an employer may condition participation on completion of more than one year of service. The maximum period for such plans is two years; however, for 401(k) plans, the maximum period is only one year (see Qs 5:4, 23:4). [IRC §§ 410(a)(1)(B), 401(k)(2)(D)]

It may be permissible to amend a qualified retirement plan to increase the service requirement from one year to two years for the purpose of delaying the participation date of a particular employee. [McGath v Auto-Body North Shore, Inc, 1993 US App Lexis 27198 (7th Cir 1993)]

Q 5:3 May a qualified retirement plan set a maximum age limit for participation?

No. A qualified retirement plan may not exclude from participation employees who are hired after reaching a specified maximum age. Previously, defined benefit and target benefit plans (see Qs 2:3, 2:5) could exclude employees who were hired within five years of the plan's normal retirement age (see Q 10:53). [IRC § 410(a)(2); Prop Reg §§ 1.410(a)-4A, 1.411(b)-2]

Although a plan may not exclude older employees by its terms, an older employee may waive plan participation, provided the waiver is knowingly and voluntarily made. A refusal to allow waivers of participation by older employees would be equivalent to imposing mandatory plan participation on that group of employees. [Finz v Schlesinger, 957 F 2d 78 (2d Cir 1992); Laniok v Advisory Committee of the Brainerd Mfg Co Pension Plan, 935 F 2d 1360 (2d Cir 1991)]

Q 5:4 May a qualified retirement plan require two consecutive years of service for participation?

Qualified retirement plans that provide for immediate 100 percent vesting and require more than one year of service, but not more than two years of service, to be eligible to participate (see Qs 5:2, 9:12) may provide that years of service preceding a one-year break in service (see Q 5:10) be disregarded if the employee has not yet met the service eligibility criterion. Thus, an employee who completes one year of service and then incurs a one-year break in service starts over again, either the next year or when the employee is rehired. However, the plan cannot require that the two years of service be consecutive. [IRC § 410(a)(5)(B); Temp Reg § 1.410(a)-8T(c)(2)]

Example. CeeKay Corp. established a profit sharing plan in 1993 that operates on a calendar year basis. The plan provides that an employee must complete two years of service before becoming a participant and that the employee will be 100 percent vested upon completion of the two-year eligibility requirement. The following three employees all became employed by CeeKay on December 31, 1992:

		Hours of Service Completed	
Plan Year	*Stephanie*	*Caroline*	*James*
1993	1,000	1,000	1,000
1994	1,000	700	500
1995	1,000	1,000	1,000
1996	1,000	1,000	700
1997	1,000	1,000	1,000

Stephanie satisfied the plan's service requirement at the end of 1994; Caroline at the end of 1995 because 1993 may not be disregarded, since she did not have a one-year break in service in 1994; and James will have satisfied the requirement at the end of 1997 because 1993 may be disregarded, since he did have a one-year break in service in 1994.

Q 5:5   May conditions other than age and service be set for participation in a qualified retirement plan?

Yes. A qualified retirement plan can impose other conditions for participation, provided that the minimum coverage and minimum participation requirements are satisfied (see Qs 5:15, 5:25). For example, a plan could require that an employee not be employed within a specified job description (e.g., sales representative) to be eligible to participate (see Q 1:23). [Treas Reg § 1.410(a)-3(d)]

The most common exclusion, other than exclusions based upon age and service, applies to union employees on whose behalf negotiations for retirement benefits have been conducted with the company. The company may exclude union employees from coverage, whether or not they are covered under a separate retirement plan, as long as retirement benefits were the subject of good-faith bargaining. Exclusions for air pilots and nonresident aliens are also permitted. [IRC § 410(b)(3)]

Plan provisions may be treated as imposing age and service requirements even though the provisions do not specifically refer to age or service. Plan provisions that have the effect of requiring an age or service requirement with the employer will be treated as if they impose an age or service requirement.

   Example. Attorney Bill, Inc. adopts a profit sharing plan that requires one year of service (see Q 5:8) to be eligible to participate but excludes part-time employees (employees who work less than 40 hours per week). The plan does not qualify because the provision could result in the exclusion by reason of a minimum service requirement of an employee who has completed a year of service. Even assuming that the exclusion from plan participation of part-time employees would not cause the plan to fail the minimum coverage requirements, the exclusion nonetheless imposes an indirect service requirement on plan participation that could exceed one year of service. A plan may not exclude any part-time employee where it is possible for that employee to complete one year of service.

   [Treas Reg §§ 1.410(a)-3(e)(1), 1.410(a)-3(e)(2); IRS Field Office Directive (Nov 22, 1994); Ltr Rul 9508003]

Q 5:6 May the company require employee contributions as a condition of plan participation?

   Yes. A company may adopt a plan—commonly called a thrift or savings plan (see Q 2:11)—that gears employer contributions on behalf of an employee to contributions made by the employee. Other types of plans may also require contributions to be made by the employees (e.g., defined benefit plans). Since participation in these plans is usually limited to those employees who contribute, if required employee contributions are so burdensome that non-highly compensated employees (see Q 3:13) cannot afford to participate, the plan may fail to satisfy the minimum coverage and participation requirements (see Qs 5:15, 5:25, 6:19).

Q 5:7 When must an employee who meets the plan's eligibility requirements begin to participate?

   An employee who meets the minimum age and service requirements of the Code (see Q 5:2), and who is otherwise eligible to participate in the qualified retirement plan, must commence participation no later than the earlier of (1) the first day of the first plan year beginning after the date the employee met the eligibility requirements or (2) the date six months after these requirements were met. [IRC § 410(a)(4)]

   Example. Ken began working for Danielle Corporation on October 1, 1995. He was 30 years old at that time. Danielle Corporation's qualified retirement plan operates on a calendar-year basis and requires that employees be at least age 21 and complete one year of service. Since Ken met the plan's eligibility requirements on October 1, 1996, he must start to participate in the plan no later than January 1, 1997. This is because January 1, 1997, the first day of the first plan year beginning after Ken has met the eligibility requirements, is earlier than April 1, 1997, the date six months after he has met these requirements.

Q 5:8 What is a year of service for a plan's service eligibility requirement?

A year of service for eligibility purposes means a calendar year, a plan year, or any other consecutive 12-month period (the eligibility computation period) specified in the qualified retirement plan during which the employee completes at least 1,000 hours of service (see Qs 5:5, 5:9). The period starts on the date employment commences. [IRC § 410(a)(3)(A)]

If the employee does not complete 1,000 hours of service during the initial eligibility computation period, the next period commences on the anniversary date of employment or, if provided in the plan, on the first day of the plan year during which the anniversary date falls. If the plan's service eligibility requirement is two years and the plan provides for the second year to start from the first day of the plan year, the employee will be credited with two years of service if 1,000 hours of service are completed during both the initial eligibility computation period and the plan year.

Example. Doctor Adam, Inc. adopted a calendar year profit sharing plan on January 1, 1995. The service eligibility requirement is two years, and the second year starts from the first day of the plan year. Caroline became employed on July 15, 1995, completed 1,000 hours of service by July 14, 1996, and completed 1,000 hours of service during calendar year 1996. Caroline is credited with two years of service and will commence participation in the plan on January 1, 1997.

Q 5:9 What is an hour of service?

An hour of service is any hour for which an employee is paid or is entitled to payment by the employer. An hour of service includes any hour for which payments are made due to an employee's vacation, sickness, holiday, disability, layoff, jury duty, military duty, or leave of absence, even if the employee no longer works for the company. An hour of service also includes any hour for which back pay is awarded. [Keleher v Dominion Insulation, Inc, 1992 US App Lexis 25561 (4th Cir 1992); DOL Reg § 2530.200b-2]

Although the general method of crediting service for an employee is based upon the actual counting of hours of service during the applicable 12-consecutive-month computation period, an alternative method, the elapsed time method, may be used to credit the service of employees for purposes of determining eligibility to participate, vesting, and benefit accrual. The elapsed time method is designed to lessen the recordkeeping burden. Under the elapsed time method of crediting service, the plan is generally required to take into account the period of time that elapses while the employee is employed with the employer *regardless* of the actual number of hours the employee completes during such period. Under this alternative method of crediting service, hours of service may be computed under any of the following methods:

1. Count 190 hours of service for each month for which the employee is paid or entitled to payment for at least one hour of service;

2. Count 95 hours of service for each semimonthly period for which the employee is paid or entitled to payment for at least one hour of service;

3. Count 45 hours of service for each week for which the employee is paid or entitled to payment for at least one hour of service; or

4. Count 10 hours of service for each day for which the employee is paid or entitled to payment for at least one hour of service.

[Treas Reg § 1.410(a)-7; DOL Reg § 2530.200b-3]

One court ruled that an employee did not receive credit for a year of service for vesting purposes (see Q 9:9) even though he was credited with 1,000 hours of service for the 12-month period under the elapsed time method adopted by the plan because the employee terminated employment before the end of the 12-month period. [Coleman v Interco Inc Divisions' Plans, No. 90-2700 (7th Cir 1991)]

Q 5:10   What is a one-year break in service?

A one-year break in service means a calendar year, a plan year, or any other consecutive 12-month period designated in the plan during which an employee does not complete more than 500 hours of service (see Qs 5:9, 5:14). [IRC §§ 410(a)(5)(C), 411(a)(6)(A); DOL Reg § 2530.200b-4]

An employee who works over 500 hours during the designated 12-month period does not incur a one-year break in service. An employee's one-year break in service has significance in terms of eligibility (see Qs 5:4, 5:12) and vesting of benefits (see Q 9:11).

Q 5:11 What years of service must be taken into account for eligibility purposes?

In general, all years of service with the employer must be counted. For the exceptions, see Q 5:12. [IRC § 410(a)(5)]

Service with a predecessor of the employer must be counted if the successor-employer maintains the predecessor's qualified retirement plan. If the successor adopts a new retirement plan, recognition of service with the predecessor-employer is supposed to be decided under as-yet-unissued IRS regulations. [IRC § 414(a)]

Service with any member of a controlled group of corporations or with a commonly controlled entity (see Q 5:31), whether or not incorporated, must be counted for eligibility purposes. Similarly, service with any member of an affiliated service group (see Q 5:37) must be counted. [IRC §§ 414(b), 414(c), 414(m)]

Q 5:12 May any years of service be disregarded for eligibility purposes?

Yes. Most qualified retirement plans may require up to two years of service as a prerequisite to participation (see Q 5:2). For plans that require two years of service as an eligibility requirement, a year of service (see Q 5:8) preceding a one-year break in service (see Q 5:10) need not be considered in determining whether an employee is eligible to participate (see Q 5:4). [IRC §§ 410(a)(1)(B), 410(a)(5)(B)]

Q 5:13 May past service with a former employer be used for eligibility purposes in the qualified retirement plan of the present employer?

If the present employer maintains the qualified retirement plan of a predecessor employer, an employee's service with the predecessor counts as service for the present employer (see Q 5:11). [Ltr Rul 9336046]

A qualified retirement plan may provide that service as an employee with a predecessor business counts for purposes of meeting the service eligibility requirement, even if the predecessor business had no qualified retirement plan (see Q 4:19). Furthermore, service as a partner of a partnership may be counted in meeting the service requirement for participation in the plan of a successor corporation. [Ltr Rul 7742003; Farley Funeral Homes, Inc, 62 TC 150 (1974)]

Q 5:14 Is a maternity or paternity period of absence treated as a break in service?

For purposes of determining whether a one-year break in service (see Q 5:10) has occurred for both participation and vesting purposes, an employee who is absent from work due to pregnancy or the birth or adoption of a child is treated as having completed, during the absence, the number of hours that normally would have been credited but for the absence, up to a maximum of 501 hours, so as to prevent a one-year break in service.

The hours of service are credited only in the year in which the absence begins (if necessary to prevent a break in service in that year) or in the following year. [IRC §§ 410(a)(5)(E), 411(a)(6)(E)]

Example. Before taking an approved maternity leave, Susan completed 750 hours of service during the 1996 plan year. Since the credit is not needed in 1996 to prevent a break in service, Susan is entitled to up to 501 hours of credited service in 1997.

Q 5:15 What coverage requirements must a retirement plan satisfy to qualify for favorable tax treatment?

A retirement plan must satisfy one of two coverage tests in order to qualify for favorable tax treatment:

1. The ratio percentage test (see Q 5:16), or

2. The average benefit test (see Q 5:17).

A plan maintained by an employer that benefits only non-highly compensated employees (see Q 3:13) or by an employer that has only highly compensated employees (see Q 3:2) will automatically satisfy the coverage requirements. [IRC §§ 410(b)(1), 410(b)(2), 410(b)(6)(F); Treas Reg §§ 1.410(b)-2(a), 1.410(b)-2(b); Rev Proc 95-34 1995-29 IRB 7; Rev Proc 93-42, 1993-2 CB 540; Ann 93-130, 1993-31 IRB 46; Ann 92-81, 1992-22 IRB 56]

A separate line of business exception may apply for the minimum coverage requirements (see Q 5:33).

Q 5:16 What is the ratio percentage test for the minimum coverage requirements?

Under the ratio percentage test, the percentage of the non-highly compensated employees (see Q 3:13) who benefit under the retirement plan must equal at least 70 percent of the percentage of the highly compensated employees (see Q 3:2) who benefit under the plan. Percentages are rounded to the nearest one-hundredth of 1 percent. [IRC § 410(b)(1); Treas Reg §§ 1.410(b)-2(b)(2), 1.410(b)-9]

> **Example 1.** For a plan year, Debi Corporation's defined benefit plan covers 60 percent of its non-highly compensated employees and 80 percent of its highly compensated employees. The plan's ratio percentage for the year is 75 percent (60% ÷ 80%) and thus satisfies the ratio percentage test.

> **Example 2.** For a plan year, Danielle Ltd.'s defined contribution plan covers 40 percent of its non-highly compensated employees and 60 percent of its highly compensated employees. The plan fails to satisfy the ratio percentage test because the ratio percentage is only 66.67 percent (40% ÷ 60%).

For purposes of satisfying the minimum coverage requirements, employees who do not meet the plan's minimum age or service requirement (see Qs 5:2, 5:5) are not counted. In addition, nonresident aliens who receive no earned income from sources within the United States and union members whose retirement benefits have been the subject of good-faith bargaining between the employer and the union do not count (see Q 5:5). [IRC §§ 410(b)(3), 410(b)(4); Treas Reg §§ 1.410(b)-6(a), 1.410(b)-6(b)(1), 1.410(b)-6(b)(2), 1.410(b)-6(c), 1.410(b)-6(d)]

Improperly characterizing employees as independent contractors could result in the failure to satisfy the ratio benefit test and the disqualification of the plan (see Q 5:1). [Kenney, 70 TCM 614 (1995)]

Q 5:17 What is the average benefit test for the minimum coverage requirements?

Under the average benefit test, (1) the plan must benefit such employees as qualify under a classification set up by the employer and found by IRS not to be discriminatory in favor of highly compensated employees (see Q 3:2), and (2) the average benefit percentage for non-highly compensated employees (see Q 3:13) of the employer must equal at least 70 percent of the average benefit percentage for highly compensated employees of the employer. [IRC § 410(b)(2); Treas Reg §§ 1.410(b)-2(b)(3), 1.410(b)-4, 1.410(b)-5]

The classification test is described in Q 5:18, and the average benefit percentage test in Q 5:19.

Q 5:18   What is the classification test?

The classification test is satisfied if, based on all the facts and circumstances, the classification set up by the employer is reasonable and is established under objective business criteria. In addition, the classification must be found to be nondiscriminatory based on either a safe harbor rule or a facts and circumstances test. The safe harbor rule is satisfied only if the plan's ratio percentage (see Q 5:16) is equal to or greater than the employer's safe harbor percentage. The safe harbor rule looks at the percentage (concentration percentage) of all of the employer's employees who are non-highly compensated employees (see Q 3:13) and then creates both a safe harbor percentage and an unsafe harbor percentage. The employer's safe harbor percentage is 50 percent reduced by .75 percent for each whole percentage point by which the concentration percentage exceeds 60 percent, and the unsafe harbor percentage is 40 percent reduced by .75 percent for each whole percentage point by which the concentration percentage exceeds 60 percent (but in no event less than 20 percent). [Treas Reg §§ 1.410(b)-4(b), 1.410(b)-4(c)]

The following table illustrates the safe harbor and unsafe harbor percentages at each concentration percentage:

Non-Highly Compensated Employee Concentration Percentage	Safe Harbor Percentage	Unsafe Harbor Percentage
0–60%	50.00%	40.00%
61	49.25	39.25
62	48.50	38.50
63	47.75	37.75
64	47.00	37.00
65	46.25	36.25
66	45.50	35.50
67	44.75	34.75
68	44.00	34.00
69	43.25	33.25
70	42.50	32.50
71	41.75	31.75
72	41.00	31.00
73	40.25	30.25
74	39.50	29.50
75	38.75	28.75

Non-Highly Compensated Employee Concentration Percentage	Safe Harbor Percentage	Unsafe Harbor Percentage
76	38.00	28.00
77	37.25	27.25
78	36.50	26.50
79	35.75	25.75
80	35.00	25.00
81	34.25	24.25
82	33.50	23.50
83	32.75	22.75
84	32.00	22.00
85	31.25	21.25
86	30.50	20.50
87	29.75	20.00
88	29.00	20.00
89	28.25	20.00
90	27.50	20.00
91	26.75	20.00
92	26.00	20.00
93	25.25	20.00
94	24.50	20.00
95	23.75	20.00
96	23.00	20.00
97	22.25	20.00
98	21.50	20.00
99	20.75	20.00

Example 1. Mikey Corp. has 200 employees; 120 are non-highly compensated employees and 80 are highly compensated employees. The non-highly compensated employee concentration percentage is 60 percent (120/200). Mikey Corp. maintains a retirement plan that excludes employees of a specified geographic location. The plan benefits 72 highly compensated employees and 60 non-highly compensated employees. The plan's ratio percentage is 55.56 percent [(60/120) ÷ (72/80) = (50% ÷ 90%)]. Since the concentration percentage is 60 percent, the safe harbor percentage is 50 percent and the unsafe harbor percentage is 40 percent. Because the ratio percentage (55.56 percent) is greater than the

safe harbor percentage (50 percent), the plan's classification satisfies the safe harbor rule.

Example 2. The facts are the same as in Example 1 except that the plan benefits 45 non-highly compensated employees. The plan's ratio percentage is 41.67 percent [(45/120) ÷ (72/80) = (37.50% ÷ 90%)]. Because the ratio percentage (41.67 percent) is below the safe harbor percentage (50 percent), but above the unsafe harbor percentage (40 percent), IRS may determine that the classification is nondiscriminatory based on all the facts and circumstances.

The exclusion from plan participation of a class of part-time employees is not an acceptable classification (see Q 5:5).

Q 5:19 What is the average benefit percentage test?

In order for a qualified retirement plan to satisfy the average benefit percentage test, the benefits provided to non-highly compensated employees (see Q 3:13) under all plans of the employer (expressed as a percentage of compensation) must generally be at least 70 percent as great, on average, as the benefits provided to the employer's highly compensated employees (see Q 3:2). [Treas Reg § 1.410(b)-5(a)]

Satisfaction of the average benefit percentage test requires that the employer determine an employee benefit percentage for each employee taken into account for testing purposes and then separately average the percentages of all employees in the highly compensated and non-highly compensated groups. Employee benefit percentages may be determined on either a contributions or a benefits basis, and employee contributions and benefits attributable to employee contributions are not taken into account. Generally, the employee benefit percentage for an employee is the rate that would be determined for that employee for purposes of applying the general nondiscrimination tests (see Qs 4:12, 4:17, 4:20). [Treas Reg §§ 1.410(b)-5(b), 1.410(b)-5(c), 1.410(b)-5(d), 1.410(b)-5(e)]

Improperly characterizing employees as independent contractors could result in the failure to satisfy the average benefit percentage test and the disqualification of the plan (see Q 5:1). [Kenney, 70 TCM 614 (1995)]

Q 5:20 When does an employee benefit under the qualified retirement plan?

For purposes of the minimum coverage rules, an employee must benefit under the qualified retirement plan to be taken into account for the percentage tests (see Qs 5:16, 5:17). An employee is treated as benefiting under the plan for a plan year:

1. In the case of a defined contribution plan (see Q 2:2), only if the employee receives an allocation of contributions or forfeitures.

2. In the case of a defined benefit plan (see Q 2:3), only if the employee receives a benefit accrual (see Q 9:2).

3. In the case of a 401(k) plan, if the employee is eligible to make an elective contribution (see Q 23:13), whether or not the employee actually does so.

4. If the employee fails to accrue a benefit solely because of the Section 415 limits on benefits and annual additions (see Qs 6:1, 6:5, 6:17), except that, in the case of a defined benefit plan, this exception does not apply if benefits in excess of the Section 415 limits are used to determine accrual rates for the general nondiscrimination test (see Q 4:17).

5. If the employee fails to accrue a benefit solely because of a uniformly applicable benefit limit under the plan.

6. If the current benefit accrual is offset by the contributions or benefits under another plan.

7. In the case of a target benefit plan (see Q 2:5), if the employee's theoretical reserve is greater than or equal to the actuarial present value of the fractional rule benefit (see Q 4:21).

8. If the employee has attained normal retirement age (see Q 10:53) under a defined benefit plan and fails to accrue a benefit solely because of the provisions regarding adjustments for delayed retirement.

9. In the case of an insurance contract plan (see Q 8:5), only if a premium is paid on behalf of the employee.

[Treas Reg §§ 1.410(b)-3(a)(1), 1.410(b)-3(a)(2)(i)-(iv); Rev Proc 93-42, 1993-2 CB 540; Ann 93-130, 1993-31 IRB 46; Ann 92-81, 1992-22 IRB 56]

In the case of a defined contribution plan, if no employee receives an allocation of contributions or forfeitures, the plan is treated as satisfying the minimum coverage requirements for the plan year because the plan benefits no highly compensated employees (see Q 3:2). Thus, a defined contribution plan for which contributions cease and for which no forfeitures can be allocated satisfies the requirements. In the case of a defined benefit plan, if no employee accrues any additional benefits under the plan, the plan is treated as satisfying the requirements for the plan year because no highly compensated employees benefit under the plan during that plan year. However, this special rule is not available with respect to a top-heavy plan that has required minimum contributions or benefit accruals (see Qs 22:37, 22:43), or to a plan where future compensation increases are taken into account in determining the accrued benefit under the plan.

An employee is treated as benefiting under a defined benefit plan for a plan year only if there is an increase in the employee's accrued benefit (see Q 9:2). Increases in the dollar amount of the accrued benefit merely because of the passage of time or because of a change in indices affecting the accrued benefit do not cause an employee to be treated as benefiting. In certain situations, however, an employee in a defined benefit plan will be treated as benefiting for a plan year even though the employee does not receive an accrual for the plan year. One of these situations is where an employee's accrued benefit would have increased if a previously accrued benefit were disregarded. An increase in covered compensation or a decrease in the employee's compensation for the plan year are other examples of situations where this might occur.

For the treatment of terminated employees, see Q 5:21; and, for a discussion of the family aggregation rule, see Q 5:22.

Q 5:21 How are employees who terminated employment during the plan year treated for minimum coverage purposes?

At the option of the employer, an employee is not taken into account for purposes of the minimum coverage tests (see Q 5:15) if:

1. The employee does not benefit (see Q 5:20) under the plan for the plan year;

2. The employee is eligible to participate in the plan;

3. The plan has a minimum hours of service requirement or a requirement that an employee be employed on the last day of the plan year (last-day requirement) in order to accrue a benefit or receive an allocation for the plan year;

4. The employee fails to accrue a benefit or receive an allocation under the plan solely because of the failure to satisfy the minimum hours of service or last-day requirement; and

5. The employee terminates employment during the plan year with not more than 500 hours of service (see Q 5:9) and the employee is not an active employee as of the last day of the plan year. (A plan that uses the elapsed time method (see Q 5:9) of determining years of service may use either 91 consecutive calendar days or three consecutive calendar months instead of 500 hours of service, provided it uses the same rule for all employees during a plan year.)

If the employer elects to use this option with respect to any employee for a plan year, it must be applied to all employees for that plan year. [Treas Reg § 1.410(b)-6(f)]

> **Example.** Norman of New Mexico, Inc. has 30 employees who are eligible under its profit sharing plan. The plan requires the employee to complete 1,000 hours of service during the plan year to receive an allocation of contributions or forfeitures. Ten employees do not receive an allocation because of their failure to complete 1,000 hours of service. Three of the ten employees completed less than 501 hours of service and terminated their employment. Two of the employees completed between 501 and 999 hours of service and terminated their employment. The remaining five employees did not terminate employment. The three terminated employees who completed less than 501 hours of service are not taken into account unless the employer elects to do so. The other seven employees who do not receive an allocation are taken into account but are treated as not benefiting under the plan.

Q 5:22   What is the family aggregation rule?

For years beginning prior to 1997, a highly compensated employee (see Q 3:2) who is a 5 percent owner (see Q 3:4) or one of the ten most highly compensated employees and all family members of such highly compensated employee who are also employees of the employer are treated as a single highly compensated employee for purposes of the minimum coverage requirements.

If any member of such group is benefiting (see Q 5:20) under the plan, the deemed single employee is treated as benefiting under the plan. If no member of such group is benefiting under the plan, the deemed single employee is treated as not benefiting under the plan.

Family includes the highly compensated employee's spouse, lineal descendants and ascendants, and spouses of lineal descendants or ascendants (see Q 3:14). [IRC §§ 410(b)(6)(A), 414(q)(6), prior to repeal by SBA '96 § 1431(b)(1); Treas Reg § 1.410(b)-8(b)]

> **Example.** Fast Ed, Inc. adopts a money purchase pension plan. The plan covers Arleen (the sole shareholder), her husband, Ed, who earns $20,000, and ten other employees. For purposes of the minimum coverage requirement, Arleen and Ed are treated as a single highly compensated employee.

For years beginning after 1996, the family aggregation rule is repealed. [SBA '96, Act § 1431(B)(1)] In the above example, Arleen and Ed will be treated as two separate employees in 1997. However, they will both be highly compensated employees because Arleen's stock ownership is attributed to Ed. [IRC §§ 416(i)(1)(B)(i)(I), 318(a)(1)(A)(i)]

Q 5:23 Must a qualified retirement plan satisfy the minimum coverage rules every day during the plan year?

No. A plan must satisfy the minimum coverage rules (see Q 5:15) for a plan year using one of three testing options. However, the annual testing option must be used in a 401(k) plan (see Q 23:1) or an employer matching or employee contribution plan (see Q 23:48), and in applying the average benefit percentage test (see Q 5:17).

The three testing options are:

1. *Daily Testing Option.* The plan must meet the coverage rules on each day of the plan year, taking into account all individuals who are employees (or former employees) on each day.

2. *Quarterly Testing Option.* The plan must satisfy the coverage rules on at least one day in each quarter of the plan year, taking into account only those individuals who are employees (or former employees) on that day, unless the four quarterly testing dates do not reasonably represent the plan's coverage over the entire plan year.

3. *Annual Testing Option.* The plan must satisfy the testing rules as of the last day of the plan year, taking into account all individuals who were employees (or former employees) at any time during the year.

[Treas Reg § 1.410(b)-8(a)]

In addition, plans may test as of a representative "snapshot" day during the year, and plans that do not experience significant change may test as infrequently as once every three years. [Rev Proc 95-34, 1995-29 IRB 7; Rev Proc 93-42, 1993-2 CB 540]

Q 5:24 When are the new minimum coverage rules effective?

The new rules (see Qs 5:15–5:22) are generally effective for plan years beginning on or after January 1, 1989. However, the final regulations published on August 31, 1993 by IRS are effective for plan years beginning on or after January 1, 1994.

For plan years beginning before January 1, 1994, the plan must be operated in accordance with a reasonable, good-faith interpretation of the minimum coverage requirements. [Treas Reg § 1.410(b)-10; Notice 92-36, 1992-2 CB 364; Ann 92-29, 1992-9 IRB 37; IRS Field Office Directive on Good-Faith Compliance (June 12, 1992); Ltr Rul 9214002]

Q 5:25   What is the minimum participation requirement?

In addition to the minimum coverage requirements (see Q 5:15), a minimum participation requirement must be met by each retirement plan of the employer in order to be qualified. *For years beginning prior to 1997,* to satisfy this latter requirement, a qualified retirement plan, whether a defined contribution plan (see Q 2:2) or a defined benefit plan (see Q 2:3), must benefit at least the lesser of (1) 50 employees, or (2) 40 percent of all employees. This requirement may not be satisfied by aggregating different plans of the employer. [IRC § 401(a)(26), prior to amendment by SBA '96 § 1432; Treas Reg §§ 1.401(a)(26)-1(a), 1.401(a)(26)-2(a)]

> **Example 1.** S&C Professional Law Corporation employs two attorneys and no other employees. Each attorney may participate in a separate qualified retirement plan because each plan will cover 40 percent or more of the employees.

> **Example 2.** SC&J Professional Law Corporation employs three attorneys and no other employees. Each attorney may not participate in a separate qualified retirement plan because each plan will cover less than 40 percent of the employees.

Among the plans that are deemed to meet the minimum participation requirements automatically are the following:

1. A plan that is not a top-heavy plan (see Qs 22:1, 22:3), benefits no highly compensated employee (see Q 3:2), and is not aggregated with any other plan to enable such other plan to satisfy the nondiscrimination requirements (see Q 4:9) or the minimum coverage requirements (see Q 5:15). [Treas Reg § 1.401(a)(26)-1(b)(1)]

2. Certain multiemployer plans (see Q 25:2). [Treas Reg § 1.401(a)(26)-1(b)(2)]

3. Certain underfunded defined benefit plans. [Treas Reg § 1.401(a)(26)-1(b)(3)]

4. Certain 401(k) plans (see Q 23:1) maintained by employers that include governmental or tax-exempt entities. [IRC § 401(k)(4)(B); Treas Reg § 1.401(a)(26)-1(b)(4)]

5. Certain plans of an employer involved in an acquisition or disposition. [Treas Reg § 1.401(a)(26)-1(b)(5)]

6. Defined contribution plans under which no employee receives an allocation of either contributions or forfeitures for the plan year. [Treas Reg § 1.401(a)(26)-2(b)]

7. Defined benefit plans under which no employee accrues any additional benefit for a plan year (other than those minimum benefits provided for non-key employees under top-heavy plans) but which

satisfy the prior benefit structure requirements (see Qs 5:27, 22:37). [Treas Reg § 1.401(a)(26)-2(b)]

Generally, an employee is deemed to benefit under the plan if the employee is deemed to benefit under the plan for the minimum coverage tests (see Q 5:20), and the family aggregation rule (see Q 5:22) does not apply for purposes of the minimum participation requirement. [Treas Reg § 1.401(a)(26)-5]

Improperly characterizing employees as independent contractors could result in the failure to satisfy the minimum participation test and the disqualification of the plan (see Q 5:1). [Kenney, 70 TCM 614 (1995)]

For years beginning after 1996, the minimum participation requirement will apply *only* to defined benefit plans. In addition, the 40 percent requirement is changed to the *greater* of (1) 40 percent of all employees, or (2) two employees (or if there is only one employee, that employee). In Example 1 above, if a plan was a defined benefit plan, that plan will not satisfy the minimum participation requirement because the plan will not cover *two* employees. In Example 2 above, if each plan is a defined contribution plan, the minimum participation requirement will not be applicable to any of the plans. [IRC § 410(a)(26)(A), as amended by SBA '96 § 1432]

Q 5:26 Which employees are not counted for the minimum participation requirements?

For purposes of applying the minimum participation test, all employees other than excludable employees must be taken into account. Generally, these requirements are applied separately to each qualified retirement plan of the employer and must be applied on a uniform and consistent basis. [Treas Reg § 1.401(a)(26)-6(a)]

An employee, if covered by one of the following exclusions, is an excludable employee:

1. The employee does not meet the plan's minimum age or service requirement (see Q 5:2).
2. The employee is a nonresident alien who receives no earned income from sources within the United States.
3. The employee is a union member whose retirement benefits have been the subject of good-faith bargaining between the employer and the union (see Q 5:5).

[Treas Reg § 1.401(a)(26)-6(b)]

Example 1. Jerry of Lawrence Ltd. maintains a defined benefit plan under which employees who have not completed one year of service are not eligible to participate. Jerry of Lawrence Ltd. has six employees. Two of the employees participate in the plan. The other four employees have not completed one year of service and are not eligible to participate. The four employees who have not completed one year of service are excludable employees and may be disregarded for purposes of applying the minimum participation test. Therefore, the test is satisfied because both of the employees who must be considered are participants in the plan.

Example 2. Busy-as-a-Bea Corporation has 100 employees and maintains two defined benefit plans, Plan A and Plan B. Plan A provides that employees who have not completed one year of service are not eligible to participate. Plan B has no minimum age or service requirement. Twenty of Busy-as-a-Bea's employees do not meet the minimum service requirement under Plan A. Each plan satisfies the ratio percentage test (see Q 5:16). In testing Plan A to determine whether it satisfies the minimum participation requirements, the 20 employees not meeting the minimum age and service requirement under Plan A are treated as excludable employees. In testing Plan B, no employees are treated as excludable employees because Plan B does not have a minimum age or service requirement.

In addition, certain terminated employees may be excluded (see Q 5:21), and a separate line of business exception may apply (see Q 5:46). [Treas Reg §§ 1.401(a)(26)-6(b)(7), 1.401(a)(26)-6(b)(8)]

Q 5:27 What is a prior benefit structure?

Defined benefit plans (see Q 2:3), but not defined contribution plans (see Q 2:2), must also satisfy the minimum participation requirements (see Q 5:25) with respect to a prior benefit structure. The prior benefit structure under a defined benefit plan for a plan year includes all benefits accrued to that time; therefore, the plan can have only one prior benefit structure. [Treas Reg §§ 1.401(a)(26)-3(a), 1.401(a)(26)-3(b)]

Generally, the prior benefit structure satisfies the minimum participation requirement if at least 50 employees or 40 percent of the employees currently accrue meaningful benefits (see Q 5:25). Whether a plan is providing meaningful benefits is determined on the basis of all the facts and circumstances. This determination is intended to ensure that a plan functions as an ongoing defined benefit plan providing meaningful benefits to at least 50 employees of the employer or 40 percent of the employer's employees. A plan does not satisfy this requirement if it exists primarily to preserve accrued benefits for a small group of employees and thereby functions more as an individual plan for the small group of employees or for the employer. The relevant factors in making this determination include, but are not limited to, the following:

1. The level of current benefit accruals;
2. The comparative rate of accruals under the current benefit formula compared to prior rates of accrual under the plan;
3. The projected accrued benefits under the current benefit formula compared to accrued benefits as of the close of the immediately preceding plan year;
4. The length of time the current benefit formula has been in effect;
5. The number of employees with accrued benefits under the plan; and
6. The length of time the plan has been in effect.

[Treas Reg § 1.401(a)(26)-3(c)]

With the change in the minimum participation requirements effective in 1997 (see Q 5:25), the new rule will apply to determine if the prior benefit structure satisfies the minimum participation requirements since a plan may have only one prior benefit structure and is based upon all benefits accrued to that time.

Q 5:28   May a retirement plan that does not satisfy the minimum participation requirements be retroactively corrected?

The minimum participation requirements (see Q 5:25) are generally effective for plan years beginning on or after January 1, 1989. [Treas Reg § 1.401(a)(26)-9(a)] The revised minimum participation requirements are effective for plan years beginning on or after January 1, 1997. [SBA '96, Act § 1432(c)]

To satisfy the requirements, the plan must satisfy the test on each day of the plan year. However, the plan will be treated as satisfying the requirements if it satisfies the test on any single day during the plan year, but only if that day is reasonably representative of the employer's workforce and the plan's coverage. A plan does not have to be tested on the same day each plan year. [Treas Reg §§ 1.401(a)(26)-7(a), 1.401(a)(26)-7(b)]

If a plan fails to satisfy the minimum participation requirements for a plan year, the plan may be retroactively amended to satisfy the requirements by expanding coverage, improving benefits or contributions, modifying eligibility conditions under the plan, or merging plans and deeming the merger to be effective retroactively to the first day of the plan year. [Treas Reg § 1.401(a)(26)-7(c); Notice 92-36, 1992-2 CB 364; IRS Field Office Directive on Good-Faith Compliance (June 12, 1992)]

Q 5:29 Can an employee's waiver of participation in the employer's qualified retirement plan jeopardize the tax-favored status of the plan?

Yes. For example, an employee who is otherwise eligible to participate in the employer's defined benefit plan that requires mandatory employee contributions as a condition of participation may be unable or unwilling to contribute and would therefore waive participation in the plan (see Qs 5:3, 5:6). That employee is included in determining whether the company's retirement plan satisfies the minimum coverage and minimum participation tests (see Qs 5:15, 5:25). Therefore, the plan may lose its tax-favored status if too many employees waive participation.

An employee's decision not to make an elective contribution (see Q 23:13) to a 401(k) plan is not a waiver of participation that would jeopardize the tax-favored status of the plan for purposes of the minimum coverage and minimum participation requirements (see Qs 5:20, 5:25). [Treas Reg §§ 1.410(b)-3(a)(2)(i), 1.401(a)(26)-5(a)(1)]

Q 5:30 What happens if a retirement plan fails to satisfy the minimum coverage or minimum participation requirements?

If a retirement plan fails to satisfy the qualification requirements of Section 401(a) (see Q 4:1), the tax-exempt status of plan earnings is revoked, employer deductions for contributions may be deferred or eliminated, and all employees must include the value of vested (see Q 9:1) plan contributions in income. [IRC § 402(b)(1); Ltr Rul 9502030]

However, if the plan fails to satisfy the minimum coverage or minimum participation requirements (see Qs 5:15, 5:25), each highly compensated employee (see Q 3:2) must include in income an amount equal to the employee's entire vested accrued benefit (see Q 9:2) not previously included in income, not just current vested plan contributions. If, however, the plan is not qualified solely because it fails to satisfy either of these requirements, no adverse tax consequences are imposed on non-highly compensated employees (see Q 3:13). [IRC § 402(b)(4); Ltr Rul 9502030]

IRS has opined that, with the integrated approach underlying the non-discrimination requirements (see Q 4:9) and the minimum coverage requirements, any failure to satisfy the nondiscrimination requirements can be viewed as failure to satisfy the minimum coverage requirements. Consequently, failure to meet the nondiscrimination requirements will subject highly compensated employees to the special sanctions. [Preamble to final regulations (Sept 19, 1991)]

Q 5:31 Do special coverage and participation rules apply to commonly controlled businesses?

For purposes of determining whether a retirement plan covers a sufficient number of employees to meet the minimum coverage requirements (see Q 5:15) and the minimum participation requirements (see Q 5:25), as well as other plan-related requirements, all employees of corporations that are members of a controlled group of corporations (see Q 5:33) are treated as if they were employed by a single employer. A comparable requirement applies to affiliated service groups (see Q 5:37), partnerships, sole proprietorships, and other businesses that are under common control. In addition, a special rule applies to owner-employees (see Qs 5:34, 5:35). [IRC §§ 414(b), 414(c), 414(m)]

However, the Tax Court has held that the employees of two failing corporations should not be aggregated with the employees of a sole proprietorship, all three of which were commonly controlled, when, under the circumstances, neither corporation was able, in good faith, to adopt a permanent retirement plan. IRS did not acquiesce in this decision. [Sutherland, 78 TC 395 (1982); *non acq*, 1986-1 CB 1]

Two related tax-exempt organizations do not constitute either a controlled group of corporations or trades or businesses under common control, ruled IRS. Both organizations were nonstock, nonprofit corporations governed by their respective boards of trustees, no individual or entity had an ownership interest in either organization, and no person served as a trustee on both boards. Four of the nine trustees on the second organization's board were employees of the first organization; this did not meet the 80 percent control test (see Q 5:33). [Ltr Rul 9442031]

A separate line of business exception may apply, for purposes of the minimum coverage and participation requirements, to commonly controlled businesses but not to affiliated service groups (see Q 5:46). [IRC §§ 401(a)(26)(G), 410(b)(5), 414(r)]

Q 5:32 If an individual owns two corporations, each of which has employees, can a qualified retirement plan be adopted by only one of the corporations?

Perhaps. For example, assume Herman owns all of the stock of Herman Corporation and Mabel Corporation. Herman Corporation maintains a retirement plan for its employees; Mabel Corporation does not.

The composition of Herman's employees is as follows:

Employee	Age	Service	Compensation
1	50	10 years	$150,000
2	35	6 years	20,000
3	30	4 years	10,000
4	28	less than 1 year	10,000

The composition of Mabel's employees is as follows:

Employee	Age	Service	Compensation
5	45	2 years	$100,000
6	43	2 years	20,000
7	18	less than 1 year	10,000

Employees 1, 2, 3, 5, and 6 satisfy the plan's eligibility requirements (age 21 and one year of service), and employees 1 and 5 are highly compensated employees (see Q 3:3). Employees 4 and 7 need not be counted for purposes of the minimum participation and minimum coverage tests since they have not satisfied the plan's age and service requirements.

Since the retirement plan covers 60 percent of the employees who satisfy the eligibility requirements (i.e., 3 ÷ 5), the plan satisfies the minimum participation requirement (see Q 5:25). In addition, the plan satisfies the ratio percentage test (see Q 5:16) because the plan's ratio percentage is 70 percent or more (i.e., the coverage percentage of non-highly compensated employees, 66.67 percent [2 ÷ 3], divided by the coverage percentage of highly compensated employees, 50 percent [1 ÷ 2]).

Q 5:33 When does common ownership result in a controlled group of corporations or businesses?

A controlled group of corporations exists if there is:

1. A parent-subsidiary group of corporations connected through at least 80 percent stock ownership; or

2. A brother-sister group in which

   a. Five or fewer people own 80 percent or more of the stock value or voting power of each corporation, and

   b. The same five or fewer people together own more than 50 percent of the stock value or voting power of each corporation, taking into account the ownership of each person only to the extent such ownership is identical with respect to each organization.

[IRC § 1563(a); United States v Vogel Fertilizer Co, 102 S Ct 821 (1982)]

Example 1. SJK Corporation owns 100 percent of the stock of SLK Corporation, 80 percent of the stock of CAK Corporation, and 70 percent of the stock of JMK Corporation. The percentage of stock not owned by SJK Corporation is owned by unrelated persons. SJK, SLK, and CAK are members of a controlled group of corporations. JMK is not a member of the group because SJK's ownership is less than 80 percent.

Example 2. Kenneth Corp. and Robert Corp. are owned by four unrelated shareholders in the following percentages:

	Percentage of Ownership	
Shareholder	Kenneth Corp.	Robert Corp.
Stanley	80%	20%
Marjorie	10	50
Kenneth	5	15
Robert	5	15
Total	100%	100%

Although the four shareholders together own 80 percent or more of the stock of each corporation, they do not own more than 50 percent of the stock of each corporation taking into account only the identical ownership as demonstrated below:

Shareholder	Identical Ownership Percentage
Stanley	20%
Marjorie	10
Kenneth	5
Robert	5
Total	40%

Consequently, Kenneth Corp. and Robert Corp. do not constitute a controlled group of corporations.

Where a corporation (Newco) was formed by the merger of six corporations (Oldcos), the plan adopted by Newco did not have to be aggregated with any plans of the Oldcos because the entities did not constitute a controlled group of corporations. [Ltr Rul 9541041]

Q 5:34 Who is an owner-employee?

An owner-employee is a self-employed individual (see Q 6:33) who is either a sole proprietor or, in the case of a partnership, a partner who owns more than 10 percent of either the capital interest or the profits interest in such partnership. [IRC § 401(c)(3); Treas Reg § 1.401-10(d)]

Q 5:35 Does any special coverage requirement apply if an owner-employee controls another business?

Yes, *but only for years beginning before 1997.* If an individual is an owner-employee (see Q 5:34) of more than one business and participates in a qualified retirement plan maintained by one of the individual's businesses (Plan X), all employees of any other business controlled by the owner-employee must be covered by a plan that gives them benefits at least as favorable as those provided for the owner-employee under Plan X. This rule also applies if two or more owner-employees together control another business as owner-employees. [IRC §§ 401(d)(1), 401(d)(2), prior to amendment by SBA '96 § 1441; Treas Reg § 1.401-12(l); see also IRC § 414(c)]

Control means (1) ownership of the entire interest in an unincorporated trade or business, or (2) ownership of more than 50 percent of either the capital interest or the profits interest in a partnership.

Example. Debi is the sole owner of a record store and is also a 51 percent partner in a hardware store. The hardware store maintains a qualified retirement plan. No contributions to the hardware store's qualified retirement plan can be made on Debi's behalf unless her record store gives its employees equal benefits under a qualified retirement plan.

This special coverage requirement was one of the few restrictions that applied to qualified retirement plans that covered owner-employees but not to corporate retirement plans. With the enactment of SBA '96 (see Q 1:21), *for years beginning after 1996,* Debi can participate in the hardware store's plan because the record store and the hardware store are not trades or businesses under common control (see Qs 5:31-5:33). However, the qualified retirement plan must provide that contributions on behalf of the owner-employee may be made only with respect to the owner-employee's earned income (see Q 6:34) derived from the trade or business adopting the plan. [IRC § 401(d), as amended by SBA '96 § 1441]

Q 5:36 What happens if the business owner sets up a management corporation?

If the business owner establishes a second corporation to perform management functions for the owner's other closely held corporation (e.g., a manufacturing corporation) and owns at least 80 percent of the stock of each corporation, both corporations will be considered to be members of a controlled group of corporations (see Qs 5:31–5:33). [IRC §§ 414(b), 1563(a)]

If the management corporation establishes a qualified retirement plan for the business owner (its only employee) and the manufacturing corporation has no plan for its employees, the plan probably will not be qualified because of inadequate coverage and participation (see Q 5:1).

In addition, even if there is no common ownership, if an organization principally performs management functions for one other organization, both such organizations are considered to be an affiliated service group (see Q 5:37).

Q 5:37   What is an affiliated service group?

An affiliated service group consists of a service organization (FSO) and one or both of the following:

1. A service organization (A-ORG) that is a shareholder or partner in the FSO and that either regularly performs services for the FSO or is regularly associated with the FSO in performing services for third persons;

2. Any other organization (B-ORG) if a significant portion of the business of the B-ORG is the performance of services for the FSO or the A-ORG (or for both) of a type historically performed in the service field of the FSO or the A-ORG by employees, and 10 percent or more of the interests in the B-ORG is held by individuals who are highly compensated employees of the FSO or A-ORG.

[IRC § 414(m); Rev Rul 81-105, 1981-1 CB 256]

Example. Medical partnership P consists of corporate partners A, B, and C. Each partner owns one-third of the partnership. The partnership employs nurses and clerical employees. Corporations A, B, and C have only one employee each, the respective shareholders. The partnership does not maintain a retirement plan. Corporations A, B, and C maintain separate retirement plans.

Partnership P may be designated as the FSO. Since Corporations A, B, and C are partners in the FSO and regularly perform services for the FSO, Corporations A, B, and C are A-ORGs. Because Corporations A, B, and C are A-ORGs for the same FSO, Corporations A, B, and C and the FSO constitute an affiliated service group. Consequently, all the employees of corporations A, B, and C and the employees of P are considered as employed by a single employer for purposes of testing the qualification of the three separate retirement plans maintained by Corporations A, B, and C.

IRS had issued proposed regulations directed at determining what types of organizational structures would be disregarded in order to prevent the avoidance of employee benefit requirements. These regulations covered affiliated service groups, leased employees (see Q 5:61), and other organizational arrangements. However, in 1993, as part of the Regulatory Burden Reduction Initiative, IRS withdrew those proposed regulations because IRS did not plan to finalize them. [TD 8474]

Where a corporation (Newco) was formed by the merger of six corporations (Oldcos), the plan adopted by Newco did not have to be aggregated with any plans of the Oldcos because the entities did not constitute an affiliated service group. [Ltr Rul 9541041]

Q 5:38 Will IRS rule on the qualified status of the retirement plan of a member of an affiliated service group?

Yes. IRS has set out procedures for obtaining determination letters on the qualification of a retirement plan established by a member of an affiliated service group, including a management organization (see Q 5:36).

An employer (1) that has adopted a new retirement plan, (2) that has amended an existing retirement plan to satisfy the affiliated service group rules, or (3) whose affiliated service group status has changed may request a determination on whether the retirement plan is qualified, taking into consideration employees of any other organization who must be treated as employees of that employer. Generally, a determination letter issued with respect to the retirement plan will cover the affiliated service group rules only if the employer submits, with the determination letter application, certain information. If IRS considers whether the retirement plan of the employer (or group of employers) satisfies the requirements of the affiliated service group rules, the determination letter issued to the employer(s) will indicate that these questions have been considered and that the retirement plan satisfies qualification requirements relating to the affiliated service group rules. Without this statement, a determination letter does not apply to any qualification issue arising by reason of the affiliated service group rules.

The application for a determination letter must include the following:

1. A description of the business of the employer, specifically discussing whether it is a service organization or an organization whose principal business is the performance of management functions.

2. Identification of other members (or possible members) of the affiliated service group.

3. A description of the nature of the business of each member (or possible member) of the affiliated service group, specifically discussing whether the member is a service organization or management organization.

4. The ownership interests between the employer and the members (or possible members) of the affiliated service group.

5. A description of services performed for the employer by the members (or possible members) of the affiliated service group, or vice versa, including financial data as to whether the services are a significant portion of the member's business and are of a type historically performed in the employer's service field by employees.

6. A description of how the employer and the members (or possible members) of the affiliated service group associate in performing services for other parties.

7. A description of management functions, if any, performed by the employer for the members (or possible members) of the affiliated service group, or received by the employer from any other members (or possible members) of the group (including data as to whether such management functions are performed on a regular and continuing basis) and whether it is not unusual for such management functions to be performed by employees of organizations in the employer's business field.

8. If management functions are performed by the employer for the members (or possible members) of the affiliated service group, a description of what part of the employer's business constitutes the performance of management functions for the members (or possible members) of the group (including the percentage of gross receipts derived from management activities as compared to the gross receipts from other activities).

9. A brief description of any other retirement plan(s) maintained by the members (or possible members) of the affiliated service group if such other retirement plan(s) is designated as a unit for qualification purposes.

10. A description of how the retirement plan(s) satisfies the coverage requirements if the members (or possible members) of the affiliated service group are considered part of an affiliated service group with the employer.

11. A copy of any ruling issued by the IRS National Office to the employer as to whether the employer is a member of an affiliated service group; a copy of any prior ruling that considered the effect of affiliated service group status on the employer's retirement plan; and, if known, a copy of any such ruling issued to any other member or possible member of the same affiliated service group, accompanied by a statement as to whether the facts upon which the ruling was based have changed.

[Rev Proc 92-6, 1992-1 CB 611; Rev Proc 85-43, 1985-2 CB 501; Rev Rul 83-36, 1983-1 CB 763; Rev Proc 80-30, 1980-1 CB 685]

Q 5:39 What is a personal service corporation?

A personal service corporation is a corporation that provides, as its principal activity, personal services substantially performed by the employee-owners (see Q 5:41). This definition is not limited to incorporated professionals but will also apply to incorporated salesmen, consultants, and other service-rendering individuals. [IRC § 269A(b)(1); Prop Reg § 1.269A-1(b)(1)]

Q 5:40 Can the income of a personal service corporation be allocated to the employee-owner?

If substantially all of the services of a personal service corporation (see Q 5:39) are performed for one other organization (see Q 5:42) and the principal purpose for forming the corporation is the avoidance of income tax by reducing the income of, or obtaining the benefit of any deduction for, any employee-owner (see Q 5:41) that would not otherwise be available, IRS may allocate income and deductions between the personal service corporation and its employee-owners. [IRC §§ 269A, 482; Prop Reg §§ 1.269A-1(a), 1.269A-1(f); Haag, 88 TC 604 (1987); Foglesong v Comm'r, 691 F 2d 848 (7th Cir 1982), *rev'g* 77 TC 1102 (1981); Achiro, 77 TC 881 (1981); Keller, 723 F 2d 58 (10th Cir 1983), *aff'g* 77 TC 1014 (1981)]

Since the personal service corporation must perform services for only one other organization and need not have any ownership interest in such organization, this provision both broadens the affiliated service group rules (see Q 5:37) and applies to other situations.

Now that parity between the amount of retirement benefits and contributions available to the employee-owner under qualified corporate retirement plans and qualified retirement plans covering self-employed individuals (see Q 6:33) has been achieved, IRS should not be able to allocate qualified retirement plan deductions to the incorporated employee-owner, since the employee-owner could then receive the same benefits without incorporating. However, if the incorporated employee-owner uses the corporation to obtain other tax benefits not available to an unincorporated employee-owner, those tax deductions may be lost (see Qs 1:9, 5:44).

Where the individual was *not* self-employed and was initially an employee of one other organization (see Q 5:42), IRS failed in its attempt to tax the individual on contributions made to the qualified retirement plan adopted by the individual's personal service corporation. The individual, a professional hockey player, entered into an employment contract with his personal service corporation, which, in turn, contracted with the hockey club to provide the individual's services. The court ruled that valid contractual relationships existed so IRS could not allocate the plan contributions to the individual as taxable income. [Sargent v Comm'r, 929 F 2d 1252 (8th Cir 1991)] However, IRS has successfully argued that the entire amount paid to a professional basketball player's personal service corporation by the basketball team was includible in the player's gross income; the corporate entity was effectively disregarded. [IRC § 482; Leavell, 104 TC 140 (1995)]

Q 5:41   Who is an employee-owner?

An employee-owner is an employee who, directly or indirectly, owns more than 10 percent of the stock of the personal service corporation. [IRC § 269A(b)(2); Prop Reg § 1.269A-1(b)(2)]

Q 5:42   What is one other organization for purposes of the personal service corporation rules?

For the potential reallocation of income and deductions between the personal service corporation and the employee-owner (see Q 5:41) to occur, substantially all of the services of the corporation must be performed for one other corporation, partnership, or other entity. [IRC § 269A(a)(1); Prop Reg § 1.269A-1(a)(1)]

All related persons are treated as one other entity. [IRC §§ 144(a)(3), 269A(b)(3); Prop Reg § 1.269A-1(b)(3)]

Q 5:43   Is there a safe harbor for a personal service corporation?

Yes. In general, a personal service corporation (see Q 5:39) will be deemed not to have been formed for the principal purpose of avoiding income tax if the federal income tax liability of no employee-owner (see Q 5:41) is reduced in a 12-month period by more than the lesser of (1) $2,500 or (2) 10 percent of the federal income tax liability of the employee-owner that would have resulted in that 12-month period had the employee-owner performed the personal services in an individual capacity. [Prop Reg § 1.269A-1(c)]

Q 5:44 Is a retirement plan considered in determining whether the principal purpose of a personal service corporation is the avoidance of income taxes?

Generally, the existence of a qualified retirement plan will not be taken into account in determining the presence or absence of a principal purpose of the personal service corporation (see Q 5:39) to avoid income tax for purposes of the safe-harbor rule (see Qs 5:40, 5:43). [Sargent v Comm'r, 929 F 2d 1252 (8th Cir 1991); Prop Reg § 1.269A-1(d)]

Q 5:45 May a director of a corporation establish a qualified retirement plan based on the director's fees?

An outside director may establish a qualified retirement plan on the basis of such fee income. Since many outside directors are in high income tax brackets, the creation of a qualified retirement plan may be an especially attractive tax-saving device for these individuals. [Rev Rul 68-595, 1968-2 CB 378]

IRS had issued proposed regulations concerning inside directors. An inside director is an individual who is both an employee and a director of the same corporation. If the inside director maintains a qualified retirement plan apart from any plan maintained by the corporation, then, to the extent that contributions, forfeitures, and benefits under the inside director's individual plan are attributable to services performed for the corporation as a director, the individual is treated as an employee of the corporation and the inside director's interest in the individual plan is treated as though it was provided under both (1) a separate qualified retirement plan maintained by the corporation and covering only the inside director, and (2) any actual plan maintained by the corporation in which the director participates. If either of these plans fails to meet the qualification requirements (see chapter 4), any plan actually maintained by the corporation that covers the inside director and the plan maintained by the inside director may be disqualified. In 1993, as part of the Regulatory Burden Reduction Initiative, IRS withdrew the proposed regulations because IRS did not plan to finalize them. [TD 8474]

The withdrawal of these proposed regulations does not constitute IRS's imprimatur for inside director plans because proposed regulations regarding leased owners and leased managers were not withdrawn, and IRS could still disqualify both plans.

An individual is a "leased owner" with respect to a recipient (e.g., the corporation) if, during the plan year of a plan maintained by a leasing organization (e.g., the inside director), the individual performs any services for a recipient other than as an employee of the recipient and is, at the time such services are performed, a more-than-5-percent owner (see Q 22:28) of the recipient (see Q 6:35). [Jacobs, 66 TCM 1470 (1993)] The fact that an individual may also perform services as an employee of the recipient does not affect the individual's status as a leased owner. [Prop Reg § 1.414(o)-1(b)]

A "leased manager" is an individual (e.g., the inside director) who during the calendar year performs any services for a recipient (e.g., the corporation) other than as an employee of the recipient, performs a significant amount of management activities or services for the recipient, including management functions performed as an employee of the recipient and in any other capacity, and is credited with at least 1,000 hours of service (see Q 5:9) for the recipient, including services performed as an employee of the recipient and in any other capacity. The fact that an individual may also perform services as an employee of the recipient does not affect the individual's status as a leased manager. [Prop Reg § 1.414(o)-1(c)]

Q 5:46   Is there a separate line of business exception to the minimum coverage and minimum participation requirements?

All employees of a single employer (see Q 5:31) are taken into account for purposes of applying the minimum coverage requirements (see Q 5:15) and the minimum participation requirements (see Q 5:25). However, if an employer is treated as operating qualified separate lines of business (see Q 5:49), the employer is permitted to apply the minimum coverage requirements separately with respect to the employees of each qualified separate line of business. A similar exception (but only with IRS consent) is provided for purposes of applying the minimum participation requirements. The separate line of business exception does not apply to an affiliated service group (see Q 5:37). [IRC §§ 410(b)(5), 401(a)(26)(G), prior to amendment by SBA '96 § 1432, 414(r)] *For years beginning after 1996,* the rule that a line of business must have at least 50 employees (see Q 5:50) does not apply in determining whether a defined benefit plan (see Q 2:3) satisfies the minimum participation requirements on a separate line of business basis. This means that the minimum participation requirements may be separately applied to an employer's line of business that has fewer than 50 employees if it otherwise qualifies as a separate line of business. [IRC §§ 401(a)(26)(A), 401(a)(26)(G), as amended by SBA '96 § 1432]

If the employer operates qualified separate lines of business, the employer need not satisfy the ratio percentage test (see Q 5:16) or the average benefit percentage test (see Q 5:19) on an employer-wide basis. However, even if an employer is treated as operating qualified separate lines of business, every plan of the employer must satisfy the nondiscriminatory classification test (see Q 5:18) on an employer-wide basis. [IRC § 410(b)(5)(B); Treas Reg §§ 1.414(r)-8, 1.414(r)-9]

An employer is treated as operating qualified separate lines of business during any year if the employer operates separate lines of business (see Q 5:48) for bona fide business reasons and satisfies certain other conditions. An employer is treated as operating qualified separate lines of business only if: (1) the employer identifies all the property and services it provides to customers and designates the property and services provided by each of its lines of business (see Q 5:47); (2) each line of business is organized and operated separately from the remainder of the employer and is therefore a separate line of business; and (3) each separate line of business meets additional statutory requirements (see Q 5:49) and thus constitutes a qualified separate line of business.

An employer is treated as operating qualified separate lines of business only if all the property and services provided by the employer to its customers are provided exclusively by qualified separate lines of business. Therefore, if an employer is treated as operating qualified separate lines of business, no portion of the employer may remain that is not included in a qualified separate line of business. [Treas Reg § 1.414(r)-1]

Q 5:47   What is a line of business?

In order to demonstrate that it maintains qualified separate lines of business (see Q 5:49), an employer must initially determine its lines of business. A line of business is a portion of an employer that is identified by the property or services it provides to customers of the employer. [Treas Reg § 1.414(r)-2]

In determining its lines of business, the employer first identifies all the property and services it provides to its customers and then designates the property and services provided by each of its lines of business. Therefore, an employer may use its discretion to determine its lines of business in a manner that conforms to its business operations.

Example 1. Rancho Krevat Corporation is a domestic conglomerate engaged in the manufacture and sale of consumer food and beverage products and the provision of data processing services to private industry. The corporation provides no other property or services to its customers. Rancho Krevat Corporation apportions all the property and services it provides to its customers among three lines of business, one providing all its consumer food products, a second providing all its consumer beverage products, and a third providing all its data processing services. Rancho Krevat Corporation has three lines of business.

Example 2. The facts are the same as in Example 1, except that Rancho Krevat Corporation determines that neither the consumer food products line of business nor the consumer beverage products line of business would satisfy the separateness criteria for recognition as a separate line of business. Accordingly, Rancho Krevat Corporation apportions all the property and services it provides to its customers between only two lines of business, one providing all its consumer food and beverage products and a second providing all its data processing services. Rancho Krevat Corporation has two lines of business.

See Q 5:48 for the rules pertaining to vertically integrated lines of business.

Q 5:48   What is a separate line of business?

In order to demonstrate that it maintains qualified separate lines of business (see Q 5:49), an employer must show that its lines of business (see Q 5:47) are organized and operated separately from one another and therefore are separate lines of business. [Treas Reg §§ 1.414(r)-3, 1.414(r)-11(b)(2), 1.414(r)-11(b)(3)]

Whether a line of business is a separate line of business is determined by satisfying each of the following objective criteria:

Separate organizational unit. Each line of business must be formally organized by the employer as a separate organizational unit within the employer (i.e., a corporation, a partnership, a division, or other similar unit).

Separate financial accountability. Each line of business must be a separate profit center within the employer. For this purpose, the employer's books and records must indicate separate revenue and expense information for each profit center comprising the line of business.

Separate workforce. Each line of business must have its own separate workforce. Satisfaction of this test will depend upon the degree to which each line shares personnel with other portions of the employer. A line of business has its own separate workforce if at least 90 percent of the employees of the employer who provide any services to the line of business are substantial-service employees (see Q 5:56) with respect to the line of business and are not substantial-service employees with respect to any other line of business.

Separate management. Each line of business must have its own separate management. A line of business has its own separate management only if at least 80 percent of the top-paid workforce who provide services to the line of business are substantial-service employees with respect to the line of business. The top-paid workforce is the top 10 percent, by compensation, of all employees who provide at least 25 percent of their services to the line of business and who are not substantial-service employees with respect to any other line of business. In addition, in determining the group of top-paid employees, the employer may choose to disregard all employees who provide less than 25 percent of their services to the line of business.

Employees of a line of business (the upstream line) that provides property or services to another line of business of the employer (the downstream line) generally are also considered to be providing services to the downstream line of business. Since this presents difficulties for vertically integrated employers desiring to satisfy the separateness tests, an optional rule permits employers to treat these employees as not necessarily providing services to the downstream line. This rule is available only if certain conditions are satisfied, including a requirement that the upstream line provide at least 25 percent of its total output to outside customers of the employer. The optional rule can now apply in the case of an upstream manufacturer that provides all of its product to a downstream line and has few, if any, outside customers. Under this alternative, the vertical integration rule will also apply if, with respect to the downstream line, the business of the upstream line consists primarily of producing or manufacturing tangible property, and the same type of tangible property is provided to unrelated customers by some entities engaged in a business similar to the upstream line. The alternative would apply also for purposes of satisfying the requirement that a line of business provide property to customers of the employer. [Treas Reg §§ 1.414(r)-2(b)(2)(i), 1.414(r)-3(d)]

Example. El Glucko Corporation operates two lines of business, one engaged in upholstery textile manufacturing and the other in furniture manufacturing. The upholstery textile line of business provides its entire output of upholstery textiles to the furniture line of business. The furniture line of business uses the upholstery textiles in the manufacture of upholstered furniture for sale to the customers of El Glucko Corporation. The furniture line of business substantially modifies the upholstery textiles provided to it by the upholstery textile line of business in providing upholstered furniture products to customers of the corporation. In addition, although the upholstery textile line of business does not provide upholstery textiles to customers of the corporation, some entities engaged in upholstery textile manufacturing provide upholstery textiles to customers outside their controlled groups. Under these facts, El Glucko Corporation's two lines of business satisfy the requirements for the optional rule. Thus, the employees of the upholstery textile line of business will be deemed to provide services only to that line of business for purposes of the separate workforce and separate management requirements, the 50-employee requirement (see Q 5:50), and the determination of the employees of each qualified separate line of business (see Q 5:56).

Q 5:49 What is a qualified separate line of business?

To demonstrate that the employer maintains qualified separate lines of business, the following requirements must be satisfied: (1) each separate line of business must have at least 50 employees (see Q 5:50); (2) the employer must notify IRS that it treats itself as operating qualified separate lines of business (see Q 5:51); and (3) the line must satisfy administrative scrutiny (see Q 5:52). [Treas Reg § 1.414(r)-1(b)(2)(iv)]

Q 5:50 What is the 50-employee requirement?

One of the requirements to establish that the employer maintains qualified separate lines of business (see Q 5:49) is that each separate line of business (see Q 5:48) must have 50 or more employees. [IRC § 414(r)(2)(A); Treas Reg § 1.414(r)-1(b)(2)(iv)(B)]

The 50-employee requirement must be satisfied on each day of the testing year (see Q 5:57). All employees who provide services exclusively to the separate line of business (see Q 5:56), *including* employees who are covered under a collective bargaining agreement, are counted. However, employees who normally work less than 17½ hours per week, who normally work six months or less during the year, who are under age 21, or who have not completed six months of service are not taken into account. [Treas Reg §§ 1.414(r)-4(b), 1.414(q)-1, Q&A 9(g)]

Q 5:51 What is the notice requirement?

To satisfy the notice requirement, the employer must notify IRS that it treats itself as operating qualified separate lines of business (see Q 5:49). [IRC § 414(r)(2)(B); Treas Reg § 1.414(r)-1(b)(2)(iv)(C)] The notice is given with respect to all the qualified separate lines of business of the employer and with respect to all retirement plans of the employer for plan years beginning in the testing year (see Q 5:57). [Treas Reg § 1.414(r)-4(c)]

Notice that the employer wishes to be treated as operating qualified separate lines of business is given by filing Form 5310-A, Notice of Merger, Consolidation or Transfer of Plan Assets or Liabilities; Notice of Qualified Separate Lines of Business.

Q 5:52 What is the administrative scrutiny requirement?

To satisfy the administrative scrutiny requirement that the employer maintains qualified separate lines of business (see Q 5:49), a separate line of business (see Q 5:48) must meet either the statutory safe harbor test (see Q 5:53) or one of the administrative safe harbors (see Q 5:54). A separate line of business that does not satisfy any of these safe harbors may still satisfy this requirement if the employer requests and receives from IRS an individual determination that the separate line of business satisfies administrative scrutiny (see Q 5:55). Each separate line of business of an employer must satisfy the administrative scrutiny requirement but need not satisfy this requirement in the same manner as the employer's other separate lines of business. [IRC § 414(r)(2)(C); Treas Reg § 1.414(r)-1(b)(2)(iv)(D)]

Q 5:53 What is the statutory safe harbor?

A qualified separate line of business (see Q 5:49) satisfies the statutory safe harbor for administrative scrutiny (see Q 5:52) if the percentage of highly compensated employees (see Q 3:2) of the separate line of business (see Q 5:48) falls within a range that is at least 50 percent but no more than 200 percent of the highly compensated employee percentage of the employer as a whole (see Q 5:56). The highly compensated employee percentage ratio of a separate line of business is calculated by determining a fraction (expressed as a percentage), the numerator of which is the percentage of the employees of the separate line of business who are highly compensated employees, and the denominator of which is the percentage of all employees of the employer who are highly compensated employees.

Additionally, if at least 10 percent of all highly compensated employees of the employer perform services exclusively for a particular separate line of business, that separate line of business will be deemed to satisfy the 50 percent requirement of the statutory safe harbor. However, a separate line of business that satisfies this special 10 percent rule still must satisfy the 200 percent requirement of the statutory safe harbor. [IRC § 414(r)(3); Treas Reg § 1.414(r)-5(b)]

Q 5:54 What are the administrative safe harbors?

There are five administrative safe harbors for the administrative scrutiny requirement (see Q 5:52). To permit the application of the minimum coverage and minimum participation standards (see Qs 5:15, 5:25) on a qualified separate line of business basis, these administrative safe harbors delineate situations that IRS has determined pass administrative scrutiny without the need for an individual determination (see Q 5:55). [IRC § 414(r)(2)(C); Treas Reg §§ 1.414(r)-5(c)–1.414(r)-5(g)]

Industry category safe harbor. This administrative safe harbor is satisfied only if the separate line of business (see Q 5:48) is in a different industry or industries from every other separate line of business of the employer. An employer may disregard foreign operations in determining whether a separate line of business is in a different industry or industries from every other separate line of business of the employer. For purposes of this administrative safe harbor, there are 12 industry categories:

1. *Food and Agriculture.* Food, beverages, tobacco, food stores, and restaurants.

2. *Textiles and Clothing.* Textile mill products, apparel and other finished products made from fabrics and other similar materials (including leather and leather products), and general merchandise stores.

3. *Forest Products.* Pulp, paper, lumber and wood products (including furniture).

4. *Transportation.* Transportation equipment and services.

5. *Finance.* Banking, insurance, and financial industries.

6. *Utilities.* Public utilities and other regulated industries and communications.

7. *Coal and Metals.* Metal industries and coal mining and production.

8. *Machinery and Electronics.* Industrial and commercial machinery; computers and other electronic and electrical equipment and components.

9. *Petroleum and Chemicals.* Oil and gas extraction, production and distribution (including gasoline service stations); petroleum refining and related industries; chemicals and allied products; rubber and miscellaneous plastic products.

10. *Construction and Real Estate.* Construction industry, real estate, stone, clay, and glass products.

11. *Leisure.* Entertainment, sports, hotels.

12. *Printing and Publishing.* Printing, publishing and allied industries.

[Rev Proc 91-64, 1991-2 CB 866]

Merger and acquisition safe harbor. This second administrative safe harbor is satisfied if (1) the employer designates the acquired business as a line of business; (2) the line of business satisfies the separateness criteria; and (3) there are not any significant changes in the workforce of the acquired separate line of business.

FAS 14 safe harbor. The third administrative safe harbor (the reportable business segments safe harbor) requires that a separate line of business be reported as one or more reportable industry segments in accordance with the Statement of Financial Accounting Standards No. 14, Financial Reporting for Segments of a Business Enterprise (FAS 14).

Average benefits safe harbor. If the highly compensated employee percentage ratio (see Q 5:53) of the separate line of business is less than 50 percent, the separate line of business will satisfy this administrative safe harbor if the actual benefit percentage of the non-highly compensated employees (see Q 3:13) of the separate line of business is at least equal to the actual benefit percentage of all other non-highly compensated employees of the employer (see Q 5:19). Similarly, if the highly compensated employee percentage ratio of the separate line of business is greater than 200 percent, the separate line of business will satisfy this safe harbor if the actual benefit percentage of the highly compensated employees (see Q 3:2) of the separate line of business does not exceed the actual benefit percentage of all other highly compensated employees of the employer.

Minimum or maximum benefits safe harbor. The fifth and last administrative safe harbor is the minimum or maximum benefits safe harbor. If the highly compensated employee percentage ratio of the separate line of business is less than 50 percent, then, under the minimum benefit requirement, at least 80 percent of the non-highly compensated employees (excluding those who do not meet the lowest age and service eligibility requirements of any plan that benefits employees in the separate line of business) in that separate line of business must benefit under a retirement plan, and each of these employees must receive at least a specified minimum benefit. The minimum benefit standard can be satisfied on the basis of the average benefit accruals or allocations provided to non-highly compensated employees; but, in contrast to the 80 percent requirement, the averaging must be based on 100 percent of such non-highly compensated employees. If the highly compensated employee percentage ratio of the separate line of business is more than 200 percent, then, under the maximum benefit requirement, each highly compensated employee who benefits under a retirement plan in that separate line of business must receive no more than a specified maximum benefit.

Q 5:55 Can the administrative scrutiny requirement be satisfied if the safe harbors are not?

Yes. A separate line of business (see Q 5:48) that does not satisfy either the statutory safe harbor (see Q 5:53) or any of the administrative safe harbors (see Q 5:54) may still satisfy the administrative scrutiny requirement if the employer requests and receives from IRS an individual determination that the separate line of business satisfies administrative scrutiny. [IRC § 414(r)(2)(C); Treas Reg § 1.414(r)-6]

This determination process applies to those situations in which the separate line of business does not satisfy any of the administrative scrutiny safe harbors (see Q 5:54). An employer cannot make a request for a testing year (see Q 5:57) that ended prior to the date of the request.

In determining whether a separate line of business will receive an individual determination, IRS will consider all relevant facts and circumstances. Among the factors that may be considered in analyzing whether separate lines of business exist are the following, no one of which will necessarily be determinative:

- Differences in property or services provided
- Separateness of organization and operation
- Nature of business competition
- History of the separate lines of business
- Geographic area in which the businesses are operated
- Degree to which the separate line of business fails to satisfy the applicable safe harbors
- Size and composition of the separate lines of business
- Allocation method used for residual shared employees (see Q 5:56)
- Level of benefits provided by each separate line of business
- Other separate lines of business
- Whether the separate line of business operates in a regulated industry

[Rev Proc 93-41, 1993-2 CB 536]

If the separate line of business does not satisfy any of the safe harbors and does not obtain a favorable individual determination, the separate line of business will not satisfy administrative scrutiny.

Q 5:56   Who are the employees of each qualified separate line of business?

For purposes of testing retirement plans (see Qs 4:9, 5:15, 5:25) benefiting employees of a qualified separate line of business (see Qs 5:48, 5:49) and for purposes of applying the statutory safe harbor (see Q 5:53) and the minimum or maximum benefits safe harbor (see Q 5:54), an employer must determine which employees are treated as employees of each qualified separate line of business. [Treas Reg § 1.414(r)-7]

All employees must be assigned among the employer's qualified separate lines of business. The employees of a qualified separate line of business consist of all employees who provide substantial services to the qualified separate line of business and all other employees who are allocated to the qualified separate line of business. An employee is a substantial-service employee with respect to a line of business (see Q 5:47) for a testing year (see Q 5:57) if at least 75 percent of the employee's services are provided to that line of business for that testing year. Employers may treat employees who provide between 50 percent and 75 percent of their services to a particular qualified separate line of business as substantial-service employees with respect to that line of business and assign those employees to that qualified separate line of business for all purposes. This option may be exercised by the employer on an employee-by-employee basis; and, if not elected, that employee is treated as a residual shared employee. [Treas Reg §§ 1.414(r)-11(b)(2), 1.414(r)-11(b)(4)]

Employees who are not substantial-service employees with respect to any line of business are referred to as residual shared employees. All residual shared employees must be assigned under the same allocation method, and each residual shared employee must be allocated to only one qualified separate line of business.

There are four permissible allocation methods:

Dominant line of business method. Under the first method for allocating residual shared employees, an employer is permitted to allocate all its residual shared employees to its dominant line of business. An employer's dominant line of business is the qualified separate line of business that has an employee assignment percentage of at least 50 percent; however, an employer is permitted to determine if it has a dominant line of business by substituting 25 percent for 50 percent if the qualified separate line of business satisfies one of the following requirements:

1. The line of business accounts for at least 60 percent of the employer's gross revenue;

2. The employee assignment percentage would be at least 60 percent if union employees were considered;

3. Each line of business meets the statutory safe harbor, the average benefits safe harbor, or the minimum or maximum benefits safe harbor; or

4. The employee assignment percentage of the line of business is at least twice the employee assignment percentage of any other line of business.

Pro rata method. The second method permits the employer to allocate residual shared employees among its qualified separate lines of business in proportion to the percentage of all substantial-service employees who provide their services to each qualified separate line of business.

HCE percentage ratio method. The third method of allocation permits the employer to allocate residual shared employees among its qualified separate lines of business in a manner generally consistent with the statutory safe harbor for satisfying administrative scrutiny (see Q 5:53).

Small group method. Under the fourth method, the employer chooses a qualified separate line of business to which each residual shared employee is allocated. The residual shared employees need not all be allocated to the same qualified separate line of business; therefore, the employer has flexibility in selecting the plans under which residual shared employees benefit. In order to prevent this allocation method from being used to provide highly compensated employees (see Q 3:2) with excessive benefits relative to the non-highly compensated employees (see Q 3:13), its use is subject to three requirements:

1. The entire group of the employer's residual shared employees cannot exceed 3 percent of the employees taken into account in applying the minimum coverage requirements.

2. The qualified separate line of business to which the employer allocates a residual shared employee must include at least 10 percent of the employer's substantial-service employees and must satisfy the administrative scrutiny safe harbor after the allocation.

3. The allocation of residual shared employees must be reasonable.

Q 5:57   What is the testing year?

For purposes of determining whether an employer operates qualified separate lines of business for bona fide business reasons (see Q 5:46), the employer must apply the requirements (see Qs 5:47–5:56) on the basis of the testing year. The testing year is the calendar year. Similarly, an employer's retirement plans are tested for discrimination (see Q 4:9), minimum coverage (see Q 5:15), and minimum participation (see Q 5:25) separately with respect to the employees of each qualified separate line of business for all plan years that begin in the testing year. [Treas Reg §§ 1.414(r)-1(d)(6), 1.414(r)-11(b)(5)–1.414(r)-11(b)(8); Rev Proc 93-42, 1993-2 CB 540; Ann 93-130, 1993-31 IRB 46]

See Q 5:23 for a discussion of testing options and snapshot testing.

Q 5:58 What are the averaging rules for the separate lines of business requirements?

For purposes of determining certain percentages (see Qs 5:48, 5:53) for testing whether lines of business satisfy separate lines of business requirements, the employer is permitted to use up to a five-year moving average, absent large fluctuations. In determining whether specific percentages have been satisfied, this rule permits the employer to average the results for the current testing year (see Q 5:57) with the results for the immediately preceding one, two, three, or four testing years. The purpose of this rule is to provide stability from year to year in the application of the separate lines of business requirements. [Treas Reg § 1.414(r)-11(c)]

Q 5:59 Is there a flowchart to show how the qualified separate lines of business requirements work?

Yes. IRS has created the flowchart on page 5-45 to show how the major provisions of the qualified separate lines of business requirements (see Qs 5:47–5:56) are applied.

Q 5:60 What is the effective date of the new qualified separate lines of business requirements?

The new qualified separate lines of business requirements (see Qs 5:47–5:56) apply to plan years beginning on or after January 1, 1994. Until the plan year beginning on or after January 1, 1994, an employer was treated as operating qualified separate lines of business if the employer reasonably determined that it met the requirements (other than the administrative scrutiny requirement; see Q 5:52). Whether an employer reasonably determined that it met these requirements was generally determined on the basis of all relevant facts and circumstances, including the extent to which the employer had resolved unclear issues in its favor. [Treas Reg § 1.414(r)-1(d)(9); Notice 92-36, 1992-2 CB 364; Ann 92-29, 1992-9 IRB 37; IRS Field Office Directive on Good-Faith Compliance (June 12, 1992)]

Q 5:61 Who is a leased employee?

A leased employee is an individual who performs services for another person (the recipient) under an arrangement between the recipient and a third person (the leasing organization) who is otherwise treated as the individual's employer. The services performed by an individual for the recipient must be of a type that is historically performed by employees (see Q 5:62). [IRC §§ 414(n)(1), 414(n)(2), prior to amendment by SBA '96 § 1454]

Qualified Separate Lines of Business (QSLOB)

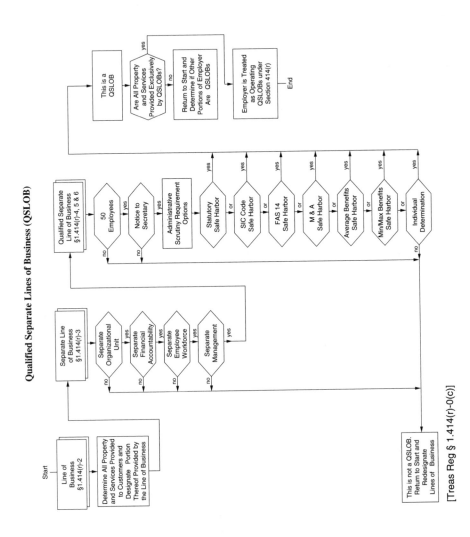

[Treas Reg § 1.414(r)-0(c)]

In 1987, IRS issued proposed regulations relating to leased employees. However, in 1993, as part of the Regulatory Burden Reduction Initiative, IRS withdrew these proposed regulations because IRS did not plan to finalize them. [TD 8474]

Q 5:62   Who is the employer of a leased employee?

The leased employee (see Q 5:61) is treated as the recipient's employee if the leased employee has performed services for the recipient pursuant to an agreement with the leasing organization on a substantially full-time basis for a period of at least one year and the services are of a type historically performed by employees in the recipient's business field. [IRC §§ 414(n)(1), 414(n)(2), prior to amendment by SBA '96 § 1454]

With the enactment of SBA '96 (see Q 1:21), the requirement that the services provided to the recipient be of a type historically performed by employees is changed to a requirement that such services be performed under primary or significant direction or control by the recipient. [IRC § 414(n)(2)(C), as amended by SBA '96 § 1454]

Factors that should be considered in determining whether an individual is under the primary direction or control of the service recipient include whether the individual is subject to the direct supervision of the recipient and whether the individual must perform services in the manner dictated by the recipient. A recipient may exercise primary direction or control by directly supervising an individual even if the recipient is not empowered to hire or fire the individual, the individual works for other companies, or another company pays the individual's wages and withholds employment and income taxes.

> **Example.** Tim works as a golf professional for MBCC, Inc. He was trained by Inwood Corporation, which also pays his wages, withholds employment taxes, and retains the authority to terminate him. However, Tim is subject to the direct supervision and day-to-day control of MBCC, Inc. and must perform services in the manner dictated by MBCC, Inc. Because Tim has worked for MBCC, Inc. on a full-time basis for over one year (see Q 5:63), he is a leased employee of MBCC, Inc.

This amendment applies to years beginning after 1996, but does not apply to any relationship determined under an IRS ruling issued before August 20, 1996 pursuant to Section 414(n)(2)(C) (as in effect on August 19, 1996) not to involve a leased employee. [SBA '96, Act § 1454(b)

Q 5:63   When is the leased employee first considered an employee of the recipient?

The leased employee (see Q 5:61) is treated as the recipient's employee after the leased employee has performed services for the recipient for a period of one year. Once this occurs, the leased employee's years of service for the recipient include the entire period for which the leased employee performed services for the recipient. [IRC § 414(n)(4)]

Q 5:64   What happens if the leased employee participates in the leasing organization's qualified retirement plan?

If the leasing organization maintains a qualified retirement plan, contributions or benefits for the leased employee (see Q 5:61) are treated as if provided by the recipient to the extent those contributions or benefits are attributable to services performed by the leased employee for the recipient. [IRC § 414(n)(1)(B)]

Q 5:65   When will the leased employee not be treated as an employee of the recipient?

A leased employee (see Q 5:61) will not be treated as the recipient's employee if leased employees do not constitute more than 20 percent of the recipient's non-highly compensated work force and each leased employee is covered by a qualified money purchase pension plan (see Q 2:4) maintained by the leasing organization that provides the following:

- Immediate participation
- Full and immediate vesting
- A nonintegrated contribution rate of 10 percent of compensation

The immediate participation requirement does not apply to (1) employees who perform substantially all of their services for the leasing organization and (2) employees whose compensation from the leasing organization for each of the four preceding plan years is less than $1,000. A money purchase pension plan meeting these requirements is referred to as a safe harbor plan. The term "non-highly compensated workforce" means the aggregate number of individuals other than highly compensated employees (see Qs 3:2, 3:13) who are employees of the recipient and have performed services for the recipient on a substantially full-time basis for one year or who are leased employees with respect to the recipient. [IRC § 414(n)(5)]

Q 5:66   Can an employer utilizing the services of leased employees obtain IRS approval of its qualified retirement plan?

Yes. An employer utilizing one or more leased employees (see Q 5:61) may be able to obtain a favorable determination letter (see Q 15:1) by following an application procedure developed by IRS. [Rev Proc 92-6, 1991-2 CB 611; Rev Proc 85-43, 1985-2 CB 501]

Chapter 6

Contribution and Benefit Limitations

ERISA set limits on the amount that could be allocated to an employee under a defined contribution plan and on the amount of the annual retirement benefit that could be provided to an employee under a defined benefit plan. These limits were subject to cost-of-living increases, and, because of the high rates of inflation in the late 1970s, these limits rose significantly. Congress reduced these limits in TEFRA and again in TRA '86. This chapter examines limitations now in effect for both defined contribution and defined benefit plans.

Q 6:1 How much may the company contribute to a defined contribution plan on behalf of a participant?

The Code sets limits on contributions and other additions made to a participant's account in a defined contribution plan (see Q 2:2). Contributions and other additions are referred to as the annual addition to a participant's account. The annual addition is the sum of the following:

1. Employer contributions;
2. Employee contributions;
3. Forfeitures;
4. Amounts allocated to an individual medical account that is part of a pension or annuity plan maintained by the employer; and
5. Amounts derived from contributions that are attributable to postretirement medical benefits allocated to the separate account of a key employee (see Q 22:24) under a welfare benefit fund maintained by the employer.

[IRC §§ 415(c)(2), 415(l), 419(e), 419A(d)]

The annual addition with respect to a participant's account during any limitation year (see Q 6:16) may not exceed the *lesser* of $30,000 (see Q 6:2) or 25 percent of the participant's compensation (see Q 6:3). [IRC § 415(c)(1)]

The annual addition limitation is best explained by an example:

Participant's compensation for 1996	$80,000
Employer contribution	16,000
Employee contribution	4,000
Forfeitures allocated to participant's account	2,000

Computation of Annual Addition

Employer contribution	$16,000
Employee contribution	4,000
Forfeitures	2,000
Annual addition	$22,000

The total amount to be allocated to the participant under the defined contribution plan will be $22,000 unless it exceeds the limitation amount, which is the lesser of $30,000 or 25 percent of the participant's compensation. Since the limitation for 1996 is $20,000 (25% of $80,000), the annual addition of $22,000 exceeds the limitation amount. The contributions and other additions to this participant's account therefore may not exceed $20,000.

IRS has ruled that a restorative payment made to a defined contribution plan in response to actual and potential claims for breach of fiduciary duty and allocated to participants' accounts was not subject to the annual addition limitation. The claims were brought after the plan incurred significant losses attributable to investments in derivatives. [Ltr Ruls 9528034, 9507030, 9506048]

Employee contributions distributed to correct an excess annual addition are treated as corrective disbursements and are not includible in the employee's gross income. However, if earnings on the returned contributions are distributed to the employee, the earnings are includible in income in the year distributed. If the plan returns employee contributions but not the earnings attributable to the returned contributions, the earnings are treated as additional employee contributions and must be taken into account for annual addition limitation purposes. For limitation years beginning after December 31, 1995, earnings attributable to returned elective deferrals (see

Q 23:28) are treated in a similar manner. [Treas Reg § 1.415-6(b)(6)(iv); Rev Proc 92-93, 1992-2 CB 505; Sherry v Central Nat'l Bank of Canajoharie, 886 F Supp 256 (ND NY 1995)]

For purposes of applying the annual addition limitation, all defined contribution plans of an employer are treated as a single plan. [IRC § 415(f); Treas Reg § 1.415-8; Ltr Rul 9325055]

Example. Mi Linda Amiga Corporation adopts a 10-percent-of-compensation money purchase pension plan and a 15-percent-of-compensation profit sharing plan. Bob, who is a participant in both plans, earns $150,000. The contribution and other additions to Bob's accounts may not, in the aggregate, exceed $30,000 in a limitation year.

Where a corporation (Newco) was formed by the merger of six corporations (Oldcos), the plan adopted by Newco did not have to be aggregated with any plans of the Oldcos for annual addition limitation purposes. [Ltr Rul 9541041]

See Q 6:31 for a discussion of the family aggregation rule.

Q 6:2   Will the $30,000 ceiling on the annual addition rise?

The $30,000 annual addition limit is subject to cost-of-living adjustments; however, an adjustment will be made only if it is $5,000 or greater and then will be made in multiples of $5,000 (i.e., rounded down to the next lowest multiple of $5,000). For example, an increase in the cost-of-living of $4,999 will result in no adjustment, and an increase of $9,999 will create an upward adjustment of $5,000. Therefore, the cost-of-living must increase by 16⅔ percent before the first adjustment to the $30,000 limit will occur (16⅔% × $30,000 = $5,000). For limitation years (see Q 6:16) ending in 1996, the dollar limitation remains unchanged at $30,000. [IRC §§ 415(c)(1)(A), 415(d); Treas Reg § 1.415-6(a)(2); Notice 95-55, 1995-45 IRB 11]

To calculate the cost-of-living increase in the $30,000 limitation for any particular year, the Consumer Price Index for All Urban Consumers (CPI-U) must be obtained from the Department of Labor (DOL) for the three months of the calendar quarter ending September 30 (i.e., July, August, and September) of the previous year. The sum of the three indices is then compared to the sum of the indices for the last three months of the base year (i.e., 1993). The quotient of these sums is rounded to four decimal places. This result is multiplied by the $30,000 limitation. Finally, if this result is an even multiple of $5,000, the result obtained is the new dollar limitation; otherwise, the result is rounded to the next lowest multiple of $5,000 to obtain the new dollar limitation. Although it will be some time before there is an increase in the $30,000 amount, the limitation cannot be reduced below $30,000 (see Q 6:25). [RPA '94, Act § 732(e)(2)]

The applicable dollar limitation is the amount in effect on the last day of the limitation year. [Treas Reg § 1.415-6(a)(2)]

Example. Assume that the dollar limitation increases from $30,000 in 1996 to $35,000 in 1997. Doctor Ric Corporation maintains a 25-percent-of-compensation money purchase pension plan with a plan year beginning on February 1 and ending on January 31. The limitation year is the same as the plan year; and Eric and Maria, who are participants in the plan, both have compensation of $150,000 for the limitation year ended January 31, 1997. The maximum annual addition for both Eric and Maria for the limitation year ended January 31, 1997 is $35,000 even though the limitation year began in 1996.

Q 6:3   What does compensation mean for purposes of the annual addition limitation?

For annual addition limitation purposes (see Q 6:1), compensation means the total compensation received from the employer for the limitation year (see Q 6:16). For a self-employed individual (see Q 6:33), compensation means earned income (see Q 6:34). This is commonly referred to as Section 415 compensation. [IRC § 415(c)(3); Treas Reg § 1.415-2(d)(4)]

Items treated as compensation include:

1. Wages, salaries, fees for professional services, and other amounts received (without regard to whether or not an amount is paid in cash) for personal services actually rendered in the course of employment to the extent that the amounts are includible in income (including, but not limited to, commissions paid to sales representatives, compensation for services on the basis of a percentage of profits, commissions on insurance premiums, tips, bonuses, fringe benefits, reimbursements, and expense allowances), whether earned from sources inside or outside the United States;

2. Employer-provided accident and health insurance benefits and medical reimbursement plan benefits, but only to the extent includible in the income of the employee [American Family Mutual Ins Co v United States, 71 AFTR 2d (WD Wis 1993)];

3. Moving expenses paid by an employer, but only to the extent not deductible by the employee under Section 217;

4. The value of a nonqualified stock option granted to an employee by the employer, but only to the extent includible in the income of the employee for the taxable year in which it was granted; and

5. The amount includible in income that results when an employee who receives restricted property makes an election to be taxed on it under Section 83(b). [Treas Reg § 1.415-2(d)(2)]

If the qualified retirement plan defines Section 415 compensation to include only those items specified in paragraph 1 of the list above and to exclude all items not treated as compensation as set forth below, the plan will contain a definition of compensation that satisfies Section 415. [Treas Reg § 1.415-2(d)(10)]

Items not treated as compensation include the following:

1. Elective or salary reduction contributions to a 401(k) plan to the extent not includible in the income of the employee for the year in which they are contributed (see Q 23:5);

2. Employer contributions to a tax-sheltered annuity (see Q 29:1) whether or not excludable from the income of the employee;

3. Certain deferred compensation payments [Licciardi v Kropp Forge Div Employees' Retirement Plan, No. 92-2731 (7th Cir 1993)];

4. SEP contributions that are excludable from the income of the employee (see Q 27:16);

5. Amounts realized from the exercise of a nonqualified stock option or when restricted stock or property held by an employee becomes freely transferable or is no longer subject to a substantial risk of forfeiture; and

6. Amounts realized from the sale, exchange, or other disposition of stock acquired under a qualified stock option. [Treas Reg § 1.415-2(d)(3)]

In lieu of defining Section 415 compensation as set forth above, a qualified retirement plan may utilize alternative definitions of Section 415 compensation (see Q 6:4). The definition of Section 415 compensation applies only to the calculation of the annual addition limitation; a different definition of compensation may be used for the allocation or crediting of contributions under a defined contribution plan (see Qs 6:37–6:45).

In a defined contribution plan (see Q 2:2), a disabled participant who is not a highly compensated employee (see Qs 3:2, 3:13) may be deemed to receive compensation at the rate of compensation paid immediately before becoming disabled. [IRC § 415(c)(3)(C), prior to amendment by SBA '96 § 1446(a)] *For years beginning after 1996*, SBA '96 (see Q 1:21) extends this benefit to highly compensated employees under certain circumstances. [IRC § 415(c)(3)(C), as amended by SBA '96 § 1446(a)]

The annual compensation of an employee taken into account under a qualified retirement plan may not exceed $150,000, with adjustments for inflation. For details, see Qs 6:23 through 6:30, and also see Q 6:31 for a discussion of the family aggregation rule.

For years beginning after 1997, Section 415 compensation will include elective deferrals under 401(k) plans, tax-sheltered annuities, SEPs, and cafeteria plans. [IRC § 415(c)(3)(D), as added by SBA '96 § 1434(a)]

Q 6:4   Can an alternative definition of Section 415 compensation be used for annual addition limitation purposes?

In lieu of defining Section 415 compensation to include and exclude certain specified forms of compensation (see Q 6:3), a qualified retirement plan may define Section 415 compensation (except in the case of self-employed individuals; see Q 6:33) using either of the following wage reporting definitions:

1. Wages under Section 3401(a) and all other payments of compensation to an employee by the employer for which the employer is required to furnish the employee a written statement under Sections 6041(d), 6051(a)(3), and 6052. This definition may be modified to exclude amounts paid or reimbursed by the employer for moving expenses incurred by an employee, but only to the extent that at the time of the payment it is reasonable to believe that these amounts are deductible by the employee under Section 217. Compensation must be determined disregarding any rules that limit remuneration based on the nature or location of employment or services performed.

2. Wages under Section 3401(a) for purposes of income tax withholding, disregarding any rules that limit remuneration based on the nature or location of employment or services performed.

[Treas Reg § 1.415-2(d)(11)]

Q 6:5   Can a qualified retirement plan include accrued compensation for annual addition limitation purposes?

For limitation years (see Q 6:16) beginning after December 31, 1991, an employer may *not* use accrued compensation. However, an employer may include in compensation amounts earned but not paid in a year because of the timing of pay periods and pay days if these amounts are paid during the first few weeks of the next year, the amounts are included on a uniform and consistent basis with respect to all similarly situated employees, and no compensation is included in more than one limitation period. No formal election is required to include the accrued compensation permitted under this *de minimis* rule. [Treas Reg § 1.415-2(d)(5)]

Q 6:6 Does a withdrawn employee voluntary contribution that is replaced during the same year constitute part of the annual addition?

Yes. If employee voluntary contributions (see Q 6:20) are withdrawn and then replaced during the same limitation year (see Q 6:16), they are treated as part of the annual addition (see Q 6:1).

> **Example.** Sallie makes employee voluntary contributions of $3,000 in January 1997 and withdraws $2,000 in June. If she replaces the $2,000 within the same limitation year of the $3,000 contribution, she will be deemed to have made a total of $5,000 of employee voluntary contributions. [Ltr Rul 8622044]

Q 6:7 Is a transfer of benefits from one qualified retirement plan to another considered an annual addition in the year of transfer?

IRS has ruled that a trustee-to-trustee transfer of plan benefits by a participant in a defined benefit plan (see Q 2:3) to a 401(k) plan (see Q 2:12) was not an annual addition (see Q 6:1). IRS has also ruled that amounts held in a trust under a frozen profit sharing plan (see Qs 2:6, 22:15) that were transferred to a second trust, which trust then held the assets of both the frozen plan and another profit sharing plan maintained by the employer, did not constitute an annual addition for the limitation year (see Q 6:16) in which the transfer occurred. [Treas Reg § 1.415-6(b)(2)(iv); Ltr Ruls 9543046, 9221045, 9111046, 9052058]

Q 6:8 What is the maximum annual retirement benefit that a defined benefit plan may provide?

The annual benefit (see Q 6:9) that may be paid to a participant under a defined benefit plan (see Q 2:3) is limited to the *lesser* of (1) $90,000, with cost-of-living adjustments, or (2) 100 percent of the participant's average compensation (see Q 6:12). [IRC §§ 415(b)(1), 415(d); Treas Reg § 1.415-3(a)(2); Ltr Rul 9543046]

Cost-of-living adjustments to the $90,000 limit are calculated in a manner similar to the annual cost-of-living increases in Social Security benefits. However, an adjustment will be made only if it is $5,000 or greater and then will be made in multiples of $5,000 (i.e., rounded down to the next lowest multiple of $5,000). For example, an increase in the cost-of-living of $4,999 will result in no adjustment, and an increase of $9,999 will create an upward adjustment of $5,000. Therefore, the cost-of-living must increase by 4⅙ percent before the next adjustment to the defined benefit dollar limit will occur ($4\frac{1}{6}\%$ × $120,000 = $5,000). [IRC §§ 415(b)(1)(A), 415(d)]

To calculate the cost-of-living increase for any particular year, the CPI-U must be obtained from DOL for the three months of the calendar quarter ending September 30 (i.e., July, August, and September) of the previous year. The sum of the three indices is then compared to the sum of the indices for the last three months of the base year (i.e., 1986). The quotient of these sums is rounded to four decimal places. This result is multiplied by $90,000. Finally, if this result is an even multiple of $5,000, the result obtained is the new dollar limitation; otherwise, the result is rounded to the next lowest multiple of $5,000 to obtain the new dollar limitation.

For example, to calculate the $90,000 limitation applicable for 1995, divide the sum of the CPI-U's for the three months of the calendar quarter ended September 30, 1994 (i.e., 446.8) by the sum of the CPI-U's for the last three months of 1986 (i.e., 331.3). The result is 1.3486. The $90,000 limitation is multiplied by 1.3486. The result is $121,374. Since this result is not an even multiple of $5,000, the result is rounded to the next lowest multiple of $5,000, which is $120,000. This final result is the dollar limitation applicable for 1995. [IR 94-117 (Dec 23, 1994)] The dollar limitation cannot be reduced below $118,800 (see Q 6:25). [RPA '94, Act § 732(e)(2)]

For limitation years (see Q 6:16) ending in 1996, the dollar limitation remains unchanged at $120,000. [Notice 95-55, 1995-45 IRB 11] For limitation years ended prior to 1995, the adjusted limit was:

Limitation Year Ending In	Adjusted Limit
1994	$118,800
1993	115,641
1992	112,221
1991	108,963
1990	102,582
1989	98,064
1988	94,023

The applicable dollar limitation is the amount in effect on the last day of the limitation year. [Treas Reg § 1.415-5(a)(2)]

Example. Assume that the dollar limitation increases from $120,000 in 1996 to $125,000 in 1997. FSB Corp. maintains a defined benefit plan with a plan year beginning on February 1 and ending on January 31. The limitation year is the same as the plan year; and Fred and Sue, who are participants in the plan, both have compensation of $150,000 for the limitation year ended January 31, 1997. The maximum annual retirement benefit for both Fred and Sue for the limitation year ended January 31, 1997 is $125,000 even though the limitation year began in 1996.

For purposes of applying the annual retirement benefit limitation, all defined benefit plans of an employer (whether or not terminated) are treated as a single plan. [IRC § 415(f); Treas Reg § 1.415-8; Ltr Rul 9325055; Ann 95-99, 1995-48 IRB 10]

Example 1. Henry's Pharmacy, Inc. adopted a defined benefit plan in 1985 and terminated the plan in 1993. In 1997, Henry's Pharmacy, Inc. adopts a new defined benefit plan. Ilene participated in the terminated plan and will participate in the new plan. Ilene's combined annual benefit from both plans cannot exceed the maximum permissible annual benefit.

Example 2. Judy Corp., Murray Corp., and Jayem Co., Inc. are members of a controlled group of corporations (see Q 5:33). Employees of all members of the controlled group are eligible to participate in a defined benefit plan, Plan A. On April 30, 1997, Jayem terminates membership in the controlled group and immediately establishes a new defined benefit plan, Plan X, for its employees. No transfers of assets and liabilities are made from Plan A to the new Plan X. For the 1997 limitation year and subsequent limitation years, benefits under both defined benefit plans (Plan A and Plan X) must be aggregated for purposes of applying the annual benefit limitations.

Where a corporation (Newco) was formed by the merger of six corporations (Oldcos), the plan adopted by Newco did not have to be aggregated with any plans of the Oldcos for annual benefit limitation purposes. [Ltr Rul 9541041]

See Q 6:31 for a discussion of the family aggregation rule.

Q 6:9   What does annual benefit mean?

The term "annual benefit" means a retirement benefit payable annually in the form of a straight life annuity (with no ancillary or incidental benefits) under a defined benefit plan (see Q 2:3) to which employees do not contribute and to which no rollover contributions are made. Under a straight life annuity, payments terminate upon the death of the annuitant. [IRC § 415(b)(2)(A)]

If benefits under a defined benefit plan are payable in a form other than a straight life annuity, the limits (see Q 6:8) are adjusted to a benefit that is equivalent to a straight life annuity; but, if benefits under the plan are payable in the form of a joint and survivor annuity (see Q 10:8), no reduction in the annual benefit is required. IRS has ruled that, if the disability benefit under a retirement plan exceeds the retirement benefit, the disability benefit is subject to the annual benefit limits. [IRC § 415(b)(2)(B); Ltr Rul 9237042]

If benefits under a defined benefit plan commence before the participant attains Social Security retirement age (SSRA; see Q 6:14), the $90,000 limit is *reduced* to the actuarial equivalent of a $90,000 annual benefit commencing at the SSRA. Similarly, if benefits commence after the SSRA, the $90,000 limit is *increased* to the actuarial equivalent of a $90,000 annual benefit commencing at the SSRA. [IRC §§ 415(b)(2)(C), 415(b)(2)(D)]

In adjusting the benefit limits for payment in a form other than a straight life annuity or for payments commencing before the SSRA, the interest rate assumption cannot be less than the *greater* of 5 percent or the interest rate specified in the plan. The interest rate for an adjustment if the payments commence after the SSRA cannot exceed the *lesser* of 5 percent or the rate specified in the plan. [IRC § 415(b)(2)(E)]

For new rules that apply for limitation years (see Q 6:16) commencing in 1995, see Qs 6:10 and 6:11. However, SBA '96 (see Q 1:21) provides that the new rules will not apply to the adjustment for payments commencing before the SSRA. [IRC §§ 415(b)(2)(E)(i), 415(b)(2)(E)(ii), as amended by SBA '96 § 1449(b)]

Q 6:10 What new limitations may apply to benefits paid under defined benefit plans?

Generally effective as of the first day of the limitation year beginning in 1995 (see Qs 6:11, 6:16), for purposes of calculating the adjustments described in Q 6:9, a mortality table must be used and, in certain circumstances, the 5 percent interest rate is replaced by the applicable interest rate (i.e., the annual interest rate on 30-year Treasury securities as specified by IRS). [IRC § 415(b)(2)(E); Rev Rul 95-29, 1995-1 CB 81 (as corrected by Rev Rul 95-29A, 1995-1 CB 85), Rev Rul 95-6, 1995-1 CB 80; Temp Reg § 1.417(e)-1T(d)]

The new interest rate applies to a benefit payable in the form of a benefit subject to the present value determination rules of Section 417(e)(3) (see Q 10:59). This includes all forms of benefit except nondecreasing annuity benefits payable for a period not less than the life of the participant or, in the case of a QPSA (see Q 10:9), the life of the surviving spouse. For this purpose, a nondecreasing annuity includes a QJSA (see Q 10:8), a QPSA, and an annuity that decreases merely because of the cessation or reduction of Social Security supplements or qualified disability payments (see Q 4:18).

To determine whether a benefit under a defined benefit plan (see Q 2:3) that is *not* payable in the form of a straight life annuity and that is *not* subject to the present value determination rules of Section 417(e)(3) satisfies the limitation on a participant's annual retirement benefit (see Q 6:8), a three-step approach is used:

Step 1: Determine the annual retirement benefit in the form of a straight life annuity commencing at the same age that is actuarially equivalent to the plan benefit. In general, the equivalent annual retirement benefit is the *greater* of the equivalent annual retirement benefit computed using the interest rate and mortality table specified in the plan for actuarial equivalence for the particular form of benefit payable or the equivalent annual retirement benefit computed using a 5 percent interest rate assumption and the IRS mortality table.

Step 2: Determine the dollar limitation that applies at the age the benefit is payable. To determine this limitation, the dollar limitation that applies at the participant's SSRA (see Q 6:14) is adjusted so that the adjusted dollar limitation equals an annual retirement benefit that is equivalent to the dollar limitation at the participant's SSRA.

If the benefit is payable at or after age 62 and before the participant's SSRA, the dollar limitation at the participant's SSRA is reduced to the age at which the benefit is payable using adjustment factors that are consistent with the factors used to reduce old-age insurance benefits under the Social Security Act. If the age at which the benefit is payable is less than age 62, the dollar limitation is further reduced so that the limitation is actuarially equivalent to the limitation at age 62. In general, the reduced dollar limitation is the *lesser* of the equivalent amount computed using the interest rate and mortality table (or other tabular factor) used for actuarial equivalence for early retirement benefits under the plan or the amount computed using 5 percent interest and the IRS mortality table. If the age at which the benefit is payable is greater than the participant's SSRA, the dollar limitation is increased so that the limitation is actuarially equivalent to the limitation at the participant's SSRA. In general, the increased dollar limitation is the *lesser* of the equivalent amount computed using the interest rate and mortality table (or other tabular factor) used for actuarial equivalence for late retirement benefits under the plan or the amount computed using 5 percent interest and the IRS mortality table.

Step 3: Determine the participant's compensation limitation (see Q 6:12).

The plan does not satisfy the limitation requirements unless the amount determined in Step 1 is no *greater* than the *lesser* of the amounts determined in Step 2 and Step 3.

If a defined benefit plan provides a benefit in a form that *is* subject to the present value determination rules of Section 417(e)(3), the determination of the equivalent annual retirement benefit is the same as in Step 1 above, except that the applicable interest rate is substituted for the 5 percent interest rate. The equivalent annual retirement benefit must be the *greater* of the equivalent annual retirement benefit computed using the interest rate and mortality table specified in the plan for actuarial equivalence for the particular form of benefit payable or the equivalent annual retirement benefit computed using the applicable interest rate and the IRS mortality table.

Example 1. Keller Kong King Corporation adopted a defined benefit plan 15 years ago. The plan provides that single sum distributions are determined as the actuarial present value of a single life annuity payable at actual retirement date. The single sum is the greater of the present value using 6 percent interest and the UP-1984 mortality table or the present value using the applicable interest rate and IRS mortality table. Thus, the single sum is not less than the actuarial present value of the normal retirement benefit using the applicable interest rate and the IRS mortality table.

In 1996, Shirley-Lou, whose SSRA is 65, retires at age 60 from the plan and elects to receive a distribution in the form of a single sum. Under the plan formula, and before the application of the limitation, the amount of the single sum is $950,000, the present value of the early retirement benefit. This benefit must be adjusted to an actuarially equivalent single life annuity commencing at age 60 in order to apply the annual retirement benefit limitation under the plan at that age. Assuming that the applicable interest rate is 8 percent, the adjustment is made as follows:

1. Divide $950,000 by an immediate single life annuity purchase rate at age 60 using the plan's interest rate and mortality table. Based on 6 percent interest and the UP-1984 mortality table, the equivalent annual benefit is $89,656 ($950,000 ÷ 10.596).

2. Divide the $950,000 by an immediate single life annuity purchase rate using the applicable interest rate and the IRS mortality table. Based on 8 percent interest and the IRS mortality table, the equivalent annual benefit is $94,078 (950,000 ÷ 10.098). The equivalent annual benefit is the greater of the two resulting amounts.

If the defined benefit plan provides a benefit payable in a form that is subject to Section 417(e)(3), and the benefit is payable before a participant's SSRA, the dollar limitation is determined in the same manner as in Step 2 on page 6-11, except that the applicable interest rate is substituted for the 5 percent interest rate.

Example 2. Assume the same facts as in Example 1, except that the plan also provides that early retirement annuity benefits are equal to the normal form of annuity benefit payable at 65, reduced by 4 percent for each year by which the early retirement age is less than 65. Shirley-Lou's retirement age is 60, and Shirley-Lou has more than ten years of plan participation at age 60. The dollar limitation at age 60 is computed as follows:

1. The dollar limitation at age 62 is determined by reducing the 1996 dollar limitation of $120,000 (see Q 6:8) at SSRA (65) by a factor of 5/9 of 1 percent for 36 months. This results in a limitation of $96,000 at age 62.

2. The resulting $96,000 limitation is further reduced as follows: Using the tabular plan reduction factor of 4 percent per year, the benefit adjustment factor at age 62 would be 88 percent [100% − (4% × 3)]. At age 60, the factor would be 80 percent [100% − (4% × 5)]. Accordingly, the dollar limitation at age 60, reduced in accordance with plan factors, is equal to $87,273 ($96,000 × 80% 88%).

3. Because Shirley-Lou's distribution is in the form of a single sum that is subject to Section 417(e)(3), the limitation at age 62 is now reduced using the applicable interest rate of 8 percent and the IRS mortality table. Assuming the mortality decrement is applied only on a postretirement basis (since plan benefits are not subject to forfeiture upon death prior to the annuity starting date), this reduced limitation is $79,541.

4. The limitation that would apply at age 60 is $79,541, the *lesser* of $87,273 or $79,541.

5. Thus, the equivalent annual benefit of $94,078 determined in Example 1 does not satisfy the limitation requirements.

In most cases, the dollar amount of a single sum payment will be significantly reduced.

For a discussion of the effect of these new rules on cash balance plans, see Q 10:59; for a discussion of the anti-cutback rule, see Qs 9:24 through 9:26.

However, SBA '96 (see Q 1:21) provides that the new rules will not apply to the adjustment for payments commencing before the SSRA. [IRC §§ 415(b)(2)(E)(i), 415(b)(2)(E)(ii), as amended by SBA '96 § 1449(b)]

Q 6:11   What is the effective date of the new limitations for defined benefit plans?

For plans adopted or effective on or after December 8, 1994, the new rules (see Q 6:10) are effective as of the first day of the first limitation year (see Q 6:16) beginning in 1995.

For plans adopted and in effect prior to December 8, 1994, the new rules were originally effective also as of the first day of the first limitation year beginning in 1995, and that effective date applied regardless of when the plan was amended to reflect changes made to the present value determination rules of Section 417(e)(3) (see Q 10:61). However, an employer could elect to treat the new rules as being effective on or after December 8, 1994. [Rev Rul 95-29, 1995-1 CB 81, Q&A-1]

Under SBA '96 (see Q 1:21), the effective date is delayed for plans adopted and in effect before December 8, 1994 until the first limitation year beginning after December 31, 1999 or, if earlier, the date a plan amendment applying the new rules is adopted or made effective. If a plan amendment applying the new rules was adopted or made effective on or before August 20, 1996, the employer may repeal the amendment on or before August 20, 1997. [SBA '96, Act § 1449(a)]

Q 6:12   What does average compensation mean for purposes of the annual retirement benefit limitation?

For purposes of the limitation on a participant's annual retirement benefit under a defined benefit plan (see Q 6:8), average compensation means the average compensation for the high three years. A participant's high three years is the period of consecutive years (not more than three) during which the participant both was an active participant in the plan and had the greatest aggregate compensation from the employer. It should be noted that IRS regulations use the high three years of service, not years of participation. [IRC § 415(b)(3); Treas Reg § 1.415-3(a)(3)]

For purposes of calculating average compensation, the definition of compensation parallels the definition of Section 415 compensation used to calculate the annual addition limitation, and the $150,000 annual compensation limitation, with adjustments for inflation, also applies (see Qs 6:3, 6:4, 6:23–6:31). The definition of Section 415 compensation applies only to the calculation of the maximum annual retirement benefit; a different definition of compensation may be used to calculate the accrued benefit (see Q 9:2) under a defined benefit plan (see Qs 6:37–6:45).

See Q 6:31 for a discussion of the family aggregation rule.

Q 6:13   Is there a minimum number of years of participation or service required before a participant in a defined benefit plan qualifies for the maximum annual benefit?

If a participant has less than ten years of participation with the employer at retirement, the dollar limitation ($90,000; see Q 6:8) is reduced by 10 percent for each year of *participation* less than ten. The maximum percentage limitation (100 percent of the participant's average compensation; see Q 6:12) is reduced by 10 percent for each year of *service* less than ten. In both cases, the reduction in the limitation is never more than 90 percent. [IRC § 415(b)(5); Rev Proc 92-42, 1992-1 CB 872; Ltr Ruls 9627029, 9547031]

Example 1. Stephanie has seven years of service but only five years of plan participation at retirement in 1996, and her average compensation is $120,000. Stephanie's maximum annual benefit is $60,000 [the lesser of $60,000 (5/10 × $120,000) or $84,000 (7/10 × 100% × $120,000)].

Example 2. If Stephanie's average compensation is $70,000, the maximum annual benefit is $49,000 [the lesser of $60,000 (5/10 × $120,000) or $49,000 (7/10 × 100% × $70,000)].

In any event, the annual benefit payable to a participant under a defined benefit plan does not exceed the limitation (see Q 6:8) if the following conditions are met:

1. The annual benefit payable to a participant under the plan (and under all other defined benefit plans of the employer) does not exceed $10,000 for the plan year or for any prior plan year; and

2. The employer has not at any time maintained a defined contribution plan in which the participant participated.

Therefore, if a participant's average compensation is less than $10,000, the annual benefit under the plan could be $10,000—more than the participant's average compensation. If the participant has less than ten years of *service* with the employer, however, the $10,000 amount is reduced by 10 percent for each year less than ten (the reduction is never more than 90 percent). [IRC § 415(b)(4)]

Years of service may include service with businesses that antedate the formation of a corporation. This applies where the transition to a corporate structure resulted in a mere formal or technical change in the employment relationship and continuity otherwise existed with respect to the substance and administration of the business operations of the previous entity and the corporation. Thus, the period during which a doctor operated his practice as a sole proprietorship prior to the business's incorporation and its sponsorship of a defined benefit plan constituted years of service with the employer. [Lear Eye Clinic, Ltd, 106 TC No. 23 (1996)] However, in a consolidated case [Brody Enterprises, Inc], an attorney who was the sole shareholder and employee of a corporation that adopted a defined benefit plan in which he participated could not include as years of service with the employer the period during which he conducted a part-time private law practice while working full-time for IRS. The practice was located in a different city, the corporation failed to show that the attorney conducted a private law practice, and the attorney maintained no records of the hours that he spent on the practice. In addition, the attorney could not include the five-year period during which he worked for a law firm that was also located in a different city. There was no indication that he had an ownership interest in the firm. Moreover, the evidence did not establish a relationship between the corporation's business operations and those of the law firm. Lastly, the plan administrator (see Q 16:1) lacked the discretion to include the disputed years as "years of service with the employer" under the plan.

To calculate the number of years of service and the number of years of participation, all years with both an acquired company and a purchasing company may be aggregated. [Ltr Rul 9336046]

Q 6:14   What is the Social Security retirement age?

For purposes of calculating adjustments to the dollar limitation ($90,000) on benefits payable under a defined benefit plan (see Qs 6:9, 6:12), Social Security retirement age (SSRA) means the age used as the retirement age under the Social Security Act (rounded to the next lower whole number) and depends on the calendar year of birth.

Year of Birth	SSRA
Before 1938	65
After 1937 but before 1955	66
After 1954	67

[IRC § 415(b)(8); Social Security Act § 216(1)]

Q 6:15   What happens if the employee's accrued benefit under a defined benefit plan exceeded the TRA '86 limitations?

If the defined benefit plan was in existence on May 6, 1986, the employee was a participant as of the first day of the first plan year beginning after 1986, and the employee's accrued benefit (see Q 9:2) as of the end of the plan year beginning before 1987 exceeded the TRA '86 maximum allowable benefit (see Qs 6:8, 6:9), the higher accrued benefit is preserved. [TRA '86 § 1106(i)]

Q 6:16   What is the limitation year?

The limitation year, with respect to any qualified retirement plan maintained by the employer, is the calendar year. However, instead of using the calendar year, an employer may elect to use any other consecutive 12-month period as the limitation year. The election is made by the adoption of a written resolution by the employer. This requirement is satisfied if the election is made in connection with the adoption of the plan or any amendments to the plan. [Treas Reg § 1.415-2(b)]

In the case of a group of employers that constitutes either a controlled group of corporations or trades or businesses (whether or not incorporated) under common control (see Q 5:31), the election to use a consecutive 12-month period other than the calendar year as the limitation year must be made by all members of the group that maintain a qualified retirement plan.

Once established, the limitation year may be changed only by making the election described above. Any change in the limitation year must be a change to a 12-month period commencing with any day within the current limitation year. The limitations are applied in the normal manner to the new limitation year and are separately applied to a limitation period that begins with the first day of the current limitation year and ends on the day before the first day of the first limitation year for which the change is effective. The dollar limitation with respect to this limitation period is determined by multiplying (1) the applicable dollar limitation for the calendar year in which the limitation period ends by (2) a fraction, the numerator of which is the number of months (including any fractional part of a month) in the limitation period, and the denominator of which is 12. This adjustment of the dollar limitation *only* applies to a defined contribution plan (see Q 2:2).

Example. In 1996, Sil-Fen, Inc., an employer with a profit sharing plan using the calendar year as the limitation year, elects to change the limitation year to a period beginning July 1 and ending June 30. Because of this change, the plan must satisfy the limitations for the limitation period beginning January 1, 1996 and ending June 30, 1996. In applying the limitations to this limitation period, the amount of compensation taken into account may include compensation only for this period. Furthermore, the dollar limitation for this period is $15,000 ($30,000 × 6/12).

Q 6:17   What happens if an employee participates in both a defined benefit plan and a defined contribution plan?

If an employee participates in both a defined benefit plan (see Q 2:3) and a defined contribution plan (see Q 2:2) that are maintained by the same employer, a special formula is used to determine the combined maximum limit on benefits and contributions. For this purpose, all defined benefit plans of the employer (whether or not terminated) are treated as a single plan and all defined contribution plans of the employer (whether or not terminated) are treated as a single plan. [IRC §§ 415(e), 415(f); Treas Reg § 1.415-8; Ltr Rul 9325055]

For an employee who participates in both plans, the sum of the defined benefit plan fraction and the defined contribution plan fraction cannot exceed 1.0. To arrive at the overall maximum limitation, take the following steps:

1. Compute a defined benefit plan fraction. The numerator of this fraction is the projected annual retirement benefit determined at year end. The denominator is the *lesser* of 1.25 times the dollar limitation for the current year or 1.4 times the percentage limitation for the current year. [IRC § 415(e)(2)]

2. Compute a defined contribution plan fraction. The numerator of this fraction is the total of the annual additions to the participant's account for all years determined at year end. The denominator is the *lesser* of 1.25 times the dollar limitation or 1.4 times the percentage limitation for the current year and all years of prior service. [IRC § 415(e)(1)]

Each plan may contain a fail-safe provision that freezes the annual addition or benefit accrual at a level that prevents the limitation from being exceeded. For purposes of the 1.0 rule, the reduction, if any, in the defined benefit plan dollar limitation is based upon years of service, not years of participation (see Q 6:13). [IRC § 415(b)(5)(B); Treas Reg §§ 1.411(d)-4, Q&A 2(b)(2)(xi), 1.415-6(b)(6)]

Example. Mr. James, age 45, incorporates his business in January 1996. The corporation adopts a 100 percent defined benefit plan and a 10-percent-of-compensation money purchase pension plan. Mr. James earns $120,000 in 1996. Here is how the 1.0 rule works:

1. The defined benefit plan fraction is .8 [$120,000/$150,000 (the lesser of 1.25 × $120,000 or 1.4 × $120,000)].

2. The defined contribution plan fraction is .32 [$12,000/$37,500 (the lesser of 1.25 × $30,000 or 1.4 × $30,000)].

3. The two fractions total 1.12.

At this point, the 1.0 rule comes into play—one of the fractions must be reduced. If the 10-percent-of-compensation contribution formula under the defined contribution plan is reduced to 6.25 percent, the defined contribution plan fraction will be .2 [$7,500/$37,500; ($7,500 = 6.25% × $120,000)]. Then, the total of the fractions will be 1.0.

The cost to fund the 100-percent-of-compensation defined benefit plan varies from participant to participant. Note that contributions under a defined benefit plan depend upon the participant's age and the actuarial assumptions, such as interest and retirement age, used by the actuary to calculate that cost. Thus, the combination of a defined benefit plan and a defined contribution plan may provide the employer with a greater tax deduction.

IRS has ruled that, if benefit accruals under a defined benefit plan are frozen (see Q 22:15), the accrued benefit (see Q 9:2) as of the date benefits are frozen becomes the projected annual retirement benefit and is, therefore, the numerator of the defined benefit plan fraction. [Ltr Rul 8936053] Where a corporation (Newco) was formed by the merger of six corporations (Oldcos), the plan adopted by Newco did not have to be aggregated with any plans of the Oldcos for purposes of the 1.0 rule. [Ltr Rul 9541041]

For details on tax deduction rules, see chapter 12; and, for details on top-heavy combined plans, see Qs 22:51 through 22:58.

For limitation years (see Q 6:16) *beginning after 1999*, the 1.0 rule is repealed. After repeal, a participant will be able to receive the maximum benefit under a defined benefit plan and the maximum contribution under a defined contribution plan at the same time. [SBA '96, Act § 1452(a)]

Q 6:18 At what level of compensation will the 1.0 rule affect an employee?

If the employee's annual compensation (see Qs 6:3, 6:4, 6:12) exceeds $107,140, the 1.0 rule requires a reduction in one of the plans (see Q 6:17). Under the rule, at $107,140 of compensation, the total of the fractions of a 100 percent defined benefit plan ($107,140 ÷ $149,996 = .714) plus a 10 percent defined contribution plan ($10,714 ÷ $37,499 = .286) equals 1.0.

If the maximum dollar limits increase (see Qs 6:1, 6:8), the threshold level of compensation for equivalency will also increase, but not necessarily in proportion to the percentage increase in the dollar limits.

Q 6:19   What limits apply to employee contributions required under a qualified retirement plan?

A special nondiscrimination test, the actual contribution percentage (ACP) test, applies to required (i.e., mandatory) employee contributions under all qualified defined contribution plans (see Qs 2:2, 23:48–23:55). If the plan satisfies the special requirements regarding such employee contributions, the plan will not be discriminatory. [Treas Reg § 1.401(a)(4)-1(b)(2)(ii)(B)]

Since a defined benefit plan does not separately account for required employee contributions (such contributions are not allocated or credited to separate accounts), the special nondiscrimination test does not apply, but the plan will generally be deemed nondiscriminatory only if such employee contributions are made at the same rate, expressed as a percentage of compensation, by all employees under the plan. [Treas Reg § 1.401(a)(4)-6]

If required employee contributions are so burdensome that non-highly compensated employees (see Q 3:13) cannot afford to participate, the plan may fail to satisfy the coverage requirements (see chapter 5) and not be a qualified retirement plan.

Required employee contributions made to a defined contribution plan are considered employee contributions that must satisfy the annual addition limitation (see Q 6:1).

Q 6:20   Is any limit set on the amount that a participant can voluntarily contribute to a qualified retirement plan?

The same special nondiscrimination test (see Q 6:19) applies to employee voluntary contributions. Since employee voluntary contributions under a defined benefit plan (see Q 2:3) will be separately accounted for, there is no limit on the amount of employee voluntary contributions made to either a defined contribution plan or a defined benefit plan as long as the ACP test and other special requirements are satisfied (see Qs 23:48–23:55).

However, under all circumstances, whether the employee voluntary contributions are made to a defined contribution plan or a defined benefit plan, these contributions are considered employee contributions that must satisfy the annual addition limitation (see Q 6:1).

Q 6:21   What tax advantages are gained when a qualified retirement plan permits participants to make voluntary contributions?

Although participants cannot deduct their voluntary contributions to the plan, they do get the advantage of having their contributions build up free of tax under the protection of the qualified retirement plan's tax shelter (see Qs 1:1, 1:6).

Q 6:22   May a qualified retirement plan permit deductible employee contributions?

The law permitting deductible employee contributions was repealed. [TRA '86 § 1101(b)]

Although deductible employee contributions are no longer permitted, separate accounting by the employer or plan administrator is required with respect to any such contributions that were ever made to the plan to ensure that an employee who later receives a distribution from the plan is able to compute the tax due correctly. However, assets purchased by the plan with deductible employee contributions need not be segregated from other plan assets. [Notice 82-13, 1982-1 CB 360]

Distributions of deductible employee contributions (including earnings) are taxed as ordinary income in the year received unless they are rolled over (that is, transferred tax-free) to an IRA or to another qualified retirement plan (see Q 28:8). Distributions of deductible employee contributions may also be subject to the early distribution tax (see Q 13:39).

Q 6:23   Is there an annual compensation limit under a qualified retirement plan?

Yes. For each employee who participates in a qualified retirement plan, an annual limit on compensation is required. [IRC § 401(a)(17); Treas Reg § 1.401(a)(17)-1]

This limit applies to a qualified retirement plan in two ways. First, a plan may not base allocations (see Q 2:6), in the case of a defined contribution plan (see Q 2:2), or benefit accruals (see Q 9:2), in the case of a defined benefit plan (see Q 2:3), on compensation in excess of the annual limit (see Q 6:30). Second, the amount of an employee's annual compensation that may be taken into account in applying certain specified nondiscrimination rules is subject to the annual limitation. [Treas Reg § 1.401(a)(17)-1(a)(1)]

The annual compensation limit was $200,000 (see Q 6:24); however, the $200,000 limitation was reduced to $150,000 for benefits accruing in plan years beginning after December 31, 1993 (see Q 6:27). [IRC § 401(a)(17); Treas Reg §§ 1.401(a)(17)-1(a)(2), 1.401(a)(17)-1(a)(3)(i)]

See Q 6:31 for a discussion of the family aggregation rule.

Q 6:24   Did the $200,000 ceiling on annual compensation rise?

Yes. The amount of the annual limit, $200,000 (see Q 6:23), was adjusted annually for increases in cost-of-living. For 1993, the annual compensation limit was $235,840. [IRC § 401(a)(17); IR 93-2 (Jan 15, 1993)] For prior years, the annual compensation limit was as follows:

Year	Annual Compensation Limit
1992	$228,860
1991	222,220
1990	209,200

The adjustment applied to plan years *beginning* in the calendar year in which the adjustment was effective. In addition, any increase in the annual limit applied only to compensation taken into account for the year of the increase and subsequent years and did not apply to compensation for prior years that were used in determining an employee's benefit (see Q 6:30).

Example. K & K Corp. maintained a defined benefit plan with a calendar-year plan year. The plan became effective on January 1, 1989 and based benefits on the average of an employee's compensation for the five highest consecutive years. For each plan year, 1989 through 1993, Leona had compensation of $235,840. The plan could not base benefits for Leona in 1993 on compensation in excess of $219,224, the average of Leona's annual compensation capped by the limit for the applicable year ($235,840 + $228,860 + $222,220 + $209,200 + $200,000). Each year used in the average is subject to the applicable annual compensation limit for that year (see Qs 6:25, 6:30).

[Treas Reg §§ 1.401(a)(17)-1(a)(2), 1.401(a)(17)-1(b)(1), 1.401(a)(17)-1(b)(2), 1.401(a)(17)-1(b)(3), 1.401(a)(17)-1(b)(6)]

Q 6:25   Will the $150,000 ceiling on annual compensation rise?

The amount of the annual limit, $150,000 (see Q 6:23), is adjusted for increases in cost-of-living. However, an adjustment will be made only if it is $10,000 or greater and then will be made in multiples of $10,000 (i.e., rounded down to the next lowest multiple of $10,000). For example, an increase in the cost-of-living of $9,999 will result in no adjustment, and an increase of $19,999 will create an upward adjustment of $10,000. Therefore, the cost-of-living must increase by 6⅔ percent before the first adjustment to the annual compensation limit will occur (6⅔% × $150,000 = $10,000). [IRC §§ 401(a)(17)(A), 401(a)(17)(B); Treas Reg § 1.401(a)(17)-1(a)(3)]

To calculate the cost-of-living increase for any particular year, the CPI-U must be obtained from DOL for the three months of the calendar quarter ending September 30 (i.e., July, August, and September) of the previous year. The sum of the three indices is then compared to the sum of the indices for the last three months of the base year (i.e., 1993). The quotient of these sums is rounded to four decimal places. This result is multiplied by the $150,000 limitation. Finally, if this result is an even multiple of $10,000, the result obtained is the new dollar limitation; otherwise, the result is rounded to the next lowest multiple of $10,000 to obtain the new dollar limitation. Since the cost-of-living increase was not 6⅔ percent or greater, the annual compensation limit remained at $150,000 for plan years that begin in 1995 and remains unchanged at $150,000 for plan years that begin in 1996. [Notice 95-55, 1995-45 IRB 11]

The table below shows how the compensation limit would change with an annual cost-of-living adjustment of 3.25 percent:

Year	3.25% COLA	New Limit
1995	$154,875	$150,000
1996	159,908	150,000
1997	165,105	160,000
1998	170,471	170,000

The adjustment applies to plan years *beginning* in the calendar year in which the adjustment is effective. In addition, any increase in the annual limit applies only to compensation taken into account for the year of the increase and subsequent years and does not apply to compensation for prior years that are used in determining an employee's benefit (see Q 6:30). [Treas Reg § 1.401(a)(17)-1(b)]

For the following examples, assume that the table above is accurate.

Example 1. C & A Corp. maintains a defined contribution plan with a plan year beginning on July 1 and ending on June 30. For the plan year ended June 30, 1997, Caroline's compensation is $160,000. Because the plan year begins in 1996, the annual compensation limit in effect on January 1, 1996 ($150,000) applies to the plan for the entire plan year and Caroline's excess compensation of $10,000 ($160,000 – $150,000) is disregarded.

Example 2. A & C Corp. maintains a defined benefit plan with a calendar-year plan year. The plan became effective on January 1, 1994 and bases benefits on the average of an employee's compensation for the five highest consecutive years. For each plan year, 1994 through 1998, Adam has compensation of $170,000. The plan cannot base benefits for Adam in 1998 on compensation in excess of $156,000, the average of Adam's annual compensation capped by the limit for the applicable year [($150,000 + $150,000 + $150,000 + $160,000 + $170,000) 5]. Each year used in the average is subject to the applicable annual compensation limit for that year.

Although the annual compensation limit can never be reduced below $150,000, it appears that an increase in the limit can be abrogated. For example, in the table above, if the cost-of-living is *reduced* in 1999 by 1 percent, the cumulative increases in the $150,000 limit will be $18,766. Since the next lowest multiple of $10,000 is $10,000, the limit would be reduced from $170,000 to $160,000 for 1999.

Q 6:26   How does the $150,000 ceiling affect plans adopted before 1994?

The best way to illustrate the effect of the reduced annual compensation limit (see Qs 6:23, 6:25) is by example.

Example 1. Ess-Ell-Kay Corp. adopted a profit sharing plan on December 1, 1993 with a plan year beginning December 1 and ending on November 30. Plan contributions are allocated in proportion to compensation (see Q 2:6); and, for the plan year ending November 30, 1994, Ess-Ell-Kay contributes the amount necessary for A, the owner, to receive an allocation of $30,000:

Employee	Compensation	Contribution
A (owner)	$235,840	$30,000
B	85,000	10,812
C	50,000	6,360
D	35,000	4,452
E	25,000	3,180
F	20,000	2,544
Total	$450,840	$57,348

Although Ess-Ell-Kay could contribute up to 15 percent of compensation (see Q 12:7), it had to contribute only 12.7 percent of compensation for A to receive the maximum $30,000 allocation (see Q 6:1). In Example 1, A receives 52.3 percent of the total contribution.

Example 2. Assume the same facts as in Example 1, except that Ess-Ell-Kay Corp. adopted the profit sharing plan on December 1, 1996.

Employee	Compensation	Contribution
A (owner)	$150,000	$22,500
B	85,000	12,750
C	50,000	7,500
D	35,000	5,250
E	25,000	3,750
F	20,000	3,000
Total	$365,000	$54,750

Because A's compensation is limited to $150,000, A will only receive an allocation of $22,500, less than the maximum annual addition. For A to receive $22,500, Ess-Ell-Kay must contribute 15 percent of compensation for all employees, and A receives only 41 percent of the total contribution.

Example 3. Because Ess-Ell-Kay Corp. wants A to receive an allocation of $30,000 for the plan year ending November 30, 1997, it adopts a 5-percent-of-compensation money purchase pension plan (see Q 2:4) for that year. With the combination of plans, A will receive an allocation of $30,000.

Employee	Compensation	Contribution
A (owner)	$150,000	$30,000
B	85,000	17,000
C	50,000	10,000
D	35,000	7,000
E	25,000	5,000
F	20,000	4,000
Total	$365,000	$73,000

To accomplish its goal, Ess-Ell-Kay must contribute 20 percent of compensation for all employees, and A still receives only 41 percent of the total contribution.

To maintain A at the $30,000 level, Ess-Ell-Kay had to increase its contribution from $54,750 to $73,000, a 33⅓ percent increase. To increase A's allocation to more than $22,500 (and possibly up to $30,000) and still keep its contribution at no more than $54,750, Ess-Ell-Kay could amend the plan to do the following:

1. Take permitted disparity into account (see Q 7:1);
2. Use both age and compensation as a basis for allocating contributions (i.e., an age-based profit sharing plan; see Qs 2:7, 2:8); or
3. Test the allocation of plan contributions on the basis of an equivalent amount of benefits (i.e., cross-testing; see Q 4:20).

Defined benefit plans (see Q 2:3) will experience the same problems. The new $150,000 annual compensation limit may cause highly compensated business owners to receive smaller future benefit accruals (see Q 6:30) or force the employer to provide greater benefits to all other employees (see Q 4:15).

Q 6:27   Can a qualified retirement plan use a 12-month period other than the plan year to determine compensation?

Yes. Alternatively, a qualified retirement plan may determine compensation used in determining allocations or benefit accruals for the plan year for all employees on the basis of a 12-consecutive-month period (or periods) ending no later than the last day of the plan year. If compensation is based on these alternative 12-month periods, the annual compensation limit (see Qs 6:23, 6:25) applies to compensation for each of those periods based on the annual compensation limit in effect for the respective calendar year in which each 12-month period *begins*. [Treas Reg § 1.401(a)(17)-1(b)(3)(ii)]

If compensation for a period of less than 12 months is used for a plan year, then the otherwise applicable annual compensation limit is reduced in the same proportion as the reduction in the 12-month period. Furthermore, if the period for determining compensation used in calculating an employee's allocation or accrual for a plan year is a short plan year (i.e., shorter than 12 months), the annual compensation limit is an amount equal to the otherwise applicable annual compensation limit multiplied by the fraction, the numerator of which is the number of months in the short plan year and the denominator of which is 12. [Treas Reg § 1.401(a)(17)-1(b)(3)(iii)(A)]

Example. B & S Corp. adopts a profit sharing plan on October 1, 1996, and the first plan year is the short period of October 1, 1996 to December 31, 1996. Barbra's compensation from B & S Corp. for calendar year 1996 is $150,000. The annual compensation limit for the plan for the short period is $37,500 (3/12 × $150,000), and Barbra's excess compensation of $112,500 ($150,000 − $37,500) is disregarded.

However, no proration is required if the plan formula provides that the allocation or accrual for each employee is based on compensation for the portion of the plan year during which the employee is a participant. [Treas Reg § 1.401(a)(17)-1(b)(3)(iii)(B)]

Example. S & B Corp. adopts a calendar-year money purchase pension plan on January 1, 1996. Steven, whose compensation is $25,000 per month, commences participation in the plan on July 1, 1996. For purposes of allocating employer contributions, only compensation earned after an employee becomes a participant is used. Steven's entire compensation of $150,000 earned from July 1, 1996 to December 31, 1996 may be used because there is no proration of the annual compensation limit.

Q 6:28 How is the annual compensation limit applied if an employee participates in a qualified retirement plan sponsored by more than one employer?

If the employers are part of a controlled group or an affiliated service group (see Qs 5:31, 5:33, 5:37), the annual compensation limit (see Q 6:23) is applied on an aggregate basis to compensation received from all members of the group; but, if the employers are not related, the annual compensation limit applies separately with respect to the compensation received by an employee from each unrelated employer maintaining the plan rather than to the total compensation from all employers maintaining the plan. [IRC §§ 413(c), 414(b), 414(c), 414(m); Treas Reg § 1.401(a)(17)-1(b)(4)]

Example. Maxine Corp., Sooper-Max Inc., and Maxfly Ltd., which are each unrelated to the others, all adopt a single profit sharing plan for calendar year 1996. Bob is employed by all three corporations and has compensation from each of $100,000. The plan is permitted to take into account the full $300,000 of Bob's compensation from the three corporations for the plan year without violating the annual compensation limit.

Although compensation need not be aggregated in the above example, for purposes of applying the annual addition limitation (see Q 6:1) and the annual retirement benefit limitation (see Q 6:8), contributions or benefits attributable to the employee from all three corporations must be taken into account. Consequently, under the profit sharing plan in the above example, Bob's annual addition limitation is $30,000 in the aggregate. [Treas Reg § 1.415-1(e)]

Q 6:29   Does the annual compensation limit affect the Code's nondiscrimination requirements?

The annual compensation limit (see Qs 6:23, 6:27) applies for purposes of applying the nondiscrimination rules under Sections 401(a)(4), 401(a)(5), 401(k)(3), 401(l), 401(m)(2), and 410(b)(2). The limit also applies in determining whether an alternative method of determining compensation impermissibly discriminates in favor of highly compensated employees (see Qs 3:2, 6:37–6:44). [Treas Reg § 1.401(a)(17)-1(c)]

Q 6:30   When is the annual compensation limit effective?

The $200,000 annual compensation limit (see Qs 6:23, 6:24) was generally effective for plan years beginning on or after January 1, 1989, and the $150,000 annual compensation limit (see Qs 6:23, 6:25) is generally effective for plan years beginning on or after January 1, 1994.

Benefits accrued (see Q 9:2) under a defined benefit plan for plan years beginning before January 1, 1994 are not subject to the new $150,000 annual compensation limit. For example, an employee's benefits accrued prior to the 1994 plan year that are based on compensation in excess of $150,000 are not required to be reduced, and these accruals based on excess compensation are not required to be offset against the employee's benefit accruals in subsequent years. [Treas Reg § 1.401(a)(17)-1(d)(5)]

To implement the reduction in the compensation limit, "fresh start" rules are provided for defined benefit plans. The fresh start rules allow benefits accrued before a reduction to be frozen under a formula; there are several available formulas, and each plan must specify the method it uses. Multiple fresh start rules are set forth, so that benefits accrued before the $200,000 limit became effective may be frozen, and benefits accrued before the $150,000 limit became effective may also be frozen. [Treas Reg §§ 1.401(a)(17)-1(d)(5)(iii), 1.401(a)(17)-1(e)(3)]

Example. On January 1, 1984, Boca Stanley Corp. adopted a calendar-year defined benefit plan providing an annual benefit for each year of service equal to 2 percent of compensation averaged over an employee's high three consecutive calendar years' compensation. As of December 31, 1988, Marjorie had five years of service and earned $250,000 each year. Marjorie's accrued benefit as of December 31, 1988 was $25,000 (2% × 5 × $250,000).

Effective January 1, 1989, the plan is amended to provide that an employee's benefit will equal the sum of the employee's accrued benefit as of December 31, 1988 (determined as though the employee terminated employment on that date and without regard to any amendments after that date) and 2 percent of compensation averaged over an employee's high three consecutive calendar years' compensation times years of service taking into account only years of service after December 31, 1988.

Marjorie earned $275,000 in each of 1989 and 1990 and $300,000 in each of 1991, 1992, and 1993. The annual compensation limit was $222,220, $228,860, and $235,840 for plan years beginning January 1, 1991, 1992, and 1993, respectively (see Q 6:24). The compensation that may be taken into account for plan benefits in 1993 cannot exceed $228,973 (the average of $222,220, $228,860, and $235,840). Therefore, as of December 31, 1993, Marjorie's accrued benefit is $47,897 [$25,000 (Marjorie's December 31, 1988 frozen accrued benefit) + $22,897 (2% × 5 × $228,973)].

As of January 1, 1994, the plan is amended to provide that an employee's benefit will equal the sum of the employee's accrued benefit as of December 31, 1993 (determined as though the employee terminated employment on that date and without regard to any amendments after that date) and 2 percent of compensation averaged over an employee's high three consecutive years' compensation times years of service taking into account only years of service after December 31, 1993.

Assume that Marjorie earns $350,000 in each of the years 1994 through 1998 and that the new $150,000 annual compensation limit is first adjusted to $160,000 for plan years beginning on or after January 1, 1997 and is not adjusted for the plan year beginning on or after January 1, 1998. The compensation that may be taken into account for the 1998 plan year cannot exceed $156,667 (the average of $150,000 for 1996, $160,000 for 1997, and $160,000 for 1998).

Therefore, on December 31, 1998, Marjorie's accrued benefit is $63,564 [$47,897 (Marjorie's December 31, 1993 frozen accrued benefit) + $15,667 (2% × 5 × $156,667)].

Q 6:31   What is the family aggregation rule?

For plan years beginning before 1997, if an individual was a member of the family of either a 5 percent owner (see Q 3:4) or a highly compensated employee (see Q 3:3) who was one of the ten most highly compensated employees, the compensation of that individual was treated as if paid to (or on behalf of) a single 5 percent owner or highly compensated employee. Family members included the employee's spouse and any lineal descendant who had not attained age 19 before the close of the year. [IRC §§ 401(a)(17), 414(q)(6), prior to repeal by SBA '96 § 1431]

Example 1. The Ezratty Golfing Group Ltd. adopts a 25-percent-of-compensation money purchase pension plan for calendar year 1996. There are two participants, Marty, who earns $150,000, and his wife, Rona, who also earns $150,000. Because of the family aggregation rule, their combined compensation cannot exceed $150,000 (see Q 6:3). The contribution for each is calculated as follows:

1. Each is deemed to earn $75,000 ($150,000 ÷ 2).
2. The contribution for each is $18,750 (25% × $75,000).
3. The total contribution is $37,500 ($18,750 + $18,750).

If the family aggregation rule did not apply, the total contribution would be $60,000 [(lesser of $30,000 or 25% × $150,000) × 2]. *For years beginning after 1996, the family aggregation rule is repealed.* [SBA '96, Act § 1431(b)(1)]

In addition to the family aggregation rule not applying to the annual addition limitation or the limitation on benefits under a defined benefit plan, the rule does *not* apply to the limit on tax-deductible contributions to a pension plan (see Qs 12:16, 12:17). Thus, the effect of the family aggregation rules can be avoided.

Example 2. Assume the same facts as in Example 1, except that The Ezratty Golfing Group Ltd. adopts a 40-percent-of-compensation money purchase pension plan for calendar year 1996. The contribution for each is calculated as follows:

1. Each is deemed to earn $75,000 ($150,000 ÷ 2).
2. The contribution for each is $30,000 (40% × $75,000).
3. The total contribution is $60,000 ($30,000 + $30,000).

The annual addition limitation is satisfied because the contribution for each of Marty and Rona does not exceed $30,000 (the lesser of $30,000 or $37,500 (25% × $150,000), and the amount of $30,000 each is the amount necessary to satisfy the minimum funding requirements (see Q 8:1).

Q 6:32   Can a self-employed individual set up a qualified retirement plan?

Yes; but, *for years beginning before 1997,* a plan covering a self-employed individual (see Q 6:33) must satisfy certain requirements in addition to the normal corporate retirement plan qualification requirements (see Q 5:35). [IRC §§ 401(c), 401(d), prior to amendment by SBA '96 § 1441]

A self-employed individual is an individual who has income (see Q 6:34) from self-employment for the taxable year (see Q 6:33). An S corporation shareholder is not a self-employed individual, and S corporation pass-through income is not income from self-employment. Therefore, an S corporation shareholder cannot establish a retirement plan and make deductible contributions thereto based upon the pass-through income. [Durando v United States, 1995 US App Lexis 32048 (9th Cir 1995)]

Q 6:33   Who is a self-employed individual?

Anyone who carries on a trade or business as a sole proprietor or who is a member of a partnership is self-employed. Although the individual need not carry on regular full-time business activities to be considered self-employed, an individual must have earned income (see Qs 6:34, 6:35). [IRC § 401(c); Treas Reg § 1.1402(c)-1] An S corporation shareholder is not a self-employed individual, and S corporation pass-through income is not earned income. [Durando v United States, 1995 US App Lexis 32048 (9th Cir 1995)]

Q 6:34   What is earned income?

The criterion for contributions to a qualified retirement plan on behalf of a self-employed individual (see Q 6:33) is earned income. This means that contributions by or for a sole proprietor or partner may be made to a qualified retirement plan only if personal services are performed. Thus, for example, inactive owners who derive income solely from investments may not participate in a qualified retirement plan. [Treas Reg § 1.401-10(c)(3); Frick, 56 TCM 1368 (1989); Pugh, 49 TCM 748 (1985); Frick, 50 TCM 1334 (1985)] Earned income is defined as the net earnings from self-employment in a trade or business in which personal services of the taxpayer are a material income-producing factor. In effect, earned income is the net profit of the business. The fact that capital is an important aspect of the self-employed individual's business is not significant in determining earned income. [IRC § 401(c)(2); see also IRS Pub 560]

Distributions of income to a limited partner are not considered net earnings from self-employment. However, guaranteed payments made to a limited partner are considered net earnings from self-employment if paid for services rendered to or for the partnership. [IRC § 1402(a)(13); Treas Reg § 1.401-11(d)(2)(ii)] Distributions in liquidation of a terminating partner's interest in a partnership are not earned income. [Kellough, 69 TCM 2998 (1995)]

An S corporation shareholder is not a self-employed individual, and S corporation pass-through income is not earned income. Therefore, an S corporation shareholder cannot establish a retirement plan and make deductible contributions thereto based upon the pass-through income. [Durando v United States, 1995 US App Lexis 32048 (9th Cir 1995)]

Payments to a former employee under a deferred compensation plan represent compensation for past services and are not considered earned income. [Ltr Rul 8522057]

For purposes of computing the limitations on deductions for contributions to a qualified retirement plan, earned income is computed after taking into account amounts contributed to the plan on behalf of the self-employed individual (i.e., the self-employed individual's earned income is reduced by the deductible contributions to the plan). Furthermore, earned income is computed after the deduction allowed to the self-employed individual for one-half of the individual's self-employment taxes (see Q 6:36). [IRC §§ 164(f), 401(c)(2)(A)(v), 401(c)(2)(A)(vi), 404(a)(8)(D), 1401]

Q 6:35   May an individual be both self-employed and an employee of another employer?

An individual may be an employee of one entity and still be self-employed with regard to another entity. With respect to the same employer, regardless of the form of entity (e.g., sole proprietorship, partnership, or corporation), the classifications as self-employed and employee are normally mutually exclusive; however, it is possible to be an employee of an entity and also be self-employed with regard to that entity. [Reese, 63 TCM 3129 (1992)]

> **Example.** Carol is employed by Billy's Ambulette Corporation as an accountant and also has her own part-time accounting practice. Even though Carol may participate in Billy's Ambulette Corporation's qualified retirement plan, she is also able to establish a qualified retirement plan for her self-employment income. [Treas Reg § 1.401-10(b)(3)(ii)]

However, where an individual was the president, the sole shareholder, and a director of a corporation, his compensation was ruled wages and not self-employment income. Consequently, the individual could not establish a qualified retirement plan. [Jacobs, 66 TCM 1470 (1993)]

Q 6:36   How much may be contributed to a qualified retirement plan on behalf of a self-employed individual?

The contribution limits that apply to corporate plans apply to plans covering self-employed individuals (see Q 6:33). Thus, the annual addition limit for defined contribution plans is the lesser of $30,000 or 25 percent of compensation (see Q 6:1). But because earned income is computed after taking into account amounts contributed to the plan on behalf of the self-employed individual and after the deduction for one-half of the individual's self-employment taxes (see Q 6:34), the effective percentage limit on the contribution is 20 percent of earned income computed after the self-employment tax deduction but before the contribution (1 ÷ 1.25 = .80; 1.0 − .80 = .20).

If the self-employed individual adopts a profit sharing plan only, the effective percentage limit on the contribution is 13.0435 percent of earned income computed after the self-employment tax deduction but before the contribution (1 ÷ 1.15 = .869565; 1.0 − .869565 = .130435).

For 1996, the self-employment tax rate is 15.3 percent (12.4 percent for Social Security and 2.9 percent for Medicare); the Social Security base is $62,700, but the Medicare base is unlimited.

Example 1. James adopted a 10-percent-of-compensation money purchase pension plan for 1996. His earned income before the deductions for the plan contribution on his behalf and one-half of his self-employment taxes is $62,700. James's deductible contribution to the plan is $5,297, determined by completing the following steps:

Step 1	Enter the rate [1.0 − (1 ÷ 1.10)]	.090909
Step 2	Enter James's net earnings	$62,700
Step 3	Enter deduction for one-half of James's self-employment taxes	4,430
Step 4	Step 2 − Step 3	58,270
Step 5	Step 1 × Step 4	5,297
Step 6	10% (plan contribution rate) × 150,000 (but not more than $30,000)	15,000
Step 7	Deductible contribution: lesser of Step 5 or Step 6	5,297

Example 2A. Caroline adopted a 15-percent-of-compensation profit sharing plan for 1996. Her earned income before the deductions for the plan contribution on her behalf and one-half of her self-employment taxes is $150,000. Caroline's maximum deductible contribution to the plan is $18,796, determined by completing the following steps:

Step 1	Enter the maximum rate [1.0 − (1 ÷ 1.15)]	.130435
Step 2	Enter Caroline's net earnings	$150,000
Step 3	Enter deduction for one-half of Caroline's self-employment taxes	5,896
Step 4	Step 2 − Step 3	144,104
Step 5	Step 1 × Step 4	18,796
Step 6	15% (plan contribution rate) × 150,000 (but not more than $30,000)Maximum dollar limitation	22,500
Step 7	Deductible contribution: lesser of Step 5 or Step 6	18,796

Example 2B. Assume the same facts as in Example 2A, except that Caroline's earned income before the deductions for the plan contribution on her behalf and one-half of her self-employment taxes is $200,000. Caroline's maximum deductible contribution to the plan is $22,500, determined by completing the following steps:

Step 1	Enter the maximum rate [1.0 − (1 ÷ 1.15)]	.130435
Step 2	Enter Caroline's net earnings	$200,000
Step 3	Enter deduction for one-half of Caroline's self-employment taxes	6,566
Step 4	Step 2 − Step 3	193,434
Step 5	Step 1 × Step 4	25,231
Step 6	15% (plan contribution rate) × 150,000 (but not more than $30,000)	22,500
Step 7	Deductible contribution: lesser of Step 5 or Step 6	22,500

Example 3A. Stephanie adopted a 25-percent-of-compensation money purchase pension plan for 1996. Her earned income before the deductions for the plan contribution on her behalf and one-half of her self-employment taxes is $150,000. Stephanie's deductible contribution to the plan IS $28,821, determined by completing the following steps:

Step 1	Enter the rate [1.0 – (1 ÷ 1.25)]	.20
Step 2	Enter Stephanie's net earnings	$150,000
Step 3	Enter deduction for one-half of Stephanie's self-employment taxes	5,896
Step 4	Step 2 – Step 3	144,104
Step 5	Step 1 × Step 4	28,821
Step 6	25% (plan contribution rate) × 150,000 (but not more than $30,000)	30,000
Step 7	Deductible contribution: lesser of Step 5 or Step 6	28,821

Example 3B. Assume the same facts as in Example 3A, except that Stephanie's earned income before the deductions for the plan contribution on her behalf and one-half of her self-employment taxes is $200,000. Stephanie's deductible contribution to the plan is $30,000, determined by completing the following steps:

Step 1	Enter the rate [1.0 – (1 ÷ 1.25)]	.20
Step 2 H	Enter Stephanie's net earnings	$200,000
Step 3	Enter deduction for one-half of Stephanie's self-employment taxes	6,566
Step 4	Step 2 – Step 3	193,434
Step 5	Step 1 × Step 4	38,687
Step 6	25% (plan contribution rate) × 150,000 (but not more than $30,000)	30,000
Step 7	Deductible contribution: lesser of Step 5 or Step 6	30,000

[Treas Reg § 1.401(a)(17)-1(b)(6), Examples 4 and 5; IRS Pub 535 and IRS Pub 560]

All of the above examples assume that the self-employed individual did not earn any salary that was subject to Social Security taxes during 1996. If the individual does earn a salary, the self-employment tax deduction will be reduced. Because the Medicare base is unlimited, the self-employment tax deduction must always be computed regardless of the individual's salary income.

Example 4. Assume the same facts as in Example 1, except that James also earned a salary of $62,700 in 1996. James's deductible contribution to the plan is $5,624, determined by completing the following steps:

Step 1	Enter the rate [1.0 – (1 ÷ 1.10)]	.090909
Step 2	Enter James's net earnings	$62,700
Step 3	Enter deduction for one-half of James's self-employment taxes	840
Step 4	Step 2 – Step 3	61,860
Step 5	Step 1 × Step 4	5,624
Step 6	10% (plan contribution rate) × 150,000 (but not more than $30,000)	15,000
Step 7	Deductible contribution: lesser of Step 5 or Step 6	5,624

The contribution limit to a defined benefit plan is based upon a maximum annual retirement benefit equal to the lesser of $90,000 or 100 percent of compensation (see Qs 6:8, 12:13).

Q 6:37 Can the definition of compensation used in a qualified retirement plan cause prohibited discrimination?

Yes. Section 414(s) provides rules for defining compensation for purposes of applying any provision that specifically refers to Section 414(s). For example, Section 414(s) is explicitly referred to in many of the nondiscrimination provisions applicable to qualified retirement plans. The amount of plan benefits or contributions, expressed as a percentage of compensation (see Qs 6:38–6:44), is generally one of the key factors in determining whether these nondiscrimination provisions are satisfied. [IRC § 414(s); Treas Reg § 1.414(s)-1(a)]

Q 6:38 May different definitions of compensation be used if an employer maintains more than one qualified retirement plan?

An employer may use any definition of compensation that satisfies Section 414(s) to determine if an applicable provision is satisfied with respect to a qualified retirement plan. This rule is designed to permit an employer, whenever possible, to use the definition used under the plan for calculating contributions or benefits to determine if an applicable nondiscrimination provision is satisfied. Consequently, an employer that maintains more than one qualified retirement plan may generally use one definition of compensation that satisfies Section 414(s) in determining whether one of the plans satisfies a particular nondiscrimination requirement (such as the general nondiscrimination requirements of Section 401(a)(4)) and use the same or a different definition of compensation in determining whether another plan satisfies the same nondiscrimination requirement. The definition of compensation selected generally must be used consistently to define the compensation of all employees taken into account in determining whether a plan satisfies the nondiscrimination provision. [Treas Reg §§ 1.414(s)-1(b)(1), 1.414(s)-1(b)(2)(i), 1.414(s)-1(b)(2)(ii)]

Q 6:39 Are there specific definitions of compensation that will satisfy Section 414(s)?

A definition of compensation that includes all compensation within the meaning of Section 415(c)(3) and excludes all other compensation will automatically satisfy Section 414(s) (see Q 6:3). In addition, Section 414(s) will be satisfied if either of the Section 415(c)(3) safe harbor definitions is used (see Q 6:4). [Treas Reg § 1.414(s)-1(c)(2)]

A safe harbor alternative definition of compensation that will automatically satisfy Section 414(s) without further testing is permitted. Under the safe harbor, compensation may be defined as set forth in the preceding paragraph but may be reduced by all of the following items (even if includible in income): (1) reimbursements or other expense allowances; (2) fringe benefits (cash and noncash); (3) moving expenses; (4) deferred compensation; and (5) welfare benefits. [Treas Reg § 1.414(s)-1(c)(3)]

A definition of compensation as set forth in either of the two preceding paragraphs will still satisfy Section 414(s) even though it is modified to include *all* elective contributions that are made by the employer on behalf of its employees that are not includible in income under Section 125, Section 402(e)(3), Section 402(h), or Section 403(b) and all compensation deferred under a Section 457 plan. [Treas Reg § 1.414(s)-1(c)(4)]

Any of the safe harbor definitions may be modified to permit additional items or amounts of compensation to be excluded from the compensation of highly compensated employees (see Q 3:2), but not from the compensation of any non-highly compensated employees (see Q 3:13). This modification is permitted to be made after the inclusion of elective contributions and deferred compensation. For example, a definition of compensation under Section 415(c)(3) could be first modified to include all elective contributions and Section 457 deferred compensation, but then be further modified to exclude Section 457 deferred compensation from the compensation of highly compensated employees. Highly compensated employees need not be treated consistently. A safe harbor definition will continue to satisfy Section 414(s) automatically even if the definition is modified to exclude any portion of the compensation of some or all of the highly compensated employees. [Treas Reg § 1.414(s)-1(c)(5)]

See Q 6:3 for proposed changes to the definition of Section 415 compensation.

Q 6:40 Are there any alternative definitions of compensation that may satisfy Section 414(s)?

A definition of compensation will satisfy Section 414(s) with respect to employees if the definition of compensation is reasonable, does not by design favor highly compensated employees (see Q 3:2), and satisfies the nondiscrimination requirement (see Q 6:41). Even if the definition is reasonable, it still must not favor the highly compensated employees or be discriminatory. A reasonable definition of compensation is permitted to exclude, on a consistent basis, all or any portion of irregular or additional compensation, including one or more of the following:

1. Any type of additional compensation for employees working outside their regularly scheduled tour of duty (such as overtime pay, premiums for shift differential, and call-in premiums);

2. Bonuses; or

3. Any type of compensation excluded under the safe harbor alternative definition (see Q 6:39).

Whether a type of compensation is irregular or additional is determined based upon all the relevant facts and circumstances. A reasonable definition of compensation is also permitted to include, on a consistent basis, all or any portion of certain types of elective contributions (see Q 6:39). [Treas Reg §§ 1.414(s)-1(d)(1), 1.414(s)-1(d)(2)(i), 1.414(s)-1(d)(2)(ii)]

A definition of compensation is not reasonable if the definition includes an item or amount not includible under a safe harbor definition (e.g., business expenses substantiated to the payor under an accountable plan). In addition, a definition is *not* reasonable if it provides that each employee's compensation is a specified portion of the employee's total compensation (such as 90 percent). However, a definition of compensation is not unreasonable merely because it excludes all compensation in excess of a specified dollar amount. [Treas Reg § 1.414(s)-1(d)(2)(iii)]

Q 6:41 Must an alternative definition of compensation be nondiscriminatory?

Yes. An alternative definition of compensation is nondiscriminatory if the average percentage of total compensation included under the alternative definition for an employer's highly compensated employees (see Q 3:2) as a group does not exceed by more than a *de minimis* amount the average percentage included under the alternative definition for the employer's non-highly compensated employees (see Q 3:13) as a group. Self-employed individuals (see Q 6:33) and employees with zero compensation (see Q 6:43) are disregarded for purposes of this nondiscrimination test (see Q 6:44). [Treas Reg §§ 1.414(s)-1(d)(3)(i), 1.414(s)-1(d)(3)(iii); Rev Proc 95-34, 1995-29 IRB 7; Rev Proc 93-42, 1993-2 CB 540; Ann 93-130, 1993-31 IRB 46; Ann 92-81, 1992-22 IRB 56]

To calculate the average percentage, total compensation means all compensation within the meaning of Section 415(c)(3) and excludes all other compensation (see Qs 6:3, 6:4). However, an employer is permitted to increase this amount by including certain types of elective contributions (see Q 6:39). If a portion of the compensation of some highly compensated employees is excluded (see Q 6:39), the total compensation of such affected highly compensated employees is reduced; but, if the exclusion applies consistently to all highly compensated employees, the adjustment is not required. Total compensation taken into account for each employee (including, if added, the elective contributions) may not exceed the annual compensation limit (see Qs 6:23, 6:25). [Treas Reg § 1.414(s)-1(d)(3)(ii)]

To determine whether the average percentage requirement is satisfied, the employer must calculate individual percentages for each employee in a group and then average the percentages (individual-percentage method). However, the employer may use any other reasonable method to determine the average percentages. Thus, an employer may calculate an aggregate compensation percentage for each group of employees by dividing the aggregate amount of compensation of all employees in that group that is included under the alternative definition by the aggregate amount of total compensation of all employees in that group (aggregate-percentage method). Alternatively, the individual-percentage method may be used for one group and the aggregate-percentage method may be used for the other group. An alternative method is considered reasonable only if the percentage is not reasonably expected to vary significantly from the average percentage produced using the individual-percentage method because of the extra weight given employees with higher compensation in the relevant group. [Treas Reg § 1.414(s)-1(d)(3)(iv)]

The determination of whether the average percentage of total compensation included for the employer's highly compensated employees as a group exceeds by more than a *de minimis* amount the average percentage of total compensation included for the employer's non-highly compensated employees as a group is based on the applicable facts and circumstances. The differences between the percentages for prior periods may be considered in determining whether the amount of the difference between the percentages for a given period is more than *de minimis*. In addition, an isolated instance of a more than *de minimis* difference between the compensation percentages that is due to an extraordinary, unforeseeable event (such as overtime payments due to a major hurricane) will be disregarded if the amount of the difference in prior determination periods was *de minimis*. [Treas Reg § 1.414(s)-1(d)(3)(v)]

Q 6:42   Can a rate-of-pay definition of compensation be used?

Rate of pay is permitted as an alternative definition of compensation (see Q 6:40). Therefore, compensation may be defined as the amount of each employee's basic or regular compensation using the employee's basic or regular *rate* of compensation rather than using the employee's *actual* basic or regular compensation. For this purpose, the employee's rate of compensation must be determined using an hourly pay scale, weekly salary, or similar unit of basic or regular compensation applicable to the employee. It is permissible to define compensation as (1) including each employee's basic or regular compensation, the amount of which is determined using each employee's basic or regular rate of compensation, plus actual amounts of irregular or additional compensation, such as overtime or bonuses, or (2) the greater of the employee's actual compensation or basic or regular compensation using the employee's basic or regular rate of compensation. Of course, the rate-of-pay definition must be nondiscriminatory. [Treas Reg § 1.414(s)-1(e)(1)]

A rate-of-pay definition cannot be used to determine if elective contributions (see Q 23:13), matching contributions (see Q 23:48), or employee contributions (see Qs 6:19, 6:20) satisfy, for example, the ADP test (see Q 23:8) or the ACP test (see Q 23:48). [Treas Reg § 1.414(s)-1(e)(2)]

The amount of each employee's basic or regular compensation for the determination period must be determined using the employee's basic or regular rate of compensation as of a designated date in the determination period. If the determination period is a calendar year, this requirement would be satisfied if the amount of each employee's basic or regular compensation for the calendar year is determined using the basic or regular rate of compensation as of January 1. Alternatively, the amount of each employee's basic or regular compensation for a determination period can be the sum of the amounts separately determined for shorter specified periods (e.g., weeks or months) within the determination period, provided that the amount of each employee's basic or regular compensation for each specified period is determined using the employee's basic or regular rate of compensation as of a designated date within the specified period. [Treas Reg §§ 1.414(s)-1(e)(3)(ii), 1.414(s)-1(h)(2)]

One or more dates may be used to determine employees' rates of compensation for a determination period or specified period provided that, if the same date is not used for all employees, the dates selected are designed to determine the rates of compensation for that period on a consistent basis for all employees taken into account for the determination period. For example, if annual compensation increases are provided to different groups of employees on different dates during the year, it would be consistent to choose a different date for each group in order to include the annual increase in the employees' rates of compensation for the determination period. [Treas Reg § 1.414(s)-1(e)(3)(iii)]

An employee's compensation may generally be determined using only the rate of compensation for employment periods during which the employer actually compensates the employee. However, if an employee terminates employment or otherwise stops performing services (such as for a leave of absence, layoff, or similar event), either without compensation or with reduced compensation during a determination period, the employer may continue to credit the employee with compensation based on the employee's rate of compensation for a period of up to 31 days after the event, but not beyond the end of the determination period (see Q 6:43). [Treas Reg § 1.414(s)-1(e)(3)(iv)]

Q 6:43   Can prior-employer compensation and imputed compensation be used?

Solely for purposes of determining whether a defined benefit plan (see Q 2:3) satisfies certain requirements (see Qs 4:9, 5:15), an alternative definition of compensation that includes prior-employer compensation or imputed compensation may be a reasonable alternative definition (see Q 6:40). Prior-employer compensation is compensation from an employer other than the employer (determined at the time that the compensation is paid) maintaining the defined benefit plan that is credited for periods prior to the employee's employment with the current employer maintaining the plan, and during which periods the employee performed services for the other employer. Imputed compensation is compensation credited for periods after an employee has commenced or recommenced participation in a defined benefit plan while the employee is not compensated by the employer maintaining the plan, or is compensated at a reduced rate by that employer because the employee is not performing services as an employee for the employer (including a period in which the employee performs services for another employer, e.g., a joint venture) or because the employee has a reduced work schedule. [Treas Reg §§ 1.414(s)-1(f)(1), 1.414(s)-1(f)(4)]

Crediting prior-employer compensation or imputed compensation must apply on the same terms to all similarly situated employees; there must be a legitimate business purpose, based on all of the relevant facts and circumstances, for crediting such compensation to an employee; and, based on all of the relevant facts and circumstances, crediting such compensation must not by design or in operation discriminate significantly in favor of highly compensated employees (see Q 3:2). Subject to certain requirements, any reasonable method may be used to determine the amount of prior-employer compensation or imputed compensation. [Treas Reg §§ 1.414(s)-1(f)(2), 1.414(s)-1(f)(3)]

Q 6:44   Are there any special rules for self-employed individuals?

If an alternative definition of compensation (see Q 6:40) is used, an equivalent alternative compensation amount must be determined for any self-employed individual (see Q 6:33) who is in the group of employees for whom the consistency requirement (see Q 6:38) requires a single definition of compensation to be used. This equivalent alternative compensation amount is determined by multiplying the self-employed individual's total earned income (see Q 6:34) by the percentage of total compensation (see Q 6:41) included under the alternative definition for the employer's non-highly compensated common-law employees as a group. For purposes of this determination, highly compensated common-law employees (see Q 3:2) must be disregarded. This equivalent alternative compensation amount will be treated as compensation determined using the alternative definition of compensation. An alternative definition may provide that compensation for some or all self-employed individuals who are highly compensated employees is a specified portion of, rather than equal to, the equivalent compensation amount. [Treas Reg §§ 1.414(s)-1(b)(3), 1.414(s)-1(g)(1)(i), 1.414(s)-1(g)(1)(iii), 1.401(a)(17)-1(c)]

If the alternative definition of compensation includes any types of elective contributions (see Q 6:39), the self-employed individual's earned income for this determination must be increased by the amount of elective contributions made by the employer on behalf of the self-employed individual, and the definition of total compensation for this determination must include all such types of elective contributions made by the employer on behalf of common-law employees (other than highly compensated employees). [Treas Reg § 1.414(s)-1(g)(1)(ii)]

Q 6:45   When are the nondiscriminatory compensation rules effective?

The rules (see Qs 6:37–6:44) are generally effective for plan years beginning on or after January 1, 1987. However, the final regulations published by IRS on September 1, 1993 are effective for plan years beginning on or after January 1, 1994. [Treas Reg § 1.414(s)-1(j)]

Chapter 7

Permitted Disparity

A company can make its qualified retirement plan part of an overall retirement scheme that includes Social Security; this combination is called permitted disparity. (Prior to TRA '86, this was called integration.) This chapter examines how permitted disparity works and the opportunity it affords a company to provide benefits favorable to shareholder-employees and key personnel without running afoul of the prohibition against discrimination.

Q 7:1   What does permitted disparity mean?

Every employer is already paying for a retirement plan for its employees—Social Security. By providing for permitted disparity in its qualified retirement plan (i.e., combining its private retirement plan with Social Security), the employer gets the benefit of its Social Security tax payments. The employer in effect makes its qualified retirement plan part of one overall scheme that combines both Social Security and the employer's private plan.

Technically, a plan that provides for permitted disparity means a qualified retirement plan that is not considered discriminatory merely because the benefits provided under the plan favor highly compensated employees (see Q 3:2), as long as the difference in benefits is attributable to what IRS refers to as permitted disparity (i.e., Social Security integration). Permitted disparity may be taken into account to demonstrate that the amount of contributions or benefits does not discriminate in favor of highly compensated employees (see Qs 4:10, 4:11, 4:13).

Permitted disparity can mean a substantial saving for the employer because the cost of the employer's qualified retirement plan can be reduced.

[IRC §§ 401(a)(5), 401(l); Treas Reg § 1.401(l)-1]

Q 7:2 What types of qualified retirement plans can provide for permitted disparity?

Both defined contribution plans (see Q 2:2) and defined benefit plans (see Q 2:3) can provide for permitted disparity.

A defined contribution excess plan is a defined contribution plan under which the rate at which employer contributions (and forfeitures) are allocated to the accounts of participants with respect to compensation above a level specified in the plan (expressed as a percentage of such compensation) is greater than the rate at which employer contributions (and forfeitures) are allocated with respect to compensation at or below such specified level (expressed as a percentage of such compensation). [Treas Reg § 1.401(l)-1(c)(16)(ii)]

A defined benefit excess plan is a defined benefit plan under which the rate at which employer-provided benefits are determined with respect to average annual compensation (see Q 7:21) above a level specified in the plan (expressed as a percentage of such compensation) is greater than the rate with respect to compensation at or below such specified level (expressed as a percentage of such compensation). [Treas Reg § 1.401(l)-1(c)(16)(i)]

A defined benefit offset plan is a defined benefit plan that is not a defined benefit excess plan and that provides that each participant's employer-provided benefit is reduced by a specified percentage of the participant's final average compensation (see Q 7:23) up to the offset level under the plan. [Treas Reg § 1.401(l)-1(c)(25)]

For purposes of the permitted disparity rules, target benefit plans (see Q 2:5) are generally treated like defined benefit plans. [Treas Reg § 1.401(l)-2(a)(1)]

Q 7:3 What general rules apply to a defined contribution excess plan?

A defined contribution excess plan (see Q 7:2) will meet the permitted disparity rules only if the excess contribution percentage (ECP; see Q 7:4) does not exceed the base contribution percentage (BCP; see Q 7:5) by more than the lesser of (1) the BCP, or (2) the greater of 5.7 percentage points, or the percentage equal to the rate of tax attributable to the old-age insurance portion of the Old-Age, Survivors, and Disability Insurance (OASDI) as of the beginning of the plan year. [IRC § 401(l)(2); Notice 89-70, 1989-1 CB 730]

For purposes of the permitted disparity rules, target benefit plans (see Q 2:5) are generally treated like defined benefit plans. [Treas Reg § 1.401(l)-2(a)(1)]

Q 7:4   What is the excess contribution percentage?

The ECP is the percentage of compensation at which employer contributions (and forfeitures) are allocated to the accounts of participants with respect to compensation of participants above the integration level (see Q 7:6) specified in the defined contribution plan (see Q 2:2) for the plan year. [IRC § 401(l)(2)(B)(i); Treas Reg § 1.401(l)-1(c)(15)]

Q 7:5   What is the base contribution percentage?

The BCP is the percentage of compensation at which employer contributions (and forfeitures) are allocated to the accounts of participants with respect to compensation of participants at or below the integration level (see Q 7:6) specified in the defined contribution plan (see Q 2:2) for the plan year. [IRC § 401(l)(2)(B)(ii); Treas Reg § 1.401(l)-1(c)(4)]

Q 7:6   What is the integration level?

The integration level is the amount of compensation specified in the defined contribution or defined benefit excess plan (see Q 7:2) at or below which the rate of contributions or benefits provided under the plan is less than the rate with respect to compensation above such level. [IRC § 401(l)(5)(A)(i); Treas Reg § 1.401(l)-1(c)(20)]

For defined contribution excess plans, the integration level must meet one of the following requirements:

1. The integration level for each participant is the taxable wage base (TWB; see Q 7:7) in effect as of the beginning of the plan year.
2. The integration level for all employees is a single dollar amount (either specified in the plan or determined under a formula specified in the plan) that does not exceed 20 percent of the TWB in effect as of the beginning of the plan year.
3. The integration level for all employees is a single dollar amount (either specified in the plan or determined under a formula specified in the plan) that is greater than the amount in (2) above and less than the TWB in effect as of the beginning of the plan year, provided the limitation of 5.7 percentage points (see Q 7:3) is reduced. If the integration level is more than 20 percent of the TWB but not more

than 80 percent of the TWB, the 5.7 percentage points factor is reduced to 4.3 percentage points. If the integration level is more than 80 percent but less than 100 percent of the TWB, the 5.7 percentage points factor is reduced to 5.4 percentage points.

[Treas Reg § 1.401(l)-2(d)]

See Q 7:15 for a discussion of the integration level in defined benefit excess plans.

Q 7:7 What is the taxable wage base?

The TWB is the maximum amount of earnings in any calendar year that may be considered wages for Social Security purposes. For 1996, this amount is $62,700.

For the five prior calendar years, the TWB was:

Year	Taxable Wage Base
1995	$61,200
1994	60,600
1993	57,600
1992	55,500
1991	53,400

Q 7:8 How are the permitted disparity rules applied to contribution formulas under defined contribution excess plans?

The following examples illustrate whether or not a defined contribution excess plan meets the permitted disparity rules (see Qs 7:2, 7:3):

Example 1. J. T. Corporation has a money purchase pension plan with a calendar year plan year. For the 1996 plan year, the plan provides that each participant will receive a contribution of 5 percent of compensation up to the TWB (see Q 7:7) and 10 percent of compensation in excess of the TWB. The plan meets the permitted disparity rules because the ECP (see Q 7:4), 10 percent, does not exceed the BCP (see Q 7:5), 5 percent, by more than the lesser of 5 percentage points or 5.7 percentage points.

Example 2. Assume the same facts as those in Example 1 except that the plan provides that, with respect to compensation in excess of the TWB, each participant will receive a contribution for the plan year of 10.7 percent of such excess compensation. The plan does not meet the permitted disparity rules because the ECP, 10.7 percent, exceeds the BCP, 5 percent, by more than the lesser of 5 percentage points or 5.7 percentage points.

Example 3. For the 1996 plan year, a profit sharing plan uses an integration level of $13,000, which is less than 80 percent of the TWB of $62,700 but more than $12,540 (20% × $62,700). Consequently, the 5.7 percentage points factor must be replaced by 4.3 percentage points.

If in Example 3 the integration level is reduced by $1,000 to $12,000, the 5.7 percentage points factor will be used. This anomaly occurs because the reduced integration level does not exceed 20 percent of the TWB [$12,540 (20% × $62,700)].

Q 7:9 What general rules apply to a defined benefit excess plan?

A defined benefit excess plan (see Q 7:2) will meet the permitted disparity rules if the excess benefit percentage (EBP; see Q 7:10) does not exceed the base benefit percentage (BBP; see Q 7:11) by more than the maximum excess allowance (MEA; see Q 7:12). Also, benefits must be based on average annual compensation (see Q 7:21).

Furthermore, any optional form of benefit, preretirement benefit, actuarial factor, or other benefit or feature provided with respect to compensation above the integration level (see Q 7:15) must also be provided with respect to compensation below the integration level. Thus, for example, if a lump-sum distribution option, calculated using particular actuarial assumptions, is available for benefits relating to compensation above the integration level, the same lump-sum option must be available on an equivalent basis for benefits based on compensation up to the integration level. [IRC § 401(l)(3); Treas Reg § 1.401(l)-3]

For purposes of the permitted disparity rules, target benefit plans (see Q 2:5) are generally treated like defined benefit plans. [Treas Reg § 1.401(l)-2(a)(1)]

Q 7:10 What is the excess benefit percentage?

The EBP is the percentage of compensation at which employer-provided benefits are determined with respect to average annual compensation (see Q 7:21) of participants above the integration level (see Q 7:15) specified in the defined benefit plan for the plan year. [IRC § 401(l)(3)(A); Treas Reg § 1.401(l)-1(c)(14)]

Q 7:11   What is the base benefit percentage?

The BBP is the percentage of compensation at which the employer-provided benefits are determined with respect to average annual compensation (see Q 7:21) of participants at or below the integration level (see Q 7:15) specified in the defined benefit plan for the plan year. [IRC § 401(l)(3)(A); Treas Reg § 1.401(l)-1(c)(3)]

Q 7:12   What is the maximum excess allowance?

The MEA for a plan year is the lesser of either the BBP (see Q 7:11) or .75 percentage point. [IRC § 401(l)(4)(A); Treas Reg § 1.401(l)-3(b)(2)]

Q 7:13   How are the permitted disparity rules applied to benefit formulas under defined benefit excess plans?

The following examples illustrate whether or not a defined benefit excess plan meets the permitted disparity rules (see Qs 7:2, 7:9):

Example 1. M. P. Corporation maintains a defined benefit excess plan. The formula is .5 percent of the participant's average annual compensation (see Q 7:21) up to covered compensation (see Q 7:22) for the plan year plus 1.25 percent of the participant's average annual compensation for the plan year in excess of the participant's covered compensation for the plan year, multiplied by the participant's years of credited service with the company up to a maximum of 35 years. The plan formula provides a benefit that exceeds the MEA (see Q 7:12) because the EBP (see Q 7:10), 1.25 percent, for the plan year exceeds the BBP (see Q 7:11), .5 percent, for the plan year by more than the BBP.

Example 2. If the BBP in Example 1 was .75 percent, the plan would meet the permitted disparity rules because the EBP (1.25 percent) would not exceed the BBP (.75 percent) by more than the MEA (.75 percentage point).

[Treas Reg § 1.401(l)-3(b)(5)]

Q 7:14   Can benefits commence prior to Social Security retirement age in a defined benefit excess plan?

Yes; but, if benefits commence prior to the Social Security retirement age (see Q 6:14), the .75 percentage point factor (see Q 7:12) is reduced depending on the age at which benefits commence and the participant's Social Security retirement age. [Treas Reg § 1.401(l)-3(e)]

Q 7:15   What integration levels can be used in a defined benefit excess plan?

For defined benefit excess plans, the integration level must meet one of the following requirements:

1. The integration level for each participant is the participant's covered compensation (see Q 7:22).

2. The integration level for each participant is a uniform percentage (greater than 100 percent) of each participant's covered compensation, and does not exceed the TWB (see Q 7:7) in effect for the plan year, and the .75 percent factor is adjusted.

3. The integration level for all participants is a single dollar amount that does not exceed the greater of $10,000 or one-half of the covered compensation of an individual who attains Social Security retirement age (see Q 6:14) in the calendar year in which the plan year begins.

4. The integration level for all participants is a single dollar amount that is greater than the amount determined in (3) above, does not exceed the TWB, and satisfies special demographic requirements, and the .75 percent factor is adjusted.

5. The integration level for all participants is a single dollar amount described in (4) above, and the .75 percent factor in the MEA (see Q 7:12) is reduced to the lesser of an adjusted factor or 80 percent of the otherwise applicable factor.

[Treas Reg § 1.401(l)-3(d)]

Q 7:16   What general rules apply to a defined benefit offset plan?

A defined benefit offset plan (see Q 7:2) will meet the permitted disparity rules if the participant's accrued benefit (see Q 9:2) is not reduced by reason of the offset by more than the maximum offset allowance (MOA; see Q 7:17) and benefits are based on average annual compensation (see Q 7:21). [IRC § 401(l)(3)(B); Treas Reg § 1.401(l)-3(b)]

A defined benefit plan may offset a participant's benefit by a percentage of the participant's primary insurance amount under Social Security. [Treas Reg § 1.401(l)-3(c)(2)(ix); Notice 92-32, 1992-2 CB 362]

For purposes of the permitted disparity rules, target benefit plans (see Q 2:5) are generally treated like defined benefit plans. [Treas Reg § 1.401(l)-2(a)(1)]

Q 7:17   What is the maximum offset allowance?

The MOA for a plan year is the lesser of (1) .75 percentage point, or (2) one-half of the gross benefit percentage, multiplied by a fraction (not to exceed one), the numerator of which is the participant's average annual compensation (see Q 7:21), and the denominator of which is the participant's final average compensation (see Q 7:23) up to the offset level (see Q 7:20). The gross benefit percentage is the percentage of employer-provided benefits (before application of the offset) with respect to a participant's average annual compensation. [IRC § 401(l)(4)(B); Treas Reg §§ 1.401(l)-1(c)(18), 1.401(l)-3(b)(3)]

Q 7:18   How are the permitted disparity rules applied to benefit formulas under defined benefit offset plans?

The following example illustrates whether or not a defined benefit offset plan meets the permitted disparity rules (see Qs 7:2, 7:16):

Example. Jill Corporation maintains a defined benefit offset plan. The formula provides that, for each year of credited service with the company up to a maximum of 35 years, a participant receives a normal retirement benefit equal to 2 percent of the participant's average annual compensation (see Q 7:21), reduced by .75 percent of the participant's final average compensation up to covered compensation (see Qs 7:22, 7:23). The plan meets the permitted disparity rules because the MOA is equal to .75 percent, the lesser of .75 percent or one-half of the gross benefit percentage [1% (½ × 2%)].

If the formula in the above example provided for a normal retirement benefit equal to 1 percent of the participant's average annual compensation, the plan would not meet the permitted disparity rules because the MOA would be equal to .5 percent, the lesser of .75 percent or one-half of the gross benefit percentage [.5% (½ × 1%)]. [Treas Reg § 1.401(l)-3(b)(5)]

Q 7:19   Can benefits commence prior to Social Security retirement age in a defined benefit offset plan?

Yes; but, if benefits commence prior to Social Security retirement age (see Q 6:14), the .75 percentage point factor (see Q 7:17) is reduced depending on the age at which benefits commence and the participant's Social Security retirement age. [Treas Reg § 1.401(l)-3(e)]

Q 7:20 What is the offset level?

The offset level is the dollar limit specified in the defined benefit offset plan (see Q 7:2) on the amount of each participant's final average compensation (see Q 7:23) taken into account in determining the offset. [Treas Reg § 1.401(l)-1(c)(23)]

For defined benefit offset plans, the offset level must meet one of the following requirements:

1. The offset level for each participant is the participant's covered compensation (see Q 7:22).

2. The offset level for each participant is a uniform percentage (greater than 100 percent) of each participant's covered compensation, and does not exceed the participant's final average compensation, and the .75 percent factor is adjusted.

3. The offset level for all participants is a single dollar amount that does not exceed the greater of $10,000 or one-half of the covered compensation of an individual who attains Social Security retirement age (see Q 6:14) in the calendar year in which the plan year begins.

4. The offset level for all participants is a single dollar amount that is greater than the amount determined in (3) above, does not exceed the participant's final average compensation, and satisfies special demographic requirements, and the .75 percent factor is adjusted.

5. The offset level for all participants is a single dollar amount described in (4) above, and the .75 percent factor in the MOA (see Q 7:17) is reduced to the lesser of an adjusted factor or 80 percent of the otherwise applicable factor.

[Treas Reg § 1.401(l)-3(d)]

Q 7:21 What is average annual compensation?

Average annual compensation means the participant's highest average annual compensation for (1) any period of at least three consecutive years, or (2) if shorter, the participant's full period of service. For this purpose, a participant's compensation history may begin at any time, but must be continuous, be no shorter than the averaging period, and end in the current plan year. [IRC § 401(l)(5)(C); Treas Reg §§ 1.401(a)(4)-3(e)(2)(i), 1.401(l)-1(c)(2)]

Q 7:22   What does covered compensation mean?

Covered compensation means the average (without indexing) of the TWB (see Q 7:7) for the 35 calendar years ending with the year an individual attains Social Security retirement age (see Q 6:14). A defined benefit plan can provide for permitted disparity on the basis of each individual employee's covered compensation. Covered compensation does not refer to the amount of compensation that the employee actually earned, but reflects the ceiling for Social Security wages (TWBs) over the years.

1996 Covered Compensation Table

Calendar Year of Birth	Year of Social Security Retirement Age	Covered Compensation
1931	1996	$27,576
1932	1997	29,232
1933	1998	30,888
1934	1999	32,532
1935	2000	34,188
1936	2001	35,796
1937	2002	37,392
1938	2004	40,536
1939	2005	42,108
1940	2006	43,668
1941	2007	45,204
1942	2008	46,692
1943	2009	48,108
1944	2010	49,488
1945	2011	50,844
1946	2012	52,164
1947	2013	53,448
1948	2014	54,588
1949	2015	55,644
1950	2016	56,580
1951	2017	57,444
1952	2018	58,224
1953	2019	58,932
1954	2020	59,592
1955	2022	60,720
1956	2023	61,224

1996 Covered Compensation Table

Calendar Year of Birth	Year of Social Security Retirement Age	Covered Compensation
1957	2024	61,644
1958	2025	61,980
1959	2026	62,244
1960	2027	62,448
1961	2028	62,592
1962	2029	62,652
1963 or later	2030 and after	62,700

In lieu of using the table set forth above, defined benefit plans may use the following table that rounds the actual amounts of covered compensation for different years of birth.

1996 Rounded Table

Year of Birth	Covered Compensation
1930–1931	$27,000
1932–1933	30,000
1934–1935	33,000
1936–1937	36,000
1938–1939	42,000
1940–1941	45,000
1942–1944	48,000
1945–1946	51,000
1947–1948	54,000
1949–1952	57,000
1953–1956	60,000
1957 or later	62,700

A plan may use an amount of covered compensation for a plan year earlier than the current plan year, provided that the earlier plan year is the same for all employees and is not earlier than the plan year that begins five years before the current plan year.

Example. In 1990, Michael Corp. adopted a defined benefit excess plan (see Q 7:2) with a calendar plan year. For the 1990 through 1995 plan years, the plan's integration level for each participant, based upon the 1990 covered compensation table, was permissible. However, the integration level must be changed for the 1996 plan year and may be the covered compensation table for the 1991 or any later plan year.

[IRC § 401(l)(5)(E); Treas Reg § 1.401(l)-1(c)(7); Rev Rul 95-75, 1995-46 IRB 8; Notice 89-70, 1989-1 CB 730]

An increase in covered compensation will result in a smaller benefit at retirement. However, a participant's accrued benefit may not be reduced because of the increase in covered compensation (see Q 9:24).

Q 7:23   What is final average compensation?

Final average compensation means the average of the participant's annual compensation for (1) the three consecutive year period ending with or within the plan year, or (2) if shorter, the participant's full period of service; but it does not include compensation for any year in excess of the TWB (see Q 7:7) in effect at the beginning of such year. [IRC § 401(l)(5)(D); Treas Reg § 1.401(l)-1(c)(17)]

Q 7:24   What does compensation mean?

Compensation means compensation as defined under the plan, provided that such definition is nondiscriminatory and satisfies Section 414(s) (see Qs 6:37–6:45). For years beginning after 1997, an employer may elect not to include as compensation elective deferrals under 401(k) plans (see Q 23:1), tax-sheltered annuities (see Q 29:1), simplified employee pensions (SEPs; see Q 27:1), and cafeteria plans. [IRC §§ 401(l)(5)(B), 414(s); Treas Reg §§ 1.401(l)-1(c)(2), 1.401(l)-1(c)(17)]

Q 7:25   What is uniform disparity?

With respect to qualified retirement plans that provide for permitted disparity (see Q 7:2), the disparity for all participants under the same plan must be uniform. [Treas Reg §§ 1.401(l)-2(a)(4), 1.401(l)-3(a)(4)]

The disparity under a defined contribution excess plan is uniform only if the plan uses the same BCP (see Q 7:5) and the same ECP (see Q 7:4) for all participants. However, an exception to this rule applies if the plan provides that, in the case of an employee for whom no FICA taxes are required to be paid, employer contributions allocated to the account of that participant are based on the participant's total plan year compensation at the ECP. [Treas Reg §§ 1.401(l)-2(c)(1), 1.401(l)-2(c)(2)(iii)]

Example. Sharon Corp. has a money purchase pension plan. For the 1996 calendar plan year, the plan provides that each participant will receive a contribution of 10 percent of compensation up to the TWB (see Q 7:7) and 15.7 percent of compensation in excess of the TWB, but that a "non-FICA" employee will receive an allocation based solely on the ECP. Mindy, a FICA employee, and Jill, a non-FICA employee, earn $100,000 each. The contribution made to Sharon Corp.'s plan on Mindy's behalf is $12,126 [$6,270 (10% × $62,700) + $5,856 (15.7% × $37,300)], and the contribution made on Jill's behalf is $15,700 (15.7% × $100,000). In this case, the disparity is considered uniform even though different BCPs are used.

The disparity provided under a defined benefit excess plan is uniform only if the plan uses the same BBP (see Q 7:11) and the same EBP (see Q 7:10) for all participants with the same number of years of service. The disparity provided under a defined benefit offset plan is uniform only if the plan uses the same gross benefit percentage and the same offset percentage (see Q 7:17) for all participants with the same number of years of service. However, an exception to these rules applies if the plan provides that, in the case of an employee for whom no FICA taxes are required to be paid, employer-provided benefits are determined with respect to the participant's total average annual compensation at the EBP or gross benefit percentage applicable to a participant with the same number of years of service. [Treas Reg §§ 1.401(l)-3(c)(1), 1.401(l)-3(c)(2)(vii)]

Q 7:26   Can the termination of a defined benefit plan affect permitted disparity?

Yes. If a defined benefit plan providing for permitted disparity is terminated and the plan assets exceed the present value of the accrued benefits (see Q 9:2), the use of the excess funds to increase benefits under the plan must not violate the permitted disparity rules. [Rev Rul 80-229, 1980-2 CB 133] The termination of a qualified retirement plan may not discriminate in favor of highly compensated employees (see Qs 3:2, 21:44). [Treas Reg § 1.401(a)(4)-5(a)(1)]

Q 7:27   What special restrictions on permitted disparity apply to top-heavy plans?

A top-heavy defined benefit plan (see Q 22:1) must provide each participant who is a non-key employee (see Q 22:29) with a minimum annual retirement benefit, and a top-heavy defined contribution plan (see Q 22:3) must provide each participant who is a non-key employee with a minimum annual contribution. A top-heavy plan cannot take into account Social Security benefits or contributions to satisfy these minimum requirements (see Qs 22:37, 22:43, 22:47). [IRC § 416(e); Treas Reg § 1.416-1, Question M-11]

Chapter 8

Funding Requirements

To ensure that sufficient money will be available to pay promised retirement benefits to employees when they retire, certain qualified retirement plans are subject to minimum funding requirements. This chapter examines the funding requirements—which qualified retirement plans must meet them, how they work, and how they are enforced.

Q 8:1 What are the minimum funding standards?

To ensure that sufficient money will be available to pay promised retirement benefits to employees when they retire, minimum funding standards have been established for defined benefit plans (see Q 2:3), money purchase pension plans (see Q 2:4), and target benefit plans (see Q 2:5). [ERISA §§ 301, 302; IRC § 412; Prop Reg § 1.412(a)-1]

For defined benefit plans, employers are required each year to fund the retirement benefits earned that year by the employees (the normal cost). In addition, formulas are established for amortizing over stated periods (1) the cost of retirement benefits for employees' services in the past for which funds have not yet been set aside (past service liabilities), (2) the cost of retroactively raising the level of benefits by plan amendments, and (3) the cost of making up experience losses (see Q 8:13) and increases in liabilities attributable to changes in actuarial assumptions.

For a money purchase pension plan, the amount required to be contributed each year is based on the plan's contribution formula. For example, if the employer has a money purchase pension plan with a 10-percent-of-compensation formula and the participants' aggregate compensation for the year totals $80,000, the employer's required contribution is $8,000.

In a target benefit plan, the required contribution is based on the participant's compensation, age, and an assumed interest rate that is specified in the plan document.

Certain qualified retirement plans are not subject to minimum funding standards (see Q 8:4).

Q 8:2 Are there funding requirements in addition to the minimum funding standards?

Yes. There is an additional funding requirement that generally applies to defined benefit plans (other than multiemployer plans or defined benefit plans having 100 or fewer participants) with assets less than their current liability for the plan year. For this purpose, current liability means all liabilities to participants and their beneficiaries under the plan.

With respect to the additional funding requirement, RPA '94 (see Q 1:19) made extensive changes that:

- Modified the calculation of the minimum required contribution
- Changed the permissible range of interest rates and required uniform mortality assumptions for the purpose of determining a plan's current liability
- Accelerated the funding of a plan's "unfunded new liability"
- Changed the calculation of the additional funding contribution required in the event of an unpredictable contingent event

A plan is not subject to the additional funding requirement if the funded current liability percentage is at least 90 percent, and for certain plans between 80 percent and 90 percent.

The additional funding charge is the sum of:

1. The excess (if any) of the deficit reduction contribution (DRC) for the year over the sum of certain plan charges reduced by the sum of certain plan credits; and
2. The unpredictable contingent event amount (if any) for that plan year.

The DRC is the sum of:

1. The unfunded new liability amount;
2. The expected increase in current liability due to benefits accruing during the plan year; and
3. The amortization amounts for certain amortization bases (i.e., unfunded old liability, unfunded existing benefit liability, additional

unfunded old liability, and the liability for unfunded mortality increase).

IRS has provided guidance on the additional funding requirements, including the election of the transition rule to phase in any increases due to the changes in law.

[ERISA § 302(d); IRC § 412(l); Rev Rul 96-21, 1996-15 IRB 7; Rev Rul 96-20, 1996-15 IRB 5; Rev Rul 95-28, 1995-1 CB 74; Ann 96-18, 1996-15 IRB 15]

See Q 21:14 regarding the participant notice requirement for certain underfunded plans.

Q 8:3   Are there special funding rules for multiple employer plans?

Yes. The minimum funding requirements for a multiple employer plan (a plan maintained by more than one employer) established after December 31, 1988 are generally determined by treating each employer as maintaining a separate plan. Multiple employer plans established before that date generally must be funded as if all participants in the plan were employed by a single employer. However, the plan administrator of a pre-1989 multiple employer plan was permitted to elect to have the new rules apply and fund the plan as if each employer maintains a separate plan. The election was required to be attached to Schedule B of Form 5500 (see Q 17:4) for the first plan year beginning after November 10, 1988. If the election was made, the funding requirements for that first plan year and all subsequent plan years are determined in accordance with the new rules. The election may be revoked only with the consent of IRS. [IRC § 413(c)(4); Ann 90-3, 1990-3 IRB 36]

Q 8:4   Which qualified retirement plans are not subject to the minimum funding standards?

The minimum funding standards do not apply to profit sharing (see Q 2:6), stock bonus (see Q 2:13), 401(k) (see chapter 23), or employee stock ownership plans (ESOPs; see chapter 24). Pension plans funded exclusively by the purchase of certain insurance contracts (insurance contract plans; see Q 8:5) are also exempt from the funding standards. [IRC §§ 412(h), 412(i)]

Other retirement plans that are not subject to the minimum funding standards include:

1. Plans that do not provide for employer contributions after September 2, 1974 (such as plans to which only employees contribute);
2. Unfunded nonqualified plans that are maintained by the employer primarily to provide deferred compensation for selected management or highly compensated employees;
3. Supplemental plans that provide benefits in excess of the limits on contributions and benefits under the Code;
4. Governmental plans; and
5. Certain church plans.

[ERISA § 301(a); IRC §§ 412(h), 414(d), 414(e)]

Q 8:5 What is an insurance contract plan?

An insurance contract plan is a pension plan that is funded exclusively by individual insurance contracts and meets the following requirements:

1. The insurance contracts provide for level annual premiums from the time the employee commences plan participation until retirement age.
2. Benefits under the plan are equal to the benefits provided under the contracts.
3. Benefits are guaranteed by an insurance company licensed to do business in the state in which the plan is located.
4. Premiums are paid timely or the contracts have been reinstated.
5. No rights under the contracts were subject to a security interest during the plan year.
6. No policy loans were outstanding during the plan year.

A pension plan that is funded exclusively by group insurance contracts having the same characteristics as those listed above is also considered to be an insurance contract plan. [ERISA § 301(b); IRC § 412(i); Treas Reg § 1.412(i)-1]

Q 8:6 Can a pension plan be converted to an insurance contract plan?

Yes. Although the conversion of an existing pension plan to a plan that is funded exclusively by insurance contracts might cause the premium payments to begin after an employee commences participation in the plan (see Q 8:5), the converted plan may be considered to be an insurance contract plan for future years if certain requirements are met. The conversion will be permitted if all future benefits are funded by level annual premium contracts, all benefits previously accrued are guaranteed, there are meaningful continuing benefit accruals for at least three years, and certain other requirements are met. [Rev Rul 94-75, 1994-2 CB 59]

Where a defined benefit plan (see Q 2:3) was terminated, all benefit accruals ceased, and the trustee purchased annuity contracts to provide plan benefits, IRS concluded that the plan had not been converted to an insurance contract plan because a conversion must provide for continued meaningful level premium accruals. [Ltr Rul 9234004]

Q 8:7 Should the employer contribute more than the amount needed to meet the minimum funding standards?

Only if the additional amount is deductible. If the additional amount is not deductible, a tax is imposed on the employer equal to 10 percent of the nondeductible contributions to the plan (see Qs 12:9, 12:17, 12:18). [IRC §§ 412(c)(6), 412(c)(7), 4972]

Q 8:8 Must actuarial assumptions used in determining plan costs be reasonable?

Yes. In the case of a defined benefit plan (see Q 2:3), all plan costs, liabilities, interest rates, and other factors must be determined on the basis of actuarial assumptions and methods (1) each of which is reasonable (taking into account the experience of the plan and reasonable expectations), or which, when taken together, produce a total contribution that is the same as if each assumption and method were reasonable; and (2) which, in combination, offer the actuary's best estimate of anticipated experience under the plan. [ERISA § 302(c)(3); IRC § 412(c)(3)]

The actuarial assumptions used to determine the cost of funding a defined benefit plan need not be set forth in the plan (see Q 2:19). However, even if the actuarial assumptions and methods are set forth in the plan, that does not mean they will always be reasonable or acceptable. [Rev Rul 78-48, 1978-1 CB 115]

In one case, the court agreed with IRS that use of a 5 percent interest rate was not reasonable and that an 8 percent interest rate was appropriate at a time when safe investments were yielding approximately 12 percent or more. The court concluded that "the reasonableness of an actuary's assumption must be evaluated in light of the plan's experience and reasonable expectations." [Jerome Mirza & Assocs, Ltd v United States, 882 F 2d 229 (7th Cir 1989); see also Ltr Ruls 9111004, 9031001]

In another case, IRS recalculated a corporation's tax deduction by rejecting the actuarial assumptions contained in its defined benefit plan. IRS concluded that the actuarial assumptions contained in the plan did not reflect current plan experience. IRS determined that a more appropriate interest rate was 8 percent (instead of the plan's assumed 5½ percent rate) and that the normal retirement age for this one-participant plan should have been age 65, rather than age 55 as provided for in the plan. As a result of these modifications by IRS, no deduction for the taxable year involved was allowable. [Ltr Rul 8552001] In a similar case, IRS determined that the plan's normal retirement age of 60 was not reasonable and, based on plan experience and other investments available at the time, the 5 percent preretirement interest rate assumption was too low; therefore, the entire deduction for two years was disallowed. [Ltr Rul 9244006]

In yet another case, IRS disallowed the entire contribution made to a defined benefit plan after recalculation of the plan's liabilities and costs. The assumed 6 percent preretirement interest rate and 6½ percent postretirement interest rate were determined to be unreasonable in the aggregate when the actual investment rate of return over a five-year period exceeded 15 percent. [Ltr Rul 9226001] Similarly, IRS determined in another case that the actuarial assumptions used were not reasonable in the aggregate in view of the experience of the plan. The assumed rate of interest was 7 percent, but the average annual investment return over the prior five plan years was over 12 percent. [Ltr Rul 9226004] In another ruling, IRS determined that a 7.5 percent assumed rate of interest was not reasonable because the plan's investment returns far exceeded 7.5 percent and could reasonably be expected to continue to do so. [Ltr Rul 9250002] IRS, in yet another ruling, determined that the funding method and actuarial assumptions used were unreasonable and therefore disallowed the entire deduction. The actuary failed to explain in any detail the funding method used and did not furnish proper evidence that the owner would likely retire at age 55. [Ltr Rul 9119007] In a different case, although IRS concluded that interest and mortality assumptions were not reasonable, the poor health of the participant justified a normal retirement age of 55. Therefore, only a portion of the contribution was disallowed. [Ltr Rul 9249003]

IRS had expanded its defined benefit plan actuarial examination program and questioned the funding of defined benefit plans if the annual contribution per participant indicated that the actuaries may have exceeded the contribution limits for any of the following reasons:

1. Using an inappropriate funding method;

2. Exceeding the maximum benefit limitation under Section 415;

3. Using an unreasonably low interest rate not supported by the facts and circumstances of the plan; or

4. Employing an unreasonably low retirement age not supported by the facts and circumstances of the plan.

However, IRS's actuarial examination program experienced major setbacks when courts, in a number of cases, ruled in favor of the employers, finding that an interest rate assumption of less than 8 percent and a retirement age assumption of below age 65 were, among other assumptions, reasonable actuarial assumptions. [Citrus Valley Estates, Inc v Comm'r, 49 F 3d 1410 (9th Cir 1995); Wachtell, Lipton, Rosen & Katz v Comm'r, 26 F 3d 291 (2d Cir 1994); Vinson & Elkins v Comm'r, 7 F 3d 1235 (5th Cir 1993); but see Rhoades, McKee & Boer v United States, 1:91-CV-540 (WD Mich 1995)]

With regard to the interest rate assumption, the courts considered the following:

1. The deference Congress gave to enrolled actuaries under ERISA for defined benefit pension plans;

2. The tendency of actuaries to be conservative in adopting actuarial assumptions;

3. That the plans were designed for a long-term time frame during which available rates of returns on plan investments were likely to fluctuate;

4. That the plans' investments were self-directed, which could reduce the rate of return;

5. That the plans, due to their recent adoption, lacked credible experience;

6. The risk that the use of too optimistic an interest rate assumption would create a funding deficit that would require increased contributions in later years;

7. The relatively slight differences between the actuarial experts' suggested ranges for proper interest rate assumptions and the rate used by the plans' actuaries; and

8. That most small defined benefit plans used interest rate assumptions of between 5 percent and 6 percent for the years at issue.

The courts also found that a retirement age earlier than age 65 was justifiable under the circumstances. Most important, the courts concluded that, since the assumptions used were not "substantially unreasonable" and represented the actuary's best estimate of anticipated experience under the plans based on actuarial assumptions used by similar plans, IRS was precluded from requiring a retroactive change of assumptions.

Q 8:9 Must a change in a plan's funding method be approved?

Generally, IRS must approve a change in a defined benefit plan's funding method. [IRC § 412(c)(5)(A)] The funding method of a plan includes not only the overall funding method used by the plan but also each specific method of computation used in applying the overall method. Therefore, for example, the funding method of a plan includes the date on which assets and liabilities are valued (the valuation date) and the definition of compensation that is used to determine the plan's normal cost or accrued liability. Furthermore, a change in a particular aspect of a funding method does not change any other aspect of that method. For example, a change in the funding method from unit credit to the level dollar individual entry age normal method does not change the current valuation date or asset valuation method used for the plan. [Treas Reg § 1.412(c)(1); Rev Proc 95-51, 1995-51 IRB 6]

Effective for plan years beginning on or after January 1, 1995, and subject to certain restrictions, automatic approval will be granted for a change to one of the following funding methods:

- Unit credit
- Level percent of compensation aggregate
- Level dollar aggregate
- Level percent of compensation individual aggregate
- Level dollar individual aggregate
- Level percent of compensation frozen initial liability
- Level dollar frozen initial liability
- Level percent of compensation individual entry age normal
- Level dollar individual entry age normal

Automatic approval will be granted for a change in the asset valuation method to the fair market value, average fair market value, and average fair market value (with phase-in) methods.

Also, automatic approval will be granted for a change in the valuation date to the first day of the plan year and for a change in the funding method used for valuing ancillary benefits to the method used for valuing retirement benefits.

Automatic approval is *not* available if:

1. A Schedule B (see Q 17:4) has been filed for the plan year using a different funding method;

2. Agreement to the change is not indicated on the Form 5500 series return/report (see Q 17:1);

3. A minimum funding waiver (see Q 8:20) has been requested or is being amortized;

4. The plan is under examination or has been notified of an impending examination; or

5. The plan is terminated (with certain exceptions).

[Rev Proc 95-51, 1995-51 IRB 6]

Furthermore, IRS must approve changes in actuarial assumptions, other than interest rate and mortality assumptions (e.g., salary scale, employee turnover), used to determine the current liability for certain defined benefit plans with significant unfunded current liability.

Approval of these changes is required if:

1. The plan is covered by Title IV of ERISA (see Qs 21:9, 21:12);

2. The aggregated unfunded vested benefits exceed $50 million as of the end of the preceding plan year; and

3. The change in assumptions (after taking into account any interest rate and mortality table changes) decreases the plan's unfunded current liability for the current plan year by either (a) more than $50 million or (b) more than $5 million and at least 5 percent of the current liability before the change.

[IRC § 412(c)(5)]

A dual funding method designed to accomplish full funding of plan liabilities that was used by a terminating defined benefit plan was held unreasonable and unacceptable by IRS because it was impermissible to use two funding methods and then select the method that resulted in the lowest cost. [Treas Reg § 1.412(c)(3)-1(b)(2); Ltr Ruls 9409002, 9409001]

Q 8:10 Is there any penalty for overstatement of pension liabilities?

Yes. Effective for returns due after December 31, 1989 (determined without regard to extensions), a penalty tax is imposed on the underpayment of tax created by a substantial overstatement of pension liabilities. A 20 percent penalty tax is imposed if the actuarial determination of pension liabilities is between 200 percent and 399 percent of the amount determined to be correct; if the actuarial determination is 400 percent or more of the correct amount, the penalty tax is increased to 40 percent. No penalty will be imposed if the underpayment attributable to the substantial overstatement is $1,000 or less. [IRC §§ 6662(a), 6662(f), 6662(h)]

Q 8:11 Can a pension plan's normal retirement age affect the minimum funding standards?

Yes. Each actuarial assumption used to determine pension plan costs should be reasonable and must offer the actuary's best estimate of antici- pated experience under the plan. [ERISA § 302(c)(3); IRC § 412(c)(3)] Therefore, an assumption that employees will retire at the normal retire- ment age specified in the plan, ignoring the fact that employees normally retire at earlier or later ages, would not be reasonable (see Q 8:8).

Q 8:12 How are past service costs funded?

If a defined benefit plan was adopted after January 1, 1974, costs relating to an employee's service before the adoption of the plan must be amortized over not more than 30 years from the date the plan was adopted. Increases or decreases in past service costs resulting from an amendment to the plan must be amortized over not more than 30 years from the time the amend- ment takes effect.

For plans in existence on January 1, 1974, past service liabilities on the first day of the plan year beginning after December 31, 1975 may be amortized over not more than 40 years. Increases or decreases in past service liabilities arising thereafter must be amortized over not more than 30 years. [IRC § 412(b)(2)]

There is an additional funding requirement for many plans (see Q 8:2) that generally requires the amortization of unfunded old liability over 18 plan years. Unfunded old liability is generally the unfunded current liability of the plan as of the beginning of the first plan year beginning after December 31, 1987. Furthermore, the amount of unfunded old liability must be increased by the amount necessary to amortize additional unfunded old liability, caused by changes of interest and mortality assumptions under RPA '94 (see Q 1:19), in equal installments over 12 years. [IRC § 412(l)(3)]

Q 8:13 Do the pension plan's investment earnings affect the funding requirement?

Yes. Experience gains and losses—that is, when the defined benefit plan's actual investment growth and earnings are either higher or lower than was actuarially estimated—must be amortized over a period of not more than five years from the time the gain or loss is determined. For experience gains and losses occurring in plan years beginning before 1988, the period for amortizing experience gains and losses was 15 years. The 15-year amortization period is retained for multiemployer plans (see Q

25:2). However, under RPA '94 (see Q 1:19), amounts necessary to amortize experience gains and losses, and gains and losses resulting from changes of actuarial assumptions, are no longer considered in the calculation of the minimum required contribution for certain defined benefit plans (see Q 8:2). The minimum required contribution for these plans is, in general, the greater of (1) the amount determined under the normal funding rules, or (2) the deficit reduction contribution plus the amount required with respect to benefits that are contingent on unpredictable events. [IRC §§ 412(b)(2)(B)(iv), 412(b)(3)(B)(ii), 412(l)(1)]

An experience gain reduces the amount of funding required, and an experience loss increases the amount of funding required. Increases or decreases in costs resulting from a change in the Social Security law or from changes in the amount of wages taken into account under a pension plan providing for permitted disparity (see Q 7:1) are treated as experience gains or losses. [IRC § 412(c)(4)]

Q 8:14   How are assets valued in a defined benefit plan?

For funding purposes, assets in a defined benefit plan (see Q 2:3) must be valued every year on the basis of any reasonable actuarial method of valuation that takes into account fair market value (see Q 8:9). To be considered a reasonable actuarial method of valuation, the method must result in an actuarial value between 80 percent and 120 percent of the current fair market value. Special rules apply to the valuation of bonds or other evidences of indebtedness. [IRC §§ 412(c)(2), 412(c)(9); Treas Reg § 1.412(c)(2)-1]

In one case, a plan's method of valuing assets that had been invested in an insurance company seized by a state was reasonable, where the valuation method used a percentage of the book value determined as the weighted average of the estimated liquidation value and estimated work-out value (as provided by the testimony of experts). [Ltr Rul 9342055]

IRS announced its intention to focus on retirement plans that improperly value nonpublicly traded assets (e.g., partnerships, real estate). The Form 5500 series, Annual Return/Report of Employee Benefit Plan (see Q 17:1), requires information regarding assets that have a fair market value that is not readily determinable on an established market and the date these assets were valued by an independent third-party appraiser. [Ann 94-101, 1994-35 IRB 53; Forms 5500 and 5500-C/R 1995]

Q 8:15 What is the funding standard account?

Each pension plan subject to the minimum funding standards (see Q 8:1) must maintain a funding standard account, which is a device used to ease the administration of the funding rules. Each year, the funding standard account is charged with amounts that must be paid to satisfy the minimum funding standards and is credited with the plan contributions made, any decrease in plan liabilities, and experience gains. If the pension plan meets the minimum funding standards (the charges equal the credits) at the end of any plan year, the funding standard account will show a zero balance. If the employer has contributed more than the minimum amount required for any year (the credits exceed the charges), the account will show a positive balance and the employer is credited with interest on the excess. If the employer contributed less than the minimum amount required for any year (the charges exceed the credits), the account will show an accumulated funding deficiency. An excise tax is imposed on that deficiency (see Q 8:18). [IRC § 412(b)]

The following examples illustrate how the funding standard account works.

Example 1. In 1995, MuMu Corporation established a defined benefit plan, with less than 100 participants, that is subject to the minimum funding requirements. For the plan's first year, the normal cost (the cost of benefits earned during the year) was $80,000. Past service costs (the cost of benefits for employees' services before the plan was adopted) are $1,000,000. The actuarially assumed rate of interest is 6 percent. MuMu contributed $148,537 to the plan. The funding standard account is charged with $80,000 of normal cost and with $68,537, which represents amortization of the past service costs of $1,000,000 at 6 percent over 30 years. Since the total charges ($148,537) equal the contribution, the funding standard account has a zero balance.

Example 2. In 1996, MuMu amended its defined benefit plan to increase benefits, so that past service costs rose by $100,000. The plan's normal cost increased to $85,000. In addition, the plan had an experience gain (the plan's actual investment growth was higher than that actuarially estimated) of $5,000. MuMu contributed $170,000 to the plan in 1996. The funding standard account for 1996 is credited with the $170,000 contribution plus $1,120 (representing amortization of the $5,000 experience gain at 6 percent over five years), for a total credit of $171,120. The funding standard account is charged with $85,000 normal cost and $68,537 for amortizing past service costs over 30 years, plus $6,854 for amortizing past service costs resulting from the plan amendment over 30 years, for a total charge of $160,391. Since the account's credits exceed the charges by $10,729 ($171,120 – $160,391), the funding standard account has a positive balance of $10,729. Add to this $644, representing interest on the $10,729 at 6 percent, and the account has a balance of $11,373 to be credited to future years.

Q 8:16   What is the full funding limitation?

The term "full funding limitation" means the excess, if any, of the lesser of (1) 150 percent of current liability or (2) the accrued liability (including normal cost) under the defined benefit plan, over the value of plan assets. If plan assets equal or exceed plan liabilities, the plan is fully funded and no contribution is required. Furthermore, because of the full funding limitation, there may be no contribution or a decreased contribution even if the accrued liability under the plan exceeds plan assets. In any case, no deduction is allowed for a contribution made when the plan is fully funded. In future years, if plan liabilities (for full funding limitation purposes) increase and exceed the value of plan assets, the employer will have to make contributions to satisfy the minimum funding requirements. RPA '94 (see Q 1:19) changed the manner in which the full funding limit is determined:

1. In order to determine the current liability, the expected increase in current liability due to benefits accruing during the plan year should be included.
2. The full funding limit may not be less than 90 percent of the plan's current liability.
3. Current liability may be determined without regard to changes in interest rate and mortality assumptions under RPA '94.

[IRC §§ 404(a)(1)(A), 412(c)(6), 412(c)(7)]

Q 8:17   Must separate funding standard accounts be maintained for each pension plan established by a controlled group of companies?

Yes. Even though identical, but separate, pension plans are established by members of a controlled group of companies (see Q 5:33), separate funding standard accounts (see Q 8:15) must be maintained for each plan. [ERISA § 302(b)(1); IRC § 412(b)(1); Rev Rul 81-137, 1981-1 CB 232]

Q 8:18   What happens if the company fails to make the required contribution to its pension plan?

There is an excise tax for failure to comply with the minimum funding standards (see Q 8:1) equal to 10 percent (5 percent for multiemployer plans; see Q 25:2) of the amount of the accumulated funding deficiency. If the accumulated funding deficiency is not corrected, an excise tax equal to 100 percent of such uncorrected amount is imposed. Accumulated funding deficiency means the excess of the total charges to the funding standard account for all plan years over the total credits to such account for such years (see Q 8:15). [IRC §§ 412(a), 4971(a), 4971(b), 4971(c)]

An accumulated funding deficiency caused by an employer's failure to make timely contributions due to its reliance on the erroneous advice of its plan consultant could not be excused even though the employer had set aside the necessary amount in a segregated checking account. The court ruled that the imposition of the excise tax was mandatory and not subject to an exception that would excuse an employer's unintentional or inadvertent failure to meet the minimum funding requirements. However, the court noted that IRS may waive the 100 percent tax and is also authorized to grant an employer any reasonable period in order to correct the accumulated funding deficiency. [DJ Lee, MD, Inc v Comm'r, 931 F 2d 418 (6th Cir 1991)] Similarly, an employer that did not make a timely contribution to its plan was liable for the tax on the accumulated funding deficiency; financial hardship and plan termination did not excuse this mandatory tax. [Lee Eng'g Supply Co, Inc, 101 TC 189 (1993)]

In other cases, no excise tax for underfunding was imposed when a bookkeeping error caused contributions to pension and profit sharing plans of the employer to be misallocated between them [Ahlberg, 780 F Supp 625 (DC Minn 1991)]; and, where a terminated plan had accumulated funding deficiencies for several years and its assets were taken over by PBGC (see Q 21:10), IRS waived the 100 percent tax, but not the 10 percent tax. [Ltr Rul 9623062; see also Ltr Ruls 962045, 9332046] IRS granted a one-year conditional waiver of the 100 percent tax in order for the employer to formulate a plan to meet its obligation. [Ltr Rul 9514002] Similarly, the 100 percent tax due to an uncorrected accumulated funding deficiency of a multiemployer pension plan was waived for certain years. [Ltr Rul 9607015]

The United States Supreme Court has ruled that excise taxes imposed by IRS for failure to meet the minimum funding standards are considered penalties (not taxes) and, therefore, do not have priority status under federal bankruptcy law. [United States v Reorganized Fabricators of Utah, Inc, No. 95-325 (S Ct 1996]

The failure to meet minimum funding standards triggers a reportable event notice requirement to PBGC if the present value of unfunded vested benefits under the pension plan equals or exceeds $250,000 (see Q 21:16). [ERISA § 4043; PBGC Reg § 2615.16]

In addition, if a quarterly payment (see Q 8:28) or any other payment required by the minimum funding standards is not made, PBGC must be notified within ten days of the due date of the payment if the unpaid balance exceeds $1 million (see Q 17:26). Furthermore, a lien is created in favor of the plan upon all property of the employer if the delinquency exceeds $1 million. [ERISA § 302(f); IRC § 412(n)]

Q 8:19   Who is liable for failure to make contributions?

Liability for contributions to a pension plan (other than a multiemployer plan; see Q 25:2) is joint and several among the employer-sponsor and the members of the controlled group (see Q 5:33) of which the employer is a member. General partners who were responsible for making contributions to the partnership's pension plan were jointly and severally liable for excise taxes (see Q 8:18) resulting from the partnership's failure to satisfy the minimum funding standards. [Ltr Rul 9414001] Also, all members of the controlled group are subject to the lien (see Q 8:18) in favor of a pension plan maintained by any member if the contributions are late. [IRC §§ 412(c)(11), 412(n)]

Furthermore, if an employer fails to make a required payment to meet minimum funding requirements or a required quarterly payment (see Qs 8:27, 8:28) within 60 days after it is due, the employer must notify each participant and beneficiary of such failure. This notice requirement does not apply to multiemployer plans or if the employer has a funding waiver request pending with IRS. This notice requirement is in addition to the requirement that participants be notified of the filing of an application for a funding waiver (see Q 8:22). [ERISA § 101(d)]

Q 8:20   May IRS waive the minimum funding standards for a particular company?

Yes. IRS may grant a waiver of the minimum funding standards for any year in which the employer is unable to make the necessary contributions without "temporary substantial business hardship" ("substantial business hardship" for multiemployer plans; see Q 25:2) and if meeting the funding requirement would harm the interests of the plan's participants. [IRC § 412(d)(1)]

IRS examines several factors in deciding whether to waive the funding standards, including the following:

1. Is the employer operating at a loss?
2. Is there substantial unemployment or underemployment in the industry?
3. Are sales and profits of the industry depressed or declining?

4. Will the pension plan be continued only if the waiver is granted?

These factors are not all-inclusive. Furthermore, IRS must be convinced that the employer's business hardship is temporary. A conditional waiver of the minimum funding standards was granted where a company experienced temporary business hardship due to flood damage but anticipated resumption of full production. [Ltr Rul 9438032] IRS has granted a conditional waiver of the minimum funding standards to a company that has experienced net losses, but whose financial situation was improving. [Ltr Ruls 9626047, 9610033, 9541033, 9517052, 9514027, 9423035, 9416040] IRS granted a conditional funding waiver, although a company had both a very large negative working capital and a negative tangible net worth, when a substantial payment—enough to pay the required pension plan contribution—was expected from the state. [Ltr Rul 9216034] In another case, IRS granted a conditional funding waiver where the employer had taken a number of steps to improve its financial condition, including expansion into new and profitable product lines and markets, consolidation of company functions to streamline operations, and refinancing its debt on longer and more favorable repayment terms. [Ltr Rul 9304032; see also Ltr Ruls 9450044, 9340058, 9313029, 9308049] IRS granted a conditional funding waiver where the company took steps to overcome business hardship that was caused by a general decline in its business and a litigation loss. Steps taken to effect recovery included a strict cost containment program, rejuvenating marketing efforts, deferring vendor payments, freezing pension accruals, and increasing employee contributions to a medical plan. [Ltr Rul 9611067] Where a company had undertaken numerous cost-cutting measures, including the elimination of an unprofitable division, IRS granted a conditional funding waiver. [Ltr Rul 9611065] Furthermore, IRS granted conditional funding waivers where the company had initiated many cost-cutting programs, including the reduction of employees and salaries. [Ltr Rul 9413048; see also Ltr Ruls 9618007, 9509045, 9449019, 9410044]

However, IRS has denied requests for waivers of the minimum funding standards to companies whose prospects of recovery were tenuous. [Ltr Ruls 9609045, 9537029, 9444046, 9349031, 9349028, 9317057] In one ruling, IRS granted waivers for two plans sponsored by a member of a controlled group but denied waivers for two other plans sponsored by another group member. The controlled group, on a consolidated basis, suffered severe business hardship; but one of the subsidiaries, considered alone, had not demonstrated economic hardship and appeared capable of satisfying the minimum funding standards. [Ltr Ruls 9226054, 9219041] In another ruling, IRS denied a request for a waiver where the companies had substantial net worth and were able to satisfy the minimum funding standards without experiencing a substantial temporary business hardship. [Ltr Rul 9423033]

The legislative history indicates that a waiver should not be granted to an employer if it appears that the employer will not recover sufficiently to make its waived contributions. Chances for a waiver are improved if the plan's assets are greater than the benefits to which the participants are entitled. [IRC § 412(d)(2)]

As a practical matter, IRS, in its efforts to avert plan terminations, generally approves a hardship waiver request if it can find reasonable grounds for doing so. In one case, a conditional funding waiver was granted; in addition, a request for approval of a retroactive plan amendment was granted with respect to contributions due for all the officers of the company, but was denied with respect to all other employees. [Ltr Rul 9416044] In another case, IRS required the owner, as a condition for granting the waiver, to reduce his accrued benefit until plan assets became sufficient to meet plan liabilities. [Ltr Rul 7945047] Furthermore, IRS granted a conditional waiver of the minimum funding standards subject to the adoption of an amendment ceasing the accrual of benefits for participants who were also shareholders. [Ltr Rul 8847079]

There are other rules with respect to funding waivers. They include:

1. The number of waivers allowed within a 15-year period is three (five for multiemployer plans).
2. If the employer applying for a funding waiver is a member of a controlled group, not only must the employer-applicant meet the standards, but the standards must be met as if all members of the controlled group are treated as a single employer.
3. The amortization period of a waived funding deficiency is five years (15 years for multiemployer plans).
4. The interest rate used for computing the amortization charge is the greater of (a) 150 percent of the federal midterm rate, or (b) the plan interest rate.
5. IRS is authorized to require security when outstanding waived amounts are $1 million or more.

[ERISA § 303(a); IRC §§ 412(b), 412(d), 412(f)]

Q 8:21   What is the procedure for obtaining a waiver of the minimum funding standards?

The request for a waiver of the minimum funding standards is made to the IRS National Office and not to the local IRS Key District Office.

The employer must furnish evidence that (1) the minimum funding standards cannot be satisfied without temporary substantial business hardship, and (2) meeting the funding standards would adversely affect the interests of the plan's participants in the aggregate. The request should include the following items:

1. A statement concerning the employer's business, its history, and its ownership, any recent or contemplated changes that might affect its financial condition, and whether the employer is to be aggregated with any other entity (see Q 5:33).

2. The current and preceding two years' financial statements (the balance sheets, profit and loss statements, and notes to the financial statements). Uncertified statements are acceptable if certified statements have not been prepared. If the employer files financial reports with the Securities and Exchange Commission, the most recent ones should be submitted. If neither the statements nor reports are available, copies of federal income tax returns may be submitted.

3. A comprehensive discussion of the nature and extent of the business hardship, including a discussion of the underlying reasons that led to the current situation (e.g., declining sales, unexpected losses, labor disputes), and statements that (a) discuss the prospects of recovery and why recovery is likely, (b) describe actions taken or planned to effect recovery, and (c) explain when and to what extent it is anticipated that required contributions can reasonably be expected to resume.

4. Facts concerning the plan and its coverage of employees, including the following:

    a. The name of the plan and the plan's identification and file folder numbers.

    b. The date the plan was adopted.

    c. The effective date of the plan.

    d. The classes of employees covered.

    e. The number of employees covered.

    f. A copy of the plan document and summary plan description (see Q 18:1).

    g. A brief description of any plan amendment during the last five years that affects plan costs.

    h. The current and preceding two years' actuarial reports.

    i. A statement of how the plan is funded (e.g., trust fund, insurance policies).

    j. The contribution history for the current plan year and prior two plan years.

    k. The plan year for which the waiver is requested.

l. The approximate contribution required to meet the minimum funding standards.

m. A copy of the most recent annual report, Form 5500 series (see Q 17:1), and for defined benefit plans, a copy of Schedule B (see Q 17:4).

n. A statement as to whether the plan is subject to PBGC jurisdiction (see Q 21:12).

o. Information concerning the granting of any prior waivers.

5. Information concerning any other plans maintained by the employer.

6. Other information, including:

a. A statement as to whether any other matters pertaining to the plan are currently pending or about to be submitted to IRS, DOL, or PBGC.

b. Details of any existing arbitration, litigation, or court procedure that involves the plan.

c. A statement as to which IRS District Office maintains files concerning the plan.

7. Although not required, a digest of certain information from the financial statements will facilitate the processing of the waiver request.

Both defined contribution plans (see Q 2:2) and defined benefit plans (see Q 2:3) must satisfy the above requirements in order to obtain a waiver of the minimum funding standards.

[Rev Proc 94-41, 1994-1 CB 711]

In addition to the above, a defined contribution plan subject to the minimum funding standards must adopt an amendment to the plan specifying how the waived contribution will be made up and allocated to the plan participants. [Rev Rul 78-223, 1978-1 CB 125; Ltr Ruls 9547030, 9438042, 9331056, 9309051] In order to provide maximum flexibility in obtaining a waiver for a defined contribution plan, the following three alternative procedures are provided:

1. The request can be for a waiver ruling only, without submission of a plan amendment. This request will require the use of a plan amendment supplied by IRS.

2. The request can be for a waiver ruling only, with the submission of a plan amendment.

3. A request can also be for a waiver ruling and a determination letter (see Q 15:1). This type of request will be treated as a request for technical advice from the IRS Key District Director and will require

payment of a user fee (see Qs 8:23, 15:2) for both the waiver request and the determination letter request. All necessary plan amendments must be included in the request.

Requests for waivers must be submitted no later than the 15th day of the third month following the close of the plan year for which the waiver is requested, and this deadline may not be extended. The application for a waiver with respect to a plan year that has not yet ended generally should not be submitted earlier than 180 days prior to the end of the plan year for which the waiver is requested, because the evidence required to support the request may not be available. [IRC § 412(d)(4); Rev Proc 94-41, 1994-1 CB 711; Ltr Ruls 9422054, 9310050]

Requests for a waiver only should be addressed to:

Assistant Commissioner
(Employee Plans and Exempt Organizations)
Attention: CP:E:EP:R
P. O. Box 14073
Washington, DC 20044

Q 8:22   Are there any notice requirements when a funding waiver request is filed?

Yes. The applicant must give advance notice of the waiver application to (1) each participant in the plan, (2) each beneficiary under the plan, (3) each alternate payee (see Q 30:3), and (4) each employee organization representing participants in the plan. The notice must be hand delivered or mailed within 14 days prior to the date of the application and must include a description of the extent to which the plan is funded for benefits that are guaranteed by PBGC and the extent to which the plan is funded for benefit liabilities. IRS has provided a model notice that the applicant may use. [ERISA § 303(e)(1); IRC § 412(f)(4)(A); Rev Proc 94-41, 1994-1 CB 711]

Q 8:23   What additional information and fees are required for the funding waiver request?

IRS charges a user fee for a request for a waiver of the minimum funding standards. Currently the user fee is $3,500 for a waiver of $1 million or more and $1,500 for a waiver of less than $1 million. [Rev Proc 96-8, 1996-1 IRB 187]

Additionally, the following procedural requirements must be met:

1. The request must be signed by the employer maintaining the plan or its authorized representative.
2. A statement attesting to the truthfulness of the statements must be attached.
3. Since the waiver request is a formal ruling request, it must comply with public disclosure requirements under Section 6110.

Furthermore, the employer must also provide a copy of the written notice (see Q 8:22) regarding the waiver application and state that such notice was mailed or hand delivered to the appropriate parties.

[Rev Proc 94-41, 1994-1 CB 711]

Q 8:24 May a pension plan be amended if a waiver of the funding standards is in effect for a particular year?

Yes, but the funding waiver automatically ends if one of the following types of plan amendments is adopted:

1. An amendment increasing plan benefits;
2. An amendment changing the accrual of benefits if the change would increase the plan's liabilities; or
3. An amendment changing the rate at which benefits become nonforfeitable if the change would increase the plan's liabilities.

These amendments will not cause a funding waiver to cease if (1) DOL decides that the amendment is reasonable and has only a small impact on plan liabilities, (2) the amendment merely repeals a retroactive plan amendment reducing benefits, or (3) the amendment must be made for the plan to remain qualified for tax-favored status. [IRC §§ 412(f)(1), 412(f)(2)]

IRS ruled that amendments increasing benefits were neither reasonable nor *de minimis*; therefore, previously granted waivers no longer applied. [Ltr Ruls 9444045, 9226075, 9224051] IRS has also ruled that an amendment increasing benefits was not reasonable merely because the amendment was agreed to in collective bargaining; and, therefore, the previously granted waivers ceased to apply. [Ltr Rul 9244040] However, in another case, IRS ruled that since a collectively bargained plan amendment that would increase disability benefits, ease retirement requirements, and provide for severance payments was reasonable and resulted in only a *de minimis* increase in plan liabilities, the plan amendment would not affect the funding waiver previously granted. [Ltr Rul 9342050]

In one case, an employer proposed that a plan that had previously been granted a waiver of the minimum funding standards be converted to a

401(k) plan. IRS ruled that, since the contributions under the new plan would represent an impermissible increase in contribution levels, the previously granted funding waiver would be revoked. [Ltr Rul 9036037] However, in another case involving a plan that had previously been granted a waiver, the employer adopted a 401(k) plan, but IRS ruled the waiver would not be revoked because the contributions to the new plan were equal to the waived amount. [Ltr Rul 9036050]

Q 8:25   What alternative is available if IRS will not waive the minimum funding standards?

To keep the pension plan in compliance with the minimum funding standards, owners of the company may have to waive their benefits irrevocably. In small pension plans, the costs attributable to the owners' benefits are usually a large portion of the required contribution. Thus, if the owners are permitted to waive their contributions or benefits, the amount that has to be contributed to the pension plan to meet the minimum funding standards may be reduced substantially. IRS has ruled that an accumulated funding deficiency could not be corrected by the waiver of a key employee's benefits upon plan termination. [Ltr Rul 9146005]

If a minimum funding waiver is not available or would be inadequate, a plan sponsor may request IRS approval to retroactively reduce accrued benefits (see Qs 9:24, 9:28). The amendment to retroactively reduce an accrued benefit to a date no earlier than the first day of the plan year to which it applies must be adopted no later than $2\frac{1}{2}$ months after the close of that plan year. In one case, IRS approved a retroactive reduction of accrued benefits because of substantial business hardship since the plan sponsor had been operating at a loss and may have been unable to continue the plan without the amendments. Furthermore, although a waiver of the minimum funding standards may have been available, it would have been inadequate because the waiver would only reduce the current year's costs, but future contributions would increase. [Ltr Rul 9614004] IRS has issued procedures for obtaining approval of plan amendments that retroactively reduce accrued benefits. [IRC § 412(c)(8); Rev Proc 94-42, 1994-1 CB 717]

Q 8:26   May an employer obtain an extension of an amortization period to help it meet the minimum funding standards?

Yes. An extension may be granted by IRS if the employer shows that the extension would provide adequate protection for participants and their beneficiaries and denial of the extension would (1) risk the continuation of the pension plan or might cause a curtailment of retirement benefits or employee compensation, and (2) be adverse to the interests of the participants. (Extending an amortization period reduces each year's pension outlay by spreading out the cost of funding benefits over a greater number of years.) [IRC § 412(e)(1); Rev Rul 79-408, 1979-2 CB 191; Rev Proc 79-61, 1979-2 CB 575]

In addition to the information required when a waiver is sought (see Q 8:21), an application for an extension must include the following information:

1. The unfunded liability (e.g., past service costs) for which the extension is sought;
2. The reasons an extension is being sought;
3. The length of the desired extension (up to a maximum of ten years); and
4. A numerical illustration showing how annual plan costs will be affected.

A request for a ten-year extension of the time to amortize the unfunded liability for a pension plan was denied where there was no indication that the hardship was temporary or that there was a fair chance of recovery. [Ltr Rul 9216029]

Q 8:27 May a contribution be timely for the minimum funding standards but not for tax deduction purposes?

Yes. Contributions made after the close of a plan year may relate back to that year if they are made within $8\frac{1}{2}$ months ($2\frac{1}{2}$ months for multiemployer plans; see Q 25:2) after the close of the plan year. This special deadline does not extend the time limit for making a contribution for tax deduction purposes; that is, payment by the due date, including extensions, for filing the employer's federal income tax return (see Q 12:3). [ERISA § 302(c)(10)(A); IRC § 412(c)(10); Treas Reg § 11.412(c)-12]

This special deadline applies only for purposes of minimum funding and the excise tax (see Q 8:18) imposed for failure to meet the funding requirements. Employer contributions to its plan after the due date for filing its federal income tax return (including extensions) but within $8\frac{1}{2}$ months after the close of the plan year are not deductible as contributions for the closed year. Although the minimum funding standards may be met, the tax deduction requirements are not. [Ltr Rul 7949018]

According to IRS, when the date for making a plan contribution falls on a weekend or holiday, the extension for filing returns until the next business day does not apply to the deadline for the minimum funding standards. *The foregoing was in answer to a question posed at a 1995 conference and should not be construed as a formal ruling.*

Q 8:28   Must quarterly contributions be made to a defined benefit plan?

Yes. Quarterly contribution payments are required to be made to a defined benefit plan (other than a multiemployer plan; see Q 25:2) that has a funded current liability percentage of less than 100 percent for the preceding plan year. The quarterly payments are due 15 days after the end of each quarter of the plan year. The percentage of each required quarterly payment is equal to 25 percent of the required annual payment. The required annual payment is the lesser of (1) 90 percent of the amount required to be contributed to the plan for the plan year in order to meet minimum funding, or (2) 100 percent of the amount so required for the preceding plan year. Quarterly contributions are not required for the first plan year. [ERISA § 302(e); IRC § 412(m); Rev Rul 95-31, 1995-1 CB 76; Notice 89-52, 1989-1 CB 692]

An underpayment of a required quarterly payment requires that the funding standard account (see Q 8:15) be charged with interest at a rate equal to the greater of (1) 175 percent of the federal midterm rate, or (2) the rate of interest used to determine costs by the plan. However, the interest is offset by the assumed interest rate under the plan. [IRC § 412(m); Notice 89-52, 1989-1 CB 692]

The required quarterly payments may result in nondeductible contributions (see Q 8:7). IRS has instituted procedures for the return of nondeductible contributions. Generally, before nondeductible contributions may be returned, the contributions must be disallowed by obtaining a ruling letter from IRS, but a formal ruling is not necessary for nondeductible contributions of less than $25,000. The procedures are effective for contributions made to satisfy the quarterly installment requirement for plan years commencing on or after January 1, 1990. [Rev Proc 90-49, 1990-2 CB 620]

A plan, subject to the quarterly contribution rules, that has more than 100 participants is required to maintain liquid plan assets at an amount approximately equal to three times the total disbursements made from the plan during the 12-month period ending on the last day of each quarter for which the plan has a required quarterly installment. If this requirement is not met, the plan is treated as failing to pay the full amount of any required quarterly contribution and the plan sponsor will be subject to a nondeductible excise tax equal to 10 percent of the liquidity shortfall. The excise tax is increased to 100 percent if the liquidity shortfall remains outstanding after four quarters. IRS may waive all or part of the excise tax if the liquidity shortfall was due to reasonable cause and not willful neglect and reasonable steps have been taken to remedy the liquidity shortfall. [IRC §§ 412(m)(5), 4971(f)(4), as added by SBA '96 § 1464(a); Rev Rul 95-31, 1995-1 CB 76]

Q 8:29 Does the minimum funding requirement cease once a pension plan terminates?

Generally, the minimum funding standards apply to a pension plan until the end of the plan year in which the plan terminates and do not apply to the plan in later years. Therefore, the funding standard account (see Q 8:15) must be maintained through the end of the plan year in which the pension plan terminates, even if the termination occurs before the last day of the plan year. [JP Jeter Co, Inc, 65 TCM 2783 (1993)] IRS has opined that Schedule B (see Q 17:4) must be filed for the plan year in which a defined benefit plan terminates but need not be filed for the plan year after the year in which the plan terminates (see Q 21:67). *The foregoing was offered as general information and is not to be construed as a ruling as to any actual case.* [Spec Rul (July 27, 1993)]

If plan assets are not distributed as soon as administratively feasible after the date of plan termination, the plan will not be treated as terminated and, therefore, such a plan remains subject to the minimum funding standards (see Q 21:67). [Rev Rul 89-87, 1989-2 CB 81; Rev Rul 79-237, 1979-2 CB 190]

For details on plan terminations, see chapter 21.

Chapter 9

Vesting

One of the major features of a qualified retirement plan is the requirement that it provide for the vesting of benefits according to one of several schedules set by law. Thus, at a certain point, an employee acquires a nonforfeitable interest in benefits under the plan. This chapter examines what vesting means, the minimum requirements set by law, and how vesting works.

Q 9:1   What does vesting mean?

Vesting represents the nonforfeitable interest of participants in their (1) account balances under a defined contribution plan (see Q 2:2), or (2) accrued benefits under a defined benefit plan (see Q 2:3).

> **Example.** Assume a participant is 40 percent vested (that is, the participant has a nonforfeitable right to 40 percent of the benefit accrued in the plan). In a defined contribution plan, the participant's vested accrued benefit is equal to 40 percent of the balance in the account. In a defined benefit plan, the participant has a nonforfeitable right to 40 percent of the normal retirement benefit that has been accrued. Thus, if the accrued normal retirement benefit is $150 a month, the participant has a nonforfeitable right to $60 a month.

Vesting is directly related to an employee's length of service with the employer or group of employers (see Q 9:3).

Special vesting rules apply to top-heavy plans (see Q 22:32).

Q 9:2 What is an accrued benefit?

A participant's accrued benefit is the benefit that has accumulated up to a particular point in employment. Earning accrued benefits does not mean that a participant has a nonforfeitable (i.e., vested) right to those benefits. The nonforfeitability of an accrued benefit is determined by the retirement plan's vesting schedule.

Defined contribution plans (see Q 2:2) must provide separate accounts with respect to each participant's accrued benefit. This means that a participant's accrued benefit is the balance of the participant's individual account (see Q 9:24). [IRC § 411(a)(7)(A)(ii)]

Defined benefit plans (other than those funded solely through insurance contracts) are required to include a procedure for determining a participant's accrued benefit that satisfies one of three alternative benefit accrual formulas. Generally, accrued benefits are determined with reference to the benefits that are payable at normal retirement age (see Q 10:53) and that accrue over the period of the employee's participation in the plan or service with the employer. The alternative formulas limit the amount of back loading (providing a higher rate for accrual of benefits for later years of service than for earlier years); however, they do not require the same rate of benefit accrual each year. Front loading (providing a higher rate for accrual of benefits for earlier years of service than for later years) is permitted, although such front loading also may be limited. [IRC § 411(b)(1); Prop Reg § 1.411(b)-2(b)(3); Rev Rul 85-131, 1985-2 CB 138; Notice 87-21, 1987-1 CB 458 (Q&A 16); Notice 89-45, 1989-1 CB 684; Jerome Mirza & Assocs, Ltd v United States, 882 F 2d 229 (7th Cir 1989)]

For a discussion of vesting and accrued benefits relating to employee contributions, see Q 9:8.

Q 9:3 Are minimum vesting standards set by law?

Yes. Two minimum vesting schedules apply to a participant's accrued benefit (see Q 9:2) derived from employer contributions. [IRC § 411(a)(2); Temp Reg §§ 1.411(a)-3T(b), 1.411(a)-3T(c), 1.411(a)-3T(e)] These schedules, either one of which may be used, are as follows:

Five-Year Vesting

Years of Service	Nonforfeitable Percentage
Less than 5	0%
5 or more	100

Seven-Year Graded Vesting

Years of Service	Nonforfeitable Percentage
Less than 3	0%
3	20
4	40
5	60
6	80
7 or more	100

Example 1. Stanley Corporation's retirement plan provides for plan participation after the completion of one year of service and provides for 100 percent vesting after five years of plan participation rather than service. The plan does not satisfy the minimum vesting standards because, under the plan, an employee becomes 100 percent vested only after completion of more than five years of service. Vesting based upon years of participation is permitted as long as the minimum vesting standards are satisfied. [Ferrara v Allentown Physician Anesthesia Assocs, Inc, 711 F Supp 206 (ED Pa 1989)]

Example 2. Marjorie Corporation's retirement plan contains the following vesting schedule:

Years of Service	Nonforfeitable Percentage
1 or less	0%
2	10
3	25
4	45
5	65
6	75
7 or more	100

The plan does not satisfy the minimum vesting standards because the nonforfeitable percentage after six years of service (75 percent) is less than the percentage required at that time (80 percent). The fact that the nonforfeitable percentage for years prior to the sixth year of service is greater than the percentage required is immaterial.

Q 9:4   Do the minimum vesting standards apply to multiemployer plans?

A multiemployer plan (see chapter 25) may use a ten-year cliff vesting schedule (that is, an employee with at least ten years of service is 100 percent vested), but only for participants covered under the plan pursuant to a collective bargaining agreement.

Employees are not covered under a collective bargaining agreement *unless* they are represented by a bona fide employee representative who is a party to the agreement. Consequently, an employee of the multiemployer plan or an employee of the union is not covered under the collective bargaining agreement, even though the employee participates in the plan pursuant to an agreement with the plan or with the union.

Plan participants not covered pursuant to a collective bargaining agreement must have a nonforfeitable right to accrued benefits derived from employer contributions under either the five-year cliff or the seven-year graded vesting schedule (see Q 9:3).

[IRC §§ 411(a)(2)(C), prior to repeal by SBA '96 § 1442(a), 414(f)(1)(B); Temp Reg §§ 1.411(a)-3T(d), 1.411(a)-3T(e)]

This special vesting rule for multiemployer plans will be eliminated so that all qualified retirement plans will be subject to the same vesting standards. This change is effective for plan years beginning on or after the earlier of (1) the later of (a) January 1, 1997 or (b) the date on which the last collective bargaining agreement under which the plan is maintained terminates, or (2) January 1, 1999, but does not apply to employees who do not have more than one hour of service under the plan on or after the effective date. [SBA '96, Act § 1442]

Q 9:5   Does the adoption of one of the minimum vesting schedules guarantee the retirement plan's qualification?

Unless there has been a pattern of abuse or actual misuse in the operation of a retirement plan, the use of one of the two minimum vesting schedules (see Q 9:3) will satisfy the plan's qualification requirements with regard to vesting. The intentional dismissal of employees to prevent vesting may indicate a pattern of abuse. See chapter 22 for details relating to vesting under a top-heavy plan. [IRC § 411(d)(1); ERISA § 510; Prop Reg § 1.411(d)-1(b); Rev Proc 89-29, 1989-1 CB 893]

When an employee was discharged by the employer shortly before his qualified retirement plan benefits would have become vested, courts have found that the proximity of the termination date and the vesting date was sufficient to infer that the employer's purpose in discharging the employee was to deprive him of his retirement benefits. [Hazen Paper Co v Biggins, No. 91-1600 (S Ct 1993); Olitsky v Spencer Gifts, Inc, No. 91-1010 (5th Cir 1992); also see Chailland v Brown & Root, Inc, No. 93-3543 (5th Cir 1995)] Another court ruled that, since an employer is prohibited from discharging an employee for the purpose of interfering with the attainment of any right that the employee may become entitled to receive under a plan, this prohibition applied to an employee who was discharged shortly before he became qualified for early retirement, even though he was fully vested in his accrued benefit (see Q 9:2). [Heath v Varity Corp, 1995 US App Lexis 33463 (7th Cir 1995)]

Other courts have ruled that the prevention of further benefit accruals or additional vesting must be a motivating factor in the employer's decision to discharge an employee. [Daughtrey v Honeywell Inc, No. 92-8221 (11th Cir 1993); Clark v Coats & Clark Inc, No. 92-8024 (11th Cir 1993)] Another court concluded that an employee who claimed he was transferred from one plant to another by the employer to avoid paying early retirement benefits could maintain an action against the employer even though the employee had not been discharged or constructively discharged. [Eret v Continental Holding Inc, 1993 US Dist Lexis 10537 (ND Ill 1993)] It has also been held that a cause of action by an employee may exist for an employer's retaliation against the employee's collection of plan benefits even where the employee applied for and received all benefits due under the plan [Kowalski v L & F Prods, 1996 US App Lexis 10090 (3rd Cir 1996); Kimbro v Atlantic Richfield Co, 889 F 2d 869 (9th Cir 1989)]; but another court held that an employer's discharge of an employee shortly after he complained about failing to receive matching contributions was not an attempt by the employer to retaliate against the employee where there was sufficient evidence to show that the actual reason for the employee's dismissal was his misconduct. [Grottkau v Sky Climber, Inc, No. 95-2132 (7th Cir 1996)]

In other cases, one court upheld the plan's vesting schedule even though a significant number of participants never became vested because of the transient nature of their employment [Phillips v Alaska Hotel and Restaurant Employees Pension Fund, Nos. 89-35735 and 90-35144 (9th Cir 1991)], and another court ruled that an employer that terminated an employee as a part of a reduction in its workforce did not unlawfully interfere with the employee's pension rights. [Card v Hercules Inc, No. 92-4169 (10th Cir 1993)]

Q 9:6 May a qualified retirement plan's vesting schedule be changed?

Yes. Like other provisions in a qualified retirement plan, the vesting schedule may be amended by the employer, even after IRS has approved the plan as initially adopted.

If the vesting schedule is amended, however, each participant in the qualified retirement plan on the date the amendment is adopted or becomes effective (whichever is later) who has completed at least three years of service may elect, during the election period (see Q 9:7), to stay under the old vesting schedule. A participant's failure to make that election means that the participant is subject to the new schedule—provided that the participant was notified of the right to elect. An amendment of the vesting schedule may not cause any participant to forfeit (directly or indirectly) vested benefits regardless of length of service. [IRC § 411(a)(10); Temp Reg § 1.411(a)-8T(b)(1)]

A new determination letter should be obtained, particularly if the plan's vesting schedule has been made less liberal (see Q 21:5). See chapter 15 for details.

Q 9:7   What is the period within which a participant may elect to stay under the old vesting schedule?

A participant must have at least 60 days to elect the old vesting schedule. In addition, the election period must begin no later than the date on which the amendment is adopted and end no earlier than 60 days after the latest of the following dates:

1. The date the amendment is adopted;
2. The date the amendment becomes effective; or
3. The date the participant "is issued written notice of the plan amendment by the employer or plan administrator."

[IRC § 411(a)(10)(B); Temp Reg § 1.411(a)-8T(b)(2)]

Q 9:8   What vesting standards apply to an employee's own contributions?

Whether contributions are mandatory or voluntary (see Qs 6:19, 6:20), the employee at all times must have a nonforfeitable right to 100 percent of the benefits derived from the employee's own contributions. [IRC § 411(a)(1); Treas Reg §§ 1.411(a)-1(a)(2), 1.411(c)-1]

Since mandatory or voluntary employee contributions under a defined contribution plan (see Q 2:2) and voluntary employee contributions under a defined benefit plan (see Q 2:3) are separately accounted for, determining the accrued benefit (see Q 9:2) derived from the employee's own contributions is not difficult. However, since a defined benefit plan does not separately account for mandatory employee contributions, the determination requires a number of calculations. To determine the employee-derived accrued benefit, IRS has issued proposed regulations effective for plan years beginning on or after January 1, 1997. [Prop Reg §§ 1.411(c)-1(c)(1), 1.411(c)-1(c)(2), 1.411(c)-1(c)(3), 1.411(c)-1(c)(5), 1.411(c)-1(c)(6), 1.411(c)-1(d), 1.411(c)-1(g)]

Example 1. Stephanie, an unmarried participant, terminates employment with William Corporation on January 1, 1997 at age 56 with 15 years of service. As of December 31, 1987, Stephanie's total accumulated mandatory employee contributions to the plan, including interest compounded annually at 5 percent for plan years beginning after 1975 and before 1988, equaled $3,021. Stephanie will receive her accrued benefit in the form of a single life annuity commencing at normal retirement age. Stephanie's annuity starting date is January 1, 2006 (the determination date). For purposes of this example, it is assumed that Stephanie's total accrued benefit under the plan in the normal form of benefit commencing at normal retirement age is $2,949 per year. Stephanie's benefit, as of January 1, 2006, would be determined as follows:

1. Determine Stephanie's total accrued benefit in the form of a single life annuity commencing at normal retirement age under the plan's formula ($2,949 per year payable at age 65).

2. Determine Stephanie's accumulated contributions with interest to January 1, 1997. As of December 31, 1987, Stephanie's accumulated contributions with interest under the plan provisions were $3,021. Stephanie's employee contributions are accumulated from December 31, 1987 to January 1, 1997 using 120 percent of the federal mid-term rate. One hundred twenty percent of the actual federal mid-term rate is used for 1988 through 1995, and it is assumed for purposes of this example that 120 percent of the federal mid-term rate is 7 percent for each year between 1996 and 2006 and that the 30-year Treasury rate for December 2005 is 8 percent. Thus, Stephanie's contributions accumulated to January 1, 1997 equal $6,480.

3. Determine Stephanie's accumulated contributions with interest to normal retirement age (January 1, 2006) using, for the 1996 plan year and for years until normal retirement age, 120 percent of the federal mid-term rate ($11,913).

4. Determine the accrued annual annuity benefit derived from Stephanie's contributions by dividing Stephanie's accumulated contributions determined in paragraph 3 by the plan's appropriate conversion factor. The plan's appropriate conversion factor at age 65 is 9.196, and the accrued benefit derived from Stephanie's contributions would be $1,295 ($11,913 ÷ 9.196).

5. Determine the accrued benefit derived from employer contributions as the excess, if any, of the employee's accrued benefit under the plan over the accrued benefit derived from employee contributions. Thus, Stephanie's accrued benefit derived from employer contributions is $1,654 ($2,949 – $1,295).

6. Determine the vested percentage of the accrued benefit derived from employer contributions under the plan's vesting schedule (100 percent).

7. Determine the vested accrued benefit derived from employer contributions by multiplying the accrued benefit derived from employer contributions by the vested percentage, $1,654 ($1,654 × 100%).

8. Determine Stephanie's vested accrued benefit in the form of a single life annuity commencing at normal retirement age by adding the accrued benefit derived from employee contributions and the vested accrued benefit derived from employer contributions, the sum of paragraphs 4 and 7, $2,949 ($1,295 + $1,654).

Example 2. Assume the same facts as Example 1, except that Stephanie's total accrued benefit under the plan in the normal form of benefit commencing at normal retirement age is $1,000 per year. Stephanie's benefit, as of January 1, 2006, would be determined as follows:

1. Determine Stephanie's total accrued benefit in the form of a single life annuity commencing at normal retirement age under the plan's formula ($1,000 per year payable at age 65).

2. Determine Stephanie's accumulated contributions with interest to January 1, 1997 ($6,480 from paragraph 2 of Example 1).

3. Determine Stephanie's accumulated contributions with interest to normal retirement age (January 1, 2006) ($11,913 from paragraph 3 of Example 1).

4. Determine the accrued annual annuity benefit derived from Stephanie's contributions by dividing Stephanie's accumulated contributions determined in paragraph 3 of this Example 2 by the plan's appropriate conversion factor ($1,295 from paragraph 4 of Example 1).

5. Determine the accrued benefit derived from employer contributions as the excess, if any, of the employee's accrued benefit under the plan over the accrued benefit derived from employee contributions. Because the accrued benefit derived from employee contributions ($1,295) is greater than the employee's accrued benefit under the plan ($1,000), the accrued benefit derived from employer contributions is zero, and Stephanie's vested accrued

benefit in the form of a single life annuity commencing at normal retirement age is $1,295 per year.

Q 9:9 What is a year of service for vesting purposes?

For purposes of determining a participant's vested benefits, a year of service means a 12-consecutive-month period specified in the qualified retirement plan during which the participant completes at least 1,000 hours of service (see Q 5:9). [IRC § 411(a)(5)]

Q 9:10 What years of service must be taken into account for vesting purposes?

In general, all years of service with the employer must be counted. For the exceptions, see Q 9:11. [IRC § 411(a)(4)]

Service with a predecessor of the employer must be counted if the successor-employer maintains the predecessor's qualified retirement plan. If the successor adopts a new retirement plan, recognition of service with the predecessor-employer is supposed to be decided under as-yet-unissued IRS regulations. IRS has said that, in the case of a predecessor-partnership, service with the partnership could be counted for vesting purposes under the successor-corporation's retirement plan, even though the corporation did not continue the partnership's retirement plan. [IRC § 414(a); Ltr Rul 7742003]

Service with any member of a controlled group of corporations or with a commonly controlled entity (see Q 5:33), whether or not incorporated, must be counted for vesting purposes. Similarly, service with any member of an affiliated service group (see Q 5:37) must be counted. [IRC §§ 414(b), 414(c), 414(m)]

A multiple-employer defined benefit plan that does not credit vesting service attributable to periods for which an employer does not make required contributions to the plan does not satisfy the minimum vesting requirements. [Rev Rul 85-130, 1985-2 CB 137]

Q 9:11 May any years of service be disregarded for vesting purposes?

Yes. There are limited exceptions to the general rule that all years of service with an employer must be counted for vesting purposes (see Q 9:10). [IRC § 411(a)(4)]

The following years of service may be disregarded:

1. Years of service before the employee reached age 18;
2. Years of service before the qualified retirement plan went into effect;
3. Years of service during which the employee declined to make required (mandatory) contributions; and
4. Years of service before a one-year break in service (see Q 5:10) if the number of consecutive one-year breaks in service equals or exceeds the greater of five or the number of prebreak years of service, and the participant did not have any nonforfeitable right to the accrued benefit (see Q 9:15).

Elective contributions (see Q 23:13) to a 401(k) plan (see Q 23:1) are considered as employer, not employee, contributions. Thus, a plan may not disregard years of service for vesting purposes because of the failure to make elective contributions; the exclusion applies only to the failure to make *mandatory* employee contributions. [Reg § 1.411(a)-5(b)(2)]

Q 9:12   Is an employee's length of service ever irrelevant in determining the degree of vesting?

Yes. In any of the following circumstances an employee is fully vested (that is, has a nonforfeitable right to 100 percent of the employer-provided account balance or accrued benefit) regardless of how many years of service the employee has completed:

1. The employee reaches normal retirement age under the plan (see Q 10:53). [IRC §§ 411(a), 411(a)(8)]
2. The qualified retirement plan is terminated, a partial termination of the plan has occurred (see Q 21:5), or plan contributions are completely discontinued. [IRC § 411(d)(3)]
3. The minimum service requirement for participation is more than one year of service (see Qs 5:4, 23:4). [IRC § 410(a)(1)(B)(i)]
4. The plan is a qualified 401(k) plan and the accrued benefit is derived from employer contributions made pursuant to the employee's election. See chapter 23 for details. [IRC § 401(k)(2)(C)]

The plan may also provide for full vesting under any of these circumstances:

1. The employee reaches the early retirement age set by the qualified retirement plan.
2. The employee becomes disabled.
3. The employee dies.

Q 9:13   What vesting schedule is best for the employer?

It depends on how long employees usually stay with the employer.

Example. Keren Corporation adopted a 5-percent-of-compensation money purchase pension plan on January 1, 1996. Sharon completes a year of service on January 1, 1997 and joins the plan. Sharon earns $20,000 a year. Below is a calculation of Sharon's benefits under the seven-year graded and five-year cliff vesting schedules (see Q 9:3):

	Seven-Year		*Five-Year*	
Plan Year	*Contribution/ Account Balance*	*Vesting Percentage/ Vested Benefits*	*Contribution/ Account Balance*	*Vesting Percentage/ Vested Benefits*
1	0 — 0		0 — 0	
2	$1,000 — $1,000	0% — $0	$1,000 — $1,000	0% — $0
3	$1,000 — $2,000	20% — $400	$1,000 — $2,000	0% — $0
4	$1,000 — $3,000	40% — $1,200	$1,000 — $3,000	0% — $0
5	$1,000 — $4,000	60% — $2,400	$1,000 — $4,000	100% — $4,000
6	$1,000 — $5,000	80% — $4,000	$1,000 — $5,000	100% — $5,000
7	$1,000 — $6,000	100% — $6,000	$1,000 — $6,000	100% — $6,000

In plan years 3 and 4, less vested benefits are provided under the five-year cliff vesting schedule; and, in plan years 5 and 6, less vested benefits are provided under the seven-year graded vesting schedule. Thus, if employees customarily leave before completing five years of service, five-year cliff vesting is more favorable to the employer; but, if they leave after completing five or six years of service, the seven-year graded schedule is more favorable to the employer. After seven years of service, both schedules provide equal benefits.

As an alternative, Keren Corporation could require employees to complete two years of service to become eligible, but then employees must be 100 percent vested immediately (see Q 9:12). With a two-year service requirement and 100 percent immediate vesting, Sharon's benefits would be as follows:

Plan Year	Contribution/ Account Balance	Vesting Percentage/ Vested Benefits
1	0 ⁄ 0	
2	0 ⁄ 0	
3	$1,000 ⁄ $1,000	100% ⁄ $1,000
4	$1,000 ⁄ $2,000	100% ⁄ $2,000
5	$1,000 ⁄ $3,000	100% ⁄ $3,000
6	$1,000 ⁄ $4,000	100% ⁄ $4,000
7	$1,000 ⁄ $5,000	100% ⁄ $5,000

In plan years 3 and 4, the least vested benefits still occur under five-year cliff; in plan year 5, the least vested benefits still occur under seven-year graded; in plan year 6, the most vested benefits are still created under five-year cliff; and, in plan year 7 and in all subsequent plan years, the least vested benefits occur with the two-year service requirement. Therefore, if employees customarily leave after completing seven or more years of service, the two-year service requirement will be most favorable to the employer.

Q 9:14 How does a one-year break in service affect an employee if the qualified retirement plan requires the employee to have more than one year of service in order to be eligible to participate?

Qualified retirement plans that provide for immediate 100 percent vesting but require more than one year of service to be eligible to participate (see Qs 5:12, 9:12) may provide that years of service preceding a one-year break in service (see Q 5:10) be disregarded if the employee has not yet met the service eligibility criterion. Thus, an employee who completes one year of service and then incurs a one-year break in service starts over again when rehired. [IRC § 410(a)(5)(B)]

Q 9:15 How does a one-year break in service affect a previously nonvested participant's right to benefits?

A nonvested participant's years of service before any period of consecutive one-year breaks in service (see Q 5:10) may be disregarded for vesting purposes if the number of consecutive one-year breaks in service equals or exceeds the greater of five or the participant's years of service before the break. [IRC § 411(a)(6)(D)]

> **Example.** KSL Corporation's profit sharing plan, which operates on a calendar-year basis, requires an employee to complete one year of service to become a participant. Under the plan's vesting provision, a participant becomes 100 percent vested after five years of service. Lauren began working for KSL on January 1, 1992, separated from service on December 15, 1993, and was rehired on January 12, 1997. Lauren's two years of service before her break in service must be counted because her consecutive one-year breaks in service are less than five.

A participant's prebreak years of service do not have to be taken into account until a year of service is completed after reemployment. [IRC § 411(a)(6)(B)]

Q 9:16 How does a one-year break in service affect a vested participant's right to benefits?

The years of service of a vested participant in a defined contribution plan (see Q 2:2) or a fully insured defined benefit plan (see Q 2:23) completed after a one-year break in service (see Q 5:10) need not be counted for purposes of computing the participant's right to benefits derived from employer contributions accruing before the one-year break in service if the participant has at least five consecutive one-year breaks in service. [IRC § 411(a)(6)(C)]

Example. Jay-Kay Corporation has a profit sharing plan in which James participated. At the time James separated from service, he had a nonforfeitable right to 20 percent of his accrued benefit, but no distribution was made. In 1997, after incurring a one-year break in service, James is rehired and becomes an active participant in the plan once again. The plan is not permitted to disregard James's postbreak service for purposes of computing the vested percentage of his prebreak accrued benefit.

If a participant's prebreak years of service are required to be taken into account, such years of service need not be counted until the participant completes a year of service after resuming employment. [IRC § 411(a)(6)(B)]

Q 9:17 What is a forfeiture of benefits?

If an employee terminates employment before becoming 100 percent vested, the employee may be entitled to some benefits. This will usually depend on the number of years the employee worked for the company. Thus, if, at the time of termination, the employee's account balance in a profit sharing plan is $10,000 and the employee is 60 percent vested, the vested benefit is $6,000 (60% × $10,000). The balance in the account that is not vested at the time of termination generally will be forfeited at the earlier of (1) when the employee receives a distribution, or (2) after the employee incurs five consecutive one-year breaks in service (see Q 5:10). [IRC § 411(a)(6)(C)]

Q 9:18 What happens to amounts forfeited by participants?

Only defined benefit plans (see Q 2:3) are restricted in the application of forfeitures. Forfeitures under a defined benefit plan must be used to reduce future employer contributions and may not be used to provide additional benefits for remaining participants. Defined contribution plans (see Q 2:2) may provide that forfeitures be used either to reduce contributions or to increase benefits provided under the plan. [IRC § 401(a)(8)]

IRS has ruled that a profit sharing plan may provide for the allocation of forfeitures to participants on the basis of their account balances provided such allocation does not discriminate in favor of highly compensated employees (see Q 3:2). [Rev Rul 81-10, 1981-1 CB 172; Treas Reg §§ 1.401-4(a)(1)(iii), 1.401(a)(4)-1(c)(10), 1.401(a)(4)-11(c)]

Q 9:19   May a nonforfeitable benefit ever be forfeited?

The courts have differed on whether forfeitures can be imposed because of employee dishonesty (so-called bad boy clauses) or violation of a promise not to compete. Some courts say such forfeitures are not permitted. Other courts have ruled that if the forfeiture provisions do not cause a forfeiture of an amount greater than what would result under the minimum vesting standards (see Q 9:3), the forfeiture is allowed. [Noell v American Design Inc Profit Sharing Plan, 764 F 2d 827 (8th Cir 1985); Montgomery v Lowe (DC ED Texas 1981); Hepple v Roberts & Dybdahl Inc (8th Cir 1980); Marshall v Edison Bros, 593 F 2d 30 (8th Cir 1979); Nedrow v MacFarlane and Hays Co (DC Mich 1979)]

According to IRS, vested benefits in excess of the benefits required to be nonforfeitable under the statutory alternatives (see Q 9:3) may be forfeited because of an employee's misconduct or dishonesty. The qualified retirement plan must provide the specific criteria for application of this bad boy clause, and its use cannot be discriminatory in operation.

Example 1. Nephew Mikey Corporation's retirement plan provides that an employee is fully vested after the completion of three years of service. The plan also provides that, if the employee works for a competitor, he forfeits his rights in the plan. Such a provision could result in a prohibited forfeiture; but, if the plan limited the forfeiture to employees who completed less than five years of service, the plan would not fail to satisfy the minimum vesting requirements.

Example 2. Aunt Sallie Corporation's retirement plan has a seven-year graded vesting provision and provides for forfeiture of benefits if an employee with less than five years of service terminates employment and works for a competitor. This is permissible because the plan could have had five-year cliff vesting.

[Temp Reg §§ 1.411(a)-4T(a), 1.411(a)-4T(c); Treas Reg § 1.411(d)-4, Q&A 6; Rev Rul 85-31, 1985-1 CB 153]

Q 9:20   Does a distribution (cash-out) of benefits affect how many years of service must be taken into account?

Yes. Upon termination of the employee's participation in a qualified retirement plan, the plan may disregard service for which the employee has received (1) an involuntary distribution of the present value of the employee's nonforfeitable benefit up to a maximum of $3,500 (see Q 10:58), or (2) a voluntary distribution of the present value of the nonforfeitable benefit. [IRC §§ 411(a)(7)(B), 411(a)(11); Treas Reg § 1.411(a)-7(d)(4)]

In order to disregard the prior service of a participant who resumes employment and participation under the qualified retirement plan and who previously received a distribution of less than the present value of the accrued benefit, the plan must provide the participant with the opportunity to repay the entire amount of the distribution (see Q 9:21). [IRC § 411(a)(7)(C); Treas Reg § 1.411(a)-7(d)(4)]

Q 9:21 How can a reemployed participant restore (buy-back) forfeited benefits?

In most situations, upon reemployment, a participant is entitled to repay a prior distribution from the qualified retirement plan and to have any forfeited benefits restored. This buy-back provision must permit the employee to pay back the full amount distributed. The plan can require repayment by the reemployed participant before the earlier of (1) five years after reemployment, or (2) when the participant incurs a period of five consecutive one-year breaks in service (see Q 5:10) commencing after the distribution. Thus, the employer is not required to offer this buy-back right to a participant who has five consecutive one-year breaks in service after the distribution. [IRC § 411(a)(7)(C)]

A defined benefit plan may require that any repayment include interest on the full amount of the distribution. The maximum interest rate that may be charged upon repayment is 120 percent of the federal midterm rate in effect on the first day of the plan year during which repayment occurs. [IRC §§ 411(a)(7)(C), 411(c)(2)(C), 1274; Treas Reg § 1.411(a)-7(d)(2)(ii)(B)]

Q 9:22 May a qualified retirement plan provide for the forfeiture of vested benefits on the death of an employee?

Yes, with the following exception: the surviving spouse of a participant in a qualified retirement plan subject to the survivor annuity requirements must be paid an annuity based on the participant's vested accrued benefit unless the participant waived the coverage with the spouse's consent (see Q 10:20). [IRC § 401(a)(11)]

A qualified retirement plan may not provide for the forfeiture of vested benefits derived from employee contributions, whether mandatory or voluntary (see Q 9:8). However, a forfeiture does not occur merely because benefits derived from contributions of both the employer and the employee are paid out in the form of an annuity that stops on the employee's death. [Treas Reg § 1.411(a)-4(b)(1)(ii)]

Q 9:23   May any years of service be disregarded for accrual purposes?

Yes. A qualified retirement plan may impose a limitation on the amount of benefits an employee may accrue or the number of years of service that will be taken into account in determining an employee's accrued benefit (see Q 9:2). Therefore, a qualified retirement plan may disregard an employee's service that occurs after the specified benefit level or the specified number of years of service has been reached. However, a retirement plan may not cease an employee's accrual of benefits (or reduce the rate of accrual) solely because the employee attains a certain age. [IRC § 411(b)(1)(H); Prop Reg § 1.411(b)-2; Atkins v Northwest Airlines Inc, No. 91-3179MN (8th Cir 1992); American Assn of Retired Persons v Farmers Group Inc, No. 90-55872 (9th Cir 1991)]

> **Example.** Stephanie Corporation maintains a defined benefit plan under which the participant's normal retirement benefit will be based on the highest annual salary earned by the participant during the time of employment. The plan further provides that each participant will accrue an interest in the benefit at the rate of 4 percent per year of service. The plan does, however, limit the number of years of service that will be taken into account in determining each participant's retirement benefit to 20. Therefore, a participant's normal retirement benefit will be limited to 80 percent of the participant's highest annual salary. This type of accrual scheme is permissible despite the fact that an older participant is more likely to be affected by the plan provision.

Q 9:24   Can a qualified retirement plan be amended to reduce accrued benefits?

Generally, no. A qualified retirement plan may not be amended to eliminate or reduce a Section 411(d)(6) protected benefit (see Q 10:42) that has already accrued (the anti-cutback rule), unless IRS approves a request to amend the plan or the elimination or reduction satisfies certain requirements (see Qs 8:25, 9:28). This is the rule even if such elimination or reduction is contingent upon the employee's consent. However, a plan may (subject to certain notice requirements) be amended to eliminate or reduce Section 411(d)(6) protected benefits with respect to benefits not yet accrued as of the later of the amendment's adoption date or effective date (see Q 9:29). [IRC §§ 411(d)(6), 412(c)(8); ERISA §§ 204(g), 302(c)(8), 4281; Treas Reg § 1.411(d)-4, Q&A 2; Smith v Nat'l Credit Union Admin Bd, 1994 US App Lexis 30390 (11th Cir 1994); Production and Maintenance Employees' Local 504 v Roadmaster Corp, Nos. 89-1464 and 90-2698 (7th Cir 1992);

Nichols v Asbestos Workers Local 24 Pension Plan, 835 F 2d 881 (Fed Cir 1987); Rev Proc 94-42, 1994-1 CB 717; Ltr Ruls 9614004, 9346012]

One court has held that a defined contribution plan (see Q 2:2) could not be retroactively amended to change the plan's valuation date where the effect of the amendment was to reduce the amount of benefits payable to a terminated plan participant. In this case, the value of the terminated participant's account balance in the plan decreased markedly from the prior valuation date. Under the plan in effect on his termination date, the terminated participant was entitled to a distribution of his account balance valued as of the nearest prior valuation date. After the participant's termination, the plan was amended (retroactive to the beginning of the plan year) to provide for interim valuation dates. An interim valuation resulted in a much smaller account balance for the terminated participant. The court held that, in a defined contribution plan, the accrued benefit is the participant's account balance (see Q 9:2). Thus, the participant's account balance could not be reduced by a retroactive plan amendment adopted after the participant terminated employment. [Pratt v Petroleum Production Mgmt, Inc Employee Savings Plan and Trust, No. 88-2190 (10th Cir 1990); Wulf v Quantum Chemical Corp, 1994 US App Lexis 14677 (6th Cir 1994); also see Kay v Thrift and Profit Sharing Plan for Employees of Boyertown Casket Co, 780 F Supp 1447 (ED Pa 1991)]

Amendments eliminating participants' rights to elect lump-sum distributions or delaying the right to payment of retirement benefits constitute prohibited elimination of or reduction in accrued benefits. [Counts v Kissack Water and Oil Service Inc Profit Sharing Plan, No. 92-8036 (10th Cir 1993); Davis v Burlington Industries, Inc, No. 91-1725 (4th Cir 1992); Auwarter v Paper Sales Corp Defined Benefit Pension Plan, No. 91-3082 (ED NY 1992)] An amendment increasing the interest rate, the effect of which reduced the amount of lump-sum payments, has been held to violate the anti-cutback rule [Costantino v TRW, Inc, Nos. 91-3768/3769 (6th Cir 1994)]; but other courts have held such an amendment not to violate the rule. [Cooke v Lynn Sand & Stone Co, 1995 US App Lexis 33252 (1st Cir 1995); Dooley v American Airlines, Inc, 1993 US Dist Lexis 15667 (ND Ill 1993)] The elimination of a postretirement cost-of-living adjustment in monthly retirement benefits constitutes a prohibited reduction in accrued benefits [Hickey v Chicago Truck Drivers, Helpers and Warehouse Workers Union, 1992 US App Lexis 30961 (7th Cir 1992)]; but other cases have held that early retirement benefits are not accrued benefits so that a reduction in such benefits does not violate the anti-cutback rule. [Meredith v Allsteel, Inc, 1993 US App Lexis 32032 (7th Cir 1993); Hunger v AB, 1993 US App Lexis 32743 (8th Cir 1993); Dade v North America Philips Corp, 1994 US Dist Lexis 11428 (DC NJ 1994)]

In a case involving the sale of a subsidiary, the court held that the inability of the affected employees to continue to participate in the seller's plan was not an amendment reducing benefits. [Andes v Ford Motor Co, 1995 US App Lexis 34438 (DC Cir 1995)] Since the merger of two defined benefit plans was a plan amendment that was subject to the notice requirements (see Q 9:29), the failure to provide notice that an amendment reducing plan benefits was being adopted entitled the affected participants to benefits at a higher accrual rate. [Koenig v Intercontinental Life Corp, No. 92-5758 (ED Pa 1995)] Another court concluded that the anti-cutback rule was not violated when an employee's pension plan benefits were reduced by workers' compensation benefits. [Huppler v Oscar Mayer Foods Corp, No. 93-3765 (7th Cir 1994)]

For a discussion of new provisions relating to the anti-cutback rule, see Qs 9:25 through 9:27.

Q 9:25 Do the new interest rate and mortality table requirements of RPA '94 violate the anti-cutback rule?

In general, a plan amendment that changes the interest rate or mortality table used to determine a participant's accrued benefit (see Q 9:2) under a defined benefit plan (see Q 2:3) is subject to the anti-cutback rules (see Q 9:24). However, under RPA '94 (see Q 1:19), a participant's accrued benefit is not considered to be reduced in violation of the anti-cutback rule merely because the plan applies the new interest rate and mortality table changes. Accordingly, a participant's accrued benefit may be reduced below the accrued benefit as of the last day of the last plan year beginning before January 1, 1995 if the reduction results solely from the application of these changes. [IRC §§ 411(d)(6), 415(b)(2)(E); RPA '94 Act §§ 767(d)(2), 767(d)(3); Rev Rul 95-29, 1995-1 CB 81; Temp Reg § 1.417(e)-1T(d)]

Although a participant's accrued benefit is permitted to be reduced in accordance with RPA '94, an accrued benefit is not required to be reduced below the accrued benefit as of the last day of the plan year beginning before January 1, 1995 (freeze date) merely because of the application of the new interest rate and mortality table changes. Thus, after the effective date of the changes, a plan will not violate the defined benefit plan limitations (see Qs 6:8–6:10) merely because the plan provides a benefit equal to the greater of (1) the participant's benefit under the terms of the plan, for the annuity starting date (see Q 10:3) and optional form and taking into account the defined benefit plan limitations as amended, and (2) the participant's protected accrued benefit as of the freeze date. The freeze date must be determined without taking into account any change in the plan or limitation year (see Q 6:16) that would delay the effective date of these changes or postpone the otherwise determined freeze date for the plan.

The participant's protected accrued benefit as of the freeze date is determined as the participant's benefit under the terms of the plan as of the freeze date, for the annuity starting date and optional form and taking into account the defined benefit plan limitations prior to these changes. For this purpose, plan amendments increasing benefits that are adopted after the freeze date are not taken into account and the accrued benefit is determined without regard to cost-of-living adjustments (see Q 6:8) that become effective after the freeze date.

Example 1. The defined benefit plan of Kay & Kay Corporation has a calendar-year plan and limitation year. Thus, the freeze date is December 31, 1994. As of that date, the plan provides a normal retirement benefit in the form of a single life annuity beginning at age 65. Early retirement benefits are available on or after age 60 with actuarial equivalence for early retirement computed using 5 percent interest and the UP-1984 mortality table. Single-sum distributions are available at any permitted retirement age. Single sums are calculated as the actuarial present value of the early retirement benefit payable at the actual retirement age computed using the PBGC (see Q 21:10) immediate interest rate and the UP-1984 mortality table. The plan further provides that any single-sum distribution must be at least as great as the actuarial present value of the participant's accrued normal retirement benefit computed using the PBGC interest rates for deferred annuities and the UP-1984 mortality table. There is no forfeiture of accrued benefits under the plan on account of death prior to the annuity starting date. Under the plan, the defined benefit plan limitations are applied after the otherwise determined benefit has been adjusted for early retirement and for any optional form of benefit.

Example 2. Sallie's Social Security retirement age (SSRA; see Q 6:14) is 65. As of the freeze date, Sallie has 10 years of participation in the plan. Under the plan formula as of the freeze date, Sallie's accrued normal retirement benefit is $110,000. This is her protected accrued benefit payable at normal retirement age. Any other optional form of benefit provided under the plan as of the freeze date (taking into account the defined benefit plan limits prior to amendment by RPA '94) is also protected.

Sallie retires in 1997 at age 60 and elects to receive a distribution in the form of a single sum. Sallie's protected single-sum distribution at retirement equals the single sum equivalent of the protected accrued benefit under the terms of the plan. Sallie's protected early retirement benefit at age 60, determined using the plan factors based on a 5 percent interest rate and the UP-1984 mortality table, is $75,242. Under the plan, the single-sum distribution at age 60 (before the application of the limitations) is equal to the greater of (1) the present value of $75,242 payable as a single life annuity commencing at age 60, determined using the PBGC immediate interest rate for 1997 and the UP-1984 mortality table, or (2) the present value as of age 60 of a deferred annuity of $110,000 payable as a single life annuity commencing at age 65, determined using the PBGC interest rates for deferred annuities and the UP-1984 mortality table. Assuming that the PBGC immediate interest rate for 1997 is equal to 7 percent, and that the PBGC interest rate used for the deferred period is 6.025 percent, the resulting single sum is $738,500, the greater of $738,500 (the present value of the immediate annuity) or $709,677 (the present value of the deferred annuity).

The plan limits effective prior to amendment by RPA '94 must now be applied. First, $738,500 is adjusted so that it is equivalent to a straight life annuity commencing at age 60. For purposes of this adjustment, the interest rate used must be 7 percent, which is the greater of the rate used under the plan to compute the single sum (in this case the PBGC immediate rate of 7 percent) or 5 percent. The mortality table is the UP-1984 table. The equivalent annual amount is equal to $75,242.

Next, the dollar limitation at age 60 must be determined. In this case, the dollar limit at age 65 taking into account Sallie's years of participation as of the freeze date and without taking into account cost-of-living increases after the freeze date is $118,800. This amount is reduced to an equivalent amount payable at age 62 by applying an adjustment factor equal to $[1 - (5/9 \times 1\%) \times 36]$, or 80 percent. The resulting amount ($95,040) is further reduced to age 60 using an interest rate that is the greater of (1) the rate used under the plan to determine actuarial equivalence for early retirement benefits, or (2) 5 percent, along with the UP-1984 mortality table. In this case, the resulting limit is $81,870.

Because $75,242 does not exceed $81,870, the protected single sum distribution is not limited. Accordingly, Sallie's protected single sum distribution is equal to $738,500.

For the effect of these new rules on cash balance plans, see Q 10:59.

Q 9:26 Can the protected accrued benefit change after the freeze date?

The protected accrued benefit can change after the freeze date (see Q 9:28) if the defined benefit plan limitations that apply to a participant prior to amendment by RPA '94 (see Q 1:19) are changed. For example, if subsequent annual additions (see Q 6:1) are credited to a participant's account in an existing defined contribution plan (see Q 2:2) of the same employer, increases in that participant's defined contribution fraction (see

Q 6:17) could result in decreases to the protected accrued benefit (depending on the terms of the plans). The protected accrued benefit could also be reduced if the interest rate generally used under the plan is changed as shown in the following examples.

Example 1. Prior to amendment for RPA '94, a defined benefit plan provided that single sum distributions were determined using the interest rates in effect prior to RPA '94 (see Q 10:59) and the UP-1984 mortality table. The plan also provided that, for purposes of computing the defined benefit plan limitations, an interest rate equal to the greater of 5 percent or the plan interest rate would be used with the UP-1984 mortality table (see Qs 6:8–6:10).

In order to reflect the present value determination rule changes (see Q 10:59), the plan is amended to substitute the applicable interest rate and the IRS mortality table for the original plan interest rate and the UP-1984 mortality table, respectively, to compute single sum distributions under the plan. These new provisions are applied to benefits accrued both before and after the amendment date.

Prior to the defined benefit plan limitation changes, the interest rate required to be used to convert a single sum distribution to an actuarially equivalent single life annuity was the greater of 5 percent or the interest rate specified in the plan. In this case, the plan has been amended to use the applicable interest rate in determining benefits accrued as of the freeze date. Therefore, in order to determine the protected accrued benefit, the accrued benefit as of the freeze date must be redetermined. If, after the amendment, the applicable interest rate that applies to the participant's distribution is more than the greater of 5 percent or the original plan interest rate, the protected accrued benefit must be reduced accordingly. Although RPA '94 protects a participant's accrued benefit from being reduced merely because of the application of the defined benefit plan limitation changes, use of the applicable interest rate in place of the original plan interest rate results from the application of the present value determination rule changes to benefits accrued as of the freeze date.

Example 2. Prior to amendment for RPA '94, a defined benefit plan provided that single-sum distributions were determined using the lesser of 6 percent or the PBGC interest rate, and the UP-1984 mortality table. The plan also provided that, for purposes of computing benefit adjustments, an interest rate equal to the greater of 5 percent or the lesser of 6 percent or the PBGC interest rate would be used with the UP-1984 mortality table.

In order to reflect the present value determination rule changes, the plan is amended after the freeze date to substitute the applicable interest rate and the IRS mortality table for the PBGC interest rate and the UP-1984 mortality table, respectively, but only with respect to benefits accruing after the amendment date. Because the amendment has no effect on the benefits accrued as of the freeze date, the protected accrued benefit will not be affected by the amendment.

[Rev Rul 95-29, 1995-1 CB 81]

For a discussion of the effective dates of these new rules, see Q 9:27 and also see Q 10:59.

Q 9:27   What effective dates apply to the new present value determination rules for defined benefit plans?

The new rules (see Qs 9:25, 9:26) are generally effective for distributions with annuity starting dates (see Q 10:3) in plan years beginning after December 31, 1994.

For a plan adopted and in effect *before* December 8, 1994, the application of the rules relating to the IRS mortality table and applicable interest rate (see Q 10:59) can be delayed *until* the first day of the plan year beginning *after* December 31, 1999, *if* the plan provisions in effect on December 7, 1994 met the present value determination rules of Section 417(e)(3) on that date. For such a plan, the present value of a distribution made before the delayed effective date is calculated under the plan provisions in effect on December 7, 1994.

The new rules can also be effective for a distribution with an annuity starting date after December 7, 1994 during a plan year beginning before January 1, 1995, *if* the employer elects, on or before the annuity starting date, to make the new rules effective as of an optional accelerated effective date.

The optional *delayed* effective date or the optional *accelerated* effective date is the later of the date a plan amendment applying both the IRS mortality table and the applicable interest rate is adopted or made effective.

[IRC § 417(e)(3)(B); Temp Reg § 1.417(e)-1T(d)(8)]

Q 9:28   Can accrued benefits be eliminated or reduced?

It is permissible to eliminate or reduce accrued benefits (see Q 9:2) if any of the following circumstances is present:

1. The amendment constitutes timely compliance with a change in law affecting plan qualification (IRS gives Section 7805(b) relief), and the

elimination or reduction is made only to the extent necessary to comply with the plan qualification rules. An amendment will not be treated as necessary if it is possible to satisfy the applicable qualification requirement through other modifications to the plan (e.g., by expanding the availability of an optional form of benefit to additional employees).

2. A qualified retirement plan that provides a range of three or more actuarially equivalent joint and survivor annuity options may be amended to eliminate any of such options, other than the options with the largest and smallest optional survivor payment percentages. The amendment is permissible even if the effect of such amendment is to change the option that is the qualified joint and survivor annuity (QJSA) (see Q 10:8).

Example. A retirement plan provides three joint and survivor annuity options with survivor payments of 50 percent, 75 percent, and 100 percent, respectively. The options are uniform with respect to age and are actuarially equivalent. The employer may eliminate the option with the 75 percent survivor payment, even if this option had been the QJSA under the plan.

3. If a qualified retirement plan includes an optional form of benefit under which benefits are distributed in specified property (other than cash), such optional form may be modified for distributions after plan termination by substituting cash for the property, but only to the extent that, on plan termination, an employee has the opportunity to receive the optional form of benefit in the specified property. However, if the employer that maintains the terminating plan also maintains another plan that provides an optional form of benefit in the specified property, this exception is not available.

Example. Ess-Kay Corporation maintains a stock bonus plan under which a participant, upon termination from employment, may elect to receive benefits in a lump-sum distribution in the company's stock. This is the only plan maintained by Ess-Kay under which distributions in employer stock are available. Ess-Kay decides to terminate the stock bonus plan. If such plan is amended to make available a lump-sum distribution in employer stock on plan termination, the plan will not fail the anti-cutback rule solely because the optional form of benefit providing a lump-sum distribution in employer stock on termination of employment is modified to provide that such distribution is available only in cash.

[Treas Reg § 1.411(d)-4, Q&A 2(b)]

Other circumstances permitting elimination or reduction of accrued benefits include amendments to provide for certain involuntary distributions, to eliminate provisions authorizing loans and certain plan-to-plan transfers, and to make a *de minimis* change in the timing of an optional form of benefit (see Q 10:33). In addition, special rules have been provided for amendments to employee stock ownership plans (ESOPs) (see Q 24:1). [Treas Reg § 1.411(d)-4, Q&A 2(d)]

For other circumstances permitting a reduction of accrued benefits, see Q 8:25.

Q 9:29 Can a qualified retirement plan be amended to reduce future accruals of benefits?

Yes. However, an amendment to a qualified retirement plan subject to the minimum funding requirements (see Q 8:1) that provides for a "significant reduction in the rate of future benefit accrual" will not be effective unless the plan administrator (see Q 16:1) provides written notice to all participants, any alternate payee under a QDRO (see Q 30:1), and each employee organization representing participants. That notice, which must set forth the amendment and its effective date, is required to be sent to such parties after adoption of the amendment and at least 15 days prior to its effective date. The reduction may result in either a termination or partial termination of the plan. See chapter 21 for details. [ERISA § 204(h)]

In a case in which an employer amended its qualified retirement plan to cease benefit accruals retroactively and gave notice of the amendment to its employees before the amendment was adopted and after the amendment's effective date, the court held that the amendment violated the prohibition against reducing accrued benefits and thus was ineffective. [Production and Maintenance Employees' Local 504 v Roadmaster Corp, Nos. 89-1464, 90-2698 (7th Cir 1992)] In another case, the court ruled that an amendment to the employer's qualified retirement plan that excluded certain income from the plan's definition of compensation, the effect of which was to reduce future benefit accruals, was ineffective because prior written notice was not given to plan participants. [Davidson v Canteen Corp, Nos. 91-1270, 91-1348 (7th Cir 1992)]

IRS has advised that written notice to participants is not required for a plan amendment that reduces further benefit accruals solely because of the new maximum compensation limit (see Q 6:23). [Rev Proc 94-13, 1994-1 CB 566; Ann 93-146, 1993-40 IRB]

The written notice is called the Section 204(h) Notice. With regard to the Section 204(h) Notice, IRS has issued temporary regulations effective for amendments adopted on or after December 15, 1995 and amendments effective by their terms on or after December 30, 1995. For details, see Qs 9:30 through 9:36.

Q 9:30   What is an amendment that affects the rate of future benefit accrual for purposes of ERISA Section 204(h)?

An amendment to a defined benefit plan (see Q 2:3) affects the rate of future benefit accrual *only* if it is reasonably expected to change the amount of the future annual benefit commencing at normal retirement age (see Q 10:53). An amendment to an individual account plan subject to the minimum funding requirements (see Qs 2:2, 8:1) affects the rate of future benefit accrual *only* if it is reasonably expected to change the amounts allocated in the future to participants' accounts. Changes in the investments or investment options under an individual account plan are not considered for this purpose. [Temp Reg § 1.411(d)-6T, Q&A-5(a)]

The rate of future benefit accrual is determined without regard to optional forms of benefit (other than the annual benefit), early retirement benefits, or retirement-type subsidies, and is also determined without regard to ancillary benefits and other rights or features (see Qs 4:18, 10:42). [Temp Reg § 1.411(d)-6T, Q&A-5(b)]

Example 1. A plan is amended with respect to future benefit accruals to eliminate a right to commencement of a benefit prior to normal retirement age. Because the amount does not affect the annual benefit commencing at normal retirement age, it does not reduce the rate of future benefit accrual for purposes of ERISA Section 204(h).

Example 2. A plan is amended to modify the assumptions used in converting an annuity form of distribution to a single sum form of distribution. The use of these modified assumptions results in a lower single sum. Because the amendment does not affect the annual benefit commencing at normal retirement age, it does not reduce the rate of future benefit accrual for purposes of ERISA Section 204(h).

Q 9:31   What plan provisions are taken into account in determining whether there has been a reduction in the rate of future benefit accrual?

All plan provisions that may affect the rate of future benefit accrual of participants or alternate payees (see Q 30:3) must be taken into account in determining whether an amendment provides for a significant reduction in the rate of future benefit accrual. Such provisions include, for example, the dollar amount or percentage of compensation on which benefit accruals are based; in the case of a plan using permitted disparity, the amount of disparity between the excess benefit percentage or excess contribution percentage and the base benefit percentage or base contribution percentage (see chapter 7); the definition of service or compensation taken into account in determining an employee's benefit accrual; the method of determining average compensation for calculating benefit accruals; the definition of normal retirement age (see Q 10:53) in a defined benefit plan (see Q 2:3); the exclusion of current participants from future participation; benefit offset provisions; minimum benefit provisions; the formula for determining the amount of contributions and forfeitures allocated to participants' accounts in an individual account plan subject to the minimum funding requirements (see Qs 2:2, 8:1); and the actuarial assumptions used to determine contributions under a target benefit plan (see Q 2:5). [Temp Reg § 1.411(d)-6T, Q&A-6(a)]

Plan provisions that do not affect the rate of future benefit accrual of participants or alternate payees are not taken into account in determining whether there has been a reduction in the rate of future benefit accrual. For example, provisions such as vesting schedules (see Qs 9:1, 9:3) or optional forms of benefit (other than the annual benefit; see Q 9:30) are not taken into account. [Temp Reg § 1.411(d)-6T, Q&A-6(b)]

Example. A defined benefit plan provides a normal retirement benefit equal to 50 percent of final average compensation times a fraction (not in excess of one), the numerator of which equals the number of years of participation in the plan and the denominator of which equals 20. A plan amendment that changes the numerator or denominator of that fraction must be taken into account in determining whether there has been a reduction in the rate of future benefit accrual.

Q 9:32 What is the basic principle used in determining whether an amendment provides for a significant reduction in the rate of future benefit accrual?

Whether an amendment provides for a significant reduction in the rate of future benefit accrual for purposes of ERISA Section 204(h) is determined based on reasonable expectations taking into account the relevant facts and circumstances at the time the amendment is adopted. [Temp Reg § 1.411(d)-6T, Q&A-7]

Q 9:33 To whom must the Section 204(h) Notice be given?

Generally, the Section 204(h) Notice (see Q 9:29) must be given to all participants, alternate payees (see Q 30:3), and each employee organization representing participants. [Temp Reg § 1.411(d)-6T, Q&A-1(a)]

Employees who have not yet become participants in a plan at the time an amendment is adopted are not taken into account. Thus, if the Section 204(h) Notice is required with respect to an amendment, the plan administrator (see Q 16:1) need not provide notice to such employees. [Temp Reg § 1.411(d)-6T, Q&A-8]

A plan administrator need not provide the Section 204(h) Notice to any participant whose rate of future benefit accrual is reasonably expected *not* to be reduced by the amendment, nor to any alternate payee whose rate of future benefit accrual is reasonably expected *not* to be reduced by the amendment. A plan administrator need not provide the Section 204(h) Notice to an employee organization unless the employee organization represents a participant to whom the notice is required to be provided. This determination is based on all relevant facts and circumstances at the time the amendment is adopted. [Temp Reg § 1.411(d)-6T, Q&A-9]

Example 1. Plan A is amended to reduce significantly the rate of future benefit accrual of all current employees who are participants in the plan. It is reasonable to expect, based on the facts and circumstances, that the amendment will not reduce the rate of future benefit accrual of former employees who are currently receiving benefits or that of former employees who are entitled to vested benefits. The plan administrator is not required to provide the Section 204(h) Notice to such former employees.

Example 2. Assume in Example 1 that Plan A also covers two groups of alternate payees. The alternate payees in the first group are entitled to a certain percentage or portion of the former spouse's accrued benefit. The accrued benefit is determined at the time the former spouse begins receiving retirement benefits under the plan. The alternate payees in the second group are entitled to a certain percentage or portion of the former spouse's accrued benefit, and the accrued benefit was determined at the time the QDRO (see Q 30:1) was issued by the court. It is reasonable to expect that the benefits to be received by the second group of alternate payees will not be affected by any reduction in a former spouse's rate of future benefit accrual. The plan administrator is not required to provide the Section 204(h) Notice to the alternate payees in the second group.

Example 3. Plan B covers hourly employees and salaried employees. Plan B provides the same rate of benefit accrual for both groups. The employer amends Plan B to reduce significantly the rate of future benefit accrual of the salaried employees only. At that time, it is reasonable to expect that only a small percentage of hourly employees will become salaried in the future. The plan administrator is not required to provide the Section 204(h) Notice to the participants who are currently hourly employees.

Example 4. Plan C covers employees in Division M and employees in Division N. Plan C provides the same rate of benefit accrual for both groups. The employer amends Plan C to reduce significantly the rate of future benefit accrual of employees in Division M. At that time, it is reasonable to expect that in the future only a small percentage of employees in Division N will be transferred to Division M. The plan administrator is not required to provide the Section 204(h) Notice to the participants who are employees in Division N.

Example 5. Assume the same facts as in Example 4 except that, at the time the amendment is adopted, it is expected that soon thereafter Division N will be merged into Division M in connection with a corporate reorganization and the employees in Division N will become subject to the plan's amended benefit formula applicable to the employees in Division M. In this instance, the plan administrator must provide the Section 204(h) Notice to the participants who are employees in Division M and to the participants who are employees in Division N.

A plan amendment that is subject to the notice requirements may also be subject to additional reporting and disclosure requirements under ERISA, such as the requirement to provide a summary description of material modifications (SMM; see Q 18:8). The Section 204(h) Notice must still be provided at least 15 days in advance of the effective date of an amendment significantly reducing the future rate of benefit accrual, even though an SMM describing the amendment is provided at a later date.

Q 9:34   May the Section 204(h) Notice contain a summary of the amendment?

The notice will not fail to comply with ERISA Section 204(h) merely because the notice contains a summary of the amendment, rather than the text of the amendment, if the summary is written in a manner calculated to be understood by the average plan participant *and* contains the effective date. The summary need not explain how the individual benefit of each participant or alternate payee (see Q 30:3) will be affected by the amendment. [Temp Reg § 1.411(d)-6T, Q&A-10]

Q 9:35   How may the Section 204(h) Notice be provided?

A plan administrator (see Q 16:1) may use any method reasonably calculated to ensure actual receipt of the notice. First-class mail to the last known address of the party is an acceptable delivery method. Likewise, hand delivery is acceptable. The Section 204(h) Notice may be enclosed along with any other notice provided by the employer or plan administrator. [Temp Reg § 1.411(d)-6T, Q&A-11]

Q 9:36   What happens if not all parties receive the Section 204(h) Notice?

If a plan administrator (see Q 16:1) fails to provide the Section 204(h) Notice to more than a *de minimis* percentage of participants and alternate payees (see Q 30:3) to whom the notice is required to be provided, the plan administrator will be considered to have complied with ERISA Section 204(h) *only* with respect to each participant and alternate payee who was provided with timely notice. In such a case, the amendment will become effective in accordance with its terms with respect to those participants and alternate payees only. [Temp Reg § 1.411(d)-6T, Q&A-12]

If the plan administrator provides the Section 204(h) Notice to all but a *de minimis* percentage of participants and alternate payees, the plan will be considered to have complied with ERISA Section 204(h) and the amendment will become effective in accordance with its terms with respect to all parties to whom the notice was required to be provided (including those who did not receive notice prior to discovery of the omission), if the plan administrator:

1. Made a good faith effort to comply with the requirements of ERISA Section 204(h);

2. Provided the Section 204(h) Notice to each employee organization that represents any participant to whom the notice is required to be provided;

3. Failed to provide the notice to no more than a *de minimis* percentage of participants and alternate payees to whom the notice is required to be provided; and

4. Provides the notice to those participants and alternate payees promptly upon discovering the oversight. [Treas Reg § 1.411(d)-6T, Q&A-13]

Q 9:37   What benefits are not Section 411(d)(6) protected benefits?

The following are examples of benefits that are not Section 411(d)(6) benefits and, therefore, may be reduced or eliminated by an amendment to a qualified retirement plan:

1. Ancillary life insurance protection;

2. Accident or health insurance benefits;

3. Social Security supplements described in Section 411(a)(9) [Cattin v General Motors Corp, Nos. 90-1016, 90-1051, 90-1052 (6th Cir 1992)];

4. The availability of loans (other than the distribution of an employee's accrued benefit upon default under a loan);

5. The right to make certain after-tax employee contributions or elective deferrals;

6. The right to direct investments;

7. The right to a particular form of investment (e.g., investment in employer stock or securities, or investment in certain types of securities, commercial paper, or other investment media);

8. The allocation dates for contributions, forfeitures, and earnings, the time for making contributions (but not the conditions for receiving an allocation of contributions or forfeitures for a plan year after such conditions have been satisfied), and the valuation dates for account balances;

9. Administrative procedures for distributing benefits, such as provisions relating to the particular dates on which notices are given and by which elections must be made; and

10. Rights that derive from administrative and operational provisions, such as mechanical procedures for allocating investment experience among accounts in defined contribution plans.

[Treas Reg § 1.411(d)-4, Q&A 1(d)]

Q 9:38 What happens to a participant's benefits if the qualified retirement plan merges with another plan?

In case of a merger or consolidation of qualified retirement plans, or a transfer of assets or liabilities from one qualified retirement plan to another, each participant must be entitled to receive a benefit after the merger that is at least equal to the value of the benefit the participant would have been entitled to receive before the merger. (The before-and-after merger benefits are determined as if the plan had been terminated.) [IRC §§ 401(a)(12), 414(l); Treas Reg §§ 1.401(a)-12, 1.414(l)-1; Ltr Rul 9422059]

Generally, the plan sponsor or plan administrator (see Q 16:1) of a merged plan must apprise the appropriate IRS District Director of the merger by completing Form 5310-A, Notice of Plan Merger or Consolidation, Spinoff, or Transfer of Plan Assets or Liabilities; Notice of Qualified Separate

Lines of Business, and filing the form, with page 1 in duplicate, at least 30 days before the event. Form 5310-A should be filed for each plan involved in the merger. Although IRS will not issue a determination letter (see Q 15:1) when a Form 5310-A is filed, an actuarial statement of valuation must be submitted, and, of course, IRS may request additional documentation with regard to any filing.

There is a penalty for late filing; the penalty is $25 a day for each day Form 5310-A is late (up to a maximum of $15,000). For exceptions to the requirement for filing Form 5310-A, see Q 9:39.

Q 9:39 Must Form 5310-A always be filed if there is a merger of qualified retirement plans?

No. Form 5310-A is *not* required to be filed in the following four situations:

1. Two or more defined contribution plans are merged, and all of the following conditions are met:
    a. The sum of the account balances (see Q 9:2) in each plan prior to the merger equals the fair market value of the entire plan assets (e.g., each plan has no unallocated suspense account or outstanding waiver balances (see Q 8:21)).
    b. The assets of each plan are combined to form the assets of the plan as merged.
    c. Immediately after the merger, each participant in the plan as merged has an account balance equal to the sum of the account balances the participant had in the plans immediately prior to the merger. [Treas Reg § 1.414(l)-1(d)]
2. There is a spinoff of a defined contribution plan, and all of the following conditions are met:
    a. The sum of the account balances in the plan prior to the spinoff equals the fair market value of the entire plan assets (e.g., the plan has no unallocated suspense account or outstanding waiver balances).
    b. The sum of the account balances for each participant in the resulting plans equals the account balance of each participant in the plan before the spinoff.
    c. The assets in each of the plans immediately after the spinoff equal the sum of the account balances for all participants in the plan (e.g., there is no unallocated suspense account or outstanding

waiver balances in any of the plans spun off). [Treas Reg § 1.414(l)-1(m)]

3. Two or more defined benefit plans (see Q 2:3) are merged into one defined benefit plan, and both of the following conditions are met:

    a. The total liabilities (the present value of benefits, whether or not vested; see Q 9:1) that are merged into the larger plan involved in the merger are less than 3 percent of the assets of the larger plan. This condition must be satisfied on at least one day in the larger plan's plan year during which the merger occurs.

    b. The provisions of the larger plan that allocate assets upon termination must provide that, in the event of a spinoff or termination of the plan within five years following the merger, plan assets will be allocated first for the benefits of the participants in the other plan(s) to the extent of the present value of their benefits as of the date of the merger. [Treas Reg § 1.414(l)-1(h)]

4. There is a spinoff of a defined benefit plan into another defined benefit plan, and both of the following conditions are met:

    a. With respect to each resulting spinoff plan, other than the spinoff plan with the greatest value of plan assets after the spinoff, the value of the assets spun off is not less than the present value of the benefits spun off (whether or not vested).

    b. The value of the assets spun off to all the resulting spinoff plans (other than the spinoff plan with the greatest value of plan assets after the spinoff) plus other assets previously spun off during the plan year in which the spinoff occurs is less than 3 percent of the assets of the plan before the spinoff as of at least one day in that plan's plan year. [Treas Reg § 1.414(l)-1(n)(2)]

A transfer of assets or liabilities is considered to be a combination of separate mergers and spinoffs, and, unless the parts of the transaction that are deemed to be a spinoff or merger conform to one of the situations described above, Form 5310-A must be filed.

Example 1. Plans A, B, and C are separate plans. A portion of the assets and liabilities of both Plan B and Plan C will be transferred to Plan A. None of the plans are excluded from filing under the exceptions. In this situation, three Forms 5310-A must be filed.

Example 2. Plans A, B, and C are separate plans. Plans A, B, and C are being merged. Assets and liabilities from each plan will be merged into Plan D, a new plan that was established for the purpose of effecting the merger. None of the plans are excluded from filing under the exceptions. In this situation, four Forms 5310-A must be filed.

A transferor plan in a spinoff of a defined contribution plan was required to account for changes in the value of assets between the previously agreed upon spinoff date and the actual date of transfer. [The John Blair Consulting, Inc Profit Sharing Plan v Telemundo Group, Inc Profit Sharing Plan, No. 93-7370 (2d Cir 1994)]

Chapter 10

General Distribution Requirements

Numerous rules govern the timing and form of benefit distributions. This chapter examines qualified joint and survivor annuity (QJSA) requirements, qualified preretirement survivor annuity (QPSA) requirements, limits on optional forms of benefit, and related matters.

Q 10:1 Must a qualified retirement plan provide benefits to a participant's surviving spouse?

If a married participant survives until the annuity starting date (see Q 10:3), all vested benefits must, with certain exceptions, be paid in the form of a QJSA (see Q 10:8). If a married participant with vested benefits dies before the annuity starting date, a QPSA (see Q 10:9) must, with certain exceptions, be provided to the participant's surviving spouse. A QPSA must be provided whether or not the participant separated from service before death. The QJSA and the QPSA must be provided by all qualified retirement plans except certain profit sharing plans (see Q 10:6), but may be waived if the applicable notice, election, and spousal consent requirements are satisfied (see Qs 10:20–10:26). Also, the automatic survivor benefit requirements do not apply to a payment of the benefit before the annuity starting date if the present value of the married participant's benefit is $3,500 or less (see Q 10:58). [IRC §§ 401(a)(11), 417]

It is possible that one portion of a married participant's benefit may be subject to a QJSA and another portion to a QPSA at the same time. For example, a participant in a money purchase pension plan (see Q 2:4) may have separate accounts for employer contributions and employee contributions. An in-service withdrawal of the employee contribution account would be subject to the QJSA. The QPSA would apply to the employer contribution account if the participant died prior to the annuity starting date. [Treas Reg § 1.401(a)-20, Q&A 9]

Q 10:2   Must a qualified retirement plan continue to pay benefits to a surviving spouse who remarries?

Yes. The remarriage of a surviving spouse does not affect a qualified retirement plan's obligation to continue to pay benefits to the surviving spouse under the QJSA (see Q 10:8) or QPSA (see Q 10:9). The plan must continue to pay benefits to the surviving spouse as long as the participant and surviving spouse are married on the date of the participant's death with respect to a QPSA, and on the annuity starting date (see Q 10:3) with respect to a QJSA (see Q 10:19). [Treas Reg § 1.401(a)-20, Q&A 25(b)]

Q 10:3   What is the annuity starting date?

The annuity starting date is the first day of the first period for which a benefit is payable as an annuity. For benefits payable in any other form, it is the first day on which all events have occurred that entitle the participant to the benefit. For example, if an annuity is scheduled to begin on January 1, 1997, the annuity starting date is January 1, 1997, even though the first payment is not made until July 1, 1997. If the benefit is a deferred annuity, the annuity starting date is the date on which the annuity payments are scheduled to commence, not the date that the deferred annuity is elected or the date the deferred annuity contract is distributed. [IRC § 417(f)(2)(A); Treas Reg § 1.401(a)-20, Q&A 10(b)]

There is a special rule that applies to disability benefits. The annuity starting date of a disability benefit is the first day of the first period for which the disability benefit becomes payable, unless it is an auxiliary benefit. An auxiliary disability benefit is disregarded in determining the annuity starting date. A disability benefit is considered auxiliary if it is not taken into account in determining the disabled participant's retirement benefit under the plan. [IRC § 417(f)(2)(B); Treas Reg § 1.401(a)-20, Q&A 10(c)]

Q 10:4   What is the significance of the annuity starting date to survivor benefit requirements?

The annuity starting date (see Q 10:3) determines whether benefits are payable as a QJSA (see Q 10:8), QPSA (see Q 10:9), or any other selected optional form of benefit. If a participant is living on the annuity starting date, the benefits must be payable as a QJSA. If the participant dies before the annuity starting date, the surviving spouse must receive a QPSA.

The annuity starting date is also relevant in determining when a participant may waive a QJSA and when a spouse may consent to the waiver. Such waivers and consents are effective only if made within 90 days before the annuity starting date (see Q 10:20). Since, under a deferred annuity, the annuity starting date is the date on which the payments are to commence (see Q 10:3), the QJSA cannot be waived until 90 days before such time. [Treas Reg § 1.401(a)-20, Q&A 10(a)]

Q 10:5   How do the automatic survivor benefit requirements apply to unmarried participants?

A QJSA (see Q 10:8) for an unmarried participant is a life annuity (i.e., payments cease on the participant's death). Thus, an unmarried participant must be provided with a life annuity unless the participant elects another form of benefit.

There is no requirement to provide a QPSA (see Q 10:9) with respect to an unmarried participant who dies before the annuity starting date (see Q 10:3). [Treas Reg § 1.401(a)-20, Q&A 25(a)]

However, one court concluded that a beneficiary designated by an unmarried participant, who later married, was entitled to the death benefit under the plan because the spousal consent requirement (see Q 10:21) was inapplicable to an unmarried participant and the marriage did not nullify the earlier designation. [Kartiganer v Bloom, No. 66606 (NY App Div, 3d Dept, 1993)]

Q 10:6   Are all qualified retirement plans required to provide automatic survivor benefits?

The automatic survivor benefit requirements (see Q 10:1) apply to defined benefit plans (see Q 2:3) and also to defined contribution plans subject to minimum funding requirements (i.e., money purchase pension and target benefit plans; see Q 8:1).

The automatic survivor benefit requirements also apply to participants in a profit sharing plan (see Q 2:6), stock bonus plan (see Q 2:13), or a 401(k) plan (see Q 2:12) *unless:*

1. The plan provides that, upon the participant's death, the participant's vested benefit (reduced by any security interest held by the plan by reason of a loan outstanding to such participant) is payable in full to the participant's surviving spouse (unless the participant has elected with spousal consent that such benefit be paid instead to a designated beneficiary) (see Q 10:18);

2. The participant does not elect the payment of benefits in the form of a life annuity; and

3. With respect to the participant, the plan is not a direct or indirect transferee plan (see Q 10:13) or a floor-offset arrangement (see Q 10:14).

[IRC § 401(a)(11); Treas Reg § 1.401(a)-20, Q&A 3(a)]

If a participant elects a life annuity option provided by a plan otherwise exempt from the automatic survivor benefit requirements, the participant's benefits under the plan will be subject to automatic survivor requirements thereafter. Generally, plans eligible to avoid the automatic survivor benefit requirements will offer benefits only in the form of a single-sum distribution or over a fixed period that is less than the participant's life expectancy. [Treas Reg § 1.401(a)-20, Q&A 4]

Q 10:7 Are there any other conditions that must be satisfied, with respect to a participant, to be exempt from the automatic survivor rules?

Yes. In order for a participant in a profit sharing plan (or other defined contribution plan not subject to the minimum funding standards) (see Q 10:6) to be exempt from the automatic survivor rules:

1. The benefit payable to the participant's surviving spouse must be available within a reasonable period after the participant's death (whether the period is reasonable will be determined on the basis of facts and circumstances; however, 90 days will be deemed to be reasonable); and

2. The benefit must be adjusted for gains or losses occurring after the participant's death in accordance with plan provisions specifying the adjustment of account balances for other plan distributions.

[Treas Reg § 1.401(a)-20, Q&A 3(b)]

Q 10:8 What is a qualified joint and survivor annuity?

A QJSA is an immediate annuity for the life of the participant, with a survivor annuity for the life of the participant's spouse. The amount of the survivor annuity may not be less than 50 percent, nor more than 100 percent, of the amount of the annuity payable during the time that the participant and spouse are both alive. The QJSA must be at least the actuarial equivalent of an annuity for the life of the participant only. [IRC § 417(b)]

A qualified retirement plan may have more than one form of joint and survivor annuity satisfying the QJSA requirements. In that event, the joint and survivor annuity with the greatest actuarial value is the QJSA. If one or more are actuarially equivalent, the plan must designate which one is the automatic form of payment. In any event, the QJSA for a married participant must be at least equal to the most valuable optional form of benefit payable to the participant at the time of the election. [IRC § 417(b); Treas Reg § 1.401(a)-20, Q&A 16]

A participant must be allowed to receive a QJSA at the participant's earliest retirement age, which is generally the earliest date on which the participant could receive a distribution from the plan. The participant (but not the participant's spouse) must consent to the distribution in the form of a QJSA before the participant's benefits are immediately distributable. A participant's benefits are immediately distributable at the later of normal retirement age (see Q 10:53) or age 62. Once benefits are immediately distributable, a QJSA may be distributed without the participant's consent (but see Qs 10:33–10:48 on optional forms of benefit). Distributions may not be made at any time in a form other than a QJSA unless the participant so elects and the participant's spouse consents. [Treas Reg §§ 1.401(a)-20, Q&A 17, 1.417(e)-1(b)]

Q 10:9   What is a qualified preretirement survivor annuity?

A QPSA is an immediate annuity for the life of the surviving spouse of a participant who dies before the annuity starting date (see Q 10:3). Under a QPSA, each payment to the surviving spouse will be the same as (or the actuarial equivalent of) the payment that would have been made to the surviving spouse under the plan's QJSA (see Q 10:8) if:

1. In the case of a participant who dies after attaining the earliest retirement age (see Q 10:8) under the plan, the participant had retired with an immediate QJSA on the day before the participant's death.

2. In the case of a participant who dies upon or before attaining the earliest retirement age under the plan, the participant had: (a) separated from service on the date of death, (b) survived to the earliest retirement age, (c) retired with an immediate QJSA at the earliest retirement age, and (d) died on the day after the day on which the earliest retirement age would have been attained. (If the participant had separated from service prior to death, the amount of the QPSA is calculated by reference to the actual date of separation from service rather than the date of death to prevent the participant from accruing benefits after separation from service.)

Example. Dan, who is married, participates in a pension plan, and early retirement age under the plan is age 50. The plan must provide automatic survivor coverage in the form of a QJSA and a QPSA. In 1997, Dan reaches age 50 but does not elect early retirement. Although Dan continues to work after age 50, a QPSA must be provided for his wife in the event that he dies before he retires.

The QPSA may be payable from a defined benefit plan (see Q 2:3) to the surviving spouse at any time, but must be available to the surviving spouse no later than the month in which the participant would have reached the earliest retirement age under the plan. A defined benefit plan may provide that the QPSA is forfeited if the surviving spouse does not survive until the QPSA is payable under the plan. Similarly, the plan may provide that the QPSA is forfeited if the surviving spouse elects to defer payment of the QPSA but does not survive until the deferred commencement date. [IRC § 417(c); Treas Reg § 1.401(a)-20, Q&A 18, 19, 22(a)]

The QPSA provided under a defined contribution plan (see Q 2:2) must be available to the surviving spouse within a reasonable time after the participant's death (see Q 10:7). The QPSA may not be less valuable than 50 percent of the vested account balance of the participant as of the date of the participant's death. A defined contribution plan may *not* provide that the QPSA is forfeited if the surviving spouse does not survive until the QPSA is payable under the plan. [IRC § 417(c)(2); Treas Reg § 1.401(a)-20, Q&A 20, 22(b)]

Q 10:10 How is a survivor annuity treated for estate tax purposes?

The value of a surviving spouse's interest in a QJSA (see Q 10:8) or QPSA (see Q 10:9) is included in the participant's gross estate for estate tax purposes. The marital deduction is allowable unless the deceased participant's executor elects not to take the deduction (see Qs 14:18, 14:20). [IRC §§ 2039, 2056(b)(7)(C)]

Q 10:11 What is the effect of a loan on the amount of a QJSA or QPSA?

In determining the amount of the QJSA (see Q 10:8) or QPSA (see Q 10:9), the accrued benefit (see Q 9:2) is reduced by any security interest held by the plan by reason of a loan outstanding to the participant if, at the date of death or benefit payment, the security interest is treated as payment of the loan under the plan. The plan may offset any loan outstanding at the participant's death that is secured by the participant's account balance against the spousal benefit. [IRC § 417(c)(3); Treas Reg § 1.401(a)-20, Q&A 24(d)]

Q 10:12 Is spousal consent necessary for plan loans?

Yes, if the participant's accrued benefit (see Q 9:2) is used as security for the loan. Consent is required even if the accrued benefit is not the primary security for the loan. Spousal consent is not required, however, if the total accrued benefit subject to the security is $3,500 or less (see Q 10:58). Spousal consent must be obtained within 90 days of the date that the loan is so secured, and in the same manner as the consent to the waiver of the QJSA (see Q 10:8) or QPSA (see Q 10:9) is obtained (see Q 10:21). For purposes of spousal consent, any renegotiation, extension, renewal, or other revision of a loan is treated as a new loan. [Treas Reg § 1.401(a)-20, Q&A 24]

Q 10:13 What is a transferee plan?

Although profit sharing plans, stock bonus plans, and 401(k) plans are generally not subject to the automatic survivor benefit requirements (see Qs 10:1, 10:6), these plans become subject to such requirements to the extent the plan is a transferee plan with respect to any participant. A plan is a transferee plan with respect to a participant if it is a direct or indirect transferee of that participant's benefits held on or after January 1, 1985 by one of the following:

- A defined benefit plan
- A defined contribution plan subject to the minimum funding standards (see Q 8:1), or
- A defined contribution plan that is subject to the automatic survivor benefit requirements with respect to that participant

Neither a transfer made before 1985 nor a rollover contribution (see Q 28:1) made by a participant at any time is treated as a transfer that subjects a plan to the survivor benefit rules with respect to the participant. Even if a plan is a transferee plan with respect to a participant, the automatic survivor benefit requirements apply only to benefits attributable to the transferred assets, as long as there is an acceptable separate accounting between the transferred assets and other plan benefits. If a separate accounting is not maintained for the transferred assets, the survivor benefit requirements apply to all benefits payable with respect to the participant under the plan. [IRC § 401(a)(11)(B)(iii)(III); Treas Reg § 1.401(a)-20, Q&A 5]

Q 10:14   Do the automatic survivor annuity requirements apply to floor-offset plans?

Yes. If benefits of a plan not otherwise subject to the survivor annuity requirements (see Qs 10:1, 10:6) are used to offset benefits that would otherwise accrue under a plan subject to the survivor annuity requirements (e.g., a defined benefit plan), the floor-offset plan (see Q 2:21) will be subject to the survivor annuity requirements. [Treas Reg § 1.401(a)-20, Q&A 5]

Q 10:15   Must annuity contracts distributed to a participant or spouse by a plan satisfy the automatic survivor benefit requirements?

Yes. If a plan is required to provide automatic survivor benefits (see Q 10:1), such benefits may not be eliminated or reduced because the plan uses annuity contracts to provide benefits or because such a contract is held by a participant or spouse instead of a plan trustee. [Treas Reg § 1.401(a)-20, Q&A 2]

Q 10:16   Must a frozen or terminated plan provide automatic survivor benefits?

Benefits under a plan that is subject to the survivor benefit requirements must be provided in the form of a QJSA (see Q 10:8) or QPSA (see Q 10:9) even if the plan is frozen or terminated. [Treas Reg § 1.401(a)-20, Q&A 6]

Q 10:17   Does it make any difference if PBGC is administering the plan?

No. If PBGC (see Q 21:10) is administering a plan, it will pay benefits in the form of a QJSA (see Q 10:8) or QPSA (see Q 10:9). [Treas Reg § 1.401(a)-20, Q&A 7]

Q 10:18   To which benefits do the automatic survivor rules apply?

Benefits derived from both employer and employee contributions are subject to the automatic survivor benefit requirements (see Q 10:1).

For defined benefit plans (see Q 2:3), the automatic survivor benefit requirements apply only to benefits in which the participant was vested immediately before death. They do not apply to benefits to which the participant's beneficiary becomes entitled by reason of death or to the proceeds of a life insurance contract maintained by the plan for the participant to the extent such proceeds exceed the present value of the participant's vested benefits existing immediately before death.

For defined contribution plans (see Q 2:2), the survivor annuity requirements apply to all vested benefits, whether vested before or upon death, including the proceeds of insurance contracts. This rule also applies in determining the vested benefits that must be paid to the surviving spouse under a defined contribution plan exempt from the survivor annuity requirements since such a plan is required to pay all death benefits to the surviving spouse (see Q 10:6). [IRC §§ 401(a)(11), 417(f)(1); Treas Reg § 1.401(a)-20, Q&A 11, 12, 13]

Q 10:19 Can a qualified retirement plan treat married participants as not married under any circumstances?

Yes. A qualified retirement plan is not required to treat a participant as married unless the participant was married throughout the one-year period ending on the earlier of the participant's annuity starting date (see Q 10:3) or date of death. The one-year marriage requirement is optional, and the plan need not contain this one-year provision. However, if the plan contains a one-year marriage requirement and if the participant marries within one year of the annuity starting date and dies after that date, the participant's spouse is still entitled to the QJSA (see Q 10:8), provided the marriage lasted for at least one year. This is true even if the spouse and the participant are not married on the date of the participant's death, except as may be provided in a qualified domestic relations order (QDRO) (see Q 30:1). [IRC § 417(d); Treas Reg § 1.401(a)-20, Q&A 25(b)(2), 25(b)(3); Hinkel v Navistar Int'l Corp, No. 90-3992 (6th Cir 1992); Kyrouac v Northern Illinois Gas Co, No. 91 C 0364 (ND Ill 1991); Enlow v Fire Protection Systems, Inc, No. 91-04080 (ED Mo Ct of App 1991)]

Also, a qualified retirement plan can refuse payment of a survivor annuity to a participant's surviving spouse who pleaded guilty to the murder of the participant. [New Orleans Electrical Pension Fund v Newman, No. 90-1935 (ED La 1992); Ltr Rul 9008079] However, one court ruled that a husband who had not waived his right to survivor benefits (see Q 10:21) was entitled to benefits upon his wife's death despite a state law under which he would forfeit all rights to his wife's property because of his allegedly adulterous conduct. The court held that the state law was preempted by ERISA. [Moore v Philip Morris Cos, Inc, 1993 US App Lexis 26601 (6th Cir 1993)]

Q 10:20   May a participant waive the automatic survivor benefits?

A plan required to provide automatic survivor benefits must also provide the participant with an opportunity to waive the QJSA (see Q 10:8) or the QPSA (see Q 10:9) during the applicable election period. In addition, the participant is permitted to revoke any election during this period. There is no limit on the number of times the participant may waive the QJSA or QPSA or revoke a waiver. [IRC § 417(a)(1)]

The applicable election period is:

1. In the case of a QJSA, the 90-day period ending on the annuity starting date (see Q 10:3), or

2. In the case of a QPSA, the period beginning on the first day of the plan year in which the participant attains age 35 and ending on the date of the participant's death.

[IRC § 417(a)(6); Treas Reg § 1.401(a)-20, Q&A 10, 33]

A plan must provide participants with a written explanation of the QJSA (see Q 10:29) no less than 30 days and no more than 90 days before the annuity starting date. However, if the participant, after having received the written explanation, affirmatively elects a form of distribution and the spouse consents to that form of distribution (see Q 10:21), a plan will not fail to satisfy the notice requirements merely because the annuity starting date is less than 30 days after the written explanation is provided to the participant, provided that the following requirements are met:

1. The plan administrator (see Q 16:1) provides information to the participant clearly indicating that the participant has a right to at least 30 days to consider whether to waive the QJSA and consent to a form of distribution other than a QJSA.

2. The participant is permitted to revoke an affirmative distribution election at least until the annuity starting date or, if later, at any time prior to the expiration of the seven-day period that begins the day after the explanation of the QJSA is provided to the participant.

3. The annuity starting date is after the date that the explanation of the QJSA is provided to the participant. However, the plan may permit the annuity starting date to be before the date that any affirmative distribution election is made by the participant and before the date that the distribution is permitted to commence.

4. Distribution in accordance with the affirmative election does not commence before the expiration of the seven-day period that begins the day after the explanation of the QJSA is provided to the participant.

[Temp Reg § 1.417(e)-IT]

The IRS temporary regulation has been codified by SBA '96 (see Q 1:21), and SBA '96 also provides that a plan is permitted to provide the written explanation of the QJSA after the annuity starting date if the distribution begins at least 30 days after the explanation is provided, subject to the same waiver of the 30-day minimum waiting period as described above. IRS may issue regulations that limit the application of this provision, except that the regulations may not limit the length of time by which the annuity starting date precedes the explanation other than by providing that the annuity starting date may not be earlier than termination of employment. These provisions are effective for plan years beginning after 1996. [IRC § 417(a)(7)(A), as added by SBA '96 § 1451]

> **Example.** Terry, a married participant in a defined benefit plan who has terminated employment, is provided with the explanation of the QJSA on November 28. Terry elects (with spousal consent) on December 2 to waive the QJSA and receive an immediate distribution in the form of a single life annuity. The plan may permit Terry to receive payments with an annuity starting date of December 1, provided that the first payment is made no earlier than December 6 and Terry does not revoke the election before that date. The plan can make the remaining monthly payments on the first day of each month thereafter in accordance with its regular payment schedule.

Q 10:21 Must the participant's spouse consent to the waiver of the QJSA or QPSA?

Yes. A spouse's consent to the participant's waiver of the QJSA (see Q 10:8) or the QPSA (see Q 10:9) is effective only if:

1. The spouse consents to the waiver in writing;
2. The election designates a beneficiary (or a form of benefit) that may not be changed without spousal consent (unless the consent expressly allows such amended designations);
3. The spouse's consent acknowledges the effect of the election; and
4. The consent is witnessed by a plan representative or notary public. [Howard v Branham & Baker Coal Co, 968 F 2d 1214 (6th Cir 1992); Farris v Farris Chemical Co Inc, No. 91-5530 (6th Cir 1992)]

One court held that the lack of notarization did not invalidate the spousal consent with regard to profit sharing plan benefits because the spouse admitted that the signature was his; thus, the benefits were payable to the deceased participant's daughter. In the same case, however, the court also held that the pension plan benefits, despite the spousal consent, were payable to the deceased participant's spouse, and not the daughter, because the plan specified that the QPSA was payable to the surviving spouse and not to a nonspouse beneficiary. [Butler v Encyclopaedia Britannica, Inc, 1994 US App Lexis 33085 (7th Cir 1994)] In another case, the court held that the spousal consent was invalid because the consent form did not acknowledge the effect of the election and was not properly witnessed or notarized. [Lasche v The George W Lasche Basic Retirement Plan, No. 93-8645-Civ (SD Fla 1994)]

The consent must be given within the applicable election period (see Q 10:20). Spousal consent is not required if the participant establishes to the satisfaction of the plan representative that there is no spouse or the spouse cannot be located, or if there is a court order stating that the participant is legally separated or has been abandoned unless a QDRO (see Q 30:1) provides otherwise. Without a court order, the estrangement of a participant and spouse is *not* sufficient reason to avoid the QPSA requirement. A participant's notarized letter alleging that his spouse could not be located was not sufficient because the plan administrator (see Q 16:1) should have protected the spouse's rights by further questioning the participant and trying to contact the spouse at her last known address or telephone number. [IRC § 417(a)(2); Treas Reg § 1.401(a)-20, Q&A 27; Lefkowitz v Arcadia Trading Co Ltd Benefit Pension Plan, 1993 US App Lexis 15138 (2d Cir 1993); Lester v Reagan Equipment Co Profit Sharing Plan & Employee Savings Plan, US Dist Lexis 12872 (ED La 1992)]

If a determination is made that spousal consent is not required, the plan is discharged from liability to the extent of previously made payments. [ERISA § 205(c)(6)] Where a plan mistakenly paid benefits to a participant in the form of a single life annuity because he falsely informed the plan administrator that he was unmarried, the court held that, after the participant's death, the widow was entitled to the payment of survivor benefits after the plan had recovered the amount of the overpayment made to the participant. [Hearn v Western Conference of Teamsters Pension Trust Fund, 1995 US App Lexis 27941 (9th Cir 1995)]

A spouse's consent to the waiver of the QJSA or QPSA is binding only on that spouse; it is not binding on a subsequent spouse of the participant. A plan may preclude a spouse from revoking the consent to the waiver once it has been given, but a plan may also permit a spouse to revoke the consent and render ineffective the participant's prior election to waive the QJSA or QPSA. [Treas Reg § 1.401(a)-20, Q&A 29, 30]

Spousal consent is also required for distributions made in the form of a direct trustee-to-trustee transfer from a qualified retirement plan to an eligible retirement plan (see Q 28:29).

IRS has requested written comments from the public on the question of what information, guidance, and language should be required to be included on the form used by the spouse of a participant in a qualified retirement plan to consent to the waiver by the participant of the requirement that the participant receive benefits in the form of a QJSA. [Notice 94-23, 1994-1 CB 340]

SBA '96 (see Q 1:21) requires IRS, not later than January 1, 1997 to develop sample language for inclusion in a spousal consent form regarding the waiver of the QJSA or QPSA. The sample language must be written in a manner calculated to be understood by the average person and must disclose in plain form whether the waiver is irrevocable or whether it may be revoked by a QDRO. [SBA '96, Act § 1457(a)]

Q 10:22 Is spousal consent contained in an antenuptial agreement effective?

An agreement entered into *prior* to marriage does not satisfy the consent requirement (see Q 10:21) even if the agreement is executed within the applicable election period (see Q 10:20). [Treas Reg § 1.401(a)-20, Q&A 28]

Courts have held the purported waiver to be invalid because the agreement was not signed by the participant's "spouse" since the agreement predated the marriage, another beneficiary was not specified (see Q 10:23), and the agreement did not acknowledge the effect of the waiver (see Q 10:21). [Pedro Enterprises, Inc v Perdue, 998 F 2d 491 (7th Cir 1993); Hurwitz v Sher, 982 F 2d 778 (2d Cir 1992); Richards v Richards, NYLJ (S Ct NY 1995); Nellis v Boeing Co, 1992 WL 122773 (D Kan 1992); but see In re Estate of Hopkins, 574 NE 2d 230 (2d Dist, App Ct of Ill 1991)] However, one court ruled that the surviving spouse would be required to pay plan benefits to the deceased spouse's estate if the surviving spouse had refused to sign a spousal consent form as required by the antenuptial agreement. [Callahan v Hutsell, Callahan & Buchino PSC Revised Profit Sharing Plan, 14 F 3d 600 (6th Cir 1993)]

Q 10:23 Must the waiver of the QJSA or QPSA specify an alternate beneficiary?

Yes. The participant's waiver of a QJSA (see Q 10:8) and QPSA (see Q 10:9), and the spouse's consent, must specify the nonspouse beneficiary (or class of beneficiaries) who will receive the benefit (see Q 10:21). For example, if the spouse consents to the participant's election to have benefits payable upon the participant's death before the annuity starting date (see Q 10:3) paid to the participant's children, the participant may not subsequently change beneficiaries (to someone other than a child) without the consent of the spouse unless the change is back to a QPSA or the spouse gave a general consent (see Q 10:26). If the spouse consents only to the designation of a trust as beneficiary, no further spousal consent to the designation of trust beneficiaries is required. [Treas Reg § 1.401(a)-20, Q&A 31(a)]

Q 10:24   Must the waiver of a QJSA specify the optional form of benefit chosen?

Yes. Both the participant's waiver of a QJSA (see Q 10:8) and the spousal consent must specify the particular optional form of benefit (see Q 10:42). A participant who has waived a QJSA with spousal consent in favor of another form of benefit may not subsequently change the optional form of benefit without the spouse's consent unless the change is back to a QJSA or the spouse gave a general consent (see Q 10:26). If the plan so provides, the participant may change the optional form of benefit after the spouse's death or a divorce (other than as provided in a QDRO; see Q 30:1). [Treas Reg § 1.401(a)-20, Q&A 31(b)(1)]

Q 10:25   Must the waiver of a QPSA specify the optional form of benefit chosen?

No. A participant's waiver of a QPSA (see Q 10:9) and the spouse's consent need not specify the optional form of any preretirement benefit. A participant may subsequently change the form of the preretirement benefit without obtaining further spousal consent. However, the participant may not change the nonspouse beneficiary without spousal consent unless there was a general consent (see Qs 10:23, 10:26). [Treas Reg § 1.401(a)-20, Q&A 31(b)(2)]

Q 10:26   May a plan allow a spouse to give general consent to waive a QJSA or QPSA?

Yes, a plan may permit a spouse to execute a general consent. A general consent will enable the participant to waive a QJSA (see Q 10:8) or QPSA (see Q 10:9) and change the optional form of benefit or a designated beneficiary without further spousal consent. Alternatively, the spouse may give a limited general consent; that is, the spouse consents only to changes with respect to certain beneficiaries or forms of benefits.

A general consent executed after October 21, 1986 will not be valid unless the general consent acknowledges that the spouse (1) has the right to limit consent to a specific beneficiary and a specific optional form of benefit, and (2) voluntarily elects to relinquish both such rights. A general consent, including a limited general consent, is effective only if it is made during the applicable election period (see Q 10:20). [Treas Reg § 1.401(a)-20, Q&A 31(c)]

Q 10:27 Does the nonparticipant spouse's consent to the waiver of a QJSA or a QPSA by the participant result in a taxable gift?

No. Such consent by the nonparticipant spouse before the participant's death does not result in a taxable transfer for purposes of the gift tax. After the participant's death, the surviving spouse may be able to disclaim the survivor benefit and avoid the gift tax. [IRC §§ 2503(f), 2518]

Q 10:28 Should the plan document specifically set forth the spousal consent rules?

It is highly recommended to ensure that plan representatives obtain valid spousal consents. One court ordered a plan to pay the QPSA (see Q 10:9) to the surviving spouse because the plan "by its own terms" did not require that spousal consent meet the requirements of the Code and ERISA. [Profit-Sharing Plan for Employees of Republic Financial Servs, Inc v MBank Dallas, NA, 683 F Supp 592 (ND Tex 1988)]

Q 10:29 Must participants be notified of the QJSA?

A plan that is required to provide a QJSA (see Qs 10:6, 10:8, 10:20) must give each participant a written explanation of:

1. The terms and conditions of the QJSA;
2. The participant's right to make, and the effect of, an election to waive the QJSA;
3. The rights of the participant's spouse; and
4. The right to make, and the effect of, a revocation of an election.

Participants must also be furnished with a general description of the eligibility conditions and other material features of the optional forms of benefit, as well as sufficient information to explain the relative values of the optional forms of benefit. This explanation must be given to the participant within a reasonable period before the annuity starting date (see Q 10:3). The plan must provide this explanation to both vested and nonvested participants. [IRC § 417(a)(3)(A); Treas Reg §§ 1.401(a)-11(c), 1.401(a)-20, Q&A 34, 36]

Q 10:30 Must participants be notified of the QPSA?

A plan that is required to provide a QPSA (see Qs 10:6, 10:9) must give each participant a written explanation of the QPSA similar to the explanation required for the QJSA (see Q 10:29). This explanation must be given to both vested and nonvested participants within whichever of the following applicable periods ends last with respect to a participant:

1. The period beginning with the first day of the plan year in which the participant attains age 32 and ending at the end of the plan year preceding the plan year in which the participant attains age 35;

2. The period beginning one year before and ending one year after the individual becomes a participant;

3. The period beginning one year before and ending one year after the survivor benefit applicable to the participant is no longer subsidized (see Q 10:31);

4. The period beginning one year before and ending one year after the survivor benefit requirements become applicable to the participant; or

5. In the case of a participant who separates from service before age 35, the period beginning one year before and ending one year after the separation.

[IRC § 417(a)(3)(B); Treas Reg § 1.401(a)-20, Q&A 35, 36]

Q 10:31 What happens if the plan fully subsidizes the cost of the QJSA or QPSA?

If a plan fully subsidizes a QJSA (see Q 10:8) or QPSA (see Q 10:9) and does not permit a participant to waive the benefit or to designate another beneficiary, it need not provide the required written explanation (see Qs 10:29, 10:30). If a plan that subsidizes the cost of the QJSA or QPSA offers such election, the plan must satisfy the election, consent, and notice requirements. [IRC § 417(a)(5); Treas Reg § 1.401(a)-20, Q&A 37]

A fully subsidized QJSA is one under which no increase in cost or decrease in benefits to the participant could possibly result from the participant's failure to elect another benefit. For example, if a plan provides a joint and survivor annuity and a lump-sum option, the plan does not fully subsidize the joint and survivor annuity (even if the actuarial value of the joint and survivor annuity is greater than the amount of the lump-sum payment) because, in the event of the participant's early death, the participant would have received less under the annuity than under the lump-sum option. Similarly, if a plan provides for a life annuity of $100 per month and a joint and 100 percent survivor benefit of $99 per month, the plan is not fully subsidizing the joint and survivor benefit.

A QPSA is fully subsidized if the participant's benefit is not reduced because of the QPSA coverage and the participant is not charged for the QPSA coverage. Therefore, a QPSA is fully subsidized in a defined contribution plan because the participant's account balance is not reduced by the QPSA coverage and no charge is made against the account for such coverage. [Treas Reg § 1.401(a)-20, Q&A 38]

Q 10:32   When did the survivor annuity benefit requirements become effective?

The survivor annuity benefit provisions generally became effective for plan years beginning after 1984, but the spousal-consent rules (see Q 10:21) became effective on January 1, 1985. Thus, a waiver by a participant made in 1985, but before the first day of the first plan year to which the survivor annuity benefit provisions apply, is not effective unless the participant's spouse subsequently consents to the election. A participant's election to waive the QPSA (see Q 10:9), and spousal consent to the waiver made before August 23, 1984 (the effective date of REA), are not valid; a new election and consent must be executed by the participant and the participant's spouse. [REA §§ 302(a), 303(c)(3); Treas Reg § 1.401(a)-20, Q&A 39, 43, 44; Ltr Rul 9008003; Lucaskevge v Mollenberg, 11 EBC 1355 (WD NY 1989); The Manitowac Eng'g and Salaried Employees' Deferred Profit Sharing Plan v Powalisz, 8 EBC 1094 (D Wis 1987)]

Q 10:33   Can a qualified retirement plan provide optional ways in which to pay benefits?

Yes. However, the optional forms of benefit provided by a qualified retirement plan must comply with IRS guidelines. Generally, each optional form of benefit must (1) be provided in a way that does not discriminate in favor of highly compensated employees (see Qs 3:2, 4:9, 4:18, 10:34–10:41), and (2) be available to eligible employees without employer discretion (see Qs 10:42–10:48). [IRC §§ 401(a)(4), 411(d)(6); Treas Reg §§ 1.401(a)(4)-4, 1.401(a)-4, 1.411(d)-4]

If a plan offers optional forms of benefit, the different forms must be actuarially equivalent and the plan must specify the actuarial assumptions to be used in calculating the equivalent benefits. [IRC § 401(a)(25); Rev Rul 79-90, 1979-1 CB 155]

Q 10:34   Can a plan permit optional forms of benefit payment that favor highly compensated employees?

No. A qualified retirement plan must provide benefits that do not discriminate in favor of highly compensated employees (see Qs 3:2, 4:9). If a plan provides for optional forms of benefit payment—for example, different forms of distribution commencing at the same time or the same form of distribution commencing at different times—the availability of each of these optional forms of benefit payment is subject to this nondiscrimination requirement (see Q 4:18). This is true whether or not the particular benefit option is the actuarial equivalent (see Qs 2:18, 2:19) of any other form of benefit under the plan. To meet the nondiscrimination requirement, the optional form of benefit must be both currently available (see Q 10:35) and effectively available (see Q 10:36) in a nondiscriminatory manner. It is not necessary, however, to apply a nondiscriminatory test to the actual receipt of each optional form of benefit. [IRC § 401(a)(4); Treas Reg §§ 1.401(a)(4)-4(b), 1.401(a)(4)-4(c), 1.401(a)-4, Q&A 1, 2]

Q 10:35   How is the determination made as to whether the current availability of an optional form of benefit is nondiscriminatory?

An optional form of benefit must be currently available to a group of employees that satisfies one of the minimum coverage tests (see Q 5:15). Generally, current availability is determined on the basis of current facts and circumstances. However, certain specified conditions on the availability of an optional form of benefit (e.g., minimum age or service, disability, hardship, vesting, family status, or waiver of rights under federal or state law) are disregarded in determining whether a benefit is currently available to an employee.

If an employer eliminates an optional form of benefit with respect to *future* benefit accruals, the current availability test is treated as satisfied for all years after the elimination if the optional form satisfied the nondiscrimination requirement immediately prior to its elimination.

Example. A profit sharing plan that provided for a lump-sum distribution available to all employees on termination of employment was amended in 1995 to eliminate the lump-sum option with respect to benefits accrued after December 31, 1995. As of December 31, 1995, the lump-sum optional form of benefit was available to a group of employees that satisfied the ratio percentage test (see Q 5:16). As of January 1, 1997, all non-highly compensated employees (see Q 3:13) who were entitled to the lump-sum optional form of benefit have terminated employment and taken a distribution of their benefits. The only remaining employees who are eligible to take a portion of their benefits in a lump sum on termination of employment are highly compensated employees (see Q 3:2). Because the availability of the lump-sum optional form of benefit satisfied the current availability test as of December 31, 1995, the availability of such optional form of benefit will be deemed to continue to satisfy the current availability test.

[Treas Reg §§ 1.401(a)(4)-4(b), 1.401(a)-4, Q&A 2(a), 2(b)]

Q 10:36 How is the determination made as to whether the effective availability of an optional form of benefit is nondiscriminatory?

This determination must be based on all the surrounding facts and circumstances of the employer maintaining the plan. A condition with respect to the availability of a particular optional form of benefit payment violates the effective availability test if it substantially favors highly compensated employees (see Q 3:2).

Example. Gaby Corporation maintains a qualified retirement plan in which all of its eligible employees participate. Under the plan, a participant is entitled to receive a retirement benefit at age 65. Also, an employee who terminates employment after age 55 with at least 30 years of service may also receive early retirement benefits. Both of Gaby Corporation's highly compensated employees, but only two of Gaby Corporation's eight non-highly compensated employees (see Q 3:13), may become eligible to receive early retirement benefits because they were hired before age 35. Even though the early retirement benefit is currently available to all participants, because age and service requirements are disregarded, it does not meet the effective availability test because the availability conditions substantially favor highly compensated employees.

[Treas Reg §§ 1.401(a)(4)-4(c), 1.401(a)-4, Q&A 2(a)(3)]

Q 10:37 May a qualified retirement plan deny a participant an optional form of benefit payment for which the participant is otherwise eligible?

No. Even though this type of provision may satisfy the nondiscrimination requirements in certain circumstances, such a provision impermissibly results in the employer or some person other than the participant having discretion as to the optional form of benefit payment (see Q 10:44). [IRC § 411(d)(6)]

Q 10:38   Will a qualified retirement plan be considered discriminatory if it requires that an involuntary distribution be made?

No. A qualified retirement plan will not be treated as discriminatory merely because it provides for an involuntary distribution if the present value of an employee's benefit is $3,500 or less (see Q 10:58). Thus, a plan may require a lump-sum distribution to terminating employees whose benefits have a present value of $3,500 or any lower amount. However, this rule does not permit employer discretion in deciding whether or not to cash out involuntarily a terminating employee and does not apply to distributions after the annuity starting date (see Q 10:3). [IRC §§ 411(a)(11), 417(e); Treas Reg §§ 1.401(a)(4)-4(b)(2)(ii)(C), 1.401(a)-4, Q&A 4, 1.411(d)-4, Q&A 2(b)(2)(v)]

Q 10:39   What are the effective dates for the optional forms of benefit payment nondiscrimination rules?

Old Treasury Regulations Section 1.401(a)-4 on discrimination in optional forms of benefit payment became effective January 30, 1986, with respect to new plans (i.e., plans either adopted or made effective on or after such date).

With respect to existing plans—i.e., plans both adopted and in effect prior to January 30, 1986—the old regulations were effective for the first day of the first plan year commencing on or after January 1, 1989. The delayed effective date for existing plans was applicable only if the optional form of benefit and any condition causing the availability of such optional form of benefit to be discriminatory were both adopted and in effect before January 30, 1986. Otherwise, the rules became effective with respect to such optional form of benefit payment as if the plan were a new plan. [Treas Reg § 1.401(a)-4, Q&A 6]

New Treasury Regulations Section 1.401(a)(4)-4 became effective for plan years beginning on or after January 1, 1994. Plans must comply with the old regulations until the 1994 plan year and the reasonable, good-faith standard (see Q 4:22) does not apply with respect to the old regulations during the transition years (1989–1993).

For plan years beginning on or after January 1, 1994, the new regulations will apply with respect to plan benefits, rights, and features. In addition to incorporating the relevant rules concerning optional forms of benefit provided in the old regulations, the new regulations require that each optional form of benefit subject to different terms affecting the value of the optional form of benefit (such as actuarial assumptions or the method of benefit calculation) separately satisfy Section 401(a)(4) with respect to its availability. This standard does not apply to the transition years. Similarly, the new regulations provide rules with respect to nondiscriminatory availability of ancillary benefits and other rights and features that are effective beginning in 1994. During the transition years, provisions relating to these benefits, rights, and features are subject to the general nondiscrimination requirements of Section 401(a)(4) and the good-faith standard is applicable. [Treas Reg § 1.401(a)(4)-13; Notice 92-36, 1992-2 CB 364; Ann 92-29, 1992-9 IRB 37; IRS Field Office Directive on Good-Faith Compliance (June 12, 1992)]

Q 10:40 Can a qualified retirement plan containing discriminatory optional forms of benefits be amended?

Yes. If the availability of an optional form of benefit in an existing qualified retirement plan is discriminatory, the plan must be amended either to eliminate the optional form or to make the availability of the optional form nondiscriminatory. The availability of an optional form of benefit may be made nondiscriminatory by making the benefit available to a sufficient number of additional non-highly compensated employees (see Q 3:13) or by imposing nondiscriminatory objective criteria on its availability so that the group of employees to whom the benefit is available is nondiscriminatory. The plan sponsor may also amend the plan in that manner if the availability of an optional form of benefit may reasonably be expected to discriminate.

The plan sponsor must have selected one of the alternatives with respect to each affected optional form on or before the applicable effective date (see Q 10:39) for the plan.

Certain corrective amendments to the availability of an optional form of benefit are permitted. Because it is difficult or impossible, in many cases, to make an optional form of benefit meaningfully available on a retroactive basis, a corrective amendment increasing availability is required only on a prospective basis. However, in order to take the correction into account for a plan year, the group of employees to whom the optional form is available (after taking the amendment into account) generally must satisfy a nondiscriminatory requirement. In addition, the amendment must remain in effect until the end of the plan year following the year in which the amendment is effective and must not be part of a pattern of amendments used to correct repeated failures. Other rules relating to retroactive correction also apply (e.g., the requirement that the correction be made no later than the 15th day of the tenth month after the close of a plan year).

As an alternative to increasing availability, an employer may make a corrective amendment by the last day of the plan year eliminating the optional form of benefit (to the extent permitted under Section 411(d)(6)). In that case, the amendment will be treated as if it were in effect throughout the plan year for purposes of nondiscrimination testing.

[Treas Reg § 1.401(a)(4)-11(g)]

Q 10:41   Should the plan administrator provide any notice that the qualified retirement plan's optional forms of benefit are being modified?

Yes. Although there is no special reporting requirement regarding modification of a qualified retirement plan's optional forms of benefit, a plan administrator (see Q 16:1) is required to file with DOL and to furnish to participants a summary of material modifications within 210 days after the close of the plan year in which the modification is adopted (see Qs 18:8, 18:9).

However, even before a modification is formally adopted, it is prudent for the plan administrator to give prompt notice of any such modification to participants. Giving prompt notice to participants would reconcile the conflict between ERISA's mandate that the plan be administered in accordance with the terms of its plan documents and IRS's operational requirement that the plan be administered consistent with a conforming plan amendment that has not yet been adopted. [ERISA §§ 104, 404(a)(1)(D); DOL Reg § 2520.104b-3]

Q 10:42   What are Section 411(d)(6) protected benefits?

Accrued benefits, early retirement benefits, retirement-type subsidies, and optional forms of benefit are Section 411(d)(6) protected benefits that may not be eliminated, reduced, or made subject to employer discretion except to the extent permitted by regulations (see Q 10:40). [IRC § 411(d)(6); Treas Reg § 1.411(d)-4, Q&A 1(a); Costantino v TRW Inc, 1993 US App Lexis 29479 (6th Cir 1993); Gillis v Hoechst Celanese Corp, 1993 US App Lexis 22527 (3d Cir 1993); Counts v Kissack Water and Oil Service, Inc, No. 92-8036 (10th Cir 1993); Davis v Burlington Industries, Inc, No. 91-1725 (4th Cir 1992); Auwarter v Donohue Paper Sales Corp Defined Benefit Pension Plan, No. 91-3082 (ED NY 1992); Rev Rul 85-6, 1985-1 CB 133; Rev Proc 92-10, 1992-1 CB 661] See Q 9:30 for examples of benefits that are not Section 411(d)(6) protected benefits; note that there appears to be a conflict among various courts.

An optional form of benefit is a form of distribution of benefits from a qualified retirement plan that is identical with respect to all features relating to the specified distribution form. The plan provides separate optional forms of benefit to the extent there are any differences in any features relating to the form of distribution, including payment schedule, timing, commencement, medium of distribution, portion of the benefit to which such distribution features apply, and election rights with respect to such features. [Treas Reg §§ 1.411(d)-4, Q&A 1(b), 1.401(a)(4)-4(e)]

Example 1. A plan permits each participant to receive a benefit under the plan as a lump-sum distribution, a level monthly distribution over ten years, a single life annuity, a joint and 50 percent survivor annuity, a joint and 75 percent survivor annuity, a joint and 50 percent survivor annuity with a benefit increase for the participant if the beneficiary dies before a specified date, or a joint and 50 percent survivor annuity with a ten-year certain feature. Each of these forms of benefit payment is an optional form of benefit, whether or not their values are actuarially equivalent.

Example 2. A plan provides a single life annuity that begins in the month of termination of employment and a single life annuity that begins after five consecutive one-year breaks in service (see Q 5:10). They are optional benefit forms because they begin at different times.

Example 3. A profit sharing plan permits loans that are secured by an employee's account balance. In the event of default on such a loan, there is an execution on the account balance. Such execution is a distribution of the employee's accrued benefit under the plan. A distribution of an accrued benefit contingent on default under a plan loan secured by such accrued benefits is an optional form of benefit under the plan.

Q 10:43 Can a pattern of plan amendments result in an optional form of benefit?

Yes. Generally, benefits are considered to be provided as an optional form of benefit only if such optional form is provided under the terms of the qualified retirement plan. If, however, an employer establishes a pattern of repeated plan amendments providing for similar benefits in similar situations for limited periods of time, those benefits may be treated as provided under the terms of the plan without regard to the limited periods of time. For example, a pattern of repeated plan amendments making single-sum distributions available only to certain participants for a limited period may result in single-sum distributions being treated as provided under the terms of the plan to all participants, without regard to any restrictions provided by the terms of the plan. However, where an employer amended its plan in each of four consecutive plan years to provide an early retirement window benefit, IRS held that the recurrence of the plan amendments did not convert this benefit to a permanent plan feature because the amendments were made in connection with the employer's efforts to reorganize its business, decrease operating costs, and reduce its workforce. [Rev Rul 92-66, 1992-2 CB 92; Treas Reg § 1.411(d)-4, Q&A 1(c)]

Q 10:44   Can a plan provide that the employer may, through the exercise of discretion, deny a participant an optional form of benefit?

Generally, no. A qualified retirement plan that permits an employer, through the exercise of discretion, to deny a participant a Section 411(d)(6) protected benefit (see Q 10:42) violates the anti-cutback rule (see Q 9:24). In other words, to the extent benefits have accrued, the discretionary denial of the optional form of the benefit is not permitted. In addition, a pension plan that permits employer discretion to deny the availability of a Section 411(d)(6) protected benefit will fail to satisfy the requirement that all benefits be definitely determinable. This is so even if the plan specifically limits the employer's discretion to choose among optional forms of benefit that are actuarially equivalent. However, a plan may permit limited administrative discretion (see Q 10:46). [Treas Reg § 1.411(d)-4, Q&A 1, 4(a)]

Q 10:45   When is the exercise of discretion by persons other than the employer treated as employer discretion?

For the purposes of determining impermissible employer discretion, the employer is considered to include a plan administrator (see Q 16:1), fiduciary (see Q 19:1), trustee, actuary, independent third party, and other persons. Thus, if a qualified retirement plan permits any person—other than the participant and the participant's spouse—to exercise discretion to limit or deny the availability of an optional form of benefit, the plan violates these rules. [IRC §§ 401(a), 411(d)(6); Treas Reg § 1.411(d)-4, Q&A 5]

Q 10:46   What is the scope of the administrative discretion exception?

A qualified retirement plan may permit limited discretion with respect to the ministerial or mechanical administration of the plan, including the application of objective plan criteria specifically set forth in the plan. The following are examples of permissible provisions of limited administrative discretion:

1. Commencement of benefit payments as soon as administratively feasible after a stated date or event;

2. Employer authority to determine whether objective criteria specified in the plan (see Q 10:47) have been satisfied; and

3. Employer authority to determine, pursuant to specific guidelines set forth in the plan, whether the participant or spouse is dead or cannot be located.

[Treas Reg § 1.411(d)-4, Q&A 4(b)]

Q 10:47   May a plan condition the availability of a Section 411(d)(6) protected benefit on objective criteria that are specifically set forth in the plan?

The availability of a Section 411(d)(6) protected benefit (see Q 10:42) may be limited to employees who satisfy certain objective conditions. The conditions must be ascertainable, clearly set forth in the qualified retirement plan, and not subject to the employer's discretion, except to the extent reasonably necessary to determine whether the objective conditions are met. In addition, the availability of the Section 411(d)(6) protected benefit must meet the nondiscrimination requirements. [Treas Reg §§ 1.411(d)-4, Q&A 6, 1.401(a)(4)-4, 1.401(a)-4]

For example, a plan may provide that the lump-sum benefit distribution option is not available to participants for whom life insurance is not available at standard rates. A plan may also provide that an otherwise permissible lump-sum distribution option may be available only in the event of extreme financial need, determined under standards specifically set forth in the plan. Another example is a provision making a lump-sum distribution available only upon the execution of a covenant not to compete, provided that the plan sets forth objective conditions with respect to employees required to execute a covenant, its terms, and the circumstances requiring execution of the covenant.

On the other hand, a plan may not condition the availability of Section 411(d)(6) protected benefits on factors that are within the employer's control. For example, the availability of an optional form of benefit payment from a defined benefit plan may not be conditioned on the level of the funding of the plan because the amount of plan funding is within the employer's discretion.

A plan may limit the availability of a Section 411(d)(6) protected benefit (e.g., a lump-sum distribution) in an objective manner. For example, a plan may provide that lump-sum distributions of $25,000 and less are available without limit, and lump-sum distributions in excess of $25,000 are available for a given year only to the extent that the total amount of such distributions for that year does not exceed $5 million. However, the plan must then also provide an objective and nondiscriminatory method for determining which particular lump-sum distributions will and will not be distributed because of the $5 million limitation.

In a case decided before the IRS regulations were issued, a "good health standard" in terms of expected mortality for determining eligibility for lump-sum payments was satisfactory. [Medei v Bethlehem Steel Corp and General Pension Bd, 617 F Supp 372 (ED Pa 1985)]

Q 10:48   May a plan be amended to add employer discretion or other conditions restricting the availability of a Section 411(d)(6) protected benefit?

No. The addition of employer discretion or restrictive conditions with respect to a Section 411(d)(6) protected benefit that has already accrued violates the anti-cutback rule (see Q 9:24). The addition of conditions or the change of any existing conditions, even if they are objective conditions, is impermissible if it results in any further restrictions. However, conditions and restrictions may be imposed prospectively to benefits accrued after the later of the adoption or effective date of the amendment. [Treas Reg § 1.411(d)-4, Q&A 7]

Q 10:49   May participants choose the way benefits will be paid to them?

Yes, if the qualified retirement plan itself provides alternatives, although the participant's spouse may have to consent (see Q 10:21). Retirement benefits are taxed when paid, not if merely made available to the participant. Thus, a deferral of the receipt of benefits also defers the taxation of the benefits. [IRC § 402(a)]

Q 10:50   Is there a limitation on the amount of benefits that may be distributed to an individual in any one year?

No. However, there is a 15 percent tax on the amount of any excess distributions (see Qs 13:27–13:38) made to any individual during any calendar year. [IRC § 4980A(a)]

Q 10:51   When must benefit payments to a participant begin?

The plan must provide that, unless the participant elects to defer payment, payment of benefits to the participant will begin not later than the sixtieth day after the close of the plan year in which the latest of the following events occurs:

1. The participant reaches the plan's normal retirement age (see Q 10:53) or age 65, whichever is earlier;

2. The tenth anniversary of the employee's participation in the plan is reached; or

3. The participant terminates service with the employer.

[IRC § 401(a)(14); Treas Reg § 1.401(a)-14(a); Rev Proc 92-16, 1992-1 CB 673; Rev Proc 92-10, 1992-1 CB 661]

If benefit payments commence after termination of employment and the employee is later reemployed, the plan may, but is not required to, suspend benefit payments. [IRC § 411(a)(3)(B)]

See chapter 11 for details on minimum distribution requirements.

Q 10:52   May a participant defer payment of benefits indefinitely?

No. The qualified retirement plan must provide that (1) the entire interest of the participant be distributed to the participant not later than the required beginning date, or (2) the participant's interest be paid out in installments that start on or before the required beginning date. The installments must be paid over (1) the life of the participant, (2) the lives of the participant and the participant's designated beneficiary, or (3) a period not extending beyond the life expectancy of the participant or the joint life expectancy of the participant and the participant's designated beneficiary. [IRC § 401(a)(9)(A)]

See chapter 11 for details on minimum distribution requirements.

Q 10:53   What does the term normal retirement age mean?

Normal retirement age means the earlier of (1) the time specified in the plan as the normal retirement age, or (2) the later of the time a participant attains age 65 or the fifth anniversary of the participant's date of initial plan participation. A qualified retirement plan must provide that an employee's right to benefits is nonforfeitable once the employee reaches the plan's normal retirement age (see Q 9:12). [IRC §§ 411(a), 411(a)(8)]

Ordinarily, a defined benefit plan uses a normal retirement age of 65. However, a plan will not fail to qualify merely because it provides for a normal retirement age earlier than 65. (Planning aspects relating to the use of a normal retirement age earlier than 65 are discussed in Q 2:36.) [Rev Rul 78-120, 1978-1 CB 117]

Unlike defined benefit plans, the normal retirement age used by a defined contribution plan (see Q 2:2) other than a target benefit plan does not affect the company's plan contribution. Thus, for example, a profit sharing plan may permit a participant to retire at age 55 and receive full benefits under the plan at that time even if employees in the particular industry involved customarily retire at a later age. [Rev Rul 80-276, 1980-2 CB 131]

Q 10:54   May benefits commence earlier than the deadlines required under the law?

Yes. The law and regulations establish only the time by which the plan must begin paying benefits (see Qs 10:51, 10:52). As long as participants are not treated in a discriminatory manner (see Qs 10:34–10:41), benefits may begin earlier.

Generally, defined benefit plans (see Q 2:3) and certain defined contribution plans, including money purchase pension plans (see Q 2:4) and target benefit plans (see Q 2:5), may not make distributions to employees who have not reached normal retirement age (see Q 10:53) or qualified for early retirement benefits (see Q 10:57). However, an employee may receive a distribution if a severance from employment has occurred. A severance from employment occurs during an employer's reorganization (e.g., sale, merger, or liquidation) only if the employee no longer works for an employer sponsoring the plan after the reorganization. An employee who works at the same job for a new employer may receive a distribution from the former employer's plan because the employee's employment has been severed, but the employee may not have had a "separation from service" for the purpose of treating the distribution as a lump-sum distribution (see Qs 13:4, 13:9). [Treas Reg § 1.401-1(b)(1)(i); GCM 39824 (July 6, 1990)]

Plan benefits are taxed only when they are paid to the employee or a beneficiary. They are not taxed if they are merely made available (see Q 10:49). It is not necessary, therefore, to draft a plan so that a participant does not have an absolute, unrestricted right to demand payment of benefits upon satisfying certain plan provisions. [IRC § 402(a)(1)]

Q 10:55   What type of election by the participant is required to postpone the commencement of benefits?

A qualified retirement plan that permits an election by a participant to postpone the receipt of benefits beyond the latest of the three dates referred to in Q 10:51 must require that the election be made by submitting to the plan administrator a written statement (signed by the participant) describing the benefit and the date payments will begin. [Treas Reg § 1.401(a)-14(b)(2)]

However, an election to postpone the payment of benefits cannot be made if it would cause benefits payable under the plan, with respect to the participant, to begin after the required beginning date or to violate the incidental death benefits rule. [Treas Reg § 1.401(a)-14(b)(3)] For details, see chapter 11.

Q 10:56 May a participant receive benefit payments from a pension plan while still employed by the plan sponsor?

Yes, provided the participant has reached the plan's normal or early retirement age. [Rev Rul 80-276, 1980-2 CB 131; Rev Rul 74-254, 1974-1 CB 91; Rev Rul 56-693, 1956-2 CB 282; Ltr Ruls 8311071, 8137048]

If a pension plan is merged into a profit sharing plan, this restriction on distributions continues to apply to the transferred pension plan assets. However, if a participant rolls over pension plan benefits to a profit sharing plan (see Q 28:29), this restriction does *not* apply to the rollover amounts and the profit sharing plan distribution rules apply (see Q 1:32). [Rev Rul 94-76, 1994-2 CB 825]

Q 10:57 Can a qualified retirement plan provide early retirement benefits?

Yes. However, if a defined benefit plan permits a participant to receive an early retirement benefit if the participant meets certain age and service requirements (e.g., age 60 and 10 years of service), the plan must also permit a former participant who fulfilled the service requirement, but separated from service before meeting the age requirement, to receive benefit payments when the former participant meets the age requirement. [IRC § 401(a)(14); Treas Reg § 1.401(a)-14(c)]

Example. The Ruthie Tennis Corporation Defined Benefit Plan provides that a normal retirement benefit will be payable to a participant upon attainment of age 65. The plan also provides that a reduced retirement benefit will be payable, upon application, to any participant who has attained age 60 and completed 10 years of service with Ruthie Tennis Corporation. When Stuart is 55 years of age and has completed 10 years of service with Ruthie Tennis Corporation, he leaves the company and does not return. The plan must provide that Stuart will be entitled to receive a reduced normal retirement benefit when he attains age 60.

A plan was permitted to pay a more valuable early retirement benefit to participants electing periodic payments than to participants electing single-sum distributions. Those electing single-sum distributions received the benefits they were entitled to, but they did not receive the supplemental payments made to the early retirees who elected to receive periodic payments. [DeNobel v Vitro Corp, 885 F 2d 1180 (4th Cir 1989)]

Q 10:58   Can a qualified retirement plan make immediate distributions without the participant's consent?

A qualified retirement plan may provide for an involuntary, immediate distribution of the present value of the benefits under either a QJSA (see Q 10:8) or a QPSA (see Q 10:9) if the present value does not exceed $3,500. The plan may pay benefits in the form of a QJSA or a QPSA at any time after the benefits are no longer immediately distributable (see Q 10:8), whether or not the present value exceeds $3,500. A plan may provide that a participant may elect a QJSA at any time without spousal consent. [IRC § 417(e); Treas Reg § 1.417(e)-1(b)(1)]

If the distribution exceeds $3,500, the participant must consent in writing before a distribution may be made. [Treas Reg §§ 1.411(a)-11(c)(3), 1.417(e)-1(b)(2); Franklin v Thornton, 1993 US App Lexis 211 (9th Cir 1993)] Written consent of the participant to the distribution must not be made before the participant receives the notice of his or her rights and must not be made more than 90 days before the date the distribution commences. A plan must provide participants with notice of their rights no less than 30 days and no more than 90 days before the date the distribution commences. However, if the participant, after having received this notice, affirmatively elects a distribution, a plan will not fail to satisfy the consent requirement merely because the distribution commences less than 30 days after the notice was provided to the participant, provided that the plan administrator (see Q 16:1), informs the participant that the participant has a right to at least 30 days to consider whether to consent to the distribution. [Temp Reg § 1.411(a)-11T(c)]

No single-sum distribution may be made after the annuity starting date (see Q 10:3) unless the participant (and spouse or surviving spouse, if applicable) consents in writing to the distribution, whether or not the present value exceeds $3,500. [IRC §§ 411(a)(11), 417(e); Treas Reg §§ 1.411(a)-11(c)(3), 1.417(e)-1(b)(2)]

For a discussion of the method used to determine present value, see Qs 10:59 and 10:61.

Q 10:59   How is the present value of benefits determined under a defined benefit plan?

A defined benefit plan (see Q 2:3) must provide that the present value of any accrued benefit (see Q 9:2) and the amount of any distribution, including a single sum, must not be less than the amount calculated using the applicable interest rate and the IRS mortality table (see Q 6:10). The present value of any optional form of benefit (see Q 10:33) cannot be less than the present value of the normal retirement benefit determined in accordance with the preceding sentence. The applicable interest rate for a month is the annual interest rate on 30-year Treasury securities as specified by the IRS for that month. [IRC §§ 411(a)(11)(B), 417(e)(3)(A); Temp Reg §§ 1.417(e)-1T(d)(1)-(3); Rev Rul 95-6, 1995-1 CB 452]

> **Example.** JMK Corporation has a defined benefit plan with a calendar-year plan year. The plan uses the IRS mortality table and provides that the applicable interest rate for the plan is the annual interest rate on 30-year Treasury securities as specified by IRS for the first full calendar month preceding the calendar month that contains the annuity starting date (see Q 10:3). Jamie was age 65 in January 1995, the month that contained his annuity starting date. Jamie had a monthly accrued benefit of $1,000 and elected to receive a distribution in the form of a single sum in January 1995. The annual interest rate on 30-year Treasury securities as published by IRS for December 1994 was 7.87 percent. Based upon the applicable interest rate and the IRS mortality table, Jamie could not receive a single-sum distribution of less than $111,351.

The applicable interest rate to be used for a distribution is the rate for the applicable look-back month. The applicable look-back month for a distribution is the look-back month for the month (or other longer stability period) that contains the annuity starting date for the distribution. The time for determining the applicable interest rate for each participant's distribution must be determined in a consistent manner that is applied uniformly to all participants in the plan. A plan must specify the period for which the applicable interest rate remains constant. This stability period may be one calendar month, one plan quarter, or one plan year. A plan must also specify the look-back month that is used to determine the applicable interest rate. The look-back month may be the first, second, third, fourth, or fifth full calendar month preceding the first day of the stability period. [Temp Reg § 1.417(e)-1T(d)(4)]

Example. Steph-Will Corporation maintains a defined benefit plan with a calendar-year plan year. Steph-Will wishes to amend the plan so that the applicable interest rate will remain fixed for each plan quarter, and so that the applicable interest rate for distributions made during each plan quarter can be determined approximately 80 days before the beginning of the plan quarter. Consequently, the plan is amended to provide that the applicable interest rate is the annual interest rate on 30-year Treasury securities as specified by IRS for the fourth calendar month preceding the first day of the plan quarter during which the annuity starting date occurs.

If a plan provides for use of an interest rate or mortality table other than the applicable interest rate or the IRS mortality table, the plan must provide that a participant's benefit must be at least as great as the benefit produced by using the applicable interest rate and the IRS mortality table. For example, where a plan provides for use of an interest rate of 7 percent and the UP-1984 mortality table in calculating single-sum distributions, the plan must provide that any single-sum distribution is calculated as the greater of the single-sum benefit calculated using this actuarial basis (i.e., 7 percent and the UP-1984 mortality table) and the single sum calculated using the applicable interest rate and the IRS mortality table. [Temp Reg § 1.417(e)-1T(d)(5)]

For a discussion of the applicable effective dates of the new present value determination rules, see Q 9:27; and, for a discussion of cash balance plans and the interaction of the new present value determination rules and the anti-cutback rule, see Qs 10:60 and 10:61.

Q 10:60   How is the present value of benefits determined under a cash balance plan?

In general terms, a cash balance plan (see Q 2:22) is a defined benefit plan that defines benefits for each employee by reference to the amount of the employee's hypothetical account balance. An employee's hypothetical account balance is credited with hypothetical allocations and hypothetical earnings determined under a formula set forth in the plan. These hypothetical allocations and hypothetical earnings are designed to mimic the allocations of actual contributions and actual earnings to an employee's account that would occur under a defined contribution plan (see Q 2:2). Cash balance plans often specify that hypothetical earnings (i.e., interest credits) are determined using an interest rate or rate of return under a variable outside index (e.g., the annual yield on one-year Treasury securities). Most cash balance plans also are designed to permit, after termination of employment, a distribution of an employee's entire accrued benefit (see Q 9:2) in the form of a single-sum distribution equal to the employee's hypothetical account balance as of the date of the distribution.

In order to comply with the present value determination rules and the anti-cutback rule in calculating the amount of a single-sum distribution under a cash balance plan, the balance of the employee's hypothetical account must be projected to normal retirement age (see Q 10:53) and then the employee must be paid at least the present value, determined in accordance with the present value determination rules, of that projected hypothetical account balance. If a cash balance plan provides interest credits using an interest rate that is higher than the applicable interest rate, payment of a single-sum distribution equal to the hypothetical account balance as a complete distribution of the employee's accrued benefit may result either in a violation of the present value determination rules or in a violation of the anti-cutback rule. This is because, in such a case, the present value of the employee's accrued benefit, determined using the applicable interest rate, will generally exceed the hypothetical account balance. The following example illustrates this potential problem.

Example. A cash balance plan provides for interest credits at a fixed rate of 8 percent per annum that are not conditioned on continued employment, and for annuity conversions using the applicable interest rate and IRS mortality table. A fully vested employee with a hypothetical account balance of $45,000 terminates employment at age 45 and elects an immediate single-sum distribution. At the time of the employee's termination, the applicable interest rate is 6.5 percent. The projected balance of the employee's hypothetical account as of normal retirement age is $209,743. If $209,743 is discounted to age 45 at 6.5 percent (the applicable interest rate), the present value equals $59,524. Accordingly, if the plan paid the hypothetical account balance of $45,000, instead of $59,524, the employee would receive $14,524 less than the amount to which the employee is entitled.

Even if a cash balance plan provides interest credits using an interest rate that exceeds the applicable interest rate, the plan can satisfy the present value determination and anti-cutback rules. Such a plan would provide that the amount of any single-sum distribution is equal to the present value of the employee's accrued benefit determined in a manner that satisfies these rules, even if the amount of the single sum exceeds the employee's hypothetical account balance. Thus, in the example above, the plan would satisfy these rules if the employee received a single-sum distribution of $59,524 (the present value of the accrued benefit) rather than $45,000 (the hypothetical account balance).

[Notice 96-8 (Jan 18, 1996)]

Q 10:61   Do the new present value determination rules violate the anti-cutback rule?

A plan amendment that changes the interest rate, the time for determining the interest rate, or the mortality assumptions used to determine present value (see Q 10:59) is subject to the anti-cutback rule (see Qs 9:24–9:26). [Temp Reg § 1.417(e)-1T(d)(10)(i)]

If a plan amendment changes the time for determining the applicable interest rate (including an indirect change as a result of a change in plan year), the amendment will not be treated as reducing accrued benefits in violation of the anti-cutback rule merely on account of this change if:

1. Any distribution for which the annuity starting date (see Q 10:3) occurs in the one-year period commencing at the time the plan amendment is effective (if the amendment is effective on or after the adoption date) must use the interest rate as provided under the terms of the plan after the effective date of the amendment, determined at either the date for determining the interest rate before the amendment or the date for determining the interest rate after the amendment, whichever results in the larger distribution.

2. If the plan amendment is adopted retroactively (i.e., the amendment is effective prior to the adoption date), the plan must use the interest rate determination date resulting in the larger distribution for the period beginning with the effective date and ending one year after the adoption date. [Temp Reg § 1.417(e)-1T(d)(10)(ii)]

A participant's accrued benefit is not considered to be reduced in violation of the anti-cutback rule merely because of a plan amendment that changes any interest rate or mortality assumption used to calculate the present value of a participant's benefit under the plan if:

1. The amendment replaces the PBGC interest rate (or an interest rate or rates based on the PBGC interest rate) as the interest rate used under the plan in determining the present value of a participant's benefit, and

2. After the amendment is effective, subject to certain exceptions, the present value of a participant's benefit under the plan cannot be less than the amount calculated using the IRS mortality table and the applicable interest rate for the first full calendar month preceding the calendar month that contains the annuity starting date. [Temp Reg §§ 1.417(e)-1T(d)(10)(iii)(A), 1.417(e)-1T(d)(10)(iii)(C)]

The anti-cutback rule, however, may be violated if a plan amendment replaces an interest rate other than the PBGC interest rate (or an interest rate or rates based on the PBGC interest rate) with another interest rate to be used under the plan in determining the present value of a participant's benefit. An interest rate is deemed based on the PBGC interest rate if the interest rate is defined as a specified percentage of the PBGC interest rate or as the PBGC interest rate minus a specified number of basis points. [Temp Reg § 1.417(e)-1T(d)(10)(iii)(B)]

Example 1. On December 31, 1994, a defined benefit plan provided that all single-sum distributions were to be calculated using the UP-1984 mortality table and the PBGC interest rate for the date of distribution. On January 4, 1995, and effective on February 1, 1995, the plan was amended to provide that all single-sum distributions are calculated using the IRS mortality table and the annual interest rate on 30-year Treasury securities for the first full calendar month preceding the calendar month that contains the annuity starting date. This amendment is not considered to reduce the accrued benefit of any participant in violation of the anti-cutback rule.

Example 2. On December 31, 1994, a defined benefit plan provided that all single-sum distributions were to be calculated using the UP-1984 mortality table and an interest rate equal to the lesser of the PBGC interest rate for the date of distribution or 6 percent. On January 4, 1995, and effective on February 1, 1995, the plan was amended to provide that all single-sum distributions are calculated using the IRS mortality table and the annual interest rate on 30-year Treasury securities for the second full calendar month preceding the calendar month that contains the annuity starting date. The 6 percent interest rate is not based on the PBGC interest rate. Therefore, the plan must provide that the single-sum distribution payable to any participant must be no less than the single-sum distribution calculated using the UP-1984 mortality table and an interest rate of 6 percent, based on the participant's benefits under the plan accrued through January 31, 1995, and based on the participant's age at the annuity starting date.

Example 3. Car-Ad Corporation maintains a defined benefit plan with a calendar-year plan year. As of December 7, 1994, the plan provided for single-sum distributions to be calculated using the PBGC interest rate as of the annuity starting date for distributions not greater than $25,000, and 120 percent of that interest rate for distributions over $25,000. Car-Ad wishes to delay the effective date of the RPA '94 rules for a year and to provide for an extended transition from the use of the PBGC interest rate to the new applicable interest rate. On December 1, 1995, and effective on January 1, 1996, Car-Ad amends the plan to provide that single-sum distributions are determined as the sum of:

    1. The single-sum distribution calculated based on the IRS mortality table and the annual interest rate on 30-year Treasury securities

for the first full calendar month preceding the calendar month that contains the annuity starting date; and

2. A transition amount. The transition amount for distributions in the years 1996–1999 is a transition percentage of the excess, if any, of the amount that the single-sum distribution would have been under the plan provisions in effect prior to this amendment over the amount of the single sum described in paragraph 1. The transition percentages are 80 percent for 1996, decreasing to 60 percent for 1997, 40 percent for 1998 and 20 percent for 1999. The amendment also provides that the transition amount is zero for plan years beginning on or after the year 2000. The plan is not considered to have reduced the accrued benefit of any participant in violation of the anti-cutback rule by reason of this plan amendment.

Q 10:62 Does a participant have to formally apply for benefits?

No. However, failure to apply for benefits would result in the participant receiving the benefit in the form of a QJSA (see Q 10:8), if applicable, or in the normal form of benefit under the terms of the plan, rather than an optional form of benefit that the participant might have preferred. If the participant has received notice of the QJSA and optional forms of benefit no less than 30 days and no more than 90 days after the annuity starting date (see Qs 10:3, 10:20), a QJSA can be distributed without the participant's consent after the participant reaches normal retirement age (see Q 10:53), or age 62, if later. [Treas Reg § 1.411(a)-11(c)(2)]

ERISA requires that every plan establish and maintain reasonable claims procedures, which must be described in the summary plan description (SPD) (see Q 18:1). DOL regulations further provide that a claim is filed when the requirements of a "reasonable claim filing procedure" of a plan have been met. [DOL Reg § 2560.503-1]

Q 10:63 What are the participant's rights if a claim for benefits is denied?

If the claim for benefits is denied, either in part or in full, the plan administrator must furnish written notice to the participant or beneficiary explaining why the claim was denied; such notice must be written in a manner calculated to be understood by the claimant. Moreover, the plan must afford a reasonable opportunity to the participant or beneficiary to have a full and fair review of that decision. [ERISA § 503; DOL Reg § 2560.503-1]

If the claim is denied after the review, the claimant can commence a court action. However, before starting a lawsuit, the claimant must exhaust the plan's administrative remedies (i.e., file a claim, request a review) unless the claimant can show that doing so would be futile. [Lindemann v Mobil Oil Corp, No. 95-2808 (7th Cir 1996); Communications Workers of America v American Telephone and Telegraph Co, 1994 US App Lexis 33043 (Fed Cir 1994); Conley v Pitney Bowes, 1994 US App Lexis 24798 (8th Cir 1994); Stumpf v Cincinnati, 1994 US Dist Lexis 13589 (SD Ohio 1994); Kimble v Int'l Brotherhood of Teamsters, Chauffeurs, Warehousemen and Helpers of America, No. 93-1569 (ED Pa 1993)]

Failure to exhaust administrative remedies may bar the claimant from pursuing judicial relief. When a claim has been denied and the participant fails to request a review within the time limit set forth in the plan, courts have ruled that judicial review of the underlying claim for benefits is precluded. [Glisson v United States Forest Service, 55 F 3d 1325 (7th Cir 1995); Petropoulos v Outbound Marine Corp, 1995 US Dist Lexis 10545 (ND Ill 1995); Graham v Federal Express Corp, 725 F Supp 429 (WD Ark 1989); Tiger v AT&T Technologies, 633 F Supp 532 (ED NY 1986)]

While an employer may have an obligation to issue a foreign language version of a plan's SPD (see Q 18:14), there is no such duty with respect to benefit denials. Therefore, there was no inadequacy in a benefit denial that excused a non-English speaking claimant from exhausting a plan's administrative remedies before bringing a suit for benefits. [Diaz v United Agric Employee Welfare Benefit Plan & Trust, 1995 US App Lexis 6112 (9th Cir 1995)]

Chapter 11

Minimum Distribution Requirements

The primary purpose of a qualified retirement plan is to provide retirement income to employees when they retire from employment. This objective will not be satisfied if employees can defer the receipt of benefits indefinitely. This chapter discusses when retirement benefits must be distributed, how much must be distributed each year, and the penalty for failure to satisfy these requirements.

Q 11:1 What plans are subject to the minimum distribution requirements?

All qualified retirement plans are subject to the minimum distribution requirements. [IRC § 401(a)(9); Prop Reg § 1.401(a)(9)-1, A-1]

The required minimum distribution rules also apply to IRAs (see Q 26:31), SEPs (see Q 27:18), and tax-sheltered annuities (see Q 29:40). [IRC §§ 403(b)(3), 408(a)(6); Prop Reg §§ 1.403(b)-2, Q&A-1–Q&A-3, 1.408-8, A-1–A-8]

Throughout this chapter reference is made to age 70½. If RRB '96 (see Q 1:22A) is enacted, age 70½ will be replaced by age 70 for all purposes relating to the minimum distribution requirements. [RRB '96, Act § 9445(b)]

Q 11:2 How must the participant's benefits be distributed?

To satisfy the minimum distribution requirements, the entire interest of a participant (1) must be distributed to the participant not later than the required beginning date (see Q 11:3), or (2) must be distributed, in installments, beginning not later than the required beginning date. The installments must be paid over (1) the life of the participant, (2) the lives of the participant and the participant's designated beneficiary (see Q 11:8), or (3) a period not extending beyond the life expectancy (see Q 11:12) of the participant or the joint life expectancy of the participant and the participant's designated beneficiary. [IRC § 401(a)(9)(A); Prop Reg § 1.401(a)(9)-1, B-1]

Q 11:3   What is the required beginning date?

For participants who reach age 70½ after 1988, the required beginning date is April 1 of the calendar year following the calendar year in which the participant reaches age 70½. [IRC § 401(a)(9)(C), prior to amendment by SBA '96 § 1404(a)]

For participants who reached age 70½ before 1989, the determination of the required beginning date depends on whether the participant was a 5 percent owner (see Q 22:28). For 5 percent owners, the required beginning date was the April 1 following the calendar year in which age 70½ was reached; for all other participants who attained age 70½ before 1988, the required beginning date is deferred until the April 1 following the calendar year in which the participant retires or becomes a 5 percent owner. A transitional rule applied to participants who were not 5 percent owners and who attained age 70½ in 1988. Those participants were treated as having retired in 1989, and their required beginning date was April 1, 1990. [Prop Reg § 1.401(a)(9)-1, B-2; Notice 89-42, 1989-1 CB 683]

A participant attains age 70½ as of the date six months after the participant's 70th birthday. For example, a participant whose date of birth is June 30, 1926 attains age 70½ on December 30, 1996, and a participant whose date of birth is August 31, 1926 attains age 70½ on February 28, 1997. [Prop Reg § 1.401(a)(9)-1, B-3]

Example. Arnold, a 5 percent owner, was born on June 30, 1926, and his 70th birthday was June 30, 1996. Arnold becomes 70½ on December 30, 1996, and must begin to take required minimum distributions by his required beginning date, April 1, 1997. Nina, who is also a 5 percent owner, was born on July 1, 1926, and she becomes age 70½ on January 1, 1997. Nina must begin to take required minimum distributions by her required beginning date, April 1, 1998.

Under SBA '96 (see Q 1:21), the required beginning date is April 1 of the calendar year following the later of the calendar year in which the participant attains age 70½ or retires. However, this change does not apply to a participant who is a 5 percent owner with respect to the plan year ending in the calendar year in which the participant attains age 70½. In the case of the non-5 percent owner who participates in a defined benefit plan (see Q 2:3) and who retires in a calendar year after the calendar year in which such participant attains age 70½, the participant's accrued benefit (see Q 9:2) will be actuarially increased to take into account the period after age 70½ in which the participant was not receiving any benefits under the plan. The actuarial adjustment rule does not apply to defined contribution plans (see Q 2:2). [IRC § 403(a)(9)(C), as amended by SBA '96 § 1404(a)]

> **Example.** Jerry, a 5 percent owner, and Linda, a non-5 percent owner, participate in the Ridge-Way Corporation defined benefit plan, and both attain age 70½ in 1997 but continue to work for Ridge-Way Corporation. Jerry must begin receiving distributions by April 1, 1998. However, Linda, a non–5 percent owner, need not commence receiving distributions until April 1 of the calendar year following the calendar year in which she retires. Linda's accrued benefit will be actuarily increased.

This provision is effective for years beginning after 1996. The Committee Report provides that a plan *may* allow a participant who is currently receiving distributions, but who would qualify for delayed distributions under the new rule, to elect to cease receiving distributions until required to begin under the new rule.

Q 11:4 Must distributions made before the required beginning date satisfy the minimum distribution requirements?

Lifetime distributions made *both* before the participant's required beginning date (see Q 11:3) and before the participant's first distribution calendar year (see Q 11:15) need *not* satisfy the minimum distribution requirements. However, if distributions commence under a particular distribution option, such as in the form of an annuity, before the participant's required beginning date for the participant's first distribution calendar year, the distribution option will fail to satisfy the minimum distribution requirements when distributions commence if, under the particular distribution option, distributions to be made for the participant's first distribution calendar year or any subsequent distribution calendar year will not satisfy the minimum distribution requirements. [Prop Reg § 1.401(a)(9)-1, B-3A]

Q 11:5 If distributions have begun before the participant's death, how must distributions be made after death?

If distribution of the participant's benefit has begun (see Q 11:6) and the participant dies before the entire benefit is distributed, the remaining portion of the participant's benefit must be distributed at least as rapidly as under the distribution method in effect on the date of the participant's death (see Q 11:14). [IRC §§ 401(a)(9)(A)(ii), 401(a)(9)(B)(i); Prop Reg § 1.401(a)(9)-1, B-4]

Example. Jane retired in 1994 and elected to receive her qualified retirement plan benefits in annual installments over 15 years. Jane dies in 1997 after receiving four installment payments (1994-1997). Jane's remaining benefit must be distributed to Jane's beneficiary over no more than the next 11 years (1998-2008).

Q 11:6 When are distributions considered to have begun?

Distributions are treated as having begun to the participant on the participant's required beginning date (see Q 11:3) even though payments may actually have been made before that date. [Prop Reg § 1.401(a)(9)-1, B-5]

Example 1. Jack retired in 1991 at age 65½ and began receiving installment distributions from a qualified retirement plan over the joint life expectancy of Jack and his wife, Jill. Distributions will not be treated as having begun until April 1, 1997 (the April 1 following 1996, the calendar year in which Jack attained age 70½). Thus, if Jack dies before April 1, 1997 (his required beginning date), distributions to Jill must be made in accordance with the rules regarding distributions that begin after a participant has died (see Q 11:7). However, if Jack made an irrevocable election at retirement to receive his distribution in the form of an annuity, distribution will be considered to have begun on the actual date payments started (see Q 11:4), even if Jack dies before his required beginning date.

Example 2. Assume the same facts as those in Example 1, except that Jack dies on July 1, 1997 without having received his required minimum distribution for 1997. If Jill elects to receive the entire remaining benefit in 1997, she may roll over the entire distribution into her own IRA, except the amount of the 1997 required minimum distribution (see Qs 28:34, 28:35). [Ltr Rul 9005071]

Q 11:7 If the participant dies before distributions are treated as having begun, how must the participant's benefit be distributed?

To satisfy the minimum distribution requirements, distributions must be made under one of two methods. The first method (the five-year rule) requires that the entire interest of the participant be distributed within five years of death regardless of to whom or to what entity the distribution is made. The second method (the exception to the five-year rule) requires that any portion of the participant's interest that is payable to a designated beneficiary (see Q 11:8) be distributed, commencing within one year of the participant's death, over the life of such beneficiary or over a period not extending beyond the life expectancy (see Q 11:12) of such beneficiary. [IRC §§ 401(a)(9)(B)(ii), 401(a)(9)(B)(iii); Prop Reg § 1.401(a)(9)-1, C-1; Ltr Ruls 9501044, 9416037]

To satisfy the five-year rule, the participant's entire interest must be distributed no later than December 31 of the calendar year that contains the fifth anniversary of the date of the participant's death. For example, if the participant died on January 1, 1992, the entire interest must be distributed by December 31, 1997. [Prop Reg § 1.401(a)(9)-1, C-2]

To satisfy the exception to the five-year rule, if the designated beneficiary is *not* the participant's surviving spouse, distributions must commence on or before December 31 of the calendar year immediately following the calendar year in which the participant died. This rule also applies if an individual is designated as a beneficiary in addition to the surviving spouse. If the designated beneficiary is the surviving spouse, distributions must commence on or before the *later* of (1) December 31 of the calendar year immediately following the calendar year in which the participant died, or (2) December 31 of the calendar year in which the participant would have attained age 70½. [IRC § 401(a)(9)(B)(iv); Prop Reg § 1.401(a)(9)-1, C-3; Ltr Ruls 9623056, 9608042, 9418034]

> **Example 1.** Harry was a participant in two qualified retirement plans, Plan A and Plan B. Harry died in 1995, and his son, Larry, is the beneficiary of both plans. Larry chose the life expectancy method with respect to Plan A but did not choose any distribution method for Plan B. Larry had to commence distributions from Plan A by December 31, 1996, and he must take the entire balance out of Plan B by December 31, 2000.

> **Example 2.** Jill, a participant in a qualified retirement plan, dies in 1997 at age 64½ having designated her husband, Jack, age 72, as beneficiary. Since Jack is the surviving spouse, distributions can be deferred until December 31, 2003, the calendar year in which Jill would have attained age 70½. This is so even though Jack will be age 78 in 2003. However, if Jill designated as beneficiary a trust created for Jack's benefit, the deferral would not be permissible (see Q 11:11). [Ltr Rul 9322005]

Generally, the surviving spouse stands in the shoes of the participant and thus can designate beneficiaries, but distribution to the beneficiaries must commence in the year following the year of the surviving spouse's death. Required minimum distributions can then be calculated based on the life expectancy of the beneficiaries. However, there is a special rule to ensure that the required minimum distributions will not be deferred again. Thus, if the original surviving spouse (surviving spouse 1) remarries and dies before required minimum distributions were to begin, any new surviving spouse (surviving spouse 2) cannot be treated as a "surviving spouse" for purposes of these rules. These rules apply to the relationship between the participant and surviving spouse 1; it is the relationship to the participant, not the relationship to surviving spouse 1, that determines the treatment of any subsequent distribution. [Ann 95-99, 1995-48 IRB 10]

Example 3. The facts are the same as those in Example 2, except that Jack marries Jane in 1998 and dies in 1999, before required minimum distributions were to begin. Jack is permitted to name his new wife, Jane, as his designated beneficiary, but distributions to Jane must begin by December 31, 2000.

The plan may adopt a provision specifying which method will apply to distributions after the participant's death. Alternatively, the plan may permit participants or beneficiaries to elect the method of distribution. If, however, the plan is silent as to which method applies if no election is made, distributions must be made in accordance with the exception to the five-year rule if the participant's beneficiary is the surviving spouse and, in all other cases, in accordance with the five-year rule. [Prop Reg § 1.401(a)(9)-1, C-4]

Q 11:8   Who is a designated beneficiary?

A person's status as a designated beneficiary is not dependent upon being selected by the participant. For example, if the terms of the plan specify the beneficiary, then whoever is so specified is the designated beneficiary and is treated as having been designated by the participant. [IRC § 401(a)(9)(E); Prop Reg § 1.401(a)(9)-1, D-1]

An individual may be designated as a beneficiary under the plan either by the terms of the plan or, if the plan provides, by an affirmative election by the participant specifying the beneficiary. A designated beneficiary need not be specified by name in the plan or by the participant to be a designated beneficiary so long as the individual who will be the beneficiary is identifiable under the plan as of the participant's required beginning date (see Q 11:3), or as of the date of the participant's death, and at all subsequent times. The members of a class of beneficiaries capable of expansion or contraction (e.g., the participant's children) will be treated as being identifiable if it is possible at the applicable time to identify the class member with the shortest life expectancy (see Qs 11:12, 11:13). [Prop Reg § 1.401(a)(9)-1, D-2]

Example. Stanley attains age 70½ in calendar year 1997. As of April 1, 1998, Stanley designates as his beneficiaries under the plan his spouse and his children. Stanley does not specify them by name. Even though Stanley did not specify his spouse, Susan, and his children, Hollie and Amy, by name, they are identifiable based on their relationship to Stanley as of his required beginning date. It is irrelevant that additional children of Stanley may be born after his required beginning date and that the class of beneficiaries is capable of expansion.

Q 11:9 May a person other than an individual be a designated beneficiary?

No. Only individuals may be designated beneficiaries (see Q 11:8) for purposes of the minimum distribution requirements. A person who is not an individual, such as the participant's estate, may not be a designated beneficiary. [Ltr Rul 9501044]

If a person other than an individual is designated as a beneficiary, the participant will be treated as having no designated beneficiary. In that event, distribution must be made over the participant's life or over a period not exceeding the participant's life expectancy (see Q 11:10). Furthermore, if, upon the participant's death, distribution has not commenced, distribution must be made in accordance with the five-year rule (see Q 11:7). [Prop Reg § 1.401(a)(9)-1, D-2A]

An individual cannot retroactively redesignate the beneficiary of a qualified retirement plan benefit in order to calculate required minimum distributions based upon the joint life expectancy of the individual and the individual's new beneficiary. The individual's designation of the estate as beneficiary causes the plan to have no designated beneficiary as of the date of the appointment. [Ltr Rul 9548031]

> **Example.** In 1991, Jack designates his wife, Beverly, as beneficiary and commences required minimum distributions over their joint life expectancy with recalculation (see Q 11:14). In 1994, Jack changes the beneficiary to his estate. Since Jack's estate is not a designated beneficiary, he can no longer use the joint life expectancy of himself and his wife, and required minimum distributions must now be made over Jack's life expectancy only. In 1997, Jack changes the beneficiary back to his wife, Beverly. Jack cannot now use Beverly's and his joint life expectancy but must continue to take distributions over his own life expectancy only.

Q 11:10 For purposes of calculating the distribution period, when is the designated beneficiary determined?

For purposes of calculating the distribution period for distributions before death, the designated beneficiary (see Q 11:8) will be determined as of the participant's required beginning date (see Q 11:3). If a designated beneficiary is added or replaces another designated beneficiary during the calendar year in which the employee's required beginning date occurs, but on or before the employee's required beginning date (January 1 through April 1 of such calendar year), the designated beneficiary of the employee for purposes of calculating the minimum distribution for the employee's first distribution calendar year (see Q 11:15) may be determined as of any date after December 31 of the employee's first distribution calendar year and before the employee's required beginning date. Thus, for purposes of determining the minimum distribution for the employee's first distribution calendar year, either designated beneficiary may be used to determine the joint life expectancy of the employee and designated beneficiary. However, for purposes of determining the minimum distribution for subsequent distribution calendar years (including the distribution calendar year in which the employee's required beginning date occurs—the second distribution calendar year), the designated beneficiary will be determined as of the employee's required beginning date. If, as of the required beginning date, there is no designated beneficiary to receive the benefit upon death, the distribution period is limited to the participant's life or a period not extending beyond the participant's life expectancy (see Q 11:12). If there is a beneficiary, such as the participant's estate, who is not designated, there is deemed to be no designated beneficiary (see Q 11:9). [Prop Reg § 1.401(a)(9)-1, D-3; Ltr Rul 9501044]

If the participant changes the beneficiary after the required beginning date, the distribution period may be shortened (see Q 11:9); it can never be lengthened. [Ltr Rul 9548031]

Example. Dick designates his wife, Jane, as his beneficiary. He chooses to recalculate both of their life expectancies (see Q 11:14), and required minimum distributions begin in 1994. In 1997, Jane dies, and Dick now designates his children as his beneficiaries. Although Dick is permitted to designate his children, they are not treated as a designated beneficiary, that is, their life expectancies cannot be used to determine the amount of the required minimum distributions. This means Dick cannot change the life expectancy and period of payout. He must take the remaining required minimum distributions over his life expectancy alone.

The designated beneficiary can be determined after the required beginning date. [Ltr Rul 9311037]

Example. Dick and his wife, Jane, are both age 73. Dick dies in 1997, and Jane rolls over the entire distribution from his qualified retirement plan to a newly established IRA. Jane designates her child as beneficiary. Even though Jane's required beginning date had passed when she established her IRA, she is not required to take a distribution until

December 31, 1998. Jane's child may be treated as a designated beneficiary because the designation occurred prior to the first required distribution date. (See chapter 28 for details on rollovers.)

For purposes of calculating the distribution period for distributions
beginning after death in accordance with the exception to the five-year rule
(see Q 11:7), the designated beneficiary will be determined as of the
participant's date of death. If, as of the date of death, there is no designated
beneficiary, distribution must be made in accordance with the five-year rule.
If there is a beneficiary, such as the participant's estate, who is not designated, there is deemed to be no designated beneficiary. [Prop Reg
§ 1.401(a)(9)-1, D-4(a); Ltr Rul 9501044]

Q 11:11   Can the beneficiary of a trust be a designated beneficiary?

If a trust is named as a beneficiary of the participant, all beneficiaries
of the trust are treated as having been designated (see Q 11:8) as
beneficiaries during the participant's lifetime if, as of the participant's
required beginning date (see Q 11:3), and as of all subsequent periods
during which the trust is named as a beneficiary, the following requirements are met:

1. The trust is a valid trust under state law, or would be but for the fact
    that there is no corpus.

2. The trust is irrevocable.

3. The beneficiaries of the trust are identifiable (see Q 11:8).

4. A copy of the trust instrument is provided to the plan.

[Prop Reg § 1.401(a)(9)-1, D-5(a); Rev Rul 89-89, 1989-2 CB 231; Ltr Ruls
9551015, 9537005, 9322005, 9052015, 9038015]

Example. Sallie names an irrevocable trust as her beneficiary under the
SWK Profit Sharing Plan. The irrevocable trust is for the benefit of Sallie's
grandchildren, and Sallie provides a copy of the trust to the plan
administrator. Since the plan administrator can determine all of the
beneficiaries of the trust and their ages, the plan administrator is
permitted to look through the trust and determine the required minimum
distributions using Sallie's life expectancy and the life expectancy of the
oldest grandchild (see Qs 11:13, 11:22).

Since only an individual may be a designated beneficiary, a trust itself
may not be the designated beneficiary even though the trust is named as a
beneficiary (see Qs 11:7, 11:9). However, if the above requirements are met,
distributions made to the trust will be treated as paid to the trust benefici-

aries. If, as of any date on or after the participant's required beginning date, a trust is named as a beneficiary and the above requirements are not met, the participant will be treated as not having a designated beneficiary. Consequently, for calendar years subsequent to such date, distribution must be made over the participant's life or over the period that would have been the participant's remaining life expectancy (see Q 11:12) determined as if no beneficiary had been designated as of the required beginning date. [Prop Reg § 1.401(a)(9)-1, D-5(b)]

With respect to distributions commencing after the participant's death and before the required beginning date, all beneficiaries of the trust will be treated as designated beneficiaries if the above requirements are satisfied as of the participant's death. However, if the above requirements are *not* satisfied, the participant will be treated as not having a designated beneficiary, and distribution must be made in accordance with the five-year rule (see Q 11:7). [Prop Reg § 1.401(a)(9)-1, D-6(a); Ltr Rul 9501044]

Q 11:12   What age is used to calculate life expectancy?

Life expectancy is calculated using the participant's and the designated beneficiary's attained ages as of the participant's birthday and the designated beneficiary's birthday in the calendar year in which the participant attains age 70½ (see Q 11:3). If life expectancy is being recalculated (see Q 11:14), the life expectancy of the participant, the life expectancy of the participant's spouse, or the joint life expectancy of the participant and spouse will be recalculated using the participant's and the spouse's attained ages as of the participant's birthday and the spouse's birthday in each succeeding calendar year in which recalculation is provided for purposes of calculating the minimum distribution for that distribution calendar year (see Q 11:15). [Prop Reg § 1.401(a)(9)-1, E-1(a)]

Example. Mary, a participant in a qualified retirement plan, retired on January 1, 1996. Her account balance on December 31, 1995 was $100,000. As of December 31, 1996, Mary was age 71, and she designated her brother, age 67, as her beneficiary. Mary elects to have the required minimum distributions made over the joint life expectancy of herself and her brother. On or before April 1, 1997, the first required minimum distribution must be made. The required minimum distribution is the account balance of $100,000 divided by the joint life expectancy of Mary and her brother, 21.7 years. The required minimum distribution is $4,608 ($100,000 ÷ 21.7).

If the participant's required beginning date (see Q 11:3) is April 1 of the year following the calendar year in which the participant retires, that calendar year is substituted for the calendar year in which the participant attains age 70½. [Prop Reg § 1.401(a)(9)-1, E-1(b)]

In the case of any installment distribution to a designated beneficiary (see Qs 11:7, 11:8), the life expectancy of the designated beneficiary is calculated based on the beneficiary's attained age as of the beneficiary's birthday in the calendar year in which distributions are required to commence to such beneficiary. [Prop Reg § 1.401(a)(9)-1, E-2]

> **Example.** An unmarried participant, Abel, died at age 50 on January 31, 1996. Abel's designated beneficiary is his brother, Cain, and Cain will receive Abel's interest over Cain's life expectancy. The date on which distributions are required to commence to Cain is December 31, 1997. Therefore, Cain's life expectancy is calculated based on his attained age as of his birthday in calendar year 1997.

Life expectancy for purposes of determining required minimum distributions must be computed by use of the expected return multiples in Tables V (single life—see Appendix A) and VI (joint lives—see Appendix B) of Treasury Regulations Section 1.72-9. [Prop Reg § 1.401(a)(9)-1, E-3, E-4]

Q 11:13   If the participant has more than one designated beneficiary, which designated beneficiary's life expectancy is used to determine the distribution period?

If more than one individual is designated as a beneficiary (e.g., the participant's children) as of the applicable date for determining the designated beneficiary (see Q 11:8), the designated beneficiary with the shortest life expectancy (see Q 11:12) will be the designated beneficiary for purposes of determining the distribution period. [Ltr Ruls 9623040, 9623039, 9623038, 9623037]

> **Example.** Stephen, age 70½, designates as beneficiaries his wife, Sallie (age 62), his daughter, Stephanie (age 29), his daughter, Caroline (age 27), and his son, James (age 26). Since Sallie is the oldest designated beneficiary and, consequently, has the shortest life expectancy, Sallie is the designated beneficiary for purposes of determining the distribution period.

If a person other than an individual is designated as a beneficiary, the participant will be treated as not having any designated beneficiaries even if there are also individuals designated as beneficiaries (see Q 11:9). The date for determining the designated beneficiary is the applicable date (see Q 11:10). The period for distributions commencing before the participant's death or for distributions over a life expectancy commencing after the participant's death, whichever is applicable, is the distribution period. [Prop Reg § 1.401(a)(9)-1, E-5(a)(1)]

Q 11:14   Can life expectancy be recalculated?

The life expectancy (see Q 11:12) of the participant and/or the participant's spouse can be recalculated *annually*. The life expectancy of a designated beneficiary (see Q 11:8) other than a spouse *cannot* be recalculated. The plan can either specify whether life expectancy will be recalculated or allow the participant to elect whether to recalculate life expectancy. The election becomes irrevocable as of the date of the first required distribution. [Prop Reg § 1.401(a)(9)-1, E-6, E-7]

Life expectancy or joint life expectancy is recalculated annually by using the appropriate table (see Q 11:12) to redetermine the life expectancy of the participant or the participant's spouse, or the joint life expectancy of the participant and the participant's spouse, using the attained ages on their birthdays in that year. Upon the death of the participant or the participant's spouse, the recalculated life expectancy of the deceased participant or deceased spouse is reduced to *zero* in the year following the year in which death occurred, *and* the participant's entire remaining interest must be distributed in the year in which the last life expectancy is reduced to zero. [IRC § 401(a)(9)(D); Prop Reg § 1.401(a)(9)-1, E-8; Ltr Rul 9604027]

Example 1. Barry attained age 70½ in 1996 and began taking required minimum distributions in that year. He designated his wife, Carrie, as his beneficiary and chose to recalculate both life expectancies. On December 1, 1997, Barry dies, after taking the required minimum distribution for that year. Payments to Carrie begin in January 1998. Carrie's required minimum distribution for 1998 is recalculated using the December 31, 1997 account balance divided by her life expectancy under the single life expectancy tables. In 1999, Carrie dies, after taking her required minimum distribution for that year. The entire remaining account balance must be paid to Carrie's beneficiary by December 31, 2000.

Example 2. Assume the same facts as those in Example 1, except that Barry chose not to recalculate either life expectancy. When Barry dies in 1997, the payments continue to Carrie at the same rate as before Barry's death (subtracting one year from their joint life expectancy for each passing year). After Carrie dies in 1999, the payments can continue to be made to Carrie's beneficiary at the same rate as before her death (again, subtracting one year from the joint life expectancy for each passing year).

If life expectancy is recalculated each year, it is referred to as the recalculation method; and, if life expectancy is *not* recalculated each year, it is referred to as the term certain method.

Q 11:15   How much must be distributed each year?

If the participant's benefit is in the form of an individual account (e.g., a defined contribution plan; see Q 2:2) and will be distributed (1) over a period not extending beyond the life expectancy (see Q 11:12) of the participant or the joint life expectancy of the participant and the designated beneficiary (see Q 11:8) or (2) over a period not extending beyond the life expectancy of the designated beneficiary, the amount required to be distributed for each calendar year, beginning with the first calendar year for which distributions are required and then for each succeeding calendar year, must at least equal the quotient obtained by dividing the participant's applicable account balance by the applicable life expectancy. The applicable account balance is the account balance as of the plan's last valuation date in the calendar year immediately preceding the calendar year for which the distribution is being made. The applicable life expectancy is the life expectancy of the participant, the joint life expectancy of the participant and the participant's designated beneficiary, or the life expectancy of the designated beneficiary. [Prop Reg § 1.401(a)(9)-1, F-1]

A year for which a distribution must be made is called a distribution calendar year. Generally, the first distribution calendar year is the year in which the participant reaches age 70½ (see Q 11:3). The distribution for the first distribution calendar year must be made by April 1 of the following year (see Q 11:3). Distributions for subsequent distribution calendar years must be made by December 31 of such year. Thus, if the participant attained age 70½ in 1996 and deferred the initial distribution until 1997, two minimum distributions must occur in 1997. The minimum distribution for 1996 must occur by April 1, 1997, and the minimum distribution for 1997 must occur by December 31, 1997. However, for purposes of calculating the December 31, 1997 minimum distribution, the applicable account balance is reduced by the amount of the required distribution for the first distribution calendar year actually made in 1997 by April 1, 1997. Taking two distributions in a single calendar year could subject the participant to the excise tax on excess distributions (see Q 13:27). [Prop Reg § 1.401(a)(9)-1, F-1, F-5]

Example 1. Stanley attains age 70½ on August 1, 1996 and thus is age 70 for the calendar year before the required beginning date.

Stanley chooses to use the term certain method (see Q 11:14) and will use only his life expectancy in determining the required minimum distribution each year. Stanley's life expectancy is 16 years, and his account balance in the plan as of December 31, 1995 was $200,000. Stanley divides $200,000 by his 16-year life expectancy. The resulting amount, $12,500, is his required minimum distribution for 1996 and must be distributed by April 1, 1997. Stanley also calculates the amount he must take by the end of 1997. His account balance as of December 31, 1996 was $205,000; but, for purposes of determining the 1997 required minimum distribution, the $12,500 payable by April 1, 1997 is subtracted from the total, leaving an account balance of $192,500 ($205,000 – $12,500). Stanley's life expectancy for the 1997 year is 15 years (the original life expectancy of 16 minus one for the one year that has passed). Stanley's required minimum distribution for 1997 is $192,500 divided by 15, or $12,833. The following year, Stanley will divide his 1997 year-end account balance by 14 to determine his required minimum distribution for 1998.

Example 2. Barbara attains age 70½ on April 1, 1996. Her required beginning date is April 1, 1997. She chooses the recalculation method (see Q 11:14) based upon her single life expectancy. Barbara will attain 71 by the end of 1996 and therefore uses age 71 to determine her life expectancy of 15.3 years (see Q 11:12). Her account balance as of December 31, 1995 was $200,000, so Barbara divides her $200,000 balance by her 15.3-year life expectancy to determine that her 1996 required minimum distribution, to be taken out by April 1, 1997, is $13,072. Barbara's December 31, 1996 account balance is $212,000. To calculate her 1997 required minimum distribution, Barbara subtracts her 1996 required minimum distribution of $13,072, payable by April 1, 1997, from this amount and uses an account balance of $198,928 to determine her 1997 required minimum distribution. Barbara's life expectancy at age 72 is 14.6 years. Barbara divides her $198,928 balance by her 14.6-year life expectancy, so that her 1997 required minimum distribution, to be taken out by December 31, 1997, is $13,625. In the following year, Barbara will divide her 1997 year-end balance by 13.9 (her life expectancy at age 73) to determine her required minimum distribution for that year.

The amount distributed in satisfaction of the minimum distribution requirement is determined annually. No credit is given for amounts distributed in previous years that exceeded the required amount. [Prop Reg § 1.401(a)(9)-1, F-2]

Annuity distributions under a defined benefit plan must be paid in periodic payments at intervals not longer than one year, over (1) the life of the participant, (2) the lives of the participant and the participant's designated beneficiary, or (3) a period certain not extending beyond the life expectancy of the participant or the joint life expectancy of the participant and the participant's designated beneficiary. Once payment begins over a period certain, the period certain cannot be extended. Payments under the annuity must either be nonincreasing or increase only under certain circumstances (e.g., in accordance with a specified cost-of-living index). The annuity may vary with the investment performance of the underlying assets. [Prop Reg § 1.401(a)(9)-1, F-3]

If an individual participates in more than one qualified retirement plan, the required minimum distribution is calculated separately for each plan, and each plan is required to make its respective minimum distribution (see Q 11:17). A different rule applies to IRAs (see Q 26:32) and tax-sheltered annuities (see Q 29:40).

Q 11:16   How does a rollover affect the required minimum distribution rules?

If an amount distributed by one plan (distributing plan) is rolled over to another plan (receiving plan), the amount distributed is still treated as a distribution by the distributing plan notwithstanding the rollover. However, a required minimum distribution may not be rolled over to another qualified retirement plan or to an IRA. [IRC § 402(c)(4)(B); Prop Reg § 1.401(a)(9)-1, G-1] (See chapter 28 for a discussion of rollovers.)

The participant's benefit under the receiving plan is increased by the amount of the rollover. However, the rollover has no impact on the minimum distribution required to be made by the receiving plan for the calendar year in which the rollover is received. But if a minimum distribution is required to be made by the receiving plan for the following calendar year, the rollover amount must be considered to be part of the participant's benefit under the receiving plan. Consequently, for purposes of determining any minimum distribution for the calendar year immediately following the calendar year in which the rollover is received by the receiving plan, the participant's benefit will be increased by the rollover amount. [Prop Reg § 1.401(a)(9)-1, G-2]

In the case of a *transfer* of the participant's benefit from one plan (transferor plan) to another (transferee plan), the transfer is not treated as a distribution by the transferor plan for required minimum distribution purposes. Instead, the benefit of the participant under the transferor plan is decreased by the amount transferred. However, if any portion of the participant's benefit is transferred in a distribution calendar year, then, in order to satisfy the minimum distribution requirement, the transferor plan must determine the amount of the minimum distribution with respect to the participant for the calendar year of the transfer using the participant's benefit under the transferor plan *before* the transfer. [Prop Reg § 1.401(a)(9)-1, G-3]

However, the participant's benefit under the transferee plan is increased by the amount transferred. The transfer has no impact on the minimum distribution required to be made by the transferee plan in the calendar year in which the transfer is received. But if a minimum distribution is required from the transferee plan for the following calendar year, the transferred amount must be considered to be part of the participant's benefit under the transferee plan. Consequently, for purposes of determining any minimum distribution for the calendar year immediately following the calendar year in which the transfer occurs, the participant's benefit under the transferee plan will be increased by the amount transferred. [Prop Reg § 1.401(a)(9)-1, G-4]

Q 11:17   What distribution rules apply if the individual is a participant in more than one plan?

If the individual is a participant in more than one qualified retirement plan, the individual must receive a minimum distribution from *each* plan. [Prop Reg § 1.401(a)(9)-1, H-1]

Separate accounts under a plan are generally aggregated for purposes of the minimum distribution requirements. Aggregation is not required if different beneficiaries are designated for each separate account; in that event, each separate account may separately satisfy the requirements. [Prop Reg § 1.401(a)(9)-1, H-2]

Q 11:18   What happens if the participant has not attained normal retirement age under the plan?

A plan will not fail to qualify solely because the plan permits distributions to commence to a participant on or after April 1 of the calendar year following the calendar year in which the participant attains age 70½ (see Q 11:3) even though the participant has not retired or attained the plan's normal retirement age (see Q 10:53) as of the date on which such distributions commence. [Prop Reg § 1.401(a)(9)-1, H-5]

Q 11:19   Can distributions be delayed until after the required beginning date?

Yes, but only if the participant made a valid election under Section 242(b)(2) of TEFRA before 1984. In that case, the participant can defer distributions until the participant actually retires. An election is valid only if it designated a distribution method that would not have disqualified the plan under pre-TEFRA law. IRS ruled that elections that deferred distributions until one year prior to the expiration of the electing participant's life expectancy or until ten years after retirement were invalid because the distribution methods did not satisfy the incidental death benefits rule (see Q 11:21). Also, elections that did not explicitly set forth the form of payment and beneficiary of death benefits were valid with regard to lifetime distributions to the electing participant but were not applicable with regard to the distribution of death benefits. [Prop Reg § 1.401(a)(9)-1, J-1; Notice 83-23, 1983-2 CB 418; Ltr Rul 9042063]

Under a Section 242(b)(2) election, a participant elected to receive a lump-sum distribution at the later of age 65 or termination of employment. The participant subsequently modified the election to increase the age from 65 to 70½, and IRS ruled that the modification caused a revocation of the Section 242(b)(2) election. [Ltr Rul 9617048] If the Section 242(b)(2) election is revoked *after* the participant's required beginning date (see Q 11:3), the total amount of distributions that would have been required by the revocation date must be distributed by the end of the calendar year after the year of revocation. [Prop Reg § 1.401(a)(9)-1, J-4; Notice 83-23, 1983-2 CB 418] Where the form of payment chosen in the Section 242(b)(2) election was a lump-sum payment and, after the participant's required beginning date, the participant changed the form of payment to one based on the joint life expectancy of the participant and his spouse, the change constituted a revocation of the election and catch-up distributions were required. [Ltr Rul 9430035]

A revocation of a Section 242(b)(2) election does not result from (1) the change in the employer's form of business from a corporation to a partnership or (2) the revocation of the election with respect to another plan within a commingled trust. An employee's Section 242(b)(2) election under a terminated profit sharing plan will not be revoked by the employer's transfer of the employee's account balance, without the employee's consent, to a segregated account in a 401(k) plan sponsored by the employer. The election will continue to apply only to the transferred account and not to the employee's other accounts in the 401(k) plan. When one plan was merged into another plan and the participant had made identical Section 242(b)(2) elections under each plan, the transferee plan could make distributions in accordance with the elections even though the transferee plan did not account separately for the transferred funds. An employee's election was not revoked when he withdrew a portion of his voluntary contributions (see Q 6:21) because the withdrawal was not inconsistent with the election and the terms of the plan both before and after the election. [Ltr Ruls 9310026, 9215040, 9052058, 9013011, 8938073]

Q 11:20 Is there a penalty for failure to make a required minimum distribution?

Yes. A nondeductible excise tax is imposed on the payee (e.g., participant or beneficiary) equal to 50 percent of the difference between the amount required to be distributed (see Q 11:15) and the amount actually distributed in any year. The tax will not apply to distributions made in accordance with a properly executed Section 242(b)(2) election (see Q 11:19). [IRC § 4974; Prop Reg § 54.4974-2, Q&A-1, Q&A-2]

> **Example 1.** Shirley should have taken a 1994 required minimum distribution of $5,000 by April 1, 1995, a 1995 required minimum distribution of $5,040 by December 31, 1995, and a 1996 required minimum distribution of $5,500 by December 31, 1996; but Shirley does not take the required minimum distributions for 1994, 1995, and 1996, until December 1, 1997. On December 1, 1997, she also takes her 1997 required minimum distribution of $5,650. In 1997, Shirley amends her 1995 income tax return to pay the 50 percent excise tax of $5,020 [($5,000 + $5,040) × 50%] and also pays any interest accumulated on that amount. Shirley amends her 1996 income tax return to pay the 50 percent excise tax of $2,750 ($5,500 × 50%) on her 1996 required minimum distribution and also pays the interest that has accumulated on that amount. For 1997, Shirley must take the required minimum distributions distributed in 1997 into income ($5,000 + $5,040 + $5,500 + $5,650). Since Shirley has taken her required minimum distribution for the 1997 year, the 50 percent excise tax does not apply to that distribution.

> **Example 2.** Ellen is the beneficiary of the profit sharing plan account balance of her aunt Helen, who died in 1993, before reaching her required beginning date. Ellen did not commence distributions by December 31, 1994, and, therefore, must take out the entire account balance by December 31, 1998. Ellen takes no distributions until March 30, 1999, at which time she takes a distribution of the entire amount. She owes an excise tax equal to 50 percent of the December 31, 1998 account balance for her 1998 tax year.

IRS may waive the excise tax if the payee establishes that the shortfall was due to reasonable error and that reasonable steps are being taken to correct the deficiency. A payee may request that IRS waive the excise tax; however, the excise tax must first be paid. The payee may then contact the appropriate IRS Service Center (the Center to which the payee's income tax return is sent) and explain why the distributions were not made in the proper amount or were not made on time. If IRS determines that the failure to take the correct distributions was due to a good faith error that has been or is being corrected, the excise tax may be refunded. The tax is shown on Form 5329, Additional Taxes Attributable to Qualified Retirement Plans

(Including IRAs), Annuities, and Modified Endowment Contracts, which is attached to the payee's income tax return. [IRC § 4974(d); Prop Reg § 54.4974-2, Q&A-8]

IRS has issued guidelines for plans that are unable to make required minimum distributions due to investments in insolvent insurance companies. [Rev Proc 92-16, 1992-1 CB 673; Rev Proc 92-10, 1992-1 CB 661]

Q 11:21   How does the incidental death benefit rule affect benefit distributions?

Any benefits payable to a beneficiary because of the participant's death must be incidental to the qualified retirement plan's primary purpose of providing retirement benefits to the participant (see Q 14:4). [Treas Reg § 1.401-1(b)(1); Prop Reg § 1.401(a)(9)-2, Q&A-1]

A qualified retirement plan is generally required to provide a QPSA (see Q 10:9) to the surviving spouse of a vested participant who dies before the annuity starting date. Since a QPSA is considered a part of the preretirement death benefit, both the QPSA and any other death benefit must be considered together to determine whether the total death benefits provided are incidental. If a plan provides a preretirement death benefit equal to both 100 times the participant's projected monthly benefit and a QPSA, the incidental death benefits rule will be violated. This problem may be remedied by:

1. Eliminating the preretirement death benefit; or

2. Offsetting the preretirement death benefit by the value of the QPSA.

[Rev Rul 85-15, 1985-1 CB 132]

Q 11:22   What is the minimum distribution incidental benefit requirement?

Distributions made during or after a participant's first distribution calendar year (see Q 11:15) must satisfy a minimum distribution incidental benefit (MDIB) requirement as well as the minimum distribution requirements. Thus, distributions must satisfy the MDIB requirement even if the amount required to be distributed under this requirement exceeds the amount required under the general minimum distribution rules. The MDIB requirement only applies to distributions during the participant's lifetime; this requirement does *not* apply to distributions after the participant's death.

For individual account and annuity distributions, the amount that must be distributed to meet the MDIB requirement is determined by dividing the participant's benefit by the applicable divisor specified below. The applicable divisor is based on the joint life expectancy (see Q 11:12) of the participant and a hypothetical individual ten years younger than the participant. However, if the participant's beneficiary on the required beginning date (see Q 11:3) is the participant's spouse, satisfaction of the minimum distribution requirement will automatically satisfy the MDIB requirement. [IRC § 401(a)(9)(G); Prop Reg § 1.401(a)(9)-2, Q&A-1–Q&A-7; Ltr Rul 9426049]

Table for Determining Applicable Divisor

Age of Employee	Applicable Divisor	Age of Employee	Applicable Divisor
70	26.2	93	8.8
71	25.3	94	8.3
72	24.4	95	7.8
73	23.5	96	7.3
74	22.7	97	6.9
75	21.8	98	6.5
76	20.9	99	6.1
77	20.1	100	5.7
78	19.2	101	5.3
79	18.4	102	5.0
80	17.6	103	4.7
81	16.8	104	4.4
82	16.0	105	4.1
83	15.3	106	3.8
84	14.5	107	3.6
85	13.8	108	3.3
86	13.1	109	3.1
87	12.4	110	2.8
88	11.8	111	2.6
89	11.1	112	2.4
90	10.5	113	2.2
91	9.9	114	2.0
92	9.4	115 and older	1.8

[Prop Reg § 1.409-2, Q&A-4(b), Q&A-5(b)]

Example 1. Bob, who has attained age 70½, is a participant in The Laitman Group Ltd. Profit Sharing Plan. Bob designates his twin daughters, Bonnie and Cathy, age 35, as his beneficiaries. The joint life expectancy of Bob and his daughters is 47.5 years. But, to satisfy the MDIB requirement, the applicable divisor is 26.2—the equivalent joint life expectancy of a 70-year-old and a 60-year-old.

Example 2. Instead of designating his daughters as beneficiaries, Bob designates his wife, Pegge, age 55, as his beneficiary. The joint life expectancy of Bob and Pegge is 29.9 years. The applicable divisor is 29.9, not 26.2, because Pegge, the designated beneficiary, is Bob's wife, and satisfaction of the minimum distribution requirement automatically satisfies the MDIB requirement.

Example 3. Carrie, age 71, named her niece, Gloria, age 35, as her designated beneficiary and chose not to recalculate her own life expectancy. Carrie's required beginning date was April 1, 1995. The joint life expectancy of Carrie and Gloria was 47.5 years. Since Gloria was more than ten years younger than Carrie and was not the spouse, the MDIB requirement applied, and the joint life expectancy became 25.3 years—the equivalent joint life expectancy of a 71-year-old and a 61-year-old. Carrie's 1994 required minimum distribution (made on March 20, 1995) was determined by dividing her December 31, 1993 plan account balance by 25.3, the smaller of the MDIB factor and regular joint life expectancy. On December 1, 1996, Carrie died, having taken the required minimum distribution for 1996. In calculating the 1997 required minimum distribution for Gloria, the December 31, 1996 account balance is divided by the joint life expectancy determined when distributions began, minus one for each year that has passed (1994, 1995, and 1996). The joint life expectancy when the distributions began was 47.5 years, so the current life expectancy under the term certain method is 44.5 years. If Carrie had chosen the recalculation method, Gloria's life expectancy for the current year would be her own life expectancy when distributions began minus one year for each year that has passed. Her life expectancy at age 35 was 47.3 years. The 1997 required minimum distribution for Gloria would then be determined by dividing the account balance by 44.3.

Q 11:23   Must a qualified retirement plan set forth the minimum distribution requirements?

A qualified retirement plan must include several written provisions reflecting the minimum distribution requirements. First, the plan must generally set forth the statutory rules, including the incidental death benefit requirement (see Q 11:22). Second, the plan must provide that distributions will be made in accordance with the proposed regulations. The plan document must also provide that these provisions override any distribution options in the plan inconsistent with the minimum distribution requirements. Finally, the plan must include any other provisions as may be prescribed in the future by IRS. [Prop Reg § 1.401(a)(9)-1, A-3]

A plan will not satisfy the general qualification requirements (see Q 4:1) unless all required minimum distributions are made for the calendar year ending with or within the plan year. However, a plan will not fail to satisfy the qualification requirements if there are isolated instances when the minimum distribution requirements are not satisfied in operation. But a pattern or regular practice of failing to meet the minimum distribution requirements with respect to one or more participants will not be considered an isolated instance even if each instance is *de minimis*. [Prop Reg § 1.401(a)(9)-1, A-5]

Example 1. Caroline receives a distribution from Plan A of $5,290. The correct minimum distribution should have been $5,920. This will not cause Plan A to fail to satisfy the minimum distribution requirements, although Caroline may be liable for the excise tax on the amount not received.

Example 2. In the last two years, five former employees attained age 70½ and should have begun receiving minimum distributions from Plan B. Plan B's plan administrator (see Q 16:1) does not maintain records adequate to identify when these five individuals reached age 70½ and, therefore, has failed to make the required distributions for the last two years. Because the plan administrator has failed to maintain adequate records and to make the required distributions, there is a pattern or regular practice of failing to satisfy the minimum distribution requirements, and the plan may be disqualified.

Chapter 12

Tax Deduction Rules

One of the primary tax advantages of a qualified retirement plan is that a current deduction is allowed for the company's contributions to a plan that provides future benefits. This chapter examines when a contribution must be made in order to be deductible on a current basis and the limits that are set on the amount of a tax-deductible contribution.

Q 12:1 What are the basic requirements for deducting employer contributions to a qualified retirement plan?

For such a contribution to be tax deductible, it must be an "ordinary and necessary" business expense and must be compensation for services actually rendered. Thus, for example, a contribution on behalf of a shareholder may be made only if the shareholder is also an employee actually rendering services to the corporation. Also, the contribution, when considered together with the employee's regular compensation, must be "reasonable in amount" for the services rendered. Reasonable current compensation and the plan contribution may include additional amounts for previously uncompensated prior services. What constitutes reasonable compensation depends upon the facts and circumstances of each particular case. [IRC §§ 162, 404; Treas Reg § 1.404(a)-1(b); RAPCO, Inc, 95-4123 (2d Cir 1996); Donald Palmer Co, Inc, No. 95-60381 (5th Cir 1996); Modernage Developers, Inc, 66 TCM 1575 (1993), *aff'd*, unpublished opinion (2d Cir 1995); RAPCO, Inc, 69 TCM 2238 (1995); Acme Constr Co Inc, 69 TCM 1596 (1995); BOCA Constr Inc, 69 TCM 1589 (1995); Comtec Systems Inc, 69 TCM 1581 (1995); Manohara, MD, Inc, 68 TCM 142 (1994); Thomas A Curtis, MD, Inc, 67 TCM 1958 (1994); Richlands Medical Assn, 60 TCM 1572 (1990), *aff'd*, unpublished opinion (4th Cir 1992); Bianchi, 66 TC 324 (1976), *aff'd*, 533 F 2d 93 (2d Cir 1977)]

A contribution on behalf of a self-employed individual (see Q 6:33) satisfies the ordinary-and-necessary business expense requirement if it does not exceed the individual's earned income for the year determined without regard to the deduction for the contribution (see Q 12:13). [IRC § 404(a)(8); Temp Reg § 1.404(a)(8)-1T; but see Gale v United States, 768 F Supp 1305 (ND Ill 1991)]

IRS has ruled that an employer could deduct in full a restorative payment made to its defined contribution plan (see Q 2:2) in response to actual and potential claims for breach of fiduciary duty because the payment was considered an ordinary and necessary business expense and was not limited by the plan deduction limits (see Qs 12:7, 12:17). The claims were brought after the plan incurred significant losses attributable to investments in derivatives. In addition, the restorative payment was not taxable income to the participants, was not subject to the excise tax on nondeductible contributions (see Q 12:8), and was not subject to the annual addition limitation (see Q 6:1). [Ltr Ruls 9528034, 9507030, 9506048]

Q 12:2   When must contributions be made to be currently deductible?

Tax-deductible contributions to a qualified retirement plan may be made at any time during the taxable year and even after the end of the taxable year up to the due date (including valid extensions) for the filing of the employer's federal income tax return for the particular year. Timely contributions made after the end of the taxable year are deductible for that taxable year if either (1) the employer designates in writing to the plan administrator or trustee that the contribution is for the preceding year, or (2) the employer claims the contribution as a deduction on its tax return for the preceding year. Such a designation, once made, is irrevocable. [IRC § 404(a)(6); Rev Rul 76-28, 1976-1 CB 106; Airborne Freight Corp v United States, C95-301R (WD Wash 1995)]

A contribution is timely if it is made before the income tax return extended due date even if it is made after the return is filed. An employer must obtain a valid extension to file the return in order to extend the time to make a contribution. IRS has ruled that a request for an automatic extension of time to file the employer's tax return was invalid because the employer failed to pay the balance of tax due shown on extension request Form 7004. An application for an extension of time to file is invalid if the employer fails to comply with all requirements of the regulations. [Rev Rul 66-144, 1966-1 CB 91; IRC § 6081(b); Treas Reg § 1.6081-3; Ltr Rul 9033005]

The employer's timely mailing of the contribution is adequate. Thus, a contribution mailed and bearing a postage cancellation date no later than the due date of the employer's tax return, including extensions, is timely even if the trust received it after such due date. [Ltr Rul 8536085]

A bookkeeping entry showing that a portion of the employer's certificate of deposit (CD) belonged to a qualified retirement plan as of the deadline for tax-deductible contributions is not timely payment of the contribution. [Rollar Homes, Inc, 53 TCM 471 (1987)]

In another case, an employer mistakenly made out and mailed its plan contribution check for the taxable year to Pension Benefit Guaranty Corporation (PBGC). The check was returned by PBGC, and the contribution was paid late. IRS ruled that the contribution was not timely made and, therefore, was not deductible for that taxable year. [Ltr Rul 9031033]

Q 12:3   May a contribution be timely for tax deduction purposes but not for the minimum funding standards?

Yes. The rules regarding timeliness for tax deduction purposes are based on the employer's taxable year and are independent of the rules regarding timeliness for purposes of the minimum funding standards (see Q 8:1), which are based on the plan year. Tax-deductible plan contributions may be made after the end of the taxable year if payment is made by the due date (including extensions) for filing the employer's federal income tax return for that taxable year (see Q 12:2). For purposes of the minimum funding standards, contributions made after the end of the plan year may relate back to that year if they are made within eight and one-half months after the end of the plan year. [IRC § 412(c)(10)(A); Rev Rul 77-82, 1977-1 CB 121]

Q 12:4   May an employer deduct the fair market value of property other than money contributed to its qualified retirement plan?

Yes. If property is contributed, the employer may deduct the fair market value of the property at the time of the contribution. However, if the fair market value exceeds the employer's basis in the property, the employer has a taxable gain equal to the excess; but, if the basis exceeds the fair market value, there is no recognizable loss to the employer. [IRC §§ 267, 1001; Rev Rul 75-498, 1975-2 CB 29; Rev Rul 73-583, 1973-2 CB 146; Rev Rul 73-345, 1973-2 CB 11]

If an employer purchases real estate from its qualified retirement plan for an amount in excess of the real estate's fair market value, such excess is considered a contribution to the plan. [Ltr Rul 8949076]

An employer's contribution of property to or the purchase of property from its qualified retirement plan may be a prohibited transaction (i.e., a transfer, sale, or exchange of assets between a party in interest and the plan) and may subject the employer to penalty taxes (see Qs 20:5, 20:10).

Q 12:5   May an employer make a timely contribution to the qualified retirement plan by check?

Yes. The contribution will be considered timely even if the plan trustee receives payment after the deadline for a deductible contribution (see Q 12:2) if the employer mails the check to the plan trustee before such deadline, the check is promptly presented for payment, and it is paid in the regular course of business. However, the contribution is not timely if the trustee delays presentation of the check because of the employer's financial problems. Also, the contribution was not considered timely in one case because the employer could not explain why the check was not negotiated until two weeks after the contribution deadline. [Flomac, Inc, 53 TCM 305 (1987); Walt Wilger Tire Co, Inc, 38 TCM 287 (1979); Cain-White & Co, Inc, 37 TCM 1829 (1978)]

If the check bounces, no contribution is deemed to have been made. [Springfield Productions, Inc, 38 TCM 74 (1979)]

Q 12:6   Is a contribution of the employer's promissory note a deductible payment?

No. The employer must make a timely contribution in cash or its equivalent to obtain a tax deduction for its contribution for the current or preceding taxable year (see Q 12:2). Since the contribution by the employer of its own promissory note is merely a promise to pay, it is not considered a payment of cash or its equivalent. [Don E Williams Co v United States, 429 US 569 (1977); Rev Rul 80-140, 1980-1 CB 89]

A contribution of the employer's own promissory note is also a prohibited transaction (see Q 20:1).

Q 12:7   What is the primary limitation on tax-deductible contributions to a profit sharing plan?

The primary limitation on tax-deductible contributions to a profit sharing plan is 15 percent of the total compensation (see Q 12:15) paid to all participants during the taxable year. [IRC § 404(a)(3)(A); Treas Reg § 1.404(a)-9(c); Ltr Rul 9548036]

Q 12:8   How are excess amounts contributed to a profit sharing plan treated for tax purposes?

There is an excise tax imposed on the employer equal to 10 percent of the portion of any contribution to any qualified retirement plan that is not deductible (see Qs 12:9–12:13, 12:18, 12:21). [IRC § 4972]

Amounts contributed in excess of the primary limitation (see Q 12:7) are generally carried forward and may be deducted in later years. However, the total amount deductible in a later taxable year, including the contribution to the profit sharing plan for that year, is limited to 15 percent of the compensation of the participants in the later taxable year. [IRC § 404(a)(3)(A); Treas Reg § 1.404(a)-9(e); Rev Rul 83-48, 1983-1 CB 93; Rev Rul 73-608, 1973-2 CB 147]

Example. Joel Corporation contributes $30,000 to its profit sharing plan in 1994, $32,000 in 1995, and $36,000 in 1996. If $27,000 is 15 percent of the total compensation paid to all participants in 1994, Joel's deduction for 1994 is limited to $27,000, and $3,000 ($30,000 – $27,000) is carried over to later years. Joel will be subject to an excise tax of $300 (10% × $3,000). If $33,000 is 15 percent of compensation in 1995, Joel's deduction for 1995 is $33,000 ($32,000 + $1,000 carried over from 1994) and the excise tax would be $200 [10% × ($3,000 – $1,000)]. If $38,000 is 15 percent of compensation in 1996, Joel's deduction for 1996 is $38,000 ($36,000 plus the remaining $2,000 carried over from 1994) and there would be no excise tax.

Q 12:9   How is the amount of nondeductible contributions computed?

Nondeductible contributions are defined as the sum of (1) amounts contributed by an employer to a qualified retirement plan for a taxable year in excess of the amount allowable as a deduction for that taxable year, plus (2) the unapplied amounts from the preceding taxable year.

The unapplied amounts from the preceding taxable year are the amounts subject to the excise tax in the preceding taxable year reduced by the sum of (1) the portion that is returned to the employer during the taxable year, plus (2) the portion that is deductible during the current taxable year.

Example. Nan Corporation makes a nondeductible contribution of $100,000 for its 1994 taxable year. Nan contributes $75,000 in 1995 when its deductible limit is $150,000. In 1996, it contributes $75,000 when its deductible limit is $100,000. Nan must pay an excise tax of $10,000 for 1994 (10% × $100,000) and $2,500 for 1995 [10% × ($100,000 + $75,000

– $150,000)]. It owes no excise tax for 1996 [10% × ($25,000 + $75,000 – $100,000)]. [IRC § 4972(c)]

The term "nondeductible contribution" does not include any contribution made for a taxable year beginning before 1987. Although the unapplied amounts in the preceding taxable year do not include nondeductible contributions made for years prior to 1987, carryforwards from pre-1987 years are applied first against the deduction limit in determining whether contributions after 1986 are subject to the excise tax. [IRC § 4972(c)(5); TRA '86 House Comm Report]

Q 12:10 When are nondeductible contributions for a given taxable year determined?

Nondeductible contributions for purposes of the excise tax are determined as of the close of the employer's taxable year. If, however, a nondeductible contribution is returned by the last day on which a deductible contribution could be made for that year (see Qs 1:36, 12:2), the returned amount is not treated as a nondeductible contribution and is not subject to the tax (see Q 12:9). [IRC § 4972(c)(3)]

Q 12:11 What happens if a deduction for plan contributions is subsequently disallowed?

The excise tax applies to contributions for which the deduction is disallowed. [General Explanation of TRA '86, Title XI, D2, p 748]

Q 12:12 Does the excise tax imposed on nondeductible contributions apply to tax-exempt organizations?

No. The 10 percent excise tax imposed on an employer for making nondeductible plan contributions (see Qs 12:8–12:11) does not apply to an employer that has, *at all times*, been exempt from tax. [IRC §§ 4972(d)(1)(B), 4980(c)(1)(A)]

IRS has ruled, however, that a tax-exempt organization that had been subject to tax on unrelated business taxable income (UBTI) was not subject to the excise tax because the portion of the nondeductible contribution attributable to the UBTI was *de minimis* [Ltr Rul 9304033]; but, where UBTI was more than *de minimis,* the excise tax was imposed. [Ltr Rul 9622037]

In other rulings, IRS concluded that plan contributions made by a tax-exempt organization, which was a member of a controlled group (see Qs 5:31, 5:33) that contained at least one nonexempt employer whose employees were covered under the plan, was subject to the 10 percent excise tax whether or not the organization had UBTI. When one of the controlled group members maintaining the plan is nonexempt, the whole group is considered nonexempt; and, therefore, the exempt organization does not qualify for the exception. [Ltr Ruls 9616003, 9236026]

Q 12:13 Do any special limitations apply to the deduction for contributions made to a qualified retirement plan on behalf of a self-employed individual?

The criterion for contributions to a qualified retirement plan on behalf of a self-employed individual (see Q 6:33) is earned income (see Q 6:35). For purposes of computing the limitations on deductions for contributions to a qualified retirement plan, earned income is computed after taking into account amounts contributed to the plan on behalf of the self-employed individual (i.e., the self-employed individual's earned income is reduced by the deductible contributions to the plan). Furthermore, earned income is computed after the deduction allowed to the self-employed individual for one-half of the individual's self-employment taxes. [IRC §§ 164(f), 401(c)(2)(A)(v), 401(c)(2)(A)(vi), 404(a)(8)(D), 1401]

The contribution limits that apply to corporate defined contribution plans apply to defined contribution plans covering self-employed individuals. Thus, the annual addition limit is the lesser of $30,000 or 25 percent of compensation (see Q 6:1). But because earned income is computed after taking into account amounts contributed to the plan on behalf of the self-employed individual and after the deduction for one-half of the individual's self-employment taxes, the effective percentage limit on the contribution is 20 percent of earned income computed after the self-employment tax deduction but before the contribution $(1 \div 1.25 = .80; 1.0 - .80 = .20)$. If the self-employed individual adopts a profit sharing plan only, the effective percentage limit on the contribution is 13.0435 percent of earned income computed after the self-employment tax deduction but before the contribution $(1 \div 1.15 = .869565; 1.0 - .869565 = .130435)$. See Q 6:34 for examples of defined contribution plans covering self-employed individuals.

However, unlike a corporate defined benefit plan to which an employer can make deductible contributions in excess of an employee's compensation if such contributions are necessary to fund the employee's benefit, an employer's deductible contribution on behalf of a self-employed individual is limited to the self-employed individual's earned income for the year (computed after the deduction for one-half of the individual's self-employment taxes, but without regard to the deduction for employer contributions made on the individual's behalf). [IRC §§ 162, 164(f), 212, 401(c)(2), 404(a)(8)(B), 404(a)(8)(C), 404(a)(8)(D); Temp Reg § 1.404(a)(8)-1T]

Example. Caroline, a sole proprietor, has net earnings (after the deduction for one-half of her self-employment taxes) of $50,000 from her business. The maximum deductible contribution she can make on her own behalf to her defined benefit plan is $50,000. (Caroline's earned income is $50,000 for deduction purposes.)

Because the annual contribution to a defined benefit plan is actuarially determined (see Qs 2:3, 2:32, 2:35), Caroline, in the above example, may be required to contribute more than $50,000 in order to satisfy the minimum funding standards (see Qs 8:1, 8:18). Even though Caroline contributes more than $50,000 and the contribution in excess of $50,000 is not deductible, the excess contribution is *not* treated as a nondeductible contribution and the 10 percent excise tax will *not* be imposed (see Qs 12:8–12:10). [IRC § 4972(c)(4)]

An S corporation shareholder is not a self-employed individual, and S corporation pass-through income is not earned income. Therefore, an S corporation shareholder cannot establish a retirement plan and make deductible contributions thereto based upon the pass-through income. [Durando v United States, 1995 US App Lexis 32048 (9th Cir 1995)]

Q 12:14   Can the employer make up a missed profit sharing plan contribution?

If an employer made less than the full 15 percent contribution (see Q 12:7) in a taxable year beginning before 1987, it may carry over the unused difference, known as the unused pre-1987 limitation carryforward, and make a larger tax-deductible contribution in a subsequent year, provided the plan is still qualified.

However, the combined regular deduction and unused pre-1987 limitation carryforward may not exceed the lesser of (1) 25 percent of that year's total compensation (see Q 12:15), or (2) 15 percent of that year's total compensation plus the amount of the unused pre-1987 limitation carryforward. Also, to avoid disqualifying the plan, the employer's contribution must be limited so that the amount allocated to any participant's account does not exceed the annual addition limitation (see Q 6:1). [IRC §§ 401(a)(16), 404(a)(3)(A)]

If the employer makes less than the maximum permissible contribution in a taxable year beginning after 1986, it may *not* carry over the unused difference. [IRC § 404(a)(3)(A)]

Q 12:15   What does compensation mean for purposes of the limits on deductible contributions to a profit sharing plan?

Compensation generally includes the total compensation of all plan participants paid or accrued during the taxable year. Even if, for purposes of allocating employer contributions, the plan defines compensation as base salary only, other forms of compensation (e.g., overtime, bonuses, and commissions) are included for purposes of the profit sharing plan deduction limitations (see Qs 6:37–6:45). Elective contributions (see Q 23:13) to a 401(k) plan (see Q 23:1) are not compensation for purposes of determining the limitation on deductible contributions. [Treas Reg § 1.404(a)-9(b); Rev Rul 80-145, 1980-1 CB 89; Ltr Rul 9225038]

The deduction for contributions to a 401(k) plan that are attributable to services rendered by participants after the end of the employer's taxable year will not be allowed because compensation must be earned before it can be deferred and contributed to the plan. [Treas Reg § 1.404(a)-1(b); Rev Rul 90-105, 1990-2 CB 69]

> **Example.** Birdie Bernie Corp.'s taxable year ended June 30, 1997, and the plan year of its 401(k) plan is the calendar year. Bea, an employee of Birdie Bernie Corp. whose salary is $1,000 per week, became a 401(k) plan participant on January 1, 1997. She elected to defer 5 percent of her salary ($50) each week. Thus, she deferred $2,600 ($50 × 52) during the 1997 plan year. However, Birdie Bernie Corp. can deduct only $1,300 ($50 × 26) on its income tax return for the taxable year ended June 30, 1997, which is the portion of the deferral attributable to Bea's services through June 30, 1997. The $1,300 deferred by Bea during the second half of 1997 will be deductible by Birdie Bernie Corp. on its income tax return for the taxable year ending June 30, 1998.

If a terminated employee does not receive a share of the employer's contribution for the year of termination, such employee's compensation is not included for deduction limitation purposes. [Dallas Dental Labs, 72 TC 117 (1979); Rev Rul 65-295, 1965-2 CB 148] Even though in a defined contribution plan (see Q 2:2) a disabled participant may be deemed to receive compensation at the rate of compensation paid immediately before becoming disabled, such "phantom" compensation is not included for deduction limitation purposes (see Q 6:3). [IRC § 415(c)(3)(C)]

For taxable years beginning on or after January 1, 1994 there is a $150,000 per participant compensation cap that applies to the computation of deductions for contributions to all qualified retirement plans. Although the $150,000 limitation is subject to cost-of-living adjustments (see Q 6:25), no adjustment occurred for the taxable year beginning in 1995 or 1996 because an adjustment will be made only if it is $10,000 or greater and then will be made in multiples of $10,000 (i.e., rounded down to the next lowest multiple of $10,000). For example, an increase in the cost-of-living of $9,999 will result in no adjustment, and an increase of $19,999 will create an upward adjustment of $10,000. Therefore, the cost-of-living must increase by 6⅔ percent before the first adjustment to the annual compensation limit will occur (6⅔% × $150,000 = $10,000). Any new adjustment will apply to taxable years *beginning* in the calendar year in which the adjustment becomes effective. [IRC § 404(l)]

See Q 12:27 for a discussion of the family aggregation rule.

Q 12:16 May a company make a deductible contribution to the profit sharing plan of an affiliated company?

Yes. Although contributions to a profit sharing plan are not required to be based on profits (see Q 2:6), a profit sharing plan may require profits in order to make a contribution. If a member of an affiliated group of corporations cannot make a contribution to its profit sharing plan because it has no current or accumulated earnings or profits, another member of the affiliated group may make a contribution for the employees of the unprofitable member. However, the contribution is deductible only if both members participate in the same profit sharing plan, and the contributing corporation has current or accumulated earnings or profits; the contribution is not deductible if they maintain separate plans. [IRC §§ 404(a)(3)(B), 1504; Treas Reg § 1.404(a)-10(a)(1)]

This rule does not apply to pension plans. However, when the common parent of an affiliated group and several of its subsidiaries made contributions to the pension plans maintained by another subsidiary of the parent, the recipient subsidiary was allowed to deduct the contributions. Contributions by other subsidiaries of the common parent were treated as distributions to the common parent, followed by contributions of capital to the recipient subsidiary and constructive contributions by the recipient subsidiary to the plans. Contributions to the recipient subsidiary's pension plans by its own subsidiaries were treated as constructive dividends to the recipient subsidiary followed by constructive contributions by the recipient subsidiary to the plans. Contributions by the common parent were treated as constructive contributions of capital to the subsidiary, followed by constructive contributions from the subsidiary to its pension plans. The contributing companies could not deduct the amounts contributed, but such amounts were deductible by the recipient subsidiary as if it had made the contributions directly. [Ltr Rul 9337025]

Q 12:17 What is the limit on tax-deductible contributions to defined contribution plans other than profit sharing plans?

Generally, the deduction for defined contribution plans that are pension plans (e.g., money purchase and target benefit plans; see Qs 2:4, 2:5) is the amount necessary to meet minimum funding standards (see Q 8:1). Thus, the deductible amount of the employer's contribution to a money purchase pension plan or a target benefit plan is ordinarily the sum of amounts required to be contributed on behalf of each plan participant. [IRC § 404(a)(1)(A); Prop Reg § 1.412(b)-1(a)]

However, in computing the amount deductible for contributions to any type of defined contribution plan (see Q 2:2), if the annual addition (see Q 6:1) of any participant under the plan is more than the amount allowed by law, the excess amount of the company contribution will not be deductible (see Q 12:24). [IRC § 404(j)(1)(B)]

Example. Villa del Sandy Corp. established a money purchase pension plan in 1996 for its only employee, Maxine. The plan provides a 25-percent-of-compensation contribution formula. Maxine's compensation is $150,000, and the contribution under the formula is $37,500. The excess portion of Villa del Sandy Corp.'s contribution for 1996 of $7,500 ($37,500 – $30,000) will not be deductible. In addition, the nondeductible contribution will be subject to a nondeductible 10 percent excise tax penalty (see Qs 12:8–12:10).

For a discussion of the per participant limitation on compensation for making tax-deductible contributions, see Q 12:15.

Q 12:18 What is the limit on tax-deductible contributions to a defined benefit plan?

Under the level cost method, the employer may deduct the amount needed to fund each employee's past and current service credits distributed as a level amount over the employee's remaining years of future service. If the amount attributable to three or fewer employees is more than 50 percent of the remaining costs, the unfunded costs for these employees must be spread over a period of at least five years. [IRC § 404(a)(1)(A)(ii)]

Under the normal cost method, the employer may deduct the normal cost of the plan plus the amount needed to amortize the unfunded portion of past service costs equally over ten years. [IRC § 404(a)(1)(A)(iii)]

If the contribution needed to satisfy the minimum funding requirement (see Q 8:1) exceeds the amount calculated under either of these two methods (whichever the plan adopts), the deductible limit is the minimum funding amount. [IRC § 404(a)(1)(A)(i)]

No deduction is allowed for any contribution to fund a retirement benefit in excess of any participant's annual benefit limit (see Q 12:25). [IRC § 404(j)(1)(A)] For a discussion of the per participant limitation on compensation for making tax-deductible contributions, see Q 12:15.

In any event, the deductible limit cannot exceed the full funding limitation (see Q 8:16). [IRC § 404(a)(1)(A)]

Nondeductible contributions to terminating single-employer defined benefit plans (see Q 25:2) with less than 101 participants for the year are not subject to the 10 percent excise tax on nondeductible contributions to the extent the contributions do not exceed the plan's unfunded current liability. This rule applies to plans that are covered under ERISA's termination provisions and terminated in a standard termination (see Q 21:17) by the end of the taxable year for which the nondeductible contribution is made. This new rule is effective for taxable years ending on or after December 8, 1994. [IRC § 4972(c)(6)]

For details, see chapter 8.

Q 12:19   How does a defined benefit plan's funding method affect its tax-deductible contributions?

The amount of deductible contributions cannot exceed the cost based on reasonable funding methods and actuarial assumptions. [IRC § 412(c)(3); Treas Reg § 1.404(a)-3(b)]

For example, a contribution calculated on the basis of an assumption that plan assets would earn interest at a rate of 5 percent was unreasonable in view of the availability of investments with a significantly higher interest rate. Further, the calculation under the normal cost method in a plan's first year of existence unreasonably failed to allocate costs between the normal cost of benefits accrued for service during the year of the contribution and the cost of benefits accrued during the year for past service, which must be amortized over no less than ten years. [Jerome Mirza & Assocs, Ltd v United States, 882 F 2d 229 (7th Cir 1989); Custom Builders, Inc, 58 TCM 696 (1989); Ltr Ruls 9119007, 9031001]

An assumption that employees will retire at the normal retirement age specified in the plan, ignoring the fact that employees normally retire later, may be unreasonable and result in a nondeductible contribution (see Q 2:18). [Rev Rul 78-331, 1978-2 CB 158]

In a number of recent cases, however, courts have concluded that, since the assumptions used were not "substantially unreasonable" and represented the actuary's best estimate of anticipated experience under the plans based on actuarial assumptions used by similar plans, IRS was precluded from requiring a retroactive change of assumptions. [Citrus Valley Estates, Inc v Comm'r, 49 F 3d 1410 (9th Cir 1995); Wachtell, Lipton, Rosen & Katz v Comm'r, 26 F 3d 291 (2d Cir 1994); Vinson & Elkins v Comm'r, 7 F 3d 1235 (5th Cir 1993); but see Rhoades, McKee & Boer v United States, 1:91-CV-540 (WD Mich 1995)] For a discussion of these cases, see Q 8:8.

An employer cannot rely on uncertified, preliminary information furnished by its actuarial firm (see Q 16:24) to support a tax-deductible contribution to its defined benefit plan. Based upon preliminary advice that utilized a 6 percent interest rate assumption, the employer contributed and deducted $60,000. Subsequently, the actuarial firm increased the interest rate assumption, the effect of which increase was to lower the deductible contribution to $20,000, and the actuarial firm certified Schedule B (see Q 17:4) setting forth this lesser amount and the interest rate change. Upon audit by IRS, a new actuarial firm advised that it would certify a revised Schedule B that would support a contribution of $60,000 based on an interest rate assumption of 6 percent. The court concluded that the employer was not entitled to file an amended Schedule B; once a Schedule B is filed, an amended Schedule B containing a different set of actuarial assumptions cannot be filed unless IRS determines that the actuarial assumptions set forth on the original Schedule B were not reasonable. [Rubin, 103 TC 200 (1994); Treas Reg § 1.404(a)-3(c)]

Q 12:20 Are excess amounts contributed to a defined benefit plan deductible in later years?

The excess contributions may be carried over and deducted in later years. For example, suppose that for 1996 the maximum deduction is $20,000 and the employer contributes $25,000 to the plan. There is a $5,000 carryover that is tax deductible only in a later year in which a full contribution is not made. So, if in 1997 the maximum deduction is $22,000 and the employer contributes $20,000 to the plan, $2,000 of the $5,000 carryover can be deducted for that year. [IRC § 404(a)(1)(E)]

Excess amounts contributed to a defined benefit plan (or any other qualified retirement plan) are subject to an excise tax equal to 10 percent of the nondeductible contributions (see Qs 12:8–12:10, 12:18). [IRC § 4972]

Q 12:21   Are there any special limits on tax-deductible contributions if an employer maintains both a defined contribution plan and a defined benefit plan?

If no employee is covered by both plans, the regular deduction limitations apply with respect to each plan. However, if at least one employee is covered by any combination of defined contribution and defined benefit plans (see Qs 2:2, 2:3) maintained by the same employer, a special deduction limitation applies: the greater of (1) 25 percent of the aggregate compensation of all participants, or (2) the amount necessary to meet the minimum funding standard for the defined benefit plan (see Q 8:1). This limitation is applied after the regular limitations have been determined for each plan. [IRC § 404(a)(7)]

> **Example.** Adam Corporation maintains a defined benefit plan and a money purchase pension plan on a calendar-year basis. Adam's employees participate in both plans. In 1997, Adam must make a contribution equal to 30 percent of the participants' aggregate compensation to fund both plans. The contribution to the defined benefit plan is an amount equal to 20 percent of the participants' aggregate compensation. Adam will not be able to deduct the full amount of both contributions on its 1997 income tax return, and the portion that is not deductible (5 percent of aggregate compensation) is subject to a 10 percent excise tax (see Qs 12:8–12:10).

To alleviate the impact of the paired plan deduction limitation and the excise tax on nondeductible contributions, the defined contribution plan may provide that required contributions will be limited to amounts that are deductible.

Aggregate compensation includes the total compensation paid or accrued during the taxable year of all employees who are participants in either the defined benefit plan or the defined contribution plan, or both (see Q 12:15). [Treas Reg § 1.404(a)-13(a)]

If an employee is covered by both a defined contribution plan and a defined benefit plan, a special rule governs the overall benefits of the employee (see Q 6:17).

A special rule applies, effective for taxable years beginning on and after January 1, 1992, if the defined benefit plan is a single-employer plan (see Q 25:2) that has more than 100 participants. Contributions to one or more defined contribution plans that are nondeductible because they exceed the combined plan deduction limits are not subject to the 10 percent excise tax (see Q 12:8). However, this exception applies only to the extent that the contributions do not exceed 6 percent of compensation in the year for which they are made. For purposes of this rule, the combined plan deduction limits are first applied to contributions to the defined benefit plan. The 6-percent-of-compensation limit is determined on an aggregate basis. If contributions exceed the 6 percent limit, only those in excess of 6 percent are subject to the excise tax. In addition, amounts that are not subject to the excise tax in the year contributed are not taken into account for purposes of applying the 6 percent limit in any future year. For example, if an employer makes contributions to two defined contribution plans, the excise tax does not apply if the contributions are less than 6 percent of the aggregate compensation of participants in both plans. [IRC § 4972(c)(6)] IRS has provided assistance to employers who may be entitled to refunds of the excise tax under this special rule. [Ann 96-26, 1996-17 IRB 13]

See Q 12:27 for a discussion of the family aggregation rule.

Q 12:22   Are there any other limitations on the deductibility of employer contributions?

Yes. For certain employers engaged in the production of property or the acquisition of property for resale, the uniform capitalization rules require the capitalization of a portion of contributions to various employee benefit plans, including qualified retirement plans. [IRC § 263A; Treas Reg § 1.263A]

Essentially, an employer that is covered by the uniform capitalization rules and maintains a qualified retirement plan must first calculate its otherwise allowable deductible contribution under the generally applicable limits under Section 404 and then allocate that amount between production or inventory costs, which must be capitalized, and other costs, which are deductible. OBRA '87 repealed an exception that had exempted past service costs from the capitalization requirements. The effective date of this change generally requires that past service costs incurred after December 31, 1987, be capitalized. [IRC § 263A(a); Treas Reg § 1.263A; General Explanation of TRA '86, Title VIII, D, p 513; Notice 88-86, 1988-2 CB 401; Ann 88-55, 1988-13 IRB 35]

Q 12:23   Will excess assets of an employer's overfunded defined benefit plan that are transferred to a defined contribution plan be considered taxable income to the employer?

Yes. However, the employer may deduct the amount transferred as a contribution to the defined contribution plan, subject to applicable deduction limits (see Qs 12:7, 12:17). [GCM 39744 (1988)]

Example. SCJ Corporation maintains two qualified retirement plans: a defined benefit plan that is overfunded and a profit sharing plan. SCJ terminates its defined benefit plan; and, after all benefits are paid to plan participants, it transfers the defined benefit plan's excess assets to the profit sharing plan. SCJ deducted all of its contributions to the defined benefit plan when made. SCJ must recognize income upon the transfer from the defined benefit plan to the profit sharing plan. SCJ will be entitled to a deduction for the transferred funds if its contribution to the profit sharing plan during the year of the transfer and the amount of transferred funds are less than or equal to 15 percent of the compensation of plan participants.

A different result will occur if the profit sharing plan is a qualified replacement plan and the transfer from the defined benefit plan is limited to 25 percent of the excess assets. See chapter 21 for details on plan terminations and the excise tax on reversions.

Q 12:24   Are excess amounts contributed to a combination of plans deductible?

If an amount is contributed by the employer to both a defined benefit plan and a defined contribution plan in excess of the deduction limitation (see Q 12:21), the excess contribution may be deducted in the succeeding taxable years. However, the total deduction in any succeeding year, including the contributions for that year, is limited to 25 percent of the compensation of the participants during that year. [IRC § 404(a)(7)(B); Treas Reg § 1.404(a)-13(c); Ltr Rul 9107033]

Example. Assume that in the example in Q 12:21, Adam Corporation makes its contribution to both plans on February 28, 1998. The contributions are timely for 1997 minimum funding standard purposes (see Q 8:1). The amount deductible in 1997 is only 25 percent of aggregate 1997 compensation, but the portion of the contributions not deductible in 1997 may be deductible in 1998.

Excess amounts contributed to any qualified retirement plan (or combination of plans) are subject to an excise tax equal to 10 percent of the nondeductible contributions (see Qs 12:8–12:10, 12:18). [IRC § 4972]

Q 12:25   May an employer deduct contributions to provide benefits to a participant in excess of Section 415 limits?

No. The deductible limit for a contribution to a defined contribution plan (see Q 2:2) is reduced to the extent the contribution produces an annual addition in excess of the Section 415 limit for the year. Similarly, no deduction is allowed for the portion of a contribution to a defined benefit plan (see Q 2:3) to fund a benefit for any participant in excess of the annual benefit limitation for the year. For details on contribution and benefit limits, see chapter 6. [IRC § 404(j)(1)]

In calculating the contribution to a defined benefit plan, anticipated cost-of-living increases in the allowable annual retirement benefit (see Q 6:8) cannot be taken into account before the year in which the increase first becomes effective. [IRC § 404(j)(2); Feichtinger, 80 TC 239 (1983)]

> **Example.** Sandi Corporation sponsors a defined benefit plan for its only employee, Steve, who is currently age 58 and has average annual compensation for plan purposes of $130,000. The plan provides an annual retirement benefit of 100 percent of compensation in the form of a straight life annuity at the normal retirement age of 65. Any portion of the company's contribution for the 1996 year that funds the excess benefit of $10,000 ($130,000 – $120,000) will not be deductible and will be subject to a 10 percent excise tax. That result is not changed by the fact that it is reasonable to project that Steve will be entitled to receive an annual benefit of $130,000 at retirement due to cost-of-living increases in the allowable annual retirement benefit.

Two doctors were the only shareholders of two corporations, which entities constituted a controlled group of corporations (see Q 5:33). Since both corporations adopted defined benefit plans (each plan provided the doctors with the maximum allowable benefit), the doctors were receiving double the permissible benefit. The deduction for the contribution made by one of the corporations was disallowed and substantial penalties were imposed (see Q 8:10). [Anesthesia Consultants, PC v United States, No. 94-WYO-419 (D Colo 1995)]

Q 12:26   Is the employer's payment of plan expenses deductible?

Many qualified retirement plans provide that general administrative expenses may be paid from plan assets unless paid by the employer. If the employer pays the administrative fees (e.g., the fees of trustees and actuaries) directly, or indirectly by reimbursing the trust, the amounts paid are deductible under Section 162 or Section 212 to the extent that they satisfy the requirements of those sections and are not considered plan contributions. [Rev Rul 84-146, 1984-2 CB 61; Ltr Ruls 9001002, 8941010, 8941009, 8940014, 8940013]

However, brokers' commissions incurred in connection with nonrecurring transactions such as the purchase and sale of plan assets, investment manager fees, and wrap fees are not separately deductible under Section 162 or Section 212. Instead, amounts paid by the employer directly to the broker or investment manager, or indirectly by payment to the trust as reimbursement for the brokers' commissions or the investment managers' fees, are treated as plan contributions and used to provide benefits. Consequently, such contributions are deductible, subject to the limits of Section 404. [Rev Rul 86-142, 1986-2 CB 60; Ltr Ruls 9124034 (modifying Ltr Rul 8941010), 9124035 (modifying Ltr Rul 8941009), 9124036 (modifying Ltr Rul 8940013), 9124037 (modifying Ltr Rul 8940014)]

Q 12:27 How does the family aggregation rule affect the employer's tax deduction?

For taxable years beginning on or after January 1, 1994, no more than $150,000 of compensation (adjusted for inflation) for each participant can be taken into account in determining the limit on deductible contributions (see Q 12:15). In addition, *for years beginning before 1997,* the compensation of an employee who was either a 5 percent owner (see Q 3:4) or a highly compensated employee (see Q 3:3) who was one of the ten most highly compensated employees of the employer was aggregated with the compensation of the family members of such employee, and the compensation limit (adjusted for inflation) was applied to the total compensation of all family members. For this purpose, the employee's family included the employee's spouse and lineal descendants who had not attained age 19 before the end of the year. [IRC §§ 404(l), prior to amendment by SBA '96 § 1431(b), 414(q)(6), prior to repeal by SBA '96 § 1431(b)]

Example. Essjaykay Enterprises Ltd. adopts a 25-percent-of-compensation money purchase pension plan for its taxable year ending December 31, 1996. There are five participants—husband Steve ($200,000), wife Sallie ($200,000), 18-year-old daughter Stephanie ($30,000), 17-year-old son James ($20,000), and 16-year-old daughter Caroline ($10,000). The maximum tax-deductible contribution is limited to $37,500 ($150,000 × 25%) (see Qs 12:15, 12:17), which will be allocated among the family members as follows:

Participant	Tax-Deductible Contribution Allocation
Steve	$16,304
Sallie	16,304
Stephanie	2,446
James	1,631
Caroline	815
Total	$37,500

The family aggregation rule does not apply to the annual addition limitation (see Q 6:1), so the total family contribution can exceed $30,000.

For years beginning after 1996, the family aggregation rule is repealed. Assuming the same facts as in the above example except that the taxable year ends December 31, 1997, Essjaykay's total contribution for that year will increase to $75,000 ($30,000 + $30,000 + $7,500 + $5,000 + $2,500). [IRC § 404(l), as amended by SBA '96 § 1431(b)]

Chapter 13

Taxation of Distributions

The form and time of payment of distributions from a qualified retirement plan depend primarily on the type of plan. Defined benefit plans generally pay benefits in the form of an annuity on the participant's early or normal retirement date. Defined contribution plans generally pay benefits in a single lump-sum payment upon the participant's termination of employment. Some retirement plans also permit participants to receive distributions prior to their retirement or termination of employment as in-service withdrawals or loans. This chapter discusses the tax treatment of the various forms of distribution.

Q 13:1   In general, how are distributions from qualified retirement plans taxed?

Generally, all distributions from qualified retirement plans are includible in the recipient's gross income when received. The taxation of certain types of distributions may be postponed through a tax-free rollover to an individual retirement account (IRA) or another qualified retirement plan; see chapter 28 for more details. In some cases, favorable tax treatment may be available for a lump-sum distribution (see Q 13:4). A distribution received from a qualified retirement plan in the form of a loan will not be taxable if certain requirements are met (see Qs 13:44–13:52). [IRC §§ 72, 402]

A transfer of funds from a qualified retirement plan to the temporary administrator of a deceased participant's estate is a distribution includible in the estate's gross income in the year of receipt. [Ltr Rul 9320006] However, the transfer of funds from a qualified retirement plan to a successor qualified retirement plan (see Q 9:39) was not a taxable event to any participant in either plan. [Ltr Rul 9438044]

Where an employee received a lump-sum distribution from a qualified retirement plan and, pursuant to a divorce decree, paid a portion of the distribution to the employee's former spouse, it has been ruled that the mere fact that the employee was required to pay over a portion of the distribution to the former spouse did not entitle the employee to exclude those funds from income. Even if the distribution is made by the plan directly to the nonemployee spouse, the distribution will be taxable to the employee unless it is made pursuant to a qualified domestic relations order (QDRO; see Q 30:1). [Rodoni, 105 TC 29 (1995); In re Boudreau, 93-9491-8G3 (Bankr MD Fla 1995); Hawkins, 102 TC 61 (1994); Powell, 101 TC 489 (1993); Karem, 100 TC 521 (1993); Darby, 97 TC 51 (1991)] In another case, the court concluded that a transfer of funds from a qualified retirement plan to a holding company was a distribution to the participant who directed the transfer because the participant could not prove that the plan was a partner with the holding company or that the funds were invested on behalf of the plan. [Federated Graphics Cos, Inc, 63 TCM 3153 (1992)] An individual who withdrew funds from his profit sharing plan to make a down payment on a home had to include the withdrawal in income. [Grow, 70 TCM 1576 (1995); see also Eagan v United States, 1996 US App Lexis 5824 (1st Cir 1996)]

A participant's waiver assigning his retirement plan benefits to the employer constituted a prohibited assignment or alienation (see Q 4:24) and resulted in his receipt of a taxable distribution. The court ruled that the waived benefits did not represent excess assets reverting to the employer. [Gallade, 106 TC No. 20 (1996)]

A profit sharing plan that allowed a participant to have elective contributions (see Q 23:13) allocated to a separate retiree medical subaccount permitted the participant, upon retirement, either to receive taxable distributions from the subaccount or to use the subaccount to pay health care premiums. IRS ruled that amounts used to pay health care premiums would be includible in the participant's gross income in the taxable year so used. [Ltr Ruls 9513027, 9405021]

In certain instances, penalty taxes are imposed on distributions that exceed certain amounts (see Q 13:27) and on distributions that commence too early (see Qs 13:39–13:42) or too late (see Q 11:20).

Distributions to beneficiaries generally are also included in the deceased participant's estate for federal estate tax purposes. Such distributions may also be subject to penalty taxes if they exceed certain amounts (see Q 13:43).

Q 13:2 Are any distributions from qualified retirement plans income tax free?

Yes, if the participant has an investment in the contract (also known as basis). [IRC §§ 72(b), as amended by SBA '96 § 1704(1), 72(c), 72(d), 72(e)(5)(E); Malbon v United States, 43 F 3d 466 (9th Cir 1994); George v United States, 30 Fed Cl 371 (1994); Montgomery v United States, 18 F 3d 500 (7th Cir 1994); Guilzon v Comm'r, 985 F 2d 819 (5th Cir 1993); Shimota v United States, 21 Cls Ct 510 (1990), *aff'd*, 943 F 2d 1312 (Fed Cir 1991); Gomez, TCM 1996-212; Grow, 70 TCM 1576 (1995); Kirkland, 67 TCM 2976 (1994); Parker v United States, 860 F Supp 657 (ED Mo 1994); Simmons, 65 TCM 1887 (1993); Twombly, 62 TCM 597 (1991); Rev Proc 92-86, 1992-2 CB 495]

A participant's investment in the contract or basis includes:

1. The participant's after-tax contributions to the qualified retirement plan (i.e., voluntary or mandatory contributions). [Ltr Rul 9310035]

2. PS-58 costs (see Qs 14:7, 14:13). [Ltr Rul 9618028]

3. Loans from the qualified retirement plan to the participant that were treated as taxable distributions (see Qs 13:44–13:52). [Ltr Rul 9122059]

IRS has ruled that, in addition to the PS-58 costs, upon the death of an insured participant, the investment in the contract includes the net death benefit of the policy (i.e., the policy proceeds in excess of the cash surrender value). [Ltr Rul 9618028]

In one case, the beneficiary of a friend's qualified retirement plan death benefits had made an oral agreement to pay the friend's debts in return for being named beneficiary. The beneficiary could not deduct the friend's debts from the amount of the taxable distribution; the assumption of the debts did not constitute basis. [Ballard, 63 TCM 2748 (1992)] In another case, an employee who, after receiving a distribution from a qualified retirement plan, made a payment to his former employer could not characterize the payment as an after-tax plan contribution. [Silver, TCM 1996-42]

Q 13:3 How are annuity payments from a qualified retirement plan taxed?

Annuity payments from a qualified retirement plan under which the participant has no investment in the contract or basis (see Q 13:2) are taxed as ordinary income in the year received by the participant or beneficiary. [IRC § 72(m)]

If a participant has basis, a portion of each distribution is considered a return of the participant's investment in the contract and is therefore not taxable. The following formula applies to determine the part of each payment that is excluded from taxable income:

$$\frac{\text{Investment in the contract}}{\text{Expected return under the annuity}} \times \text{Annual annuity payment}$$

If payments commenced before November 19, 1996, the expected return was determined at the time of commencement on the basis of unisex life expectancy tables. The ratio of the participant's investment in the contract to the expected return under the contract was then applied to each annuity payment to derive the nontaxable portion. [IRC §§ 72(b)(1), 72(e)(8); Treas Reg § 1.72-9; Malbon v United States, 43 F 3d 466 (9th Cir 1994); George v United States, 30 Fed Cl 371 (1994); Montgomery v United States, 18 F 3d 500 (7th Cir 1994); Guilzon v Comm'r, 985 F 2d 819 (5th Cir 1993); Shimota v United States, 21 Cls Ct 510 (1990), aff'd, 943 F 2d 1312 (Fed Cir 1991); Gomez, TCM 1996-212; Green, 68 TCM 167 (1994); Kirkland, 67 TCM 2976 (1994); Parker v United States, 860 F Supp 657 (ED Mo 1994); Simmons, 65 TCM 1887 (1993); Twombly, 62 TCM 597 (1991); Ltr Rul 9618028]

The participant may not exclude from income an amount greater than the participant's investment in the contract. Thus, once the participant recovers the entire basis, all remaining payments are fully taxable. If the participant dies before recovering the entire investment in the contract, the unrecovered basis can be deducted on the participant's last income tax return. [IRC §§ 72(b)(2), 72(b)(3), 72(b)(4)]

> **Example 1.** Able, an individual age 65, has a 20-year life expectancy. Able's monthly pension is $1,000, and he has basis of $24,000. The expected return is $240,000 ($1,000 × 12 × 20). The exclusion ratio is 10 percent ($24,000 ÷ $240,000), and $100 of the monthly payment (10% × $1,000) represents recovery of basis and is nontaxable. After 240 payments, 100 percent of each payment will be taxable. If Able died after 15 years, the unrecovered basis of $6,000 ($24,000 − $18,000) will be deductible on Able's last income tax return.

If payments commenced before November 19, 1996, then, instead of using the unisex life expectancy tables, a simplified safe-harbor method could have been used. [Notice 88-118, 1988-2 CB 450] Under the simplified method, the following table is used:

Age at Annuity Starting Date	Number of Payments
55 and under	300
56–60	260
61–65	240
66–70	170
71 and over	120

Example 2. If Able elected to use the simplified method, he would have the same total payments projection of $240,000 (240 × $1,000), and his exclusion ratio would still be 10 percent ($24,000 ÷ $240,000). However, if Able were 63, his exclusion ratio under the regular method would have only been 9.3 percent (expected return multiple of 21.6 × $12,000 = $259,200; $24,000 ÷ $259,200 = 9.3%).

Under SBA '96 (see Q 1:21), a different simplified method is adopted to derive the nontaxable portion of each payment. Under this simplified method, the portion of each payment that is nontaxable is generally equal to the employee's basis as of the date payments commence, divided by the number of anticipated monthly payments, using the following table:

Age at Annuity Starting Date	Number of Payments
55 and under	360
56–60	310
61–65	260
66–70	210
71 and over	160

Example 3. If Able commences receipt of payments on January 1, 1997, under this simplified method, the nontaxable portion of each monthly payment will be $92.31 ($24,000 ÷ 260).

If the number of payments is fixed, that number is used rather than the number of anticipated payments listed in the table. The simplified method does not apply if the individual has attained age 75 on the annuity starting date unless there are fewer than five years of guaranteed payments under the annuity.

The simplified method is effective if the annuity starting date is on or after November 19, 1996. [IRC § 72(d), as amended by SBA '96 § 1403(a)]

Q 13:4 What is a lump-sum distribution?

A lump-sum distribution is a distribution from a qualified retirement plan of the balance to the credit of an employee (see Q 13:5) made within one taxable year of the recipient. The distribution must be made on account of the employee's death, attainment of age 59½, separation from service (except for self-employed individuals; see Q 6:33), or disability (self-employed individuals only). [IRC § 402(d)(4)(A); Clark, 101 TC 215 (1993); Acquisto, 62 TCM 44 (1991); Baskovich, 61 TCM 2628 (1991); Ltr Rul 9248047]

The distribution must be made from a qualified retirement plan (see Q 13:23); a distribution from the employer's general funds is not a lump-sum distribution. [Gruber, 68 TCM 923 (1994)]

A distribution will not qualify as a lump-sum distribution unless the employee was a plan participant for at least five of the employee's taxable years prior to the year of distribution, and IRS has ruled that plan participants who have their entire account balances transferred directly from an old plan to a new plan may include years of participation in both plans to satisfy the five-year participation requirement. This five-year participation requirement does not apply to a beneficiary receiving a distribution after the participant's death (see Q 13:13). [IRC § 402(d)(4)(F); Prop Reg § 1.402(e)-2(e)(3); Deisenroth, 58 TCM 838 (1989); Ltr Ruls 9425042, 9423032, 9221045, 9114059, 9114058]

Lump-sum distributions may qualify for favorable income tax treatment (see Q 13:13). Further, the participant (or surviving spouse) may elect to defer payment of taxes by rolling over the distribution into an IRA or another qualified retirement plan. See chapter 28 for details.

Q 13:5 What does the term "balance to the credit of an employee" mean?

Balance to the credit of an employee means either the vested (nonforfeitable) account balance (see Q 9:2) that will be distributed from a defined contribution plan (see Q 2:2) or the vested (nonforfeitable) accrued benefit (see Q 9:2) that will be distributed from a defined benefit plan (see Q 2:3). [Emmons, TCM 1996-265; Powell, TCM 1996-264; Pumphrey, 70 TCM 882 (1995); Humberson, 70 TCM 886 (1995)]

In determining whether a distribution is the balance to the credit of the employee, all qualified profit sharing plans must be aggregated, all qualified stock bonus plans must be aggregated, and all qualified pension plans (defined benefit, money purchase, and target benefit plans) must be aggregated. Because only similar plans of the employer are required to be aggregated, a distribution to the employee from a profit sharing plan may qualify as a lump-sum distribution even though the employee still has an interest in a pension plan maintained by the employer. [IRC § 402(d)(4)(C); Brown, 69 TCM 2028 (1995)]

Only the vested portion of an employee's account balance or accrued benefit is taken into account in determining the balance to the credit. For this purpose, amounts attributable to deductible employee contributions (see Q 13:26) are ignored. Accordingly, a partially vested employee who receives a distribution of the entire vested balance may qualify for lump-sum distribution tax treatment. However, if the employee is reemployed and is credited with additional vesting with respect to the employee's preseparation benefits, the tax benefits the employee received earlier will be recaptured. [IRC §§ 402(d)(4)(A), 402(d)(6)(B)]

Two beneficiaries were permitted to elect lump-sum distribution treatment with respect to their deceased mother's qualified retirement plan benefits because the account balance of the mother's predeceased husband was not included in calculating the balance to her credit. The mother's election, as beneficiary of her predeceased husband's benefits, to receive annual distributions after his death, did not preclude her beneficiaries from electing lump-sum distribution treatment with regard to the mother's own account. [Ltr Rul 9541036]

The balance to the credit does not include amounts payable to an alternate payee under a QDRO. See chapter 30. [IRC § 402(d)(4)(H)]

To qualify as a lump-sum distribution, the balance to the credit of the employee must be paid within one taxable year of the recipient. Thus, if more than one payment is planned, all the payments must be made within the same calendar year (most individuals are calendar-year taxpayers). However, if an individual receives lump-sum distributions from both a pension plan and a profit sharing plan of the same employer in the same taxable year, the individual must elect forward averaging treatment for both distributions or neither will qualify for forward averaging. The same rule applies if an individual receives lump-sum distributions from qualified retirement plans of different employers in the same taxable year. [IRC §§ 402(d)(4)(A), 402(d)(4)(B); Sites v United States, Civ 94-820 (D Md 1995); Middleton v United States, 822 F Supp 1549 (SD Ala 1993); Fowler, 98 TC 503 (1992); Blyler, 67 TC 878 (1977); Ltr Rul 9003061]

Even if the distribution represents the balance to the credit of the employee, if a prior distribution from the plan or any other plan required to be aggregated with it was rolled over, five-year forward averaging treatment will *not* be available (see Qs 13:13, 13:18, 28:1). [IRC § 402(c)(10)] This provision, as is five-year forward averaging, is repealed for taxable years beginning *after* 1999. [SBA '96, Act §§ 1401(a), 1401(b)(2)]

If a portion of a participant's benefits in an existing qualified retirement plan (Plan A) is transferred to a new plan (Plan B), and Plan A is terminated soon thereafter, IRS has ruled that the distribution of the remaining benefits in Plan A does not constitute the balance to the credit of the employee and, therefore, is not a lump-sum distribution. [Rev Rul 72-242, 1972-1 CB 116; Ltr Rul 9139031]

Q 13:6 How are frozen plan assets treated for the balance to the credit requirement?

In order to determine whether a qualified retirement plan distribution is a lump-sum distribution (see Q 13:4), the employee's balance to the credit (see Q 13:5) in the plan must be determined.

When the distribution of plan assets invested in group annuity contracts was contingent upon their release pursuant to court-authorized proceedings, IRS ruled that a plan participant's balance to the credit may be determined by excluding the portion of the participant's benefit that was attributable to amounts that were not being paid to the plan by the insurance company because of the court-authorized proceedings. [IRS Special Ruling (Oct 3, 1991); Rev Rul 83-57, 1983-1 CB 92; Ltr Rul 9219042]

However, when complete distribution of plan assets could not be made within one taxable year because a portion of the plan assets was in a frozen real estate fund, IRS ruled that the distribution of all other plan assets would not be a lump-sum distribution. [Ltr Ruls 9316047, 9137046] But, if a qualified retirement plan holds illiquid, nonmarketable assets, IRS has ruled that a distribution of both liquid assets and an interest in the illiquid assets can constitute a lump-sum distribution. An independent, nonqualified trust is established, and the illiquid assets are transferred to the nonqualified trust. Each participant, in addition to receiving a distribution of liquid assets, receives a transferable certificate representing the participant's interest in the nonqualified trust. This total distribution may qualify for favorable income tax treatment (see Q 13:13). [Ltr Ruls 9507032, 9418028, 9226066, 9108049, 9104038] Even though the final distribution may be a lump-sum distribution, it will *not* qualify for five-year forward averaging treatment (see Q 13:13) if the employee rolled over any prior distribution from the plan or from any plan required to be aggregated with the distributing plan (see Qs 13:5, 28:8–28:31). [IRC § 402(c)(10)]

Q 13:7 Can an employee who received installment payments later receive a lump-sum distribution from the same qualified retirement plan?

No. If an employee separates from service, receives benefits in installment payments, and then takes the balance to the employee's credit under the qualified retirement plan in a subsequent taxable year in lieu of the remaining installment payments, the payout will not qualify as a lump-sum distribution. [Prop Reg § 1.402(e)-2(d)(1)(ii)(C); Ltr Ruls 9137037, 8917020]

However, if an employee commences receiving distributions while still employed and subsequently terminates employment and receives the balance to the employee's credit under the plan within a single taxable year, IRS has ruled that the final distribution will qualify as a lump-sum distribution. [Ltr Ruls 9143078, 9052058] But, if any prior distribution from the plan was rolled over, the employee will *not* be eligible for five-year forward averaging treatment (see Qs 13:5, 28:8–28:31). [IRC § 402(c)(10)]

Q 13:8   **Are the tax benefits of a lump-sum distribution lost when an additional distribution is made in a subsequent taxable year?**

Not necessarily. If a distribution constituted the balance to the credit of the employee at the time it was made and all other requirements are satisfied (see Qs 13:4, 13:5), it is treated as a lump-sum distribution even if additional amounts are credited and distributed to the employee in a later taxable year. The additional distribution, however, is not a lump-sum distribution. [Campbell, 64 TCM 1117 (1992); Prop Reg § 1.402(e)-2(d)(1)(ii)(B); Rev Rul 69-190, 1969-1 CB 131; Rev Rul 56-558, 1956-2 CB 290; Ltr Ruls 9009055, 8952010; but see Ltr Rul 9252034]

Q 13:9   **What does separation from service mean?**

Separation from service and termination of employment are synonymous. Separation from service does not occur when the employee continues on the same job for a different employer as a result of a corporate transaction (e.g., merger or sale) or continues on the same job for the same employer after the sale of a shareholder's shares, or when the individual's status changes from an employee and sole shareholder of a professional corporation to a sole proprietor (see Q 2:20). Separation from service occurs only upon death, retirement, resignation, or discharge, and not when the employee continues in the same job for a different employer. [GCM 39824; Vidrine, 66 TCM 123 (1993); Burton, 99 TC 622 (1992); Dickson, 59 TCM 314 (1990); Edwards v Comm'r, 906 F 2d 114 (4th Cir 1990); United States v Johnson, 331 F 2d 943 (5th Cir 1964); Rev Rul 81-141, 1981-1 CB 204; Rev Rul 81-26, 1981-1 CB 200; Rev Rul 80-129, 1980-1 CB 86; Rev Rul 79-336, 1979-2 CB 187; Ltr Ruls 9443041, 9243048, 8441071] However, IRS has ruled that separation from service did occur notwithstanding continued employment with another employer that had assumed certain functions performed previously by the first employer. Both employers were unrelated; ownership of both employers did not change; and the transfer of functions was not incident to an asset transfer, exchange of stock, merger, or consolidation. [Ltr Rul 9325045]

Distribution need not be made in the year of the employee's termination of employment to be considered made "on account of" the employee's separation from service. Thus, distributions from qualified retirement plans that permit distributions to be deferred until a specified age or time may qualify as lump-sum distributions. [Ltr Ruls 8949102, 8541094, 8541116] An individual received a distribution from a state retirement system when he elected to transfer the balance of his benefits to the state pension system. The individual retired at about the same time. Even though the distribution was made because of the transfer from one system to the other and not because of the individual's retirement, the court concluded that the distribution was made "on account of" his separation from service. [Adler, 95-2348 (4th Cir 1996)]

A distribution to a self-employed individual (see Q 6:33) cannot qualify as a lump-sum distribution solely by reason of separation from service (see Q 13:4). [IRC § 402(d)(4)(A); Ltr Rul 8945053]

Q 13:10 Can a distribution from a qualified retirement plan to a disabled employee qualify as a lump-sum distribution?

No, unless the employee terminates employment at that time (see Q 13:9). On the other hand, a distribution from a qualified retirement plan to a disabled (see Q 26:41) self-employed individual (see Q 6:33) can be a lump-sum distribution (see Q 13:4). [IRC §§ 72(m)(7), 402(d)(4)(A)]

Although some courts [Berner v United States, No. 79-1485 (WD Pa 1981); Wood, 590 F 2d 321 (9th Cir 1979); Masterson v United States, 478 F Supp 454 (DC Ill 1979)] have ruled that amounts paid to a disabled employee under the disability retirement provisions of a qualified retirement plan are tax-free disability payments, IRS and most other courts have ruled that such amounts are taxable. [IRC § 105(c); Rev Rul 85-105, 1985-2 CB 53; IRS Litigation Guideline Memorandum (TL-60); Estate of Hall, TCM 1996-93; Dorroh, 68 TCM 337 (1994); Burnside, 67 TCM 2557 (1994); Berman v Comm'r, 925 F 2d 936 (6th Cir 1991); Beisler v Comm'r, 787 F 2d 1325 (9th Cir 1986); Gordon, 88 TC 630 (1987); Mabry, 50 TCM 336 (1985); Caplin v United States, 718 F 2d 544 (2d Cir 1983); Christensen v United States, 7 EBC 1110 (D Minn 1986); Gibson v United States, 643 F Supp 181 (WD Tenn 1986); Ltr Rul 9504041]

Q 13:11 How is a lump-sum distribution from a qualified retirement plan to the beneficiary of a deceased participant taxed?

If the beneficiary is the surviving spouse of the deceased participant, the same options that would have been available to the participant (see Q

13:13) are available to the spouse. Other beneficiaries have the same options, except they cannot take advantage of a tax-free rollover to an IRA (see Q 28:36). [IRC §§ 402(c)(9), 402(d)(4)]

The five-year participation requirement (see Qs 13:4, 13:13) for electing forward averaging does not apply to distributions due to death. [IRC § 402(d)(4)(F)]

Q 13:12   Can the beneficiary of a deceased participant who received annuity payments from a qualified retirement plan receive a lump-sum distribution?

Yes. A distribution to an employee before the employee's death, in the form of annuity payments after retirement, will not prevent the employee's beneficiary from receiving a lump-sum distribution. [Prop Reg § 1.402(e)-2(d)(1)(ii)(B); Rev Rul 69-495, 1969-2 CB 100] However, if the employee rolled over any of the annuity payments, the beneficiary will *not* be eligible to elect five-year forward averaging treatment (see Qs 13:5, 13:7). [IRC § 402(c)(10)]

Q 13:13   How is a lump-sum distribution from a qualified retirement plan to an employee taxed?

An employee who has attained age 59½ and who has completed at least five years of plan participation prior to the year of distribution (see Q 13:4) has five income tax options:

1. The ordinary income portion of the distribution (amount attributable to post-1973 plan participation) might qualify for five-year forward averaging or ten-year forward averaging, and the rest of the distribution (amount attributable to pre-1974 plan participation) might qualify as long-term capital gain (see Qs 13:14, 13:18, 13:19, 13:21).

2. The entire distribution may be reported as ordinary income and might qualify for five-year forward averaging (see Q 13:18).

3. The entire distribution may be reported as ordinary income and might qualify for ten-year forward averaging (see Qs 13:14, 13:19).

4. The entire distribution may be reported as ordinary income without electing either five-year forward averaging or ten-year forward averaging. [IRC § 402(a)]

5. All or part of the distribution may be rolled over to an IRA or to another qualified retirement plan; no tax is paid on the amount rolled over; and the rest is taxed as ordinary income without the availability of electing five-year forward averaging or ten-year forward averaging (see Qs 28:8–28:31). [IRC § 402(d)(4)(K); Barrett, 64 TCM 1080 (1992)]

To qualify for five-year forward averaging, the employee must have attained age 59½. [Orgera, 70 TCM 1488 (1995)] This requirement applies if the employee dies prior to age 59½ even though a lump-sum distribution is made to the deceased employee's beneficiary. Thus, even if the beneficiary has attained age 59½, five-year forward averaging is not available if the employee died prior to age 59½. [Cebula, 101 TC 70 (1993); IRC § 402(d)(4)(B)] For options available when the participant has not satisfied the five-year participation requirement, see Q 13:15.

An individual who receives a lump-sum distribution and who attained age 50 before January 1, 1986 is eligible to elect special tax treatment (see Q 13:14).

If more than one lump-sum distribution is received in a single taxable year, all such distributions received that year must be aggregated, and the election to use forward averaging will apply to the aggregate amount. Only one election to use forward averaging treatment is permitted after the employee has attained age 59½. If the employer maintains more than one qualified retirement plan, special rules apply (see Q 13:5). [IRC §§ 402(d)(4)(A), 402(d)(4)(B), 402(d)(4)(C); Hegarty, 63 TCM 2335 (1992)]

If any prior distribution from the qualified retirement plan or any other plan required to be aggregated with the distributing plan was rolled over, five-year forward averaging will *not* be available for the distribution from the distributing plan or any aggregated plan (see Qs 13:5, 13:7). [IRC § 402(c)(10)]

SBA '96 (see Q 1:21) repeals five-year forward averaging for taxable years beginning *after* 1999. [SBA '96, Act § 1401(a)] Even though RRB '96 (see Q 1:22A) contains a provision replacing age 59½ with age 59, the provision will not apply to either the definition of a lump-sum distribution or the ability to elect five-year forward averaging if otherwise available. [RRB '96, Act § 9445(a)]

Q 13:14 What special rules apply to a lump-sum distribution with regard to an individual who had attained age 50 before January 1, 1986?

If an individual who had attained age 50 before January 1, 1986 receives a lump-sum distribution, the requirement that an individual be at least age 59½ (see Q 13:13) to use forward averaging tax treatment will not apply, and the individual may elect capital gains treatment for the pre-1974 portion of the distribution (see Q 13:21). [Ltr Rul 9221045]

Forward averaging can be either five-year averaging at the rates in effect at the time of distribution or ten-year averaging at the rates in effect during 1986 (see Q 13:20). Under either alternative, capital gains will be taxed at a flat 20 percent rate. Alternatively, the individual can elect either five-year averaging or ten-year averaging on the entire distribution.

Only one election to use forward averaging (and capital gains treatment) is permitted. Thus, an individual who makes an election under the special rule for individuals who attained age 50 before January 1, 1986 will be unable to make another election under the general rule after attaining age 59½. [TRA '86 §§ 1122(h)(5), 1122(h)(3)(A)(ii), 1122(h)(3)(B)(ii); Ltr Rul 9226076]

Even though five-year forward averaging is repealed for taxable years beginning after 1999 (see Q 13:13), ten-year forward averaging and capital gains treatment will remain available to those individuals eligible to elect the special rules.

Even though five-year forward averaging is unavailable if a prior distribution was rolled over (see Q 13:13), ten-year averaging and capital gains treatment should remain available. [IRC § 402(c)(10)]

Q 13:15   What tax options are available when a participant does not satisfy the five-year participation requirement?

Forward averaging is not an option (see Q 13:4), so only two tax choices are available:

1. A tax-free rollover into an IRA or another qualified retirement plan (see Q 28:8); or
2. Inclusion of the distribution in gross income for the year of receipt.

Q 13:16   What portion of a lump-sum distribution is taxable?

Several adjustments that reduce the taxable amount of a lump-sum distribution are made before any tax is computed. The amount of the employee's investment in the contract (see Q 13:2) is subtracted from the distribution in computing the taxable amount. If any part of the distribution is made in employer securities, special rules apply (see Q 13:17).

If the recipient elects to use forward averaging, a minimum distribution allowance reduces the tax on relatively small distributions. The allowance, which is subtracted in computing the taxable amount of the payout, is the lesser of $10,000 or one-half of the total taxable amount of the payout, reduced by 20 percent of the excess of the total amount over $20,000. In effect, there is no minimum distribution allowance if the total taxable amount is $70,000 or more. [IRC § 402(d)(1)(C)]

Example. Assume that Sallie receives a lump-sum distribution of $50,000 in cash from a qualified retirement plan, has no basis, and the entire payment is ordinary income (i.e., attributable to post-1973 plan participation). The minimum distribution allowance is the lesser of $10,000 or one-half the total taxable amount. Because it is less than $25,000 (i.e., one-half of $50,000), the $10,000 figure applies. The $10,000 figure is then reduced by 20 percent of the excess of the taxable amount of the payment over $20,000, or $6,000 (20 percent of $30,000). This makes the minimum distribution allowance $4,000 and the taxable amount of the distribution $46,000.

Q 13:17   What is the tax treatment of a lump-sum distribution made in the form of employer securities?

Special rules apply to appreciated stock or other securities of the employer that are included in a lump-sum distribution. These rules apply to employer securities distributed from an employee stock ownership plan (ESOP; see Q 24:1) or from any other type of qualified retirement plan. The gain on the securities while they were held by the qualified retirement plan (the net unrealized appreciation) is not subject to tax until the securities are sold by the recipient, at which time the gain is eligible for capital gains treatment. The basis of the securities (the value when contributed to the plan) is includible in income upon distribution. If the value of the securities at the time of distribution is less than basis, the total value of the securities is taxable in accordance with the general rules applicable to lump-sum distributions. The net unrealized appreciation, however, may be subject to the excess distributions tax (see Qs 13:27, 13:29). [IRC §§ 402(d)(4)(D), 402(e)(4), 402(j); Prop Reg § 1.402(a)-1(b)(1); Treas Reg § 1.402(a)-1(b)(2); Rev Rul 75-125, 1975-1 CB 254, Rev Rul 69-297, 1969-1 CB 131; Ltr Ruls 9619079, 9448045, 9438044, 9233052, 9222055, 9222048]

The recipient of a distribution that includes employer securities may elect to have the net unrealized appreciation included in income at the time the distribution is received rather than taxed as a capital gain at the time the securities are sold. This election is made on the recipient's tax return for the year in which the distribution is received. [IRC § 402(e)(4)(B); Notice 89-25 (Q&A 1), 1989-1 CB 662]

An employee's novel contention that his receipt of employer securities from an ESOP was not taxable because it represented a mere name change from the ESOP trustee to the employee was rejected. [Stoddard, 66 TCM 585 (1993)]

Q 13:18   How is the tax on a lump-sum distribution computed using the five-year averaging method?

The tax computed using the five-year averaging method is separate from and in addition to the regular income tax. To avoid double taxation, the ordinary income portion is deducted from the recipient's gross income. The tax on lump-sum distributions for which five-year averaging is elected is computed using IRS Form 4972 (see Q 13:24).

There are three basic steps in computing the tax on ordinary income using five-year averaging:

Step 1: Subtract the minimum distribution allowance (see Q 13:16) from the ordinary income portion of the distribution.

Step 2: Divide the net amount determined in Step 1 by five and compute the initial separate tax on this figure using the rate table for single individuals (regardless of the recipient's marital status).

Step 3: Multiply the initial separate tax determined in Step 2 by five.

For 1996, the following schedule (which takes into account the minimum distribution allowance) may be used to calculate the tax on a lump-sum distribution for which this averaging method is elected:

If ⅕ of the Adjusted Total Taxable Amount Is		The Five-Year Averaging Tax Is 5 Times		
Over	*But Not Over*	*This Amount*	*Plus This %*	*Of the Excess Over*
. . .	$ 24,000	Zero	15.0	Zero
$ 24,000	58,150	$ 3,600.00	28.0	$ 24,000
58,150	121,300	13,162.00	31.0	58,150
121,300	263,750	32,738.50	36.0	121,300
263,750	. . .	84,020.50	39.6	263,750

Multiple lump-sum distributions received during the taxable year are added together in computing the tax using the five-year averaging method. Only one election to use forward averaging may be made after 1986. [IRC §§ 402(d)(1)(B), 402(d)(3), 402(d)(4)(B); Ltr Rul 9231046]

Five-year forward averaging is repealed for taxable years beginning *after* 1999. [SBA '96, Act § 1401(a)]

Q 13:19   How is the tax on a lump-sum distribution computed using the ten-year averaging method?

Ten-year forward averaging is available only if the participant had attained age 50 before January 1, 1986 (see Q 13:14). Since ten-year forward averaging remains keyed to the 1986 income tax rates, the following schedule (which takes into account the minimum distribution allowance; see Q 13:16) may be used to calculate the tax on a lump-sum distribution for which this averaging method is elected:

If ¹⁄₁₀ of the Adjusted Total Taxable Amount Is		The Ten-Year Averaging Tax Is 10 Times		
Over	But Not Over	This Amount	Plus This %	Of the Excess Over
. . .	$ 1,190	Zero	11	Zero
$ 1,190	2,270	$ 130.90	12	$ 1,190
2,270	4,530	260.50	14	2,270
4,530	6,690	576.90	15	4,530
6,690	9,170	900.90	16	6,690
9,170	11,440	1,297.70	18	9,170
11,440	13,710	1,706.30	20	11,440
13,710	17,160	2,160.30	23	13,710
17,160	22,880	2,953.80	26	17,160
22,880	28,600	4,441.00	30	22,880
28,600	34,320	6,157.00	34	28,600
34,320	42,300	8,101.80	38	34,320
42,300	57,190	11,134.20	42	42,300
57,190	85,790	17,388.00	48	57,190
85,790	. . .	31,116.00	50	85,790

Even though five-year forward averaging is repealed for taxable years beginning after 1999 (see Q 13:18), ten-year forward averaging will remain available to those individuals eligible to elect the special rule.

Q 13:20   Is ten-year averaging always more favorable than five-year averaging?

No, because ten-year forward averaging remains keyed to the 1986 income tax rates. For a lump-sum distribution received during calendar year 1996, the ten-year averaging method is more favorable than five-year forward averaging only if the adjusted total taxable amount is $358,220 or less. Above $358,220, the ten-year averaging method results in a greater income tax than the five-year averaging method.

If the individual is not eligible to elect ten-year forward averaging (see Qs 13:13, 13:14), the five-year averaging method is more favorable than regular ordinary income treatment, unless the individual has tax-deductible expenses to offset the income or the five-year averaging tax bracket (see Q 13:18) is greater than the individual's personal federal income tax bracket.

Q 13:21 What portion of a lump-sum distribution from a qualified retirement plan may be eligible for capital gains treatment?

Generally, no portion of a lump-sum distribution from a qualified retirement plan is eligible to be taxed under separate tax rates applicable to capital gains. [IRC § 402(a)(2) before repeal by TRA '86 § 1122(b)(1)(A)]

However, an individual who attained age 50 before January 1, 1986 may elect to treat the capital gain portion of a lump-sum distribution under the 1986 tax provisions. This means that the capital gain portion will be taxed at a flat 20 percent rate (see Q 13:14). [Ltr Rul 9221045]

An employee (or the employee's beneficiaries) who is able to treat the portion attributable to pre-1974 participation as long-term capital gain may also irrevocably elect to use forward averaging on the entire distribution. This election is significant because, as a capital gain, part of a lump-sum distribution might otherwise be subject to the alternative minimum tax. [IRC § 402(e)(4)(L) before repeal by TAMRA § 1011(A)(b)(8)(G); Brown, 93 TC 736 (1989)]

The allocation between the capital gain portion and the ordinary income portion is made on the basis of the number of months of active participation before 1974 as compared with the total number of months of plan participation (see Q 13:22). The portion of the taxable amount of a distribution that is taxed as long-term capital gain is determined as follows:

$$\text{Taxable amount} \times \frac{\text{Number of months of plan participation before 1974}}{\text{Number of months of plan participation}}$$

[IRC § 402(a)(2) before repeal by TRA '86 § 1122(b)(1)(A)]

If the qualified retirement plan from which the distribution is made had assets transferred to it from another qualified retirement plan or if the distributee plan was merged into the plan making the distribution, the period of active participation includes both participation in the distributing plan and participation in the distributee plan. Although IRS has previously ruled that plan participants who have their entire account balances transferred directly from one plan to another may treat pre-1974 participation in the distributee plan as pre-1974 participation in the distributing plan for purposes of determining the capital gain portion of the distribution [Ltr Ruls

9114059, 8934051, 8535116], it has more recently ruled that pre-1974 participation would apply only to the transferred account balances [Ltr Rul
9425042].

Q 13:22 How is the number of months of plan participation computed?

To compute an employee's number of months of participation (see Q
13:21), any part of a calendar year prior to 1974 in which the employee
participated in the qualified retirement plan is counted as 12 months, and
any part of a calendar month after 1973 in which the employee participated
in the plan is counted as one month. [Prop Reg § 1.402(e)-2(d)(3)(ii)]

Example. If an employee commenced participation in a plan on December 22, 1970 and terminated employment on May 2, 1997, the employee
would have 48 (12 × 4) months of pre-1974 participation and 281 [(12 ×
23) + 5] months of post-1973 participation, for a total of 329 months of
participation. If the total taxable amount of the distribution received by
the employee is $658,000, the capital gain portion is $96,000 (48 ÷ 329
× $658,000) and the ordinary income portion is $562,000 (281 ÷ 329 ×
$658,000).

Q 13:23 How is the distribution taxed if the retirement plan loses its qualified status?

If IRS revokes the favorable determination letter (see Q 15:1) previously issued to the retirement plan, the plan is no longer qualified, and
a distribution from the retirement plan will not be eligible for favorable
tax treatment (see Q 13:13) or qualify as an eligible rollover distribution
(see Q 28:8). [Treas Reg §§ 1.402(a)-1(a)(1)(ii), 1.402(a)-1(a)(1)(v),
1.402(b)-1(b); Meyers v Comm'r, Nos. 95-1521 and 4943-94 (7th Cir
1996); Cass v Comm'r, 774 F 2d 740 (7th Cir 1985); Baetens v Comm'r,
777 F 2d 1160 (6th Cir 1985); Woodson v Comm'r, 651 F 2d 1094 (5th Cir
1981); Weddel, TCM 1996-36; Fazi, 105 TC No. 29 (1995); Fazi, 102 TC
695 (1994); Meyers, 68 TCM 1354 (1994); but see Greenwald v Comm'r,
366 F 2d 538 (2d Cir 1966)]

Q 13:24 How does a recipient elect special forward averaging for a lump-sum distribution?

Form 4972, Tax on Lump-Sum Distributions, is used for electing five-year
and ten-year averaging and computing the tax. The form must be attached

to the individual's tax return for the year in which the distribution is received. [Prop Reg § 1.402(e)-3(c)(2)]

Plan administrators must issue Form 1099-R (Distributions from Pensions, Annuities, Retirement or Profit-Sharing Plans, IRAs, Insurance Contracts, etc.) to let the recipient know the amount of the distribution and the breakdown between ordinary income and capital gain. This statement must be issued to the recipient by January 31 of the year following the distribution, and a copy must be sent to IRS by the end of February.

Q 13:25 Must all recipients of a single lump-sum distribution elect to use forward averaging?

No. When more than one person receives a payment qualifying as a lump-sum distribution (e.g., if the payments are made to several beneficiaries on the participant's death), any eligible recipient may elect to use forward averaging even if the others do not. Similarly, any recipient may decide to treat amounts attributable to pre-1974 participation as ordinary income instead of capital gain (see Q 13:21). [TIR-1426, Dec 15, 1975; Ann 76-51, 1976-15 IRB 30]

Form 4972 (see Q 13:24) is used to make the election and compute the tax.

Q 13:26 What is the income tax treatment of distributions of deductible employee contributions made by a participant?

Distributions of deductible employee contributions (see Q 6:22), including earnings, are taxed as ordinary income in the year received. They do not qualify for forward averaging tax treatment as a lump-sum distribution (see Q 13:4) or the $5,000 income tax exemption for death benefits (see Q 14:18). If a distribution is premature (i.e., made before the participant reaches age 59½, dies, or is disabled), a penalty tax equal to 10 percent of the amount distributed may be imposed (see Qs 13:39–13:42). [IRC §§ 72(o), 72(t)]

Distributions of deductible employee contributions may be rolled over to an IRA or another qualified retirement plan on a tax-free basis. See chapter 28.

Q 13:27 May any additional taxes be imposed on the recipient of a distribution from a qualified retirement plan?

In addition to penalty taxes imposed on distributions that commence too early (see Qs 13:39–13:42) or too late (see Q 11:20), a 15 percent excise tax is imposed on excess distributions (see Q 13:28). The individual with respect to whom the excess distributions are made is liable for this additional tax. [IRC §§ 4980A(a), 4980A(b); Temp Reg § 54.4981A-1T, Q&A a-1; Emmons, TCM 1996-265; Montgomery, TCM 1996-263; Wittstadt, Jr, 70 TCM 994 (1995); Ltr Rul 9041041]

This 15 percent excise tax is suspended for a three-year period—1997, 1998, and 1999—and any distributions received during that period are treated as made first from the non-grandfather amount (see Qs 13:31-13:36). [IRC § 4980A(g), as added by SBA '96 § 1452(b)]

Q 13:28   What are excess distributions?

The term "excess distributions" means the aggregate amount of retirement plan distributions (see Q 13:29) made with respect to any individual during any calendar year to the extent that such amount exceeds either (1) $112,500 (as adjusted for inflation), or (2) $150,000. This is known as the threshold amount. The $112,500 adjusted threshold amount is used by individuals who elected the special grandfather rule, and the $150,000 unadjusted threshold amount is used by individuals who did not elect or were ineligible to elect the special grandfather rule (see Q 13:31). For 1996, the $112,500 amount has increased to $155,000. Since the adjusted threshold amount now exceeds the $150,000 unadjusted amount, the $155,000 threshold amount is available to all individuals whether or not the special grandfather rule was elected. [IRC § 4980A(c)(1); Temp Reg § 54.4981A-1T, Q&A a-2, a-9; Notice 95-55, 1995-45 IRB 11] For prior years, the adjusted amounts were as follows:

Year	Adjusted Amount
1995	$150,000
1994	148,500
1993	144,551
1992	140,276
1991	136,204
1990	128,228
1989	122,580
1988	117,529

Example. Stella commences receiving annual distributions from three retirement plans in 1996: $90,000 from a defined benefit plan; $55,000 from a profit sharing plan; and $30,000 from an IRA. Stella did not make a grandfather election (see Q 13:31). Since Stella's total retirement distributions ($175,000) in 1996 exceed the $155,000 threshold amount by $20,000, the excise tax will be $3,000 (15% × $20,000).

The threshold amount is adjusted at the same time and in the same manner as under Section 415(d) (see Qs 6:2, 6:8). However, an adjustment will be made only if it is $5,000 or greater and then will be made in multiples of $5,000 (i.e., rounded down to the next lowest multiple of $5,000). For example, an increase in the cost-of-living of $4,999 will result in no adjustment, and an increase of $9,999 will create an upward adjustment of $5,000. Although an increase in the threshold amount can be abrogated (see Q 6:25), it cannot be reduced below the 1994 amount. [IRC § 415(d); RPA '94, Act § 732(e)(2)]

The table below shows, in a general way, how the threshold amount would change with an annual cost-of-living adjustment of 2.5 percent:

Year	2.5% COLA	New Limit
1997	$158,875	$155,000
1998	162,847	160,000
1999	166,918	165,000
2000	171,091	170,000

Even though the excess distribution tax is suspended for 1997, 1998, and 1999 (see Q 13:27), there is *no* suspension for increases to the threshold amount during these years.

See Q 13:30 regarding special treatment of lump-sum distributions.

Q 13:29   What distributions are taken into account to compute the individual's excess distributions?

All distributions from qualified retirement plans, tax-sheltered annuities (see Q 29:1), and IRAs (see Q 26:1) must be taken into account in determining the amount of excess distributions for the calendar year. [Temp Reg § 54.4981A-1T, Q&A a-3, a-6]

The following amounts, whether or not they are actually distributed during the year or currently includible in income, are also included:

1. Amounts payable to an alternate payee under a QDRO (see Q 30:1) if not taxable to the alternate payee (e.g., a child);

2. Payments received under an annuity contract previously distributed from a plan;

3. PS-58 costs (see Qs 14:7, 14:13);

4. Loans that are treated as taxable distributions (see Qs 13:44–13:52);

5. Amounts includible in income because of plan disqualification (see Q 4:23); and

6. Net unrealized appreciation in employer securities (see Q 13:17) when distributed.

[IRC § 4980A(e); Temp Reg § 54.4981A-1T, Q&A a-5, a-8]

The following amounts, however, are not included:

1. Amounts received by any person as a result of the participant's death;

2. Amounts payable to an alternate payee under a QDRO (see Q 30:1) if taxable to the alternate payee (e.g., spouse or former spouse);

3. Amounts attributable to the individual's investment in the contract (e.g., a distribution that is excluded from gross income because it is treated as a recovery of nondeductible contributions from an IRA) (see Q 13:2);

4. Any amount rolled over into an IRA or another qualified retirement plan (see chapter 28);

5. The distribution of an annuity contract from a plan;

6. Certain inherited benefits;

7. Any health coverage or any distribution of medical benefits provided to retirees under a pension or certain other plans to the extent that the coverage or distribution is excludable from an individual's gross income; and

8. Distributions of excess deferrals, excess contributions, excess aggregate contributions, and excess IRA contributions, including any income attributable to such amounts.

[IRC §§ 401(k)(8), 401(m)(6), 402(g)(2), 408(d)(4), 408(d)(5), 4980A(c)(2); Temp Reg § 54.4981A-1T, Q&A a-4, a-5, a-7, a-8, d-10; Ltr Ruls 9416037, 9402022, 9303023, 9138004, 9013008, 9013020]

Post-death distributions may be disregarded for purposes of the tax on excess distributions. Thus, a beneficiary who is receiving distributions with respect to a participant after the participant's death is not required to aggregate those amounts with any other retirement distributions except for a surviving spouse who made a spousal election (see Q 14:26). If the surviving spouse did not make a spousal election and rolled over the distribution, then post-death distributions will be disregarded only if the surviving spouse did not commingle the rollover with any other IRA funds. IRS has determined that this rule applies even if the rollover by the surviving spouse occurred prior to the enactment of the tax on excess distributions. Prior to August 1, 1986, the surviving spouse rolled over her deceased husband's qualified retirement plan and IRA benefits to a newly established IRA in her own name. IRS ruled that distributions from the IRA will be disregarded for purposes of the taxes on both excess distributions during the surviving spouse's lifetime and excess retirement accumulations upon her death. [Ltr Rul 9619072]

If RRB '95 (see Q 1:22A) is enacted, distributions from an American Dream IRA (see Q 26:13) will not be included in determining the amount of excess distributions for the calendar year. [RRB '95, Act § 11015(c)]

Q 13:30 Is there a special rule regarding excess distributions when the individual receives a lump-sum distribution?

Yes. If the retirement distributions with respect to any individual include a lump-sum distribution (see Q 13:4) for which the individual elects forward averaging or capital gains tax treatment (see Qs 13:13, 13:14), the lump-sum distribution is treated separately from the other distributions and is subject to a threshold amount that is five times the threshold amount that applies to non-lump-sum distributions [$775,000 for 1996 (5 × $155,000); see Q 13:28]. [IRC § 4980A(c)(4); Temp Reg § 54.4981A-1T, Q&A c-1; Ltr Rul 9328034]

> **Example 1.** In 1996, Stephanie, age 60, receives a lump-sum distribution of $775,000 from a qualified retirement plan and elects five-year income averaging. Whether or not Stephanie made a grandfather election (see Q 13:31), her threshold amount is $155,000. Stephanie's distribution consists solely of an amount in the lump-sum category. Stephanie's threshold amount equals $775,000 (5 × $155,000). Because Stephanie's threshold amount ($775,000) equals the amount of her distribution from the plan ($775,000), no part of her lump-sum distribution is treated as an excess distribution subject to the 15 percent excise tax.

> **Example 2.** Assume the same facts, except that Stephanie receives an additional distribution from an IRA of $155,000. Stephanie's distributions consist of two categories: the lump-sum category (qualified retirement plan—$775,000) and the non-lump-sum category (IRA—$155,000). A separate threshold amount is subtracted from Stephanie's IRA distribution. This threshold amount equals $155,000, the same initial threshold amount that is applied against the lump-sum distribution prior to the multiplication by five. Because Stephanie's threshold amount ($155,000) equals the amount of her distribution from the IRA ($155,000), no part of her distribution from the IRA is treated as an excess distribution subject to the 15 percent excise tax.

If a distribution from a qualified retirement plan is rolled over, five-year forward averaging treatment will not be available for any subsequent distribution to the employee from the distributing plan or from any other qualified retirement plan aggregated with the distributing plan (see Qs 13:5, 13:13). Therefore, if five-year averaging is unavailable and the employee is ineligible to elect ten-year averaging or capital gains treatment, there will be no increase in the threshold amount. Assuming, in Example 1, that Stephanie could not elect favorable tax treatment, she would pay an excise tax of $93,000 [15% × ($775,000 – $155,000)]. [IRC § 402(c)(10)]

Even with the repeal of five-year forward averaging (see Q 13:13), the increased threshold amount will still be available if the individual receives a lump-sum distribution and makes an election; such an election may be made only once. [IRC § 4980A(c)(4), as amended by SBA '96 § 1401(b)(12) for taxable years beginning after 1999]

Q 13:31 What is the grandfather rule?

An individual whose total benefits in all retirement plans (see Q 13:29) on August 1, 1986 (the initial grandfather amount) had a value in excess of $562,500 was eligible to elect the special grandfather rule. The special grandfather rule permits an individual to offset distributions by the portion of the initial grandfather amount recovered during the year of distribution. The election had to be made no later than the due date of the individual's timely filed 1988 income tax return.

The $112,500 indexed threshold amount is used by individuals who elected the special grandfather rule. The $150,000 unindexed threshold amount is used by individuals who did not elect or were ineligible to elect the special grandfather rule. Since the indexed $112,500 amount ($155,000 for 1996) now exceeds the unindexed $150,000 amount, the $155,000 amount is available to all individuals, whether or not the grandfather election was made (see Q 13:28).

If an individual elected the special grandfather rule, the individual also had to elect one of two alternative grandfather recovery methods (see Qs 13:33, 13:34) to determine the rate at which the initial grandfather amount would be recovered. Where the special grandfather rule was elected but the individual failed to elect a grandfather recovery method, IRS permitted the individual to use the discretionary method. [Ltr Rul 9443040]

The excess distribution tax does not apply to the portion of the distribution that represents the recovery of the initial grandfather amount. The initial grandfather amount is then reduced by the amount that is treated as a recovery thereof. When an individual's initial grandfather amount has been reduced to zero, the special rule no longer applies, and the entire amount of any subsequent excess distributions will be subject to the 15 percent excise tax. [IRC § 4980A(f); Temp Reg § 54.4981A-1T, Q&A b-1 through b-14 and c-1; Ltr Rul 9615042]

See Q 13:32 for the effect of SBA '96 on the recovery of the grandfather amount.

Q 13:32   What portion of a distribution is treated as the recovery of an individual's initial grandfather amount?

The total amount of all retirement distributions received between August 1 and December 31, 1986 is treated as a recovery of the initial grandfather amount. The portion of retirement distributions received after December 31, 1986 that is treated as a recovery of the initial grandfather amount is calculated under the method of recovery elected (see Q 13:31).

The amount that is treated as a recovery of the initial grandfather amount is then applied, on a dollar-for-dollar basis, as a reduction from the remaining unrecovered grandfather amount. After the entire initial grandfather amount has been recovered, the excise tax rules apply to excess distributions without regard to any grandfather amount.

[IRC § 4980A(f); Temp Reg § 54.4981A-1T, Q&A b-1; Ltr Rul 9615042]

The 15 percent excise tax is suspended for a three-year period—1997, 1998, and 1999 (see Q 13:27). Any distributions received during this three-year period are treated as made first from the non-grandfather amount. [IRC § 4980A(g), as added by SBA '96 § 1452(b)]

As illustrated by the following example, it is unclear as to how this will work if more than the non-grandfather amount is distributed during the three-year period.

Example. Norman has a profit sharing plan account valued at $1 million and, on December 31, 1996, has an unrecovered grandfather amount of $600,000. During each of 1997, 1998, and 1999, Norman receives a distribution of $150,000. The 1997 distribution reduces the non-grandfather amount from $400,000 ($1,000,000 – $600,000) to $250,000, and the 1998 distribution further reduces the amount to $100,000. In 1999, the first $100,000 of that year's distribution reduces the remaining non-grandfather amount to zero.

Assuming Norman elected the discretionary method of recovery (see Q 13:33), how is the $50,000 amount (the excess over the non-grandfather amount) treated?

1. Is the unrecovered grandfather amount reduced by $5,000 (10% of $50,000) under the discretionary method?
2. Is the unrecovered grandfather amount reduced by $50,000 if Norman had previously made an acceleration election (see Q 13:33)?
3. Is the unrecovered grandfather amount reduced by $50,000 even if Norman had not made an acceleration election?

Q 13:33 What is the discretionary method?

Under the discretionary method, 10 percent of the total retirement distributions (see Q 13:29) received by an individual during a calendar year will be treated as a recovery of the initial grandfather amount. This method also allows an individual to elect to accelerate the rate of recovery to 100 percent of the distributions received. [Temp Reg § 54.4981A-1T, Q&A b-12; Ltr Ruls 9615042, 9443040]

Example. Bill had, as of December 31, 1986, a grandfather amount of $800,000. He made the required election to use the special grandfather rule and chose the discretionary method of recovery. In 1995, Bill received total retirement distributions of $100,000. With regard to his 1995 distributions, 10 percent, or $10,000, was treated as a recovery of his initial grandfather amount. In 1996, Bill received $200,000 of distributions. With his 1996 tax return, Bill files Form 5329 electing to accelerate his recovery rate to 100 percent. This election will cause the entire $200,000 of 1996 retirement distributions to be treated as a recovery of Bill's initial grandfather amount. By making this election, Bill avoids the excise tax on the excess portion of his 1996 distributions [$45,000 ($200,000 – $155,000)] because the entire $200,000 represents a recovery of a portion of his initial grandfather amount.

The acceleration election will also be effective for all years subsequent to the election. The election may be made (or revoked retroactively) on an individual's (amended) tax return. However, with respect to deceased individuals, the acceleration election may *not* be made on an amended return filed after the individual's death for a year for which a return was filed before the individual's death, but may be made after the individual's death on either the final tax return or on a return for a prior year that was *not* filed prior to the individual's death. [IRC § 4980A(f); Temp Reg § 54.4981A-1T, Q&A b-12; Ltr Rul 9246027]

If an election is made by the surviving spouse (see Q 14:26), the surviving spouse is allowed to use the deceased spouse's unrecovered grandfather amount (see Q 13:32) and is also deemed to have elected the same method of recovery that had been elected by the deceased participant (see Q 13:31). [Ltr Ruls 9450042, 9311039, 9246026]

See Q 13:32 for the effect of SBA '96 on the recovery of the grandfather amount.

Q 13:34   What is the attained age method?

Under the attained age method, the rate of recovery is calculated based on a formula that takes into account the individual's age both on August 1, 1986 and at the end of the year in which the retirement distributions are received. The recovery rate is derived from a fraction whose numerator is the difference between the individual's attained age in months on August 1, 1986 and the individual's age in months at age 35 (420 months). The denominator of this fraction is the difference between the individual's attained age in months on December 31 of the calendar year in which the retirement distributions are received and the individual's age in months at age 35 (420 months). As a result, the rate of recovery diminishes as the individual ages. [IRC § 4980A(f); Temp Reg § 54.4981A-1T, Q&A b-13]

Example. Christopher had an unrecovered grandfather amount of $1 million as of December 31, 1995. Christopher elected the special grandfather rule and the attained age method of recovery. If Christopher was born on December 1, 1944, his attained age on August 1, 1986 was 500 months. In 1996, Christopher received total distributions of $300,000. His attained age on December 31, 1996 was 625 months. Therefore, of the $300,000 distributed in 1996, $117,073 [$300,000 × (500 – 420) (625 – 420)] represents a recovery of Christopher's initial grandfather amount.

See Q 13:32 for the effect of SBA '96 on the recovery of the grandfather amount.

Q 13:35   How is the amount of the excess distribution tax calculated when the special grandfather rule applies?

The 15 percent excise tax is applied to the amount by which the total retirement distributions received during the calendar year exceed the greater of (1) the threshold amount (see Q 13:28) applicable for the year in which the distribution is made or (2) the initial grandfather amount recovered in that year. This means there is no tax benefit for the recovered grandfather amount up to the threshold amount. [IRC § 4980A(f); Temp Reg § 54.4981A-1T, Q&A b-4; Ltr Rul 9615042]

Example. Peter's unrecovered initial grandfather amount on December 31, 1995 is $600,000. Peter elected the discretionary method (see Q 13:33) of recovery. In 1996, Peter receives IRA distributions totaling $755,000 and makes an acceleration election (see Q 13:33). Even though the grandfather amount recovered ($600,000) is exempt from the excise tax, the remaining $155,000 is subject to the tax. The amount exempt from the excise tax is the greater of (1) the grandfather amount recovered or (2) the threshold amount, not the total of both amounts.

See Q 13:32 for the effect of SBA '96 on the recovery of the grandfather amount.

Q 13:36 How is the special grandfather rule applied if an individual receives both a lump-sum distribution and a non-lump-sum distribution in the same year?

If, in any calendar year, an individual receives both a lump-sum distribution and a non-lump-sum distribution, the grandfather amount will be recovered ratably from each of the two categories of distributions. The ratable recovery is required even if the distribution in one category is less than that category's threshold amount while the distribution in the other category exceeds the applicable threshold amount. [Temp Reg § 54.4981A-1T, Q&A c-1(b), c-1(c), c-1(d)]

See Q 13:32 for the effect of SBA '96 on the recovery of the grandfather amount.

Q 13:37 Is the excess distribution tax reduced by the early distribution tax?

Yes, the 15 percent excess distribution tax is offset by the 10 percent early distribution tax (see Q 13:39), but only to the extent that the early distribution tax is applied to the excess distribution. The early distribution tax is still applicable to the amount of the distribution that is not an excess distribution. [IRC § 4980A(b); Temp Reg § 54.4981A-1T, Q&A c-4; Wittstadt, Jr, 70 TCM 994 (1995)]

> **Example.** In 1996, Sharon, age 35, receives total distributions of $200,000. Her threshold amount is $155,000. The excess distribution tax is $6,750 (15% × $45,000). The entire distribution is subject to an early distribution tax of $20,000 (10% × $200,000). Of that amount, $4,500 (10% × $45,000) may be offset against the excess distribution tax because $4,500 represents the early distribution tax applicable to the excess portion of the distribution. Therefore, Sharon will owe a total of $22,250 [$20,000 + ($6,750 − $4,500)] in additional taxes on her 1996 distribution.

Q 13:38 Can a qualified retirement plan be amended to avoid the excess distribution tax?

If a plan sponsor chooses, it can amend a qualified retirement plan to limit future benefit accruals provided certain notice requirements are satisfied (see Q 9:29). [Temp Reg § 54.4981A-1T, Q&A c-2; ERISA § 204(h)]

However, a qualified retirement plan may not be amended to reduce accrued benefits in order to avoid the excess distribution tax. An amendment reducing accrued benefits generally is a violation of plan qualification requirements (see Q 9:24). [Temp Reg § 54.4981A-1T, Q&A c-3]

Q 13:39 May participants be subject to a penalty for early distribution of benefits?

Yes. The tax of an employee who participates in a qualified retirement plan is increased by 10 percent of the amount that is distributed from the plan and includible in the employee's income, unless the distribution is:

1. Made on or after the date the employee attained age 59½;

2. Made to a beneficiary (or to the estate of the employee) after the death of the employee [Ltr Ruls 9608042, 9418034];

3. Attributable to the employee's disability (see Q 26:41);

4. Part of a series of substantially equal periodic payments (not less frequently than annually) made for the life (or life expectancy) of the employee, or the joint lives (or joint life expectancy) of such employee and the employee's beneficiary, and that begin after the employee separates from service (see Qs 13:40, 13:41);

5. Made to an employee after separation from service after attainment of age 55 (see Q 13:42);

6. A dividend paid with respect to certain stock held by an employee stock ownership plan (ESOP) (see Q 24:14);

7. A payment to an alternate payee pursuant to a QDRO (see Q 30:1); or

8. An amount not in excess of the total medical expenses deductible for the year under Section 213 by the employee (determined without regard to whether the employee itemizes deductions for the relevant taxable year).

[IRC § 72(t); Hobson, TCM 1996-272; Montgomery, TCM 1996-263; Ross, 70 TCM 1596 (1995); Grow, 70 TCM 1576 (1995); Orgera, 70 TCM 1488 (1995); Wittstadt, Jr, 70 TCM 994 (1995); Roundy, 70 TCM 6 (1995)]

Exceptions 5, 7, and 8 above are not applicable to a distribution from an individual retirement plan; and, for exception 4 to apply to an individual retirement plan, separation from service is not required. (For rules governing early distributions from individual retirement plans, see Q 26:41.)

The penalty tax applies only to distributions from qualified retirement plans, individual retirement plans, and tax-sheltered annuities (see Q 29:46). In one ruling, excess plan assets from a terminated plan were returned to the employer (see Q 21:53). After former participants started an action against the employer claiming that some of the excess plan assets should have been allocated to them, the employer placed some of the assets in an escrow account. Distributions from the escrow account to the former participants following settlement of the suit were not distributions from a qualified retirement plan, so the 10 percent penalty tax was not imposed. [Ltr Rul 9006055; but see O'Connor, 67 TCM 2708 (1994)]

The 10 percent penalty tax applies only to the portion of the distribution subject to income tax and is in addition to the income tax. Thus, the 10 percent penalty tax does not apply to the portion of the distribution that is income tax-free (see Q 13:2). The penalty tax applies to a participant who made an irrevocable election to defer receipt of the distribution prior to both the effective date and the date of enactment of the penalty tax, and then received the distribution thereafter. [O'Connor, 67 TCM 2708 (1994); Bullard, 65 TCM 1844 (1993); Shimota v United States, 21 Cls Ct 510 (1990), aff'd, 943 F 2d 1312 (Fed Cir 1991); Panos, 64 TCM 542 (1992)]

One court ruled that the 10 percent penalty tax applies to voluntary distributions and not to involuntary withdrawals. Hence, the court did not apply the penalty tax when IRS levied against an individual's qualified retirement plan account (see Q 4:26). [Larotonda, 89 TC 287 (1987)]

The additional tax on early distributions is treated as a penalty, not a tax, for bankruptcy law purposes. Thus, IRS does not have priority status over other creditors. [In re Cassidy, Jr, Nos. 91-1180 and 91-1244 (10th Cir 1992); and see Q 8:18]

The 10 percent penalty tax can be avoided if the early distribution qualifies for rollover treatment and it is rolled over into another qualified plan or an IRA. See chapter 28 for more information on rollovers.

In this question and Qs 13:40, 13:41, reference is made to age 59½. If RRB '96 (see Q 1:22A) is enacted, age 59½ will be replaced by age 59 for purposes of the 10 percent penalty tax. [RRB '96, Act § 9445(a)]

Q 13:40   What are substantially equal periodic payments?

One of the exceptions to the 10 percent penalty tax (see Q 13:39) is for a distribution from a qualified retirement plan that commences after the employee separates from service and is part of a series of substantially equal periodic payments (not less frequently than annually) made over the life (or life expectancy) of the employee or the joint lives (or joint life expectancy) of the employee and the employee's designated beneficiary. [IRC §§ 72(t)(2)(A)(iv), 72(t)(3)(B)]

According to IRS, payments will be considered to be substantially equal periodic payments if they are made according to one of the methods set forth below:

1. Payments will be treated as satisfying this requirement if the annual payment is determined using a method that would be acceptable for purposes of calculating required minimum distributions. See chapter 11 for details.

2. Payments will also be treated as substantially equal periodic payments if the amount to be distributed annually is determined by amortizing the employee's account balance over a number of years equal to the employee's life expectancy (or the joint life and last survivor expectancy of the employee and the employee's beneficiary) at an interest rate that does not exceed a reasonable interest rate on the date that payments commence.

   Example 1. V & S Corporation established a profit sharing plan many years ago. Vicente, age 50, has an account balance in the plan of $1,000,000 and has terminated employment. If Vicente receives $86,790 a year from the plan, the annual payments will be considered substantially equal periodic payments and will not be subject to the 10 percent penalty tax. This is because Vicente has a life expectancy of 33.1 years and amortizing $1,000,000 over 33.1 years at an interest rate of 8 percent results in an annual payment of $86,790.

3. As a third permissible method, payments will be treated as substantially equal periodic payments if the amount to be distributed annually is determined by dividing the employee's account balance by an annuity factor (the present value of an annuity of $1 per year beginning at the employee's age attained in the first distribution year and continuing for the life of the employee), with such annuity factor derived using a reasonable mortality table and an interest rate that does not exceed a reasonable interest rate on the date that payments commence.

   Example 2. S & V Corporation established a money purchase pension plan many years ago. Sabine, age 50, has an account balance in the plan of $900,000 and has terminated employment. If the annuity factor for a $1 per year annuity for Sabine is 11.109 (assuming an interest rate of 8 percent and using the UP-1984 mortality table), Sabine would receive an annual distribution of $81,015 ($900,000 ÷ 11.109). As substantially equal periodic payments, no 10 percent penalty tax would apply.

[Notice 89-25, 1989-1 CB 662, Q&A 12; Ltr Ruls 9401040, 9310054, 9223049, 9152045, 9152044, 9152041]

Under the above examples, the annual payment remains constant (at least until Vicente and Sabine attain age 59½; see Q 13:41). However, IRS has approved a method whereby the annual payments may increase from year to year, as illustrated in the example below. [Ltr Rul 9047043]

Example 3. In Example 2, assume that the first year of distribution was 1993 when the dollar limitation for the annual benefit under a defined benefit plan was $115,641 (see Q 6:8). In 1994, the dollar limitation increased to $118,800 and, in 1995, to $120,000. In 1994, Sabine could receive an annual distribution of $83,228 ($81,015 × $118,800 ÷ $115,641); and, in 1995, Sabine can receive an annual distribution of $84,069 ($81,015 × $120,000 ÷ $115,641).

Q 13:41   What happens if the substantially equal periodic payments are modified?

There is a special recapture provision. If the amount of the periodic payments is modified (other than by reason of death or disability) before the later of (1) the end of the five-year period beginning with the date of the first payment or (2) the employee's attainment of age 59½, the 10 percent penalty tax that would have been imposed on all payments, plus interest, is imposed. [IRC § 72(t)(4)]

Example 1. Harriet commences receiving substantially equal annual payments from her qualified retirement plan after retirement at age 40. Harriet ceases receiving payments at age 48 after eight annual payments. The recapture tax will apply because, even though Harriet has received more than five annual payments, she is not age 59½. Harriet must pay the recapture tax in the year in which she reaches age 48. The recapture amount will be 10 percent of the total of the eight annual payments. Interest will also be imposed.

Example 2. Harriet terminated employment at age 54 and commenced receiving substantially equal annual payments from her qualified retirement plan at age 58. Harriet ceases receiving payments at age 61 after three annual payments. The recapture tax will apply because, even though Harriet has attained age 59½, she ceased receiving payments before the end of the five-year period. Harriet must pay the recapture tax in the year in which she reaches age 61. The recapture amount will be 10 percent of the total of the three annual payments. Interest will also be imposed.

A change in the monthly distribution date is ministerial and not a modification of the periodic payment method; therefore, the 10 percent penalty tax will not be imposed on either the current or prior distributions. [Ltr Rul 9514026]

Q 13:42   How does the age 55 requirement work?

If an employee receives a distribution from a qualified retirement plan after separation from service and separation occurs during or after the calendar year in which the employee attains age 55, the 10 percent penalty tax (see Q 13:39) will not apply. Thus, it appears that a 54-year-old employee will not be subject to the penalty tax on a distribution made after separation from service as long as the employee attains age 55 during the calendar year in which separation occurs. [IRC § 72(t)(2)(A)(v); Notice 87-13, 1987-1 CB 432, Q&A 20; Ltr Ruls 9429026, 9224056; but see Ltr Rul 9135060 (the employee retired at age 50) and replaced by Ltr Rul 9241063 (based on different facts)]

Example. Monroe participated in a profit sharing plan until 1995 when he retired at age 55. In 1997, at age 57, Monroe received a lump-sum distribution of his plan benefits. Since Monroe separated from service during or after the calendar year in which he attained age 55, his receipt of benefits will not be subject to the 10 percent penalty tax.

Q 13:43   May an additional estate tax be imposed at the participant's death?

Amounts accumulated in a decedent's retirement plans as of the date of death may be subject to an additional 15 percent estate tax on excess retirement accumulations (see Qs 14:21–14:29 for details). There is no three-year suspension of this tax (see Q 13:27).

Q 13:44   Are there any limitations on loans from qualified retirement plans?

Yes. Loans from qualified retirement plans are subject to a number of limitations and requirements (see Qs 13:45–13:52).

An amount received by a participant (or beneficiary) as a loan from a qualified retirement plan is treated as having been received as a distribution from the plan (a deemed distribution), unless the loan satisfies the applicable limitations and requirements. A loan made from a contract (e.g., insurance policy) that has been purchased under a plan is considered a loan made under the plan. If a participant assigns or pledges any portion of the participant's interest in a plan as security for a loan, the portion of the interest assigned or pledged is treated as a loan from the plan. Any assignment or pledge by a participant of any portion of the participant's interest in a contract that has been purchased under a plan is considered an assignment or pledge of an interest in the plan. However, if all or a portion of a participant's interest in a plan is pledged or assigned as security for a loan from the plan to the participant, only the amount of the loan received by the participant, not the amount pledged or assigned, is treated as a loan. [IRC §§ 72(p)(1), 72(p)(5); Prop Reg § 1.72(p)-1, Q&A-1].

IRS has ruled that when a plan participant's account balance is transferred directly from one plan to another and the transfer includes an outstanding loan of the participant, the participant will not be considered to have received a distribution or to have renegotiated or modified the loan. [Ltr Ruls 9617046, 9043018; Rev Rul 67-213, 1967-2 CB 149] The rules regarding plan loans apply to both direct and indirect loans to a participant. IRS has ruled that bank loans to participants that were contingent upon the plan making deposits of plan funds in the bank equal to the amounts of the loans were indirect participant loans and, consequently, would be treated as if the plan had made the loans directly to the participants. [IRS Spec Rul (Aug 12, 1992)]

Q 13:45 Is there a dollar limitation on loans from qualified retirement plans?

A loan from a qualified retirement plan to a participant or beneficiary is not treated as a taxable distribution to the extent the loan (when added to the outstanding balance of all other loans from the plan) does not exceed the *lesser* of:

1. $50,000 reduced by the excess (if any) of:

   a. The highest outstanding balance of loans from the plan during the one-year period ending on the day before the date on which such loan was made, over

   b. The outstanding balance of loans from the plan on the date such loan was made; or

2. The greater of:

a. 50 percent of the present value of the participant's vested benefit (see Q 9:1) under the plan (determined without regard to any deductible employee contributions; see Q 6:22), or

b. $10,000.

[IRC § 72(p)(2)(A)]

For the purpose of applying the loan limits, all qualified retirement plans maintained by the same employer and all qualified retirement plans maintained by a member of a controlled group (see Q 5:33) or an affiliated service group (see Q 5:37) are treated as one plan. [IRC § 72(p)(2)(D)]

Example. On April 4, 1996, Dan borrowed $40,000 from his employer's qualified retirement plan, and he repaid $30,000 on December 5, 1996. On March 6, 1997, Dan's vested interest under the plan is $150,000, and he wishes to make another loan. Until December 6, 1997, Dan can borrow only $10,000 more. Here's why:

Highest outstanding loan balance	$40,000
Balance on March 6, 1997	−10,000
Reduction in maximum loan amount	$30,000
Maximum loan amount	$50,000
Reduction	−30,000
Reduced loan limit	$20,000
Balance on March 6, 1997	−10,000
Maximum loan not a distribution	$10,000

Q 13:46 How are loans made pursuant to a residential mortgage loan program treated?

Residential mortgage loans made by a qualified retirement plan in the ordinary course of an investment program are not subject to the limitations and restrictions on plan loans if the property acquired with the loans is the primary security for such loans and the amount loaned does not exceed the fair market value of the property. An investment program exists only if the plan has established, in advance of a specific investment under the program, that a certain percentage or amount of plan assets will be invested in residential mortgages available to persons purchasing the property who satisfy commercially customary financial criteria. Loans will not be considered as made under an investment program if the loans are only made available to, or any loan is earmarked for, any person or persons who are participants or beneficiaries in the plan, or if such loans mature upon a participant's termination from employment. In addition, no loan that benefits an officer, director, or owner of the employer maintaining the plan, or such person's beneficiaries, will be treated as made under an investment program. [Prop Reg § 1.72(p)-1, Q&A-18]

IRS has ruled that mortgages given to plan participants under a qualified retirement plan's residential mortgage investment program would be deemed loans to the plan participants and not plan investments because over 90 percent of the persons eligible for mortgages under the program were plan participants. [Ltr Rul 9110039]

Q 13:47   Is there a maximum repayment period for a loan from a qualified retirement plan?

A loan to a participant from a qualified retirement plan must be required to be repaid within five years or it is treated as a taxable distribution at the time the loan is made (see Qs 13:48, 13:49). However, the five-year repayment period does not apply to a loan used to acquire any dwelling unit that within a reasonable time is to be used (determined at the time the loan is made) as the principal residence of the participant (a principal residence plan loan). [IRC § 72(p)(2)(B)]

A principal residence has the same meaning as a principal residence under Section 1034. A loan is not required to be secured by the dwelling unit that will within a reasonable time be used as the participant's principal residence in order to satisfy the requirements for a principal residence plan loan. The tracing rules established under Section 163(h)(3)(B) apply to determining whether a loan is treated as for the acquisition of a principal residence in order to qualify as a principal residence plan loan. Generally, a refinancing will not qualify as a principal residence plan loan. However, a loan from a plan used to repay a loan from a third party will qualify as a principal residence plan loan if the plan loan qualifies as a principal residence plan loan without regard to the loan from the third party.

> **Example.** On July 1, 1997, Steve requests a $50,000 plan loan to be repaid in level monthly installments over 15 years. On August 1, 1997, Steve acquires a principal residence and pays a portion of the purchase price with a $50,000 bank loan. On September 1, 1997, the plan loans $50,000 to Steve, which Steve uses to pay the bank loan. Because the loan satisfies the requirements to qualify as a principal residence plan loan (taking into account the tracing rules), the plan loan qualifies for the exception to the five-year repayment period. [Prop Reg § 1.72(p)-1, Q&A-5–Q&A-8]

The loan repayment schedule must provide for level amortization. That is, repayment must be made in substantially equal installments consisting of principal and interest and must be made not less frequently than quarterly over the term of the loan. Accordingly, the participant cannot repay the loan in one balloon payment at the end of the loan term. [IRC § 72(p)(2)(C)] An individual made a loan from his pension plan and signed a note requiring that interest be paid annually with the loan principal being payable on demand. Even though the individual made quarterly interest and principal payments and the loan was repaid over a five-year period, because the note, by its terms, did not require level amortization, the loan was a taxable distribution (see Qs 13:48, 13:49). [Estate of Gray, 70 TCM 556 (1995)]

The level amortization requirement does not apply for a period, not longer than one year, that a participant is on a leave of absence, either without pay from the employer or at a rate of pay (after income and employment tax withholding) that is less than the amount of the installment payments required under the terms of the loan. However, the loan must be repaid by the latest date permitted, and the installments due after the leave ends (or, if earlier, after the first year of the leave) must not be less than those required under the terms of the original loan.

Example. On July 1, 1997, Sallie borrows $40,000 to be repaid in level monthly installments over five years. The loan is not a principal residence plan loan. Sallie makes nine monthly payments and commences an unpaid leave of absence that lasts for 12 months. Thereafter, Sallie resumes active employment and resumes making repayments on the loan until the loan is repaid. The amount of each monthly installment is increased in order to repay the loan by June 30, 2002. Because the loan satisfies the plan loan requirements, Sallie does not have a deemed distribution (see Q 13:48). Alternatively, Sallie could continue to pay the monthly installments in the original amount after resuming active employment and, on June 30, 2002, repay the full balance remaining due.

Loans renewed, renegotiated, redefined, or extended may be treated as new loans. [TRA '86, Act § 1134(e); Ltr Rul 9344001]

Q 13:48   What is a deemed distribution, when does it occur, and how much is it?

A loan to a participant or beneficiary from a qualified retirement plan will not be a deemed distribution to the participant or beneficiary if the loan satisfies the repayment term requirement (see Q 13:47), the level amortization requirement (see Q 13:47), and the enforceable agreement requirement, but only to the extent the loan satisfies the amount limitations (see Q: 13:45).

A loan does not satisfy these requirements *unless* the loan is evidenced by a legally enforceable agreement (which may include more than one document) set forth in writing or in such other form as may be approved by IRS, and the terms of the agreement demonstrate compliance with the requirements for plan loans. Thus, the agreement must specify the amount of the loan, the term of the loan, and the repayment schedule.

A deemed distribution occurs at the first time that the requirements for plan loans are not satisfied, in form or in operation, with respect to that amount. This may occur at the time the loan is made or at a later date. If the terms of the loan do not require repayments that satisfy the repayment term requirement or the level amortization requirement, or the loan is not evidenced by an enforceable agreement, the entire amount of the loan is a deemed distribution at the time the loan is made. [Estate of Gray, 70 TCM 556 (1995)] If the loan satisfies the plan loan requirements except that the amount loaned exceeds the dollar limitations, the amount of the loan in excess of the applicable limitation is a deemed distribution at the time the loan is made. [W L Miller, PSC v Comm'r, No. 93-2432 (6th Cir 1994)] If the loan initially satisfies the plan loan requirements and the enforceable agreement requirement, but payments are not made in accordance with the terms of the loan, a deemed distribution occurs as a result of the failure to make such payments.

Example 1. Caroline has a vested account balance of $200,000 and receives $70,000 as a loan repayable in level quarterly installments over five years. Caroline has a deemed distribution of $20,000 (the excess of $70,000 over $50,000) at the time of the loan because the loan exceeds the $50,000 limit. The remaining $50,000 is not a deemed distribution.

Example 2. James has a vested account balance of $30,000 and borrows $20,000 as a loan repayable in level monthly installments over five years. Because the amount of the loan is $5,000 more than 50 percent of James's vested account balance [$20,000 − (50% × $30,000)], James has a deemed distribution of $5,000 at the time of the loan. The remaining $15,000 is not a deemed distribution. (Note also that, if the loan is secured solely by James's account balance, the loan may be a prohibited transaction; see Q 13:52).

Example 3. Adam's vested account balance is $100,000, and a $50,000 loan is made to Adam repayable in level quarterly installments over seven years. The loan is not a principal residence loan. Because the repayment period exceeds the maximum five-year period, Adam has a deemed distribution of $50,000 at the time the loan is made.

Example 4. On August 1, 1997, Bill has a vested account balance of $45,000 and borrows $20,000 from the plan to be repaid over five years in level monthly installments due at the end of each month. After making monthly payments through July 1999, Bill fails to make any of the payments due thereafter. As a result of the failure to satisfy the requirement that the loan be repaid in level monthly installments, Bill has a deemed distribution on August 31, 1999, the date of the first missed payment.

Failure to make any installment payment when due in accordance with the terms of the loan results in a deemed distribution at the time of such failure. However, the plan administrator (see Q 16:1) may allow a grace period, and a violation will not occur until the last day of the grace period. A grace period will be given effect only to the extent it does not continue beyond the last day of the calendar quarter following the calendar quarter in which the required installment payment was due. If there is a failure to pay the installment payments required under the terms of the loan (taking into account any grace period allowed), then the amount of the deemed distribution equals the entire outstanding balance of the loan at the time of such failure.

Example 5. Assume the same facts as in Example 4, except that the plan administrator allows a three-month grace period. As a result of the failure to satisfy the requirement that the loan be repaid in level installments, Bill has a deemed distribution on November 30, 1999, which is the last day of the three-month grace period for the August 31, 1999 installment. The amount of the deemed distribution is the outstanding balance on the loan at November 30, 1999. Alternatively, if the plan administrator had allowed a grace period through the end of the next calendar quarter, there would be a deemed distribution on December 31, 1999 equal to the outstanding balance of the loan at December 31, 1999.

[Prop Reg § 1.72(p)-1, Q&A-4, Q&A-10]

Q 13:49   What are the tax consequences of a deemed distribution?

A deemed distribution is includible in gross income. However, if the participant has basis (see Q 13:2), all or a portion of the deemed distribution may not be taxable. [Prop Reg § 1.72(p)-1, Q&A-11]

In addition, a taxable plan loan may also be subject to the early distribution tax (see Q 13:39) and the excess distributions tax (see Qs 13:27, 13:29). [Prop Reg § 1.72(p)-1, Q&A-11; Estate of Gray, 70 TCM 556 (1995); Earnshaw, 69 TCM 2353 (1995); Caton, 69 TCM 1937 (1995)]

A bankruptcy court has ruled that it did not have jurisdiction to determine if plan loans were taxable distributions. [In re Somma, 585-648 (Bankr ND Ohio 1992)]

If there is an express or tacit understanding that a plan loan will not be repaid or, for any reason, the transaction does not create a debtor-creditor relationship, then the amount transferred is treated as an actual distribution from the plan, includible in gross income, and is not treated as a loan or as a deemed distribution. [Prop Reg § 1.72(p)-1, Q&A-17]

For a further discussion of the consequences of a deemed distribution, see Qs 16:15, 28:14–28:16.

Q 13:50　Is interest paid on loans from qualified retirement plans deductible?

The deductibility of interest on a loan from a qualified retirement plan is first determined under the general rules governing the deductibility of interest. Notwithstanding the general rules, interest on plan loans is never deductible if the loan is made to a key employee (see Q 22:24), whether or not the plan is top-heavy, or if the loan is secured by elective contributions made under a 401(k) plan (see Q 23:1). [IRC §§ 72(p)(3), 163; Ltr Rul 8933018]

Q 13:51　Is it necessary to obtain spousal consent for a loan from a qualified retirement plan?

A qualified retirement plan that is subject to the automatic survivor benefit requirements (see Q 10:1) must provide that no portion of a participant's accrued benefit (see Q 9:2) may be used as security for a plan loan unless the participant's spouse consents to the loan within the 90-day period ending on the date the security agreement becomes effective. The consent must satisfy the requirements applicable to the qualified preretirement survivor annuity (QPSA) and qualified joint and survivor annuity (QJSA) election procedures (see Q 10:21). However, spousal consent is not required if the accrued benefit subject to the security is $3,500 or less. [IRC § 417(a)(4); Treas Reg § 1.401(a)-20, Q&A 24]

Q 13:52　Are there any other requirements applicable to loans from qualified retirement plans?

Yes. Another set of requirements must be met to avoid a plan loan from being subject to an excise tax. An excise tax is imposed on certain prohibited transactions (e.g., loans) between a plan and a disqualified person (see chapter 20 for details). However, an exemption is provided for any loan by a qualified retirement plan to a participant or beneficiary who is a disqualified person if the following requirements are met:

1. The loan must be available to all participants and beneficiaries on a reasonably equivalent basis;

2. Loans must not be made available to highly compensated employees (see Q 3:2) in amounts greater than the amounts made available to other employees;

3. The loan must be made in accordance with specific provisions in the plan;

4. The loan must bear a reasonable rate of interest; and

5. The loan must be adequately secured.

[IRC §§ 4975(c), 4975(d); ERISA § 408(b)(1); Rev Rul 89-14, 1989-1 CB 111]

A shareholder-employee of an S corporation may not borrow from the corporation's qualified retirement plan, and the law prohibits a qualified retirement plan from lending to an owner-employee (see Q 5:34). [IRC §§ 401(a)(13), 4975(d)] The term "shareholder-employee" means an individual who owns, on any day during the S corporation's taxable year, more than 5 percent of the outstanding stock of the S corporation, and includes the individual's spouse, children, grandchildren, and parents. The term "owner-employee" includes the individual's spouse, lineal descendants, ancestors, brothers, and sisters. [IRC §§ 1379(d) (prior to repeal), 318(a)(1), 401(c)(3), 267(c)(4)]

According to IRS, the loan may be secured by the participant's vested accrued benefit (see Qs 9:1, 9:2); but, according to DOL, no more than one-half of the vested accrued benefit may be used to secure the loan. [IRC § 401(a)(13)(A); Treas Reg § 1.401(a)-13(d)(2); DOL Reg § 2550.408b-1; DOL Adv Op 89-30A]

Chapter 14

Life Insurance and Death Benefits

Although the primary purpose of a qualified retirement plan is to pay retirement benefits, the plan may also provide life insurance coverage for participants. This chapter examines the limits on life insurance coverage and the tax consequences of including insurance in a qualified retirement plan. A discussion of how death benefit payments by qualified retirement plans are taxed is also included.

Q 14:1 Must a qualified retirement plan provide a death benefit to participants?

Generally, a qualified retirement plan is not required to provide a death benefit with respect to employer contributions if the employee dies while a participant in the plan. However, in the case of married participants, a qualified retirement plan is required to provide a death benefit to the participant's surviving spouse unless an election and consent to waive such benefits have been made. [IRC §§ 401(a)(11), 411(a)(3), 417(a)]

For details on preretirement survivor annuities and joint and survivor annuities, see chapter 10.

Q 14:2 May a qualified retirement plan provide life insurance coverage for participants?

Yes, but the primary purpose of a company's qualified retirement plan must be to pay retirement benefits to participants. Any life insurance coverage provided under the qualified retirement plan must be incidental to the provision of retirement benefits (see Q 14:4).

Q 14:3   Is a company allowed a deduction for life insurance purchased under a qualified retirement plan?

The portion of employer contributions to its qualified retirement plan that is used to purchase life insurance on behalf of plan participants is deductible.

However, if life insurance is provided under a qualified retirement plan for a self-employed individual (see Q 6:33), the cost of current life insurance protection (see Qs 14:6–14:8) is neither deductible nor considered as contributions for purposes of determining the maximum amount of contributions that may be made on behalf of an owner-employee (see Q 5:34). [IRC § 404(e); Treas Reg § 1.404(e)-1A(g)]

Q 14:4   What limits apply to the amount of life insurance that can be purchased for participants under a qualified retirement plan?

The basic restriction is that the amount of life insurance coverage must be incidental to the plan's retirement benefits. [Treas Reg § 1.401-1(b)(1)]

For a defined contribution plan (see Q 2:2), life insurance coverage is considered incidental if less than 50 percent of the company's contributions to the plan on behalf of the participant is used to purchase whole life insurance, or no more than 25 percent is used to purchase term life insurance. [Rev Rul 54-51, 1954-1 CB 147; Rev Rul 57-213, 1957-1 CB 157; Rev Rul 60-83, 1960-1 CB 157; Rev Rul 66-143, 1966-1 CB 79; Rev Rul 76-353, 1976-2 CB 112; Ltr Rul 8725088]

Although there is no limit if the life insurance is purchased with company contributions accumulated in a profit sharing plan for two years or longer (see Q 1:32), IRS has never addressed if doing so would cause the excess premium payment to be includible in the insured participant's income. The author understands that IRS withdrew a proposed letter to that effect.

For a defined benefit plan (see Q 2:3), life insurance coverage is generally considered incidental if the amount of the insurance does not exceed 100 times the participant's projected monthly benefit. For example, if a participant can expect a $1,000 monthly benefit, life insurance coverage of up to $100,000 can be provided for the participant under the defined benefit plan. However, life insurance coverage may exceed the 100 times limit and still be considered incidental. [Rev Rul 60-83, 1960-1 CB 157; Rev Rul 61-121, 1961-2 CB 65; Rev Rul 68-31, 1968-1 CB 151; Rev Rul 68-453, 1968-2 CB 163; Rev Rul 74-307, 1974-2 CB 126]

The incidental limitations do not apply to life insurance purchased with voluntary employee contributions (see Q 1:33). [Rev Rul 69-408, 1969-2 CB 58]

Q 14:5   Does the purchase of life insurance affect retirement benefits?

If part of the company's contributions to its defined contribution plan (see Q 2:2) goes toward the purchase of life insurance coverage, there may be less available for participants at retirement. This will be so if the return on the investment in life insurance is less than the return on the trust fund investments. Although retirement benefits may be reduced, death benefits will be substantially increased.

Using company contributions to pay for life insurance under a defined benefit plan (see Q 2:3) does not affect the amount of a participant's retirement benefit. However, because participants are promised a fixed level of benefits at retirement, the company may have to increase its contributions to cover any shortfall in funding for those benefits resulting from the use of company contributions to pay insurance premiums.

Q 14:6   What are the tax consequences to participants when their employer's qualified retirement plan provides life insurance protection?

The tax law allows participants to postpone payment of income taxes on retirement benefits payable to them from a qualified retirement plan. Participants pay no tax until they receive those benefits. They do, however, incur some tax cost when their employer's qualified retirement plan provides life insurance protection. Because participants receive a present benefit—current life insurance protection—they must include the value of that benefit in their gross incomes for the year in which employer contributions or trust earnings are used to pay life insurance premiums.

A participant must pay tax on the term cost of insurance protection paid for with employer contributions or trust earnings if, upon death, the proceeds of the life insurance policy on the participant's life are payable to either (1) the participant's estate or beneficiary, or (2) the trustee of the plan if the trustee is required by the plan's provisions to pay such proceeds to the participant's estate or beneficiary. [IRC § 72(m)(3)(B); Treas Reg § 1.72-16(b)]

The amount included in a participant's gross income, which is determined under special IRS tables that contain the PS-58 costs (see Q 14:7), is often well below the premium paid by the plan for the insurance. [Rev Rul 55-747, 1955-2 CB 228; Rev Rul 66-110, 1966-1 CB 12]

If a self-employed individual (see Q 6:33) is covered by a life insurance policy under a qualified retirement plan, the individual will not be taxed with PS-58 costs because the cost of the current life insurance protection is not deductible by the employer (see Q 14:3). [IRC §§ 72(m)(3)(B), 404(e); Treas Reg § 1.404(e)-1A(g)]

Q 14:7   What are PS-58 costs?

IRS rulings set forth the method of calculating the amount of a participant's current taxable income as a result of receiving life insurance protection under a company's qualified retirement plan (see Q 14:6). [Rev Rul 55-747, 1955-2 CB 228; Rev Rul 66-110, 1966-1 CB 12]

The participant's current taxable amount is determined by applying the one-year premium term rate (the PS-58 rates) at the participant's age to the difference between the face amount of the policy and its cash surrender value at the end of the year.

The PS-58 rates are shown in the chart on page 14-5.

Example. Keren, age 35, is a participant in her company's qualified retirement plan. The plan provides Keren with a life insurance policy in the face amount of $40,000. At year-end, the policy had a cash surrender value of $2,000. Keren must include $121.98 in her current taxable income [($40,000 – $2,000) multiplied by $3.21, divided by 1,000].

Q 14:8   Must the PS-58 rates be used to determine the cost of pure life insurance included in a participant's gross income?

No. If the insurance company's rates for individual one-year term policies available to all standard risks on an initial issue insurance basis are lower, the lower rates may be utilized. [Rev Rul 66-110, 1966-1 CB 12; Rev Rul 67-154, 1967-1 CB 11; Ltr Rul 9023044]

The rate tables published by the parent corporation of an insurance company that issued the policy could not be used because the parent corporation and the issuing company were not the same insurer and the parent corporation's rate tables were not available to all standard risks and were developed for five-year term insurance. [Ltr Rul 9452004]

One-Year Term Premiums for $1,000 of Life Insurance Protection

Age	Premium	Age	Premium	Age	Premium
15	$1.27	38	$ 3.87	60	$ 20.73
16	1.38	39	4.14	61	22.53
17	1.48	40	4.42	62	24.50
18	1.52	41	4.73	63	26.63
19	1.56	42	5.07	64	28.98
20	1.61	43	5.44	65	31.51
21	1.67	44	5.85	66	34.28
22	1.73	45	6.30	67	37.31
23	1.79	46	6.78	68	40.59
24	1.86	47	7.32	69	44.17
25	1.93	48	7.89	70	48.06
26	2.02	49	8.53	71	52.29
27	2.11	50	9.22	72	56.89
28	2.20	51	9.97	73	61.89
29	2.31	52	10.79	74	67.33
30	2.43	53	11.69	75	73.23
31	2.57	54	12.67	76	79.63
32	2.70	55	13.74	77	86.57
33	2.86	56	14.91	78	94.09
34	3.02	57	16.18	79	102.23
35	3.21	58	17.56	80	111.04
36	3.41	59	19.08	81	120.57
37	3.63				

Q 14:9　Are loans from insurance policies purchased under qualified retirement plans taxable?

If a participant receives a loan from an insurance policy purchased under a qualified retirement plan (as well as any assignment or pledge of the policy), it is treated as a loan made from the plan.

Generally, such loans are not taxable. However, if the policy loan exceeds the Code limitations on loans from qualified retirement plans, the loan is treated as a taxable distribution to the participant (see Qs 13:2, 13:44–13:52). [IRC §§ 72(p)(2), 72(p)(5)]

Q 14:10   Who receives the proceeds from life insurance purchased under a qualified retirement plan when a participant dies before retirement?

Generally, if a participant dies while working for the company, the proceeds from life insurance purchased under a qualified retirement plan will be paid to designated beneficiaries. If the participant fails to designate a beneficiary or if the sole designated beneficiary predeceases the participant, the life insurance proceeds generally will be paid to the participant's estate in accordance with the provisions of the policy. When a widow named her daughter as beneficiary of a life insurance policy under her employer's profit sharing plan and subsequently remarried, the court ruled that the surviving spouse, and not the daughter, was entitled to the insurance proceeds. [Howard v Branham & Baker Coal Co, 968 F 2d 1214 (6th Cir 1992)] (See Qs 10:1 through 10:32 for a discussion of the automatic survivor annuity requirements and their effect on the participant's right to designate a beneficiary.)

If there is a death benefit under the plan (other than life insurance) and there is no designated beneficiary, the provisions of the plan will determine who will receive the death benefit. [Jensen v Estate of McGowan, 697 P 2d 1380 (1985)] One court ruled that the death benefit could be paid to the persons designated by a deceased participant on an unsigned beneficiary designation form. [O'Shea v First Manhattan Co Thrift Plan & Trust, No. 94-9004 (2d Cir 1995)] In a case in which a deceased participant had not removed the former spouse as the designated beneficiary, the court ruled that ERISA preempted a state statute that purported to nullify the former spouse's right to receive the death benefit, and the beneficiary designation remained effective. [Iron Workers Mid-South Pensions Fund v Stoll, No. 91-0513 (ED La 1991)] However, in other cases in which the deceased participant did not remove the former spouse as the designated beneficiary, the court held that the former spouse had waived her interest as a beneficiary in the separation agreement incorporated in the divorce decree. [Estate of Altobelli v IBM Corp, 1996 US App Lexis 3207 (4th Cir 1996); Czarski v Estate of Bonk, 1996 US Dist Lexis 4808 (ED Mi 1996)]

One court concluded that a nonparticipant spouse who predeceased the participant spouse could not bequeath her community property interest in his pension plan to a third party [Albamis v Rogers, 937 F 2d 1450 (9th Cir 1991); but another court ruled otherwise. [Boggs v Boggs, 1996 US App Lexis 8664 (5th Cir 1996)]

Q 14:11   How are proceeds from life insurance purchased under a qualified retirement plan taxed for income tax purposes?

The amount of the proceeds that is equal to the cash surrender value of the policy is included in the beneficiary's gross income. Any proceeds in excess of the cash surrender value of the insurance policy are not subject to federal income tax. However, the beneficiary's taxable amount is subject to a $5,000 death benefit exclusion and is reduced further by the PS-58 costs that were included in the deceased participant's gross income during such participant's lifetime (see Qs 13:2, 14:6; the PS-58 costs are treated as a tax-free return of the participant's investment). The $5,000 death benefit exclusion has been repealed with respect to decedents dying after August 20, 1996. [IRC § 101(b), repealed by SBA '96 § 1402(a); Treas Reg § 1.72-16(b)]

If the participant's surviving spouse receives the proceeds, payment of income tax may be postponed by rolling over the taxable amount of the proceeds to an individual retirement account (IRA). In that case, the surviving spouse will not incur income tax liability until withdrawals are made from the IRA. For details on rollovers, see chapter 28.

If all of the benefits payable under the qualified retirement plan—including the life insurance proceeds—are distributed within one taxable year, the recipient may be able to elect forward averaging income tax treatment for the entire distribution. See chapter 13 for more details.

Q 14:12   Are proceeds from life insurance purchased under a qualified retirement plan included in the participant's estate for tax purposes?

Yes. Life insurance proceeds (and other death benefits) paid under a qualified retirement plan are included in the participant's gross estate. [IRC § 2039] (See Qs 14:21 through 14:28 regarding additional estate tax liability that may apply to a deceased participant.)

Q 14:13   Can a participant recover PS-58 costs tax-free when qualified retirement plan benefits are distributed?

Yes. When an insurance policy purchased under a qualified retirement plan is distributed to a participant who had reported PS-58 costs as income (see Q 14:6), the total PS-58 costs that were included in gross income can be recovered tax-free from the benefits received under the plan (see Q 13:2). However, these costs can be recovered only if the original insurance policy is distributed to the employee. If the life insurance is surrendered and the cash value and investment fund are used to purchase an annuity, the PS-58 costs are not part of the participant's cost for the annuity because the benefits will not be provided under the same contract. However, if the participant elects an annuity settlement option under the original policy, the

PS-58 costs are recoverable. [IRC § 72; Treas Reg § 1.72-16(b); Rev Rul 67-336, 1967-2 CB 66]

In addition, if the policy is surrendered by the plan's trustee and the cash surrender value is distributed to the participant, the participant's PS-58 costs are not recoverable.

Q 14:14   Are PS-58 costs recovered tax-free by a deceased participant's beneficiary?

Yes. PS-58 costs can be recovered tax-free by the beneficiary of the life insurance proceeds in the event of the participant's death (see Q 14:11). [Treas Reg § 1.72-16(c); Rev Rul 63-76, 1963-1 CB 23]

Q 14:15   What advantage does a participant gain when the company's qualified retirement plan provides life insurance protection?

By purchasing life insurance protection through the company's qualified retirement plan, the participant is able to shift a personal expense (not tax-deductible) to the plan without adverse tax consequences (see Q 14:3).

The income tax advantage of buying life insurance through the company's qualified retirement plan is even greater for a participant who could otherwise buy insurance only by paying a very high premium because of ill health. Instead of making large out-of-pocket premium payments, the participant merely includes the PS-58 costs (see Q 14:6) in gross income.

Q 14:16   May a qualified retirement plan purchase a life insurance policy from a plan participant or from the employer?

Generally, a prohibited transaction (see Q 20:1) occurs if there is a sale of property between a qualified retirement plan and a party in interest (see Q 20:3). Thus, a purchase by a qualified retirement plan of a life insurance policy from a plan participant or from the participant's employer would constitute a prohibited transaction. However, the Department of Labor (DOL) is authorized to grant a class exemption (see Q 20:17) under which a party in interest or disqualified person (see Q 20:4) who meets the requirements of the class exemption will automatically be entitled to relief from the prohibited transaction rules.

DOL has granted a class exemption so that the prohibited transaction rules do not apply to the sale of a life insurance policy to a qualified retirement plan from a plan participant on whose life the policy was issued, or from an employer, any of whose employees are covered by the plan, if:

1. The plan pays no more than the lesser of:

   a. The cash surrender value of the policy;

   b. If the plan is a defined benefit plan (see Q 2:3), the value of the participant's accrued benefit (see Q 9:2) at the time of the sale (determined under any reasonable actuarial method); or

   c. If the plan is a defined contribution plan (see Q 2:2), the value of the participant's account balance (see Q 9:2);

2. The sale does not involve any policy that is subject to a loan that the plan assumes; and

3. The sale does not contravene any provision of the plan.

The exemption is also available for plan participants who are owner-employees (see Q 5:34) or shareholder-employees (i.e., a more-than-5 percent shareholder) of an S corporation.

[PTCE 92-5 (57 FR 5019)]

Q 14:17   May a qualified retirement plan sell a life insurance policy to a plan participant or to the employer?

Generally, a prohibited transaction (see Q 20:1) occurs if there is a sale of property between a qualified retirement plan and a party in interest (see Q 20:3). Thus, a sale by a qualified retirement plan of a life insurance policy to a plan participant or to the participant's employer would constitute a prohibited transaction. However, DOL is authorized to grant a class exemption (see Q 20:17) under which a party in interest or disqualified person (see Q 20:4) who meets the requirements of the class exemption will automatically be entitled to relief from the prohibited transaction rules.

DOL has granted a class exemption so that the prohibited transaction rules do not apply to the sale of a life insurance policy by a qualified retirement plan to (1) a participant under the plan; (2) a relative of the participant; (3) an employer, any of whose employees are covered by the plan; or (4) another qualified retirement plan, if:

1. The participant is the insured under the policy;

2. The relative is the beneficiary under the policy;

3. The policy would, but for the sale, be surrendered by the plan;

4. With respect to a sale of the policy to the employer, a relative, or another plan, the insured participant is first informed of the proposed sale and is given the opportunity to purchase the policy from the plan but delivers to the plan a written election not to purchase the policy and a written consent to the sale by the plan; and

5. The amount received by the plan as consideration for the sale is at least equal to the amount necessary to put the plan in the same cash position as it would have been in had it retained the policy, surrendered it, and made a distribution to the participant of the participant's vested (see Q 9:1) interest under the plan.

The exemption is also available for plan participants who are owner-employees (see Q 5:34) or shareholder-employees (i.e., a more-than-5 percent shareholder) of an S corporation.

[PTCE 92-6 (57 FR 5189)]

Q 14:18   How are death benefit payments under a qualified retirement plan taxed?

Death benefits payable under a qualified retirement plan are generally included in the deceased participant's gross estate. For the exceptions, see Q 14:19. [IRC § 2039]

The participant's beneficiary is subject to income tax on death benefit payments. The income tax treatment depends on how the beneficiary receives the death benefit payments. Forward averaging treatment may be available for a lump-sum distribution (see Q 13:11). If an annuity is purchased, ordinary income tax rates apply to amounts received under the annuity contract. A transfer of funds from a qualified retirement plan to the temporary administrator of a deceased participant's estate is a distribution includible in the estate's gross income in the year of receipt. [Ltr Rul 9320006]

Death benefit payments up to $5,000 are exempt from income tax. The $5,000 exemption is not available if the participant had a nonforfeitable right to receive the payment while the participant was alive. However, the exemption is available in any event for a lump-sum distribution. If there are two or more beneficiaries, the exemption is still $5,000 and must be apportioned between or among them. The $5,000 death benefit exclusion has been repealed with respect to decedents dying after August 20, 1996. [IRC § 101(b), repealed by SBA '96 § 1402(a); Treas Reg §§ 1.101-2(a), 1.101-2(c); Rev Rul 71-146, 1971-1 CB 34]

For rules on the taxation of life insurance proceeds, see Qs 14:11 and 14:14.

Q 14:19 Are any death benefit payments received from a qualified retirement plan excluded from estate tax?

Yes. The repeal of the $100,000 estate tax exclusion by TRA '84 does not apply to a participant who was receiving benefit payments (i.e., was in pay status) under the plan prior to 1985 and who, prior to July 18, 1984, irrevocably elected the form of the benefit that the beneficiary would receive.

Furthermore, the total estate tax exclusion previously available if the participant had died before 1983 continues to apply if the participant was receiving benefit payments (i.e., was in pay status) under the plan prior to 1983, and had already irrevocably elected the form of benefit that the beneficiary would receive.

The estate tax exclusion remains available if the participant terminated employment before 1985 (in the case of the $100,000 exclusion) or 1983 (in the case of the total exclusion), irrevocably elected the form of benefit to be paid in the future, and was not in pay status as of the applicable date. [IRC § 2039; TEFRA § 245(c) as amended by TRA '84 § 525; Temp Reg § 20.2039-1T, Q&A-1; Ltr Rul 8630028] This exclusion applies only to qualified retirement plans and *not* to IRAs. [Rev Rul 92-22, 1992-1 CB 313; Ltr Ruls 9221030, 9144046; Senate Report, 1986-3 (Vol 3) CB 1019]

A participant was in pay status on the applicable date with respect to an interest in the plan if the participant irrevocably elected the form of benefit and received at least one payment under such form of benefit. [Temp Reg § 20.2039-1T, Q&A-2]

As of the applicable date, an election of the form of benefit is irrevocable if, as of such date, a written election had been made specifying the form of distribution (e.g., lump sum, annuity) and the period over which the distribution would be made (e.g., life annuity, term certain). An election is considered revocable if the form or period of the distribution could be determined or altered after the applicable date, but it will not be considered revocable just because the beneficiaries were not designated as of such date or could be changed thereafter. [Temp Reg § 20.2039-1T, Q&A-3]

Q 14:20 Is a deceased participant's estate entitled to a marital deduction for death benefit payments received by the surviving spouse from a qualified retirement plan?

A marital deduction is allowed for any property included in the deceased participant's estate that passes from the decedent to the surviving spouse. [IRC § 2056]

Death benefit payments from a qualified retirement plan to a deceased participant's surviving spouse will qualify for the marital deduction and will be deducted from the deceased participant's gross estate for estate tax purposes (see Q 26:37). This deduction will also be available if the surviving spouse receives the death benefit payments in the form of a qualified preretirement survivor annuity (see Q 10:9) and the deceased participant's executor does not elect to forgo the deduction. [IRC §§ 2039, 2056(b)(7)(C); Treas Reg § 301.9100-8; Ltr Ruls 9245033, 9232036, 9204017, 9008003; see also Rev Rul 89-89, 1989-2 CB 231; Ltr Ruls 9052015, 9038015; but see Ltr Rul 9220007]

Q 14:21 May any additional taxes be imposed on the estate of a decedent?

The estate of a participant may be subject to an additional estate tax equal to 15 percent of the deceased participant's excess retirement accumulation (see Q 14:22). Neither the unified credit nor the credit for state death taxes allowable in the computation of the estate tax may be used to offset this additional estate tax. Further, neither the marital deduction (see Q 14:20) nor the charitable deduction for estate tax purposes is available. [IRC §§ 4980A(d)(1), 4980A(d)(2); Temp Reg § 54.4981A-1T, Q&A d-1, d-8]

The excess distribution tax is suspended for 1997, 1998, and 1997 (see Q 13:27). This suspension will allow a participant to receive distributions during the suspension period without incurring the 15 percent excise tax on excess distributions. In this way, a participant could eliminate an excess retirement accumulation and avoid the 15 percent additional estate tax.

Q 14:22 What is an excess retirement accumulation?

For purposes of determining the additional estate tax (see Q 14:21), an excess retirement accumulation generally means the excess (if any) of:

1. The value of the deceased participant's aggregate interests (see Q 14:23) in qualified retirement plans, tax-sheltered annuities (see Q 29:1), and IRAs (see Q 26:1) as of the date of death (or, in the case of any alternate valuation election, the applicable valuation date), over

2. The present value of a single life annuity (see Q 14:24) with annual payments equal to the excess distribution threshold amount (see Q 13:28).

[IRC §§ 4980A(c)(1), 4980A(d)(3); Temp Reg § 54.4981A-1T, Q&A d-2]

Q 14:23 How are the deceased participant's aggregate interests calculated?

Generally, the aggregate interests include all amounts payable to beneficiaries under any qualified retirement plan (including payments under a joint and survivor annuity or preretirement survivor annuity), tax-sheltered annuity (see Q 29:1), or IRA (see Q 26:1). [IRC § 4980A(d)(3)(A); Temp Reg § 54.4981A-1T, Q&A d-5]

However, the deceased participant's aggregate interests do not include (1) benefits that represent the participant's investment in the contract (e.g., PS-58 costs, nondeductible employee contributions, nondeductible IRA contributions) (see Q 13:2); (2) amounts payable to an alternate payee spouse or former spouse pursuant to a qualified domestic relations order (QDRO) (see Qs 30:1, 30:3); (3) life insurance proceeds reduced by the cash surrender value of the policy immediately before the deceased participant's death; and (4) amounts inherited from other deceased individuals (see Q 14:29). [IRC §§ 4980A(d)(3)(A), 4980A(d)(4); Temp Reg § 54.4981A-1T, Q&A d-6]

In addition, the excess retirement accumulation is computed without regard to any community property law. Consequently, a deceased spouse's community property interest in the surviving spouse's qualified retirement plan benefits was disregarded, as was the surviving spouse's community property interest in the deceased spouse's plan benefits. [IRC § 4980A(d)(4); Temp Reg § 54.4981A-1T, Q&A c-8; Ltr Rul 9441004]

If RRB '95 (see Q 1:22A) is enacted, it appears that the earnings on contributions to an American Dream IRA (see Q 26:13) will be included in the decedent's aggregate interests. [RRB '95, Act § 11015(c)]

Q 14:24 How is the present value of the single life annuity calculated for purposes of determining the amount of the participant's excess retirement accumulation?

The present value of the single life annuity is calculated using the applicable interest rate and mortality assumptions in effect on the date of the participant's death. [IRC §§ 4980A(d)(3)(B), 7520; Temp Reg § 54.4981A-1T, Q&A d-7(c); Treas Reg § 20.2031-7; IRS Pub 1457 (Actuarial Values–Alpha Volume)]

For purposes of this calculation, the amount of each annual payment under the single life annuity is equal to the greater of $150,000 (unindexed) or $112,500 (indexed). If the special grandfather rule (see Q 13:31) is applicable, each annual payment is $112,500 (indexed) even if no grandfather amount remains. For 1996, the indexed amount is $155,000, greater than the unindexed amount. [Notice 95-55, 1995-45 IRB 11] Since the indexed $112,500 amount is now greater than the unindexed $150,000, the $155,000 amount is available to all individuals, whether or not the grandfather election was made. For prior years, the indexed amount was:

Year	Indexed Amount
1995	$150,000
1994	148,500
1993	144,551
1992	140,276
1991	136,204
1990	128,228
1989	122,580
1988	117,529

The applicable interest rate is equal to 120 percent of the federal midterm rate rounded to the nearest .2 percent for the month in which the participant's death occurs. The applicable interest rate used to calculate present value may change each month; the mortality assumption will change at least once every ten years. [IRC § 7520]

For individuals whose date of death occurred in 1996, set forth below is the present value (PV) of a single life annuity (SLA) for ages 40 to 85 based upon different interest rates (Table S—single life annuity factors) and using the most current mortality table (Table 80CNSMT—mortality table based on the 1980 census):

Age at Death	PV/SLA at 7%	PV/SLA at 8.6%	PV/SLA at 10%
40	$1,932,804	$1,638,164	$1,440,648
41	1,917,722	1,627,996	1,433,208
42	1,902,005	1,617,317	1,425,365
43	1,885,637	1,606,110	1,417,072
44	1,868,572	1,594,346	1,408,315
45	1,850,824	1,582,008	1,399,092
46	1,832,379	1,569,096	1,389,374
47	1,813,221	1,555,580	1,379,159
48	1,793,412	1,541,506	1,368,449
49	1,772,983	1,526,905	1,357,289
50	1,751,919	1,511,762	1,345,679
51	1,730,219	1,496,060	1,333,574
52	1,707,806	1,479,723	1,320,910
53	1,684,649	1,462,735	1,307,658

Age at Death	PV/SLA at 7%	PV/SLA at 8.6%	PV/SLA at 10%
54	1,660,810	1,445,127	1,293,878
55	1,636,289	1,426,884	1,279,525
56	1,611,070	1,408,005	1,264,583
57	1,585,092	1,388,413	1,249,006
58	1,558,386	1,368,154	1,232,808
59	1,530,982	1,347,198	1,215,960
60	1,502,973	1,325,653	1,198,553
61	1,474,407	1,303,550	1,180,620
62	1,445,344	1,280,936	1,162,190
63	1,415,832	1,257,825	1,143,280
64	1,385,809	1,234,188	1,123,859
65	1,355,181	1,209,930	1,103,802
66	1,323,902	1,184,975	1,083,078
67	1,291,925	1,159,292	1,061,626
68	1,259,282	1,132,911	1,039,477
69	1,226,159	1,105,941	1,016,723
70	1,192,617	1,078,475	993,442
71	1,158,827	1,050,668	969,742
72	1,124,804	1,022,473	945,640
73	1,090,518	993,907	921,088
74	1,055,845	964,844	895,978
75	1,020,691	935,193	870,232
76	985,025	904,906	843,774
77	948,941	874,030	816,680
78	912,578	842,735	789,043
79	876,231	811,239	761,097
80	840,147	779,805	733,073
81	804,683	748,743	705,266
82	770,009	718,208	677,815
83	736,266	688,371	650,892
84	703,421	659,184	624,449
85	671,352	630,556	598,424

As can be gleaned from the above tables, the higher the interest rate, the lower the present value. For single life annuity factors at other interest rates, see IRS Publication 1457 (Actuarial Values—Alpha Volume). An upward adjustment of present value may be appropriate since the single life annuity is deemed to commence on the date of the decedent's death. If an annuity is payable at the beginning of the year, the value of the annuity is the sum of the first payment plus the present value of a similar annuity, the first payment of which is not to be made until the end of the year. Since the Table S single life annuity factors assume that payments are made at the end of the year, it appears that the present value of a single life annuity should be increased by $155,000 for an individual whose date of death occurred in 1996. [Treas Reg § 20.2031-7(d)(2)(iv); Temp Reg § 54.4981A-1T, Q&A d-7(a)]

The decedent's age as of the date of death is the decedent's attained age (in whole years) as of the date of death. For example, if the decedent was born on December 23, 1930, and died on December 21, 1996, the decedent's age for purposes of valuing the single life annuity is 65. [Temp Reg § 54.4981A-1T, Q&A d-7(b)]

Q 14:25   Is the special grandfather rule applicable in determining the amount of a deceased participant's excess retirement accumulation?

Yes. If the grandfather election (see Q 13:31) was made, the excess retirement accumulation is equal to the deceased participant's aggregate interests (see Q 14:23) minus the *greater* of (1) the unrecovered grandfather amount on the date of death, or (2) the present value of the single life annuity (see Q 14:24). [IRC § 4980A(f)(2)(B); Temp Reg § 54.4981A-1T, Q&A d-3, d-4]

The unrecovered grandfather amount is the portion of the grandfather amount not previously recovered by the participant as of the date of death (see Q 13:32). [Temp Reg § 54.4981A-1T, Q&A b-11–b-14]

Q 14:26   Is there a special rule if the surviving spouse is the beneficiary of the deceased participant's aggregate interests?

Yes. If the surviving spouse is the beneficiary of at least 99 percent of the deceased participant's aggregate interests (see Q 14:23), the surviving spouse may elect to have such interests and any retirement distribution attributable to such interests treated as belonging to the surviving spouse. [IRC § 4980A(d)(5)]

If the surviving spouse makes the election, no additional estate tax will be imposed on the deceased participant's estate. [Ltr Ruls 9450042, 9426049, 9350040, 9335051, 9335050] However, the surviving spouse may, upon receipt of such interests, be subject to the excess distributions tax (see Q 13:27) unless the distribution is rolled over to an IRA (see Qs 28:6, 28:36). Even if the distribution is rolled over, distributions from the IRA to the surviving spouse may be subject to the excess distributions tax during the surviving spouse's lifetime and/or the excess retirement accumulation tax upon the surviving spouse's death (see Q 14:29). [Temp Reg § 54.4981A-1T, Q&A d-10]

If the election is made by the surviving spouse, the surviving spouse is allowed to use the deceased participant's unrecovered grandfather amount (see Q 13:32) and is also deemed to have elected the same method of recovery that had been elected by the deceased participant (see Qs 13:31, 13:33, 13:34). [Ltr Ruls 9450042, 9311039, 9246026]

The election is made on Schedule S, Form 706, United States Estate (and Generation-Skipping Transfer) Tax Return. Although no specific time period is set forth for making the election, IRS has ruled that a three-year election period applies because the election is part of the estate tax return, so the election period should be the same as that allowed for filing an amended estate tax return. [IRS §§ 6018(a)(4), 6511(a); Ltr Rul 9437041]

Q 14:27   Is the excess retirement accumulation tax deductible?

The additional estate tax is deductible for estate tax purposes or, alternatively, may be deductible for income tax purposes on a fiduciary income tax return if the estate or a trust is the beneficiary of the excess retirement accumulation. If the beneficiary is other than the deceased participant's estate or a trust, the tax is deductible only for estate tax purposes. [IRC §§ 642(g), 2053(c)(1)(B)]

Q 14:28   Who is liable for the excess retirement accumulation tax?

The deceased participant's estate is liable for the excise tax. [IRC § 4980A(d)(1)]

Additionally, the rules generally applicable for purposes of determining the apportionment of the estate tax apply to the apportionment of the excess retirement accumulation tax. The deceased participant's will or the applicable state apportionment law may provide that the estate is entitled to recover the tax. However, absent such a provision either in the will or under applicable state law, the estate is not entitled to recover the tax from the beneficiary. [Temp Reg § 54.4981A-1T, Q&A d-8A]

At least three states have estate tax apportionment laws that specifically refer to the excess retirement accumulation tax. [Cal Probate Code § 20114.5(b); NY EPTL §§ 2-1.8(a), 2-1.8(c), 2-1.8(d-1); Wash RCW § 83.110.020(2)]

Q 14:29 Whether or not the estate tax on an excess retirement accumulation is imposed, are postdeath distributions subject to the taxes on excess distributions or excess retirement accumulations?

Whether or not the additional estate tax is imposed (see Q 14:21), postdeath distributions may be disregarded for purposes of the taxes on both excess distributions and excess retirement accumulations. Thus, a beneficiary who is receiving distributions with respect to a participant after the participant's death is not required to aggregate those amounts with any other retirement distributions or accumulations except for a surviving spouse who made a spousal election (see Q 14:26). If the surviving spouse did not make a spousal election and rolled over the distribution, then postdeath distributions will be disregarded only if the surviving spouse did not commingle the rollover with any other IRA funds. [IRC § 4980A(d)(3)(A); Temp Reg § 54.4981A-1T, Q&A d-10; Ltr Ruls 9402022, 9013076, 9013020, 9013008]

IRS has determined that this rule applies even if the rollover by the surviving spouse occurred prior to the enactment of the tax on excess retirement accumulations. Prior to August 1, 1986, a surviving spouse rolled over her deceased husband's qualified retirement plan and IRA benefits to a newly established IRA in her own name. IRS ruled that distributions from the IRA will be disregarded for purposes of the taxes on both excess distributions during the surviving spouse's lifetime and excess retirement accumulations upon her death. [Ltr Rul 9619072]

Chapter 15

Determination Letters

Before a company commits itself to making substantial contributions to a retirement plan, it must be certain that the plan qualifies for favorable tax treatment. This chapter discusses the procedure for submitting the retirement plan to IRS for an advance ruling on the plan's tax status.

Q 15:1   What is an IRS determination letter?

Although it is not required, an employer has the option of seeking an advance determination as to the qualified status of its retirement plan by IRS, rather than waiting for IRS to review the plan in connection with an audit. This written advance determination is called a determination letter. A favorable determination letter indicates that, in the opinion of IRS, the terms of the plan conform to the requirements of the Code. For more details, see chapter 4. [Rev Proc 96-6, 1996-1 IRB 151; IRS Pub 794 (Apr 1994)]

A determination letter may also be requested when the retirement plan is amended or terminated.

Q 15:2   Is a fee charged for a request for a determination letter?

Yes. IRS charges a user fee for each request for a determination letter (as well as for letter rulings, opinion letters, and other similar rulings or determinations). The user fee program, which was to end September 30, 1995, has been extended for requests made before October 1, 2000. [OBRA '87 § 10511, as amended by RPA '94, Act § 743] Both RRB '95 (see Q 1:21) and RRB '96 (see Q 1:22) contain provisions extending the user fee program to October 1, 2002. [RRB '95, Act § 11118; RRB '96, Act § 9593]

Each request must be accompanied by payment of the user fee (check or money order) attached to IRS Form 8717, User Fee for Employee Plan Determination Letter Request. Any determination letter request not accompanied by full payment will be returned to the applicant for resubmission. The fee is refundable only in certain situations (e.g., if IRS refuses to rule on an issue properly requested, or issues an erroneous ruling, or if the ruling issued is not responsive).

The amount of the user fee depends on the type of request, whether a multiple employer plan is involved, whether a master and prototype plan or a volume submitter plan is involved, and whether the request covers the average benefit test (see Q 5:17) or any general test (see Qs 4:12, 4:17). Some examples are listed below:

Determination Request Without
General or Average Benefit Test

Individually designed plans (Form 5300)	$ 700
Collectively bargained plans (Form 5303)	$ 700
Adopters of master and prototype plans, volume submitter plans (including a collectively bargained plan covering only collectively bargained employees) (Form 5307)	$ 125
Terminations (Form 5310)	$ 225

Determination Request with
General or Average Benefit Test

Individually designed plans (Form 5300)	$1,250
Collectively bargained plans (Form 5303)	$1,250
Adopters of master and prototype plans, volume submitter plans (including a collectively bargained plan covering only collectively bargained employees) (Form 5307)	$1,000
Terminations (Form 5310)	$ 375

[OBRA '87 § 10511, as amended by RPA '94, Act § 743; Rev Proc 96-8, 1996-1 IRB 187; Form 8717 (Rev Jan 1994)]

Q 15:3   Must an employer apply for a determination letter?

No. However, the advantage of obtaining a favorable determination letter is that the employer is afforded some assurance that its retirement plan is qualified and will remain so if it qualifies in operation (see Q 15:4), if it is not amended (other than as may be required by IRS), and if there is no change in law. Receipt of a favorable determination letter allows the employer to make contributions to the retirement plan with the knowledge that its deductions for those contributions will most likely be allowed should IRS audit its tax returns.

See Q 4:6 for a discussion of timely filed determination letter requests and an employer's ability to recover its contributions to a disqualified retirement plan.

Q 15:4   What does the term "qualifies in operation" mean?

Generally, a retirement plan qualifies in operation if it is maintained according to the terms on which the favorable determination letter was issued. However, conditions may develop in operation that may jeopardize the qualification of the retirement plan. Examples of common operational features that arise after issuance of a favorable determination letter and that may adversely affect the favorable determination include the following:

- Failure to meet nondiscrimination requirements (see Q 4:9)
- Rapid turnover of lower-paid employees (see Q 9:5)
- Contributions or benefits in excess of the limitations under Section 415 (see chapter 6)
- Not providing top-heavy minimums (see chapter 22)

Q 15:5   What are the limitations of a favorable determination letter?

A determination letter applies only to qualification requirements regarding the form of the retirement plan. For example, a determination letter does not consider whether actuarial assumptions are reasonable for funding purposes (see Qs 2:19, 8:8) or whether a specific contribution is deductible. The determination as to whether a retirement plan qualifies is made from the information in the written plan document and the supporting information submitted by the employer. Therefore, the determination letter may not be relied upon if:

1. There has been a misstatement or omission of material facts;
2. The facts subsequently developed are materially different from the facts on which the determination was made; or
3. There is a change in applicable law.

IRS revoked a previously issued favorable determination letter on a prospective, rather than a retroactive, basis because IRS had all of the necessary information when it made its favorable determination, and the employer had relied in good faith on the determination letter. [Ltr Rul

9508003; IRC § 7805(b)] Similarly, where a determination letter was subsequently revoked by IRS, the revocation was applied prospectively. With respect to the original request, there was no misstatement or omission of material facts, the facts at the time of the transaction were not materially different from the facts on which the determination was based, and there had been no change in applicable law. [Ltr Rul 9519001]

Also, the determination letter applies only to the employer and its participants on whose behalf the determination letter was issued. A determination letter may include one or more caveats that affect the scope of reliance represented by the letter (see Q 15:13).

A plan sponsor has a certain amount of flexibility in determining the scope of the determination letter to be issued for its plan since the sponsor is given the option to elect whether the determination letter should consider certain requirements. Specifically, a plan sponsor may choose whether a plan that relies on a general test or a nondesign-based safe harbor test (see Qs 4:12, 4:17) will be reviewed for compliance with the nondiscrimination in amount requirement (see Q 4:10), and whether a plan that relies on the average benefit test (see Q 5:17) will be reviewed for compliance with the minimum coverage requirements. A plan sponsor may also request IRS to determine whether specific benefits, rights, or features under the plan satisfy the current availability requirement (see Q 4:18). [Rev Proc 96-6, 1996-1 IRB 151]

Q 15:6   When should a retirement plan be submitted for IRS approval?

A retirement plan should be submitted for IRS approval as early as possible. Amendments needed to qualify a retirement plan can be made retroactively until the company's federal income tax return for the year is due (including extensions) or at a later time if allowed by IRS. If the retirement plan is submitted to IRS before the tax return is due, IRS will extend the time limit for amending the plan. If the retirement plan is submitted after the company's tax return is due, IRS may not allow the company to amend its plan retroactively, particularly if the changes that need to be made are significant. [IRC § 401(b); Treas Reg § 1.401(b)-1]

Generally, qualified retirement plans must have been amended to comply with the requirements of TRA '86 (and other laws) by the last day of the plan year beginning in 1994. IRS gave employers maintaining plans with remedial amendment periods that expired before April 1, 1995 an additional three months to file determination letter applications, provided they timely adopted the TRA '86 amendments. Furthermore, the plan must have complied in operation with the new rules as of each rule's effective date; and plan amendments, when made, must have been retroactive to the applicable effective date (see Qs 4:6, 4:7). [Rev Proc 94-13, 1994-1 CB 566, *modified by* Rev Proc 95-12, 1995-3 IRB 24; Ann 94-136, 1994-49 IRB 14; Notice 92-36, 1992-2 CB 364; Ann 92-29, 1992-9 IRB 37; IRS Field Office Directive on Good-Faith Compliance, June 12, 1992]

IRS has indicated that it will extend the period of time by which plan sponsors could retroactively amend their plans to comply with the requirements of GATT. Until further notice is given by IRS, determination letters, other than those issued for terminating plans, will not include consideration of any requirements made by GATT. However, favorable determination letters issued by IRS for such plans may not be relied upon with respect to whether such provisions satisfy the qualification requirements as amended by GATT. [Rev Proc 96-6, 1996-1 IRB 151]

IRS extended the deadline for employers to adopt certain regional prototype, master and prototype, and volume submitter plans to comply with TRA '86 and for filing determination letter applications. Generally, the deadline for employers adopting prototype or volume plans expired at the end of the sixth month beginning after the date on which a favorable TRA '86 notification/advisory letter was issued by IRS for the plan and the following requirements were satisfied:

- The prototype/specimen plan was submitted to IRS prior to July 1, 1994
- A favorable IRS notification/advisory letter was not issued by IRS prior to July 1, 1994
- The employer and sponsor executed a written certification
- The employer adopted such plan within six months of IRS approval

IRS also extended the deadline for a plan to be retroactively amended to comply with the $150,000 compensation limit (see Q 6:23) until the later of the last day of the 1994 plan year or the time (including extensions) for filing the employer's 1994 income tax return. [Rev Proc 95-12, 1995-3 IRB 24]

Furthermore, the remedial amendment period has been extended for plans maintained by tax-exempt organizations to the last day of the first plan year beginning on or after January 1, 1997. [Ann 95-48, 1995-23 IRB 13]

IRS has provided an extended reliance period for certain retirement plans. Extended reliance generally means that the retirement plan will not have to be amended to reflect subsequent regulations or administrative guidance issued by IRS after the date of the determination letter until the earlier of (1) the last day of the last plan year commencing prior to January 1, 1999, or (2) the date for plan amendment as set by legislation. Employers who adopted master, prototype, or regional prototype plans submitted and approved before April 1, 1991, and who requested a determination letter on or before December 31, 1993, are eligible for the extended reliance; sponsors of individually designed plans who requested a determination letter on or before June 30, 1994 are eligible for the extended reliance; and sponsors of volume submitter plans whose advisory letter for the specimen plan was requested by June 30, 1994, and who requested a determination letter on or before December 31, 1994, are eligible for the extended reliance.

[Rev Proc 93-39, 1993-2 CB 513; Rev Proc 93-9, 1993-1 CB 474; Ann 94-85, 1994-26 IRB 23]

Generally, qualified retirement plans must be amended to comply with the requirements of SBA '96 (see Q 1:21) by the first day of the plan year beginning in 1998. However, the plan must comply in operation with the new rules as of each rule's effective date, and plan amendments, when made, must be retroactive to the applicable effective date. [SBA '96, Act § 1465]

Q 15:7   What are the filing requirements for obtaining a favorable determination letter?

Before the actual application may be filed, notice of the filing must first be given to all interested parties (see Q 15:8). The application should then be sent to the District Director of the key district (see Q 15:9) that covers the employer's principal place of business. Documents that should accompany the request include the following:

- Copies of the plan and trust
- Executed power of attorney (if the application is made on behalf of the employer)
- IRS application Form 5300, 5307, or 5303 (for both defined benefit and defined contribution plans); each of these forms was revised in 1996
- Form 8717 and applicable user fee (see Q 15:2)
- Copy of latest favorable determination letter, if any
- Schedule Q (Form 5300), Nondiscrimination Requirements

IRS accepted determination letter applications that were filed on a 5300 series form with a revision date prior to 1996 and that did not include Schedule Q through October 1, 1996, provided the application satisfied the procedures for a determination letter application that were in effect prior to 1996.

[Ann 96-53, 1996-23 IRB 12; Rev Proc 96-6, 1996-1 IRB 151; Rev Proc 93-39, 1993-2 CB 513, *modified by* Rev Proc 94-37, 1994-1 CB 683]

In the case of certain minor amendments to a retirement plan, Form 6406 may be filed as an alternative to Form 5300 provided the plan has received a favorable determination letter under TRA '86. This form can be filed for amendments to individually designed plans (including volume submitter plans) or permitted changes to adoption agreement elections in master or prototype or regional prototype plans provided the changes constitute minor amendments. Form 6406 was revised in 1996. IRS accepted determination letter applications that were filed on a Form 6406 with a revision date prior to 1996 through October 1, 1996, provided the application satisfied the procedures for a determination letter application that were in effect prior to 1996. The instructions to Form 6406 require that only the actual amendments, along with various explanatory information, and not the entire plan document, be included with Form 6406. Form 6406 cannot be used to request determination letters for terminated plans, restated plans or plans initially amended to comply with TRA '86. [Ann 96-53, 1996-23 IRB 12; Rev Proc 96-6, 1996-1 IRB 151]

If an employer has adopted an interim amendment before the execution of a volume submitter, regional prototype, master, or prototype plan, Form 5300 must be submitted instead of Form 5307, except where:

1. The interim amendment was a simple amendment that could have been submitted on Form 6406; or

2. The interim amendment consists of an adoption agreement of an earlier version of a subsequently approved and adopted master, prototype, or regional prototype plan. [EP/EO Dallas Key District Newsletter, Winter 1992]

Form 5309, Application for Determination of Employee Stock Ownership Plan, should be filed together with Form 5300, Application for Determination for Employee Benefit Plan (or Form 5303, if applicable), if the application relates to an employee stock ownership plan (ESOP; see chapter 24). [Rev Proc 96-6, 1996-1 IRB 151]

Form 5310, Application for Determination Upon Termination, should be used when the employer intends to terminate a retirement plan, other than a multiemployer plan covered by the PBGC (see Qs 21:12, 25:2). Form 5303, Application for Determination for Collectively Bargained Plan, should be filed in the case of the termination of a multiemployer plan covered by PBGC. Schedule Q, Nondiscrimination Requirements, is required to be included as an attachment to Form 5310 or 5303. Form 6088, Distributable Benefits From Employee Pension Benefit Plans, is required to be included with the filing of the termination of a defined benefit plan or an *under-*

funded defined contribution plan and for a collectively bargained plan if the plan benefits employees who are not collectively bargained employees. A separate Form 6088 is required for each employer employing covered employees. Generally, IRS will not issue a determination letter with respect to the termination unless the retirement plan has been amended to comply with the applicable provisions of law that are in effect at the time of termination (see Q 21:66). [Rev Proc 96-6, 1996-1 IRB 151; Instructions to Form 6088 (Rev July 1994)]

For details with regard to requesting a determination letter for an affiliated service group, see Q 5:38.

Q 15:8   What are the requirements regarding notice to employees?

All interested parties must be given notice that an application for a determination letter will be made. Generally, this means that all current employees eligible to participate in the retirement plan must be notified. If that notice is given by posting or in person, it must be given not less than seven days, and not more than 21 days, before the application is filed. If notice is given by mail, it must be given not less than ten days, and not more than 24 days, before the application is filed. (The postmark date is what counts.) [IRC § 7476(b); Treas Reg §§ 1.7476-1, 1.7476-2, 601.201(o)(3)(xv); Rev Proc 96-6, 1996-1 IRB 151; Rev Proc 80-30 (§ 7.02), 1980-1 CB 685] An employer that mailed notice of an impending determination letter request to the last known address of each interested party fulfilled the notice requirement. [Halliburton Co, 64 TCM 713 (1992)]

The notice must contain the following information:

1. Brief description of the class of interested parties to whom the notice is addressed;

2. Name of plan, plan identification number, and name of plan administrator;

3. Name and identification number of the applicant;

4. Description of class of employees eligible to participate;

5. Description of the procedures for employees to submit comments to IRS or to request DOL to do so;

6. That an application for a determination letter will be sent to IRS, the address of the IRS office, and the purpose of the application (e.g., initial qualification);

7. Statement of whether IRS has ever issued a determination letter as to the qualified status of the plan; and

8. The procedure whereby certain additional information may be obtained by the interested parties. This additional information consists of:

   a. An updated copy of the plan and related trust agreement;

   b. A copy of the application;

   c. Other documents, whether sent to or from IRS in connection with this application; and

   d. Any other information that affects the rights of the interested parties.

An employer that fails to give proper notice to interested parties is barred from appealing IRS's refusal to issue a determination letter to the Tax Court. [IRC § 7476(b); Treas Reg §§ 601.201(o)(3)(xviii)–601.201(o)(3)(xx); Rev Proc 96-6, 1996-1 IRB 151; Rev Proc 80-30, 1980-1 CB 685]

Q 15:9   Where is an application for a determination letter sent?

Seven IRS districts are designated as key districts. Each key district has a division known as the Employee Plans/Exempt Organizations (EP/EO) Division. The other districts are associate districts.

The application for a determination letter with all supporting documents and forms (see Q 15:7) should be sent to the IRS key district that has jurisdiction over the employer. For example, an employer based in Albany, New York, files its application with the Brooklyn (New York) district because the Brooklyn district is the key district for Albany, New York.

If Entity Is In:	*Send Application to:*
Connecticut, Maine, Massachusetts, New Hampshire, New York, Rhode Island, Vermont	Internal Revenue Service EP/EO Division P.O. Box 1680, GPO Brooklyn, NY 11202
Delaware, District of Columbia, Maryland, New Jersey, Pennsylvania, Virginia, any U.S. possession or foreign country	Internal Revenue Service EP/EO Division P.O. Box 17288 Baltimore, MD 21203

If Entity Is In:	*Send Application to*:
Indiana, Kentucky, Michigan, Ohio, West Virginia	Internal Revenue Service EP/EO Division P.O. Box 3159 Cincinnati, OH 45201
Arizona, Colorado, Kansas, Oklahoma, New Mexico, Texas, Utah, Wyoming	Internal Revenue Service EP/EO Division Mail Code 4950 DAL 1100 Commerce Street Dallas, TX 75242
Alabama, Arkansas, Florida, Georgia, Louisiana, Mississippi, North Carolina, South Carolina, Tennessee	Internal Revenue Service EP/EO Division P.O. Box 941 Atlanta, GA 30370
Alaska, California, Hawaii, Idaho, Nevada, Oregon, Washington	Internal Revenue Service EP Application EP/EO Division McCaslin Industrial Park 2 Cupania Circle Monterey Park, CA 91754-7406
Illinois, Iowa, Minnesota, Missouri, Montana, Nebraska, North Dakota, South Dakota, Wisconsin	Internal Revenue Service EP/EO Division 230 S. Dearborn DPN 20-6 Chicago, IL 60604

[Rev Proc 96-8, 1996-1 IRB 187; Instructions to IRS Form 5300 (Rev Jan 1996); Instructions to IRS Form 8717 (Rev Jan 1994)]

IRS has announced that it will centralize the determination letter program in the Cincinnati key district. Until IRS gives advance notice, requests for determination letters should continue to be submitted to the appropriate key district as under current rules. [Ann 95-51, 1995-25 IRB 132]

Q 15:10 What happens to an application for a determination letter after it is sent to IRS?

After the application is stamped "received," it is reviewed by an individual known as a perfecter. The perfecter reviews the application and related documents for completeness and to ensure that it has been sent to the proper district. If the application is incomplete, it may be returned to the employer.

Once the perfecter is satisfied that the application is complete, case and file folder numbers are assigned to the application. The file folder number has nine digits; the case number has nine digits followed by the letters EP. In each instance, the first two digits reflect the district code; thus, for example, an application of a Brooklyn employer bears case and file folder numbers beginning with 11, the Brooklyn district code.

Data are then fed from the application through a computer terminal to one of the IRS Service Centers. The Service Center, in turn, performs the following two functions with those data:

1. The Service Center issues Form 2693, which is an acknowledgment to the applicant of IRS's receipt of the application. In addition to identifying data regarding the applicant, this acknowledgment contains the case and file folder numbers and the IRS control date, which starts the 270-day review period (see Q 15:11).

2. The Service Center generates preaddressed labels that are affixed to the annual reporting forms that are sent to the applicant.

The application is then either screened out for the early issuance of a favorable determination letter or winds its way through clerical functions and is assigned to a group. The group manager assigns the application to an employee plans specialist, depending on the degree of difficulty, the size of the applicant, and the workload of the specialists in the group. The application is assigned about 60 to 90 days after the control date.

The specialist reviews the application and contacts the applicant or authorized representative if additional information is needed. If everything is in order, the specialist recommends the issuance of a favorable determination letter. If the group manager agrees with the recommendation, the file is sent to the Review Staff. Not all applications receive this second level of review. Although some applications are subject to mandatory review, most are subjected to a random sampling review.

If everything is in order and the reviewer agrees with the specialist, the district apprises the Service Center of its recommendation and a computer-generated favorable determination letter is issued to the applicant. The applicant's authorized representative receives a copy of the determination letter.

The Chicago key district has adopted new procedures comprised of three stages that are expected to expedite the review process. Initially, a clerical review is performed for such common errors as missing documents or failure to sign forms. Although an application is generally returned when such errors are discovered, the applicant will have 90 days to make a correction without having to pay a new filing fee. The filing is next reviewed by the technical screening unit for minor technical problems with the plan document, application forms, and accompanying demonstrations that can be corrected by the IRS's receipt of information from the applicant within three business days. The third stage is a more detailed review by a group agent who will contact the applicant regarding questions on complex aspects of a plan such as average benefit testing (see Q 5:17). IRS emphasized that it will attempt to close out review of a plan at the earliest possible stage.

Q 15:11   How long does it take to obtain a determination letter?

Generally, a determination letter is issued within 180 days after the application is filed. Form 2693 (see Q 15:10) generally provides an estimate of the time period required to process the application (typically, 145 days).

IRS has a maximum of 270 days to rule after it receives an application for a determination. If IRS fails to act within this period, the employer can ask the Tax Court for a favorable ruling (technically, a declaratory judgment) notwithstanding IRS's inaction (see Q 15:12).

On the other hand, IRS must wait at least 60 days after it receives the application before it can issue a determination letter. This gives IRS a chance to review any comments made by interested parties (see Q 15:8).

[IRC § 7476; Rev Proc 96-6, 1996-1 IRB 151; Rev Proc 80-30, 1980-1 CB 685]

Q 15:12   What alternatives are available to an applicant if IRS proposes to issue an adverse determination letter?

Generally, IRS is inclined to issue a favorable determination letter to an applicant even if this means accepting amendments in proposed form as a basis for closing a case. There are circumstances, however, in which the applicant cannot satisfy the employee plans specialist (by amendment or otherwise) that a favorable determination letter should be issued. Three courses of action are then available to the applicant. The applicant can:

1. Request the employee plans specialist to seek technical advice from IRS's National Office;
2. Withdraw the application; or
3. Appeal the proposed adverse determination letter.

Requests for technical advice are made only when the issue involved satisfies certain criteria established by IRS. Chances of going this route are remote.

Withdrawal of an application at best restores the status quo. On occasion, withdrawal might even lead the employee plans specialist to issue an information report to the Examination Division (formerly the Audit Division) to consider selecting the employer's tax return for examination to see whether a tax deduction was claimed for the employer's contribution to the plan.

Appeal is the usual course of action. An appeal may be taken to an IRS Regional Office within time limits established by IRS. If the Appeals Officer sustains the district's position, the next appeal is to the IRS National Office. Finally, if that office sustains the district's position, the applicant must petition the Tax Court for a declaratory judgment that its retirement plan is qualified on or before the 91st day after the date of issuance of the final adverse determination. [Hamlin Development Co, 65 TCM 2071 (1993)] Failure to exhaust all IRS administrative remedies bars an applicant from proceeding in the Tax Court. [Joseph P Clawson, MD, Inc, PS, Profit and Pension Trusts, 65 TCM 2452 (1993)] However, an employer whose plan qualification request is unduly delayed by IRS is deemed to have exhausted administrative remedies. [IRC § 7476; Tipton and Kalmbach, Inc, 43 TCM 1345 (1982)]

Q 15:13 Once a favorable determination letter is issued, may IRS subsequently revoke such qualification?

Courts have generally held that in order for IRS to revoke a prior favorable determination letter, a material change of fact must have occurred since the time of the initial IRS review of the employer's retirement plan (see Q 15:5). However, the failure to amend a retirement plan on a timely basis after initial IRS approval may cause the plan to lose its qualified status (see Q 4:7). [Boggs v Comm'r, 784 F 2d 1166 (4th Cir 1986); Lansons, Inc, 622 F 2d 774 (5th Cir 1980); Mills, Mitchell & Turner, 65 TCM 2127 (1993); Hamlin Development Co, 65 TCM 2071 (1993); Kollipara Rajsheker, MD, Inc, 64 TCM 1153 (1992); Attardo, 62 TCM 313 (1991); Stark Truss Co, Inc, 62 TCM 169 (1991); Basch Eng'g, Inc, 59 TCM 482 (1990); Halligan, 51 TCM 1203 (1986)]

In one case, a favorable determination letter was conditioned on limiting the deduction for contributions to the retirement plan and requiring the participant to include a corresponding amount in his income; the participant, however, refused to include the amount in his income. The court found that the plan was not qualified because the participant did not comply with the conditions of the determination letter. [TCS Mfg, Inc Employees Pension Trust, 60 TCM 1312 (1990)]

Q 15:14   Will a retirement plan with disqualifying defects be disqualified?

In order to qualify, a retirement plan must meet certain requirements (see Q 4:1). A plan that does not meet these requirements both in form and operation has a disqualifying defect and may be disqualified. However, IRS has implemented three programs—the Employee Plans Closing Agreements Pilot Program (see Q 15:15), the Administrative Policy Regarding Sanctions (see Q 15:16), and the Voluntary Compliance Resolution Program (see Q 15:17)—to resolve disqualifying plan defects without the sanction of plan disqualification. [Rev Proc 94-62, 1994-2 CB 778; Rev Proc 94-16, 1994-1 CB 576; IRS Memoranda, Dec 21, 1990 and Mar 26, 1991]

Q 15:15   What is the Employee Plans Closing Agreements Pilot Program (CAP)?

The CAP program provides a mechanism for resolution of issues in dispute between IRS and plan sponsors where the issues would normally result in plan disqualification. The CAP program applies to both form and operational plan defects. Closing agreements will only be issued in those cases in which the plan sponsor will make (1) retroactive and prospective corrections of all plan defects, and (2) payment based on the outstanding tax liability as if the plan had been disqualified. The determination of whether to enter into a closing agreement and the amount of the tax sanction may be affected by the equities of the case. The CAP program, initiated in December 1990, is now a permanent program.

Originally, the CAP program applied to the following four areas:

1. Failure to amend the plan timely for TEFRA, TRA '84, and REA;
2. Improper application of an integration formula;
3. Failure to apply full vesting on partial termination; and
4. Operational violation of top-heavy rules.

The CAP program has been expanded to include cases involving all qualification issues. However, the CAP program will not apply in cases where the exclusive benefit rule has been violated (see Q 4:1), where there is significant discrimination in favor of highly compensated employees (see Q 3:2), or where there are repeated, deliberate, or intentional violations. CAP is available both to plan sponsors with a plan under examination and to plan sponsors that discover plan defects before being examined. While the CAP program is designed to resolve matters at the key district office level, it is recommended that the key district consult with the National

Office in cases involving 500 or more participants or more than $1 million in potential tax liability. [IRS Memoranda, Oct 9, 1991 and Dec 21, 1990]

IRS has advised that, subject to very limited exceptions, CAP sanctions should be paid by parties other than the plan, such as the employer or fiduciary responsible for the disqualifying defect.

The exceptions where plan assets can be used to satisfy the dollar sanction are the following:

1. The employer is unable to pay the sanctions, the employer's tax liability upon disqualification would be nominal, and the adverse consequences of plan disqualification would fall on non-highly compensated employees (see Q 3:13);

2. An employee's accrued benefit (see Q 9:2) can be used if, in general, the employee (a) is the party responsible for the disqualifying defect, (b) is a plan participant, and (c) agrees to a distribution of the accrued benefit for the purpose of paying the sanction; or

3. In the case of multiemployer plans and accountable third-party fiduciaries where it is often difficult to secure payment, plan assets can be used only after IRS has sought the assistance of DOL in identifying the source of payment and has tried to obtain payment from a specific party without success.

[IRS Field Directive, Feb 21, 1995]

In one case, the Tax Court ruled that the taxpayer was not entitled to relief under the CAP program because the program was discretionary, may not have applied in the taxpayer's key district, and was not available as an alternative to disqualification at the time the taxpayer's plan was disqualified. [Mills, Mitchell & Turner, 65 TCM 2127 (1993)]

IRS provides another option for resolution of cases that are unable to take advantage of the current CAP program or that are ineligible for the VCRP (see Q 15:17). Several key elements to this program, referred to as "walk-in CAP," include:

1. The program applies to plans with form or operational defects, including those not eligible under the VCRP or CAP (e.g., plans without determination letters for TEFRA, TRA '84, and REA; plans with repeated, deliberate, and flagrant violations; plans with violations that are considered to be "egregious").

2. A plan is not eligible under the "walk-in CAP" if it is eligible under the VCRP or it is the subject of a key district office employee plan examination.

3. The program is available when a plan sponsor voluntarily approaches a key district office and requests in writing a resolution of specific defects.

4. Correction of all defects must be made for all years in which the defects occurred.

5. A monetary sanction generally will be imposed at a significantly lower amount than under the current CAP program and is limited to 40 percent of the approximate tax liability that would have been assessed had the plan been disqualified.

[Rev Proc 94-16, 1994-1 CB 576]

IRS has established procedures for plans that were not amended for TRA '86 and subsequent legislation, up to and including OBRA '93, by the end of the remedial amendment period (see Q 15:6). If it is discovered during an IRS examination that a plan was not amended in a timely fashion, existing CAP procedures will be used. Under a special program, plans that are voluntarily submitted under walk-in CAP within 15 months after the end of the remedial amendment period will be exposed to a much smaller penalty (between a minimum of $1,000 and a maximum of 20 percent of the approximate tax liability that would have been assessed had the plan been disqualified). If the submission is made after 15 months, the upper end is increased from 20 percent to 40 percent.

If it is discovered during the determination letter process that a plan was not amended in a timely fashion, a favorable determination letter will not be issued unless:

1. Appropriate amendments are made, along with a statement from the plan sponsor that benefits of both current and former participants will be restored to the levels they would have been had the plan been timely amended; and

2. The appropriate dollar sanction is paid.

If the determination letter request was filed within 15 months after the end of the remedial amendment period, the sanction will be between $1,000 and 40 percent of the approximate tax liability that would have been assessed had the plan been disqualified. If the determination letter request was filed more than 15 months after the end of the remedial amendment period, the 40 percent ceiling will not apply.

The above procedures establish a range of permissible sanctions. The exact amount of the dollar sanction will depend upon a number of factors and will be based on the facts and circumstances of the specific case. These factors include:

- The nature of the defects in the plan

- The timeliness of the required amendments
- Good faith on the part of the plan sponsor
- The extent of the disclosure by the plan sponsor that the plan has not been amended timely (for determination letter cases)

If a plan has been amended timely for all qualification requirements other than amendments required by UCA '92 (the direct transfer provisions of Section 401(a)(31)) and OBRA '93 (the $150,000 compensation limitation of Section 401(a)(17)), the plan sponsor will be subject to a penalty at the low end of the penalty range. [IRS Memorandum, Oct 26, 1995]

Q 15:16 What is the Administrative Policy Regarding Sanctions?

The Administrative Policy recognizes that even though a retirement plan may have an operational disqualifying defect, it may not need to be disqualified if the error is so minor that disqualification is not productive. The Administrative Policy applies only to operational defects, and no tax sanctions will be applied. An operational defect may not result in plan disqualification if the following six criteria are met:

1. The error is an isolated one;
2. There is a history of compliance;
3. Procedures to ensure compliance have been established;
4. The operational defect occurred through an oversight or mistake;
5. The dollar amount resulting from the defect is not substantial; and
6. The taxpayer makes an immediate and complete correction.

The Administrative Policy will not be available in cases involving exclusive benefit violations (see Q 4:1) and disqualification due to late statutory plan amendments (see Qs 15:13, 15:15).

[IRS Memorandum, Mar 26, 1991]

IRS has informally advised that it intends to expand the Administrative Policy to include a wider range of plan defects.

Q 15:17 What is the Voluntary Compliance Resolution Program (VCRP)?

VCRP permits plan sponsors to voluntarily correct operational defects in their retirement plans and to obtain a compliance statement that provides that the corrections are acceptable and that the IRS will not pursue plan disqualification (see Q 15:18). Consideration under VCRP does not preclude an examination of the employer or the plan by IRS with respect to matters outside the compliance statement.

A request for a compliance statement should be made to the National Office and contain a description of the defects, a description of the proposed method of correction, a description of the measures that have been or will be implemented to ensure that the same operational defects will not occur, and other procedural items and supporting information. The submission must be accompanied by a copy of the first two pages of the most recently filed Form 5500 series return (see Q 17:2), a copy of a determination letter, opinion letter, or notification letter that considered TRA '86, and a copy of the relevant portions of the plan document. The plan sponsor must pay a fixed voluntary compliance fee that is based on the number of plan partici-pants and amount of plan assets. The voluntary compliance fees are:

1. $500 for a plan with assets of less than $500,000, and no more than 1,000 participants;

2. $1,250 for a plan with assets of at least $500,000, and no more than 1,000 participants;

3. $5,000 for a plan with more than 1,000, but fewer than 10,000 participants; and

4. $10,000 for a plan with 10,000 or more participants.

With respect to requests submitted prior to January 1, 1996, VCRP only applied to plans that had received a favorable determination letter for TEFRA, TRA '84, and REA; and, with respect to requests submitted on or after January 1, 1996, VCRP only applies to plans that have received a favorable determination letter for TRA '86. The program is not available in cases involving exclusive benefit violations (see Q 4:1), egregious viola-tions, where trusts were not created or maintained, where terminated plans no longer have plan assets, or where the plan is under examination. [Rev Proc 96-8, 1996-1 IRB 187; Rev Proc 94-62, 1994-2 CB 778; Rev Proc 94-16, 1994-1 CB 576]

Q 15:18 What are the correction principles and requirements of VCRP?

A request for a compliance statement must contain the specific informa-tion necessary to support the suggested correction method. This includes the number of employees affected (and how this number was determined), the expected cost of correction, the years involved, and any calculations or assumptions the plan sponsor used to determine the amounts needed for correction. The submission must state the interest rate (and the method for determining the interest rate) that will apply to any corrective contributions or distributions. As a general rule, the interest rate earned by the plan during the applicable periods should be used in determining the earnings for corrective contributions or distributions. The submission should also provide the proposed method of locating and notifying former participants who become entitled to additional benefits.

The request for a compliance statement must give a description of the method for correcting the defect that the plan sponsor has implemented or proposes to implement. The following general principles should be used in suggesting an acceptable correction method:

1. The correction method should restore both current and former participants to the benefit level they would have had if the defect had not occurred. Actions must be taken to find former participants who are due additional benefits;

2. The correct method should restore the plan to the position it would have been in had the defect not occurred;

3. To the extent possible, the correction should conform the operation of the plan to the actual plan language. Amending the plan to conform the plan document to the way the plan was operated is not an acceptable VCRP correction;

4. The correction method should not violate another qualification requirement;

5. The correction method should, to the extent possible, resemble one already provided for in the Code, regulations, or other publications;

6. The correction method should keep the assets in the plan, except to the extent the Code, regulations, or other publications provide for a distribution;

7. Corrective allocations to a defined contribution plan (see Q 2:2) must be adjusted for earnings and forfeitures that would have been allocated during the applicable period. Corrective allocations must be based on the compensation or earnings that would have been used in the period for which the allocation is made;

8. The corrective contributions should come only from employer contributions (including forfeitures, if the plan permits forfeitures to reduce employer contributions (see Q 9:18));

9. A corrective allocation to a participant's account because of a failure to make a required allocation in a prior limitation year (see Q 6:16) will not be considered an annual addition (see Q 6:1) with respect to the participant for the limitation year in which the correction is made. It will be considered an annual addition for the limitation year in which it relates. This rule does not apply to the limitation regarding deductions; and

10. Any distributions from the plan should be properly reported.

VCRP has been extended indefinitely.

[Rev Proc 94-62, 1994-2 CB 778; Rev Proc 94-16, 1994-1 CB 576]

Q 15:19 What is the Standardized Voluntary Compliance Resolution Program (SVP)?

VCRP (see Q 15:17) was modified by the addition of SVP. SVP is available to a plan sponsor if a listed defect (but no more than two) is corrected using a permitted correction method. If the plan sponsor wishes to propose a correction method other than one permitted in SVP, the plan sponsor should enter the VCRP. The general correction principles of VCRP must be followed in a SVP correction (see Q 15:18).

The listed defects and their permitted correction methods include:

1. Failure to provide top-heavy minimums (see Qs 22:37, 22:43). In a defined contribution plan (see Q 2:2), the permitted correction method is to contribute and allocate the required top-heavy minimums in the manner provided for in the plan on behalf of non-key employees (see Q 22:29) (and any other employee required to receive top-heavy allocations under the plan). In a defined benefit plan (see Q 2:3) the minimum required benefit must be accrued in the manner provided in the plan.

2. Failure to satisfy the ADP test, the ACP test, or the multiple use test (see Qs 23:8, 23:48, 23:56). The permitted correction method is to make qualified nonelective contributions or qualified matching contributions (see Q 23:14) on behalf of the non-highly compensated employees (see Q 3:13) to the extent necessary to raise the actual deferral percentage or actual contribution percentage of the non-highly compensated employees to the percentage needed to pass the test or tests. The contributions must be made on behalf of all eligible non-highly compensated employees and must be either the same flat dollar amount or the same percentage of compensation.

3. Failure to distribute excess deferrals (see Q 23:28). The permitted correction method is to distribute the excess deferral to the employee and to report the amount as taxable in the year of deferral and the year distributed. A distribution to a highly compensated employee (see Q 3:3) is included in the ADP test (see Q 23:8); a distribution to a non-highly compensated employee is not included in the ADP test.

4. Failure to include an eligible employee as a participant in the plan (see chapter 5). The permitted correction method is to make a contribution to the plan on behalf of employees excluded from a

defined contribution plan or to provide benefit accruals for the employees excluded from a defined benefit plan. If an employee was denied eligibility in a 401(k) plan, the employer must make a qualified nonelective contribution to the plan on behalf of the employee that is equal to the average deferral percentage of the employee's group (either highly compensated or non-highly compensated). The qualified nonelective contribution is treated as an elective contribution (see Q 23:13), and any match that would have been applied to the elective contribution must be applied to the qualified nonelective contribution. If an employee was denied the opportunity to make employee contributions or receive a matching contribution, the employer must make a qualified nonelective contribution to the plan on behalf of the employee that is equal to the average contribution percentage (see Q 23:48) of the employee's group (either highly compensated or non-highly compensated). If the qualified nonelective contribution is contributed in lieu of an employee contribution, any match that would have applied to an employee contribution must be applied to the qualified nonelective contribution.

5. Failure to timely pay required minimum distributions (see chapter 11). The permitted correction method is to distribute the required minimum distribution amounts and any applicable gains or losses for all prior years. The employer must also agree to pay 100 percent of the excise tax (see Q 11:20) that would apply because of the failure to distribute.

6. Failure to obtain participant and/or spousal consent for certain distributions (see chapter 10). The permitted correction method is to give the affected employees a choice between providing informed consent for the distribution actually made or receiving a qualified joint and survivor annuity (QJSA; see Q 10:8). If participant consent cannot be obtained, the participant must receive a QJSA. This annuity may be offset for any amounts already received by the participant. If spousal consent cannot be obtained, the employer must provide a survivor annuity. A spousal survivor annuity may not be offset by any amount received by the participant.

7. Failure to limit annual additions (see Q 6:1). The permitted correction method is to place the excess annual addition into an unallocated suspense account to be used as an employer contribution in the succeeding years. The permitted correction for failure to limit annual additions that are elective deferrals is to distribute the elective deferral.

The voluntary compliance fee under SVP is $350 regardless of the number of participants.

[Rev Proc 96-8, 1996-1 IRB 187; Rev Proc 94-62, 1994-39 IRB 11]

Chapter 16

Operating the Plan

By clearly placing the responsibility for administering a qualified retirement plan with the plan administrator, ERISA gave that role considerable significance. This chapter explains who the plan administrator is, what the plan administrator's responsibilities are, and which records must be maintained.

Q 16:1   Who is the plan administrator?

Generally, the plan administrator is a person specifically designated by the qualified retirement plan as the administrator (1) by name, (2) by reference to the person or group holding a named position, (3) by reference to a procedure for designating an administrator, or (4) by reference to the person or group charged with the specific responsibilities of plan administrator. If no person or group is designated, the employer is the administrator (in the case of a qualified retirement plan maintained by a single employer). The employer's board of directors (in the case of a corporation) may authorize a person or group to fulfill the responsibilities of administrator. In any case, if a plan administrator cannot be determined, the plan administrator is the person or persons actually responsible for control, disposition, or management of the property received by the qualified retirement plan. [ERISA § 3(16)(A); IRC § 414(g); Treas Reg § 1.414(g)-1]

The employer was held liable as plan administrator where the named administrator was inactive or was not solely responsible for plan administration, and where the employer retained some control over benefit decisions. [Rosen v TRW, Inc, 979 F 2d 191 (11th Cir 1992); Law v Ernst & Young, 956 F 2d 364 (1st Cir 1992)] However, where a retirement plan specifically designated an administrator, the employer, who was not the named administrator, could not be held liable for failure to provide requested information.

[Jones v Allied Signal Inc, 16 F 3d 141 (7th Cir 1994); McKinsey v Sentry Ins, No. 92-3194 (10th Cir 1993)] (See Q 16:6.)

Q 16:2 Can officers or owners of the company function as the plan administrator?

Yes. In small companies, a company officer or owner usually is designated as plan administrator. In large companies, three or more people (a committee) may be designated collectively as plan administrator.

Q 16:3 What are the basic responsibilities of the plan administrator?

The plan administrator is responsible for managing the day-to-day affairs of the qualified retirement plan. Specifically, these responsibilities include the following:

1. Hiring attorneys, accountants, consultants, and, for certain qualified retirement plans, actuaries;
2. Determining eligibility for plan participation, vesting, and accrual of benefits;
3. Advising participants or beneficiaries of their rights and settlement options;
4. Ruling on claims for benefits;
5. Directing distribution of benefits;
6. Preparing reports for IRS, DOL, and PBGC (see chapter 17);
7. Preparing reports for participants and responding to information requests by participants (see Q 18:13); and
8. Keeping service records, benefit records, vesting records, and participant information.

Q 16:4 Which records should a plan administrator maintain?

The plan administrator is required to maintain records relating to the operation of the qualified retirement plan that will provide in sufficient detail the necessary information from which required reports (to IRS, DOL, and PBGC) may be verified, explained, or clarified. These records must be kept available for at least six years after the filing date of the reports. [ERISA § 107]

The plan administrator must also maintain records to determine the benefits due or that may become due in order to be able to report that information to any plan participant who:

1. Requests the information (but not more than once in any 12-month period);

2. Terminates service with the company; or

3. Has a break in service (see Q 5:10).

[ERISA § 209]

Thus, a plan administrator should maintain the following records:

Service: Precise records must be kept of time worked by all employees so that determinations of eligibility, vesting, or benefit accrual may be substantiated. These records have to be maintained for many years, even though a participant may have terminated employment and distributions may have been made.

Benefits: Detailed records should be maintained to project benefits for highly paid participants to ensure that their benefits do not exceed the limitations provided by law. These records should also be maintained if a qualified retirement plan provides for deferred payment of benefits. For example, a participant who terminates employment at a young age might not receive benefits until a later age.

Vesting: The vesting alternatives under ERISA and the Code require calculations under specific formulas. In some cases, participants may be under different vesting schedules, requiring meticulous administrative records. For example, if a vesting schedule is changed by amendment, certain participants may elect to remain under the old vesting schedule (see Q 9:6). See also Qs 22:32 through 22:36 regarding vesting under top-heavy plans, which may require dual recordkeeping for vesting purposes.

Deductible employee contributions: Although no longer permitted, separate accounting for past contributions, if any, is still required (see Q 6:22).

Plan administrators are also required to retain all plan records necessary to support or validate PBGC premium payments. The records, which include actuarial calculations, must be kept for six years after the filing due date. For the consequences of a plan administrator's failure to maintain those records, see Q 16:6. [PBGC Reg § 2610.11]

Q 16:5 May the plan administrator rely on information gathered by those performing ministerial functions?

Yes, provided the plan administrator has exercised prudence in selecting and retaining these people. The plan administrator should consider whether those gathering information are competent, honest, and responsible. [DOL Reg § 2509.75-8, FR-11]

Q 16:6 What penalty is imposed for failure to comply with recordkeeping requirements?

If a plan administrator does not maintain records necessary to make required benefit status reports to participants (see Q 16:4), DOL may impose a penalty of $10 for each affected participant unless there is reasonable cause for the failure. [ERISA § 209(b)] Furthermore, a plan administrator who fails to comply with a request for information that is required to be furnished to a participant may be liable for penalties of up to $100 a day from the date of failure to comply (see Q 16:19). [ERISA § 502(c)(1)] In one case, the court assessed a penalty of $100 per day per document, but only for one participant, for failure to supply requested information to over 70 participants; the penalty was divided among all such participants. The district court's basis for its ruling that there had been no showing of prejudice or bad faith was not an abuse of discretion. [Bartling v Fruehauf Corp, 29 F 3d 1062 (6th Cir 1994)] However, in another case, although the court agreed that the participant was entitled to receive a detailed breakdown of his monthly benefit, it did not penalize the plan administrator for failing to provide such information because the court had no reliable evidence that the administrator knew it was obligated to provide this data. [Maiuro v Federal Express Corp, No. 92-4518 (D NJ 1994)] In another case, the court held that a plan administrator who failed to provide plan documents in a timely manner to a participant could be assessed penalties even though the participant was not prejudiced by the delay and the delay was not due to the plan administrator's bad faith if the cause of the failure was not beyond the control of the plan administrator. [Glocker v WR Grace & Co, 1995 US App Lexis 33874 (4th Cir 1995)] In yet another case, a court's failure to assess a penalty against a government agency for failing to comply with a request for a plan document was not considered an abuse of power because an award of monetary damages is a matter within the court's discretion. [Hennessy v Federal Deposit Ins Corp, 58 F 3d 908 (3d Cir 1995)]

For more details, see Q 18:13.

Also, PBGC may audit the records of a defined benefit plan covered by PBGC (see Qs 21:12, 21:13) regarding the calculation of the premium owed each year to the agency. If it is determined that the plan's records do not support the amount of unfunded vested benefits reported in the PBGC forms, PBGC will "deem" the variable-rate portion of the premium to be the maximum amount per participant ($53; see Q 21:14). [PBGC Reg § 2610.11]

Q 16:7   Is withholding required on the distribution of benefits from a retirement plan?

An eligible rollover distribution (see Q 28:8) is subject to automatic 20 percent withholding unless the distribution is transferred by a direct rollover (see Q 28:20) to an eligible retirement plan (see Q 28:19) that permits the acceptance of rollover distributions. [IRC §§ 401(a)(31), 3405(c); Treas Reg §§ 1.401(a)(31)-1, Q&A 1(b)(1), 1.402(c)-2, Q&A 1(b)(3), 31.3405(c)-1, Q&A 1(a), 8]

Distributions other than eligible rollover distributions are subject to elective withholding provisions and are *not* subject to the mandatory 20 percent withholding. Form W-4P, Withholding Certificate for Pension or Annuity Payments, is used to inform payors whether income tax is to be withheld and on what basis. The elective withholding rules apply to both periodic payments (e.g., annuities) and nonperiodic payments (e.g., lump-sum distributions) that are not eligible rollover distributions. The option to elect out of withholding is not available if the payment is delivered outside the United States or its possessions, unless the payee certifies to the payor that the payee is not (1) a U.S. citizen or resident alien, or (2) a tax-avoiding expatriate under Section 877. [IRC §§ 3405(a), 3405(b), 3405(e); Treas Reg § 31.3405(c)-1, Q&A 1(a); Notice 87-7, 1987-1 CB 420] However, IRS has ruled that plan administrators (see Q 16:1) are not required to withhold tax on installment distributions to nonresident aliens to the extent that the distributions are in substantially equal payments if the nonresident alien performed services for the employer outside the United States and at least 90 percent of the plan's participants are citizens of the United States. [IRC §§ 871(f), 1441(c)(7); Ltr Rul 9537028]

In addition to withholding, plan administrators are also subject to recordkeeping and reporting responsibilities (see Q 17:17).

Q 16:8   Does 20 percent automatic withholding apply if a participant elects to receive only a portion of the distribution?

If a participant elects to have a portion of the distribution paid to an eligible retirement plan (see Q 28:19) in a direct rollover (see Q 28:20) and to receive the remainder of the distribution, the 20 percent withholding requirement (see Q 16:7) applies only to the portion of the distribution that the participant receives. There is no 20 percent withholding for the portion of the distribution that is paid to an eligible retirement plan in a direct rollover. [Treas Reg § 31.3405(c)-1, Q&A 6]

Q 16:9   May a participant elect to have more than 20 percent withheld from an eligible rollover distribution?

Yes. A participant and a plan administrator (see Q 16:1) may enter into an agreement to withhold more than 20 percent of the eligible rollover distribution (see Qs 16:7, 28:8). [IRC § 3402(p); Treas Reg § 31.3405(c)-1, Q&A 3]

Q 16:10   Is there any liability for failure to withhold income taxes?

Yes. Generally, the plan administrator (see Q 16:1) or payor will be liable for the tax that should have been withheld as well as any penalties if a taxable distribution is made from a retirement plan and the recipient of the distribution does not elect out of the withholding or if automatic withholding applies (see Q 16:7). [IRC §§ 3405(d), 6672(a); Temp Reg § 35.3405-1, G-2, G-20] With respect to an eligible rollover distribution (see Q 28:8), if the plan administrator reasonably relies on information provided by the participant, the plan administrator will not be liable for any taxes that should have been withheld solely because the distribution is paid to a plan that is not an eligible retirement plan (see Q 28:19). Although the plan administrator is not required to verify independently the accuracy of information provided by the distributee, the plan administrator's reliance on the information furnished must be reasonable. [Treas Reg § 31.3405(c)-1, Q&A 7]

Q 16:11   Which types of retirement plans are subject to the withholding rules on distributions?

All qualified and nonqualified retirement plans—including individual retirement accounts (IRAs) of any type—are subject to the general withholding rules. Only an eligible rollover distribution (see Q 28:8) is subject to automatic 20 percent withholding (see Q 16:7). [IRC § 3405]

Q 16:12   If property other than cash is distributed, how is withholding accomplished?

The plan administrator (or payor) must withhold on distributions of property even if this requires selling all or part of the property. However, the participant may remit to the administrator sufficient cash to satisfy the withholding obligation. [Treas Reg §§ 31.3405(c)-1, Q&A 9, 35.3405-1, Q&A F-2, F-3]

Q 16:13 Is there an exception from withholding for distributions of employer securities?

Yes. The maximum amount withheld on any distribution (including any eligible rollover distribution; see Q 28:8) may not exceed the sum of the cash and the fair market value of other property (excluding employer securities and plan loan offset amounts; see Q 16:15) received in the distribution. Thus, although employer securities must be included in the aggregate amount that is subject to 20 percent withholding, the total amount required to be withheld from an eligible rollover distribution is limited to the sum of cash and the fair market value of property received by the participant, excluding any amount of the distribution that is an employer security. If the distribution consists solely of employer securities or of employer securities and cash (not in excess of $200) in lieu of fractional shares, no amount is required to be withheld. [IRC §§ 402(e)(4)(E), 3405(e)(8); Treas Reg § 31.3405(c)-1, Q&A 11]

Q 16:14 If the amount of an eligible rollover distribution is less than $200, must tax be withheld?

No. If the amount of the eligible rollover distribution (see Q 28:8) is less than $200, the plan administrator (see Q 16:1) need not withhold tax. However, all eligible rollover distributions received within one taxable year of the distributee under the same plan must be aggregated for purposes of determining whether the $200 floor is reached. If the plan administrator (or payor) does not know at the time of the first distribution (that is less than $200) whether there will be additional eligible rollover distributions during the year for which aggregation is required, the plan administrator need not withhold from the first distribution. If distributions are made within one taxable year under more than one plan of an employer, the plan administrator (or payor) may, but need not, aggregate distributions for purposes of determining whether the $200 floor is reached. However, once the $200 floor is reached, the sum of all payments during the year must be used to determine the amount required to be withheld. [Treas Reg § 31.3405(c)-1, Q&A 14]

Q 16:15   How are participant loans treated for the withholding rules?

With respect to a participant loan from a qualified retirement plan that is an offset amount (see Qs 28:14–28:16) and an eligible rollover distribution (see Q 28:8), the automatic withholding rules are applied in a manner similar to a distribution of employer securities (see Q 16:13). In other words, although the offset amount must be included in the aggregate amount that is subject to 20 percent withholding, the total amount required to be withheld from an eligible rollover distribution does not exceed the sum of the cash and the fair market value of property received by the participant, excluding any amount of the distribution that is an offset amount.

Example 1. In 1997, Julie, a participant in Kenneth Corporation's profit sharing plan, has an account balance of $10,000, of which $3,000 is represented by a plan loan secured by her account balance. Upon termination of employment in 1997, Julie elects a distribution of her entire account balance, and the outstanding loan is offset against the account balance on distribution. Julie elects a direct rollover of the distribution, and $7,000 is paid to an eligible retirement plan. When Julie's account balance was offset by the amount of the $3,000 unpaid loan balance, she received an offset amount (equivalent to $3,000) that is an eligible rollover distribution. No withholding is required on account of the distribution of the $3,000 offset amount because no cash or other property (other than the offset amount) is received by Julie from which to satisfy the withholding.

Example 2. The facts are the same as those in Example 1, except that Julie elects to receive a distribution of her account balance that remains after the $3,000 offset. In this case, the amount of the distribution received by Julie is $10,000, not $3,000. Because the amount of the $3,000 offset attributable to the loan is included in determining the amount that equals 20 percent of the eligible rollover distribution received by Julie, withholding in the amount of $2,000 (20% × $10,000) is required. The $2,000 is required to be withheld from the $7,000 to be distributed to Julie in cash, so that Julie actually receives a check for $5,000.

[Treas Reg § 31.3405(c)-1, Q&A 11]

Q 16:16   When did the new automatic withholding rules become effective?

The new rules are applicable to eligible rollover distributions (see Q 28:8) made *after* December 31, 1992, even if the event giving rise to the distribution occurs *before* January 1, 1993, or even if the eligible rollover distribution is part of a series of payments that began *before* January 1, 1993. [Treas Reg §§ 1.401(a)(31)-1, Q&A 1(c), 1.402(c)-2, Q&A 1(c), 31.3405(c)-1, Q&A 1(c)]

Example 1. Richie terminated employment with The Greatest Sandusky Corporation in 1992 but does not receive his pension plan benefits until 1997. Even though Richie's employment was terminated in 1992 (before the new rules became effective), the distribution of his benefits in 1997 is subject to the new automatic withholding rules.

Example 2. Helaine terminated employment with The Greatest Sandusky Corporation in 1991 and elected to receive her pension plan benefits in 72 equal monthly payments beginning January 1, 1992. Helaine's monthly payments, starting with the January 1, 1993 payment, are subject to the new automatic withholding rules even though the series of payments commenced before 1993.

Q 16:17 Must a recipient receive an explanation of the tax effects of a distribution from a qualified retirement plan?

The plan administrator (see Q 16:1) is required, within a reasonable time before making an eligible rollover distribution (see Q 28:8), to provide the distributee with a written explanation of the direct rollover provisions and other special tax rules. This explanation is known as the Section 402(f) Notice. The posting of a Section 402(f) Notice does not satisfy this requirement. The notice must be provided, individually, to each distributee.

A participant's consent to a distribution is not valid unless the participant receives a notice of the participant's rights under the plan no more than 90 days and no less than 30 days prior to the annuity starting date (see Q 10:3). However, a participant may waive the 30-day requirement and, therefore, need not wait 30 days after receipt of the Section 402(f) Notice for a direct rollover (see Q 28:20) to be made if:

1. The participant is given the opportunity to consider the decision of whether or not to elect a direct rollover for at least 30 days after the notice is provided; and

2. The plan administrator provides information to the participant clearly indicating that the participant has a right to this period for making the decision.

IRS has provided a model amendment that plan sponsors may adopt in order to allow participants to waive the 30-day notice requirement. The waiver *does not* apply to the qualified joint and survivor annuity (QJSA) notice (see Q 10:29). Therefore, waivers are only available to profit sharing, stock bonus, and 401(k) plans that are exempt from the automatic survivor benefit requirements (see Q 10:6).

[IRC § 402(f); Treas Reg §§ 1.401(a)(31)-1, Q&A 1(b)(2), 1.402(f)-1, Q&A 1 through Q&A 4; Rev Proc 93-47, 1993-2 CB 578; Notice 93-26, 1993-1 CB 308]

There is a penalty of $10 for each recipient who is not given timely notice unless there is reasonable cause for the failure. [IRC § 6652(i)]

In one case, the court held that the administrator had a duty to provide tax information to the participant, but that the administrator did not have a duty to ensure that the participant actually read the material and was not required to give advice regarding every possible investment option and tax consequence. [Bouteiller v Vulcan Iron Works, Inc, 834 F Supp 207 (ED Mi 1993)] Courts have held that a participant could not recover money damages for failure of the plan administrator to give notice of the rollover option upon distribution of the participant's benefits, even though the participant, because he failed to roll over the distribution, was taxed on the distribution. [Fraser v Lintas:Campbell-Ewald, 56 F 3d 722 (6th Cir 1995); Novak v Andersen Corp, No. 91-1957MN (8th Cir 1992)]

IRS has announced that plan administrators can satisfy the notice requirement by providing each recipient of an eligible rollover distribution with a copy of the model IRS notice. However, IRS encourages plan administrators to supplement the model IRS notice with language that addresses specific subjects not addressed in the current model notice.

The complete model notice is lengthy, and the following is the summary portion of the notice:

SPECIAL TAX NOTICE REGARDING PLAN PAYMENTS

This notice contains information you will need before you decide how to receive your benefits from [INSERT NAME OF PLAN] (the "Plan").

SUMMARY

A payment from the Plan that is eligible for "rollover" can be taken in two ways. You can have *all or any portion* of your payment either (1) PAID IN A "DIRECT ROLLOVER" or (2) PAID TO YOU. A rollover is a payment of your Plan benefits to your individual retirement arrangement (IRA) or to another employer plan. This choice will affect the tax you owe.

If you choose a DIRECT ROLLOVER

- Your payment will not be taxed in the current year and no income tax will be withheld.
- Your payment will be made directly to your IRA or, if you choose, to another employer plan that accepts your rollover.
- Your payment will be taxed later when you take it out of the IRA or the employer plan.

If you choose to have your Plan benefits PAID TO YOU

- You will receive only 80% of the payment, because the Plan administrator is required to withhold 20% of the payment and send it to the IRS as income tax withholding to be credited against your taxes.
- Your payment will be taxed in the current year unless you roll it over. You may be able to use special tax rules that could reduce the tax you owe. However, if you receive the payment before age $59\frac{1}{2}$, you also may have to pay an additional 10% tax.
- You can roll over the payment by paying it to your IRA or to another employer plan that accepts your rollover within 60 days of receiving the payment. The amount rolled over will not be taxed until you take it out of the IRA or employer plan.
- If you want to roll over 100% of the payment to an IRA or an employer plan, *you must find other money to replace the 20% that was withheld.* If you roll over only the 80% that you received, you will be taxed on the 20% that was withheld and that is not rolled over.

[Notice 92-48, 1992-2 CB 377]

Q 16:18   Must a separate Section 402(f) Notice be given for each distribution in a series of periodic payments?

No. The plan administrator (see Q 16:1) can satisfy the Section 402(f) Notice requirement (see Q 16:17) with respect to each payment in the series by providing the notice to the distributee prior to the first payment, and then providing the notice at least once annually for as long as the payments continue. [Treas Reg § 1.402(f)-1, Q&A 3]

Q 16:19   What documents can a participant obtain?

A participant is entitled to obtain, without charge and without request, a summary plan description (SPD; see Q 18:1), a summary of material modifications (see Q 18:8) to the plan, and a summary annual report. Upon request, other documents must be furnished to a participant by the plan administrator (see Q 16:1). [ERISA § 104(b)(4)] One court held that participants were entitled to receive copies of a plan's actuarial reports because they were necessary for the operation of a pension plan and these were other instruments under which the plan was established or operated. [Bartling v Fruehauf Corp, 1994 US App Lexis 26568 (6th Cir 1994)] Another court held that a list of plan participants was not an instrument under which the plan was operated; and, therefore, the plan administrator was not required to provide the list to a committee representing retired participants because participants only have a right to obtain documents that provide information regarding plan benefits. [Hughes Salaried Retirees Action Committee v Adm'r of the Hughes Non-Bargaining Retirement Plan, 1995 US App Lexis 35262 (9th Cir 1995)] Since former employees are not participants, former employees are not entitled to plan documents unless they have an expectation of returning to covered employment or have a colorable claim for benefits. [Szoke v Deloitte & Touche LLP, 1995 US Dist Lexis 2517 (SD NY 1995)]

For more details, see Q 18:13.

Q 16:20 How should a plan administrator handle oral inquiries from participants?

Numerous questions by participants can be expected. The plan administrator can insist that inquiries be in writing unless the effect of that request is to make it difficult for participants to inquire about the plan (e.g., if the participants are not fluent in English). One court ruled that the obligation to issue a foreign language version of a plan's SPD does not extend to the denial of benefit claims made by participants (see Q 18:14). [Diaz v United Agric Employee Welfare Benefit Plan & Trust, 50 F 3d 1478 (9th Cir 1995)]

The danger, of course, in responding orally to complex questions about the plan is that since there is no record of what was said, a participant may claim at a later date that the information provided by the plan administrator was misleading. Thus, the plan administrator should limit the number of individuals authorized by the plan to answer questions concerning the plan or its benefits. Such a policy should be strictly adhered to and conveyed to participants. Those authorized to answer questions should maintain a log for recording inquiries. They should also respond in writing to inquiries that they believe may affect an individual's benefits in order to have a record of what was said.

Q 16:21 May the plan administrator or trustee choose the form of distribution that will be made to a participant?

No. See Qs 10:42 through 10:49 regarding discretion with respect to distributions from a qualified retirement plan.

Q 16:22   Can innocent errors in the operation of a qualified retirement plan result in disqualification of the plan?

Yes. One qualified retirement plan, for example, was disqualified (i.e., lost its tax-favored status) after IRS determined that the plan was discriminatory because contributions had been allocated solely for the benefit of a shareholder-employee when, in fact, five additional employees were eligible for coverage. It did not matter that this situation resulted from an honest mistake. Furthermore, the company's offer to cure the discrimination retroactively was rejected. Although the Code authorizes retroactive corrections for defects in the retirement plan itself (see Q 15:6), there is no statutory authority for a retroactive correction of a mistake in the operation of the retirement plan. However, IRS has announced that it may not seek plan disqualification for operational errors under certain circumstances (see Qs 15:14–15:17). [IRC § 401(b); Myron v United States, 550 F 2d 1145 (9th Cir 1977); see also Buzzetta Constr Corp, 92 TC 641 (1989)]

Q 16:23   Can a qualified retirement plan be amended?

Yes, but ERISA requires that a plan provide a procedure for amending the plan and for identifying the persons who have authority to amend the plan. [ERISA § 402(b)(3)] The Supreme Court held that a plan provision stating that the company reserves the right to modify or amend the plan was a sufficient amendment procedure so that the employer could amend its plan. [Curtiss-Wright Corp v Schoonejongen, No. 93-1935 (S Ct 1995)]

Q 16:24   What is the actuary's role in administering a qualified retirement plan?

The actuary's primary function is to determine the amount needed by an employer's defined benefit plan (see Q 2:3) to pay promised retirement benefits to participants. Assumptions and methods used by the actuary are basic to the application of the minimum funding standards (see Q 8:1). The actuary is called upon to certify the amount of tax-deductible dollars the employer must contribute to its defined benefit plan.

If a defined benefit plan is not funded solely through insurance, the services of an enrolled actuary—that is, an actuary licensed to practice before the government agencies responsible for administering ERISA—are required. Some enrolled actuaries may work for insurance companies, and others may be employed by accounting firms or firms specializing in actuarial services. [ERISA §§ 3041, 3042, 3043; IRC § 7701(a)(35)]

Q 16:25 What is the trustee's role in administering a qualified retirement plan?

The trustee holds title to plan assets and is responsible for managing them unless this responsibility has been delegated to an investment manager. For details on the trustee's investment responsibilities, see chapter 19.

Q 16:26 What is the accountant's role in administering a qualified retirement plan?

The accountant's role may entail preparing statements of plan assets, auditing the plan's books and records, and preparing reports to government agencies. A plan with 100 or more participants requires special reports by an independent qualified public accountant (see Q 17:14).

Q 16:27 Which plan officials must be bonded?

Generally, every fiduciary (anyone who has some discretionary authority or control over the plan or its assets; see chapter 19), and anyone who handles funds or other property of the plan, must be bonded. The bond must cover at least 10 percent of the amount handled by the bonded individual; it may not be for less than $1,000 and need not be for more than $500,000. [ERISA §§ 3(21), 412]

Q 16:28 What are funds or other property for purposes of the bonding requirement?

The term funds or other property is intended to encompass all property that is or may be used as a source for the payment of benefits to plan participants. It includes property in the "nature of quick assets" (e.g., cash, checks, negotiable instruments) and property that is readily convertible into cash for distribution as benefits.

Although the term does not include permanent assets used in plan operation (land, buildings, furniture, and fixtures), land and buildings that are investments of a qualified retirement plan will be covered by the term other property. [DOL Reg § 2580.412-4]

Q 16:29   What is handling of funds?

A person handles funds or other property of a qualified retirement plan whenever that person's duties or activities are such that there is risk that the funds or other property could be lost if that person, acting alone or with others, engaged in dishonest or fraudulent conduct. Under this definition, handling is generally considered to include situations in which there is:

1. Physical contact with cash, checks, or property;
2. The power to secure physical possession of the cash, checks, or similar property;
3. The authority to cause a transfer of property such as mortgages or securities to oneself or another; or
4. Disbursement of funds or other property including the power to sign or endorse checks.

[DOL Reg § 2580.412-6]

Q 16:30   Are any fiduciaries exempt from the bonding requirements?

Yes. A bond generally is not required from:

1. A bank that is subject to federal regulation and federally insured;
2. A savings and loan association subject to federal regulation if it is the plan administrator; and
3. An insurance company that provides or underwrites, in accordance with state law, plan benefits for any plan other than one established or maintained for the insurance company's employees.

[ERISA § 412(a); DOL Reg §§ 2580.412-23 through 2580.412-32]

Q 16:31   May a party in interest provide a bond in satisfaction of the bonding requirements?

Generally, a bond may not be procured from a party in interest (see Q 20:3) or from any entity in which the qualified retirement plan or a party in interest, directly or indirectly, has any significant control or financial interest. However, a bond can be procured from a party in interest where the financial interest or control is not incompatible with an unbiased exercise of judgment. Thus, a bond may be obtained from a party in interest providing multiple services to plans. For example, if an insurance company providing life insurance for a plan is affiliated with a surety company, a bond may be obtained from the surety company. [ERISA § 412(c); DOL Reg §§ 2580.412-33 through 2580.412-36]

Q 16:32   Is bonding required for a plan with only one participant?

In the case of a qualified retirement plan covering only the owner (i.e., the shareholder or sole proprietor), or the owner and the owner's spouse, the qualified retirement plan is not subject to the bonding requirements. However, if the plan's only participant is not the owner, this exception does not apply. Furthermore, if a partnership's qualified retirement plan covers only partners (or partners and their spouses), the qualified retirement plan is not subject to the bonding requirements (see Q 19:7). [DOL Reg § 2510.3-3]

Chapter 17

Reporting to Government Agencies

Once a qualified retirement plan has been put into operation, the plan administrator has the responsibility of filing certain information returns, reports, and statements with the agencies that administer the federal pension laws: IRS, DOL, and PBGC. This chapter sets forth guidelines for the plan administrator to follow in meeting these reporting requirements.

Q 17:1   What are IRS's reporting requirements?

Each employer (subject to a limited exception (see Q 17:2)) that maintains a qualified retirement plan is required to file an annual report. The annual report is commonly referred to as the Form 5500 series return/report.

The appropriate Form 5500 series return/report (Form 5500, 5500-C/R, or 5500-EZ) must be filed for each qualified retirement plan (see Q 17:2) for each plan year in which the plan has assets. Therefore, the year of complete distribution of all plan assets is the last year for which a return/report must be filed (see Q 17:5). [IRC §§ 6058, 6059]

Q 17:2   Which Form 5500 series return/report is required for a particular qualified retirement plan?

Qualified retirement plans with 100 or more participants must file Form 5500, Annual Return/Report of Employee Benefit Plan (With 100 or more participants), each year. Qualified retirement plans with fewer than 100 participants generally must file Form 5500-C/R, Return/Report of Employee Benefit Plan (With fewer than 100 participants). The Form 5500-C/R must be filed as Form 5500-C for the first plan year, at least once every three plan years thereafter, and for the final plan year. For the plan years that Form 5500-C is not required, Form 5500-C/R may be filed as Form 5500-R, a brief registration statement.

According to the instructions to Form 5500 and DOL regulations, if the plan has between 80 and 120 participants (inclusive) at the beginning of the plan year (year 2), the plan may file the same series of forms (Form 5500 or 5500-C/R) that it filed for the previous year (year 1). This rule appears to create an anomaly if the number of plan participants increases from below 100 in year 1 to between 100 and 120 in year 2 and subsequent years. For example, a qualified retirement plan with 95 participants in year 1 files Form 5500-C/R; and, in year 2, if the plan has 105 participants, it may again file Form 5500-C/R. Each year thereafter, if the plan has between 100 and 120 participants, it appears that the plan could file Form 5500-C/R for each such year. [DOL Reg § 2520.103-1(d); Instructions to 1995 IRS Forms 5500 and 5500-C/R]

Form 5500-C is enforcement-oriented and, according to IRS, PBGC, and DOL, "will provide the information necessary for each Agency to monitor compliance with ERISA. The 5500-R is designed to ensure that the Agencies receive annually certain minimal information to permit the continuous review of small plans." [Notice of Adoption of Revised Forms, filed with the Federal Register of July 31, 1980] Certain questions on the 1995 Form 5500-C/R relating to participant contributions have been modified to enable more effective monitoring of the handling of participant contributions by employers. Specifically, the 1995 Form 5500-C/R includes a question whether any participant contributions were transmitted to the plan more than 31 days after receipt or withholding by the employer (see Qs 19:24, 20:7). [PWBA Notice of Change, published in the Federal Register on Feb 1, 1996]

IRS has ruled that only the employer designated as plan sponsor or plan administrator (see Q 16:1) of a multiple employer plan adopted by other unrelated employers must annually file the complete Form 5500 or Form 5500-C/R, whichever is appropriate. The other unrelated employers must file Form 5500-C/R with only certain items completed. A plan is a multiple employer plan for this purpose only if the contributions of all employers are available to pay benefits to all participants. Therefore, if each employer's contributions are available to pay benefits only for that employer's employees, a completed annual return/report must be filed for each participating employer. [Ltr Rul 8930050; Instructions to 1995 IRS Forms 5500 and 5500-C/R]

Form 5500-EZ, Annual Return of One-Participant (Owners and Their Spouses) Retirement Plan, may be used for certain qualified retirement plans. A one-participant plan is defined as a qualified retirement plan that covers only:

1. The owner of a business or both the owner and spouse; and the business, whether or not incorporated, is wholly owned by the owner, or both the owner and spouse; or

2. Partners (or the partners and their spouses) in a business partnership.

Form 5500-EZ cannot be used if the plan sponsor is a member of an affiliated service group (see Q 5:37), controlled group of corporations (see Q 5:33), or group of businesses under common control (see Q 5:31), or if it leases employees (see Q 5:62). In addition, if the plan satisfies the coverage requirements (see Q 5:15) only when combined with another plan, Form 5500-EZ cannot be used. A qualified retirement plan that cannot use Form 5500-EZ must use Form 5500-C/R.

For 1995 and later years, employers with one or more one-participant plans that have total assets in excess of $100,000 at the end of any plan year beginning on or after January 1, 1994, must file Form 5500-EZ for the year that assets exceed $100,000 and each year thereafter, even if total plan assets are subsequently reduced to $100,000 or less. For example, if plan assets in a plan that otherwise satisfies the requirements for filing Form 5500-EZ totaled $110,000 at the end of the 1995 plan year, and a distribution occurred in 1996 so that plan assets totaled $85,000 at the end of the 1996 plan year, Form 5500-EZ must be filed for the 1996 plan year. A one-participant plan must also file Form 5500-EZ for its final plan year even though plan assets have always been less than $100,000. [Instructions to 1995 IRS Form 5500-EZ]

Q 17:3 Does the plan administrator have the option of filing Form 5500-C/R as Form 5500-C annually instead of as Form 5500-R?

Yes. Plan administrators (see Q 16:1) and sponsors may file a Form 5500-C for any year in which a Form 5500-R registration statement could have been filed. If the Form 5500-C is filed, the three-year filing cycle starts again (see Q 17:2). [Instructions to 1995 IRS Form 5500-C/R]

Q 17:4 Must any special schedules accompany the employer's Form 5500 series return/report?

Yes. Schedule A (Form 5500), Insurance Information, must be attached to Forms 5500 and 5500-C/R if any benefits under the qualified retirement plan are provided by an insurance company. However, Schedule A is not needed if Form 5500-EZ is filed, or if a Form 5500-C/R is filed, but the plan covers only a sole owner of a trade or business (or owner and owner's spouse) or partners (or partners and their spouses). [ERISA § 103(e); Instructions to 1995 IRS Forms 5500 and 5500-C/R]

Schedule B (Form 5500), Actuarial Information, must be attached to the Form 5500 series return/report of most defined benefit plans (see Q 2:3). [IRC § 6059] IRS has opined that Schedule B must be filed for the plan year in which a defined benefit plan terminates, but need not be filed for the plan year after the year in which the plan terminates (see Qs 8:29, 21:67). *The foregoing was offered as general information and was not to be construed as a ruling as to any actual case.* [IRS Spec Rul, July 27, 1993]

Schedule C (Form 5500), Service Provider and Trustee Information, must be attached to Form 5500 to report the following:

1. Service providers receiving, directly or indirectly, $5,000 or more in compensation for services rendered to the plan during a plan year (see Instructions to 1995 Schedule C to IRS Form 5500 for exceptions);

2. Trustee information; and

3. Information relating to the termination of all persons who acted as accountants, enrolled actuaries, insurance carriers, custodians, administrators, investment managers, and trustees of the plan during the plan year.

[Instructions to 1995 Schedule C to IRS Form 5500]

Schedule E (Form 5500), ESOP Annual Information, must be completed by an employer or plan administrator (see Q 16:1) of a qualified retirement plan that includes employee stock ownership plan (ESOP) benefits (see Q 24:1). If applicable, the completed Schedule E must be filed as an attachment to Form 5500, 5500-C/R, or 5500-EZ. [Instructions to 1995 Schedule E to IRS Form 5500]

Schedule G (Form 5500), Financial Schedules, is not required to be attached to Form 5500 to report certain investment information. Schedule G was developed to provide uniformity in the reporting of assets; and, although the filing of the form is not mandatory, the information required by the schedule is nonetheless required to be included as part of the Form 5500 filing. [PWBA Notice, May 17, 1994; Instructions to 1995 IRS Form 5500]

Schedule P (Form 5500), Annual Return of Fiduciary of Employee Benefit Trust, may be completed by a fiduciary (trustee or custodian) and filed as an attachment to Form 5500, 5500-C/R, or 5500-EZ. It is strongly recommended that Schedule P be filed because it starts the running of the statute of limitations under Section 6501 (a) for the trust (see Q 17:12). [Instructions to 1995 Schedule P to IRS Form 5500]

Schedule SSA (Form 5500), Annual Registration Statement Identifying Separated Participants With Deferred Vested Benefits, is used to inform IRS of plan participants who separated from service but were not paid retirement benefits. The Instructions to the 1995 IRS Form 5500 Schedule SSA describe when a separated participant must be reported on Schedule SSA but contain a material error. The instructions incorrectly state that a separated plan participant with deferred vested benefits must be reported on Schedule SSA filed for the plan year during which separation occurred; however, the instructions should state that such a separated plan participant must be reported on Schedule SSA filed for the plan year *following* the plan year in which the separation occurred. [IRC § 6057; Ann 96-38, 1996-19 IRB]

Q 17:5   When is a Form 5500 series return/report due?

Unless an extension is granted (see Qs 17:6, 17:7), the appropriate Form 5500 series return/report is due by the last day of the seventh month following the close of the plan year (July 31 for calendar-year plans). Note that the due date relates to the plan year and not to the employer's taxable year. [ERISA § 104]

> **Example.** Allaire Corporation files its federal income tax return on a calendar-year basis. Allaire maintains a qualified retirement plan with a plan year end of January 31. For the plan year ending January 31, 1997, the Form 5500 series return/report is due September 2, 1997 (August 31, 1997 is a Sunday, and September 1, 1997 is a federal holiday).

For a short plan year, the Form 5500 series return/report is due by the last day of the seventh month after the short plan year ends. A short plan year ends on the date of a change in a plan's accounting period or upon the complete distribution of assets with respect to a plan termination (see chapter 21). If a current Form 5500 series return/report is not available before the due date for the short plan year return, the latest form available should be used and the date printed on the return should be changed to the current year. In addition, the dates the short plan year began and ended should be included on the return. [Instructions to 1995 IRS Forms 5500, 5500-C/R, 5500-EZ]

Q 17:6   May the due date for filing a Form 5500 series return/report be extended?

Yes. An extension of up to two and one-half months may be granted for filing the Form 5500 series return/report. Form 5558, Application for Extension of Time To File Certain Employee Plan Returns, must be filed in sufficient time before the regular due date to permit IRS to consider and act on the application. A detailed statement of the reason for an extension must be attached to the application (see Q 17:7).

Q 17:7 Is the extension of time for filing the Form 5500 series return/report ever automatic?

Yes. An automatic extension of the due date for filing is available to an employer if all of the following conditions are met:

1. The plan year coincides with the employer's taxable year;
2. The employer has been granted an extension of time to file its federal income tax return to a date later than the due date for its Form 5500 series return/report; and
3. A copy of the income tax extension is attached to the Form 5500 series return/report.

Example. Susan Corporation files its federal income tax return on a calendar-year basis. Susan maintains a qualified retirement plan with a plan year end of January 31. Susan receives extensions to file its federal income tax return through September 15, 1997. Is the September 2, 1997 (August 31, 1997 is a Sunday, and September 1, 1997 is a federal holiday) due date for filing the Form 5500 series return/report automatically extended? No, it is not, because the plan year does not coincide with the tax year. However, if the plan year was a calendar year, the due date would have been extended from July 31, 1997 to September 15, 1997.

Q 17:8 What penalties may be imposed for late filing of the Form 5500 series return/report?

One or more of the following five penalties may be imposed or assessed for late or incomplete filings after the date they are due unless there was reasonable cause for the improper filing:

1. DOL may assess a civil penalty against a plan administrator (see Q 16:1) of up to $1,000 a day for the late filing of a Form 5500 series return/report. In addition, a Form 5500 series return/report rejected by DOL because it lacks material information will be treated as if it had not been filed. In other words, the plan administrator can be assessed a penalty for an incomplete as well as an untimely but complete filing.
2. A penalty of $25 a day (up to a maximum of $15,000) is imposed for each day a Form 5500 series return/report is overdue.

3. A plan administrator who fails to include all required separated participants in a timely filed annual registration statement (Schedule SSA; see Q 17:4) is subject to a penalty of $1 a day for each separated participant (the maximum penalty is $5,000).

4. A penalty of $1,000 is imposed if an actuarial report (Schedule B; see Q 17:4) is not filed for a defined benefit plan.

5. A penalty of $1 a day (up to a maximum of $1,000) is imposed if a notification of change of status of a plan is not filed on time.

[ERISA §§ 104(a)(4), 502(c)(2); IRC §§ 6652(d)(1), 6652(d)(2), 6652(e), 6692]

Penalties assessed against a plan administrator were within DOL's discretion where subsequent to DOL's initial rejection of Form 5500, the plan administrator mistakenly sent a corrected form to IRS, not DOL. DOL waived 90 percent of the penalty, but assessed the remaining 10 percent because the plan administrator failed to show reasonable cause. [US DOL, PWBA v Rhode Island Bricklayers & Allied Craftsmen Pension Fund, DOL/ALJ (Boston, Ma), No. 94-RIS-64 (May 30, 1995)] Also, DOL's assessment of a penalty for failure to file a correct annual report (Form 5500) despite numerous opportunities to correct errors in the form was upheld by an administrative law judge. [US DOL, PWBA v Northwestern Institute of Psychiatry, DOL/ALJ (Camden, NJ), No. 93-RIS-23 (Dec 21, 1993)] In another case, IRS could not collect penalties from a plan sponsor for failure to file returns where the plan sponsor established that it had mailed them, and IRS was unable to rebut the presumption that it had received the returns. [In re Boedecker, 1993 Bankr Lexis 1873 (Bankr DC Mt 1993)]

DOL has opined that a penalty for the late filing of Form 5500 does not constitute a reasonable expense of administering a plan; and, therefore, the penalty is a liability of the plan administrator and not a liability of the plan. [DOL Info Ltr, Feb 23, 1996]

See Q 17:9 regarding the DFVC program.

Q 17:9 What is the Delinquent Filer Voluntary Compliance Program?

DOL established the Delinquent Filer Voluntary Compliance (DFVC) program to encourage, through the assessment of reduced civil penalties (see Q 17:8), delinquent plan administrators (see Q 16:1) to comply with the annual reporting requirements (see Q 17:1). The DFVC program is *not* available to plan administrators who have been notified of a failure to file the annual report at issue.

Plan administrators electing to be covered under the program must file with IRS a complete Form 5500 or Form 5500-C (not Form 5500-R), as appropriate, with all required attachments and include at the top center of the first page in red, bold print "DFVC Program." A signed and dated copy of the first page of the appropriate Form 5500 with a check payable to the "U.S. Department of Labor" in the amount of the applicable penalty should be sent to:

DFVC Program
Pension and Welfare Benefits Administration
P. O. Box 277025
Atlanta, Georgia 30384-7025

Under DFVC, the penalty is $50 per day. For an annual report filed up to 12 months late (without regard to any extensions), the maximum is $2,500 for Form 5500 filers, and $1,000 for Form 5500-C filers; for an annual report filed more than 12 months late (without regard to any extensions), the maximum is $5,000 for Form 5500 filers, and $2,000 for Form 5500-C filers. The penalty paid under the DFVC program may not be paid from plan assets, does not preclude the assessment of non-filing or late-filing penalties by IRS, and does not cover criminal penalties (see Q 7:10).

[DOL Notice, 60 FR 20874 (Apr 27, 1995)]

Q 17:10   Are there any criminal penalties for violations of the reporting requirements?

Yes. Willful violations of the reporting and disclosure requirements of ERISA can result in penalties up to a maximum of $5,000 in the case of an individual ($100,000 for any other entity), one-year imprisonment, or both. [ERISA § 501]

In addition, it is a criminal offense to knowingly make a false statement, or conceal or fail to disclose any fact needed to prepare reports required by Title I of ERISA. The maximum penalties are a $10,000 fine, five-year imprisonment, or both. [18 USC § 1027] This provision has been applied to the following:

1. A service provider who provided the plan with false information regarding his profits, which the plan needed to complete its Form 5500. [United States v Martorano, 767 F 2d 63 (3d Cir 1985)]

2. A participant who submitted false information to his plan. [United States v Bartkus, 816 F 2d 255 (6th Cir 1987)]

Q 17:11   Does a plan administrator's reliance on a third party to timely file the Form 5500 series return/report constitute reasonable cause for late filing?

No. One court has upheld the imposition by IRS of a $5,000 penalty against an employer for the late filing of Form 5500-C, even though the employer relied on a bank to file the return on time, because the responsibility for timely filing remains with the employer or plan administrator (see Q 16:1). [IRC § 6058(a); Alton Ob-Gyn, Ltd v United States, 789 F 2d 515 (7th Cir 1986)]

Q 17:12   Does the statute of limitations apply to the Form 5500 series return/report?

The filing of Schedule P (Form 5500), Annual Return of Fiduciary of Employee Benefit Trust (see Q 17:4), with the Form 5500 series return/report starts the running of the statute of limitations for any tax-exempt trust that is part of a qualified retirement plan. [IRC §§ 6033(a), 6501(a)]

One court has held that the filing of Form 5500-C for 1980 without Schedule P attached started the running of the statute of limitations because the form disclosed the plan's trustees and was signed by a trustee under penalty of perjury. However, the 1979 Form 5500-C did not start the running of the statute of limitations because it did not disclose the plan's trustees. [Martin Fireproofing Profit Sharing Plan and Trust, 92 TC 1173 (1989)]

Q 17:13   Does the filing of the Form 5500 series return/report start the statute of limitations running with regard to a prohibited transaction?

Yes, it does, if it discloses the transaction. Although Form 5330 is the appropriate form to report a prohibited transaction for the purpose of computing any excise taxes that may be owed (see Qs 17:16, 20:5), IRS conceded in one case that the filing of a Form 5500 series return/report that adequately discloses the facts of the transaction is sufficient to start the three-year statute of limitations running for prohibited transactions. [Rutland, 89 TC 1137 (1987)] In one case, the trustee of a pension plan paid excise taxes on a prohibited transaction and filed Form 5330 some years after Form 5500 had been filed. Subsequently, the trustee filed for a refund when it discovered that the transaction was not prohibited. IRS denied the refund because the claim was made more than three years after Form 5500 had been filed even though the claim was made within three years of the Form 5330 filing. The court concluded that the filing of Form 5500, and not the filing of Form 5330, started the three-year statute of limitations applicable to refund claims. [Imperial Plan, Inc v United States (CD Cal 1994)]

However, the six-year statute of limitations may be applicable if the Form 5500 series return/report does not disclose a prohibited transaction. [Thoburn, 95 TC 132 (1990)]

Q 17:14   Must a plan engage an independent accountant when it files its Form 5500 series return/report?

If a plan files Form 5500 (see Q 17:2), a certified public accountant or licensed public accountant (or an individual certified by DOL) must, in most cases, conduct an audit of the plan's books and records and issue an opinion, which is to be included in the annual report, covering:

1. The financial statements and schedules covered by the annual report;

2. The accounting principles and practices reflected in the report;

3. The consistency of the application of those principles and practices; and

4. Any changes in accounting principles having a material effect on the financial statements.

[ERISA §§ 103(a)(3), 109(b); DOL Reg § 2520.103-1(b)(5)]

If a plan does not file Form 5500 (see Q 17:2), an accountant's audit and opinion are not required. [DOL Reg § 2520.104-46]

[Instructions to 1995 IRS Forms 5500, 5500-C/R, 5500-EZ]

DOL has stated that both Form 5500 and Form 5500-C/R filers must use current value to determine realized and unrealized gains and losses, not the historical cost method. [DOL Notice, Jan 26, 1990; DOL News Rel 91-2 (1991)]

Q 17:15   Where are the Form 5500 series returns/reports filed?

Returns should be filed at the IRS Service Center indicated below:

Location of the Principal Office of the Plan Sponsor or Plan Administrator	*Internal Revenue Service Center Address*
Connecticut, Delaware, District of Columbia, Maine, Maryland, Massachusetts, New Hampshire, New Jersey, New York, Pennsylvania, Puerto Rico, Rhode Island, Vermont, Virginia, and foreign addresses	Holtsville, NY 00501
Alabama, Alaska, Arkansas, California, Florida, Georgia, Hawaii, Idaho, Louisiana, Mississippi, Nevada, North Carolina, Oregon, South Carolina, Tennessee, and Washington	Atlanta, GA 39901
Arizona, Colorado, Illinois, Indiana, Iowa, Kansas, Kentucky, Michigan, Minnesota, Missouri, Montana, Nebraska, New Mexico, North Dakota, Ohio, Oklahoma, South Dakota, Texas, Utah, West Virginia, Wisconsin, and Wyoming	Memphis, TN 37501
All Form 5500-EZ filers	Memphis, TN 37501-0024

The four digits -0044 should be inserted after the applicable zip code and used with Form 5500 filings, and the four digits -0020 should be inserted after the applicable zip code and used with Form 5500-C/R filings.

[Instructions to 1995 IRS Forms 5500, 5500-C/R, 5500-EZ]

Q 17:16   Which special returns must be filed with IRS?

Form 5310, Application for Determination for Terminating Plan, is filed as part of an application for a determination letter from IRS concerning the termination of a qualified retirement plan. Although there is no legal requirement to file for a determination letter regarding a plan's termination, it is strongly suggested that Form 5310 be filed with IRS (see Q 21:67).

Form 5310-A, Notice of Plan Merger or Consolidation, Spinoff, or Transfer of Plan Assets or Liabilities; Notice of Qualified Separate Lines of Business, is filed to notify IRS of a consolidation, merger, spinoff, or transfer of plan assets and liabilities. Form 5310-A must be filed at least 30 days before the event. See Q 9:38 for details and Q 9:39 for filing exceptions. Form 5310-A is also filed to notify the IRS that the employer treats itself as operating qualified separate lines of business (see Qs 5:49, 5:51).

Another special return is Form 5330, Return of Excise Taxes Related to Employee Benefit Plans. Form 5330 is used to report and pay the tax on the following:

- Prohibited transactions (see Q 17:13 and chapter 20)
- Failure to meet minimum funding standards (see Q 8:1)
- Certain ESOP dispositions (see chapter 24)
- Nondeductible contributions to qualified retirement plans (see chapter 12)
- Excess contributions to 401(k) plans (see Qs 23:16, 23:18)
- Certain prohibited allocations of qualified securities by an ESOP (see chapter 24)
- Reversions of qualified retirement plan assets to employers (see Q 21:56)

[IRC §§ 4971, as amended by SBA '96 § 1464(a), 4972, as amended by SBA '96 § 1421(b), 4975, as amended by SBA '96 § 1453(a), 4978, as amended by SBA '96 § 1602(b), 4978B, prior to repeal by SBA '96 § 1602(b), 4979, 4979A, 4980; Instructions to IRS Form 5330 (revised May 1993)]

Form 5330 is generally due on or before the last day of the seventh month after the end of the taxable year of the employer or other person required to file Form 5330. An extension of up to six months may be requested by filing Form 5558 (see Q 17:6). However, Form 5558 does not extend the time to pay taxes. To report reversions, Form 5330 must be filed by the last day of the month following the month in which the reversion occurred. To report excess contributions to 401(k) plans, Form 5330 must be filed by the last day of the 15th month after the close of the plan year to which the excess contributions relate.

Another special return, Form 5329, Additional Taxes Attributable to Qualified Retirement Plans (Including IRAs), Annuities, and Modified Endowment Contracts, is used to report any excise tax or additional tax owed in connection with a qualified retirement plan or IRA. Form 5329 is used to report and pay the tax on the following:

- Excess contributions to an IRA (see Q 26:6)
- Early distributions (see Qs 13:39, 26:41)
- Excess accumulations (failure to make a required minimum distribution; see Qs 11:20, 26:33)
- Excess distributions (this 15 percent excise tax is suspended for a three-year period—1997, 1998, and 1999; see Qs 13:27–13:29)

Form 5329 should generally be attached to and filed by the same due date (including extensions) as the taxpayer's Form 1040, U.S. Individual Income Tax Return. If a taxpayer is subject *only* to the tax on early distributions (and distribution code 1 is correctly shown in Box 7 of Form

1099-R; see Q 17:17), Form 5329 need not be filed and the tax should be reported on Form 1040.

[IRC §§ 72(t), as amended by SBA '96 § 1421(b) and HIPA '96 § 361, 4973, 4974, 4980A, as amended by SBA '96 § 1452(b); Instructions to 1995 IRS Form 5329]

Q 17:17   Which form is used to report qualified retirement plan distributions?

Form 1099-R, Distributions From Pensions, Annuities, Retirement or Profit-Sharing Plans, IRAs, Insurance Contracts, etc., is used to report distributions from qualified retirement plans, including periodic payments, nonperiodic payments that are not total distributions, and total distributions. [Rev Proc 92-86, 1992-2 CB 495]

To implement the requirements that payors report direct rollovers (see Q 28:20) from qualified retirement plans, a direct rollover to an IRA should be reported on Form 1099-R using code G in Box 7 and a direct rollover to a qualified retirement plan should be reported on Form 1099-R using code H in Box 7. [Ann 93-20, 1993-6 IRB 65]

Those receiving qualified retirement plan payments must receive Form 1099-R by January 31 of the year after the payment. Form 1099-R information is summarized on Form 1096, Annual Summary and Transmittal of U.S. Information Returns, which must be filed with IRS by the last day in February. Note: If magnetic media are used to transmit Forms 1099-R to IRS, Form 4804, Transmittal of Information Returns Reported Magnetically/Electronically (not Form 1096), must accompany such submission. [Instructions to 1996 IRS Form 1096]

The failure to timely file a required report can result in a $25 per day penalty up to a maximum of $15,000. [IRC § 6652(e), as amended by SBA '96 § 1455(d)]

Form 1099-R is also used to report corrective distributions of excess deferrals and excess contributions to 401(k) plans (see Qs 23:28, 23:17). [Notice 89-32, 1989-1 CB 671, *corrected by* Ann 89-69, 1989-24 IRB 78]

Generally, the filing of Form 1099-R with respect to each payee satisfies information reporting requirements with respect to income tax withholding. For failing to report withholding taxes or to keep necessary records, IRS may impose a penalty of $50 for each affected individual, up to a maximum of $50,000 in a calendar year. [IRC §§ 6047(d), as amended by SBA '96 § 1455(b), 6704; Treas Reg § 35.3405-1, Q&A E-9]

[Instructions to 1996 IRS Form 1099-R]

Form 945, Annual Return of Withheld Federal Income Tax, is used to report nonpayroll items, including pension withholding. Semiweekly depositors are required to complete and file Form 945-A, Annual Record of Federal Tax Liability, with Form 945. Form 945 must be filed only for a calendar year in which withholding is required. [Temp Reg § 31.6011(a)-4T(b); Ann 94-13, 1994-5 IRB 50; Instructions to IRS Forms 945 and 945-A]

Q 17:18   What are DOL reporting requirements?

Unless a qualified retirement plan is exempt from the reporting and disclosure requirements of ERISA (see Q 17:19), the following reports are required:

1. Annual reports (Form 5500 series return/report; see Q 17:2);
2. Summary plan descriptions (SPDs; see Q 18:1);
3. Summary description of material modifications (sometimes referred to as SMMs; see Q 18:8) to the plan or SPD; and
4. Supplementary or terminal reports.

[ERISA §§ 101, 104]

To avoid duplicate reporting, annual reports are filed only with IRS. Copies of the reports are supplied to DOL by IRS. See Q 17:9 regarding the DFVC program.

Some of these reports must also be distributed to participants. See chapter 18 for more details.

Q 17:19   Which types of plans are exempt from the reporting requirements of DOL?

There is a general exemption for individual retirement accounts (IRAs; see chapter 26), governmental plans, church plans, and excess benefit plans (unfunded plans providing benefits above the limits on contributions and benefits for tax purposes). [ERISA § 4(b)]

There is also an exemption for "plans without employees"—that is, plans in which the only participants are either an individual and the individual's spouse if that individual is the only owner of the business (whether incorporated or not), or the partners in a partnership and the partners' spouses. In the case of any other family relationship, the exemption does not apply. For example, if the only plan participants are brothers, or father and son, the reporting requirements apply unless they are partners. This exemption does not apply to the requirement to file the Form 5500 series return/report with IRS (see Q 17:2). [DOL Reg § 2510.3-3]

Q 17:20   Which forms must be filed with PBGC?

PBGC Form 1, Annual Premium Payment (including Schedule A, Single-Employer Plan Variable Rate Portion of the Premium), and PBGC Form 1-ES, Estimated Premium Payment, are used to report premiums due to the PBGC. Qualified retirement plans with fewer than 500 participants file only PBGC Form 1, along with their total premium payment, by the final filing due date (see Q 17:21).

The plan administrator of any qualified retirement plan (single-employer or multiemployer) that reported 500 or more participants on its PBGC Form 1 for the prior year must file a PBGC Form 1-ES to make its premium payment initially (the flat-rate portion of the premium for single-employer plans) on the basis of an estimated participant count. This filing and payment must be made by the first filing due date (see Q 17:21). Using the actual participant count, such single-employer and multiemployer plans must thereafter file PBGC Form 1 to make a reconciliation filing and pay the final fixed per-participant premium. In addition, all single-employer plans must file a Schedule A with PBGC Form 1 and pay the variable-rate portion of the premium (see Q 21:14). If plan participants are required to be notified of the plan's funded status (see Q 8:12), the plan administrator must certify on Schedule A (PBGC Form 1) whether such notice was issued. (It should be noted that if all the information needed to file PBGC Form 1 is known before the first filing due date, PBGC Form 1 should be filed instead of Form 1-ES. If Form 1-ES is filed, it will be necessary to file PBGC Form 1 by the final filing due date.) [Instructions to 1996 Premium Payment Package]

A plan that was at the full funding limitation (see Q 8:16) for the preceding plan year is not liable for the variable-rate portion of the premium. [PBGC Reg § 4006.5(a)(5)]

Q 17:21   When are the PBGC premium forms due?

If the plan has 500 or more participants for the plan year, the plan sponsor must file a PBGC Form 1-ES by the last day of the second full calendar month following the close of the preceding plan year (first filing due date). For single-employer plans, only the flat-rate portion of the premium is due by the first filing due date; the variable-rate portion is due and PBGC Form 1 must be filed by the final filing due date. For multiemployer plans, the entire premium is due by the first filing due date.

If the plan has fewer than 500 participants for the plan year, the plan sponsor must file Form 1 (single-employer plans must also file Schedule A to Form 1) and pay the entire premium by the 15th day of the eighth full calendar month following the month in which the plan year began (final filing due date). If the full amount due is not paid by the applicable date(s), the plan will be subject to late payment interest and penalty charges (see Q 17:24). [PBGC Reg § 4007.11]

Example 1. A single-employer plan has a plan year beginning July 1 and ending June 30. It had 950 participants as of the first day of its first plan year, July 1, 1995. For its second plan year beginning July 1, 1996, the plan should have filed a PBGC Form 1-ES on the first filing due date, September 3, 1996 (August 31, 1996 was a Saturday, and September 2, 1996 was a federal holiday), using an estimated participant count to determine the flat-rate portion of the premium. The plan must file its PBGC Form 1 and pay any outstanding balance of the flat-rate portion of the premium plus the variable-rate portion by the final filing due date, March 17, 1997 (March 15, 1997 is a Saturday).

Example 2. A multiemployer plan has a July 15 to July 14 plan year. It had 1,500 participants as of the first day of the plan's first year, July 15, 1995. The first filing due date for the plan's second plan year beginning July 15, 1996, was September 30, 1996, and the plan should have filed a PBGC Form 1-ES on that date, using an estimated participant count to determine the amount of the premium. The plan must make a final reconciliation filing on PBGC Form 1 by the final filing due date, March 17, 1997 (March 15, 1997 is a Saturday).

New and newly covered single-employer and multiemployer plans, regardless of the number of plan participants, are not required to pay estimated premiums. Such plans are required to file and pay the applicable premium for the first time by the latest of the following dates:

1. The 15th day of the eighth full calendar month following the later of the month in which the plan year began or the month in which the plan first became effective for benefit accruals for future service;
2. The 90th day after the date of the plan's adoption; or
3. The 90th day after the date on which the plan became covered under Title IV of ERISA.

[PBGC Reg § 4007.11]

Example 1. A new plan has a plan year beginning January 1, 1996, and ending December 31, 1996. The plan was adopted on October 1, 1995, but became effective for benefit accruals on January 1, 1996. The filing due date was September 16, 1996 (September 15, 1996 was a Sunday).

Example 2. A professional service employer maintains a plan with a plan year beginning on January 1, 1996, and ending December 31, 1996. If this plan has always had no more than 25 participants, it is not a covered plan under ERISA Section 4021. On October 15, 1996, the plan has 26 participants for the first time. It is now a covered plan and will continue to be a covered plan regardless of the plan's future participant count. The filing due date is January 13, 1997, the date 90 days after the plan became covered under Title IV.

An extension of the due date granted by IRS for filing the Form 5500 series return/report does not extend the due date for filing PBGC Form 1.

PBGC Form 1-ES and Form 1 should be mailed with premium payments to:

Pension Benefit Guaranty Corporation
P. O. Box 64880
Baltimore, MD 21264-4880

PBGC Form 1-ES and Form 1, along with premium payments, may be hand delivered to:

First National Bank of Maryland
110 South Paca Street
Mail Code: 109-320/Lockbox # 64880
Baltimore, MD 21201

[PBGC Reg § 4007.4; Instructions to 1996 Premium Payment Package]

Q 17:22   How does a change in the plan year affect the due dates for filing the PBGC premium forms?

If the plan year is changed, two sets of PBGC forms must be filed: one for the old plan year and another for the new plan year. Each filing and premium payment must reflect a full 12-month plan year.

Plans that change their plan years as a result of a plan amendment must follow the due date rules for the short year as though it were a regular plan year (see Q 17:21).

For the plan year following the short year, the first filing due date is the later of (1) the last day of the second full calendar month following the close of the short plan year, or (2) 30 days after the date the amendment changing the plan year was adopted. The final filing due date is the later of (1) the 15th day of the eighth full calendar month following the month in which the plan year begins, or (2) 30 days after the date the amendment changing the plan year was adopted. [PBGC Reg § 4007.1(a)(3)]

Example 1. A plan amendment adopted on October 1, 1996, and made effective retroactively to February 1, 1996, changes a calendar-year plan to one with a plan year beginning February 1. The plan's 1995 Form 1 reported 350 plan participants. The final filing due date for the plan year that began on January 1, 1996, was September 16, 1996 (September 15, 1996 was a Sunday). The final filing due date for the new plan year, which began on February 1, 1996, was October 31, 1996.

Example 2. A plan changes its plan year from one that begins January 1 to one that begins June 1. The change was adopted on December 1, 1995. This resulted in a short plan year that began January 1, 1996, and ended May 31, 1996. The plan's 1995 Form 1 reported 100 plan participants. The final filing due date was September 16, 1996 (September 15, 1996 was a Sunday), for the plan year that began January 1, 1996, and would have otherwise ended December 31, 1996. The final filing due date is February 18, 1997 (February 15, 1997 is a Saturday, and February 17, 1997 is a federal holiday), for the new plan year beginning June 1, 1996, and ending May 31, 1997.

Refunds for duplicate premium payments for overlapping periods must be requested by writing to:

Pension Benefit Guaranty Corporation
P. O. Box 64916
Baltimore, MD 21264-4916

The employer must include copies of the relevant PBGC Forms 1, and the PBGC will calculate the amount of the refund and send it to the employer. [PBGC Reg § 4006.5(f)]

Q 17:23 Must PBGC Form 1 be filed after the plan is terminated?

The obligation to file PBGC Form 1 and make the required premium payment continues until the end of the plan year in which either the plan's assets are distributed or a trustee is appointed under ERISA. Any required premium payments will be for a full plan year and may not be prorated. However, a refund for premium payments applicable to the months after final distribution may be obtained by using the procedure for overlapping payments resulting from a change of plan year (see Q 17:22). [PBGC Reg § 4007.1(d)]

A pension plan was not required to pay premiums to the PBGC for the plan year following the plan year in which the plan filed for a standard termination (see Q 21:17) and distributed plan benefits and all surplus assets under the first six categories of ERISA Section 4044(a) (see Q 21:42), except for assets attributable to employee contributions and subject to a lawsuit. [PBGC Op Ltr No. 93-1]

Q 17:24   What happens if the premium payment is late?

Late payment charges are assessed if PBGC receives a premium payment after the due date. The interest charge is based on the number of days the payment is late. The late filing penalty is the greater of 5 percent of the late payment for each late month (or part thereof), or $25, but not more than 100 percent of the unpaid premiums. [PBGC Reg § 2610.8]

Q 17:25   Can the late penalty charges be waived?

Generally, if the plan administrator (see Q 16:1) can show substantial hardship or otherwise demonstrate good cause, PBGC may waive the penalty (but not interest) charge. [PBGC Reg § 4007.8(b)]

Q 17:26   Are there any other notification requirements to PBGC?

Yes. PBGC must be notified by filing Form 200, Notice of Failure to Make Required Contributions, within ten days of the due date for a required plan contribution (see Q 8:18) if the aggregate unpaid balance, including interest, exceeds $1 million. [ERISA § 302(f)(4)]

Also, the plan sponsor is required to provide PBGC with certain additional information if (1) the aggregate unfunded vested benefits of all underfunded plans sponsored by the controlled group (see Q 5:33) exceed $50 million, (2) the conditions for imposing a lien for missed plan contributions exceeding $1 million have been met, or (3) any portion of minimum funding waivers exceeding $1 million remains unpaid (see Qs 8:18, 8:20). [ERISA § 4010; PBGC Reg §§ 4010.1–4010.14]

Chapter 18

Summary Plan Descriptions

One of the major obligations of a plan administrator is the preparation of a summary of the plan for distribution to participants and beneficiaries. This chapter examines summary plan descriptions (SPDs)—what they are, the information they must contain, and how to avoid their legal pitfalls.

Q 18:1   What is a summary plan description?

An SPD is a booklet that describes the plan's provisions and the participants' benefits, rights, and obligations in simple language. The SPD is the primary source of supplying information regarding the plan document, and plan administrators (see Q 16:1) must provide the SPD to each plan participant and each beneficiary receiving benefits under the plan (see Q 18:2). [ERISA §§ 101(a), 102(a)(1), 104(b)]

An SPD must contain certain information (see Q 18:4), and many courts have ruled that it is a legally binding document (see Q 18:5).

Q 18:2   When must an SPD be furnished to a participant?

An SPD must be furnished to each participant and beneficiary no later than (1) 90 days after becoming a participant or first receiving benefits, as the case may be, or (2) within 120 days after the plan first becomes subject to the reporting and disclosure requirements of ERISA. [ERISA § 104(b)]

In the case of a new plan that provides that it is effective only upon IRS approval, the 120-day period does not begin until the day after such condition is satisfied (i.e., the day after IRS issues a favorable determination letter; see Q 15:1). [DOL Reg § 2520.104b-2(a)(3)] Conversely, if the plan is adopted retroactively, the 120-day period begins to run at the time of adoption.

In one case, penalties were assessed against a plan administrator (see Q 16:1) for failure to provide plan participants and beneficiaries with an SPD. [ERISA § 502(c); Sacks v Gross, Sklar & Metzger, PC, No. 88-5009 (ED Pa 1992)] Sending an SPD to a participant via first-class mail is acceptable. If a dispute arises as to whether or not an SPD was provided by mail to a participant, the plan administrator must prove that the SPD was mailed; the plan administrator is not required to prove that the SPD was received. Evidence that an SPD was always sent by first-class mail to a participant's last known address was satisfactory proof. [Campbell v Emery Air Freight Corp, No. 93-6568 (ED Pa 1995)]

In another case, the court determined that the failure of an employer to provide an SPD did not negate the knowing waiver of ERISA claims by an employee who was aware of his potential eligibility for benefits at the time he signed the release. [Finz v Schlesinger, 957 F 2d 78 (2d Cir 1992)]

A plan administrator can refuse to provide an SPD to a deceased participant's son who was not a beneficiary. [Keys v Eastman Kodak Co, 739 F Supp 135 (WD NY 1990)]

Q 18:3   Where is the SPD filed?

The SPD must be filed with DOL no later than the time it is furnished to plan participants and beneficiaries. The SPD is filed at the following address:

SPD, Pension and Welfare Benefits Administration
Room N-5644
U. S. Department of Labor
200 Constitution Avenue, N.W.
Washington, DC 20210

[DOL Reg § 2520.104a-3]

Q 18:4   What information must an SPD contain?

An SPD must contain the following information:

1. Name of the plan;
2. Name and address of the employer whose employees are covered by the plan;

3. Employer identification number (EIN) assigned by IRS to the employer;

4. Plan number;

5. Type of plan (e.g., defined benefit plan, money purchase pension plan, profit sharing plan);

6. Type of administration of the plan (e.g., employer self-administration, contract administration, insurer administration);

7. Name, business address, and business telephone number of the plan administrator;

8. Name of the person designated as agent for the service of legal process and the address at which the agent may be served (and a statement that a plan trustee or administrator may also be served);

9. Name, title, and business address of each trustee;

10. Plan's requirements regarding eligibility for participation and benefits, including the plan's normal retirement age;

11. Statement describing any joint and survivor benefits;

12. Description of the benefits and vesting provisions of the plan, including contingent top-heavy provisions, and circumstances that may result in disqualification, ineligibility, or denial, loss, forfeiture, or suspension of benefits;

13. Statement as to whether the plan is maintained pursuant to one or more collective bargaining agreements and, if so, a statement that copies of such agreement are available to participants and beneficiaries;

14. Statement as to whether the plan is covered by termination insurance from PBGC and, if so, a description of the guaranty provisions;

15. Plan's fiscal year end;

16. Source of contributions to the plan (employer and/or employee contributions) and the method used to calculate the amount of the contributions (a defined benefit plan need only state that the contribution is actuarially determined);

17. Identity of any funding medium (e.g., insurance company, trust fund) used for the accumulation of assets to provide benefits;

18. Plan's provisions governing termination of the plan, including the rights and benefits of participants and the disposition of assets;

19. Plan's procedures regarding claims for benefits and the remedies available for disputing denied claims; and

20. Statement of ERISA rights available to plan participants.

One court has ruled that a plan description that did not include all of the items enumerated above was still an SPD. [Intl Union of Operating Engrs-Employers Const Indus Pension, Welfare and Training Funds v Karr, No. 91-38546 (9th Cir 1993)]

Bear in mind that technical jargon is out—the idea is simplicity and the goal is clarity. The SPD should be understood by the average plan participant. Clarifying examples and illustrations are recommended. The SPD must not mislead or misinform (see Q 18:5). Benefits should not be exaggerated, and restrictions and limitations should be described and not be minimized. [ERISA § 102(b); DOL Reg §§ 2520.102-2, 2520.102-3; DOL ERISA Tech Rel 84-1; DOL Op Ltr 85-05A]

Q 18:5   Is an SPD a legally binding document?

Since an SPD is the primary source of information concerning the terms of the plan (see Q 18:1), the trend is to permit employees to rely on the SPD when it conflicts with the terms of the plan document. Plan administrators (see Q 16:1) must make sure that they do not make any false or misleading representations in an SPD because the plan may be bound by a statement in the SPD that is inconsistent with the plan, even if the inconsistency is inadvertent (see Q 18:6). [Curcio v John Hancock Mut Life Ins Co, 1994 US App Lexis 21935 (3d Cir 1994); Nelson v EG&G Energy Measurements Group, Inc, 1994 US App Lexis 27853 (9th Cir 1994); Aiken v Policy Mgmt Systems Corp, 1993 US App Lexis 34398 (4th Cir 1993); Brumm v Bert Bell NFL Retirement Plan, No. 92-3346 (8th Cir 1993); Pierce v Security Trust Life Ins Co, 1992 US App Lexis 15562 (4th Cir 1992); Hansen v Continental Ins Co, 940 F 2d 971 (5th Cir 1991); Heidgerd v Olin Corp, No. 89-7869 (2d Cir 1990); Edwards v State Farm Mutual Automobile Ins Co, 851 F 2d 134 (6th Cir 1988); McKnight v Southern Life and Health Ins Co, 758 F 2d 1566 (11th Cir 1985); Gregory v Texasgulf, Inc, No. B-84-88 (WWE) (D Ct 1990)]

However, some courts have ruled that a participant must show reliance on a faulty SPD in order to recover denied benefits. [Maxa v John Alden Life Ins Co, No. 91-2203MN (8th Cir 1992); Bachelder v Communications Satellite Corp, 837 F 2d 519 (1st Cir 1988); Govoni v Bricklayers, Masons, and Plasterers Pension Fund, 732 F 2d 250 (1st Cir 1984); Thompson v Federal Express Corp, 1992 US Dist Lexis 19334 (MD Ga 1992); Freund v Gerson, 610 F Supp 69 (SD Fla 1985)] One court ruled that a participant must show *either* reliance upon or prejudice flowing from a faulty SPD, but not both. [Aiken v Policy Mgmt Systems Corp, 1993 US App Lexis 34398 (4th Cir 1993)] However, in another case, the same court previously ruled that a participant could not have relied on the SPD to his detriment, even though the SPD and the plan language conflicted with respect to the amount of his distribution. [Fuller v FMC Corp, 1993 US App Lexis 19448 (4th Cir 1993)]

An SPD gave adequate notice that a participant may receive only benefits guaranteed by PBGC (see Q 21:20) upon the termination of an underfunded defined benefit plan; therefore, the participant was not improperly denied benefits under the plan when reduced benefits were received. [Arnold v Arrow Transportation Co, No. 89-35280 (9th Cir 1991)] Where an SPD did not expressly set forth whether severance payments were included in the definition of compensation for plan purposes, the plan administrator was permitted to look to extrinsic evidence to determine that such payments were not included. [Krawczyk v Harnischfeger Corp, 1994 US App Lexis 32973 (7th Cir 1994)]

One court ruled that an employer is not bound by an erroneous statement in a separate booklet distributed to employees with the SPD, because the SPD was consistent with the plan. However, the court implied that an employer might be bound by an erroneous statement in the SPD. [Alday v Container Corp of America, No. 89-3476 (11th Cir 1990)] Another court held that a booklet describing plan benefits did not contain sufficient information to rise to the status of an SPD (see Q 18:4). Therefore, even though the booklet was in conflict with the actual plan document, the employee could not rely upon the booklet. [Hicks v Fleming Cos, Inc, 961 F 2d 537 (5th Cir 1992)]

Q 18:6   What is the purpose of a disclaimer clause?

Disclaimer language (see below) is a possible, though unreliable, means of insulating plan assets and the plan administrator (see Q 16:1) from liability should the SPD prove to be misleading, incomplete, or contradictory to the provisions of the plan. Participants and their beneficiaries are placed on notice that the plan itself is the controlling document and that they should not rely solely upon the representations in the SPD. [Kolentus v Avco Corp, 798 F 2d 949 (7th Cir 1986)]

The following is a sample disclaimer clause:

> Please read this summary carefully. This summary is written in simple, nontechnical language, and it is intended to help you to understand how this plan will benefit you and your loved ones. The plan and trust documents are also available for you to read. Although these documents are written in technical language, they may be helpful to you.

> If it appears to you that any of the provisions of the plan or trust documents is not in agreement with the statements made in this summary, please bring this to the attention of the plan administrator. Keep in mind that, if there is any conflict between this summary and the provisions of the plan or trust documents, the

terms of the plan or trust will govern. You should rely solely on the provisions of the plan and trust documents.

However, it has been held that employees can rely on an SPD despite a disclaimer where the SPD favors the employees [Pierce v Security Trust Life Ins Co, 1992 US App Lexis 15562 (4th Cir 1992)] and that an employer cannot disavow a disclaimer when the SPD favors the employer but the plan favors the employees. [Glocker v W R Grace & Co, No. 91-2262 (4th Cir 1992)]

Q 18:7 Will a disclaimer in an SPD be recognized in a lawsuit?

At present, there are no governmental prohibitions against the use of a disclaimer in an SPD. Nothing is risked, therefore, by including the disclaimer (see Q 18:6).

The courts have held that a participant or beneficiary cannot use an SPD to sue for relief under ERISA unless the lawsuit also asserts a claim arising under the plan itself. However, the courts have left the door open for a participant to sue on other than ERISA grounds on the basis of inaccurate or misleading statements in the SPD. In any event, it is reasonable to expect that a claim based on willful or negligent misrepresentations in an SPD would be upheld even when a disclaimer is included in the SPD. [O'Brien v Sperry Univac, 458 F Supp 1179 (D DC 1978); McKnight v Southern Life and Health Ins Co, 758 F 2d 1566 (11th Cir 1985)]

Q 18:8 What happens if the plan is changed?

Any change in the provisions of the plan or in the administration of the plan that constitutes a material modification (see Q 18:9) must be disclosed to participants and beneficiaries in the form of a summary description of material modifications (SMM) to the plan. The SMM must be distributed within 210 days after the close of the plan year in which the material modification is adopted. [DOL Reg § 2520.104b-3]

The SMM must also be filed with DOL within the same 210-day period, at the following address:

SMM, Pension and Welfare Benefits Administration
Room N-5644
U.S. Department of Labor
200 Constitution Avenue, N.W.
Washington, DC 20210

[DOL Reg § 2520.104a-4]

Q 18:9   What constitutes a reportable material modification?

Basically, a material modification exists when there is a change or modification to any of the information required to be included in the SPD (see Q 18:4). [DOL Reg § 2520.104b-3]

For example, the elimination of a special retirement benefit that allowed participants not eligible for normal retirement benefits to qualify for reduced retirement benefits was held to be a material modification of a plan. [Baker v Lukens Steel Co, 793 F 2d 509 (3d Cir 1986)]

Q 18:10   How often is an updated SPD due?

Generally, every five years the plan administrator (see Q 16:1) is required to furnish to each participant and each beneficiary receiving benefits under the plan an updated SPD that incorporates all plan amendments made within that five-year period. The updated SPD must be furnished no later than 210 days after the end of the fifth plan year after the previous SPD. This requirement for an updated SPD must be met even if SMMs have been issued (see Q 18:8). However, even if there have been no amendments to the plan, another copy of the original SPD must be distributed every ten years. [ERISA § 104(b); DOL Reg § 2520.104b-2]

Q 18:11   How is the five-year period for an updated SPD measured?

Each time an SPD is distributed and filed with DOL, the five-year period begins anew. If the plan distributes an updated SPD less than five years after the previous one was distributed, a new five-year period begins at that time. [DOL Reg § 2520.104b-2(b)]

Example. The plan administrator of the Ess-Cee-Jay Corporation profit sharing plan distributed the first SPD on March 1, 1991. On January 3, 1992, the vesting provisions of the calendar-year plan were amended and an SMM (see Q 18:8) was timely filed on July 29, 1993 (210 days after the end of the plan year of the amendment). An updated SPD will be due on July 29, 1997 (210 days after December 31, 1996, the end of the plan year of the fifth anniversary of the original SPD). If a new SPD (instead of the SMM) had been distributed on July 29, 1993, the next SPD would be due July 29, 1999.

Q 18:12   What happens if the plan is terminated?

If the plan terminates before the date by which an original or an updated SPD is required, the SPD requirement is waived if, and only if, all distributions to participants and beneficiaries have been completed. [DOL Reg § 2520.104a-3(c)]

Q 18:13   What documents other than an SPD can a participant obtain?

Other than an SPD, a participant is entitled to obtain, without charge and without request, a summary of material modifications (see Q 18:8) to the plan and a summary annual report.

Upon request, other documents must be furnished to a participant by the plan administrator (see Q 16:1). These include:

1. A statement of the participant's total accrued benefits;
2. The plan instrument;
3. The latest annual report (Form 5500 series return);
4. The trust agreement; and
5. The collective bargaining agreement or any other document under which the plan is established.

A reasonable charge (not to exceed $.25 per page) may be imposed for copies of these items (other than the annual benefit statement). [ERISA § 105(a); DOL Reg § 2520.104b-30] The plan administrator's failure to provide these documents within 30 days after the participant's request may subject the plan administrator to fines, attorney's fees, and costs (see Q 19:43). [ERISA §§ 502(c)(1), 502(g)(1); Boone v Leavenworth Anesthesia, Inc, No. 92-3349 (10th Cir 1994); Lee v Benefit Plans Administrator of ARMCO, Inc, No. H-90-3642 (SD Tex 1992)] In addition, the failure may result in a participant's complaint to the local DOL field office, with the possibility of an ensuing investigation of the plan. [Thomas v Jeep-Eagle Corp, 746 F Supp 863 (ED Wis 1990)]

In one case, no penalty was imposed on the employer for a ten-month delay in providing plan information, because the employee did not show that any damage resulted from the delay or that bad faith or intentional delay existed on the part of the employer. [Plotkin v Bearings Ltd, 1992 US Dist Lexis 7787 (ED NY 1992)] However, in another case, the court held that a showing of injury or prejudice was not required and a substantial penalty was assessed against the employer. [Moothart v Bell, No. 21 F 3d 1499 (10th Cir 1994)] Where an employee received inaccurate written benefit statements and oral communications, the employer was not bound by the inaccurate representations, because the terms of the plan controlled. [Miller v Coastal Corp, No. 92-3030 (10th Cir 1992)]

An employee was dismissed and received her plan benefits; ten years later, she requested plan documents and commenced an action. The court ruled that the employee was not entitled to the documents, because she had no expectation of returning to employment with the employer and had no colorable claim for benefits. In addition, the court concluded that the state law six-year statute of limitations had expired. [Szoke v Deloitte & Touche LLP, 1995 US Dist Lexis 2517 (SD NY 1995)]

Q 18:14   Is there any special requirement if many plan participants cannot read English?

Yes. If a sufficient number of plan participants (generally, 25 percent for plans with less than 100 participants, 10 percent for plans with 100 or more participants) are literate only in the same non-English language, then the plan administrator (see Qs 16:1, 18:1) must give these participants an SPD with a notice written in their own language. This notice must inform such participants of the availability of assistance sufficient to enable them to become informed as to their rights under the plan. [DOL Reg § 2520.102-2(c)] One court has ruled that the foreign language notice rules do not extend to the denial of benefit claims made by participants (see Q 10:63). [Diaz v United Agric Employee Welfare Benefit Plan & Trust, 1995 US App Lexis 6112 (9th Cir 1995)]

Chapter 19

Fiduciary Responsibilities

Plan administrators, trustees, and fiduciaries must take special care to carry out their responsibilities properly. Carelessness in the investment of plan assets, for example, can mean financial ruin for these individuals. This chapter examines the meaning of fiduciary responsibility under ERISA, when a fiduciary can be held personally liable for losses sustained by the plan, how liability can be avoided, and guidelines for investing plan assets.

Q 19:1 Who is a fiduciary under ERISA?

A fiduciary under ERISA is any person who:

1. Exercises any discretionary authority or control over the plan's management;
2. Exercises any authority or control over the management or disposition of the plan's assets;
3. Renders investment advice for a fee or other compensation with respect to plan funds or property; or
4. Has any discretionary authority or responsibility in the plan's administration.

[ERISA § 3(21)(A)]

The test for determining fiduciary status is a functional one; if a person or entity has or may exercise any of the functions described in ERISA Section 3(21)(A), the person or entity will be deemed to be a fiduciary. [Mid-Atlantic Perfusion Assocs, Inc v Professional Assn Consulting Services, Inc, No. 94-1863 (3d Cir 1995); Blatt v Marshall and Lassman, 812 F 2d 810 (2d Cir 1987); Eaves v Penn, 587 F 2d 453 (10th Cir 1978); Reich v Hosking, 1996

US Dist Lexis 5975 (ED Mich 1996); Daniels v Nat'l Employee Benefit Services, Inc, 1994 US Dist Lexis 9485 (ND Ohio 1994)] A person may be a fiduciary for a limited purpose and also perform other, nonfiduciary roles with regard to the same plan. [John Hancock Mutual Life Ins Co v Harris Trust and Savings Bank, 114 S Ct 517 (1993)] Fiduciary status may involve a question of fact; a provision of an oral agreement that a broker was not to be considered an ERISA fiduciary was not dispositive of the issue. [Schiffli Embroidery Workers Pension Fund v Ryan, Beck & Co, No. 91-5433 (D NJ 1994]

In the *John Hancock Mutual Life Insurance Co. v. Harris Trust and Savings Bank* case cited in the preceding paragraph, the United States Supreme Court ruled that certain pension plan assets held in the general accounts of insurance companies constituted plan assets and were therefore subject to the fiduciary responsibility rules of ERISA, including the rules prohibiting certain transactions involving the assets of an employee benefit plan.

SBA '96 (see Q 1:21) requires that the Department of Labor (DOL) issue proposed regulations no later than June 30, 1997, clarifying the status of plan assets held in insurance company general accounts under ERISA and the Code. The proposed regulations will be subject to public notice and comment until September 30, 1997, and DOL will be required to issue final regulations by December 31, 1997. The regulations will only apply with respect to a policy issued by an insurer on or before December 31, 1998. In the case of such a policy, the regulations will take effect at the end of the 18-month period following the date the regulations become final. New policies issued after December 31, 1998 will be subject to the fiduciary responsibility rules of ERISA.

The regulations are required to be administratively feasible and to protect the interests and rights of the plan and its participants and beneficiaries. In addition, in connection with any policy (other than a guaranteed benefit policy) issued by an insurer to or for the benefit of an employee benefit plan, the regulations must require that:

1. A plan fiduciary totally independent of the insurer authorize the purchase of the policy (unless it is the purchase of a life insurance, health insurance, or annuity contract exempt from ERISA's prohibited transaction rules; see Q 20:1);

2. After the date final regulations are issued, the insurer provide periodic reports to the policyholder disclosing the method by which any income or expenses of the insurer's general account are allocated to the policy and disclosing the actual return to the plan under the policy and such other financial information as DOL may deem appropriate;

3. The insurer disclose to the plan fiduciary the extent to which alternative arrangements supported by assets of separate accounts of the insurer (which generally hold plan assets) are available, whether there is a right under the policy to transfer funds to a separate account and terms governing any such right, and the extent to which support by assets of the insurer's general account and support by assets of separate accounts of the insurer might pose differing risks to the plan; and

4. The insurer manage general account assets (irrespective of whether the assets are plan assets) with the level of care, skill, prudence, and diligence that a prudent man acting in like capacity and familiar with such matters would use in the conduct of an enterprise of like character and like aims, taking into account all obligations supported by such enterprise.

Compliance by the insurer with the DOL regulations will be deemed compliance by the insurer with ERISA's provisions on fiduciary responsibility, including the provisions on prohibited transactions and limitations on holding employer securities (see Q 19:56) and employer real property (see Q 19:55).

No person will be liable under ERISA or the Code for conduct that occurred prior to the date that is 18 months following the effective date of the final regulations, except as provided by DOL in order to prevent avoidance of the guidance in the regulations, or as provided in an action brought by DOL under ERISA's enforcement provisions for a breach of fiduciary responsibility that would also constitute a violation of federal or state criminal law. DOL is authorized to commence an action if a participant, beneficiary, or fiduciary demonstrates that a breach of fiduciary responsibility has occurred. SBA '96 does not preclude the application of any federal criminal law.

These rules are generally effective on January 1, 1975. However, they will not apply to any civil action commenced before November 7, 1995. [ERISA § 401(c) as added by SBA '96 § 1460(a)]

Q 19:2 Are all actions by fiduciaries that affect a plan within the definition of fiduciary duties?

No. Courts have held that various actions by plan fiduciaries that affect a plan, such as plan amendment or termination, are employer or settlor functions not falling within the purview of ERISA Section 3(21)(A) and, accordingly, not subject to fiduciary duties to participants. [Siskind v The Sperry Retirement Program, UNYSIS, 47 F 3d 498 (2d Cir 1995); Akers v Palmer, Nos. 94-5740 and 94-5743 (6th Cir 1995); Haberern v Kaupp

Vascular Surgeons Ltd, 1994 US App Lexis 11953 (3d Cir 1994); Nazay v Miller, 949 F 2d 1323 (3d Cir 1991); Sutton v Weirton Steel, Div of Nat'l Steel Corp, 724 F 406 (4th Cir 1983)] Although a decision to terminate a plan may be a business decision that is not regulated by ERISA, misrepresentations in response to specific questions regarding future benefits do fall within ERISA and may state a claim thereunder. [Pocchia v NYNEX Corp, 1996 US App Lexis 6980 (2d Cir 1996); Vartanian v Monsanto Co, Nos. 92-30223 and 93-30075 (D Mass 1995)]

An amendment to a plan that benefited an employer by increasing the reversion of surplus assets (see Q 21:54) was not considered a breach of fiduciary duty; the amendment related to the design of plan benefits and not the administration of the plan. Accordingly, it was not subject to ERISA's fiduciary duty standards. [Engelhart v Consolidated Rail Corp, No. 92-7056 (ED Pa 1993)] Amendments to multiemployer plans, however, may be subject to ERISA's fiduciary duties if inherently unfair, not rationally related to the plan's overall purposes, and enacted to further other, nonpension fund interests. [Walling v Brady, 1996 US Dist Lexis 2260 (D Del 1996)]

Q 19:3   Does a person who performs ministerial duties within guidelines furnished by others acquire fiduciary status?

No. Those performing purely ministerial functions within guidelines established by others are not plan fiduciaries. Department of Labor (DOL) regulations list the following job categories as ministerial:

1. Application of rules to determine eligibility for participation or benefits;
2. Calculation of service and compensation for benefit purposes;
3. Preparing communications to employees;
4. Maintaining participants' service and employment records;
5. Preparing reports required by government agencies;
6. Calculating benefits;
7. Explaining the plan to new participants and advising participants of their rights and options under the plan;
8. Collecting contributions and applying them as specified in the plan;
9. Preparing reports covering participants' benefits;
10. Processing claims; and
11. Making recommendations to others for decisions with respect to plan administration.

[DOL Reg § 2509.75-8, D-2; Flacche v Sun Life Assurance Co of Canada, No. 91-3462 (6th Cir 1992); Demaio v Cigna Corp, No. 89-0724 (ED Pa 1993); Reichling v Continental Bank, 813 F Supp 197 (ED NY 1993)]

Trustees were not fiduciaries to the extent they lacked discretion over the investment of plan assets, so they did not violate their fiduciary duties by investing all plan assets in group annuity contracts because the plan itself required such investment and the trustees had no discretion. [Arakelian v Nat'l Western Life Ins Co, No. 84-1953 (D DC 1990)]

A broker or dealer registered under the Securities Exchange Act of 1934 is not deemed to be a fiduciary solely because the broker-dealer executes securities transactions on behalf of the plan in the ordinary course of its business, provided:

1. The broker-dealer is not affiliated with a plan fiduciary; and
2. The plan fiduciary specifies:
   a. The security to be purchased or sold;
   b. The price range within which the security may be purchased or sold;
   c. The time span (not exceeding five days) during which the security may be purchased or sold; and
   d. The minimum or maximum quantity of the security that may be purchased or sold within such price range.

[DOL Reg § 2510.3-21(d)(1)]

Q 19:4   What is rendering investment advice for the purpose of determining fiduciary status?

A person is rendering investment advice to a plan only if such person (1) makes recommendations as to valuing, buying, holding, or selling securities or other property, and (2) has, directly or indirectly, (a) discretionary authority or control over buying or selling securities or other property for the plan, whether or not pursuant to an agreement, arrangement, or understanding, or (b) regularly renders advice to the plan pursuant to a mutual agreement, arrangement, or understanding that such advice will serve as a primary basis for plan investment decisions and that such advice will be based on the particular needs of the plan regarding such matters as investment policies or strategy, overall portfolio composition, or diversification of plan investments. [DOL Reg § 2510.3-21(c)(1); DOL Op Ltr 95-17A]

A broker's practice of recommending investments will not make that broker a fiduciary in the absence of any agreement, arrangement, or understanding referred to in item (2)(b) above. [Thomas, Head & Greisen Employees Trust v Buster, 24 F 3d 1114 (9th Cir 1994); Farm King Supply, Inc Integrated Profit Sharing Plan and Trust v Edward D Jones & Co, 884 F 2d 288 (7th Cir 1989)] However, a broker may be considered a fiduciary if the broker engages in unauthorized buying and selling of plan assets. [Olson v E F Hutton & Co, Inc, No. 91-1416MN (8th Cir 1992)]

Although a broker may be a fiduciary because it rendered advice for a fee, the broker's fiduciary duty is limited to those fiduciary duties it performed; thus, the broker had no duty to inform a fund client regarding the reasons a dishonest employee's employment was terminated. [Glaziers and Glassworkers Union Local 252 Annuity Fund v Newbridge Securities, Inc (ED Pa 1995)] The person rendering investment advice can be a fiduciary even though compensated on a commission basis since commissions constitute a fee or other compensation (see Q 19:1). [Reich v McManus, 1995 US Dist Lexis 5661 (ND Ill 1995)]

Q 19:5 What is a named fiduciary?

Every plan is required to have at least one named fiduciary. A named fiduciary is one or more persons designated in the plan by name or title as responsible for operating the plan. The purpose of the requirement is to enable employees and other interested parties to ascertain the person responsible for plan operations. A plan covering employees of a corporation can designate the corporation as the named fiduciary. However, DOL regulations suggest that "a plan instrument which designates a corporation as 'named fiduciary' should provide for designation by the corporation of specified individuals or other persons to carry out specified fiduciary responsibilities under the plan. . . ." [ERISA § 402(a)(1); DOL Reg § 2509.75-5, FR-1, FR-3] There is a conflict among the circuit courts as to whether officer-shareholders of the named fiduciary may be held to be fiduciaries. [Compare Kayes v Pacific Lumber Co, 1995 US App Lexis 7854 (9th Cir 1995) (finding fiduciary status) with Confer v Custom Eng'g Co, 952 F 2d 34 (3d Cir 1991)(rejecting fiduciary status)]

Q 19:6 Are attorneys, accountants, actuaries, insurance agents, insurers, and consultants who provide services to a plan considered plan fiduciaries?

No. They are not considered plan fiduciaries solely because they render such services. However, they will be regarded as fiduciaries if they exercise discretionary authority or control over the management or administration of the plan or some authority or control over plan assets even if such activities are unauthorized. [DOL Reg § 2509.75-5, D-1; John Hancock

Mutual Life Ins Co v Harris Trust and Savings Bank, 114 S Ct 517 (1993); Reich v Lancaster, 55 F 3d 1034 (5th Cir 1995); Sheldon Co Profit-Sharing Plan and Trust v Smith, 1995 US App Lexis 20708 (6th Cir 1995); Libby-Owens-Ford Co v Blue Cross & Blue Shield Mutual of Ohio, 982 F 2d 1061 (6th Cir 1993); Olson v E F Hutton & Co, Inc, No. 91-1416MN (8th Cir 1992); Bouton v Thompson, 764 F Supp 20 (D Conn 1991); Brock v Self, 632 F Supp 1509 (WD La 1986)]

Recent cases have held that attorneys, accountants, actuaries, and consultants do not possess or exert the necessary discretionary authority or control respecting management of the plan to cause them to be fiduciaries under ERISA. [Chapman v Klemick, 3 F 3d 1508 (11th Cir 1993) (attorney); Kaniewski v Equitable Life Assurance Soc, No. 92-3604 (6th Cir 1993) (insurance company); Schloegel v Boswell, 994 F 2d 266 (5th Cir 1993) (insurance agent); Kyle Railways, Inc v Pacific Administration Svcs, Inc, 1993 US App Lexis (9th Cir 1993) (third party administrator); Useden v Acker, No. 90-5445 (11th Cir 1991) (attorneys and bank); Mertens v Hewitt Assocs, 948 F 2d 607 (9th Cir 1991), *aff'd*, 113 S Ct 2063 (1993) (actuaries); Consolidated Beef Indus, Inc v New York Life Ins Co, Nos. 90-5131 and 90-5164 (8th Cir 1991) (insurance company and agent); Pappas v Buck Consultants, Inc, 923 F 2d 531 (7th Cir 1991) (actuaries); Anoka Orthopaedic Assocs, PA v Lechner, 910 F 2d 514 (8th Cir 1990) (attorneys and consultants); Pension Plan of Public Svc Co of NH v KPMG Peat Marwick, 1993 US Dist Lexis 2254 (D NH 1993) (accountants); Painters of Philadelphia District Council No. 21 Welfare Fund v Price Waterhouse, 879 F 2d 1146 (3d Cir 1989) (accountants)]

Although not fiduciaries, they may be liable to the plan or plan sponsors based upon traditional theories of negligence or malpractice. [Steiner Corp Retirement Plan v Johnson & Higgins of California, 1994 US App Lexis 16716 (10th Cir 1994); Padeh v Zagoria, 1995 US Dist Lexis 14255 (SD Fla 1995); Clayton v KPMG Peat Marwick, No. 94-2005 (CD Cal 1994); Berlin City Ford, Inc v Roberts Planning Group, 864 F Supp 292 (D NH 1994); Horton v Cigna Individual Financial Svcs Co, 1993 US Dist Lexis 8639 (ND Ill 1993); Hanovi Corp v San Francisco Pension Corp, 1993 US Dist Lexis 18314 (ND Cal 1993); Mazur v Gaudet, 826 F Supp 188 (ED La 1992)]

See Q 19:1 for a discussion of the new ERISA Section 401(c).

Q 19:7   Do the fiduciary responsibility rules of ERISA apply to a Keogh plan?

Generally, if the plan covers self-employed individuals as well as common-law employees, the fiduciary responsibility provisions of ERISA are applicable. However, the fiduciary responsibility provisions of ERISA do not apply to plans that cover only self-employed individuals. A plan covering only the owner-employee (see Q 5:34) and the owner-employee's spouse is not a plan providing retirement income to employees. Plans in which only sole proprietors or partners participate are not considered employee benefit plans, and sole proprietors, partners, and their spouses are not considered employees for ERISA's fiduciary responsibility rules. [ERISA § 3(3); DOL Reg §§ 2510.3-3(b), 2510.3-3(c); Robertson v Alexander Grant & Co, 798 F 2d 868 (5th Cir 1986); Schwartz v Gordon, 761 F 2d 864 (2d Cir 1985); Olsavsky v Casey, 1992 US Dist Lexis 18495 (D Conn 1992)]

Q 19:8   What is a self-directed account plan?

A self-directed account plan is an individual account plan described in ERISA Section 3(34) that permits a participant to make an independent choice from a broad range of investment alternatives regarding the manner in which any portion of the assets in the participant's individual account is invested. [ERISA § 404(c); DOL Reg § 2550.404c-1(b)(1)]

According to DOL, a self-directed account plan must:

1. Include at least three investment options with materially different risk and return characteristics;

2. Provide enough information to allow the participant to make informed investment decisions for every investment alternative offered;

3. Enable diversification of investments; and

4. Allow participants independent control to change investments at least quarterly, and more frequently if volatile investments are offered.

A participant will not be considered to have sufficient information to make informed investment decisions unless provided with an explanation that the plan is intended to constitute an ERISA Section 404(c) plan and a description of the investment alternatives available under the plan, including their investment objectives and risk and return characteristics. A participant must be provided, either directly or on request, with the following information (based on the latest information available to the plan):

• A description of the annual operating expenses of each investment alternative, and the aggregate amount of these expenses expressed as a percentage of average net assets

• Copies of any prospectuses, financial statements, and reports available to the plan

• List of the assets in the portfolio of each alternative, and, for any asset that is a fixed rate investment contract, the name of the issuer, the term, and the rate of return

- Information on the value of shares of the alternatives available under the plan, as well as the past and current investment performance determined (net of expenses) on a reasonable and consistent basis

A plan offers a broad range of investment alternatives only if the available investment alternatives are sufficient to provide the participant with a reasonable opportunity to affect materially both the potential return on amounts in the account and the degree of risk to which these amounts are subject, and to permit the participant to choose from at least three investment alternatives, each of which is diversified; each of which has materially different risk and return characteristics, which, in the aggregate, enable the participant to achieve a portfolio with aggregate risk and return characteristics within the range normally appropriate for the participant; and each of which, when combined with the others, tends to minimize the overall risk of a portfolio through diversification.

Participants must also be advised that, if DOL requirements are satisfied, the plan's fiduciaries may be protected against liability for investment losses incurred as a result of the investment instructions given by participants to the fiduciaries.

[DOL Reg § 2550.404c-1(d)(2)]

The final ERISA Section 404(c) regulations are effective as of the first day of the first plan year beginning on or after October 13, 1993. For a calendar-year plan year, the effective date is January 1, 1994.

DOL has provided guidance concerning educational materials that may be circulated to participants by employers without such employers being considered investment advisors. [DOL Reg § 2509.961]

A fiduciary has the burden of showing that it complied with ERISA Section 404(c). [In re Unisys Savings Plan Litigation, Nos. 95-1156, 95-1157, and 95-1186 (3d Cir 1996)]

Q 19:9 Is a participant or beneficiary who self-directs an individual account considered a fiduciary?

No. If the plan permits self-directed accounts (see Q 19:8), participants will not be considered fiduciaries solely because they exercise control over assets in their individual accounts. The consequences are twofold. First, other plan fiduciaries generally would have no co-fiduciary liability on account of participants' investment decisions. Second, because the participants are not fiduciaries, no prohibited transaction under ERISA would result if their exercise of control over the assets in their accounts caused the trust to engage in transactions with parties in interest (see Q 20:3). [ERISA § 404(c); DOL Reg §§ 2550.404c-1(a), 2550.404c-1(d)]

Q 19:10   Are any individuals prohibited from serving as fiduciaries?

Yes. A person who has been convicted of any of a wide range of crimes, including robbery, bribery, extortion, and fraud, cannot serve as a plan fiduciary for a period of 13 years after the conviction or after the end of imprisonment, whichever is later. A person who knowingly violates the rule is subject to a maximum fine of $10,000 or five years' imprisonment, or both. [ERISA § 411]

One court has gone further and permanently barred former plan fiduciaries from acting as fiduciaries or providing services to plans in the future. [Beck v Levering, No. 91-6174 (2d Cir 1991)]

Q 19:11   Can a trustee be appointed for life?

No. DOL has ruled that the appointment of a trustee for life, or the ability to remove a trustee only upon misfeasance or incapacity to perform the duties of the position, is inconsistent with ERISA's fiduciary responsibility provisions. [DOL Adv Op No. 85-41A; Levy v Local Union No. 810, 20 F 3d 516 (2d Cir 1994); Mobile, Alabama-Pensacola, Florida Bldg & Constr Trades Council v Daugherty, 684 F Supp 270 (SD Ala 1989)]

Trustees did not breach their fiduciary duty by approving a trust amendment that transferred the power to appoint and remove trustees from a single joint council of local unions to three joint councils. The amendment only affected the distribution of power among the various unions and did not entrench current trustees. [Int'l Brotherhood of Teamsters v New York State Teamsters Council Health and Hospital Fund, 1990 US App Lexis 8409 (2d Cir 1990)]

Q 19:12   What is a fiduciary's basic duty?

The basic duty of a fiduciary is to act solely in the interest of the plan's participants and beneficiaries and for the exclusive purpose of providing benefits for participants and their beneficiaries. [Waller v Blue Cross of California, 1994 US App Lexis 16490 (9th Cir 1994)] A fiduciary must also act prudently, diversify the investment of the plan's assets, and act in a manner consistent with the plan's documents. A trustee did not breach its fiduciary duty when it invested all plan funds in employer stock because the plan itself required such investment upon the direction of the plan administrator (see Q 16:1) and the trustee had no discretion; and an employer did not breach its fiduciary duty when former employee stock ownership plan (ESOP; see Q 24:1) participants who elected cash distributions, rather than employer stock, were not advised by the employer that it had commenced preliminary discussions to sell the company at a price substantially in excess of the current market price. [ERISA § 404(a); Ershick v United Missouri Bank of Kansas City, NA, No. 90-3283 (10th Cir 1991); Sweeney v The Kroger Co, 773 F Supp 1266 (ED Mo 1991)] However, misleading communications or misrepresentations to participants may constitute a breach of fiduciary duty. [Curcio v John Hancock Mutual Life Ins Co, 1994 US App Lexis 21935 (3d Cir 1994); Fischer v The Philadelphia Electric Co, 994 F 2d 130 (3d Cir 1993); Kurz v The Philadelphia Electric Co, 994 F 2d 136 (3d Cir 1993); Drennan v General Motors Corp, 977 F 2d 246 (6th Cir 1992)] In certain circumstances, such misleading communications or misrepresentations may constitute fraud under state law on the theory that they do not relate to an ERISA plan and, accordingly, are not preempted by ERISA. [Farr v US West, Inc, 1995 US App Lexis 15706 (9th Cir 1995)]

A trustee's transfer of excess plan assets to the employer before participants received all their benefits violated the trustee's fiduciary duty to the participants (see Q 21:53). [PBGC v Fletcher, No. MO-89-CA-179 (WD Tex 1990)] Trustees breached their fiduciary duty to a participant's widow by failing to distribute plan benefits to her as soon as the amount payable was determined as required by the plan, and a company breached its fiduciary duty when it unreasonably delayed implementing a plan participant's request to transfer his plan account from a common stock fund to a fixed income investment fund. [Carich v James River Corp, No. 90-35567 (9th Cir 1992); Sherwood Group, Inc v Meselsohn, No. 88 Civ 3650 (SD NY 1990)]

Q 19:13   What is the applicable standard of care for a fiduciary?

A fiduciary is subject to the prudent man standard of care; that is, the fiduciary must act "with the care, skill, prudence, and diligence under the circumstances then prevailing that a prudent man acting in a like capacity and familiar with such matters would use in the conduct of an enterprise of a like character and with like aims." [ERISA § 404(a)(1)(B); Kowalewski v Detweiler, 770 F Supp 290 (D Md 1991)] A good faith reliance upon expert advice later found erroneous has been held not to be a breach of the standard. [Riley v Murdock, No. 92-442-CV-5-BR (ED NC 1995); Morgan v Ind Drivers Assn Pension Plan, 1992 US App Lexis 22927 (10th Cir 1992)]

ERISA does not, however, prohibit dual loyalties. Accordingly, a bank serving as trustee did not breach its fiduciary duty to the plan by refusing to continue to extend credit to an unrelated corporation in which the plan had invested plan assets. [Friend v Sanwa Bank California, 1994 US App Lexis 24805 (9th Cir 1994)]

Q 19:14   How does the prudent man standard apply to trustees or investment managers?

A trustee or other fiduciary responsible for investing the plan's assets must, in order to satisfy the prudent man standard, consider the following factors:

1. The composition of the portfolio with regard to diversification;
2. The liquidity and current return of the portfolio relative to the anticipated cash flow requirements of the plan; and
3. The projected return of the portfolio relative to the funding objectives of the plan.

In addition, the trustee or other fiduciary must determine that the particular investment or investment strategy is reasonably designed to further the purposes of the plan, taking into consideration the risk of loss and the opportunity for gain (or other return) associated with the investment or the investment strategy. [DOL Reg § 2550.404a-1] DOL has reviewed fiduciary responsibility rules relating to investments in derivatives. [DOL Info Ltr, May 21, 1996]

Q 19:15   Would a transaction involving the plan that benefits the employer result in a breach of fiduciary duty?

Not necessarily. A transaction that incidentally benefits the employer will not violate the rule that a fiduciary act solely in the interest of the plan's participants and beneficiaries as long as the fiduciary correctly concludes, on the basis of a careful, thorough, and impartial inquiry, that the transaction is in the interests of participants and beneficiaries. [Donovan v Bierwirth, 680 F 2d 263 (2d Cir 1982); Andrade v The Parsons Corp, No. 90-56202 (9th Cir 1992); see also Phillips v Amoco Oil Co, 799 F 2d 1464 (11th Cir 1986)]

However, management trustees of an ESOP (see Q 24:1) breached their fiduciary duty by not voting the ESOP shares at a shareholder meeting. If their conflicting loyalties to the company and the participants prevented them from properly representing the participants, they should have sought advice from a competent, independent advisor (see Q 24:40). [Newton v Van Otterloo, No. S89-610 (ND Ind 1991)]

Q 19:16   Must the assets of the plan be segregated?

Yes. The plan's assets must be segregated from the employer's property and held in trust. [ERISA § 403(a)]

Q 19:17   What are plan assets when a plan invests in another entity?

Generally, the plan's assets will include its investment in an entity but not any of the underlying assets of such entity. However, if the plan's equity interest in an entity is neither a publicly offered security nor a security issued by an investment company registered under the Investment Company Act of 1940, the plan's assets will include both the equity interest and an undivided interest in each of the underlying assets (the look-through rule; see Q 19:18). In that event, any person who has any authority or control over the management of the underlying assets or provides investment advice for a fee with respect to such assets is a fiduciary of the investing plan (see Q 19:1). [DOL Reg § 2510.3-101(a)]

Q 19:18   Are there any exceptions to the look-through rule?

The look-through rule (see Q 19:17) will not apply if:

1. The equity interest (see Q 19:19) is in an operating company (see Q 19:20); or
2. The amount of equity participation in the entity by benefit plan investors is not significant (see Qs 19:21, 19:22).

[DOL Reg § 2510.3-101(a)(2)]

Q 19:19   What is an equity interest and a publicly offered security?

An equity interest is any interest in an entity other than an instrument that is treated as indebtedness under applicable local law and that does not have substantial equity features. Examples of equity interests include an interest in profits of a partnership, an undivided interest in property, and a beneficial interest in a trust.

A publicly offered security is a security that is freely transferable, is part of a widely held class of securities, and is covered under certain federal securities registration rules.

Example 1. A plan acquires debentures issued by the Jaykay Corporation pursuant to a private offering. All of Jaykay's shareholders are benefit plan investors. Jaykay is engaged primarily in investing and reinvesting in precious metals on behalf of its shareholders, so it is not an operating company. By their terms, the plan's debentures are convertible into common stock of Jaykay at the plan's option. At the time of the plan's acquisition of the debentures, the conversion feature is incidental to Jaykay's obligation to pay interest and principal. The plan's assets do not include an interest in the underlying assets of Jaykay because the plan has not acquired an equity interest in Jaykay.

Example 2. Assume the same facts as in Example 1, except the plan exercises its option to convert the debentures into common stock, thereby acquiring an equity interest in Jaykay. Assuming that the common stock is not a publicly traded security and that there has been no change in the composition of the other equity investors in Jaykay, the plan's assets would then include an undivided interest in the underlying assets of Jaykay. As a result, employees of Jaykay with authority or control over the assets of Jaykay would be fiduciaries of the plan.

[DOL Reg §§ 2510.3-101(b), 2510.3-101(j)(1)]

DOL has issued an interpretive bulletin concerning the duty to vote publicly held securities. [DOL Interpretive Bulletin 94-2; DOL Reg § 2509.94-2] The Securities and Exchange Commission (SEC) has approved a proposed rule change allowing any member of the National Association of Security Dealers (NASD) who is designated by a named fiduciary (see Q 19:5) as an investment manager of equity securities to vote proxies in accordance with fiduciary responsibilities. [SEC Order Approving Proposed Rule Change by Nat'l Assn of Security Dealers, 60 FR 25749]

Q 19:20 What is an operating company?

An operating company is generally an entity that is primarily engaged, directly or through subsidiaries, in the production or sale of a product or services other than the investment of capital. Also, a venture capital operating company or a real estate operating company will be treated as an operating company. [DOL Reg § 2510.3-101(c)]

An entity is a venture capital operating company if at least 50 percent of its assets (other than short-term investments made pending long-term commitments) are invested in an operating company (other than a venture capital operating company) as to which the investing entity has and exercises the right to participate substantially in or influence the management of the operating company. [DOL Reg § 2510.3-101(d)]

An entity is a real estate operating company if at least 50 percent of its assets are invested in managed or developed real estate and the investing entity has the right to participate substantially and directly in the management or development activities. In addition, the investing entity, in the ordinary course of its business, must actually engage in real estate management or development activities. [DOL Reg § 2510.3-101(e)]

Q 19:21 What level of participation of benefit plan investors is considered significant?

Equity participation in an entity is significant on any date if, immediately after the most recent acquisition or redemption of any equity interest (see Q 19:19) in the entity, 25 percent or more of the value of any class of equity interest in the entity is held by benefit plan investors (see Q 19:22). [DOL Reg § 2510.3-101(f)(1); DOL Adv Op No. 89-05A]

Q 19:22 What is a benefit plan investor?

The term "benefit plan investor" includes:

1. An employee benefit plan as defined by ERISA;

2. A qualified retirement plan, individual retirement account, or individual retirement annuity; or

3. Any entity whose underlying assets include plan assets as a result of a plan's investment in that entity.

[DOL Reg § 2510.3-101(f)(2)]

Q 19:23 Are there any investments by a plan that may never satisfy the exceptions to the look-through rule?

Yes. If a plan acquires or holds an interest in any entity (other than a licensed insurance company) established or maintained to provide any pension or welfare benefit to participants or beneficiaries of the investing plan, none of the exceptions may apply (see Qs 19:17, 19:18). As a result, the assets of the plan will include its investment and an undivided interest in the underlying assets of that entity.

Example. A qualified retirement plan acquires a beneficial interest in a trust that is not an insurance company licensed to do business in a state. Under this arrangement, the trust will provide the plan benefits that are promised to the participants and beneficiaries under the terms of the plan. The plan's assets include its beneficial interest in the trust and an undivided interest in each of the trust's underlying assets. Thus, persons with authority or control over trust assets would be fiduciaries of the qualified retirement plan.

[DOL Reg §§ 2510.3-101(h)(2), 2510.3-101(j)(12)]

Q 19:24   When are participant contributions considered plan assets?

Amounts paid by participants, or withheld by the employer from participants' wages, as contributions to a plan will be considered plan assets as of the earliest date on which the contributions can reasonably be segregated from the general assets of the employer. That date can be no later than 90 days after the date on which the contributions are received by the employer or would have been paid to the employee in cash if not withheld from wages. [DOL Reg § 2510.3-102(a)]

Example. Cee & Ess Company employs a small number of people at a single payroll location. Cee & Ess maintains a contributory profit sharing plan in which there is 100 percent participation. Because the small number of participants are all in a single location, the company could reasonably be expected to transmit participant contributions to the trust within ten days of the close of each pay period. Therefore, the assets of the plan would include the participants' contributions as of that date. [DOL Reg § 2510.3-102(b)(2)]

DOL has published proposed regulations that, if adopted, would shorten the 90-day period described above to a maximum period identical to the period in which an employer must deposit withheld income taxes and employment taxes under applicable IRS regulations. [DOL Prop Reg § 2510.3-102]

The president of an employer was liable to a multiemployer plan for unpaid contributions after the employer stopped making contributions and filed for bankruptcy since such unpaid contributions were deemed plan assets over which the president exercised discretionary authority and committed a breach of fiduciary duty to the plan by paying corporate expenses instead of making the required plan contributions (see Q 25:4). [PMTA-ILA Containerization Fund v Rose, 1995 US Dist Lexis 10877 (ED Pa 1995)]

Q 19:25   What expenses relating to the plan may be paid out of plan assets?

Generally, plan assets are held exclusively to provide benefits to participants or beneficiaries and to defray reasonable expenses of administering the plan (see Q 19:12). Plan assets may therefore be used to pay plan expenses that are reasonably related to plan administration and authorized by the plan.

Services provided in conjunction with establishing the plan, terminating the plan, and other plan design functions would not properly be paid out of the plan. Payment of PBGC premiums is proper if the plan is silent or explicitly states that the plan may pay the premiums. However, the payment would be improper if the document indicates that the plan sponsor will pay them. [ERISA §§ 403(c)(1), 404(a)(1); DOL Information Letter, Mar 2, 1987]

Q 19:26   What are the consequences if plan assets are used improperly?

An improper payment of plan assets for expenses other than reasonable plan administration expenses would be a breach of fiduciary duty and would subject the fiduciary to personal liability for the breach (see Q 19:27). In addition, the payment may be a prohibited transaction if the payment is made to, on behalf of, or for the benefit of, a party in interest (see Qs 20:3, 20:5) and does not qualify for a statutory or administrative exemption under ERISA or the Code (see Qs 20:9–20:11). Finally, the payment may be considered a violation of the exclusive benefit provision of the Code and result in plan disqualification (see Q 4:1).

Q 19:27   Can a fiduciary be held liable for a breach of duty?

Yes. ERISA permits a civil action to be brought by a participant, beneficiary, or other fiduciary against a fiduciary for a breach of duty. The fiduciary is personally liable for any losses to the plan resulting from the breach of duty, and any profits obtained by the fiduciary through the use of plan assets must be turned over to the plan. The court may require other appropriate relief, including removal of the fiduciary. [ERISA §§ 409, 502(a)(2); Oscar A Samos, MD, Inc v Dean Witter Reynolds, Inc, No. 91-0209 (D RI 1991)] There is a question whether fiduciaries are liable to third parties if their breach may be considered in the best interests of plan beneficiaries. [General American Life Ins Co v Castonguay, 984 F 2d 1518 (9th Cir 1993)]

Q 19:28   May an individual sue a fiduciary for a personal wrong with respect to an ERISA plan?

Yes. ERISA Section 502(a)(3) permits plan participants to sue on their own behalf when harmed by a fiduciary's breach of duty. [Howe v Varity Corp, 1996 US Lexis 1954 (S Ct 1996)] The United States Supreme Court resolved a conflict among the circuit courts, supporting *Bixler v. Central Pennsylvania Teachers Health & Welfare Fund* [12 F 3d 1292 (3d Cir 1993)], *Anweiler v. American Elec. Power. Svcs. Corp.* [3 F 3d 986 (7th Cir 1993)], *Roche v. Matteson* [1995 US Dist Lexis 5939 (ND Ill 1995)], and *Iwans v. Aetna Life Ins. Corp.* [1994 US Dist Lexis 8490 (D Ct 1994)], all of which permitted such an action, and rejecting *McLeod v. Oregon Lithoprint Inc.* [46 F 3d 956 (9th Cir 1995)], *Watkins v. Westinghouse Hanford Co.* [1993 US App Lexis 33816 (9th Cir 1993)], and *Richards v. General Motors Corp.* [1994 US Dist Lexis 4045 (ED Mich 1994)], all of which denied a direct action.

A representative of a subclass of participants where less than all participants were damaged may sue on behalf of that subclass. [Kuper v Iovenko, 1995 US App Lexis 27764 (6th Cir 1995)]

An earlier case held that a participant who had received all benefits due from a plan does not have standing to sue as such individual is no longer a participant or beneficiary. [Crawford v Lamantia, No. 93-2241 (1st Cir 1994)] However, under PPA '94 (see Q 1:18), a former participant who receives an annuity upon termination of a plan has standing to sue if the purchase of the annuity violated fiduciary standards. DOL has stated that fiduciaries must justify their actions in purchasing anything other than the safest annuity available (see Q 21:41). [DOL Interpretive Bulletin 95-1]

Q 19:29 May a plan sue to redress an ERISA violation?

Courts are divided as to whether a plan, as opposed to the plan fiduciaries, may sue under ERISA. One court has permitted a plan to sue under ERISA for unpaid contributions; whereas another court dismissed a suit by a plan for breach of fiduciary duty and restitution of profits unjustly retained, concluding that the plan did not have standing to assert an ERISA violation. [Chicago Graphics Arts Health and Welfare Fund v Jefferson Smurfit Corp, 1995 US Dist Lexis 14228 (ND Ill 1995); Pedre Co v Robins, 1995 US Dist Lexis 14253 (SD NY 1995)]

Q 19:30 Can fiduciaries of a transferee plan sue fiduciaries of a transferor plan?

Yes. One court has held that fiduciaries of a transferee plan have standing to sue the fiduciaries of a transferor plan in connection with a breach of fiduciary duties. [Modern Woodcrafts, Inc v Hawley, 354 F Supp 1000 (D Ct 1982)] Another court agreed and also extended the right to sue to the purchaser of the business that sponsored the transferee plan. [Pilkington PLC v Perelman, 1995 US App Lexis 36632 (9th Cir 1995)]

Q 19:31 Is a jury trial available in an action against a fiduciary?

Courts have generally determined that a jury trial is not available in an action alleging breach of fiduciary duty, especially when the relief sought is equitable in nature. [Pane v RCA Corp, 36 F 3d 1508 (5th Cir 1995); Houghton v SIPCO, 38 F 3d 953 (8th Cir 1994); Spinelli v Gaughan, 12 F 3d 853 (9th Cir 1993); Blake v Union Mutual Stock Life Ins Co of America, 906 F 2d 1525 (11th Cir 1990); Richards v General Motors Corp, 1994 US Dist Lexis 4045 (ED Mich 1994); Chilton v Savannah Foods & Industries, Inc, 814 F 2d 620 (11th Cir 1986); Henley v Lokey Oldsmobile-Countryside, Inc, 1993 US Dist Lexis 3742 (MD Fla 1993); Landry v Air Line Pilots Assoc, International, AFL-CIO, No. 86-3196 (ED La 1991); but see Algie v RCA Global Communication, Inc, 1994 US Dist Lexis 10139 (SD NY 1994); Sullivan v LTV Aerospace and Defense Co, 1994 US Dist Lexis 5061 (WD NY 1994); and McDonald v Artcraft Electric Supply Co, 774 F Supp 29 (D DC 1991)] A jury trial was permitted in a case alleging that an employer failed to notify an employee of a new early retirement program since the relief sought was not equitable in nature. [Mullins v Pfizer, 1995 US Dist Lexis 13574 (DC Ct 1995)]

A jury trial may be available when an ERISA claim is combined with either a common law or statutory claim where the plaintiff is entitled to a jury trial under the United States Constitution. [Stewart v KHD Deutz of American Corp, 1996 US App Lexis 3243 (8th Cir 1996)]

Q 19:32 Is an ERISA claim subject to arbitration?

An agreement between a trustee and investment advisor to arbitrate an ERISA claim of breach of fiduciary duty may be enforced; ERISA does not require that ERISA claims be decided only by courts. [Kramer v Smith Barney, 1996 US App Lexis 8861 (5th Cir 1996); Pritzker v Merrill Lynch Pierce Fenner & Smith, Inc, 7 F 3d 1110 (3d Cir 1993); Bird v Shearson Lehman/American Express, Inc, 926 F 2d 116 (2d Cir 1991); Bevere v Oppenheimer & Co, 1994 US Dist Lexis 17703 (D NJ 1994); Witkowski v Welch, No. 90-0924 (ED Pa 1993); Fabian Financial Services v The Kurt H Volk Inc Profit Sharing Plan, 768 F Supp 728 (CD Cal 1991); but see International Assn of Machinists, Dist 10 v Waukesha Engine Div, 17 F 3d 1994 (7th Cir 1994) and Johnson v Francis Xavier Cabrini Hospital of Seattle, 910 F 2d 594 (9th Cir 1990)] In certain circumstances, arbitration may be ordered with respect to a claim against a party to an arbitration agreement while the court stays the action with regard to other defendants who are not parties to the arbitration agreement. [Schorr v GB Resources, 1992 WL 183392 (SD NY 1992)]

Q 19:33 Can a fiduciary be liable for a breach of fiduciary duty that occurred prior to the fiduciary's appointment?

No. A fiduciary cannot be held liable for a breach of fiduciary duty that was committed prior to the fiduciary becoming a fiduciary. Although the fiduciary may not be liable for the original breach, if the fiduciary knows about the breach, the fiduciary should take steps to remedy the situation. Failure to do so may constitute a subsequent independent breach of fiduciary duty by the successor fiduciary.

> **Example.** Esther has no existing relationship with the plan. She negotiates an agreement to provide investment advice to the plan that will render her a fiduciary. She will not be liable for any investment decisions made prior to her becoming a fiduciary that are held to have been imprudent and, consequently, a fiduciary breach. [ERISA § 409(b); Barker v American Mobile Power Corp, 1995 US App Lexis 31979 (9th Cir 1995); Baeten v Van Ess, 446 F Supp 868 (ED Wis 1977); DOL Op Ltr 76-95]

Q 19:34 Can a fiduciary be liable for failing to act?

Yes. A breach of fiduciary duty can occur by reason of omission as well as commission. A plan administrator was held to have breached his fiduciary duty by not investing plan assets, liquidating assets only to pay benefits, not making an effort to collect obligations owed to the plan, and holding an unspecified sum of plan funds in cash at his home. [Newport v Elms, 1992 US Dist Lexis 9130 (ED La 1992)] A fiduciary may also be liable for not investigating his suspicions that a plan was not being operated properly by other fiduciaries. [Barker v American Mobil Power Corp, 1995 US App Lexis 31979 (9th Cir 1995)]

Q 19:35 Can a qualified retirement plan set off a fiduciary's liability to a plan for breach of fiduciary duty against the fiduciary's benefits from the plan?

A qualified retirement plan can set off a fiduciary's liability to a plan for breach of fiduciary duty against the fiduciary's benefits from the plan, notwithstanding ERISA's anti-alienation provision (see Qs 4:24, 4:25). [Coar v Kazimir, 1993 US App Lexis 7817 (3d Cir 1993); United States v Gaudet, No. 91-3647 (5th Cir 1992); Friedlander v Doherty, 1994 US Dist Lexis 6369 (ND NY 1994); but see Guidry v Sheet Metal Workers Natl Pension Fund, 493 US 365 (1990) and Herberger v Shanbaum, 897 F 2d 801 (5th Cir 1990)]

Q 19:36 Does DOL impose a penalty for breaches of fiduciary duty?

Yes. For breaches of fiduciary duties (or knowing participation therein) on or after December 19, 1989, DOL imposes a penalty of 20 percent of the amount payable pursuant to a court order or settlement agreement with DOL. DOL may waive or reduce the penalty if the fiduciary or other person (1) acted responsibly and in good faith, or (2) will not otherwise be able to restore all plan losses without severe financial hardship. [ERISA § 502(l)]

Q 19:37   Can a nonfiduciary be held liable for a breach of fiduciary duty?

No. ERISA does not authorize suits by plan participants for money damages against nonfiduciaries who knowingly participate in a fiduciary's breach of fiduciary duty. [Mertens v Hewitt Associates, 113 S Ct 2063 (1993); Buckley Dement, Inc v Travelers Plan Administrators of Illinois, Inc, 39 F 3d 784 (7th Cir 1994); Reich v Continental Casualty Co, 33 F 3d 754 (7th Cir 1994); Slice v Sons of Norway, No. 93-2301 (8th Cir 1994); Reich v Rowe, 20 F 3d 25 (1st Cir 1994); Colleton Regional Hospital v MRS Medical Review Systems, Inc, 866 F Supp 896 (D SC 1994); Blevins Screw Products, Inc v Prudential Bache Securities, Inc, 835 F Supp 984 (ED Mi 1993)] At least two courts, however, have concluded that the language in the Mertens case cited above to the effect that a nonfiduciary is not liable for participating in a breach of fiduciary duties was dictum, not precedent they were required to follow. Accordingly, they permitted an action based upon a nonfiduciary's knowing participation in a fiduciary's breach. [DeLaurentis v Job-Shop Technical Services, Inc, 1996 US Dist Lexis 593 (ED NY 1996); Carpenters Local Union No. 64 Pension Fund v Silverman, 1995 US Dist Lexis 8663 (SD NY 1995)]

Claims for restitution, as opposed to damages, against nonfiduciaries may be permitted under ERISA, as may claims based upon the non-fiduciary's own conduct of engaging in the prohibited transaction, such as improperly receiving monies from the plan. [Harris Trust and Savings Bank v Salomon Bros, Inc, 832 F Supp 1169 (ND Ill 1993); Landwehr v Dupree, 1995 US App Lexis 35023 (9th Cir 1995)]

The DOL 20 percent penalty tax (see Q 19:36) may, however, be imposed against nonfiduciaries. Nonfiduciaries may be liable for participating in a prohibited transaction (see Q 20:3). [Reich v Compton, 1995 US App Lexis 13619 (3d Cir 1995)]

Certain earlier cases imposed liability on nonfiduciaries who partici-pated in a fiduciary's breach when the nonfiduciaries:

1. Had actual knowledge that a breach was occurring; and

2. Participated or took action that furthered or completed the breach.

[Diduck v Kaszycki & Sons Contractors, Inc, 974 F 2d 270 (2d Cir 1992); Brock v Hendershott, 840 F 2d 339 (6th Cir 1988); Thornton v Evans, 692 F

2d 1064 (7th Cir 1982); Bouton v Thompson, 764 F Supp 20 (D Conn 1991); Weir v Northwestern Nat'l Life Ins Co, 1992 US Dist Lexis 9653 (ED Pa 1992); PBGC v Ross, 733 F Supp 1005 (MD NC 1990); Mid-Jersey Trucking Industry-Local 701 v Omni Funding Group, 731 F Supp 161 (D NJ 1990); Brock v Gerace, 635 F Supp 563 (D NJ 1986); Freund v Marshall & Isley Bank, 485 F Supp 629 (WD Wi 1979)]

Individuals controlling a fiduciary, however, can be jointly and severally liable for a fiduciary's breach of duty. [Lowen v Tower Asset Mgmt, Inc, 829 F 2d 1209 (2d Cir 1987); but see Confer v Custom Eng'g Co, 952 F 2d 34 (3d Cir 1991)] A nonfiduciary insurance company was not liable for breach of fiduciary duty by its soliciting agent, admittedly a fiduciary, where the agent acted outside the scope of his employment without the knowledge or participation of the insurance company. [Kral, Inc v Southwestern Life Ins Co, 1993 US App Lexis 20656 (5th Cir 1993)] Fiduciaries may also be liable for the actions of nonfiduciaries acting as agents for fiduciaries. [Taylor v Peoples Natural Gas Co, 49 F 3d 982 (3d Cir 1995)] Such liability may be determined under a federal common law of agency rule of imputing the knowledge of an agent to its principal. [Steinberg v Mikkelsen, 1995 US Dist Lexis 15588 (ED Wi 1995)]

Q 19:38   Can a nonfiduciary be liable on a rationale outside of ERISA?

Yes. A plan administrator who was not an ERISA fiduciary may be liable for negligence under traditional theories not preempted by ERISA (see Q 19:6). [Zandi-Dulabi v Pacific Retirement Plans Inc, 1993 US Dist Lexis 8700 (ND Ca 1993)]

Q 19:39   May a fiduciary be held liable for breaches committed by a co-fiduciary?

Yes, if the fiduciary:

1. Knowingly participates in or tries to conceal a co-fiduciary's breach;

2. Enables a co-fiduciary to commit a breach by failing to meet the fiduciary's specific responsibilities; or

3. Knowing of a co-fiduciary's breach, fails to make a reasonable effort to remedy it. [ERISA § 405(a)]

Example. Anna and Amy are co-trustees. The trust specifies that they cannot invest in commodity futures. If Anna suggests to Amy that she invest part of the plan assets in commodity futures and Amy does so, both Anna and Amy may be held personally liable for any losses sustained by the plan. Similarly, if Amy invests in commodity futures and tells Anna about it, Anna could be held personally liable for any losses if she conceals the investment or fails to make a reasonable effort to correct it.

The co-fiduciary may be liable by virtue of failing to perform the co-fiduciary's fiduciary duties, even if the co-fiduciary is not aware of the other fiduciary's breach of duty. [Russo v Unger, No. 86 Civ 9741 (SD NY 1991)] Fiduciaries may also be liable where, by not following the procedures set forth in the plan, they enable a co-fiduciary to embezzle plan assets. [Mazur v Gaudet, 826 F Supp 188 (ED La 1992)]

Q 19:40   What should a fiduciary do if a co-fiduciary commits a breach of duty?

The fiduciary must try to remedy the breach. For example, if an improper investment was made, the fiduciary might consider disposing of the asset. Alternatively, the fiduciary might notify the company of the breach, institute a lawsuit against the co-fiduciary, or bring the matter before DOL. The fiduciary's resignation as a protest against the breach, without making reasonable efforts to prevent it, will not relieve the fiduciary of liability. [ERISA § 405(a)(3); DOL Reg § 2509.75-5, FR-10] A fiduciary may also remain liable after an effective resignation if the fiduciary fails to make adequate provision for the continued prudent management of plan assets. [Ream v Frey, 1996 US Dist Lexis 3820 (ED Pa 1996)]

Q 19:41   Can a breaching fiduciary obtain contribution or indemnity from other breaching co-fiduciaries?

There is a split among the courts as to whether there is a right of contribution or indemnity among fiduciaries in plans governed by ERISA so that a passive trustee can seek indemnification from an active trustee. Some cases hold that no such right exists. [Call v Sumitomo Bank of California, 881 F 2d 626 (9th Cir 1989); Kim v Fujikawa, 871 F 2d 1427 (9th Cir 1989); Daniels v Nat'l Employee Benefit Services, Inc, 877 F Supp 1067 (ND Ohio 1995); Physicians Healthchoice, Inc v Trustees of the Automotive Employee Benefit Trust, 764 F Supp 1360 (D Minn 1991)].

Other cases, however, hold that a fiduciary's right to seek contribution and indemnity is a fundamental principle of the law governing trusts and that those remedies should be incorporated into a federal common law of ERISA. [Chemung Canal Trust Co v Sovran Bank/Maryland, 939 F 2d 12 (2d Cir 1991); Free v Briody, 732 F 2d 1331 (7th Cir 1984); Duncan v Santaniello,

1995 US Dist Lexis 14381 (D Mass 1995); Cohen v Baker, 1994 US Dist Lexis 1595 (ED Pa 1994); Maher v Strachan Shipping Co, 817 F Supp 43 (ED La 1993), rev'd on other grounds, 1995 US App Lexis 32042 (5th Cir 1995)] Such federal common law would include a system of proportional fault among fiduciaries. [In re Masters, Mates & Pilots Pension Plan and IRAP Litigation, 957 F 2d 1020 (2d Cir 1993)]

A right of contribution under ERISA may also have been endorsed by implication in a decision that resolved a conflict among the circuits by holding that defendants in an action under Section 10(b) of the Securities Exchange Act of 1934 have a right to seek contribution as a matter of federal law. [Musick, Peeler & Garrett v Employers Ins of Wausau, No. 92-34 (S Ct 1993)]

Q 19:42   Does ERISA authorize punitive damages to a beneficiary for breach of fiduciary duty?

No. The Supreme Court has held that punitive damages are not available to a beneficiary in an action against the plan fiduciary for an alleged breach of fiduciary duty when the alleged breach was the untimely processing of the beneficiary's claim for benefits. Remedies available to the beneficiary in such instances would include only recovery of the benefits owed, clarification of the beneficiary's right to present or future benefits, or removal of the breaching fiduciary. [Mass Mutual Life Ins Co v Russell, 473 US 134 (1985)] Extra-contractual compensatory damages are also not available in a suit against a fiduciary under ERISA. [Shih v Commercial Assn for Security and Health, 809 F Supp 80 (D Col 1992)]

However, the Supreme Court expressly left open certain issues—for instance, whether a plan, as opposed to a participant or beneficiary, could recover punitive damages, and whether a participant or beneficiary could recover such damages when the injurious conduct was not a breach of fiduciary duty but a violation of other sections of ERISA or of the terms of the plan. Most courts since the *Russell* decision have concluded that punitive damages under such circumstances are similarly unavailable under ERISA. [Fraser v Lintas: Campbell-Ewald, 56 F 3d 722 (6th Cir 1995); Medina v Anthem Life Ins Co, 1993 US App Lexis 1317 (5th Cir 1993); Lafoy v HMO Colorado, 988 F 2d 97 (10th Cir 1993); Diduck v Kaszycki & Sons Contractors, Inc, 974 F 2d 270 (2d Cir 1992); Novak v Andersen Corp, 962 F 2d 757 (8th Cir 1992); Harsch v Eisenberg, 956 F 2d 651 (7th Cir 1992); McRae v Seafarers' Welfare Plan, 920 F 2d 819 (11th Cir 1991); Reinking v Philadelphia American Life Ins Co, 910 F 2d 1210 (4th Cir 1990); Drinkwater v Metropolitan Life Ins Co, 846 F 2d 821 (1st Cir 1988); Varhola v Doe, 820 F 2d 809 (6th Cir 1987); Powell v Chesapeake and Potomac Tel Co of Va, 780 F 2d 419 (4th Cir 1985); Bone v Assn Management Servs, Inc, 632 F

Supp 493 (SD Miss 1986); but see D'Amore v Stangle and Denigris Inc, 1995 US Dist Lexis 18313 (D Ct 1995) and California Digital Defined Benefit Pension Plan v Union Bank, 705 F Supp 489 (CD Cal 1989)] However, one court concluded that a fiduciary could recover punitive damages from another fiduciary who was guilty of malicious conduct. [Ampere Automotive Corp v Employee Benefit Plans, Inc, No. 92 C 2580 (ND Ill 1993)] Another court upheld an arbitrator's award of punitive damages in favor of a plan against its investment manager, although acknowledging that the arbitrators may have misinterpreted applicable law. [Shearson Lehman Bros v Neurosurgical Associates of Indiana, 1995 US Dist Lexis 12161 (SD Ind 1995)]

Q 19:43　Does ERISA authorize the recovery of attorneys' fees and costs?

Yes. A court may, in its discretion, award reasonable attorneys' fees and costs to either party in an action by a participant, beneficiary, or fiduciary. [ERISA § 502(g)]

Courts have examined the following factors in deciding whether to award fees and costs, not all of which must be present to justify an award:

- Opponent's bad faith
- Opponent's ability to pay
- Deterrent effect on others in similar circumstances
- Whether action benefited all plan participants
- Relative merits of parties' positions

[Denzler v Questech, Inc, No. 94-2109 (4th Cir 1996); Eddy v Colonial Life Ins Co of America, 59 F 3d 201 (DC Cir 1995); McPherson v Employees' Pension Plan of American Re-Insurance Co, Inc, 1994 US App Lexis 22777 (3d Cir 1994); Commercial Electric, Inc v IBEW Local 1168, No. 92-15268 (9th Cir 1993); Meredith v Navistar Int'l Transp Co, 935 F 2d 124 (7th Cir 1991); Eaves v Penn, 587 F 2d 453 (10th Cir 1978); Trustees of the Pension, Welfare and Vacation Fringe Benefit Funds of IBEW Local 701 v Favia Electric Co, 1994 US Dist Lexis 2566 (ND Ill 1994); Maryland Electric Industry Health Fund v Triangle Sign & Service Div of Lok-Tite Ind, Inc, 1993 US Dist Lexis 2606 (D Md 1993); St Laurent v New Haven Terminal, Inc, 1993 US Dist Lexis 17331 (D Ct 1993); Plotkin v Bearings Ltd, 1992 US Dist Lexis 7787 (ED NY 1992); Lanning v Maxwell, 1992 US Dist Lexis 14089 (D Kan 1992)]

The "lodestar/multiplier" method has been used to determine reasonable attorneys' fees. The lodestar is a reasonable hourly rate multiplied by the number of hours reasonably spent on the case. The multiplier is then applied to increase or decrease the lodestar amount on the basis of other relevant factors, including whether the attorneys had a sure source of compensation for their services. [Florin v Nationsbank of Georgia, 1994 US App Lexis 24337 (7th Cir 1994); D'Emanuele v Montgomery Ward & Co, 904 F 2d 1379 (9th Cir 1990)]

Attorneys' fees may be denied to a prevailing party after trial, awarded even though all substantive issues are settled out of court, and awarded in suits seeking injunctive relief and not monetary damages. [Sheldon Co Profit-Sharing Plan and Trust v Smith, 1995 US App Lexis 20708 (6th Cir 1995); Freeman v Continental Ins Co, No. 92-8316 (11th Cir 1993); Spain v Aetna Life Ins Co, 1993 US App Lexis 33975 (9th Cir 1993); Cefali v Buffalo Brass Co, Inc, No. 87-102L (WD NY 1990)]

Courts are divided as to whether attorneys' fees are recoverable for administrative proceedings. [Thomke v Connecticut General Life Ins Co, 1994 US App Lexis 2972 (9th Cir 1994)(refusing to award attorneys' fees); Cann v Carpenters' Pension Trust Fund of Northern California, 989 F 2d 313 (9th Cir 1993)(refusing to award attorneys' fees); Hamilton v Bank of New York, 1995 US Dist Lexis 10464 (D Del 1995)(awarding attorneys' fees); Chicago Graphic Arts Health and Welfare Fund v Jefferson Smurfit Corp, 1995 US Dist Lexis 18203 (ND Ill 1995)(awarding attorneys' fees)]

Once a fiduciary breach has been established, the burden may shift to the defendant fiduciary to show why costs, including attorneys' fees, should not be awarded. [The New York State Teamsters Council Health and Hospital Fund v Estate of De Perno, Nos. 93-7870 and 93-7896 (2d Cir 1994)]

A prevailing party may be awarded what it would have paid to independent attorneys if the party was represented by its in-house staff counsel. [Central States, Southeast and Southwest Areas Pension Fund v Central Cartage Co, 1996 US App Lexis 756 (7th Cir 1996)]

An award of attorneys' fees to a defendant, who was a consultant to a plan, in an action brought by the plan was improper since the plan was not a participant, beneficiary, or fiduciary as required under ERISA Section 502(g). [Corder v Howard Johnson & Co, 53 F 3d 225 (9th Cir 1994)] Also, an award of attorneys' fees to an association successfully challenging a state law as preempted by ERISA was denied for the same reason. [Self-Insurance Institute of America, Inc v Korioth, 53 F 3d 694 (5th Cir 1995)]

The trial court may also award simple or compound prejudgment interest. [Diduck v Kaszycki & Sons Contractors, Inc, 974 F 2d 270 (2d Cir 1992); Russo v Unger, 1994 US Dist Lexis 758 (SD NY 1994)]

Q 19:44 Can the plan contain a provision relieving a fiduciary of personal liability?

No. [Martin v NationsBank of Georgia, NA, 1993 US Dist Lexis 6322 (ND Ga 1993)] The plan may, however, buy insurance to cover liability or losses due to acts or omissions of fiduciaries if the insurance company is given a right to sue the breaching fiduciary. [ERISA § 410] If misrepresentations are made in the insurance application by one fiduciary, the policy may be voided as against all fiduciaries, some of whom may be without coverage through no fault of their own; otherwise, the insurance company would suffer hardship by providing coverage for a risk it never meant to insure. A fiduciary may buy insurance to cover the fiduciary's own liability. [Mazur v Gaudet, 825 F Supp 188 (ED La 1992)] The fiduciary may also be indemnified from a nonplan source, such as the plan sponsor. [DOL Reg § 2509.75-4]

Q 19:45 Can a plan contain a provision permitting indemnification of a fiduciary?

A plan may provide for indemnification of expenses of a fiduciary who successfully defends against a claim of breach of fiduciary duty. [Packer Eng'g, Inc v Kratville, No. 91-2976 (7th Cir 1992)]

Q 19:46 Is a release executed by a plan beneficiary freeing plan fiduciaries from past liability under ERISA valid?

Yes. A release that is part of a settlement of a bona fide dispute over past fiduciary breaches is valid, but not where entitlement is clear and without doubt or relating to the performance of future fiduciary duties. [Blessing v Struthers-Dunn, Inc, 1985 WL 3569 (ED Pa 1985)]

Q 19:47 Can fiduciary responsibility be delegated?

Yes. For example, the trust instrument can provide that one trustee has responsibility for one-half of the plan assets and a second trustee has responsibility for the other half of the plan assets. Neither trustee would be liable for the acts of the other except under the co-fiduciary liability rule of ERISA Section 405(a) (see Q 19:39). [ERISA § 405(b)]

If the plan expressly so provides, the named fiduciaries can allocate among themselves or delegate to others their fiduciary duties, other than the management or control of the plan's assets. The management or control of the plan's assets can be delegated only to an investment manager. [ERISA §§ 405(c)(1), 402(c)(3)]

An effective allocation or delegation will generally relieve the named fiduciary from liability for the acts of the person to whom such duties are allocated or delegated. The named fiduciary, however, is not relieved of liability under the co-fiduciary rules of ERISA Section 405(a). [ERISA § 405(c)(2)]

Q 19:48   What is the liability of an investment manager for its decisions regarding investment of plan assets?

An investment manager is a bank, insurance company, or registered investment advisor that acknowledges in writing that it is a fiduciary with respect to the plan (see Q 19:1). Therefore, any failure to comply with fiduciary standards may result in a breach of fiduciary duty, and the investment manager will be liable for any losses to the plan resulting from the breach. In addition, the investment manager may be required to disgorge any profits derived from the breach.

An investment manager who bought and sold on behalf of a plan was found to have engaged in churning the plan's portfolio when the manager directed approximately 94 transactions over 17 months. The churning transactions resulted in a loss of $47,000, while the broker received commissions of $9,700 in one three-month period. The investment manager was held liable for the losses to the plan and was ordered to return the commissions to the plan. [Dasler v E F Hutton and Co, Inc, 694 F Supp 624 (D Minn 1988)] A bank trustee whose duties were limited to following the directions of another fiduciary was not liable for losses to the plan. [Maniace v Commerce Bank of Kansas City, 40 F 3d 264 (8th Cir 1994), but see also FirsTier Bank, NA v Zeller, 16 F 3d 907 (8th Cir 1994); Moench v Robertson, 62 F 3d 553 (3d Cir 1995); Kuper v Iovenko, 1995 US App Lexis 27764 (6th Cir 1995)]

Q 19:49   Are there any limits on the investments a qualified retirement plan can make?

There are no specific dollar or percentage limits placed on the amount a qualified retirement plan can invest in any particular type of asset (other than qualifying employer securities or qualifying employer real property; see Q 19:54). Nor are there any limits on the types of investments that can be made. Investments in such tangible assets as real estate, gold, art, or diamonds are permitted, even though these investments may not generate current income for the plan and generally lack liquidity. However, see the discussion regarding a fiduciary's standard of care at Qs 19:12 and 19:13.

Limits on investments in qualifying employer securities or qualifying employer real property are discussed at Q 19:54. The consequences of investments by self-directed accounts in collectibles are discussed at Q 19:57.

Q 19:50 May a qualified retirement plan borrow to make investments?

Yes. There is no prohibition against any particular method by which a qualified retirement plan invests its assets. However, securities purchased on margin are considered acquisition indebtedness, subject to the unrelated business income tax on the income—both dividends and gains—resulting from its acquisition indebtedness. [IRC §§ 511, 514; Ocean Cove Corp Retirement Plan and Trust v United States, 657 F Supp 776 (SD Fla 1987); Elliot Knitwear Profit Sharing Plan v Comm'r, 614 F 2d 347 (3d Cir 1980), aff'g, 71 TC 765 (1979)] Gains realized from the short sale of publicly traded securities through a broker are not income derived from acquisition indebtedness and, hence, are not unrelated business taxable income. [Rev Rul 95-8, 1995-1 CB 293] Trading in commodity futures contracts does not constitute debt-financed property and also does not constitute unrelated business taxable income. [Ltr Ruls 8338138, 8110164, 8107114, 8104998, 8044023]

When a plan borrows money to acquire or improve real estate, the debt generally is not considered acquisition indebtedness, so the income or gain from the real estate is not treated as unrelated business taxable income. [IRC § 514(c)(9)]

Q 19:51 What is the diversification requirement?

A trustee (or any other fiduciary responsible for investing plan assets) is required to discharge the trustee's duties "by diversifying the investments of the plan so as to minimize the risk of large losses, unless under the circumstances it is clearly not prudent to do so." [ERISA § 404(a)(1)(C)]

The degree of investment concentration that would violate the diversification rule cannot be stated as a fixed percentage but depends on the facts and circumstances of each case, including the following factors:

- The purposes of the plan
- The amount of plan assets

- Financial and industrial conditions
- The type of investment made
- Diversification along geographic lines
- Diversification along industry lines
- The date the investment matures

For example, if the trustee is investing in real estate mortgages, the trustee should not invest a disproportionate amount in mortgages within a particular area or on a particular type of property even if that investment would result in social gains to a particular community. [H Conf Rep No. 1280, 93d Cong, 2d Sess, reprinted in 1974 US Code Cong & Admin News 5038, 5084, 5085]

One court held that trustees violated the diversification rule when over 65 percent of the plan's assets were invested in commercial first mortgages secured by property located in one area. The lack of diversification caused too much risk that the value of the assets would decline in the event of a severe economic downturn in the area where the property securing the mortgages was located. As a result, the investments in the aggregate were held to be imprudent. [Brock v Citizens Bank of Clovis, 841 F 2d 344 (10th Cir 1988)] Another court held that investing over 70 percent of a plan's assets in real estate did not necessarily mean that the investments were imprudent. [Reich v King, 1994 US Dist Lexis 16763 (DC Md 1994)]

Another court held that an investment company that invested over 70 percent of a plan's assets in long-term government bonds did not properly diversify plan assets because the investment company failed to determine the plan's particular cash flow needs and was forced to sell some bonds at a loss to meet the plan's need for cash. [GIW Inds, Inc v Trevor, Stewart, Burton & Jacobsen, Inc, 845 F 2d 729 (11th Cir 1990)] However, other courts have found that no violation occurred with an investment of almost 90 percent of a plan's assets in one profitable investment or that the failure to diversify was not an imprudent act. [Etter v J Pease Const Co, Inc, 963 F 2d 1005 (7th Cir 1992); Lanka v O'Higgins, No. 88-CV-922 (ND NY 1992)]

It is possible to meet the diversification requirement by investing plan assets in a bank's pooled investment fund (see Q 19:58), a mutual fund (see Q 19:59), or insurance or annuity contracts if the bank, mutual fund, or insurance company diversifies its investments.

The diversification requirement generally does not apply to an investment in employer securities by an ESOP (see Q 24:1), depending on the exact language of the ESOP. Where it does not apply, there may still be a presumption that an ESOP fiduciary did not violate ERISA by investing plan assets in employer securities. [Moench v Robertson, 1995 US App Lexis

21546 (3d Cir 1995); Ershick v United Missouri Bank of Kansas City, NA, No. 90-3283 (10th Cir 1991)] However, an ESOP must offer certain participants the right to elect to diversify the stock acquired after 1986 and allocated to their accounts (see Qs 24:41–24:51).

Q 19:52 Must a plan make only blue chip investments?

No. DOL says, "[A]lthough securities issued by a small or new company may be a riskier investment than securities issued by a blue chip company, the investment in the former company may be entirely proper under . . . [the] prudence rule." [Preamble to DOL Reg § 2550.404a-1]

The degree of risk that the trustee takes in making investments depends in part on the type of plan the employer maintains. In a defined contribution plan (see Q 2:2), benefits received by a plan participant are based on the employer's contributions, increased or decreased by the return on plan investments. Thus, it may be appropriate to consider some speculative investments in a defined contribution plan.

In a defined benefit plan (see Q 2:3), a rate of return on investments above that assumed by the actuary reduces required contributions, and a rate of return below the assumed rate increases required contributions. Thus, investments will normally be of a nature that will return at least as much as the actuary has assumed. It is likely, therefore, that speculative investments in a defined benefit plan will have less appeal than in a defined contribution plan.

Q 19:53 How can a trustee or other plan fiduciary be protected from lawsuits for failure to meet the prudent man rule?

In acting prudently, trustees or other fiduciaries should also act defensively, building a record to defend their actions. Fiduciaries should, for example:

1. Keep detailed records of the actions taken and the factors that went into the decisions;

2. Make sure these records describe in detail the relevant circumstances prevailing at the time—that is, outline the conditions under which the action was taken; and

3. Make sure all reasonable steps have been taken to acquire the information needed to make informed decisions.

Q 19:54　May a qualified retirement plan invest in employer securities or employer real property?

A plan subject to ERISA generally may not acquire or hold qualifying employer securities (see Q 19:56) or qualifying employer real property (see Q 19:55) if the total fair market value of such assets exceeds 10 percent of the fair market value of the plan's assets at the time of acquisition. The 10 percent limitation does not apply to an eligible individual account plan that specifically authorizes such investments. An eligible individual account plan is defined as:

1. A profit sharing, stock bonus, thrift, or savings plan;

2. An ESOP; or

3. A money purchase pension plan in existence on the date of ERISA's enactment that invested primarily in qualifying employer securities at that time. [ERISA § 407]

Individual account plans that are part of a floor offset arrangement—an arrangement under which the plan's benefits are taken into account in determining a participant's benefits under a defined benefit plan—established after December 17, 1987 do not fall within this exception. [ERISA § 407(d)(3)(C)]

In addition, the two plans that constitute the floor offset arrangement will be treated as a single plan for purposes of the 10 percent limit.

Example. Samsin Corporation and Tasha Corporation each have floor offset arrangements with assets of $200,000 divided equally between their defined benefit and profit sharing plans. Samsin Corporation established its floor offset arrangement in 1985; Tasha Corporation's was established in 1988. Up to $10,000 of the assets of Samsin Corporation's defined benefit plan and up to $100,000 (which is 100 percent of the assets) of Samsin Corporation's profit sharing plan can be invested in qualifying employer securities—for a total of $110,000. In contrast, the amount of Tasha Corporation's qualifying employer securities held by the floor offset arrangement may not exceed $20,000 (10 percent of its assets in the aggregate). [ERISA § 407(d)(9)]

Q 19:55　What is qualifying employer real property?

Employer real property is real property leased to an employer of employees covered by the plan or an affiliate of the employer. Such real property is qualifying only if it is dispersed geographically, suitable for more than one use, and held without violation of the other ERISA fiduciary rules (except the diversification and prohibited transaction rules, which do not apply). [ERISA §§ 406(d)(2), 406(d)(4)]

Q 19:56 What are qualifying employer securities?

Employer securities are stock, marketable obligations, or certain publicly traded partnership interests issued by an employer of employees covered by the plan or an affiliate of the employer. Stock or partnership interests acquired by a plan other than an eligible individual account plan after December 17, 1987 will be qualifying employer securities only if (1) not more than 25 percent of the aggregate amount of stock of the same class issued and outstanding at the time of acquisition is held by the plan, and (2) at least 50 percent of such aggregate amount is held by persons independent of the issuer. For stock acquired on or before December 17, 1989, plans had until December 31, 1992 to comply with the new rules. [ERISA §§ 407(d)(5), 407(f)]

Q 19:57 What does earmarking investments mean?

Earmarking in a defined contribution plan (see Q 2:2) allows each participant, on a nondiscriminatory basis, an opportunity to invest funds contributed to the plan on the participant's behalf as the participant sees fit in any investment vehicle that the trustees are willing to administer. Traditional retirement plan investments—blue chip stocks, bonds, and real estate—can be passed over in favor of more speculative investments such as new stock issues, diamonds, gold, art, and antiques. However, amounts invested in collectibles under an earmarked plan will be treated as distributions for tax purposes. Collectibles are defined as works of art, rugs, antiques, precious metals, stamps, coins, and any other tangible property specified as a collectible by IRS. [IRC § 408(m)]

There is no place for earmarking of employer contributions in a defined benefit plan (see Q 2:3) since there are no individual accounts and investment gains or losses affect the amount the employer must contribute to the plan rather than the level of benefits payable to participants. However, earmarking of voluntary or rollover contributions by participants may be appropriate. Earmarking in a self-directed account plan (see Q 19:8 has the added advantage of possibly relieving the plan's trustees of liability for poor investment decisions made by the participant.

Q 19:58 What are pooled investment funds?

Pooled investment funds are commingled funds maintained by a bank on behalf of many qualified retirement plans. When a bank is appointed as trustee and the qualified retirement plan's assets are invested by the bank, the company retains only a limited choice in directing the investment of the plan's assets.

Generally, the bank has a dual fund arrangement—a fixed-income fund and a common stock fund—that permits the company to direct the proportion of its contributions invested in each fund.

The pooling of funds makes it possible to offer small plans the economies and security of a large plan. This investment vehicle may be particularly attractive to small and medium-sized plans, such as plans in which the annual contribution is below $100,000.

To participate in a pooled investment fund, the company maintaining the plan must adopt the bank's collective trust as part of its own trust and authorize investments in the bank's trust.

A trustee must, of course, be prudent in selecting and retaining the bank that directs the plan's investments.

Q 19:59   Can plan assets be invested in a mutual fund?

Yes. Mutual funds are a common investment vehicle, especially for small plans desiring professional investment management but not wishing to retain a bank's trusteeship or for plans that are too small to participate in a bank's pooled investment fund. A trustee must, of course, be prudent in selecting and retaining the mutual fund in which plan assets are invested, taking into account the wide variety of funds available with different investment goals.

Chapter 20

Prohibited Transactions

Both ERISA and the Code prohibit certain classes of transactions between a retirement plan and parties in interest to the plan, regardless of the fairness of the particular transaction involved or the benefit to the plan. In addition, fiduciaries are prohibited from engaging in certain conduct that would affect their duty of loyalty to the plan. This chapter examines the nature of prohibited transactions, the penalties that apply when a prohibited transaction occurs, and the statutory, administrative, and class exemptions to the prohibited-transaction rules.

Q 20:1 What is a prohibited transaction?

A prohibited transaction occurs under ERISA if a plan fiduciary (see Q 19:1) causes the retirement plan (see Q 20:4) to engage in a transaction that the fiduciary knows or should know constitutes a *direct* or *indirect*:

1. Sale, exchange, or lease of any property between the plan and a party in interest (see Q 20:3);

2. Loan or other extension of credit between the plan and a party in interest; [Ltr Rul 9238003]

3. Furnishing of goods, services, or facilities between the plan and a party in interest;

4. Transfer of plan assets to a party in interest or the use of plan assets by or for the benefit of a party in interest; or

5. Acquisition of employer securities or employer real property in excess of the limits set by law (see Q 19:54). [ERISA § 406(a)(1)]

There are three key concepts in the area of prohibited transactions. First, a prohibited transaction may be either direct or indirect. Second, a prohibited transaction involves both a plan and a party in interest. Third, a prohibited transaction occurs between a plan and a party in interest in either direction. For example, a prohibited transaction might consist of a transfer of assets from a party in interest to a plan or a transfer of assets from a plan to a party in interest.

In addition, ERISA prohibits a fiduciary from:

1. Dealing with plan assets (see Q 19:17) in the fiduciary's own interest or for the fiduciary's own account;

2. Acting in any transaction involving the plan on behalf of a party whose interests are adverse to the interests of the plan or its participants or beneficiaries; or

3. Receiving any consideration for the fiduciary's own personal account from any person dealing with the plan in connection with any transaction involving plan assets. [ERISA § 406(b)]

In one case, a party in interest sold publicly traded securities of an unrelated corporation for cash and a noninterest bearing, demand promissory note to a qualified retirement plan established by the professional corporation through which the individual conducted his practice. The individual conceded that the sale of the stock constituted a prohibited transaction but contended that the excise tax (see Q 20:5) should not apply because the transaction would qualify as a prudent investment if judged under the highest fiduciary standards. The court upheld the imposition of the excise tax and affirmed the principle that the prohibited-transaction restrictions were *per se* prohibitions with specifically defined exemptions and that no good-faith exception exists. [Leib, 88 TC 1474 (1987)] In another case, the individuals who were parties in interest also argued that they should not be subject to the excise tax because they acted in good faith and on the advice of their attorneys and investment counselors in engaging in the prohibited transactions and further argued that the plan was not harmed and in fact was better off as a result of the transactions. The court rejected these arguments as irrelevant and noted that the language and the legislative history of the statutory provisions at issue indicated a congressional intention to create a blanket prohibition against certain transactions whether the transaction was entered into prudently or in good faith, or whether the plan benefited as a result. In essence, "good intentions and a pure heart are no defense." [Rutland, 89 TC 1137 (1987); see also Donovan v Cunningham, 716 F 2d 1455 (5th Cir 1983); M & R Investment Co v Fitzsimmons, 685 F 2d 283 (9th Cir 1982); and Cutair v Marshall, 590 F 2d 523 (3d Cir 1979)]

In a case of potentially far-reaching consequences, the United States Supreme Court held that a prohibited transaction did not occur when an employer conditioned eligibility for plan benefits under a special early retirement program on the employee's execution of a broad waiver covering potential Age Discrimination in Employment Act (ADEA) and other employment-related claims against the employer. [Spink v Lockheed Corp, No. 95-809 (S Ct 1996)]

Receipt of commissions by a fiduciary's wholly owned subsidiary on loans from a plan to unrelated borrowers is a prohibited transaction. [Murphy v Dawson, No. 88-2992 (4th Cir 1989)] A plan's payment of legal fees to the attorneys defending a trustee in a criminal prosecution is a prohibited transaction between the plan and the trustee. [O'Malley v Comm'r, 972 F 2d 150 (7th Cir 1992), *aff'g* 96 TC 644 (1991)] Loans from a law firm's qualified retirement plan to clients of the law firm pending settlement of their lawsuits are prohibited transactions because the loans benefit the law firm's business. [Ltr Ruls 9238001, 9118001] Similarly, a loan from a plan to a partnership in which a trustee had a 39 percent interest was a prohibited transaction between the plan and the trustee because of the loan's benefit to the partnership in which the trustee had a significant interest. [Ltr Rul 9119002] An investment by a qualified retirement plan in a participating mortgage loan made to a limited partnership in which the plan investment advisor held a 7.5 percent interest was a prohibited transaction because the ownership interest created a conflict of interest resulting in the advisor's having divided loyalties. [Ltr Rul 9208001]

The mere retention of an investment management company—a party in interest because it was half-owned by a corporation that also wholly owned a company sponsoring the qualified retirement plan—to manage the plan's assets did not result in a prohibited transaction because the sponsoring company, not the plan, paid the investment management fees. [DOL Op Ltr 91-44A] A bank trustee that purchased the stock of its parent corporation at the direction of an unaffiliated named fiduciary did not engage in a prohibited transaction. [DOL Op Ltr 92-23A] However, a trustee's receiving income from the float on benefit checks it issues to plan participants is a prohibited transaction. [DOL Op Ltr 93-24A]

Bank fees paid by qualified retirement plans for certain services provided to mutual funds, and not for investment advisory services, are not prohibited transactions, the Department of Labor (DOL) opined. [DOL Op Ltr 93-12A; PTE 77-4] The payment of fees to a plan trustee by plans investing in mutual funds, and the waiver of investment advisory fees by the mutual funds' investment advisor, meet the requirements of a prohibited transaction exemption. [DOL Op Ltr 93-13A; PTE 77-4] To satisfy the requirements of PTE 77-4, a prospectus must be furnished to an independent plan fiduciary. If a prospectus is not available, this requirement will be met if all the information required under the form used to register an open-end investment company and certain additional information are provided to the fiduciary. [DOL Op Ltr 94-34A]

An employer and an individual who was the employer's president, controlling shareholder, and a plan trustee were found jointly and severally liable for the excise tax on a series of prohibited transactions. Plan assets were taken without loan agreements and used to repay employer debts; a trust checking account was used as an expense account to pay the individual's wife, relatives, and other persons; and loans by the plan to third parties were repaid to the employer. These transactions violated both the proscription on self-dealing by a plan fiduciary and the prohibition on any direct or indirect transfer to, or use by or for the benefit of, a disqualified person (see Q 20:4) of the income or assets of a plan. [Ltr Rul 9424001]

For a discussion of statutory, administrative, and class exemptions, see Qs 20:9, 20:11, and 20:17.

Q 20:2 Can one event give rise to more than one prohibited transaction?

One case involved the sale of property by disqualified persons (see Q 20:4) to a qualified retirement plan. The disqualified persons included the corporation that maintained the plan, officers, directors, and employees of the corporation, and participants of the plan. In 1976, disqualified persons sold property owned by them to the plan for $430,000. The plan paid cash, assumed an outstanding mortgage on the property, and issued a promissory note to the parties as consideration for the purchase. In 1977, the plan leased the property to the corporation for use as its corporate headquarters. The plan failed to report the transactions as prohibited transactions (see Q 17:13). In 1978, the parties filed an application for exemption from the prohibited-transaction restrictions with DOL (see Qs 20:11, 20:15). After the application was denied, two of the parties purchased the property from the plan for $430,000 in June 1980 and paid an additional $20,000 as additional consideration for the purchase in December 1982.

The court determined that the parties engaged in three separate prohibited transactions: (1) the sale of the property to the plan; (2) the issuance of the promissory note to the parties by the plan; and (3) the lease of the property by the plan to the corporation.

The parties argued that they should not be subjected to double taxation in having both the sale of the property to the plan and the plan's issuance of the promissory note treated as separate prohibited transactions. Alternatively, the parties argued that the amount involved (see Q 20:6) in the sale transaction should be reduced by the amount of the promissory note. The court held that each of the enumerated prohibited transactions was designed to guard against particular instances of overreaching by a person able to exert influence over the affairs of a plan. Further, the court found no indication in ERISA or in the legislative history that the prohibited-transaction restrictions were intended to be mutually exclusive. [Rutland, 89 TC 1137 (1987)]

Q 20:3 Who is a party in interest?

Under ERISA, the following are parties in interest with respect to a plan:

1. Any fiduciary, counsel, or employee of the plan;
2. A person providing services to the plan;
3. An employer any of whose employees are covered by the plan, and any direct or indirect owner of 50 percent or more of such employer;
4. A relative (i.e., spouse, ancestor, lineal descendant, or spouse of a lineal descendant) of any of the persons described in (1), (2), or (3) above;
5. An employee organization, any of whose members are covered by the plan;
6. A corporation, partnership, estate, or trust of which at least 50 percent is owned by any person or organization described in (1), (2), (3), (4), or (5) above;
7. Officers, directors, 10-percent-or-more shareholders, and employees of any person or organization described in (2), (3), (5), or (6) above; and
8. A 10-percent-or-more partner of or joint venturer with any person or organization described in (2), (3), (5), or (6) above.

[ERISA §§ 3(14), 3(15)]

In one case, a court rejected DOL's contention that a corporation was the alter ego of a labor union that was a party in interest to a pension plan and found that the plan's loan and sale of a mortgage note to the corporation was not a prohibited transaction; however, the court also ruled that DOL could bring a civil action against a nonfiduciary who participated in a prohibited transaction (see Q 19:37). [Reich v Compton, 1993 US App Lexis 13619 (3d Cir 1995)] Another court ruled that a nonfiduciary who unknowingly violated the prohibited-transaction rules by receiving money that his employer had wrongfully taken from the company's plan could be held liable for the violation as a party in interest and could also be ordered to make restitution to the plan. [Landwehr v Dupree, 1995 US App Lexis 35023 (9th Cir 1995)]

DOL has opined that an international union that owned less than 10 percent of the stock of a holding company whose wholly owned subsidiary administered welfare and pension plans that were managed by employers and local unions affiliated with the international union was not a party in interest solely because of the stock ownership. [PWBA Gen Info Ltr, June 3, 1993]

In another case, a plan that covered employees of corporation A loaned funds to corporation B that was formed by children of the majority owners of A. The plan received guarantees from two of the children; but, within a year of the loan transaction and with most of the loan unpaid, the plan released the guarantors from their guarantees. The court concluded that the guarantors were parties in interest since they were related to the majority owners of A and that the release of the guarantors was a direct or indirect transfer of plan assets to, or for the benefit of, a party in interest and, hence, a prohibited transaction. The release of the guarantees benefited the guarantors at the expense of the plan in that the plan no longer had the same security to enable it to collect on the outstanding amount of its loan and the guarantees were assets of the plan. [Reich v Polera Building Corp, 1996 US Dist Lexis 1365 (SD NY 1996)]

Q 20:4   How do the prohibited-transaction provisions under the Code differ from the prohibited-transaction provisions under ERISA?

The prohibited-transaction provisions under the Code are in many respects the same as those under ERISA. However, the Code uses the term "disqualified person" rather than "party in interest" (see Q 20:3) and does not require knowledge on the part of a fiduciary that the transaction or conduct is prohibited. The definitions of the term "party in interest" under ERISA and "disqualified person" under the Code are nearly identical, but the term "party in interest" is slightly more inclusive (i.e., the ERISA, but not the Code, definition includes counsel to and employees of the plan, and all employees—not only highly compensated employees (see Q 3:2)—of the employer). [IRC § 4975(e)(2)] A disqualified person is:

1. A fiduciary;

2. A person providing services to the plan;

3. An employer any of whose employees are covered by the plan;

4. An employee organization any of whose members are covered by the plan;

5. An owner, direct or indirect, of 50 percent or more of the employer or employee organization, whether a partnership, corporation, trust, or unincorporated enterprise;

6. A member of the family (i.e., spouse, ancestor, lineal descendant, or spouse of a lineal descendant) of any individual described in (1), (2), (3), or (5) above;

7. A corporation, partnership, or trust or estate of which (or in which) 50 percent or more is owned directly or indirectly by persons described in (1), (2), (3), (4), or (5) above;

8. An officer, director (or an individual having powers or responsibilities similar to those of officers or directors), a 10-percent-or-more shareholder, or a highly compensated employee (earning 10 percent or more of the yearly wages of an employer) of a person described in (3), (4), (5), or (7) above; or

9. A 10-percent-or-more partner or joint venturer of a person described in (3), (4), (5), or (7) above.

Plans that cover only a sole shareholder and/or the shareholder's spouse and plans that cover only partners are not subject to ERISA and, therefore, are not subject to ERISA's prohibited-transaction provisions. However, such plans are subject to the prohibited-transaction provisions of the Code. [DOL Reg §§ 2510.3-3(b), 2510.3-3(c)] In addition, the prohibited-transaction provisions under the Code apply to individual retirement accounts (IRAs), while ERISA's prohibited-transaction provisions do not. [IRC §§ 4975(c), 4975(e)(1)]

A partnership that received a loan from its defined contribution plans was a disqualified person because the general partners, who were fiduciaries of the plans, owned, directly or indirectly, 50 percent or more of the partnership. The general partners, husband and wife, each owned a one-third interest in the partnership. Under the attribution rules, each spouse was deemed to own two-thirds; thus, each spouse owned 50 percent or more of the partnership (see Q 20:3). [Davis v United States, 93-2047 (4th Cir 1995)]

Once a disqualified person enters into a prohibited transaction, the person remains liable for any excise taxes (see Q 20:5) until correction of the prohibited transaction is completed (see Q 20:6). A person's status at the time of the prohibited transaction determines whether the person has a relationship to the plan or the employer or related parties that fits within one of the definitions of disqualified person. One court reasoned that it would not serve the purpose of ERISA to allow an otherwise disqualified person to avoid liability by merely changing his legal status after he had engaged in the prohibited transaction. Thus, an individual who had terminated his employment and stockholdings in the employer before the prohibited transaction occurred should not be treated as a disqualified person; whereas, an individual who divested himself of stockholdings by the date of the prohibited transaction, but did not terminate employment until after the prohibited transaction occurred, was a disqualified person. [Rutland, 89 TC 1137 (1987)]

Q 20:5　What penalties may be imposed on a party in interest or disqualified person for engaging in a prohibited transaction?

Under the Code, a penalty tax equal to 5 percent of the amount involved in the transaction is imposed on the disqualified person (see Q 20:4) (other than a fiduciary acting solely in that capacity) for each year or part thereof that the transaction remains uncorrected. The amount involved is determined by considering the transaction to be separate and continuing prohibited transactions on the day it occurred and on the first day of each subsequent taxable year. Thus, the 5 percent penalty tax carries over from year to year *and* a new 5 percent penalty tax is imposed each year. Because it is *both* a continuing transaction and a new transaction each year, the penalty tax pyramids. An additional tax equal to 100 percent of the amount involved is imposed if the prohibited transaction is not timely corrected (see Q 20:6). [IRC §§ 4975(a), prior to amendment by SBA '96 § 1453(a), 4975(b); Davis v United States, 93-2047 (4th Cir 1995); Lambos, 88 TC 1440 (1987)] Moreover, parties who engage in a prohibited transaction can be liable, in addition to the penalty tax, for another penalty for failure to file Form 5330 (see Q 17:16). [Janpol, 102 TC 499 (1994); Janpol, 101 TC 518 (1993)]

The 5 percent penalty tax is increased to 10 percent for prohibited transactions occurring after August 20, 1996. [IRC § 4975(a), as amended by SBA '96 § 1453(a)] Because the amount involved is determined by considering the transaction to be separate and continuing prohibited transactions on the day it occurred and on the first day of each subsequent taxable year, it appears that, if the prohibited transaction first occurred prior to August 20, 1996 and continues into the next taxable year, the penalty tax will be 10 percent of the amount involved for such subsequent taxable year.

The amount involved in a prohibited transaction generally means the greater of the amount of money and the fair market value of the other property given, or the amount of money and the fair market value of the other property received. Fair market value must be determined as of the date on which the prohibited transaction occurs. If the use of money or other property is involved, the amount involved is the greater of the amount paid for the use or the fair market value of the use for the period for which the money or other property is used. In addition, as previously stated, transactions involving the use of money or other property are treated as giving rise to a prohibited transaction occurring on the date of the actual transaction plus a new prohibited transaction on the first day of each succeeding taxable year or portion of a succeeding taxable year that is within the taxable period. The taxable period is the period of time beginning with the date of the prohibited transaction and ending with the earliest of: (1) the date correction is completed; (2) the date of mailing of a notice of deficiency; or (3) the date on which the tax is assessed.

Example. A disqualified person borrowed money from a plan in a prohibited transaction. The fair market value of the use of the money and the actual interest on the loan is $1,000 per month. The loan was made on July 1, 1995 and repaid on December 31, 1996 (date of correction). The disqualified person's taxable year is the calendar year. On July 31, 1997, the disqualified person files a delinquent Form 5330 for the 1995 plan year and a timely Form 5330 for the 1996 plan year (see Q 17:16). No notice of deficiency with respect to the tax has been mailed to the disqualified person, and no assessment of the tax has been made before the time the disqualified person files Forms 5330.

When a loan is a prohibited transaction, the loan is treated as giving rise to a prohibited transaction on the date the transaction occurs, and an additional prohibited transaction occurs on the first day of each succeeding taxable year within the taxable period. Each prohibited transaction has its own separate taxable period that begins on the date the prohibited transaction occurred or is deemed to occur and ends on the date of the correction. The taxable period that begins on the date the loan occurs runs from July 1, 1995 (date of loan) through December 31, 1996 (date of correction). Therefore, in this example, there are two prohibited transactions, the first occurring on July 1, 1995 and the second occurring on January 1, 1996. A 5 percent tax is imposed on the amount involved for each taxable year or part thereof in the taxable period of each prohibited transaction.

The amount involved to be reported on Form 5330 filed for 1995 is $6,000 (6 months × $1,000 of interest). The amount of tax due is $300 (5% × $6,000). Any interest and penalties imposed for the delinquent filing of Form 5330 for 1995 will be billed separately to the disqualified person.

The taxable period for the second prohibited transaction runs from January 1, 1996 through December 31, 1996 (date of correction). Because there are two prohibited transactions with taxable periods running during 1996, the penalty tax is due for the 1996 taxable year for both prohibited transactions. The penalty tax to be reported on Form 5330 filed for 1996 includes both the prohibited transaction of July 1, 1995, with an amount involved of $6,000, resulting in a tax due of $300 (5% × $6,000) and the second prohibited transaction of January 1, 1996, with an amount involved of $12,000 (12 months × $1,000 of interest), resulting in a tax due of $600 (5% × $12,000). The total penalty tax for 1996 is $900 ($300 + $600).

If the loan is not repaid until December 31, 1997, it appears that the penalty tax to be reported on Form 5330 filed for 1997 will include the prohibited transaction of July 1, 1995, with an amount involved of $6,000, resulting in a tax due of $300 (5% × $6,000); the second prohibited transaction of January 1, 1996, with an amount involved of $12,000 (12 months × $1,000 of interest), resulting in a tax due of $600 (5% × $12,000); and a third prohibited transaction of January 1, 1997, with an amount involved of $12,000 (12 months × $1,000 of interest), resulting in a tax due of $1,200 (10% × 12,000). The total penalty tax for 1997 would be $2,100 ($300 + $600 + $1,200).

IRS has authority to abate the 5 percent penalty tax. [IRC § 4962]

Under ERISA, any fiduciary (see Q 19:1) who engages in a prohibited transaction is personally liable for any losses to the plan and must restore to the plan any profit made by the fiduciary through the use of the plan's assets. Also, the civil penalty imposed by DOL for certain breaches of fiduciary duty applies to prohibited transactions (see Q 19:27), but the penalty is reduced by any penalty tax imposed under Code Section 4975. [ERISA §§ 409(a), 502(l)] One court has ruled that the Double Jeopardy Clause of the United States Constitution does not bar the imposition of the civil penalty against a plan trustee who was convicted of embezzling funds from qualified retirement plans. [DOL v Rutledge, No. 92-7011 (11th Cir 1993)]

Q 20:6 How is a prohibited transaction corrected?

A prohibited transaction is corrected by undoing the transaction to the extent possible, but in any event placing the plan in a financial position no worse than the position it would have been in had the party in interest (see Q 20:3) acted under the highest fiduciary standards. [IRC § 4975(f)(5)]

If a prohibited transaction is not corrected during the correction period, an additional tax equal to 100 percent of the amount involved may be imposed. The term "correction period" means, with respect to a prohibited transaction, the period beginning on the date on which the prohibited transaction occurs and ending 90 days after the date of mailing of a notice of deficiency with respect to the 100 percent tax imposed on the prohibited transaction, extended by:

1. Any period in which a deficiency cannot be assessed under Section 6213(a), and

2. Any other period that IRS determines is reasonable and necessary to bring about correction of the prohibited transaction. [IRC § 4963]

If a prohibited transaction is corrected during the correction period, then the 100 percent tax imposed with respect to the prohibited transaction (including interest, additions to the tax, and additional amounts) will not be assessed, and if assessed will be abated, and if collected will be credited or refunded as an overpayment. The goal, if possible, is correction of the prohibited transaction, rather than the collection of the 100 percent tax. [IRC § 4961; IRS Litigation Guideline Memorandum (TL-83)]

A subsidiary that sold customer loans to its parent corporation's profit sharing plan was not entitled to an exemption from the 5 percent tax on prohibited transactions (see Q 20:5) because no class exemption (see Q 20:17) was available since the plan trustee was also the sole shareholder and president of the parent corporation and president of the subsidiary. The plan could not cure the prohibited transaction by retroactively appointing an unrelated co-trustee (see Q 20:15). However, the subsidiary was not assessed the 100 percent tax because the plan timely sold the loans. [Westoak Realty and Investment Co, Inc v Comm'r, 999 F 2d 308 (8th Cir 1993), *aff'g* 63 TCM 2502 (1992)]

A sole shareholder's transfer of assets from the employer's two retirement plans to the employer's checking account constituted a prohibited transaction. Furthermore, the sole shareholder's payments to former participants from the employer's assets and from his own funds did not correct the prohibited transaction because the plans were not restored to the same financial position they would have been in had the prohibited transaction not occurred. The employer and the shareholder were found jointly and severally liable for both the 5 percent and the additional 100 percent penalty taxes (see Q 20:5). [Ltr Rul 9316001]

One court ruled that a prohibited transaction corrected itself because it was an extremely successful investment, thereby enabling the disqualified persons (see Q 20:4) to avoid additional assessments of both the 5 percent tax and the 100 percent tax. [Zabolotny v Comm'r, 7 F 3d 774 (8th Cir 1993)] IRS disagrees that the prohibited transaction was self-correcting and has announced that although it will follow the decision in cases arising within the Eighth Circuit, it will not adhere to the decision on a nationwide basis. [*Non-acq,* 1994-1 CB 1; AOD 1994-004 (May 31, 1994)]

On occasion, a prohibited transaction is required to correct a prohibited transaction. For example, a sale of assets to a plan by the plan sponsor is a prohibited transaction (see Q 20:1); and if to undo the transaction the plan sponsor wishes to purchase those assets from the plan, that, too, is a prohibited transaction. Therefore, to undo the transaction, an exemption must be obtained (see Q 20:11). DOL has issued a class exemption (see Q 20:17) that covers transactions specifically authorized by DOL under a settlement agreement and thus permits the proposed corrective action to be taken without an individual exemption. To be exempt, the following conditions must be met:

1. The transaction (i.e., corrective action) must have been authorized by DOL pursuant to a settlement agreement and must follow a DOL investigation.

2. The transaction must be described in writing by the terms of the settlement agreement.

3. The parties in interest must give advance written notice of the transaction to all affected participants and beneficiaries at least 30 days before the settlement agreement.

4. The notice and method of distribution must be approved in advance by the DOL office that negotiated the settlement.

5. The notice must include a description of the transaction, the approximate date on which the transaction will occur, the address of the DOL office that negotiated the settlement agreement, and a statement informing participants and beneficiaries of their right to forward comments to the DOL office.

[PTCE 94-71 (59 FR 51216)]

Q 20:7 What is the Pension Payback Program?

DOL instituted a voluntary compliance program for employers that withheld contributions to a 401(k) plan (see Q 23:1) or other qualified retirement plan and failed to timely make the contributions to the plan. This Pension Payback Program provided a limited opportunity for employers to repay employee contributions, with earnings, and escape civil penalties that could be imposed by DOL. The program was coordinated with a proposed prohibited-transaction class exemption (see Q 20:17) that allowed employers to make restitution of employee contributions, plus earnings, to qualified retirement plans. Under the proposed class exemption, employers who withheld employee contributions, but did not timely deposit them, had until September 7, 1996 to make the corrected contributions. The exemption was not available to employers who engaged in egregious conduct, such as excessive withholding of contributions, or those who were under criminal investigation or maintained plans that were under examination by a federal agency. The program could be used to repay unpaid contributions withheld before April 6, 1996, but was not available for unpaid contributions withheld after that date. [Notice of Adoption of Voluntary Compliance Program for Restoration of Delinquent Participant Contributions (Feb 29, 1996); Proposed Prohibited Transaction Class Exemption (61 FR 9199); DOL News Rel 96-82 (March 6, 1996)]

IRS also announced that it would not impose prohibited-transaction excise taxes (see Q 20:5) that employers may otherwise owe for the late deposit of participant contributions as long as the employer participated in, and met the requirements of, the Pension Payback Program. As part of the announcement, IRS advised that it would treat the contributions as corrective annual additions (see Q 6:1) for the limitation year (see Q 6:16) in which the contributions should have been made. [Ann 96-15, 1996-13 IRB 22]

Q 20:8   May a plan purchase insurance to cover any losses to the plan resulting from a prohibited transaction?

Yes, a plan may carry insurance to protect itself from loss due to the conduct of a fiduciary (see Q 19:1). However, a plan cannot contain a provision relieving a fiduciary from liability for actions taken with respect to a prohibited transaction. [ERISA § 410]

Q 20:9   Are there any statutory exceptions to the prohibited-transaction provisions?

There are numerous statutory exceptions to the prohibited-transaction provisions. Some of the most common are as follows:

1. Loans made by a plan to a party in interest (see Q 20:3) who is a plan participant or beneficiary if such loans (1) are available to all participants and beneficiaries on a reasonably equivalent basis, (2) are not made available to highly compensated employees (see Q 3:2) in an amount greater than the amount made available to other employees, (3) are made in accordance with specific provisions regarding such loans set forth in the plan, (4) bear a reasonable rate of interest, and (5) are adequately secured. For more details on plan loans, see Qs 13:44 through 13:52.

2. Services rendered by a party in interest to a plan that are necessary for the establishment or operation of the plan if no more than reasonable compensation is paid. DOL has found no violation when a fiduciary received investment management fees from a plan. [DOL Op Ltrs 93-06A, 92-08A]

3. A loan to an employee stock ownership plan (ESOP), provided the loan is primarily for the benefit of plan participants and beneficiaries and the interest rate is not in excess of a reasonable interest rate (see Q 24:4).

4. Ancillary services provided by a federal or state supervised bank or similar financial institution that is a fiduciary (see Q 19:1) to the plan, provided (1) the bank or similar financial institution has adopted adequate internal safeguards to ensure that provision of the ancillary service is consistent with sound banking and financial practice, and (2) no more than reasonable compensation is paid for such services.

5. The acquisition or sale by a plan of qualifying employer securities (see Q 19:56) or the acquisition, sale, or lease by a plan of qualifying employer real property (see Q 19:55) if (1) the acquisition, sale, or lease is for adequate consideration; (2) no commission is charged; and (3) the restrictions and limitations of ERISA Section 407 are satisfied. In one case, disqualified persons (see Q 20:4) sold their interest in land including mineral rights to an ESOP (see Q 24:1). Because the mineral rights were not leased to the employer and, with respect to the land leased, such properties were not dispersed geographically, the land did not constitute qualifying employer real property and the exemption did not apply. [Zabolotny, 97 TC 385 (1991); but see Zabolotny v Comm'r, 7 F 3d 774 (8th Cir 1993), non-acq, 1994-1 CB 1; AOD 1994-004 (May 31, 1994)] In another case, a real estate transaction between a disqualified person and a profit sharing plan did not satisfy the requirements for an exemption because the property was never leased to the corporation sponsoring the plan or to an affiliate and was not composed of a substantial number of land parcels dispersed geographically. [Pearland Investment Co, 62 TCM 1221 (1991); see also Rutland, 89 TC 1137 (1987) and Lambos 88 TC 1440 (1987)]

[ERISA §§ 408(b), 408(e); IRC § 4975(d); DOL Op Ltr 90-04A]

DOL has opined that loans from plans that are made available to participants of different bargaining units only after their collective bargaining agreements are renegotiated will be treated as being available to participants on a reasonably equivalent basis, as long as all bargaining units approve the loan feature within a reasonable period of time. Therefore, the loans will be exempt from ERISA's prohibited-transaction provisions. [DOL Op Ltr 95-19A] DOL has also opined that a plan's agreement to settle a lawsuit against a service provider, arising out of the underlying service arrangement, could qualify for ERISA's exemption from the prohibited-transaction rules for plans that reasonably contract with parties in interest for services necessary for the operation of the plan, provided that certain conditions are satisfied. [DOL Op Ltr 95-26A]

Q 20:10 Can an employer's contribution of property to a qualified retirement plan be a prohibited transaction?

According to DOL and IRS, the contribution of property to a pension plan (e.g., defined benefit or money purchase pension plan; see Qs 2:3, 2:4) is a prohibited transaction because the contribution discharges the employer's legal obligation to contribute cash to the plan. On the other hand, if the plan is not a pension plan (e.g., profit sharing plan; see Q 2:6), the contribution of property is not a prohibited transaction because it is purely voluntary and does not relieve the employer of an obligation to make cash contributions to the plan. However, if the employer is obligated to contribute a percentage of net profit to a profit sharing plan, a contribution of property will be a prohibited transaction. No matter what type of plan is involved, a transfer of encumbered property will be treated as a sale or exchange (i.e., prohibited transaction). [DOL Interpretive Bulletin 94-3; DOL Op Ltrs 90-05A, 81-69A; see also Ltr Rul 9145006]

The United States Supreme Court, agreeing with both DOL and IRS, ruled that the transfer of unencumbered property to a defined benefit plan is a prohibited transaction because it constitutes a sale or exchange within the meaning of the Code. [Comm'r v Keystone Consolidated Ind, Inc, 113 S Ct 2006 (1993)]

Q 20:11 Can a party in interest obtain an exemption from the prohibited-transaction restrictions?

DOL may grant an exemption from the prohibited-transaction rules if the exemption is (1) administratively feasible, (2) in the interests of the plan and of its participants and beneficiaries, and (3) protective of the rights of the plan's participants and beneficiaries. [ERISA § 408(a); IRC § 4975(c)(2)]

IRS has granted DOL primary authority to issue rulings and regulations on, and grant exemptions from, the prohibited-transaction restrictions. A specific statement explaining how the proposed exemption satisfies the requirements listed above and detailed information concerning the proposed transaction are required. [DOL Reg §§ 2570.30–2570.52]

To comply with the provisions of a qualified domestic relations order (QDRO; see Q 30:1), a participant was permitted to make a loan to the plan because the plan contained insufficient liquid assets to effect a transfer to the IRA (see Q 26:1) of the alternate payee (see Q 30:3). [DOL Op Ltr 94-29A; PTCE 80-26 (45 FR 28545)]

DOL has provided, in a booklet, examples of common transactions for which exemptions are requested and has set forth the factors that DOL ordinarily would consider and that should be addressed by the applicants. [Exemption Procedures Under Federal Pension Law (DOL 1995)]

Example 1. Esskay-H Corporation sponsors a qualified retirement plan. The plan owns a parcel of real property that it wishes to sell to Esskay-H Corporation. These are the factors that DOL ordinarily would consider and that should be addressed by the applicants:

1. The plan pays no commissions or other expenses in connection with the sale.

2. If there is no generally recognized market for the property, the fair market value of the property must be determined by a qualified independent appraiser (see Q 20:12) and reflected in a qualified appraisal report (see Q 20:13). If there is a generally recognized market for the property, the fair market value of the property is the value objectively determined by reference to the price on such market on the date of the transaction.

3. If the party in interest (see Q 20:3) engaging in the transaction (or a related entity) caused the plan to invest in the property, then the plan should receive no less than the greater of its cost of acquiring and holding the property (e.g., original purchase price, insurance, real estate taxes) or the current fair market value of the property at the time of the sale, provided, however, that a purchase price in excess of such fair market value may not be required if the applicant provides sufficient documentation that the plan's original investment was consistent with ERISA's fiduciary standards, or the sale is made from a one-participant plan, an individual retirement account (IRA; see Q 26:1) not subject to Title I of ERISA, or an individual account or accounts in the plan and the affected participant voluntarily consents to the sale. In order to complete consideration of the application, DOL needs to know the background history of the property: from whom was it acquired (party in interest), date of acquisition, and price paid. Information must also be furnished concerning whether the property has been used by or leased to anyone, including parties in interest, since its acquisition by the plan. DOL also needs to know why the plan proposes to sell the property, and whether it has made any efforts to sell the property to an unrelated third party.

4. Where the sale of property eliminates an ongoing prohibited transaction (such as a prohibited lease to a party in interest), DOL will not grant an exemption unless the prohibited transaction is corrected (see Q 20:6) and the party in interest pays the appropriate excise taxes (see Q 20:5).

5. If the sale of the property will result in a contribution to the plan under the Code, the applicant must represent that such contribution will not result in any violation of the requirements for qualification or, if there would be a violation, that it will be remedied without any adverse consequences for the plan (see chapter 4).

Example 2. UU-Pee-H Corporation wishes to borrow $100,000 from its plan. These are the factors that DOL would ordinarily consider and that should be addressed by the applicants:

1. At the time the loan is made, the sum of the principal amount of the loan, plus the amount of all other plan loans and leases to the party in interest (or a related entity), does not exceed 25 percent of the aggregate fair market value of the assets of the plan (or self-directed account; see Qs 19:8, 19:57). The aggregate fair market value is determined as of the plan's most recent valuation date (no more than 12 months before the transaction). This 25 percent limitation is a continuing requirement that must be met throughout the term of the loan.

2. The exemption request must include a statement that the terms of the loan (e.g., interest rate, repayment schedule, duration of the loan) are not less favorable to the plan than those obtainable in an arm's length transaction between unrelated parties. The exemption request must also set forth the basis for this determination. To assure comparability with arm's-length loans, a statement from a third party in the business of lending money under similar circumstances may be required.

3. The loan is secured by collateral having a fair market value at the time the loan is made that is at least 150 percent of the principal amount of the loan if the collateral is real property, and at least 200 percent of the principal amount of the loan if the collateral is personal property or accounts receivable.

4. The collateral securing the loan has been appraised by a qualified independent appraiser who has issued a qualified appraisal report. The property securing the loan is insured against casualty loss in an amount not less than the amount of the outstanding principal of the loan (plus accrued but unpaid interest), and the plan is a named beneficiary of the policy.

5. The plan's security interest must be perfected in the manner required by applicable state law. For example, if recording is required for perfection, the security agreement must be recorded with the appropriate government officials.

6. Unless the loan is from a self-directed account or an IRA, a qualified independent fiduciary (see Q 20:14) who has the experience necessary to effectively review and monitor loans of this type:

   a. Reviewed the terms of the loan and compared the terms with the terms for similar loans between unrelated parties;

   b. Examined the plan's overall investment portfolio, considered the plan's liquidity and diversification requirements, in light of the proposed transaction, and determined whether the proposed transaction complies with the plan's investment objectives and policies;

   c. Stated that such fiduciary believes that the proposed transaction is in the best interests of the plan and its participants and beneficiaries and explained in detail the reasons for such opinion; and

   d. Agreed to monitor the loan and the conditions of the exemption on behalf of the plan throughout the term of the loan, taking all appropriate actions to safeguard the interests of the plan and has stated that such fiduciary will be given the authority to so act.

Example 3. Ceekayell Corporation sponsors a plan for its employees. Ceekayell Corporation wishes to sell a parcel of land to the plan which then will be leased back to it. These are the factors that DOL ordinarily would consider and that should be addressed by the applicants:

1. At the time when the sale and leaseback transactions are effectuated, the sum of the fair market value of the property, plus the amount of all other plan loans and leases to such party in interest (or a related entity), does not exceed 25 percent of the aggregate fair market value of the plan's assets. The aggregate fair market value is determined as of the plan's most recent valuation date (no more than 12 months before the transaction). This 25 percent limitation is a continuing requirement which must be met throughout the term of the lease.

2. Both the fair market value of the property acquired by the plan and the fair market rental value of the property to be leased to the party in interest have been appraised by a qualified independent appraiser and reflected in a qualified appraisal report.

3. The exemption request must include a representation that the terms of the lease (e.g., rent, duration, allocation of expenses) are not less favorable to the plan than those obtainable in an arm's-length transaction between unrelated parties. The exemption

request must also set forth the basis for this determination (e.g., comparable to the terms of similar leases between unrelated parties).

4. A qualified independent fiduciary who has the experience necessary to effectively review and monitor transactions of this type reviewed the terms of the purchase by the plan and of the lease and compared them with the terms of similar transactions involving unrelated parties and must have satisfied the other requirements of paragraph 6 of Example 2.

5. The lease must provide for periodic adjustments (no less frequently than every year) to the rents payable thereunder, so that the rents will be no less than the fair market rental value of the leased premises at the time of the adjustment. Generally, the initial rent will be the floor rental during the term of the lease, even if the fair market rental value has decreased. The adjustment may be made by using the consumer price index, or by retaining a qualified independent appraiser satisfactory to the qualified independent fiduciary. The qualified independent fiduciary will determine which method is appropriate for making such adjustment; the method need not be the same for all periods.

Example 4. A-Essell Corporation wishes to raise capital by issuing, to all holders of its stock, rights that will entitle such shareholders to acquire additional shares. A-Essell Corporation's profit sharing plan currently owns shares of stock of the corporation and, thus, is entitled to acquire these rights. This prohibited transaction involves stock rights that are not considered qualifying employer securities (see Q 19:56). Although the plan is a holder of stock of the employer that is a qualifying employer security, when a business decision is made to issue stock rights to all shareholders of the employer, the plan's acquisition and holding of such rights would be prohibited in the absence of an administrative exemption. These are the factors that DOL would ordinarily consider and that should be addressed by the applicants:

1. The plan's acquisition of the stock rights results from a business decision on behalf of the plan's sponsor in its capacity as issuer of the securities, rather than in its capacity as plan fiduciary.

2. The plan is treated in the same manner as any other holder of the affected class of securities.

3. If the plan provides for self-directed investment of the assets in each participant's account, all decisions with respect to the plan's acquisition, holding, and control of the rights are made by the individual plan participants.

4. With respect to plans other than those providing for self-directed accounts, a qualified independent fiduciary who is qualified to review and monitor transactions of this type:

   a. Examined the plan's overall investment portfolio, considered the plan's liquidity and diversification requirements, and considered the plan's investment objectives and policies in light of the receipt of the stock rights; and

   b. Will exercise the authority for all decisions regarding the acquisition, holding, and control of the rights, including the decision as to whether the plan should exercise or sell the rights acquired through the offering.

5. If the employer securities to be received upon exercise of the stock rights would otherwise violate ERISA Section 407, the exemption will include additional relief for the receipt and holding of such securities provided that the securities are disposed of by the plan within an agreed upon period of time from their receipt by the plan or another prohibited transaction exemption is obtained. There is a general prohibition on the acquisition of additional employer securities by a defined benefit plan (see Q 2:3) if the plan already holds qualifying employer securities up to the limit imposed under ERISA (see Q 19:54).

Example 5. Jayemkay Corporation sponsors a defined benefit plan and wishes to lease a parcel of land owned by the plan to use as a parking lot. These are the factors that DOL ordinarily would consider and that should be addressed by the applicants:

1. At the time the lease is entered into, the sum of the fair market value of the leased property, plus the amount of all other plan loans and leases to such party in interest (or a related entity) does not exceed 25 percent of the aggregate fair market value of the plan's assets, such aggregate fair market value to be determined as of the plan's most recent valuation date (but no more than 12 months before the transaction). This 25 percent limitation is a continuing requirement that must be met throughout the term of the lease.

2. The other factors set forth in Example 3 regarding the lease.

Q 20:12   Who is a qualified independent appraiser?

A qualified independent appraiser is any individual or entity that is qualified to serve in that capacity and that is independent of the party in interest (see Q 20:3) engaging in the transaction and its affiliates. The qualified independent appraiser must represent in writing its qualifications to serve in that capacity and must also detail any relationship it may have with the party in interest engaging in the transaction with the plan, or its affiliates, that could enable the party in interest or its affiliates to control or materially influence the actions of the appraiser, or vice versa.

If the property in question is real property, the appraiser should be an M.A.I., or a member of a similar sanctioning body. If the property is an asset other than real property, the appraiser must demonstrate that it has experience in valuing assets of that type.

If an individual is to serve as the qualified independent appraiser, less than 1 percent of the appraiser's annual income (generally measured on the basis of the prior year's income, but including amounts received for performing the appraisal) may be derived from the party in interest and its affiliates. If an entity is to serve as the qualified independent appraiser, less than 1 percent of the entity's annual income (generally measured on the basis of the prior year's income, but including amounts received for performing the appraisal) may come from business derived from the party in interest and its affiliates. [Exemption Procedures Under Federal Pension Law (DOL 1995)]

Q 20:13 What is a qualified appraisal report?

The appraisal must be in writing and set forth the methods used in determining the fair market value and the reasons used for the valuation in light of those methods. The appraisal should be no more than one year old; if an appraisal report older than one year is submitted, there must be a written update by the qualified independent appraiser (see Q 20:12) reaffirming the prior appraisal as of the date of the transaction. The document submitted by the qualified independent appraiser should describe the methodology used to determine the fair market value of the property and explain why such methodology best represented the fair market of the property. The appraisal must take into account any special benefit that the party in interest (see Q 20:3) may derive from the property such as the fact that it owns an adjacent parcel of property or would gain voting control over a company. [Exemption Procedures Under Federal Pension Law (DOL 1995)]

Q 20:14 Who is a qualified independent fiduciary?

A qualified independent fiduciary is any individual or entity that is qualified (i.e., knowledgeable as to its duties and responsibilities as an ERISA fiduciary (see Qs 19:1, 19:13) and knowledgeable as to the subject transaction) to serve in that capacity and that is independent of the party in interest (see Q 20:3) engaging in the transaction and its affiliates. Thus, for example, the independent fiduciary cannot be an affiliate of the person engaging in the transaction under the exemption.

The qualified independent fiduciary must represent in writing its quali- fications to serve in that capacity and must also detail any relationship it may have with the party in interest engaging in the transaction with the plan, or its affiliates, in order to determine whether such fiduciary may be subject to improper influence by a party to the transaction other than the plan, or whether such fiduciary has an interest that may conflict with the interests of the plan for which it acts. In addition, the qualified independent fiduciary must represent that it understands its ERISA duties and responsi- bilities in acting as a fiduciary with respect to the plan.

The general rule for individual exemption requests involving a financial institution serving as the qualified independent fiduciary is that less than 1 percent of the financial institution's deposits and less than 1 percent of its outstanding loans (both in dollar amounts) are attributable to the deposits and loans of the party in interest and its affiliates.

If an individual is to serve as the qualified independent fiduciary, less than 1 percent of the fiduciary's annual income (generally measured on the basis of the prior year's income) may be derived from the party in interest and its affiliates. Fixed, nondiscretionary retirement income would not be included for purposes of this test. If an entity is to serve as the qualified independent fiduciary, less than 1 percent of the entity's annual income (generally measured on the basis of the prior year's income) may come from business derived from the party in interest and its affiliates. While in certain cases DOL has permitted an independent fiduciary to receive as much as 5 percent of its annual income from the party in interest and its affiliates, these cases have involved unusual circumstances, and the general standard of independence remains a 1 percent test.

[Exemption Procedures Under Federal Pension Law (DOL 1995)]

Q 20:15   Can a prohibited-transaction exemption be granted retroactively?

Yes, but only under very limited circumstances. DOL generally will grant a retroactive exemption only if the applicant acted in good faith and the safeguards necessary for the grant of a prospective exemption were in place when the prohibited transaction occurred. DOL generally will not grant a retroactive exemption if the transaction resulted in a loss to the plan or was inconsistent with the general fiduciary responsibility provisions of ERISA Sections 403 and 404. [DOL Tech Rel 85-1]

Q 20:16   Can a prohibited-transaction exemption be used to benefit the owner of a closely held corporation?

Yes. Although the continued well-being of the plan is the prime consideration in qualifying for an exemption from the prohibited-transaction restrictions, the fact that the corporation or a shareholder also benefits from the transaction will not preclude the granting of an exemption. For example, it may be possible for the corporation to borrow from its cash-rich qualified retirement plan or to sell assets to the plan to improve the business's cash flow without incurring a penalty. As the following case histories illustrate, DOL is willing to approve an exemption even if the corporation or shareholder will reap a substantial benefit from the transaction with the qualified retirement plan.

Business financing: Leep Homes, a corporation engaged in building homes in California, received approval from DOL to enter into a sale-lease-back arrangement for its model homes with its profit sharing and defined benefit plans. Investments in the corporation's model homes were estimated to yield the plans a net return of 10 percent and would be limited to 25 percent of each plan's assets. Leep would buy the land and incur all development expenses. The purchase price was set at Leep's costs for building the homes.

An independent real estate investment advisor was to check out the model homes and have the power to reject any home offered to the plans. Leep was to pay all maintenance expenses and taxes. The plan's trustee was to have an option to sell the homes back to Leep at cost or fair market value, whichever was greater. Any offers to buy from third parties would be reviewed by the real estate advisor; Leep, however, would have a right of first refusal. Elwood J. Leep, sole stockholder of Leep Homes, was to personally guarantee the corporation's lease payments. [PTE 80-61]

Loan to corporation: DOL granted a New York law firm an exemption that permitted the corporation's defined benefit plan to make loans to the law firm on a recurring basis over a five-year period. The proceeds of the loans were to be used by the corporation to buy automobiles. [PTE 82-125]

Selling an unwanted asset: A doctor's professional corporation had a profit sharing plan that permitted him (as well as all other participants) to direct the investment of funds for his own account. Several years earlier, he had the plan invest in residential farmland. The land cost the plan $55,000 plus $30,000 spent on improvements. Since the land supported only subsistence agricultural activities and yielded little or no income, the land was not helping to build much of a nest egg for the doctor's retirement.

The plan received approval from DOL to sell the land to the doctor for $88,000, its then current value. After selling the land, which represented a substantial part of the assets in the doctor's account, the plan was able to invest in other assets yielding a much higher return. [PTE 80-38]

Sale by parties in interest to plan: DOL granted an exemption to participants in a medical corporation's profit sharing plan that enabled the participants to sell promissory notes to their respective individual plan accounts. The promissory notes, which were issued by an unrelated third party, were held by the participants and sold for cash to their respective fully vested individual plan accounts at fair market value. [PTE 82-143]

Lease of facilities: A professional corporation's profit sharing and money purchase pension plans acquired medical facilities and then sought to lease them to the plans' sponsor. Based on evidence that the terms of the lease were at least as favorable to the plans as those they could obtain from an unrelated party, the transaction was exempted. [PTE 83-124]

Loan to plan: DOL granted an exemption, on both a retroactive and a prospective basis, to loans by an insurance company to a qualified retirement plan of the maximum loan values of life insurance policies held by the plan on the lives of the plan participants. [PTE 86-13]

Q 20:17   What is a prohibited-transaction class exemption?

In addition to the statutory and administrative exemptions from the prohibited-transaction rules, DOL can grant a class exemption under which a party in interest or disqualified person (see Qs 20:3, 20:4) who meets the requirements of the class exemption will automatically be entitled to relief from the prohibited-transaction rules.

The following is a brief summary of some of the transactions for which prohibited-transaction class exemptions (PTCEs) have been issued. Many of these exemptions have detailed requirements that are not summarized here.

PTCE 96-23: PTCE 96-23 allows in-house asset managers (INHAMs) to engage in a wide variety of party in interest transactions without violating ERISA Section 406(a)(1)(A) (see Qs 20:1, 20:3). INHAMs are exempted from transactions in which either affiliates of the employer or the parent corporation are involved, so long as they are service providers to the plan. Transactions between an INHAM and individuals who are not service providers would still be prohibited. Thus, for example, an INHAM would still be prohibited from doing an individual transaction with the president of the plan sponsor. The transaction cannot be designed to specifically favor a party in interest.

An INHAM is an organization that is:

1. Either (a) a direct or indirect wholly owned subsidiary of an employer or of a parent organization of the employer, or (b) a membership nonprofit corporation, a majority of whose members are officers or directors of such an employer or parent corporation, and
2. A registered investment adviser that has under its management and control total assets attributable to plans maintained by affiliates of the INHAM in excess of $50 million.

The employer or parent corporation's plans must have at least $250 million in plan assets. The INHAM must have discretionary authority to negotiate the transactions, although the plan sponsor may retain the right to veto or approve transactions involving amounts of $5 million or more. [61 FR 15975]

PTCE 95-60: PTCE 95-60 allows (prospectively and retroactively to January 1, 1975) certain transactions engaged in by insurance company general accounts in which an employee benefit plan has an interest if certain specified conditions are met. An additional exemption is provided for plans to engage in transactions with persons who provide services to insurance company general accounts. The exemption also permits transactions relating to the origination and operation of certain asset pool investment trusts in which a general account has an interest as a result of the acquisition of certificates issued by the trust. The exemption affects participants and beneficiaries of employee benefit plans, insurance company general accounts, and other persons engaging in the described transactions. [60 FR 35925]

PTCE 94-20: PTCE 94-20 permits an employee benefit plan and a broker-dealer or bank or any affiliate that is a party in interest to enter into a foreign currency exchange transaction if the transaction is directed by an independent fiduciary and meets certain arm's-length tests. [59 FR 8022]

PTCE 93-33: PTCE 93-33 allows banks to offer services at reduced or no cost to persons who maintain IRAs, SEPs, and Keogh plans, provided that the services offered are the same as those offered by the bank in the ordinary course of business to customers who do not maintain such plans or IRAs (see Q 26:23). The exemption covers investments in securities for which market quotations are readily available, but excludes investments in securities offered by a bank exclusively to IRAs and Keogh plans.

PTCE 93-1: PTCE 93-1 permits banks, credit unions, and other financial institutions to give cash or other premiums as an incentive to open, or make contributions to, an IRA or Keogh plan (see Q 26:23).

PTCE 86-128: PTCE 86-128 allows broker-dealers who are plan fiduciaries to effect or execute securities transactions for a fee paid by the plan, if certain requirements are satisfied. The exemption also allows sponsors of pooled separate accounts and other pooled investment funds to use their affiliates to effect or execute securities transactions for such accounts if certain conditions are met. [51 FR 41686]

PTCE 84-14: PTCE 84-14 permits parties in interest to engage in various transactions involving plan assets that would otherwise be prohibited transactions if, among other conditions, the plan assets are managed by persons defined in the exemption as qualified professional asset managers (QPAMs). QPAMs can be banks, savings and loans, insurance companies, and investment managers that are regulated by applicable state or federal law and meet certain financial standards. A major condition of the exemption is the requirement that the QPAM maintain independence from the entities in which the plan invests by retaining full authority over the terms of transactions and investment decisions. [49 FR 9494, as amended by 50 FR 41430]

PTCE 81-6: Securities lending arrangements between a security owner and a broker-dealer may enable the owner to increase its return on its assets. PTCE 81-6 permits such arrangements provided neither the borrower nor any affiliate of the borrower has any discretionary authority with respect to the investment of plan assets involved in the transaction. [46 FR 7527, as amended by 52 FR 18754]

PTCE 79-13: PTCE 79-13 permits the acquisition and sale of shares of a closed-end mutual fund that is registered under the Investment Company Act of 1940 by an employee benefit plan covering only employees of the mutual fund, the investment advisor of the fund, or any affiliate thereof (whether or not the mutual fund, investment advisor, or affiliate is a fiduciary of the plan). [44 FR 25533]

PTCE 77-3: PTCE 77-3 permits the acquisition and sale of shares of an open-end mutual fund registered under the Investment Company Act of 1940 by an employee benefit plan covering only employees of the mutual fund, the investment advisor, or principal underwriter of the mutual fund, or any affiliate thereof (whether or not such mutual fund, investment advisor, principal underwriter, or affiliate is a fiduciary of the plan). [42 FR 18734]

PTCE 75-1: PTCE 75-1 permits certain transactions among employee benefit plans, broker-dealers, reporting dealers, and banks. Under this exemption, the prohibited-transaction provisions of ERISA will not apply to the purchase or sale of securities between a broker-dealer registered under the Securities and Exchange Act of 1934, an employee benefit plan during the existence of an underwriting or selling syndicate with respect to such securities, or a reporting dealer who is a market maker. The exemption also allows the extension of credit between a broker-dealer and a plan. [40 FR 50845]

DOL has proposed a class exemption from the prohibited transaction rules for certain prospective transactions that are substantially similar to transactions for which exemptions have been granted within the last five years. Consideration of these requests for exemption would be made under expedited procedures and as class exemptions, rather than as an individual exemption, if certain conditions are met. [60 FR 58376]

See Qs 14:16 and 14:17 for PTCEs regarding the purchase and sale of life insurance policies and Q 26:22 regarding application of the prohibited-transaction rules to IRAs.

Chapter 21

Termination of the Plan

To qualify for tax-favored status, an employer's qualified retirement plan must be permanent. Nevertheless, an employer may amend the plan, terminate the plan, or stop contributing to the plan. This chapter examines how these actions may affect plan participants and the plan status, and discusses the rules regarding the termination of qualified retirement plans.

Q 21:1 Once a qualified retirement plan is established, may the employer terminate it?

Yes. Although the employer must have intended the plan to be permanent, it may be terminated if the plan permits it. In addition, in the case of a defined benefit plan (see Q 2:3) covered by Title IV of ERISA (see Qs 21:9, 21:12, 21:13), the applicable termination rules must be satisfied.

Defined contribution plans (see Q 2:2) and defined benefit plans not covered by Title IV of ERISA are not subject to these rules. However, not less than 15 days before the effective date of a plan amendment that significantly reduces the rate of future benefit accruals, the plan administrator must provide a written notice to each participant and beneficiary in the pension plan. This written notice is called the Section 204(h) Notice, and IRS has issued temporary regulations with regard to this Notice (see Qs 9:29–9:36). [ERISA § 204(h)]

In one case, a plan covered by Title IV of ERISA was terminated by the adoption of a board resolution and not by a plan amendment (see Q 21:2). Since the employer complied with the requirements for a standard termination (see Q 21:17), the court ruled that the plan was not required to be amended to cease benefit accruals prior to its termination. [Aldridge v

Lily-Tulip, Inc Salary Retirement Plan Benefits Committee, 1994 US App Lexis 36300 (11th Cir 1994)]

See Q 21:65 regarding the application of ERISA Section 204(h) to a terminated plan covered by Title IV of ERISA.

Q 21:2 May a qualified retirement plan be terminated by a formal declaration of the plan sponsor's board of directors?

Although the plan sponsor's board of directors should adopt a resolution authorizing the termination of a qualified retirement plan, certain substantive and/or notice requirements must also be met to implement a plan termination (see Qs 21:1, 21:17, 21:19, 21:64, 21:67).

The date that a plan subject to PBGC jurisdiction is deemed to terminate can be no earlier than the date determined under applicable PBGC provisions (see Q 21:32). Where a plan sponsor never notified PBGC of its intention to terminate its defined benefit plan, PBGC properly established the date on which the sponsor ceased operations as the plan's involuntary termination date, not the date ten years earlier when the plan sponsor informed its employees that the plan was being terminated. [PBGC v Mize Company, Inc, No. 92-1351 (4th Cir 1993)] In the case of any other qualified retirement plan, the date of termination is generally established by the terms of the plan and by the actions of the company officials (e.g., a meeting of the board of directors). [ERISA § 4041(a)(1); Treas Reg § 1.411(d)-2; Phillips v Bebber, Nos. 89-2184 and 89-2189 (4th Cir 1990); Rev Rul 89-87, 1989-2 CB 81; Rev Rul 79-237, 1979-2 CB 190]

An independent plan administrator may terminate a pension plan despite the plan sponsor's desire to continue the plan. [Delgrosso v Spang and Co, No. 82-2672 (WD Pa 1991); ERISA § 4041(a)] Pension plan trustees who terminated a plan after a plan sponsor changed the plan's funding method acted in good faith and did not breach their fiduciary duties (see Qs 19:12, 19:13). [Morgan v Ind Drivers Assn Pension Plan, Nos. 91-1029, 91-1310 (10th Cir 1992)] In another case, a bankruptcy trustee who assumed the position of the employer-debtor was ordered by the court to terminate the company's defined benefit plan. Upon reconsideration, the court ruled that only the plan administrator had authority to terminate the plan and, because the employer-debtor was not the plan administrator, the bankruptcy trustee did not have this authority. [In re Esco Mfg Co, No. 93-1681 (5th Cir 1995)]

However, IRS has declared that a termination will not occur if plan assets are not distributed as soon as administratively feasible, even if the plan has been terminated in accordance with Title IV of ERISA (see Q 21:67).

Q 21:3   Which factors may cause a qualified retirement plan to be terminated?

A defined benefit plan covered by the Title IV program (see Qs 21:12, 21:13) will be considered to be terminated only if the conditions and procedures prescribed by PBGC are satisfied (see Qs 21:2, 21:17, 21:19).

Whether a defined contribution plan (see Q 2:2) is terminated is generally a question to be determined with regard to all the facts and circumstances in a particular case. For example, a plan may be terminated when, in connection with the winding up of the company's trade or business, the company begins to discharge its employees (see Q 21:5). However, a plan is not terminated merely because a company consolidates or replaces that plan with a comparable plan (see Q 21:6). [Treas Reg § 1.401-6(b)] Similarly, a plan is not terminated merely because the company sells or otherwise disposes of its trade or business if the acquiring company continues the plan as a separate and distinct plan of its own or consolidates or replaces that plan with a comparable plan.

Q 21:4   What is the effect of a plan termination on a participant's accrued benefit?

A qualified retirement plan must provide that (1) upon its full or partial termination, or (2) in the case of a profit sharing plan upon complete discontinuance of contributions under the plan "the rights of all affected employees to benefits accrued to the date of such termination, partial termination, or discontinuance, to the extent funded as of such date, or the amounts credited to the employees' accounts, are nonforfeitable" (see Q 9:14). [IRC § 411(d)(3)]

The practical effect of a plan termination, therefore, is that each affected participant becomes 100 percent vested in the participant's accrued benefit (see Q 9:2) as of the date of termination if the plan has sufficient assets to cover the benefit. In one case, where there was a partial termination (see Q 21:5) of an employee stock ownership plan (ESOP; see Q 24:1), the court held that the terminated participants were not required to be vested in unallocated assets held in a suspense account because these assets were not accrued benefits. [Rummel v Consolidated Freightways, Inc, 1992 US Dist Lexis 15144 (ND Cal 1992)]

Generally, a participant who is partially vested need not become 100 percent vested upon termination of the plan if the participant separates from service and is paid the vested accrued benefit prior to the date of termination. However, a partially vested participant who terminates service, is not paid the vested accrued benefit, and does not incur a one-year break in service (see Q 5:10) prior to the date of termination must become 100 percent vested upon termination of the plan. Some IRS district offices have interpreted the above rule to require that all nonvested former participants with breaks in service of less than five years who have not been paid their vested accrued benefits be fully vested (see Q 9:16). [IRC §§ 411(a)(6)(B), 411(a)(6)(C); Penn v Howe-Baker Eng'rs, Inc, No. 89-2257 (5th Cir 1990); GCM 39310 (Nov 29, 1984)]

In one case, the court upheld a plan administrator's decision to deny full credit to employees who were laid off prior to a plan's termination. The court reasoned that "a person is unaffected by a plan's termination unless either he or she was employed by the plan-sponsoring employer at the time of the plan's termination or his or her discharge was directly linked to the plan's termination." [Bayer v Holcroft/Loftus, Inc, 769 F Supp 225 (ED Mich 1991)]

An issue that has not been clearly resolved by IRS involves whether converting a money purchase pension plan (see Q 2:4) to a profit sharing plan (see Q 2:6) requires full vesting of benefits. According to an IRS Technical Advisor, the conversion is not a termination and, therefore, full vesting is not required. *The foregoing was in answer to a question posed at a 1995 conference and should not be construed as a formal ruling.*

See Q 21:5 regarding partial terminations and Q 21:6 regarding conversions.

Q 21:5   What is a partial termination?

Generally, whether or not a partial termination of a qualified retirement plan has occurred will be determined on the basis of all the facts and circumstances. Under applicable regulations, a partial termination may be found to have occurred when a significant group of employees covered by the plan is excluded from coverage, as a result of either an amendment to the plan or their discharge by the employer. Similarly, a partial termination may be held to have occurred when benefits or employer contributions are reduced or the eligibility or vesting requirements under the plan are made less liberal. However, according to IRS, a reduction in future benefit accruals or employer contributions, or a situation in which the eligibility or vesting requirements under the plan are made less liberal, does not necessarily constitute a partial termination. Instead, in order to bring about a partial termination in such a situation: (1) a potential for reversion (see Q 21:53) must have been created or increased, (2) prohibited discrimination has occurred or the potential for discrimination has been increased (see Q 4:9), and/or (3) situations similar to those noted above are found. [IRS Document 6678(4-81), Explanation for Worksheet, Form 6677, Plan Termination Standards] If a partial termination of a qualified retirement plan occurs, the provisions of the Code and regulations apply only to the part of the plan that is terminated. [Treas Reg §§ 1.401-6(b)(2), 1.411(d)-2(b)(3)]

Example 1. An amendment to a defined benefit plan that eliminated an after-tax contributory feature resulting in the loss of contributory benefits for certain participants did not create a partial termination. Although between 29 percent and 39 percent of all plan participants suffered a decrease in future benefit accruals following the amendment, a determination of whether a defined benefit plan ceases or decreases future benefit accruals under the plan must be made by reference to the plan as a whole and not to a part of the plan. Since the impact of the amendment on the entire plan was to increase future benefit accruals in the aggregate for all plan participants, there was no reduction in future benefit accruals. The court found that there was no partial termination because there was no decrease in future benefit accruals as a result of the amendment and no increase in the potential for a reversion to the employer. [Gluck v Unisys Corp, No. 90-1510 (ED Pa 1995)]

Example 2. A partial termination occurred when the employees of two subsidiaries became participants in a union plan, were no longer active participants in the company's plan, and the number of participants decreased to 958 from 1,564. [Ltr Rul 9523025]

Example 3. A profit sharing plan was not partially terminated where layoffs due to a sharp decline in the company's business resulted in a 19.85 percent reduction in the number of plan participants. The facts did not show employer abuse, bad faith, or misconduct (i.e., no reversion was created, the financial health of the plan was not adversely affected, and there was no discrimination in favor of highly compensated participants). Furthermore, the employer rehired a significant number of terminated employees in succeeding years. [Halliburton Co, 100 TC 216 (1993), aff'd, unpublished opinion (5th Cir 1994); see also, Baker, 68 TCM 48 (1994)(same record as Halliburton)] However, a partial termination did occur when a company sold most of its operating assets and did not make continued employment available to 83 percent of its employees. [Collingnon v Reporting Services Co, 1992 US Dist Lexis 10070 (CD Ill 1992)]

Example 4. Where between 40 and 70 percent of employees were laid off after completion of a project, and the union pension plan defined "partial termination" as a layoff of more than 20 percent of employees, the terminated employees became 100 percent vested. [Duncan v Northern Alaska Carpenters Retirement Fund, No. 90-133-DA (DC Or 1992)] Similarly, a partial termination occurred when a multiemployer plan experienced two reductions of over 50 percent in participation. [Thayer v Alaska Teamster-Employer Pension Trust, No. A90-147 (DC Alas 1992)]

Example 5. An employer discharged 132 of the 395 employees participating in its qualified retirement plan. Of the discharged employees, 65 were not fully vested. The court originally held that no partial termination occurred because the 65 nonvested discharged participants represented only 16.4 percent of all 395 participants. Upon reconsideration, the court held that all discharged plan participants must be taken into account, including vested participants. Thus, a partial termination occurred because 33.4 percent of all plan participants, a significant group, were discharged. [Weil v Retirement Plan Administrative Committee of the Terson Co, Inc, 913 F 2d 1045 (2d Cir 1991)]

Example 6. Two major oil companies (Gulf and Chevron) merged their operations in 1984 and merged their pension plans in 1986. The merger of operations resulted in a partial termination with respect to the significant number of Gulf plan participants (almost 10,000) who were discharged (prior to the merger of the plans) because of the merger of operations. A second partial termination occurred with respect to Gulf plan participants who were still employed by Chevron at the time of the merger of the plans. That merger resulted in a substantial reduction in future benefit accruals to those employees, thereby increasing the potential reversion to Chevron upon termination of the plan. [In re Gulf Pension Litigation, No. 86-4365 (SD Tex 1991)]

Example 7. A partial termination of a qualified retirement plan occurred when the employer's business was closed and 12 of the 15 participating employees were discharged upon refusing the opportunity to transfer to the employer's new business location. [Rev Rul 73-284, 1973-1 CB 139; see also Rev Rul 81-27, 1981-1 CB 228]

Example 8. In two successive years, an employer experienced reductions in its workforce of 34 percent and 51 percent, respectively, as a result of adverse economic conditions. The Tax Court ruled that, based on all the facts and circumstances, a partial termination occurred in each year. [Tipton & Kalmbach, Inc, 83 TC 154 (1984)]

Example 9. A corporation maintaining pension and profit sharing plans operated two divisions: one manufactured paint, and the other produced other types of wall coverings. As a result of a split-off of one of the divisions to a new corporation, 16 employees (representing 14.7 percent of the participating employees) were transferred and were no longer eligible to participate in the original corporation's plans. In reviewing these facts, a court held that there was not a "significant percentage" of participants affected by the corporation's actions and that a partial termination of the plans did not occur. [Babb v Olney Paint Co, 764 F 2d 240 (4th Cir 1985); see also Kreis v Charles O. Townley, MD & Assocs, PC, 833 F 2d 74 (6th Cir 1987)]

If a determination letter on the continued qualification of the plan after a possible partial termination is desired, Form 5300 (see Q 15:7) should be filed with IRS.

Q 21:6 Does the adoption of a new qualified retirement plan to replace another plan result in a termination of the original plan?

Not necessarily. A qualified retirement plan is not considered to be terminated if it is either replaced by or converted into a comparable plan. For this purpose, a comparable plan is defined as a qualified retirement plan covered by the same limitations on deductions as the original plan. Since stock bonus plans, ESOPs, and profit sharing plans are generally covered by the same limitations on deductions, these plans are considered to be comparable (see Q 21:4). [Treas Reg §§ 1.381(c)(11)-1(d)(4), 1.401-6(b)(1)]

On the other hand, a defined benefit plan covered by Title IV is considered to be terminated if an amendment is adopted to convert the plan to a defined contribution plan, such as a profit sharing plan, an ESOP, or a stock bonus plan. However, the amendment will not take effect unless and until the requirements for a standard or distress termination under Title IV are satisfied (see Qs 21:17, 21:19). [ERISA § 4041(e)]

Furthermore, an employer's transfer of excess assets from its terminated defined benefit plan to its defined contribution plan constitutes a reversion resulting in taxable income and excise tax, followed by a contribution to the defined contribution plan (see Qs 21:53, 21:56, 21:57). [Lee Eng'g Supply Co, Inc, 101 TC 189 (1993); Notice 88-58, 1988-1 CB 546; GCM 39744 (July 14, 1988)]

Q 21:7 Can termination of a qualified retirement plan affect its tax-favored status for earlier years?

Yes. The termination of a plan, or the complete discontinuance of contributions to a profit sharing plan, can result in the retroactive disqualification of the plan, causing the disallowance of tax deductions for the employer. This will depend on whether the plan was intended as a permanent program for the exclusive benefit of employees or a temporary device to set aside funds for the benefit of highly compensated employees (see Q 3:2), and whether the plan was discriminatory in operation.

Generally, IRS will not treat the termination as a device to benefit highly compensated employees (see Q 4:19) if the termination is caused by a change in circumstances that would make it financially impractical to continue the plan. When termination of the plan occurs within a few years of its adoption, the reasons for termination will be examined closely. IRS will assume the plan was not temporary if the termination is for a "valid business reason" or on account of "business necessity."

Form 5310, Application for Determination for Terminating Plan, provides some insight into IRS's views as to what reasons for plan termination it considers valid, notwithstanding the presumed permanence of the plan. The listed reasons include:

- A change in ownership by merger
- The liquidation or dissolution of the employer
- A change in ownership by sale or transfer
- The existence of adverse business conditions
- The adoption of a new plan

If the plan termination is due to adverse business conditions, IRS requires an explanation of why such adverse conditions require the plan's termination.

When the termination occurs after ten years of active operation, IRS will usually not challenge the plan on these grounds even though a valid business reason for the termination is lacking. [Rev Rul 72-239, 1972-1 CB 107]

A qualified retirement plan will not satisfy Section 401(a)(4) if the plan's termination discriminates significantly in favor of highly compensated employees (see Qs 3:2, 4:19). The determination of discrimination is based on all relevant facts and circumstances. [Treas Reg § 1.401(a)(4)-5(a)]

Q 21:8   Is there a limit on the annual amount that a pension plan may pay to certain participants?

With respect to distributions commencing in a plan year beginning on or after January 1, 1994, a defined benefit plan (and a money purchase pension plan with an accumulated funding deficiency; see Q 8:18) must provide that the annual payments to an employee are restricted to an amount equal to a straight life annuity that is the actuarial equivalent of the accrued benefit and other benefits to which the employee is entitled under the plan (other than a Social Security supplement) plus the amount an employee would be entitled to receive under a Social Security supplement. The restrictions apply to distributions to all highly compensated employees (see Q 3:2) and highly compensated former employees. However, in any given year, the plan may limit the preceding restricted group to those 25 highly compensated employees whose compensation was the highest.

The above restrictions are not applicable if:

1. The distribution to a restricted highly compensated employee is less than 1 percent of plan assets after the payment of the benefit;

2. The value of the plan assets is at least 110 percent of the plan's current liabilities; or

3. The value of the benefit payable to the restricted highly compensated employee does not exceed $3,500 (the amount described in Section 411(a)(11)(A)).

Distributions in excess of the limit will be permitted if the participant enters into an escrow agreement.

[Treas Reg § 1.401(a)(4)-5(b); Rev Rul 92-76, 1992-2 CB 76]

A repayment agreement that was part of an IRA arrangement into which restricted distributions from a defined benefit plan were transferred satisfied the repayment (escrow) requirements where the participant agreed to repay the restricted amount if the plan terminated and repayment was necessary. [Ltr Rul 9514028]

Prior to the issuance of regulations under Section 401(a)(4), a plan that substantially funded benefits for older, higher-paid employees at a more rapid pace than for younger, lower-paid employees (e.g., a defined benefit plan) was limited in the amount that it could pay out. [Treas Reg § 1.401-4(c)]

Similar to the current rules, the full benefit was allowed to be paid if there was adequate provision for repayment of any part of the distribution representing the restricted portion. A participant, part of the restricted group, who was to receive a large distribution, agreed to provide the plan trustee with a security agreement and letter of credit to fund his obligation to repay the plan if necessary. The agreement did not violate the restriction. [Rev Rul 81-135, 1981-1 CB 203; Ltr Rul 9210037] An escrow agreement imposed on a highly compensated employee's IRA as a result of a pre-1994 distribution could be released where the value of plan assets exceeded 110 percent of the plan's liabilities. [Ltr Ruls 9419040, 9417031]

Q 21:9   What is Title IV of ERISA?

Title IV of ERISA established the rules regarding the termination of many defined benefit plans (see Q 2:3). In addition, it established an insurance program to guarantee that participants and beneficiaries will receive certain pension benefits promised under an employer's defined benefit plan if the plan does not have sufficient assets to cover certain benefits in the event of the plan's termination. The program was designed to be self-financed, funded with premiums paid by sponsors of covered plans.

Q 21:10   What is the Pension Benefit Guaranty Corporation (PBGC)?

ERISA established PBGC as a wholly owned government corporation to administer the termination rules and to establish the mechanism for insuring benefits under Title IV. [ERISA § 4002]

Q 21:11   What are the Single Employer Pension Plan Amendments Act, the Pension Annuitants Protection Act, and the Retirement Protection Act of 1994?

The Single Employer Pension Plan Amendments Act (SEPPAA) was enacted as a sweeping reform of the single-employer defined benefit plan termination rules of Title IV. It was designed to bolster an increasingly overburdened plan termination insurance program and to correct a system that, in some instances, encouraged employers to terminate a plan, avoid their obligations to pay benefits, and shift unfunded pension liabilities to PBGC.

The Pension Annuitants Protection Act (PPA '94; see Q 1:18) was designed to protect the fiscal integrity of the Title IV program, for example, by increasing premium rates and limiting the circumstances in which an employer may terminate its defined benefit plan (see Q 2:3).

The Retirement Protection Act (RPA '94; see Q 1:19) includes provisions to strengthen funding in underfunded plans, remove impediments to funding certain plans, phase out the PBGC variable-rate premium cap (see Q 21:14), and prohibit benefit increases during bankruptcy proceedings.

As a result of SEPPAA, PPA '94, and RPA '94, a defined benefit plan covered by Title IV of ERISA may be voluntarily terminated (i.e., terminated by the plan administrator) only if the conditions for either a standard or a distress termination are satisfied (see Qs 21:17, 21:19). In addition, these laws expanded the employer's liability upon termination if the plan is underfunded (see Q 21:52).

Q 21:12 What pension plans are insured by PBGC?

To be entitled to coverage, the plan must be a defined benefit plan (see Q 2:3). In addition, the plan must:

1. Have been in effect for at least one year;

2. Be maintained by an employer engaged in commerce or in an industry or activity that affects commerce, or by a labor organization that represents employees who are engaged in commerce or in activities affecting commerce; and

3. Be a qualified pension plan, or have been operated in practice as a qualified pension plan for the five plan years prior to the termination.

[ERISA § 4021(a)]

In one case, the court ruled that an employer was not liable to the PBGC for its terminated pension plan's underfunding because the plan was not qualified and, thus, was not insured by PBGC. [PBGC v Artra Group Inc, No. 90 C 5358 (ND Ill 1991)]

PBGC has stated that with respect to defined benefit plans that terminated prior to September 26, 1980 and were not amended to comply with the minimum vesting schedules, benefits are guaranteed only to the extent that they were vested under the express terms of the plan. [Policy Submission of Board of Directors of PBGC, Jan 14, 1993; also see Page v PBGC, 968 F 2d 1310 (DC Cir 1992)]

Q 21:13 Are any qualified defined benefit plans exempt from PBGC coverage?

Excluded from plan termination insurance coverage are defined benefit plans (see Q 2:3) that are established and maintained:

1. For government employees (or to which the Railroad Retirement Acts apply);

2. For church employees, unless the plan elects under Section 410(d) to be covered and has notified PBGC that it wishes to have this section of the law apply to it;

3. Outside the United States for nonresident aliens;

4. Exclusively for one or more substantial owners (i.e., the sole owner of the trade or business, a more-than-10 percent partner, or a more-than-10 percent shareholder); or

5. By professional service employers that at no time have had more than 25 active participants.

In addition to the aforementioned plans, all defined contribution plans (e.g., profit sharing, money purchase pension, ESOPs, stock bonus) as well as certain nonqualified plans are excluded from Title IV coverage. [ERISA § 4021(b)]

A defined benefit plan becomes exempt as exclusively for the benefit of the substantial owner when (1) all nonowner employees have retired and received their plan benefits and (2) the owner remains as the only plan participant. [PBGC Op Ltr No. 90-6]

Q 21:14 What must plan sponsors pay as an insurance premium to PBGC?

The basic annual premium rate is $19 for each participant in a single-employer pension plan during the plan year. [ERISA § 4006(a)(3)(A)(i)] In addition, each plan year, a variable-rate component must be paid for underfunded plans equal to $9 for every $1,000 of unfunded vested benefits, divided by the number of participants for whom premiums are being paid as of the close of the preceding plan year. For plan years beginning prior to July 1, 1994, the variable-rate premium could not exceed $53 per participant and, therefore, the total premium amount for each participant could not exceed $72. RPA '94 eliminated the cap on the variable-rate premium; but, under a special transition rule, the cap was phased out over a three-year period. For plan years beginning on or after July 1, 1996, there is no maximum limit on the amount of the variable-rate premium. The variable-rate component does not apply to a plan if, for the prior plan year, contributions were made in an amount not less than the full funding limitation (see Q 8:16). [ERISA § 4006(a)(3)(E); PBGC Reg §§ 4006.3, 4006.5]

> **Example.** For the plan year beginning September 1, 1996, and ending August 31, 1997, a defined benefit plan with 100 participants has unfunded vested benefits of $1,000,000. For purposes of computing the variable-rate premium, the amount based on the unfunded vested benefits is $9,000 [($1,000,000 ÷ $1,000) × $9]. The variable rate for the plan is $90 per participant ($9,000 ÷ 100). The total premium due for this year is $109 per participant. This consists of the $19 flat rate and the full $90 variable-rate portion.

Generally, for each plan year for which a variable-rate premium is payable, plan participants must be notified of the plan's funded status and the limits on PBGC's guarantee. A plan that is a least 90 percent funded for either the current or prior plan year is generally exempt from having to provide the notice. Also exempt are plans that meet certain transition or other special rules, and most new and newly covered plans. The notice is due two months after the Form 5500 series return/report is due (including extensions) (see Q 17:5). The plan administrator (see Q 16:1) must certify on Schedule A to PBGC Form 1 (see Q 17:20) whether the notice was issued as required or was not required to be issued. If the required notice was not issued or was issued late, the plan administrator must provide an explanation. PBGC has issued a sample notice that when completed satisfies the requirements of PBGC regulations. [ERISA § 4011; PBGC Reg §§ 4011.1–4011.11, including Appendices A and B; PBGC Tech Update 96-5]

PBGC has issued an opinion letter stating that, with respect to a terminated pension plan, it would hold an individual who acted as plan administrator personally liable for unpaid PBGC insurance premiums, as well as penalties and interest on the premiums, where the plan sponsor has ceased operations, gone bankrupt, and been liquidated. [PBGC Letter; PBGC Reg § 4041.27; preamble to PBGC Reg § 2617.28 prior to renumbering]

For multiemployer plans—that is, plans maintained under a collective bargaining agreement to which two or more employers contribute—the annual PBGC premium is $2.60 per participant (see Q 25:2). [ERISA § 4006(a)(3)(A)(iii)]

The total amount of premiums is determined on the basis of the number of plan participants (see Q 21:15).

Q 21:15 How is the number of participants determined for insurance premium purposes?

The participant count is made as of the last day of the prior plan year, except that, for a new plan, the count is made as of the date on which the plan becomes subject to PBGC jurisdiction. [PBGC Reg §§ 4006.3, 4006.5(d)]

The following categories of individuals are considered participants:

- All individuals accruing benefits or retaining or earning credited service under the plan
- Former employees with vested rights to either immediate or deferred benefits
- Retirees receiving or eligible to receive benefits
- Deceased participants whose beneficiaries are receiving benefits
- Any other "participants" as defined under the plan

Certain individuals to whom an insurance company has made an irrevocable commitment to pay benefits are not considered participants. The number of participants in the above categories should equal the total number reported on the Form 5500 series return/report (see Q 17:1) for the plan for the prior plan year. [PBGC Reg § 4006.2]

Q 21:16 Must PBGC be notified when certain significant events affecting a single-employer defined benefit plan occur?

Yes. The plan administrator (see Q 16:1) or contributing sponsor may be required to notify PBGC within 30 days after the plan administrator or sponsor knows or has reason to know of a reportable event. ERISA Section 4043 and PBGC regulations include a list of reportable events.

The 30-day notice is always required for the following:

- Inability to pay benefits when due
- Failure to meet minimum funding standards (see Q 8:1) if the present value of unfunded vested benefits equals or exceeds $250,000 (unless PBGC Form 200 is filed; see Q 17:26)
- Bankruptcy, liquidation, or dissolution of a plan sponsor
- Certain transactions involving a change of employer

Also by regulation, PBGC has waived the notice requirement for those reportable events that would have minimal impact on the plan, the employer, or PBGC, and for those reportable events about which IRS or DOL is required by ERISA to notify PBGC. Examples of these events include:

- Plan disqualification
- Decrease in benefits
- DOL finding of an ERISA violation
- Plan merger, consolidation, or transfer
- Certain corporate reorganizations
- A determination by IRS that there has been a complete or partial termination

RPA '94 added four new reportable events that apply when:

1. As a result of an event such as a sale of a subsidiary, a controlled group member ceases to be a member of the controlled group.
2. A contributing sponsor or member of a contributing sponsor's controlled group liquidates.
3. In any 12-month period, a contributing sponsor or controlled group member (a) declares an extraordinary dividend, or (b) redeems 10 percent or more of the total combined voting power or total value of shares of all classes of all stock of the entire controlled group.

4. In any 12-month period, 3 percent or more of a plan's benefit liabilities are transferred to a plan maintained by a sponsor who is outside the controlled group.

In the case of events that are both new reportable events and existing reportable events, the existing waivers will not apply. For example, on May 21, 1996, Plan A transferred assets and benefit liabilities to Plan B, a plan maintained by a sponsor outside Plan A's controlled group. The liabilities transferred represent 10 percent of Plan A's benefit liabilities. A reportable event occurred, but PBGC waived the notification requirement. [PBGC Reg § 4043.19] The waiver, however, does not apply because this is a new reportable event.

In certain circumstances, the contributing sponsor (but *not* the plan administrator) must notify PBGC at least 30 days *before* the occurrence of a new reportable event. This advance notice applies only to privately held companies that are members of a controlled group that maintain plans with aggregate unfunded vested benefits of more than $50 million and an aggregate funded vested benefit percentage of less than 90 percent.

PBGC has advised that it will not impose a penalty for failure to satisfy the new reportable event requirements if (1) a plan is fully funded and (2) the notice is due after the event. [ERISA §§ 4043(a), 4043(b), 4043(c); PBGC Reg § 4043; PBGC Tech Update 95-3] However, PBGC has advised that failure to provide advance notice of a reportable event will generally result in a penalty of $1,000 per day. [PBGC Statement of Policy, 60 FR 36837 (July 18, 1995)]

PBGC Form 10-SP, Optional Reportable Event Form for Small Plans, may be used by defined benefit plans with fewer than 500 participants to notify PBGC of reportable events. Rather than submitting extensive documentation, contributing sponsors and plan administrators are able to check a box on this one-page form. [PBGC News Release 95-43; Instructions to PBGC Form 10-SP]

Q 21:17   What is a standard termination?

A single-employer defined benefit plan may be voluntarily terminated under Title IV's standard termination procedures only if it is determined that when the final distributions are made, the assets of the plan will be sufficient to cover all benefit liabilities (see Q 21:18) as of the termination date. In addition:

1. The plan administrator (see Q 16:1) must provide a 60-day advance notice of termination to affected parties (see Qs 21:29, 21:33);

2. A notice containing specified information (completed by the plan administrator), together with an enrolled actuary's certification, must be filed with PBGC (see Q 21:34);

3. A notice containing required information must be provided to participants and beneficiaries regarding benefits to be paid (see Q 21:35); and

4. PBGC must not have issued a notice of noncompliance stating that it has reason to believe that the standard termination requirements have not been met or that the plan does not have sufficient assets for benefit liabilities (see Q 21:37).

[ERISA § 4041(b)]

Q 21:18   What are benefit liabilities?

Benefit liabilities under a single-employer defined benefit plan are defined as "the benefits of employees and their beneficiaries under the plan (within the meaning of § 401(a)(2) of the Internal Revenue Code of 1986)." [ERISA § 4001(a)(16)]

If a plan does not have sufficient assets for benefit liabilities, the plan sponsor may consider making a contribution to the plan. Also, a contributing sponsor, or a member of a controlled group (see Q 5:33) of a contributing sponsor, may make a commitment to contribute any additional sums necessary to make the plan sufficient. [PBGC Reg § 4041.7(a)] However, because of the rules relating to deductibility of contributions and funding requirements, the contribution may not be deductible. In this circumstance, some limited relief is offered whereby contributions made to a plan under a standard termination are deductible, but only to the extent that they are guaranteed by PBGC. [IRC § 404(g), clarified by OBRA '89 § 11841]

Alternatively, in order to facilitate the termination of a plan in a standard termination, a majority owner (i.e., an individual who owns 50 percent or more of the company) may agree to forgo receipt of all or part of the majority owner's benefit. To be valid:

1. The agreement must be in writing;

2. If the benefit is greater than $3,500, the spouse, if any, must consent in writing; and

3. The agreement must not be inconsistent with a qualified domestic relations order (QDRO) (see Q 30:1).

[PBGC Reg § 4041.7(b)]

Q 21:19   What is a distress termination?

If a defined benefit plan (see Q 2:3) cannot satisfy the conditions for a standard termination (see Q 21:17), it can be voluntarily terminated only if the conditions for a distress termination of a single-employer plan are satisfied. This type of termination may occur if the employer contributing to the plan and each member of its controlled group (see Q 5:33) meet at least one of the following conditions:

1. Liquidation in bankruptcy or insolvency proceeding.

2. Reorganization in bankruptcy or insolvency proceeding. In addition, the bankruptcy petition must be filed prior to the proposed date of plan termination, and the bankruptcy or other appropriate court must determine that, unless the plan is terminated, the employer and all the members of the controlled group will be unable to pay their debts under a reorganization plan and unable to continue without a reorganization.

3. Termination of the plan is required to enable payment of debts while staying in business or to avoid unreasonably burdensome pension costs caused by a decline of the employer's covered workforce.

A bankruptcy court held that an employer did not have to submit a reorganization plan and disclosure statement before the court could determine whether it was financially necessary for the employer to terminate its defined benefit plan under the distress termination procedures. [In re Sewell Mfg Co Inc, 1996 Bankr Lexis 468 (Bankr ND Ga 1996)]

If PBGC determines that the requirements of a distress termination have been met, additional information may be required of the plan administrator and the enrolled actuary in order to determine the sufficiency of plan assets. PBGC must then notify the plan administrator as soon as possible after reaching its determination. [ERISA § 4041(c)]

Q 21:20   What benefits under a single-employer defined benefit plan are guaranteed by PBGC?

When a single-employer defined benefit plan terminates under the distress termination procedures, PBGC will guarantee the payment of "certain benefits." The characteristics of this type of benefit are that:

1. It is a pension benefit;

2. It is nonforfeitable (see Q 21:21) on the date of plan termination; and

3. A participant must be entitled to the benefit. The benefit will be guaranteed to the extent that it does not exceed the limitations set

forth in ERISA and its regulations (see Qs 21:22–21:25). [ERISA §§ 4022(a), 4022(b); PBGC Reg § 4022.3]

Under a special rule, a qualified preretirement survivor annuity is not treated as forfeitable solely because the participant has not died as of the termination date. [ERISA § 4022(e)]

Q 21:21   Does PBGC guarantee a benefit that becomes nonforfeitable solely as a result of the plan's termination?

No. Although the plan must provide for 100 percent vesting upon termination (see Q 21:4), a benefit that vests because of this rule is not a guaranteed benefit. [ERISA § 4022(a)]

Q 21:22   Are there any limitations on the amount of the benefit PBGC will guarantee?

Yes. PBGC's guarantee may be subject to one or more statutorily pre-scribed benefit limitations (see Qs 21:23–21:25). For example, the guarantee may not exceed the maximum monthly benefit limitation amount, which is expressed in terms of an annuity that is payable for the life of the participant commencing at age 65. The maximum guaranteed benefit is adjusted annually to reflect cost-of-living increases (see Q 21:23).

Furthermore, the guaranteed benefit may not exceed the actuarial equivalent of a monthly benefit in the form of a life annuity commencing at age 65. Accordingly, if a benefit is payable at an earlier age, the maximum guaranteed benefit is actuarially reduced to reflect the earlier commence-ment of the receipt of the benefit. This reduction does not apply to a disability benefit. [ERISA § 4022(b); PBGC Reg § 4022.23]

Q 21:23   What is the maximum guaranteed monthly benefit?

The maximum guaranteed monthly benefit for plans terminating in 1996 is $2,642.05. This amount applies even though a participant may not retire and receive the benefit until years after the termination of the plan. [ERISA § 4022(b)(3); PBGC News Release No. 96-17 (Dec 12, 1995); Appendix to 29 CFR Part 4022]

The maximum guaranteed benefit has been adjusted for inflation and was initially $750.00 in 1974. For the prior five years, the adjusted amounts were as follows:

Year	Adjusted Amount
1995	$2,573.86
1994	2,556.82
1993	2,437.50
1992	2,352.27
1991	2,250.00

Q 21:24 What is the effect on PBGC's guarantees of a plan amendment prior to the plan's termination?

If an amendment is adopted within five years of the termination and adds a new benefit or increases the value of a benefit for any participant who is not a substantial owner (see Q 21:13), PBGC's guarantee will be subject to a phase-in rule. Such increases include any changes that advance a participant's entitlement (such as liberalization of the participation or vesting requirement), a reduction in the normal or early retirement ages, or a change in the form of benefit. Increases due to salary increases or additional years of service are not subject to this rule. Under this five-year phase-in rule, a benefit increase will be subject to the following formula: multiply the number of years a benefit increase has been in effect by the greater of 20 percent of the monthly increase or $20 per month (but not in excess of the actual increase). [ERISA § 4022(b)(7); PBGC Reg §§ 4022.2, 4022.25]

Any benefits provided under a plan to a participant who is a substantial owner, and thereafter any amendment benefiting a substantial owner, will be subject to a 30-year phase-in rule. [ERISA § 4022(b)(5); PBGC Reg § 4022.26] In one case, a substantial owner was precluded from receiving PBGC benefits after amendment and termination of the plan, because, under the original plan, the substantial owner would not have received any benefits. [Brown v PBGC, 1993 US Dist Lexis 6764 (D DC 1993)]

A defined benefit plan subject to PBGC coverage (see Q 21:12) cannot be amended to increase plan liabilities while the employer is in bankruptcy. Exceptions to this prohibition allow any plan amendment that either:

1. Provides *de minimis* increases;
2. Would leave the plan with a funded current liability percentage of 100 percent or more;
3. Only repeals a retroactive plan amendment under Code Section 412(c)(8); or
4. Is required as a condition of qualification.

[IRC § 401(a)(33); ERISA §§ 204(i), 4022(f)]

Q 21:25   What is the effect of the plan's disqualification on the guaranteed benefit?

PBGC will not guarantee any benefits that accrue after IRS has disqualified a plan or an amendment. [ERISA § 4022(b)(6); PBGC Reg § 4022.27]

Q 21:26   Can PBGC initiate the termination of a plan?

Yes. PBGC may institute termination proceedings in federal court if it finds that:

1. Minimum funding standards (see Q 8:1) have not been satisfied;
2. The plan will be unable to pay benefits when due;
3. A distribution of more than $10,000 was made to a substantial owner in any 24-month period for reasons other than death and, after the distribution, there are unfunded vested liabilities; or
4. The possible long-run liability of the employer to PBGC is expected to increase unreasonably if the plan is not terminated.

[ERISA § 4042(a)]

Where PBGC determined that its liability would increase unreasonably if a company's defined benefit plans were terminated after bankruptcy reorganization, PBGC was allowed to terminate the plans prior to reorganization. [PBGC v Fel, 798 F Supp 239 (D NJ 1992)] In another case, the court upheld the decision of PBGC to terminate defined benefit plans where the record included reports that the plans were underfunded and there was no prospect that the plans would be properly funded in the future. [Pan American World Airways, Inc Cooperative Retirement Income Plan v The Pension Committee of Pan American World Airways, Inc, Nos. 91 Civ 5016 (MBM) and 91 Civ 5017 (MBM) (SD NY 1991)]

However, PBGC must institute termination proceedings whenever it determines that a single-employer defined benefit plan does not have enough assets to pay benefits that are currently due. [ERISA § 4042(a)]

Furthermore, PBGC may cease the termination of a plan and restore the plan to its status prior to termination if circumstances change. In a much publicized case, the United States Supreme Court allowed PBGC to restore terminated defined benefit plans. LTV Corporation (LTV) filed for bankruptcy. At that time, LTV maintained three underfunded defined benefit plans all covered by PBGC. PBGC instituted proceedings to involuntarily terminate the plans. Subsequently, LTV established new plans that provided benefits lost by the termination. In effect, the new "follow-on" plans provided benefits equal to the difference between the promised benefits under the terminated plans and PBGC guaranteed benefits. PBGC objected and determined to restore the plans. The Supreme Court upheld PBGC's authority to return responsibility for funding the terminated plans to the plan sponsor. [PBGC v LTV Corp, No. 89-390 (S Ct 1990)] The PBGC restoration order was held enforceable because PBGC was not required to consider whether restoration would lead to the retermination of the plans or whether the bankruptcy court would approve contributions to the restored plans. [PBGC v LTV Corp, No. 87 Civ 7261 (RJS)(SD NY 1990)] Employers may now be discouraged from using "follow-on" plans to shift the burden of paying benefits from the plan sponsor to PBGC. [ERISA § 4047]

Since the minimum funding standards (see Q 8:1) do not apply between the dates of termination and restoration and the plan will be underfunded, or become more underfunded, during this period, PBGC will issue a restoration payment schedule that provides for the amortization of the restored plan's unfunded liabilities over a period of up to 30 years after the PBGC restoration order. The restoration payment schedule is used to determine the minimum funding standards for the unfunded prerestoration plan liabilities. Restored plans must reimburse PBGC for any guaranteed benefit payments (see Q 21:20) made by PBGC while the plan was terminated, and PBGC insurance premiums (see Q 21:14) must be paid on behalf of restored plans. [PBGC Reg § 4047; Temp Reg § 1.412(c)(1)-3T]

Q 21:27   Can a plan covered by Title IV be terminated if the termination would violate an existing collective bargaining agreement?

The authority of PBGC to terminate a plan under these circumstances will depend on whether the termination is initiated by the plan administrator (see Q 16:1) or PBGC. If the plan administrator attempts to terminate the plan under the standard or distress termination provisions (see Qs 21:17, 21:19), PBGC may not proceed with the termination. However, PBGC's authority to institute involuntary termination proceedings for such a plan is not limited by the fact that the termination would violate the collective bargaining agreement. [ERISA § 4041(a)(3); PBGC Op Ltr No. 87-4]

Q 21:28   Is there any restriction on the form of a benefit paid by a terminating defined benefit plan?

Yes. The general rule is that a benefit be paid in annuity form, unless the participant elects an optional form of benefit under the terms of the plan. [ERISA § 4041(b)(3)(A)(i); PBGC Reg § 4041.4] However, an exception exists for small amounts of benefits. PBGC and any other plan administrator of a terminating plan may choose to pay a benefit in a single payment without the consent of the participant if the present value of the benefit is $3,500 or less. [PBGC Reg §§ 4022.7, 4041.6; PBGC Op Ltr No. 90-5]

See Qs 21:40, 21:46–21:50 regarding missing participants.

Q 21:29 Who must be notified of the company's intention to terminate a defined benefit plan covered by Title IV—and when must this notice be given?

The plan administrator (see Q 16:1) must provide to all affected parties (see Q 21:33) written notice of the company's intention to terminate a defined benefit plan covered by Title IV (Notice of Intent to Terminate—NOIT) at least 60 days and no more than 90 days before the proposed date of termination. [ERISA § 4041(a)(2); PBGC Reg §§ 4041.3(b)(1), 4041.21(a)]

Q 21:30 What information must be included in the NOIT?

According to regulations issued by PBGC, the plan administrator (see Q 16:1) must issue the NOIT (see Q 21:29) to each affected party (see Q 21:33) individually. Each notice must be either hand delivered or delivered by first-class mail or courier service to the affected party's last known address.

The plan administrator must include in the NOIT the following information:

1. The name of the plan and sponsor;
2. The sponsor's employer identification number and the plan number;
3. The name, address, and telephone number of the person who may be contacted with questions concerning the plan's termination;
4. A statement that the plan administrator expects to terminate the plan in a standard termination on a proposed termination date;
5. If the proposed termination date is dependent on the occurrence of a future event, a description of the nature of the event, when the event is expected to occur, and when the termination will occur in relation to the event;
6. A statement that benefit and service accruals will continue until the date of termination or, if applicable, that benefit accruals were or will be frozen as of a specific date;
7. A statement that, in order to terminate in a standard termination, plan assets must be sufficient to provide all benefit liabilities under the plan;

8. A statement that, after plan assets have been distributed to provide all benefit liabilities, either by the purchase of irrevocable commitments from an insurer or by an alternative form of distribution provided for under the plan, the PBGC's guarantee ends;

9. If distribution of benefits under the plan may be wholly or partially provided by the purchase of irrevocable commitments from an insurer:

   a. The name and address of the insurer or insurers from whom the plan administrator intends to purchase the irrevocable commitments; or

   b. If the plan administrator has not identified an insurer or insurers at the time the NOIT is issued, a statement that (i) irrevocable commitments may be purchased from an insurer to provide some or all of the benefits under the plan, (ii) the insurer or insurers have not yet been identified, and (iii) affected parties will be notified of the name and address of the insurer or insurers at a later date (but no later than 45 days before the date of distribution);

10. A statement that if the termination does not occur, the plan administrator will notify the affected parties in writing of that fact;

11. A statement that each affected party, other than an employee organization, will be receiving a written notification of the benefits that the party will receive; and

12. For retirees only, a statement that their monthly (or other periodic) benefit amounts will not be affected by the plan's termination.

[PBGC Reg § 4041.21]

Q 21:31 What is the relevance of the date of plan termination?

The termination date is critical for determining the rights of the participants and beneficiaries to the benefits under the plan that are guaranteed by PBGC, the employer's liability to PBGC for any underfunding, and PBGC's exposure for guaranteed benefits. [ERISA § 4048; Audio Fidelity Corp v PBGC, 624 F 2d 513 (4th Cir 1980)]

Q 21:32 What factors are considered by PBGC in establishing a defined benefit plan's termination date?

The date of termination will depend on whether the termination is filed by the plan administrator (see Q 16:1) under the standard or distress termination procedures (see Qs 21:17, 21:19) or whether PBGC has initiated the termination (see Q 21:26). However, in a termination other than one initiated by PBGC, the date must be prospective and at least 60 days after the NOIT is issued to affected parties (see Qs 21:2, 21:29, 21:33). [ERISA § 4041(a)(2); Phillips v Bebber, Nos. 89-2184 and 89-2189 (4th Cir 1990)]

Q 21:33　Who is an affected party?

An affected party, for purposes of a termination subject to PBGC's jurisdiction, is:

- A participant

- A beneficiary of a deceased participant

- A beneficiary who is an alternate payee under a QDRO (see chapter 30)

- Any employee organization that represents plan participants or that represented plan participants within five years prior to the issuance of the NOIT (see Q 21:29)

- PBGC (in the case of a distress termination; see Q 21:19), or

- Any person designated in writing to receive notice on behalf of an affected party

[ERISA §§ 4001(a)(21), 4041(a)(2), 4041(c)(1)(A); PBGC Reg § 4001.2]

Q 21:34　Are there any other notice requirements if the company intends to terminate a defined benefit plan in a standard termination?

Yes. Notice must be provided to PBGC by filing PBGC Form 500, Standard Termination Notice Single-Employer Plan Termination. Schedule EA-S, Standard Termination Certification of Sufficiency, attached to Form 500, must be used by the enrolled actuary to certify that the plan is projected to have sufficient assets to provide all benefit liabilities. [ERISA § 4041(b)(2)(A)]

Form 500 should be filed no later than 120 days after the proposed termination date. [PBGC Reg § 4041.24(a)]

In addition, no later than the date on which the notice is filed with PBGC, the plan administrator (see Q 16:1) must provide each participant and beneficiary with a Notice of Plan Benefits (see Q 21:35). [ERISA § 4041(b)(2)(B)]

Q 21:35   What information must be included in the Notice of Plan Benefits?

The plan administrator (see Q 16:1) must issue a notice to each affected party (other than an employee organization; see Q 21:33) that (1) specifies the amount of the individual's benefits as of the proposed termination date and the form of benefit on the basis of which the amount was determined, and (2) includes the following information used in determining the individual's benefits:

- Length of service
- Age of the participant or beneficiary
- Wages
- Assumptions (including the interest rate)
- Such other information as PBGC may require

[ERISA § 4041(b)(2)(B); PBGC Reg §§ 4041.22, 4041.23]

Q 21:36   Are there any special rules regarding the purchase of annuity contracts?

Yes. PBGC has issued regulations requiring plan administrators (see Q 16:1) to inform both participants and PBGC of the identity of the insurer or insurers from whom irrevocable commitments (i.e., annuity contracts) may be purchased prior to the distribution of plan assets. This information must be included in the NOIT (see Q 21:29) and must be included with the filing of the standard termination with PBGC (see Q 21:34). If the identity of the insurer is not known, the information must be provided to participants and PBGC no later than 45 days prior to the date of distribution. [PBGC Reg §§ 4041.21(e), 4041.24(b)]

See Q 21:41 regarding the selection of an annuity.

Q 21:37   After the notice is filed with PBGC, does PBGC have to act within designated time limits?

Yes. Within 60 days after the plan administrator (see Q 16:1) notifies PBGC (see Q 21:34), PBGC must issue to the plan administrator a notice of noncompliance if it determines (1) based on the notice provided by filing Form 500 (see Q 21:34), or based on information provided by affected parties (see Q 21:33) or otherwise obtained by PBGC, that there is reason to believe that the plan assets are not sufficient for benefit liabilities (see Q 21:18); or (2) that any of the notice requirements (see Qs 21:29, 21:34, 21:35) have not been met. PBGC is no longer required to issue a notice of noncompliance for failure to satisfy the procedural requirements in (2) above and may elect not to if it determines that issuance of the notice would be inconsistent with the interests of participants and beneficiaries. [ERISA § 4041(b)(2)(C); PBGC Reg §§ 4041.25, 4041.26]

Q 21:38   May the 60-day period for PBGC to issue a notice of noncompliance be extended?

Yes. PBGC and the plan administrator (see Q 16:1) may extend the 60-day period (see Q 21:37) for the noncompliance notice by jointly signing a written agreement before expiration of the initial 60-day period. Additional extensions are also permitted. [ERISA § 4041(b)(2)(C); PBGC Reg § 4041.25(a)(2)]

Q 21:39   Assuming that PBGC does not issue a notice of noncompliance, when should final distribution of assets occur?

The plan administrator (see Q 16:1) must complete the distribution of assets, pursuant to a standard termination, no later than 180 days after expiration of the 60-day (or extended) period (see Qs 21:37, 21:38), assuming that plan assets are sufficient to meet benefit liabilities (see Q 21:18), determined as of the termination date, when the final distribution occurs. [ERISA § 4041(b)(2)(D); PBGC Reg § 4041.27(a)]

The distribution deadline will automatically be extended until the 60th day after the plan's receipt of a favorable IRS determination letter (see Q 15:1), if:

1. On or before the date that the plan administrator files Form 500, the plan administrator submitted to IRS a request for a determination letter with respect to the plan's termination;

2. The plan administrator does not receive the IRS's determination letter at least 60 days before the expiration of the 180-day period for distribution; and

3. On or before the expiration of the 180-day period, the plan administrator notifies PBGC in writing that an extension of the distribution deadline is required and certifies that the conditions in 1 and 2 above have been met.

[PBGC Reg § 4041.27(e)]

If the plan administrator will be unable to complete the distribution of plan assets within the 180-day period, PBGC may grant a discretionary extension only if PBGC is satisfied that the delay in making the distribution is not due to the action or inaction of the plan administrator or the contributing sponsor, and that distribution can in fact be completed by the date requested. The request must be filed no later than 30 days before the expiration of the 180-day period, must explain the reason for the request, and must provide a date certain by which the distribution will be made. PBGC will not grant any request based on:

1. Insufficient plan assets to provide all benefit liabilities;
2. Failure to meet the requirements for an automatic extension; or
3. Failure to locate all participants and beneficiaries.

[PBGC Reg § 4041.27(f)]

Q 21:40   What is the method for the final distribution of assets?

The plan administrator (see Q 16:1) must distribute the plan's assets, pursuant to a standard termination (see Q 21:17), in accordance with the required allocation of assets (see Q 21:42). In distributing the assets, the plan administrator must:

1. Purchase irrevocable commitments from an insurer to provide for all benefit liabilities (and any other benefits to which assets are required to be allocated) (see Q 21:41); or
2. Otherwise fully provide the benefit liabilities (and any other benefits to which assets are required to be allocated) in accordance with the plan's provisions and any applicable PBGC regulations, including the transfer of assets to PBGC on behalf of a missing participant.

[ERISA §§ 4041(b)(3), 4050]

See Qs 21:46 through 21:50 regarding missing participants.

In order to have a valid termination, the benefits of all participants must be distributed. Before a reversion of excess assets occurs (see Q 21:53), all plan liabilities must first be satisfied. [IRC § 401(a)(2); ERISA § 4044(d)]

Q 21:41   Is PBGC or the employer liable to participants if an insurer fails to make payments under annuity contracts?

When irrevocable commitments (i.e., annuity contracts) have been purchased to pay all benefit liabilities, the plan termination process is completed and the PBGC guarantee obligation ends. [PBGC Op Ltr No. 91-1]

Similarly, employers are not liable to participants if an insurer fails to meet its obligations under the annuity contracts. The purchase of annuity contracts that irrevocably provide for the payment of all benefit liabilities satisfies the employer's obligation with respect to the termination. [PBGC Op Ltr No. 91-4]

However, fiduciaries must select the insurer that issues the annuity contracts in a way that satisfies their fiduciary duty to plan participants (see Q 19:12). Fiduciaries of defined benefit plans may be liable for purchasing annuities without adequately evaluating the insurer's financial condition. [DOL News Rel 91-281] Plan fiduciaries have a duty to select the safest annuity provider available unless it is in the interests of participants and beneficiaries to do otherwise. For example, when the safest available annuity is only marginally safer but disproportionately more expensive than competing annuities, the participants are likely to bear a significant portion of the increased cost. [PWBA Interpretive Bulletin 95-1] In one case, the court held that an employer may have breached its fiduciary duty by not acting prudently when it selected a company to provide annuities for a terminated pension plan. [Waller v Blue Cross of California, 1994 US App Lexis 16490 (9th Cir 1994)] In another case, a company agreed to pay $4.07 million to DOL as part of a settlement involving the improper selection of a group annuity provider to fund pension benefits. The money will be distributed to the participants and beneficiaries of the terminated pension plan. [DOL News Rel 95-143]

A qualified retirement plan participant, beneficiary, or fiduciary can bring an action for appropriate relief if the purchase of an insurance or annuity contract in connection with the termination of a person's status as a plan participant would violate fiduciary standards. [ERISA § 502(a)(9)]

See Q 21:36 regarding notice requirements with respect to insurers providing annuity benefits for terminating plans.

Q 21:42 How are plan assets allocated when a defined benefit plan is terminated?

There are six categories into which plan assets must be divided upon termination of a single-employer defined benefit plan. The assets are assigned to these categories, starting with the first category, until the value of the assets has been exhausted. On termination of a defined benefit plan, the assets are allocated in the following order:

1. Employee voluntary contributions;
2. Employee mandatory contributions;

3. Annuity payments in pay status at least three years before the termination of the plan (including annuity payments that would have been in pay status for at least three years if the employee had retired then) based on the provisions of the plan in effect during the five years before termination of the plan under which the benefit would be the least;

4. All other guaranteed insured benefits, determined without regard to the aggregate limit on benefits guaranteed with respect to a participant under all multiemployer and single-employer plans;

5. All other vested benefits; and

6. All other benefits under the plan (see Q 21:43).

[ERISA § 4044(a)]

Q 21:43   What does the phrase "all other benefits under the plan" cover?

According to PBGC and IRS, the statutory language in ERISA Section 4044(a)(6) encompasses only those benefits that participants have accrued as of the date of termination (or in the case of benefit subsidies protected by REA, benefits to which participants may become entitled in the future). [PBGC Op Ltr No. 87-11; GCM 39665]

The Supreme Court has agreed with the PBGC and IRS positions and held that the "all other accrued benefits" category under ERISA Section 4044(a)(6) covers participants' accrued forfeitable benefits, but not unaccrued benefits. [Mead Corp v Tilley, 109 S Ct 2156 (1989); see also May v The Houston Post Pension Plan, No. 89-2249 (5th Cir 1990) and Blessitt v Retirement Plan for Employees of Dixie Engine Co, 848 F 2d 1164 (11th Cir 1988)] After remand by the Supreme Court, the Fourth Circuit ruled that the unaccrued subsidized early retirement benefits of participants who satisfied the service requirement but not the age requirement to be eligible for the subsidized benefits at the time of plan termination constituted contingent liabilities that the plan required to be satisfied before excess assets could be returned to the employer (see Q 21:53). [Tilley v Mead Corp, No. 86-3858 (4th Cir 1991)]

One court held that unaccrued early retirement subsidies did not automatically vest upon plan termination where the participants did not meet the age and service eligibility requirements for early retirement subsidies. [Berard v Royal Electric, Inc, 795 F Supp 519 (D RI 1992)]

Another court held that a plan sponsor was not required to place additional funds in the pension plan upon the plan's termination in 1986 in order to satisfy the "participants' contingent, forfeitable right to subsidized early retirement benefits." However, the court noted that, for terminations initiated after October 16, 1987, the law changed, and a plan sponsor would be prevented from limiting its liability upon its own failure to fund. [Aldridge v Lily-Tulip, Inc Salary Retirement Plan Benefits Committee, No. 90-8686 (11th Cir 1992)]

Q 21:44   Can a distribution of plan assets be reallocated?

Yes. The traditional rules provide that if the asset allocation discriminates in favor of highly compensated employees (see Q 3:2), the allocation (see Q 21:42) may be changed to the extent necessary to avoid the prohibited discrimination (see Q 21:8).

A qualified retirement plan will be considered discriminatory if a plan amendment or series of plan amendments discriminates significantly in favor of highly compensated employees. For this purpose, a plan amendment includes the termination of a plan and any change in the benefits, rights, or features under a plan (see Qs 4:18, 4:19). [Treas Reg § 1.401(a)(4)-5(a)(1)]

However, the law also provides that a defined benefit plan cannot terminate in a standard termination (see Q 21:17) unless it has sufficient assets to cover all benefit liabilities of the plan, which would obviate any such reallocation. [ERISA § 4041(b)(1)(D)]

One court upheld a reallocation of excess plan assets solely to 13 management employee-participants upon a plan termination that occurred after 102 plan participants terminated employment and received annuity contracts in satisfaction of their entire plan benefits. Those 102 former employees were not entitled to share in the reallocation because they were not plan participants when the plan was terminated. [Teagardener v Republic-Franklin, Inc, No. 89-3865 (6th Cir 1990)]

Q 21:45   Must PBGC be notified once final distribution of assets is completed?

Yes. Within 30 days after the final distribution of assets is completed, the plan administrator (see Q 16:1) must file with PBGC a notice certifying that the assets have been distributed in accordance with the required order of allocation of assets and that all benefits have been distributed in accordance with either method of distribution described in Q 21:40. PBGC Form 501, Post-Distribution Certification for Standard Termination, has been designed for this purpose. Form 501 also requires information regarding the insurers, if any, from whom annuity contracts have been purchased and the forms and amounts of distributions. [ERISA § 4041(b)(3)(B); PBGC Reg § 4041.27(h)]

See Q 21:49 regarding missing participants.

PBGC may assess a penalty, not to exceed $1,000 a day, for failure to provide any required notice or other material information. [ERISA § 4071] However, according to PBGC, the penalty for failure to file Form 501 should not exceed $25 per day for the first 90 days of delinquency, and $50 per day thereafter. For plans with fewer than 100 participants, the penalty will be proportionately reduced with a minimum penalty of $5 per day. In general, the total penalty should not exceed $100 multiplied by the number of participants. PBGC may reduce or eliminate the penalty where reasonable cause is shown. [PBGC Statement of Policy, 60 FR 36837 (July 18, 1995)]

Q 21:46 May benefits due missing participants be paid to PBGC?

Yes. Administrators (see Q 16:1) of plans that terminate under the standard termination procedures (see Q 21:17) may provide benefits for a participant or beneficiary who cannot be located either through the purchase of an annuity from an insurer or by paying funds on behalf of the missing individual to PBGC (see Q 21:48). If funds are paid to PBGC, PBGC will search for the participant or beneficiary and pay benefits to those who are located. Terminating plans are subject to the new rules for distributions made in plan years beginning on or after January 1, 1996. [ERISA § 4050; Preamble to PBGC Reg § 2629 prior to renumbering]

Q 21:47 Is a diligent search required before paying a missing participant's benefit to PBGC?

Yes. A diligent search must be made for each missing participant before the designated benefit is paid to PBGC. A search is diligent only if the search:

1. Begins not more than six months before the NOIT (see Q 21:29) is issued;
2. Includes inquiry of any plan participants and beneficiaries of the missing participant; and
3. Includes use of a commercial locator service to search for the missing participant.

[PBGC Reg § 4050.4]

If a participant cannot be located, a request can be sent to IRS or the Social Security Administration. IRS has issued instructions and information on the use of its letter-forwarding program. Written requests should explain the need for letter forwarding, list the Social Security number of the individual being sought, and include the letter to be forwarded. There is no charge for requests involving less than 50 potential recipients. [Rev Proc 94-22, 1994-1 CB 608]

Q 21:48   What is the method of distribution for missing participants?

The plan administrator (see Q 16:1) must purchase an irrevocable commitment from an insurer or pay PBGC a designated benefit, and provide PBGC with certain information and certifications. The amount of the designated benefit is determined under special rules and will depend on whether the benefit required under the plan is a mandatory lump-sum, *de minimis* lump-sum, no lump-sum, or elective lump-sum. [ERISA § 4050(a); PBGC Reg § 4050.5]

An additional $300 must be added to each designated benefit greater than $3,500 as an adjustment for expenses. [PBGC Reg § 4050.2]

Q 21:49   What procedures apply with respect to missing participants?

PBGC has revised the forms and applicable instructions thereto with respect to its standard termination procedures (see Q 21:17). Specifically, Form 501 (see Q 21:45) now may be filed as a preliminary filing or amended filing if participants cannot be located. Form 501 is filed as a preliminary filing if distributions for missing participants have not been completed as of its due date. If the plan has missing participants, Schedule MP (with certain attachments) must be filed with Form 501.

Generally, payments to PBGC for missing participants and filing Form 501 with PBGC must be made no later than 120 days after the deemed distribution date (see Q 21:39).

Q 21:50   If PBGC locates a missing participant, how is distribution made?

If a missing participant is located, PBGC will pay a single sum if this amount is $3,500 or less and no participant or spousal consent is required. If the single-sum benefit is greater than $3,500, PBGC will pay the benefit, subject to actuarial assumptions set by PBGC at the time of the transfer, in the same forms and at the same times as a guaranteed benefit, including a single sum, if the plan had provided for payment in this form. [PBGC Reg §§ 4050.7(b), 4050.8–4050.12]

Q 21:51 Does PBGC perform post-termination audits for compliance with the Title IV requirements?

Yes. PBGC selectively conducts post-termination compliance audits. The data request may include copies of the following:

- The plan and trust documents
- Applicable labor contracts
- Applicable insurance contracts to fund the plan
- Actuarial reports and enrolled actuary's worksheets
- The plan's financial statement as of the termination date
- Benefit data for each participant
- Election and spousal consent forms

The plan administrator (see Q 16:1) or sponsor should maintain records relating to the plan's termination for six years after Form 501 (see Q 21:45) is filed with PBGC. [PBGC Reg § 4041.11]

Q 21:52 Does an employer incur any liability to PBGC for the payment of benefits to plan participants of an underfunded terminated plan?

Yes. When PBGC incurs liabilities for benefits in the case of a distress termination (see Q 21:19) or a termination instituted by the PBGC (see Q 21:26), it can obtain reimbursement from the contributing employer or a member of its controlled group (see Q 5:33). If more than one employer jointly sponsors a plan, the liability to PBGC is separately applicable to each such entity.

Any trade or business, whether or not incorporated, can be a member of the contributing employer's controlled group if a prescribed control or ownership test is satisfied. In that case, it will be jointly and severally liable to reimburse PBGC. [ERISA §§ 4001(b), 4062(b)] Although a company did not control the operation of its subsidiary's business at the time of the subsidiary's plan termination, it did own at least 80 percent of the subsidiary's stock and therefore was liable to PBGC for the plan's unfunded benefit liabilities. [PBGC v East Dayton Tool and Die Co, No. 93-3185 (6th Cir 1994)]

The liability of a contributing employer or member of its controlled group generally is the total amount of the unfunded benefit liabilities to all participants and beneficiaries as of the termination date, plus interest at a reasonable rate calculated from the termination date. [ERISA § 4062(b)]

If the liability to PBGC is not paid, a lien in favor of PBGC arises in an amount equal to the lesser of (1) the unfunded benefit liabilities or (2) 30 percent of the collective net worth of the contributing employers of a plan and members of the controlled group (but treating as zero any negative net worth). [ERISA §§ 4062(d)(1), 4068(a)]

Q 21:53   May excess assets remaining after the standard termination of a defined benefit plan be returned to the employer after payment of all plan benefit liabilities?

Yes, provided that the distribution does not contravene any other provision of law, the excess was the result of an "erroneous actuarial computation," and the plan specifically permits the distribution of excess assets in this situation (see Qs 21:40, 21:54–21:56). [ERISA § 4044(d); Treas Reg § 1.401-2; Int'l Union of Elec Workers v Murata Erie N Amer, Inc, No. 94-3267 (3d Cir 1994)]

In one case, the employer received $3.5 million of excess funds as a result of actuarial error. The section of the plan containing a general prohibition against reversion of funds had to be read in conjunction with another section that contained a specific exception allowing for a reversion after the satisfaction of all liabilities. [Parrett v American Ship Building Co, 990 F 2d 854 (6th Cir 1993)] In another case, an employer recovered $275 million to use in expanding and improving its ongoing business [Walsh v The Great Atlantic & Pacific Tea Co, 4 EBC 2577 (3d Cir 1983)]; and, in another, the court held that a reversion of $600,000 of excess assets to the receiver of the insolvent employer did not violate ERISA's "exclusive benefit" rule. [Outzen v Federal Deposit Insurance Corp, No. 90-8077 (10th Cir 1991)]

In another case, the court held that a 1959 plan provision that "in no event and under no circumstances" could plan assets be returned to the employer precluded any subsequent amendment to the plan to allow such a reversion upon termination of the plan [Bryant v Int'l Fruit Products, Inc, 793 F 2d 118 (6th Cir 1986)]; and another court held that plan participants were entitled to excess assets upon plan termination because an amendment providing for a reversion of excess assets to the employer was not properly executed according to plan procedures. [Albedyll v Wisconsin Porcelain Co Revised Retirement Plan, 947 F 2d 246 (7th Cir 1991)] Similarly, the employer was not entitled to the excess assets upon plan termination where the plan did not specifically provide for a reversion even though the reversion provision had existed in an earlier version of the plan and was provided for in the trust agreement. [Rinard v Eastern Co, 978 F 2d 265 (6th Cir 1992)]

In yet another case, a board resolution required that all assets be distributed to participants, although the plan permitted reversions. The court determined that this resolution informally amended the plan to require that excess assets be distributed to plan participants. [Horn v Berdon, Inc Defined Benefit Pension Plan, No. 89-55391 (9th Cir 1991)] However, in another case, former employees were not entitled to a pro rata share of excess assets recouped by their former employer when the employer terminated its retirement plan because the employees, who were laid off before they reached the plan's early retirement age, were not entitled to retirement benefits. [Fuller v FMC Corp, Nos. 92-1738 and 92-2248 (4th Cir 1993)]

A participant's waiver assigning his pension plan benefits to the employer constituted a prohibited assignment or alienation (see Q 4:24) and resulted in his receipt of a taxable distribution (see Q 13:1). The court ruled that the waived benefits did not represent excess assets reverting to the employer. [Gallade, 106 TC No. 20 (1996)]

Further, if an overfunded plan with mandatory employee contributions is terminated, certain assets attributable to such contributions must be distributed to participants and beneficiaries. [ERISA § 4044(d)(3)(B)]

Q 21:54 May a defined benefit plan that did not originally provide for distribution of excess assets to the employer be amended to authorize such a distribution?

Yes. However, for defined benefit plans covered by PBGC (see Qs 21:12, 21:13), any amendment providing for a reversion, or increasing the amount that may revert to the employer, is not effective before the fifth calendar year following the date of the adoption of such an amendment. A special rule provides that a distribution to the employer will not be treated as failing to satisfy this rule if the plan has been in effect for fewer than five years.

For plans that, as of December 17, 1987, had no provision relating to the distribution of plan assets to the employer, the new rule applies to such amendments that were adopted more than one year after the effective date of the new law. For plans that, as of December 17, 1987, provided for the distribution of plan assets to the employer, the new law applies to any amendment made after December 17, 1987. [ERISA § 4044(d)(2)]

In one case, participants in one plan that was merged into a plan of another employer were not entitled to any portion of the surplus assets of the merged plan at the time of the merger because the merged plan reserved the employer's right to amend the plan to allow for the reversion of surplus assets on plan termination. The fact that the merger resulted in a partial termination (see Q 21:5) of the merged plan did not prevent amendment of the surviving plan to allow for the reversion of the surplus assets at the time of the merger. However, two other plans that were simultaneously merged into the surviving plan did provide an irrevocable provision for the reallo- cation of excess assets to plan participants upon plan termination. Thus, the surviving plan could not be amended to allow reversion of the surplus assets of those plans at the time of the merger. Although the surplus assets were not required to be distributed until complete termination, the court consid- ered the two merged plans as terminated as of the day prior to the merger and ordered the distribution of the surplus assets to the participants. [Borst v Chevron Corp, US App Lexis 29473 (5th Cir 1994); In re Gulf Pension Litigation, No. 86-4365 (SD Tex 1991)]

Q 21:55   May an employer terminate a defined benefit plan to recover any excess assets and adopt a new defined benefit plan covering the same employees?

Yes, if the plan specifically permits the recovery of excess assets and:

1. All employees covered by the original plan are given notice of the termination and adoption;
2. All accrued benefits are vested as of the termination date and annuities are purchased to cover those benefits;
3. The plan's funding method is changed to take into consideration the termination and adoption, and IRS approves the change in funding method;
4. No other termination and adoption will be made in the next 15 years; and
5. The new plan is intended to be permanent.

[PBGC News Rel 84-23, on the Joint Implementation Guidelines for Termination of Defined Benefit Plans]

Legislation has sought to deter employers from terminating plans in order to recover excess assets (see Q 21:56).

Q 21:56   Is the employer liable for any taxes on the reversion?

Yes. The amount of the reversion is taxable to the employer as ordinary income. Furthermore, a nondeductible excise tax equal to 50 percent of the amount of the reversion is imposed upon the employer; however, the excise tax is reduced from 50 percent to 20 percent if the employer either establishes a qualified replacement plan (see Q 21:57) or amends the plan to provide pro rata benefit increases (see Q 21:58). For an exception to the excise tax, see Q 21:59. [IRC §§ 4980(a), 4980(d)(1)]

The excise tax applies to direct and indirect reversions. An indirect reversion includes the use of plan assets for the benefit of the employer on plan termination and, therefore, would include the use of plan assets to satisfy an obligation of the employer. [IRC § 4980(c)(2)(A); Ltr Rul 9136017]

A reversion received by a tax-exempt organization from its terminated defined benefit plan is generally not subject to the excise tax on reversions [IRC § 4980(c)(1)(A); Ltr Ruls 9320050, 9120029], and an exception to the excise tax exists for certain reversions transferred to an ESOP (see chapter 24). [IRC § 4980(c)(3); Ltr Rul 9138065]

An employer's transfer of liabilities from an underfunded defined benefit plan to an overfunded defined benefit plan did not constitute a reversion of plan assets to the employer [Ltr Rul 9318035], and the merger of three overfunded defined benefit plans sponsored by a parent company's subsidiaries into the parent company's underfunded defined benefit plan did not constitute a reversion of plan assets. [Ltr Rul 9224032] Furthermore, an employer's transfer of a portion of the assets and liabilities of its defined benefit plan to a new defined benefit plan for certain former employees was not a termination of the original defined benefit plan, and the transfer of plan assets was not considered a reversion of plan assets. [Ltr Rul 9046046]

Courts have ruled that the excise tax imposed on a reversion is not considered a penalty for bankruptcy purposes and, therefore, has priority status over the claims of unsecured creditors. [In re C-T of Virginia, Inc, No. 91-2397 (4th Cir 1992); In re Juvenile Shoe Corp of America, (ED Mo 1995)] However, see Q 8:18 regarding the excise tax relating to the minimum funding standards.

Form 5330 (see Q 17:16) is used to report the reversion and pay the excise tax. If the 20 percent rate is used, the employer must explain why it qualifies for the lower rate.

Q 21:57   What is a qualified replacement plan?

The 50 percent excise tax on reversions is reduced to 20 percent if the employer, in connection with the termination of its defined benefit plan, establishes or maintains a qualified replacement plan (see Q 21:56). [IRC § 4980(d)(2)]

Qualified replacement plans must satisfy the following requirements:

1. At least 95 percent of the active participants in the terminated plan who remain as employees of the employer after the termination must be active participants in the replacement plan.

2. The replacement plan must receive a transfer from the terminated plan of an amount equal to 25 percent (no more and no less) of the maximum amount of the reversion (less the present value of any benefit increases due to plan amendments within the 60-day period prior to plan termination). The amount that is transferred to the replacement plan is not includible in the employer's income and is not subject to the excise tax on reversions; and, concomitantly, the employer is not permitted a tax deduction for the transfer.

   Example. Lauren, Inc. maintains a defined benefit plan that has excess assets of $200,000. As part of the termination of this plan, it establishes a qualified replacement plan funded with $50,000. Lauren's excise tax on the reversion is $30,000 (20% × $150,000), and Lauren also reports $150,000 of income. Assuming that Lauren is taxed at 34 percent on its income, it will owe $51,000 in income tax on the reversion and end up with $69,000 [$200,000 − ($50,000 + $30,000 + $51,000)] after paying both taxes and funding the replacement plan.

3. If the replacement plan is a defined contribution plan, the amount transferred to it must be allocated to the accounts of participants in the plan year in which the transfer occurs or be credited to a suspense account and allocated from the account to the participant accounts no less rapidly than ratably over seven plan years beginning with the year of the transfer. If the limitation on annual additions to defined contribution plans (see Q 6:1) prevents any amount in the suspense account from being allocated to a participant by the end of the seven-year period, that amount will be allocated to the accounts of other participants. If any amount credited to the suspense account is not allocated as of the termination date of a replacement plan, it must be allocated to the accounts of participants as of such date. Any amount that cannot be so allocated will be treated as an employer reversion subject to the excise tax. [Ltr Rul 9224033]

An existing plan constituted a qualified replacement plan where at least 95 percent of the active participants in the terminated defined benefit plan who remained employees of the company after the termination were active participants in the existing plan and the requirements of 2 and 3 above were met. [Ltr Rul 9627030] Because certain employees elected out of the predecessor defined benefit plan and were not accruing benefits on the plan's termination date, they were not considered active participants as of the termination date and, therefore, were not considered in determining whether the plan satisfied the 95 percent requirement in 1 above. [Ltr Rul 9252035] Amounts transferred to a qualified replacement plan can be used as matching contributions (see Q 23:50) if the requirements of 3 above are satisfied. [Ltr Rul 9302027]

In order to qualify, the asset transfer must be a "direct transfer from the terminated plan to the replacement plan . . . before any employer reversion." [IRC § 4980(d)(2)(B)(i)] In one case, the employer deposited funds from the terminated plan into its own account and subsequently transferred those funds into a replacement profit sharing plan. The court ruled that the new plan did not satisfy the requirements of a qualified replacement plan because the transfer was an "indirect transfer." [Southern Aluminum Castings Co v United States, Civ 90-0235-P-C (SD Ala 1991)]

Q 21:58 What is a pro rata benefit increase?

If, in connection with the termination of its defined benefit plan, the employer amends the plan, effective as of the date of termination, to provide pro rata benefit increases in the accrued benefits (see Q 9:2) of qualified participants equal to at least 20 percent of the amount of the reversion, the 50 percent excise tax on the reversion will be reduced to 20 percent (see Q 21:56). [IRC § 4980(d)(3); Ltr Rul 9236043]

The pro rata increase must benefit all qualified participants. Qualified participants include active participants, participants in pay status, certain beneficiaries, and individuals who have a nonforfeitable right to an accrued benefit under the terminated plan as of the termination date and whose service terminated during the period beginning three years before the termination date. The 20 percent excise tax, rather than the 50 percent tax, was imposed on an employer reversion at plan termination because the employer provided for pro rata benefit increases to qualified participants equal to 20 percent of the surplus assets remaining after satisfaction of plan obligations. [Ltr Rul 9335047]

Q 21:59 Are there any exceptions to the imposition of the excise tax on defined benefit plan reversions?

If a defined benefit plan (see Q 2:3) is overfunded and the plan termination would expose the employer to the excise tax on reversions (see Q 21:56), the amount of the excess assets can be reduced by a qualified transfer of assets to a postretirement health benefits account that is part of the plan. The amount transferred is not considered a reversion subject to either income or excise taxes. One qualified transfer can be made during each tax year beginning after 1990 and before 2001 of the amount reasonably estimated to be required to pay qualified current retiree health liabilities for the year. The amount of a qualified transfer, however, cannot exceed the amount of excess plan assets as of the last valuation date before the transfer. All accrued benefits (see Q 9:2) of all plan participants must become fully vested (see Q 21:4) as if the plan terminated at the time of a qualified transfer. [IRC §§ 401(h), 420; Ltr Rul 9419037; ERISA Tech Rel No. 91-1]

The IRS has issued procedures for requesting determination letters regarding the effect on the qualified plan status of a transfer of excess pension assets to a retiree health benefit account. [Rev Proc 92-24, 1992-1 CB 739]

Q 21:60   If an employer wants to withdraw from a plan maintained by two or more unrelated employers, would the withdrawal be considered a plan termination?

No. The general rule is that such a withdrawal would not constitute a plan termination. However, the withdrawal of one or more employers may result in a partial termination of the plan (see Q 21:5). [Treas Reg § 1.411(d)-2(b)]

Q 21:61   What is a complete discontinuance of contributions under a profit sharing plan?

Instead of directly defining a complete discontinuance, IRS describes what it is and what it is not.

First, IRS regulations distinguish a complete discontinuance from a suspension of contributions under a plan that is "merely a temporary cessation of contributions by the employer." The regulations provide that "a complete discontinuance of contributions may occur although some amounts are contributed by the employer under the plan if such amounts are not substantial enough to reflect the intent on the part of the employer to continue to maintain the plan. The determination of whether a complete discontinuance of contributions under the plan has occurred will be made with regard to all the facts and circumstances in the particular case, and without regard to the amount of any contributions made under the plan by employees." [Treas Reg § 1.411(d)-2(d)]

Second, the regulations state that, in any case in which a suspension of a profit sharing plan is considered a discontinuance, the discontinuance becomes effective no later than the last day of the taxable year that follows the last taxable year for which a substantial contribution was made under the profit sharing plan. [Treas Reg § 1.411(d)-2(d)(2)]

Example. SOS Corporation maintains a calendar-year profit sharing plan. The last "substantial" contribution made by the corporation was on July 2, 1996. If a discontinuance of contributions is deemed to occur, it will become effective no later than December 31, 1997.

Employees who become eligible to enter a plan subsequent to its discontinuance receive no benefits, nor do any additional benefits accrue to any of the participants unless employer contributions are resumed. IRS, therefore, takes the position that discontinuance of contributions is equivalent to a plan termination.

What if an employer has no profits? IRS says that the failure of an employer to make contributions to its profit sharing plan for five consecutive years due solely to the absence of current or accumulated earnings and profits is not a discontinuance of contributions if the plan requires the employer to resume contributions as soon as it has profits. [Rev Rul 80-146, 1980-1 CB 90] Since current or accumulated profits are no longer required for the employer to make tax deductible contributions to a profit sharing plan, such failure to make contributions may ripen into a discontinuance. [IRC § 401(a)(27)]

Q 21:62 Must a profit sharing plan provide for full vesting of benefits upon a complete discontinuance of contributions?

Yes. A Tax Court decision upheld IRS's position that a profit sharing plan did not qualify merely because it did not provide for full vesting of participants' accrued benefits on complete discontinuance of contributions. Even though IRS conceded that there never was a discontinuance of contributions, and that no employee's rights to benefits were ever adversely affected, the absence of such a provision from a plan was, according to the court, a sufficient defect in the instrument to disqualify the plan, resulting in the disallowance of the employer deduction. [Tionesta Sand and Gravel, Inc, 73 TC 758 (1980), *aff'd*, 3d Cir in unpublished opinion (Feb 27, 1981)]

Q 21:63 Can a plan amendment result in the termination of the plan?

Yes. If benefits or employer contributions to the plan are reduced, or vesting or eligibility requirements are made less liberal, the plan is considered to be curtailed. Full vesting of a portion of the benefits may be required if IRS decides that the curtailment is a partial termination of the plan (see Q 21:5).

If an employer seeks to amend a defined benefit plan covered by Title IV to convert it to a defined contribution plan, the termination rules of Title IV must be satisfied first before the former plan is treated as terminated (see Q 21:6). [ERISA § 4041(e)]

Q 21:64   Can a plan be amended to reduce or stop benefit accruals?

Yes, but if the amendment provides for a significant reduction in the rate of future benefit accrual, certain notice requirements must be satisfied. After adoption of the amendment and no less than 15 days before the effective date of a plan amendment that significantly reduces future accruals, each participant, beneficiary who is an alternate payee under a QDRO (see chapter 30), and labor organization representing plan participants must be provided with written notice of the amendment and its effective date. This written notice is called the Section 204(h) Notice (see Qs 9:29–9:36, 21:1). This rule applies to amendments to defined benefit plans and to defined contribution plans subject to the funding standards of ERISA Section 302, namely, money purchase pension plans and target benefit plans. [ERISA § 204(h)]

In one case, the court ruled that a company's notice violated ERISA Section 204(h) when the notice came before the plan amendment was adopted and after the amendment's effective date—exactly the opposite of what ERISA requires. By posting the notice, the company also failed to provide individual written notice to each plan participant (see Q 21:30). [Production and Maintenance Employees' Local 504 v Roadmaster Corp, Nos. 89-1464 and 90-2698 (7th Cir 1992)]

Q 21:65   How does ERISA Section 204(h) apply to terminated plans covered by Title IV of ERISA?

A defined benefit plan (see Q 2:3) covered by Title IV of ERISA (see Q 21:9) that is terminated in accordance with the applicable rules (see Q 21:17) is deemed to satisfy ERISA Section 204(h) (see Qs 9:29–9:36) not later than the date of termination. Accordingly, additional benefit accruals are not required after the date of termination. [Temp Reg § 1.411(d)-6T, Q&A-14(a)]

If an amendment that is effective before the termination date provides for a significant reduction in the rate of future benefit accrual, the Section 204(h) Notice must be provided. The notice may be provided either separately, or with, or as part of the NOIT (see Qs 21:29, 21:30). If the plan is not amended to significantly reduce the rate of future benefit accruals before the termination date, the Section 204(h) Notice is not required. [Temp Reg § 1.411(d)-6T, Q&A-14(b)]

However, if the date of termination is deferred, benefits continue to accrue until the deferred date of termination unless accruals ceased as of an earlier date. [Preamble to Temp Reg § 1.411(d)-6T]

Q 21:66 Must terminating plans be amended for changes in the law?

Yes. A plan that terminates after the effective date of a change in law, but prior to the date that amendments are otherwise required (see Q 4:7), must still be amended to comply with the applicable provisions of law that are in effect at the time of plan termination. Because such a terminated plan would no longer be in existence by the required amendment date and therefore could not be amended on that date, the plan must be amended in connection with the plan termination. [Rev Proc 96-6, 1996-1 IRB 151]

Q 21:67 Must IRS be notified when a plan terminates?

Just as there is no legal requirement to file a request for a favorable determination letter (see Q 15:1) with IRS with regard to a new or amended plan, there is no requirement regarding a plan's termination. However, a plan administrator (see Q 16:1) must notify IRS on the Form 5500 series return/report (see Q 17:1) for the year in which the plan terminates. In addition, a Form 5500 series return/report must be filed every year (even after a plan terminates) until all assets are distributed from the trust. IRS has opined that Schedule B (see Qs 8:29, 17:4) must be filed for the plan year in which a defined benefit plan (see Q 2:3) terminates, but need not be filed for the plan year after the year in which the plan terminates. *The foregoing was offered as general information and was not to be construed as a ruling as to any actual case.* [Spec Rul (July 27, 1993)]

It is strongly suggested that plan administrators file Form 5310 (see Q 15:7) with IRS requesting a favorable determination letter with regard to a plan's termination. Form 6088, Distributable Benefits From Employee Pension Benefit Plans, must be attached to Form 5310 with respect to the termination of a defined benefit plan or an *underfunded* defined contribution plan (see Q 15:7). [Rev Proc 96-6, 1996-1 IRB 151; Instructions to Form 6088 (Feb 1996)] IRS has developed guidelines when examining plans for compliance with qualification requirements (see Q 4:1) where a plan was terminated and a determination letter request was not submitted to IRS. [Ann 94-101, 1994-35 IRB 53]

IRS has issued a revenue ruling explaining that a termination of a qualified retirement plan is not complete until the final distribution of plan assets. However, if the "terminated" retirement plan fails to distribute its assets as soon as administratively feasible following the established plan termination date, IRS will not treat the plan as being terminated. [Rev Rul 89-87, 1989-2 CB 81]

The ruling provides that whether a distribution is made as soon as administratively feasible will be determined under all the facts and circumstances of the given case; but, generally, a distribution that is not completed within one year following the date of plan termination specified by the employer will be presumed not to have been completed as soon as administratively feasible. If a plan's assets are not distributed as soon as administratively feasible, the plan is considered to be an ongoing plan and must meet the requirements of Section 401(a) in order to maintain its qualified status. For example, such a plan remains subject to the minimum funding requirements under Section 412 (see Q 8:1) and the information reporting requirements of Sections 6057 and 6058 (and, in the case of a defined benefit plan, the actuarial reporting requirements of Section 6059). It is not clear under the ruling whether a pending determination letter request on the plan's termination or a delay caused by the termination procedures of Title IV of ERISA (applicable to certain defined benefit plans) will excuse a distribution delay of more than one year. However, one IRS key district (see Q 15:9) has advised that, if the determination letter request is submitted timely, distributions completed within six months after the issuance of the determination letter will be treated as having been made as soon as administratively feasible. [EP/EO Baltimore Key District Newsletter, April 1991]

Chapter 22

Top-Heavy Plans

A qualified retirement plan that primarily benefits key employees—a top-heavy plan—can qualify for tax-favored status only if, in addition to the regular qualification requirements, it meets several special requirements. This chapter examines what top-heavy plans are and the special requirements these plans must satisfy.

Q 22:1 What is a top-heavy defined benefit plan?

A defined benefit plan (see Q 2:3) is top-heavy if, as of the determination date (see Q 22:21), the present value of the accrued benefits of all key employees (see Q 22:24) exceeds 60 percent of the present value of the accrued benefits of all employees. [IRC § 416(g)(1)(A)(i); Treas Reg § 1.416-1, Question T-1(c)]

Q 22:2 How are accrued benefits calculated for purposes of determining whether a qualified retirement plan is top-heavy?

Solely for determining whether the present value of cumulative accrued benefits for key employees (see Q 22:24) exceeds 60 percent of the present value of cumulative accrued benefits for all employees (90 percent for purposes of the super-top-heavy plan rules, see Q 22:57), the accrued benefit of an employee (other than a key employee) is determined by the method that is used for benefit accrual purposes under all qualified retirement plans maintained by the employer or, if there is no such single method used under all the plans, as if the benefit accrues no more rapidly than the slowest permitted rate under the fractional accrual rule. [IRC § 416(g)(4)(F)]

Q 22:3 What is a top-heavy defined contribution plan?

A defined contribution plan (see Q 2:2) is top-heavy if, as of the determination date (see Q 22:21), the total of the accounts of all key employees (see Q 22:24) exceeds 60 percent of the total of the accounts of all employees. [IRC § 416(g)(1)(A)(ii); Treas Reg § 1.416-1, Questions T-1(c) and M-16]

Q 22:4 Which qualified retirement plans are subject to the top-heavy rules?

Generally, all defined benefit plans (see Q 2:3) and defined contribution plans (see Q 2:2) are subject to the top-heavy rules. A simplified employee pension (SEP) is also subject to the top-heavy rules (see Qs 22:7, 27:1). [Treas Reg § 1.416-1, Question G-1] SIMPLE plans (see Q 27:30) are not subject to the top-heavy rules. [IRC § 416(g)(4)(G), as added by SBA '96 § 1421(b)(7)]

Q 22:5 Is a multiple employer plan subject to the top-heavy rules?

Yes. A multiple employer plan is subject to the top-heavy rules. A multiple employer plan is a qualified retirement plan to which more than one employer contributes and that is not the subject of a collective bargaining agreement.

If five employers contribute to a multiple employer plan and the accrued benefits of the key employees (see Q 22:24) of one employer exceed 60 percent of the accrued benefits of all employees of that employer, the plan is top-heavy with respect to that employer. If the retirement plan fails to satisfy the top-heavy rules for the employees of that employer, all five employers will be maintaining a retirement plan that is not qualified. [IRC § 413(c); Treas Reg § 1.416-1, Questions G-2, T-2]

Q 22:6 Are qualified nonelective contributions under a 401(k) plan taken into account for top-heavy purposes?

Yes. Qualified nonelective contributions to a 401(k) plan (see Q 23:14) may be taken into account for the purpose of satisfying the minimum top-heavy contribution requirement. Also, matching contributions to a 401(k) plan may not be treated as elective contributions in order to satisfy the actual deferral percentage (ADP) test (see Q 23:12) if they are allocated to non-key employees in order to satisfy the minimum top-heavy contribution requirement (see Qs 22:43, 22:46, 22:48). [Treas Reg §§ 1.401(k)-1(e)(7), 1.416-1, Questions M-18, M-19]

Q 22:7   What is a top-heavy simplified employee pension?

A SEP (see Q 27:1) is top-heavy if, as of the determination date (see Q 22:21), the total of the accounts of all key employees (see Q 22:24) exceeds 60 percent of the total of the accounts of all employees. However, at the employer's election, top-heavy status may be determined by taking into account only the total employer contributions (rather than account balances) to the SEP. [IRC §§ 408(k)(1), 416(i)(6)]

Q 22:8   Which factors must be considered in determining whether a qualified retirement plan is top-heavy?

To determine whether a qualified retirement plan is top-heavy, it is necessary to consider:

1. Which employers must be treated as a single employer (see Q 22:13);

2. What the determination date is for the plan year (see Q 22:21);

3. Which employees are or formerly were key employees (see Q 22:24);

4. Which former employees have not performed any services for the employer during the five-year period ending on the determination date;

5. Which plans of such employers are required or permitted to be aggregated in determining top-heavy status (see Qs 22:9, 22:10); and

6. The present value of the accrued benefits (under a defined benefit plan) or the account balances (under a defined contribution plan) of key employees, former key employees, and non-key employees (see Qs 22:1, 22:3).

[Treas Reg § 1.416-1, Question T-1(a)]

Q 22:9   What is a required aggregation group?

A required aggregation group consists of each retirement plan of the employer in which a key employee (see Q 22:24) is a participant in the plan year containing the determination date (see Q 22:21) or any of the four preceding plan years, and any other retirement plan of the employer that enables a retirement plan covering a key employee to satisfy the coverage and nondiscriminatory benefit requirements (see Qs 5:15, 4:9). [IRC § 416(g)(2)(A); Treas Reg § 1.416-1, Question T-6]

Example 1. Elaine Corporation maintains a defined benefit plan covering key employees and other salaried employees and also maintains a second defined benefit plan covering hourly employees. The first defined benefit plan by itself does not satisfy the coverage or nondiscriminatory benefit requirements, but does so when the two plans are considered together. The two defined benefit plans constitute a required aggregation group. If the first plan by itself satisfies the coverage and nondiscriminatory benefit requirements, the second plan would not be part of the required aggregation group.

Example 2. Jamie, a sole proprietor, terminated her qualified retirement plan in 1996. In 1997, Jamie incorporates and establishes a corporate qualified retirement plan. In determining whether the corporate plan is top-heavy, Jamie's terminated retirement plan and the corporate retirement plan are part of a required aggregation group.

Q 22:10   What is a permissive aggregation group?

A permissive aggregation group consists of each retirement plan of the employer that is required to be aggregated (see Q 22:9) and any other retirement plan of the employer that is not part of the required aggregation group but that satisfies the coverage and nondiscriminatory benefit requirements (see Qs 5:15, 4:9) when considered together with the required aggregation group. [IRC § 416(g)(2)(A)(ii); Treas Reg § 1.416-1, Question T-7]

In Example 1 in Q 22:9, suppose that the second defined benefit plan was not part of the required aggregation group. If so, the second plan could be permissively aggregated with the first retirement plan only if the benefits or contributions under the second retirement plan were comparable to those under the first plan.

Q 22:11   Must collectively bargained retirement plans be aggregated with other retirement plans of the employer?

Collectively bargained retirement plans that include a key employee (see Q 22:24) must be included in the required aggregation group for the employer (see Q 22:9). Collectively bargained retirement plans that do not include a key employee may be included in a permissive aggregation group (see Q 22:10). However, the special qualification requirements applicable to top-heavy plans (see Q 22:23) generally do not apply to collectively bargained retirement plans, whether or not they include a key employee. [IRC §§ 416(i)(4), 7701(a)(46); Treas Reg § 1.416-1, Questions T-3, T-7, T-8]

Q 22:12   What is a top-heavy group?

If a required aggregation group (see Q 22:9) is a top-heavy group, each retirement plan that is required to be included in the aggregation group is treated as a top-heavy plan. If, however, the group is not top-heavy, no retirement plan in the required aggregation group is treated as a top-heavy plan.

If a permissive aggregation group (see Q 22:10) is top-heavy, only those retirement plans that are part of the required aggregation group are subject to the special qualification requirements (see Q 22:23) placed on top-heavy plans. Retirement plans that are not part of the required aggregation group are not subject to these added requirements. If a permissive aggregation group is not top-heavy, on the other hand, the top-heavy requirements do not apply to any retirement plan in the group.

An aggregation group is a top-heavy group if, as of the determination date (see Q 22:21), the sum of (1) the present value of the accumulated accrued benefits for key employees (see Q 22:24) under all defined benefit plans included in the group and (2) the account balances of key employees under all defined contribution plans included in the group exceeds 60 percent of the same amount determined for all employees under all retirement plans included in the group. [IRC § 416(g)(2)(B); Treas Reg § 1.416-1, Questions T-9, T-10, T-11]

> **Example.** Nat Corporation maintains a defined benefit plan covering key employees and other salaried employees and also maintains a second defined benefit plan covering hourly employees that enables the first plan to satisfy the coverage and nondiscriminatory benefit requirements. If the present value of the total accrued benefits for all key employees exceeds 60 percent of the present value of the total accrued benefits for all employees under both plans, both plans are considered top-heavy plans. If, however, the first plan satisfied the coverage and nondiscriminatory benefit requirements by itself, the two plans would not constitute an aggregation group and only the first plan would be a top-heavy plan.

Q 22:13   How are separate retirement plans of related employers treated for purposes of the top-heavy rules?

The aggregation group rules (see Qs 22:9, 22:10) and the top-heavy group rules (see Q 22:12) apply to all retirement plans of related employers if the related employers are treated as a single employer for retirement plan purposes. [IRC §§ 414(b), 414(c), 414(m); Treas Reg § 1.416-1, Question T-1(b)]

Q 22:14   How is a terminated retirement plan treated for purposes of the top-heavy rules?

A terminated retirement plan must be aggregated with the employer's other retirement plans if it (1) was maintained within the five-year period ending on the determination date (see Q 22:21) for the plan year in question and (2) would be part of a required aggregation group (see Q 22:9) for that plan year had it not been terminated. (A terminated retirement plan is a retirement plan that has formally terminated, has ceased crediting service for benefit accruals and vesting, and has been or is distributing plan assets to the participants.)

No additional vesting, benefit accruals, or contributions must be provided for participants in a terminated retirement plan. [IRC § 416(g)(3); Treas Reg § 1.416-1, Question T-4]

Q 22:15   How is a frozen retirement plan treated for purposes of the top-heavy rules?

A frozen retirement plan must provide minimum benefits or contributions (see Qs 22:37, 22:43) and provide top-heavy vesting (see Q 22:32). (A frozen retirement plan is a retirement plan that has ceased crediting service for benefit accruals, but has not distributed all assets to the participants.) [Treas Reg § 1.416-1, Question T-5]

Q 22:16   What happens if an employee ceases to be a key employee?

If an employee ceases to be a key employee (see Q 22:24) and continues to work for the employer, that employee is treated as a non-key employee and the employee's accrued benefit under the defined benefit plan and account balance under the defined contribution plan are disregarded for purposes of determining whether the retirement plan is top-heavy for each plan year following the last plan year for which the employee was a key employee. [IRC § 416(g)(4)(B); Treas Reg § 1.416-1, Questions T-1(d), T-12]

Q 22:17   How are plan distributions to employees treated for purposes of determining whether the qualified retirement plan is top-heavy?

The present value of the accrued benefit of an employee in a defined benefit plan, or the account balance of an employee in a defined contribution plan, includes any amount distributed with respect to the employee under the plan within the five-year period ending on the determination date (see Q 22:21). This rule applies whether or not the employee is a key employee (see Q 22:24) and applies to distributions made to a beneficiary of an employee (see Q 22:31). [IRC § 416(g)(3); Treas Reg § 1.416-1, Question T-30]

If the employee does not render any services to the employer at any time during the five-year period ending on the determination date (see Q 22:21), the present value of the employee's accrued benefit or account balance is not taken into account for purposes of top-heavy plan testing. [IRC § 416(g)(4)(E); Treas Reg § 1.416-1, Question T-1(d)]

Q 22:18 Are death benefits treated as distributions for purposes of determining whether a qualified retirement plan is top-heavy?

Death benefits up to the present value of the deceased participant's accrued benefit immediately prior to death are treated as distributions for top-heavy testing purposes, but any death benefits in excess of this amount are not taken into account. For example, the distribution from a defined contribution plan, including the cash value of life insurance policies, of a participant's account balance on account of the participant's death is treated as a distribution for top-heavy testing purposes. [Treas Reg § 1.416-1, Question T-31]

Q 22:19 How are rollovers and transfers treated for purposes of determining whether a retirement plan is top-heavy?

The rules for handling rollovers and plan-to-plan transfers depend on whether the rollovers and transfers are unrelated (both initiated by the employee and made from a qualified retirement plan maintained by one employer to a qualified retirement plan maintained by another employer) or related (either not initiated by the employee or made to a qualified retirement plan maintained by the same or a related employer).

In the case of unrelated rollovers or transfers, (1) the qualified retirement plan making the distribution always counts the distribution (see Q 22:17) and (2) the qualified retirement plan accepting the rollover or transfer does not consider it if it was accepted after 1983, but considers it if it was accepted prior to 1984.

In the case of related rollovers or transfers, the qualified retirement plan making the rollover or transfer does not count it as a distribution, but the qualified retirement plan accepting the rollover or transfer counts it. The rules for related rollovers do not depend on whether the rollover or transfer was accepted prior to 1984. [IRC § 416(g)(4)(A); Treas Reg § 1.416-1, Question T-32]

IRS has opined that if a participant does a direct rollover (see Q 28:20) of a distribution from a terminated retirement plan to another plan of the same employer, the amount rolled over will be counted in the recipient plan's top-heavy determination because it is a related rollover. However, IRS also opined that if a participant rolls over a distribution from a terminated retirement plan to an IRA and later rolls over the IRA assets into another plan of the same employer (see Q 28:40), the amount rolled over will *not* be counted in the recipient plan's top-heavy determination because it is an unrelated rollover. *The foregoing was in answer to a question posed at a 1995 conference and should not be construed as a formal ruling.*

Q 22:20 How are employee contributions treated for purposes of determining whether a qualified retirement plan is top-heavy?

For purposes of determining the present value of accumulated accrued benefits under a defined benefit plan and the sum of the account balances under a defined contribution plan, benefits derived from both employer contributions and employee contributions (whether mandatory or voluntary) are taken into account. However, accumulated deductible employee contributions (see Q 6:22) under a qualified retirement plan are disregarded. [Treas Reg § 1.416-1, Question T-28]

Q 22:21 When is the determination date?

The date on which a qualified retirement plan is determined to be top-heavy is called the determination date. The determination date for a new retirement plan is the last day of the first plan year; for an existing plan, it is the last day of the preceding plan year. [IRC § 416(g)(4)(C); Treas Reg § 1.416-1, Question T-22]

> **Example.** Charles Corporation established a calendar-year defined contribution plan on January 1, 1997. On December 31, 1997 (the last day of the first plan year), the accounts of the key employees exceed 60 percent of all employees' accounts under the plan. For 1997, the plan is top-heavy. The plan will also be top-heavy for the 1998 plan year because the determination date for the 1998 plan year is the last day of the 1997 plan year.

Q 22:22 If the employer has more than one qualified retirement plan, when is the top-heavy determination made?

When two or more retirement plans are aggregated (see Qs 22:9, 22:10), the present value of the accrued benefits or account balances is determined separately for each plan as of each plan's determination date (see Q 22:21).

The retirement plans are then aggregated by adding the results of each plan as of the determination dates that fall within the same calendar year. The combined results indicate whether or not the retirement plans are top-heavy. [Treas Reg § 1.416-1, Question T-23]

> **Example.** David Corporation maintains two qualified retirement plans, Plan A and Plan B, each covering a key employee. Plan A's plan year commences July 1 and ends June 30. Plan B's plan year is the calendar year. For Plan A's plan year commencing July 1, 1996, the determination date is June 30, 1996. For Plan B's 1997 plan year, the determination date is December 31, 1996. These plans must be aggregated.

On the respective determination dates of each plan, separate calculations of the present value of the accrued benefits of all employees are made. The determination dates, June 30, 1996 and December 31, 1996, fall within the same calendar year. Accordingly, the present values of accrued benefits or account balances with respect to each of these determination dates are combined for purposes of determining whether the plans are top-heavy. If, after combining the two, the total results show that the plans are top-heavy, Plan A will be top-heavy for the plan year commencing July 1, 1996, and Plan B will be top-heavy for the 1997 calendar plan year.

Q 22:23 Are there special qualification requirements that apply to top-heavy plans?

Yes. In addition to the qualification requirements that apply to all retirement plans, a top-heavy plan must satisfy the following requirements:

1. Minimum vesting (see Q 22:32); and
2. Minimum benefits or contributions (see Qs 22:37, 22:43).

[IRC § 416(a); Treas Reg § 1.416-1, Questions T-35, T-36, T-37]

Q 22:24 Who is a key employee?

A key employee is an employee who, at any time during the plan year containing the determination date (see Q 22:21) or any of the four preceding plan years, is (or was):

1. An officer having annual compensation in excess of 50 percent of the annual dollar limitation for defined benefit plans in effect for such plan year (see Qs 22:25, 6:8);
2. One of the ten largest owners of the employer having annual compensation in excess of the annual addition limitation in effect for such plan year (see Qs 22:27, 6:1);

3. A 5 percent owner (see Q 22:28); or

4. A 1 percent owner whose annual compensation exceeds $150,000 (see Q 22:28).

[IRC § 416(i)(1)(A); Treas Reg § 1.416-1, Question T-12]

Q 22:25 Who is an officer of the employer for top-heavy plan purposes?

The determination as to whether an employee is an officer is made on the basis of all the facts and circumstances—including, for example, the source of the employee's authority, the term for which the employee was elected or appointed, and the nature and extent of the employee's duties. As generally accepted in connection with corporations, the term "officer" means an administrative executive who is in regular and continued service. It implies continuity of service and excludes those employed for a special and single transaction, or those with only nominal administrative duties. So, for example, all the employees of a bank who have the title of vice-president or assistant vice-president are not automatically considered officers. An employee who does not have the title of an officer but has the authority of an officer is an officer for purposes of the key employee test. [Rev Rul 80-314, 1980-2 CB 152; Treas Reg § 1.416-1, Question T-13]

The number of employees that can be considered officers is equal to 10 percent of all employees, or three, whichever is greater. In no case, however, can the total number of officers exceed 50. Thus, if the employer has fewer than 30 employees, no more than three can be considered officers. [IRC § 416(i)(1)(A); Treas Reg § 1.416-1, Question T-14]

Q 22:26 Do any organizations other than corporations have officers?

Sole proprietorships, partnerships, unincorporated associations, trusts, and labor organizations may have officers. [Treas Reg § 1.416-1, Question T-15]

Q 22:27 Who is one of the ten largest owners of the employer?

The ten largest owners are the ten employees owning the largest interest in the employer. An employee who has some ownership interest is considered to be one of the top ten owners unless at least ten other employees own a greater interest than the employee owns.

In determining the ten employees owning the largest interests in the employer, only employees with annual compensation in excess of the annual addition limitation for such plan year (see Q 6:1) and having more than a ½ percent ownership interest are taken into account as key employees. If two employees have the same interest in the employer, the employee with the greater annual compensation is treated as having a larger interest. [IRC § 416(i)(1); Treas Reg § 1.416-1, Question T-19]

> **Example.** Twenty-five employees at Allyson Corporation have a 4 percent interest in the employer. Compensation for 15 of these employees ranges from $25,000 to $45,000. Compensation for the other ten employees ranges from $60,000 to $75,000. Only the latter ten employees are considered key employees for top-heavy plan testing purposes.

Q 22:28 Who is a 5 percent owner or a 1 percent owner for top-heavy plan purposes?

A 5 percent owner is a person who owns, directly or indirectly, more than 5 percent of the shares of stock of the corporation. A 1 percent owner is a person who owns, directly or indirectly, more than 1 percent of the shares of stock of the corporation. A 1 percent owner is a key employee (see Q 22:24) only if such owner's annual compensation from the employer is more than $150,000.

If the employer is not a corporation, the ownership test is applied to the person's capital or profits interest in the employer. In determining ownership percentages, each employer, whether related or unrelated (see Q 5:33), is treated as a separate entity. But for purposes of determining whether an employee has compensation of more than $150,000, compensation from each related entity is aggregated. [IRC §§ 416(i)(1)(B), 416(i)(1)(C); Treas Reg § 1.416-1, Questions T-16, T-17, T-18, T-20, T-21]

For purposes of determining ownership, an individual is considered as owning the shares of stock owned by his or her spouse, children, grandchildren, and parents. In addition, shares of stock owned by a corporation, partnership, estate, or trust can be attributed to the individual, and vice versa. If the employer is not a corporation, similar principles apply. [IRC §§ 318(a), 416(i)(1)(B)(iii); Treas Reg §§ 1.318-1 through 1.318-4, 1.416-1, Question T-18]

Q 22:29 Who is a non-key employee?

Any employee who is not a key employee (see Q 22:24) is a non-key employee. [IRC § 416(i)(2)]

Q 22:30   Who is a former key employee?

A former key employee is an individual who, when employed by the employer, was once a key employee (see Q 22:24).

> **Example.** Melanie, who was a 5 percent owner of Whitney Corp. in 1996, sold all of her interest in the corporation before the end of the year and retired. Even though Melanie is no longer an employee or owner, she will be treated as a key employee for each plan year through the 2001 plan year. For the 2002 plan year and subsequent plan years, Melanie will be treated as a former key employee.

Former key employees are non-key employees and are excluded entirely from the calculation in determining top-heaviness. [Treas Reg § 1.416-1, Questions T-1(d), T-12]

Q 22:31   How is a beneficiary treated under the top-heavy plan rules?

For purposes of the top-heavy plan rules, the terms "key employee," "former key employee," and "non-key employee" include their beneficiaries. [IRC § 416(i)(5); Treas Reg § 1.416-1, Question T-12]

Q 22:32   What is the minimum vesting requirement for a top-heavy plan?

A top-heavy plan must contain either a three-year vesting provision or a six-year graded vesting provision. [IRC § 416(b)(1); Treas Reg § 1.416-1, Question V-1]

Under three-year vesting, an employee who completes at least three years of service (see Q 22:33) must be 100 percent vested. Under six-year graded vesting, an employee must become vested as determined by the following table:

Completed Years of Service	Vested Percentage
2	20
3	40
4	60
5	80
6 or more	100

Q 22:33 Which years of service must be taken into account for minimum vesting purposes?

The rules for determining an employee's years of service for vesting under non-top-heavy plans (see chapter 9) also apply for the minimum vesting requirements under top-heavy plans. Thus, years of service completed before 1984 (the year the top-heavy rules went into effect) and years of service completed after 1983 (including years when the plan is not top-heavy) are counted for minimum vesting purposes. [IRC § 416(b)(2); Treas Reg § 1.416-1, Question V-2]

Q 22:34 Which benefits must be subject to the minimum top-heavy vesting requirement?

All benefits must be subject to the minimum top-heavy vesting requirement. These benefits include benefits accrued before a retirement plan becomes top-heavy. However, when a retirement plan becomes top-heavy, the accrued benefit of an employee who does not have an hour of service after the plan becomes top-heavy is not required to be subject to the minimum vesting requirement. [Treas Reg § 1.416-1, Question V-3]

Q 22:35 When a top-heavy plan ceases to be top-heavy, may the vesting schedule be changed?

Yes. When a top-heavy plan ceases to be top-heavy, the vesting schedule may be changed to one that would otherwise be permitted. However, in changing the vesting schedule, any portion of the benefit that was nonforfeitable before the plan ceased to be top-heavy must remain nonforfeitable, and any employee with three or more years of service must be given the option of remaining under the prior (i.e., top-heavy) vesting schedule (see Q 9:6). [IRC § 411(a)(10); Treas Reg § 1.416-1, Question V-7]

Q 22:36 Which top-heavy vesting schedule is more favorable to the employer?

It depends on how long the employees usually stay with the employer.

Example. Rena Corporation adopted a 10-percent-of-compensation money purchase pension plan on January 1, 1996. Bob completes a year of service on January 1, 1997 and enters the plan. Bob earns $10,000 a year. Set forth below is a calculation of Bob's benefits under the six-year graded and three-year cliff vesting schedules (see Q 22:32):

| | 6-Year | | 3-Year | |
| | | | | |
Plan Year	Contribution/ Account Balance	Vesting Percentage/ Vested Benefits	Contribution/ Account Balance	Vesting Percentage/ Vested Benefits
1	0 / 0		0 / 0	
2	$1,000 / $1,000	20% / $200	$1,000 / $1,000	0% / $0
3	$1,000 / $2,000	40% / $800	$1,000 / $2,000	100% / $2,000
4	$1,000 / $3,000	60% / $1,800	$1,000 / $3,000	100% / $3,000
5	$1,000 / $4,000	80% / $3,200	$1,000 / $4,000	100% / $4,000
6	$1,000 / $5,000	100% / $5,000	$1,000 / $5,000	100% / $5,000

In plan year 2, less vested benefits are provided under the three-year cliff vesting schedule; in plan years 3, 4, and 5, less vested benefits are provided under the six-year graded vesting schedule. Thus, if employees customarily leave before completing three years of service, three-year cliff vesting is more favorable to the employer; if they leave after completing three years of service, the six-year graded schedule is more favorable to the employer. After six years of service, both schedules provide equal benefits.

As an alternative, Rena Corporation could require employees to complete two years of service to become eligible, but then employees must be 100 percent vested immediately (see Q 9:12). With a two-year service requirement and 100 percent immediate vesting, Bob's benefits would be as follows:

Plan Year	Contribution/ Account Balance	Vesting Percentage/ Vested Benefits
1	$\dfrac{0}{0}$	
2	$\dfrac{0}{0}$	
3	$\dfrac{\$1,000}{\$1,000}$	100% $\$1,000$
4	$\dfrac{\$1,000}{\$2,000}$	100% $\$2,000$
5	$\dfrac{\$1,000}{\$3,000}$	100% $\$3,000$
6	$\dfrac{\$1,000}{\$4,000}$	100% $\$4,000$

In plan year 2, the least vested benefits occur under three-year cliff or with the two-year service requirement; in plan years 3 and 4, the least vested benefits occur under six-year graded; in plan years 5 and 6, and in all subsequent plan years, the least vested benefits occur with the two-year service requirement. Therefore, if employees customarily leave after completing five or more years of service, the two-year service requirement will be most favorable to the employer maintaining a top-heavy plan.

Q 22:37   What is the minimum benefit requirement for a top-heavy defined benefit plan?

Under a top-heavy defined benefit plan, the annual retirement benefit (see Q 22:38) of a non-key employee (see Q 22:29) must not be less than the employee's average compensation (see Q 22:40) multiplied by the lesser of:

1. 2 percent times the number of years of service (see Q 22:41); or

2. 20 percent.

Benefits attributable to employer contributions are considered, but benefits attributable to employee contributions must be ignored.

[IRC §§ 416(c)(1)(A), 416(c)(1)(B); Treas Reg § 1.416-1, Questions M-1, M-2, M-5, M-6]

Q 22:38 What does annual retirement benefit mean for the minimum benefit requirement?

Annual retirement benefit means a benefit attributable to employer contributions payable annually in the form of a single life annuity (with no ancillary benefits) beginning at the retirement plan's normal retirement age (see Q 10:55). [IRC § 416(c)(1)(E); Treas Reg § 1.416-1, Question M-2(d)]

If benefits under the defined benefit plan are payable in a form other than a straight life annuity (under a straight life annuity, payments terminate upon the death of the annuitant), the minimum benefit is adjusted downward to a benefit that is equivalent to a straight life annuity. For example, if the annuity payments under the defined benefit plan are guaranteed for a period of ten years (that is, if the participant dies within the ten-year period, payments will be made to the participant's beneficiary for the rest of the period), the minimum annual retirement benefit (see Q 22:37) is reduced by 10 percent. [Treas Reg § 1.416-1, Question M-3]

Q 22:39 What is the minimum benefit required if the employee receives benefits other than at normal retirement age?

If the benefit commences at a date other than at normal retirement age (see Q 10:53), the employee must receive an amount that is at least the actuarial equivalent of the minimum single life annuity benefit (see Qs 22:37, 22:38) commencing at normal retirement age. The employee may receive a lower benefit if the benefit commences before normal retirement age and must receive a higher benefit if the benefit commences after normal retirement age. [Treas Reg § 1.416-1, Question M-3]

Q 22:40 What does the term participant's average compensation mean for the minimum benefit requirement?

A participant's average compensation means the participant's compensation averaged over a period of no more than five consecutive years (the testing period) during which the participant had the greatest aggregate compensation from the employer. [IRC § 416(c)(1)(D)(i); Treas Reg § 1.416-1, Questions M-2(c), T-21]

A year need not be taken into account during the testing period if it ends in a plan year beginning before 1984 or begins after the close of the last plan year in which the plan was a top-heavy plan. [IRC § 416(c)(1)(D)(iii); Treas Reg § 1.416-1, Question M-2(c)]

Q 22:41 Which years of service are taken into account in determining the minimum annual benefit under a top-heavy defined benefit plan?

A year of service generally means a year during which the employee completes 1,000 hours of service. The rules for determining years of service parallel those for calculating vesting (see Qs 9:3, 9:9–9:11). However, the following years of service are not taken into account for determining the minimum annual retirement benefit:

1. A year of service within which ends a plan year for which the defined benefit plan is not top-heavy; and

2. A year of service completed in a plan year beginning before 1984.

[IRC § 416(c)(1)(C); Treas Reg § 1.416-1, Question M-2(b)]

The minimum annual benefit under a top-heavy defined benefit plan (see Q 22:37) is the lesser of (1) 2 percent of the employee's compensation multiplied by the employee's years of service, or (2) 20 percent of the employee's compensation. This determination of the employee's total years of service is important only if the total is less than ten, because if years of service equal or exceed ten, the 20 percent minimum can be used.

In one circumstance, IRS allowed the top-heavy minimum accrued benefit to start to accrue when the employee became a participant. According to the facts, a non-key employee was hired January 1, 1985 and became eligible to participate in the company's defined benefit plan on January 1, 1988. For purposes of the top-heavy rules, IRS stated that the minimum accrued benefit starts to accrue when an employee becomes a participant, so that in the circumstances of the above case, the accrued benefit as of January 1, 1988 was zero. *The foregoing was offered as general information and was not to be construed as a ruling relating to any actual case.*

Q 22:42 Which employees must receive a minimum benefit in a top-heavy defined benefit plan?

Each non-key employee (see Q 22:29) who is a participant and who has at least 1,000 hours of service during the year must receive a minimum benefit in a top-heavy defined benefit plan for that period. A non-key employee may not fail to receive a minimum benefit merely because the employee was not employed on a specified date (e.g., the last day of the plan year). Similarly, a non-key employee who is excluded from participation (or who accrues no benefit) because either (1) the employee's compensation is below a stated amount or (2) the employee fails to make mandatory employee contributions must nevertheless accrue a minimum benefit. [Treas Reg § 1.416-1, Questions M-1, M-4]

Q 22:43 What is the minimum contribution requirement for a top-heavy defined contribution plan?

Under a top-heavy defined contribution plan, the employer's contribution for each non-key employee (see Q 22:29) must not be less than 3 percent of compensation (see Q 22:45). However, if the highest contribution percentage rate for a key employee (see Q 22:24) is less than 3 percent of compensation, the 3 percent minimum contribution rate is reduced to the rate that applies to the key employee. [IRC §§ 416(c)(2)(A), 416(c)(2)(B); Treas Reg § 1.416-1, Questions M-1, M-7, M-8, M-9]

> **Example.** Aviva Corporation established a calendar-year defined contribution plan (see Q 2:2) on January 1, 1996. The plan is top-heavy and contains a contribution formula of 2 percent of compensation below the taxable wage base (see Q 7:7) and 4 percent of compensation in excess of the taxable wage base. Andrea, the highest-paid key employee, earns $70,000, and the contribution on her behalf is $1,546 [(2% × $62,700) + 4% × ($70,000 – $62,700)]. Because her contribution rate is 2.21 percent ($1,546 ÷ $70,000), Aviva Corporation has to contribute only 2.21 percent of compensation for each non-key employee.

Q 22:44 Do forfeitures affect the minimum contribution requirement?

Under the minimum contribution rules (see Q 22:43), reallocated forfeitures are considered as employer contributions. For example, if no amount is contributed by the employer under a profit sharing plan for any key employee but forfeitures are allocated to key employees, contributions may be required under the minimum contribution rules for non-key employees. [Treas Reg § 1.416-1, Question M-7]

Q 22:45 What does participant's compensation mean for purposes of the minimum contribution requirement?

The term "participant's compensation" means the participant's total compensation from the employer during the year (see Q 6:3)—even though compensation, as defined in the plan, may exclude certain forms of compensation (e.g., bonuses). [IRC §§ 415(c)(3), 416(c)(2)(A); Treas Reg § 1.416-1, Questions M-7, T-21]

Q 22:46 Which employees must receive the top-heavy defined contribution plan minimum contribution?

Those non-key employees (see Q 22:29) who are participants and have not separated from service at the end of the plan year, whether or not they have completed 1,000 hours of service, must receive the top-heavy defined contribution plan minimum contribution. A non-key employee who is excluded from participation (or who accrues no benefit) because (1) the employee declines to make mandatory contributions to the plan or (2) the employee declines to make elective contributions under a 401(k) plan (see Qs 22:48, 23:13) is considered an employee covered by the plan for purposes of the minimum contribution requirement. [Treas Reg § 1.416-1, Question M-10]

Q 22:47 Can Social Security benefits or contributions be used to satisfy the minimum benefit and contribution requirements?

No. A top-heavy plan cannot take benefits or contributions under Social Security into account to satisfy the minimum benefit requirement (see Q 22:37) or the minimum contribution requirement (see Q 22:43). Thus, the required minimum benefit or contribution for a non-key employee may not be eliminated or reduced by providing for permitted disparity (see Q 7:1) in the plan. [IRC § 416(e); Treas Reg § 1.416-1, Question M-11]

Q 22:48 Can elective contributions under a 401(k) plan be used to satisfy the top-heavy minimum contribution rules?

No. Elective contributions to a 401(k) plan (see Q 23:13) on behalf of non-key employees may not be treated as employer contributions for the purpose of satisfying the top-heavy minimum contribution requirement. However, in determining the percentage at which contributions are made for the key employee with the highest percentage, elective contributions on behalf of key employees are taken into account (see Qs 22:6, 22:43, 22:46). [Treas Reg §§ 1.401(k)-1(e)(7), 1.416-1, Question M-20]

Q 22:49   Must an employer that has both a top-heavy defined benefit plan and a top-heavy defined contribution plan provide both a minimum benefit and a minimum contribution for non-key employees?

No. If a non-key employee (see Q 22:29) participates in both a top-heavy defined benefit plan and a top-heavy defined contribution plan maintained by an employer, the employer is not required to provide the non-key employee with both the minimum benefit and the minimum contribution.

There are four safe-harbor rules a top-heavy plan may use in determining which minimum an employee must receive. Because the defined benefit minimums are generally more valuable, if each employee covered under both a top-heavy defined benefit plan and a top-heavy defined contribution plan receives the defined benefit minimum, receipt of that minimum will satisfy the standards. A safe-harbor defined contribution minimum is provided by IRS. If the contributions and forfeitures under the defined contribution plan equal 5 percent of compensation in each year the plan is top-heavy, that minimum will also satisfy the standards.

The other two safe-harbor rules are:

1. Using a floor offset under which the defined benefit minimum is provided in the defined benefit plan and is offset by the benefits provided under the defined contribution plan (see Q 2:21); and

2. Proving by use of a comparability analysis that the plans provide aggregate benefits at least equal to the defined benefit minimum.

[IRC § 416(f); Treas Reg § 1.416-1, Questions M-12, M-13, M-15; Rev Rul 76-259, 1976-2 CB 111]

Example. Alicia, a non-key employee, participates in a top-heavy money purchase pension plan that provides an annual contribution rate of 5 percent of compensation and a top-heavy defined benefit plan that provides a retirement benefit equal to 8 percent of compensation. The employer is not required to provide an additional retirement benefit for Alicia under the defined benefit plan.

Q 22:50   What is the limitation on compensation that may be taken into account under a top-heavy plan?

Only the first $150,000 (adjusted for cost-of-living increases) of an employee's compensation (see Qs 6:23, 6:25) may be taken into account, regardless of whether the plan is top-heavy. The compensation limit was $200,000 (adjusted for cost-of-living increases) for plan years beginning prior to 1994 (see Q 6:24). [IRC § 401(a)(17)]

An adjustment to the annual compensation limit will be made only if it is $10,000 or greater and then is made in multiples of $10,000 (i.e., rounded down to the next-lowest multiple of $10,000). For example, an increase in the cost-of-living of $9,999 will result in no adjustment, and an increase of $19,999 will create an upward adjustment of $10,000. Therefore, the cost of living must increase by $6\frac{2}{3}$ percent before the first adjustment to the annual compensation limit will occur ($6\frac{2}{3}\% \times \$150,000 = \$10,000$). [IRC §§ 401(a)(17)(A), 401(a)(17)(B); Treas Reg § 1.401(a)(17)-1(a)(3)]

Q 22:51 What happens if a key employee participates in both a defined benefit plan and a defined contribution plan?

For limitation years (see Q 6:16) *beginning before 2000,* if a key employee (see Q 22:24) participates in both a defined benefit plan and a defined contribution plan that are included in a top-heavy group (see Q 22:12), the overall maximum limitation for the key employee is computed under a more restrictive formula unless certain requirements are met (see Q 22:56).

For combined plans in a top-heavy group, the sum of the defined benefit plan fraction and the defined contribution plan fraction cannot exceed 1.0 (the same rule that applies in a non-top-heavy situation; see Q 6:17). However, the denominator of each fraction is calculated differently.

To arrive at the overall maximum limitation, take the following steps:

Step 1: Compute a defined benefit plan fraction. The numerator of this fraction is the projected annual retirement benefit determined at year end. The denominator is the lesser of 1.0 (instead of 1.25) times the dollar limitation for the current year or 1.4 times the percentage limitation for the current year (see Q 6:8). [IRC §§ 415(e)(2), prior to repeal by SBA '96 § 1452(a), 416(h)(1), prior to repeal by SBA '96 § 1452(c)(7)]

Step 2: Compute a defined contribution plan fraction. The numerator of this fraction is the total of the annual additions to the participant's account for all years determined at year end. The denominator is the lesser of 1.0 (instead of 1.25) times the dollar limitation or 1.4 times the percentage limitation for the current year and all years of prior service (see Q 6:1). [IRC §§ 415(e)(3), 416(h)(1); Treas Reg § 1.416-1, Question T-33]

Step 3: Add the two fractions. The total may not exceed 1.0.

[IRC § 415(e)(1), prior to repeal by SBA '96 § 1452(a)]

Each plan may contain a fail-safe provision (see Q 6:17).

Example. Mr. Jason incorporates his business in January 1996. The corporation adopts a 100 percent defined benefit plan and a 10-percent-of-compensation money purchase pension plan that are included in a top-heavy group. Mr. Jason earns $106,679 in 1996. Here is how the top-heavy 1.0 rule works:

1. The defined benefit plan fraction is .889 [$106,679 ÷ $120,000 (i.e., the lesser of 1.0 × $120,000 or 1.4 × $106,679)].

2. The defined contribution plan fraction is .356 [$10,668 ÷ $30,000 (i.e., the lesser of 1.0 × $30,000 or 1.4 × $26,670)].

3. The two fractions total 1.245.

At this point, the top-heavy 1.0 rule comes into play so that one of the fractions must be reduced. If the 10-percent-of-compensation contribution formula under the defined contribution plan is reduced to 3.12 percent, the defined contribution plan fraction will be .111 [$3,328 (i.e., 3.12% × $106,679) ÷ $30,000]. Then, the total of the fractions will be 1.0.

For limitation years beginning after 1999, the 1.0 rule is repealed. [SBA '96, Act §§ 1452(a), 1452(c)(7)]

Q 22:52 At what level of compensation is a key employee excluded from participating in a second plan?

For limitation years (see Q 6:16) *beginning before 2000,* if either the defined benefit plan fraction or the defined contribution plan fraction is 1.0, the key employee is excluded from participating in a second plan.

If the key employee's annual compensation is $120,000 or more and the key employee's annual retirement benefit under the defined benefit plan is $120,000 (the current maximum; see Q 6:8), the defined benefit plan fraction is 1.0 [$120,000 ÷ $120,000 (i.e., the lesser of 1.0 × $120,000 or 1.4 × $120,000)].

If the key employee's annual compensation is $120,000 or more and the annual addition (see Q 6:1) under the defined contribution plan is $30,000 (the current maximum; see Q 6:1), the defined contribution plan fraction is 1.0 [$30,000 ÷ $30,000 (i.e., the lesser of 1.0 × $30,000 or 1.4 × $30,000)].

If the maximum dollar limits increase (see Qs 6:2, 6:8), the level of compensation at which a key employee is excluded from a second plan will also increase.

For limitation years beginning after 1999, the 1.0 rule is repealed. [SBA '96, Act §§ 1452(a), 1452(c)(7)]

Q 22:53   At what level of compensation will the top-heavy 1.0 rule have an effect on a key employee?

For limitation years (see Q 6:16) *beginning in 1996,* if the employee's annual compensation exceeds $85,714, the top-heavy 1.0 rule requires a reduction in one of the plans (see Q 22:51). At $85,714 or less, the 1.0 rule as applied to combined plans in a non-top-heavy group will be equivalent to the top-heavy 1.0 rule.

Under the non-top-heavy rule, at $85,714 of compensation, the total of the fractions of a 100 percent defined benefit plan ($85,714 ÷ $120,000 = .714) plus a 10 percent defined contribution plan ($8,571 ÷ $30,000 = .286) equals 1.0. Under the top-heavy rule, at $85,714 of compensation, the total of the fractions of the same 100 percent defined benefit plan ($85,714 ÷ $120,000 = .714) plus the same 10 percent defined contribution plan ($8,571 ÷ $30,000 = .286) also equals 1.0.

If the maximum dollar limits increase (see Qs 6:2, 6:8), the threshold level of compensation for equivalency will also increase, but not necessarily in proportion to the percentage increase in the dollar limits.

For limitation years beginning after 1999, the 1.0 rule is repealed. [SBA '96, Act §§ 1452(a), 1452(c)(7)]

Q 22:54   What is the special rule if two qualified retirement plans were adopted prior to 1984?

If the employer adopted both a defined benefit plan and a defined contribution plan prior to 1984 (the defined contribution plan must have been in existence on or before July 1, 1982), the plan administrator may make a special election to calculate the denominator of the defined contribution plan fraction for each participant for all limitation years (see Q 6:16) ending before 1983.

This calculation is made in two steps. First, the denominator of the fraction for the 1982 limitation year is determined. Then, the denominator is multiplied by a transition fraction.

The numerator of the transition fraction is the lesser of:

1. $41,500 (instead of $51,875—the amount used in a non-top-heavy situation); or

2. 1.4 times 25 percent of the participant's compensation for the 1981 limitation year.

The denominator of the fraction is the lesser of:

1. $41,500; or

2. 25 percent of the participant's compensation for the 1981 limitation year.

[IRC §§ 415(e)(6), prior to repeal by SBA '96 § 1452(a), 416(h)(4), prior to repeal by SBA '96 § 1452(c)(7)]

Example. Dr. Saul incorporated his medical practice in January 1975. His compensation for each of the years 1975 through 1982 was $185,000. The corporation adopted a 25-percent-of-compensation money purchase pension plan (a defined contribution plan) in 1977 and a defined benefit plan in 1982.

The denominator of the defined contribution plan fraction for 1982 was $266,600, and Dr. Saul earned $185,000 in 1981. The numerator of the transition fraction is $41,500 [the lesser of $41,500 or $64,750 (i.e., 1.4 × 25% × $185,000)]; the denominator is also $41,500 [the lesser of $41,500 or $46,250 (i.e., 25% × $185,000)]. The transition fraction is 1.0 (i.e., $41,500 ÷ $41,500), and the adjusted denominator of the defined contribution plan fraction remains $266,600 (i.e., 1.0 × $266,600). In this example, electing the transition rule is of no value.

If Dr. Saul earned less than $166,000 in 1981, the transition fraction would exceed 1.0 and Dr. Saul would therefore benefit by electing to use the transition fraction.

Q 22:55 What happens if a key employee's combined fractions exceed 1.0?

In some cases *in a limitation year* (see Q 6:16), *beginning before 2000,* the total of a key employee's defined benefit plan fraction and defined contribution plan fraction may exceed 1.0 at the time the key employee becomes subject to this rule. In that event, the key employee is permitted no further benefit accruals under the defined benefit plan and no additional employer contributions (including forfeitures and voluntary nondeductible contributions) under the defined contribution plan until the total of these fractions becomes less than 1.0. [IRC § 416(h)(3), prior to repeal by SBA '96 § 1452(c)(7)]

For limitation years beginning after 1999, the 1.0 rule is repealed. [SBA '96, Act §§ 1452(a), 1452(c)(7)]

Q 22:56 If a key employee participates in both a defined benefit plan and a defined contribution plan, can the overall maximum limitation be computed under the regular 1.0 rule?

For limitation years (see Q 6:16) *beginning before 2000,* the 1.0 rule (see Q 6:17), which applies to an employee covered by two qualified retirement plans that are not top-heavy, also applies to a key employee covered by two qualified retirement plans in a top-heavy group (rather than the more restrictive rule that is usually applied; see Q 22:51) if these additional requirements are met:

1. A concentration test is satisfied (see Q 22:57); and

2. An extra minimum benefit or extra minimum contribution is given to non-key employees (see Q 22:58).

[IRC § 416(h)(2), prior to repeal by SBA '96 § 1452(c)(7); Treas Reg § 1.416-1, Questions T-33, M-14]

For limitation years beginning after 1999, the 1.0 rule is repealed. [SBA '96, Act §§ 1452(a), 1452(c)(7)]

Q 22:57 What is the concentration test for purposes of the 1.0 rule?

For limitation years (see Q 6:16) *beginning before 2000,* one of the two requirements (see Q 22:56) that must be satisfied before a key employee is subject to the less restrictive 1.0 rule (see Q 6:17) is the concentration test. This test is generally satisfied with respect to a key employee for a year if, as of the last determination date (see Q 22:21), (1) the present value of the accumulated accrued benefits for key employees under the defined benefit plan, plus (2) the sum of the account balances of key employees under the defined contribution plan is not greater than 90 percent of the same amount determined for all participants under the retirement plans. [IRC § 416(h)(2)(B), prior to repeal by SBA '96 § 1452(c)(7); Treas Reg § 1.416-1, Question T-33]

Qualified retirement plans may be permissively aggregated to avoid exceeding the 90 percent amount (see Q 22:10). [Treas Reg § 1.416-1, Question T-34]

For limitation years beginning after 1999, the 1.0 rule is repealed. [SBA '96, Act §§ 1452(a), 1452(c)(7)]

Q 22:58   What is an extra minimum benefit or extra minimum contribution for purposes of the 1.0 rule?

For limitation years (see Q 6:16) *beginning before 2000,* the second requirement (see Q 22:56) that must be satisfied before a key employee is subject to the less restrictive 1.0 rule (see Q 6:17) is that non-key employees must be given an extra minimum benefit or an extra minimum contribution.

To satisfy this requirement, any one of the four safe-harbor rules (see Q 22:49) may be used with the following modifications. Each non-key employee in the defined benefit plan accrues an extra benefit, which is not less than:

1. One percent of the employee's average annual compensation multiplied by years of service with the employer; or

2. Ten percent of the employee's average annual compensation, whichever is less.

This extra minimum benefit generally is determined in the same manner as the minimum benefit required for a top-heavy defined benefit plan (see Q 22:37).

The defined contribution minimum is increased to $7\frac{1}{2}$ percent of compensation. If the floor offset or comparability analysis approach is used, each non-key employee in the defined benefit plan will accrue the extra 1 percent benefit discussed above. [IRC § 416(h)(2)(A)(ii), prior to repeal by SBA '96 § 1452(c)(7); Treas Reg § 1.416-1, Questions T-33, M-14, M-15]

For limitation years beginning after 1999, the 1.0 rule is repealed. [SBA '96, Act §§ 1452(a), 1452(c)(7)]

Q 22:59   Must every qualified retirement plan be amended to incorporate the top-heavy plan requirements?

The additional rules for top-heavy plans are tax-qualification requirements. A top-heavy plan will be a qualified retirement plan, and a trust forming part of a top-heavy plan will be a qualified trust, only if the additional requirements are met. Other than governmental plans and collectively bargained plans that are not top-heavy, any retirement plan qualifies for tax-favored status only if the plan includes provisions that will automatically take effect if the plan becomes a top-heavy plan and also has provisions that will meet the additional qualification requirements for top-heavy plans. [IRC § 401(a)(10)(B); Treas Reg § 1.416-1, Questions G-1, T-38]

Chapter 23

401(k) Plans

Qualified plans containing cash-or-deferred arrangements, commonly known as 401(k) plans, are one of the most popular and widely offered employee benefit plans. This chapter describes how a 401(k) plan operates and the special qualification requirements that must be satisfied. Also discussed are the special qualification requirements applicable to qualified retirement plans that provide for employer matching contributions and/or employee voluntary contributions.

Q 23:1 What is a 401(k) plan?

A 401(k) plan is a qualified profit sharing or stock bonus plan (see Qs 2:6, 2:13) that contains a cash-or-deferred arrangement (CODA). Under a CODA, an eligible employee may make a cash-or-deferred election (see Q 23:2) to have the employer make a contribution to the plan on the employee's behalf or pay an equivalent amount to the employee in cash. The amount contributed to the plan under the CODA on behalf of the employee is called an elective contribution (see Q 23:13). Subject to certain limitations (see Qs 23:8, 23:26), elective contributions are excluded from the employee's gross income for the year in which they are made and are not subject to taxation until distributed. For purposes of many of the rules applicable to 401(k) plans, elective contributions are considered employer contributions.

A 401(k) plan may be a stand-alone plan (permitting elective contributions only) or may also permit other types of employer contributions and/or employee voluntary contributions. However, a 401(k) plan is the only method available under which employees may defer compensation on an elective, pretax basis to a qualified retirement plan. Technically, a 401(k) plan means a plan consisting solely of elective contributions under a CODA (i.e., a stand-alone plan); however, references in *The Pension Answer Book* to a 401(k) plan include a plan containing a CODA that also permits other types of contributions. [IRC § 401(k); Treas Reg §§ 1.401(k)-1(a), 1.401(k)-1(e), 1.401(k)-1(g)(3), 1.401(k)-1(g)(15), 1.410(b)-9]

For years beginning before 1997, state and local governments and tax-exempt organizations were prohibited from maintaining 401(k) plans, unless the plan was established prior to May 6, 1986, in the case of a plan sponsored by a state or local government, or prior to July 2, 1986, in the case of a plan sponsored by a tax-exempt organization. This prohibition did not apply to a rural cooperative plan. [IRC § 401(k)(4)(B), prior to amendment by SBA '96 § 1426; Treas Reg § 1.401(k)-1(e)(4); Ltr Ruls 9625053, 9612029, 9550030, 9449021] *For years beginning after 1996,* 401(k) plans are available to tax-exempt organizations, but remain unavailable to state and local governments other than a rural cooperative plan. [IRC § 401(k)(4)(B), as amended by SBA '96 § 1426]

IRS has begun a program of auditing 401(k) plans in an effort to gather data that will assist in determining problem areas regarding compliance. IRS has advised that it is targeting 550 plans of various sizes for examination. This will represent a cross-section of the 401(k) plan population. IRS hopes to spot recurring problems so it can issue more guidance to practitioners in the form of regulations, and plans on staggering the audits, looking to complete them by December 1997. [Ann 94-101, 1994-35 IRB 53]

Q 23:2   What is a cash-or-deferred election?

Under a 401(k) plan, an employee can elect either to have the employer make an elective contribution to the plan on the employee's behalf or to receive an equivalent amount in cash. This is known as a cash-or-deferred election. The election may take the form of a compensation reduction agreement between the employee and the employer, under which the employee elects to reduce cash compensation or to forgo an increase in cash compensation and to have the employer contribute such amount to the plan on the employee's behalf. A cash-or-deferred election may be made at any time permitted under the plan, but may be made only with respect to amounts that are not currently available (see Q 23:3) to the electing employee as of the date of the election. [IRC § 401(k)(2)(A); Treas Reg §§ 1.401(k)-1(a)(2), 1.401(k)-1(a)(3)(i), 1.401(k)-1(a)(3)(iii)]

Example 1. Adam Corporation gives each employee an annual bonus of 10 percent of compensation payable on January 30 each year with respect to the previous calendar year. Under Adam Corporation's profit sharing plan, each eligible employee may elect prior to January 30 to receive all or part of the bonus in cash or to have Adam Corporation contribute such amount to the plan on the employee's behalf. This constitutes a cash-or-deferred election under a CODA.

Example 2. Dana Corporation maintains a profit sharing plan under which each eligible employee may elect to have Dana Corporation contribute up to 10 percent of the employee's compensation for each payroll period during the plan year or to receive an equivalent amount in cash. The election must be made prior to the date on which such compensation will be paid to the employee. This constitutes a cash-or-deferred election under a CODA.

Q 23:3 When is an employee's election a cash-or-deferred election?

A qualified cash-or-deferred election does not occur if amounts contributed to a plan at the employee's election are either currently available to the employee or designated as after-tax employee voluntary contributions. Compensation is currently available if it has been paid to the employee or if the employee is able currently to receive the cash at his or her discretion. An amount is not currently available if there is a significant restriction on the employee's right to receive the amount currently, or if the employee may under no circumstances receive the amount before a particular time in the future. Contributions of amounts that were currently available to the employee at the time of the election are treated as employee voluntary contributions and are included in the employee's gross income at the time they are contributed to the plan. [Treas Reg §§ 1.401(k)-1(a)(2)(ii), 1.401(k)-1(a)(3)(i), 1.401(k)-1(a)(3)(iii), 1.401(k)-1(a)(5)(ii), 1.402(a)-1(d)(2)]

In addition, an employee's elective contributions are treated as not having been made pursuant to a cash-or-deferred election if they are made pursuant to a one-time irrevocable election by the employee to have a specified amount or percentage of compensation (including no amount of compensation) contributed by the employer to the plan for the duration of the employee's employment or, in the case of a defined benefit plan (see Q 2:3), to receive accruals or other benefits (including no benefits) under the plan. The election must be available either at the employee's inception of employment or when the employee first becomes eligible under any plan of the employer and must relate to all plans of the employer, including those not in existence at the time the election is made. In no event is an election made after December 23, 1994 treated as a one-time irrevocable election if the election is made by an employee who *previously* became eligible under another plan (whether or not terminated) of the employer (see Q 23:7). [Treas Reg § 1.401(k)-1(a)(3)(iv)]

IRS has approved an arrangement under which a highly compensated employee (see Q 3:3) may defer compensation under a nonqualified plan (see Qs 1:11–1:14) and retain the amounts in that plan until the employer performs the actual deferral percentage test (see Q 23:8) and the actual contribution percentage test (see Q 23:48) to determine the maximum amount of elective contributions (see Q 23:13) that can be made for that plan year under the employer's qualified 401(k) plan. Once the employer determines the maximum amount of elective contributions that can be made for the plan year, an appropriate amount of funds will be transferred to the qualified 401(k) plan from the nonqualified plan so that the maximum amount allowable can be deferred. [Ltr Rul 9530038]

Q 23:4　Does a 401(k) plan qualify for favorable tax treatment?

Yes, provided certain special qualification requirements are met in addition to the regular plan qualification requirements (see chapter 4 for details). The special qualification requirements are the following:

1. The plan must permit the employee to elect either to have the employer make a contribution to the plan on the employee's behalf or to receive an equivalent amount in cash (see Q 23:1).

2. The plan must not allow distributions to employees with respect to amounts attributable to elective contributions merely because of the completion of a stated period of plan participation or the passage of a fixed number of years (see Q 23:33).

3. Employees' rights to their benefits derived from elective contributions must be nonforfeitable (i.e., 100 percent vested) (see Q 23:31).

4. The employer must not condition the availability of any other benefit (except for employer matching contributions) on the employee's electing, or not electing, to make elective contributions under a CODA in lieu of receiving cash. [IRC § 401(k)(4)(A); Treas Reg § 1.401(k)-1(e)(6)]

5. The plan meets the special nondiscrimination test with respect to the amount of elective contributions made to the plan each plan year (see Q 23:8). [IRC § 401(k)(3), as amended by SBA '96 §§ 1433(c)(1), 1433(d)(1), 1459(a); Treas Reg § 1.401(k)-1(b)(2)(i)]

6. The plan does not condition participation on completion of more than one year of service with the employer. [IRC § 401(k)(2)(D); Treas Reg § 1.401(k)-1(e)(5)]

7. The amount of elective contributions made to the plan on behalf of each employee does not exceed the applicable limit (see Q 23:26). [IRC §§ 401(a)(30), 402(g)(1); Treas Reg §§ 1.401(a)-30, 1.402(g)-1(d)]

A plan will not qualify as a 401(k) plan if other benefits are contingent on an employee's electing to make or not to make elective contributions under the plan. IRS ruled that the contingent benefit rule was not violated where a company established a nonqualified supplemental retirement plan to provide additional benefits to employees whose contributions to its 401(k) plan were limited and an employee could only defer amounts into the supplemental plan if the maximum elective contributions and employer matching contributions were made to the 401(k) plan. [Ltr Rul 9612027]

Q 23:5 Are elective contributions to a 401(k) plan taxable to the employee?

Elective contributions (see Q 23:13) made to a plan under a qualified CODA are not includible in the employee's gross income. Income taxes are postponed until the employee receives a distribution from the plan. In addition, earnings on elective contributions are accumulated tax-free until distributed. [IRC § 402(e)(3); Treas Reg §§ 1.401(k)-1(a)(4), 1.402(a)-1(d)(2)]

A plan that includes a CODA that is not qualified (the arrangement does not satisfy the special requirements; see Q 23:4) may, nevertheless, be a qualified plan under the regular plan qualification requirements (see chapter 4). However, if the plan satisfies only the regular requirements, contributions to the plan made at the election of the employee for the plan year are considered employee voluntary contributions and are includible in the employee's gross income. [Treas Reg §§ 1.401(k)-1(a)(5), 1.402(a)-1(d)(1)]

Q 23:6 Must a cash-or-deferred plan be a profit sharing plan?

Generally, a CODA must be part of a profit sharing or stock bonus plan (see Qs 2:6, 2:13) and cannot be part of a pension plan. There is a limited exception for pre-ERISA money purchase pension plans and rural cooperative plans. [IRC §§ 401(k)(1), 401(k)(2), 401(k)(6), 401(k)(7); Treas Reg §§ 1.401(k)-1(a)(1), 1.401(k)-1(g)(12), 1.401(k)-1(g)(14), 1.401(k)-1(h)(3)]

Elective contributions to profit sharing plans may be made without regard to whether or not the employer has current or accumulated profits. [IRC § 401(a)(27)]

Q 23:7 May a self-employed individual, including a partner, participate in a 401(k) plan?

Yes. The term "employee" for purposes of 401(k) plans includes a self-employed individual (see Q 6:33). If the self-employed individual is a sole proprietor, the individual is treated as the individual's own employee. If the self-employed individual is a partner, the individual is treated as an employee of the partnership. The compensation of a self-employed individual is earned income (see Q 6:34). [IRC § 401(c)(1); Treas Reg §§ 1.401(k)-1(g)(5), 1.410(b)-9]

Special rules apply to a profit sharing plan of a partnership that includes a CODA (see Q 23:1). A partnership may maintain a CODA, and individual partners may make cash-or-deferred elections (see Q 23:2) with respect to compensation attributable to services rendered to the partnership. Generally, the same qualification rules apply to a partnership CODA as apply to any other CODA (see Q 23:4). [Treas Reg § 1.401(k)-1(a)(6)(i)]

A CODA includes any arrangement that directly or indirectly permits individual partners to vary the amount of contributions made on their behalf. However, a partnership, like any other employer, may allow each of its employees (including partners, who are treated as employees) to make a one-time irrevocable election (see Q 23:3), upon commencement of employment or initial eligibility under any plan of the employer, to have a specified amount or percentage of compensation (including no amount) contributed by the employer throughout the employee's employment or, in the case of a defined benefit plan (see Q 2:3), to receive accruals or other benefits (including no benefits) under the plan. This permits partners to elect different rates of employer contributions; however, since this arrangement is not treated as a CODA, these employer contributions must satisfy Section 401(a)(4) (see Qs 4:9–4:23) without relying on the actual deferral percentage (ADP) test (see Q 23:8). [Treas Reg §§ 1.401(k)-1(a)(3)(iv), 1.401(k)-1(a)(6)(ii)(A), 1.401(k)-1(a)(6)(ii)(C)]

A partner's compensation is deemed currently available on the last day of the partnership taxable year (see Q 23:3). Accordingly, an individual partner may not make a cash-or-deferred election with respect to compensation for a partnership taxable year after the last day of that year. [Treas Reg §§ 1.401(k)-1(a)(6)(ii)(B), 1.401(k)-1(b)(4)(iii)]

If a partnership makes matching contributions (see Q 23:14) with respect to an individual partner's elective contributions (see Q 23:13) or employee contributions, then the matching contributions are treated as elective contributions made on behalf of the partner. [Treas Reg § 1.401(k)-1(a)(6)(iii)]

Q 23:8   What are the special nondiscrimination tests for a 401(k) plan?

A qualified 401(k) plan must meet a special actual deferral percentage (ADP) test, which is designed to limit the extent to which elective contributions (see Q 23:13) made on behalf of highly compensated employees (see Q 3:3) may exceed the elective contributions made on behalf of non-highly compensated employees (see Q 3:13). A 401(k) plan will not fail the ADP test if all of the eligible employees are highly compensated employees. [IRC § 401(k)(3)(C)]

For years beginning before 1997, the ADP test for the plan year was satisfied if:

1. The ADP for the plan year for highly compensated employees did not exceed the ADP for such plan year for non-highly compensated employees multiplied by 1.25; or

2. The ADP for the plan year for highly compensated employees did not exceed the ADP for such plan year for non-highly compensated employees multiplied by 2.0, provided that the ADP for the highly compensated employees did not exceed the ADP for the non-highly compensated employees by more than two percentage points. [IRC § 401(k)(3), prior to amendment by SBA '96 § 1433; Treas Reg § 1.401(k)-1(b)(2)(i)]

Example 1. Ellen of New City Corporation's 401(k) plan has a 12 percent ADP for highly compensated employees and an 8 percent ADP for non-highly compensated employees for the 1996 plan year. The plan does not meet the ADP test because (1) 12 percent exceeds 8 percent multiplied by 1.25, and (2) the ADP of highly compensated employees exceeds the ADP of non-highly compensated employees by more than two percentage points.

For years beginning after 1996, satisfaction of the ADP test is simplified:

1. For the *first plan year* of a 401(k) plan, the ADP for the non-highly compensated employees can be the *greater* of (a) 3 percent, or (b) if the employer elects, the actual ADP for the first plan year; and

2. After the first plan year, the ADP of the highly compensated employees for the *current* plan year may be tested against the ADP of the non-highly compensated employees for the *preceding* plan year.

Example 2. Ellen of New City Corporation's 401(k) plan has a 10 percent ADP for highly compensated employees and a 6 percent ADP for non-highly compensated employees for the 1997 plan year. The plan would not meet the ADP test because (1) 10 percent exceeds 6 percent multiplied by 1.25, and (2) the ADP of highly compensated employees exceeds the ADP of non-highly compensated employees by more than two percentage points. However, because the ADP of the non-highly compensated employees for the *1996* plan year, 8 percent, is now used, the plan will meet the ADP test because (1) 10 percent does not exceed 8 percent multiplied by 1.25, and, alternatively, (2) the ADP of highly compensated employees does not exceed the ADP of non-highly compensated employees by more than two percentage points.

Example 3. Ellen of New City Corporation's 401(k) plan has a 10 percent ADP for highly compensated employees and an 8 percent ADP for non-highly compensated employees for the 1998 plan year. The plan does not meet the ADP test because (1) 10 percent exceeds 6 percent (the ADP for non-highly compensated employees for 1997, the *preceding* plan year) multiplied by 1.25, and (2) the ADP of highly compensated employees exceeds the *preceding* plan year's ADP of non-highly compensated employees by more than two percentage points. However, Ellen of New City Corporation may elect to base the 1998 ADP test on the ADP for non-highly compensated employees for the *current* plan year, 1998. If this election is made, the plan will meet the ADP test because (1) 10 percent does not exceed 8 percent multiplied by 1.25, and (2) the ADP of highly compensated employees does not exceed the ADP of non-highly compensated employees by more than two percentage points. Once this election is made, it can only be changed as will be provided by IRS.

[IRC §§ 401(k)(3)(A), as amended by SBA '96 § 1433(c)(1), 401(k)(3)(E), as added by SBA '96 § 1433(d)(1)]

For years beginning after 1998, the ADP test will be further simplified because the test will automatically be satisfied if the employer either:

1. Makes a matching contribution (see Q 23:14) of 100 percent of the employee's elective contributions up to 3 percent of the employee's compensation (see Q 23:11) *and* 50 percent of the elective contributions between 3 and 5 percent of compensation, or

2. Makes a contribution to a defined contribution plan of at least 3 percent of each non-highly compensated employee's compensation whether or not the employee makes elective contributions.

To qualify under this safe harbor rule, the matching or nonelective contributions must satisfy the vesting (see Q 23:31) and distribution (see Q 23:33) requirements applicable to elective contributions, and the employer must give written notice to each eligible employee prior to the plan year of the employee's rights and obligations under the CODA. It is intended that employer matching and nonelective contributions used to satisfy the contribution requirements of the safe harbor rules can be used to satisfy other nondiscrimination rules *except* the ACP test (see Q 23:48) applicable to employer matching contributions. For example, a cross-tested defined contribution plan (see Qs 4:10, 4:20) that includes a CODA can consider such employer matching and nonelective contributions in testing.

Under the safe harbor matching contribution rule, the match rate for highly compensated employees cannot be greater than the match rate for non-highly compensated employees at any level of compensation. If the matching contribution requirement is not satisfied, an alternative method of meeting the contribution requirement is available. Under this alternative, the requirement is deemed to be satisfied if:

1. The rate of an employer's matching contribution does not increase as an employee's rate of elective contribution increases, and

2. The aggregate amount of matching contributions at such rate of elective contribution at least equals the aggregate amount of matching contributions that would be made if matching contributions satisfied the above percentage requirements.

For example, the alternative test will be satisfied if an employer matches 125 percent of an employee's elective contributions up to the first 3 percent of compensation, 25 percent of elective deferrals from 3 to 4 percent of compensation, and provides no match thereafter. However, the alternative test will not be satisfied if an employer matches 80 percent of an employee's elective contributions up to the first 5 percent of compensation. The former example satisfies the alternative test because the employer match does not increase and the aggregate amount of matching contributions at any rate of elective contribution is at least equal to the aggregate amount of matching contributions required under the safe harbor rule.

[IRC § 401(k)(12), as added by SBA '96 § 1433(a)]

Lastly, *for years beginning after 1998*, a 401(k) plan may elect to disregard non-highly compensated employees eligible to participate in the plan before they complete one year of service and attain age 21. To make this election, the plan must satisfy the minimum coverage rules (see Q 5:15) taking into account only those employees who do not meet the plan's minimum age and service requirements. Instead of applying two separate tests, a plan can adopt a single ADP test that compares the ADP for highly compensated employees who are eligible to participate (including those who have not satisfied the plan's minimum age and service requirements) and the ADP for non-highly compensated employees who are eligible to participate and who have met the plan's minimum age and service requirements. [IRC § 401(k)(3)(F), as added by SBA '96 § 1459(a)]

Q 23:9   How is the ADP calculated for purposes of applying the ADP test?

The ADP is calculated by first determining the actual deferral ratio (ADR) (expressed as a percentage) of each eligible employee's elective contributions (including qualified nonelective contributions and qualified matching contributions that are treated as elective contributions; see Qs 23:13, 23:14) for the plan year to the employee's compensation (see Q 23:11) for the plan year. For example, if Gerri's compensation is $50,000 and she made elective contributions of $3,000, her ADR is 6 percent ($3,000 ÷ $50,000).

The ADP for the highly compensated employees (see Q 3:3) is then determined by taking the average of the ADRs (expressed as a percentage) for all eligible highly compensated employees. For example, if there are three highly compensated employees with ADRs of 5, 7, and 3 percent, respectively, the ADP is 5 percent [(5% + 7% + 3%) ÷ 3]. This procedure is then performed for the group of eligible non-highly compensated employees (see Q 3:13). The ADP test (see Q 23:8), comparing the ADP of the highly compensated employees to the ADP of the non-highly compensated employees, is then applied. The ADRs and ADP for each group are calculated to the nearest one-hundredth of 1 percent. [IRC § 401(k)(3)(B); Treas Reg § 1.401(k)-1(g)(1)]

Example. Lenny of Lido Corp., with six eligible employees, maintains a 401(k) plan. Each employee may elect to receive up to 15 percent of compensation (or $7,000, adjusted for inflation, if less) in cash or to have part or all of this amount contributed to the plan as an elective contribution. The employees make the following elections:

Highly Compensated	Compensation	Elective Contribution	Percentage of Compensation
A	$70,000	$7,000	10.0
B	65,000	4,875	7.5
			17.5

Non-Highly Compensated	Compensation	Elective Contribution	Percentage of Compensation
C	$20,000	$1,000	5.0
D	15,000	0	0.0
E	10,000	350	3.5
F	10,000	350	3.5
			12.0

The ADP for the highly compensated employees is 8.75 percent (17.5% ÷ 2); the ADP for the non-highly compensated employees is

3 percent (12% ÷ 4). The plan fails the ADP test (see Q 23:8) because the ADP of the highly compensated employees is more than the ADP of the non-highly compensated employees multiplied by 1.25 and the ADP of the highly compensated employees exceeds the ADP of the non-highly compensated employees by more than two percentage points.

See Qs 23:56 and 23:57 for discussions of the multiple use limitation and the family aggregation rules.

Q 23:10   How is the ADR of an employee calculated if an employer maintains more than one 401(k) plan?

For purposes of the ADP test, if a highly compensated employee (see Q 3:3) is eligible to participate in more than one 401(k) plan of the employer, the ADR is generally calculated by treating all such plans in which the highly compensated employee may participate as one plan. If the plans have different plan years, all plans having plan years ending with or within the same calendar year are combined. [IRC § 401(k)(3)(A), as amended by SBA '96 § 1433(c)(1); Treas Reg § 1.401(k)-1(g)(1)(ii)(B)]

> **Example.** Steve, who earns $100,000, may make elective contributions under two of Dolly Corporation's 401(k) plans. If Steve makes elective contributions of $5,000 to one and $1,000 to the other, Steve's ADR is 6 percent [($5,000 + $1,000) ÷ $100,000].

Q 23:11   What does compensation mean for purposes of the ADP test?

For purposes of determining the availability of making elective contributions (see Q 23:13) by an employee, the term "compensation" must satisfy a general nondiscriminatory definition—that is, the definition cannot discriminate in favor of highly compensated employees (see Q 3:3). An employer may elect to include or exclude elective contributions in the definition of compensation (see Qs 6:37–6:41). [IRC §§ 401(k)(9), 414(s), as amended by SBA '96 § 1434(b)(2); Treas Reg §§ 1.401(k)-1(g)(2)(i), 1.414(s)-1]

The period used to determine an employee's compensation for a plan year must be either the plan year or the calendar year ending within the plan year. Whichever period is selected must be applied uniformly to determine the compensation of every eligible employee under the plan for that plan year. An employer may, however, limit the period taken into account under either method to that portion of the plan year or calendar year in which the employee was an eligible employee, provided that this limit is applied uniformly to all eligible employees under the plan for that plan year. [Treas Reg § 1.401(k)-1(g)(2)(i)]

For plan years beginning on or after January 1, 1994, the amount of compensation used for purposes of the ADP test cannot exceed $150,000 (adjusted for inflation). Although the first cost-of-living adjustment could have occurred in the plan year beginning in 1995, it did not because an adjustment will be made only if it is $10,000 or greater and then will be made in multiples of $10,000 (i.e., rounded down to the next lowest multiple of $10,000). For example, an increase in the cost-of-living of $9,999 will result in no adjustment, and an increase of $19,999 will create an upward adjustment of $10,000. Therefore, the cost-of-living must increase by 6⅔ percent before the first adjustment to the annual compensation limit will occur (6⅔% × $150,000 = $10,000) (see Q 6:23). The adjustment applies to plan years *beginning* in the calendar year in which the adjustment is effective. For the plan beginning in 1996, the compensation limitation remained at $150,000. [IRC § 401(a)(17); Notice 95-55, 1995-45 IRB 11]

Example. Lillian Limited adopted a 401(k) plan on January 1, 1996. In 1996, A, B, and C are highly compensated employees, and D, E, and F are non-highly compensated employees.

Compensation and Deferrals

Employee	Compensation	Deferral	ADR	Average
A	$150,000	$9,500	6.33%	
B	150,000	9,500	6.33	8.22%
C	70,000	8,400	12.00	
D	40,000	4,800	12.00	
E	35,000	2,100	6.00	6.00%
F	20,000	0	0.00	

The ADP test is not satisfied in 1996 (see Q 23:8). See Q 23:16 for a discussion of the leveling method.

Had the compensation limitation increased to $160,000 in 1996, the ADP test would have been satisfied.

Employee	Compensation	Deferral	ADR	Average
		Compensation and Deferrals		
A	$160,000	$9,500	5.94%	
B	160,000	9,500	5.94	7.96%
C	70,000	8,400	12.00	
D	40,000	4,800	12.00	
E	35,000	2,100	6.00	6.00%
F	20,000	0	0.00	

Q 23:12 What contributions are counted for purposes of the ADP test?

In applying the ADP test, a participant's elective contributions (see Q 23:13) are taken into account, but only if the following two requirements are satisfied:

1. The elective contribution is allocated to the employee as of a date within the plan year; and

2. The elective contribution relates to compensation that either (a) would have been received by the employee in the plan year but for the employee's cash-or-deferred election (see Q 23:2), or (b) is attributable to services performed by the employee in the plan year and, but for the employee's cash-or-deferred election, would have been received by the employee within 2½ months after the close of the plan year.

For purposes of the first requirement, an elective contribution is considered to be allocated to the employee as of a date within the plan year if the allocation is not contingent upon the employee's participation in the plan or performance of services on any later date, and the elective contribution is actually paid to the plan no later than the end of the 12-month period immediately following the plan year to which it relates (see Q 19:24). [Treas Reg § 1.401(k)-1(b)(4)(i); Ltr Rul 9317037] Failure by the employer to pay over elective contributions to the plan in a timely manner may subject the employer to prohibited transaction excise taxes (see Q 20:7).

Elective contributions that do not meet these requirements may not be taken into account in applying the ADP test for the plan year for which they are made or for any other plan year. Instead, they must satisfy the nondiscrimination requirements of Section 401(a)(4) (without the application of the ADP test; see Qs 4:9–4:23) for the plan year for which they are allocated as if they were the only employer contributions for that plan year. [Treas Reg § 1.401(k)-1(b)(4)(iv)]

In addition, for purposes of applying the ADP test, all or any part of qualified nonelective contributions and qualified matching contributions (see Q 23:14) made to any plan of the employer with respect to those employees who are eligible under the 401(k) plan being tested may, if the plan so provides, be treated as elective contributions. [IRC § 401(k)(3)(D); Treas Reg § 1.401(k)-1(b)(5)]

Qualified nonelective contributions may be used to satisfy the ADP test even though they are also used to satisfy the actual contribution percentage (ACP) test (see Q 23:48). However, if qualified matching contributions are used to satisfy the ADP test, they may not also be used to satisfy the ACP test, nor are they subject to that test. Qualified matching contributions made on behalf of non-key employees (see Q 22:29) may be used to satisfy the top-heavy minimum contribution requirement (see Qs 22:6, 22:48); but, if applied for this purpose, the matching contributions cannot be used to satisfy the ADP or ACP test. [Treas Reg §§ 1.401(m)-1(b)(5), 1.416-1, Question M-10]

Q 23:13 What are elective contributions?

Elective contributions are those contributions made to a plan by the employer on an employee's behalf pursuant to the employee's cash-or-deferred election (see Q 23:2). Any amount that is contributed to the plan pursuant to a special one-time irrevocable election, that is designated as an employee voluntary contribution, or that is currently available to the employee at the time of the employee's election is not treated as an elective contribution (see Qs 23:3, 23:7). [Treas Reg §§ 1.401(k)-1(a)(2), 1.401(k)-1(a)(3), 1.401(k)-1(g)(3)]

Elective contributions cannot be used to satisfy the top-heavy minimum contribution requirement (see Q 22:48).

Q 23:14 What are qualified nonelective contributions and qualified matching contributions?

A nonelective contribution is an employer contribution made to the plan (other than a matching contribution) that the employee could not have elected to receive in cash. [Treas Reg § 1.401(k)-1(g)(10)]

A matching contribution is an employer contribution made to the plan on behalf of an employee because of an after-tax voluntary contribution or an elective contribution made by or on behalf of such employee. [Treas Reg §§ 1.401(k)-1(g)(9), 1.401(m)-1(f)(12)]

To be qualified, nonelective contributions and matching contributions must satisfy the vesting (see Q 23:31) and distribution (see Q 23:33) requirements as though they were elective contributions. [Treas Reg §§ 1.401(k)-1(g)(13)(i)-1.401(k)-1(g)(13)(iii)]

To be qualified, the following requirements must also be satisfied to the extent applicable:

1. The nonelective contributions, including those qualified nonelective contributions treated as elective contributions for purposes of the ADP test, must satisfy the nondiscrimination requirements of Section 401(a)(4) (see Qs 4:9–4:23).

2. The nonelective contributions, excluding those qualified nonelective contributions treated as elective contributions for purposes of the ADP test and those qualified nonelective contributions treated as matching contributions for purposes of the ACP test, must satisfy the nondiscrimination requirements of Section 401(a)(4).

3. The qualified nonelective contributions and qualified matching contributions must satisfy the allocation rules (see Q 23:12).

4. The plan year of the plan that includes the CODA and takes qualified nonelective contributions and qualified matching contributions into account in determining whether elective contributions satisfy the ADP test must be the same as the plan year of the plan or plans to which the qualified nonelective contributions and qualified matching contributions are made.

[Treas Reg § 1.401(k)-1(b)(5)]

Q 23:15   Is there a simple rule to follow in determining whether the ADP test is satisfied?

Yes. If the ADP (see Qs 23:8, 23:9) for the non-highly compensated employees (see Q 3:13) is less than 2 percent, the ADP for the highly compensated employees (see Q 3:3) can be up to two times higher. If the ADP for the non-highly compensated employees is between 2 percent and 8 percent, the ADP for the highly compensated employees can be two percentage points higher. If the ADP for the non-highly compensated employees is more than 8 percent, the ADP for the highly compensated employees can be up to 1.25 times higher.

For example, a 4 percent ADP for the non-highly compensated employees means that an ADP of 6 percent (4% + two percentage points) for the highly compensated employees is not discriminatory. Likewise, an ADP of 10 percent for the non-highly compensated employees permits an ADP of 12.5 percent (10% × 1.25) for the highly compensated group. [IRC § 401(k)(3); Treas Reg § 1.401(k)-1(b)(2)(i)]

See Q 23:8 for a discussion of new rules that apply or will apply to the satisfaction of the ADP test.

Q 23:16 What are excess contributions?

An excess contribution for a plan year is the excess of the elective contributions (including qualified nonelective and matching contributions that are treated as elective contributions; see Qs 23:13, 23:14) made on behalf of highly compensated employees (see Q 3:3) for the plan year over the maximum amount of such contributions permitted under the ADP test (see Q 23:8) for such plan year. [IRC § 401(k)(8)(B); Treas Reg § 1.401(k)-1(g)(7)(i)]

The ADP test compares the elective contribution percentage for highly compensated employees with the elective contribution percentage for non-highly compensated employees (see Q 3:13). If the ADP test is failed, there is an excess contribution made to the plan. However, correction of the excess contribution (see Q 23:17) is done on an individual employee basis. [IRC § 401(k)(8)(C), prior to amendment by SBA '96 § 1433(e)(1)]

For years beginning before 1997, the amount of the excess contribution allocated to a highly compensated employee for a plan year was determined by the following leveling method, under which the ADR of the highly compensated employee with the highest ADR was reduced to the extent required to:

1. Enable the plan to satisfy the ADP test; or
2. Cause such highly compensated employee's ADR to equal the ratio of the highly compensated employee with the next highest ADR.

This process was repeated until the plan satisfied the ADP test. For each highly compensated employee, the amount of excess contributions was equal to (1) the total elective contributions made on behalf of the employee (determined without regard to the above described reduction), minus (2) the amount determined by multiplying the employee's ADR (as reduced under the above described procedure) by the employee's compensation used in determining the ADR.

The total elective contributions in (1) above ordinarily include qualified nonelective contributions and qualified matching contributions that were treated as elective contributions. However, if a highly compensated employee's share of excess contributions was recharacterized for a plan year in order to correct the excess contribution (see Q 23:17), that share could not exceed the actual amount of elective contributions made on the employee's behalf for that plan year. [Treas Reg § 1.401(k)-1(f)(2)]

In the Example in Q 23:11, C has the highest ADR (12%). Even though the compensation of A and B is greater than C's, to enable the plan to satisfy the ADP test, C's deferral would be reduced to $7,938 or 11.34 percent [(6.33% + 6.33% + 11.34%) ÷ 3 = 8%].

For years beginning after 1996, the leveling method is changed so that the highly compensated employee with the greatest elective contribution *amount* will incur a reduction even if that employee does not have the highest ADR. Therefore, in the Example in Q 23:11, in 1997, the deferrals of both A and B would be reduced to $9,000 or 6 percent and C's deferral would not be reduced [(6% + 6% + 12%) ÷ 3 = 8%]. [IRC § 401(k)(8)(C), as amended by SBA '96 § 1433(e)(1)]

See Qs 23:56 and 23:57 for discussions of the multiple use limitation and the family aggregation rules.

Q 23:17   How are excess contributions corrected?

A 401(k) plan will not be considered as failing the ADP test (see Q 23:8) for any plan year (and, therefore, will maintain its qualification) if:

1. The amount of the excess contributions for such plan year (plus any income allocable to such contributions) is distributed to the appropriate highly compensated employees (see Q 3:3) within 12 months after the close of the applicable plan year; or

2. The highly compensated employee elects to treat the amount of the excess contributions as an amount distributed to the employee and then contributed by the employee to the plan as an after-tax employee voluntary contribution. This is known as recharacterization. [IRC § 401(k)(8)(A); Treas Reg §§ 1.401(k)-1(f)(3), 1.401(k)-1(f)(4)]

A plan may use qualified nonelective contributions, qualified matching contributions, the recharacterization method, the corrective distribution method, or a combination of these methods, to avoid or correct excess contributions (see Qs 23:14, 23:16, 23:19, 23:24). [Treas Reg § 1.401(k)-1(f)(1); Ann 93-105, 1993-27 IRB 15]

Q 23:18 What happens if a 401(k) plan fails to correct excess contributions?

If a 401(k) plan does not correct excess contributions (see Q 23:17) within 2½ months after the end of the plan year for which they were made, the employer is subject to a 10 percent penalty tax on the amount of the excess contributions. Qualified nonelective contributions and qualified matching contributions (see Q 23:14) properly taken into account for a plan year may permit a plan to avoid having excess contributions even if such contributions are made after the close of the 2½-month period. [IRC § 4979(f); Treas Reg §§ 1.401(k)-1(f)(6)(i), 54.4979-1; Ann 91-50, 1991-13 IRB 50]

If excess contributions are not corrected before the end of the plan year following the plan year for which the excess contributions were made, the 401(k) plan will fail to qualify for the plan year for which the excess contributions were made and for all subsequent plan years during which the excess contributions remain in the plan. [IRC § 401(k)(8), as amended by SBA '96 § 1433(e)(1); Treas Reg § 1.401(k)-1(f)(6)(ii)]

Q 23:19 How are excess contributions recharacterized?

The recharacterization (see Q 23:17) of all or a portion of a highly compensated employee's (see Q 3:3) share of excess contributions is done in the following manner:

1. The payor or plan administrator (see Q 16:1) must report the recharacterized excess contribution as an employee voluntary contribution to IRS and the employee. This is done by timely providing the employer and the employee whose contribution is recharacterized with such forms as IRS may designate for this purpose and taking such other action as IRS may prescribe.

2. The plan administrator must account for the recharacterized amounts as an employee voluntary contribution for purposes of Section 72 (relating to rules under which distributions from qualified retirement plans are taxed) and Section 6047 (relating to information returns with respect to owner-employees). [Notice 89-32, 1989-1 CB 671; Treas Reg § 1.401(k)-1(f)(3)(ii)]

Excess contributions may not be recharacterized unless they are recharacterized under the plan with respect to which the excess contributions were made or under a plan that may be combined with that plan for minimum coverage purposes (see Q 5:15). [Treas Reg § 1.401(k)-1(f)(3)(iii)(C)]

Q 23:20   What are the tax consequences of the recharacterization of excess contributions?

A recharacterized excess contribution (see Q 23:17) is included in the employee's gross income on the earliest date it would have been received by the employee if the employee had originally elected to receive the elective contribution in cash (see Q 23:1). [Treas Reg § 1.401(k)-1(f)(3)(ii)]

A recharacterized amount is treated as an employee voluntary contribution for purposes of Sections 72 and 6047 (see Q 23:19), the ACP test (see Q 23:51), and the nondiscrimination requirements of Section 401(a)(4) (see Qs 4:9–4:23). For all other purposes under the Code, a recharacterized excess contribution is treated as an employer contribution that is an elective contribution. Thus, for example, it is so treated for purposes of the vesting (see Q 23:31) and distribution (see Q 23:33) requirements applicable to elective contributions (see Q 23:13). [Treas Reg § 1.401(k)-1(f)(3)(ii)]

Q 23:21   When must the recharacterization of excess contributions occur?

Recharacterization must be accomplished no later than 2½ months after the close of the plan year to which the excess contribution relates. For purposes of this rule, recharacterization occurs on the date on which the last of the highly compensated employees (see Q 3:3) with excess contributions to be recharacterized is notified (see Q 23:19). [Treas Reg § 1.401(k)-1(f)(3)(iii)(A)]

Q 23:22   Does the recharacterization of excess contributions result in a penalty tax to the employee?

No. If a timely recharacterization of excess contributions is made, no penalty tax is imposed on the employee. [IRC §§ 72(t), 401(k)(8)(A), 401(k)(8)(D), 4980A(c)(2)(F); Treas Reg § 1.401(k)-1(f)(4)(v)]

Q 23:23   Is there an excise tax on recharacterized excess contributions?

A 10 percent excise tax is imposed on the employer for excess contributions made to a plan. If excess contributions are recharacterized within 2½ months after the end of the plan year for which they were made, they are not treated as excess contributions for purposes of the excise tax. [IRC §§ 4979(a), 4979(f); Treas Reg §§ 1.401(k)-1(f)(6)(i), 54.4979-1]

Q 23:24   How is an excess contribution corrected by distribution?

In addition to recharacterization, another method of correcting a highly compensated employee's (see Q 3:3) share of excess contributions for a plan year is for the plan to distribute such amount plus any allocable income to the highly compensated employee.

For a distribution to effectively correct an excess contribution, it must be designated as a distribution of an excess contribution, and allocable income and the distribution must be made to the appropriate highly compensated employee within 12 months after the close of the plan year in which the excess contribution arose. [Treas Reg § 1.401(k)-1(f)(4)(i)]

The plan may use any reasonable method for computing the income allocable to the excess contribution, provided that the method is nondiscriminatory, is used consistently for all participants and for all corrective distributions under the plan for the plan year, and is used by the plan for allocating income to participants' accounts. [Treas Reg § 1.401(k)-1(f)(4)(ii)]

IRS has indicated that it would approve an arrangement whereby an excess contribution could be transferred to a nonqualified plan (see Qs 1:11–1:14), provided that both the cash-or-deferred election and the election to transfer the excess contribution to the nonqualified plan are made before the beginning of the plan year (i.e., before the participant earns the contributed funds).

Q 23:25   How is a distribution of an excess contribution taxed?

If the distribution is made within 2½ months following the close of the plan year to which the excess contribution relates, it is included in the highly compensated employee's (see Q 3:3) gross income on the earliest date any elective contribution (see Q 23:13) made by the employee during that plan year would have been received had the employee originally elected to receive it in cash. If the distribution is made after the 2½ month period, it is included in the employee's gross income for the taxable year of the employee in which it is distributed. A corrective distribution of less than $100, however, is includible in gross income in the year of distribution rather than in the year deferred even if it occurs within the 2½ month period. [IRC § 4979(f)(2)(B); Treas Reg § 1.401(k)-1(f)(4)(v)]

If the plan year coincides with the calendar year, then a distribution on or before March 15 of the current year is taxable to the participant in the prior year. However, if the plan year is a noncalendar year, distributions of excess contributions made within 2½ months after the plan year are taxable to the participant under the following procedures:

1. It is taxable to the highly compensated employee in the calendar year that contains the first day of the plan year. For example, assume that a plan with a plan year ending on October 31, 1996 fails the ADP test (see Q 23:8). To correct the test, a distribution of $500 is made to the employee. If the distribution is made on or before January 15, 1997, the employee must include the distribution in taxable income for calendar year 1995 (November 1, 1995 is the first day of the plan year). This would require the employee to amend an already filed income tax return, possibly subjecting the employee to penalties and interest. In addition, if the distribution is made to the employee within 2½ months following the close of the plan year to which the excess contribution relates, the 10 percent excise tax on excess contributions imposed on the employer does not apply. [IRC § 4979(f); Treas Reg §§ 1.401(k)-1(f)(6)(i), 54.4979-1]

2. Distributions made more than 2½ months after the year-end are taxed in the year of distribution. The employer also pays the 10 percent excise tax on the excess contribution. If the employer in this example delays the distribution until after January 15, 1997, the distribution is taxable in the 1997 calendar year. If the distribution is not completed by the end of the next plan year (October 31, 1997), the plan could be disqualified (see Q 23:18).

A corrective distribution of excess contributions is not subject to the 10 percent excise tax on early distributions imposed by Section 72(t) (see Q 13:39), the 15 percent excise tax on excess distributions imposed by Section 4980A (see Q 13:27), or the spousal consent requirements (see Q 10:21). [IRC §§ 401(k)(8)(A), 401(k)(8)(D); Treas Reg §§ 1.401(k)-1(f)(4)(iii), 1.401(k)-1(f)(4)(v)]

A corrective distribution is not considered a distribution for purposes of the minimum distribution requirements of Section 401(a)(9) (see chapter 11). Therefore, any distribution that must be made to the employee to satisfy the minimum distribution requirements is not satisfied by the corrective distribution. [Treas Reg § 1.401(k)-1(f)(4)(vi)]

Q 23:26 Is there a dollar limitation on the amount of elective contributions?

An employee's elective contributions (see Q 23:13) under all plans in which the employee participates (even if not maintained by the same employer) during any taxable year (including simplified employee pensions (SEPs) that offer salary reduction arrangements and SIMPLE plans) are limited to $7,000, and the amount of the elective contributions in excess of

$7,000 (excess deferrals) is included in such individual's gross income. [IRC § 402(g)(1); Treas Reg §§ 1.402(g)-1(a), 1.402(g)-1(d)(1)]

The $7,000 limit on elective contributions is adjusted annually at the same time and in the same manner as the dollar limit on benefits payable under a defined benefit plan (see Q 6:8). Although the $7,000 limitation is adjusted for inflation, new rules apply for years beginning on and after January 1, 1995. Under the new rules, an adjustment will be made only if it is $500 or greater and then will be made in multiples of $500 (i.e., rounded down to the next lowest multiple of $500). For example, an increase in the cost-of-living of $499 will result in no adjustment, and an increase of $999 will create an upward adjustment of $500. Although an increase in the limitation can be abrogated (see Q 6:25), it cannot be reduced below the 1994 amount ($9,240). [IRC § 402(g)(5); Treas Reg § 1.402(g)-1(d)(1); RPA '94 Act §§ 732(c), 732(e)(2)]

For 1996, the limitation on the amount of a participant's elective contributions has increased to $9,500. [Notice 95-55, 1995-45 IRB 11] For years prior to 1996, the elective contribution limits were:

Year	Elective Contribution Limit
1995	$9,240
1994	9,240
1993	8,994
1992	8,728
1991	8,475
1990	7,979
1989	7,627
1988	7,313

Since a CODA is part of a defined contribution plan, the amount of a participant's elective contributions is also subject to the limitation on annual additions (see Q 6:1). For example, a participant with compensation of $30,000 could not make an elective contribution of $9,500 in 1996, because the 25-percent-of-compensation limitation would be violated [25% × ($30,000 – $9,500) = $5,125]. The maximum deferral would be $6,000 [25% × ($30,000 – $6,000)]. [Treas Reg § 1.415-6(b)(6)(iv); Rev Proc 92-93, 1992-2 CB 505] However, *for years beginning after 1997,* for annual addition limitation purposes, compensation will include elective deferrals so that an elective deferral of $7,500 could be made [25% × $30,000 = $7,500]. [IRC § 415(c)(3)(D), as added by SBA '96 § 1434(a)]

A 401(k) plan is not qualified unless the plan provides that the elective contributions on behalf of an employee under the plan and all other plans of the employer may not exceed the applicable limit for the employee's taxable year *beginning* in the calendar year. The plan may incorporate the applicable limit by reference. [IRC § 401(a)(30); Treas Reg § 1.401(a)-30(a)]

Q 23:27 To what time period does the dollar limitation on elective contributions apply?

The limitation on elective contributions applies on the basis of the participant's tax year. In most cases, this is the calendar year. The limitation applies without regard to:

1. The plan year of the plan under which the elective contributions are made;

2. When the participant elects to make the contributions; or

3. When the elective contributions are made to the plan.

[IRC §§ 401(a)(30), 402(g)(1); Treas Reg §§ 1.401(a)-30(a), 1.402(g)-1(a)]

Q 23:28 How are excess deferrals corrected?

If an excess deferral is included in a participant's gross income for any taxable year, then, not later than March 1 following the close of the taxable year, the participant may allocate the amount of the excess deferral among the plans under which it arose (assuming more than one plan) and may notify each such plan of the portion allocated to it. Regulations issued by IRS extend the March 1 date to April 15. A plan may provide that the participant is deemed to have notified the plan of excess deferrals to the extent the participant has excess deferrals for the taxable year calculated by taking into account only elective deferrals under the plan and other plans of the same employer. A plan may instead provide that the employer may notify the plan on behalf of the individual under these circumstances. [IRC § 402(g)(2)(A)(i); Treas Reg § 1.402(g)-1(e)(2)(i)]

Not later than April 15 following the close of the taxable year in which the excess deferral arose, the plan may distribute to the participant the amount allocated to it by the participant plus any income allocable to that amount. This distribution may be made notwithstanding any other provision of law. [IRC § 402(g)(2)(A)(ii); Treas Reg § 1.402(g)-1(e)(2)(ii)]

A corrective distribution of an excess deferral may also be made during the same year in which the excess deferral arose. Such a distribution may be made only if the following conditions are satisfied:

1. The participant designates the distribution as an excess deferral;
2. The corrective distribution is made after the date on which the plan received the excess deferral; and
3. The plan designates the distribution as a distribution of an excess deferral.

[Treas Reg § 1.402(g)-1(e)(3)]

Corrective distributions must be provided for under the terms of the plan. A plan may require that the notification and designations referred to above must be in writing, and may also require that the participant certify or otherwise establish that the specified amount is an excess deferral. [Treas Reg § 1.402(g)-1(e)(4)]

Q 23:29   What are the tax consequences of making excess deferrals?

Excess deferrals for a taxable year are included in the employee's gross income for the taxable year in which they were made. However, the income allocable to excess deferrals is included in the employee's gross income for the taxable year in which it is distributed. [IRC §§ 402(g)(1), 402(g)(2)(C)(ii); Treas Reg § 1.402(g)-1(a)]

Example. In 1996, Susan defers $9,760 under a 401(k) plan. Earnings attributable to the excess deferral [$260 ($9,760 – $9,500)] are $10. If Susan withdraws $270 ($260 + $10) by April 15, 1997, $260 is taxable in 1996 and $10 in 1997.

The 10 percent penalty tax on early distributions (see Q 13:39) does not apply to a corrective distribution of an excess deferral. Similarly, it is not treated as a distribution for purposes of the 15 percent excise tax on excess distributions, nor is it subject to the spousal consent requirements (see Qs 13:27, 10:21). [Treas Reg §§ 1.402(g)-1(e)(7), 1.402(g)-1(e)(8)(i)]

If excess deferrals are not timely distributed, the amount of the excess deferrals is included in the employee's gross income for the taxable year in which the excess deferrals arose *and* will again be included in the employee's gross income in the year when they are actually distributed. Accordingly, failure to make a corrective distribution of excess deferrals within the specified period causes double taxation on such deferrals. [Treas Reg § 1.402(g)-1(e)(8)(iii)]

A plan may use any reasonable method for computing the income allocable to excess deferrals, provided that the method is nondiscriminatory, is used consistently for all participants and for all corrective distributions under the plan for the plan year, and is used by the plan for allocating income to participants' accounts. IRS has provided a safe-harbor procedure for calculating the income. Under this method, the income for the plan year allocated to the excess deferral is determined by multiplying the income allocable to all deferrals in the taxable year by the employee's excess deferral for the taxable year and then dividing the result by the sum of (1) the employee's total account balance attributable to deferrals at the start of the year and (2) the employee's new deferrals during the taxable year. [Treas Reg § 1.402(g)-1(e)(5)]

Q 23:30 Are excess deferrals distributed after year-end to an employee nevertheless counted for purposes of the ADP test?

Whether or not excess deferrals are timely distributed to an employee after the end of the employee's taxable year, any excess deferrals of highly compensated employees (see Q 3:3) are still counted for purposes of the ADP test (see Q 23:8); excess deferrals of non-highly compensated employees (see Q 3:13) are not taken into account. [IRC § 402(g)(2)(B); Treas Reg § 1.402(g)-1(e)(1)(ii)]

Q 23:31 Must all contributions under a 401(k) plan be nonforfeitable?

A 401(k) plan is not qualified unless the employee's rights to benefits derived from elective contributions, as well as from qualified matching and qualified nonelective contributions (see Q 23:12) used to satisfy the ADP test (see Q 23:8), are nonforfeitable (i.e., 100 percent vested immediately). [IRC §§ 401(k)(2)(C), 401(k)(3)(D); Treas Reg § 1.401(k)-1(c)]

Nonelective contributions and/or matching contributions not used to satisfy the ADP test may be forfeitable (i.e., subject to a vesting schedule). See chapter 9.

Q 23:32 What is a combined 401(k) plan?

A combined 401(k) plan is a plan that permits both elective contributions (those contributions that are made pursuant to a cash-or-deferred arrangement; see Qs 23:2, 23:13) and other types of employer contributions. By establishing a combined plan, the employer can failsafe the 401(k) plan so that it will always satisfy the ADP test (see Q 23:8). [Treas Reg § 1.401(k)-1(b)(6)]

> **Example.** Cindy-Joe Corporation has a profit sharing plan with a CODA. Each employee may elect to receive up to 2 percent of compensation in cash or to have that amount contributed to the plan as an elective contribution. In 1997, all highly compensated employees (see Q 3:3) elect to have 2 percent of their compensation contributed to the plan, and all other employees elect to receive cash. Cindy-Joe Corporation also makes a nonelective contribution to the plan equal to 2 percent of each employee's compensation. The nonelective contribution is qualified because it is subject to the same nonforfeitability and distribution provisions as the elective contributions (see Q 23:14).

The elective contributions, taken alone, do not satisfy the ADP test. Nevertheless, the 2 percent nonelective contributions may be taken into account in applying the ADP test because such contributions satisfy the nonforfeitability and distribution requirements. When these contributions are considered, the ADP for the highly compensated employees is 4 percent (2% + 2%), and the ADP for the non-highly compensated employees (see Q 3:13) is 2 percent (0% + 2%). Because 4 percent is not more than two percentage points greater than 2 percent and not more than 2 percent multiplied by 2.0, the ADP test is now satisfied. Because the ADP for the non-highly compensated employees will never be less than 2 percent, this enables the plan to pass the ADP test in a year when it would otherwise fail—when the difference between the ADP for the highly compensated employees and the ADP for the non-highly compensated employees exceeds the permissible spread.

See Q 23:8 for a discussion of the effect of SBA '96.

Q 23:33 When may distributions be made under a 401(k) plan?

Contrary to the usual rule for a profit sharing or stock bonus plan (see Qs 2:6, 2:13), a qualified 401(k) plan may not permit a distribution from the plan of amounts attributable to elective contributions (see Q 23:13) merely because of the completion of a stated period of participation or the lapse of a fixed number of years (see Q 1:32). [IRC § 401(k)(2)(B)(ii); Treas Reg § 1.401(k)-1(d)(6)(i)]

A qualified 401(k) plan must provide that amounts attributable to elective contributions (including qualified nonelective contributions and qualified matching contributions that are treated as elective contributions; see Q 23:14) may not be distributed to a participant or beneficiary before the occurrence of one of the following events:

1. The participant's retirement, death, disability, or other termination of service (see Q 13:9);

2. The termination of the plan without the establishment of a successor defined contribution plan (other than an employee stock ownership plan (ESOP); see Q 24:1) or a SEP (see Q 27:1));

3. The date of the sale by a transferor corporation to an unrelated transferee corporation of substantially all of the assets used by the transferor corporation in a trade or business of the transferor corporation with respect to an employee who continues employment with the transferee corporation acquiring such assets;

4. The date of the sale or other disposition by a corporation of such corporation's interest in a subsidiary to an unrelated entity with respect to an employee who continues employment with such subsidiary;

5. The participant's attainment of age $59\frac{1}{2}$ if the CODA is part of a profit sharing or stock bonus plan; or

6. The participant's hardship (see Q 23:34) if the CODA is part of a profit sharing or stock bonus plan.

[IRC §§ 401(k)(2)(B), 401(k)(10); Treas Reg §§ 1.401(k)-1(d)(1), 1.401(k)-1(d)(3), 1.401(k)-1(d)(4); Ltr Ruls 9618025, 9601051, 9445028, 9445023, 9443041]

Where the transferee entity was a partnership and not a corporation, IRS ruled that the requirements of item 3 were not satisfied. [IRC § 401(k)(10)(A)(ii); Ltr Rul 9102044]

If the amounts attributable to elective contributions (including qualified nonelective and qualified matching contributions) are transferred to another qualified retirement plan of any employer, the distribution limitations continue to apply to the transferred amounts. Thus, such other plan will not be qualified if the transferred amounts are distributed before the occurrence of one of the events specified above. [Treas Reg § 1.401(k)-1(d)(6)(iv)]

A partial termination (see Q 21:5) is not tantamount to a plan termination so that affected participants who did not terminate employment could not receive a distribution from the employer's 401(k) plans. [Ltr Rul 9523025]

If RRB '95 (see Q 1:22A) is enacted, distributions of amounts attributable to elective contributions will be permitted to be made to the employee if used for the payment of premiums for long-term care insurance coverage for the employee and/or the employee's spouse, and such distributions will not be subject to the 10 percent premature penalty tax (see Q 13:39). [RRB '95, Act § 11044] If RRB '96 (see Q 1:22A) is enacted, age $59\frac{1}{2}$ will be replaced with age 59 for purposes of permissible in-service distributions. [RRB '96, Act § 9445(a)]

Q 23:34 What amounts may be distributed in the case of a participant's hardship?

Prior to attaining age 59½, participants in a 401(k) plan are permitted to make in-service withdrawals only in the case of a hardship (see Qs 23:35–23:39). RRB '96 would replace age 59½ with age 59 (see Q 23:33).

A distribution on account of hardship must be limited to the distributable amount. The distributable amount is equal to the employee's total elective contributions (see Q 23:13) as of the date of distribution, reduced by the amount of previous distributions on account of hardship. If the plan so provides, the employee's total elective contributions used in determining the distributable amount may be increased by earnings thereon, and by qualified matching contributions and qualified nonelective contributions (see Q 23:14) used to satisfy the ADP test (see Q 23:8) and earnings thereon. The distributable amount may include only amounts that were credited to the employee's account as of a date specified in the plan that is no later than December 31, 1988, or, if later, the end of the last plan year ending before July 1, 1989. Thus, the maximum amount available to a participant for a hardship withdrawal consists of the amount of all such contributions and earnings thereon as of the applicable date, plus elective contributions made thereafter. [IRC § 401(k)(2)(B)(i)(IV); Treas Reg §§ 1.401(k)-1(d)(1)(ii), 1.401(k)-1(d)(2)(ii)]

If the participant does not qualify for a hardship withdrawal, the participant may be permitted to make a loan from the plan (see Qs 13:44–13:52).

A hardship distribution is an eligible rollover distribution (see Q 28:8) and is, therefore, subject to the 20 percent income tax withholding rules (see Qs 16:7, 23:38, 23:39).

Q 23:35 What constitutes hardship?

For a withdrawal to qualify as having been made on account of hardship, it must satisfy the following two-part test:

Part 1: The withdrawal must be made on account of the participant's immediate and heavy financial need; and

Part 2: The withdrawal must be necessary to satisfy such need.

Under the regulations, two methods are available for granting hardship withdrawals from qualified 401(k) plans. Under the first method, a determination of whether a participant qualifies for a hardship withdrawal under the two-part test specified above is based on a review of all the relevant facts and circumstances in each individual situation. This is known as the facts-and-circumstances test.

Under the second method, if the plan uses certain types of expenditures and specific requirements as set forth in the regulations as a basis for granting hardship withdrawals, the withdrawal will be conclusively considered to have satisfied the two-part test specified above. This is known as the safe-harbor test.

A 401(k) plan may use the safe-harbor test for Part 1 and the facts-and-circumstances test for Part 2 and vice versa, or it may use the same test for both parts. [Treas Reg §§ 1.401(k)-1(d)(2)(iii), 1.401(k)-1(d)(2)(iv)]

Q 23:36 How is an immediate and heavy financial need (Part 1) determined under the facts-and-circumstances test?

The determination of whether a participant has an immediate and heavy financial need is made on the basis of all relevant facts and circumstances. Thus, a plan that uses the facts-and-circumstances test for Part 1 will have to establish rules regarding the purposes for which hardship withdrawals will be permitted. The plan can allow hardship withdrawals for any reason, provided the surrounding facts and circumstances create an immediate and heavy financial need. In this regard, the regulations note that, generally, the need to pay funeral expenses for a family member would constitute an immediate and heavy financial need, but that the need to purchase a boat or television would not. Additionally, the regulations provide that a financial need will not fail to qualify as immediate and heavy merely because such need was reasonably foreseeable or voluntarily incurred by the participant—for example, the need to purchase a home or send a child to college. [Treas Reg § 1.401(k)-1(d)(2)(iii)(A)]

Q 23:37 How is an immediate and heavy financial need (Part 1) determined under the safe-harbor test?

Under the safe-harbor test, a hardship withdrawal will be deemed to be made on account of an immediate and heavy financial need of the participant if the withdrawal is made for any of the following reasons:

1. Payment of medical fees incurred by the participant, the participant's spouse, or any dependents of the participant; or obtainment of medical care if the withdrawal is necessary for these persons to obtain medical care;

2. Purchase of the participant's principal residence (excluding mortgage payments);

3. Payment of tuition, related educational fees, and room and board expenses for the next 12 months of postsecondary education for the participant or the participant's spouse, children, or dependents;

4. Payment of amounts necessary to prevent the eviction of the participant from the participant's principal residence or foreclosure on the mortgage of the participant's principal residence; or

5. Any additional events that may be prescribed by IRS in the future.

[Treas Reg §§ 1.401(k)-1(d)(2)(iv)(A), 1.401(k)-1(d)(2)(iv)(C)]

Q 23:38 How is a hardship withdrawal determined to be necessary (Part 2) under the facts-and-circumstances test?

A withdrawal will be treated as necessary to satisfy an immediate and heavy need of the participant if the amount of the withdrawal does not exceed the amount necessary to relieve the financial need and such need cannot be satisfied from other sources that are reasonably available to the participant. This determination is made on the basis of all relevant facts and circumstances. For these purposes, a participant's resources are deemed to include assets of the participant's spouse and minor children that are reasonably available to the participant. For example, a vacation home owned by the participant and the participant's spouse as community property, joint tenants, tenants by the entirety, or tenants in common is deemed a resource of the participant, whereas property held for a participant's child under the Uniform Gifts to Minors Act is not treated as a resource of the participant. The amount of an immediate and heavy financial need may include any amounts necessary to pay any federal, state, or local income taxes or penalties reasonably anticipated to result from the distribution and may also include mandatory income tax withholding (see Q 23:34).

A withdrawal generally may be treated as necessary to satisfy an immediate and heavy financial need if the employer relies on the participant's written representation, unless the employer has actual knowledge to the contrary, that the need cannot reasonably be relieved:

1. Through reimbursement or compensation by insurance or otherwise;

2. By liquidation of the participant's assets;

3. By the participant's cessation of elective and voluntary contributions under the plan; or

4. By the participant's making other withdrawals or nontaxable loans from all plans in which the participant participates or by borrowing from commercial sources on reasonable commercial terms in an amount sufficient to satisfy such need.

A need cannot reasonably be relieved by one of the actions listed above if the effect would be to increase the amount of the need. For example, the need for funds to purchase a principal residence cannot reasonably be relieved by a plan loan if the loan would disqualify the employee from obtaining other necessary financing.

[Treas Reg § 1.401(k)-1(d)(2)(iii)(B)]

Q 23:39 How is a hardship withdrawal determined to be necessary (Part 2) under the safe-harbor test?

Under the safe-harbor test, a withdrawal will be deemed to be necessary to satisfy an immediate and heavy financial need if the employer relies on the participant's representation that the amount of the withdrawal does not exceed the amount necessary to satisfy the participant's financial need (including any amounts necessary to pay any federal, state, or local income taxes or penalties reasonably anticipated to result from the distribution and possibly including mandatory income tax withholding; see Q 23:34) and all of the following requirements are satisfied:

1. The participant has made all withdrawals (other than hardship withdrawals) and all nontaxable loans currently available under all plans maintained by the employer.

2. The plan and all other plans maintained by the employer provide that the maximum elective contribution that a participant may make in the next taxable year is reduced by the amount of the elective contribution the participant made in the year in which the participant received a hardship withdrawal.

3. The plan and all other plans maintained by the employer provide that the participant will not be permitted to make any contributions (elective and voluntary) to the plan for at least 12 months after receipt of the hardship withdrawal. However, the participant is still counted as an eligible employee for purposes of the ADP test. All other plans maintained by the employer means all qualified and nonqualified plans of deferred compensation maintained by the employer, including a stock option, stock purchase, or similar plan, or a cash-or-deferred arrangement that is part of a cafeteria plan within the meaning of Section 125.

4. Any additional methods of distribution that may be prescribed by IRS in the future.

[Treas Reg §§ 1.401(k)-1(d)(2)(iv)(B), 1.401(k)-1(d)(2)(iv)(C), 1.401(k)-1(g)(4)(i)]

Q 23:40 Are matching contributions and nonelective contributions subject to the nonforfeitability and distribution requirements applicable to elective contributions?

Employer matching contributions and nonelective contributions under a 401(k) plan need not be subject to the special nonforfeitability and distribution requirements (see Qs 23:31, 23:33) applicable to elective contributions unless they are needed to satisfy the ADP test (see Q 23:12). However, if elective contributions are not accounted for separately (see Q 23:41), the nonforfeitability and distribution requirements will also apply to all matching contributions and nonelective contributions, whether or not they are used to satisfy the ADP test. [Treas Reg § 1.401(k)-1(e)(3)]

A matching contribution is not forfeitable for minimum vesting purposes (see Q 9:3) merely because it is forfeitable if the related contribution is treated as an excess contribution (see Q 23:16), excess deferral (see Q 23:26), or excess aggregate contribution (see Q 23:53). [IRC § 411(a)(3)(G)]

Q 23:41 What is a separate accounting under a 401(k) plan?

The portion of an employee's benefit that is attributable to elective contributions (see Q 23:13) (including qualified matching and qualified nonelective contributions used to satisfy the ADP test; see Q 23:12) must be determined by an acceptable separate accounting between such portion and any other benefits of the employee under the plan by allocating investment gains and losses on a reasonable and consistent basis and by adjusting account balances for withdrawals and contributions. [Treas Reg § 1.401(k)-1(e)(3)]

Q 23:42 Can an employer maintain two or more 401(k) plans?

Yes. But an employer that maintains two or more plans with CODAs and aggregates the plans for purposes of meeting the minimum coverage requirements (see Q 5:15) must also aggregate the plans for purposes of the ADP test (see Q 23:8). [Treas Reg §§ 1.401(k)-1(b)(3)(i), 1.401(k)-1(b)(3)(ii), 1.401(k)-1(g)(1)(ii), 1.401(k)-1(g)(11)] For purposes of the ADP test, a highly compensated employee's elective contributions are aggregated (see Q 23:10).

Contributions and allocations under an ESOP (see Q 24:1) may not be combined with contributions or allocations under any plan that is not an ESOP for purposes of determining whether either the ESOP or the non-ESOP satisfies the minimum coverage requirements and the ADP test. This rule applies even if the ESOP and CODA are part of the same plan. [Treas Reg §§ 1.401(k)-1(g)(1)(ii)(B)(1), 1.410(b)-7(c)(2); see also Treas Reg §§ 54.4975-11(a)(5), 54.4975-11(e)]

An employer may, however, treat a plan benefiting otherwise excludable employees (see Q 5:26) as two separate plans. [Treas Reg §§ 1.401(k)-1(b)(3)(ii), 1.410(b)-6(b)(3), 1.410(b)-7(c)(3)]

Q 23:43 Can a CODA be part of a thrift or savings plan?

Yes. A thrift or savings plan (see Q 2:11) is a plan in which employee or elective contributions and employer contributions are made on a matching basis. The matching contributions by the employer encourage greater participation by the non-highly compensated employees (see Q 3:13) and may be important in satisfying the ADP test (see Qs 23:8, 23:48).

For example, if the employer makes a $.50 matching contribution for every $1.00 of elective contributions made by the employee, the employee receives an immediate 50 percent return on the investment and has a greater incentive to participate in the plan.

See Q 23:8 for a discussion of the effect of SBA '96.

Q 23:44 How does a CODA affect the employer's tax-deductible contributions?

Since a CODA must be part of a profit sharing or stock bonus plan (see Q 23:6), the limitation on an employer's tax-deductible contributions to such type of plan applies—15 percent of total compensation paid to all participants (see Qs 12:7, 12:15). [IRC § 404(a)(3)(A); Ltr Rul 9225038]

If any employee of the employer is covered by both a defined contribution plan and a defined benefit plan, a special tax-deduction limitation applies (see Q 12:21). [IRC § 404(a)(7)]

The deduction for contributions to a 401(k) plan that are attributable to services rendered by participants after the end of the employer's taxable year will not be allowed because compensation must be earned before it can be deferred and contributed to the plan. [Treas Reg § 1.404(a)-1(b); Rev Rul 90-105, 1990-2 CB 69]

> **Example.** JMK Corporation files its federal income tax return on a June 30 fiscal-year basis and maintains a 401(k) plan with a plan year end of December 31. By December 31, 1997, JMK contributes to the plan elective deferrals attributable to participants' compensation earned both before and after the end of its June 30, 1997, taxable year. The plan contributions attributable to compensation earned after June 30, 1997 cannot be deducted on JMK's tax return for its taxable year ended June 30, 1997.

Q 23:45 How does a CODA affect the annual addition limitation?

Since a CODA must be part of a profit sharing or stock bonus plan (see Q 23:6), the limitation on annual additions to defined contribution plans applies (see Qs 6:1, 23:26). In computing the annual addition, elective contributions made under a qualified CODA are considered employer contributions. [IRC § 415(c); Treas Reg § 1.401(k)-1(a)(4)(ii)]

If the employee also participates in a defined benefit plan of the employer, a combined plan contribution limit applies (see Q 6:17). [IRC § 415(e)]

Q 23:46 Are elective contributions subject to payroll taxes?

Yes. Elective contributions (see Q 23:13) made under a CODA are included in the Social Security taxable wage base for both employer and employee withholding purposes. Elective contributions are also subject to the Federal Unemployment Taxes Act (FUTA). [Social Security Act Amendments of 1983 § 324(d)]

Elective contributions are also included for purposes of measuring the annual increases in Social Security average wages, which will affect the calculation of both the taxable earnings base and benefit computations. [Social Security Act § 209]

Q 23:47 Does a 401(k) plan require registration with the Securities and Exchange Commission?

The Securities and Exchange Commission (SEC) has expressed its opinion that CODAs do not require registration of plan interests or employer stock purchased by the plan, but that a salary reduction plan under which an employee accepts a reduction in salary to obtain a contribution of a like amount by the employer to a qualified profit sharing plan may create plan interests that are securities. [SEC Rel No. 33-6281; Diasonics, Inc, SEC, Div of Corp Fin, Dec 23, 1982]

In a case in which the employer adopted a wage reduction program that consisted of eligibility to participate in an ESOP (see Q 24:1) and profit sharing plan in return for a reduction in wages, the court held that, in order to be considered an investment contract subject to protection under the Securities Acts of 1933 and 1934, there must be (1) an investment of money (2) in a common enterprise (3) with profits derived from the efforts of other persons. Since the wage reduction program constituted an investment of money, the ESOP is a common enterprise, and profits (i.e., dividends and appreciation in value) would result primarily from efforts of management and employees, each employee's interest in the ESOP was an investment contract. [Uselton v Commercial Lovelace Motor Freight, Inc, Nos. 88-1253 and 88-1750 (10th Cir 1991); see also International Brotherhood of Teamsters v Daniel, 439 US 551 (1979); SEC v W J Howey Co, 328 US 293 (1946)]

In another case, the court ruled that the Securities Acts applied to employee claims involving an ESOP because (1) the plan, as an ESOP, lacked the primary indicia of a pension plan (i.e., payment of benefits only upon retirement), (2) participation was voluntary, (3) the ESOP was contributory because participants gave up a percentage of income, and (4) participants acquired common stock, a security specifically enumerated in the Securities Act of 1933. [Hood v Smith's Transfer Corp, 762 F Supp 1274 (1991)]

Q 23:48   What is the special nondiscrimination test for qualified plans with employer matching contributions and/or employee contributions?

A special nondiscrimination test, the actual contribution percentage (ACP) test, applies to employer matching contributions and employee contributions under all qualified defined contribution plans (see Q 2:2). The ACP test also applies to employee contributions under a defined benefit plan to the extent they are allocated to a separate account for each individual participant. The ACP test is essentially the same as the ADP test that is applied to elective contributions (see Q 23:8).

A plan will be treated as meeting the nondiscrimination requirements of Section 401(a)(4) (see Qs 4:9-4:23) as to the amount of matching contributions and/or employee contributions only if the plan satisfies the ACP test. Satisfaction of the ACP test is the exclusive method of satisfying Section 401(a)(4) with respect to matching and employee contributions. [IRC § 401(m); Treas Reg §§ 1.401(m)-1(a)(1), 1.401(m)-1(a)(2)]

For years beginning before 1997, the ACP test for the plan year was satisfied if:

1. The ACP (see Q 23:49) for the plan year for highly compensated employees (see Q 3:3) did not exceed the ACP for such plan year for non-highly compensated employees (see Q 3:13) multiplied by 1.25; or

2. The ACP for the plan year for highly compensated employees did not exceed the ACP for such plan year for non-highly compensated employees multiplied by 2.0, provided that the ACP for highly compensated employees did not exceed the ACP for non-highly compensated employees by more than two percentage points. [IRC § 401(m)(2)(A), prior to amendment by SBA '96 § 1433; Treas Reg § 1.401(m)-1(b)(1)]

For years beginning after 1996, satisfaction of the ACP test is simplified:

1. For the *first* plan year of a plan, the ACP for the non-highly compensated employees can be the *greater* of (a) 3 percent, or (b) if the employer elects, the actual ACP for the first plan year; and

2. After the first plan year, the ACP of the highly compensated employees for the *current* plan year may be tested against the ACP of the non-highly compensated employees for the *preceding* plan year. With regard to the ACP of the non-highly compensated employees, the employer may elect to use the ACP for the *current* plan year instead of the ACP for the *preceding* plan year. However, if this election is made, it can be changed only as will be provided by IRS [IRC §§ 401(m)(2)(A), as amended by SBA '96 § 1433(c)(2), 401(m)(3), as amended by SBA '96 § 1433(d)(2)]

For years beginning after 1998, the ACP test will be further simplified because the test will automatically be satisfied if the employer either:

1. Makes a matching contribution of 100 percent of the employee's elective contributions up to 3 percent of the employee's compensation (see Q 23:11) *and* 50 percent of the elective contributions between 3 and 5 percent of compensation, *or*

2. Makes a contribution to a defined contribution plan of at least 3 percent of each non-highly compensated employee's compensation whether or not the employee makes elective contributions, *and*

3. The plan satisfies a special limitation on matching contributions.

To qualify under this safe harbor rule, the employer must give written notice to each eligible employee prior to the plan year of the employee's rights and obligations under the plan. The special limitation on matching contributions is satisfied if:

1. The employer matching contributions on behalf of any employee may not be made with respect to employee contributions or elective deferrals in excess of 6 percent of compensation;

2. The rate of an employer's matching contribution does not increase as the rate of an employee's contributions or elective deferrals increases; and

3. The matching contribution with respect to any highly compensated employee at any rate of employee contribution or elective deferral is not greater than that with respect to a non-highly compensated employee.

Any employee contributions made under the CODA will continue to be tested under the ACP test. Employer matching and nonelective contributions used to satisfy the safe harbor rules for a CODA cannot be considered in calculating the ACP test. However, employer matching and nonelective contributions in excess of the amount required to satisfy the safe harbor rules can be taken into account in calculating the ACP test.

[IRC § 401(m)(11), as added by SBA '96 § 1433(b)]

Lastly, *for years beginning after 1998*, a plan may elect to disregard non-highly compensated employees eligible to participate in the plan before they complete one year of service and attain age 21. To make this election, the plan must satisfy the minimum coverage rules (see Q 5:15) taking into account only those employees who do not meet the plan's minimum age and service requirements. Instead of applying two separate ACP tests, a plan can adopt a single ACP test that compares the ACP for highly compensated employees who are eligible to participate (including those who have not satisfied the plan's minimum age and service requirement) and the ACP for non-highly compensated employees who are eligible to participate and who have met the plan's minimum age and service requirements. [IRC § 401(m)(5)(C), as added by SBA '96 § 1459(b)]

See Qs 23:56 and 23:57 for discussions of the multiple use limitation and the family aggregation rules.

Q 23:49   How is the ACP calculated for purposes of applying the ACP test?

The ACP is calculated by first determining the actual contribution ratio (ACR) (expressed as a percentage) for each employee. This is the ratio of the sum of the employee's employee contributions and matching contributions to the employee's compensation for the year. [IRC § 401(m)(3); Treas Reg § 1.401(m)-1(f)(1)]

For example, an employee whose compensation is $60,000 and who makes employee contributions of $5,000, which are matched by $1,000 of employer contributions, has an ACR of 10 percent [($5,000 + $1,000) ÷ $60,000]. The ACP of the highly compensated employees (see Q 3:3) is determined by taking the average of the ACRs for all highly compensated employees. If there are three highly compensated employees with ACRs of 5, 7, and 3 percent, respectively, the ACP is 5 percent [(5% + 7% + 3%) 3]. The same procedure is followed for the group of non-highly compensated employees (see Q 3:13). The ACP test is applied by comparing the ACP of the highly compensated employees to the ACP of the non-highly compensated employees. ACRs and ACPs are calculated to the nearest one-hundredth of 1 percent. [Treas Reg § 1.401(m)-1(f)(1)(i)]

Q 23:50   What contributions may be included for purposes of the ACP test?

A plan is generally required to apply the ACP test with respect to matching contributions and employee contributions. However, if qualified matching contributions are treated as elective contributions for purposes of satisfying the ADP test (see Q 23:12), then they do not have to satisfy the ACP test (see Q 23:48) and may not be used to help employee contributions and other matching contributions satisfy the ACP test. The matching contributions that are eliminated from the ACP test under this rule are only those contributions used to satisfy the ADP test. [Treas Reg § 1.401(m)-1(b)(4)(ii)(B)]

If the ACP test cannot be met with respect to matching and employee contributions, the plan has the option of treating as matching contributions all or any part of any qualified nonelective contributions (see Q 23:14) and elective contributions (see Q 23:13) made to any plan of the employer with respect to those employees who are eligible employees under the plan being tested. A qualified nonelective contribution that is treated as an elective contribution for purposes of the ADP test cannot be used for the ACP test. In other words, the same qualified nonelective contributions cannot be used to satisfy both the ADP and ACP tests. The plan year of the plan that uses qualified nonelective contributions and/or elective contributions to meet the ACP test must be the same as the plan year of the plans to which the qualified elective and nonelective contributions are made. An employer may, however, treat a plan benefiting otherwise excludable employees (see Q 5:26) as two separate plans. [IRC § 401(m)(3); Treas Reg §§ 1.401(m)-1(b)(3)(ii), 1.401(m)-1(b)(4)(ii)(B), 1.401(m)-1(b)(5)(v), 1.401(m)-1(d), 1.410(b)-6(b)(3), 1.410(b)-7(c)(3)]

Example. The Hepner Corporation maintains a profit sharing plan that permits elective and employee contributions. The plan permits elective contributions made by non-highly compensated employees to be treated as employee contributions if required to meet the ACP test. The following contributions, as a percentage of compensation, are made to the plan:

	Elective Contributions	Employee Contributions
Highly compensated employees	10%	10%
Non-highly compensated employees	10%	6%

The plan does not satisfy the ACP test with respect to employee contributions because the 10 percent ACP for the highly compensated employees is both more than two percentage points greater than the ACP for the non-highly compensated employees and more than such ACP multiplied by 1.25. If one-fifth of the non-highly compensated employees' elective contributions are treated as employee contributions, the elective contributions and employee contributions for the non-highly compensated employees each becomes 8 percent. The plan can then meet the ACP test because the 10 percent ACP for the highly compensated employees is not more than the 8 percent ACP for the non-highly compensated employees multiplied by 1.25.

Matching contributions made on behalf of non-key employees (see Q 22:29) may be used to satisfy the top-heavy minimum contribution requirement (see Qs 22:6, 22:48); but, if applied for this purpose, the matching contributions cannot be used to satisfy the ADP or ACP test. [Treas Reg §§ 1.401(m)-1(b)(5); 1.416-1, Question M-10]

If an overfunded defined benefit plan (see Q 2:3) is terminated and a portion of the overfunding is transferred to a qualified replacement plan (see Qs 21:56, 21:57), the amount transferred may be used as matching contributions. [Ltr Rul 9302027]

Q 23:51 When are contributions counted for purposes of applying the ACP test?

For purposes of the ACP test (see Q 23:48), an employee contribution is taken into account for the plan year in which it is made. Payment to an agent of the plan is treated as a contribution if the funds are transmitted to the plan within a reasonable time. Failure by the employer to pay over employee contributions to the plan in a timely manner may subject the employer to prohibited transaction excise taxes (see Q 20:7).

If an excess contribution under a 401(k) plan is recharacterized as an employee contribution, then such recharacterized contribution is taken into account for the plan year in which it is included in the employee's gross income (see Q 23:17).

A matching contribution is taken into account for the plan year in which it is allocated to the participant's account under the terms of the plan, provided that:

1. It is actually paid to the plan no later than the end of the 12-month period beginning after the close of that plan year (see Q 19:24); and

2. It is made on account of the employee's voluntary or elective contributions for that plan year.

If a matching contribution does not satisfy these conditions, it may not be taken into account for purposes of the ACP test for the plan year in which it is made or any other plan year. Instead, it must satisfy the nondiscrimination requirements of Section 401(a)(4) (see Q 4:9–4:23) (without application of the ACP test) for the plan year for which it is allocated as if it were the only employer contribution for that year. [Treas Reg § 1.401(m)-1(b)(4)(ii)(A)]

Q 23:52 What other requirements must a plan subject to the ACP test meet?

To satisfy the nondiscrimination requirements of Section 401(m), a plan must maintain the records necessary to demonstrate compliance with those requirements. Among other things, the records must be adequate to show that the ACP test (see Q 23:48) has been met and must include information regarding the extent to which elective and nonelective contributions were taken into account to satisfy the ACP test. [Treas Reg § 1.401(m)-1(c)(2)]

To be a qualified retirement plan, it is not sufficient that a plan to which employee and/or matching contributions are made satisfy the ACP test. In addition, the plan must not discriminate in favor of highly compensated employees (see Q 3:2) with respect to other benefits or rights of the plan, including the availability (as opposed to the amount) of voluntary and matching contributions. The determination of whether a rate of matching contributions discriminates in favor of highly compensated employees is made after correction of excess deferrals, excess contributions, and excess aggregate contributions. [Treas Reg § 1.401(m)-1(a)(2)]

Q 23:53 What are excess aggregate contributions under the ACP test?

Excess aggregate contributions are the excess of the aggregate amount of employee contributions and matching contributions made on behalf of highly compensated employees (see Q 3:3) for a plan year over the maximum amount of such contributions that are permitted under the ACP test (see Q 23:48). Any qualified nonelective contributions and elective contributions treated as matching contributions for purposes of the ACP test are treated as matching contributions under this definition. However, qualified matching contributions that are treated as elective contributions for purposes of meeting the ADP test (see Q 23:8) are not treated as matching contributions under this definition. [IRC § 401(m)(6)(B); Treas Reg § 1.401(m)-1(f)(8)]

If the ACP test is failed, there are excess aggregate contributions in the plan. However, correction of the excess aggregate contributions must be done on an individual employee basis. Allocation of the excess aggregate contributions among the highly compensated employees is done under the same leveling method that is used in allocating excess contributions under a 401(k) plan to individual highly compensated employees (see Q 23:16). [IRC § 401(m)(6)(C), prior to amendment by SBA '96 § 1433(e)(2); Treas Reg §§ 1.401(m)-1(e)(1)(i), 1.401(m)-1(e)(2)(i)]

For years beginning after 1996, the same leveling method that is used to allocate excess contributions will be used to allocate excess aggregate contributions (see Q 23:16).

Q 23:54   How are excess aggregate contributions corrected?

The principal method of correcting a highly compensated employee's (see Q 3:3) share of excess aggregate contributions for a plan year is for the plan to distribute the share plus any allocable income to the employee. However, to the extent that excess aggregate contributions are forfeitable (i.e., not vested) under the terms of the plan, they may be forfeited rather than distributed. [IRC § 401(m)(6)(A); Treas Reg §§ 1.401(m)-1(e)(1)(i), 1.401(m)-1(e)(1)(ii), 1.401(m)-1(e)(3), 1.415-6(b)(6)(iv); Rev Proc 92-93, 1992-2 CB 505]

The following are *not* permissible methods of correcting an excess aggregate contribution:

1. Recharacterization (see Q 23:17);
2. Failing to make matching contributions for highly compensated employees that are required under the terms of the plan; and
3. Forfeiting vested matching contributions made on behalf of highly compensated employees. [Treas Reg §§ 1.401(m)-1(e)(1)(iii), 1.411(a)-4(b)(7)]

For a distribution to effectively correct an employee's share of excess aggregate contributions and allocable income, it must be designated as a distribution of an excess aggregate contribution and must be made within 12 months after the close of the plan year in which the excess contribution arose. However, if the excess aggregate contributions are not distributed within $2\frac{1}{2}$ months following the close of the plan year in which they arose, a 10 percent penalty tax will be imposed on the employer. [IRC §§ 401(m)(6)(A), 4979(f); Treas Reg §§ 1.401(m)-1(e)(3)(i), 1.401(m)-1(e)(5), 54.4979-1; Ann 91-50, 1991-13 IRB 50]

Q 23:55   What is the tax treatment of excess aggregate contributions?

Amounts attributable to excess aggregate contributions are generally included in the gross income of a highly compensated employee (see Q 3:3). However, amounts attributable to employee contributions are includible only to the extent of the income on such contributions. [IRC § 401(m)(7)(B)]

If the distribution is made within the first $2\frac{1}{2}$ months after the close of the plan year for which the excess aggregate contributions were made, the year of inclusion is the taxable year of the employee ending with or within that plan year. If the distribution is made at a later date, the year of inclusion is the taxable year of the employee in which the distribution occurs. A corrective distribution of less than $100, however, is includible in gross income in the year of distribution even if it occurs within the $2\frac{1}{2}$-month period. [IRC § 4979(f)(2)(B); Treas Reg § 1.401(m)-1(e)(3)(v)]

A corrective distribution of excess aggregate contributions is not subject to the 10 percent excise tax on early distributions imposed by Section 72(t) (see Q 13:39), nor is it treated as a distribution for purposes of the 15 percent excise tax on excess distributions imposed by Section 4980A (see Q 13:27). [IRC § 401(m)(7)(A); Treas Reg § 1.401(m)-1(e)(3)(v)(A)]

A corrective distribution may be made without regard to the spousal consent requirements of Sections 401(a)(11) and 417 (see Q 10:21) and is not regarded as a distribution for purposes of the minimum distribution requirements of Section 401(a)(9) (see chapter 11). Therefore, any distribution required under Section 401(a)(9) is not satisfied by a corrective distribution. [Treas Reg §§ 1.401(m)-1(e)(3)(iii), 1.401(m)-1(e)(3)(vi)]

Q 23:56   What is the multiple use limitation?

The multiple use of the alternative limitation with respect to any highly compensated employee (see Q 3:3) is prohibited. The alternative limitation is the 2.0/two percentage point limitation (see Qs 23:8, 23:48). [IRC § 401(m)(9)(B); Treas Reg §§ 1.401(m)-2(a), 1.401(m)-2(b)(2)]

Multiple use of the alternative limitation does not occur unless the ADP and ACP of the highly compensated employees each exceeds 1.25 times the corresponding percentage of the non-highly compensated employees (see Q

3:13). Furthermore, multiple use of the alternative limitation does not occur unless (1) one or more highly compensated employees are eligible to participate in both a CODA and a plan to which employee contributions or matching contributions are made, and (2) the percentage obtained by adding the ADP and the ACP of the highly compensated employees exceeds an aggregate limit. The aggregate limit is the greater of:

1. The sum of (a) 1.25 times the greater of the ADP or the ACP of the non-highly compensated employees, and (b) two percentage points plus the lesser of the ADP or the ACP of the non-highly compensated employees, but this latter amount cannot exceed 2.0 times the lesser of the ADP or the ACP of the non-highly compensated employees; or

2. The sum of (a) 1.25 times the lesser of the ADP or the ACP of the non-highly compensated employees and (b) two percentage points plus the greater of the ADP or the ACP of the non-highly compensated employees, but this latter amount cannot exceed 2.0 times the greater of the ADP or the ACP of the non-highly compensated employees.

If the sum of the ADP and ACP of the highly compensated employees exceeds this aggregate limit, there is prohibited multiple use. [Treas Reg §§ 1.401(m)-2(b)(1), 1.401(m)-2(b)(3)]

Example. Under SBK Corporation's 401(k) plan, which provides for matching contributions, the ADPs for highly compensated employees and non-highly compensated employees are 3.9 percent and 2.0 percent, respectively, while the ACPs for the two groups are 1.3 percent and 1.0 percent, respectively. The sum of the ADP and ACP for the highly compensated employees is 5.2 percent, and the prohibited multiple use does not occur because the limitation is 5.25 percent, as follows:

1.	Greater of ADP or ACP of non-highly compensated employees	2.0
2.	1.25 × 2.0	2.5
3.	Lesser of ADP or ACP of non-highly compensated employees	1.0
4.	2.0 × 1.0	2.0
5.	First limit (2.5 + 2.0)	4.5
6.	Lesser of ADP or ACP of non-highly compensated employees	1.0
7.	1.25 × 1.0	1.25
8.	Greater of ADP or ACP of non-highly compensated employees	2.0
9.	2.0 × 2.0	4.0
10.	Second limit (1.25 + 4.0)	5.25
11.	Aggregate limit: greater of first limit or second limit	5.25

When prohibited multiple use of the alternative limitation occurs, the ADP and/or ACP of the highly compensated employees is reduced by use of the leveling met alternative limitation occurs, the ADP and/or ACP of the highly compensated employees is reduced by use of the leveling method (see Qs 23:16, 23:53) so that the combined ADP and ACP does not exceed the aggregate limit. The amount of the reduction must be distributed to the highly compensated employees according to the allocation produced by the leveling method; or, at the employer's election, the reduction may be allocated among all highly compensated employees under the plan or CODA that is being reduced or among only those highly compensated employees who are eligible under both the CODA and the plan for which employee contributions or employee and matching contributions are made. [Treas Reg §§ 1.401(m)-2(c)(1), 1.401(m)-2(c)(3)]

See Qs 23:8, 23:48 for discussions of the new rules that apply or will apply to the satisfaction of the ADP and ACP tests.

Q 23:57   What are the family aggregation rules?

For years beginning before 1997, if an individual was a member of the family of a 5 percent owner (see Q 3:4), or a member of the family of a highly compensated employee (see Q 3:3) who was one of the ten most highly compensated employees, that individual was not treated as a separate employee and the compensation of the individual (and any applicable contribution or benefit on his or her behalf) was treated as if paid to (or on behalf of) a single 5 percent owner or highly compensated employee. Family members included the employee's spouse, lineal descendants or ascendants, and spouses of such lineal descendants or ascendants. [IRC §§ 401(k)(5), 414(q)(6), 416(i)(1)(B)(i); Treas Reg § 1.401(k)-1(g)(1)(ii)(C)]

For such a family group, which was treated as one highly compensated employee, the combined ADR (see Q 23:9) was the ADR determined by combining the elective contributions, compensation, and amounts treated as elective contributions of all the eligible family members. Generally, the elective contributions, compensation, and amounts treated as elective contributions of all family members were disregarded in determining the ADP (see Q 23:9) of the non-highly compensated employees. [Treas Reg § 1.401(k)-1(g)(1)(ii)(C)(2)]

Example. Shirley has a child, Ellen. Both participate in a 401(k) plan maintained by EMK Corporation. Shirley is one of the ten most highly compensated employees, and Ellen is a non-highly compensated employee. Shirley has compensation of $100,000 and defers $7,000 under the 401(k) arrangement; Ellen has compensation of $40,000 and defers $4,000 under the arrangement. The ADR of the family unit is 7.86

percent, calculated by aggregating the contributions and compensation of Shirley and Ellen [($7,000 + $4,000) ÷ ($100,000 + $40,000)].

If the ADR of the family unit created an excess contribution (see Q 23:16), the reduction was applied in proportion to both Shirley's and Ellen's contributions. [Treas Reg §§ 1.401(k)-1(f)(5)(ii), 1.401(k)-1(f)(7), Example 3]

The family aggregation rules also applied for purposes of the ACP test (see Q 23:48) and correcting excess aggregate contributions (see Q 23:54). [Treas Reg §§ 1.401(m)-1(e)(2)(iii), 1.401(m)-1(f)(1)(ii)(C)]

For years beginning after 1996, the family aggregation rule is repealed. [SBA '96, Act § 1431(b)(1)]

Q 23:58 Are 401(k) plan benefits exempt from the participants' creditors?

In 1992, the United States Supreme Court held that a participant's interest in a qualified retirement plan is exempt from the claims of creditors in a bankruptcy proceeding, thereby resolving the conflict among the courts of appeals. [Patterson v Shumate, 112 S Ct 2242 (1992)]

See Qs 4:24 through 4:27 for more details.

Chapter 24

Employee Stock Ownership Plans

An employee stock ownership plan (ESOP) is a special breed of qualified retirement plan. In addition to providing retirement benefits for employees, an ESOP can be used as a market for company stock, as a method of increasing the company's cash flow, as an estate planning tool for the owner of a closely held corporation, and as a means of financing the company's growth. This chapter examines the requirements for establishing and maintaining an ESOP and explains how an ESOP works.

Q 24:1 What is an employee stock ownership plan?

An ESOP is essentially a defined contribution plan (see Q 2:2) whose funds must be invested primarily in employer securities (see Q 24:15). Generally, the funds may come from any or all of the following sources: (1) company contributions of cash or employer securities, (2) an exempt loan to the ESOP (see Q 24:3), or (3) a defined contribution plan converted to an ESOP (see Q 24:19). The amount of tax deductible contributions to an ESOP is generally determined in the same manner as for other defined contribution plans (see Qs 12:1–12:17), although there is a special rule increasing the deductible amount of employer contributions used to repay exempt loans to the ESOP (see Q 24:10). [IRC §§ 404(a)(3), 404(a)(9), 409, 4975(e)(7)]

The funds are held in trust for the benefit of employees and their beneficiaries and are used to buy employer securities from shareholders or from the company itself. When a participant retires or leaves, the participant receives the vested interest in the ESOP in the form of cash or employer securities. However, an ESOP may preclude a participant from obtaining a distribution of employer securities if the company's corporate charter or bylaws restrict the ownership of substantially all employer securities to employees or the ESOP. [IRC § 409(h)(2)]

Participants can exercise a put option and put the employer securities back to the company for their fair market value if the securities are not readily tradable on an established market (see Q 24:55). To keep the employer securities from falling into the hands of competitors, either the ESOP or the company may be given the right of first refusal if the participant attempts to sell the securities. However, a participant generally can demand a distribution of benefits in the form of employer securities and cannot be required to sell the securities back to the company. [IRC § 409(h)(1); Treas Reg § 54.4975-7(b)(9)]

The basic purpose of an ESOP is the investment of plan assets in employer securities. Courts have ruled that an ESOP trustee did not breach its fiduciary duty (see Q 19:12) to plan participants by investing plan assets in employer securities even though the employer was in serious financial decline because the trustee had no discretion and was required to act upon the direction of the company's ESOP committee. [Maniace v Commerce Bank of Kansas City, 40 F 3d 264 (8th Cir 1994); Ershick v United Missouri Bank of Kansas City, NA, No. 90-3283 (10th Cir 1991)] However, another court ruled that a bank trustee violated its fiduciary duty when the ESOP purchased employer stock for more than fair market value even though the trustee had relied on an outside valuation report and informal DOL opinion. [Reich v Valley National Bank of Arizona, No. 89 Civ 8361 (SD NY 1993)] In another case, the court ruled that the trustees of an ESOP violated their fiduciary duties when they established a competing business knowing that the new business would decrease the value of the ESOP's assets. [Neyer, Tiseo & Hindo, Ltd v Russell, 1993 US Dist Lexis 12011 (ED Pa 1993)] Another court ruled that fiduciaries of an ESOP did not breach their fiduciary duty when they failed to diversify the ESOP's assets during an 18-month period in which the value of employer securities declined by 80 percent. The court stated that an ESOP fiduciary is presumed to have acted prudently in investing in employer securities but that this presumption can be overcome by a showing that the fiduciary abused its discretion. [Kuper v Iovenko, 1995 US App Lexis 27764 (6th Cir 1995); see also Moench v Robertson, 1995 US App Lexis 21546 (3d Cir 1995)]

A terminated ESOP participant received all shares of employer stock credited to his ESOP account and promptly sold the shares. Seven months later the employer was sold, and the buyer purchased the ESOP shares for a significantly greater price per share. The court held that the employer did not commit a fiduciary breach by failing to inform the participant that a sale of the employer was being considered. [Olson v Chem-Trend, Inc, 1995 US Dist Lexis 11016 (ED Mich 1995)]

Q 24:2   How is an ESOP different from a stock bonus plan?

A stock bonus plan (see Q 2:13) permits, but does not require, current investments in employer securities (see Q 24:9). An ESOP must invest primarily in employer securities. Further, an ESOP, but not a stock bonus plan, may borrow from the employer or use the employer's credit to acquire employer securities. [ERISA § 407(d)(6); IRC § 4975(d)(3)]

Q 24:3   What is an exempt loan?

Generally, the lending of money by the employer to a qualified retirement plan is a prohibited transaction (see Q 20:1). However, an employer's loan or guarantee of a loan to an ESOP will not be a prohibited transaction if the loan satisfies the requirements for being an exempt loan. The exempt loan requirements include the following:

1. The loan must be primarily for the benefit of participants and beneficiaries of the ESOP;

2. The proceeds of the loan must be used to acquire qualifying employer securities (see Q 24:9) or to repay an exempt loan or a prior exempt loan;

3. The interest rate of the loan must be reasonable;

4. The loan must be without recourse against the ESOP and without collateral other than qualifying employer securities acquired (or refinanced) with the proceeds of the exempt loan; and

5. The loan must provide for the release from encumbrance of employer securities used as collateral as the loan is repaid.

[IRC § 4975(d)(3); Treas Reg § 54.4975-7(b); Ltr Ruls 9431055, 9417033, 9417032]

The refinancing of an exempt loan will not create a prohibited transaction if the refinancing is carried out primarily for the benefit of the ESOP participants and beneficiaries and satisfies the other requirements set forth above. [Ltr Ruls 9610028, 9530015] IRS concluded that a loan continued to be an exempt loan after the ESOP acquired common stock of its new parent corporation after a merger. [Ltr Rul 9608040] A subsidiary's exempt loan incurred to acquire its parent company's ESOP stock did not create a prohibited transaction when, once the subsidiary was sold, the parent redeemed the subsidiary's unallocated ESOP stock held in the plan suspense account as security for the ESOP loan repayment and used the proceeds received from the redemption to repay the loan. IRS also ruled that the redemption proceeds were a permissible source for the loan repayment. [Ltr Rul 9621034]

DOL has opined that a loan to an ESOP is an exempt loan even if ESOP assets other than those pledged as collateral are used to repay the loan. However, if the employer securities purchased with the proceeds of the loan were not pledged as collateral, repayment of the loan could violate ERISA's general fiduciary responsibility rules. [DOL Op Ltr 93-35A; ERISA § 408(b)(3); DOL Reg § 2550.408b-3(e)]

The sale of employer securities held in a suspense account (i.e., employer securities not yet allocated to participants) under the ESOP in order to repay an exempt loan with any excess funds being allocated to the participants just prior to the termination of the ESOP satisfied the requirement that the transaction be for the primary benefit of participants and beneficiaries. [Ltr Ruls 9624002, 9437035]

The amendment of an ESOP and the write-down of loans to the ESOP because of the decline in value of the employer securities did not cause the remaining ESOP loan to fail to qualify as an exempt loan. [Ltr Ruls 9506030, 9437039, 9237037] However, IRS has ruled that the accelerated release of employer securities held in a suspense account under the ESOP can cause the loan to fail to satisfy the requirements of an exempt loan. [Ltr Rul 9447057; Treas Reg § 54.4975-7(b)(8)(i)]

IRS has ruled that salary reduction contributions to a 401(k) plan (see Q 23:1) are *employer* contributions and may be used to repay an exempt loan [Ltr Rul 9503002], but DOL has suggested that these contributions are *employee* contributions and, as such, may cause a prohibited transaction to occur.

Q 24:4   Do commercial lenders have a tax incentive to make loans to ESOPs?

Yes. If a commercial lender (see Q 24:6) makes a securities acquisition loan (see Q 24:5) that enables the ESOP to acquire employer securities (see Q 24:9), then 50 percent of the interest received by the commercial lender during the excludable period (see Q 24:8) is not subject to income tax. The commercial lender may make the loan directly to the ESOP or to the employer (which in turn lends the money to the ESOP). Loans between related persons do not qualify for the exclusion. [IRC §§ 133(a), 133(b), prior to repeal by SBA '96 § 1602(a); Rev Rul 89-76, 1989-1 CB 24; Ltr Rul 8941071]

The 50 percent interest exclusion has been repealed. The repeal is effective with respect to loans made after August 20, 1996, but the repeal does not apply to loans made pursuant to a written binding contract in effect before June 10, 1996, and at all times thereafter before the loan is made. In addition, the repeal of the 50 percent interest exclusion does not apply to the refinancing of an ESOP loan originally made on or before August 20, 1996 or pursuant to a binding contract in effect before June 10, 1996, provided: (1) such refinancing loan otherwise meets the requirements of Section 133 prior to repeal; (2) the outstanding principal amount of the loan is not increased; and (3) the term of the refinancing loan does not extend beyond the term of the original ESOP loan. [SBA '96, Act §§ 1602(a), 1602(c)]

Q 24:5   What is a securities acquisition loan?

A securities acquisition loan is:

1. Any loan to an ESOP that qualifies as an exempt loan (see Q 24:3) to the extent the proceeds are used to acquire employer securities (see Q 24:9) for the ESOP or are used to refinance an exempt loan that was used to acquire employer securities [Ltr Ruls 9406009, 9314007]; or

2. An immediate allocation loan to an employer that, within 30 days, transfers employer securities to the ESOP in an amount equal to the proceeds of the loan and such securities are allocable to accounts of participants within one year of the date of the loan.

A loan made to an employer sponsoring an ESOP may also qualify as a securities acquisition loan if the employer then, in turn, uses the proceeds to make an exempt loan to the ESOP with substantially similar repayment terms as the loan from the lender to the employer. If the repayment terms of the two loans are not substantially similar, the loan to the sponsoring employer will still qualify as a securities acquisition loan if (1) the loan to the ESOP provides for more rapid payment of principal or interest than the loan to the sponsoring employer, and (2) the allocations of employer securities within the ESOP attributable to the difference in payment schedules do not result in discrimination in favor of highly compensated employees (see Q 3:2).

A loan made after July 10, 1989 will be treated as a securities acquisition loan only if the ESOP owns more than 50 percent of the issuing corporation's stock immediately after the ESOP receives the employer securities acquired with the loan proceeds. For purposes of the 50 percent test, certain nonvoting, nonconvertible preferred stock is disregarded, and IRS may provide that warrants, options, and convertible debt interests may be treated as stock. Also, the commercial lender's 50 percent exclusion does not apply to interest income received during a period in which the ESOP's stock ownership percentage falls to 50 percent or less. The 50 percent ESOP stock ownership requirement is reduced to 30 percent for loans made after

July 10, 1989 but before November 18, 1989. The 50 percent interest exclusion has been repealed (see Q 24:4).

The term of a securities acquisition loan made after July 10, 1989 cannot exceed 15 years. Also, the ESOP must permit participants to vote stock allocated to their accounts that was acquired with a post-July 10, 1989 securities acquisition loan on a "one share/one vote" basis on all issues put to a shareholder vote.

A 10 percent nondeductible excise tax is imposed on the employer with respect to the amount realized on dispositions of employer securities acquired with a securities acquisition loan made after July 10, 1989 in a transaction to which Section 133 applied if:

1. Within three years, the total amount of employer securities held by the ESOP decreases;

2. Within three years, the value of the ESOP's employer securities drops below 50 percent of the value of all employer securities; or

3. The ESOP disposes of employer securities not allocated to participants and does not allocate the proceeds to participants.

Certain distributions to participants, including distributions pursuant to a diversification election (see Q 24:41), exchanges in corporate reorganizations, and dispositions required by state law, are not treated as dispositions for purposes of the excise tax. [IRC §§ 133, prior to repeal by SBA '96 § 1602(a), 4978B, prior to repeal by SBA '96 § 1602(b); Treas Reg §§ 54.4975-7, 54.4975-11; Temp Reg § 1.133-1T, Q&A 1; Ltr Ruls 9621034, 8821021]

Q 24:6 Which commercial lenders are eligible for the 50 percent interest exclusion?

A bank, an insurance company, a regulated investment company, or a corporation actively engaged in the business of lending money is eligible to exclude from gross income 50 percent of the interest received with respect to a securities acquisition loan (see Qs 24:4, 24:5). Entities eligible for the 50 percent interest exclusion are often referred to as qualified lenders. [IRC § 133(a), prior to repeal by SBA '96 § 1602(a)]

A corporation is actively engaged in the business of lending money if:

1. It is not an S corporation;

2. It lends money to the public on a regular and continuing basis (other than in connection with the purchase by the public of goods and services from the lender or a related party); and

3. A predominant share of such loans is not securities acquisition loans.

[Temp Reg § 1.133-1T, Q&A 2; Ltr Ruls 9119065, 8951027]

The 50 percent interest exclusion has been repealed (see Q 24:4).

Q 24:7 May loans that qualify for the 50 percent interest exclusion be transferred to other lending institutions?

Yes. A holder of a securities acquisition loan (see Q 24:5) may sell or transfer such loan to another lending institution. A subsequent holder of the debt instrument may qualify for the interest exclusion if the holder is a qualified lender (see Q 24:6). Further, a qualified lender will be eligible for the 50 percent interest exclusion even if a previous holder of the debt instrument was not a qualified lender (see Q 24:4). [IRC § 133, prior to repeal by SBA '96 § 1602(a); Rev Rul 89-76, 1989-1 CB 24]

The 50 percent interest exclusion has been repealed (see Q 24:4).

Q 24:8 Is there a limit on the time period for which the 50 percent interest exclusion applies?

Yes. The interest exclusion is allowable for the excludable period measured with respect to the date of the original securities acquisition loan. The excludable period generally is seven years or the term of the original securities acquisition loan, if longer. However, the excludable period is only seven years for immediate allocation loans and back-to-back loans with more rapid repayment provisions for the ESOP than the employer (see Q 24:6). Also, the refinancing of an original securities acquisition loan does not extend the excludable period with respect to the original securities acquisition loan and does not affect the partial excludability for interest paid (see Q 24:4) under the remaining portion of the original loan. [IRC § 133(e), prior to repeal by SBA '96 § 1602(a); Ltr Ruls 9610028, 9427011]

The 50 percent interest exclusion has been repealed (see Q 24:4).

Q 24:9 What are employer securities?

Employer securities include common stock issued by the employer that is readily tradable on an established securities market. If the employer has no readily tradable common stock, employer securities include employer-issued common stock that has a combination of voting power and dividend rights at least the equal of the class of common stock with the greatest voting power and the class of common stock with the greatest dividend rights. Noncallable preferred stock that is convertible into common stock that meets the requirements of employer securities also qualifies if the conversion price is reasonable. Nonvoting common stock of an employer is treated as employer securities if the employer has a class of nonvoting common stock outstanding and the specific shares that the plan acquires have been issued and outstanding for at least 24 months. [IRC § 409(l)]

IRS has ruled that common stock of a corporation held by its subsidiary's ESOP that is traded on the National Association of Securities Dealers Automated Quotation (NASDAQ) SmallCap Market qualifies as employer securities readily tradable on an established securities market. [Ltr Rul 9529043]

Employer securities also include stock issued by a member of a controlled group of corporations (see Q 5:33) that includes the employer if the stock meets the same requirements as qualifying employer-issued stock. If a U.S. corporation is a wholly owned subsidiary of a foreign corporation whose stock is not tradable on an established U.S. securities market, the U.S. subsidiary is deemed to have no readily tradable common stock and employer securities may include both stock of the foreign parent and stock of the U.S. subsidiary. [IRC § 409(l); Ltr Ruls 9219038, 9135059, 8610082] Common stock of a parent corporation does not constitute employer securities with respect to the employees of a partnership partially owned by the parent's subsidiary because a partnership cannot be a member of a controlled group of corporations. Consequently, the employees of the partnership could not participate in the ESOP maintained by the parent corporation. [GCM 39880; Ltr Rul 9236042]

Q 24:10 What is the limitation on tax-deductible contributions to an ESOP?

Generally, the limitation on deductions for employer contributions to an ESOP is 15 percent of covered compensation. However, money purchase pension ESOPs have a 25 percent limitation. In addition, the overall limitation on deductible contributions to all defined contribution plans in combination is 25 percent of covered compensation (see Qs 12:7, 12:17, 12:21). [IRC §§ 404(a)(3), 404(a)(7)]

The employer may deduct up to 25 percent of covered compensation for contributions to a leveraged ESOP (an ESOP that borrows to acquire employer securities) used to repay loan principal, and an unlimited amount for contributions used to pay interest on the loan. [IRC § 404(a)(9); Ltr Rul 9548036]

Q 24:11   Are dividends paid on employer securities held by an ESOP ever deductible by the employer?

Yes. The employer may be allowed to deduct dividends it pays on employer securities (see Q 24:9) held by an ESOP that it maintains or held by an ESOP maintained by another member of a controlled group (see Q 5:33) that includes the employer.

To be deductible, the dividend must be:

1. Paid in cash to the ESOP participants or their beneficiaries;
2. Paid to the ESOP and distributed to the participants or beneficiaries not later than 90 days after the close of the plan year in which paid; or
3. Used to make payments on an exempt loan. (For employer securities acquired by the ESOP after August 4, 1989, the deduction for dividends used for loan repayment is applicable only if the dividends are on employer securities acquired with the proceeds of the loan being repaid.)

The deduction is allowed for the taxable year of the employer during which the dividend is paid, distributed, or used to repay an exempt loan. [IRC §§ 404(k), 409(l)(4); Ltr Ruls 9626002, 9619078, 9619066, 9618009, 9610028, 9610026]

If dividends on employer securities allocated to a participant are used to repay an exempt loan, the ESOP must provide that employer securities with a fair market value equal to the dividends be allocated to such participant in lieu of the dividends. [IRC § 404(k)(2)(B); Ltr Rul 9132024]

An employer's cash distribution to an ESOP in redemption of a portion of the ESOP's stock may be considered a dividend and deductible by the employer. [IRC §§ 301, 302, 316; Ltr Rul 9211006] However, IRS has also ruled that amounts paid by an employer to redeem stock from its ESOP pursuant to a participant's election are payments in exchange for stock and not deductible dividends. [Ltr Rul 9612001]

It is important to note that IRS has authority to disallow the deduction if the dividends constitute an evasion of taxation or are unreasonably excessive in amount. [IRC § 404(k)(5)(A); Steel Balls, Inc, 95-3431 (8th Cir 1996); Ltr Rul 9304003]

Although dividends paid on employer securities held by an ESOP may be deductible by the employer from gross income, they are not deductible for alternative minimum tax purposes. [Snap-Drape, Inc, 105 TC 16 (1995); Illinois Cereal Mills, Inc, 93-2223 (CD Ill 1994); Treas Reg § 1.56(g)-1(d)(3)(iii)(E)]

Q 24:12 Are dividends paid to participants deductible even if participants can elect whether or not to receive them in a current cash payment?

Yes. Dividends actually paid in cash to plan participants are deductible despite a plan provision that permits participants to elect to receive or not to receive payment of dividends. [IRC § 404(k); Temp Reg § 1.404(k)-1T, Q&A 2; Ltr Rul 9618009]

Q 24:13 How are dividends paid to ESOP participants taxed?

Dividends paid in cash directly to ESOP participants by the employer and dividends paid to the ESOP and then distributed in cash to participants are treated as paid separately from any other payments from the ESOP. Thus, a deductible dividend is treated as a plan distribution and as paid under a separate contract providing only for payment of deductible dividends. A deductible dividend is a taxable distribution even though an employee has basis (see Q 13:2), but the distribution is not subject to the 10 percent tax on early distributions (see Q 13:39). [IRC §§ 72(e)(5)(D), 72(t)(2)(A)(vi), 402; Temp Reg § 1.404(k)-1T, Q&A 3]

A distribution of a participant's entire account balance from an ESOP is eligible for treatment as a lump-sum distribution (see Q 13:4) even if the participant received dividend distributions with respect to employer securities held by the ESOP in earlier years. [Ltr Ruls 9045048, 9024083]

Employers must report deductible dividends on Form 1099-DIV; but, if the dividend is paid in the same year that a total distribution is made to the participant, the entire amount should be reported on Form 1099-R. Participants must report the dividend distribution on their tax returns as a plan distribution and not as investment income. IRS is directed to establish procedures for information returns and reports with respect to deductible dividend payments. [IRC § 6047(e); Ann 85-168, 1985-48 IRB 40; Ann 85-180, 1985-51 IRB 24]

Q 24:14 What is the limit on the amount that may be added to an ESOP participant's account each year?

The amount that can be added to a participant's account (the annual addition) is limited to the lesser of $30,000 or 25 percent of the participant's compensation (see Qs 6:1, 6:2). [IRC §§ 415(c)(1), 415(c)(2)]

If no more than one-third of the employer's contributions for the year are allocated to highly compensated employees (see Q 3:3), contributions applied to pay interest on a loan, as well as forfeitures of ESOP stock acquired through a loan, are disregarded for purposes of computing the annual addition. [IRC § 415(c)(6)]

Dividends on employer securities (see Q 24:9) held by an ESOP may not be considered part of the annual addition so that contributions to an ESOP might be effectively increased; however, in one case, the dividends were so excessive in amount that the court agreed with IRS that the dividends were part of the annual addition and disqualified the ESOP. [IRC § 404(k); Treas Reg § 1.415-6(b)(2)(i); Steel Balls, Inc, 95-3431 (8th Cir 1996)]

Q 24:15   Can a company obtain a tax deduction for stock contributions to its ESOP?

Yes. One of the basic advantages of using an ESOP is the ability to use either cash or employer securities (see Q 24:9) for the company's contributions. A company strapped for cash can make its contributions in authorized but unissued securities and still get a tax deduction for the full amount of the contribution. Thus, for example, a company with an annual payroll of $500,000 that contributes $75,000 (15 percent of $500,000) to its ESOP in the form of employer securities is allowed a tax deduction of $75,000. The contribution in the form of employer securities not only keeps cash in the company but also provides a cash flow from the tax savings realized by the deduction.

The amount of the contribution is the fair market value of the employer securities even though there is no cost to the company.

Note, however, that a contribution of employer securities to a money purchase pension ESOP could be a prohibited transaction (see Q 20:10).

Q 24:16   Can an ESOP provide for permitted disparity?

A qualified retirement plan designated as an ESOP after November 1, 1977 may not provide for permitted disparity (i.e., integration with Social Security; see chapter 7). An ESOP providing for permitted disparity before that date can continue to do so, but the plan cannot be amended to increase the integration level or the integration percentage. [Treas Reg § 54.4975-11(a)(7)(ii)]

Q 24:17   How can a company use an ESOP to help finance the acquisition of another company?

A purchasing company that needs cash to acquire another company (the target) may obtain the necessary cash by arranging a bank loan to its ESOP.

The ESOP gets the borrowed cash to the purchasing company by buying employer securities (see Q 24:9) of the purchasing company. The purchasing company then buys the target's assets or stock with the cash. The bank loan is paid off through tax-deductible cash contributions by the purchasing company to the ESOP.

Another approach is to have the ESOP itself buy the stock of the target with the borrowed funds, and then exchange the target stock for newly issued stock of its own company. This approach is riskier, however, because the exchange of stock may be considered a prohibited transaction under ERISA (see Q 20:1). Before proceeding in this way, a DOL exemption request should be considered (see Q 20:11).

A third approach is for the company itself to borrow the cash and buy the target directly, using the cash flow created by a tax deduction for the stock contributions to the ESOP to help finance the purchase. This approach has the advantages of avoiding prohibited transaction problems and producing less dilution of the purchasing company's stock.

Q 24:18   Are ESOPs used by publicly traded companies to defend against unwanted takeovers?

Yes. By establishing an ESOP that purchases stock on the open market, management hopes to place a block of stock in the presumably friendly hands of its employees. However, to the extent that publicly traded stock (i.e., a registration-type class of securities) is allocated to participants, each participant must be given the opportunity to direct the ESOP as to the voting of the allocated shares. With respect to unallocated stock, the trustees and other fiduciaries must take special care to be sure they are acting solely in the interest of ESOP participants and beneficiaries (see Q 24:40). [IRC § 409(e)]

Shareholders of the target company and the potential acquiring company may challenge the voting of the ESOP's stock. In one case, an ESOP that acquired 14 percent of the stock of a publicly traded company in response to a takeover threat was upheld as fundamentally fair to the shareholders of the public company. The ESOP required that unallocated stock be voted in the same proportion as allocated stock. [Shamrock Holdings v Polaroid, 559 A 2d 257 (Del Ch 1989)]

However, the trustees of NCR's leveraged ESOP, established in the midst of AT&T's takeover threat, were enjoined from voting the ESOP's convertible preferred NCR stock in a special shareholders' meeting at which AT&T was expected to try to replace NCR's board of directors. Even though the ESOP required the trustees to vote unallocated stock in the same proportion as allocated stock, NCR's directors approved the establishment of the ESOP without adequate information about its fairness to NCR shareholders. The ESOP's purpose was to entrench management and prevent AT&T's takeover. [NCR v AT&T, No. C-3-91-78 (SD Ohio 1991); Menowitz v NCR, No. C-3-91-12 (SD Ohio 1991)]

Q 24:19   Can a profit sharing plan be converted to an ESOP?

Yes. If the company currently has a profit sharing plan and wants to replace it with an ESOP, the company has three alternatives. It can:

1. Continue the profit sharing plan and make future contributions to both the profit sharing plan and the ESOP.

2. Terminate the profit sharing plan. This results in the immediate 100 percent vesting of all the accounts of plan participants (see Q 21:4). The assets under the profit sharing plan can be either distributed currently or maintained in the plan for distribution as employees retire or separate from service.

3. Adopt the ESOP as a continuation of the profit sharing plan. Replacement of the profit sharing plan will not be considered a termination of the plan for vesting purposes. Employer securities must be purchased with plan assets because an ESOP must invest primarily in employer securities (see Qs 24:1, 24:9).

Plan fiduciaries must beware that the conversion of a profit sharing plan into an ESOP may, depending on the purpose and financial consequences of the conversion, be a violation of the prudent man rule. In other words, if the business goes sour after the conversion, it is likely that participants will bring a claim against the fiduciaries for making an imprudent investment. The courts have been sympathetic to such claims. [Eaves v Penn, 587 F 2d 453 (10th Cir 1978); Bradshaw v Jenkins, No. C83-771R (DC Wash 1984); Baker and Goss v Smith, 2 EBC 1380 (DC Pa 1981); but see Andrade v The Parsons Corp, No. CV 85-3344-RJK (CD Cal 1990)]

Q 24:20   How can an ESOP be used as an estate planning tool for the owner of a closely held corporation?

The bulk of an owner's estate frequently consists of the value of the stock in the owner's corporation. If the value of that stock is not established before the owner's death, an arbitrary figure—one based on a compromise between an IRS valuation expert and the estate's expert—may be used to determine the amount of estate taxes due. The establishment of an ESOP before the owner's death may ease this burden on the estate because the fair market value of the stock acquired by the ESOP would be determined by an independent (see Q 24:57) appraiser beforehand, reducing the chances of a dispute with IRS. [IRC § 401(a)(28)]

The ESOP can also provide cash to pay the estate taxes and administration expenses of a deceased majority shareholder. The tax law provides various solutions to the liquidity problems of an estate that consists mostly of the stock of a closely held corporation. If the estate fails to qualify for this special treatment, it may be able to raise the cash through the sale of stock to the ESOP.

For example, assume that the estate of a deceased shareholder fails to meet the requirements that permit it to pay the estate tax in installments over a period of up to 15 years. The estate tax is then due within nine months of the shareholder's death. By selling the deceased shareholder's stock to the ESOP, the estate can raise the cash it needs. However, one court has indicated that a premium price paid by the ESOP to purchase a majority of a corporation's stock from the estates of two shareholders may be unreasonable corporate waste. [RCM Securities Fund v Stanton, No. 90-7047 (2d Cir 1991)]

The ESOP can also rescue an estate of a deceased shareholder that cannot avail itself of the benefits of a Section 303 redemption. This provision of the Code permits the redemption of a portion of a deceased shareholder's stock for the express purpose of paying estate taxes and administration expenses. If an estate fails to qualify, the proceeds of a redemption of the deceased shareholder's stock are likely to be subject to income tax as a dividend. This result can be avoided by having the ESOP buy the stock from the estate. The sale to the ESOP does not have the danger of being treated as a dividend.

Generally, a sale to the corporation or to the ESOP will result in no gain at all because the estate's basis for the stock it sells will equal the fair market value of the stock on the deceased shareholder's date of death, and the purchase price paid by the corporation or the ESOP will likely be this amount. [IRC §§ 302, 303, 1014, 6166]

Q 24:21   How can an ESOP be used to provide a market for the stock of controlling shareholders in a closely held corporation?

An ESOP is a mechanism that enables controlling shareholders to sell all or a portion of their shares to the employees, who would be the logical buyers if they could obtain the financing.

The transaction clearly benefits the shareholders by allowing them to cash out their interests in the corporation. It also benefits the corporation because the shares may be purchased with pretax dollars (i.e., annual cash contributions to the ESOP), resulting in a substantial reduction in the cash required to finance the transaction. Further, a commercial lender may be eligible to exclude from its taxable income 50 percent of the interest received on the loan to purchase the shares of a selling shareholder, so the lender may charge a reduced rate of interest (see Qs 24:4, 24:8).

Another advantage of this type of transaction is that it provides for the continuity of management by enabling new employees to acquire stock as older employees and shareholders retire without diluting the equity of the remaining shareholders. That is, the ESOP, by purchasing outstanding shares from existing shareholders, avoids the diluting effect that would be involved if the ESOP purchased newly issued shares from the corporation.

There may, however, be some dilution of earnings to the extent that the ESOP creates expenses that the corporation would not otherwise have. Even this may not be the case if the corporation previously had a profit sharing plan and the ESOP is installed simply as a replacement for the profit sharing plan (see Q 24:19).

An existing buy-sell agreement between two controlling shareholders, a father and son, giving each the option to buy the other's shares at a below-market price, may pose a problem. IRS ruled that the father's sale of some of his shares to an ESOP at market value (after the son's waiver of his rights under the agreement) would be a taxable gift by the son to his father to the extent the ESOP's purchase price exceeds the option price under the buy-sell agreement. [Ltr Rul 9117035]

Q 24:22   May gain on the sale of securities to an ESOP be deferred?

Yes. A shareholder who sells qualified securities (see Q 24:24) to an ESOP may elect to defer recognition of all or part of the gain, which would otherwise be recognized as long-term capital gain, by purchasing qualified replacement property (see Q 24:25) within the replacement period (see Q 24:26). If the shareholder makes an election (see Q 24:28), gain is immediately taxable only to the extent that the amount realized on the sale exceeds the cost of the replacement property. If the sale to the ESOP is an installment sale, any taxable gain (that is, the gain relating to the portion of the proceeds not invested in qualified replacement property within the replacement period) must be reported on the installment basis, unless the seller elects otherwise. [IRC §§ 453, 1042; Temp Reg § 1.1042-1T, Q&A 1; Ltr Ruls 9102021, 9102017]

Note: If the selling shareholders' interests in the ESOP are in excess of 20 percent of the total account balances for all employees, IRS may consider the sale to the ESOP to be a distribution under Section 301 and not a sale. [Rev Proc 87-22, 1987-1 CB 718]

Q 24:23　Are all taxpayers eligible to elect deferral of gain upon the sale of securities to an ESOP?

All taxpayers (including grantor trusts) other than C corporations (see the Glossary) can make the election (see Q 24:29). [IRC § 1042(c)(7); Ltr Ruls 9442015, 9141046, 9041027]

However, only the taxpayer who sells the qualified securities (see Q 24:24) is eligible to make the election. A trust with eight individual beneficiaries sold its stock to an ESOP, elected to defer recognition of the gain, and purchased qualified replacement property (see Q 24:25) with a portion of the proceeds. Soon thereafter, the trust was divided into eight equal separate trusts, one for each beneficiary. The separate trusts are not eligible to defer gain by acquiring replacement property with the remaining proceeds because the original trust and the resulting eight separate trusts are not the same taxpayer. [Ltr Rul 9143013]

Where a partnership sold the qualified securities, the election was a partnership decision; therefore, no individual partner was eligible to elect deferral of gain. [Ltr Rul 9508001]

Q 24:24　What are qualified securities?

Qualified securities are employer securities (see Q 24:9) that (1) are issued by a domestic corporation that for one year before and immediately after the sale has no readily tradable stock outstanding, (2) have not been received by the seller as a distribution from a qualified retirement plan or pursuant to an option or other right to acquire stock granted by the employer, and (3) as of the time of the sale, have been held by the seller for more than one year. Shares of common stock are not qualified securities if the employer's stock had been traded over the counter on NASDAQ within one year of the sale to the ESOP (see Q 24:9). [IRC § 1042(c)(1); Temp Reg § 1.1042-1T, Q&A 1(b); Ltr Ruls 9215026, 9036039]

For taxable years beginning *after* 1997, the domestic corporation must be a domestic C corporation. [IRC § 1042(c)(1)(A), as amended by SBA '96 § 1316(d)(3)]

Q 24:25   What is qualified replacement property?

Qualified replacement property is any security issued by a domestic operating corporation that did not have passive investment income (e.g., rents, royalties, dividends, or interest) that exceeded 25 percent of its gross receipts in its taxable year preceding the purchase. Securities of the corporation that issued the employer securities (see Q 24:9), and of any corporation that is a member of a controlled group of corporations with such corporation (see Q 5:33), cannot be qualified replacement property. An operating corporation is a corporation that uses more than 50 percent of its assets in the active conduct of a trade or business. Banks and insurance companies are considered operating corporations. [IRC §§ 409(l), 1042(c)(4); Ltr Rul 9432009]

A sale of employer securities to an ESOP in exchange for a promissory note, followed by a transfer of the note to an unrelated corporation in exchange for shares of its stock, qualifies for deferral treatment (see Q 24:22) because the stock of the unrelated corporation constitutes qualified replacement property. [Ltr Rul 9321067]

Q 24:26   What is the replacement period?

The replacement period is the period beginning three months before the date of sale to the ESOP and ending 12 months after the sale. The qualified replacement property (see Q 24:25) must be purchased during this period. [IRC § 1042(c)(3); Temp Reg § 1.1042-1T, Q&A 3(c)]

Q 24:27   What other conditions apply before the deferral of gain is permitted?

After the sale, the ESOP must own at least 30 percent of either (1) each class of outstanding stock of the corporation or (2) the total value of all outstanding stock of the corporation. Also, for sales after July 10, 1989, the selling shareholder must have held the stock for at least three years. As part of the election (see Q 24:28), the selling shareholder must file with IRS a verified written statement of the corporation sponsoring the ESOP consenting to the application of the excise taxes on early dispositions and prohibited allocations of the qualified securities (see Qs 24:33–24:35). [IRC § 1042(b); Temp Reg § 1.1042-1T, Q&A 2(a)]

Q 24:28 How does the selling shareholder elect not to recognize gain?

The election not to recognize the gain realized upon the sale of qualified securities (see Q 24:24) is made in a statement of election attached to the selling shareholder's income tax return filed on or before the due date (including extensions) for the taxable year in which the sale occurs. The election is irrevocable. If the selling shareholder does not make a timely election, the shareholder may not subsequently make an election on an amended return or otherwise. No discretionary extension of time to file the election can be granted by IRS because the deadline for filing an election to defer gain on sales of qualified securities is prescribed by statute. [IRC § 1042(c)(6); Ltr Ruls 9438016, 8932048]

The statement of election must provide that the selling shareholder elects to treat the sale of securities as a sale of qualified securities and must contain the following information:

- Description of the qualified securities sold, including the type and number of shares
- Date of the sale of the qualified securities
- Adjusted basis of the qualified securities
- Amount realized upon the sale of the qualified securities
- Identity of the ESOP to which the qualified securities were sold, and
- Names and taxpayer identification numbers of the others involved if the sale was part of a single interrelated transaction including other sales of qualified securities, and the number of shares sold by the other sellers

If the selling shareholder has purchased qualified replacement property (see Q 24:25) at the time of the election, a statement of purchase must be attached to the statement of election. The statement of purchase must describe the qualified replacement property, give the date of the purchase and the cost of the property, declare such property to be the qualified replacement property, and be notarized within 30 days after the purchase of the qualified replacement property.

If the selling shareholder has not purchased qualified replacement property at the time of the filing of the statement of election, the notarized statement of purchase described above must be attached to the shareholder's income tax return filed for the following taxable year. The statement of purchase must be filed with the IRS district where the election was originally filed if the return is not filed with such district. [IRC § 1042(a)(1); Temp Reg § 1.1042-1T, Q&A 3]

IRS has ruled that notarization after the 30-day period did not invalidate the election and that an election that substantially complied with the rules was valid even though the notarized statement did not declare that the property purchased with the sales proceeds was intended to be qualified replacement property. [Ltr Ruls 9550014, 9429017, 9028082]

Q 24:29 What is the basis of qualified replacement property?

If the selling shareholder makes an election not to recognize the gain (see Q 24:28), the basis of the qualified replacement property (see Q 24:25) purchased during the replacement period (see Q 24:26) is reduced by an amount equal to the amount of gain that was not recognized. If more than one item of qualified replacement property is purchased, the basis of each item is reduced by an amount determined by multiplying the total gain not recognized by a fraction whose numerator is the cost of such item of property and whose denominator is the total cost of all such items of property. [IRC § 1042(d); Temp Reg § 1.1042-1T, Q&A 4; Ltr Ruls 9102021, 9102017]

If the selling shareholder dies, the basis of the qualified replacement property becomes the property's fair market value at the date of the selling shareholder's death. [Ltr Rul 9339005]

Q 24:30 What happens if the taxpayer who elects nonrecognition treatment later disposes of the qualified replacement property?

If the taxpayer disposes of any qualified replacement property (see Q 24:25), gain must be recognized unless exempted (see Q 24:31) to the extent not previously recognized in connection with the acquisition of the qualified replacement property, notwithstanding any other provision of the law that might defer recognition. A special recapture rule applies if the taxpayer controls the corporation that issued the qualified replacement property and the corporation disposes of a substantial portion of its assets other than in the ordinary course of its trade or business. [IRC § 1042(e)]

A taxpayer's transfer of qualified replacement property to a revocable trust created by the taxpayer is not a disposition, and the division of a trust that acquired qualified replacement property into eight separate trusts is not a disposition (see Q 24:23). Furthermore, the distribution of qualified replacement property by a trust to its beneficiary is not a disposition. [Ltr Ruls 9533038, 9411003, 9327080, 9226027, 9143013, 9141046]

Contributions of qualified replacement property to a charitable remainder trust constitute a disposition of such property but do not result in a recapture of the deferred gain because of the nature of the trust. [Ltr Ruls 9547023, 9547022, 9234023] The same result occurs if the contribution is made directly to a charitable organization. [Ltr Ruls 9533038, 9515002]

Q 24:31   Do all dispositions of qualified replacement property result in the recapture of gain?

No. The following dispositions are exempted from the recapture provisions:

- Dispositions upon death
- Dispositions by gift
- Subsequent sales of the qualified replacement property to an ESOP pursuant to Section 1042, and
- Transfers in a corporate reorganization, provided no corporation involved in the reorganization is controlled by the taxpayer holding the qualified replacement property

[IRC § 1042(e)(3); Ltr Ruls 9533038, 9515002, 9339005]

Q 24:32   What is the statute of limitations when a selling shareholder elects nonrecognition of the gain on the sale of qualified securities?

If any gain is realized, but not recognized, by the selling shareholder on the sale of any qualified securities (see Q 24:24), the statute of limitations with respect to such nonrecognized gain will not expire until three years from the date of IRS receipt of:

1. A notarized statement of purchase that includes the cost of the qualified replacement property (see Q 24:28);
2. A written statement of the selling shareholder's intent not to purchase qualified replacement property (see Q 24:25) within the replacement period (see Q 24:26); or
3. A written statement of the selling shareholder's failure to purchase qualified replacement property within the replacement period.

If the selling shareholder files a statement of intent not to purchase or failure to purchase qualified replacement property, the statement must be accompanied, if appropriate, by an amended return for the taxable year in which the gain from the sale of the qualified securities was realized. The amended return must report any gain from the sale of qualified securities that is required to be recognized in the taxable year in which the gain was realized due to a failure to meet the nonrecognition requirements. [IRC § 1042(f); Temp Reg § 1.1042-1T, Q&A 5]

Q 24:33   What happens if the ESOP disposes of qualified securities within three years of their acquisition?

An excise tax is imposed on the amount realized on the disposition (see Q 24:34) of qualified securities (see Q 24:24) if:

1. The ESOP acquires any qualified securities in a sale for which nonrecognition treatment was elected (see Q 24:28);

2. The ESOP disposes of any of such qualified securities during the three-year period after the date on which any qualified securities were acquired; and

3. Either (a) the total number of shares of employer securities (see Q 24:9) held by the ESOP after such disposition is less than the total number of shares of employer securities held immediately after the sale for which nonrecognition treatment was elected, or (b) the value of the employer securities held by the ESOP immediately after such disposition is less than 30 percent of the total value of all employer securities outstanding at that time.

[IRC § 4978(a); Temp Reg § 54.4978-1T, Q&A 1]

Q 24:34   What is the amount of the excise tax on the disposition of qualified securities?

The tax is 10 percent of the amount realized on the disposition that is allocable to qualified securities acquired within the three-year period following their acquisition. [IRC § 4978(b), as amended by SBA '96 § 1602(b)(4); Temp Reg § 54.4978-1T, Q&A 2]

A disposition is any sale, exchange, or distribution. However, the excise tax will not apply to any disposition of qualified securities that is made by reason of:

- Death of the employee
- Retirement of the employee after the employee has attained age 59½
- Disability of the employee (see Q 26:41), or

- Separation from service by the employee for any period that results in a one-year break in service (see Q 5:10)

In addition, dispositions necessary to comply with the diversification requirements (see Q 24:41) and exchanges pursuant to corporate reorganizations will not trigger the excise tax. [IRC § 4978(d); Temp Reg § 54.4978-1T, Q&A 3]

The excise tax is imposed on the corporation or corporations that made the verified written statement of consent to the application of such excise tax on the disposition of employer securities (see Q 24:28). [IRC § 4978(c); Temp Reg § 54.4978-1T, Q&A 4]

If RRB '96 (see Q 1:22A) is enacted, age 59½ will be replaced with age 59. [RRB '96, Act § 9445(a)]

Q 24:35   Are there any restrictions on the allocation of qualified securities acquired by the ESOP in a transaction in which the seller elected nonrecognition of gain?

Yes. None of the employer securities (see Q 24:9) acquired by the ESOP in a nonrecognition transaction may be directly or indirectly allocated to or accrue to the benefit of the selling shareholder or a member of the shareholder's family during the nonallocation period (see Q 24:36), or to an owner of more than 25 percent of any class of employer stock at any time. The family-member restriction does not apply if the family member is a lineal descendant of the shareholder and the total amount allocated to all such lineal descendants does not exceed more than 5 percent of the employer securities held by the plan that are attributable to the sale to the plan by a person related to such descendants. In addition, a person will not be treated as a 25 percent shareholder if such person was not a 25 percent shareholder at any time during the one-year period ending on the date of sale of the employer securities to the plan or on the date the employer securities are allocated to participants. [IRC §§ 409(n)(1), 409(n)(3)]

For purposes of determining whether the prohibition against an accrual of qualified securities (see Q 24:24) is satisfied, the allocation of any contributions or other assets that are not attributable to qualified securities sold to the ESOP must be made without regard to the allocation of the qualified securities. In effect, this allocation restriction operates to prohibit any direct or indirect accrual of benefits under all qualified retirement plans of an employer. [IRC § 409(n)(1); Temp Reg § 1.1042-1T, Q&A 2(c); Ltr Rul 9041071]

Example. Stephanie, Caroline, and James own 50, 25, and 25 shares, respectively, of the 100 outstanding shares of common stock of Ess & Ess

Corporation. The corporation establishes an ESOP that obtains a loan, and the loan proceeds are used to purchase the 100 shares of qualified securities from Stephanie, Caroline, and James, all of whom elect nonrecognition treatment with respect to the gain realized on their sale of such securities. No part of the assets of the ESOP attributable to the 100 shares of qualified securities may accrue under the ESOP for the benefit of Caroline or James during the nonallocation period or to Stephanie at any time. These restrictions also generally apply to any person who is a member of any of their families. Furthermore, no other assets of the ESOP may accrue to the benefit of such individuals in lieu of the receipt of assets attributable to such qualified securities.

The prohibited allocation is treated as a distribution to the person receiving such allocation. Also, there is an excise tax imposed on the employer equal to 50 percent of the amount involved in a prohibited allocation of qualified securities acquired by an ESOP after October 23, 1986. [IRC §§ 409(n)(2), 4979A]

Q 24:36   What is the nonallocation period?

The nonallocation period, for purposes of the nonrecognition provisions regarding sales of stock to an ESOP (see Qs 24:22–24:35), is the period beginning on the date of sale and ending on the later of (1) the date that is ten years after the date of sale, or (2) the date of the plan allocation attributable to the final payment of acquisition indebtedness incurred in connection with the sale. [IRC § 409(n)(3)(C)]

Q 24:37   How can an ESOP be used to facilitate a buyout of shareholders in a closely held corporation?

An ESOP can be used to purchase all or a portion of the stock of minority shareholders, inactive shareholders, and outside shareholders. In these instances, the primary advantage is that the corporation purchases the shares with pretax dollars. From the minority shareholder's point of view, it is generally irrelevant whether the shares are purchased by the corporation or by the ESOP, since the shareholder would generally be entitled to the same tax treatment in either case. However, the sale of the stock to the ESOP is more likely to be treated as a sale (and not a distribution of property) than a sale of stock to the corporation. [Ltr Rul 8931040]

The purchase of stock from existing shareholders can be financed in a number of ways, depending on the size of the payroll, the assets of the ESOP, and the needs and objectives of the selling shareholder. If the selling shareholder needs immediate liquidity, the ESOP may use any cash on hand

and borrow funds either from the corporation or from an outside lender to purchase the shareholder's stock for cash.

If the selling shareholder does not need immediate liquidity, the shareholder may prefer to receive interest by selling the stock to the ESOP on an installment-sale basis in return for an interest-bearing note. An installment sale has the advantages of spreading out the tax over a number of years and fixing the price of the shares at the time of the sale.

Finally, the shareholder may simply sell a portion of the shares each year on a serial-sale basis. This is the approach usually taken when the shareholder is not yet ready to sell a block of stock at one time.

Note: In order to meet qualification requirements and avoid a prohibited transaction (see Q 20:1), an independent appraiser (see Q 24:57) must determine the purchase price in each transaction on the basis of the stock's fair market value at the time of sale. [IRC §§ 401(a)(28)(C), 4975(d)(13); ERISA § 408(e)] One court ruled that a sale of stock by the majority shareholder to an ESOP was a prohibited transaction because the shareholder did not prove that the purchase price was equal to fair market value or that the price was determined in good faith after a prudent investigation. [Eyeler v Comm'r, 95-2482 (7th Cir 1996)]

Q 24:38   How can an ESOP be used to finance a business?

Under conventional financing, a corporation that needs to raise $1 million for working capital or expansion purposes borrows the funds from a bank or other lender and repays the loan with after-tax dollars. Although the interest component of each debt payment is a deductible expense to the corporation, the principal repayment is not deductible and is, therefore, considered an after-tax payment.

By use of an ESOP, it is possible to arrange the financing so that both the interest and principal repayments are tax deductible. This is accomplished either by having the ESOP rather than the corporation borrow the $1 million or by having the corporation reloan the proceeds to the ESOP. The ESOP uses the loan proceeds to purchase $1 million worth of newly issued stock from the corporation. The corporation has the $1 million needed for working capital or expansion purposes, and the ESOP owns $1 million worth of the corporation's stock. Thereafter, the corporation may make an annual tax-deductible contribution to the plan consisting of (1) an amount of up to 25 percent of covered payroll for the purpose of repaying the loan principal, plus (2) an unlimited amount used to pay interest on the loan (see Q 24:10). [IRC § 404(a)(9)]

In the case of a typical private corporation, the lender may demand both a pledge agreement, pledging the shares of stock as collateral for the loan, and a guarantee agreement from the corporation. Under the guarantee agreement, the corporation agrees to make annual contributions to the ESOP sufficient to amortize the loan and, in the event that the corporation fails to make such contributions, to pay the loan directly.

See Qs 24:4 through 24:8 for a discussion of the 50 percent interest exclusion available to certain lenders.

Q 24:39   May an ESOP enter into an agreement obligating itself to purchase stock when a shareholder dies?

No. An ESOP may, however, be given an option to buy stock when the shareholder dies. [Treas Reg § 54.4975-11(a)(7)(i)]

Q 24:40   Must plan participants be given voting rights with respect to their stock?

If the employer securities (see Q 24:9) are registered with the Securities and Exchange Commission (SEC), participants must be given full voting rights with respect to stock allocated to their accounts. DOL has opined that fiduciaries of a collectively bargained ESOP must pass through decisions concerning tender offers or proxy voting to the plan's participants and vote as directed, unless doing so would violate ERISA. According to DOL, even if the plan provides the trustees with the discretion to vote shares and circumstances justify not voting as directed, trustees cannot disregard the participants' directions unless obeying the directions would violate ERISA. [DOL Ltr Rul, Sept 28, 1995]

An ESOP maintained by an employer that does not have registration-type securities (e.g., a closely held corporation) is required to pass through voting rights to participants with stock allocated to their accounts only with respect to any corporate merger or consolidation, recapitalization, reclassification, liquidation, dissolution, sale of substantially all assets of a trade or business, or other similar transaction prescribed by regulations. The plan may authorize the trustees of an ESOP maintained by such an employer to vote such allocated stock on a one vote per participant basis. [IRC §§ 133(b)(7), 409(e)]

These voting requirements do not apply to stock held by the ESOP in a suspense account (i.e., stock not yet allocated to participants). The trustees have discretion in voting unallocated stock and allocated stock not subject to the pass-through rule, but they must vote such stock in accordance with their fiduciary duty to plan participants and beneficiaries (see Q 19:12). [The Central Trust Co, NA v American Advents Corp, 771 F Supp 871 (SD Ohio 1991)]

The pass-through voting requirements are not violated when trustees vote the shares of stock that are allocated to participants' accounts and for which no voting directions are timely received. The participants were entitled to direct the votes but failed to timely communicate their directions to the trustees. [Rev Rul 95-57, 1995-35 IRB 5]

Q 24:41   What is diversification of investments in an ESOP?

A qualified participant (see Q 24:42) in an ESOP must be permitted to direct the ESOP as to the investment of up to 25 percent of the participant's account during the 90-day period following each plan year in the qualified election period (see Q 24:43). With the final diversification election during the qualified election period, the participant may elect to diversify up to 50 percent of the participant's account. [IRC § 401(a)(28)(B)]

Q 24:42   Who is a qualified participant?

A qualified participant is any employee who has completed at least ten years of participation in the ESOP and has attained age 55. [IRC § 401(a)(28)(B)(iii)]

When an ESOP is terminated and a successor ESOP adopted, a participant's years of participation in both ESOPs can be aggregated for purposes of the ten-year requirement. [Ltr Rul 9213006]

Q 24:43   What is the qualified election period?

The qualified election period is the six-plan-year period beginning with the plan year after the first plan year in which the employee is a qualified participant (see Q 24:42). [IRC § 401(a)(28)(B)(iv)]

Example. Joe of Rockville Centre Ltd. maintains an ESOP with a calendar-year plan year. Mitzi completes ten years of participation in the ESOP in 1997 when she is age 56. Thus, Mitzi becomes a qualified participant in the plan year beginning January 1, 1997. Mitzi will be eligible to make diversification elections during the election periods in 1998, 1999, 2000, 2001, 2002, and 2003.

Q 24:44 What must an ESOP do to satisfy the diversification requirements?

A qualified participant (see Q 24:42) must be given the opportunity to make a diversification election within 90 days after the close of each plan year within the qualified election period (see Q 24:43) with respect to a cumulative amount of at least 25 percent of the participant's account (50 percent for the last election period). The ESOP can satisfy this requirement by offering any of the following:

1. To distribute all or part of the amount subject to the diversification election;

2. At least three other distinct investment options; or

3. To transfer the portion of the account balance subject to the diversification election to another qualified defined contribution plan (see Q 2:2) of the employer that offers at least three investment options.

The ESOP must complete diversification in accordance with a diversification election within 90 days after the end of the period during which the election could be made for the plan year. [IRC § 401(a)(28)(B)(ii); Notice 88-56, 1988-1 CB 540, Q 13]

If this requirement is satisfied by the distribution of all or part of the amount subject to the diversification election, the distribution will be an eligible rollover distribution (see Q 28:8) subject to the 20 percent income tax withholding rules (see Q 16:7).

Q 24:45 What is the effect of the diversification or distribution of a participant's employer securities?

Amounts diversified pursuant to a diversification election are generally treated as amounts not held by an ESOP and are no longer subject to the statutory provisions governing amounts held by an ESOP. Thus, for example, a qualified participant (see Q 24:42) cannot demand that the distribution of diversified amounts be made in the form of employer securities (see Q 24:9). [Notice 88-56, 1988-1 CB 540, Q 16]

Amounts distributed in satisfaction of the diversification requirements that consist of employer securities are subject to a participant's put option (see Q 24:55). Distributions in satisfaction of the diversification requirements do not violate the restrictions regarding distributions before a participant's termination of employment or certain other events. [Notice 88-56, 1988-1 CB 540, Q 14; IRC § 409(h)]

Q 24:46   Are all employer securities held by an ESOP subject to diversification?

No. Only employer securities (see Q 24:9) acquired by or contributed to an ESOP after December 31, 1986 are subject to the diversification requirements. Therefore, employer securities allocated to participant accounts after December 31, 1986 will not be subject to diversification if they were acquired or contributed before that date. [Notice 88-56, 1988-1 CB 540, Q 1]

Also, if an ESOP received cash contributions prior to January 1, 1987 and thereafter—but within certain time limits—used the contributions to acquire employer securities, those securities will be deemed to have been acquired before January 1, 1987 and will not be subject to the diversification rules. [Notice 88-56, 1988-1 CB 540, Q 3]

An ESOP acquired employer securities prior to January 1, 1987, received cash for the securities after a tender offer, and then used the proceeds of the tender offer to acquire stock of the new parent corporation. IRS ruled that the new parent corporation's stock was deemed to have been acquired prior to January 1, 1987 and, therefore, not subject to the diversification requirements. [Ltr Rul 9608040]

Q 24:47   Are dividends paid to an ESOP subject to the diversification rules?

Yes. Dividends paid after December 31, 1986 in the form of employer securities (see Q 24:9), or in cash or other property used to acquire employer securities (see Q 24:11), are subject to the diversification rules. This is true even though the dividends are paid with respect to employer securities acquired by the ESOP before January 1, 1987. [Notice 88-56, 1988-1 CB 540, Q 1]

However, the diversification rules will not apply to securities acquired with cash dividends paid before January 1, 1987 if the acquisition occurred within 60 days of the date of payment of the dividend. [Notice 88-56, 1988-1 CB 540, Q 1 and Q 3]

Q 24:48   How is the determination made as to which employer securities are subject to diversification?

An ESOP may separately account for employer securities (see Q 24:9) contributed or acquired after December 31, 1986 and those contributed before January 1, 1987. If the ESOP does not maintain separate accounts for securities based on the date of acquisition, any securities allocated after

1986 will be presumed to consist, first, of securities acquired or contributed after 1986 and, second, of securities acquired or contributed before 1987. [Notice 88-56, 1988-1 CB 540, Q 4]

An ESOP may, under certain circumstances, use an alternative formula to determine the portion of a qualified participant's (see Q 24:42) account attributable to employer securities acquired or contributed after December 31, 1986. Under this formula, the number of securities in a qualified participant's account deemed acquired or contributed after December 31, 1986 is determined by multiplying the number of shares allocated to a qualified participant's account by a fraction representing, as of the plan valuation date closest to the date on which the individual becomes a qualified participant, the portion of the total shares that were acquired by or contributed to the ESOP after December 31, 1986. This formula is available only if the IRS model plan amendments to conform to the TRA '86 changes were adopted by the ESOP sponsor on or before January 1, 1989. [Notice 88-56, 1988-1 CB 540, Q 5; Notice 87-2, 1987-1 CB 396]

Example. Floyd Corporation adopted the model plan amendments with respect to its ESOP. On January 1, 1995—the plan's valuation date—the ESOP held 100,000 shares of Floyd Corporation's stock. Of those 100,000 shares, 75,000 were acquired by the ESOP after December 31, 1986. Michelle, a participant in the ESOP with 40 shares allocated to her account, became a qualified participant on January 18, 1996. The number of shares allocated to Michelle's account that are subject to the diversification requirements is 30 (75,000 ÷ 100,000 × 40). If Michelle does not elect to diversify within 90 days after the close of the 1996 plan year, and eight more shares are allocated to her account on January 1, 1997, the number of shares in her account subject to diversification increases to 36 [(75,000 ÷ 100,000) × (40 + 8)]. [Notice 88-56, 1988-1 CB 540, Q 9]

Q 24:49 May any qualified participants in ESOPs that hold employer securities acquired after December 31, 1986 be excluded from making the diversification election?

Yes. If an ESOP holds and allocates to a qualified participant's (see Q 24:42) account a *de minimis* amount of employer securities (see Q 24:9) acquired after December 31, 1986 (see Qs 24:47, 24:49), it will not be required to offer diversification to that participant. A fair market value of $500 or less will be considered to be a *de minimis* amount for this purpose, although an ESOP may elect to use a lower threshold. If the *de minimis* level is exceeded later in the qualified election period (see Q 24:43), then all employer securities allocated to the qualified participant that were acquired or contributed after December 31, 1986 are subject to diversification. [Notice 88-56, 1988-1 CB 540, Q 7 and Q 8]

Q 24:50   May employer securities acquired before 1987 be diversified?

Yes. The shares diversified need not be those actually acquired after 1986 (see Qs 24:46, 24:48). The number of shares that must be available for diversification is nevertheless determined by the number of shares acquired or contributed after December 31, 1986. The diversified shares, however, must be employer securities (see Q 24:9) that, immediately prior to diversification, were subject to the put option and right to demand requirements of Section 409(h) (see Qs 24:1, 24:55). [Notice 88-56, 1988-1 CB 540, Q 10]

Q 24:51   May an ESOP permit a qualified participant to elect diversification of amounts in excess of that required by statute?

Yes, an ESOP may permit diversification of amounts in excess of the minimum requirements (see Q 24:44). However, such amounts are not treated as available for diversification or as diversified in accordance with Section 401(a)(28)(B). Amounts in excess of the minimum diversification requirements remain subject to the participant's right under Section 409(h) to demand distribution in the form of employer securities (see Q 24:9). [Notice 88-56, 1988-1 CB 540, Q 11]

Q 24:52   Is a loan from a shareholder to an ESOP a prohibited transaction?

Not necessarily. Although ERISA generally prohibits loans (or loan guarantees) between a qualified retirement plan and a disqualified person (a 10 percent or more shareholder, for example), a loan (or a loan guarantee) by a disqualified person to an ESOP is not a prohibited transaction (see Q 20:1) if the loan qualifies as an exempt loan (see Q 24:3). [ERISA § 408(b)(3); IRC § 4975(d)(3)]

Q 24:53   Must distributions under an ESOP commence by specified dates?

Yes. As a qualification requirement, with regard to distributions attributable to stock acquired after December 31, 1986, an ESOP must provide that, if a participant elects (and, if applicable, the participant's spouse consents), the distribution of the participant's account balance will begin not later than one year after the end of the plan year:

1.   In which the individual terminates employment by reason of reaching retirement age, disability (see Q 26:41), or death; or

2.   That is the fifth plan year following the plan year in which the individual otherwise terminates employment (unless the individual is reemployed by the employer before such time).

For purposes of this rule, the individual's account balance is deemed not to include any employer securities (see Q 24:9) acquired with the proceeds of an exempt loan (see Q 24:3) until the end of the plan year in which such loan is repaid in full. In addition to these requirements, the ESOP must comply with the minimum distribution requirements (see chapter 11). [IRC §§ 401(a)(9), 409(o)(1)(A), 409(o)(1)(B)]

Q 24:54   Must distributions under an ESOP be made at certain intervals?

With regard to distributions attributable to stock acquired after December 31, 1986, an ESOP must provide that (unless the participant elects otherwise) the distribution of the participant's account balance will be in substantially equal periodic payments (not less frequently than annually) over a period not longer than five years. If the participant's account balance exceeds $500,000, the distribution period may be extended one year for each $100,000 (or part thereof) by which the account balance exceeds $500,000. However, the distribution period cannot exceed ten years. [IRC § 409(o)(1)(C)]

Both of the dollar amounts are adjusted for inflation. However, an adjustment will be made only if it is $5,000 or greater and then will be made in multiples of $5,000 (i.e., rounded down to the next lowest multiple of $5,000). For example, an increase in the cost-of-living of $4,999 will result in no adjustment, and an increase of $9,999 will create an upward adjustment of $5,000. For 1996, the respective amounts are $690,000 and $135,000. [Notice 95-55, 1995-45 IRB 11; IRC §§ 409(o)(2), 415(d); RPA '94 Act § 732(e)(2)]

Q 24:55   When can participants exercise their put option?

Participants can exercise a put option and put the employer securities (see Q 24:9) back to the company for their fair market value if the securities are not readily tradable on an established market.

The put option must last for a period of at least 60 days following the date of distribution of employer securities. If the option is not exercised, the participant must be given the opportunity to sell the stock to the employer during an additional 60-day period in the following plan year. [IRC § 409(h)(4)]

If a put option is exercised with respect to stock distributed in a total distribution, the employer must pay for the stock in substantially equal periodic payments (not less frequently than annually) over a period beginning no later than 30 days after the exercise of the put option and ending no later than five years thereafter. Reasonable interest and adequate security must be provided for unpaid amounts. For this purpose, a total distribution is a distribution of the balance of the recipient's account within one calendar year. [IRC § 409(h)(5); Treas Reg § 54.4975-7(b)(12)(iv)] The employer's unsecured promissory notes are not adequate security. [Ltr Rul 9438002]

If the stock is distributed in installments, the employer must pay for the stock no later than 30 days after the put option is exercised. [IRC § 409(h)(6)]

One court ruled that ESOP participants whose put options were not honored by the sponsoring company could not sue the ESOP trustees under ERISA because the put options were binding on the company and not the ESOP. [Flynn v Ballinger, No. C94-0190 SBA (ND Cal 1994)]

A company maintained an ESOP that contained a put option provision. When exercised, the option required the company to repurchase its stock from the retirees. Two employees retired and exercised their put options. The ESOP purchased the stock, instead of the company, in exchange for a promissory note payable over a period of years that was secured by the stock sold. Shortly thereafter, the company went bankrupt, rendering the stock worthless. The court held that the ESOP trustees may be liable for breach of fiduciary duty because the decline in value of the stock due to the company's bankruptcy constituted a loss to the plan that was brought about by the trustees' decisions. [Roth v Sawyer-Cleaton Lumber Co, 1995 US App Lexis 19919 (8th Cir 1995)]

Q 24:56   How are distributions from an ESOP taxed?

Distributions from an ESOP are generally taxed like any other distribution from a qualified retirement plan (see chapter 13). If appreciated employer securities (see Q 24:9) are included in a lump-sum distribution, the recipient may defer tax on the net unrealized appreciation until the securities are sold (see Q 13:17). [Ltr Ruls 9438043, 9147053]

Distributions from ESOPs may be subject to the 10 percent additional tax on early distributions (see Q 13:39), and net unrealized appreciation on employer securities is an includible distribution for excess distribution tax purposes (see Q 13:29).

ESOP assets will be considered invested in employer securities in a variety of circumstances. If an ESOP receives cash or other assets for employer securities as part of a reorganization, the assets will satisfy the requirement if they are invested in employer securities within 90 days (or an extended period if granted by IRS) of the acquisition of cash or other assets. Cash received by an ESOP as the result of an exempt loan, earnings, dividends, or other cash contributions will satisfy the requirement if invested in employer securities within 60 days of the contribution. Cash or cash equivalents allocated to a participant's account will be deemed to be invested in employer securities if the value of those benefits does not exceed 2 percent of the value of the allocated securities. Also, amounts transferred to an ESOP following a reversion from a terminated defined benefit plan will meet the investment requirement if the amounts are invested in employer securities within 90 days of the transfer, and such amounts will not be subject to the excise tax on employer reversions (see Q 21:56). The 90-day period may be extended by IRS. [IRC § 4980(c)(3); Notice 88-56, 1988-1 CB 540, Q 18; Ltr Ruls 9452045, 9448045, 9419030, 9402021]

An ESOP that holds in a suspense account the stock of a subsidiary company spun off from the parent company sponsoring the ESOP, which stock was purchased with a reversion amount from a terminated defined benefit plan, can sell the stock of the subsidiary and use the proceeds to buy stock of the sponsoring parent company. The ESOP cannot, however, use the proceeds to buy any assets other than the sponsoring parent's stock, because such a transaction would be a violation of the ESOP exception to the tax on employer reversions. [Ltr Rul 9411038] Participants in an ESOP are permitted to make elective deferrals under the plan's cash-or-deferred arrangement (see Q 23:1) prior to the allocation of all stock held in a suspense account purchased with reversion amounts from a terminated defined benefit plan, provided the elective deferrals are not made until after required allocations are made from the suspense account for the plan year and the combined amounts do not exceed the annual addition limitation (see Q 24:14). In addition, stock held in the suspense account could be used for matching contributions, subject to the annual addition limitation. [IRC § 4980(c)(3)(C); Ltr Rul 9350025]

Q 24:57   Which factors are used to value employer securities that are not readily tradable?

Employer securities (see Q 24:9) that are not readily tradable must be valued by an independent appraiser. [IRC § 401(a)(28)(C)]

The valuation of employer securities must be reasonable, written, made in good faith, and based on all relevant factors used to determine fair market value. Relevant factors include:

- Nature of the business and history of the enterprise
- Economic outlook in general and condition of specific industry
- Book value of the securities and financial condition of the business
- Earning capacity of the company
- Dividend-paying capacity of the company
- Existence of goodwill
- Market price of similar stocks
- Marketability of securities, including an assessment of the company's ability to meet its put obligations, and
- Existence of a control premium, which means a block of security that provides actual control of the company (control must be actual control that is not dissipated within a short period of time)

[DOL Prop Reg § 2510.3-18]

Q 24:58 Can employees' interests in an ESOP be investment contracts under the Securities Acts of 1933 and 1934?

Yes, says one court. The company solicited new employees to participate in its wage reduction program, which constituted eligibility to participate in the company's ESOP and profit sharing plan in return for a reduction in wages. The court held that, in order to be considered an investment contract subject to protection under the Securities Acts of 1933 and 1934, there must be (1) an investment of money (2) in a common enterprise (3) with profit derived from the efforts of other persons. Since the wage reduction program constituted an investment of money, the ESOP is a common enterprise, and profits (i.e., dividends and appreciation in value) would result primarily from efforts of management and employees, each employee's interest in the ESOP was an investment contract. [Uselton v Commercial Lovelace Motor Freight, Inc, Nos. 88-1253 and 88-1750 (10th Cir 1991); see also Int'l Brotherhood of Teamsters v Daniel, 439 US 551 (1979); SEC v WJ Howey Co, 328 US 293 (1946)]

Another court has ruled that the Securities Acts applied to employee claims involving an ESOP because (1) the plan, as an ESOP, lacked the primary indicia of a pension plan (i.e., payment of benefits only upon retirement), (2) participation was voluntary, (3) the ESOP was contributory because participants gave up a percentage of income, and (4) participants acquired common stock, a security specifically enumerated in the Securities Act of 1933. [Hood v Smith's Transfer Corp, 762 F Supp 1274 (1991)]

Q 24:59   Is a participant's interest in an ESOP exempt from bankruptcy?

In 1992, the United States Supreme Court held that a participant's interest in a qualified retirement plan is exempt from the claims of creditors in a bankruptcy proceeding, thereby resolving the conflict among the Courts of Appeals. [Patterson v Shumate, 112 S Ct 2242 (1992)]

See Qs 4:24 through 4:27 for more details.

Chapter 25

Multiemployer Plans

Many companies maintain qualified retirement plans established under collective bargaining agreements. Frequently, more than one employer is required to contribute to the plan. How these multiemployer plans work, their basic advantages, and the system for guaranteeing benefits are examined in this chapter.

Q 25:1 What kind of retirement plan is used to provide retirement benefits for union workers?

Retirement plans are subject to collective bargaining. Often a retirement plan negotiated by a union is set up on an industrywide (sometimes regional) basis. An employer, out of necessity or voluntarily, will negotiate to join this industrywide retirement plan. In other cases, the employer may find it possible or desirable to have a separate (individual) retirement plan for its own employees as a result of negotiations with the union.

If the employer decides to go with an individual retirement plan, the plan is virtually identical to those plans adopted in nonunion situations. The only differences are that the retirement plan covers union workers and that the benefits result from the collective bargaining process. All of the requirements for qualification as a tax-favored retirement plan that apply to retirement plans that do not cover union employees apply to the individual collectively bargained retirement plan.

If, on the other hand, the employer decides to provide benefits under an industrywide or areawide retirement plan, commonly referred to as a multiemployer plan, an entirely different set of rules applies (in addition to some of the basic requirements). [IRC §§ 413(a), 413(b); see also ERISA §§ 4201–4225] For example, hours of service that are credited to a participant for purposes of eligibility, vesting, and accrual of benefits are determined under different rules. [IRC § 413(b)] The minimum funding require-ments applicable to qualified retirement plans are modified, and the time to adopt certain retroactive plan amendments is extended. [IRC §§ 412(b)(7), 412(c)(8)] Also, the provisions governing plan termination differ greatly from the rules for single-employer plans. [Compare ERISA §§ 4041, 4041A]

Q 25:2 What is a multiemployer plan?

Generally, a multiemployer plan is a plan established under a collective bargaining agreement that is maintained by two or more unrelated employ-ers. From a technical or legal standpoint, however, the multiemployer plan is defined as a plan:

1. To which more than one employer is required to contribute;

2. That is maintained under a collective bargaining agreement between an employee organization and more than one employer; and

3. That meets any additional requirements that may be issued by DOL.

[ERISA § 3(37); IRC § 414(f)]

The multiemployer plan should be distinguished from the single-em-ployer plan. Although the multiemployer plan is established through nego-tiations between employers, an association of employers, or a trade association and the union representing the plan participants, the single-em-ployer plan is established or maintained by only one employer, either unilaterally or through a collective bargaining agreement. Generally, the sponsoring single employer has the ultimate responsibility for the admini-stration of the plan. In contrast, responsibility for a multiemployer plan lies with a board of trustees composed of both union and employer repre-sentatives. [ERISA § 3(37)(A); Labor-Management Relations Act § 302(c)(5)]

The refusal to comply with the request of a participating employer in a multiemployer plan that the plan's trustees transfer the plan's liability to pay benefits for the employer's employees and an amount of funds equal to the employer's contributions to a new single employer plan has been upheld because a multiemployer plan is not *required* to permit an asset transfer to another plan. [ERISA § 4234; Ganton Technologies, Inc v Nat'l Industrial Group Pension Plan, 1996 US App Lexis 1758 (2d Cir 1996); Caterino v Barry, 8 F 3d 878 (1st Cir 1993); Vornado, Inc v Trustees of the Retail Store Employees' Union Local 1262, 829 F 2d 416 (3d Cir 1987)]

Q 25:3   What are the basic advantages of a multiemployer plan?

The multiemployer plan has been developed to meet the needs of industries (e.g., construction, transportation, mining) that usually use craftsmen and draw their employees from a limited pool of workers within a specific geographical area. A multiemployer plan can benefit a particular industry because it:

1. Permits mobile employees to take their pension benefits with them when they move from one participating employer to another within the same industry;

2. Stabilizes pension costs among participating employers, reducing competitive wrangling for select employees;

3. Makes possible economies of scale because of the pooling of pension resources, either increasing benefits or reducing employer costs; and

4. Reduces administrative costs through use of experienced and knowledgeable administrators and trustees.

Q 25:4   Must an employer contribute to a multiemployer plan?

Every employer who is obligated to make contributions to a multiemployer plan under the terms of the plan or under the terms of a collective bargaining agreement must make contributions in accordance with the terms and conditions of the plan or the agreement. [ERISA § 515]

In an action by a multiemployer plan to enforce ERISA Section 515, if a judgment in favor of the plan is awarded, the court shall award to the plan:

1. The unpaid contributions;

2. Interest on the unpaid contributions;

3. An amount equal to the greater of (a) interest on the unpaid contributions, or (b) liquidated damages provided for under the plan in an amount not in excess of 20 percent (or such higher percentage as may be permitted under federal or state law) of the amount determined by the court under paragraph 1;

4. Reasonable attorneys' fees and costs of the action, to be paid by the employer; and

5. Such other legal or equitable relief as the court deems appropriate.

[ERISA § 502(g)(2)]

An employer cannot escape liability for interest, liquidated damages or double interest, attorneys' fees, and costs by paying delinquent contributions before the entry of a judgment, as long as plan contributions were unpaid at the time the suit was filed. [Iron Workers District Council of Western New York and Vicinity Welfare and Pension Funds v Hudson Steel Fabricators & Erectors, Inc, 1995 US App Lexis 30924 (2d Cir 1995)]

Even if a collective bargaining agreement is declared void from its inception by the National Labor Relations Board, it is not void from inception for purposes of ERISA. Consequently, contributions to the multiemployer plan required by the agreement must be made from the date of the agreement until the date the agreement is declared void. [Mackillop v Lowe's Market, Inc, 1995 US App Lexis 16769 (9th Cir 1995)]

One court held that the president of an employer that was obligated to contribute to a multiemployer plan was personally liable for unpaid plan contributions even though he was not provided with copies of the collective bargaining or trust agreements before signing a counterpart agreement. [Employee Painters' Trust v J & B Finishes, 1996 US App Lexis 3416 (9th Cir 1996)] Another court held that an employer's president committed a fiduciary breach by failing to make plan contributions and was personally liable to the plan for the unpaid contributions. The court concluded that the unpaid contributions became plan assets when they became due and owing to the plan. Because the president exercised discretionary authority over these amounts, he was a fiduciary (see Q 19:1) and, therefore, committed a breach when he used the amounts to pay corporate expenses rather than plan contributions. Thus, he was liable to the plan for the losses caused by his breach (see Q 19:17). [ERISA § 409(a); PMTA-ILA Containerization Fund v Rose, 1995 US Dist Lexis 10877 (ED Pa 1995)] However, one court declined to impose personal liability on a corporate officer because, in New York, an agent who signs an agreement on behalf of a disclosed principal is not individually bound to the terms of the agreement unless there is clear and explicit evidence of the agent's intention to substitute or add the officer's personal liability for, or to, that of the principal. [Cement and Concrete Workers District Council Welfare Fund, Pension Fund, Legal Services Fund and Security Fund v Lollo, 35 F 3d 29 (2d Cir 1994)]

Q 25:5 How are hours of service credited to an employee under a multiemployer plan?

For purposes of participation and vesting, a multiemployer plan is treated as if all participating employers constitute a single employer. Thus, with certain exceptions, all covered service with an employer participating in the plan as well as all contiguous noncovered service with that same employer are taken into account. For purposes of the accrual of benefits, only covered service is counted. [DOL Reg § 2530.210; IRC §§ 413(a), 413(b); Gauer v Connors, 953 F 2d 97 (4th Cir 1991); Rev Rul 85-130, 1985-2 CB 137]

The determination of covered service is functional. Full-time employees performed covered service even though their employers claimed they were casual employees under the collective bargaining agreement. [Central States, Southeast & Southwest Areas Pension Fund v Independent Fruit & Produce Co, No. 89-1927 (8th Cir 1990)]

Q 25:6   Is a retirement plan maintained by two or more affiliated companies considered a multiemployer plan?

No. In considering whether more than one employer is required to contribute to the plan, employers that are under common control (see Q 5:33) are considered as only one employer. Thus, a plan that requires contributions from two or more companies that are controlled by the same interests is not a multiemployer plan because only one employer is required to contribute to the plan; multiemployer plans require more than one unrelated employer (see Q 25:2). [ERISA § 3(37)(B)]

Q 25:7   Are benefits under a multiemployer plan guaranteed?

Yes. PBGC has the authority to insure the benefits of a defined benefit multiemployer plan. Although a multiemployer plan usually combines the features of a defined benefit plan (see Q 2:3) and a defined contribution plan (see Q 2:2) (i.e., both benefits and contributions are fixed) the courts have said that a multiemployer plan is a defined benefit plan. Therefore, the benefits under a multiemployer plan are guaranteed by PBGC. [Connolly v PBGC, 581 F 2d 729 (9th Cir 1978); PBGC v Defoe Shipbuilding Co, 639 F 2d 311 (6th Cir 1981)]

Note, however, that the benefits under a multiemployer plan are guaranteed only if the plan becomes insolvent (see Q 25:8). [ERISA § 4022A(a)(2)]

Q 25:8   When is a multiemployer plan insolvent?

A multiemployer plan is considered insolvent when its available resources are insufficient to pay benefits when due for the plan year or when the plan is determined by the plan sponsor to be insolvent while the plan is in reorganization. The plan's available resources include cash, marketable securities, earnings, payments due from withdrawn employers, and employer contributions, minus reasonable administration expenses and amounts owed to PBGC for financial assistance. [ERISA § 4245]

Q 25:9   What level of benefits is guaranteed?

The level of guaranteed benefits is generally lower than the guarantees provided under single-employer defined benefit plans. However, benefits accrued through July 29, 1980 that are payable to retirees or beneficiaries as of that date or to vested participants who were within three years of normal retirement age as of that date are guaranteed in accordance with the higher ERISA single-employer rules. [ERISA §§ 4022A(a), 4022A(c), 4022A(h)]

PBGC now guarantees 100 percent of the first $5 of monthly benefits per year of service. The next $15 of monthly benefits or, if less, the accrual rate over $5 per month per year of service is guaranteed at 75 percent for strong plans and 65 percent for weaker plans. [ERISA § 4022A(c)]

Q 25:10   What benefits are not guaranteed by PBGC?

PBGC will not guarantee benefits that have been in effect under the multiemployer plan for less than 60 months. Also, benefit improvements that have not been in effect for at least 60 months are not guaranteed.

This differs from coverage provided for single-employer plans, which phase in benefit guarantees of 20 percent a year, with a minimum phase-in of $20 each month, during the five-year period following the implementation of a benefit improvement (see Q 21:24). [ERISA §§ 4022(b), 4022A(b)]

Q 25:11   What is the financial liability of an employer that withdraws from a multiemployer plan?

An employer that withdraws from a multiemployer plan is liable for its proportionate share of unfunded vested benefits (UVBs), determined as of the date of withdrawal. The liability is imposed upon withdrawal without reference to the plan's termination.

The employer's withdrawal liability is based on the plan's total unfunded liability for vested benefits, not the lesser guaranteed benefits that apply to single-employer terminations. The method used to determine the employer's share can vary from plan to plan (see Q 25:23).

The result is that an employer that withdraws from an underfunded multiemployer plan may have to continue to contribute to the plan at approximately the same dollar level after withdrawal as before withdrawal until the liability is fully paid. In some cases, the withdrawing employer can make payments over a 20-year period (see Q 25:34).

Q 25:12 Can withdrawal liability be assessed against any employer that withdraws from a multiemployer plan?

Withdrawal liability applies only to withdrawals that occur on or after September 26, 1980. The United States Supreme Court has ruled that the withdrawal liability provisions of ERISA are constitutional. [Connolly v PBGC, 475 US 211 (1986)]

When an employer temporarily ceased contributions to a multiemployer plan prior to September 26, 1980, but a complete withdrawal (see Q 25:14) did not occur until thereafter, the employer was assessed withdrawal liability, and the United States Supreme Court ruled that the assessment did not violate the employer's right to due process of law and did not constitute an unconstitutional taking of property without just compensation. [Concrete Pipe and Products of California, Inc v Construction Laborers Pension Trust for Southern California, 113 S Ct 2264 (1993)] However, an employer who, prior to September 26, 1980, entered into a binding agreement to withdraw and ceased business operations before the end of 1980 was not assessed withdrawal liability. [Crown Cork & Seal Co, Inc v Central States, Southeast and Southwest Areas Pension Fund, 982 F 2d 857 (3d Cir 1992)]

Q 25:13 What steps are involved in determining multiemployer plan withdrawal liability?

The withdrawal liability process consists of five phases:

1. Determining whether the employer has withdrawn;
2. Computing the withdrawn employer's share of the plan's UVBs;
3. Determining whether any reductions apply to the withdrawal liability;
4. Notifying the employer of the amount of the withdrawal liability; and
5. Collecting the liability.

[ERISA §§ 4201, 4202]

Q 25:14 When is a participating employer considered to have withdrawn from a multiemployer plan?

An employer is considered to have withdrawn, and therefore is subject to withdrawal liability, when it (1) permanently ceases to have an obligation to contribute to the multiemployer plan, or (2) permanently ceases all covered operations under the plan.

Special rules apply for determining whether there is a complete or partial withdrawal (see Q 25:16) of employers in the following industries:

- Building and construction
- Trucking
- Household goods moving
- Public warehousing
- Retail food
- Certain segments of the entertainment industry

[ERISA § 4203]

The key issue is whether the employer's obligation to contribute has ceased. [Connors v Barrick Gold Exploration, Inc, 962 F 2d 1076 (DC Cir 1992)] If the employer is no longer obligated to make contributions to the multiemployer plan, it cannot escape withdrawal by either continuing to make payments or getting another company to agree to make contributions on its behalf. [Connors v B&W Coal Co, 646 F Supp 164 (D DC 1986)] However, the result may be different if another company signs an agreement undertaking the obligation on behalf of the original employer. [ILGWU Nat'l Retirement Fund v Distinctive Coat Co, 6 EBC 2631 (SD NY 1985)]

In an arbitration, it was held that although the passage of some time may be necessary for a determination of whether a cessation of covered operations is permanent, once it is determined to be permanent, the date of withdrawal will relate back to the date when contributions ceased. [E H Hatfield Enters, Inc v UMW 1950 and 1974 Pension Plans, 9 EBC 1980 (1988) (Jaffe, Arb)] In another case, a general contractor was not required to continue making contributions after it subcontracted the covered employees' work to a non-union employer. [Board of Trustees of the Chicago Plastering Inst Pension Trust Fund v William A Duguid Co, No. 87 C 10768 (ND Ill 1991)]

Q 25:15   Can an employer be held liable for withdrawal liability as a result of circumstances such as decertification of the union or a plant closing?

Yes. The issue is whether the employer's obligation to contribute to the multiemployer plan has ceased or whether all covered operations under the plan have ceased. If the answer is yes to either, then the circumstances that led to the cessation of the obligation to contribute or to the cessation of all covered operations are irrelevant. For example, an employer may be subject to withdrawal liability if the employer's employees vote to decertify the union representing them. Similarly, withdrawal liability may be triggered by a plant closing or merger of a facility. [ERISA §§ 4203, 4205, 4212]

Q 25:16   Does a participating employer have any liability if there is a partial withdrawal from the multiemployer plan?

Yes. Withdrawal liability applies when a participating employer partially withdraws from the multiemployer plan. Generally, a partial withdrawal occurs when:

1. There is at least a 70 percent decline in the employer's contribution base units (e.g., hours worked) [PBGC Op Ltr 93-2];

2. The employer ceases to have an obligation to contribute to the plan under at least one, but not all, of its collective bargaining agreements and continues the same type of work in the geographical area covered by the agreement; or

3. The employer ceases to have an obligation to contribute to the plan for work performed at one or more, but fewer than all, of its facilities (see Q 25:17) covered under the agreement.

A 70 percent decline in contribution base units occurs if, during the plan year and each of the preceding two plan years (the three-year testing period), the number of contribution base units for which the employer was required to make plan contributions did not exceed 30 percent of the number of contribution base units for the high base year. The high base year is determined by averaging the employer's contribution base units for the two plan years for which such units were the highest within the five plan years preceding the three-year testing period.

[ERISA §§ 4205, 4208; Chicago Truck Drivers, Helpers and Warehouse Workers Union (Ind) Pension Fund v Leaseway Trans Corp, 1996 US App Lexis 1858 (7th Cir 1996)]

Q 25:17   What is a facility for purposes of a partial withdrawal?

The term "facility" has been determined by PBGC to be a discrete economic unit of an employer. For example, the term will ordinarily apply to a single retail store rather than to a group of stores in a metropolitan area. [PBGC Op Ltr Nos. 86-2, 82-33, 82-22; May Stern & Co v Western Pennsylvania Teamsters and Employers Pension Fund, 8 EBC 2202 (1987) (Nagle, Arb)]

Q 25:18   Is withdrawal liability affected if employers are under common control?

Employers under common control (see Qs 5:31, 5:33) are considered as only one employer. Withdrawal liability can be assessed against all members of the commonly controlled group, even if only one member of the commonly controlled group is required to contribute to the multiemployer plan. [ERISA § 4001(b); DOL Op Ltr 82-13; Central States, Southeast and Southwest Areas Pension Fund v Slotky, 956 F 2d 1369 (7th Cir 1992); Central States, Southeast and Southwest Areas Pension Fund v Newbury Transport Corp, 1992 US Dist Lexis 1757 (ND Ill 1992); Central States, Southeast and Southwest Areas Pension Fund v Chatham Properties, 929 F 2d 260 (6th Cir 1991); IUE AFL-CIO Pension Fund v Barker & Williamson, Inc, 788 F 2d 118 (3d Cir 1986); O'Connor v DeBolt Transfer, Inc, 737 F Supp 1430 (WD Pa 1990); Board of Trustees of the W Conference of Teamsters Pension Trust Fund v Salt Creek Terminals, Inc, No. C85-2270R (WD Wash 1986); Connors v Calvert Dev Co, 622 F Supp 877 (D DC 1985)] One court ruled that, in determining whether a partnership and a withdrawing employer are jointly liable for withdrawal liability, the lack of an economic nexus between them is irrelevant; the proper inquiry is whether they are under common control. [Connor v Incoal, Inc, 1993 US App Lexis 13168 (DC Cir 1993)] In another case, an acquiring corporation was liable for the withdrawal liability payments of the acquired corporation even after the acquired corporation was discharged in bankruptcy because of the acquiring corporation's control both before and after the bankruptcy reorganization. [Teamsters Joint Council No. 83 v Centra, Inc, No. 90-1815 (4th Cir 1991)] However, a public entity that hired a private company to manage a marine terminal was not considered the employer of the private company's employees. [Seaway Port Auth of Duluth v Duluth-Superior ILA Marine Assoc Restated Pension Plan, 920 F 2d 503 (8th Cir 1990)]

The employer of leased employees for withdrawal liability purposes is not necessarily the same as under the Code (see Qs 5:61–5:66). In one case, a company leased truck drivers to another company and made interim withdrawal liability payments (see Q 25:39) after the lease ended. Although both companies may be considered employers, the issue of each company's withdrawal liability to the plan is subject to arbitration (see Q 25:38). [Global Leasing, Inc v Henkel Corp, 744 F Supp 595 (D NJ 1990)] In another case, a company that leased truck drivers from another company was held not to be an employer for withdrawal liability purposes since it had no contractual liability to contribute to the plan. [Rheem Mfg Co v Central States, Southeast and Southwest Areas Pension Fund, No. 95-1073 (8th Cir 1995)] In determining whether a corporation was the employer, one court applied a contributing obligor test. Under this test, only a party that is obligated to contribute to a plan is an employer. The court noted that the corporation was not contractually bound to contribute to the plan and, therefore, was not subject to withdrawal liability. [Tampa Bay Int'l Terminals, Inc v Tampa Maritime Assn-Int'l Longshoremen's Assn Pension Plan and Trust, No. 95-2776 (11th Cir 1996)]

Where the shareholders of a bankrupt company also operated a real estate business that leased property to the company and the leasing of property was considered a trade or business, the shareholders were liable for the withdrawal liability of the company as members of a commonly controlled group. [Central States, Southeast and Southwest Areas Pension Fund v Ditello, 974 F 2d 887 (7th Cir 1992)] In other cases, sole proprietors were found personally liable for the withdrawal liability of their failed companies because their real estate investments constituted a business and the individuals had common control over both the failed company and the sole proprietorship. [Central States, Southeast and Southwest Areas Pension Fund v Personnel, Inc, 974 F 2d 789 (7th Cir 1992); Central States, Southeast and Southwest Areas Pension Fund v Koder, 970 F 2d 1067 (7th Cir 1992); Central States, Southeast and Southwest Areas Pension Fund v Landvatter, 1993 US Dist Lexis (ND Ill 1993)]

One court ruled that an individual's estate planning trust was jointly and severally liable for the withdrawal liability of a company owned by the individual who established the trust. The trust had leased property to the company and another entity under the individual's control and was thus a trade or business under common control. [Vaughn v Sexton, 975 F 2d 498 (8th Cir 1992)]

Q 25:19 Does a withdrawal occur if there is a change in business structure?

No, provided the change in corporate structure does not cause an interruption in the employer's contributions or obligations under the multiemployer plan. [ERISA § 4218]

Changes in corporate structure include the following:

- Reorganization involving a mere change in identity, form, or place of organization
- Liquidation into a parent corporation
- Merger, consolidation, or division; and
- Change to an unincorporated form of business enterprise

[ERISA § 4069(b)]

The incorporation of a sole proprietorship or partnership does not constitute a withdrawal if the successor corporation continues to have an obligation to contribute and does so. [PBGC Op Ltr No. 83-18] One court ruled that a successor corporation was automatically liable for a predecessor sole proprietorship's delinquent contributions to a multiemployer plan because the successor corporation had the same ownership, management, and type of business as the predecessor sole proprietorship and was therefore the alter ego of the predecessor sole proprietorship. [Downey v General Interiors, Inc, Nos. 92-16711 and 92-16797 (9th Cir 1994); see also UA Local 343 of the United Assoc of Journeymen & Apprentices of the Plumbing and Pipefitting Ind of the United States and Canada, AFL-CI0 v Nor-Cal Plumbing, Inc, No. 92-15749 (9th Cir 1994)]

Similarly, changes in the composition of an employer-partnership (e.g., sale of partnership interests to new partners) do not result in a withdrawal if the partnership continues to have an obligation to contribute and continues to honor that obligation. [Park S Hotel Corp v New York Hotel Trades Council, 851 F 2d 578 (2d Cir 1988); Connors v B&W Coal Co, Inc, 646 F Supp 164 (D DC 1986); but see E H Hatfield Enters, Inc v UMW 1950 and 1974 Pension Plans, 9 EBC 1980 (1988) (Jaffe, Arb)] Assignees of a partnership interest were not subject to withdrawal liability because they were assignees and not partners. [Connors v Middle Fork Corp, No. 89-0698(GHR) (D DC 1992)]

A sale of one subsidiary in a corporate group did not result in a complete withdrawal of that corporate group from a multiemployer plan because another subsidiary in the group continued to contribute to the plan, and withdrawal liability was not imposed. [Central States, Southeast and Southwest Areas Pension Fund v Sherwin-Williams Co, 1995 US App Lexis 35273 (7th Cir 1995)] Similarly, withdrawal liability was not imposed when two of three subsidiaries of a parent corporation ceased operations because the parent continued to contribute to the fund on behalf of the third subsidiary. However, the parent's withdrawal liability was triggered when it sold the third subsidiary to an unrelated purchaser even though the purchaser continued to make contributions to the plan. The court held that the corporate restructuring exception applies only when the withdrawal does not result *solely* because of a change in corporate restructuring. The alleged corporate restructuring was the sale of the third subsidiary. Refusing to view the sale of the third subsidiary in isolation, the court found that the parent's withdrawal did not result *solely* because of the sale of the third subsidiary. Instead, withdrawal was the net effect of a series of transactions (the second subsidiary ceasing operations four years after the first subsidiary, and the third subsidiary being sold ten months afterwards) that altogether resulted in the severance of the parent's common ownership of all three corporations. [Penn Central Corp v Western Conf of Teamsters Pension Trust Fund, 1996 US App Lexis 1143 (9th Cir 1996)]

Where two U.S. shipping companies that contributed to a multiemployer plan withdrew from certain shipping operations and entered into a joint venture establishing a new company to handle those operations, the court held that the joint venture creation of a new company, where the two companies continued to exist in the same corporate form, did not qualify under the corporate restructuring exception. [Bowers v Andrew Weir Shipping, Ltd, 1994 US App Lexis 15524 (2d Cir 1994)]

Q 25:20 Does a withdrawal occur if there is a suspension of contributions during a labor dispute?

No withdrawal occurs as a result of the temporary suspension of contributions during a labor dispute. However, a withdrawal may occur if the cessation of contributions is permanent even though the cessation occurred during a labor dispute. [ERISA § 4218; PBGC Op Ltr Nos. 82-2 and 82-21; Combs v Adkins Coal Co, Inc, 597 F Supp 122 (D DC 1984)]

Q 25:21 Who determines when a withdrawal from a multiemployer plan occurs?

The plan sponsor determines whether and when an employer has withdrawn from the multiemployer plan. [ERISA §§ 3(16)(B), 4202]

Q 25:22 Is a sale of employer assets considered a withdrawal from a multiemployer plan?

If the assets sold by the employer represent all of its covered operations, there may be a complete withdrawal. However, if only part of the employer's operation is sold, a partial withdrawal (see Q 25:16) may result. The withdrawal liability of the selling employer is limited to a maximum amount. [ERISA § 4225]

The selling employer is relieved of primary withdrawal liability only if the following conditions are satisfied:

1. The purchasing company is an unrelated party that assumes substantially the same contribution obligation;

2. The purchasing company posts a bond for the following five plan years; and

3. The contract of sale provides that the selling employer is secondarily liable if the purchasing company completely or partially withdraws during the following five plan years and fails to pay its withdrawal liability.

If the above conditions are not satisfied, the purchasing company is not responsible for any of the seller's withdrawal liability. However, PBGC is authorized to grant individual or class exemptions or variances from the requirement that the purchasing company post a bond if it determines that the request for exemption or variance would more effectively or equitably carry out the purposes of Title IV of ERISA and would not significantly increase the risk of financial loss to the plan. [ERISA § 4204(c); PBGC Reg § 2643.3(b); PBGC Notice of Exemption, 58 FR 60707 (Nov 17, 1993); PBGC Notice of Exemption, 57 FR 7408 (Mar 2, 1992)] Also, if the purchaser withdraws after the sale, the determination of the purchaser's withdrawal liability takes into account the seller's required contribution for the year of the sale and the four preceding years. [ERISA § 4204]

If the selling employer distributes all or substantially all of its assets or liquidates before the expiration of the five-year period, it must post a bond or establish an escrow account. [ERISA § 4204(a)(3)] When a selling employer converted its assets to cash before the expiration of the five-year period, it did not incur withdrawal liability even though it failed to post the required bond, because the purchasing company had not failed to make contributions during the period. The plan's sole remedy was to enforce the bond requirement. [Central States, Southeast and Southwest Areas Pension Fund v Bell Transit Co, No. 93-2519 (7th Cir 1994)]

In one case, the purchasing company continued to contribute on behalf of the selling company's employees pursuant to its own collective bargaining agreement, which was essentially identical to that of the selling employer. The court held that no withdrawal had occurred. [Dorns Transp, Inc v Teamsters Pension Trust Fund of Philadelphia and Vicinity, 787 F 2d 897 (3d Cir 1986)] In another case, the court ruled that when the purchasing company assumed substantially the same contribution obligation as the seller and subsequent events caused a reduction in workforce and contributions, withdrawal liability could not be assessed against the selling employer because the sale of assets did not cause the reduction in contributions and the reduction was neither abusive nor significantly harmful to the plan. [IAM Nat'l Pension Fund Benefit Plan A v Dravo Corp, 7 EBC 1892 (D DC 1986)]

A parent company sold one of its subsidiaries to an unrelated entity, relieving the parent of primary withdrawal liability. Subsequently, the parent closed facilities owned by two other subsidiaries. In calculating the parent's withdrawal liability, the contribution history of the previously sold subsidiary could not be considered. [Borden, Inc v Bakery & Confectionery Union & Industry International Pension, 974 F 2d 528 (4th Cir 1992)] However, where a parent corporation sold all of its shares of stock in a subsidiary and not the assets of the subsidiary, the court concluded that since the primary purpose of the sale was avoidance of withdrawal liability, the parent remained liable for the subsidiary's withdrawal liability. [Santa Fe Pacific Corp v Central States, Southeast and Southwest Areas Pension Fund, Nos. 93-2736 and 93-2899 (7th Cir 1994)]

Also, at least one court has held that a company that purchased a selling company's assets for cash may still be liable for the selling company's delinquent contributions in some circumstances. [Upholsterer's Int'l Union Pension Fund v Artistic Furniture of Pontiac, 920 F 2d 1323 (7th Cir 1990)] Moreover, where a pension fund agreement provided that participants' service with a withdrawing employer would include service with a predecessor employer, the withdrawing employer was required to pay the withdrawal liability of the predecessor employer from whom it had purchased assets. [Artistic Carton Co v Paper Industry Union-Management Pension Fund, 971 F 2d 1346 (7th Cir 1992)]

Q 25:23   How is a withdrawing employer's share of the multiemployer plan's UVBs computed?

The withdrawing employer's share of the multiemployer plan's UVBs (see Q 25:11) may be computed under a statutory method or a PBGC-approved alternative method. The four statutory methods are:

1. The presumptive method;
2. The modified presumptive method;
3. The rolling-five method;
4. The direct attribution method.

The presumptive method is generally used to determine withdrawal liability unless the plan is amended to permit the use of an alternative method. [ERISA § 4211; PBGC Reg § 2642.1]

The plan may adopt a statutory alternative method, but such an alternative may not be applied to an employer without its consent if it withdrew before the adoption of the alternative method. An assessment of withdrawal liability was found to be erroneous and unenforceable where the fund used a calculation method adopted after the employer had withdrawn. [ERISA § 4214(a); Jos Schlitz Brewing Co v Milwaukee Brewery Workers' Pension Plan, 1993 US App Lexis 20658 (7th Cir 1993); Sigmund Cohn Corp v District No. 15 Machinists Pension Fund, No. CV 91-2691 (RJD) (ED NY 1992)]

PBGC has issued a final regulation modifying the presumptive and modified presumptive methods of allocating UVBs, and plans may adopt these modifications without prior PBGC approval. [PBGC Reg § 2642.5(1)] In addition, final PBGC regulations contain rules for determining the allocation of UVBs for an employer that withdraws from a multiemployer plan after the plan has merged with another multiemployer plan and rules concerning the partial withdrawal of an employer from a multiemployer plan and its subsequent reentry into the plan. [PBGC Reg §§ 2640.4, 2642.1, 2642.21–2642.27]

One court ruled that death, disability, and early retirement benefits provided in a defined benefit multiemployer plan are nonforfeitable under ERISA and are therefore properly included in calculations used to determine an employer's withdrawal liability. [United Foods, Inc v The Western Conference of Teamsters Pension Trust Fund, Nos. 93-15765 et al (9th Cir 1994)] Another court ruled that, for purposes of assessing withdrawal liability, benefits credited to participants for service with the employer before the employer began contributing to the plan were nonforfeitable, even though the past service credits were subject to cancellation by the trustees if the employer withdrew from the plan. [Almacs, Inc v New England Teamsters & Trucking Ind Pension Fund, 1993 US Dist Lexis 10977 (D RI 1993)]

Q 25:24   Can withdrawal liability be imposed if the multiemployer plan has no UVBs?

Yes. Even if a multiemployer plan as a whole has no UVBs (see Q 25:11), each of the statutory methods of calculating withdrawal liability except the rolling-five method (see Q 25:23) may result in liability for a withdrawing employer. Under the statutory methods, the withdrawing employer is deemed responsible for the vested benefits of its employees. Accordingly, withdrawal liability may be imposed even if plan assets would be sufficient to fund this liability. [RXDC, Inc v Oil, Chemical and Atomic Workers Union-Industry Pension Fund, No. 781 F Supp 1516 (D Col 1992); Wise v Ruffin, 914 F 2d 570 (4th Cir 1990); Ben Hur Constr Co v Goodwin, 784 F 2d 876 (8th Cir 1986); PBGC Withdrawal of Notice of Interpretation, 56 FR 12288 (Mar 22, 1991); but see Berkshire Hathaway, Inc v Textile Workers Pension Fund, 874 F 2d 53 (1st Cir 1989)]

Q 25:25   May multiemployer plan withdrawal liability be waived or reduced?

There are numerous circumstances under which multiemployer plan withdrawal liability can be either waived or reduced. These waivers are designed to protect small employers and employers in certain industries.

For example, an employer's liability is waived in full if its share is less than the lesser of $50,000 or .75 percent of the total unfunded liability of the plan. If the employer's share is between $50,000 and $150,000, it is reduced but not eliminated. The plan may increase the $50,000 and $150,000 limits to $100,000 and $250,000, respectively. [ERISA § 4209]

Also, waivers of withdrawal liabilities are provided in the construction industry on a mandatory basis when the employer leaves the area. A similar waiver is provided in certain cases for plans covering the entertainment industry. In both cases, there is no withdrawal liability unless the employer either continues to perform the same work in the same jurisdiction or resumes the same work in the same jurisdiction within five years and does not renew its obligation to contribute to the plan. PBGC may exclude certain employers in the entertainment industry from the waiver provision if PBGC determines that it is necessary to protect the plan's participants. [ERISA §§ 4203(b), 4203(c)]

Plans in industries other than construction or entertainment may be amended to provide for special withdrawal liability rules if PBGC finds that the rules apply to an industry in which the characteristics that make use of the special rules appropriate are clearly shown and that the rules would not pose a significant risk to PBGC. [PBGC Notice of Approval, 56 FR 49804 (Oct 1, 1991)]

Employers that withdraw from a plan that receives substantially all its contributions from employers in the trucking, public warehousing, or household goods moving industries may post a five-year bond instead of making withdrawal liability payments. If the withdrawal of an employer that posted a bond substantially damages the plan, PBGC may require that the bond be paid to the plan. A bond could not be posted by an employer that withdrew from a plan that received approximately 62 percent of its contributions from employers primarily involved in the trucking business; the plan does not receive substantially all its contributions from truckers. [ERISA § 4203(d); Continental Can Co v Chicago Truck Drivers, Helpers and Warehouse Workers Union Pension Fund, 916 F 2d 1154 (7th Cir 1990)]

Q 25:26   What happens if an employer reenters a plan after a prior withdrawal?

PBGC has issued regulations providing for the reduction or abatement of withdrawal liability under certain circumstances. A reentering employer that seeks an abatement of its complete withdrawal liability must formally apply for the waiver by the date of the first scheduled withdrawal liability payment falling due after the employer resumes covered operations or, if later, at least 15 days from the date the employer resumes covered operations under the multiemployer plan. The application must:

1. Identify the withdrawn employer and the date it withdrew;

2. Identify the reentered employer and all trades and businesses under common control with the employer as of both the date of withdrawal and the date of resumption of covered operations;

3. Set forth the list of operations for which the employer is obligated to contribute to the plan; and

4. Include the date the employer resumes covered operations.

[ERISA § 4207(a); PBGC Reg § 2647.2]

PBGC has issued regulations that allow multiemployer plans to adopt alternative rules for reduction or waiver of complete withdrawal liability. A plan sponsor is required to submit a written request for PBGC approval of a plan amendment adopting the alternative rules. The request must contain the following information:

1. The name and address of the plan and the telephone number of the plan sponsor or its duly authorized representative.

2. The sponsor's nine-digit employer identification number (EIN) and the three-digit plan identification number (PIN).

3. A copy of the executed amendment, including the date on which the amendment was adopted, its proposed effective date, and the full text of the alternative rules.

4. A copy of the plan's most recent actuarial valuation report.

5. A certification that notice of the adoption of the amendment and of the request for PBGC approval has been given to all employers with an obligation to contribute to the plan and to all employee organizations representing employees covered by the plan.

6. In addition, the plan may submit any other information that it believes is pertinent to its request. PBGC may require the plan sponsor to submit any other information that it may need to review the request.

PBGC will approve a plan amendment if it determines that the alternative rules contained therein are consistent with the purposes of ERISA. However, PBGC will not approve an abatement rule if its implementation would be adverse to the interest of plan participants and beneficiaries or the rule would increase PBGC's risk of loss with respect to the plan.

[ERISA § 4207(b); PBGC Reg § 2647.9]

Q 25:27   What withdrawal liability payments must the employer make while the abatement determination is made?

The reentering employer may post a bond or establish an escrow account equal to 70 percent of the required withdrawal liability payments, in which case, pending the abatement determination, no withdrawal liability payments need be made. [PBGC Reg § 2647.3]

Q 25:28 What is required for abatement of an employer's withdrawal liability upon reentry to the multiemployer plan?

An employer that completely withdraws from a multiemployer plan and subsequently reenters the plan will have its liability abated if it resumes covered operations under the plan and assumes a post-entry level of contribution base units (see Q 25:16) that exceeds 30 percent of the employer's prewithdrawal amount. [PBGC Reg § 2647.4]

Q 25:29 What are the effects of an abatement?

If the plan sponsor determines that the reentering employer is eligible for abatement:

1. The employer has no obligation to make future withdrawal liability payments to the multiemployer plan with respect to its complete withdrawal;
2. The employer's liability for a subsequent withdrawal will be calculated under modified rules;
3. The bond will be canceled or amounts held in the escrow account (see Q 25:27) will be returned to the employer; and
4. Any withdrawal liability payments made by the employer will be refunded by the plan.

[PBGC Reg § 2647.2(c)]

Q 25:30 What are the effects of a nonabatement?

If the plan sponsor determines that the employer is not eligible for abatement:

1. The sponsor notifies the employer of its determination;
2. Within 30 days of the sponsor's notice, the bond posted or the escrow account established by the employer (see Q 25:27) must be paid to the multiemployer plan;
3. Within 30 days of the sponsor's notice, the employer must make the balance of the withdrawal liability payment not covered by the bond or escrow account;

4. The employer must resume its withdrawal liability payments under the plan schedule; and

5. The employer will be treated as a new employer for purposes of any future application rules.

[PBGC Reg § 2647.2(d)]

Q 25:31   How can a reentering employer elect nonabatement?

A reentering employer can elect nonabatement by not filing the application for a waiver of its withdrawal liability (see Q 25:26) upon its reentry to the multiemployer plan. [PBGC Reg § 2647.2]

Q 25:32   Does the value of the employer affect the amount of its withdrawal liability?

Yes. If all, or substantially all, of the employer's assets are sold in an arm's-length transaction to an unrelated party and the purchasing company does not assume the withdrawal liability (see Q 25:22), the employer's withdrawal liability is limited to the greater of (1) the UVBs (see Qs 25:11, 25:23) attributable to its employees or (2) a percentage of the employer's liquidation or dissolution value, as determined under the following table:

Liquidation or Dissolution Value of Employer After Sale	Percentage
Not more than $2,000,000	30% of the amount
More than $2,000,000, but not more than $4,000,000	$600,000, plus 35% of the amount in excess of $2,000,000
More than $4,000,000, but not more than $6,000,000	$1,300,000, plus 40% of the amount in excess of $4,000,000
More than $6,000,000, but not more than $7,000,000	$2,100,000, plus 45% of the amount in excess of $6,000,000
More than $7,000,000, but not more than $8,000,000	$2,550,000, plus 50% of the amount in excess of $7,000,000
More than $8,000,000, but not more than $9,000,000	$3,050,000, plus 60% of the amount in excess of $8,000,000
More than $9,000,000, but not more than $10,000,000	$3,650,000, plus 70% of the amount in excess of $9,000,000
More than $10,000,000	$4,350,000, plus 80% of the amount in excess of $10,000,000

However, the withdrawal liability is not included in determining the liquidation or dissolution value of the employer. [ERISA § 4225; PBGC Op Ltr 93-3]

Q 25:33   Does an insolvent employer have withdrawal liability?

Yes, but that liability may be limited. An insolvent employer in liquidation or dissolution is liable for the first 50 percent of its normal withdrawal liability, and the remainder of its liability is limited to the employer's value, as of the commencement of liquidation or dissolution, reduced by the first 50 percent. [ERISA § 4225(b); PBGC Op Ltr 93-3]

An employer is insolvent if its liabilities, including withdrawal liability, exceed its assets as of the commencement of liquidation or dissolution. However, the employer's liquidation or dissolution value is determined without regard to withdrawal liability. [ERISA § 4225(d); Trustees of Amalgamated Ins Fund v Geltman Indus, Inc, 784 F 2d 926 (9th Cir 1986)] An employer in Chapter 11 reorganization, however, is not said to be in liquidation or dissolution and so may not have its withdrawal liability cut in half. [Granada Wines, Inc v New England Teamsters & Trucking Indus Pension Fund, 748 F 2d 42 (1st Cir 1984)]

Q 25:34   What is the 20-year cap on a withdrawing employer's liability?

The withdrawing employer's liability is paid over the number of years required to amortize the liability in level annual installments. The annual liability payments are basically equal to the annual payments of the employer's plan contributions before withdrawal. If the annual payments will not amortize the withdrawal liability in 20 years, the withdrawal liability is reduced to the amount that can be paid off in the 20-year period. [ERISA § 4219(c)]

The United States Supreme Court has ruled that the word "amortize" assumes interest charges and that interest begins to accrue on the first day of the plan year following withdrawal. [ERISA §§ 4219(c)(1)(A)(i), 4219(c)(4); Milwaukee Brewery Workers' Pension Plan v Jos Schlitz Brewing Co, No. 93-768 (S Ct 1995)]

Q 25:35   When is the employer notified of its liability for withdrawal from a multiemployer plan?

The plan sponsor must notify the employer of the amount of its liability "as soon as practicable" after the employer's withdrawal. At the same time, the plan sponsor will demand payment in accordance with a schedule of payments. In one case, a notice given to an employer two years after the withdrawal liability arose was considered timely. In another case, timely notice was given 12 years after withdrawal because the withdrawing employer never notified the plan sponsor and, for some reason, continued to make contributions to the plan. [ERISA § 4219(b); Brentwood Financial Corp v Western Conference of Teamsters Pension Fund, 902 F 2d 1456 (9th Cir 1990); Giroux Bros Trans, Inc v New England Teamsters & Trucking Indus Pension Fund, No. 95-1032 (1st Cir 1996)] In other cases, notice given five and one-half and six years after the withdrawal liability arose was not considered timely. [Teamsters Pension Trust Fund of Philadelphia and Vicinity v Custom Cartage, Co, 1991 US Dist Lexis 11566 (ED Pa 1991); Bay Area Laundry & Dry Cleaning Pension Trust Fund v Ferbar Corp of Cal, Inc, No. 94-15976 (9th Cir 1996)]

Notice of, and demand for, withdrawal liability made to one member of a commonly controlled group is sufficient to constitute notice and demand to all members of the group. Thus, courts have held an entity within a commonly controlled group liable for the withdrawal liability of another group member even though only the withdrawing employer received actual notice of the withdrawal liability. The rationale for this is that all trades or businesses under common control are treated as a single employer and, thus, notice to one is notice to all (see Q 25:18). [IAM Nat'l Fund v Slyman Indus, Inc, 901 F 2d 127 (DC Cir 1990); Teamsters Pension Trust Fund-Board of the W Conference v Allyn Transp Co, 832 F 2d 502 (9th Cir 1987); IUE AFL-CIO Pension Fund v Barker & Williamson, Inc, 788 F 2d 118 (3d Cir 1986); Central States, Southeast and Southwest Areas Pension Fund v Landvatter, 1993 US Dist Lexis 13 (ND Ill 1993); Central States, Southeast and Southwest Areas Pension Fund v Bay, 684 F Supp 483 (ED Mich 1988); Board of Trustees of the W Conference of Teamsters Pension Trust Fund v Salt Creek Terminals, Inc, No. C85-2270R (WD Wash 1986); Connors v Calvert Dev Co, 622 F Supp 877 (D DC 1985)]

The date when one employer in a commonly controlled group receives notice of withdrawal liability is used to determine the timeliness of any group member's request to arbitrate disputes concerning the withdrawal liability (see Q 25:37). [McDonald v Centra, No. S 89-1734 (D Md 1990); Teamster Pension Trust Fund of Philadelphia v Laidlaw Indus, Inc, 745 F Supp 1016 (D Del 1990)] However, one court permitted a husband and wife who jointly owned an unincorporated farm to arbitrate the amount of withdrawal liability assessed against the husband's manufacturing company. The plan sponsor's notice of withdrawal liability demanded payment only from the husband's corporation and other commonly controlled corporations. [ILGWU Nat'l Retirement Fund v Minotola Indus, Inc, 88 Civ 9131 (RJW) (SD NY 1991)]

ERISA Section 4301 imposes a three- or six-year statute of limitations on civil actions with respect to multiemployer plans, including issues of withdrawal liability. Because the statute of limitations begins to run when notice and demand for payment of withdrawal liability is not met by the withdrawing employer, an action brought more than six years thereafter is not timely. [Central States, Southeast and Southwest Areas Pension Fund v Navco, 1993 US App Lexis 20367 (7th Cir 1993); Joyce v Clyde Sandoz Masonry, 871 F 2d 1119 (Fed Cir 1989); Central States, Southeast and Southwest Areas Pension Fund v Mississippi Warehouse Corp, 1994 US Dist Lexis 5888 (ND Ill 1994); Central States, Southeast and Southwest Areas Pension Fund v Van Vorst Industries, Inc, 1992 US Dist Lexis 1867 (ND Ill 1992)]

However, one court held that the six-year statute of limitations began to run when an employer in the construction industry withdrew from the plan (i.e., the date on which the employer resumed covered work within five years from the date on which it ceased making plan contributions; see Q 25:25). [Board of Trustees of the Construction Laborers Pension Trust for Southern California v Thibodo, 1994 US App Lexis 24499 (9th Cir 1994)] Other courts have held that the six-year statute of limitations commences with each withdrawal liability payment due date; that is, each scheduled payment is a separate obligation that has its own statute of limitations period. [Board of Trustees of the District No. 15 Machinists' Pension Trust v Kahle Eng'g Corp, 1994 US App Lexis 36945 (3d Cir 1994); Carriers Container Council v Mobile SS Assn, 948 F 2d 1219 (11th Cir 1991)]

A plan's action to collect withdrawal liability from an employer that stopped making payments in 1982 was not barred by the statute of limitations. The statute did not start running until the plan demanded payment in 1987. [ILGWU Nat'l Retirement Fund v Smart Modes of California, Inc, 735 F Supp 103 (SD NY 1990)]

Q 25:36   Is the initial determination of a withdrawing employer's liability presumptively correct?

When an employer withdraws from a multiemployer plan, the plan sponsor determines the amount of the withdrawing employer's liability (see Qs 25:11, 25:13). The initial determination is presumed to be correct. To overcome this presumption, the employer must demonstrate, by a preponderance of evidence, that the actuarial assumptions and methods used by the plan's actuary are unreasonable or that a significant error has been made in applying the assumptions or methods. In one case, a plan's actuarial calculations were not unreasonable in the aggregate even though the interest rate assumption may have been unreasonably low. [ERISA § 4221(a)(3); Combs v Classic Coal Corp, 931 F 2d 96 (DC Cir 1991)]

A number of employers have raised unsuccessful constitutional challenges to the presumption of correctness accorded plan sponsors' determinations of withdrawal liability. [Keith Fulton & Sons, Inc v New England Teamsters and Trucking Indus Pension Fund, 762 F 2d 1137 (1st Cir 1985); Board of Trustees of the W Conference of Teamsters Pension Trust Fund v Thompson Bldg Materials, Inc, 749 F 2d 1396 (9th Cir 1984); Washington Star Co v International Typographical Union Negotiated Pension Plan, 729 F 2d 1502 (DC Cir 1984); Textile Workers Pension Fund v Standard Dye & Finishing Co, 725 F 2d 843 (2d Cir 1984); Republic Indus, Inc v Teamsters Joint Council No. 83 of Virginia Pension Fund, 718 F 2d 628 (4th Cir 1983); Centennial State Carpenters Pension Trust Fund v Woodworkers of Denver, Inc, 615 F Supp 1063 (D Col 1985)]

However, two courts have held that the presumption of correctness of the determination of the amount of the withdrawing employer's liability by plan sponsors who owe a fiduciary duty to the plan and who are therefore biased in favor of the plan is unconstitutional. [United Retail & Wholesale Employees Teamsters Union Local No. 115 Pension Plan v Yahn & McDonnell, Inc, 787 F 2d 128 (3d Cir 1986), *aff'd per curiam sub nom*, PBGC v Yahn & McDonnell, Inc, 481 US 735 (1987); Robbins v Pepsi-Cola Metropolitan Bottling Co, 636 F Supp 641 (ND Ill 1986)] In affirming the Third Circuit's decision that the presumption in favor of the correctness of a plan sponsor's initial determination regarding withdrawal liability is unconstitutional, the Supreme Court split four to four. Thus, the decision is binding only with respect to the parties in the case. As a result, the conflict among the circuits continues.

Q 25:37 May an employer contest the determination of its liability for withdrawing from a multiemployer plan?

Yes. When the employer receives notice of its withdrawal liability (see Q 25:35) from the plan sponsor, it may, within 90 days of its receipt of such notice, ask the plan sponsor to review any specific matter relating to its determination, point out any inaccuracy in its determination, or provide additional information to the trustees bearing on their determination. The plan sponsor must also comply with an employer's request for an explanation of its calculation of the employer's withdrawal liability even if the employer has not yet requested arbitration. [ERISA §§ 4219(b)(2), 4221(e); John J Nissen Baking Co, Inc v New England Teamsters and Trucking Indus Pension Fund, 737 F Supp 679 (D Me 1990)]

The plan sponsor has 120 days to respond to an employer's request that it reconsider its earlier determination of withdrawal liability. If it takes no action, then the employer must request arbitration within 60 days after the expiration of the 120-day period or it may be estopped from disputing the amounts owed in a later court action to collect the withdrawal liability (see Q 25:38). The plan sponsor, however, is required to undertake a "reasonable review" of the employer's contentions and notify the employer of its decision, setting forth the basis for its decision and the reasons behind any change in its liability determination. The employer must request arbitration within 60 days of its receipt of this second notice even though 120 days may not have lapsed since the employer requested a review of its withdrawal liability. [ERISA § 4221(a)(1)]

The plan sponsor, too, may request arbitration within 60 days of either (1) notification to the employer of its decision after review of the employer's dispute of the liability determination or (2) the expiration of 120 days after the employer requests review of the plan sponsor's initial determination. Alternatively, both the plan sponsor and the employer may jointly request arbitration within 180 days of the initial demand for payment of withdrawal liability. [ERISA §§ 4219(b), 4221(a); PBGC Reg § 2641.2]

The time limits set forth above are strictly enforced. In one case, an employer erroneously mailed its timely arbitration request to the plan sponsor, not to the arbitration association as required under the plan. The court refused to order arbitration, even though the arbitration request was hand delivered to the arbitration association immediately upon discovery of the error two days after the deadline. [Central States, Southeast and Southwest Areas Pension Fund v TW Servs, No. 89 C 7415 (ND Ill 1989)]

Q 25:38 Does the employer run any risk if it does not demand arbitration of the plan sponsor's claim for withdrawal liability?

Yes. An employer that fails to initiate arbitration within the statutory periods (see Q 25:37) risks being barred from disputing the plan's determination of withdrawal liability in a subsequent court action by the plan sponsor to recover that liability. [Chicago Truck Drivers, Helpers and Warehouse Workers Union (Ind) Pension Fund v R Sumner Trucking Co, Inc, 1992 US Dist Lexis 1877 (ND Ill 1992); Trustees of the Colorado Pipe Indus Pension Trust v Howard Elec & Mechanical, Inc, 909 F 2d 1379 (10th Cir 1990); New York State Teamsters Conference Pension & Retirement Fund v McNicholas Transp Co, 848 F 2d 20 (2d Cir 1988); ILGWU Nat'l Retirement Fund v Levy Bros Frocks, Inc, 846 F 2d 879 (2d Cir 1988); Robbins v Admiral Merchants Motor Freight, Inc, 846 F 2d 1054 (7th Cir 1988); Teamsters Pension Trust Fund-Bd of Trustees v Allyn Transp Co, 832 F 2d 502 (9th Cir 1987); IAM Nat'l Pension Fund v Clinton Engines Corp, 825 F 2d 415 (DC Cir 1987)]

Additionally, courts will generally dismiss an employer's action to challenge a determination of withdrawal liability when arbitration has been bypassed. [McDonald v Centra, Inc, No. 90-2483 (4th Cir 1991); Caleb v Smith & Son of Ohio, Inc, 946 F 2d 1059 (SD NY 1991); Mason and Dixon Tank Lines, Inc v Central States, Southeast and Southwest Areas Pension Fund, 852 F 2d 156 (6th Cir 1988); Flying Tiger Line v Teamsters Pension Trust Fund, 830 F 2d 1241 (3d Cir 1987); Central States, Southeast and Southwest Areas Pension Fund v Conaway, 1991 US Dist Lexis 5096 (ND Ill 1991)] However, an employer has been permitted to proceed in court in the absence of arbitration when only statutory or constitutional issues, not factual issues, were raised. [IAM Nat'l Pension Fund Benefit Plan C v Stockton Tri Indus, 727 F 2d 1204 (DC Cir 1984); Central States, Southeast and Southwest Areas Pension Fund v Skyland Leasing Co, 691 F Supp 6 (WD Mich 1987)] There is no right to a jury trial in a suit contesting the enforcement of withdrawal liability because the arbitrator is the fact finder. [Connors v Ryan's Coal Co, Inc, 923 F 2d 1461 (11th Cir 1991)]

Even if the employer attempts to initiate arbitration but does not do so properly—that is, in accordance with the rules of the plan—it may be held to have waived its right to contest the claim. For example, merely expressing a desire for arbitration and requesting information on how to proceed is not the equivalent of initiation of arbitration within the meaning of the plan's rules. [Robbins v Braver Lumber and Supply Co, No. 85 C 08332 (ND Ill 1987)]

Q 25:39   When are withdrawal liability payments due?

The plan sponsor sets the schedule of payments. The first payment is due no later than 60 days after demand (see Q 25:35), and subsequent payments are usually made quarterly.

Even if the employer contests the determination of liability either with the plan sponsor or through arbitration, the employer is not relieved of its obligation to begin payment of the withdrawal liability. [ERISA §§ 4219(c)(2), 4219(c)(3), 4221(d); Central States, Southeast and Southwest Areas Pension Fund v Ten D, Inc, 1992 US Dist Lexis 5524 (ND Ill 1992); DeBreceni v Merchants Terminal Corp, 889 F 2d 1 (1st Cir 1989)] Further, courts have ordered an employer that refused to make withdrawal liability payments pending arbitration to pay the plan's attorneys' fees and costs. [Trustees of the Plumbers and Pipefitters Nat'l Pension Fund v Mar-Len, Inc, 1994 US App Lexis 23919 (5th Cir 1994); Retirement Fund of the Fur Mfg Indus v Getto & Getto, Inc, 714 F Supp 651 (SD NY 1989)] In addition, one court ordered an employer that was not subject to withdrawal liability to pay liquidated damages for its failure to make interim payments while challenging the withdrawal liability assessment. [Central States, Southeast and Southwest Areas Pension Fund v Lady Baltimore Foods, Inc, 960 F 2d 1339 (7th Cir 1992)]

In limited situations, an employer may be relieved from making withdrawal liability payments pending arbitration upon a showing of the employer's likelihood of success in arbitration and irreparable harm to be suffered due to payment. [Robbins v McNicholas Transportation Co, 819 F 2d 682 (7th Cir 1987)] The employer must provide evidence of irreparable harm after first demonstrating that the pension fund lacks a "colorable claim" for the assessment of withdrawal liability. [Trustees of the Plumbers and Pipefitters Nat'l Pension Fund v Mar-Len, Inc, 1994 US App Lexis 23919 (5th Cir 1994); Trustees of the Chicago Truck Drivers, Helpers and Warehouse Workers Union (Ind) Pension Fund v Rentar Indus, Inc, 951 F 2d 152 (7th Cir 1991)] However, in a case where an arbitration proceeding initiated by the employer was still pending, the court ruled that it was premature for the plan to request payment of the total amount of the employer's withdrawal liability. [New York State Teamsters Conference Pension and Retirement Fund v CDC Haulage Corp, 1996 US Dist Lexis 2706 (ND NY 1996)]

The bankruptcy or insolvency of the parent member of a controlled group does not relieve the subsidiary controlled group members of their obligation to make withdrawal liability payments (see Q 25:18) even if the liquidation or dissolution of the insolvent parent may reduce the amount of the withdrawal liability (see Q 25:33). [Central States, Southeast and Southwest Areas Pension Fund v Chatham Properties, 929 F 2d 260 (6th Cir 1991)]

A default will not occur, however, until 60 days after a demand for payment is made (see Q 25:40).

If, after review, the plan sponsor or arbitrator determines that the employer has overpaid, the employer is entitled to a lump-sum refund with interest. [PBGC Reg § 2644.2(d); Huber v Casablanca 916 F 2d 85 (3d Cir 1990)] A multiemployer plan that mistakenly overcharged withdrawing employers for withdrawal liability can refund the overcharged amounts to the employers as long as the refunds are made within six months of the discovery of the error. [ERISA § 403(c)(2)(A)(ii); DOL Op Ltr 95-24A]

Q 25:40 What happens if a withdrawal liability payment is missed?

If a payment is not made by the due date, interest is charged from that date until the payment is actually made. [ERISA § 4219(c)(3); Carriers Container Council, Inc, v Mobile Steamship Assoc, Inc, 896 F 2d 1330 (11th Cir 1990)] A default generally occurs 60 days after the employer gets written notice from the plan sponsor of failure to make a payment when due. If the payment is not made within the 60 days, the entire amount of the withdrawal liability plus interest becomes due immediately. [ERISA

§ 4219(c)(5); PBGC Reg §§ 2644.2, 2644.3; Huber v Casablanca Indus, Inc, 916 F 2d 85 (3d Cir 1990); Local 807 Labor-Management Pension Fund v ABC Fast Freight Forwarding Corp, No. 82 C 3356 (ED NY 1984)]

An employer must make withdrawal liability payments even if the National Labor Relations Board has exclusive jurisdiction to determine whether the employer must continue to make plan contributions after the expiration of the collective bargaining agreement. [Trustees of the Colorado Pipe Indus Pension Trust v Howard Electrical & Mechanical, Inc, 909 F 2d 1379 (10th Cir 1990)]

Q 25:41   Are owners of the employer personally liable for withdrawal liability?

Generally, shareholders of corporations are not personally liable for amounts the employer cannot pay. [Operating Eng'r Pension Trust v Reed, 726 F 2d 513 (9th Cir 1984); but see Laborers Clean-Up Contract Admin Trust Fund v Uriarte Clean-Up Serv, Inc, 736 F 2d 516 (9th Cir 1984)] Controlling or dominant shareholders are not considered employers for withdrawal liability purposes. [Scarbrough v Perez, 870 F 2d 1079 (6th Cir 1989); DeBreceni v Graf Bros Leasing, Inc, 828 F 2d 877 (1st Cir 1987); Connors v P & M Coal Co, 801 F 2d 1373 (DC Cir 1986)] However, shareholders were held personally liable when they did not observe corporate formalities and removed assets from the corporation. [Plumbers' Pension Fund, Local 130, UA v A-Best Plumbing & Sewer, Inc, US Dist Lexis 3110 (ND Ill 1992); see also Schaffer, Jr v Charles Benjamin, Inc, No. 92-1312 (3d Cir 1992)]

However, a shareholder of a dissolved corporation may be personally liable to the extent of corporate assets distributed to the shareholder upon dissolution. [Retirement Fund of the Fur Manufacturing Indus v Robert Goldberg Furs, Inc, 88 Civ 6033 (JES) (SD NY 1991); Central States, Southeast and Southwest Areas Pension Fund v Minneapolis Van & Warehouse Co, 764 F Supp 1289 (ND Ill 1991); Retirement Fund of the Fur Manufacturing Indus v Strassberg and Tama, Inc, 88 Civ 6034 (MBM) (SD NY 1989)] Also, a state law under which the ten largest shareholders of a closely held corporation can be held liable for unpaid plan contributions was held not to be preempted by ERISA. [Sasso v Vachris, 66 NY 2d 28 (1985)]

A corporate officer is not personally liable for withdrawal liability payments solely by virtue of the individual's capacity as an officer of the withdrawing employer. [Cement and Concrete Workers Dist Council Welfare Fund, Pension Fund, Legal Services Fund and Security Fund v Lollo, 35 F 3d 29 (2d Cir 1994); Blankenship v Omni Catering, Inc, No. 92-55871 (9th Cir 1994); Seymour v Hull & Moreland Eng'g, Inc, 605 F 2d 1105 (9th Cir

1979); Connors v BMC Coal Co, 634 F Supp 74 (D DC 1986); Connors v Darryll Waggle Constr, Inc, 631 F Supp 1188 (D DC 1986)]

Partners or sole proprietors are personally liable, but assets that would be exempt under bankruptcy law are also exempt from satisfaction of the withdrawal liability obligation. Furthermore, a husband and wife who jointly operated a farm were personally liable for the unpaid withdrawal liability of a corporation controlled by the husband because the farm and corporation were under common control (see Q 25:18). [ERISA § 4225(c); Connors v Ryan's Coal Co, Inc, 923 F 2d 1461 (11th Cir 1991); Board of Trustees of the W Conference of Teamsters Pension Trust Fund v H F Johnson, Inc, 830 F 2d 1009 (9th Cir 1987)] However, the spouse of an unincorporated business owner is not personally liable for the business owner's withdrawal liability unless it can be shown that she intended to form a partnership with her husband with respect to the business. [Chicago Truck Drivers, Helpers and Warehouse Union (Ind) Pension Fund v Steinberg, 32 F 3d 269 (7th Cir 1994); Central States, Southeast and Southwest Areas Pension Fund v Johnson, 991 F 2d 387 (7th Cir 1993); Chicago Truck Drivers, Helpers and Warehouse Workers Union (Ind) Pension Fund v Slotky, 9 F 3d 1251 (7th Cir 1993)]

Q 25:42 Are withdrawal liability claims entitled to priority in bankruptcy proceedings?

It has been held that withdrawal liability is considered a general unsecured claim and is not entitled to priority in bankruptcy proceedings because it is not an administrative expense claim. [Trustees of the Amalgamated Ins Fund v McFarlin's, Inc, 789 F 2d 98 (2d Cir 1986)] However, the discharge in bankruptcy of a corporation that owed contributions and withdrawal liability to a multiemployer plan did not preclude the plan from later seeking recovery from a new corporation that had acquired the assets of the old corporation. [Chicago Truck Drivers, Helpers and Warehouse Workers Union (Ind) Pension Fund v Tasemkin, Inc, 59 F 3d 48 (7th Cir 1995)]

Q 25:43 What is a mass withdrawal from a multiemployer plan?

A mass withdrawal is one form of multiemployer plan termination (see Q 25:44). A mass withdrawal occurs if:

1. Every employer withdraws from the plan; or

2. The obligation of all employers to contribute to the plan ceases.

[ERISA § 4041A(a)(2)]

If a mass withdrawal occurs, all withdrawing employers lose the benefit of the waiver or reduction of small liabilities (see Q 25:25) and the 20-year cap (see Q 25:34), and the plan's unfunded vested benefits are fully allocated among all of the withdrawing employers. For this purpose, the withdrawal of substantially all employers by agreement or arrangement is considered a mass withdrawal. [ERISA §§ 4209, 4219(c); PBGC Reg §§ 2640.7, 2648.1–2648.5]

PBGC has given guidance as to the administration of multiemployer plans that have terminated by mass withdrawal. Generally, the plan sponsor must periodically determine whether the value of nonforfeitable benefits exceeds the value of plan assets. If so, the plan sponsor must reduce benefits other than accrued benefits guaranteed by PBGC (see Q 25:9), suspend certain benefit payments, or seek financial assistance in the form of a PBGC loan (see Q 25:44) to the extent necessary to ensure the plan's sufficiency. Under these circumstances, the reduction of accrued benefits does not cause plan disqualification (see Q 9:24). [ERISA § 4281; IRC § 411(a)(3)(F); PBGC Reg §§ 2675.1–2675.44]

Generally, the plan sponsor of a plan that terminates by mass withdrawal can only pay benefits that were nonforfeitable at plan termination without first obtaining PBGC approval. Thus, PBGC approval is not needed to pay a qualified preretirement survivor annuity (QPSA; see Q 10:9) to the surviving spouse of a participant who died before the plan termination date. Further, the plan sponsor does not need PBGC approval to pay the QPSA for a participant who died after the plan termination date unless the plan sponsor has determined that plan assets are not sufficient to pay all nonforfeitable plan benefits. [ERISA § 4041A(c); PBGC Op Ltr No. 91-2]

Q 25:44   What is the liability of an employer upon termination of a multiemployer defined benefit plan?

For multiemployer plans, plan termination does not mean dissolution of the plan, nor does it result in PBGC involvement as the provider of benefits. Instead, termination means mass withdrawal (see Q 25:43), the amendment of the plan to freeze vested benefits and to give no credit for further service, or the conversion of the plan into a defined contribution plan. Employers must continue to contribute to the frozen plan in order to fund the plan's unfunded liabilities. The plan administrator must notify PBGC after the effective date of termination and follow PBGC reporting requirements and rules regarding administration of terminated multiemployer plans. [ERISA § 4041A; PBGC Reg §§ 2673.2, 2675.1, 2675.2]

PBGC funds are available only if a plan becomes insolvent (see Q 25:8). These PBGC funds are only loans and must be repaid. [ERISA §§ 4022A(a), 4261]

If, upon termination of a multiemployer plan, there are excess assets, such excess cannot revert to the employers. [ERISA § 403(c)(1); DOL Op Ltr 94-39A] One court concluded that the reversion of surplus employer contributions from a multiemployer plan to one of the contributing employers would also violate ERISA's exclusive benefit rule. [Resolution Trust Corp v Financial Institutions Retirement Fund, No. 95-5016 (10th Cir 1995)]

Q 25:45   May a multiemployer plan exclude some newly adopting employers from withdrawal liability?

Yes. A multiemployer plan may adopt a rule under which an employer may withdraw from the plan without liability within six years after joining the plan or, if less, the number of years required for vesting under the plan. This free-look rule is applicable to the employer only if it (1) contributes less than 2 percent of all employer contributions to the plan each year, and (2) has not previously used this rule with respect to the plan.

In addition, for the free-look rule to be enforceable, the plan must (1) be amended to permit the rule, (2) have an eight-to-one assets-to-benefits payable ratio in the year before the employer joins the plan, and (3) provide that an employee's service before the employer joined the plan will not be counted in determining benefits. Plans primarily covering employees in the building and construction industry are not permitted to adopt the free-look rule. [ERISA § 4210]

One court held that the free-look rule did not apply to an employer after it was acquired by another employer because both employers were then under common control and the acquiring employer was ineligible to use the free-look rule (see Q 25:18). [Central States, Southeast and Southwest Areas Pension Fund v Hoosier Dairy, Inc, No. 90 C 3795 (ND Ill 1991)]

Chapter 26

Individual Retirement Plans

Anyone who receives compensation may set aside a modest amount of money each year for retirement in a tax-deferred account known as an individual retirement plan (IRA). However, not all IRA contributions are deductible. Both the Administration and Congress have introduced legislation dramatically affecting IRAs. This chapter examines how IRAs work and also discusses the important provisions of the proposed legislation.

Q 26:1   What is an individual retirement plan?

An individual retirement plan is a personal retirement plan. This type of plan allows employees, self-employed individuals (see Q 6:33), and certain other individuals, whether or not they participate in qualified retirement plans (including Keogh plans, simplified employee pensions (SEPs), SIMPLE plans, tax-sheltered annuities, and government plans), to establish IRAs and make annual contributions to them. For active plan participants, however, these contributions might not be deductible (see Q 26:7). [IRC §§ 219, 408]

There are two types of individual retirement plans: (1) individual retirement accounts (see Q 26:2) and (2) individual retirement annuities (see Q 26:3). Both types are commonly referred to as IRAs.

A working spouse may set up an IRA for the nonworking spouse (see Q 26:18). In addition, certain divorced or separated persons may make deductible contributions to IRAs even though they receive no wages or salary (see Q 26:5).

Deductible contributions to an IRA are tax deductible whether or not the individual itemizes deductions. [IRC § 62(a)(7)]

Earnings on all amounts contributed to any IRA accumulate on a tax-deferred basis. [IRC § 408(e)]

If enacted, RRB '95 and RRB '96 (see Q 1:22A) will change many of the rules relating to IRAs. The effects of these proposed Acts will be discussed, where appropriate, in the remaining questions of this chapter.

Q 26:2 What are the basic characteristics of an individual retirement account?

An IRA is a trust or custodial account established for the exclusive benefit of an individual and the individual's beneficiaries. The trustee (or custodian) must be a bank, thrift institution, insurance company, brokerage firm, or other person who demonstrates to IRS that such person will administer the account in a manner consistent with the requirements of the law. No part of the account funds can be invested in life insurance contracts. Assets of the account cannot be commingled with other property except if there is a common trust fund or common investment fund. [IRC § 408(a); Nichola, 63 TCM 2150 (1992)]

An IRA cannot be a shareholder of an S corporation, and IRA assets should not be invested in collectibles (works of art, rugs, antiques, metals, gems, stamps, coins, or other items of tangible personal property specified by IRS). Amounts invested in collectibles are treated as distributions for tax purposes (that is, taxed as current income; if the individual is under age $59\frac{1}{2}$, a 10 percent penalty tax for a premature withdrawal also applies (see Q 26:41)). However, gold or silver coins issued by the U.S. government or any type of coin issued under the laws of any state will not be considered collectibles. An interest in a portion of a gold coin portfolio is not considered a collectible. [IRC §§ 408(m), 1361; Rev Rul 92-73, 1992-2 CB 224; Ltr Rul 8940067]

The individual's interest in the IRA must be nonforfeitable. Distributions must satisfy the minimum distribution requirements in order to avoid penalties for insufficient distributions (see Qs 26:32, 26:33). [IRC §§ 408(a)(4), 408(a)(6)]

An account that is identified as an IRA and meets the statutory requirements is treated as an IRA, even if the owner later claims it is not an IRA because the owner made an untimely rollover contribution that is an excess contribution (see Q 26:6). [Michel, 58 TCM 1019 (1989)]

Q 26:3 What are the basic characteristics of an individual retirement annuity?

An individual retirement annuity is an annuity contract or endowment contract issued by an insurance company. However, an endowment contract issued after November 6, 1978 cannot qualify. The contract must be non-transferable and nonforfeitable. Premiums may not be fixed, nor may they exceed $2,000 a year (see Q 26:5). Distributions must satisfy the minimum distribution requirements and must be made by specified dates in order to avoid penalties for insufficient distributions (see Qs 26:32, 26:33). [IRC § 408(b); Treas Reg § 1.408-3(e)(1)(ix)]

Participation in a group annuity may be used instead of an individual annuity contract. Only part of the premium for an endowment contract builds an annuity; the rest buys current life insurance protection. The part of the premium that pays for current life insurance protection is not tax deductible. [IRC §§ 219(d)(3), 408(a)(3), 408(b); Ltr Rul 8439026]

If an individual borrows any money from or against an individual retirement annuity, the annuity contract ceases to be a qualified individual retirement annuity as of the first day of the year. Because of the borrowing, the individual must include in gross income for the year the fair market value of the annuity as of the first day of such year. [IRC § 408(e)(3); Griswold, 85 TC 869 (1985)]

Q 26:4   Who is eligible to set up an IRA?

Any individual under age 70½ receiving compensation may establish an IRA (also see Q 26:5). [IRC § 219(d)(1)]

An IRA may also be established as a vehicle for deferring taxes on eligible rollover distributions from qualified retirement plans and tax-sheltered annuities (see Q 29:1), including distributions received after attainment of age 70½ and distributions to surviving spouses of plan participants. For details, see chapter 28.

If enacted, RRB '95 (see Q 1:22A) would permit an individual over age 70½ to contribute to an American Dream IRA (AD IRA) (see Q 26:13) and to make a rollover to an AD IRA (see Q 26:35). [RRB '95, Act § 11015(a)]

If enacted, RRB '96 (see Q 1:22A) would not permit an individual over age 70½ to contribute to a Special Individual Retirement Account (Special IRA) (see Q 26:13); however, a rollover to a Special IRA would be permissible after age 70½ (see Q 26:36). [RRB '96, Act § 9211(a)] RRB '96 would also replace age 70½ with age 70. [RRB '96, Act § 9445(b)]

Q 26:5   How much can be contributed to an IRA?

Each year an individual may contribute 100 percent of compensation up to a maximum of $2,000 to an IRA. [IRC §§ 219(b)(1), 408(a), 408(b)] *For years beginning before 1997,* the contribution limit is $2,250 if a spousal IRA is also established (see Q 26:18). [IRC § 219(c)(2), prior to amendment by SBA '96 § 1427(a)] However, there is no dollar limit with respect to a rollover contribution (see Q 28:2).

IRS has provided a safe-harbor definition of compensation for the purpose of determining eligibility to make an IRA contribution. Under the safe harbor, compensation is the amount properly shown on Form W-2, Box 1 (wages, tips, and other compensation) less the amount properly shown in Box 11 (nonqualified plans). [IRC § 219(f)(1); Rev Proc 91-18, 1991-1 CB 522]

Compensation includes taxable alimony and separate maintenance payments. A divorced or separated spouse who receives taxable alimony, but no other compensation, is able to make contributions to an IRA. Unemployment compensation benefits are not compensation for purposes of calculating IRA contributions. Where an individual's only income consisted of interest, dividends, and pension distributions, he had no compensation to support the deduction of his IRA contribution. Deferred compensation and amounts received as a pension or annuity are not treated as compensation and cannot be used as a basis for contributions to an IRA even if the safe-harbor definition of compensation is used. A separation pay allowance received by an employee is considered deferred compensation for this purpose. Also, a fee paid by a husband to his wife for services rendered in connection with their jointly held investments is not compensation to her, nor is a payment by a husband to his wife where, in fact, the wife did not render any services to the husband's business. [IRC § 219(f)(1); Treas Reg § 1.219-1(c); Russell, TCM 1996-278; King, TCM 1996-231; Shelley, 68 TCM 584 (1994); Bingo, 61 TCM 2782 (1991); Ltr Ruls 8535001, 8519051]

In a novel ruling, a farmer transferred hogs to his wife, who was a bona fide employee, as compensation for her services to his farming business. IRS ruled that the hogs constituted compensation and could be used as a basis for contributions to an IRA. [Ltr Rul 9202003]

A contribution made to an IRA for the year in which an individual attains age 70½, or any year thereafter, is a nondeductible excess contribution (see Q 26:6) that cannot be treated as a designated nondeductible IRA contribution (see Q 26:14). [IRC §§ 219(d)(1), 408(o)] RRB '96 (see Q 1:22A) would replace age 70½ with age 70. [RRB '96, Act § 9445(b)]

An estate cannot make an IRA contribution on behalf of the decedent or to the spousal IRA of the decedent's spouse for the year in which the decedent died. [Ltr Rul 8439066]

Under both RRB '95 (see Q 1:22A) and RRB '96, the $2,000 amount would be adjusted for cost-of-living increases. However, an adjustment to the $2,000 amount would be made only if it is $500 or greater and then would be made in multiples of $500 (i.e., rounded down to the next lowest multiple of $500). For example, an increase of $499 would result in no adjustment, and an increase of $999 would create an upward adjustment of $500. [RRB '95, Act § 11012(a); RRB '96, Act § 9202(a)]

Under RRB '96, however, the IRA deduction limit would be coordinated with the limit on elective deferrals (see Q 23:26) so that the maximum allowable IRA deduction for a year could not exceed the excess of the elective deferral limit over the amount of elective deferrals made by the individual. Elective deferrals include elective contributions to a 401(k) plan (see Q 23:13), salary reduction contributions to a simplified employee pension (SEP; see Q 27:10), and elective deferrals contributed to a tax-sheltered annuity under a salary reduction agreement (see Q 29:27). [RRB '96, Act § 9203(a)]

Q 26:6 What penalty is imposed on an excess contribution to an IRA?

If an individual contributes more to an IRA than the amount allowable (see Q 26:5), the excess contribution is subject to a 6 percent excise tax. Further, the penalty will be charged each year the excess contribution remains in the IRA. [IRC § 4973; Rodoni, 105 TC 29 (1995); Wittstadt, Jr, 70 TCM 994 (1995); Conway v United States, Civ MJG-93-1707 (D Md 1995); Adler, 69 TCM 2314 (1995); Dorsey, 69 TCM 2041 (1995); Brown, 69 TCM 2028 (1995); Shelley, 68 TCM 584 (1994); Martin, 67 TCM 2960 (1994)]

The individual can avoid the penalty by withdrawing the excess contribution, along with the net income allocable to the excess, before the due date (including extensions) of the individual's federal income tax return for the year of the excess contribution. The net income on the excess contribution is treated as gross income for the taxable year in which the excess contribution was made. [IRC §§ 408(d)(4), 4973(b)] Where excess contributions were not withdrawn timely because of errors made by the IRA custodian, excise taxes were not imposed. [Childs, TCM 1996-267; Thompson, TCM 1996-266]

If the individual does not withdraw the excess contribution before such filing deadline, the 6 percent excise tax must be paid for the year of the excess contribution. To avoid the 6 percent excise tax for the following year, the remaining excess contribution can be eliminated by either withdrawing such amount from the IRA or making a contribution for such year equal to the maximum allowable amount (see Q 26:5) reduced by the remaining excess contribution. [IRC § 4973(b)]

Under both RRB '95 (see Q 1:21) and RRB '96 (see Q 1:22A), the excess contribution rules would apply to AD IRAs and to Special IRAs (see Q 26:13). For this purpose, a contribution to a regular IRA would be aggregated with the contribution to the AD IRA or to the Special IRA. [RRB '95, Act §§ 11015(a), 11015(d); RRB '96, Act §§ 9211(a), 9211(c)]

Q 26:7 Can active participants in qualified retirement plans also make deductible IRA contributions?

Not necessarily. If an individual is an active participant in a qualified retirement plan (see Qs 26:8, 26:9) for any part of a plan year ending with or within the individual's taxable year, IRA contributions cannot be deducted if the individual's adjusted gross income exceeds certain specified amounts (see Qs 26:10, 26:11). For married couples, if either spouse is an active participant, both are treated as active participants (see Qs 26:9, 26:10). [IRC § 219(g)] These rules apply even if the individual is unaware that the individual is an active participant in the employer's qualified retirement plan. [Baumann, 70 TCM 61 (1995)]

Q 26:8 What is active participation?

Generally, active participation refers to participation in a qualified retirement plan, SEP (see chapter 27), SIMPLE plan (see chapter 27), tax-sheltered annuity (see Q 29:1), or governmental plan (see Q 26:9). [IRC § 219(g)(5), as amended by SBA '96 § 1421(b); Freese, TCM 1996-224] An individual's status as an active participant must be reported on Form W-2.

Q 26:9 Who is an active participant?

An active participant in a defined benefit plan (see Q 2:3) is an individual who participates or meets the eligibility requirements for participation at any time during the plan year ending with or within the individual's taxable year. Thus, an individual is an active participant if the individual is eligible but declines to participate or fails to complete the minimum period of service or to make an employee contribution necessary to accrue a benefit. However, an individual who elects pursuant to the plan not to participate will be considered to be ineligible for participation for the period to which the election applies; but, in the case of a defined benefit plan, such an election is effective no earlier than the first plan year commencing after the date of the election. An individual is not an active participant if the employer has frozen benefit accruals (unless pre-freeze benefit accruals increase as compensation increases). An individual who accrues no additional benefits in a plan year ending with or within the individual's taxable year by reason of attaining a specified age is not an active participant by reason of participation in the plan. [Treas Reg § 1.219-2(b); Prop Reg § 1.219-2(f)(1); Wartes, 65 TCM 2058 (1993); Ann 91-11, 1991-4 IRB 80; Notice 88-131, 1988-2 CB 546; Notice 87-16, 1987-1 CB 446; Ltr Rul 8948008]

An individual is an active participant in a money purchase pension or target benefit plan (see Qs 2:4, 2:5) if an employer contribution or forfeiture is required to be allocated to the individual's account for the plan year ending with or within the individual's taxable year. Thus, an individual who separates from service before the beginning of a calendar year may still be an active participant for such calendar year if, under the terms of the plan, the individual is eligible to receive an allocation for the plan year ending in such calendar year. [Treas Reg § 1.219-2(c)]

An individual is treated as an active participant under a profit sharing or stock bonus plan (see Qs 2:6, 2:13) if any employer contribution is added or any forfeiture is allocated to the individual's account during the individual's taxable year. A contribution is added to the individual's account on the later of the date the contribution is made or allocated. [Treas Reg § 1.219-2(d)]

An individual is not an active participant in a defined contribution plan (see Q 2:2) if only earnings (rather than contributions or forfeitures) are allocated to the individual's account.

An individual is treated as an active participant for any taxable year in which the individual makes a voluntary or mandatory employee contribution or an elective contribution under a 401(k) plan (see Q 23:1). However, an individual is not an active participant merely because the individual is eligible but chooses not to make such elective contribution. [Treas Reg § 1.219-2(e); Prop Reg § 1.219-2(f)(1)]

The determination of whether an individual is an active participant is made without regard as to whether the individual's rights are nonforfeitable. [IRC § 219(g); Freese, TCM 1996-224; Morales-Caban, 66 TCM 995 (1993); Wartes, 65 TCM 2058 (1993)]

An individual was treated as an active participant in her employer's qualified retirement plan even though she was unaware of her eligibility to participate, and actual inclusion, in the plan. [Baumann, 70 TCM 61 (1995)]

For married couples filing jointly, if either spouse is an active participant under the rules described above, both spouses are treated as active participants for purposes of determining the amount that each may contribute to an IRA. However, in the case of a married couple filing separate tax returns who do not live together at any time during the taxable year, the active participant status of one spouse will not affect the status of the other spouse; each spouse is treated as a single individual. [IRC § 219(g)(4); Baumann, 70 TCM 61 (1995); Bermingham, 67 TCM 2200 (1994); Wartes, 65 TCM 2058 (1993); Felber, 64 TCM 261 (1992)] If RRB '95 (see Q 1:22A) is enacted, the active participation of one spouse will not cause the other spouse to be treated as an active participant. [RRB '95, Act § 11011(b)]

Q 26:10   What level of income affects an active participant's deduction limitation?

Adjusted gross income over the applicable dollar amount results in a limit on the IRA deduction for active participants (see Q 26:9). The applicable dollar amounts are:

1. $40,000 for taxpayers filing a joint return;
2. $25,000 for any unmarried taxpayer; and
3. Zero for married individuals filing separate returns.

However, married individuals filing separately who live apart during the entire year are treated as not married for this purpose so that the applicable dollar amount is $25,000 for each individual. [IRC §§ 219(g)(3)(B), 219(g)(4); Notice 87-16, 1987-1 CB 446] If RRB '95 (see Q 1:22A) is enacted, the active participation of one spouse will not cause the other spouse to be treated as an active participant. However, it is unclear whether the applicable dollar amount for the active participant spouse would be the higher amount for a taxpayer filing a joint return or the lower amount for an unmarried taxpayer. It is also unclear as to how the adjusted gross income of the active participant spouse would be calculated. For example, if the married individuals earn interest on a jointly held bank account, what portion of the interest should be allocated to the active participant spouse? [RRB '95, Act §§ 11011(a), 11011(b)]

For purposes of the IRA deduction limit, adjusted gross income is calculated without taking into account any deductible IRA contributions made for the taxable year or certain exclusions for foreign earned income and U.S. savings bond redemptions, but taking into account any taxable Social Security benefits and passive loss limitations applicable to the taxpayer (see Q 26:12). [IRC § 219(g)(3)(A), prior to amendment by SBA '96 § 1807(c)]

For taxable years beginning after 1996, adjusted gross income is calculated without taking into account the exclusion for amounts paid to the individual or expenses incurred by the individual's employer for qualified adoption expenses. [IRC § 219(g)(3)(A), as amended by SBA '96 § 1807(c)]

If enacted, RRB '95 would increase the applicable dollar amounts both for individuals filing a joint return and for an unmarried individual by $5,000 a year for 12 years. For individuals filing a joint return, the applicable dollar amount would reach $100,000 and for an unmarried individual, $85,000. In addition, these new phased-in applicable dollar amounts would be adjusted for cost-of-living increases commencing in the 13th year. However, an adjustment would be made only if it is $1,000 or greater and then would be made in multiples of $1,000 (i.e., rounded down to the next lowest multiple of $1,000). For example, an increase in the cost-of-living of $999 would result in no adjustment, and an increase of $1,999 would create an upward adjustment of 1,000. [RRB '95, Act §§ 11011(a)(1), 11011(a)(3)]

If enacted, RRB '96 (see Q 1:22A) would increase the applicable dollar amounts to $70,000 for the first three years, and then $80,000 for the fourth year, for individuals filing a joint return and to $45,000 for the first three years, and then $50,000 for the fourth year, for any unmarried individual. In addition, these new applicable dollar amounts would be adjusted for cost-of-living increases commencing in the fifth year. However, an adjustment would be made only if it is $5,000 or greater and then would be made in multiples of $5,000 (i.e., rounded down to the next lowest multiple of $5,000). For example, an increase in the cost-of-living of $4,999 would result in no adjustment, and an increase of $9,999 would create an upward adjustment of $5,000. [RRB '96, Act §§ 9201(a), 9202(a)]

Q 26:11   If an individual is an active participant in a qualified retirement plan, what are the applicable IRA deduction limits?

The amount that may be deducted will be the contribution limitation (see Q 26:5) reduced by an amount that bears the same ratio to the contribution limitation as the amount by which the taxpayer's adjusted gross income exceeds the applicable dollar amount (see Q 26:10) bears to $10,000. Thus, a married couple with at least one active participant spouse and adjusted gross income of at least $50,000 cannot make a deductible IRA contribution. [Freese, TCM 1996-224; Baumann, 70 TCM 61 (1995); Rogers, 69 TCM 2263 (1995); Bermingham, 67 TCM 2200 (1994); Morales-Cabʿn, 66 TCM 995 (1993); Wartes, 65 TCM 2058 (1993); Felber, 64 TCM 261 (1992)]

Example 1. Ed, an active participant in his employer's qualified retirement plan, is married to Lois, and they file a joint return. Their adjusted gross income for 1996 is $47,500, and each earns over $2,000. Both Ed and Lois may make a deductible IRA contribution of up to $500, computed as follows:

Adjusted gross income	$47,500
Less: Applicable dollar amount	40,000
Difference	$ 7,500
Reduction in $2,000 limitation	$ 1,500
($2,000 × $7,500/$10,000)	
Maximum deductible IRA contribution	$ 500
($2,000 – $1,500)	

[IRC § 219(g)(2)(A); Notice 87-16, 1987-1 CB 446]

If RRB '95 (see Q 1:22A) is enacted, the active participation of one spouse will not cause the other spouse to be treated as an active participant (see Q 26:10).

The reduction in the $2,000 limitation is rounded to the next lowest $10 in the case of a reduction that is not a multiple of $10. [IRC § 219(g)(2)(C)]

For individuals whose adjusted gross income is not above the level that would totally eliminate a deductible IRA contribution, there is a $200 minimum IRA deduction allowable.

Example 2. Norman, an unmarried individual who is an active participant in his employer's qualified retirement plan, has adjusted gross income of $34,900. He may make a deductible IRA contribution of $200.

[IRC § 219(g)(2)(B)]

If RRB '95 is enacted, the phaseout amount for married individuals filing a joint return would increase by $2,500 a year to a maximum of $20,000. It appears that there would be no phaseout amount for any other individual so that, if the adjusted gross income of an unmarried individual equalled the applicable dollar amount, a deductible IRA contribution could not be made. [RRB '95, Act § 11011(a)]

If enacted, RRB '96 (see Q 1:22A) would increase the $10,000 phaseout amount to 10 times the IRA deduction limit (see Q 26:5). If the IRA deduction limit remained at $2,000, the phaseout amount would increase to $20,000; if the limit increased to $2,500, the phaseout amount would increase to $25,000. [RRB '96, Act §§ 9201(b), 9202(a)]

Q 26:12   Does the receipt of Social Security benefits affect deductible IRA contributions?

If an individual is an active participant in a qualified retirement plan (see Qs 26:8, 26:9), the deduction for IRA contributions is subject to a phaseout if adjusted gross income exceeds certain specified amounts (see Qs 26:10, 26:11). An individual's adjusted gross income includes the taxable portion of Social Security benefits. [IRC §§ 219(g)(3)(A)(i), 219(g)(3)(B)]

The determination of the taxable portion of Social Security benefits depends in part upon the individual's modified adjusted gross income. In determining modified adjusted gross income, the individual may subtract deductible IRA contributions. Therefore, a deductible IRA contribution may cause a reduction in the taxable portion of Social Security benefits, and the individual must compute taxable Social Security benefits twice. The first computation is for the purpose of determining the tentative amount of Social Security benefits that must be included in gross income if the individual did not make any IRA contribution. This first computation determines the amount of hypothetical adjusted gross income for purposes of the IRA phaseout provision. The second computation actually determines the amount of taxable Social Security benefits by taking into account the deductible IRA contribution that was determined under the first computation. [IRC § 86(b)(2); Ann 88-38, 1988-10 IRB 60; Conf Rpt No. 99-841, 1986-3 (Vol 4) CB 377; IRS Publ 590 (for use in preparing 1995 returns)]

Q 26:13   May an individual who is ineligible to make a fully deductible IRA contribution make a nondeductible IRA contribution?

Yes. An individual who is ineligible to make a deductible IRA contribution to the full extent of the contribution limitation (see Q 26:5) may make a designated nondeductible IRA contribution (see Q 26:14). [IRC § 408(o)]

If enacted, RRB '95 (see Q 1:22A) would replace nondeductible IRAs with new AD IRAs to which individuals could make nondeductible contributions. An AD IRA would be an IRA that is designated at the time of establishment as an AD IRA. The maximum annual contribution that could be made to an AD IRA would be the lesser of $2,000 or 100 percent of the individual's compensation for the year. The maximum annual contribution to an AD IRA would be reduced by any contributions made for that year to a deductible IRA (see Qs 26:5–26:7). In the case of a married couple, the aggregate compensation of the couple would be taken into account in determining the maximum permitted contribution. Thus, for example, each spouse in a married couple could make an AD IRA contribution of $2,000 (for a total contribution by the couple of $4,000), provided the couple had at least $4,000 in compensation. The $2,000 contribution limit would be adjusted annually for cost-of-living increases (see Q 26:5). If an AD IRA is established, new rules would apply to:

- Taxation of distributions (see Qs 26:34, 26:35)
- Rollovers (see Q 26:35)
- Imposition of the premature penalty tax (see Q 26:42)

[RRB '95, Act §§ 11013(a), 11015(a), 11015(b)]

If enacted, RRB '96 (see Q 1:22A) would permit the establishment of a Special IRA. A Special IRA would be an IRA that is designated at the time of establishment as a Special IRA. No deduction would be allowed for a contribution to a Special IRA, and the maximum amount that could be contributed for any taxable year would be the excess, if any, of the IRA deduction limit applicable to the individual over the amount of all other IRA contributions for that taxable year. A nondeductible IRA would still be available. If a Special IRA is established, new rules would apply to:

- Taxation of distributions (see Q 26:36)
- Rollovers (see Q 26:36)
- Imposition of the premature penalty tax (see Q 26:43)

[RRB '96, Act § 9211(a)]

Q 26:14 What is a designated nondeductible IRA contribution?

A designated nondeductible IRA contribution is a nondeductible IRA contribution to the extent of the excess of (1) the lesser of $2,000 (or an increased amount when a spousal IRA is also involved; see Q 26:18) or 100 percent of compensation over (2) the IRA deduction limit with respect to the individual (but see Q 26:15). [IRC § 408(o)]

Under RRB '95, a designated nondeductible IRA contribution would not be permitted, but a designated nondeductible IRA contribution would be permitted under RRB '96 (see Q 26:13).

Q 26:15 May an individual who is eligible to make a deductible IRA contribution elect to treat such a contribution as nondeductible?

Yes. An individual is permitted to make such an election and might do so if, for example, the individual had no taxable income for the year after taking into account other deductions. [IRC § 408(o)(2)(B)(ii)]

Under RRB '95, an individual who would be eligible to make a deductible IRA contribution would be permitted to make a nondeductible contribution to an AD IRA, but only to the extent that a deductible IRA contribution was not made for that year. (see Q 26:13).

If a Special IRA (see Q 26:13) is established, an individual would still be permitted to elect to treat an IRA contribution as nondeductible. However, the contribution limit to the Special IRA would be reduced by the amount of the designated nondeductible IRA contribution.

Q 26:16   Is an individual required to report a designated nondeductible contribution on the tax return?

Yes. An individual who makes a designated nondeductible contribution (see Q 26:14) to an IRA (or who receives any amount from an IRA) must include the following information on the income tax return for the applicable taxable year:

1. The amount of designated nondeductible contributions for the year;

2. The amount of distributions from IRAs for the year;

3. The excess (if any) of (a) the aggregate amount of designated nondeductible contributions for all preceding taxable years, over (b) the aggregate amount of distributions from IRAs that were excludable from gross income for such taxable years;

4. The aggregate balance of all IRAs of the individual as of the end of the taxable year; and

5. Such other information as IRS may prescribe.

[IRC § 408(o)(4)]

If the required information is not provided on the individual's tax return for a taxable year, all IRA contributions are considered to have been deductible and, therefore, are taxable upon withdrawal from the IRA. However, an individual may change a designation of a contribution from deductible to nondeductible (or vice versa) by filing an amended return before the expiration of the statute of limitations on assessment of tax for such year. [Notice 87-16, 1987-1 CB 446]

There is a $50 penalty for failure to report the required information, and a $100 penalty for overstating the amount of designated nondeductible contributions—unless the taxpayer can demonstrate that the error was due to reasonable cause. [IRC §§ 408(o)(4), 6693(b)]

Under RRB '95 (see Q 1:22A), a designated nondeductible IRA contribution would not be permitted (see Q 26:13).

There is no requirement in either RRB '95 or RRB '96 (see Q 1:22A) for an individual who contributed to an AD IRA or a Special IRA (see 26:13) to report any information on the individual's income tax return for that taxable year.

Q 26:17   What is the tax treatment of IRA withdrawals by an individual who has previously made both deductible and nondeductible contributions?

The amount includible in an individual's income is determined by subtracting from the amount of the IRA withdrawal an amount that bears the same ratio to the amount withdrawn as the individual's aggregate nondeductible IRA contributions bear to the aggregate balance of all IRAs of the individual (including rollover IRAs and SEPs).

The formula for determining the nontaxable portion of an IRA distribution is:

$$\frac{\text{Total nondeductible contributions}}{\substack{\text{Aggregate IRA year-end} \\ \text{account balances plus amount} \\ \text{of IRA distributions}}} \times \substack{\text{IRA} \\ \text{distributions}} = \substack{\text{Nontaxable portion} \\ \text{of distribution}}$$

[Notice 87-16, 1987-1 CB 446]

Example. Assume that Anne has made aggregate deductible IRA contributions into two IRAs for 1994 and 1995 of $1,800 and aggregate nondeductible IRA contributions of $2,200 during those two years. In January 1996, Anne withdrew $1,000 from one IRA. At the end of 1996, the account balance of both IRAs is $4,500. Of the $1,000 withdrawn during 1996, $400 is treated as a partial return of nondeductible contributions, calculated as follows:

$$\frac{\substack{\text{Total nondeductible} \\ \text{contributions (\$2,200)}}}{\substack{\text{Aggregate IRA year-end} \\ \text{account balances (\$4,500)} \\ \text{plus amount of IRA} \\ \text{distributions during year} \\ \text{(\$1,000)}}} = \frac{\$2,200}{\$5,500} \times \$1,000 = \$400$$

The balance of the withdrawn amount ($1,000 – $400 = $600) is includible in income on Anne's 1996 tax return.

Since both an AD IRA and a Special IRA (see Q 26:13) are discrete accounts, the above rules would not apply to distributions from either type of new IRA. For further discussion of the taxability of withdrawals from IRAs, AD IRAs, and Special IRAs, see Qs 26:34 through 26:36.

Q 26:18   What is a spousal IRA?

If only one spouse is working, the working spouse may make an additional contribution to an IRA (a spousal IRA) on behalf of the nonworking spouse (provided a joint income tax return is filed). A spousal IRA is available even if both spouses work if the spouse for whom the spousal IRA is set up consents to being treated as having no compensation, for IRA purposes, for the taxable year. *For taxable years beginning before 1997,* the total amount of allowable annual contributions to the working spouse's IRA and to the spousal IRA is $2,250 (or 100 percent of the working spouse's earnings if less). The contributions to both IRAs need not be split equally between the spouses. However, the maximum IRA contribution on behalf of either spouse is $2,000. [IRC § 219(c), prior to amendment by SBA '96 § 1427(a); Bingo, 61 TCM 2782 (1991); Harris, 51 TCM 1154 (1986)]

For taxable years beginning after 1996, the total amount of allowable annual contributions to the working spouse's IRA and to the spousal IRA is $4,000 (or 100 percent of the working spouse's earnings if less). As with prior law, the contributions to both IRAs need not be split equally between the spouses. However, the maximum IRA contribution on behalf of either spouse is $2,000. [IRC § 219(c), as amended by SBA '96 § 1427(a)]

> **Example 1.** Caroline is married to Adam, and they file a joint return. Their adjusted gross income for 1997 is $40,000, all of which is earned by Caroline. Caroline and Adam may each make a deductible IRA contribution of up to $2,000.

If either spouse is an active participant in a qualified retirement plan (see Qs 26:8, 26:9), the allowable contributions are not fully deductible if the couple's adjusted gross income is more than $40,000 (see Q 26:10). If the couple's adjusted gross income is between $40,000 and $50,000, the deductible portion of the allowable contributions ($2,250 in 1996, and $4,000 in 1997) is proportionately reduced (see Q 26:11). None of the contribution is deductible if the couple's adjusted gross income is $50,000 or more. [IRC § 219(g); Freese, TCM 1996-224; Baumann, 70 TCM 61 (1995); Morales-Caban, 66 TCM 995 (1993); Wartes, 65 TCM 2058 (1993); Felber, 64 TCM 261 (1992)] If RRB '95 (see Q 1:22A) is enacted, the active participation of one spouse will not cause the other spouse to be treated as an active participant. [RRB '95, Act § 11011(b)]

> **Example 2.** Stephanie, an active participant in her employer's qualified retirement plan, is married to Bill, and they file a joint return. Their adjusted gross income for 1997 is $42,500, all of which is earned by Stephanie. Stephanie and Bill may each make a deductible IRA contribution of up to $1,500, computed as follows:

Adjusted gross income	$42,500
Less: Applicable dollar amount	40,000
Difference	$ 2,500
Reduction in $2,000 limitation	$ 500
($2,000 × $2,500/$10,000)	
Maximum deductible IRA contribution	$ 1,500
($2,000 – $500)	

[IRC § 219(g)(2)(A); Notice 87-16, 1987-1 CB 446]

What happens if the working spouse has reached age 70½? As long as the working spouse continues to receive compensation, the working spouse can make deductible contributions to the nonworking spouse's IRA. The nonworking spouse must, however, be less than age 70½, and the maximum contribution on behalf of the nonworking spouse is $2,000. [IRC § 219(d)(1)] RRB '96 (see Q 1:22A) would replace age 70½ with age 70. [RRB '96, Act § 9445(b)]

What happens if the working spouse dies? A contribution may be made to a spousal IRA by the surviving spouse if a joint income tax return is filed for the year for which the contribution was made. [Ltr Rul 8527083]

Q 26:19   When must IRA contributions be made?

A deductible or nondeductible contribution to an IRA must be made by the due date, not including extensions, for filing the return. [IRC § 219(f)(3)]

> **Example.** Betty wants to make a contribution to her IRA for 1996. Betty can do so any time in 1996, or she can wait until her 1996 tax return is due, April 15, 1997. Even if Betty obtains an extension to file her return to August 15, 1997, her IRA contribution is due by April 15, 1997.

An IRA contribution is timely if it is received by the IRA sponsor in an envelope bearing a post office cancellation date no later than the due date of the individual's federal income tax return, not including extensions. [Ltr Ruls 8628047, 8611090, 8551065, 8536085]

Since, in most cases, both an AD IRA and a Special IRA (see Q 26:13) would be treated in the same manner as an IRA, the same rule will apply. [RRB '95, Act § 11015(a); RRB '96, Act § 9211(a)]

Q 26:20   Can an IRA deduction be claimed before the contribution is actually made?

Yes, as long as the contribution is made by the due date, not including extensions, for filing the return. [Rev Rul 84-18, 1984-1 CB 88]

Example. Danielle files her 1996 return on February 5, 1997, and claims a deduction of $2,000 for an IRA contribution that she has not made. If she makes the contribution by the due date of the return, April 15, 1997, the deduction is allowed.

Q 26:21   Does the payment of a fee to the trustee of an IRA reduce the amount otherwise allowable as a contribution to the IRA?

No. The payment of a fee to the trustee for the establishment and maintenance of an IRA, or for various other administrative services performed, is not considered a contribution to an IRA for purposes of the annual contribution limit (see Q 26:5) or the excess contribution penalty (see Q 26:6). Moreover, the trustee fees may be deductible as expenses incurred for the production of income. [IRC § 212; Rev Rul 84-146, 1984-2 CB 61; Ltr Ruls 8432109, 8329049]

However, the payment of brokerage commissions incurred for the purchase or sale of IRA assets is considered a contribution to the IRA subject to the annual contribution limit. [Rev Rul 86-142, 1986-2 CB 60; Ltr Rul 8711095] This rule also applies to commissions paid to insurance agents attributable to the purchase of individual retirement annuities. [Ltr Rul 8747072]

Q 26:22   What happens if an individual engages in a prohibited transaction with regard to the IRA?

A retirement account is not treated as an IRA if an individual engages in a prohibited transaction (see Q 20:1) with respect to the retirement account. The account is treated as having distributed all its assets to the individual on the first day of the taxable year in which the prohibited transaction occurs. [IRC § 408(e)(2)] Since, in most cases, both an AD IRA and a Special IRA (see Q 26:13) would be treated in the same manner as an IRA, the same rule should apply.

An individual is a disqualified person (see Q 20:4) with respect to the individual's IRA, so the individual's guarantee of a loan to the IRA is a prohibited transaction. [IRC §§ 4975(c)(1), 4975(e)(2); DOL Adv Op No. 90-23A] DOL also opined that a proposed sale and leaseback of a building and land to an IRA by members of the IRA holder's family would be a prohibited transaction. [DOL Adv Op No. 93-33A] The use of an IRA to purchase a personal residence is a prohibited transaction resulting in a taxable distribution to the IRA holder. [Harris, 67 TCM 1983 (1994)]

An individual established an IRA and contributed shares of stock of a corporation formed by the individual and of which he was a director. The payment of dividends by the corporation to the IRA did not constitute a prohibited transaction. [Swanson, 106 TC No. 3 (1996)]

DOL has granted a class exemption permitting purchases and sales by IRAs of American Eagle bullion coins from or to authorized purchasers even if the authorized purchasers are disqualified persons (see Qs 20:3, 20:4). [PTCE 91-55 (56 FR 49209)]

Q 26:23   Will the receipt of reduced or no-cost services by a customer who directs the IRA to invest in a bank's financial products constitute a prohibited transaction?

Effective May 11, 1993, banks are permitted to provide IRA holders or their family members with institutional services either at reduced costs or at no cost, such as free checking. The services offered must be the same as those offered by the bank in the ordinary course of its business to customers who do not maintain IRAs at the bank. Therefore, a prohibited transaction (see Q 20:1) will not occur when an IRA holder, who is a fiduciary with respect to the IRA, uses IRA assets to obtain services from the bank. [IRC § 4975(c)(1); PTCE 93-33 (59 FR 22686, 58 FR 31053)]

Retroactively effective to 1975, banks and other financial institutions can offer cash or other premiums as incentives for opening IRAs or for making additional IRA contributions. The value of the premium on deposits up to $5,000 is limited to $10 and on deposits in excess of $5,000 is limited to $20. Free group-term life insurance can be offered to IRA holders annually if the face amount of the insurance does not exceed the lesser of $5,000 or the value of the account. [PTCE 93-1 (58 FR 3567)]

Q 26:24   May an individual borrow money to fund an IRA?

Yes. The deductibility of the interest paid on the loan is determined under the general rules applicable to interest payments. The interest payments are not subject to the rule prohibiting interest deductions on loans incurred to purchase or carry tax-exempt assets because the income earned on the IRA is tax deferred, not tax exempt. [IRC § 163; Ltr Rul 8527082]

Q 26:25   May an individual make a contribution to an IRA with a credit card?

Yes, according to IRS. An individual established an IRA at a bank and funded the IRA with a cash advance drawn on his bank credit card. The bank executed the transaction pursuant to written instructions of the individual. IRS ruled that if, by April 15, a cash advance was drawn on the individual's credit card, credited to the IRA, and designated as a contribution for the previous year, the individual could deduct the contribution for the previous year, provided the bank honored its obligation to make payment on the credit card cash advance. [Ltr Rul 8622051]

Q 26:26   What is an employer-sponsored IRA?

An employer may establish IRAs for its employees (and for the nonworking spouses of these employees). The contributions are deductible by the employer and includible as compensation income by the employee, subject to Social Security and unemployment taxes. Whether the employee can deduct the contribution is determined under the rules generally applicable to IRA contributions (see Qs 26:7–26:11). The assets of the employer-sponsored IRAs may be held in a common trust fund. [IRC §§ 219(f)(5), 408(c)]

If the employer contributes less than the maximum allowed (100 percent of compensation up to $2,000; increased to $2,250 in 1996 and to $4,000 in 1997 in the case of a spousal IRA), the employee can contribute the difference (see Qs 26:5, 26:18).

Example. Jim's employer contributes $1,500 to an IRA on his behalf. Because Jim earns more than $2,000 a year, the maximum allowable contribution is $2,000. Jim, who is not married, can contribute an additional $500 to the IRA.

There is no requirement that an employer-sponsored IRA cover a certain number or group of employees. In fact, the employer may discriminate in favor of highly compensated employees (see Q 3:3). [IRC § 408(c)]

An IRA is not considered employer sponsored merely because the employer acts as trustee or custodian of its employees' IRAs. However, the employer is a disqualified person (see Qs 20:3, 20:4) with respect to the IRA, so the employer must be careful to avoid engaging in a prohibited transaction (see Q 20:1) that would disqualify the IRA (see Q 26:22). For example, the purchase of stock of the employer's parent company by the employer as IRA custodian may be considered a prohibited transaction. [DOL Adv Op No. 90-20A]

Q 26:27 Can employer-sponsored IRAs help an employer that has a qualified retirement plan satisfy coverage requirements?

No. An employer maintaining a qualified retirement plan cannot satisfy the coverage requirements that must be met by taking into consideration the fact that employees not covered under the plan are covered by an employer-sponsored IRA.

For details on coverage requirements, see chapter 5.

Q 26:28 What is a payroll-deduction IRA?

An employer may choose to play a limited role in promoting retirement savings (IRAs) for its employees by establishing a payroll-deduction program in conjunction with a financial institution (e.g., a bank, insurance company, mutual fund, or brokerage firm). Each employee is allowed to set up an IRA with the sponsoring institution, and the amount the employee wishes to contribute to the IRA each pay period is deducted from the employee's paycheck by the employer.

Q 26:29 Does a payroll-deduction IRA expose the employer to ERISA liabilities and compliance requirements?

A payroll-deduction IRA is not considered a pension plan subject to ERISA as long as the employer does not endorse the program. The employer will not be considered to have endorsed the program and will be free of ERISA responsibilities if all of the following conditions are met:

1. Materials distributed to the employees, either by the employer or by the IRA sponsor, clearly say that:
   a. The program is completely voluntary;
   b. The employer is not endorsing the sponsor or its investment program;

   c. There are other IRA investments available to employees outside the payroll-deduction program;

   d. An IRA may not be appropriate for everyone; and

   e. The tax consequences are the same whether or not payroll deductions are used to make the IRA contributions.

2. The employer is not the IRA sponsor or an affiliate of the sponsor.

3. No significant investments will be made in securities of the employer.

4. If the payroll-deduction IRA is the result of a collective bargaining agreement, no investments designed to provide more jobs, loans, or similar direct benefits to union members are permitted.

In addition, the employer must promptly transfer the funds it deducts from its employees' paychecks to the IRA sponsor or it risks the imposition of some ERISA responsibilities. [DOL Adv Op No. 81-80A]

Q 26:30 How does a simplified employee pension differ from an employer-sponsored IRA?

A SEP allows a company to contribute the lesser of $30,000 or 15 percent of an eligible employee's compensation (see Q 6:23) to an IRA established by the employee. The employer-sponsored IRA limit is the lesser of $2,000 ($2,250 in 1996 and $4,000 in 1997 for a spousal IRA) or 100 percent of compensation (see Q 26:5). SEPs must comply with coverage and nondiscrimination requirements, while an employer-sponsored IRA may discriminate in favor of highly compensated employees (see Q 3:3).

For details on how a SEP and the new SIMPLE plan work, see chapter 27.

Q 26:31 Are there restrictions on IRA distributions?

No. Unlike qualified retirement plans, an individual may withdraw all or any part of an IRA at any time. Also, spousal consent to a withdrawal is not necessary, and there are no limitations as to the form of distribution.

However, minimum annual distributions must start by April 1 of the year after the year in which the individual reaches age $70\frac{1}{2}$ (see Q 26:32), and a penalty tax is imposed for insufficient distributions (see Q 26:33). [IRC §§ 408(a)(6), 408(b)(3); see also IRC § 401(a)(9)]

Also, additional taxes may apply to distributions before an individual reaches age $59\frac{1}{2}$ (see Q 26:41) and to distributions in excess of certain limits (see Q 13:27).

RRB '96 (see Q 1:22A) would replace ages 70½ and 59½ with ages 70 and 59, respectively. [RRB '96, Act §§ 9445(a), 9445(b)]

Q 26:32   What is the minimum distribution requirement?

Once distributions from an IRA are required to begin (see Q 26:31), the owner must withdraw a certain amount during each year or be subject to a penalty for insufficient distributions (see Q 26:33).

IRS has issued proposed regulations detailing the methods for satisfying the minimum distribution requirement. The proposed regulations indicate that distributions from an IRA are subject to requirements similar to those governing minimum distributions from qualified retirement plans, including the minimum distribution incidental benefit requirement. [Prop Reg § 1.408-8, Q&A A-1, B-13] See chapter 11 for details.

Generally, the minimum required distribution for a year is calculated by dividing the account balance of the IRA as of December 31 of the previous year by the owner's life expectancy (or by the joint life expectancy of the owner and the owner's designated beneficiary). [Prop Reg § 1.401(a)(9)-1, Q&A F-1]

An individual who is the owner or beneficiary of more than one IRA must calculate the required minimum distribution with respect to each IRA. However, the amounts required to be distributed may then be aggregated and the distribution taken from any one or more of the IRAs. [Notice 88-38, 1988-1 CB 524; Ltr Rul 9416037]

Example. Norman, age 71, has three IRAs and has named his estate as beneficiary of each IRA. IRA 1 has an account balance of $200,000; IRA 2, $20,000; and IRA 3, $10,000. The required minimum distribution for each IRA is separately calculated. The required minimum distribution for IRA 1 is $13,071.90; for IRA 2, $1,307.19; and for IRA 3, $653.59. Norman can take $15,032.68 from IRA 1, IRA 2, or any combination of the IRAs to satisfy his required minimum distributions for the year.

The minimum distribution for a year is not reduced even if a portion of the IRA assets is transferred to a former spouse pursuant to a divorce decree during the year (see Q 26:44). The minimum distribution is still based on the IRA balance on December 31 of the year before the transfer. [Ltr Rul 9011031]

The minimum distribution requirements would not apply to an AD IRA (see Q 26:13) during the lifetime of the individual. [RRB '95, Act § 11015(a)]

See Q 26:40 for the minimum distribution requirements after the death of the IRA owner.

Q 26:33 What is the penalty imposed for insufficient distributions from an IRA?

An annual nondeductible 50 percent excise tax is imposed on the difference between the minimum required distribution from an IRA (see Q 26:32) and the amount distributed. [IRC § 4974]

IRS can waive the penalty tax if the shortfall resulted from a reasonable error and the individual is taking steps to correct the situation (see Q 11:22). [IRC § 4974(d)]

Since the minimum distribution requirements would not apply to an AD IRA (see Q 26:13) during the lifetime of the individual (see Q 26:32), no excise tax could be imposed.

Q 26:34 How are distributions from an IRA taxed?

Generally, a recipient of a payment or distribution from an IRA must include the amount received in gross income for the year of receipt. [Copley, 70 TCM 1040 (1995)] The naming of a trust as the beneficiary of an individual's IRA does not constitute a distribution from the IRA even though the individual is the creator, trustee, and sole beneficiary of the trust because no amount was actually distributed from the IRA to either the individual or the trust. Amounts embezzled from an IRA by an officer of the IRA trustee and then restored to the IRA by the trustee are not taxable distributions. [GCM 39858; Ltr Ruls 9253054, 9234016]

IRA distributions are taxed as ordinary income. IRA distributions are not eligible for capital gains treatment or the forward averaging method that may apply to lump-sum distributions from qualified retirement plans (see Q 13:13). [IRC § 408(d)(1); Costanza, 50 TCM 280 (1985)] However, IRA distributions made upon an individual's death to a charitable organization or to a charitable remainder trust are not subject to income tax because the charitable beneficiary is exempt from tax. [IRC §§ 501(a), 664(c); Ltr Ruls 9341008, 9237020]

If the IRA is paid out all in one year, the individual pays income tax on the entire amount in one year. If distributions are received as an annuity or over a period of years, tax payments are spread over several years. If the individual has made only deductible IRA contributions, the entire amount of each IRA distribution is fully taxable. If, however, the individual has made nondeductible contributions to any IRA, a portion of all IRA distributions, even distributions made from an IRA to which only deductible contributions have been made, will be considered a tax-free return of the individual's nondeductible contributions (see Q 26:17). For purposes of determining what portion of an IRA distribution is taxable, the following special rules apply:

1. All IRAs and SEPs (see Q 27:1) maintained by the individual are aggregated;
2. All distributions during the year are treated as one distribution;
3. The aggregate account balance is determined as of the end of the year, and includes distributions made during the year; and
4. The individual's overall nondeductible contributions are determined as of the end of the year.

[IRC § 408(d)(2)]

A distribution from a rollover IRA (see Q 28:2) established by a surviving spouse with a distribution from the deceased spouse's tax-sheltered annuity (see Q 29:1) is fully taxable. The surviving spouse does not receive a basis (see Q 13:2) equal to the fair market value of the amount rolled over. [Ltr Rul 9031046] However, when an individual rolled over the entire distribution to an IRA and was informed the following year by the trustee of the qualified retirement plan that the individual's benefits had been erroneously overvalued, IRS ruled that the amount distributed to the individual to repay the employer would not be includible in the individual's income. [Ltr Rul 9118020]

If a distribution from an IRA is premature, the amount distributed is taxed as ordinary income and a penalty tax may be imposed (see Q 26:41). [IRC § 72(t)] IRA distributions may also be subject to the penalty tax on excess distributions (see Qs 13:27, 26:35). A distribution from an IRA is not taxable if there is a valid rollover of the distribution to another IRA, or to the same IRA (see Qs 28:3, 28:4).

A sale of assets held in an individual's IRA is not a distribution to the individual when the sale proceeds are retained by the IRA custodian. [Ltr Rul 9331055] The payment of a fee directly from the IRA to a company for services in connection with transferring IRA assets between mutual funds is not a taxable distribution to the IRA owner. [Ltr Rul 8747072]

A disclaimer of IRA benefits by the beneficiary of a deceased IRA owner that satisfies the requirements of state law and the Code is not an assignment of income, does not violate the nonforfeitability requirement (see Q 26:2) or the nontransferability requirement (see Q 26:3), and will be taxable to the actual recipient and not to the disclaiming beneficiary. [GCM 39858; IRC §§ 408(a)(4), 408(b)(1), 2518(b)] A married couple's agreement to divide the husband's IRA, a community property asset, into separate equal shares that could be disposed of separately by each spouse did not constitute a distribution or transfer of amounts from the IRA for income tax purposes so that no amount was includible in either individual's gross income because the reclassification of community property into separate property did not constitute an actual distribution or payment from the IRA. [Ltr Rul 9439020]

A levy by IRS on an individual's IRA to satisfy the individual's tax liabilities is a constructive receipt of income and, therefore, a taxable distribution to the individual. [IRC §§ 72(e)(2), 408(d)(1); Pilipski, 66 TCM 984 (1993)] A withdrawal from an IRA that was applied toward the purchase of a residence constituted a taxable distribution to the individual. [Clarke, 68 TCM 398 (1994)]

For a discussion of the taxation of distributions from an AD IRA or a Special IRA, see Qs 26:35 and 26:36.

Q 26:35   Are distributions from an AD IRA taxable?

Qualified distributions from an AD IRA (see Q 26:13) would not be includible in gross income. A qualified distribution would be a distribution that is made after the five-taxable-year period beginning with the first taxable year for which the individual made a contribution to an AD IRA and that is:

1. Made on or after the date on which the individual attains age 59½;

2. Made to a beneficiary (or to the individual's estate) on or after the death of the individual;

3. Attributable to the individual's being disabled (see Q 26:41); or

4. A qualified special purpose distribution (see Q 26:42).

[RRB '95, Act § 11015(a)]

The five-year holding period would run from the taxable year for which the individual is deemed to make the contribution; and, in the case of qualified rollover contributions (see Q 28:45) that are not from another AD IRA, the five-year holding period would begin with the taxable year in which the rollover was made. For example, an individual could contribute $100 to an AD IRA on December 31 of year one (actually, up to April 15 of year two), and then make annual $2,000 contributions for each of years two through five. In year six, the five-year holding period will have been met with respect to the entire AD IRA. [RRB '95, Act § 11015(a)]

If the distribution from the AD IRA is not a qualified distribution, only the portion of the distribution allocable to earnings on the contributions will be includible in the individual's income.

Distributions from an AD IRA could be rolled over tax free to another AD IRA, and the 10 percent penalty tax would not apply (see Q 26:42).

If a rollover is made from an IRA to an AD IRA, the entire amount transferred would be includible in gross income (except to the extent attributable to nondeductible IRA contributions), but the 10 percent penalty tax would not apply. If the rollover from the IRA occurred during a two-year window period, the amount includible in gross income would be includible ratably over the four-taxable year period beginning in the taxable year in which the amount was distributed from the IRA. For an example, see Q 28:45. [RRB '95, Act § 11015(a)]

Distributions from an AD IRA would not be taken into account for purposes of the penalty tax on excess distributions (see Q 13:27). [RRB '95, Act § 11015(c)]

Q 26:36   Are distributions from a Special IRA taxable?

Generally, any amount distributed from a Special IRA (see Q 26:13) would not be included in the gross income of the distributee. However, any amount distributed from a Special IRA that consisted of earnings allocable to contributions made to the Special IRA during the five-year period ending on the day before distribution would be included in the gross income of the distributee for the taxable year in which the distribution occurred. Distributions would be treated as having been made (1) first from the earliest contribution (and earnings allocable thereto) remaining in the Special IRA at the time of the distribution, and (2) then from other contributions (and earnings allocable thereto) in the order in which made. Any portion of a distribution allocated to a contribution (and earnings allocable thereto) would be treated as allocated first to the earnings and then to the contribution, and earnings would be allocated to a contribution in such manner as IRS will subsequently determine. Also as IRS will subsequently determine, all contributions made during the same taxable year and all contributions made before the expiration of the five-year period may be treated as one contribution for purposes of these rules. In general, distributions from a Special IRA would not be includible in income to the extent attributable to contributions that had been in the Special IRA for at least five years, and withdrawals of earnings from a Special IRA before five years would be subject to income tax. [RRB '96, Act § 9211(a)]

Special rules would apply to qualified transfers. A qualified transfer would be a transfer to a Special IRA from another Special IRA or from an IRA that satisfied the rollover rules (see Q 28:3). A transfer from an IRA to a Special IRA would be a qualified transfer only if the individual's adjusted gross income did not exceed the aggregate of the applicable dollar amount (see Q 26:10) and the phaseout amount (see Q 26:11). Under a special rule for the first two years, the dollar limitation would be $100,000 for a married individual filing a joint return, $70,000 for an unmarried individual, and zero for a married individual filing a separate return. Adjusted gross income would take into account any deductible IRA contributions. [RRB '96, Act § 9211(a)]

No rollover could be made to a Special IRA unless it constituted a qualified transfer, and there would be no dollar limit on the amount of a qualified transfer. If a qualified transfer is made from an IRA to a Special IRA, the entire amount transferred would be includible in gross income (except to the extent attributable to nondeductible IRA contributions), but the 10 percent penalty tax (see Q 26:43) would not apply. If the qualified transfer occurred during a one-year window period, the amount includible in gross income would be includible ratably over the four-taxable-year period beginning in the taxable year in which the amount was distributed from the IRA. For an example, see Q 28:45. [RRB '96, Act § 9211(a)]

Q 26:37   Are amounts remaining in an IRA at death subject to federal estate taxes?

The entire amount in the IRA is included in the decedent's gross estate. [IRC § 2039] Amounts accumulated in a decedent's IRA as of the date of death may be subject to the 15 percent excise tax on excess retirement accumulations (see Qs 14:21, 14:22).

An IRA may constitute qualified terminable interest property (QTIP) for which an estate tax marital deduction may be elected (see Q 14:20). IRS has allowed a QTIP election when all IRA income is paid to a QTIP trust that, in turn, pays out all such income received from the IRA, plus all trust income, to the surviving spouse annually during lifetime. IRS also allowed a QTIP election for an IRA that pays the greater of all IRA income or the required minimum distribution (see Q 26:40) to a QTIP trust that then pays an amount equal to the IRA income and all trust income to the surviving spouse. [IRC § 2056(b)(7); Rev Rul 89-89, 1989-2 CB 231; Ltr Ruls 9551015, 9537005, 9442032, 9439020, 9420034, 9418026] Where a decedent designated a qualified domestic trust (QDOT) for the benefit of his noncitizen spouse as the beneficiary of his IRA, IRS permitted a QTIP election to be made. [Ltr Rul 9544038] Where a decedent designated his noncitizen spouse as beneficiary of his IRA, the spouse created a QDOT for her own benefit, and the spouse then designated the QDOT as beneficiary of the IRA, IRS ruled that the IRA qualified for the estate tax marital deduction. [Ltr Rul 9623063]

The entire amount in either an AD IRA or a Special IRA (see Q 26:13) would be included in the decedent's gross estate. However, even though under RRB '95 (see Q 1:22A) distributions from an AD IRA would not be subject to the 15 percent excise tax on excess distributions (see Q 26:35), the amount in an AD IRA attributable to earnings as of the date of an individual's death may be subject to the 15 percent excise tax on excess retirement accumulations. [RRB '95, Act § 11015(c)]

Q 26:38   What is an inherited IRA?

An IRA becomes an inherited IRA after the death of the IRA owner unless the beneficiary is the IRA owner's surviving spouse (see Q 26:39). The nonspouse beneficiary cannot make a tax-deductible contribution to an inherited IRA, and distributions from an inherited IRA do not qualify for rollover treatment. If a trust is named as beneficiary of an IRA, the IRA will be an inherited IRA even if the surviving spouse is the sole trust beneficiary; and, since an inherited IRA cannot be rolled over, distributions from the IRA will be taxable to the beneficiary. (See Q 26:40 for the applicable minimum distribution requirements.) [IRC §§ 219(d)(4), 408(d)(3)(C); Ltr Ruls 9416037, 9322005, 9321032; Rev Rul 92-47, 1992-1 CB 198]

The beneficiary of an inherited IRA can have the IRA funds transferred directly to a new IRA (see Q 28:5) *if* the new IRA is maintained in the name of the decedent. This type of transfer is not a rollover and does not result in a taxable distribution to the beneficiary. [Ltr Ruls 9504005, 9433032]

Q 26:39   Do special rules apply if the beneficiary is the IRA owner's surviving spouse?

Yes. A surviving spouse who inherits an IRA from a deceased spouse can elect to treat the IRA as that of the surviving spouse. In that event, the surviving spouse can make contributions to the IRA, and the minimum distribution requirements during the surviving spouse's lifetime (see Q 26:32) and after the surviving spouse's death (see Q 26:40) apply exactly as if the surviving spouse were the original owner of the IRA. The surviving spouse may make such election even if the deceased spouse had started taking distributions from the IRA. However, if the surviving spouse dies before the election is made, the surviving spouse's estate cannot make the election. [IRC § 408(d)(3); Prop Reg § 1.408-8, Q&A A-4; Ltr Ruls 9534027, 9237038]

Alternatively, a surviving spouse who is the beneficiary of a deceased spouse's IRA may roll the IRA distribution into the surviving spouse's own IRA. [Ltr Ruls 9534027, 9433031] Such rollover was allowed when the deceased spouse named his estate as beneficiary of his IRA, and his surviving spouse was the sole beneficiary of the estate (see Q 28:6). [IRC § 402(c)(9)]

Q 26:40 What minimum distribution requirements apply after the IRA owner's death?

Generally, the minimum distribution rules applicable to qualified retirement plans apply to distributions from IRAs (see Qs 11:5, 11:7). [IRC §§ 408(a)(6), 408(b)(3)]

Thus, if a decedent who died after the required beginning date (see Q 11:3) had been receiving lifetime distributions, post-death distributions must be made at least as rapidly as under the lifetime distribution method. [IRC § 401(a)(9)(B)(i); Ltr Ruls 9450040, 9119067] If distributions had not begun or had begun but the decedent died before the required beginning date, the IRA must be distributed in one of two methods:

1. The entire IRA must be distributed by December 31 of the year that includes the fifth anniversary of the decedent's death; or
2. Distributions may be made over a period not extending beyond the life expectancy of the designated beneficiary if distributions begin by December 31 of the year that includes the first anniversary of the decedent's death.

[IRC §§ 401(a)(9)(B)(ii), 401(a)(9)(B)(iii); Ltr Ruls 9504045, 9501044, 9416037, 9322005]

If the designated beneficiary is the surviving spouse, distribution may be deferred until the decedent would have reached age 70½. Alternatively, the surviving spouse may choose to treat the IRA as that of the surviving spouse (see Q 26:39). [IRC § 401(a)(9)(B)(iv)] RRB '96 (see Q 1:22) would replace age 70½ with age 70. [RRB '96, Act § 9445(b)]

Although under RRB '95 (see Q 1:22A) the minimum distribution requirements would not apply to an AD IRA during the lifetime of the individual (see Q 26:32), the minimum distribution rules would apply after the individual's death. [RRB '95, Act § 11015(a)]

For details on minimum distribution requirements, see chapter 11.

Q 26:41 What is the penalty imposed on a premature distribution from an IRA?

A distribution from an IRA before the individual for whose benefit the IRA was established reaches age 59½ is subject to a 10 percent penalty tax (i.e., the tax is increased by an amount equal to 10 percent of the amount includible in gross income). [Copley, 70 TCM 1040 (1995); Huff, 68 TCM 674 (1994)] The penalty tax does not apply, however, if an early distribution is made because of the IRA owner's death or disability. [IRC § 72(t); Ltr Ruls 9621043, 9608042, 9418034, 9106044, 9043063]

To come within the exception for disability:

1. The individual must be unable to engage in any substantial gainful activity due to a medically determinable physical or mental impairment;

2. The disability must be expected to result in death or be of a long-continued and indefinite duration; and

3. The individual must furnish proof of the disability in the form and manner required by IRS.

[IRC § 72(m)(7); Treas Reg § 1.72-17A(f); Dwyer, 106 TC No. 18 (1996); Kovacevic, 64 TCM 1076 (1992); Kane, 63 TCM 2753 (1992); Ltr Ruls 9318043, 9249034] Distributions from a wife's IRA to pay household expenses after her husband became disabled did not come within the exception for disability and, therefore, were subject to the penalty tax. [Boulden, 70 TCM 216 (1995), *aff'd*, unpublished opinion (4th Cir 1996)]

In addition, the penalty tax does not apply if the payment is part of a series of substantially equal periodic payments (not less frequently than annually) made over the life (or life expectancy) of the IRA owner or the joint lives (or joint life expectancy) of the IRA owner and the owner's designated beneficiary (see Qs 13:39, 13:40). However, if the amount of the periodic payments is modified (other than by reason of death or disability) before the *later* of (1) the end of the five-year period beginning with the date of the first payment, or (2) the owner's attainment of age 59½, the penalty tax that would have been imposed on all payments, plus interest, is imposed in the year in which the modification occurs (see Q 13:41). IRS has provided acceptable methods of calculating substantially equal periodic payments. [Notice 89-25, 1989-1 CB 662, Q&A 12; Ltr Ruls 9615042, 9604028, 9601052, 9545018, 9541034, 9531039] IRS has ruled that IRA distributions constituted a series of substantially equal periodic payments even though the annual distribution amount would be increased by a 3 percent adjustment in each subsequent year. [Ltr Rul 9536031] A change in the monthly distribution date is ministerial and not a modification of the periodic payment method; therefore, the 10 percent penalty tax will not be imposed on either the current or prior distributions. [Ltr Rul 9514026]

An individual with more than one IRA can take periodic payments from one IRA without taking periodic payments from the others. Also, the account balances of the other IRAs need not be considered in calculating the amount of the periodic payment from the distributing IRA. However, the individual can consider the account balances of all IRAs, calculate the amount of the periodic payments from each IRA, and then take the periodic payments from only one IRA. [Notice 88-38, 1988-1 CB 524; Ltr Ruls 9505022, 9243054, 9050030, 8946045]

A married couple who were both under age 59½ and who used their IRAs to make a down payment on a personal residence were subject to the penalty tax. [Harris, 67 TCM 1983 (1994)]

For taxable years beginning after 1996, the 10 percent penalty tax will not apply to early distributions from an IRA that are used to pay medical expenses in excess of 7½ percent of adjusted gross income. In addition, the 10 percent penalty tax will not apply to distributions to an individual from an IRA for the payment of health insurance premiums with respect to the individual and the individual's spouse and dependents after the individual has separated from service. For this latter exception to apply, the individual must have received unemployment compensation for 12 consecutive weeks under federal or state law, and the distributions must be made during a taxable year in which the unemployment compensation is paid or during the next year. This exception does not apply to distributions made after an individual's reemployment if the individual has been employed for at least 60 days after the initial separation from service. A self-employed individual (see Q 6:33) is treated as meeting the requirements for unemployment compensation if the individual would have received the compensation except for the fact that the individual had been self-employed. [IRC §§ 72(t)(2)(B), 72(t)(3)(A), as amended by HIPA '96 § 361(a), 72(t)(2)(D), as added by HIPA '96 § 361(b)]

RRB '96 (see Q 1:22A) would replace age 59½ with age 59. [RRB '96, Act § 9445(a)]

For a discussion of proposed modifications by RRB '95 to the imposition of the 10 percent penalty tax on distributions from IRAs and AD IRAs, see Q 26:42; and, for a discussion of proposed modifications by RRB '96 to the imposition of the 10 percent penalty tax on distributions from IRAs and Special IRAs, see Q 26:43.

Q 26:42 How would RRB '95 affect the imposition of the premature penalty tax on IRA and AD IRA distributions?

Qualified distributions from an AD IRA (see Q 26:35) would not be subject to the 10 percent premature penalty tax (see Q 26:41), and qualified special purpose distributions (whether or not qualified distributions) would not be subject to the penalty tax. For example, a distribution within the five-year holding period would not be a qualified distribution but could still be a qualified special purpose distribution. Distributions from an AD IRA that are not qualified distributions or qualified special purpose distributions would be subject to the penalty tax.

In general, qualified special purpose distributions would be distributions to certain unemployed individuals or distributions to other individuals for:

1. The purchase or acquisition of a principal residence of a first-time homebuyer;

2. Qualified higher education expenses; or

3. Medical expenses of the individual or the individual's spouse and certain other persons.

These same exceptions to the imposition of the 10 percent premature penalty tax would also apply to distributions from regular IRAs.

First-time homebuyers would be individuals who did not own an interest in a principal residence during the two years prior to the purchase of a home and who were not in an extended period for filing with respect to the gain from the sale of a principal residence. Penalty-free withdrawals could be made for the acquisition, construction, or reconstruction costs of a principal residence for a first-time homebuyer who is the individual or the individual's spouse, or a child, grandchild, or ancestor of the individual or the individual's spouse. In order to qualify as a first-time homebuyer distribution, the distribution would have to be used within 60 days to pay the costs of acquiring, contracting, or reconstructing a residence. If there is a delay in acquisition, construction, or reconstruction, the distribution could be redeposited in an IRA or an AD IRA, as applicable, within 120 days without imposition of income or penalty taxes. This exception is subject to a $10,000 lifetime limitation.

Qualified higher education expenses would be tuition, fees, books, supplies, and equipment required for the enrollment or attendance of the individual, the individual's spouse, or a child, grandchild, or ancestor of the individual or the individual's spouse at an eligible educational institution. The amount of qualified higher education expenses would be reduced by any amount excludable from income under the rules relating to education savings bonds.

RRB '95 would extend to IRAs and AD IRAs the exception to the penalty tax for premature distributions from qualified retirement plans for medical care expenses exceeding 7½ percent of adjusted gross income. The exception would also apply to medical expenses of a child, grandchild, or ancestor of the individual or the individual's spouse, regardless of whether such person would otherwise qualify as the individual's dependent. Penalty-free withdrawals could also be made to individuals who have been receiving unemployment compensation for at least 12 consecutive weeks. This latter exception could also apply to self-employed individuals (see Q 6:33).

An additional exception would apply to distributions for premium payments for a qualified long-term care insurance contract for the individual or the individual's spouse; however, it is unclear as to whether this exception applies only to IRA distributions or to distributions from both an IRA and an AD IRA.

If a qualified rollover is made from an IRA to an AD IRA, the 10 percent penalty tax would not apply (see Q 26:35).

[RRB '95, Act §§ 11015(a), 11016, 11044(a)]

Q 26:43 How would RRB '96 affect the imposition of the premature penalty tax on IRA and Special IRA distributions?

RRB '96 (see Q 1:22A) expands both the types of IRA distributions that would be subject to the 10 percent premature penalty tax (see Q 26:41) and the type of IRA distributions that would be exempted from the tax.

The penalty tax exception for IRA distributions on or after attainment of age 59½ (see Q 26:41) would *not* apply to any amount distributed from an IRA (other than a Special IRA; see Q 26:13) that is allocable to contributions made to the IRA during the five-year period ending on the date of distribution (and earnings on such contributions). If amounts are transferred from one IRA to another (see Q 28:3), the period during which the funds were held in the transferring IRA would be utilized for purposes of calculating the five-year period. Distributions would be treated as having been made (1) first from the earliest contribution (and earnings allocable thereto) remaining in the IRA at the time of the distribution, and (2) then from other contributions (and earnings allocable thereto) in the order in which made. Earnings would be allocated to contributions in such manner as IRS would subsequently determine. The 10 percent penalty tax, however, would not be imposed on IRA distributions attributable to rollovers from qualified retirement plans and tax-sheltered annuities (see Qs 28:34, 29:42).

Withdrawals of earnings from Special IRAs before five years (see Q 26:35) would be subject to the 10 percent penalty tax (even if made after reaching age 59½), unless used for one of the qualified purposes described below.

RRB '96 provides exceptions from the 10 percent penalty tax for distributions from IRAs and Special IRAs used for certain purposes. Penalty-free withdrawals could be made for (1) qualified higher education expenses, (2) acquisition of a principal residence for a first-time homebuyer, and (3) distributions to individuals who have been receiving unemployment compensation for at least 12 consecutive weeks. RRB '96 would also extend to IRAs and Special IRAs the exception for distributions from qualified retirement plans for extraordinary medical expenses and would expand the scope of the exception (see Q 13:39).

Qualified higher education expenses generally would be tuition and fees at an institution of higher education for an eligible student who is the individual, the individual's spouse, the individual's dependent, or any child or grandchild of the individual (even if not a dependent for income tax purposes). The amount of qualified higher education expenses would be reduced by any amount excludable from income under the rules relating to education savings bonds but would include distributions to purchase a state prepaid tuition program instrument.

First-time homebuyers would be individuals who did not own an interest in a principal residence during the three years prior to the purchase of a home and who were not in an extended period for filing with respect to the gain from the sale of a principal residence. Penalty-free withdrawals could be made for the acquisition, construction, or reconstruction costs of a principal residence for a first-time homebuyer who is the individual or the individual's spouse, child, or grandchild. The distribution would have to be used within 60 days to pay the costs of acquiring, contracting, or reconstructing a residence. If there is a delay in acquisition, construction, or reconstruction, the distribution could be redeposited in an IRA or Special IRA, as applicable, within 120 days without imposition of income or penalty taxes.

An unemployed individual would be permitted to make a penalty-free withdrawal if the individual has received unemployment compensation for at least 12 consecutive weeks during the taxable year in which the withdrawal is made or the preceding taxable year.

RRB '96 would extend to IRAs and Special IRAs the exception to the penalty tax for distributions from qualified retirement plans for medical care expenses exceeding $7\frac{1}{2}$ percent of adjusted gross income. The exception would also apply to medical expenses of a child, grandchild, or ancestor of the individual or the individual's spouse, regardless of whether such person would otherwise qualify as the individual's dependent. In addition, for this purpose, the definition of medical care would include qualified long-term care services for incapacitated individuals. Qualified long-term care services generally would be services that are required by an incapacitated individual if the primary purpose of the services is to provide needed assistance with any activity of daily living or protection from threats to health and safety due to severe cognitive impairment. An incapacitated individual generally would be a person who is certified by a licensed professional within the preceding 12-month period as being unable to perform (without substantial assistance) at least two activities of daily living, or as having severe cognitive impairment.

If a qualified transfer is made from an IRA to a Special IRA, the 10 percent penalty tax would not apply (see Q 26:36).

[RRB '96, Act §§ 9102, 9211, 9221, 9222, 9223]

Q 26:44   May an IRA be transferred incident to divorce?

Yes. A transfer of an individual's interest in an IRA to the individual's spouse or former spouse under a divorce decree or a written instrument incident to the divorce is not a taxable distribution or transfer (see Q 30:5). After the transfer, the transferred interest is treated as the IRA of the transferee spouse or former spouse. [IRC § 408(d)(6); Ltr Rul 9006066] However, when an individual and his spouse entered into a private separation agreement providing for a division of the individual's IRA, the transfer to the spouse was taxable to the individual because the agreement was not incident to a decree of divorce or legal separation. [Ltr Ruls 9422060, 9344027] Furthermore, if funds are withdrawn from an IRA and paid over to the former spouse by the IRA owner to satisfy a divorce decree, the withdrawal will be taxable to the IRA owner. [Harris, 62 TCM 406 (1991)]

If an individual, incident to a divorce, is required to transfer some or all of the assets in an IRA to a spouse or former spouse, there are two methods commonly used to make the transfer:

1. *Changing the Name on the IRA.* If all the assets in an IRA are to be transferred, the individual can make the transfer by changing the name on the IRA from the individual's name to the name of the spouse or former spouse.

2. *Direct Transfer.* The individual directs the trustee (or custodian) of the IRA to transfer the affected assets directly to the trustee of a new or existing IRA set up in the name of the spouse or former spouse; or, if the spouse or former spouse is allowed to keep his or her portion of the IRA assets in the individual's existing IRA, the individual can direct the trustee to transfer the assets permitted to be kept by the individual directly to a new or existing IRA set up in the individual's name. The name on the IRA containing the spouse's or former spouse's portion of the assets would then be changed to show the spouse's ownership.

[IRS Pub 590 (for use in preparing 1995 returns)]

When a decedent had designated his wife as the beneficiary of his IRA and failed to change the beneficiary after their divorce, the court ruled that the ex-spouse released her interest in the IRA when she executed a divorce settlement agreement stating that any IRAs were the sole and exclusive property of the depositor. [Kruse v Todd, Nos. S89A0554 and S89A0555 (Ga Sup Ct 1990)] However, another court ruled otherwise because the settlement agreement contained only a general waiver provision and did not express a specific intention to surrender any rights as the beneficiary of the IRA. [Maccabees Mutual Life Ins Co v Morton, No. 90-8618 (11th Cir 1991)]

Q 26:45 Can an IRA be reached by judgment creditors?

It depends on state law because ERISA does not apply to IRAs. [In re Nelson, No. WW-94-1446 (9th Cir 1995)] Some courts have ruled that an IRA can be reached by all judgment creditors because the money deposited in the IRA is contributed voluntarily, set aside for the depositor's own benefit, and subject to the depositor's control, and the IRA is revocable at will. Additionally, some courts will consider the special needs of the depositor. [In re Meehan, 1993 Bankr Lexis 1899 (Bankr SD Ga 1993); In re Brewer, No. 92-25198-BM (Bankr WD Pa 1993); In re Huebner, No. C 91-3067 (ND Ia 1992); Velis v Kardanis, 949 F 2d 78 (3d Cir 1991); In re Swenson, No. 90A-04222 (Bankr D Utah 1991); In re Damast, No. 90-1815 (Bankr D NH 1991); In re Ree, No. 89-00723-W (ND Okla 1990); In re Lownsberry, No. 89-B-07144-J (DC Colo 1989); Schoneman v Schoneman, No. 62-852 (Kan Ct of App 1989); In re Gillett, 46 BR 642 (SD Fla 1985); In re Montavon, 52 BR 99 (D Minn 1985)]

Conversely, other courts have ruled that an IRA is exempt property under state law. [In re Solomon, 1995 US App Lexis 29795 (4th Cir 1995); In re Nelson, No. WW-94-1446 (9th Cir 1995); In re Bates, 1994 Bankr Lexis 1977 (Bankr D Me 1994); In re Walker, No. 90-5171 (10th Cir 1992); In re Templeton, Jr, No. 92 B04870 (Bankr ND Ill 1992); In re Kulp, No. 90-1190 (10th Cir 1991); Reliance Ins Co v Ziegler, Nos. 90-1628, 90-1799, and 90-2068 (7th Cir 1991); In the Matter of Volpe, No. 90-8496 (5th Cir 1991); In re Suarez, No. 90-18947 BKC-AJC (Bankr SD Fla 1991); In re Shumaker, 124 BR 820 (Bankr D Mont 1991); In re Volpe, 120 BR 843 (Bankr WD Tex 1990); In re Galvin, No. 89-21638-7 (D Kan 1990); In re Herrscher, No. B-88-07650-PHX-RGM (D Ariz 1990); In re Ewell, No. 89-1736-8P7 (Bankr MD Fla 1989); In re Maitin, No. 3-88-02890 (Bankr ED Tenn 1989); In re Laxson, 102 Bankr 85 (ND Tex 1989)]

One court has held that an IRA, upon the depositor's death, passed directly to the named beneficiary and did not become part of the deceased depositor's estate subject to the claims of creditors. [Estate of Davis, 6 EBC 2491 (Cal Apps Ct 1985)]

Although state law may exempt an IRA from judgment creditors [NY CPLR § 5205(c)(2); Md Cts § Jud Proc Code Ann § 11-504(h)], an exemption provided by state law is ineffective against the execution and creation of statutory liens of the United States for federal taxes. [In re Jacobs, 147 BR 106 (Bankr WD Pa 1992); Leuschner v First Western Bank & Trust Co, 261 F 2d 705 (9th Cir 1958); Knox v Great West Life Assur Co, 212 F 2d 784 (8th Cir 1954)] Consequently, IRS can levy on an individual's IRA to satisfy the individual's liability for taxes and can also assert a tax lien against an individual's IRA (see Q 26:34). [IRC § 6321; Treas Reg § 1.401(a)-13(b)(2); In re Deming, 92-17755F (Bankr ED Pa 1994); In re Schreiber, 1994 Bankr Lexis 49 (ND Ill 1994); Pilipski, 66 TCM 984 (1993)]

See Q 28:44 for a discussion of rollover IRAs.

Q 26:46   What are the IRA reporting requirements?

The reporting requirements by IRA trustees apply to contributions to and distributions from IRAs, even if the IRA is revoked. Thus, Form 5498, Individual Retirement Arrangement Information, must be filed to report a contribution to an IRA even if the IRA is later revoked. An exception is made for amounts transferred from one IRA to another IRA. In this case, the transferor IRA trustee will generally have reported an IRA contribution on Form 5498 when the IRA was established (and when additional contributions were made). Therefore, the transferee IRA trustee should not file a Form 5498 upon the establishment of the transferred IRA.

In addition, Form 1099-R, Distribution From Pensions, Annuities, Retirement or Profit-Sharing Plans, IRAs, Insurance Contracts, etc., must be filed for all distributions, even those made on account of revocation. Distributions should be reported as taxable in the year distributed.

Form 5498 is used both to report any contributions made to an IRA and to report the fair market value of any IRA balance as of December 31 of the tax year. In addition, the IRA trustee is required to report the fair market value of the IRA as of December 31 to the IRA owner by the following January 31. Generally, if the fair market value of the IRA is zero on December 31, no reporting of the fair market value is required. However, the IRA trustee may still be required to file a Form 5498 to report any contribution made for the year.

If both an IRA contribution and revocation of the IRA occur in the same calendar year, the contribution must be reported. The fair market value on December 31 need not be reported because the account balance is zero on that day. However, if the IRA is revoked in the year after it is established, both the contribution and the fair market value must be reported. [Rev Proc 91-70, 1991-2 CB 899; IRC §§ 408(i), 6047(d)]

The reporting requirements will also apply to AD IRAs and Special IRAs (see Q 26:13). [RRB '95, Act § 11015(a); RRB '96, Act § 9211(a)]

Chapter 27

Simplified Employee Pensions and Savings Incentive Match Plans for Employees

Complex and burdensome rules may cause the owner of a small business to think twice before adopting a qualified retirement plan. But then both the company and the owner forgo significant tax benefits. Both the simplified employee pension (SEP) and the savings incentive match plan for employees (SIMPLE plan) offer a practical alternative with respect to the institution of a retirement program. Requirements for establishing and maintaining each of these plans are explained in this chapter.

Q 27:1   What is a simplified employee pension?

A SEP is an individual retirement account or individual retirement annuity (IRA) established for an employee to which the employer makes direct tax-deductible contributions. [IRC § 408(k), as amended by SBA '96 § 1421(c)]

For a discussion on IRAs, see chapter 26.

Q 27:2   Who is eligible to participate in a SEP?

Each employee age 21 or over who, for 1996, earns at least $400 during the year (adjusted for cost-of-living increases) and has performed services for the employer in at least three of the immediately preceding five calendar years must participate in the SEP. Employees covered by a collective bargaining agreement in which retirement benefits were the subject of good-faith bargaining and employees who are nonresident aliens may be excluded from participation. All employees, including part-time employees, not excluded under one of the above statutory exclusions must participate in the SEP. [IRC § 408(k)(2); Prop Reg § 1.408-7(d); Notice 95-55, 1995-45 IRB 11]

Example. JTS Corporation, a calendar year corporation, maintains a SEP. Mindy commenced employment on October 1, 1993. Mindy worked 250 hours in 1993 and 900 hours each year in 1994, 1995, and 1996. If Mindy is at least age 21 and earns $400 or more, she must participate in the SEP in 1996.

The compensation requirement amount of $400 for 1996, which remains unchanged since 1995, has been adjusted for inflation and was initially $300. [IRC §§ 408(k)(2)(C), 408(k)(8)] For the four years prior to 1995, the adjusted amount was:

Year	Adjusted Amount
1994	$396
1993	385
1992	374
1991	363

An adjustment to the $400 compensation requirement will be made only if it is $50 or greater and then will be made in multiples of $50 (i.e., rounded down to the next-lowest multiple of $50). For example, an increase in the cost-of-living of $49 will result in no adjustment, and an increase of $99 will create an upward adjustment of $50. [IRC § 408(k)(8)] Although it may be some time before there is an increase in the $400 amount, the compensation requirement cannot be reduced below $396, the 1994 amount. [RPA '94, Act § 732(e)(2)]

Contributions must be made on behalf of all employees who meet the participation requirements during the calendar year, whether or not they are employed as of a particular date. [Prop Reg § 1.408-7(d)(3)]

Contributions must also be made on behalf of eligible employees over age 70½, even though the employees may already have started to receive required distributions from the SEP and may not make contributions to their own IRAs (see chapter 11 and Q 26:4). [IRC § 219(b)(2)]

For purposes of participation in a SEP, the rules regarding controlled businesses, affiliated service groups, and leased employees are applicable (see Qs 5:31, 5:37, 5:61). [IRC §§ 414(b), 414(c), 414(m)(4), 414(n)(3); Ltr Rul 9026056]

Q 27:3 Does the prohibition against discrimination in favor of highly compensated employees apply to a SEP?

Yes. A SEP may not discriminate in favor of highly compensated employees (see Q 3:2). Contributions must bear a uniform relationship to the compensation of each employee. However, the amount of employee compensation that may be taken into account in computing the employer's annual contribution in 1996 may not exceed $150,000 (adjusted for cost-of-living increases). [IRC §§ 408(k)(3), 408(k)(8)] The compensation limit was $200,000 (adjusted for cost-of-living increases) prior to 1994 (see Q 6:24 regarding the compensation limit for prior years).

Example. In 1996, Jill Corporation has three employees: the business owner earning $250,000 and two other employees earning $20,000 each. Since all three employees meet the eligibility requirements and the SEP may take into account only the first $150,000 of compensation paid to an employee, only $190,000 ($150,000 plus $40,000) would be counted for purposes of determining the amount of the contribution to the SEP. Assuming Jill Corporation wants to contribute the maximum amount allowed on behalf of the owner (see Q 27:6), it must use a 15 percent formula for its contribution. The contribution on behalf of the owner would be $22,500 (15% × $150,000), and the contribution for the other two employees would be $3,000 each (15% × $20,000).

The amount of the annual limit, $150,000 (see Q 6:23), is adjusted for increases in cost-of-living. However, an adjustment will be made only if it is $10,000 or greater and then is made in multiples of $10,000 (i.e., rounded down to the next-lowest multiple of $10,000). For example, an increase in the cost-of-living of $9,999 will result in no adjustment, and an increase of $19,999 will create an upward adjustment of $10,000. Therefore, the cost-of-living must increase by 6⅔ percent before the first adjustment to the annual compensation limit will occur (6⅔% × $150,000 = $10,000) (see Q 6:25). [IRC §§ 401(a)(17)(A), 401(a)(17)(B), 408(k)(8); Treas Reg § 1.401(a)(17)-1(a)(3)]

For years beginning before 1997, the family aggregation rule applicable to the $150,000 compensation limit applied to SEPs (see Q 6:31). *For years beginning after 1996,* the family aggregation rule is repealed. [IRC § 401(a)(17)(A), as amended by SBA '96 § 1431(b)(2)]

If the SEP is top-heavy, the employer contributions on behalf of each eligible non-key employee must generally be at least 3 percent of compensation. [IRC §§ 408(k)(1)(B), 416(c)(2), 416(e)] For details on top-heavy plans, see chapter 22.

Q 27:4　May a SEP provide for permitted disparity?

Yes. The permitted disparity (or integration) rules applicable to defined contribution plans also apply to employer contributions to SEPs. These rules permit a limited disparity between the contribution percentages applicable to compensation below and above the integration level (see Q 7:6). Generally, the integration level is the taxable wage base (TWB; see Q 7:7), or some percentage of the TWB, in effect as of the beginning of the plan year. [IRC §§ 401(l)(2), 408(k)(3)(D)]

A SEP will not be considered discriminatory if the excess contribution percentage (ECP; see Q 7:4) does not exceed the base contribution percentage (BCP; see Q 7:5) by more than the lesser of (1) the BCP, or (2) the greater of 5.7 percentage points, or the percentage equal to the rate of tax attributable to the old age insurance portion of the Old-Age, Survivors, and Disability Insurance (OASDI) as of the beginning of the plan year (see Qs 7:3–7:8). [IRC § 401(l)(2)]

> **Example.** Sharon Corporation establishes a SEP for the 1996 calendar year. The SEP provides that each participant will receive an allocation of 5 percent of compensation up to the taxable wage base ($62,700 in 1996) and 10.7 percent of compensation in excess of the taxable wage base. The SEP does not meet the permitted disparity requirements, because the ECP, 10.7 percent, exceeds the BCP, 5 percent, by more than the lesser of 5 percentage points or 5.7 percentage points. However, if the ECP was reduced to 10 percent, the plan would meet the permitted disparity requirements.

Whether or not permitted disparity is taken into account, no participant can receive an allocation of more than $22,500 in 1996 (see Q 27:6).

For details on permitted disparity, see chapter 7.

Q 27:5　Are contributions made to a SEP on an employee's behalf forfeitable?

No. Employer contributions under a SEP must fully vest when made and are nonforfeitable. Employers may not condition any contribution to a SEP on the employee's retaining any portion of the contribution in the account and may not prohibit withdrawals from a SEP. The employee may take a distribution from the SEP at any time and at the employee's discretion, but the distribution must then be included in income (see Q 27:18). [IRC § 408(k)(4)]

Q 27:6 How much may be contributed to an employee's IRA through a SEP?

The employer's annual contribution to a SEP on behalf of each employee is limited to the lesser of (1) 15 percent of the employee's compensation (not including the SEP contribution), or (2) $30,000. The $30,000 amount is subject to cost-of-living adjustments; however, an adjustment will be made only if it is $5,000 or greater and then will be made in multiples of $5,000 (see Q 6:2). If the employer's contribution exceeds the above limitation, the excess contribution is includible in the employee's income and regarded as having been contributed by the employee to the IRA under the SEP. [IRC § 402(h)(2)]

A 6 percent excise tax is imposed on an excess contribution to an IRA, and this tax is applicable to SEPs. [IRC § 4973]

The employee may contribute an additional $2,000 to a personal IRA, even though the employee is a participant in a SEP. However, for the purpose of determining the deductibility of the IRA contribution, the employee will be considered an active participant because of the employee's participation in the SEP (see Q 26:9). [IRC §§ 219(g)(5)(A)(v), 408(j); Notice 87-16, 1987-1 CB 446]

The maximum contribution to a SEP on behalf of an employee for 1996 (see Q 27:3) is $22,500 (15% × $150,000). Thus, increases in the $150,000 compensation limitation are more important than increases in the $30,000 contribution limitation. If the compensation limitation increases to $200,000 and the contribution limitation increases to $40,000, the maximum contribution is still $30,000 (15% × $200,000).

Q 27:7 How much can an employer deduct for contributions to a SEP?

Subject to the $30,000 annual addition limitation for each employee (see Q 27:6), the employer may deduct no more than 15 percent of the total compensation (see Q 12:15) paid to all participating employees during the calendar year ending with or within the employer's taxable year (or during the taxable year in the case of a SEP maintained on the basis of the employer's taxable year). [IRC § 404(h)(1)(C)]

An excess contribution is deductible in succeeding taxable years in order of time, subject to the 15 percent limitation. If the employer maintains both a SEP and a profit sharing plan, the deduction limitation for the profit sharing plan contribution is reduced by the amount of the allowable deduction for the SEP contribution with respect to the participants in such plan. [IRC § 404(h)(2)]

Q 27:8 When are contributions to a SEP deductible?

Contributions to a SEP are deductible:

1. In the case of a SEP maintained on a calendar-year basis, for the taxable year within which the calendar year ends; or
2. In the case of a SEP maintained on the basis of the taxable year of the employer (that is not a calendar year), for such taxable year.

[IRC § 404(h)(1)(A)]

The contribution must be made no later than the due date of the employer's return for the taxable year (including extensions). [IRC § 404(h)(1)(B)]

Q 27:9 May an employer adopt a salary reduction SEP?

For years beginning before 1997, an employer that had fewer than 26 employees who were eligible to participate at any time during the preceding calendar year could have established a SEP whereby each employee was permitted to elect to have contributions made to the SEP or to receive the contributions in cash under procedures similar to a 401(k) plan. At least 50 percent of the eligible employees of the employer must have elected to defer part of their compensation to the SEP. [IRC § 408(k)(6), prior to amendment by SBA '96 § 1421(c)]

For years beginning after 1996, an employer may not establish a salary reduction SEP. However, an employer may continue to make contributions to a salary reduction SEP that was established in a year beginning before 1997, and employees hired in a year beginning after 1996 may participate in the salary reduction SEP. [IRC § 408(k)(6), as amended by SBA '96 § 1421(c)]

A state or local government or a tax-exempt organization was not permitted to maintain a salary reduction SEP. [IRC § 408(k)(6)(E); Ltr Rul 9030014]

Q 27:10 What are the limits on elective deferrals to a SEP?

Elective deferrals under a SEP (see Q 27:9) are treated like elective deferrals under a 401(k) plan and are subject to an annual $7,000 limitation for an employee. The $7,000 amount is adjusted for cost-of-living increases; and, for 1996, the maximum deferral amount is $9,500 (see Q 23:26 regarding the adjusted amount for prior years and the method for calculating future adjustments). [IRC §§ 401(a)(30), 402(g), 408(k)(6)(A)(iv); Notice 95-55, 1995-45 IRB 11]

Q 27:11   Is there a special nondiscrimination test for salary reduction SEPs?

Yes. Under a salary reduction SEP (see Q 27:9), the deferral percentage for each highly compensated employee (see Q 3:3) cannot exceed 125 percent of the average deferral percentage for all eligible non-highly compensated employees (see Q 3:13). The deferral percentage for an employee for a year is the ratio of (1) the amount of elective employer contributions actually paid over to the SEP on behalf of the employee for the year, to (2) the employee's compensation for the year. [IRC §§ 408(k)(6)(A)(iii), 408(k)(6)(D)]

The above calculation is different from the calculation applicable to a 401(k) plan (see Qs 23:8, 23:9). Under a 401(k) plan, after the actual deferral percentage (ADP) is calculated separately for each employee, the *average* of the ADP for all highly compensated employees cannot exceed 125 percent of the average of the ADP for all non-highly compensated employees. Also, an alternative test is available under a 401(k) plan. If the average ADP for highly compensated employees does not exceed the average ADP for non-highly compensated employees multiplied by 2, and the average ADP for highly compensated employees does not exceed the average ADP for the non-highly compensated employees by more than two percentage points, then the ADP test will be satisfied even if the first test is not satisfied.

> **Example.** L&S Corporation establishes a salary reduction SEP. The deferral percentage for each highly compensated employee equals 5.5 percent. The average deferral percentage for the non-highly compensated employees equals 4 percent. The special nondiscrimination test is not satisfied, because 5.5 percent is greater than 5 percent (125% × 4%). If the salary reduction SEP was a 401(k) plan, the requirement would be met because 5.5 percent does not exceed 4 percent by more than two percentage points and 5.5 percent is less than 4 percent multiplied by 2.

Q 27:12   How is a SEP established?

Generally, any employer may establish a SEP. SEPs are available to both C and S corporations, partnerships, and sole proprietorships. In one case, the court determined that a SEP was not established by an individual or by an employer on his behalf where the contribution was not made by an employer on his behalf, but was made by the individual who was not self-employed and, therefore, not eligible to establish a SEP. [Ramsey, TCM 1996-189]

In order to establish a SEP, the employer must execute a written instrument within the time prescribed for making deductible contributions (see

Q 27:8). This instrument must include the name of the employer, the participation requirements, the allocation formula, and the signature of a responsible official. [IRC § 408(k)(5); Prop Reg § 1.408-7(b)]

The SEP may be set up in one of three ways:

1. By executing Form 5305-SEP or Form 5305A-SEP in the case of a salary reduction SEP (see Q 27:9);

2. By a master or prototype plan for which a favorable opinion letter has been issued; or

3. By an individually designed plan.

Q 27:13   When may an employer use a model SEP?

IRS has designed a model SEP agreement to be used by employers wishing to implement SEPs with relatively little paperwork. This is done by completing Form 5305-SEP or 5305A-SEP for salary reduction SEPs. The form is not filed with IRS, but is retained by the employer and distributed to all participating employees. This fulfills the employer's reporting and disclosure obligations relating to the adoption of the agreement and also satisfies the notification requirements. However, a model SEP may not be used:

1. By an employer currently maintaining another qualified retirement plan;

2. By an employer that has ever maintained a defined benefit plan (even if it has been subsequently terminated);

3. By members of an affiliated service group, a controlled group of corporations, or trades or businesses under common control, unless all eligible employees of all members participate in the SEP;

4. By an employer that uses the services of leased employees;

5. If any eligible employee has not established an IRA;

6. If the contribution formula considers permitted disparity; or

7. By an employer with no non-highly compensated employees (this applies only to a salary reduction SEP).

To adopt a model SEP or model salary reduction SEP, the plan must be maintained on a calendar-year basis. [See Instructions to Forms 5305-SEP and 5305A-SEP]

Use of a nonmodel SEP requires the employer to distribute certain other summaries regarding the SEP. Once an employee becomes eligible to participate in the SEP, the employer must furnish certain specific information to the employee, including an explanation of participation requirements, the formula allocating employer contributions, the name of the person designated to supply any additional SEP information, and an explanation of the terms of the IRA accepting the SEP contribution.

Q 27:14   Can a dissolved partnership's SEP be continued by its successor sole proprietors?

No. A SEP adopted by a partnership is not considered a plan covering its employees after the partnership is dissolved, even though the former partners continue to operate the same business as sole proprietors. A sole proprietor must adopt a new SEP in order to continue making deductible contributions for the employees. [Ltr Rul 8450051]

Q 27:15   What are the annual reporting requirements of a SEP?

Once a SEP is established, there is limited annual reporting to both IRS and participants. There is no requirement that the employer file the Form 5500 series for the SEP (see Q 17:1). The trustee or issuer of the IRA is required to furnish annual information regarding contributions to the SEP and the fair market value of assets in the SEP. For this purpose, Form 5498 must be filed with IRS by May 31. [Prop Reg § 1.408-5]

The information on Form 5498 must also be supplied to the participants. The employer maintaining the SEP must notify each participant of the SEP contribution made on the employee's behalf on Form W-2 by the later of January 31 following the contribution year or 30 days after the contribution. [IRC § 408(l); Prop Reg § 1.408-9]

Q 27:16   Are SEP contributions taxable to the employee?

No. Both employer contributions and employee elective deferrals under the SEP (see Q 27:9) are excludible from the employee's gross income. [IRC § 402(h)]

Notwithstanding the exclusion from gross income, SEP contributions made under a salary reduction agreement are subject to the Federal Insurance Contributions Act (FICA) and the Federal Unemployment Taxes Act (FUTA) taxes, but SEP contributions under a non-salary reduction arrangement are not subject to such taxes. [IRC §§ 3121(a)(5)(C), 3306(b)(5)(C)]

Q 27:17   How are SEP assets managed?

The assets of a SEP are managed by a financial institution and not by individual trustees, although the employee may be permitted to direct the investment of the employee's account. The SEP must be established with a bank, thrift institution, insurance company, brokerage firm, or other entity that is eligible to be an IRA custodian. Each individual who participates in the SEP may set up or use a personal IRA for investment purposes. If the participant does not have an IRA, the employer *must* establish one for the participant.

Similar to an individual's personal IRA, the participant may make trustee-to-trustee transfers and change the investment manager of the SEP. Since IRA rules govern the types of investments in a SEP, SEP assets cannot be lent to participants or invested in life insurance contracts, collectibles, or any other assets in which IRAs may not invest (see Qs 26:2, 26:23). [IRC §§ 408(a)(3), 408(e)(4), 408(m)]

Q 27:18   How are distributions from a SEP taxed?

Generally, the same rules that apply to IRA distributions apply to distributions from a SEP. Distributions from a SEP are includible in ordinary income in the year received; and, as with an IRA, favorable tax elections (e.g., special averaging) are not available for distributions from a SEP.

If a withdrawal from a SEP is premature (that is, a distribution is made before the individual reaches age 59½, becomes disabled, or dies), the amount withdrawn, in addition to ordinary income tax, is subject to a 10 percent penalty tax. Similar to distributions from an IRA, an exception to the 10 percent penalty tax exists if the individual receives a distribution from the SEP in substantially equal periodic payments. [IRC §§ 72(t)(1), 72(t)(2)(A)(iv)] See Q 26:41 for details.

Distributions from a SEP must begin no later than April 1 of the calendar year following the year in which the participant reaches age 70½. If the required minimum distribution is not made, a penalty tax is imposed equal to 50 percent of the amount by which such minimum required distribution exceeds the actual amount distributed during the taxable year (see Q 26:32). [IRC §§ 401(a)(9), 4974(a)]

If the employee has at any time made nondeductible IRA contributions, the amount includible in income upon a distribution from a SEP is determined in accordance with an allocation formula (see Q 26:17). [IRC §§ 402(h)(3), 408(d)]

The assets of a decedent's SEP are included in the decedent's gross estate. [IRC § 2039]

The 15 percent excise tax on excess distributions from qualified retirement plans and excess accumulations upon the employee's death is also applicable to SEPs (see Qs 13:27, 13:43). The excise tax on excess distributions is suspended for a three-year period—1997, 1998, and 1999. [IRC § 4980A, as amended by SBA '96 § 1452(b)]

Q 27:19 How may assets be moved from a SEP without penalty?

An employee may wish to move funds from an IRA under the SEP to another IRA for higher interest rates, different investment alternatives, or more favorable withdrawal and transfer terms. Similar to IRAs, there are two ways to move assets from the SEP without penalty. One method is through a rollover, whereby the employee withdraws all or part of the amount from the SEP account and rolls over that amount to another IRA, or even the same IRA, within 60 days. Assets withdrawn, but not timely rolled over, will be included in the employee's income and may be subject to penalty taxes. Also, such rollovers may not be made more frequently than once every 12 months; otherwise, the subsequent rollover will be included in the employee's income and may be subject to penalty taxes. [IRC § 408(d)(3)]

The second, and more advisable, way to move funds from an IRA under a SEP to another IRA is through a trustee-to-trustee transfer of funds. Under this method, the employee directs the trustee of the IRA to transfer the IRA funds directly to the trustee of a second IRA. There are no restrictions on the number of trustee-to-trustee transfers that may be made to or from a SEP.

For more details, see chapter 28.

Q 27:20 May a distribution from a qualified retirement plan be rolled over into a SEP?

Yes. If, within 60 days after receipt, a participant rolls over an eligible rollover distribution (see Q 28:8) from a qualified retirement plan to an IRA funded as a SEP, the rollover amount will not be includible in income. [IRC § 402(c); Ltr Rul 8630068]

However, if a participant wishes to retain the ability to roll the distribution back into another qualified retirement plan, a conduit IRA must be used (see Q 28:40).

Q 27:21   What advantages does a SEP offer to the business owner?

The greatest advantage a SEP offers over qualified retirement plans is the minimal amount of paperwork and bookkeeping necessary to start and maintain the plan. Costs for consultants (lawyers, accountants, or actuaries) are sharply reduced, possibly even eliminated. Another advantage of a SEP is the flexibility it affords with respect to contributions. The employer can contribute any amount it wishes, up to a maximum set by law (see Q 27:6), or it can choose not to make any contribution at all. Although this is generally true for profit sharing plans also, it is not true for pension plans. In addition, the employer's fiduciary duty (see chapter 19) is reduced because participants in a SEP choose their own investments when they establish IRAs. Furthermore, a SEP may be established after the end of the employer's taxable year (see Qs 27:8, 27:12).

Q 27:22   What are the drawbacks to the adoption of a SEP?

Eligibility rules for a SEP tend to be less restrictive than the rules for qualified retirement plans, and this can increase the employer's costs. Many of the employees who need not be covered under a qualified retirement plan must be covered under a SEP. For example, a SEP must include part-time and seasonal workers, regardless of how few hours they worked during the year (assuming they satisfy the compensation requirement and have worked for the employer in at least three of the previous five years; see Q 27:2).

Another drawback to a SEP is that employees must be fully vested at all times (see Q 27:5). A qualified retirement plan does not operate this way; vesting can be gradually phased in to favor longer-term employees (see chapter 9).

In addition, the maximum contribution to a SEP on behalf of an employee is limited to $22,500 (see Q 27:6), whereas the maximum contribution under a defined contribution plan is $30,000 (see Q 6:1).

Also, although SEPs are subject to fewer reporting requirements, employers may not be aware of many of the rules applicable to SEPs. For example, the employer must determine which employees are eligible, which are highly compensated employees, and which are key employees. In addition, ADP and top-heavy tests may need to be performed. (See Qs 27:2, 27:3, 27:11.)

Furthermore, the extent to which assets in a SEP are protected from creditors may not be as great as under a qualified retirement plan (see Qs 26:45, 4:25). In one case, the court allowed the assets in a SEP to be attached. Although, under state law, exemptions existed for qualified retirement plans and IRA rollover accounts, SEPs were not included in the list of exemptions. [European American Bank v H Frenkel, Ltd, 555 NYS 2d 1016 (1990)] In another case, the court determined that a SEP was not an ERISA qualified plan subject to the anti-alienation rules and, therefore, the SEP assets were not exempt in bankruptcy. [In re Taft, No. 190-13220-352 (Bankr ED NY 1994)] Since a SEP is an IRA, the bankruptcy rules applicable to IRAs may be important (see Q 26:45).

Q 27:23   What is the savings incentive match plan for employees?

The SIMPLE plan is a new simplified retirement plan that small businesses may adopt *for years beginning after 1996.* The SIMPLE plan allows employees to make elective contributions and requires employers to make matching or nonelective contributions. The SIMPLE plan may be structured as an IRA (see chapter 26) or as a 401(k) plan (see chapter 23). SIMPLE plans are not subject to nondiscrimination rules generally applicable to qualified retirement plans, including the top-heavy rules (see chapter 22). [IRC §§ 401(k)(11), as added by SBA '96 § 1422(a), 408(p), as amended by SBA '96 § 1421(a), 416(g)(4)(G), as added by SBA '96 § 1421(b)(7)]

Q 27:24   Who may adopt a SIMPLE IRA?

Employers who employed 100 or fewer employees earning at least $5,000 in compensation for the preceding year may adopt a SIMPLE IRA. A SIMPLE IRA may not be established if the employer maintains another qualified retirement plan, tax-sheltered annuity (see Q 29:1), or SEP (see Q 27:1). The rules regarding controlled businesses (see Q 5:31), affiliated service groups (see Q 5:37), and leased employees (see Q 5:61) are applicable. [IRC §§ 408(p)(2)(C), as amended by SBA '96 § 1421(a), 408(p)(2)(D), as amended by SBA '96 § 1421(a)]

An employer who maintains a SIMPLE IRA for at least one year, but who fails to be eligible for any subsequent year may continue to maintain the plan for two years following the last year in which the employer was eligible. [IRC § 408(p)(2)(C), as amended by SBA '96 § 1421(a)]

Example. Sharon Corp. employed 95 employees in 1996 earning at least $5,000 and, in 1997, establishes a SIMPLE IRA. In 1997 and thereafter, Sharon Corp. employs more than 100 employees earning at least $5,000. Sharon Corp. may continue to maintain the SIMPLE IRA in 1998 and 1999.

Q 27:25   Who is eligible to participate in a SIMPLE IRA?

Each employee who received at least $5,000 in compensation during any two preceding years and who is reasonably expected to receive at least $5,000 in compensation during the year must be eligible to participate in the SIMPLE IRA. An employer may elect to exclude from participation union employees (as long as retirement benefits were the subject of good-faith bargaining), air pilots, and nonresident aliens. The rules regarding controlled businesses, affiliated service groups, and leased employees are applicable (see Q 27:24). [IRC §§ 408(p)(4), as amended by SBA '96 § 1421(a)]

Q 27:26   What contributions may be made to a SIMPLE IRA?

Contributions to a SIMPLE IRA are limited to employee elective contributions and required employer matching contributions and nonelective contributions. An employee may make elective contributions (expressed as a percentage of compensation) of up to $6,000 a year. The $6,000 limit is adjusted for inflation; however, an adjustment will be made only if it is $500 or greater and then will be made in multiples of $500 (i.e., rounded down to the next lowest multiple of $500).

Employers must satisfy one of two contribution requirements: (1) a matching contribution, or (2) a nonelective contribution.

Under the matching contribution requirement, employers are generally required to match the employee elective contributions in an amount up to 3 percent of the employee's compensation for the year. However, an employer may instead elect to match contributions for all eligible employees for a given year at a rate lower than 3 percent (but not lower than 1 percent) of each employee's compensation. In order to utilize the lower matching percentage, the employer must notify employees of the lower percentage within a reasonable time before the 60-day election period during which employees are allowed to determine whether to participate in the SIMPLE plan (see Q 27:27). In addition, the lower percentage may not be elected for a year if it would cause the matching percentage to drop below 3 percent of employee compensation in more than two years in a five-year period ending with that year.

As an alternative, in lieu of making matching contributions, an employer may elect to make a nonelective contribution of 2 percent of compensation for each eligible employee who has earned at least $5,000 in compensation from the employer during the year. The employer is required to notify each eligible employee of the nonelective contributions within a reasonable period of time before the 60-day election period.

[IRC § 408(p)(2), as amended by SBA '96 § 1421(a)]

All contributions made to an employee's SIMPLE IRA must be nonforfeitable. Thus, contributions made by the employer vest immediately. [IRC § 408(p)(3), as amended by SBA '96 § 1421(a)]

Q 27:27 What are the administrative requirements regarding SIMPLE IRAs?

Employers must contribute an employee's elective deferrals to the employee's SIMPLE IRA no later than 30 days after the last day of the month for which the contributions are made. An employer must make matching contributions by the date that its tax return for the tax year is due (including extensions). [IRC §§ 404(m), as added by SBA '96 § 1421(b), 408(p)(5)(A), as amended by SBA '96 § 1421(a)]

An employee may terminate participation in the SIMPLE plan by discontinuing contributions at any time during the year. However, a plan may prohibit the employee from resuming participation until the beginning of the following year. [IRC § 408(p)(5)(B), as amended by SBA '96 § 1421(a)]

An eligible employee may elect to participate in the SIMPLE plan during the 60-day period before the beginning of the year (or the 60-day period before the employee becomes eligible to participate). During this period, the employee may also modify the contribution amount previously elected. The plan may also allow a participant to reduce the contribution percentage or to otherwise change the salary reduction contribution election during the year. [IRC § 408(p)(5)(C), as amended by SBA '96 § 1421(a)]

An employer may make contributions on behalf of eligible employees to a designated trustee or annuity contract issuer. Plan participants must be notified in writing that the account balance may be transferred without cost or penalty to another individual account or annuity. [IRC § 408(p)(7), as amended by SBA '96 § 1421(a)]

Q 27:28 How are SIMPLE IRA contributions and distributions treated?

Employers may generally deduct contributions (including employee elective deferrals) to the SIMPLE account for the employer's taxable year with or within which the calendar year for which the contributions were made ends. An employer may deduct the contributions for its taxable year only if the contributions are made by the date the employer's tax return is due (including extensions). [IRC § 404(m), as added by SBA '96 § 1421(b)(2)]

Contributions to a SIMPLE account are excludable from an employee's income, and distributions from a SIMPLE account are generally taxed like distributions from an IRA. Accordingly, distributions are includible in a participant's income when withdrawn from the account.

Participants may roll over distributions from one SIMPLE account to another and may also roll over a distribution from a SIMPLE account to an IRA tax free, without penalty, if the individual has participated in the SIMPLE plan for two years. However, distributions may *not* be rolled over to a qualified retirement plan. [IRC §§ 72(t)(6), as added by SBA '96 § 1421(b)(4), 408(d)(3)(G), as added by SBA '96 § 1421(b)(3)] The procedures for rolling over distributions from the SIMPLE account must be fully disclosed in the summary description provided by the trustee to the employer (see Q 27:29).

A participant who takes a distribution from a SIMPLE account before age 59½ may be subject to the 10 percent penalty tax applicable to IRAs (see Q 26:41). However, a participant who takes a distribution during the two-year period beginning on the date the participant began participating in the SIMPLE plan will be assessed a *25 percent* penalty tax. [IRC § 72(t)(6), as added by SBA '96 § 1421(b)(4)]

Q 27:29   What are the reporting requirements for a SIMPLE IRA?

The trustee of a SIMPLE IRA must, on an annual basis, provide the employer maintaining the plan with a summary description containing the following information:

1. The name and address of the employer and trustee;
2. The requirements for eligibility for participation;
3. The benefits provided under the plan;
4. The time and method of making elections; and
5. The procedures for, and effect of, withdrawals (including rollovers) from the plan account.

[IRC § 408(l), as amended by SBA '96 § 1421(b)(5); ERISA § 101(g), as amended by SBA '96 § 1421(d)(1)]

The trustee must also provide an account statement to each individual for whom the SIMPLE account is maintained within 30 days after each calendar year. The statement must reflect the account balance at the end of the year and the account activity during the year. The trustee must also file a report each calendar year with IRS. [IRC § 408(i), as amended by SBA '96 § 1421(b)(6)] Trustees who fail to provide the summary description, the account statement, or the annual report are subject to a penalty of $50 for each day such failure continues. The penalty may be waived if the failure was due to reasonable cause. [IRC §§ 6693(a), as amended by SBA '96 § 1455(d)(3) and HIPA § 301(g)(1), 6693(c), as amended by SBA '96 § 1421(b)(4)(B)]

Employers maintaining a SIMPLE plan are not required to file annual reports. However, employers must notify each employee of the employee's right to make salary reduction contributions under the plan, as well as the contribution alternative elected by the employer (see Q 27:26). The notice must include a copy of the summary description prepared by the trustee for the employer and must be provided immediately before the period during which an employee may make an election (see Q 27:27). [IRC § 408(l), as amended by SBA '96 § 1421(b)(6)] Employers who fail to provide such notice are subject to a penalty of $50 for each day such failure continues. The penalty may be waived if the failure was due to reasonable cause. [IRC § 6693(c), as amended by SBA '96 § 1421(b)(4)(B)]

Q 27:30   What special rules apply to a SIMPLE 401(k) plan?

Employers who employed 100 or fewer employees earning at least $5,000 in compensation for the preceding year may adopt a SIMPLE plan as part of a 401(k) arrangement. The nondiscrimination rules generally applicable to elective deferrals (ADP test; see Q 23:8) and employer matching contributions (ACP test; see Q 23:48) under a 401(k) plan are deemed to be met if:

1. No contributions are made or benefits accrue on behalf of any eligible employee under any other retirement plan of the employer;

2. Contributions made under the SIMPLE plan are fully vested; and

3. With respect to contributions:

   a. An employee's elective deferrals for the year, expressed as a percentage of compensation, do not exceed $6,000 (there appears to be no adjustments for inflation; see Q 27:26);

   b. The employer makes contributions matching the employee's elective deferrals in an amount up to 3 percent of the employee's compensation for the year or makes a nonelective contribution of 2 percent of compensation for each eligible employee who has earned at least $5,000 in compensation from the employer for the year; and

   c. No other contributions are made under the arrangement.

Under a SIMPLE 401(k) plan, the employer does not have the option available under a SIMPLE IRA of reducing the matching contribution to less than 3 percent of an employee's compensation (see Q 27:26).

Employers who decide to make the 2 percent nonelective contribution must notify employees of the election within a reasonable period of time before the 60th day before the beginning of the plan year (see Q 27:27).

Although a SIMPLE 401(k) plan is not subject to the top-heavy rules (see chapter 22), the arrangement is subject to the other rules governing qualified retirement plans.

[IRC § 401(k)(11), as added by SBA '96 § 1422(a)]

Chapter 28

Rollovers

It is possible to postpone payment of taxes on certain distributions from a qualified retirement plan by transferring (rolling over) all or part of the distribution to an individual retirement account (IRA) or to another qualified retirement plan. In addition, money contributed to one IRA can be withdrawn and transferred to another IRA without tax or penalty. This chapter examines how rollovers work and describes the tax advantages and drawbacks involved.

Q 28:1 What is a rollover?

A rollover is a tax-free transfer of cash or other property from a qualified retirement plan to an individual and then from the individual to another qualified retirement plan. There are two types of rollovers to an IRA. First, amounts may be transferred from one IRA to another. Second, amounts may be transferred from a qualified retirement plan to an IRA. A rollover from one qualified retirement plan to another is also possible, as is a rollover to a qualified retirement plan from an IRA if all amounts in the IRA are attributable to an earlier rollover contribution from a qualified retirement plan (see Q 28:40). However, an individual cannot roll over a distribution from a qualified retirement plan to an IRA of the individual's spouse (see Q 28:19). [IRC §§ 402(c), 408(d); Rodoni, 105 TC 29 (1995); Ltr Rul 9315031]

An individual who received a distribution from a qualified retirement plan and used the distribution to improve his residence and pay off a portion of his mortgage was taxable on the entire distribution. His argument that applying the distribution in this manner was akin to rolling over the distribution into his own private retirement plan was without merit. [Luke, 66 TCM 615 (1993); see also Grow, 70 TCM 1576 (1995)]

The distribution of the entire amount credited to an individual under an annuity contract that had been distributed to the individual from a previously terminated qualified retirement plan was eligible to be rolled over into an IRA. [Ltr Rul 9338041; Notice 93-26, 1993-1 CB 308]

If a distribution from a qualified retirement plan is rolled over, five-year forward averaging treatment will *not* be available for any subsequent distribution to the employee from the distributing plan or from any other qualified retirement plan aggregated with the distributing plan (see Qs 13:5, 13:13). [IRC § 402(c)(10)]

For new rules that may apply to a rollover made from an IRA to an American Dream IRA (AD IRA) or to a Special Individual Retirement Account (Special IRA), see Q 28:45.

Q 28:2 What are IRA rollover accounts?

An IRA rollover account is an individual retirement plan to which certain distributions from a qualified retirement plan or from another individual retirement plan have been transferred. The transfer is on a tax-free basis. There is no dollar limit on the amount that may be transferred into an IRA rollover account. [IRC §§ 402(c)(2), 408(d)(3)]

A distribution from a qualified retirement plan may be rolled over to any type of individual retirement plan except an endowment contract (see Q 26:3). [IRC §§ 402(c)(8)(B)(i), 402(c)(8)(B)(ii)]

Nondeductible employee contributions to a qualified retirement plan that are included in the distribution may not be rolled over to an IRA. Instead, they are returned to the employee tax-free. Any distribution that represents a participant's investment in the contract or basis (see Q 13:2) may not be rolled over and is received tax-free. See Q 28:42 for details of a conduit IRA.

Q 28:3 How does a rollover from one IRA to another work?

All or part of the money contributed to a particular IRA may be withdrawn and transferred (rolled over) to another IRA without tax or penalty. This gives the IRA participant flexibility by enabling the participant to shift investments. For example, the participant may shift from one annuity IRA to another or, seeking higher interest or dividends, from one trusteed IRA to another.

To make the switch, certain requirements must be met. To qualify for a tax-free rollover:

1. The amount distributed to the individual from the old account must be transferred to the new account not later than 60 days after receipt (see Q 28:39). [Duralia, 67 TCM 3084 (1994)]

2. If property, other than cash, is received from the old account, that same property must be transferred to the new account.

3. If a tax-free rollover of a particular IRA has been made during the preceding 12-month period, a second (tax-free) rollover from that IRA is not permitted (see Q 28:5). [IRC § 408(d)(3); Treas Reg § 1.402(c)-2, Q&A 16; Martin, 63 TCM 3122 (1992); Ltr Rul 8502044]

Example 1. On January 10, 1997, Paul receives a first distribution from IRA X and, on January 23, 1997, deposits the distribution in IRA Y. Since Paul did not receive any distributions from IRA X during the preceding 12-month period, the rollover from IRA X to IRA Y is permitted.

Example 2. On January 30, 1997, Paul receives a second distribution from IRA X and, on March 6, 1997, deposits this distribution in IRA Y. Even though the distribution is rolled over within the 60-day period, this rollover is *not* permitted because Paul received the first rollover distribution from IRA X within the preceding 12-month period. [Ltr Rul 9308050]

To avoid the adverse consequences resulting to Paul in Example 2, Paul could have had the funds in IRA X transferred directly to IRA Y (see Q 28:5).

Involuntary distributions made by the Resolution Trust Corporation from an IRA held in an insolvent financial institution may be rolled over to another IRA even if the amount had been rolled over to the IRA within the preceding 12-month period. [IRS Spec Rul, Feb 5, 1991]

For new rules that may apply to a rollover made from an IRA to an AD IRA or to a Special IRA, see Q 28:45.

Q 28:4   May an individual borrow from an IRA?

No, but IRS has ruled that the requirements for a valid rollover are met when an individual receives a distribution from an IRA and the distribution is redeposited in the same IRA within 60 days. Such a transaction will constitute a tax-free rollover and not be subject to the excess contribution limits (see Q 26:6). [IRC §§ 408(e), 4975(d); Ltr Ruls 9010007, 8826009]

Example. Susan has a $10,000 certificate of deposit (CD) maturing in 45 days. Susan has a $4,000 tuition payment due now and does not want to cash in the CD early. Susan withdraws $4,000 from her IRA and makes the tuition payment. When the CD matures, Susan immediately repays the $4,000 to her IRA. The withdrawal and redeposit are tax-free.

Q 28:5 May more than one tax-free transfer between IRAs be made during a 12-month period?

Yes, but only if the individual has the funds in an IRA transferred from the IRA *directly* to another IRA. Because this type of transfer is not considered a rollover, the 12-month waiting period (see Q 28:3) does not apply. [Ltr Ruls 9438019, 9416037, 9106044, 9034068; IRS Pub 590 (for use in preparing 1995 returns); see Martin, 63 TCM 3122 (1992) and Martin, 67 TCM 2960 (1994); Ltr Rul 9308050]

Further, if the individual has more than one IRA, a separate 12-month waiting period applies for each IRA. [Prop Reg § 1.408-4(b)(4)(ii)]

A rollover from a qualified retirement plan to an IRA (see Q 28:37) is not treated as a rollover contribution for purposes of the 12-month waiting period rule. [Treas Reg § 1.402(c)-2, Q&A 16]

Q 28:6 May a beneficiary of an IRA roll over the proceeds at the death of the owner of the IRA?

Yes, but only if the beneficiary is the *surviving spouse* of the IRA's owner. [IRC § 408(d)(3)(C)(ii)(II); Ltr Ruls 9426049, 9011035]

IRS has ruled that a surviving spouse may roll over funds received from the deceased spouse's IRA if the funds were paid to the surviving spouse under the laws of intestacy (i.e., the decedent died without a will), as a beneficiary of the decedent's estate, as the result of a disclaimer (see Q 4:24), or as a beneficiary of a trust created by the decedent, rather than as the designated beneficiary of the IRA. Generally, a rollover by the surviving spouse is permitted where there is no discretion on the part of someone other than the surviving spouse (e.g., the surviving spouse is the sole beneficiary of the estate or the surviving spouse may withdraw the funds from the trust). [Ltr Ruls 9626049, 9623064, 9623056, 9620038, 9615043, 9611057, 9609052]

An IRA acquired by a beneficiary upon the death of a nonspouse is an inherited IRA and does not qualify for rollover treatment (see Q 26:38). [IRC § 408(d)(3)(C); Ltr Ruls 9504045, 9305025, 9250040, 9014071, 8623054] IRS has ruled that a surviving spouse could *not* roll over an IRA distribution from a trust created by the deceased spouse. Because the surviving spouse had no discretionary control over the trust, the IRA was considered an inherited IRA, ineligible for rollover treatment. [Ltr Ruls 9445029, 9416045, 9303031]

Q 28:7   What types of distributions from a qualified retirement plan may be rolled over?

For qualified retirement plan distributions made after 1992, only an eligible rollover distribution (see Q 28:8) may be rolled over. [IRC § 402(c)]

Q 28:8   What is an eligible rollover distribution?

An eligible rollover distribution is any distribution to an employee of all or any portion of the employee's qualified retirement plan benefit *except*:

1. A required minimum distribution (see Q 28:11);

2. A distribution that is one of a series of substantially equal periodic payments (at least annually) made (a) over the life or life expectancy of the employee or over the joint lives or joint life expectancy of the employee and the employee's beneficiary or (b) over a specified period of *ten* or more years (see Q 28:9);

3. The portion of any distribution that is not includible in gross income (determined without regard to the exclusion for net unrealized appreciation) (see Qs 13:2, 13:17);

4. Elective contributions (see Q 23:13) that are returned as a result of Section 415 limitations (see Q 23:26), together with the income allocable to these corrective distributions;

5. Corrective distributions of excess contributions (see Q 23:17) and excess deferrals (see Q 23:28) and corrective distributions of excess aggregate contributions (see Q 23:54), together with the income allocable to these corrective distributions;

6. Loans in default that are deemed distributions (see Qs 28:14–28:16);

7. Dividends paid on employee stock ownership plan (ESOP) employer securities (see Q 24:13); and

8. The costs of life insurance coverage (PS-58 costs; see Q 14:7).

[IRC § 402(c)(4); Treas Reg § 1.402(c)-2, Q&A 3, Q&A 4]

An eligible rollover distribution is subject to automatic 20 percent withholding unless the distribution is transferred by a direct rollover (see Q 28:20) to an eligible retirement plan (see Q 28:19) that permits the acceptance of rollover distributions (see Q 16:7). To be a qualified retirement plan, the plan *must* provide that if the distributee of an eligible rollover distribution elects to have the distribution paid directly to an eligible retirement plan, and specifies the eligible retirement plan to which the distribution will be paid, then the distribution will be paid to that eligible retirement plan in a direct rollover. Thus, the plan *must* give the distributee the option of having the distribution paid in a direct rollover to an eligible retirement plan specified by the distributee. [IRC §§ 401(a)(31), 3405(c); Treas Reg §§ 1.401(a)(31)-1, Q&A 1(a), 1.402(c)-2, Q&A 1(a)]

An individual participated in a qualified retirement plan that was terminated, and the individual received the distribution of his entire benefits in the form of an annuity contract. Subsequently, the individual received a distribution of the entire amount credited under the annuity contract and rolled the distribution over to an IRA. IRS ruled that the distribution from the annuity contract was an eligible rollover distribution. [Ltr Rul 9338041; Notice 93-26, 1993-1 CB 308]

If a qualified retirement plan holds illiquid, nonmarketable assets, IRS has ruled that a distribution of both liquid assets and an interest in the illiquid assets can constitute an eligible rollover distribution. An independent, nonqualified trust is established, and the illiquid assets are transferred to the nonqualified trust. Each participant, in addition to receiving a distribution of liquid assets, receives a transferable certificate representing the participant's interest in the nonqualified trust. This total distribution may also qualify for favorable income tax treatment (see Q 13:6). [Ltr Ruls 9507032, 9421041, 9418028, 9417041]

Q 28:9   What is a series of substantially equal periodic payments?

One of the exceptions to the 10 percent penalty tax (see Q 13:39) is for a distribution that is part of a series of substantially equal periodic payments. To determine whether a series of payments is a series of substantially equal periodic payments, and therefore not an eligible rollover distribution (see Q 28:8), generally the same principles are followed (see Q 13:40). Whether the series is one of substantially equal periodic payments over a specified period of *ten* or more years is generally determined at the time payments begin without regard to contingencies or modifications that have not yet occurred. For example, a joint and survivor annuity with a 50 percent survivor annuity to the participant's spouse will be treated as a series of substantially equal payments at the time payments commence, as will a joint and survivor annuity that provides for increased payments to the participant if the participant's spouse dies before the participant. [IRC §§ 72(t)(2)(A)(iv), 402(c)(4)(A); Treas Reg § 1.402(c)-2, Q&A 5(a)]

For purposes of determining whether a distribution is one of a series of payments that are substantially equal, Social Security supplements are disregarded. Similarly, a series of payments that is not substantially equal but that generally produces a series of substantially equal payments when expected Social Security payments are taken into account, is treated as substantially equal for purposes of determining whether a distribution is an eligible rollover distribution.

> **Example.** Judy will receive a life annuity from the PJK Corp. pension plan of $500 per month, plus a Social Security supplement consisting of payments of $200 per month until Judy reaches the age at which Social Security benefits begin. The $200 supplemental payments are disregarded so that each monthly payment of $700 made before the Social Security age and each monthly payment of $500 made after the Social Security age will be treated as one of a series of substantially equal periodic payments for life. Therefore, each monthly payment to Judy will not be an eligible rollover distribution. [Treas Reg § 1.402(c)-2, Q&A 5(b); Ltr Rul 9601054]

If the amount (or, if applicable, the method of calculating the amount) of the payments changes so that subsequent payments are not substantially equal to prior payments, a new determination must be made as to whether the remaining payments are a series of substantially equal periodic payments over a period specified in paragraph 2 of Q 28:8. This determination is made without taking into account payments made or the years of payment that elapsed prior to the change. However, a new determination is not made merely because, upon the death of the employee, the spouse of the employee becomes the distributee. Thus, once distributions commence over a period that is at least as long as either the employee's life or ten years (e.g., as provided by a life annuity with a five-year or ten-year-certain guarantee), then substantially equal payments to the survivor are not eligible rollover distributions (see Q 28:18) even though the payment period remaining after the death of the employee is or may be less than ten years. For example, substantially equal periodic payments made under a life annuity with a five-year term certain would not be an eligible rollover distribution even when paid after the death of the employee with only three years remaining under the term certain. [Treas Reg § 1.402(c)-2, Q&A 5(c)]

The following rules apply to determining whether a series of payments from a defined contribution plan (see Q 2:2) constitute substantially equal periodic payments for a period of at least ten years:

1. *Declining balance of years.* A series of payments from an account balance under a defined contribution plan will be considered substantially equal payments over a period, if, for each year, the amount of the distribution is calculated by dividing the account balance by the number of years remaining in the period. For example, a series of payments will be considered substantially equal payments over ten years if the series is determined as follows: in year 1, the annual payment is the account balance

divided by 10; in year 2, the annual payment is the remaining account balance divided by 9; and so on until year 10 when the entire remaining balance is distributed.

2. *Reasonable actuarial assumptions.* If an employee's account balance under a defined contribution plan will be distributed in annual installments of a specified amount until the account balance is exhausted, then, for purposes of determining if the period of distribution is at least ten years, the period of years over which the installments will be distributed must be determined using reasonable actuarial assumptions. For example, if an employee has an account balance of $100,000, elects distributions of $12,000 per year until the account balance is exhausted, and the future rate of return is assumed to be 8 percent per year, the account balance will be exhausted in approximately 14 years. Similarly, if the same employee elects a fixed annual distribution amount and the fixed annual amount is less than or equal to $10,000, it is reasonable to assume that a future rate of return will be greater than zero percent and, thus, the account will not be exhausted in less than ten years. [Treas Reg § 1.402(c)-2, Q&A 5(d)]

If a series of periodic payments began before January 1, 1993, the determination of whether the post-December 31, 1992 payments are a series of substantially equal periodic payments over a specified period of *ten* or more years is made by taking into account all payments made, including payments made before January 1, 1993. [Treas Reg § 1.402(c)-2, Q&A 5(e)]

Example 1. Paul commenced receiving a series of substantially equal periodic payments on January 1, 1984, which were scheduled to be paid over a period of 15 years. Payments in the series that are made after December 31, 1992 will not be eligible rollover distributions even though they will continue for only six years after December 31, 1992, because the pre-January 1, 1993 payments are taken into account in determining the specified period.

Example 2. If the series commenced on January 1, 1991 and were scheduled to be paid over seven years, each payment made in the series after December 31, 1992 will be an eligible rollover distribution because the total specified period is less than ten years.

Where an individual elected to receive monthly payments from a qualified retirement plan over six years, each monthly payment was an eligible rollover distribution. [Ltr Rul 9429026]

Q 28:10 If a payment is independent of a series of substantially equal periodic payments that are not eligible rollover distributions, can that payment be an eligible rollover distribution?

Yes. A payment is treated as independent of the payments in a series if the payment is substantially larger or smaller than the other payments in the series (see Q 28:9). An independent payment is an eligible rollover distribution (see Q 28:8) if it is not otherwise excepted from the definition of eligible rollover distributions. This is the case regardless of whether the payment is made before, with, or after payments in the series. [Treas Reg § 1.402(c)-2, Q&A 6(a)]

Example 1. Bob elects a single payment of half of his account balance under The Gordons of Chappaqua, Inc. profit sharing plan, with the remainder of his account balance to be paid over his life expectancy. The single payment is treated as independent of the payments in the series and is an eligible rollover distribution unless otherwise excepted.

Example 2. If a participant's surviving spouse receives a survivor life annuity of $1,000 per month plus a single payment of $5,000, the single payment is treated as independent of the annuity payments and is an eligible rollover distribution unless otherwise excepted.

If, due solely to reasonable administrative error or delay in payment, there is an adjustment after the annuity starting date (see Q 10:3) to the amount of any payment in a series of payments that otherwise would constitute a series of substantially equal payments, the adjusted payment or payments will be treated as part of the series of substantially equal periodic payments and will not be treated as independent of the payments in the series. For example, if, due solely to reasonable administrative delay, the first payment of a life annuity is delayed by two months and reflects an additional two months worth of benefits, that payment will be treated as a substantially equal payment in the series rather than as an independent payment. The result will not change merely because the amount of the adjustment is paid in a separate supplemental payment. [Treas Reg § 1.402(c)-2, Q&A 6(b)(1)]

A supplemental payment from a defined benefit plan (see Q 2:3) to annuitants (e.g., retirees or beneficiaries) will be treated as part of a series of substantially equal payments, rather than as an independent payment, provided that the following conditions are met:

1. The supplement is a benefit increase for annuitants;

2. The amount of the supplement is determined in a consistent manner for all similarly situated annuitants;

3. The supplement is paid to annuitants who are otherwise receiving payments that would constitute substantially equal periodic payments; and

4. The aggregate supplement is less than or equal to the greater of 10 percent of the annual rate of payment for the annuity or $750 (or any higher amount prescribed by IRS). [Treas Reg § 1.402(c)-2, Q&A 6(b)(2)]

If a payment in a series of payments from an account balance under a defined contribution plan (see Q 2:2) represents the remaining balance to the credit and is substantially less than the other payments in the series, the final payment must nevertheless be treated as a payment in the series of substantially equal payments and may not be treated as an independent payment if the other payments in the series are substantially equal and the payments are for a period of at least ten years. Thus, such final payment will not be an eligible rollover distribution. [Treas Reg § 1.402(c)-2, Q&A 6(b)(3)]

Q 28:11   When is a distribution from a plan a required minimum distribution?

A required minimum distribution is not an eligible rollover distribution (see Q 28:8). If a minimum distribution is required for a calendar year, all amounts distributed during that calendar year are treated as required minimum distributions as long as the total required minimum distribution for that calendar year has not been made. [Treas Reg § 1.402(c)-2, Q&A 7(a)]

Example. Linda is required to receive a minimum distribution from The Gordons of Chappaqua, Inc. profit sharing plan in 1997 of $21,000. During 1997, Linda receives four quarterly distributions of $7,500 each. The first two distributions and $6,000 of the third distribution are required minimum distributions. However, the remaining $1,500 of the third distribution and all of the fourth distribution are not required minimum distributions because these are the amounts by which the total of the distributions exceeds the required minimum distribution.

If the total amount that is required to be distributed for a calendar year in order to satisfy the minimum distribution requirements is not distributed in that calendar year, the amount that was required but not distributed is added to the amount required to be distributed for the next calendar year in determining the portion of any distribution in the next calendar year that is a required distribution.

Example. Bob should have received, but did not receive, a minimum distribution in 1996 of $8,000. For 1997, Bob should receive a minimum distribution of $6,000. Bob's required minimum distribution for 1997 is $14,000.

Any amount paid before January 1 of the year in which the employee attains age 70½ will not be treated as a required minimum distribution and, thus, is an eligible rollover distribution if it otherwise qualifies. Conversely, any amount paid on or after January 1 of the year in which the employee attains age 70½ will be treated as a required minimum distribution and, hence, not an eligible rollover distribution. [Treas Reg § 1.402(c)-2, Q&A 7(b)]

Example. Shirley attains age 70½ on December 30, 1997 and has a required beginning date of April 1, 1998 (see Q 11:3). Shirley's required minimum distribution to be made on or before April 1, 1998 is $20,000, and she is paid that amount on June 21, 1997. Even though Shirley is only age 69 on June 21, 1997, the distribution is a required minimum distribution and, thus, is not an eligible rollover distribution.

Proposed regulations issued by IRS in 1987 imply that annuity payments from a defined benefit plan (see Q 2:3) may be required minimum distributions even if annuity payments are made before the employee attains age 70½ and for a period of less than ten years (see Qs 11:4, 11:6). To clarify this issue, IRS has provided two rules:

1. Annuity payments made in or after the year in which the employee is 70½ are required minimum distributions and, hence, not eligible rollover distributions.

2. Annuity payments made before the year in which the employee is 70½ are not required minimum distributions and, hence, are eligible rollover distributions.

[Treas Reg § 1.402(c)-2, Q&A 7(c)]

If the required minimum distribution has not yet been made to an employee, a distribution is then made to the employee that exceeds the required minimum distribution, and a portion of that distribution is excludible from gross income (see Q 13:2), the following rule applies for purposes of determining the amount of the distribution that is an eligible rollover distribution. The portion of the distribution that is excludible from gross income is first allocated toward satisfaction of the required minimum distribution and then the remaining portion of the required minimum distribution, if any, is satisfied from the portion of the distribution that is includible in gross income. [Treas Reg § 1.402(c)-2, Q&A 8]

Example. Norman is required to receive a minimum distribution of $4,000, and he receives a $4,800 distribution, of which $1,000 is excludible from income as a return of basis. First, the $1,000 return of basis is allocated toward satisfying the required minimum distribution. Then, the remaining $3,000 of the required minimum distribution is satisfied from the $3,800 of the distribution that is includible in gross income, so that the remaining balance of the distribution, $800, is an eligible rollover distribution if it otherwise qualifies.

For a detailed discussion of the minimum distribution requirements, see chapter 11.

Q 28:12 How is the $5,000 death benefit exclusion treated for purposes of determining the amount that is an eligible rollover distribution?

To the extent that a death benefit is a distribution from a qualified retirement plan, is paid to the deceased employee's surviving spouse, and qualifies for the $5,000 death benefit exclusion, the portion of the distribution that is excluded from gross income is not an eligible rollover distribution (see Q 28:8). [IRC § 101(b); Treas Reg § 1.402(c)-2, Q&A 14]

A plan administrator (see Q 16:1) is permitted to assume that a distribution from the plan that qualifies for the $5,000 death benefit exclusion is the only death benefit being paid with respect to a deceased employee that qualifies for that exclusion. Thus, to the extent that such a distribution would be excludable from gross income based on this assumption, the plan administrator is permitted to assume that it is not an eligible rollover distribution. However, even though the plan administrator assumes that the distribution is the only death benefit that qualifies for the $5,000 death benefit exclusion, to the extent that the death benefit exclusion is allocated to a different death benefit, a greater portion of the distribution may actually be includible in gross income and, thus, be an eligible rollover distribution, so that the surviving spouse may roll over the additional amount if it otherwise qualifies. [Treas Reg §§ 1.401(a)(31)-1, Q&A 17, 1.402(c)-2, Q&A 15]

The $5,000 death benefit exlusion has been repealed with respect to decedents dying after August 20, 1996 (see Q 14:11).

Q 28:13 May an employee roll over more than the plan administrator determines to be an eligible rollover distribution?

A plan administrator (see Q 16:1) may make certain assumptions in determining the amount of a distribution that is an eligible rollover distribution (see Q 28:8). In addition to the assumption concerning the $5,000 death benefit exclusion (see Q 28:12), the plan administrator may assume that, for the purpose of determining the required minimum distribution amount, there is no designated beneficiary (see Q 11:8). [Treas Reg § 1.401(a)(31)-1, Q&A 17]

Even though the plan administrator calculates the portion of a distribution that is a required minimum distribution (and thus not an eligible rollover distribution) by assuming that there is no designated beneficiary, the portion of the distribution that is actually a required minimum distribution is determined by taking into account the designated beneficiary, if any. If, by taking into account the designated beneficiary, a greater portion of the distribution is an eligible rollover distribution, the employee may roll over the additional amount. [Treas Reg § 1.402(c)-2, Q&A 15]

Q 28:14   How are participant loans treated?

Loans to a participant from a qualified retirement plan can give rise to two types of distributions:

1. A deemed distribution (see Qs 13:44–13:52), and

2. A distribution of a plan loan offset amount.

A deemed distribution occurs when certain requirements are not satisfied, either when the loan is made or at a later time, such as when the loan is in default. A deemed distribution is treated as a distribution to the participant only for income tax purposes and is not a distribution of the participant's accrued benefit (see Q 9:2).

A distribution of a plan loan offset amount occurs when the participant's accrued benefit is reduced (offset) in order to repay the loan. A distribution of a plan loan offset amount can occur in a variety of circumstances, such as where the plan requires that, in the event of the participant's termination of employment, a loan be repaid immediately or treated as in default. A distribution of a plan loan offset amount also occurs when the loan is cancelled, accelerated, or treated as if it were in default (e.g., where the plan treats a loan as in default upon an employee's termination of employment or within a specified period thereafter). A distribution of a plan loan offset amount is an actual distribution, not a deemed distribution. [Treas Reg § 1.402(c)-2, Q&A 4, Q&A 9(b); Caton, 69 TCM 1937 (1995)]

Q 28:15 When is a distribution attributable to a plan loan an eligible rollover distribution?

The only type of distribution related to a plan loan that cannot be an eligible rollover distribution (see Q 28:8) is a deemed distribution (see Q 28:14). In contrast, when a participant terminates employment and the participant's accrued benefit (see Q 9:2) is offset by the amount of an unpaid plan loan balance, the plan loan offset amount (see Q 28:14) can be an eligible rollover distribution (see Q 28:16). Thus, an amount equal to the plan loan offset amount can be rolled over by the employee (or spousal distributee) to an eligible retirement plan within the 60-day period (see Q 28:37) unless the plan loan offset amount fails to be an eligible rollover distribution for another reason.

An offset amount to repay a plan loan can be an eligible rollover distribution whether or not the offset occurs after the participant's employment has terminated. Similarly, a plan loan offset amount can be an eligible rollover distribution even if the offset occurs because the loan is accelerated or is treated as if it were in default (e.g., where the plan treats a loan as in default upon termination of employment or within a specified period thereafter). [Treas Reg § 1.402(c)-2, Q&A 9(a), Q&A 9(b)]

Q 28:16 Must a direct rollover option be provided for an offset amount that is an eligible rollover distribution?

A plan will *not* fail to satisfy the direct rollover requirement (see Q 28:8) merely because the plan does not permit a participant to elect a direct rollover (see Q 28:20) of a plan loan offset amount (see Q 28:14) that is an eligible rollover distribution (see Q 28:8). Nevertheless, the amount by which a participant's accrued benefit (see Q 9:2) is offset to repay a plan loan can be an eligible rollover distribution (see Q 28:15). Thus, an amount equal to the plan loan offset amount can be rolled over by the participant to an eligible retirement plan (see Q 28:19) within 60 days (see Q 28:37) unless the plan loan offset amount fails to be an eligible rollover distribution for another reason. [Treas Reg §§ 1.401(a)(31)-1, Q&A 15, 1.402(c)-2, Q&A 9]

> **Example 1.** In 1997, Dale has an account balance of $10,000 in Stu 'N Dale Corporation's profit sharing plan, of which $3,000 is represented by a plan loan secured by her account balance. The plan does not provide any direct rollover option with respect to plan loans. Upon termination of employment in 1997, Dale, who is under age 70½, elects a distribution of her entire account balance, and her outstanding loan is offset against the account balance on distribution. Dale elects a direct rollover of $7,000. When Dale's account balance was offset by the amount of the

$3,000 unpaid loan balance, she received a plan loan offset amount (equivalent to $3,000) that is an eligible rollover distribution. Dale may roll over $3,000 to an eligible retirement plan within 60 days.

Example 2. The facts are the same as in Example 1, except that the plan provides that, upon termination of employment, Dale's account balance is automatically offset by the amount of the unpaid loan balance. Dale terminates employment but does not request a distribution from the plan. The $3,000 offset amount attributable to the plan loan in this example is treated in the same manner as the $3,000 offset amount in Example 1.

Example 3. The facts are the same as in Example 2, except that, instead of providing for an automatic offset upon termination of employment, the plan requires full repayment of the loan by Dale within 30 days of termination. Dale terminates employment, does not elect a distribution from the plan, and also fails to repay the plan loan within 30 days. The plan declares the plan loan in default and executes on the loan by offsetting Dale's account balance by $3,000. The $3,000 offset amount in this example is treated in the same manner as the $3,000 offset amount in Examples 1 and 2. The result in this example is the same even though the plan treats the loan as in default before offsetting Dale's accrued benefit by the amount of the unpaid loan.

Example 4. Stuart, who is age 50, has an account balance in the Lori-Dana Corp. 401(k) plan. In 1994, Stuart made a plan loan that is secured by elective contributions; and, in 1997, Stuart stops repayment. In 1997, Stuart is taxed on a deemed distribution equal to the amount of the unpaid loan balance. The deemed distribution is *not* an eligible rollover distribution. Because Stuart has not separated from service or experienced any other event that permits the distribution of his elective contributions that secure the loan, the plan is prohibited from executing on the loan. Accordingly, Stuart's account balance is not offset by the amount of the unpaid loan balance at the time he stops repayment on the loan. Thus, there is no distribution of an offset amount that is an eligible rollover distribution in 1997. However, Stuart has basis (see Q 13:2) in his account balance to the extent of the deemed distribution. In 1998, Stuart separates from service and is eligible, and elects, to receive a total distribution of his account balance. As part of the distribution to Stuart, his account balance is offset by the amount of the unpaid loan balance. Although an offset amount can generally be part of an eligible rollover distribution, the portion of the distribution to Stuart that equals the amount of the prior deemed distribution will not be eligible for rollover because it is not includible in his gross income.

Q 28:17   How is a qualified retirement plan distributed annuity contract treated?

A qualified retirement plan distributed annuity contract is an annuity contract purchased for a participant, and distributed to the participant, by a qualified retirement plan. [Treas Reg § 1.402(c)-2, Q&A 10(a)]

Amounts paid under a qualified retirement plan distributed annuity contract are eligible rollover distributions if they otherwise qualify (see Q 28:8). For example, if the employee surrenders the contract for a single-sum payment of its cash surrender value, the payment would be an eligible rollover distribution to the extent it is includible in gross income and not a required minimum distribution. This rule applies even if the annuity contract is distributed in connection with a plan termination. If any amount to be distributed under a qualified retirement plan distributed annuity contract is an eligible rollover distribution, the annuity contract must satisfy the direct rollover requirements in the same manner as a qualified retirement plan. In the case of a qualified retirement plan distributed annuity contract, the payor under the contract is treated as the plan administrator (see Q 16:1). [Treas Reg §§ 1.401(a)(31)-1, Q&A 16, 1.402(c)-2, Q&A 10(b); Ltr Rul 9338041; Notice 93-26, 1993-1 CB 308]

Q 28:18   Can a person other than an employee receive an eligible rollover distribution?

If a distribution attributable to an employee is paid to the employee's surviving spouse, the rollover rules apply to the distribution in the same manner as if the spouse were the employee. The same rules apply if a distribution is paid to a spouse or former spouse as an alternate payee (see Q 30:3) under a qualified domestic relations order (QDRO; see Q 30:1). Therefore, a distribution to the surviving spouse of an employee (or to a spouse or former spouse as an alternate payee under a QDRO) can be an eligible rollover distribution (see Q 28:8). However, a qualified retirement plan is *not* treated as an eligible retirement plan (see Q 28:19) with respect to the distribution to a surviving spouse; only an IRA is treated as an eligible retirement plan for the surviving spouse's eligible rollover distribution. [IRC § 402(c)(9); Treas Reg § 1.402(c)-2, Q&A 12(a)]

Distributions from a qualified retirement plan to a distributee other than the employee or the employee's surviving spouse (or spouse or former spouse as an alternate payee under a QDRO) cannot be rolled over and, therefore, do not constitute eligible rollover distributions. [Treas Reg § 1.402(c)-2, Q&A 12(b)]

Q 28:19   What is an eligible retirement plan?

For *regular* rollover purposes (see Q 28:1), an eligible retirement plan means an IRA or a qualified retirement plan. [IRC 402(c)(8)(B); Treas Reg § 1.402(c)-2, Q&A 2]

For *direct* rollover purposes (see Q 28:20), an eligible retirement plan means an IRA or a qualified defined contribution plan (see Q 2:2) but *not* a defined benefit plan (see Q 2:3). [IRC §§ 401(a)(31)(D), 402(c)(8)(B)] However, IRS has advised that a qualified retirement plan *must* permit direct rollovers to defined contribution plans and *may* permit (but is not required to permit) direct rollovers to defined benefit plans. [Treas Reg § 1.401(a)(31)-1, Q&A 2]

An individual cannot roll over a distribution from a qualified retirement plan to an IRA of the individual's spouse because the spouse's IRA is not an eligible retirement plan. [Rodoni, 105 TC 29 (1995); Ltr Rul 9315031]

Q 28:20   What is a direct rollover?

A direct rollover is an eligible rollover distribution (see Q 28:8) that is paid directly to an eligible retirement plan (see Q 28:19) for the benefit of the distributee (i.e., the distribution is made in the form of a direct trustee-to-trustee transfer from a qualified retirement plan to the eligible retirement plan). [IRC § 401(a)(31); Treas Reg § 1.401(a)(31)-1, Q&A 3; Ltr Ruls 9617043, 9428042, 9331055]

A direct rollover may be accomplished by any reasonable means of direct payment to an eligible retirement plan. Reasonable means include a wire transfer or the mailing of a check to the eligible retirement plan. If the payment is made by wire transfer, the wire transfer must be directed only to the trustee of the eligible retirement plan. If payment is made by check, the check must be negotiable only by the trustee of the eligible retirement plan (see Q 28:21). In the case of an eligible retirement plan that does not have a trustee (e.g., an individual retirement annuity), the custodian of the plan or issuer of the contract under the plan, as appropriate, should be substituted for the trustee. [Treas Reg § 1.401(a)(31)-1, Q&A 3]

Q 28:21   Is providing a distributee with a check for delivery to an eligible retirement plan a reasonable means of accomplishing a direct rollover?

Giving the distributee a check and instructing the distributee to deliver the check to the eligible retirement plan (see Q 28:19) is a reasonable means of direct payment (see Q 28:20), *provided* that the check is made payable as follows: [Name of the trustee] as trustee of [name of eligible retirement plan]. For example, if the name of the eligible retirement plan is "Individual Retirement Account of Jack N. Jill" and the name of the trustee is "ABC Bank," the payee line of the check should read "ABC Bank as trustee of Individual Retirement Account of Jack N. Jill."

Unless the name of the distributee is included in the name of the eligible retirement plan, the check also must indicate that it is for the benefit of the distributee. If the eligible retirement plan is not an IRA, the payee line of the check need not identify the trustee by name and may read "Trustee of the XYZ Corporation Savings Plan FBO Jane Plane." [Treas Reg § 1.401(a)(31)-1, Q&A 4]

If the plan does not make out the check to the trustee, a distribution, not a rollover, has occurred. [Ann 95-99, 1995-48 IRB 10]

Q 28:22   Is an eligible rollover distribution that is paid to an eligible retirement plan in a direct rollover includible in gross income?

No. An eligible rollover distribution (see Q 28:8) that is paid to an eligible retirement plan (see Q 28:19) in a direct rollover (see Q 28:20) is not currently includible in the distributee's gross income. However, when any portion of the eligible rollover distribution is subsequently distributed from the eligible retirement plan, that portion will be includible in gross income. [IRC § 402(c)(1); Treas Reg § 1.401(a)(31)-1, Q&A 5; Ltr Rul 9428042]

Q 28:23   What procedures may a plan administrator prescribe for electing a direct rollover?

The plan administrator (see Q 16:1) may prescribe any reasonable procedure for a distributee to elect a direct rollover (see Q 28:20). The procedure may include any reasonable requirement for information or documentation from the distributee. For example, it would be reasonable for the plan administrator to require the distributee to provide a statement from the plan designated by the distributee that it is, or is intended to be, an IRA or a qualified retirement plan, and that it will accept the direct rollover for the benefit of the distributee. In the case of a designated recipient qualified retirement plan, it also would be reasonable for the plan administrator to require a statement that the plan is not excepted from the definition of an eligible retirement plan (i.e., is not a defined benefit plan; see Q 28:19). It would not be reasonable, however, for the plan administrator to require information or documentation or to establish procedures that effectively eliminate or substantially impair the distributee's ability to elect a direct rollover. For example, it would not be reasonable for the plan administrator to require the distributee to obtain an opinion from the distributee's attorney that the eligible retirement plan receiving the rollover is a qualified retirement plan or IRA. As another example, the plan administrator cannot require the trustee of an eligible retirement plan receiving a direct rollover to agree to return, upon demand, any portion of the distribution that the plan administrator subsequently claims was paid incorrectly. Likewise, the plan administrator cannot require a letter from the recipient plan indemnifying the distributing plan for any liability arising from the distribution. [Treas Reg § 1.401(a)(31)-1, Q&A 6; IRS Spec Rul (June 3, 1993)]

The plan administrator may establish a default procedure whereby a distributee who fails to make an affirmative election is treated as having either made or not made a direct rollover election. However, the plan administrator may not make a distribution under any default procedure unless the distributee has received an explanation of the default procedures and an explanation of the direct rollover option on a timely basis (see Q 28:30). [Treas Reg § 1.401(a)(31)-1, Q&A 7]

The plan administrator may establish a deadline after which the distributee may not revoke an election to make or not to make a direct rollover, but the plan administrator is not permitted to prescribe any deadline or time period that is more restrictive for the distributee than that which otherwise applies under the plan to a revocation of the form of distribution elected by the distributee. [Treas Reg § 1.401(a)(31)-1, Q&A 8]

Q 28:24   Can a distributee elect a partial direct rollover?

Yes. The plan administrator (see Q 16:1) must permit a distributee to elect to have a portion of an eligible rollover distribution (see Q 28:8) paid to an eligible retirement plan (see Q 28:19) in a direct rollover (see Q 28:20) and to have the remainder paid to the distributee. The plan administrator is permitted to require that, if the distributee elects to have only a portion of an eligible rollover distribution paid to an eligible retirement plan in a direct rollover, that portion be equal to at least $500. If the entire amount of the eligible rollover distribution is $500 or less, the plan administrator need not allow the distributee to divide the distribution. [Treas Reg § 1.401(a)(31)-1, Q&A 9]

Q 28:25   Can a direct rollover be paid to two or more eligible retirement plans?

The plan administrator (see Q 16:1) is not required (but is permitted) to allow the distributee to divide an eligible rollover distribution (see Q 28:8) into separate distributions to be paid to two or more eligible retirement plans (see Q 28:19) in direct rollovers (see Q 28:20). The plan administrator may require that the distributee select a single eligible retirement plan to which the eligible rollover distribution (or portion thereof) will be distributed in a direct rollover. [Treas Reg § 1.401(a)(31)-1, Q&A 10]

Q 28:26   Can there be a dollar limitation on a direct rollover?

Yes. A qualified retirement plan will satisfy the direct rollover requirement (see Qs 28:8, 28:20) even though the plan does not permit a distributee to elect a direct rollover with respect to eligible rollover distributions during a year that are reasonably expected to total less than $200 or any lower minimum amount specified by the plan administrator (see Q 16:1). [Treas Reg § 1.401(a)(31)-1, Q&A 11]

Q 28:27   How many elections are required for a series of periodic payments?

Each distribution in a series of substantially equal periodic payments may be an eligible rollover distribution (see Qs 28:8, 28:9).

Example. Joe participates in The Golfing Grace Corporation's money purchase pension plan. Joe retires and elects to receive payment of his account balance in 60 substantially equal monthly payments. Each of the 60 monthly payments is an eligible rollover distribution, and Joe may make a direct rollover election.

A qualified retirement plan is permitted to treat a distributee's election to make or not to make a direct rollover with respect to one payment in a series of periodic payments as applying to all subsequent payments in the series, provided that:

1. The employee is permitted at any time to change, with respect to subsequent payments, a previous election to make or not to make a direct rollover, and

2. The written explanation (see Q 28:30) explains that the election to make or not to make a direct rollover will apply to all future payments unless the employee subsequently changes the election. [Treas Reg § 1.401(a)(31)-1, Q&A 12]

Q 28:28   Must a plan accept a direct rollover?

No. Although qualified retirement plans are required to provide distributees with the option to make a direct rollover (see Q 28:20) of their eligible rollover distributions (see Q 28:8) to an eligible retirement plan (see Q 28:19), there is no requirement that an eligible retirement plan accept rollovers. Thus, an eligible retirement plan can refuse to accept rollovers. Alternatively, a plan can limit the circumstances under which it will accept rollovers. For example, a plan can limit the types of plans from which it will accept a rollover or limit the types of assets it will accept in a rollover (such as only cash or its equivalent). [Treas Reg § 1.401(a)(31)-1, Q&A 13(a)]

A plan that accepts a direct rollover from another plan will not be disqualified merely because the plan making the distribution is, in fact, not qualified at the time of the distribution, if, prior to accepting the rollover, the receiving plan reasonably concluded that the distributing plan was qualified. For example, the receiving plan may reasonably conclude that the distributing plan was qualified if, prior to accepting the rollover, the plan administrator (see Q 16:1) of the distributing plan provided the receiving plan with a statement that the distributing plan had received a favorable determination letter (see Q 15:1). [Treas Reg § 1.401(a)(31)-1, Q&A 13(b)]

Q 28:29   Is a direct rollover a distribution and rollover or a transfer of assets and liabilities?

A direct rollover (see Q 28:20) is a distribution and rollover of the eligible rollover distribution (see Q 28:8) and not a transfer of assets and liabilities. If the spousal consent requirements (see Q 10:21) apply to the distribution, the requirements must be satisfied before the eligible rollover distribution may be distributed in a direct rollover. Similarly, the direct rollover is not a transfer of assets and liabilities that must satisfy the merger or consolidation requirements (see Q 9:38). Finally, a direct rollover is not a transfer of benefits for purposes of applying the optional forms of benefits requirement (see Q 10:42). Therefore, the eligible retirement plan (see Q 28:19) is not required to provide, with respect to amounts paid to it in a direct rollover, the same optional forms of benefits that were provided under the qualified retirement plan that made the direct rollover. [Treas Reg § 1.401(a)(31)-1, Q&A 14]

Q 28:30   Must distributees receive a written explanation of the rollover rules?

The plan administrator (see Q 16:1) is required, within a reasonable period of time (see Qs 16:17, 16:18) before making an eligible rollover distribution (see Q 28:8), to provide the distributee with a written explanation known as a Section 402(f) Notice. The Section 402(f) Notice must be designed to be easily understood and must explain the following:

1. The rules under which the distributee may have the distribution paid in a direct rollover (see Q 28:20) to an eligible retirement plan (see Q 28:19);

2. The rules that require the withholding of tax on the distribution if it is not paid in a direct rollover (see Qs 16:7–16:15);

3. The rules under which the distributee will not be subject to tax if the distribution is contributed in a rollover to an eligible retirement plan within 60 days of the distribution (see Q 28:37);

4. If applicable, certain special rules regarding the taxation of the distribution (see chapter 13); and

5. If the plan administrator has established a default procedure whereby a distributee who fails to make an affirmative election is treated as having either made or not made a direct rollover election (see Q 28:23).

[IRC § 402(f); Treas Reg §§ 1.401(a)(31)-1, Q&A 1(b)(2), Q&A 7, 1.402(c)-2, Q&A 1(b)(2), 1.402(f)-2, Q&A 1 through Q&A 4; Notice 93-26, 1993-1 CB 308]

IRS has issued a model Section 402(f) Notice (see Q 16:17). [Notice 92-48, 1992-2 CB 377]

One court has ruled that the failure of the plan administrator to give the Section 402(f) Notice to the recipient of a distribution did not entitle the recipient to money damages. [Fraser v Lintas: Campbell-Ewald, 56 F 3d 722 (6th Cir 1995)] A former participant who rolled over a plan distribution into an IRA and then withdrew a portion of the rollover could not hold the plan administrator responsible for not informing him that a subsequent distribution from the rollover IRA would be taxable. [Bouteiller v Vulcan Iron Works, Inc, 834 F Supp 207 (ED Mich 1993)]

Q 28:31 When did the new eligible rollover distribution rules become effective?

The new rules are applicable to eligible rollover distributions (see Q 28:8) made after December 31, 1992, even if the event giving rise to the distribution occurs before January 1, 1993, or if the eligible rollover distribution is part of a series of payments that began before January 1, 1993. [Treas Reg §§ 1.401(a)(31)-1, Q&A 1(c), 1.402(c)-2, Q&A 1(c)]

Example 1. Phil terminated employment with The Rollin' Dolen Corporation in 1992 but does not receive his pension plan benefits until 1997. Even though Phil's employment was terminated in 1992 (before the new rules became effective), the distribution of his benefits in 1997 is subject to the new eligible rollover distribution rules.

Example 2. Linda terminated employment with The Rollin' Dolen Corporation in 1991 and elected to receive her pension plan benefits in 84 equal monthly payments beginning January 1, 1992. Linda's monthly payments, starting with the January 1, 1993 payment, are subject to the new eligible rollover distribution rules even though the series of payments commenced before 1993.

Q 28:32 When must qualified retirement plans be amended to incorporate the direct rollover provisions?

Even though the direct rollover provisions apply to distributions from qualified retirement plans made after December 31, 1992, a qualified retirement plan is not required to be amended before the last day of the first plan year beginning on or after January 1, 1994 (or, if later, the last day by which amendments must be made to comply with TRA '86 and related provisions, as permitted in other administrative guidance of general applicability), provided that:

1. In the interim period between January 1, 1993, and the date on which the plan is amended, the plan is operated in compliance with the new requirements, and

2. The amendment applies retroactively to January 1, 1993.

[Treas Reg § 1.401(a)(31)-1, Q&A 18]

IRS has issued a model amendment, which may be adopted by plan sponsors. [Rev Proc 93-12, 1993-1 CB 479]

Q 28:33 How is a direct rollover reported to IRS?

IRS has advised that a direct rollover to an IRA should be reported on Form 1099-R (see Q 17:17) using code G in Box 7, and that a direct rollover to a qualified retirement plan should be reported using code H in Box 7. [Ann 95-99, 1995-48 IRB 10; Ann 94-40, 1994-12 IRB 7; Rev Proc 93-31, 1993-2 CB 355; Ann 93-20, 1993-6 IRB 65]

If an individual receives from a qualified retirement plan both a required minimum distribution and a direct rollover within the same taxable year, two Forms 1099-R must be filed—one for the required minimum distribution and one for the direct rollover. [Ann 94-46, 1994-13 IRB 22]

Q 28:34 Is a rollover available for a distribution from a terminated retirement plan?

A participant who has not separated from service but who receives a distribution from a qualified retirement plan because of the plan's termination can roll over all or part of the distribution to postpone the payment of tax if it is an eligible rollover distribution (see Q 28:8). The distribution can be an eligible rollover distribution even if the participant continues to participate in another qualified retirement plan of the same employer (see Q 28:10). [IRC § 402(c); Ltr Ruls 9615042, 9507032, 9418028, 9338041; Notice 93-26, 1993-1 CB 308]

Q 28:35 May a person who is over age 70½ roll over a qualified retirement plan distribution?

An individual over age 70½ may roll over a distribution from a qualified retirement plan except to the extent that such distribution is a required minimum distribution (see Qs 11:2, 28:8, 28:11). [IRC §§ 401(a)(9), 402(c)(4)(B); Rev Rul 82-153, 1982-2 CB 86; Ltr Rul 9143078]

Q 28:36 Is a rollover of qualified retirement plan benefits available to the spouse of a deceased employee?

Yes. The spouse of an employee who receives an eligible rollover distribution (see Qs 28:8, 28:18) from a qualified retirement plan on account of the employee's death is permitted to roll over all or part of the distribution to an IRA. This applies only to a surviving spouse and not to a nonspouse beneficiary. [IRC § 402(c)(9); Ltr Ruls 9402023, 9351041, 9005071] IRS has also ruled that, if the deceased spouse's qualified retirement plan benefits are paid to a trust and the trust distributes the benefits to the surviving spouse, the surviving spouse may roll over the distribution. [Ltr Ruls 9533042, 9509028, 9234032, 9232041, 9047060; but see Ltr Ruls 9437042, 9145041]

If the deceased spouse's qualified retirement plan benefits are paid to the decedent's estate and the surviving spouse is the sole beneficiary of the decedent's residuary estate, IRS has ruled that the surviving spouse may roll over the distribution to an IRA [Ltr Ruls 9402023, 9351041, 9229022, 9138067]; but the surviving spouse cannot roll over any part of the distribution that represents a required minimum distribution (see Qs 11:2, 28:8,

28:11). [Ltr Rul 9211059] IRS has also ruled that qualified retirement plan death benefits paid to the surviving spouse in satisfaction of her elective share rights under state law could be rolled over to an IRA. [Ltr Rul 9524020]

The surviving spouse was permitted to roll over the benefit to an IRA when the deceased spouse named a trust as the beneficiary of the death benefit payable from a qualified retirement plan, the trust beneficiaries disclaimed the benefit, and, as a result of the disclaimer, the benefit was paid to the surviving spouse (see Q 4:24). [Ltr Ruls 9450041, 9247026]

Generally, a rollover by the surviving spouse is permitted where there is no discretion on the part of someone other than the surviving spouse (e.g., the surviving spouse is the sole beneficiary of the estate or the surviving spouse may withdraw the funds from the trust).

The spouse may establish an IRA rollover account even if the spouse would not be eligible to establish a regular IRA. However, the surviving spouse may not roll over the distribution to another qualified retirement plan or from the rollover IRA to another qualified retirement plan in which the spouse is a participant. [IRC § 402(c)(9)] IRS has ruled that the surviving spouse could roll over the deceased spouse's plan benefits to an IRA of the deceased spouse. By rolling over the benefits to the deceased spouse's IRA, the surviving spouse, who had not yet attained age 59½, could commence distributions from that IRA without imposition of the 10 percent penalty tax (see Q 26:41). [Ltr Rul 9608042]

Since the distribution to a surviving spouse is an eligible rollover distribution, the distribution will be subject to automatic 20 percent withholding unless transferred by a direct rollover to an IRA. [Ltr Ruls 9402023, 9351041]

Q 28:37   How does a rollover from a qualified retirement plan to an IRA work?

The payout must be transferred into one or more IRAs within 60 days after receipt (see Q 28:38). It is not necessary, however, to transfer the entire amount into the IRA; but the portion not rolled over is taxed as ordinary income in the year received. No special tax treatment (e.g., forward averaging) is available with respect to the portion of the distribution that is currently taxed. [IRC §§ 402(c)(3), 402(d)(4)(K); Orgera, 70 TCM 1488 (1995); Barrett, 64 TCM 1080 (1992); Tassinari, 48 TCM 915 (1984); Ltr Rul 9243054]

However, unless the distribution is transferred by a direct rollover (see Q 28:20) to the IRA, the distribution would be subject to automatic 20 percent withholding (see Qs 16:7, 28:8). [Treas Reg § 1.402(c)-2, Q&A 11]

Example. Fran is entitled to a distribution of $20,000 from her employer's profit sharing plan and is undecided about rolling over the distribution to her IRA. Since the distribution to Fran is an eligible rollover distribution, the plan will withhold $4,000 and distribute to Fran only $16,000; however, Fran is deemed to have received a distribution of $20,000. If Fran then decides to roll over the distribution, she must transfer an additional $4,000 to her IRA from her other funds within the 60-day period; otherwise, the withheld amount ($4,000) will be includible in her gross income.

A distribution from a qualified retirement plan may be rolled over into an IRA that has previously been established by a participant for purposes of the participant's annual contributions; but, when the rollover is made into this type of IRA, the participant cannot later roll over the amount of the original distribution into a second qualified retirement plan maintained by the same or a new employer. The only way around this pitfall is to set up a separate IRA (a conduit IRA) to receive the rollover (see Q 28:40). [IRC § 408(d)(3)(A)]

If a qualified retirement plan distribution is rolled over, five-year forward averaging treatment will *not* be available for any later distribution to the employee from the distributing plan or from any other qualified retirement plan aggregated with the distributing plan (see Qs 13:5, 13:13). [IRC § 402(c)(10)]

Q 28:38   When does the 60-day rollover period begin?

IRS has held that if a distribution qualifying for rollover treatment is received by an individual in more than one payment, for purposes of the 60-day rollover period, that individual is deemed to have received all distributions on the day the last payment is received. [Ltr Ruls 9318044, 8434052] It was doubtful that this rule would remain effective because, in the example in Q 28:27, Joe should not be permitted to roll over all 60 payments within the 60-day period following the last payment. IRS has now stated that, if more than one distribution is received by an employee from a qualified retirement plan during a taxable year, the 60-day rule applies separately to each distribution. [Treas Reg § 1.402(c)-2, Q&A 11]

The distribution need not occur in any particular year. An individual who receives an eligible rollover distribution (see Q 28:8) a number of years after termination of employment may still roll over the distribution. [Ltr Ruls 9604029, 9152041, 9049047]

Q 28:39   Can the 60-day rollover period be extended?

According to IRS, the 60-day rollover period may not be extended under any circumstances. IRS has held that transfers not completed within 60 days of the date of distribution are not valid rollovers, even though they were caused by clerical error and not the fault of the individual. IRS says that neither the statute nor the regulations grant IRS the authority to waive or extend the 60-day period. [Orgera, 70 TCM 1488 (1995); Ltr Ruls 9537017, 9211035, 9145036, 9013078, 8824047, 8819074]

But, when an individual received a distribution of cash and shares of stock, delivered the distribution to a brokerage company with instructions to deposit the distribution into his IRA, and the brokerage company mistakenly credited the shares of stock to the individual's personal account, the bookkeeping error was disregarded and the IRA rollover was ruled timely. [Wood, 93 TC 114 (1989)]

When a state agency, as receiver of an insolvent financial institution, distributed IRA proceeds and the individual failed to roll over the proceeds within 60 days of receipt of the funds, the distribution was includible in the individual's income. [Aronson, 98 TC 283 (1992)]

Q 28:40   Can amounts in a rollover IRA be transferred to a qualified retirement plan?

An IRA that contains only assets attributable to a rollover contribution from a qualified retirement plan may be rolled over to a second qualified retirement plan or to the original plan. This type of IRA is called a conduit IRA. Also, the recipient qualified retirement plan must provide for the acceptance of rollovers. However, a required minimum distribution from a conduit IRA cannot be rolled over to either the original or any other qualified retirement plan (see Qs 28:8, 28:11). [IRC §§ 402(c)(5), 408(d)(3)(A)(ii); Ltr Ruls 9530037, 9518019, 9505023, 9108057]

Transferring money from one qualified retirement plan to another through a conduit IRA may provide a big tax advantage. The amount rolled over might remain eligible for special tax treatment (e.g., electing forward averaging tax treatment for a lump-sum distribution received from the second qualified retirement plan), although generally a trust-to-trust transfer provides more assurance of retaining eligibility for favorable tax treatment (see Q 13:4). [Ltr Ruls 9226076, 9151024, 9146045]

An individual rolled over a distribution from a terminated qualified retirement plan into an IRA that had previously been established with contributions from other sources. Subsequently, the individual transferred the rollover funds to a new retirement plan. Because the IRA was not a conduit IRA, the new plan was disqualified (see Qs 1:5, 1:6, 4:1, 4:23). [Ltr Rul 9604028]

Q 28:41 Can a distribution from a disqualified retirement plan be rolled over?

A distribution from a retirement plan that is retroactively disqualified is includible in income and is not eligible for a rollover to an IRA or a qualified retirement plan. Rollover treatment is permitted for a distribution from a retirement plan that is qualified at the time of distribution, not at the time when contributions by the employer were made. [Treas Reg §§ 1.402(a)-1(a)(1)(ii), 1.402(a)-1(a)(1)(v), 1.402(b)-1(b); Weddel, TCM 1996-36; Fazi, 105 TC No. 29 (1995); Fazi, 102 TC 695 (1994); Cass v Comm'r, 774 F 2d 740 (7th Cir 1985); Baetens v Comm'r, 777 F 2d 1160 (6th Cir 1985); Woodson v Comm'r, 651 F 2d 1094 (5th Cir 1981); but see Greenwald v Comm'r, 366 F 2d 538 (2d Cir 1966)]

A payment made to an employee in settlement of the employee's claim for benefits from a qualified retirement plan was not eligible for rollover treatment because the settlement payment was made from the employer's general assets and not from a qualified retirement plan. [Ltr Rul 9241008]

Q 28:42 What are the tax advantages and disadvantages of rolling over a qualified retirement plan distribution to an IRA?

A rollover of a qualified retirement plan distribution to an IRA provides three distinct tax advantages:

1. Postponement of tax payments;
2. Possible reduction of tax liability on the eventual payout; and
3. Continued tax-free build up of retirement savings.

The rollover defers tax on the qualified retirement plan payout and on the income earned in the IRA. Subsequently, tax liability on amounts in the IRA can be spread out by making withdrawals over a period of years.

Nevertheless, an IRA rollover has drawbacks. First, amounts in the IRA generally cannot be withdrawn without penalty before age 59½ (see Q 26:41). Second, IRA withdrawals are taxed as ordinary income with no special tax-reducing rules available (e.g., forward averaging). Third, any subsequent distributions from the qualified retirement plan will not be eligible for five-year forward averaging treatment (see Qs 28:1, 28:36). [IRC §§ 72(t), 402(c)(10), 408(d); Costanza v Comm'r, 50 TCM 280 (1985)]

Whether the advantages of a rollover will outweigh the disadvantages depends on each individual situation.

Q 28:43   Can an IRA rollover be revoked?

Upon receipt of a lump-sum distribution from a qualified retirement plan, an individual has the option of electing to roll over the distribution to another eligible retirement plan or to have the tax on such distribution computed by using the forward averaging method (see Qs 13:13, 13:14). Once the individual elects to roll over the distribution into an IRA, those funds become part of the IRA and are then subject to the rules governing IRAs. The amount timely rolled over to an IRA cannot be considered an excess contribution (see Q 26:6) and, therefore, cannot be withdrawn as such. [IRC §§ 402(c)(5), 4973(b)] An individual cannot recharacterize a rollover contribution made to an IRA once the rollover has been made. Once an individual has chosen the form of a transaction for tax purposes, the individual cannot later disavow the form of the transaction merely because the tax consequences of the form chosen have become disadvantageous. [Barnes, Jr, 67 TCM 2341; Barrett, 64 TCM 1080 (1992); Hall, 61 TCM 2236 (1991); Ltr Ruls 8536098, 8536097]

For the IRA rollover to be tax-free, the individual must irrevocably elect to treat the IRA contribution as a rollover contribution. Once any portion of the lump-sum distribution is irrevocably designated as a rollover contribution, the amount rolled over is not taxable and no part of the distribution is eligible for special income tax treatment. An irrevocable election is made by a written designation to the IRA sponsor (at the time of contribution) that it is a rollover contribution. In the case of a direct rollover (see Q 28:20), the individual is deemed to have irrevocably designated that the direct rollover is a rollover contribution. These same rules apply to a rollover by a surviving spouse (see Q 28:36). [Treas Reg § 1.402(c)-2, Q&A 13; Ltr Rul 8815035]

However, when an individual rolled over the entire distribution to an IRA and was informed the following year by the trustee of the qualified retirement plan that the individual's benefits had been erroneously overvalued, IRS ruled that the amount distributed to the individual to repay the employer would not be includible in the individual's income. [Ltr Rul 9118020]

Q 28:44   Can a rollover IRA be reached by judgment creditors?

Courts have ruled that a rollover IRA (see Qs 28:37, 28:40) is exempt from execution by judgment creditors under state law because ERISA does not apply to IRAs and the state elected to opt out of the federal scheme. [Youngblood v Fed Deposit Ins Co, No. 93-1403 (5th Cir 1994); In re Mann, No. 889-92426 (ED NY 1992); NY CPLR § 5205(c)] One court concluded that a rollover IRA is not exempt from creditors [In re Cesare, 1994 Bankr Lexis 1028 (Bankr DC Ct 1994)]; but other courts have ruled that even though an IRA may not be exempt from bankruptcy (see Q 26:45), the portion of the IRA attributable to a rollover from a qualified retirement plan retains its exempt status. [In re Sheldon Modansky, No. 92 B 21976 (SD NY 1993); In the Matter of Woods, 59 Bankr 221 (WD Wis 1986)]

Q 28:45 Does proposed legislation affect rollovers to IRAs?

Both RRB '95 and RRB '96 (see Q 1:22A) contain provisions affecting rollovers.

Under RRB '95, distributions from an AD IRA could be rolled over tax-free to another AD IRA. In addition, amounts distributed from an IRA could be rolled over within 60 days (see Q 28:3) to an AD IRA; or, alternatively, an IRA could be converted into an AD IRA. During a two-year window period, if an IRA is rolled over or converted into an AD IRA, the amount otherwise includible in gross income due to the IRA distribution or conversion would be includible in gross income ratably over the four-taxable-year period beginning with the taxable year in which the distribution or conversion is made. After the two-year window period, the IRA rollover or conversion would be includible in gross income in the year of distribution or conversion. The early distribution penalty tax (see Q 26:41) would not apply to such qualified rollovers. Qualified retirement plan distributions, even eligible rollover distributions (see Q 28:8), could *not* be rolled over to an AD IRA. [RRB '95, Act § 11015] (See Qs 26:36, 26:43.)

Similar provisions are included in RRB '96. However, rollovers from an IRA to a Special IRA (RRB '96's version of the AD IRA) could be made only if an individual's adjusted gross income (see Q 26:10) is below a specified dollar amount. In addition, only a one-year window period would apply for the four-taxable-year ratable inclusion in gross income, and this ratable inclusion would also apply for purposes of the excess distributions tax (see Q 13:27). [RRB '96, Act § 9211] (See Qs 26:35, 26:42.)

Example. In 1997, Abraham rolls over a $40,000 IRA distribution to an AD IRA or Special IRA. The amount of $10,000 will be includible is Abraham's gross income in each year of 1997, 1998, 1999, and 2000. Neither RRB '95 nor RRB '96 contains a provision concerning Abraham's death prior to 2000. Assuming Abraham dies in 1998, is the remaining $30,000 includible in gross income that year; is the legal representative of Abraham's estate required to file income tax returns on Abraham's behalf for 1999 and 2000; does Abraham's estate include the untaxed amounts on its 1999 and 2000 income tax returns; if Abraham was married, must his surviving spouse include the untaxed amounts on her 1999 and 2000 income tax returns?

For a discussion of AD IRAs and Special IRAs, see chapter 26.

Chapter 29

Tax-Sheltered Annuities

One way for employees of certain organizations to accumulate funds for retirement is through a tax-sheltered annuity. A tax-sheltered annuity is a tax-favored deferred compensation arrangement that enables employees to exclude from income amounts contributed toward the purchase of annuity contracts. This chapter examines tax-sheltered annuities—what they are, their tax advantages, and the myriad rules and requirements that apply to them.

Q 29:1 What is a tax-sheltered annuity?

A tax-sheltered annuity is a special type of deferred compensation arrangement that is available only to employees of certain organizations (see Q 29:2). The annuity contract is purchased by the employer on behalf of the employee, but a tax-sheltered annuity must satisfy a number of requirements (see Q 29:11). [IRC § 403(b)(1); Treas Reg § 1.403(b)-1(b)]

The employee can exclude from gross income, within certain specified limits, the amounts contributed toward the purchase of the annuity contract, and the employee does not have taxable income until payments under the contract are received (see Qs 29:21, 29:44). In addition, earnings within the annuity contract accumulate tax-free. A tax-sheltered annuity has many of the same advantages as a qualified retirement plan. With the plethora of rules and requirements applicable to tax-sheltered annuities, a violation of any one of them can cause the loss of the tax advantages. Because of this, IRS has released guidelines designed to assist its agents in determining whether colleges and universities are complying with all applicable rules and requirements [Ann 94-112, 1994-37 IRB 36] and has also announced a new voluntary compliance program for tax-sheltered annuities, the Tax

Sheltered Annuity Voluntary Correction Program. See Qs 29:52 through 29:57 for details.

Tax-sheltered annuities are also commonly referred to as TSAs, Section 403(b) annuities, Section 403(b) plans, or tax-deferred annuities. Throughout this chapter, tax-sheltered annuities are referred to as TSAs.

Q 29:2   What types of organizations can establish TSA programs?

Employees of only two types of organizations may participate in a TSA:

1. Employees of tax-exempt organizations described in Section 501(c)(3) (see Q 29:3), or

2. Employees of public educational systems (see Q 29:4).

[IRC §§ 170(b)(1)(A)(ii), 403(b)(1)(A); Treas Reg § 1.403(b)-1(b)(1)]

These organizations are referred to as eligible employers.

Q 29:3   What is a Section 501(c)(3) organization?

A Section 501(c)(3) organization is a nonprofit organization (a corporation, and any community chest, fund, or foundation) that meets the following conditions:

1. It is organized and operated exclusively for religious, charitable, scientific, testing for public safety, literary, or educational purposes; to foster national or international amateur sports competition (but only if no part of its activities involves the provision of athletic facilities or equipment); or for the prevention of cruelty to children or animals;

2. No part of the net earnings of the organization may inure to the benefit of any private shareholder or individual;

3. No substantial part of the activities of the organization may consist of carrying on propaganda, or otherwise attempting, to influence legislation (except for certain lobbying activities by public charities); and

4. It does not participate in, or intervene in (including the publishing or distributing of statements), any political campaign on behalf of (or in opposition to) any candidate for public office.

[IRC § 501(c)(3)]

A cooperative hospital service organization established under Section 501(e) is treated as a Section 501(c)(3) organization and, therefore, may establish a TSA on behalf of its employees. [Rev Rul 72-329, 1972-2 CB 226]

State and municipal agencies and instrumentalities generally do not qualify as Section 501(c)(3) organizations; but, if an organization serves the exclusive purposes described above and is a separate entity from the government, then it may establish a TSA for its employees. [Rev Rul 60-384, 1960-2 CB 172; Rev Rul 67-290, 1967-2 CB 183]

An institution operated exclusively for educational purposes by a separate educational instrumentality may qualify both as a Section 501(c)(3) organization and as a public school (see Q 29:4). [Estate of Johnson, 56 TC 944 (1971); Ltr Rul 7817098]

Q 29:4   What is a public educational system?

A public educational system is an educational organization that normally maintains a regular faculty and curriculum, normally has a regularly enrolled body of pupils or students in attendance at the place where its educational activities are regularly carried on, and is operated by a state, a political subdivision of a state, or an agency or instrumentality thereof. The term includes a federal public-supported school. [IRC §§ 403(b)(1)(A)(ii), 170(b)(1)(A)(ii); Treas Reg § 1.170A-9(b)]

The term "educational organization" includes primary, secondary, preparatory, and high schools, colleges, and universities. If the organization engages in both educational and noneducational activities, it will qualify as an educational organization only if the noneducational activities are incidental to the primary educational purpose. [Treas Reg § 1.170A-9(b)(1)]

A state department of education may qualify as a part of a public school system if its services involve the operation or direction of the state's public school program. [Rev Rul 73-607, 1973-2 CB 145] A state agency created as part of a state educational department, which consists of accredited colleges and universities, community colleges, and junior colleges, is a public educational institution. [Ltr Rul 9438031]

Teachers in private and parochial schools are employees of Section 501(c)(3) organizations (see Q 29:3).

Q 29:5   Must there be an employer-employee relationship?

Whether an individual is associated with a Section 501(c)(3) organization (see Q 29:3) or a public educational system (see Q 29:4), the individual must be an *employee*, not an independent contractor, to be eligible to participate in a TSA program. Thus, it is necessary to determine that an employer-employee relationship exists between the organization and the individual (see Q 5:1). [IRC § 403(b)(1)(A); Treas Reg § 1.403(b)-1(b)(1)]

IRS has provided guidelines for classifying individuals as either employees or independent contractors and has listed 20 factors to be considered in establishing the existence of an employer-employee relationship. These guidelines do not specifically relate to TSAs; however, they do provide guidance even though certain factors clearly may be inapplicable to eligible employers (see Q 29:2). Control is the important element: if the organization controls the relationship, the individual is an employee; if the individual controls the relationship, the individual is an independent contractor. The 20 factors are described below:

1. *Instructions.* Is the individual subject to another person's instructions as to when, where, and how the work is to be performed? [Rev Rul 68-598, 1968-2 CB 464; Rev Rul 66-381, 1966-2 CB 449]

2. *Training.* Is the individual required to work with an experienced worker, to attend meetings, and to perform services in a particular manner? [Rev Rul 70-630, 1970-2 CB 229]

3. *Integration.* Are the individual's services integrated into business operations? [United States v Silk, 331 US 704 (1947)]

4. *Services rendered personally.* Must the services rendered by the individual be rendered personally? [Rev Rul 55-695, 1955-2 CB 410]

5. *Hiring, supervising, and paying assistants.* Does the individual have this responsibility? [Rev Rul 63-115, 1963-1 CB 178; Rev Rul 55-593, 1955-2 CB 610]

6. *Continuing relationship.* Are the individual's services of a temporary or permanent nature? [United States v Silk, 331 US 704 (1947)]

7. *Set hours of work.* Does the organization set the work hours of the individual? [Rev Rul 73-591, 1973-2 CB 337]

8. *Full time required.* Must the individual work substantially full time for the organization? [Rev Rul 56-694, 1956-2 CB 694]

9. *Doing work on employer's premises.* Who controls the place of work? [Rev Rul 56-694, 1956-2 CB 694]

10. *Order or sequence set.* Must the individual perform services in the order or sequence set by the organization? [Rev Rul 56-694, 1956-2 CB 694]

11. *Oral or written reports.* Is the individual required to submit regular reports? [Rev Rul 70-309, 1970-1 CB 199; Rev Rul 68-248, 1968-1 CB 431]

12. *Method of payment.* Is the individual paid by the hour or week, by the job, or by straight commission? [Rev Rul 74-389, 1974-2 CB 330]

13. *Expenses.* Are business and travel expenses paid by the individual or the organization? [Rev Rul 55-144, 1955-1 CB 483]

14. *Furnishing of tools and materials.* Who furnishes the tools, materials, and equipment? [Rev Rul 71-524, 1971-2 CB 346]

15. *Significant investment.* Who makes the investment in facilities used by the individual? [Rev Rul 71-524, 1971-2 CB 346]

16. *Realization of profit or loss.* Can the individual realize a profit or suffer a loss as a result of the work performed? [Rev Rul 70-309, 1970-1 CB 199]

17. *More than one organization.* Does the individual perform more than *de minimis* services for more than one unrelated organization at the same time? [Rev Rul 70-572, 1970-2 CB 221]

18. *General public.* Are the individual's services available to the general public on a regular and consistent basis? [Rev Rul 56-660, 1956-2 CB 693]

19. *Right to discharge.* Does the organization have the right to fire the individual? [Rev Rul 75-41, 1975-1 CB 323]

20. *Right to terminate.* Can the individual terminate the relationship without incurring liability? [Rev Rul 70-309, 1970-1 CB 179]

[Rev Rul 87-41, 1987-1 CB 296; Rev Rul 70-136, 1970-1 CB 12; Rev Rul 66-274, 1966-2 CB 446; Azad v United States, 388 F 2d 74 (8th Cir 1968); Haugen, 30 TCM 1247 (1971); Ravel, 26 TCM 885 (1967); Ltr Ruls 9443002, 9429010, 9428012, 9149001]

An individual performs services for an educational organization if the individual is performing services as an employee directly or indirectly for such an institution. The principal, clerical employees, custodial employees, and teachers at a public elementary school are employees performing services *directly* for the educational institution. An employee who performs services involving the operation or direction of a state's or political subdivision's education program as carried on through educational institutions is an employee performing services *indirectly* for the institutions. An employee participating in an in-home teaching program is included since the program is merely an extension of the activities carried on by the educational institutions. [Treas Reg § 1.403(b)-1(b)(5); Ltr Ruls 9613013, 9613011, 9613005, 7801019, 7747057]

IRS has ruled that employees of a state teachers' retirement system do not perform services directly or indirectly for an educational organization and neither does a state employee who works in a department that is not part of an educational institution but supervises payroll and timekeeping for public schools. [Rev Rul 80-139, 1980-1 CB 88; Rev Rul 72-390, 1972-2 CB 227]

A person occupying an elective or appointive public office is not an employee performing services for an educational institution unless such office is one to which an individual is elected or appointed only if the individual has received training, or is experienced, in the field of education. The term "public office" includes any elective or appointive office of a state, a political subdivision of a state, or an agency or instrumentality thereof. For example, a regent or trustee of a state university or a member of a board of education is not an employee performing services for an educational institution; however, a commissioner or superintendent of education will generally be considered an employee performing services for an educational institution. [Treas Reg § 1.403(b)-1(b)(5)]

Janitorial, custodial, and general clerical employees of a state department of education who are appointed by the commissioner of education are not persons occupying appointed public office, but are employees providing indirect services for an educational institution. Also, if an individual has a significant degree of executive or policymaking authority and the individual's position is based on educational training or experience, the individual will be considered to perform indirect services. [Rev Rul 73-607, 1973-2 CB 145]

An individual can be both an employee of an organization and an independent contractor with regard to the same organization (see Q 6:35). [Reese, 63 TCM 3129 (1992)]

IRS has issued proposed examination guidelines for use during examinations of colleges and universities for TSA qualification. The guidelines are intended to provide a framework that agents may follow in conducting their examinations and provide factors to be considered in determining how the college or university is structured. [Ann 93-2, 1993-2 IRB 39]

Q 29:6   Must an insurance company annuity contract be used for a TSA?

For the TSA rules to apply, an annuity contract must be purchased for the employee; however, the term "annuity contract" is not defined. [IRC § 403(b)(1)(A)]

An annuity contract, as that term is commonly understood, must be purchased from an insurance company. The annuity contract may be an individual contract for each employee or a group contract under which each employee has a separate account. The annuity contract may provide a fixed retirement benefit or a variable benefit that is based upon the performance of the underlying investments (i.e., a variable annuity contract). [Treas Reg § 1.403(b)-1(c)(3); Rev Rul 82-102, 1982-1 CB 62; Rev Rul 68-116, 1968-1 CB 177; Ltr Rul 9415016]

Contributions for an employee to a *custodial account* that are invested solely in regulated investment company stock (i.e., mutual fund) are treated as amounts contributed by an employer for an annuity contract. The custodian must be a bank or any other party satisfactory to IRS. [IRC §§ 401(f)(2), 403(b)(7), 408(n), 851(a); Treas Reg § 1.408-2(b)(2); Ltr Ruls 9525067, 9525060, 9522056, 9415016]

A single group annuity contract may be used to fund benefits of both a qualified retirement plan and a TSA program of an eligible employer (see Q 29:2), provided that the assets of both plans are separately accounted for and subaccounts are created for each employee to identify each plan's contributions. [Ltr Rul 9422053] IRS has also ruled that a single trust or custodial account may be used to fund benefits of both a qualified retirement plan and a TSA program. [Ltr Rul 9540061; see also Rev Rul 81-100, 1981-1 CB 326]

The term "annuity" also includes a face-amount certificate but does not include any contract or certificate that is transferable if a person other than a trustee is the owner of the contract or certificate. [IRC § 401(g); Investment Company Act of 1940 § 2(a)(15)]

Contributions on behalf of employees to a credit union that maintains separate nonforfeitable special share accounts for each employee do not constitute the purchase of annuity contracts, and neither do contributions to a state teachers' retirement system or to a separately funded employee retirement reserve subject to state insurance department supervision. [Rev Rul 82-102, 1982-1 CB 62; Corbin v United States, 760 F 2d 234 (8th Cir 1985); Ltr Rul 9511040]

Q 29:7 Can a TSA provide life insurance protection?

Yes, provided that the life insurance protection is incidental to the retirement annuity. To determine if the life insurance protection is incidental, the rules applicable to qualified retirement plans also apply to TSAs (see Q 14:4). [Treas Reg § 1.403(b)-1(c)(3); Ltr Ruls 9626042, 9617042, 9601053]

A separate insurance policy may be purchased as part of a TSA, but the policy must satisfy all of the requirements of a TSA (see Q 29:11). It is not required that both the annuity contract and the insurance policy be issued by the same insurance company. [Treas Reg §§ 1.403(b)-1(b)(4), 1.403(b)-1(c)(3); Ltr Ruls 9617042, 9336054, 9336053, 9327025, 9324044]

If life insurance is provided as part of the TSA, the portion of the contribution providing current life insurance protection—the PS-58 cost—is includible in the employee's gross income (see Qs 14:6–14:8).

Q 29:8 Must a TSA be part of a plan or trust?

Although there appears to be no statutory requirement that a plan be established, Section 403(b) contains numerous references to the word "plan." [IRC §§ 403(b)(1)(D), 403(b)(7)(B), 403(b)(12)(A)] In this context, the word "plan" implies a written document. If the employer makes contributions to a TSA for the benefit of an employee, a written plan document will be required. [ERISA § 402(a)(1)] However, if the TSA is established solely pursuant to a salary reduction agreement (see Q 29:10), the agreement itself may constitute the written plan document.

Since TSAs are funded, in whole or in part, through individual annuity contracts, group annuity contracts, life insurance policies, and custodial accounts that must satisfy a number of requirements (see Qs 29:6, 29:7), a trust is not required. As an example, the employee will usually own and hold an individual annuity contract. However, a trust may be established for the purpose of making annuity contracts available to eligible employees. [Ltr Rul 9423031]

Q 29:9　How are contributions made to a TSA?

A TSA must be purchased by the employer (see Q 29:2) so, in all cases, it is the employer that makes the contribution to the TSA. However, there are two main sources from which contributions are made:

1. Elective deferrals by the employee through salary reduction agreements (see Q 29:10).

2. Employer contributions that are made without regard to the employee's elective deferral or that match in some proportion the employee's elective deferral (see Qs 29:12, 29:19).

[IRC §§ 403(b)(1)(A), 403(b)(1)(E); Treas Reg §§ 1.403(b)-1(b)(1), 1.403(b)-1(b)(3)]

In some cases, employees may be permitted to make voluntary, nondeductible contributions (see Qs 1:33, 23:49–23:55, 29:19).

Q 29:10　What is a salary reduction agreement?

The primary method for making contributions to a TSA is by the employee taking a reduction in salary or forgoing an increase in salary. In either case, this is referred to as a salary reduction agreement. Amounts contributed by the employer to a TSA by reason of a salary reduction agreement are referred to as elective deferrals. [IRC § 402(g)(3)(C); Treas Reg § 1.403(b)-1(b)(3)]

A salary reduction agreement must be legally binding, apply only to compensation earned by the employee after the agreement becomes effective, and be irrevocable with respect to compensation earned while the agreement is in effect. *For years beginning before 1996,* the employee could not make more than one agreement with the same employer during the employee's taxable year but could be permitted to terminate the agreement with respect to compensation not yet earned. Salary reductions are of a fixed dollar amount or a fixed percentage of compensation. The fact that the amount of the contribution could change under the percentage formula because of increases or decreases in compensation did not constitute a new agreement, nor did the purchase of an annuity contract from an insurance company other than the one specified in the original agreement. If an employee entered into a salary reduction agreement for an indefinite period during one tax year, the employee could make a new agreement in a subsequent tax year. [Treas Reg § 1.403(b)-1(b)(3); Bollotin v United States, No. 76-6187 (2d Cir 1977); Rev Rul 87-114, 1987-2 CB 116; Rev Rul 68-179, 1968-1 CB 179; Rev Rul 68-58, 1968-1 CB 176; Ltr Ruls 9610009, 9610008, 9610007, 9546029, 9525067, 9525060; GCM 39659]

For years beginning after 1995, multiple salary reduction agreements are permitted so that the frequency with which an employee can enter into a salary reduction agreement, the salary to which the agreement may apply, and the ability to revoke the agreement is determined under the rules applicable to cash-or-deferred elections under 401(k) plans (see Q 23:2). [SBA '96, Act § 1450(a)(1)]

Example. Jamie is a teacher at Christie University. His monthly salary is $3,000; and, for 1995, he entered into a 4 percent salary reduction agreement. On July 1, 1995, he entered into a second salary reduction agreement for an additional 3 percent. The amounts contributed from the second TSA salary reduction agreement were includible in Jamie's gross income for 1995. If Jamie makes the same arrangements in 1996, his TSA contribution from the second salary reduction agreement for the last six months of 1996 will not be includible in his compensation.

A contribution is not treated as made pursuant to a salary reduction agreement if it is made pursuant to a one-time irrevocable election by the employee at the time of initial eligibility to participate in the plan (see Q 23:3). [IRC § 403(b)(12)(A); Notice 89-23, Part III, 1989-1 CB 654]

Q 29:11   What requirements must a TSA satisfy?

In addition to the requirement that a TSA be purchased only by certain types of employers (see Q 29:2), a number of other requirements must be met:

1. The employee's rights under the TSA must be nonforfeitable (see Q 29:12). [IRC § 403(b)(1)(C)]

2. The TSA must be nontransferable (see Q 29:13). [IRC § 401(g)]

3. The TSA must provide for required minimum distributions (see Q 29:40). [IRC § 403(b)(10)]

4. No distributions may be made from an *annuity contract* (as opposed to a custodial account) attributable to contributions made pursuant to a salary reduction agreement until the occurrence of certain specified events (see Q 29:38). [IRC § 403(b)(11)]

5. No distributions may be made from a *custodial account* (as opposed to an annuity contract) before the occurrence of certain specified events (see Q 29:38). [IRC § 403(b)(7)(A)(ii)]

6. The TSA must be purchased under a plan that satisfies minimum coverage, minimum participation, and nondiscrimination requirements and that limits the amount of compensation that may be considered (see Qs 29:14–29:18). [IRC §§ 403(b)(1)(D), 403(b)(12)]

7. Elective deferrals cannot exceed a specified amount (see Q 29:27). [IRC § 403(b)(1)(E)]

8. The TSA must provide for direct rollovers (see Q 29:42). [IRC § 403(b)(10)]

[Ltr Ruls 9522056, 9442026]

Each TSA *contract*, not the TSA *plan*, must provide that elective deferrals made under the contract may not exceed the annual limit on elective deferrals. [IRC § 403(b)(1)(E), as amended by SBA § 1450(c)(1)] It is intended that the contract terms be given effect in order for this requirement to be satisfied. Thus, for example, if the contract issuer takes no steps to ensure that deferrals under the contract do not exceed the applicable limit, then the contract will not be treated as satisfying Section 403(b). This provision is intended to make clear that the exclusion of elective deferrals from gross income by employees who have not exceeded the annual limit on elective deferrals will not be affected to the extent other employees exceed the annual limit. However, if the occurrence of an uncorrected elective deferral made by an employee is attributable to reasonable error, the contract will not fail to satisfy Section 403(b), and only the portion of the elective deferral in excess of the annual limit will be includible in gross income.

This new provision is effective for years beginning *after* 1995, except that an annuity contract is not required to meet any change in any requirement by reason of this provision before November 18, 1996. [SBA '96, Act § 1450(c)(2)]

Q 29:12 Must an employee's rights under a TSA be nonforfeitable?

Except for the failure to pay future premiums, the employee's rights under the TSA must be nonforfeitable at the time of the contributions for the purchase of the annuity contract. Nonforfeitable means being 100 percent vested (see Q 9:1). [IRC § 403(b)(1)(C)]

If the employee's rights under the TSA are forfeitable, some portion of the contributions may be includible in gross income for the employee's taxable year. However, if the employee's rights change from forfeitable to nonforfeitable during the employee's taxable year, none of the contributions will be includible in the employee's gross income for that year unless the employer is not an eligible employer (see Q 29:2) at the time of the change or the contributions exceed the exclusion allowance (see Q 29:22) for that year. Because the contributions are deemed to be made by the employer at the time the change occurs, it is immaterial whether the employer was an eligible employer at the time the actual contributions were made. [IRC §§ 403(b)(6), 403(c); Treas Reg § 1.403(b)-1(b)(2)]

The nonforfeitability requirement is not violated if the TSA permits a return of contributions made as a result of a mistake of fact. [GCM 38992]

IRS has ruled that employer nonmatching contributions to a TSA program are not required to be 100 percent vested immediately and may be subject to a vesting schedule (see Q 9:3). [Ltr Rul 9529006]

Q 29:13   Must the TSA be nontransferable?

A TSA purchased after 1962 must be nontransferable. A TSA is transferable if the employee can transfer any portion of his or her interest in the TSA to any person other than the insurance company. Accordingly, a TSA is transferable if the employee can sell, assign, discount, or pledge as collateral for a loan or as security for the performance of an obligation or for any other purpose the employee's interest in the TSA to any person other than the insurance company. A written agreement between the employee and the employer that the employee will not transfer the TSA is insufficient; the nontransferability provision must be part of the TSA itself. [IRC § 401(g); Treas Reg § 1.401-9; Rev Rul 74-458, 1974-2 CB 138]

The nontransferability requirement is not violated even though the employee can surrender the TSA to the insurance company, make a loan against the TSA (see Q 29:47), designate a beneficiary, elect an optional method of settlement (e.g., a joint and survivor annuity), transfer amounts held under the TSA from one insurance company to another (see Q 29:41), or roll over a TSA distribution to another TSA or an IRA (see Q 29:42).

Q 29:14   Are TSAs subject to the minimum coverage and minimum participation requirements?

Both the minimum coverage and minimum participation requirements must be satisfied by the TSA program unless the program allows only elective deferrals (see Q 29:10). Thus, these requirements must be met if the program provides for contributions other than, or in addition to, elective deferrals (see Q 29:9). [IRC §§ 403(b)(1)(D), 403(b)(12)(A)(i), 403(b)(12)(A)(ii)]

For a discussion of these requirements, see Qs 5:15 through 5:28.

A TSA program may require an employee to reach age 21 and to complete one year of service before becoming eligible to participate. If the employee's rights under the TSA are immediately nonforfeitable, as is usually the case (see Q 29:12), the service eligibility requirement may be increased to up to two years. If the TSA program is adopted by a tax-exempt educational institution (see Q 29:2), the service eligibility requirement is no more than one year, and the employee's rights are immediately nonforfeitable, the age requirement may be increased to age 26. [IRC §§ 410(a)(1), 170(b)(1)(A)(ii)]

In many cases, an individual TSA is purchased by the employer for each employee. For purposes of satisfying the minimum coverage and minimum participation requirements, all of the individual TSAs are referred to as an "aggregated 403(b) annuity program," and all of the individual TSAs will be treated as satisfying these requirements only if the aggregated 403(b) annuity program satisfies the requirements. If the employer makes contributions to only a group TSA contract, the aggregated 403(b) annuity program is that single contract. [Notice 89-23, Part V, 1989-1 CB 654]

See Q 29:17 for a discussion of the safe harbors that generally replace the separate testing for the minimum coverage and minimum participation requirements.

Q 29:15   Do the nondiscrimination requirements applicable to qualified retirement plans also apply to TSAs?

Contributions to an aggregated 403(b) annuity program (see Q 29:14) may not discriminate in favor of highly compensated employees (see Q 3:2); therefore, the same general nondiscrimination requirements that apply to qualified retirement plans will also be applicable to TSAs. However, if the program allows only elective deferrals (see Q 29:10), the general nondiscrimination requirements are replaced by a single nondiscrimination requirement (see Q 29:16). [IRC §§ 403(b)(1)(D), 403(b)(12)(A)(i), 403(b)(12)(A)(ii)]

For a discussion of the nondiscrimination requirements, see Qs 4:9 through 4:22, and also see Q 29:17 for a discussion of the safe harbors that may be used to satisfy these requirements.

The nondiscrimination requirements are effective for plan years beginning on and after January 1, 1997. For plan years beginning before January 1, 1997, a TSA program must be operated in accordance with a reasonable, good-faith interpretation of the nondiscrimination requirements. [Ann 95-48, 1995-23 IRB 13]

Q 29:16 Is there a special nondiscrimination requirement if an employee may enter into a salary reduction agreement?

If any one employee may elect to have the employer make contributions to a TSA pursuant to a salary reduction agreement (see Q 29:10), then all employees of the employer must be permitted to elect to have the employer make salary reduction contributions of more than $200. This is the *only* nondiscrimination requirement that applies if the TSA allows just elective deferrals. [IRC §§ 403(b)(1)(D), 403(b)(12)(A)(ii)]

In other words, the aggregated 403(b) annuity program (see Q 29:14) is deemed to satisfy the nondiscrimination requirements for a plan year only if each employee is eligible to defer annually more than $200 pursuant to a salary reduction agreement and the opportunity to make such contributions is available to all employees on the same basis. If an employer historically has treated its various geographically distinct units as separate for employee benefit purposes, then each unit, rather than the employer, may be considered a separate organization for purposes of this nondiscrimination requirement, so long as the units are, on a day-to-day basis, operated independently. Units of the same employer are not geographically distinct if such units are located within the same Standard Metropolitan Statistical Area. [Notice 89-23, Parts II and III, 1989-1 CB 654]

If a TSA provides for both elective deferrals and other contributions (i.e., employer contributions or employee contributions (see Q 29:9)), the nondiscrimination requirement discussed in this question applies to the elective deferrals, and the nondiscrimination requirements discussed in Qs 29:14, 29:15, and 29:19 apply to the other contributions.

Q 29:17 What safe harbors are available to satisfy the nondiscrimination requirements applicable to employer contributions to TSAs?

The employer's aggregated 403(b) annuity program (see Q 29:14) will satisfy the nondiscrimination requirements, including the minimum coverage and minimum participation requirements (see Q 29:15), if the program satisfies any one of the following three safe harbors:

Maximum disparity safe harbor (180 percent rule). This safe harbor is satisfied if:

1. The highest percentage of compensation (see Qs 6:37, 29:18) for a year contributed on behalf of any highly compensated employee (see Q 3:3) currently accruing benefits under the program is not more than 180 percent of the lowest percentage of compensation for a year

contributed on behalf of any non-highly compensated employee (see Q 3:13) currently accruing benefits;

2. At least 50 percent of the non-highly compensated employees are currently accruing benefits under the program; and

3. The percentage of employees currently accruing benefits under the program who are non-highly compensated employees is at least 70 percent.

Lesser disparity safe harbor (140 percent rule). This safe harbor is satisfied if:

1. The highest percentage of compensation for a year contributed on behalf of a highly compensated employee currently accruing benefits under the program is not more than 140 percent of the lowest percentage of compensation for a year contributed on behalf of any non-highly compensated employee currently accruing benefits;

2. At least 30 percent of the non-highly compensated employees are currently accruing benefits under the program; and

3. The percentage of employees who are currently accruing benefits under the program who are non-highly compensated employees is at least 50 percent.

No disparity safe harbor. This safe harbor is satisfied if the highest percentage of compensation for a year contributed on behalf of any highly compensated employee currently accruing benefits under the program is not higher than the lowest percentage of compensation for a year contributed on behalf of any non-highly compensated employee currently accruing benefits, and either one of the following two tests is satisfied:

1. At least 20 percent of the non-highly compensated employees are currently accruing benefits under the program and the percentage of participants in the program who are non-highly compensated employees is at least 70 percent, or

2. At least 80 percent of the non-highly compensated employees are currently accruing benefits under the program and the percentage of participants in the program who are non-highly compensated employees is at least 30 percent.

The safe harbors are illustrated in the chart below. The numbers in the blocks represent the benefit disparity (i.e., the ratio of the highest percentage of compensation contributed on behalf of any highly compensated employee currently accruing benefits under the program to the lowest percentage of compensation contributed on behalf of any non-highly compensated employee currently accruing benefits) permitted under the safe harbors.

Percentage of non-highly compensated employees of the employer currently accruing benefits under the program.

	90	80	70	60	50	40	30	20	10	0
0										
10										
20	0	0	0							
30	140	140	140	140	140					
40	140	140	140	140	140					
50	180	180	180	140	140					
60	180	180	180	140	140					
70	180	180	180	140	140					
80	180	180	180	140	140	0	0			
90	180	180	180	140	140	0	0			
100										

Percentage of all employees of the employer currently accruing benefits under the program who are non-highly compensated.

Example. If 55 percent of an employer's non-highly compensated employees are currently accruing benefits under the program and 50 percent of the employees currently accruing benefits thereunder are non-highly compensated employees, the program satisfies the lesser disparity safe harbor as long as the highest percentage of compensation for a year contributed on behalf of any highly compensated employee currently accruing benefits is not more than 140 percent of the lowest percentage of compensation for a year contributed on behalf of any non-highly compensated employee currently accruing benefits.

[Notice 89-23, Part IV, 1989-1 CB 654; Notice 90-73, 1990-2 CB 353; Notice 92-36, 1992-2 CB 364]

An employer may elect to include in its class of highly compensated employees only those employees who, during the plan year, are 5 percent owners (see Q 22:28) or receive compensation in excess of $50,000, adjusted for inflation (see Qs 3:3, 3:9). The safe harbors are applied as of the last day of the plan year, taking into account employees who are employed by the employer on that day. However, highly compensated employees who accrue benefits under the program during the plan year but terminate employment during the last quarter of the year are considered to be currently accruing benefits and are included for purposes of determining the highly compensated employee with the highest percentage of contributions.

In applying the safe harbors, the following employees may be excluded:

1. Nonresident aliens.

2. Certain student-employees.

3. Employees who normally work less than 20 hours per week.

4. Employees who make a one-time election to participate in a governmental plan instead of a TSA.

5. Certain professors.

6. Certain members of a religious order who have taken a vow of poverty.

7. Union employees (see Q 1:30).

If any employee in categories 1 through 6 above is included in the program, then no other employee in that category will be considered an excludable employee. [Notice 89-23, Parts IV and V, 1989-1 CB 654]

Example. The Wagger Furniture Foundation, an eligible employer, has offices in New York, North Carolina, Ohio, and Michigan. Wagger sponsors a separate TSA plan for its salaried employees at each office. Under each plan, an employee becomes a participant upon completion of one year of service. Wagger contributes 8 percent of compensation to the TSA plan for its New York employees; and, to each other plan, Wagger contributes 5 percent of compensation. The number of participants in each plan, the classifications of such participants, and the number of nonexcludable employees who are ineligible because they are non-salaried (all of whom are non-highly compensated employees) are set forth below.

	Highly Compensated Employees	Non-Highly Compensated Employees	Ineligible Employees
New York plan	19	45	55
North Carolina plan	2	15	15
Ohio plan	3	20	15
Michigan plan	3	23	15
	27	103	100

The aggregated 403(b) annuity program sponsored by The Wagger Furniture Foundation satisfies the maximum disparity safe harbor because the highest percentage of compensation contributed on behalf of any highly compensated employee is not more than 180 percent of that contributed on behalf of any non-highly compensated employee currently accruing benefits (8% ÷ 5% = 160%); at least 50 percent of the non-highly compensated employees are currently accruing benefits (103 ÷ 203 = 50.74%); and the percentage of participants who are non-highly compensated employees is at least 70 percent (103 ÷ 130 = 79.23%).

The safe harbors do not apply to employer matching contributions or employee contributions (see Q 29:19).

The nondiscrimination requirements are effective for plan years beginning on and after January 1, 1997. For plan years beginning before January 1, 1997, a TSA program must be operated in accordance with a reasonable, good-faith interpretation of the nondiscrimination requirements. [Ann 95-48, 1995-23 IRB 13]

Q 29:18   Is there a limitation on the amount of compensation that may be taken into account under a TSA?

The same $150,000 compensation limitation that applies to qualified retirement plans also applies to TSAs. [IRC §§ 401(a)(17), 403(b)(1)(D), 403(b)(12)(A)(i); Treas Reg § 1.401(a)(17)-1(a)(3)]

In the case of plans maintained by tax-exempt organizations, the regulatory effective date is the first plan year beginning on or after January 1, 1996. Hence, for plan years beginning before 1996, the plan must be operated in accordance with a reasonable, good-faith interpretation of the annual compensation limitation. [Treas Reg §§ 1.401(a)(17)-1(d)(2), 1.401(a)(17)-1(d)(3)]

For a discussion of the limitation on the amount of compensation that may be considered, see Qs 6:23 through 6:26.

Q 29:19   Can employer matching contributions and employee contributions be made to a TSA?

Yes, but the special nondiscrimination test applies as if the TSA were a qualified retirement plan. [IRC §§ 403(b)(1)(D), 403(b)(12)(A)(i); Ltr Rul 9541038]

For a discussion of this special test, see Qs 23:48 through 23:55.

The safe harbors (see Q 29:17) do not apply to employer matching contributions and employee contributions; and, if a plan included in an aggregated 403(b) annuity program (see Q 29:14) provides for such contributions, the plan must satisfy the special test. For purposes of satisfying the special test, contributions made pursuant to a salary reduction agreement (see Q 29:10) to a TSA may not be considered. [Notice 89-23, Part IV, 1989-1 CB 654]

Q 29:20   Can a TSA program take permitted disparity into account?

Yes; however, an employer may not take into account any Social Security benefits or contributions or permitted disparity for purposes of satisfying the safe harbors (see Q 29:17). [Notice 89-23, Part IV, 1989-1 CB 654]

For a discussion of permitted disparity, see chapter 7.

Q 29:21   Is there a limit on the amount of contributions to a TSA that will be excludable from the employee's income?

The amount of contributions to a TSA that the employee may exclude from gross income for the taxable year (usually, the calendar year) is subject to three separate restrictions, each of which is applied on an annual basis:

1. The exclusion allowance (see Q 29:22). [IRC § 403(b)(2)]
2. The limit on elective deferrals (see Q 29:27). [IRC §§ 401(a)(30), 402(g), 403(b)(1)(E)]
3. The overall limitation (see Q 29:29). [IRC § 415(a)(2)(B)]

Generally, the employee can exclude from gross income for the taxable year employer contributions to a TSA equal to the *least* of:

1. The exclusion allowance for the *taxable* year;
2. The limit on elective deferrals for the *calendar* year; or
3. The overall limitation for the *limitation* year ending with or within the employee's taxable year.

The limitation year is the calendar year, but the employee may elect to change the limitation year to another 12-month period. To do this, the employee must attach a statement to his or her income tax return filed for the taxable year in which the change is made. However, if the employee is in control (see Q 29:32) of an employer, the limitation year is the limitation year (see Q 6:16) of that employer. [Treas Reg § 1.415-2(b)(7)]

Q 29:22   What is the exclusion allowance?

An employee's exclusion allowance for the taxable year (usually, the calendar year) is (1) 20 percent of the employee's includible compensation (see Q 29:23) multiplied by the employee's number of years of service (see Q 29:24), and reduced by (2) the aggregate amounts previously excludable from the employee's gross income for prior taxable years (see Q 29:25). [IRC § 403(b)(2)(A); Treas Reg § 1.403(b)-1(d)(1); Rev Rul 84-149, 1984-2 CB 97; Rev Rul 68-304, 1968-1 CB 179]

Rollover contributions from another TSA (see Q 29:42) or from a conduit IRA (see Q 28:40) are not considered for purposes of calculating the exclusion allowance. [IRC § 403(b)(1)]

If an employee participates in TSAs of two or more employers, a separate exclusion allowance is computed with respect to each employer. Therefore, in computing the exclusion allowance with respect to one employer, the includible compensation received by the employee from any other employer, the employee's years of service with any other employer, and amounts contributed by any other employer are not taken into account. [Treas Reg § 1.403(b)-1(d)(2); Rev Rul 69-629, 1969-2 CB 101]

To the extent that the current year's contribution does not exceed the employee's exclusion allowance or any other applicable limitation (see Qs 29:27, 29:29), the amount contributed will not be includible in the employee's gross income for the taxable year and will not be taxable until distributed (see Q 29:44).

Example. On January 1, 1997, Gary became an employee of The Klein Music Foundation, a tax-exempt organization. Gary earns $30,000 during 1997, and the foundation contributes $6,000 to a TSA purchased for Gary. Gary's exclusion allowance and the amount, if any, includible in his gross income for 1997 are calculated as follows:

1.	20% × $30,000 (includible compensation) × 1 (number of years of service)	$6,000
2.	Less: amounts previously excludable	0
3.	Exclusion allowance	$6,000
4.	1997 contribution	$6,000
5.	Less: exclusion allowance	$6,000
6.	Amount includible in gross income	0

IRS has ruled that forfeitable contributions (see Q 29:12) are included in calculating the exclusion allowance when the contributions become nonforfeitable. [Ltr Ruls 9610009, 9610008, 9610007]

Q 29:23   What does includible compensation mean?

Includible compensation means the amount of compensation received by the employee from an eligible employer (see Q 29:2) that is includible in gross income for the most recent period (ending not later than the close of the employee's taxable year for which the exclusion allowance (see Q 29:22) is being determined) that may be counted as one year of service (see Q 29:24). [IRC § 403(b)(3); Treas Reg § 1.403(b)-1(e)(1)]

In addition, the following items are *included*:

1. Certain foreign income even if not includible in gross income.

2. Compensation received from an eligible employer that has lost its tax-exempt status but was earned by the employee before the loss of such status.

The following items are *excluded* for the purposes of determining an employee's includible compensation:

1. Employer contributions to the TSA, including contributions includible in gross income because in excess of the exclusion allowance.

2. Employer contributions to a qualified retirement plan for the benefit of the employee.

3. PS-58 costs (see Q 29:7).

4. Compensation earned while the employer is not an eligible employer.

[Treas Reg §§ 1.403(b)-1(e)(2), 1.403(b)-1(e)(4); Rev Rul 79-221, 1979-2 CB 188; Rev Rul 68-304, 1968-1 CB 179]

For purposes of computing an employee's exclusion allowance for a taxable year, any compensation earned by the employee during a taxable year ending after the taxable year for which the exclusion allowance is being determined cannot be taken into account as includible compensation. On the other hand, an employee's includible compensation may include all or part of the compensation earned during a taxable year prior to the taxable year for which the exclusion allowance is being determined. Such a situation can occur, for example, when an employer purchases a TSA for a part-time employee whose most recent one-year period of service extends over more than one taxable year of the employee. Post-retirement payments to a former employee for earlier services are part of includible compensation, and this can permit an employer to make post-retirement contributions to its TSA program for employees who accept an early retirement offer. [Treas Reg § 1.403(b)-1(e)(3); Ltr Rul 9625043]

In determining an employee's most recent one-year period of service, all service performed by the employee during the taxable year for which the exclusion allowance is being determined is first taken into account, but an employee's most recent one-year period of service may not be the same as the employer's most recent annual work period.

Example. Bonnie, a contract bridge professor who reports her income on a calendar-year basis, is employed by Klein State University on a full-time basis during the university's 1996–1997 and 1997–1998 academic years (October through May). For purposes of computing Bonnie's exclusion allowance for her 1997 taxable year, her most recent one-year period of service consists of her service performed during January through May 1997 (which is part of the 1996–1997 academic year), and her service performed during October through December 1997 (which is part of the 1997–1998 academic year).

In the case of a part-time employee or a full-time employee who is employed for only part of a year, it is necessary to aggregate the most recent periods of service to determine the most recent one-year period of service. In such a case, service during the taxable year for which the exclusion allowance is being determined is first taken into account, then service during the next preceding taxable year is taken into account, and so forth until service equals, in the aggregate, one year of service.

Example. If an employee, who reports his income on a calendar year basis, is employed on a full-time basis during the months July through December 1995 (½ year of service), July through December 1996 (½ year of service), and October through December 1997 (¼ year of service), his most recent one-year period of service for purposes of computing his exclusion allowance for 1997 consists of his service during 1997 (¼ year of service), his service during 1996 (½ year of service), and his service during the months October through December 1995 (¼ year of service).

[Treas Reg § 1.403(b)-1(f)(7)]

Q 29:24 How is a year of service determined?

To compute an employee's exclusion allowance (see Q 29:22) for a taxable year, the employee's number of years of service for the employer as of the close of the taxable year must be determined. [IRC § 403(b)(4); Treas Reg § 1.403(b)-1(f)(1)]

An employee can earn a year of service only during a period in which the organization is an eligible employer (see Q 29:2). A teacher who changes employment from one school system to another in the same state cannot include years of service with the first school system for purposes of computing the exclusion allowance for the second. In determining an employee's number of years of service, all service performed by the employee as of the close of the taxable year may be taken into account. Whenever possible, service performed during each of the employee's taxable years should be considered separately in arriving at the total number of years of service. For example, if an employee who reports income on a calendar year basis is employed on a full-time basis on July 1, 1996 and continues on a full-time basis through December 31, 1997, the number of years of service as of the close of the 1997 taxable year is computed as follows:

1. Number of years of service performed during 1996 taxable year	½
2. Number of years of service performed during 1997 taxable year	1
3. Total number of years of service as of close of 1997 taxable year [(1) + (2)]	1½

However, in determining what constitutes a full year of service, the employer's annual work period, and not the employee's taxable year, is the standard of measurement. For example, in determining whether a professor is employed full time, the number of months in the school's academic year is the standard of measurement. [Treas Reg §§ 1.403(b)-1(f)(2), 1.403(b)-1(f)(3); Rev Rul 69-629, 1969-2 CB 101]

Each full year during which an individual is employed full time is considered as one year of service. In determining whether an individual is employed full time, the amount of work required to be performed is compared with the amount of work normally required of individuals who hold the same position with the same employer and generally derive the major portion of their personal service income from such position. In determining whether positions with the same employer are the same, all of the facts and circumstances concerning the positions are considered, including the work performed, the methods by which compensation is computed, and the descriptions (or titles) of the positions. For example, an assistant professor employed in the English department of a university is considered a full-time employee if the amount of work that the individual is required to perform is the same as the amount of work normally required of assistant professors of English at that university who derive the main portion of their personal service income from such position. A full year of service for a particular position means the usual annual work period of individuals employed full time in that general type of employment at the place of employment. For example, if a doctor employed by a hospital works throughout the 12 months of a year except for a one-month vacation, the doctor is considered as being employed for a full year if the other doctors at that hospital work 11 months of the year with a one-month vacation. Similarly, if the usual annual work period at a university consists of the fall and spring semesters, an instructor at that university who teaches those semesters is considered as working a full year. [Treas Reg § 1.403(b)-1(f)(4); Ravel, 26 TCM 885 (1967)]

Full-time employees who work only part of the year and employees who work part time are treated as having fractional years of service and these fractional years are aggregated to determine the employee's years of service. [Treas Reg § 1.403(b)-1(f)(5)(i)]

In determining the fraction that represents the fractional year of service for an individual employed full time for part of a year, the numerator is the number of weeks (or months) during which the individual was a full-time employee in a position during that year, and the denominator is the number of weeks (or months) that is considered as the usual annual work period for that position. For example, if an instructor is employed full time by a university for the 1997 spring semester (which lasts from February 1997 through May 1997), and the academic year of the university is eight months long, beginning in October 1996, and ending in May 1997, the individual is considered as having completed $\frac{4}{8}$ of a year of service. [Treas Reg § 1.403(b)-1(f)(5)(ii)]

In determining the fraction that represents the fractional year of service of an individual who is employed part time for a full year, the numerator is the amount of work required to be performed by the individual, and the denominator is the amount of work normally required of individuals who hold the same position. Thus, if a practicing physician teaches one course at a local medical school three hours per week for two semesters and other faculty members at that medical school teach nine hours per week for two semesters, the practicing physician is considered as having completed $\frac{3}{9}$ of a year of service. [Treas Reg § 1.403(b)-1(f)(5)(iii)]

In determining the fraction representing the fractional year of service of an individual who is employed part time for part of a year, it is necessary to compute the fractional year of service as if the individual were a part-time employee for a full year and as if the individual were a full-time employee for part of a year. The two fractions are multiplied, and the product is the fractional year of service of the individual. For example, if an attorney who is a specialist in a subject teaches a course in that subject for three hours per week for one semester at a nearby law school, and the full-time instructors at that law school teach 12 hours per week for two semesters, then the fractional part of a year of service for such part-time instructor is computed as follows:

1. The fractional year of service if the instructor was a part-time employee for a full year is $\frac{3}{12}$ (number of hours employed divided by the usual number of hours of work required for that position).

2. The fractional year of service if the instructor was a full-time employee for part of a year is $\frac{1}{2}$ (period worked or one semester, divided by usual work period, or two semesters).

3. These fractions are multiplied to obtain the fractional year of service $(\frac{3}{12} \times \frac{1}{2} = \frac{3}{24} = \frac{1}{8})$.

[Treas Reg § 1.403(b)-1(f)(5)(iv)]

If, at the close of a taxable year, an employee has a period of service of less than one year, the employee is nevertheless considered to have one year of service for purposes of computing the exclusion allowance for that taxable year. Such period of service of less than one year is also considered to be the employee's most recent one-year period of service for purposes of determining includible compensation (see Q 29:23).

[Treas Reg § 1.403(b)-1(f)(6)]

Q 29:25 How are the aggregate amounts previously excludable from the employee's gross income for prior taxable years determined?

To calculate an employee's exclusion allowance (see Q 29:22) for the taxable year, the initial calculation is *reduced* by the amounts previously excludable from gross income for *prior* years. These previously excludable amounts are aggregated. [IRC § 403(b)(2)(A)(ii)]

These amounts include the following:

1. Employer contributions to TSAs, including contributions made pursuant to salary reduction agreements, that were excludable from gross income (see Qs 29:9, 29:10);

2. Employer contributions to a qualified retirement plan that were excludable from gross income;

3. Employer contributions to a qualified bond purchase plan that were excludable from gross income even though such plans are no longer permissible;

4. Compensation deferred under a Section 457 plan even if the employer sponsoring the plan differs from the employer purchasing the TSA;

5. Employer contributions that were excludable from gross income solely because the employee's rights were forfeitable at that time, that subsequently became nonforfeitable in a prior year, and that were not includible in gross income for the year in which the employee's rights became nonforfeitable (see Q 29:12); and

6. Employer contributions to a TSA for a prior taxable year that exceeded the annual addition limitation (see Q 29:29).

[Treas Reg §§ 1.403(b)-1(d)(1), 1.403(b)-1(d)(3); Rev Rul 84-149, 1984-2 CB 97; Rev Rul 79-221, 1979-2 CB 188; Rev Rul 69-629, 1969-2 CB 101]

If the contribution to a TSA exceeds the annual addition limitation (see paragraph 6 above), the excess amount is considered a previously excludable amount in determining the exclusion allowance for future taxable years, even though the excess amount was not excludable from gross income in the taxable year when made. [Treas Reg §§ 1.403(b)-1(d)(3)(v), 1.415-6(e)(1)(ii)]

Employer contributions to a defined contribution plan (see Q 2:2) on behalf of an employee can be easily calculated for purposes of determining previously excludable amounts; however, employer contributions to a defined benefit plan (see Q 2:3) are not readily calculated. A formula, converting benefits into contributions, may be used to calculate employer contributions to a defined benefit plan that were previously excludable from the employee's gross income. [Treas Reg § 1.403(b)-1(d)(4)]

Q 29:26   Is there an alternative exclusion allowance calculation?

An employee of an educational organization, a hospital, a home health service agency, or a health and welfare service agency may elect to have a special limitation apply for a taxable year. If the employee so elects, the exclusion allowance (see Q 29:22) is the maximum amount that could be contributed by the employer for the benefit of the employee if the TSA were treated as a defined contribution plan (see Q 2:2) maintained by the employer. Thus, the exclusion allowance for the taxable year of an employee who makes the election may not exceed the annual addition limitation (see Q 29:29). [IRC §§ 403(b)(2)(B), 415(c)(4)(C), 415(c)(4)(D); Social Security Act § 1861(o); Treas Reg § 1.403(b)-1(d)(5)]

Q 29:27   Is there a dollar limit on the amount of elective deferrals under a TSA?

Elective deferrals relate to amounts contributed to (1) a TSA under a salary reduction agreement (see Q 29:10), (2) a 401(k) plan pursuant to a cash-or-deferred arrangement (see Q 23:1), (3) a SEP under a salary reduction agreement (see Q 27:9), and (4) a SIMPLE plan under a salary reduction agreement (see Q 27:23). [IRC § 402(g)(3), as amended by SBA '96 § 1421(b)(9)(B); Treas Reg § 1.402(g)-1(b)]

Although the aggregate annual limit on elective deferrals under a 401(k) plan and a SEP is $7,000, adjusted for inflation (see Qs 23:26, 27:10), and under a SIMPLE plan is $6,000, adjusted for inflation (see Q 27:26), the limit under a TSA is $9,500. However, all of the employee's elective deferrals for the taxable year are aggregated, so that if the employee makes an elective deferral to a TSA of $9,500 for the taxable year, no amount may be contributed to a 401(k) plan, a SEP, or a SIMPLE plan under salary reduction agreements for that year. [IRC §§ 401(a)(30), 402(g)(1), 402(g)(4),

403(b)(1)(E); Treas Reg §§ 1.402(g)-1(d)(2), 1.402(g)-1(d)(4); Notice 87-13, 1989-1 CB 432]

> **Example.** The Wagger State University, an eligible employer, offers its employees TSAs to which elective deferrals may be made. For the 1996 taxable year, two of Wagger's employees, Harold and Renee, contribute $3,500 and $8,500, respectively, to the TSA. Harold and Renee also participate in another employer's 401(k) plan for 1996. The maximum amounts that Harold and Renee may contribute under the 401(k) plan for their 1996 taxable year are $6,000 ($9,500 – $3,500) and $1,000 ($9,500 – $8,500), respectively.

The amount of the elective deferrals excludable from gross income for a taxable year may be less than the dollar limit if the amount exceeds the lesser of the exclusion allowance (see Q 29:22) or the overall limitation (see Q 29:29). However, required contributions made by employees under a TSA program are not subject to the limit on elective deferrals or treated as made pursuant to a salary reduction agreement if the required contributions are a condition of employment when made. [Ltr Ruls 9610009, 9610008, 9610007]

When the dollar limit for 401(k) plans and SEPs increases to more than $9,500, the dollar limit for elective deferrals under TSAs will also increase. [TRA '86 Comm Reports, II-405]

An employee who has completed 15 years of service (see Q 29:24) with an educational organization, a hospital, a home health service agency, or a health and welfare service agency is eligible for a special catch-up rule, which increases the dollar limit to more than $9,500. Under the catch-up rule, the dollar limit for the employee's taxable year is increased by the *least* of the following amounts:

1. $3,000;
2. $15,000 reduced by amounts previously excluded from gross income in prior taxable years under this catch-up rule; or
3. $5,000 multiplied by the employee's number of years of service (see Q 29:24) with the employer, reduced by all prior elective deferrals under all plans of the employer and certain prior deferrals under a Section 457 plan.

[IRC §§ 402(g)(8), 457(c)(2); Treas Reg § 1.402(g)-1(d)(3)]

Based upon the above limitation, under the catch-up rule, the dollar limit for any taxable year cannot be increased by more than $3,000. As with the regular dollar limit, the exclusion from gross income cannot exceed the lesser of the exclusion allowance or the overall limitation. [TRA '86 Comm Reports, II-404]

For a discussion of correcting excess deferrals and the tax consequences of making excess deferrals, see Qs 23:28 and 23:29.

Q 29:28 Are elective deferrals subject to payroll taxes?

Yes. Elective deferrals made under a salary reduction agreement (see Q 29:10) are included in the Social Security taxable wage base (see Q 7:7) for both employer and employee withholding purposes. Elective deferrals are also subject to the Federal Unemployment Taxes Act (FUTA). [Rev Rul 65-208, 1965-2 CB 383; Social Security Act Amendments of 1983 § 324(d)]

Elective deferrals are also included for purposes of measuring the annual increases in Social Security average wages, which will affect the calculation of both the taxable earnings base and benefit computations. [Social Security Act § 209]

Q 29:29 What is the overall limitation?

A TSA is treated as a defined contribution plan (see Q 2:2) for purposes of the limitations on contributions and, thus, is subject to the rules regarding the amount of annual additions (see Q 6:1) that may be made to a participant's account for a limitation year (see Qs 6:16, 29:21). In other words, the annual addition with respect to any limitation year may not exceed the *lesser* of $30,000 (see Q 6:2) or 25 percent of compensation (see Q 6:3). [IRC §§ 415(a)(2)(B), 415(c)(1); Treas Reg § 1.415-6(a)(1)(i); Ltr Rul 9529006]

If the amount of contributions for an employee under a TSA for a taxable year exceeds the annual addition limitation, then, for purposes of computing the exclusion allowance (see Q 29:22) for future taxable years, the excess contribution is considered as an amount contributed by the employer for a TSA that was excludable from the employee's gross income for a prior taxable year (see Q 29:25). Therefore, for future taxable years, the exclusion allowance is reduced by the amount of the excess contribution even though that amount was *not* excludable from the employee's gross income in the taxable year when it was made. For purposes of the annual addition limitation, the amount contributed toward the purchase of a TSA is treated as allocated to the employee's account as of the last day of the limitation year ending with or within the taxable year during which the contribution is made. [Treas Reg §§ 1.415-6(e)(1)(ii), 1.415-6(e)(1)(iii)]

Excess elective deferrals distributed within the correction period (see Q 23:28) are not considered annual additions, but excess deferrals distributed after the correction period are counted. [Treas Reg §§ 1.402(g)-1(e)(1)(ii), 1.402(g)-1(e)(8)(iii)]

A special election available to certain employees may permit a higher overall limit than the annual addition limitation (see Q 29:30).

Q 29:30 May a special election be made to increase the overall limitation?

Yes, but the special election is available only to an employee of an educational organization, a hospital, a home health service agency, or a health and welfare service agency. [IRC § 415(c)(4)]

There are three alternative limitations that may be elected, which are referred to respectively as the (A) election limitation, the (B) election limitation, and the (C) election limitation. [Treas Reg § 1.415-6(e)(2)]

The (A) election limitation may be used *only* once and *only* when the employee separates from service. This limitation allows an employee to make a greater contribution (i.e., catch-up) for the last year of employment. For the limitation year (see Q 29:21) ending with or within the year of separation, the employee's exclusion allowance (see Q 29:22) may be calculated without the 25-percent-of-compensation limitation; however, the dollar limitation ($30,000, adjusted for inflation) continues to apply (see Q 29:29). The calculation of the exclusion allowance is modified to include only years of service and employer contributions during the ten-year period ending on the date of separation. If the contribution for the last year is by elective deferrals, that limitation will apply (see Q 29:27). [IRC § 415(c)(4)(A); Treas Reg § 1.415-6(e)(3)]

> **Example.** Leonard, executive director of Eisner Hospital, plans to retire on December 31, 1996, after 15 years of service. Leonard's compensation for 1996 will be $100,000; and, during the ten-year period prior to retirement, Eisner Hospital contributed $80,000 to the TSA. Leonard's modified exclusion allowance is $120,000 [(20% × $100,000 × 10) − $80,000]. If Leonard elects this alternative, Eisner Hospital could contribute $30,000 (the dollar limitation continues to apply) to the TSA for his last year of employment.

The second alternative, the (B) election limitation, can be used each year by the employee and substitutes for the annual addition limitation the *least* of:

1. $4,000, plus 25 percent of the employee's includible compensation (see Q 29:23) for the taxable year with or within which the limitation year ends;

2. The exclusion allowance for the taxable year with or within which the limitation year ends; or

3. $15,000.

As with the (A) election limitation, if the contribution for the year is by elective deferrals, that limitation will apply. [IRC § 415(c)(4)(B); Treas Reg § 1.415-6(e)(4)]

Example. Marlene, assistant executive director of Eisner Hospital, will earn $29,000 (before reduction for elective deferrals) during 1997. Assume that Marlene's exclusion allowance for 1997 is $12,000 and she desires to make elective deferrals of $9,000 during 1997. The (B) election limitation will allow Marlene to make elective deferrals for 1997 of $9,000, calculated as follows:

1.	$4,000 + [25% × ($29,000 − $9,000)]	$ 9,000
2.	Exclusion allowance	$12,000
3.	$15,000	$15,000
4.	Least of 1, 2, or 3	$ 9,000

The (C) election limitation is the same as the overall limitation (see Q 29:29) and permits the employee to use the annual addition limitation as the employee's exclusion allowance. [IRC § 415(c)(4)(C); Treas Reg § 1.415-6(e)(5)]

Q 29:31   How is the special election made?

An employee's election to use one of the three alternative limitations (see Q 29:30) is made by calculating the employee's income tax liability for that year by using any one of the alternatives. However, an employee is only considered to have made an election for a taxable year when the use of one of the alternative limitations is necessary to support the exclusion from gross income reflected in the employee's income tax return for that taxable year. [Treas Reg § 1.415-6(e)(6)(i)]

An election to use an alternative limitation is irrevocable once made. An employee can only make the (A) election limitation once. If the (B) election limitation or the (C) election limitation is made, the employee can *never* use either of the other two alternatives for any subsequent year. For example, if an employee uses the (B) election limitation, neither the (A) nor (C) election limitation may ever be used by the employee, but the employee is not required to elect the (B) election limitation in every succeeding year. [IRC § 415(c)(4)(D)(i)]

Q 29:32   What happens if an employee participates in a TSA and a qualified retirement plan?

The answer depends upon whether the TSA must be combined or aggregated with the qualified retirement plan. If the TSA is combined with a defined contribution plan (see Q 2:2), the annual addition limitation (see Qs 6:1, 29:29) applies to the combined plans; and, if the TSA is aggregated with a defined benefit plan (see Q 2:3), the 1.0 rule (see Q 6:17) applies. For these purposes, a TSA is treated as a defined contribution plan. *For limitation years* (see Q 6:16) *beginning after 1999,* the 1.0 rule is repealed. [SBA '96, Act § 1452(a)]

Generally, in the case of a TSA, the employee on whose behalf the TSA is purchased is considered to have exclusive control of the TSA; and, accordingly, the employee, *not the employer*, is deemed to maintain the TSA. However, if the employee has elected the (C) election limitation (see Q 29:30) for a taxable year, the TSA is treated as a defined contribution plan maintained by *both* the employer that purchased the TSA and the employee on whose behalf it was purchased for the limitation year (see Q 29:21) that ends during such taxable year. Even if the (C) election limitation is not made, where an employee on whose behalf a TSA is purchased is in control of any employer, the TSA is treated as a defined contribution plan maintained by *both* the controlled employer and the employee for that limitation year. For example, if a doctor is employed by an educational organization that provides him with a TSA, and the doctor also maintains a private practice as a shareholder owning more than 50 percent of a professional corporation, any defined contribution plan of the professional corporation must be combined with the TSA for purposes of applying the annual addition limitation. It is immaterial whether the TSA is purchased as a result of a salary reduction agreement (see Q 29:10) between the employer and the employee. [IRC §§ 414(b), 414(c), 415(c), 415(e)(5) prior to repeal by SBA '96 § 1452(a), 415(f), 415(g), 415(h); Treas Reg § 1.415-8(d)]

If the employee has elected the (C) election limitation for a taxable year, or if the employee is in control of any employer, the TSA is treated as a defined contribution plan maintained by *both* the controlled employer and the employee for the limitation year, and any contributions made for the TSA are taken into account in computing the defined contribution plan fraction applicable to the employee for the limitation year. As with a defined contribution plan, if a doctor is employed by an educational organization that provides him with a TSA, and the doctor also maintains a private practice as a shareholder owning more than 50 percent of a professional corporation, any defined benefit plan of the professional corporation must be aggregated with the TSA for purposes of applying the 1.0 rule, and it is again immaterial whether the TSA is purchased pursuant to a salary reduction agreement. Where a TSA is aggregated with a defined benefit plan, all contributions made to the TSA in *prior* limitation years are taken into account in computing the employee's defined contribution plan fraction; but, if the aggregation is *solely* attributable to the election of the (C) election limitation, all contributions made to the TSA in *prior* limitation years do not have to be taken into account in computing the defined contribution plan fraction. However, any contributions made to a TSA in any limitation year for which the (C) election limitation is applicable will be taken into account in *subsequent* limitation years even though the (C) election limitation is not made for the subsequent limitation year (see Q 29:31). [Treas Reg § 1.415-7(h); Ann 95-33, 1995-19 IRB 14]

> **Example 1.** Carl is employed by a hospital that purchases a TSA on Carl's behalf for the current limitation year. The hospital also maintains a defined benefit plan in which Carl is a participant during that limitation year. Carl does not elect the (C) election limitation for the current limitation year and is not in control of any employer. Since Carl is considered to have exclusive control of the TSA, Carl (and not the hospital) is treated as maintaining the TSA and the 1.0 rule does not apply for the current limitation year.

> **Example 2.** Assume the same facts as in Example 1, except that the hospital also maintains a defined contribution plan during the limitation year in which Carl is a participant. Because the hospital is not considered to be maintaining the TSA, contributions made to the TSA on behalf of Carl during the current limitation year by the hospital are not taken into account in computing the defined contribution plan fraction applicable to Carl for the plans maintained by the hospital for that limitation year.

> **Example 3.** Assume the same facts as in Example 1, except that Carl has elected the (C) election limitation for the current limitation year. Because of this election, the TSA is treated as a defined contribution plan maintained by the hospital as well as a defined contribution plan maintained by Carl. Accordingly, because the hospital is also maintaining a defined benefit plan, the 1.0 rule is applicable to Carl for the TSA and the defined benefit plan maintained by the hospital in the current limitation year.

> **Example 4.** Arleen is employed by a hospital that purchases a TSA on Arleen's behalf for the current limitation year. The hospital does not maintain any qualified retirement plans during that limitation year. However, for the limitation year, Arleen is in control of Corky Corporation, and Corky Corporation maintains a defined benefit plan during that limitation year. Because the TSA is treated as a defined contribution plan maintained by Corky Corporation (the controlled employer) as well as a defined contribution plan maintained by Arleen, and because Corky

Corporation is also maintaining a defined benefit plan, the 1.0 rule is applicable to Arleen for the TSA and the defined benefit plan maintained by Corky Corporation in the current limitation year.

See Q 29:33 for a discussion of special rules relating to the calculation of the defined contribution plan fraction.

Q 29:33   If a TSA is aggregated with a defined benefit plan, how is the defined contribution plan fraction calculated?

Under the normal rule, the denominator of the defined contribution plan fraction (see Qs 6:17, 29:32) is the sum of the maximum amount of annual additions (see Q 6:1) that could have been made for the limitation year (see Q 6:16) and for each prior limitation year of the employee's service with the employer (regardless of whether a defined contribution plan was in existence during those years). [Treas Reg § 1.415-7(c)(1)(ii)]

There are two special rules applicable to TSAs. First, in computing the defined contribution plan fraction applicable to an employee on whose behalf a TSA has been purchased, the amount included in the denominator of the fraction for a particular limitation year (see Q 29:21) is the maximum amount that could have been contributed under the annual addition limitation applicable to the employee for that particular limitation year. However, if the employee elects either the (A) or (B) election limitation (see Q 29:30) for a particular limitation year, the denominator for that particular limitation year is the maximum amount that could have been contributed under the annual addition limitation, as modified by the alternative elected. [Treas Reg § 1.415-7(c)(2)(i)]

The second special rule applies to an employee on whose behalf a TSA has been purchased prior to commencing employment with a controlled employer (see Q 29:32) that maintains a defined benefit plan (see Q 2:3). In this situation, the controlled employer is considered to be maintaining the TSA as a defined contribution plan. However, for all years prior to commencing employment with the controlled employer, the employee does not have any years of service with that employer. Thus, for each limitation year in which the employee did not have a year of service with the controlled employer, the denominator of the defined contribution plan fraction applicable to the employee is deemed to equal the numerator of that fraction. [Treas Reg § 1.415-7(c)(2)(ii)]

For limitation years beginning after 1999, the 1.0 rule is repealed. [SBA '96, Act § 1452(a)]

Q 29:34 What happens if aggregating or combining a TSA and a qualified retirement plan causes the applicable limitation to be exceeded?

If this occurs, the exclusion allowance (see Q 29:22) is adjusted first to the extent necessary to satisfy such limitations. [Treas Reg § 1.415-9(c)(1)]

If combining a TSA and a defined contribution plan causes the annual addition limitation (see Qs 6:1, 29:29) to be exceeded for the limitation year (see Qs 6:16, 29:21), the excess of (1) the contributions to the TSA plus the annual additions to the plan, over (2) the limitation is treated as a disqualified contribution to the TSA and therefore includible in the gross income of the employee for the taxable year with or within which that limitation year ends. Furthermore, for purposes of computing the exclusion allowance for future taxable years, the disqualified contribution is treated as an amount contributed by the employer for a TSA that was excludable from the employee's gross income (see Q 29:25). Thus, for future taxable years, the exclusion allowance will be reduced by the amount of the disqualified contribution even though such amount was not excludable from the employee's gross income in the taxable year when it was made. [Treas Reg § 1.415-9(c)(3)]

> **Example.** Shirley is employed by a hospital that purchases a TSA on Shirley's behalf during the limitation year, which is Shirley's first year of service with the hospital. Assume that Shirley is in control of the hospital so that the TSA is treated as a defined contribution plan maintained by the hospital and Shirley. The hospital also maintains a defined contribution plan in which Shirley participates. Shirley's compensation from the hospital for the limitation year is $20,000, and she does not elect any alternative limitation. For the limitation year, the hospital contributes $3,000 for the TSA and $3,000 to the plan on Shirley's behalf. Because the hospital is considered to be maintaining only one defined contribution plan (all contributions to the TSA and to the plan must be combined) and because the total combined contributions ($6,000) exceed the annual addition limitation applicable to Shirley [$5,000 (25% × $20,000)], $1,000 of the $3,000 contributed to the TSA is considered a disqualified contribution currently includible in Shirley's gross income. Furthermore, in computing Shirley's exclusion allowance for future taxable years, besides the $3,000 contributed to the plan, the $3,000 contributed for the TSA is also considered an amount contributed by the employer and excludable from Shirley's gross income, even though only $2,000 of this latter amount was actually excludable from Shirley's gross income.

If aggregating a TSA and a defined benefit plan causes the 1.0 rule (see Q 6:17) to be exceeded, the amount of the excess contribution to the TSA is treated as a disqualified contribution and therefore includible in the gross income of the employee for the taxable year with or within which that limitation year ends. Furthermore, for purposes of computing the exclusion allowance for future taxable years with respect to the employee, the disqualified contribution is treated as an amount contributed by the employer for a TSA that was excludable from the employee's gross income. Thus, for future taxable years, the exclusion allowance will be reduced by the amount of the disqualified contribution, even though such amount was not excludable from the employee's gross income in the taxable year when it was made. [Treas Reg § 1.415-9(c)(2)]

> **Example.** Assume the same facts as in the above example, except that, instead of the defined contribution plan, the hospital maintains a defined benefit plan in which Shirley participates. Because the hospital is considered to be maintaining a defined contribution plan (in the form of a TSA) in addition to its defined benefit plan, the 1.0 rule applies. Assume that, under the 1.0 rule, only $2,000 could have been contributed to the TSA on Shirley's behalf for the limitation year. Because the hospital contributed $3,000 to the TSA, $1,000 of this amount is considered a disqualified contribution currently includible in Shirley's gross income. Furthermore, in computing Shirley's exclusion allowance for future taxable years, the $3,000 contributed to the TSA is considered the amount contributed by the employer and excludable from Shirley's gross income, even though only $2,000 of this amount was actually excludable from Shirley's gross income.

For limitation years (see Q 6:16) *beginning after 1999*, the 1.0 rule is repealed. [SBA '96, Act § 1452(a)]

See Q 29:35 for the excise tax imposed upon excess contributions to a custodial account.

Q 29:35 What is an excess contribution?

An excess contribution is (1) the amount by which the contributions to a *custodial account* (see Q 29:6) for the employee's taxable year exceed the *lesser* of the exclusion allowance (see Q 29:22) or the overall limitation (see Q 29:29), plus (2) any excess carried over from the preceding taxable year. Rollover contributions are not included (see Q 29:42). [IRC §§ 4973(c)(1), 4973(c)(2); Prop Reg § 54.4973-1(d)]

If an excess contribution is made to a custodial account, the excess account is subject to a 6 percent excise tax, and the penalty will be charged each year the excess contribution remains in the custodial account. The excise tax is determined as of the close of the taxable year and cannot exceed 6 percent of the value of the custodial account. The excise tax is imposed on the employee, not on the employer. [IRC § 4973(a); Prop Reg § 54.4973-1(e)]

An excess contribution can be corrected by either one or both of the following methods:

1. Making taxable distributions to the employee from the custodial account, or

2. Contributing in a subsequent taxable year less than the lower of the exclusion allowance or overall limitation applicable to the employee for that year.

[IRS Pub 571 (for use in preparing 1995 returns)]

Form 5330, Return of Excise Taxes Related to Employee Benefit Plans, is used to report the excise tax and must be filed by the employer no later than the last day of the seventh month following the close of the taxable year.

This excise tax does *not* apply to contributions made to *annuity contracts*; it only applies with respect to *custodial accounts*.

Q 29:36 What are excess aggregate contributions?

Excess aggregate contributions are the excess of the aggregate amount of employee contributions and employer matching contributions (see Q 29:19) made on behalf of highly compensated employees (see Q 3:3) for a plan year over the maximum amount of such contributions that are permitted under a special nondiscrimination test. [IRC § 401(m)(6)(B)]

If excess aggregate contributions are made to any type of TSA, the excess amount is subject to a 10 percent excise tax. The excise tax is imposed on the employer, not on the highly compensated employees. However, excess aggregate contributions can be corrected to avoid the 10 percent tax. [IRC §§ 4979(a), 4979(f)]

Form 5330, Return of Excise Taxes Related to Employee Benefit Plans, is used to report the excise tax and must be filed by the employer no later than the last day of the 15th month following the close of the plan year to which the excess aggregate contributions relate.

For a discussion of the special nondiscrimination test and method of correction, see Qs 23:48 through 23:55.

Q 29:37 What special rules apply to TSAs purchased for church employees?

Certain rules that apply to TSAs purchased for employees of churches also apply to employees of other specified organizations; however, some special rules apply only to church employees.

A retirement income account is treated as a TSA, and amounts paid by an employer to a retirement income account are treated as amounts contributed by the employer for a TSA for the employee on whose behalf the account is maintained. The term "retirement income account" means a defined contribution program established or maintained by a church or a convention or association of churches to provide benefits under a TSA for an employee. [IRC §§ 403(b)(9), 414(e), 414(i); Ltr Ruls 9625044, 9530031, 9451082, 9451063, 9419039] Retirement income accounts, annuity contracts, and custodial accounts can be used by church employees. [Ltr Ruls 9613024, 9531034, 9415016, 9414047, 9414046]

Generally, TSAs purchased by churches need not satisfy the minimum participation, minimum coverage, and nondiscrimination requirements (see Qs 29:14, 29:15). [IRC §§ 403(b)(1)(D), 403(b)(12), 414(e), 3121(w)(3); Notice 89-23, Part I, 1989-1 CB 654; Ann 95-48, 1995-23 IRB 13]

For the purpose of determining years of service (see Q 29:24) in order to calculate the exclusion allowance (see Q 29:22) of a duly ordained, commissioned, or licensed minister of a church, or a layperson, as an employee of a church or a convention or association of churches, all years of service with related church organizations are treated as years of service with a single employer. In addition, all amounts contributed for TSAs by each church or convention or association of churches during those years of service for the minister or layperson are treated as contributed by a single employer for purposes of calculating the exclusion allowance. The alternative exclusion allowance calculation may also be elected (see Q 29:26). [IRC §§ 403(b)(2)(C), 403(b)(2)(D); Ltr Ruls 9451082, 9451063]

In addition to being eligible to elect any of the three alternative exclusion allowance calculations (see Q 29:30), in any year that a church employee's adjusted gross income does not exceed $17,000, the employee is permitted a minimum exclusion allowance equal to the lesser of (1) $3,000 or (2) the employee's includible compensation (see Q 29:23). This amount will not be considered to exceed the overall limitation (see Q 29:29). [IRC §§ 403(b)(2)(D), 415(c)(7)(A)]

A further election may be made by a church employee to increase the annual addition limitation (see Q 6:1). This election allows a contribution to a TSA in any year to be as much as $10,000 even if this amount is more than the 25-percent-of-compensation limit. Under this election, contributions in excess of the compensation limit may not exceed $40,000 for the lifetime of the employee. However, this election cannot be used in the same year in which the (A) election limitation is used. [IRC § 415(c)(7)(B)]

A church employee with 15 years of service is eligible for the special catch-up election relating to the increased dollar amount of elective deferrals (see Q 29:27). [IRC § 402(g)(8)]

A church employee is also eligible for the deferred required beginning date relating to required minimum distributions (see Q 29:40). [IRC § 401(a)(9)(C)]

SBA '96 (see Q 1:21) makes a number of changes with regard to participation in church plans that are effective for years beginning *after* 1996. [IRC §§ 404(a)(10), as added by SBA '96 § 1461(b), 414(e)(5), as added by SBA '96 § 1461(a)]

Self-employed ministers and ministers, such as chaplains, who are employed by organizations that are not Section 501(c)(3) organizations (see Q 29:3) may participate in church plans. SBA '96 expands eligibility to participate in church plans to include ministers who are self-employed in connection with the exercise of their ministry. A self-employed individual is someone who has net earnings from self-employment (see Qs 6:33, 6:34). A self-employed minister is treated as the minister's own employer that is a Section 501(c)(3) organization. The self-employed minister's includible compensation is determined on the basis of the minister's net earnings from self-employment, instead of the amount of compensation received from an employer. In determining the number of years of service, the years and portions of years in which the minister was self-employed with respect to the ministry must be included.

In addition to self-employed ministers, ministers who are employed by organizations other than Section 501(c)(3) organizations can participate in church plans. Such ministers are treated as if they were employed by churches and may, therefore, participate in church plans. To be eligible for this treatment as a church employee, the minister's employment by such an organization must be in connection with the exercise of the ministry.

An employer that is not eligible to participate in a church pan may exclude a minister who participates in a church plan and who is employed in the exercise of the ministry from being treated as an employee for purposes of the employer's nondiscrimination testing for nondenominational plans. Such nondenominational plans include a qualified retirement plan, a TSA, and a retirement income account. Compensation that is taken into account for purposes of determining contributions or benefits with respect to a church plan may not also be taken into account for purposes of determining contributions or benefits under a non-church plan; the compensation may be considered only once.

SBA '96 also expands eligibility to participate in retirement income accounts to ministers who are self-employed or are employed by entities other than Section 501(c)(3) organizations (such as chaplains). The contributions made by such ministers to retirement income accounts are deductible, subject to (1) the limit on elective deferrals, (2) the exclusion allowance, or (3) the limit on annual additions.

Q 29:38 Are there any prohibitions on TSA distributions?

Yes, but different rules apply depending upon whether the funding vehicle is an annuity contract or a custodial account (see Q 29:6).

If the funding vehicle is an annuity contract, distributions attributable to contributions made pursuant to a salary reduction agreement (see Q 29:10) may be paid only:

1. After the employee attains age 59½;
2. After separation from service (see Q 13:9);
3. Upon the employee's death;
4. Because the employee becomes disabled (see Q 26:41); or
5. In the case of hardship (but excluding any earnings on such contributions).

[IRC § 403(b)(11)]

These restrictions do not apply to assets held under the annuity contract as of the end of the last year beginning before 1989. [TAMRA § 1011A(c)(11)] Furthermore, since these restrictions apply only to contributions made pursuant to a salary reduction agreement, there are no restrictions on distributions attributable to nonelective contributions (i.e., employer or employee contributions). In either case, distributions made prior to the employee's attainment of age 59½, even in the case of hardship, may be subject to the 10 percent premature penalty tax (see Q 13:39).

If the funding vehicle is a custodial account, distributions may not be paid or made available before the employee:

1. Dies;
2. Attains age 59½;
3. Separates from service (see Q 13:9);
4. Becomes disabled (see Q 26:41); or

5. In case of contributions made pursuant to a salary reduction agreement, encounters financial hardship.

[IRC § 403(b)(7)(A)(ii)]

The restriction on financial hardship distributions applies only to salary reduction contributions made in years beginning after 1988 and the earnings on all salary reduction contributions whenever made. Effectively, hardship distributions may be made only from the custodial account assets as of the end of the last year beginning before 1989, plus all subsequent salary reduction contributions. [TAMRA § 1011A(c)(1)] As with annuity contracts, hardship distributions may be subject to the 10 percent premature penalty tax.

Neither hardship nor financial hardship has been defined; however, the rules regarding hardship distributions from 401(k) plans can probably be used for guidance (see Qs 23:35–23:39). A hardship distribution made after 1992 is an eligible rollover distribution and is, therefore, subject to the 20 percent excise tax withholding rules (see Q 28:8).

The payment of fees from a TSA to an investment advisor who was responsible for managing the assets was neither a distribution nor a prohibited withdrawal. [Ltr Rul 9332040]

The restrictions on distributions from annuity contracts and custodial accounts do not prohibit distributions to an alternate payee pursuant to a qualified domestic relations order (QDRO) (see Qs 30:1, 30:12). [IRC § 414(p)(10); Blatt, 66 TCM 1409 (1993); Ltr Rul 9619040]

Q 29:39   Are TSAs subject to the QJSA and QPSA requirements?

Although the QJSA and QPSA requirements contained in the Code are not applicable to TSAs, parallel provisions contained in ERISA make these survivor annuity requirements applicable if the TSA is an employee pension benefit plan (see Q 29:49). Thus, if the TSA is exempt from Title I of ERISA, the QJSA and QPSA requirements do *not* apply. [ERISA §§ 3(2), 3(3), 205(a), 205(d), 205(e)]

If the TSA is not exempt from Title I, the survivor annuity requirements apply to a defined benefit plan (see Q 2:3), any individual account plan (see Q 2:2) subject to minimum funding requirements (see Q 8:1), and any participant under any other individual account plan unless:

1. The plan provides that, upon the participant's death, the participant's nonforfeitable benefit (reduced by any security interest held by the plan by reason of a loan outstanding to such participant) is payable in full to the participant's surviving spouse (unless the participant

has elected with spousal consent that such benefit be paid instead to a designated beneficiary);

2. The participant does not elect the payment of benefits in the form of a life annuity; and

3. With respect to the participant, the plan is not a direct or indirect transferee plan.

[ERISA §§ 3(34), 3(35), 205(b)]

Since a TSA is usually not a defined benefit plan or an individual account plan subject to the minimum funding requirements, it appears that, if the TSA is not exempt from Title I, the QJSA requirement may only apply if the employee elects benefit payments in the form of a life annuity, and the QPSA requirement may only apply if the death benefit is not payable in full to the surviving spouse.

For a detailed discussion of the survivor annuity rules, see Qs 10:1 through 10:32.

Q 29:40   Do the minimum distribution requirements apply to TSAs?

Effective for benefits accruing after 1986, TSAs must satisfy both the minimum distribution rules and the minimum distribution incidental benefit (MDIB) requirement. These requirements relate to both the time by which distributions from the TSA must begin and the amount that must be distributed from the TSA, and these requirements are similar to those that apply to qualified retirement plans and IRAs. [IRC § 403(b)(10); Prop Reg § 1.403(b)-2, Q&A-1]

For a complete discussion of the required minimum distribution rules and MDIB requirement, see chapter 11 and Qs 26:32, 26:33, and 26:40.

There is at least one notable exception applicable to the required minimum distribution rules. Since these rules apply only to benefits accruing after 1986, one rule applies to the employee's pre-1987 benefits and a second rule applies to the employee's post-1986 benefits (including earnings on the pre-1987 benefits). [Prop Reg § 1.403(b)-2, Q&A-2]

Prior to the enactment of TRA '86, there was no specific time by which TSA distributions were required to begin. On an administrative basis, IRS required TSA distributions to commence by age 75. Thus, with regard to the pre-1987 benefits, distributions need not commence until the employee attains age 75. However, this exception applies *only* if records have been maintained to identify the pre-1987 benefits; if not, the entire benefit will be subject to the new minimum distribution requirements. [Ltr Ruls 9442030, 9345044, 7913129, 7825010; Notice 88-39, 1988-1 CB 525; Prop Reg

§ 1.403(b)-2, Q&A-2] If the pre-1987 benefits are rolled over to an IRA (see Q 29:42), the delayed distribution date will no longer be available.

There appears to be another exception to the required minimum distribution rules applicable to post-1986 benefits of government or church employees. This exception defers the required beginning date to April 1 of the calendar year following the calendar year in which the employee retires; however, IRS has ruled that the commencement of distributions cannot be deferred beyond age 75. [IRC § 401(a)(9)(C); Ltr Rul 9345044]

The MDIB requirement applies alike to both the pre-1987 and post-1986 benefits. [Prop Reg § 1.403(b)-2, Q&A-3]

As with IRAs (see Q 26:32), an employee with more than one TSA must calculate the required minimum distribution with respect to each TSA. However, the amounts required to be distributed may then be aggregated and the distribution taken from any one or more of the TSAs. [Notice 88-39, 1988-1 CB 525; Ltr Rul 9442030]

A violation of the minimum distribution requirements will not occur if distributions are not made because the insurance company that issued the TSA is in delinquency proceedings. [Rev Proc 92-16, 1992-1 CB 673; Rev Proc 92-10, 1992-1 CB 661]

For years beginning after 1996, the required beginning date is April 1 of the calendar year following the later of the calendar year in which the employee attains age 70½ or retires (see Q 11:3). However, this change does not apply to an employee who is a 5 percent owner (see Q 22:28) with respect to the plan year ending in the calendar year in which the employee attains age 70½. If the employee is deemed to maintain the TSA (see Q 29:32), the question arises as to whether or not such an employee would be considered a 5 percent owner. [IRC § 401(a)(9)(C), as amended by SBA '96 § 1404(a)]] In addition, if RRB '96 (see Q 1:22A) is enacted, age 70½ will be replaced by age 70 for purposes of the minimum distribution requirements. [RRB '96, Act § 9445(b)]

Q 29:41   Can the funds be transferred directly from one investment vehicle to another?

If an individual transfers an interest in an annuity contract not subject to early distribution restrictions (see Q 29:38) to another annuity contract or to a custodial account, the transfer is not an actual distribution and, consequently, is not a taxable transfer. If an individual transfers funds from a custodial account to an annuity contract or to another custodial account and the transferred funds continue to be subject to the early distribution restrictions applicable to custodial accounts, the transfer is not an actual distribution and, consequently, is not a taxable transfer. If an individual transfers funds from an annuity contract containing funds subject to early distribution restrictions to another annuity contract or to a custodial account and the transferred funds continue to be subject to the same or more stringent distribution restrictions, the transfer is not an actual distribution and, consequently, is not a taxable transfer.

In determining whether any of the above transfers constitutes an actual distribution, it is irrelevant whether a complete interest or a partial interest is transferred, and whether the transferring individual is a current employee, a former employee, or a beneficiary of a former employee.

[Rev Rul 90-24, 1990-1 CB 97; GCM 38992; Ltr Ruls 9442030, 9423031, 9339024]

If cash is distributed from an annuity contract and the proceeds are reinvested in another annuity contract or in a custodial account, the distribution will not be a taxable transfer if:

1. The contract is issued by an insurance company that is subject to a rehabilitation, conservatorship, insolvency, or similar state proceeding at the time of the cash distribution;

2. The individual withdraws 100 percent of the cash distribution to which the individual is entitled under the annuity contract or, if less, the maximum amount permitted to be withdrawn under the terms of the state proceeding;

3. An exchange of the old annuity contract for the new annuity contract would qualify for tax-free treatment under Section 1035(a) or as a tax-free transfer under Revenue Ruling 90-24; and

4. The reinvestment is made within 60 days after receipt of the cash distribution and, if the cash distribution is restricted by the state proceeding to an amount less than the individual is entitled to, the individual assigns all rights to any future distributions to the issuer of the new annuity contract.

[Rev Proc 92-44, 1992-1 CB 875]

Additionally, an individual's exchange of an annuity contract issued by a life insurance company that has become subject to a rehabilitation, conservatorship, or similar state proceeding for an annuity contract issued by another life insurance company will qualify as a tax-free exchange if the new contract is funded by a series of two or more payments from the old annuity contract. [Rev Rul 92-43, 1992-1 CB 288; Ltr Rul 9348051]

Q 29:42 Can TSA distributions be rolled over?

The rules relating to the rollover of qualified retirement plan distributions also pertain to distributions from TSAs, except that a TSA distribution may be rolled over *only* to another TSA or to an IRA (see Q 26:1) and *cannot* be rolled over to a qualified retirement plan. [IRC §§ 403(b)(8), 403(b)(10); Treas Reg § 1.403(b)-2, Q&A 1; Tolliver, 62 TCM 770 (1991)] A distribution from a TSA that is invested in a personal certificate of deposit is not a rollover. [Adamcewicz, 68 TCM 276 (1994)]

If a distribution from a TSA is rolled over to an IRA and the IRA contains only assets attributable to the amounts rolled over (i.e., a conduit IRA; see Q 28:40), the employee may roll over the conduit IRA assets to another TSA. [IRC §§ 403(b)(1), 408(d)(3)(A)(iii)]

A TSA is required to provide that, if the distributee of an eligible rollover distribution elects to have the distribution paid directly to another TSA or IRA and specifies the plan to which the distribution will be paid, then the distribution must be paid to that plan in a direct rollover. [Ltr Rul 9415016] A direct rollover from a TSA to another TSA is a distribution and a rollover and not a transfer of funds between TSAs and, thus, does not affect the applicable law governing transfers of funds between TSAs. According to IRS, if a TSA is subject to restrictions regarding distributions (see Q 29:38), a rollover cannot be made while those restrictions apply. However, a transfer of funds between IRAs may be permissible (see Q 29:41). [Treas Reg § 1.403(b)-2, Q&A 2(a); IRS Spec Rul (May 19, 1995)]

As in the case of an eligible rollover distribution from a qualified retirement plan, if a distributee of an eligible rollover distribution from a TSA does not elect to have the eligible rollover distribution paid to another TSA or an IRA in a direct rollover, the eligible rollover distribution is subject to 20 percent income tax withholding.

To ensure that the distributee of an eligible rollover distribution from a TSA has a meaningful right to elect a direct rollover, the distributee must be informed of the option. Thus, within a reasonable time period before making an eligible rollover distribution, the payor must provide an explanation to the distributee of the right to elect a direct rollover and the income tax withholding consequences of not electing a direct rollover. [Treas Reg § 1.403(b)-2, Q&A 2(b) and 3]

An alternate payee spouse or former spouse under a QDRO (see Q 30:1) can roll over a TSA distribution to either an IRA or a TSA. [IRC § 402(e)(1); Blatt, 66 TCM 1409 (1993)]

See chapter 28 for a detailed discussion of rollovers.

Q 29:43 Is a rollover of TSA benefits available to the spouse of a deceased employee?

Yes. The spouse of an employee who receives an eligible rollover distribution (see Q 28:8) from a TSA on account of the employee's death is permitted to roll over all or part of the distribution to an IRA. This applies only to a surviving spouse and not to a nonspouse beneficiary.

The spouse may establish an IRA rollover account even if the spouse would not be eligible to establish a regular IRA. The surviving spouse may not roll over the distribution to another TSA or to a qualified retirement plan or from the rollover IRA to another qualified retirement plan in which the spouse is a participant. [IRC § 402(c)(9); Treas Reg §§ 1.402(c)-2, Q&A 12, 1.403(b)-2, Q&A 1]

Q 29:44 How are TSA distributions taxed?

The amounts received by an employee under a TSA are included in the employee's income for the taxable year in which received. [IRC §§ 72(m), 403(b)(1); Treas Reg § 1.403(b)-1(c)(1); Ltr Ruls 9617043, 9342056]

If the employee has an investment in the contract (also known as basis), a portion of the TSA distribution will be recovered tax-free. [IRC §§ 72(b), 72(c)]

An employee's investment in the contract (basis) includes:

1. The employee's voluntary contributions (see Qs 1:33, 29:19).
2. PS-58 costs (see Q 29:7).
3. Employer contributions previously includible in the employee's income (see Qs 29:25, 29:29).
4. Loans from the TSA to the employee that were treated as taxable distributions (see Q 29:47).

If amounts are received by the employee before the annuity starting date (see Q 10:3) and the employee has basis, a portion of the distribution bearing the same ratio as the basis bears to the employee's accrued benefit (see Q 9:2) as of the date of distribution is excludable from the employee's taxable income. If, on May 5, 1986, the TSA permitted the employee to withdraw voluntary contributions, pre-1987 basis will be recovered first and the pro rata recovery rule will apply only to the extent that amounts received exceed the employee's basis as of December 1, 1986. [IRC § 72(e)]

If the employee has basis and receives annuity payments from the TSA, basis will be recovered under the annuity rules applicable to qualified retirement plans (see Q 13:3).

If the employee receives the full value of the TSA in a lump-sum payment, the entire amount (less basis) will be taxable as ordinary income; the special averaging methods that may be available for a lump-sum distribution from a qualified retirement plan (see Q 13:13) are *not* available for a lump-sum payment from a TSA. [IRC §§ 402(d)(4)(A), 403(b)(1); Adamcewicz, 68 TCM 276 (1994)]

If dividends are paid to the employee under a TSA, the dividends constitute taxable income except to the extent excludable under the pro rata basis recovery rule.

The payment of fees from a TSA to an investment advisor who is responsible for managing the assets is not a taxable distribution. [Ltr Rul 9332040]

Q 29:45   How are death benefit payments under a TSA taxed?

Death benefits payable under a TSA are generally included in the deceased employee's estate. For the exceptions, see Q 14:19. [IRC § 2039]

Death benefit payments from a TSA to a deceased employee's surviving spouse will qualify for the marital deduction and will be deducted from the decedent's gross estate for estate tax purposes (see Q 14:20). [IRC § 2056]

For income tax purposes, the death benefit payable under a TSA will be taxed to the beneficiary in the same manner as the lifetime benefit would have been taxed to the employee. However, a $5,000 death benefit exclusion may be available to the beneficiary if the employer is a tax-exempt religious or non-public educational organization, or a tax-exempt organization normally receiving a substantial portion of its support from the government or general public. This death benefit exclusion applies to (1) annuity payments received by the beneficiary *unless* the employee had a nonforfeitable right to receive the payments while alive, and (2) a lump-sum payment if the entire death benefit is paid within one taxable year. [IRC §§ 101 (b)(1), 101(b)(2); Treas Reg § 1.403(b)-1(c)(2); Estate of Johnson, 56 TC 944 (1971), *acq* 1973-2 CB 2]

The $5,000 death benefit exclusion has been repealed with respect to decedents dying after August 20, 1996. [IRC § 101(b), repealed by SBA '96 § 1402(a)]

Q 29:46   May any additional taxes be imposed on the recipient of a distribution from a TSA?

The penalty and excise taxes that may apply to distributions from qualified retirement plans also apply to TSA distributions and are the following:

1. 10 percent premature penalty tax (see Qs 13:39–13:42).

2. 15 percent excess distributions tax (see Qs 13:27–13:37).

3. 15 percent excess accumulation tax (see Qs 14:21–14:29).

4. 50 percent penalty tax for failure to make a required minimum distribution (see Q 11:20).

The 15 percent excess distributions tax is suspended for a three-year period—1997, 1998, and 1999—and any distributions made during that period will be treated as first made from the nongrandfather amount. [IRC § 4980A(g), as added by SBA '96 § 1452(b)]

Q 29:47   Can an employee make a loan from a TSA?

Yes, but loans from TSAs are subject to the same limitations and requirements that apply to loans from qualified retirement plans. [IRC § 72(p)(4)(A)(i)(III)] Interest paid by an employee on a loan from a TSA secured by amounts attributable to elective deferrals (see Q 29:27) is not deductible. [IRC §§ 72(p)(3)(A), 72(p)(3)(B)(ii)]

When an employee who had previously made loans from a TSA terminated the TSA without having repaid the loans, the outstanding loan balance was includible in income in the year of termination. Also, a taxable distribution occurs when an employee defaults on a loan under a TSA and the insurance company forecloses on the cash value of the annuity contract as used for security on the loan. [Dean, 65 TCM 2757 (1993); IRS Spec Rul (Jan 26, 1994)]

For a discussion of the rules relating to loans, see Qs 13:44 through 13:51, 28:14 through 28:16, and 29:48.

Q 29:48   Can a loan from a TSA be a prohibited transaction?

Although IRS and DOL share jurisdiction with regard to prohibited transactions, the Code restrictions and penalties imposed upon prohibited transactions do *not* apply to TSAs. Consequently, a loan to an employee from a TSA can never be a prohibited transaction for purposes of the Code (see Q 13:52). [IRC § 4975(e)]

If the TSA is an employee pension benefit plan subject to ERISA (see Q 29:49), then the ERISA restrictions and penalties imposed upon prohibited transactions will apply to a loan to an employee from a TSA (see Qs 20:1, 20:9). [ERISA §§ 406, 408(b)]

Q 29:49 Are TSAs subject to the reporting and disclosure requirements of ERISA?

The answer to this question is dependent upon whether or not the TSA program is subject to Title I of ERISA, and the TSA program will be subject to Title I if it is an employee benefit pension plan. The term "employee benefit pension plan" means any plan, fund, or program established or maintained by an employer or by an employee organization, or by both, to the extent that such plan, fund, or program:

1. Provides retirement income to employees, or
2. Results in a deferral of income by employees for periods extending to the termination of covered employment or beyond.

[ERISA §§ 3(2), 3(3)]

A TSA established pursuant to salary reduction agreements will *not* be "established or maintained by an employer" and, hence, *not* subject to Title I, if the following requirements are satisfied:

1. Participation is completely voluntary for employees;
2. All rights under the TSA are enforceable solely by the employee, by a beneficiary of such employee, or by their authorized representative;
3. The sole involvement of the employer is limited to any of the following:
   a. Permitting annuity contractors (e.g., insurance companies, mutual fund brokers) to publicize their products to employees;
   b. Requesting information concerning proposed funding media, products, or annuity contractors;
   c. Summarizing the information provided with respect to the proposed funding media or products made available, or the annuity contractors whose services are provided, in order to facilitate review and analysis by the employees;
   d. Collecting TSA contributions as required by salary reduction agreements, remitting the contributions to annuity contractors, and maintaining records of the contributions;
   e. Holding in the employer's name one or more group annuity contracts covering its employees;
   f. Limiting the funding media or products available to employees, or the annuity contractors who may approach employees, to a number and selection designed to afford employees a reasonable choice in light of all relevant circumstances; and
4. The employer receives no compensation other than reasonable compensation to cover expenses properly and actually incurred in the

performance of the employer's duties pursuant to the salary reduction agreements.

[DOL Reg § 2510.3-2(f)]

Consequently, unless the TSA program comes within the above-mentioned exceptions, the program will be subject to the reporting and disclosure requirements of ERISA. If the TSA program is subject to such requirements:

1. Form 5500 must be filed each year (see Qs 17:1–17:15).
2. A summary plan description (SPD) must be distributed to employees and beneficiaries (see Q 18:1).
3. A summary annual report must be distributed to employees and beneficiaries (see Q 18:13).
4. An employee may request a statement of benefits (see Q 18:13).

Where an employer ceased making contributions to a TSA program on February 28, 1989 and only the employees continued to make contributions thereafter, DOL ruled that the program was an employee benefit pension plan subject to Title I. [DOL Op Ltr No. 94-30A] Church plans (see Q 29:37) are excluded from the requirements of Title I (see Q 17:19). [DOL Op Ltr No. 94-18A]

Q 29:50   Do the fiduciary responsibility rules apply to TSAs?

ERISA sets forth numerous rules relating to the duties, responsibilities, and liability of fiduciaries with respect to employee pension benefit plans (see Q 29:49). If a TSA is an employee pension benefit plan, the fiduciary responsibility rules of Title I of ERISA will apply. However, even if the TSA is covered by Title I, government plans are excluded from coverage, and this, by extension, excludes a TSA maintained by a public educational organization (see Q 29:4) from the fiduciary responsibility rules. [ERISA § 3(32)]

A fiduciary of a TSA that is subject to Title I is prohibited from causing the TSA to engage in certain transactions with a party in interest and from engaging in other conduct in the fiduciary's own interest with regard to the TSA. Violation of the proscription against engaging in prohibited transactions can result in substantial penalties being imposed on the offending fiduciary. [ERISA §§ 406, 502(i)]

A TSA may be a self-directed account plan—that is, a plan that permits an employee to make an independent choice, from a broad range of investment alternatives, regarding the manner in which the assets in the employee's TSA are invested. If the TSA permits a self-directed account, the employee will not be considered a fiduciary solely because the employee exercises control over assets in the TSA. The consequences of this are twofold. First, other fiduciaries generally would have no co-fiduciary liability on account of the employee's investment decisions. Second, because the employee is not a fiduciary, no prohibited transaction under ERISA would result if the exercise of control over the assets caused the TSA to engage in transactions with parties in interest. [ERISA § 404(c); DOL Reg §§ 2550.404c-1(a), 2550.404(c)-1(b)(1), 2550.404c-1(d)]

See chapter 19 for a discussion of fiduciary responsibilities and chapter 20 for a discussion of prohibited transactions.

Q 29:51   Are TSA benefits exempt from claims of creditors?

In 1992, the United States Supreme Court held that a participant's interest in a qualified retirement plan is exempt from the claims of creditors in a bankruptcy proceeding, which, hopefully, resolved the conflict among the courts of appeals. [Patterson v Shumate, 112 S Ct 2242 (1992)]

ERISA and the Code require every qualified retirement plan to prohibit the assignment or alienation of benefits under the plan. [ERISA § 206(d)(1); IRC § 401(a)(13)] Federal Bankruptcy Code Section 541(c)(2) excludes from the bankruptcy estate property of the debtor that is subject to a restriction on transfer enforceable under applicable nonbankruptcy law. The Supreme Court ruled that the anti-alienation provision contained in a qualified retirement plan constitutes a restriction on transfer enforceable under applicable nonbankruptcy law; and, accordingly, a debtor may exclude his interest in such a plan from the property of the bankruptcy estate. The Supreme Court referred to an "ERISA qualified" plan.

Not all TSA programs are subject to Title I of ERISA (see Q 29:49). Two courts held that TSA benefits were not subject to creditor claims; neither court relied upon the Supreme Court decision; and, in at least one case, the TSA was not subject to ERISA. [In re Macintyre, 74 F 3d 186 (9th Cir 1996); In re Johnson, 191 BR 75 (MD Pa 1996)]

Q 29:52   What is the Tax Sheltered Annuity Voluntary Correction Program (TVC)?

The TVC program permits an employer that offers a TSA program to voluntarily identify and correct defects. Employers that request consideration under the TVC program, agree to correct the identified defects, and pay the negotiated sanction will receive written assurance that the corrections are acceptable and that IRS will not pursue revocation of the income tax exclusion with respect to the violations identified and corrected. The TVC program is not available to waive or reduce any applicable excise taxes and does not alter an employer's obligations to satisfy FICA and FUTA requirements (see Q 29:28).

The TVC program became effective on May 1, 1995 and will be available until October 31, 1996.

Under the TVC program, the employer will pay a correction fee and a negotiated sanction (see Q 29:55).

IRS will not make any finding under the TVC program concerning the existence of defects. Thus, each item to be considered under the program must be identified by the employer as a defect. Since the TVC program is a compliance program, not based upon an examination of the plan by IRS, IRS will generally rely upon the statements of the employer in identifying the plan's defects. Only the defects raised by the employer, related issues, and other issues presented by the employer in written or oral statements are addressed under the program, and only those issues will be covered in the correction statement (see Q 29:57).

Under the TVC program, the employer must correct the identified defects for all years for which the defects exist, even closed tax years (see Q 29:54). IRS must be assured that the employer has initiated or will initiate procedures for paying the appropriate employment tax obligations.

If IRS discovers an unrelated plan defect while considering the voluntary request, that violation may be outside the scope of the voluntary request for consideration because it was not voluntarily brought forward by the employer. In most cases, the defect will be added to the correction statement. However, if the additional defect is significant, all aspects of the plan may be forwarded to the appropriate key district (see Q 15:9) for consideration for an examination.

[Rev Proc 95-24, 1995-1 CB 694]

DOL has confirmed for IRS its position that an employer, by participating in the TVC program, will not generally subject the TSA to the requirements of Title 1 of ERISA (see Q 29:49). Accordingly, employers may be required, incident to the TVC program, to negotiate with IRS, reform administrative procedures, pay correction fees and negotiated sanctions, or remit a one-time make-up correction to the TSA, without forcing the TSA to comply with Title I. However, an employer may risk establishing and maintaining a plan that will become subject to ERISA if it either corrects the actions of third parties for whom the employer is not responsible under the TSA or assumes ongoing duties for the TSA. [DOL Ltr (Feb 27, 1996)]

Q 29:53   What is the scope of the TVC program?

The TVC program is available only to employers that are eligible to offer TSAs to their employees (see Q 29:2).

The following defects and plans *cannot* be corrected in the TVC program:

1. Plans in which there are defects relating to the misuse or diversion of plan assets (cases in which DOL may also have jurisdiction);
2. Plans for which a custodial account (see Q 29:6), although required, was not created or was not maintained;
3. Plans for which the employer does not have sufficient information to determine the nature or extent of the defect or does not have sufficient information to effect reasonable correction;
4. Plans in which annuity contracts (see Q 29:6) were purchased from an entity other than an insurance company (if the purchase was not grandfathered);
5. Plans in which there is no initial purchase of annuity contracts (and the contributions were not made to a custodial account) or the contributions are not invested in a proper custodial account (or a retirement income account in a church plan; see Q 29:37);
6. Annuity contracts purchased or custodial accounts established on behalf of ineligible employees or independent contractors (see Q 29:5); and
7. Plans in which the defects are egregious.

In addition, the TVC program is not available for operational defects that are subject to an excise tax, a penalty tax, or additional income tax, because the Code already provides sanctions for those defects. For example, failure to file the Form 5500 series return/report (see Q 17:1) cannot be corrected in the TVC program. However, if a defect results in both loss of TSA status (or other loss of the income tax exclusion) and the imposition of an excise tax or an additional income tax, the TVC program will be available to correct the defect.

A TSA plan that is under an IRS examination is not eligible for the program.

The defects for which an employer may request a correction statement (see Q 29:57) under TVC are as follows:

1. Failure to satisfy the nondiscrimination requirements (see Q 29:15), including a failure to satisfy the nondiscrimination requirements for matching contributions (see Q 29:19) and the failure to offer the opportunity to make salary reduction contributions universally (see Q 29:16);

2. Failure to comply with the distribution restrictions (see Q 29:38), such as improper hardship distributions, distributions on termination of the plan, or improper withdrawal of salary reduction amounts contributed after January 1, 1988 or of post-1988 earnings;

3. Failure to satisfy the incidental death benefit rules (see Q 29:40);

4. Failure to pay minimum required distributions (see Q 29:40);

5. Failure to give employees the right to elect a direct rollover (including the failure to give an information notice to employees) (see Q 29:42);

6. Failure to satisfy the elective deferral rules, such as treatment of amounts as being subject to a one-time irrevocable election when the election is revocable (see Qs 29:10, 29:21, 29:27);

7. Contributions in excess of the exclusion allowance (see Q 29:22);

8. Failure to satisfy the nontransferability requirements (see Q 29:13);

9. Failure to satisfy the salary reduction agreements requirements (see Q 29:10); and

10. Failure to satisfy the Section 415 limitations (see Qs 29:29, 29:32, 29:33, 29:34).

[Rev Proc 95-24, §§ 5 and 7, 1995-1 CB 694]

Q 29:54 What are the correction principles of the TVC program?

In the request for a correction statement (see Q 29:57), the employer must give a description of the method for correcting the defect that the employer has implemented or proposes to implement. The following general principles should be used in suggesting acceptable corrections:

1. The correction method should restore both active and former employees to the benefit levels they would have had if the defect had not occurred.

2. The correction method should restore the TSA plan to the position it would have been in had the defect not occurred.

3. The correction method should generally keep the assets in the plan.

4. Corrective allocations must be adjusted for earnings and forfeitures that would have been allocated during the applicable period. In addition, increases in allocations that would have occurred due to changes in compensation must be taken into account.

5. Corrective contributions should come only from employer contributions.

6. A corrective contribution on behalf of a participant because of a failure to allocate the contribution in a prior year will generally be

subject to the exclusion allowance (see Q 29:22) as a contribution for the year in which the corrective contribution is made and a contribution amount (for purposes of the Section 415 limitations; see Qs 29:29, 29:32, 29:33, 29:34) for the year to which it relates.

7. The correction method should not, in general, reduce the benefit to which the participant is entitled.

8. Any plan corrections should be properly reported on Form 1099-R or Form W-2, as appropriate.

[Rev Proc 95-24, § 6, 1995-1 CB 694]

Q 29:55 What are the voluntary correction fees and sanction limitations?

The voluntary correction fee depends on the number of employees of the employer. If the employer has:

1. Fewer than 25 employees, the fee is $500.

2. At least 25 and no more than 1,000 employees, the fee is $1,250.

3. More than 1,000 employees but less than 10,000 employees, the fee is $5,000.

4. 10,000 or more employees, the fee is $10,000.

[Rev Proc 95-24, § 8, 1995-1 CB 694]

In addition to the voluntary correction fee, the employer pays a sanction with respect to the corrected defects. The sanction will be limited to a percentage of the Total Sanction Amount and will be determined using the facts and circumstances in the case. The sanction will be offset by the correction fee but will not be less than the correction fee.

The Total Sanction Amount for a TSA plan for the defects that affect the entire TSA plan (generally defects 1 and 6; see Q 29:53) is approximately equal to the tax IRS could apply to the defects. It is the sum of:

1. The tax on the earnings on amounts in the custodial accounts for all open years;

2. The amount that should have been included in income by the highly compensated employees (see Q 3:2) covered under the plan, calculated at the 28 percent rate, for all open years; and

3. The income tax required to have been withheld on amounts contributed to the plan, calculated at the 20 percent rate, on behalf of the non-highly compensated employees (see Q 3:13) for all open years.

The Total Sanction Amount for a TSA plan for the defects that cause amounts contributed to the affected annuity contracts (or a portion thereof) to lose TSA status is approximately equal to the tax IRS could apply to those defects. It is the sum of:

1. The amount that should have been included in income by the highly compensated employees covered by the affected annuity contracts, calculated at the 28 percent rate, to the extent that the contributions fail to satisfy the requirements of Section 403(b), for all open years; and

2. The income tax required to have been withheld on amounts contributed to the plan on behalf of the non-highly compensated employees covered by the affected annuity contracts, calculated at the 20 percent rate, to the extent that contributions fail to satisfy the requirements of Section 403(b), for all open years.

The highest percentage of the Total Sanction Amount that may be applied as a monetary sanction for defects for which the employer voluntarily requested consideration under the TVC program is 40 percent.

Depending on the factors, the actual monetary sanction may range from 40 percent of the Total Sanction Amount to as little as the correction fee. Factors considered in determining the actual sanction include (but are not limited to) the severity of the defect, the number and type of employees affected by the defect, the number of rank and file employees that would be hurt if the income tax exclusion were lost, the extent to which the employer's own procedures found the error, and the cost of correction. Cases with less severe defects may be subject to small monetary sanctions.

The sanction is not a tax. Thus, no interest or penalties apply in determining the Total Sanction Amount. In addition, neither employment tax obligations nor excise tax obligations (see Q 29:52) are satisfied by the payment of the sanction. The sanction is not deductible.

[Rev Proc 95-24, § 9, 1995-1 CB 694]

Q 29:56   What are the TVC submission requirements?

In general, a request for a correction statement (see Q 29:57) consists of a letter from the employer to the IRS that contains a description of the defect(s) (see Q 29:55), a description of the proposed method(s) of correction (see Q 29:54), and other procedural items and includes supporting information and documentation.

A request for consideration under the TVC program must contain the specific information needed to support the suggested correction method.

This includes, for example, the number of employees affected, the number of contracts held by employees of the employer, and the number of related organizations affected by the defect(s). This also includes the applicable earnings (and the method of determining the earnings) that will apply to any corrective contributions to the plan, the years involved, and any calculations or assumptions the employer used to determine the amounts needed for correction. The submission must state the earnings (and the method of determining the earnings) that will apply to any corrective distributions.

The request for consideration under the TVC program must contain the following:

1. A complete description of the defects and the years in which the defects occurred, including closed years (i.e., years for which the statutory period has elapsed);

2. A description of the current administrative procedures for the plan;

3. An explanation of how and why the defects arose;

4. A detailed description of the methods for correcting the defects that the employer has implemented or proposes to implement, including specific calculations for each affected employee, where applicable;

5. A calculation of the Total Sanction Amount (see Q 29:55);

6. A description of the measures that have been or will be implemented to ensure that the same defect will not recur;

7. A list of any other TSA plans, qualified retirement plans, or SEPs (see Q 27:1) maintained by the employer;

8. A statement that, to the best of the employer's knowledge, the plan is not currently under an IRS examination (see Q 29:53);

9. The location of the key district (see Q 15:9) that has jurisdiction over the employer; and

10. A statement that the employer has contacted all other entities involved in the plan and has been assured of cooperation, to the extent necessary.

The submission must be accompanied by the following documentation:

1. A copy of the first two pages of the most recently filed Form 5500 series return/report (if applicable). If a Form 5500 is not applicable, the employer must furnish the name of the plan, the employer identification number, and the other information generally required of tax-exempt organizations filing the Form 5500.

2. A copy of the pertinent portion of any relevant TSA documents, including plan documents (see Q 29:8), written descriptions of the plan, and salary reduction agreements (see Q 29:10).

3. A statement that the employer is eligible to offer a TSA plan (see Q 29:2).

The submission must include the voluntary correction fee (see Q 29:55).

The letter to IRS should be marked "TVC PROGRAM" in the upper right hand corner of the letter and mailed to:

Internal Revenue Service
Attention: CP:E:EP:TVC
P. O. Box 14073
Ben Franklin Station
Washington, DC 20044

[Rev Proc 95-24, § 10, 1995-1 CB 694]

Q 29:57   What is the correction statement?

At the favorable completion of the TVC process, the employer will receive a correction statement from IRS. The correction statement will state the defects identified, the required corrections (see Q 29:54), the sanction amount (see Q 29:55), and any revision to administrative procedures or employment tax procedures upon which the statement is conditioned. The statement will also state the time frame in which the corrections and procedures must be implemented.

If the correction statement is properly implemented, and all conditions satisfied, IRS will not pursue revocation of the income tax exclusion or the inclusion in income.

With the correction statement, the employer will receive an acknowledgment letter. Within 25 days after the correction statement is issued, the employer must sign and send the acknowledgment letter to the IRS, agreeing to the terms of the correction statement, and paying the sanction amount.

[Rev Proc 95-24, § 4, 1995-1 CB 694]

Chapter 30

Qualified Domestic Relations Orders

The rate of divorce in the United States continues to increase; and, in many cases, qualified retirement plan benefits represent the major marital asset. The Retirement Equity Act of 1984 established a new category of plan benefit recipients—alternate payees under qualified domestic relations orders (QDROs). This chapter analyzes the requirements for QDROs and their tax consequences.

Q 30:1   What is a qualified domestic relations order?

A QDRO is a domestic relations order (DRO; see Q 30:2) that creates or recognizes the existence of an alternate payee's (see Q 30:3) right to, or assigns to an alternate payee the right to, receive all or a portion of the benefits payable with respect to a participant under a qualified retirement plan, and that complies with certain special requirements (see Q 30:2). [IRC § 414(p)(1)(A); ERISA § 206(d)(3); Treas Reg § 1.401(a)-13(g)(1); Hawkins v Comm'r, 94-9011, 94-9009 (10th Cir 1996); Brotman, 105 TC 141 (1995); In re Norfleet, No. 4-92-0780 (Ill Ct of App, 4th Dist, 1993); Brotman v Molitch, No. 88-9876 (ED Pa 1989)]

Federal courts and state courts have concurrent jurisdiction to rule on the validity of QDROs. [Board of Trustees of the Laborers Pension Trust Fund for Northern California v Levingston, 816 F Supp 1496 (ND Cal 1993); In re Marriage of Levingston, No. A057164 (Cal Ct of App, 1st App Dist, Div Five, 1993); ERISA §§ 502(a)(1)(B), 502(e)(1)] If the terms of a QDRO are ambiguous, the proper forum for resolving the dispute is at the trial level, not at the appellate level. [Hullett v Towers, Perrin, Forster & Crosby, Inc, No. 94-1517 (3d Cir 1994)]

In one case, a husband received a lump-sum distribution (see Q 13:4) from a qualified retirement plan and transferred the distribution to an IRA established in his wife's name. Because the distribution and transfer were not made pursuant to a QDRO, the distribution was includible in the husband's gross income and penalties were assessed against both the husband and the wife (see Qs 13:27, 13:39, 26:6). [Rodoni, 105 TC 29 (1995)]

One court has ruled that a QDRO could be created in favor of the participant's first spouse even though (1) eight years had passed since the divorce, (2) the participant had remarried, and (3) the participant had commenced receiving retirement benefits in the form of a qualified joint and survivor annuity (QJSA; see Q 10:8). [Hopkins v AT&T Global Information Solutions Co, 1996 US Dist Lexis 1978 (SD W Va 1996)]

The rules relating to QDROs generally became effective on January 1, 1985. However, a plan administrator (see Q 16:1) may treat a DRO entered before 1985 as a QDRO, whether or not it meets the above definition, but must treat it as a QDRO if, on January 1, 1985, the plan administrator was paying benefits in compliance therewith. If a plan administrator chooses not to treat a pre-1985 order as a QDRO, the alternate payee should try to have the DRO amended to satisfy the requirements for a QDRO. [Layton v TDS Healthcare Systems Corp, No. C-93-1827-MHP (9th Cir 1994); Reineke v Reineke, No. 92-3333 (Fla DC of App, 1st Dist, 1993)]

SBA '96 (see Q 1:21) requires IRS, not later than January 1, 1997, to develop sample language for inclusion in a form for a QDRO that satisfies the legal requirements for a QDRO and that focuses attention on the need to consider the treatment of a lump-sum payment, qualified joint and survivor annuity (QJSA; see Q 10:8), or qualified preretirement survivor annuity (QPSA; see Q 10:9). [SBA '96, Act § 1457(a)]

Q 30:2 What is a domestic relations order?

A DRO is a judgment, decree, or order (including approval of a property settlement agreement) made pursuant to a state domestic relations law (including a community property law) that relates to the provision of child support, alimony payments, or marital property rights to an alternate payee (see Q 30:3). [IRC § 414(p)(1)(B); ERISA § 206(d)(3)(B)(ii)]

A DRO must also satisfy certain special requirements. The DRO must clearly specify:

1. The name and last known mailing address (if any) of the participant and the name and mailing address of each alternate payee covered by the order;

2. The amount or percentage of the participant's benefits to be paid by the qualified retirement plan to each such alternate payee or the manner in which such amount or percentage is to be determined;

3. The number of payments or period to which the order applies; and

4. The qualified retirement plan to which the order applies.

[IRC § 414(p)(2); ERISA § 206(d)(3)(C)]

In addition, a DRO may not require:

1. The qualified retirement plan to provide any type or form of benefit, or any option, not otherwise provided under the plan (see Q 30:8);

2. The qualified retirement plan to provide increased benefits (determined on the basis of actuarial value); or

3. The payment of benefits to an alternate payee that are required to be paid to another alternate payee under another order previously determined to be a QDRO (see Q 30:1).

[IRC § 414(p)(3); ERISA § 206(d)(3)(D)]

An order will not be disqualified merely because it does not specify the current mailing address of the participant and each alternate payee, as long as the plan administrator (see Q 16:1) has reason to know the addresses independently of the order (for example, the alternate payee is also a plan participant and the plan records include a current address for each participant). [REA Senate Comm Report]

An order will not be treated as providing increased benefits unless it provides for the payment of benefits in excess of those to which the participant would be entitled in the absence of the order. A DRO will remain qualified with respect to a successor qualified retirement plan of the same employer or a qualified retirement plan of a successor employer. [REA Senate Comm Report]

An order will not fail to be a QDRO even if the form of the benefit does not continue to be a form permitted under the qualified retirement plan because of a plan amendment or a change of law. In the case of a plan amendment, an alternate payee remains entitled to receive benefits in the form specified in the order. In the case of a law change that makes the benefit form specified in the order impermissible, the plan must permit the alternate payee to select a form of benefit specified in the plan. In either case, the elected form cannot affect, in any way, the amount or form of benefits payable to the participant. [TRA '86 Comm Reports]

If a DRO satisfies all of the above requirements, then the order will satisfy the special requirements of a QDRO (see Q 30:1).

Q 30:3   Who is an alternate payee?

An alternate payee is a spouse, former spouse, child, or other dependent of a participant who is recognized by a DRO (see Q 30:2) as having a right to receive all or a portion of the benefits payable under the qualified retirement plan with respect to the participant. [IRC § 414(p)(8); ERISA § 206(d)]

Whether the alternate payee is the spouse or a former spouse of the participant, as opposed to a child or other dependent of the participant, affects the tax consequences of a distribution from the qualified retirement plan pursuant to a QDRO (see Q 30:1). See Qs 30:17 through 30:19 for details.

Q 30:4   Does a QDRO violate the anti-assignment rule?

Generally, a retirement plan will not be a qualified retirement plan unless the plan provides that plan benefits may not be assigned or alienated. However, this prohibition against the assignment of plan benefits does not apply to the creation, assignment, or recognition of a right to any benefit payable with respect to a participant pursuant to a QDRO (see Qs 4:24, 30:1). [IRC § 401(a)(13); Temp Reg § 1.401(a)-13(g); Ltr Rul 9234014; but see Estate of Altobelli v IBM Corp, 1996 US App Lexis 3207 (4th Cir 1996); Fox Valley & Vicinity Construction Workers Pension Fund v Brown, 879 F 2d 249 (7th Cir 1990); Czarski v Estate of Bonk, 1996 US Dist Lexis 4808 (ED Mich 1996)]

A postnuptial agreement requiring that a portion of the husband's benefits in a qualified retirement plan be segregated in a separate plan account for the wife caused the plan to be disqualified. Because the post-nuptial agreement was not a QDRO, the segregation violated the anti-assign-ment rule. [Merchant v Kelly, Haglund, Garnsey & Kahn, 874 F Supp 300 (D Colo 1995)]

Q 30:5   Do the QDRO rules apply to all qualified retirement plans?

Yes. The QDRO (see Q 30:1) requirements apply to all qualified retire-ment plans and also apply to tax-sheltered annuities (see Q 29:1). [IRC §§ 401(a)(13), 414(p)(9)]

The QDRO rules have also been extended to governmental plans and church plans; however, distributions from such plans are treated as made pursuant to a QDRO without the necessity of satisfying the special QDRO requirements (see Qs 30:1, 30:2). If these types of plans provide that plan benefits may not be assigned or alienated (see Q 30:4) and such a provision is enforceable under state law, it is possible that plan benefits may not be reachable even with a QDRO. [IRC §§ 414(d), 414(e), 414(p)(11)]

Although the QDRO rules do not apply to IRAs (see Q 26:1), the transfer of an individual's interest in an IRA to the individual's spouse or former spouse under a divorce or separation agreement is not considered a taxable transfer made by such individual; and, thereafter, the IRA is treated as maintained for the benefit of the spouse or former spouse (see Q 26:44). It is also possible for a QDRO to require a distribution of benefits to the participant and then a transfer of a portion or all of the distribution to an IRA for the benefit of the former spouse. [IRC § 408(d)(6); Ltr Rul 9016077]

An IRA may also be used to implement a QDRO if a direct transfer of the participant's interest in a retirement plan to the participant's spouse is otherwise prohibited. When a QDRO required a participant–contract holder to transfer his interest in a tax-sheltered annuity to his spouse, but the terms of the annuity prevented a transfer to anyone other than the contract holder, the participant–contract holder could surrender the tax-sheltered annuity for its cash surrender value, roll over the distribution to an IRA, and then transfer the IRA to his spouse. [IRC § 408(d)(6); Ltr Rul 8916083]

The QDRO rules do not apply to nonqualified plans. [Ltr Rul 9340032] However, one court has ruled that life insurance benefits under an employer-sponsored nonqualified plan, an ERISA welfare benefit plan, are subject to the QDRO rules if the divorce decree specifies how the life insurance benefits must be distributed. [Metropolitan Life Ins Co v Wheaton, No. 94-1362 (7th Cir 1994); but see Equitable Life Assurance Soc'y of the US v Crysler, 1995 US App Lexis 27605 (8th Cir 1995)]

Q 30:6   Does a QDRO affect the qualification of a retirement plan?

A qualified retirement plan will not be treated as failing to satisfy the general qualification requirements (see Q 4:1) and the restriction on distributions under a 401(k) plan (see Q 23:33) solely because of a payment to an alternate payee (see Q 30:3) pursuant to a QDRO (see Q 30:1). This is the case even if the plan provides for payments pursuant to a QDRO to an alternate payee prior to the time the plan may make payments to a participant. For example, a qualified retirement plan may pay an alternate payee even though the participant may not receive a distribution because the participant continues to be employed by the employer (see Q 30:8). [IRC § 414(p)(10); Treas Reg § 1.401(a)-13(g)(3)]

Where there were insufficient liquid assets in a qualified retirement plan to make a payment to an alternate payee pursuant to a QDRO, DOL ruled that a loan to the plan from the participant spouse to enable the plan to comply with the QDRO was exempt from the prohibited transaction rules (see Q 20:1). [DOL Op Ltr 94-28A; PTCE 80-26; ERISA § 206(d)(3)]

Q 30:7 Must a qualified retirement plan include provisions regarding QDROs?

No. A qualified retirement plan need not include provisions with regard to QDROs (see Q 30:1), and this exclusion will not cause the retirement plan to fail to satisfy the general qualification requirements. [Treas Reg § 1.401(a)-13(g)(2)]

Q 30:8 What is the earliest retirement age rule?

A DRO may not require a qualified retirement plan to provide any type or form of benefit, or any option, not otherwise provided under the plan (see Q 30:2). [IRC § 414(p)(3)(A)]

A DRO will not fail to satisfy the above requirement solely because the DRO requires that payment of benefits be made to an alternate payee (see Q 30:3):

1. In the case of any payment before the participant has separated from service, on or after the date on which the participant attains (or would have attained) the earliest retirement age (see Q 30:9);
2. As if the participant had retired on the date on which such payment is to begin under the DRO; and
3. In any form in which such benefits may be paid under the qualified retirement plan to the participant.

[IRC § 414(p)(4)(A)]

A DRO will be a QDRO (see Q 30:1) even though the order provides that payments to the alternate payee may begin on or after the date on which the participant attains the earliest retirement age under the qualified retirement plan, whether or not the participant actually retires on that date. Therefore, a participant cannot delay an alternate payee's receipt of benefits by failing to take advantage of an early retirement option provided by the plan. [IRC § 414(p)(4)(A)(i)] For an exception to the earliest retirement age rule, see Q 30:10.

Payments of benefits prior to a participant's separation from service, but after earliest retirement age, must be made as if the participant had actually retired on the date payments are to begin under the QDRO. Only benefits actually accrued on that date are taken into account, and any employer subsidy for early retirement is not taken into account. An employer subsidizes an early retirement benefit to the extent that the benefit provided is greater than the actuarial equivalent of a retirement benefit commencing at normal retirement age. For example, if a participant would be entitled to a monthly retirement benefit under a qualified retirement plan of $1,000 at age 65 and the plan permits the participant to retire at age 62 with the full $1,000 monthly retirement benefit, the employer is subsidizing the early retirement benefit. Actuarial equivalency is computed using the interest rate specified in the qualified retirement plan. If the plan does not specify an interest rate for determining actuarial equivalency (as would be the case if the employer were subsidizing the benefit), a 5 percent interest rate is used. [IRC § 414(p)(4)(A)(ii)]

Benefit payments to an alternate payee after the earliest retirement age generally may be in any form allowed under the qualified retirement plan; however, benefits may not be paid in the form of a joint and survivor annuity with respect to the alternate payee and the alternate payee's subsequent spouse. [IRC § 414(p)(4)(A)(iii); Treas Reg § 1.401(a)-13(g)(4)(iii)(B)]

The amount payable under a QDRO following the participant's earliest retirement age cannot exceed the amount that the participant would be entitled to receive at such time. For example, assume that a profit sharing plan provides that a participant may withdraw some, but not all, of the participant's account balance (see Q 9:2) before separation from service. A QDRO may provide for payment to an alternate payee up to the amount that the participant may withdraw. [REA Senate Comm Report]

Q 30:9 What does earliest retirement age mean?

Earliest retirement age means the earlier of:

1. The earliest date on which the participant is entitled to a distribution under the qualified retirement plan; or

2. The later of (a) the date on which the participant attains age 50, or (b) the earliest date on which the participant could begin receiving a distribution from the plan if the participant separated from service. [IRC § 414(p)(4)(B)]

If the plan permits distributions to be made to the employee while an active participant (in-service distributions), the QDRO (see Q 30:1) can require that payments be made to the alternate payee (see Q 30:3) at any time when the participant qualifies for an in-service distribution. If the plan does not permit in-service distributions but distributions may begin at any time after separation from service, the earliest retirement age will be the earlier of age 50 or the date of separation from service. If the plan does not permit in-service distributions and does not permit distributions until the attainment of a specified age (age 65, for example), the earliest retirement age will, in this case, be age 65. One court enforced a QDRO that required a distribution to be made to an alternate payee even though, before the QDRO became final, the plan was retroactively amended to prohibit any distributions prior to age 65. [Stephen Allen Lynn, PC Employee Profit Sharing Plan v Stephen Allen Lynn, PC, No. 93-1501 (5th Cir 1994)]

Q 30:10   Can a distribution to an alternate payee be made before the earliest retirement age?

Yes. If the qualified retirement plan so permits, a QDRO (see Q 30:1) may require that payments be made to the alternate payee (see Q 30:3) prior to the participant's earliest retirement age (see Q 30:9). If the plan does not contain such a provision, the plan must be amended to permit a pre-earliest retirement age distribution. [TRA '86 Comm Reports; Ltr Ruls 8837013, 8744023]

Q 30:11   Must a qualified retirement plan establish a procedure to determine the qualified status of a DRO?

A qualified retirement plan must establish reasonable procedures to determine the qualified status of DROs (see Q 30:2) and to administer distributions made pursuant to QDROs (see Q 30:1). [IRC § 414(p)(6)(B)]

Although a qualified retirement plan need not include provisions regarding QDROs (see Q 30:7), the plan procedures must be in writing and the procedures must permit an alternate payee (see Q 30:3) to designate a representative to receive copies of the notices sent to the alternate payee with respect to a DRO. [REA Senate Comm Report]

Where a plan required that a "hold" be placed on a participant's account *after* receipt of a DRO, but the hold was placed *before* receipt because the plan administrator (see Q 16:1) had been informed that a DRO would be issued, the court ruled that the hold violated ERISA because it was contrary to the plan's written procedures. [Schoonmaker v Employee Savings Plan of Amoco Corp and Participating Cos, No. 91-2944 (7th Cir 1993)]

Q 30:12   What happens when a qualified retirement plan receives a DRO?

If a DRO (see Q 30:2) is received by a qualified retirement plan, the plan administrator (see Q 16:1) must promptly notify the participant and each alternate payee (see Q 30:3) of the receipt of the DRO and the plan's procedures (see Q 30:11) for determining its qualified status. In addition, the plan administrator must determine whether the DRO is a QDRO (see Q 30:1) and notify the participant and each alternate payee of the determination within a reasonable period after receipt of the DRO. After the DRO is issued, it is not the responsibility of the plan administrator to determine if an individual is, in fact, the spouse, former spouse, child, or other dependent of the participant. [IRC § 414(p)(6)(A); Sippe v Sippe, 101 NC App 194 (1990); DOL Adv Op 92-17A]

During the period in which the determination of whether a DRO is a QDRO is being made (by the plan administrator, by a court of competent jurisdiction, or otherwise), the plan administrator must separately account for the amounts (segregated amounts) that would have been payable to the alternate payee during such period if the DRO had been determined to be a QDRO. [IRC § 414(p)(7)(A); Board of Trustees of the Laborers Pension Trust Fund for Northern California v Levingston, 816 F Supp 1496 (ND Cal 1993)]

If, within the 18-month period beginning with the date on which the first payment under the DRO would be required, the DRO (or any modification thereof) is determined to be a QDRO, the plan administrator must pay the segregated amounts (including any interest thereon) to the alternate payee or payees. [IRC §§ 414(p)(7)(B), 414(p)(7)(E)]

If, within the 18-month period, it is determined that the DRO is not a QDRO or the determination is not made, then the plan administrator must pay the segregated amounts (including any interest thereon) to the person or persons who would have been entitled to such amounts if there had been no DRO. If a determination that a DRO is a QDRO is made after the 18-month period, it may be applied prospectively only. Therefore, the qualified retirement plan should not be liable to the alternate payee for payments for the period prior to the determination if the qualification is determined after the 18-month period. However, if a DRO is determined to be a QDRO after the 18-month period, the alternate payee may have a cause of action against the participant under state law for the amounts that were paid to the participant but that otherwise should have been paid to the alternate payee. [IRC §§ 414(p)(7)(C), 414(p)(7)(D); REA Senate Comm Report]

If the plan administrator fails to notify the participant and each alternate payee promptly of the procedures for determining the qualified status of the DRO, or fails to complete the determination process within a reasonable period after receipt, the plan administrator may be liable for breach of fiduciary duty. One court ruled that a state law that allowed a party to recover attorneys' fees from plan fiduciaries for their alleged unreasonable refusal to qualify a DRO was preempted by ERISA. [AT&T Mgmt Pension Plan v Tucker, No. CV 95-2263 (CD Cal 1995)]

DOL has ruled that a plan administrator may not charge fees to a plan participant or alternate payee or against a plan account for determining and administering a QDRO. [DOL Op Ltr 94-32A]

IRS has ruled that, in a salary-reduction-only tax-sheltered annuity (see Qs 29:1, 29:10), it is the employee-participant who determines that a DRO is a QDRO. [Ltr Rul 9619040]

Q 30:13   Can the amounts segregated for an alternate payee under a QDRO be forfeited?

If an alternate payee (see Q 30:3) cannot be located, the qualified retirement plan is not permitted to provide for the forfeiture of the alternate payee's segregated amounts (see Q 30:12) unless the plan provides for the segregated amounts to be fully reinstated when the alternate payee is located. [REA Senate Comm Report]

Q 30:14   How does a QDRO affect the qualified preretirement survivor annuity and qualified joint and survivor annuity requirements?

A QDRO (see Q 30:1) may provide that a former spouse will be treated as the participant's current spouse for some or all of the QPSA (see Q 10:9) and QJSA (see Q 10:8) requirements. [IRC § 414(p)(5); Treas Reg §§ 1.401(a)-13(g)(4)(i)(A), 1.401(a)-13(g)(4)(ii)]

To the extent a former spouse is treated as the participant's current spouse by reason of a QDRO, the actual current spouse will not be treated as the participant's current spouse. [IRC § 414(p)(5); Treas Reg § 1.401(a)-13(g)(4)(i)(B)]

Example 1. Assume Barrie is divorced from Larry, but a QDRO provides that Barrie shall be treated as Larry's current spouse with respect to all of Larry's benefits under a qualified retirement plan. Barrie will be treated as the surviving spouse under the QPSA and QJSA unless Larry obtains Barrie's consent to waive the QPSA or QJSA or both. The fact that Larry married Carrie after Larry's divorce from Barrie is disregarded. If, however, the QDRO had provided that Barrie would be treated as Larry's current spouse only with respect to benefits that accrued prior to the divorce, then Larry would need Barrie's consent to waive the QPSA or QJSA with respect to benefits accrued before the divorce, and Carrie's consent would be required with respect to the remainder of the benefits.

Example 2. Assume the same facts as in Example 1, except that the QDRO ordered that a portion of Larry's benefit must be distributed to Barrie rather than ordering that Barrie be treated as Larry's spouse. The QPSA and QJSA requirements would not apply to the part of Larry's benefit awarded Barrie. Instead, the QDRO would determine how Barrie's portion of Larry's benefit would be paid. Larry would be required to obtain Carrie's consent if Larry wanted to elect to waive either the QPSA or QJSA with respect to the remaining portion of his benefit.

Example 3. Assume the same facts as in Example 1, except that there was no QDRO and Larry died after marrying Carrie but never removed Barrie as his designated beneficiary. One court ruled that Carrie was entitled to one-half of Larry's plan benefits as his surviving spouse, but that Barrie was entitled to the other half (see Q 14:10). [McMillan v Parrott, 913 F 2d 310 (6th Cir 1990)]

If, because of a QDRO, more than one individual is treated as the surviving spouse, the qualified retirement plan may provide that the total amount to be paid in the form of a QPSA or survivor portion of a QJSA may not exceed the amount that would be paid if there were only one surviving spouse. The QPSA or survivor portion of the QJSA payable to each surviving spouse must be paid as an annuity based on the life expectancy of each respective spouse. If the QDRO splits the participant's benefit between the participant and a former spouse (either through separate accounts or percentage of the benefit), the surviving actual current spouse of the participant would be entitled to a QPSA or QJSA based on the participant's benefit reduced by the separate account or percentage payable to the former spouse. The calculation is made as if the separate account or percentage had been distributed to the participant. [Treas Reg § 1.401(a)-13(g)(4)(i)(C)]

If an alternate payee is treated pursuant to a QDRO as having an interest in the plan benefit, including a separate account or percentage of the participant's benefit, then the QDRO cannot provide the alternate payee with a greater right to designate a beneficiary for the alternate payee's benefit amount than the participant's right. The QPSA or QJSA provisions do not apply to the spouse of an alternate payee. If the former spouse who is treated as a current spouse should die prior to the participant's annuity starting date (see Q 10:3), then any actual current spouse of the participant would be treated as the current spouse, except as otherwise provided in the QDRO. [Treas Reg § 1.401(a)-13(g)(4)(iii)]

Q 30:15 Must an alternate payee consent to a distribution from a qualified retirement plan?

The general rules that apply to the distribution of benefits to a participant from a qualified retirement plan also apply to the distribution of benefits to an alternate payee (see Q 30:3) pursuant to a QDRO (see Q 30:1). (For exceptions, see Qs 30:6, 30:8, 30:14.)

If the distribution to the alternate payee does not exceed $3,500, the alternate payee's consent is not required. However, if the distribution exceeds $3,500, the alternate payee's consent is required (see Q 10:58).

In determining whether the present value of the benefit payable to the alternate payee exceeds $3,500, the present value of the participant's remaining benefit is disregarded. Similarly, for purposes of determining whether the present value of the benefit payable to the participant exceeds $3,500, the present value of the benefit payable to the alternate payee under a QDRO is disregarded. [TRA '86 Comm Reports]

Q 30:16 Does a QDRO affect the maximum amount of the participant's benefits under a qualified retirement plan?

Even though a participant's benefits are awarded to an alternate payee (see Q 30:3) pursuant to a QDRO (see Q 30:1), the benefits awarded to the alternate payee are still considered benefits of the participant for purposes of applying the limitations of Section 415 to the participant's benefits. See chapter 6 for details. [Treas Reg § 1.401(a)-13(g)(4)(iv)]

Q 30:17 What are the income tax consequences of a QDRO to the participant?

If the alternate payee (see Q 30:3) pursuant to a QDRO (see Q 30:1) is other than the participant's spouse or former spouse (e.g., a child), any distribution from a qualified retirement plan to such alternate payee will be included in the participant's gross income for the year of distribution. If, however, any portion of the distribution represents a recovery of the participant's investment in the contract (see Q 13:2), that portion will be excluded from the participant's gross income. [IRC §§ 402(a), 402(e)(1)(A)]

The balance to the credit of an employee (see Q 13:5) does not include an amount payable to an alternate payee under a QDRO. So, an alternate payee's decision to receive payments in a form other than a lump sum will not affect the participant's eligibility for the special tax treatment afforded a lump-sum distribution (see Q 13:4) or the participant's eligibility to roll over a distribution from the qualified retirement plan. [IRC § 402(d)(4)(H); Ltr Ruls 8935041, 8743102]

See chapters 13 and 28 for details on taxation of distributions and rollovers.

Q 30:18 What are the income tax consequences of a QDRO to an alternate payee spouse or former spouse?

If the alternate payee (see Q 30:3) is the spouse or former spouse of the participant, any distribution from a qualified retirement plan to such alternate payee pursuant to a QDRO (see Q 30:1) will be included in the alternate payee's gross income for the year of distribution. The participant's investment in the contract (see Q 13:2) must be apportioned between the participant and such alternate payee. The investment in the contract will be allocated on a pro rata basis between the present value of the distribution to the alternate payee and the present value of all other benefits payable with respect to the participant. [IRC §§ 72(m)(10), 402(e)(1)(A); Hawkins v Comm'r, 94-9011, 94-9009 (10th Cir 1996); Brotman, 105 TC 141 (1995); Rudzin, 69 TCM 1649 (1995); Powell, 101 TC 489 (1993); Ltr Ruls 9138004, 9013007]

If a distribution of the balance to the credit of an employee (see Q 13:5) would be treated as a lump-sum distribution (see Q 13:4), then the payment under a QDRO of the balance to the credit of an alternate payee spouse or former spouse of the participant will be treated as a lump-sum distribution. The balance to the credit of the alternate payee does not include any amount payable to the participant. [IRC § 402(d)(4)(J)]

If there is no QDRO, the spouse or former spouse is not an alternate payee, and a distribution from the plan to the participant, who then gives the payment to such spouse, or from the plan directly to the spouse or former spouse, is included in the participant's gross income (see Qs 13:1, 30:1). Pursuant to a QDRO, a participant's ex-spouse was entitled to a portion of his qualified retirement plan benefits. Subsequently, however, the participant received a distribution of the entire plan benefit, rolled over the distribution to an IRA, and designated his new spouse as beneficiary. Upon the participant's death, the new spouse received the IRA proceeds and paid income tax on the proceeds. After a lawsuit was commenced by the ex-spouse, she received a settlement payment from the new spouse. IRS concluded that the settlement payment did not constitute a taxable distribution from either a qualified retirement plan or an IRA, but did not rule on whether the payment was taxable under other Code sections. [Ltr Rul 9327083]

For details on taxation of distributions, see chapter 13.

Q 30:19 Can an alternate payee roll over a distribution pursuant to a QDRO from a qualified retirement plan?

A distribution from a qualified retirement plan pursuant to a QDRO (see Q 30:1) to an alternate payee (see Q 30:3) who is not the spouse or former spouse of the participant (e.g., a child) may not be rolled over to another qualified retirement plan or to an IRA.

Since such alternate payee pays no income tax on the distribution, the ineligibility of the alternate payee to roll over the distribution is of no importance to the alternate payee. However, because the participant remains taxable on a distribution to a nonspouse or non–former spouse alternate payee, this ineligibility to roll over will cause the participant to include the distribution in income. This remains true even if the participant receives, at the same time, a distribution from the plan eligible to be rolled over and does roll over such distribution (see Q 30:17).

If, however, the alternate payee is the spouse or former spouse of the participant and receives an eligible rollover distribution (see Q 28:8) pursuant to a QDRO, the alternate payee is eligible to roll over any portion or all of the distribution to an eligible retirement plan (see Q 28:19). [IRC §§ 402(c), 402(e)(1)(B); Ltr Ruls 9109052, 9013007]

An eligible rollover distribution made to an alternate payee spouse or former spouse may be subject to mandatory 20 percent income tax withholding (see Q 16:7). Since an alternate payee nonspouse or non–former spouse pays no income tax on the distribution, the distribution will not be subject to the automatic withholding rules. [IRC § 3405(c)]

For details on rollovers, see chapter 28.

Q 30:20   Does the 10 percent early distribution tax apply to a distribution made to an alternate payee pursuant to a QDRO?

The 10 percent tax on early distributions (see Q 13:39) from qualified retirement plans does not apply to any distribution to any alternate payee (see Q 30:3) pursuant to a QDRO (see Q 30:1). [IRC § 72(t)(2)(C); Ltr Ruls 9051041, 9013007, 8935041]

Because of this exception, the 10 percent early distribution tax will not be imposed on the participant if the alternate payee is a nonspouse or non–former spouse (e.g., a child) (see Q 30:17) and will not be imposed on a spouse or former spouse alternate payee (see Q 30:18).

If a spouse or former spouse alternate payee rolls over to an IRA a distribution pursuant to a QDRO from a qualified retirement plan (see Q 30:19), the alternate payee can commence distributions from the IRA prior to age 59½ in a series of substantially equal periodic payments and avoid the 10 percent tax on early distributions (see Qs 13:40, 26:41). [IRC § 72(t)(2)(A)(iv); Ltr Rul 9109052]

Q 30:21   How does a QDRO affect the excess distribution tax and the excess accumulation tax?

To calculate an individual's distributions for excess distribution tax purposes, amounts paid to an alternate payee (see Q 30:3) who is not the spouse or former spouse of the individual (e.g., a child) from a qualified retirement plan pursuant to a QDRO (see Q 30:1) are included, but amounts paid to an alternate payee spouse or former spouse are disregarded. Any amounts paid to an alternate payee spouse or former spouse from a qualified retirement plan pursuant to a QDRO are includible distributions of the alternate payee for excess distribution tax purposes (see Qs 13:27–13:30). [Ltr Ruls 9338040, 9138004]

To calculate a decedent's aggregate interests for excess accumulation tax purposes, amounts paid to an alternate payee who is not the spouse or former spouse of the decedent (e.g., a child) from a qualified retirement plan pursuant to a QDRO are included, but amounts paid to an alternate payee spouse or former spouse are disregarded. Any amounts paid to an alternate payee spouse or former spouse from a qualified retirement plan pursuant to a QDRO will be includible distributions of the alternate payee for excess distribution tax purposes and, if rolled over to an eligible retirement plan (see Q 30:19), will be includible, to the extent not withdrawn during the alternate payee's lifetime, in the alternate payee's calculation of aggregate interests for excess accumulation tax purposes. However, if the alternate payee is the spouse, as opposed to the former spouse, of the decedent, a special spousal election will be available (see Qs 14:21–14:28). [Ltr Rul 9138004]

An individual whose total benefits in all retirement plans (see Q 13:31) on August 1, 1986 had a value in excess of $562,500 was eligible to elect a special grandfather rule. The grandfather election permits the individual to offset distributions received during the individual's lifetime by the portion of the initial grandfather amount recovered during the year of distribution. Furthermore, if the grandfather election was made, the decedent's aggregate interests may be reduced by the unrecovered grandfather amount on the date of the decedent's death. The effect of the special grandfather rule is the potential reduction of the excess distribution tax and/or the excess accumulation tax (see Qs 13:31–13:36, 14:24–14:26).

IRS has ruled that, if a portion or all of a participant's qualified retirement plan benefits are awarded to the participant's spouse or former spouse pursuant to a QDRO, there is no statutory authority for allocating to the alternate payee any portion, pro rata or otherwise, of the participant's unrecovered grandfather amount. Since there is no statutory authority for an allocation of the unrecovered grandfather amount, the participant's unrecovered grandfather amount is not reduced because of the distribution required by the QDRO. [Ltr Ruls 9338040, 9138004]

> **Example.** Larry had qualified retirement plan benefits of $2,000,000 on August 1, 1986 and made the grandfather election. In 1997, Larry and Carrie are divorced and, under a QDRO, $1,000,000 of Larry's benefits is allocated to Carrie. If Larry has not recovered any portion of his initial grandfather amount, he retains the entire $2,000,000 initial grandfather amount.

Q 30:22   Are qualified retirement plan benefits subject to equitable distribution?

Some portion or all of a participant's benefits under a qualified retirement plan may be awarded to the participant's spouse pursuant to a QDRO (see Q 30:1). [Hamstead v Hamstead, No. 19529 (SCA W Va 1990); Givler v Givler, No. Ca-181 (CA Tenn, ED, 1990)] One court ruled that benefits could be awarded to the participant's spouse even though she had executed an antenuptial agreement waiving her rights, because the waiver was ineffective (see Q 10:22). [Richards v Richards, NYLJ (S Ct NY 1995)]

At least one court has ruled that qualified retirement plan benefits accrued prior to the marriage are not subject to an equitable distribution of marital assets absent evidence of a gift or conveyance. [Zaborowski v Zaborowski, No. 88-1802 (DCA Fla, 5th District, 1989)] However, another court ruled that plan benefits accrued during the time a couple lived together before marriage were subject to division upon divorce. [Bays v Bays, No. 5-3635 (SC Alaska 1991)]

In a matter in which a couple separated and, during the separation but prior to the divorce, one spouse became covered under a new plan, the court ruled that the new retirement benefits were separate property and not community property and therefore the nonparticipant spouse had no entitlement to the benefits. [In re the Matter of the Marriage of Manry, 60 Wn App 146 (1991)] In another case, to accomplish a division of marital property, the court ruled that the value of the spouse's pension benefits should be based on present value and not the projected value at age 65. [In re the Marriage of Keedy, No. 90-598 (SC Mont 1991)]

An enhanced pension benefit elected by an employee as part of an early retirement incentive program that occurred after divorce was held to be marital property subject to equitable distribution because it was a modification of a marital asset and not the creation of a new asset. [Olivo v Olivo, 82 NY 2d 202 (CA NY 1993)] Another court ruled that benefit increases not attributable to the employee's efforts between the marital separation date and the benefit commencement date would be shared by the spouse, but increases resulting from the employee's efforts (e.g., salary increases) would not be shared. [Berrington v Berrington, No. 20 WD Appeal Docket (S Ct Pa 1993)]

Q 30:23 Can a QDRO be enforced by an attachment of the participant's monthly retirement benefits?

One court has held that an order made pursuant to the state domestic relations law that relates to alimony payments is a QDRO (see Q 30:1), which may be enforced by attachment of the participant's (husband's) qualified retirement plan benefits. The court determined that, since the state domestic law allowed attachment of the husband's income in any form, the attachment order against his qualified retirement plan benefits was a QDRO, which allowed the wife to recover amounts for alimony. [Taylor v Taylor, 44 Ohio St 3d 61 (1989)] Another court ruled that a garnishment judgment against a plan participant for failure to make required alimony and child support payments must satisfy the QDRO requirements. [Arizona Laborers, etc. Local 385 Pension Fund v Nevarez, 8 EBC 2227 (D Ariz 1987)]

Even though an award of attorney's fees incurred by a spouse to obtain a QDRO for spousal support was not itself a QDRO, a court ruled that qualified retirement plan benefits could be used to satisfy the award. [In re the Marriage of Olivarez, 8 EBC 1263 (Cal Ct App 1986)]

Q 30:24 Can a QDRO be discharged in bankruptcy?

One court has held that a participant's obligation to pay one-half of his qualified retirement plan benefits to his former spouse as part of a divorce decree's property settlement was a "debt" under the U.S. Bankruptcy Code that was dischargeable in bankruptcy. The property settlement awarded the former spouse one-half of the participant's qualified retirement plan benefits as he received them. The participant filed a Chapter 7 bankruptcy petition and listed that obligation as a dischargeable debt. The Bankruptcy Code defines a debt as a liability on a claim and a claim as a right to payment, whether or not such right is contingent or unmatured. The court held that the former spouse had a claim for a share of future qualified retirement plan payments, however contingent or unmatured that claim might be. Although a debt for alimony, maintenance, or support is not dischargeable under the Bankruptcy Code, the obligation in this case was a property settlement and, therefore, a debt that was dischargeable in bankruptcy. [Bush v Taylor, No. 88-2145 (8th Cir 1990); see also In re Ellis, 1995 US App Lexis 35337 (8th Cir 1995); Anderson v Lifeline Healthcare Group, Ltd, No. 92-5076 (10th Cir 1993)]

However, other courts have ruled that since the wife had been awarded a part of the husband's pension fund, it had become her property and was not a dischargeable debt of the participant-husband when he filed a bankruptcy petition. [In re Gendreau, 1995 Bankr Lexis 1964 (9th Cir 1995); In re Bennett, 1994 Bankr Lexis 1942 (Bankr ED Pa 1994); In re Zick, No. 89-02388 (Bankr ED Wis 1990)]

Appendix A

Ordinary Life Annuities, One Life—Expected Return Multiples

Age	Multiple	Age	Multiple
5	76.6	61	23.3
6	75.6	62	22.5
7	74.7	63	21.6
8	73.7	64	20.8
9	72.7	65	20.0
10	71.7	66	19.2
11	70.7	67	18.4
12	69.7	68	17.6
13	68.8	69	16.8
14	67.8	70	16.0
15	66.8	71	15.3
16	65.8	72	14.6
17	64.8	73	13.9
18	63.9	74	13.2
19	62.9	75	12.5
20	61.9	76	11.9
21	60.9	77	11.2
22	59.9	78	10.6
23	59.0	79	10.0
24	58.0	80	9.5
25	57.0	81	8.9
26	56.0	82	8.4
27	55.1	83	7.9
28	54.1	84	7.4
29	53.1	85	6.9
30	52.2	86	6.5
31	51.2	87	6.1
32	50.2	88	5.7
33	49.3	89	5.3
34	48.3	90	5.0
35	47.3	91	4.7
36	46.4	92	4.4
37	45.4	93	4.1
38	44.4	94	3.9
39	43.5	95	3.7
40	42.5	96	3.4
41	41.5	97	3.2
42	40.6	98	3.0
43	39.6	99	2.8
44	38.7	100	2.7
45	37.7	101	2.5
46	36.8	102	2.3
47	35.9	103	2.1
48	34.9	104	1.9
49	34.0	105	1.8
50	33.1	106	1.6
51	32.2	107	1.4
52	31.3	108	1.3
53	30.4	109	1.1
54	29.5	110	1.0
55	28.6	111	.9
56	27.7	112	.8
57	26.8	113	.7
58	25.9	114	.6
59	25.0	115	.5
60	24.2		

Appendix B

Ordinary Joint Life Annuities, Two Lives—Expected Return Multiples

Ages	5	6	7	8	9	10	11	12	13	14
5	83.8	83.3	82.8	82.4	82.0	81.6	81.2	80.9	80.6	80.3
6	83.3	82.8	82.3	81.8	81.4	81.0	80.6	80.3	79.9	79.6
7	82.8	82.3	81.8	81.3	80.9	80.4	80.0	79.6	79.3	78.9
8	82.4	81.8	81.3	80.8	80.3	79.9	79.4	79.0	78.6	78.3
9	82.0	81.4	80.9	80.3	79.8	79.3	78.9	78.4	78.0	77.6
10	81.6	81.0	80.4	79.9	79.3	78.8	78.3	77.9	77.4	77.0
11	81.2	80.6	80.0	79.4	78.9	78.3	77.8	77.3	76.9	76.4
12	80.9	80.3	79.6	79.0	78.4	77.9	77.3	76.8	76.3	75.9
13	80.6	79.9	79.3	78.6	78.0	77.4	76.9	76.3	75.8	75.3
14	80.3	79.6	78.9	78.3	77.6	77.0	76.4	75.9	75.3	74.8
15	80.0	79.3	78.6	77.9	77.3	76.6	76.0	75.4	74.9	74.3
16	79.8	79.0	78.3	77.6	76.9	76.3	75.6	75.0	74.4	73.9
17	79.5	78.8	78.0	77.3	76.6	75.9	75.3	74.6	74.0	73.4
18	79.3	78.5	77.8	77.0	76.3	75.6	74.9	74.3	73.6	73.0
19	79.1	78.3	77.5	76.8	76.0	75.3	74.6	73.9	73.3	72.6
20	78.9	78.1	77.3	76.5	75.8	75.0	74.3	73.6	72.9	72.3
21	78.7	77.9	77.1	76.3	75.5	74.8	74.0	73.3	72.6	71.9
22	78.6	77.7	76.9	76.1	75.3	74.5	73.8	73.0	72.3	71.6
23	78.4	77.6	76.7	75.9	75.1	74.3	73.5	72.8	72.0	71.3
24	78.3	77.4	76.6	75.7	74.9	74.1	73.3	72.6	71.8	71.1
25	78.2	77.3	76.4	75.6	74.8	73.9	73.1	72.3	71.6	70.8
26	78.0	77.2	76.3	75.4	74.6	73.8	72.9	72.1	71.3	70.6
27	77.9	77.1	76.2	75.3	74.4	73.6	72.8	71.9	71.1	70.3
28	77.8	76.9	76.1	75.2	74.3	73.4	72.6	71.8	70.9	70.1
29	77.7	76.8	76.0	75.1	74.2	73.3	72.5	71.6	70.8	70.0
30	77.7	76.8	75.9	75.0	74.1	73.2	72.3	71.5	70.6	69.8
31	77.6	76.7	75.8	74.9	74.0	73.1	72.2	71.3	70.5	69.6
32	77.5	76.6	75.7	74.8	73.9	73.0	72.1	71.2	70.3	69.5
33	77.5	76.5	75.6	74.7	73.8	72.9	72.0	71.1	70.2	69.3
34	77.4	76.5	75.5	74.6	73.7	72.8	71.9	71.0	70.1	69.2
35	77.3	76.4	75.5	74.5	73.6	72.7	71.8	70.9	70.0	69.1
36	77.3	76.3	75.4	74.5	73.5	72.6	71.7	70.8	69.9	69.0
37	77.2	76.3	75.4	74.4	73.5	72.6	71.6	70.7	69.8	68.9
38	77.2	76.2	75.3	74.4	73.4	72.5	71.6	70.6	69.7	68.8
39	77.2	76.2	75.2	74.3	73.4	72.4	71.5	70.6	69.6	68.7
40	77.1	76.2	75.2	74.3	73.3	72.4	71.4	70.5	69.6	68.6
41	77.1	76.1	75.2	74.2	73.3	72.3	71.4	70.4	69.5	68.6
42	77.0	76.1	75.1	74.2	73.2	72.3	71.3	70.4	69.4	68.5
43	77.0	76.1	75.1	74.1	73.2	72.2	71.3	70.3	69.4	68.5
44	77.0	76.0	75.1	74.1	73.1	72.2	71.2	70.3	69.3	68.4
45	77.0	76.0	75.0	74.1	73.1	72.2	71.2	70.2	69.3	68.4
46	76.9	76.0	75.0	74.0	73.1	72.1	71.2	70.2	69.3	68.3
47	76.9	75.9	75.0	74.0	73.1	72.1	71.1	70.2	69.2	68.3
48	76.9	75.9	75.0	74.0	73.0	72.1	71.1	70.1	69.2	68.2
49	76.9	75.9	74.9	74.0	73.0	72.0	71.1	70.1	69.1	68.2
50	76.9	75.9	74.9	73.9	73.0	72.0	71.0	70.1	69.1	68.2
51	76.8	75.9	74.9	73.9	73.0	72.0	71.0	70.1	69.1	68.1
52	76.8	75.9	74.9	73.9	72.9	72.0	71.0	70.0	69.1	68.1
53	76.8	75.8	74.9	73.9	72.9	71.9	71.0	70.0	69.0	68.1
54	76.8	75.8	74.8	73.9	72.9	71.9	71.0	70.0	69.0	68.1
55	76.8	75.8	74.8	73.9	72.9	71.9	70.9	70.0	69.0	68.0
56	76.8	75.8	74.8	73.8	72.9	71.9	70.9	69.9	69.0	68.0

Ages	5	6	7	8	9	10	11	12	13	14
57	76.8	75.8	74.8	73.8	72.9	71.9	70.9	69.9	69.0	68.0
58	76.8	75.8	74.8	73.8	72.8	71.9	70.9	69.9	68.9	68.0
59	76.7	75.8	74.8	73.8	72.8	71.9	70.9	69.9	68.9	68.0
60	76.7	75.8	74.8	73.8	72.8	71.8	70.9	69.9	68.9	67.9
61	76.7	75.7	74.8	73.8	72.8	71.8	70.9	69.9	68.9	67.9
62	76.7	75.7	74.8	73.8	72.8	71.8	70.8	69.9	68.9	67.9
63	76.7	75.7	74.8	73.8	72.8	71.8	70.8	69.8	68.9	67.9
64	76.7	75.7	74.7	73.8	72.8	71.8	70.8	69.8	68.9	67.9
65	76.7	75.7	74.7	73.8	72.8	71.8	70.8	69.8	68.9	67.9
66	76.7	75.7	74.7	73.7	72.8	71.8	70.8	69.8	68.9	67.9
67	76.7	75.7	74.7	73.7	72.8	71.8	70.8	69.8	68.8	67.9
68	76.7	75.7	74.7	73.7	72.8	71.8	70.8	69.8	68.8	67.8
69	76.7	75.7	74.7	73.7	72.7	71.8	70.8	69.8	68.8	67.8
70	76.7	75.7	74.7	73.7	72.7	71.8	70.8	69.8	68.8	67.8
71	76.7	75.7	74.7	73.7	72.7	71.8	70.8	69.8	68.8	67.8
72	76.7	75.7	74.7	73.7	72.7	71.8	70.8	69.8	68.8	67.8
73	76.7	75.7	74.7	73.7	72.7	71.7	70.8	69.8	68.8	67.8
74	76.7	75.7	74.7	73.7	72.7	71.7	70.8	69.8	68.8	67.8
75	76.7	75.7	74.7	73.7	72.7	71.7	70.8	69.8	68.8	67.8
76	76.6	75.7	74.7	73.7	72.7	71.7	70.8	69.8	68.8	67.8
77	76.6	75.7	74.7	73.7	72.7	71.7	70.8	69.8	68.8	67.8
78	76.6	75.7	74.7	73.7	72.7	71.7	70.7	69.8	68.8	67.8
79	76.6	75.7	74.7	73.7	72.7	71.7	70.7	69.8	68.8	67.8
80	76.6	75.7	74.7	73.7	72.7	71.7	70.7	69.8	68.8	67.8
81	76.6	75.7	74.7	73.7	72.7	71.7	70.7	69.8	68.8	67.8
82	76.6	75.7	74.7	73.7	72.7	71.7	70.7	69.8	68.8	67.8
83	76.6	75.7	74.7	73.7	72.7	71.7	70.7	69.8	68.8	67.8
84	76.6	75.7	74.7	73.7	72.7	71.7	70.7	69.8	68.8	67.8
85	76.6	75.7	74.7	73.7	72.7	71.7	70.7	69.8	68.8	67.8
86	76.6	75.7	74.7	73.7	72.7	71.7	70.7	69.8	68.8	67.8
87	76.6	75.7	74.7	73.7	72.7	71.7	70.7	69.8	68.8	67.8
88	76.6	75.7	74.7	73.7	72.7	71.7	70.7	69.7	68.8	67.8
89	76.6	75.7	74.7	73.7	72.7	71.7	70.7	69.7	68.8	67.8
90	76.6	75.6	74.7	73.7	72.7	71.7	70.7	69.7	68.8	67.8
91	76.6	75.6	74.7	73.7	72.7	71.7	70.7	69.7	68.8	67.8
92	76.6	75.6	74.7	73.7	72.7	71.7	70.7	69.7	68.8	67.8
93	76.6	75.6	74.7	73.7	72.7	71.7	70.7	69.7	68.8	67.8
94	76.6	75.6	74.7	73.7	72.7	71.7	70.7	69.7	68.8	67.8
95	76.6	75.6	74.7	73.7	72.7	71.7	70.7	69.7	68.8	67.8
96	76.6	75.6	74.7	73.7	72.7	71.7	70.7	69.7	68.8	67.8
97	76.6	75.6	74.7	73.7	72.7	71.7	70.7	69.7	68.8	67.8
98	76.6	75.6	74.7	73.7	72.7	71.7	70.7	69.7	68.8	67.8
99	76.6	75.6	74.7	73.7	72.7	71.7	70.7	69.7	68.8	67.8
100	76.6	75.6	74.7	73.7	72.7	71.7	70.7	69.7	68.8	67.8
101	76.6	75.6	74.7	73.7	72.7	71.7	70.7	69.7	68.8	67.8
102	76.6	75.6	74.7	73.7	72.7	71.7	70.7	69.7	68.8	67.8
103	76.6	75.6	74.7	73.7	72.7	71.7	70.7	69.7	68.8	67.8
104	76.6	75.6	74.7	73.7	72.7	71.7	70.7	69.7	68.8	67.8
105	76.6	75.6	74.7	73.7	72.7	71.7	70.7	69.7	68.8	67.8
106	76.6	75.6	74.7	73.7	72.7	71.7	70.7	69.7	68.8	67.8
107	76.6	75.6	74.7	73.7	72.7	71.7	70.7	69.7	68.8	67.8
108	76.6	75.6	74.7	73.7	72.7	71.7	70.7	69.7	68.8	67.8
109	76.6	75.6	74.7	73.7	72.7	71.7	70.7	69.7	68.8	67.8
110	76.6	75.6	74.7	73.7	72.7	71.7	70.7	69.7	68.8	67.8
111	76.6	75.6	74.7	73.7	72.7	71.7	70.7	69.7	68.8	67.8
112	76.6	75.6	74.7	73.7	72.7	71.7	70.7	69.7	68.8	67.8
113	76.6	75.6	74.7	73.7	72.7	71.7	70.7	69.7	68.8	67.8
114	76.6	75.6	74.7	73.7	72.7	71.7	70.7	69.7	68.8	67.8
115	76.6	75.6	74.7	73.7	72.7	71.7	70.7	69.7	68.8	67.8

Ages	15	16	17	18	19	20	21	22	23	24
15	73.8	73.3	72.9	72.4	72.0	71.6	71.3	70.9	70.6	70.3
16	73.3	72.8	72.3	71.9	71.4	71.0	70.7	70.3	70.0	69.6
17	72.9	72.3	71.8	71.3	70.9	70.5	70.0	69.7	69.3	69.0
18	72.4	71.9	71.3	70.8	70.4	70.0	69.5	69.1	68.7	68.3
19	72.0	71.4	70.9	70.4	69.8	69.4	68.9	68.5	68.1	67.7
20	71.6	71.0	70.5	69.9	69.4	68.8	68.4	67.9	67.5	67.1
21	71.3	70.7	70.0	69.5	68.9	68.4	67.9	67.4	66.9	66.5
22	70.9	70.3	69.7	69.0	68.5	67.9	67.4	66.9	66.4	65.9
23	70.6	70.0	69.3	68.7	68.1	67.5	66.9	66.4	65.9	65.4
24	70.3	69.6	69.0	68.3	67.7	67.1	66.5	65.9	65.4	64.9
25	70.1	69.3	68.6	68.0	67.3	66.7	66.1	65.5	64.9	64.4
26	69.8	69.1	68.3	67.6	67.0	66.3	65.7	65.1	64.5	63.9
27	69.6	68.8	68.1	67.3	66.7	66.0	65.3	64.7	64.1	63.5
28	69.3	68.6	67.8	67.1	66.4	65.7	65.0	64.3	63.7	63.1
29	69.1	68.4	67.6	66.8	66.1	65.4	64.7	64.0	63.3	62.7
30	69.0	68.2	67.4	66.6	65.8	65.1	64.4	63.7	63.0	62.3
31	68.8	68.0	67.2	66.4	65.6	64.8	64.1	63.4	62.7	62.0
32	68.6	67.8	67.0	66.2	65.4	64.6	63.8	63.1	62.4	61.7
33	68.5	67.6	66.8	66.0	65.2	64.4	63.6	62.8	62.1	61.4
34	68.3	67.5	66.6	65.8	65.0	64.2	63.4	62.6	61.9	61.1
35	68.2	67.4	66.5	65.6	64.8	64.0	63.2	62.4	61.6	60.9
36	68.1	67.2	66.4	65.5	64.7	63.8	63.0	62.2	61.4	60.6
37	68.0	67.1	66.2	65.4	64.5	63.7	62.8	62.0	61.2	60.4
38	67.9	67.0	66.1	65.2	64.4	63.5	62.7	61.8	61.0	60.2
39	67.8	66.9	66.0	65.1	64.2	63.4	62.5	61.7	60.8	60.0
40	67.7	66.8	65.9	65.0	64.1	63.3	62.4	61.5	60.7	59.9
41	67.7	66.7	65.8	64.9	64.0	63.1	62.3	61.4	60.5	59.7
42	67.6	66.7	65.7	64.8	63.9	63.0	62.2	61.3	60.4	59.6
43	67.5	66.6	65.7	64.8	63.8	62.9	62.1	61.2	60.3	59.4
44	67.5	66.5	65.6	64.7	63.8	62.9	62.0	61.1	60.2	59.3
45	67.4	66.5	65.5	64.6	63.7	62.8	61.9	61.0	60.1	59.2
46	67.4	66.4	65.4	64.6	63.6	62.7	61.8	60.9	60.0	59.1
47	67.3	66.4	65.4	64.5	63.6	62.6	61.7	60.8	59.9	59.0
48	67.3	66.3	65.4	64.4	63.5	62.6	61.6	60.7	59.8	58.9
49	67.2	66.3	65.3	64.4	63.5	62.5	61.6	60.7	59.7	58.8
50	67.2	66.2	65.3	64.3	63.4	62.5	61.5	60.6	59.7	58.8
51	67.1	66.2	65.3	64.3	63.4	62.4	61.5	60.5	59.6	58.7
52	67.1	66.2	65.2	64.3	63.3	62.4	61.4	60.5	59.6	58.6
53	67.1	66.2	65.2	64.2	63.3	62.3	61.4	60.4	59.5	58.6
54	67.1	66.1	65.2	64.2	63.2	62.3	61.3	60.4	59.5	58.5
55	67.1	66.1	65.1	64.2	63.2	62.3	61.3	60.4	59.4	58.5
56	67.0	66.1	65.1	64.1	63.2	62.2	61.3	60.3	59.4	58.4
57	67.0	66.1	65.1	64.1	63.2	62.2	61.2	60.3	59.3	58.4
58	67.0	66.0	65.1	64.1	63.1	62.2	61.2	60.3	59.3	58.4
59	67.0	66.0	65.0	64.1	63.1	62.1	61.2	60.2	59.3	58.3
60	67.0	66.0	65.0	64.1	63.1	62.1	61.2	60.2	59.2	58.3
61	67.0	66.0	65.0	64.0	63.1	62.1	61.1	60.2	59.2	58.3
62	66.9	66.0	65.0	64.0	63.1	62.1	61.1	60.2	59.2	58.2
63	66.9	66.0	65.0	64.0	63.0	62.1	61.1	60.1	59.2	58.2
64	66.9	65.9	65.0	64.0	63.0	62.1	61.1	60.1	59.2	58.2
65	66.9	65.9	65.0	64.0	63.0	62.0	61.1	60.1	59.1	58.2
66	66.9	65.9	64.9	64.0	63.0	62.0	61.1	60.1	59.1	58.2
67	66.9	65.9	64.9	64.0	63.0	62.0	61.1	60.1	59.1	58.1

Ages	15	16	17	18	19	20	21	22	23	24
68	66.9	65.9	64.9	64.0	63.0	62.0	61.0	60.1	59.1	58.1
69	66.9	65.9	64.9	63.9	63.0	62.0	61.0	60.0	59.1	58.1
70	66.9	65.9	64.9	63.9	63.0	62.0	61.0	60.0	59.1	58.1
71	66.9	65.9	64.9	63.9	62.9	62.0	61.0	60.0	59.1	58.1
72	66.9	65.9	64.9	63.9	62.9	62.0	61.0	60.0	59.0	58.1
73	66.8	65.9	64.9	63.9	62.9	62.0	61.0	60.0	59.0	58.1
74	66.8	65.9	64.9	63.9	62.9	62.0	61.0	60.0	59.0	58.1
75	66.8	65.9	64.9	63.9	62.9	61.9	61.0	60.0	59.0	58.1
76	66.8	65.9	64.9	63.9	62.9	61.9	61.0	60.0	59.0	58.0
77	66.8	65.9	64.9	63.9	63.9	62.9	61.0	60.0	59.0	58.0
78	66.8	65.8	64.9	63.9	62.9	61.9	61.0	60.0	59.0	58.0
79	66.8	65.8	64.9	63.9	62.9	61.9	61.0	60.0	59.0	58.0
80	66.8	65.9	64.9	63.9	62.9	61.9	60.9	60.0	59.0	58.0
81	66.8	65.8	64.9	63.9	62.9	61.9	60.9	60.0	59.0	58.0
82	66.8	65.8	64.9	63.9	62.9	61.9	60.9	60.0	59.0	58.0
83	66.8	65.8	64.9	63.9	62.9	61.9	60.9	60.0	59.0	58.0
84	66.8	65.8	64.8	63.9	62.9	61.9	60.9	60.0	59.0	58.0
85	66.8	65.8	64.8	63.9	62.9	61.9	60.9	60.0	59.0	58.0
86	66.8	65.8	64.8	63.9	62.9	61.9	60.9	60.0	59.0	58.0
87	66.8	65.8	64.8	63.9	62.9	61.9	60.9	60.0	59.0	58.0
88	66.8	65.8	64.8	63.9	62.9	61.9	60.9	60.0	59.0	58.0
89	66.8	65.8	64.8	63.9	62.9	61.9	60.9	60.0	59.0	58.0
90	66.8	65.8	64.8	63.9	62.9	61.9	60.9	60.0	59.0	58.0
91	66.8	65.8	64.8	63.9	62.9	61.9	60.9	60.0	59.0	58.0
92	66.8	65.8	64.8	63.9	62.9	61.9	60.9	59.9	59.0	58.0
93	66.8	65.8	64.8	63.9	62.9	61.9	60.9	59.9	59.0	58.0
94	66.8	65.8	64.8	63.9	62.9	61.9	60.9	59.9	59.0	58.0
95	66.8	65.8	64.8	63.9	62.9	61.9	60.9	59.9	59.0	58.0
96	66.8	65.8	64.8	63.9	62.9	61.9	60.9	59.9	59.0	58.0
97	66.8	65.8	64.8	63.9	62.9	61.9	60.9	59.9	59.0	58.0
98	66.8	65.8	64.8	63.9	62.9	61.9	60.9	59.9	59.0	58.0
99	66.8	65.8	64.8	63.9	62.9	61.9	60.9	59.9	59.0	58.0
100	66.8	65.8	64.8	63.9	62.9	61.9	60.9	59.9	59.0	58.0
101	66.8	65.8	64.8	63.9	62.9	61.9	60.9	59.9	59.0	58.0
102	66.8	65.8	64.8	63.9	62.9	61.9	60.9	59.9	59.0	58.0
103	66.8	65.8	64.8	63.9	62.9	61.9	60.9	59.9	59.0	58.0
104	66.8	65.8	64.8	63.9	62.9	61.9	60.9	59.9	59.0	58.0
105	66.8	65.8	64.8	63.9	62.9	61.9	60.9	59.9	59.0	58.0
106	66.8	65.8	64.8	63.9	62.9	61.9	60.9	59.9	59.0	58.0
107	66.8	65.8	64.8	63.9	62.9	61.9	60.9	59.9	59.0	58.0
108	66.8	65.8	64.8	63.9	62.9	61.9	60.9	59.9	59.0	58.0
109	66.8	65.8	64.8	63.9	62.9	61.9	60.9	59.9	59.0	58.0
110	66.8	65.8	64.8	63.9	62.9	61.9	60.9	59.9	59.0	58.0
111	66.8	65.8	64.8	63.9	62.9	61.9	60.9	59.9	59.0	58.0
112	66.8	65.8	64.8	63.9	62.9	61.9	60.9	59.9	59.0	58.0
113	66.8	65.8	64.8	63.9	62.9	61.9	60.9	59.9	59.0	58.0
114	66.8	65.8	64.8	63.9	62.9	61.9	60.9	59.9	59.0	58.0
115	66.8	65.8	64.8	63.9	62.9	61.9	60.9	59.9	59.0	58.0

Ages	25	26	27	28	29	30	31	32	33	34
25	63.9	63.4	62.9	62.5	62.1	61.7	61.3	61.0	60.7	60.4
26	63.4	62.9	62.4	61.9	61.5	61.1	60.7	60.4	60.0	59.7
27	62.9	62.4	61.9	61.4	60.9	60.5	60.1	59.7	59.4	59.0
28	62.5	61.9	61.4	60.9	60.4	60.0	59.5	59.1	58.7	58.4
29	62.1	61.5	60.9	60.4	59.9	59.4	59.0	58.5	58.1	57.7
30	61.7	61.1	60.5	60.0	59.4	58.9	58.4	58.0	57.5	57.1
31	61.3	60.7	60.1	59.5	59.0	58.4	57.9	57.4	57.0	56.5
32	61.0	60.4	59.7	59.1	58.5	58.0	57.4	56.9	56.4	56.0
33	60.7	60.0	59.4	58.7	58.1	57.5	57.0	56.4	55.9	55.5
34	60.4	59.7	59.0	58.4	57.7	57.1	56.5	56.0	55.5	54.9
35	60.1	59.4	58.7	58.0	57.4	56.7	56.1	55.6	55.0	54.5
36	59.9	59.1	58.4	57.7	57.0	56.4	55.8	55.1	54.6	54.0
37	59.6	58.9	58.1	57.4	56.7	56.0	55.4	54.8	54.2	53.6
38	59.4	58.6	57.9	57.1	56.4	55.7	55.1	54.4	53.8	53.2
39	59.2	58.4	57.7	56.9	56.2	55.4	54.7	54.1	53.4	52.8
40	59.0	58.2	57.4	56.7	55.9	55.2	54.5	53.8	53.1	52.4
41	58.9	58.0	57.2	56.4	55.7	54.9	54.2	53.5	52.8	52.1
42	58.7	57.9	57.1	56.2	55.5	54.7	53.9	53.2	52.5	51.8
43	58.6	57.7	56.9	56.1	55.3	54.5	53.7	52.9	52.2	51.5
44	58.4	57.6	56.7	55.9	55.1	54.3	53.5	52.7	52.0	51.2
45	58.3	57.4	56.6	55.7	54.9	54.1	53.3	52.5	51.7	51.0
46	58.2	57.3	56.5	55.6	54.8	53.9	53.1	52.3	51.5	50.7
47	58.1	57.2	56.3	55.5	54.6	53.8	52.9	52.1	51.3	50.5
48	58.0	57.1	56.2	55.3	54.5	53.6	52.8	51.9	51.1	50.3
49	57.9	57.0	56.1	55.2	54.4	53.5	52.6	51.8	51.0	50.1
50	57.8	56.9	56.0	55.1	54.2	53.4	52.5	51.7	50.8	50.0
51	57.8	56.9	55.9	55.0	54.1	53.3	52.4	51.5	50.7	49.8
52	57.7	56.8	55.9	55.0	54.1	53.2	52.3	51.4	50.5	49.7
53	57.6	56.7	55.8	54.9	54.0	53.1	52.2	51.3	50.4	49.6
54	57.6	56.7	55.7	54.8	53.9	53.0	52.1	51.2	50.3	49.4
55	57.5	56.6	55.7	54.7	53.8	52.9	52.0	51.1	40.2	49.3
56	57.5	56.5	55.6	54.7	53.8	52.8	51.9	51.0	50.1	49.2
57	57.4	56.5	55.6	54.6	53.7	52.8	51.9	50.9	50.0	49.1
58	57.4	56.5	55.5	54.6	53.6	52.7	51.8	50.9	50.0	49.1
59	57.4	56.4	55.5	54.5	53.6	52.7	51.7	50.8	49.9	49.0
60	57.3	56.4	55.4	54.5	53.6	52.6	51.7	50.8	49.8	48.9
61	57.3	56.4	55.4	54.5	53.5	52.6	51.6	50.7	49.8	48.9
62	57.3	56.3	55.4	54.4	53.5	52.5	51.6	50.7	49.7	48.8
63	57.3	56.3	55.3	54.4	53.4	52.5	51.6	50.6	49.7	48.7
64	57.2	56.3	55.3	54.4	53.4	52.5	51.5	50.6	49.6	48.7
65	57.2	56.3	55.3	54.3	53.4	52.4	51.5	50.5	49.6	48.7
66	57.2	56.2	55.3	54.3	53.4	52.4	51.5	50.5	49.6	48.6
67	57.2	56.2	55.3	54.3	53.3	52.4	51.4	50.5	49.5	48.6
68	57.2	56.2	55.2	54.3	53.3	52.4	51.4	50.4	49.5	48.6
69	57.1	56.2	55.2	54.3	53.3	52.3	51.4	50.4	49.5	48.5

Ages	25	26	27	28	29	30	31	32	33	34
70	57.1	56.2	55.2	54.2	53.3	52.3	51.4	50.4	49.4	48.5
71	57.1	56.2	55.2	54.2	53.3	52.3	51.3	50.4	49.4	48.5
72	57.1	56.1	55.2	54.2	53.2	52.3	51.3	50.4	49.4	48.5
73	57.1	56.1	55.2	54.2	53.2	52.3	51.3	50.3	49.4	48.4
74	57.1	56.1	55.2	54.2	53.2	52.3	51.3	50.3	49.4	48.4
75	57.1	56.1	55.1	54.2	53.2	52.2	51.3	50.3	49.4	48.4
76	57.1	56.1	55.1	54.2	53.2	52.2	51.3	50.3	49.3	48.4
77	57.1	56.1	55.1	54.2	53.2	52.2	51.3	50.3	49.3	48.4
78	57.1	56.1	55.1	54.2	53.2	52.2	51.3	50.3	49.3	48.4
79	57.1	56.1	55.1	54.1	53.2	52.2	51.2	50.3	49.3	48.4
80	57.1	56.1	55.1	54.1	53.2	52.2	51.2	50.3	49.3	48.3
81	57.0	56.1	55.1	54.1	53.2	52.2	51.2	50.3	49.3	48.3
82	57.0	56.1	55.1	54.1	53.2	52.2	51.2	50.3	49.3	48.3
83	57.0	56.1	55.1	54.1	53.2	52.2	51.2	50.3	49.3	48.3
84	57.0	56.1	55.1	54.1	53.2	52.2	51.2	50.3	49.3	48.3
85	57.0	56.1	55.1	54.1	53.2	52.2	51.2	50.2	49.3	48.3
86	57.0	56.1	55.1	54.1	53.1	52.2	51.2	50.2	49.3	48.3
87	57.0	56.1	55.1	54.1	53.1	52.2	51.2	50.2	49.3	48.3
88	57.0	56.1	55.1	54.1	53.1	52.2	51.2	50.2	49.3	48.3
89	57.0	56.1	55.1	54.1	53.1	52.2	51.2	50.2	49.3	48.3
90	57.0	56.1	55.1	54.1	53.1	52.2	51.2	50.2	49.3	48.3
91	57.0	56.1	55.1	54.1	53.1	52.2	51.2	50.2	49.3	48.3
92	57.0	56.1	55.1	54.1	53.1	52.2	51.2	50.2	49.3	48.3
93	57.0	56.1	55.1	54.1	53.1	52.2	51.2	50.2	49.3	48.3
94	57.0	56.0	55.1	54.1	53.1	52.2	51.2	50.2	49.3	48.3
95	57.0	56.0	55.1	54.1	53.1	52.2	51.2	50.2	49.3	48.3
96	57.0	56.0	55.1	54.1	53.1	52.2	51.2	50.2	49.3	48.3
97	57.0	56.0	55.1	54.1	53.1	52.2	51.2	50.2	49.3	48.3
98	57.0	56.0	55.1	54.1	53.1	52.2	51.2	50.2	49.3	48.3
99	57.0	56.0	55.1	54.1	53.1	52.2	51.2	50.2	49.3	48.3
100	57.0	56.0	55.1	54.1	53.1	52.2	51.2	50.2	49.3	48.3
101	57.0	56.0	55.1	54.1	53.1	52.2	51.2	50.2	49.3	48.3
102	57.0	56.0	55.1	54.1	53.1	52.2	51.2	50.2	49.3	48.3
103	57.0	56.0	55.1	54.1	53.1	52.2	51.2	50.2	49.3	48.3
104	57.0	56.0	55.1	54.1	53.1	52.2	51.2	50.2	49.3	48.3
105	57.0	56.0	55.1	54.1	53.1	52.2	51.2	50.2	49.3	48.3
106	57.0	56.0	55.1	54.1	53.1	52.2	51.2	50.2	49.3	48.3
107	57.0	56.0	55.1	54.1	53.1	52.2	51.2	50.2	49.3	48.3
108	57.0	56.0	55.1	54.1	53.1	52.2	51.2	50.2	49.3	48.3
109	57.0	56.0	55.1	54.1	53.1	52.2	51.2	50.2	49.3	48.3
110	57.0	56.0	55.1	54.1	53.1	52.2	51.2	50.2	49.3	48.3
111	57.0	56.0	55.1	54.1	53.1	52.2	51.2	50.2	49.3	48.3
112	57.0	56.0	55.1	54.1	53.1	52.2	51.2	50.2	49.3	48.3
113	57.0	56.0	55.1	54.1	53.1	52.2	51.2	50.2	49.3	48.3
114	57.0	56.0	55.1	54.1	53.1	52.2	51.2	50.2	49.3	48.3
115	57.0	56.0	55.1	54.1	53.1	52.2	51.2	50.2	49.3	48.3

Ages	35	36	37	38	39	40	41	42	43	44
35	54.0	53.5	53.0	52.6	52.2	51.8	51.4	51.1	50.8	50.5
36	53.5	53.0	52.5	52.0	51.6	51.2	50.8	50.4	50.1	49.8
37	53.0	52.5	52.0	51.5	51.0	50.6	50.2	49.8	49.5	49.1
38	52.6	52.0	51.5	51.0	50.5	50.0	49.6	49.2	48.8	48.5
39	52.2	51.6	51.0	50.5	50.0	49.5	49.1	48.6	48.2	47.8
40	51.8	51.2	50.6	50.0	49.5	49.0	48.5	48.1	47.6	47.2
41	51.4	50.8	50.2	49.6	49.1	48.5	48.0	47.5	47.1	46.7
42	51.1	50.4	49.8	49.2	48.6	48.1	47.5	47.0	46.6	46.1
43	50.8	50.1	49.5	48.8	48.2	47.6	47.1	46.6	46.0	45.6
44	50.5	49.8	49.1	48.5	47.8	47.2	46.7	46.1	45.6	45.1
45	50.2	49.5	48.8	48.1	47.5	46.9	46.3	45.7	45.1	44.6
46	50.0	49.2	48.5	47.8	47.2	46.5	45.9	45.3	44.7	44.1
47	49.7	49.0	48.3	47.5	46.8	46.2	45.5	44.9	44.3	43.7
48	49.5	48.8	48.0	47.3	46.6	45.9	45.2	44.5	43.9	43.3
49	49.3	48.5	47.8	47.0	46.3	45.6	44.9	44.2	43.6	42.9
50	49.2	48.4	47.6	46.8	46.0	45.3	44.6	43.9	43.2	42.6
51	49.0	48.2	47.4	46.6	45.8	45.1	44.3	43.6	42.9	44.2
52	48.8	48.0	47.2	46.4	45.6	44.8	44.1	43.3	42.6	41.9
53	48.7	47.9	47.0	46.2	45.4	44.6	43.9	43.1	42.4	41.7
54	48.6	47.7	46.9	46.0	45.2	44.4	43.6	42.9	42.1	41.4
55	48.5	47.6	46.7	45.9	45.1	44.2	43.4	42.7	41.9	41.2
56	48.3	47.5	46.6	45.8	44.9	44.1	43.3	42.5	41.7	40.9
57	48.3	47.4	46.5	45.6	44.8	43.9	43.1	42.3	41.5	40.7
58	48.2	47.3	46.4	45.5	44.7	43.8	43.0	42.1	41.3	40.5
59	48.1	47.2	46.3	45.4	44.5	43.7	42.8	42.0	41.2	40.4
60	48.0	47.1	46.2	45.3	44.4	43.6	42.7	41.9	41.0	40.2
61	47.9	47.0	46.1	45.2	44.3	43.5	42.6	41.7	40.9	40.0
62	47.9	47.0	46.0	45.1	44.2	43.4	42.5	41.6	40.8	39.9
63	47.8	46.9	46.0	45.1	44.2	43.3	42.4	41.5	40.6	39.8
64	47.8	46.8	45.9	45.0	44.1	43.2	42.3	41.4	40.5	39.7
65	47.7	46.8	45.9	44.9	44.0	43.1	42.2	41.3	40.4	39.6
66	47.7	46.7	45.8	44.9	44.0	43.1	42.2	41.3	40.4	39.5
67	47.6	46.7	45.8	44.8	43.9	43.0	42.1	41.2	40.3	39.4
68	47.6	46.7	45.7	44.8	43.9	42.9	42.0	41.1	40.2	39.3
69	47.6	46.6	45.7	44.8	43.8	42.9	42.0	41.1	40.2	39.3
70	47.5	46.6	45.7	44.7	43.8	42.9	41.9	41.0	40.1	39.2
71	47.5	46.6	45.6	44.7	43.8	42.8	41.9	41.0	40.1	39.1
72	47.5	46.6	45.6	44.7	43.7	42.8	41.9	40.9	40.0	39.1
73	47.5	46.5	45.6	44.6	43.7	42.8	41.8	40.9	40.0	39.0
74	47.5	46.5	45.6	44.6	43.7	42.7	41.8	40.9	39.9	39.0
75	47.4	46.5	45.5	44.6	43.6	42.7	41.8	40.8	39.9	39.0

Ages	35	36	37	38	39	40	41	42	43	44
76	47.4	46.5	45.5	44.6	43.6	42.7	41.7	40.8	39.9	38.9
77	47.4	46.5	45.5	44.6	43.6	42.7	41.7	40.8	39.8	38.9
78	47.4	46.4	45.5	44.5	43.6	42.6	41.7	40.7	39.8	38.9
79	47.4	46.4	45.5	44.5	43.6	42.6	41.7	40.7	39.8	38.9
80	47.4	46.4	45.5	44.5	43.6	42.6	41.7	40.7	39.8	38.8
81	47.4	46.4	45.5	44.5	43.5	42.6	41.6	40.7	39.8	38.8
82	47.4	46.4	45.4	44.5	43.5	42.6	41.6	40.7	39.7	38.8
83	47.4	46.4	45.4	44.5	43.5	42.6	41.6	40.7	39.7	38.8
84	47.4	46.4	45.4	44.5	43.5	42.6	41.6	40.7	39.7	38.8
85	47.4	46.4	45.4	44.5	43.5	42.6	41.6	40.7	39.7	38.8
86	47.3	46.4	45.4	44.5	43.5	42.5	41.6	40.6	39.7	38.8
87	47.3	46.4	45.4	44.5	43.5	42.5	41.6	40.6	39.7	38.7
88	47.3	46.4	45.4	44.5	43.5	42.5	41.6	40.6	39.7	38.7
89	47.3	46.4	45.4	44.4	43.5	42.5	41.6	40.6	39.7	38.7
90	47.3	46.4	45.4	44.4	43.5	42.5	41.6	40.6	39.7	38.7
91	47.3	46.4	45.4	44.4	43.5	42.5	41.6	40.6	39.7	39.7
92	47.3	46.4	45.4	44.4	44.4	43.5	42.5	41.6	40.6	38.7
						[42.5]	[41.6]	[40.6]	[39.7]	
93	47.3	46.4	45.4	43.5	42.5	41.6	40.6	39.7	39.7	38.7
				[44.4]	[43.5]	[42.5]	[41.6]	[40.6]		
94	47.3	46.4	45.4	44.4	43.5	42.5	41.6	40.6	39.7	38.7
95	47.3	46.4	45.4	44.4	43.5	42.5	41.6	40.6	39.7	38.7
96	47.3	46.4	45.4	44.4	43.5	42.5	41.6	40.6	39.7	38.7
97	47.3	46.4	45.4	44.4	43.5	42.5	41.6	40.6	39.7	38.7
98	47.3	46.4	45.4	44.4	43.5	42.5	41.6	40.6	39.6	38.7
99	47.3	46.4	45.4	44.4	43.5	42.5	41.6	40.6	39.6	38.7
100	47.3	46.4	45.4	44.4	43.5	42.5	41.5	40.6	39.6	38.7
101	47.3	46.4	45.4	44.4	43.5	42.5	41.5	40.6	39.6	38.7
102	47.3	46.4	45.4	44.4	43.5	42.5	41.5	40.6	39.6	38.7
103	47.3	46.4	45.4	44.4	43.5	42.5	41.5	40.6	39.6	38.7
104	47.3	46.4	45.4	44.4	43.5	42.5	41.5	40.6	39.6	38.7
105	47.3	46.4	45.4	44.4	43.5	42.5	41.5	40.6	39.6	38.7
106	47.3	46.4	45.4	44.4	43.5	42.5	41.5	40.6	39.6	38.7
107	47.3	46.4	45.4	44.4	43.5	42.5	41.5	40.6	39.6	38.7
108	47.3	46.4	45.4	44.4	43.5	42.5	41.5	40.6	39.6	38.7
109	47.3	46.4	45.4	44.4	43.5	42.5	41.5	40.6	39.6	38.7
110	47.3	46.4	45.4	44.4	43.5	42.5	41.5	40.6	39.6	38.7
111	47.3	46.4	45.4	44.4	43.5	42.5	41.5	40.6	39.6	38.7
112	47.3	46.4	45.4	44.4	43.5	42.5	41.5	40.6	39.6	38.7
113	47.3	46.4	45.4	44.4	43.5	42.5	41.5	40.6	39.6	38.7
114	47.3	46.4	45.4	44.4	43.5	42.5	41.5	40.6	39.6	38.7
115	47.3	46.4	45.4	44.4	43.5	42.5	41.5	40.6	39.6	38.7

Ages	45	46	47	48	49	50	51	52	53	54
45	44.1	43.6	43.2	42.7	42.3	42.0	41.6	41.3	41.0	40.7
46	43.6	43.1	42.6	42.2	41.8	41.4	41.0	40.6	40.3	40.0
47	43.2	42.6	42.1	41.7	41.2	40.8	40.4	40.0	39.7	39.3
48	42.7	42.2	41.7	41.2	40.7	40.2	39.8	39.4	39.0	38.7
49	42.3	41.8	41.2	40.7	40.2	39.7	39.3	38.8	38.4	38.1
50	42.0	41.4	40.8	40.2	39.7	39.2	38.7	38.3	37.9	37.5
51	41.6	41.0	40.4	39.8	39.3	38.7	38.2	37.8	37.3	36.9
52	41.3	40.6	40.0	39.4	38.8	38.3	37.8	37.3	36.8	36.4
53	41.0	40.3	39.7	39.0	38.4	37.9	37.3	36.8	36.3	35.8
54	40.7	40.0	39.3	38.7	38.1	37.5	36.9	36.4	35.8	35.3
55	40.4	39.7	39.0	38.4	37.7	37.1	36.5	35.9	35.4	34.9
56	40.2	39.5	38.7	38.1	37.4	36.8	36.1	35.6	35.0	34.4
57	40.0	39.2	38.5	37.8	37.1	36.4	35.8	35.2	34.6	34.0
58	39.7	39.0	38.2	37.5	36.8	36.1	35.5	34.8	34.2	33.6
59	39.6	38.8	38.0	37.3	36.6	35.9	35.2	34.5	33.9	33.3
60	39.4	38.6	37.8	37.1	36.3	35.6	34.9	34.2	33.6	32.9
61	39.2	38.4	37.6	36.9	36.1	35.4	34.6	33.9	33.3	32.6
62	39.1	38.3	37.5	36.7	35.9	35.1	34.4	33.7	33.0	32.3
63	38.9	38.1	37.3	36.5	35.7	34.9	34.2	33.5	32.7	32.0
64	38.8	38.0	37.2	36.3	35.5	34.8	34.0	33.2	32.5	31.8
65	38.7	37.9	37.0	36.2	35.4	34.6	33.8	33.0	32.3	31.6
66	38.6	37.8	36.9	36.1	35.2	34.4	33.6	32.9	32.1	31.4
67	38.5	37.7	36.8	36.0	35.1	34.3	33.5	32.7	31.9	31.2
68	38.4	37.6	36.7	35.8	35.0	34.2	33.4	32.5	31.8	31.0
69	38.4	37.5	36.6	35.7	34.9	34.1	33.2	32.4	31.6	30.8
70	38.3	37.4	36.5	35.7	34.8	34.0	33.1	32.3	31.5	30.7
71	38.2	37.3	36.5	35.6	34.7	33.9	33.0	32.2	31.4	30.5
72	38.2	37.3	36.4	35.5	34.6	33.8	32.9	32.1	31.2	30.4
73	38.1	37.2	36.3	35.4	34.6	33.7	32.8	32.0	31.1	30.3
74	38.1	37.2	36.3	35.4	34.5	33.6	32.8	31.9	31.1	30.2
75	38.1	37.1	36.2	35.3	34.5	33.6	32.7	31.8	31.0	30.1
76	38.0	37.1	36.2	35.3	34.4	33.5	32.6	31.8	30.9	30.1
77	38.0	37.1	36.2	35.3	34.4	33.5	32.6	31.7	30.8	30.0
78	38.0	37.0	36.1	35.2	34.3	33.4	32.5	31.7	30.8	29.9
79	37.9	37.0	36.1	35.2	34.3	33.4	32.5	31.6	30.7	29.9
80	37.9	37.0	36.1	35.2	34.2	33.4	32.5	31.6	30.7	29.8
81	37.9	37.0	36.0	35.1	34.2	33.3	32.4	31.5	30.7	29.8
82	37.9	36.9	36.0	35.1	34.2	33.3	32.4	31.5	30.6	29.7
83	37.9	36.9	36.0	35.1	34.2	33.3	32.4	31.5	30.6	29.7
84	37.8	36.9	36.9	35.0	34.2	33.2	32.3	31.4	30.6	29.7
85	37.8	36.9	36.0	35.1	34.1	33.2	32.3	31.4	30.5	29.6
86	38.8	36.9	36.0	35.0	34.1	33.2	32.3	31.4	30.5	29.6
87	37.8	36.9	35.9	35.0	34.1	33.2	32.3	31.4	30.5	29.6
88	37.8	36.9	35.9	35.0	34.1	33.2	32.3	31.4	30.5	29.6
89	37.8	36.9	35.9	35.0	34.1	33.2	32.3	31.4	30.5	29.6
90	37.8	36.9	35.9	35.0	34.1	33.2	32.3	31.3	30.5	29.6
91	37.8	36.8	35.9	35.0	34.1	33.2	32.2	31.3	30.4	29.5
92	37.8	36.8	35.9	35.0	34.1	33.2	32.2	31.3	30.4	29.5
93	37.8	36.8	35.9	35.0	34.1	33.1	32.2	31.3	30.4	29.5
94	37.8	36.8	35.9	35.0	34.1	33.1	32.2	31.3	30.4	29.5
95	37.8	36.8	35.9	35.0	34.0	33.1	32.2	31.3	30.4	29.5
96	37.8	36.8	35.9	35.0	34.0	33.1	32.2	31.3	30.4	29.5
97	37.8	36.8	35.9	35.0	34.0	33.1	32.2	31.3	30.4	29.5
98	37.8	36.8	35.9	35.0	34.0	33.1	32.2	31.3	30.4	29.5
99	37.8	36.8	35.9	35.0	34.0	33.1	32.2	31.3	30.4	29.5
101	37.8	36.8	35.9	35.0	34.0	33.1	32.2	31.3	30.4	29.5
102	37.8	36.8	35.9	35.0	34.0	33.1	32.2	31.3	30.4	29.5
103	37.7	36.8	35.9	34.9	34.0	33.1	32.2	31.3	30.4	29.5
104	37.7	36.8	35.9	34.9	34.0	33.1	32.2	31.3	30.4	29.5
105	37.7	36.8	35.9	34.9	34.0	33.1	32.2	31.3	30.4	29.5
106	37.7	36.8	35.9	34.9	34.0	33.1	32.2	31.3	30.4	29.5
107	37.7	36.8	35.9	34.9	34.0	33.1	32.2	31.3	30.4	29.5
108	37.7	36.8	35.9	34.9	34.0	33.1	32.2	31.3	30.4	29.5
109	37.7	36.8	35.9	34.9	34.0	33.1	32.2	31.3	30.4	29.5
110	37.7	36.8	35.9	34.9	34.0	33.1	32.2	31.3	30.4	29.5
111	37.7	36.8	35.9	34.9	34.0	33.1	32.2	31.3	30.4	29.5
112	37.7	36.8	35.9	34.9	34.0	33.1	32.2	31.3	30.4	29.5
113	37.7	36.8	35.9	34.9	34.0	33.1	32.2	31.3	30.4	29.5
114	37.7	36.8	35.9	34.9	34.0	33.1	32.2	31.3	30.4	29.5
115	37.7	36.8	35.9	34.9	34.0	33.1	32.2	31.3	30.4	29.5

Ages	55	56	57	58	59	60	61	62	63	64
55	34.4	33.9	33.5	33.1	32.7	32.3	32.0	31.7	31.4	31.1
56	33.9	33.4	33.0	32.5	32.1	31.7	31.4	31.0	30.7	30.4
57	33.5	33.0	32.5	32.0	31.6	31.2	30.8	30.4	30.1	29.8
58	33.1	32.5	32.0	31.5	31.1	30.6	30.2	29.9	29.5	29.2
59	32.7	32.1	31.6	31.1	30.6	30.1	29.7	29.3	28.9	28.6
60	32.3	31.7	31.2	30.6	30.1	29.7	29.2	28.8	28.4	28.0
61	32.0	31.4	30.8	30.2	29.7	29.2	28.7	28.3	27.8	27.4
62	31.7	31.0	30.4	29.9	29.3	28.8	28.3	27.8	27.3	26.9
63	31.4	30.7	30.1	29.5	28.9	28.4	27.6	27.3	26.9	26.4
64	31.1	30.4	29.8	29.2	28.6	28.0	27.4	26.9	26.4	25.9
65	30.9	30.2	29.5	28.9	28.2	27.6	27.1	26.5	26.0	25.5
66	30.6	29.9	29.2	28.6	27.9	27.3	26.7	26.1	25.6	25.1
67	30.4	29.7	29.0	28.3	27.6	27.0	26.4	25.8	25.2	24.7
68	30.2	29.5	28.8	28.1	27.4	26.7	26.1	25.5	24.9	24.3
69	30.1	29.3	28.6	27.8	27.1	26.5	25.8	25.2	24.6	24.0
70	29.9	29.1	28.4	27.6	26.9	26.2	25.6	24.9	24.3	23.7
71	29.7	29.0	28.2	27.5	26.7	26.0	25.3	24.7	24.0	23.4
72	29.6	28.8	28.1	27.3	26.5	25.8	25.1	24.4	23.8	23.1
73	29.5	28.7	27.9	27.1	26.4	25.6	24.9	24.2	23.5	22.9
74	29.4	28.6	27.8	27.0	26.2	25.5	24.7	24.0	23.3	22.7
75	29.3	28.5	27.7	26.9	26.1	25.3	24.6	23.8	23.1	22.4
76	29.2	28.4	27.6	26.8	26.0	25.2	24.4	23.7	23.0	22.3
77	29.1	28.3	27.5	26.7	25.9	25.1	24.3	23.6	22.8	22.1
78	29.1	28.2	27.4	26.6	25.8	25.0	24.2	23.4	22.7	21.9
79	29.0	28.2	27.3	26.5	25.7	24.9	24.1	23.3	22.6	21.8
80	29.0	28.1	27.3	26.4	25.6	24.8	24.0	23.2	22.4	21.7
81	28.9	28.1	27.2	26.4	25.5	24.7	23.9	23.1	22.3	21.6
82	28.9	28.0	27.2	26.3	25.5	24.6	23.8	23.0	22.3	21.5
83	28.8	28.0	27.1	26.3	25.4	24.6	23.8	23.0	22.2	21.4
84	28.8	27.9	27.1	26.2	25.4	24.5	23.7	22.9	22.1	21.3
85	28.8	27.9	27.0	26.2	25.3	24.5	23.7	22.8	22.0	21.3
86	28.7	27.9	27.0	26.1	25.3	24.5	23.6	22.8	22.0	21.2
87	28.7	27.8	27.0	26.1	25.3	24.4	23.6	22.8	21.9	21.1
88	28.7	27.8	27.0	26.1	25.2	24.4	23.5	22.7	21.9	21.1
89	28.7	27.8	26.9	26.1	25.2	24.4	23.5	22.7	21.9	21.1
90	28.7	27.8	26.9	26.1	25.2	24.3	23.5	22.7	21.8	21.0
91	28.7	27.8	26.9	26.0	25.2	24.3	23.5	22.6	21.8	21.0
92	28.6	27.8	26.9	26.0	25.2	24.3	23.5	22.6	21.8	21.0
93	28.6	27.8	26.9	26.0	25.1	24.3	23.4	22.6	21.8	20.9
94	28.6	27.7	26.9	26.0	25.1	24.3	23.4	22.6	21.7	20.9
95	28.6	27.7	26.9	26.0	25.1	24.3	23.4	22.6	21.7	20.9
96	28.6	27.7	26.9	26.0	25.1	24.2	23.4	22.6	21.7	20.9
97	28.6	27.7	26.8	26.0	25.1	24.2	23.4	22.5	21.7	20.9
98	28.6	27.7	26.8	26.0	25.1	24.2	23.4	22.5	21.7	20.9
99	28.6	27.7	26.8	26.0	25.1	24.2	23.4	22.5	21.7	20.9
100	28.6	27.7	26.8	26.0	25.1	24.2	23.4	22.5	21.7	20.8
101	28.6	27.7	26.8	25.9	25.1	24.2	23.3	22.5	21.7	20.8
102	28.6	27.7	26.8	25.9	25.1	24.2	23.3	22.5	21.7	20.8
103	28.6	27.7	26.8	25.9	25.1	24.2	23.3	22.5	21.7	20.8
104	28.6	27.7	26.8	25.9	25.1	24.2	23.3	22.5	21.6	20.8
105	28.6	27.7	26.8	25.9	25.1	24.2	23.3	22.5	21.6	20.8
106	28.6	27.7	26.8	25.9	25.1	24.2	23.3	22.5	21.6	20.8
107	28.6	27.7	26.8	25.9	25.1	24.2	23.3	22.5	21.6	20.8
108	28.6	27.7	26.8	25.9	25.1	24.2	23.3	22.5	21.6	20.8
109	28.6	27.7	26.8	25.9	25.1	24.2	23.3	22.5	21.6	20.8
110	28.6	27.7	26.8	25.9	25.1	24.2	23.3	22.5	21.6	20.8
111	28.6	27.7	26.8	25.9	25.0	24.2	23.3	22.5	21.6	20.8
112	28.6	27.7	26.8	25.9	25.0	24.2	23.3	22.5	21.6	20.8
113	28.6	27.7	26.8	25.9	25.0	24.2	23.3	22.5	21.6	20.8
114	28.6	27.7	26.8	25.9	25.0	24.2	23.3	22.5	21.6	20.8
115	28.6	27.7	26.8	25.9	25.0	24.2	23.3	22.5	21.6	20.8

Ages	65	66	67	68	69	70	71	72	73	74
65	25.0	24.6	24.2	23.8	23.4	23.1	22.8	22.5	22.2	22.0
66	24.6	24.1	23.7	23.3	22.9	22.5	22.2	21.9	21.6	21.4
67	24.2	23.7	23.2	22.8	22.4	22.0	21.7	21.3	21.0	20.8
68	23.8	23.3	22.8	22.3	21.9	21.5	21.2	20.8	20.5	20.2
69	23.4	22.9	22.4	21.9	21.5	21.1	20.7	20.3	20.0	19.6
70	23.1	22.5	22.0	21.5	21.1	20.6	20.2	19.8	19.4	19.1
71	22.8	22.2	21.7	21.2	20.7	20.2	19.8	19.4	19.0	18.6
72	22.5	21.9	21.3	20.8	20.3	19.8	19.4	18.9	18.5	18.2
73	22.2	21.6	21.0	20.5	20.0	19.4	19.0	18.5	18.1	17.7
74	22.0	21.4	20.8	20.2	19.6	19.1	18.6	18.2	17.7	17.3
75	21.8	21.1	20.5	19.9	19.3	18.8	18.3	17.8	17.3	16.9
76	21.6	20.9	20.3	19.7	19.1	18.5	18.0	17.5	17.0	16.5
77	21.4	20.7	20.1	19.4	18.8	18.3	17.7	17.2	16.7	16.2
78	21.2	20.5	19.9	19.2	18.6	18.0	17.5	16.9	16.4	15.9
79	21.1	20.4	19.7	19.0	18.4	17.8	17.2	16.7	16.1	15.6
80	21.0	20.2	19.5	18.9	18.2	17.6	17.0	16.4	15.9	15.4
81	20.8	20.1	19.4	18.7	18.1	17.4	16.8	16.2	15.7	15.1
82	20.7	20.0	19.3	18.6	17.9	17.3	16.6	16.0	15.5	14.9
83	20.6	19.9	19.2	18.5	17.8	17.1	16.5	15.9	15.3	14.7
84	20.5	19.8	19.1	18.4	17.7	17.0	16.3	15.7	15.1	14.5
85	20.5	19.7	19.0	18.3	17.6	16.9	16.2	15.6	15.0	14.4
86	20.4	19.6	18.9	18.2	17.5	16.8	16.1	15.5	14.8	14.2
87	20.4	19.6	18.8	18.1	17.4	16.7	16.0	15.4	14.7	14.1
88	20.3	19.5	18.8	18.0	17.3	16.6	15.9	15.3	14.6	14.0
89	20.3	19.5	18.7	18.0	17.2	16.5	15.8	15.2	14.5	13.9
90	20.2	19.4	18.7	17.9	17.2	16.5	15.8	15.1	14.5	13.8
91	20.2	19.4	18.6	17.9	17.1	16.4	15.7	15.0	14.4	13.7
92	20.2	19.4	18.6	17.8	17.1	16.4	15.7	15.0	14.3	13.7
93	20.1	19.3	18.6	17.8	17.1	16.3	15.6	14.9	14.3	13.6
94	20.1	19.3	18.5	17.8	17.0	16.3	15.6	14.9	14.2	13.6
95	20.1	19.3	18.5	17.8	17.0	16.3	15.6	14.9	14.2	13.5
96	20.1	19.3	18.5	17.7	17.0	16.2	15.5	14.8	14.2	13.5
97	20.1	19.3	18.5	17.7	17.0	16.2	15.5	14.8	14.1	13.5
98	20.1	19.3	18.5	17.7	16.9	16.2	15.5	14.8	14.1	13.4
99	20.0	19.2	18.5	17.7	16.9	16.2	15.5	14.7	14.1	13.4
100	20.0	19.2	18.4	17.7	16.9	16.2	15.4	14.7	14.0	13.4
101	20.0	19.2	18.4	17.7	16.9	16.1	15.4	14.7	14.0	13.3
102	20.0	19.2	18.4	17.6	16.9	16.1	15.4	14.7	14.0	13.3
103	20.0	19.2	18.4	17.6	16.9	16.1	15.4	14.7	14.0	13.3
104	20.0	19.2	18.4	17.6	16.9	16.1	15.4	14.6	14.0	13.3
105	20.0	19.2	18.4	17.6	16.8	16.1	15.4	14.6	13.9	13.3
106	20.0	19.2	18.4	17.6	16.8	16.1	15.3	14.6	13.9	13.2
107	20.0	19.2	18.4	17.6	16.8	16.1	15.3	14.6	13.9	13.2
108	20.0	19.2	18.4	17.6	16.8	16.1	15.3	14.6	13.9	13.2
109	20.0	19.2	18.4	17.6	16.8	16.1	15.3	14.6	13.9	13.2
110	20.0	19.2	18.4	17.6	16.8	16.1	15.3	14.6	13.9	13.2
111	20.0	19.2	18.4	17.6	16.8	16.0	15.3	14.6	13.9	13.2
112	20.0	19.2	18.4	17.6	16.8	16.0	15.3	14.6	13.9	13.2
113	20.0	19.2	18.4	17.6	16.8	16.0	15.3	14.6	13.9	13.2
114	20.0	19.2	18.4	17.6	16.8	16.0	15.3	14.6	13.9	13.2
115	20.0	19.2	18.4	17.6	16.8	16.0	15.3	14.6	13.9	13.2

Ages	75	76	77	78	79	80	81	82	83	84
75	16.5	16.1	15.8	15.4	15.1	14.9	14.6	14.4	14.2	14.0
76	16.1	15.7	15.4	15.0	14.7	14.4	14.1	13.9	13.7	13.5
77	15.8	15.4	15.0	14.6	14.3	14.0	13.7	13.4	13.2	13.0
78	15.4	15.0	14.6	14.2	13.9	13.5	13.2	13.0	12.7	12.5
79	15.1	14.7	14.3	13.9	13.5	13.2	12.8	12.5	12.3	12.0
80	14.9	14.4	14.0	13.5	13.2	12.8	12.5	12.2	11.9	11.6
81	14.6	14.1	13.7	13.2	12.8	12.5	12.1	11.8	11.5	11.2
82	14.4	13.9	13.4	13.0	12.5	12.2	11.8	11.5	11.1	10.9
83	14.2	13.7	13.2	12.7	12.3	11.9	11.5	11.1	10.8	10.5
84	14.0	13.5	13.0	12.5	12.0	11.6	11.2	10.9	10.5	10.2
85	13.8	13.3	12.8	12.3	11.8	11.4	11.0	10.6	10.2	9.9
86	13.7	13.1	12.6	12.1	11.6	11.2	10.8	10.4	10.0	9.7
87	13.5	13.0	12.4	11.9	11.4	11.0	10.6	10.1	9.8	9.4
88	13.4	12.8	12.3	11.8	11.3	10.8	10.4	10.0	9.6	9.2
89	13.3	12.7	12.2	11.6	11.1	10.7	10.2	9.8	9.4	9.0
90	13.2	12.6	12.1	11.5	11.0	10.5	10.1	9.6	9.2	8.8
91	13.1	12.5	12.0	11.4	10.9	10.4	9.9	9.5	9.1	8.7
92	13.1	12.5	11.9	11.3	10.8	10.3	9.8	9.4	8.9	8.5
93	13.0	12.4	11.8	11.3	10.7	10.2	9.7	9.3	8.8	8.4
94	12.9	12.3	11.7	11.2	10.6	10.1	9.6	9.2	8.7	8.3
95	12.9	12.3	11.7	11.1	10.6	10.1	9.6	9.1	8.6	8.2
96	12.9	12.2	11.6	11.1	10.5	10.0	9.5	9.0	8.5	8.1
97	12.8	12.2	11.6	11.0	10.5	9.9	9.4	9.0	8.5	8.1
98	12.8	12.2	11.5	11.0	10.5	9.9	9.4	8.9	8.5	8.0
99	12.7	12.1	11.5	10.9	10.4	9.9	9.4	8.9	8.4	8.0
100	12.7	12.1	11.5	10.9	10.4	9.8	9.3	8.8	8.3	7.9
101	12.7	12.1	11.4	10.9	10.3	9.8	9.2	8.7	8.3	7.8
102	12.7	12.0	11.4	10.8	10.3	9.7	9.2	8.7	8.2	7.8
103	12.6	12.0	11.4	10.8	10.2	9.7	9.2	8.7	8.2	7.7
104	12.6	12.0	11.4	10.8	10.2	9.7	9.1	8.6	8.1	7.7
105	12.6	12.0	11.3	10.7	10.2	9.6	9.1	8.6	8.1	7.6
106	12.6	11.9	11.3	10.7	10.2	9.6	9.1	8.5	8.0	7.6
107	12.6	11.9	11.3	10.7	10.1	9.6	9.0	8.5	8.0	7.5
108	12.6	11.9	11.3	10.7	10.1	9.6	9.0	8.5	8.0	7.5
109	12.6	11.9	11.3	10.7	10.1	9.5	9.0	8.5	8.0	7.5
110	12.6	11.9	11.3	10.7	10.1	9.5	9.0	8.4	7.9	7.5
111	12.5	11.9	11.3	10.7	10.1	9.5	9.0	8.4	7.9	7.4
112	12.5	11.9	11.3	10.7	10.1	9.5	8.9	8.4	7.9	7.4
113	12.5	11.9	11.2	10.6	10.0	9.5	8.9	8.4	7.9	7.4
114	12.5	11.9	11.2	10.6	10.0	9.5	8.9	8.4	7.9	7.4
115	12.5	11.9	11.2	10.6	10.0	9.5	8.9	8.4	7.9	7.4

Ages	85	86	87	88	89	90	91	92	93	94
85	9.6	9.3	9.1	8.9	8.7	8.5	8.3	8.2	8.0	7.9
86	9.3	9.1	8.8	8.6	8.3	8.2	8.0	7.8	7.7	7.6
87	9.1	8.8	8.5	8.3	8.1	7.9	7.7	7.5	7.4	7.2
88	8.9	8.6	8.3	8.0	7.8	7.6	7.4	7.2	7.1	6.9
89	8.7	8.3	8.1	7.8	7.5	7.3	7.1	6.9	6.8	6.6
90	8.5	8.2	7.9	7.6	7.3	7.1	6.9	6.7	6.5	6.4
91	8.3	8.0	7.7	7.4	7.1	6.9	6.7	6.5	6.3	6.2
92	8.2	7.8	7.5	7.2	6.9	6.7	6.5	6.3	6.1	5.9
93	8.0	7.7	7.4	7.1	6.8	6.5	6.3	6.1	5.9	5.8
94	7.9	7.6	7.2	6.9	6.6	6.4	6.2	5.9	5.8	5.6
95	7.8	7.5	7.1	6.8	6.5	6.3	6.0	5.8	5.6	5.4
96	7.7	7.3	7.0	6.7	6.4	6.1	5.9	5.7	5.5	5.3
97	7.6	7.3	6.9	6.6	6.3	6.0	5.8	5.5	5.3	5.1
98	7.6	7.2	6.8	6.5	6.2	5.9	5.6	5.4	5.2	5.0
99	7.5	7.1	6.7	6.4	6.1	5.8	5.5	5.3	5.1	5.0
100	7.4	7.0	6.6	6.3	6.0	5.7	5.5	5.3	5.1	4.9
101	7.3	6.9	6.6	6.2	5.9	5.6	5.4	5.2	5.0	4.8
102	7.3	6.9	6.5	6.2	5.8	5.5	5.3	5.1	4.9	4.7
103	7.2	6.8	6.4	6.1	5.8	5.5	5.3	5.0	4.8	4.6
104	7.2	6.8	6.4	6.0	5.7	5.5	5.2	4.9	4.7	4.5
105	7.1	6.7	6.3	6.0	5.6	5.4	5.1	4.8	4.6	4.4
106	7.1	6.7	6.3	5.9	5.6	5.3	5.0	4.8	4.5	4.3
107	7.1	6.6	6.2	5.9	5.5	5.3	5.0	4.7	4.5	4.2
108	7.0	6.6	6.2	5.9	5.5	5.2	4.9	4.6	4.4	4.2
109	7.0	6.6	6.2	5.8	5.5	5.2	4.9	4.6	4.3	4.1
110	7.0	6.6	6.2	5.8	5.5	5.1	4.8	4.5	4.3	4.1
111	7.0	6.6	6.2	5.8	5.4	5.1	4.8	4.5	4.3	4.0
112	7.0	6.5	6.1	5.7	5.4	5.1	4.8	4.5	4.2	4.0
113	6.9	6.5	6.1	5.7	5.4	5.0	4.7	4.4	4.2	3.9
114	6.9	6.5	6.1	5.7	5.4	5.0	4.7	4.4	4.2	3.9
115	6.9	6.5	6.1	5.7	5.3	5.0	4.7	4.4	4.1	3.9

Ages	95	96	97	98	99	100	101	102	103	104
95	5.3	5.1	5.0	4.8	4.7	4.6	4.5	4.4	4.3	4.2
96	5.1	5.0	4.8	4.7	4.5	4.4	4.3	4.2	4.1	4.0
97	5.0	4.8	4.7	4.5	4.4	4.3	4.1	4.0	3.9	3.8
98	4.8	4.7	4.5	4.4	4.2	4.1	4.0	3.9	3.8	3.7
99	4.7	4.5	4.4	4.2	4.1	4.0	3.8	3.7	3.6	3.5
100	4.6	4.4	4.3	4.1	4.0	3.8	3.7	3.6	3.5	3.3
101	4.5	4.3	4.1	4.0	3.8	3.7	3.6	3.4	3.3	3.2
102	4.4	4.2	4.0	3.9	3.7	3.6	3.4	3.3	3.2	3.1
103	4.3	4.1	3.9	3.8	3.6	3.5	3.3	3.2	3.0	2.9
104	4.2	4.0	3.8	3.7	3.5	3.3	3.2	3.1	2.9	2.8
105	4.1	3.9	3.7	3.6	3.4	3.2	3.1	2.9	2.8	2.7
106	4.0	3.8	3.6	3.5	3.3	3.1	3.0	2.8	2.7	2.5
107	4.0	3.8	3.6	3.4	3.2	3.1	2.9	2.7	2.6	2.4
108	3.9	3.7	3.5	3.3	3.1	3.0	2.8	2.7	2.5	2.3
109	3.8	3.6	3.4	3.3	3.1	2.9	2.7	2.6	2.4	2.3
110	3.8	3.6	3.4	3.2	3.0	2.8	2.7	2.5	2.3	2.2
111	3.8	3.5	3.3	3.2	3.0	2.8	2.6	2.4	2.3	2.1
112	3.7	3.5	3.3	3.1	2.9	2.8	2.6	2.4	2.2	2.1
113	3.7	3.5	3.3	3.1	2.9	2.7	2.5	2.4	2.2	2.0
114	3.7	3.5	3.3	3.1	2.9	2.7	2.5	2.3	2.1	2.0
115	3.7	3.4	3.2	3.0	2.8	2.7	2.5	2.3	2.1	1.9

Ages	105	106	107	108	109	110	111	112	113	114	115
105	2.5	2.4	2.3	2.2	2.1	2.0	2.0	1.9	1.8	1.8	1.8
106	2.4	2.3	2.2	2.1	2.0	1.9	1.8	1.7	1.7	1.6	1.6
107	2.3	2.2	2.1	1.9	1.8	1.7	1.7	1.6	1.5	1.5	1.4
108	2.2	2.1	1.9	1.8	1.7	1.6	1.5	1.5	1.4	1.3	1.3
109	2.1	2.0	1.8	1.7	1.6	1.5	1.4	1.3	1.3	1.2	1.1
110	2.0	1.9	1.7	1.6	1.5	1.4	1.3	1.2	1.1	1.1	1.0
111	2.0	1.8	1.7	1.5	1.4	1.3	1.2	1.1	1.0	.9	.9
112	1.9	1.7	1.6	1.5	1.3	1.2	1.1	1.0	.9	.8	.8
113	1.8	1.7	1.5	1.4	1.3	1.1	1.0	.9	.8	.7	.7
114	1.8	1.6	1.5	1.3	1.2	1.1	.9	.8	.7	.6	.6
115	1.8	1.6	1.4	1.3	1.1	1.0	.9	.8	.7	.6	.5

TABLE VIA.—ANNUITIES FOR JOINT LIFE ONLY; TWO LIVES—EXPECTED RETURN MULTIPLES

Ages	5	6	7	8	9	10	11	12	13	14
5	69.5	69.0	68.4	67.9	67.3	66.7	66.1	65.5	64.8	64.1
6	69.0	68.5	68.0	67.5	66.9	66.4	65.8	65.1	64.5	63.8
7	68.4	68.0	67.5	67.0	66.5	66.0	65.4	64.8	64.2	63.5
8	67.9	67.5	67.0	66.6	66.1	65.5	65.0	64.4	63.8	63.2
9	67.3	66.9	66.5	66.1	65.6	65.1	64.6	64.0	63.4	62.8
10	66.7	66.4	66.0	65.5	65.1	64.6	64.1	63.6	63.0	62.5
11	66.1	65.8	65.4	65.0	64.6	64.1	63.6	63.1	62.6	62.1
12	65.5	65.1	64.8	64.4	64.0	63.6	63.1	62.7	62.2	61.7
13	64.8	64.5	64.2	63.8	63.4	63.0	62.6	62.2	61.7	61.2
14	64.1	63.8	63.5	63.2	62.8	62.5	62.1	61.7	61.2	60.7
15	63.4	63.1	62.9	62.6	62.2	61.9	61.5	61.1	60.7	60.2
16	62.7	62.4	62.2	61.9	61.6	61.3	60.9	60.5	60.1	59.7
17	61.9	61.7	61.5	61.2	60.9	60.6	60.3	59.9	59.6	59.2
18	61.2	61.0	60.7	60.5	60.2	60.0	59.7	59.3	59.0	58.6
19	60.4	60.2	60.0	59.8	59.5	59.3	59.0	58.7	58.4	58.0
20	59.6	59.4	59.2	59.0	58.8	58.6	58.3	58.0	57.7	57.4
21	58.8	58.7	58.5	58.3	58.1	57.8	57.6	57.3	57.1	56.8
22	58.0	57.8	57.7	57.5	57.3	57.1	56.9	56.6	56.4	56.1
23	57.2	57.0	56.9	56.7	56.5	56.4	56.1	55.9	55.7	55.4
24	56.3	56.2	56.1	55.9	55.8	55.6	55.4	55.2	55.0	54.7
25	55.5	55.4	55.2	55.1	55.0	54.8	54.6	54.4	54.2	54.0
26	54.6	54.5	54.4	54.3	54.1	54.0	53.8	53.7	53.5	53.3
27	53.8	53.7	53.6	53.4	53.3	53.2	53.0	52.9	52.8	52.5
28	52.9	52.8	52.7	52.6	52.5	52.4	52.2	52.1	51.9	51.7
29	52.0	51.9	51.8	51.7	51.6	51.5	51.4	51.3	51.1	51.0
30	51.1	51.0	51.0	50.9	50.8	50.7	50.6	50.4	50.3	50.2
31	50.2	50.2	50.1	50.0	49.9	49.8	49.7	49.6	49.5	49.3
32	49.3	49.3	49.2	49.1	49.0	49.0	48.9	48.8	48.6	48.5
33	48.4	48.4	48.3	48.2	48.2	48.1	48.0	47.9	47.8	47.7
34	47.5	47.5	47.4	47.4	47.3	47.2	47.1	47.0	47.0	46.8
35	46.6	46.6	46.5	46.5	46.4	46.3	46.3	46.2	46.1	46.0
36	45.7	45.7	45.6	45.6	45.5	45.4	45.4	45.3	45.2	45.1
37	44.8	44.7	44.7	44.6	44.6	44.5	44.5	44.4	44.3	44.3
38	43.9	43.8	43.8	43.7	43.7	43.6	43.6	43.5	43.5	43.4
39	42.9	42.9	42.9	42.8	42.8	42.7	42.7	42.6	42.6	42.5
40	42.0	42.0	42.0	41.9	41.9	41.8	41.8	41.7	41.7	41.6
41	41.1	41.1	41.0	41.0	41.0	40.9	40.9	40.8	40.8	40.7
42	40.2	40.1	40.1	40.1	40.1	40.0	40.0	39.9	39.9	39.8

Ages	5	6	7	8	9	10	11	12	13	14
43	39.2	39.2	39.2	39.2	39.1	39.1	39.1	39.0	39.0	39.0
44	38.3	38.3	38.3	38.3	38.2	38.2	38.2	38.1	38.1	38.1
45	37.4	37.4	37.4	37.3	37.3	37.3	37.3	37.2	37.2	37.2
46	36.5	36.5	36.5	36.4	36.4	36.4	36.4	36.3	36.3	36.3
47	35.6	35.6	35.5	35.5	35.5	35.5	35.5	35.4	35.4	35.4
48	34.7	34.7	34.6	34.6	34.6	34.6	34.6	34.5	34.5	34.5
49	33.8	33.8	33.7	33.7	33.7	33.7	33.7	33.7	33.6	33.6
50	32.9	32.9	32.8	32.8	32.8	32.8	32.8	32.8	32.7	32.7
51	32.0	32.0	31.9	31.9	31.9	31.9	31.9	31.9	31.9	31.8
52	31.1	31.1	31.1	31.0	31.0	31.0	31.0	31.0	31.0	30.9
53	30.2	30.2	30.2	30.2	30.1	30.1	30.1	30.1	30.1	30.1
54	29.3	29.3	29.3	29.3	29.3	29.2	29.2	29.2	29.2	29.2
55	28.4	28.4	28.4	28.4	28.4	28.4	28.4	28.3	28.3	28.3
56	27.5	27.5	27.5	27.5	27.5	27.5	27.5	27.5	27.5	27.5
57	26.7	26.7	26.7	26.6	26.6	26.6	26.6	26.6	26.6	26.6
58	25.8	25.8	25.8	25.8	25.8	25.8	25.8	25.7	25.7	25.7
59	24.9	24.9	24.9	24.9	24.9	24.9	24.9	24.9	24.9	24.9
60	24.1	24.1	24.1	24.1	24.1	24.0	24.0	24.0	24.0	24.0
61	23.2	23.2	23.2	23.2	23.2	23.2	23.2	23.2	23.2	23.2
62	22.4	22.4	22.4	22.4	22.4	22.4	22.4	22.3	22.3	22.3
63	21.5	21.5	21.5	21.5	21.5	21.5	21.5	21.5	21.5	21.5
64	20.7	20.7	20.7	20.7	20.7	20.7	20.7	20.7	20.7	20.7
65	19.9	19.9	19.9	19.9	19.9	19.9	19.9	19.9	19.9	19.9
66	19.1	19.1	19.1	19.1	19.1	19.1	19.1	19.1	19.1	19.1
67	18.3	18.3	18.3	18.3	18.3	18.3	18.3	18.3	18.3	18.3
68	17.5	17.5	17.5	17.5	17.5	17.5	17.5	17.5	17.5	17.5
69	16.8	16.8	16.8	16.7	16.7	16.7	16.7	16.7	16.7	16.7
70	16.0	16.0	16.0	16.0	16.0	16.0	16.0	16.0	16.0	16.0
71	15.3	15.3	15.3	15.3	15.3	15.3	15.3	15.3	15.3	15.2
72	14.6	14.6	14.5	14.5	14.5	14.5	14.5	14.5	14.5	14.5
73	13.9	13.9	13.8	13.8	13.8	13.8	13.8	13.8	13.8	13.8
74	13.2	13.2	13.2	13.2	13.2	13.2	13.2	13.2	13.2	13.2
75	12.5	12.5	12.5	12.5	12.5	12.5	12.5	12.5	12.5	12.5
76	11.9	11.9	11.8	11.8	11.8	11.8	11.8	11.8	11.8	11.8
77	11.2	11.2	11.2	11.2	11.2	11.2	11.2	11.2	11.2	11.2
78	10.6	10.6	10.6	10.6	10.6	10.6	10.6	10.6	10.6	10.6
79	10.0	10.0	10.0	10.0	10.0	10.0	10.0	10.0	10.0	10.0
80	9.5	9.5	9.5	9.5	9.5	9.5	9.5	9.5	9.4	9.4
81	8.9	8.9	8.9	8.9	8.9	8.9	8.9	8.9	8.9	8.9
82	8.4	8.4	8.4	8.4	8.4	8.4	8.4	8.4	8.4	8.4
83	7.9	7.9	7.9	7.9	7.9	7.9	7.9	7.9	7.9	7.9
84	7.4	7.4	7.4	7.4	7.4	7.4	7.4	7.4	7.4	7.4
85	6.9	6.9	6.9	6.9	6.9	6.9	6.9	6.9	6.9	6.9
86	6.5	6.5	6.5	6.5	6.5	6.5	6.5	6.5	6.5	6.5
87	6.1	6.1	6.1	6.1	6.1	6.1	6.1	6.1	6.1	6.1
88	5.7	5.7	5.7	5.7	5.7	5.7	5.7	5.7	5.7	5.7
89	5.3	5.3	5.3	5.3	5.3	5.3	5.3	5.3	5.3	5.3
90	5.0	5.0	5.0	5.0	5.0	5.0	5.0	5.0	5.0	5.0
91	4.7	4.7	4.7	4.7	4.7	4.7	4.7	4.7	4.7	4.7
92	4.4	4.4	4.4	4.4	4.4	4.4	4.4	4.4	4.4	4.4
93	4.1	4.1	4.1	4.1	4.1	4.1	4.1	4.1	4.1	4.1
94	3.9	3.9	3.9	3.9	3.9	3.9	3.9	3.9	3.9	3.9
95	3.7	3.7	3.7	3.7	3.7	3.7	3.7	3.6	3.6	3.6
96	3.4	3.4	3.4	3.4	3.4	3.4	3.4	3.4	3.4	3.4
97	3.2	3.2	3.2	3.2	3.2	3.2	3.2	3.2	3.2	3.2
98	3.0	3.0	3.0	3.0	3.0	3.0	3.0	3.0	3.0	3.0
99	2.8	2.8	2.8	2.8	2.8	2.8	2.8	2.8	2.8	2.8
100	2.7	2.7	2.7	2.7	2.7	2.7	2.7	2.7	2.7	2.7
101	2.5	2.5	2.5	2.5	2.5	2.5	2.5	2.5	2.5	2.5
102	2.3	2.3	2.3	2.3	2.3	2.3	2.3	2.3	2.3	2.3
103	2.1	2.1	2.1	2.1	2.1	2.1	2.1	2.1	2.1	2.1
104	1.9	1.9	1.9	1.9	1.9	1.9	1.9	1.9	1.9	1.9
105	1.8	1.8	1.8	1.8	1.8	1.8	1.8	1.8	1.8	1.8
106	1.6	1.6	1.6	1.6	1.6	1.6	1.6	1.6	1.6	1.6
107	1.4	1.4	1.4	1.4	1.4	1.4	1.4	1.4	1.4	1.4
108	1.3	1.3	1.3	1.3	1.3	1.3	1.3	1.3	1.3	1.3
109	1.1	1.1	1.1	1.1	1.1	1.1	1.1	1.1	1.1	1.1
110	1.0	1.0	1.0	1.0	1.0	1.0	1.0	1.0	1.0	1.0
111	.9	.9	.9	.9	.9	.9	.9	.9	.9	.9
112	.8	.8	.8	.8	.8	.8	.8	.8	.8	.8
113	.7	.7	.7	.7	.7	.7	.7	.7	.7	.7
114	.6	.6	.6	.6	.6	.6	.6	.6	.6	.6
115	.5	.5	.5	.5	.5	.5	.5	.5	.5	.5

Table of
Internal Revenue Code Sections

[References are to question numbers.]

[References are to question numbers.]

[References are to question numbers.]

[References are to question numbers.]

[References are to question numbers.]

[References are to question numbers.]

[References are to question numbers.]

Internal Revenue Code Sections

[References are to question numbers.]

[References are to question numbers.]

Internal Revenue Code Sections

[References are to question numbers.]

Internal Revenue Code Sections

[References are to question numbers.]

Table of Treasury Regulations

[*References are to question numbers.*]

[References are to question numbers.]

[References are to question numbers.]

[References are to question numbers.]

[References are to question numbers.]

[*References are to question numbers.*]

[References are to question numbers.]

[References are to question numbers.]

[References are to question numbers.]

Treasury Regulations

[References are to question numbers.]

[References are to question numbers.]

[References are to question numbers.]

Treasury Regulations

Table of ERISA Sections

[References are to question numbers.]

ERISA Sections

[References are to question numbers.]

[References are to question numbers.]

Table of DOL Regulations

[References are to question numbers.]

[References are to question numbers.]

Table of Revenue Rulings

[References are to question numbers.]

[References are to question numbers.]

[References are to question numbers.]

Rev Rul

85-31, 1985-1 CB 153 . . . . . . 9:19

85-105, 1985-2 CB 53 . . . . . 13:10

85-130, 1985-2 CB 137 . . 9:10, 25:5

85-131, 1985-2 CB 138 . . . . . . 9:1

86-142, 1986-2 CB 60 . . 12:26, 26:21

87-41, 1987-1 CB 296 . . . . . . 29:5

87-114, 1987-2 CB 116 . . . . . 29:10

89-14, 1989-1 CB 111 . . . . . 13:52

89-76, 1989-1 CB 24 . . . 24:4, 24:7

89-87, 1989-2 CB 81 . . . . 8:29, 21:2, 21:67

89-89, 1989-2 CB 231 . . 11:11, 14:20, 26:37

89-97, 1989-2 CB 81 . . . . 1:10

90-105, 1990-2 CB 69 . . 12:15, 23:44

91-4, 1991-1 CB 57 . . . . 1:37

92-22, 1992-1 CB 313 . . . . . 14:19

Rev Rul

92-47, 1992-1 CB 198 . . . . . 26:38

92-66, 1992-2 CB 92 . . . . . . 10:43

92-73, 1992-2 CB 224 . . . . . . 26:2

92-76, 1992-2 CB 76 . . . . 21:8

94-75, 1994-2 CB 591 . . . . . . 8:6

94-76, 1994-2 CB 46 . . . 1:32, 10:56

95-6, 1995-1 CB 80 . . . 6:10, 10:59

95-8, 1995-1 CB 293 . . . . . . 19:50

95-28, 1995-1 CB 76 . . . . 8:2

95-29, 1995-1 CB 81 . . . . 6:10, 6:11, 9:25, 9:26

95-29A, 1995-1 CB 85 . . . . . . 6:10

95-31, 1995-1 CB 76 . . . . 8:28

95-57, 1995-24 IRB 5 . . . . . . 24:40

95-75, 1995-46 IRB 8 . . . . 7:22

96-20, 1996-15 IRB 5 . . . . 8:2

96-21, 1996-15 IRB 7 . . . . 8:2

Table of Revenue Procedures

[*References are to question numbers.*]

[References are to question numbers.]

Rev Proc

96-6, 1996-1 IRB 151 .   15:1, 15:5-15:8,
15:11, 21:66

Rev Proc

96-8, 1996-1 IRB 187 . . .   8:23, 15:2,
15:17, 15:19

Table of Letter Rulings

[References are to question numbers.]

Ltr Rul		Ltr Rul	
962045	8:18	8522057	6:34
7742003	5:13, 9:10	8527082	26:24
7747057	29:5	8527083	26:18
7801019	29:5	8535001	26:5
7817098	29:3	8535116	13:21
7825010	29:40	8536085	12:2, 26:19
7913129	29:40	8536097	28:43
7945047	8:20	8536098	28:43
7949018	8:27	8541094	13:9
8044023	19:50	8541116	13:9
8104998	19:50	8551065	26:19
8107114	19:50	8552001	2:36, 8:8
8110164	19:50	8610002	2:36
8137048	10:56	8610082	24:9
8311071	10:56	8611090	26:19
8338138	19:50	8622044	6:6
8432109	26:21	8622051	26:25
8434052	28:38	8623054	28:6
8439026	26:3	8628047	26:19
8439066	26:5	8630028	14:19
8441071	13:9	8630068	27:20
8450051	27:14	8711095	26:21
8502044	28:3	8725088	14:4
8519051	26:5	8743102	30:17

[References are to question numbers.]

[References are to question numbers.]

[References are to question numbers.]

[References are to question numbers.]

Ltr Rul	
9303023	13:29
9303031	28:6
9304003	24:11
9304032	8:20
9304033	12:12
9305025	28:6
9308049	8:20
9308050	28:3, 28:5
9309051	8:21
9310026	11:19
9310035	13:2
9310050	8:21
9310054	13:40
9311037	11:10
9311039	13:33, 14:26
9313029	8:20
9314007	24:5
9315031	28:1, 28:19
9316001	20:6
9316047	13:6
9317037	23:12
9317057	8:20
9318035	21:56
9318043	26:41
9318044	28:38
9320006	13:1, 14:18
9320050	21:56
9321032	26:38
9321067	24:25
9322005	11:7, 11:11, 26:38, 26:40
9324044	29:7
9325045	13:9
9325055	6:1, 6:8, 6:17

Ltr Rul	
9327025	29:7
9327080	24:30
9327083	30:18
9328034	13:30
9329049	26:21
9331055	26:34, 28:20
9331056	8:21
9332040	29:38, 29:44
9332046	8:18
9335047	21:58
9335050	14:26
9335051	14:26
9336046	5:13, 6:13
9336053	29:7
9336054	29:7
9337025	12:16
9338040	30:21, 30:21
9338041	28:1, 28:8, 28:17, 28:34
9339005	24:29, 24:31
9339024	29:41
9340032	30:5
9340059	8:20
9341008	26:34
9342050	8:24
9342055	8:14
9342056	29:44
9344001	13:47
9344027	26:44
9345044	29:40
9346012	9:24
9348051	29:41
9349028	8:20
9349031	8:20
9350025	24:56

[References are to question numbers.]

Letter Rulings

[References are to question numbers.]

Ltr Rul		Ltr Rul	
9438031	29:4	9504005	26:38
9438032	8:20	9504041	13:10
9438042	8:21	9504045	26:40, 28:6
9438043	24:56	9505022	26:41
9438044	13:1, 13:17	9505023	28:40
9439020	26:34, 26:37	9506030	24:3
9441004	14:23	9506048	6:1, 12:1
9442015	24:23	9507030	6:1, 12:1
9442026	29:11	9507032	13:6, 28:8, 28:34
9442030	29:40, 29:41		
9442031	5:31	9508001	24:23
9442032	26:37	9508003	5:5, 15:5
9443002	29:5	9509028	28:36
9443040	13:31, 13:33	9509045	8:20
9443041	13:9, 23:33	9511040	29:6
9444045	8:24	9513027	13:1
9444046	8:20	9514002	8:18
9445023	23:33	9514026	13:41, 26:41
9445028	23:33	9514027	8:20
9445029	28:6	9514028	21:8
9447075	24:3	9515002	24:30, 24:31
9448045	13:17, 24:56	9517052	8:20
9449019	8:20	9518019	28:40
9449021	23:1	9519001	15:5
9450040	26:40	9522056	29:6, 29:11
9450041	28:36	9523025	21:5, 23:33
9450042	13:33, 14:26	9524020	28:36
9450044	8:20	9525060	29:6, 29:10
9451063	29:37	9525067	29:6, 29:10
9451082	29:37	9528034	6:1, 12:1
9452004	14:8	9529006	29:12, 29:29
9452045	24:56	9529043	24:9
9501044	11:7, 11:9, 11:10, 11:11, 26:40	9530015	24:3
		9530031	29:37
9502030	4:23, 5:30	9530037	28:40

[References are to question numbers.]

Letter Rulings

Table of
Notices and Announcements
[References are to question numbers.]

[References are to question numbers.]

Table of Cases

[References are to question numbers.]

[References are to question numbers.]

Cases

[References are to question numbers.]

[References are to question numbers.]

Cases

[References are to question numbers.]

Cases

Connors v B&W Coal Co, 646
F Supp 164 (D DC
1986) 25:14, 25:19

Connors v Barrick Gold Exploration, Inc, 962 F 2d 1076
(DC Cir 1992) 25:14

Connors v Calvert Dev Co,
622 F Supp 877 (D DC
1985) 25:18, 25:35

Connors v Middle Fork Corp,
No. 89-0698(GHR), (D DC
1992) 25:19

Consolidated Beef Indus, Inc
v New York Life Ins Co,
Nos. 90-5131/90-5164 (8th
Cir 1991) 19:6

Continental Can Co v Chicago
Truck Drivers, Helpers and
Warehouse Workers Union
Pension Fund, 916 F 2d
1154 (7th Cir 1990) 25:25

Conway v United States, Civ
MJG-93-1707 (D Md 1995) . . 26:6

Cooke v Lynn Sand & Stone
Co, 1995 US App Lexis
33252 (1st Cir 1995) 9:24

Copley, 70 TCM 1040 (1995)26:34, 26:41

Corbin v United States, 760 F
2d 234 (8th Cir 1985) 29:6

Corder v Howard Johnson &
Co, 53 F 3d 225 (9th Cir
1994) 19:43

Costantino v TRW, Inc, Nos.
91-3768/3769 (6th Cir 1994) . 9:24

Costantino v TRW Inc, 1993
US App Lexis 29479 (6th
Cir 1993) 10:42

Costanza, 50 TCM 280 (1985) . 26:34

Costanza v Comm'r, 50 TCM
280 (1985) 28:42

Cottrill v Sparrow, Johnson &
Ursillo, Inc, Nos. 95-1363
and 95-1434 (1st Cir 1996) . . 4:24

Counts v Kissack Water and
Oil Service Inc Profit Shar-
ing Plan, No. 92-8036 (10th
Cir 1993) 9:24, 10:42

Crawford v Lamantia, No. 93-
224 (1st Cir 1994) 19:28

Crown Cork & Seal Co, Inc v
Central States, SE and SW
Areas Pension Fund, 982 F
2d 857 (3d Cir 1992) 25:12

C-T of Virginia, Inc, In re, No.
91-2397 (4th Cir 1992) . . . 21:56

Curcio v John Hancock Mu-
tual Life Ins Co, 1994 US
App Lexis 21935 (3d Cir
1994) 18:5, 19:12

Curtiss-Wright Corp v
Schoonejongen, No. 93-
1935 (S Ct 1995) 16:23

Custom Builders, Inc, 58 TCM
696 (1989) 12:19

Cutair v Marshall, 590 F 2d
523 (3d Cir 1979) 20:1

Czarski v Estate of Bonk,
1996 US Dist Lexis 4808
(ED Mich 1996) 14:10, 30:4

D

Dade v North America Philips
Corp, 1994 US Dist Lexis
11428 (DC NJ 1994) 9:24

Dallas Dental Labs, 72 TC 117
(1979) 12:15

[References are to question numbers.]

[References are to question numbers.]

[References are to question numbers.]

[References are to question numbers.]

Cases

[References are to question numbers.]

[References are to question numbers.]

[References are to question numbers.]

Cases

Park S Hotel Corp v NY Hotel Trades Council, 851 F 2d 578 (2d Cir 1988) 25:19

Parrett v Am Ship Building Co, 990 F 2d 854 (6th Cir 1993) 21:53

Patterson v Shumate, 112 S Ct 2242 (1992) 4:25, 23:58, 24:59, 29:51

PBGC v Artra Group Inc, No. 90 C 5358 (ND Ill 1991) . . 21:12

PBGC v Defoe Shipbuilding Co, 639 F 2d 311 (6th Cir 1981) 25:7

PBGC v East Dayton Tool and Die Co, No. 93-3185 (6th Cir 1994) 21:52

PBGC v Fel, 798 F Supp 239 (D NJ 1992) 21:26

PBGC v Fletcher, No. MO-89-CA-179 (WD Tex 1990) . . . 19:12

PBGC v LTV Corp, No. 87 Civ 7261 (RJS) . . . D NY 1990), 21:26

PBGC v LTV Corp, No. 89-390 (S Ct 1990) 21:26

PBGC v Mize Company, Inc, No. 92-1351 (4th Cir 1993) . . 21:2

PBGC v Ross, 733 F Supp 1005 (MD NC 1990) 19:37

Pearland Investment Co, 62 TCM 1221 (1991) 20:9

Pedre Co v Robins, 1995 US Dist Lexis 14253 (SD NY 1995) 19:29

Pedro Enterprises, Inc v Perdue, 998 F 2d 491 (7th Cir 1993) 10:22

Penn v Howe-Baker Eng'rs, Inc, No. 89-2257 (5th Cir 1990) 21:4

Penn Central Corp v W Conf of Teamsters Pension Trust Fund, 1996 US App Lexis 1143 (9th Cir 1996) 25:19

Pension Plan of Public Svc Co of NH v KPMG Peat Marwick, 1993 US Dist Lexis 2254 (D NH 1993) 19:6

Petropoulos v Outbound Marine Corp, 1995 US Dist Lexis 10545 (ND Ill 1995) . . 10:63

Phillips v Alaska Hotel and Restaurant Employees Pension Fund, Nos. 89-35735/90-35144 (9th Cir 1991) 9:5

Phillips v Amoco Oil Co, 799 F 2d 1464 (11th Cir 1986) . . 19:15

Phillips v Bebber, Nos. 89-2184 and 89-2189 (4th Cir 1990) 21:2, 21:32

Physicians Healthchoice, Inc v Trustees of the Automotive Employee Benefit Trust, 764 F Supp 1360 (D Minn 1991) 19:41

Pierce v Security Trust Life Ins Co, 1992 US App Lexis 15562 (4th Cir 1992) . . 18:5, 18:6

Pilipski, 66 TCM 984 (1993) 26:34, 26:45

Pilkington PLC v Perelman, 1995 US App Lexis 36632 (9th Cir 1995) 19:30

[References are to question numbers.]

[References are to question numbers.]

[*References are to question numbers.*]

Sheldon Co Profit-Sharing
Plan and Trust v Smith,
1995 US App Lexis 20708
(6th Cir 1995) 19:6, 19:43

Sheldon Modansky, In re, No.
92 B 21976 (SD NY 1993) . . 28:44

Shelley, 68 TCM 584
(1994) 26:5, 26:6

Sherry v Central Natl Bank of
Canajoharie, 886 F Supp
256 (ND NY 1995) 6:1

Sherwood Group, Inc v Meselsohn, No. 88 Civ 3650 (SD
NY 1990) 19:12

Shih v Commercial Assn for
Security and Health, 809 F
Supp 80 (D Col 1992) . . . 19:42

Shimota v United States, 21
Cls Ct 510 (1990), *aff'd*,
943 F 2d 1312 (Fed Cir
1991) 13:2, 13:3,
13:39

Shumaker, 124 BR 820 (Bankr
D Mont 1991) 26:45

Sigmund Cohn Corp v Dist
No. 15 Machinists Pension
Fund, No. CV 91-2691
(RJD) (ED NY 1992) 25:23

Silk, United States v, 331 US
704 (1947) 29:5

Silver, TCM 1996-42 . . . . . . 13:2

Simmons, 65 TCM 1887
(1993) 13:2, 13:3

Sippe v Sippe, 101 NC App
194 (1990) 30:12

Siskind v The Sperry Retirement Program, UNYSIS, 47
F 3d 498 (2d Cir 1995) 19:2

Sites v United States, Civ 94-
820 (D Md 1995) 13:5

Slice v Sons of Norway, No.
93-2301 (9th Cir 1994) . . . 19:37

Smith v Nat'l Credit Union
Admin Bd, 1994 US App
Lexis 30390 (11th Cir 1994) . . 9:24

Smith, United States v, 1995
US App Lexis 4151 (4th Cir
1995) 4:27

Snap-Drape, Inc, 105 TC 16
(1995) 24:11

Solomon, In re, 1995 US App
Lexis 29795 (4th Cir 1995) . 26:45

Somma, In re, 585-648 (Bankr
ND Ohio 1992) 13:49

Southern Aluminum Castings
Co v United States, Civ 90-
0235-P-C (SD Ala 1991) . . . 21:57

Spain v Aetna Life Ins Co,
1993 US App Lexis 33975
(9th Cir 1993) 19:43

Spinelli v Gaughan, 12 F 3d
853 (9th Cir 1993) 19:31

Spink v Lockheed Corp, No.
95-809 (S Ct 1996) 20:1

Springfield Productions, Inc,
38 TCM 74 (1979) 12:5

Stark Truss Co, Inc, 62 TCM
169 (1991) 4:7, 15:13

Steel Balls, Inc, 95-3431 (8th
Cir 1996) 24:11, 24:14

Steinberg v Mikkelsen, 1995
US Dist Lexis 155880 (ED
Wis 1995) 19:37

Steiner Corp Retirement Plan
v Johnson & Higgins of
California, 1994 US App
Lexis 16716 (10th Cir 1994) . . 19:6

[References are to question numbers.]

[References are to question numbers.]

Cases

Glossary

The following is a list of terms (arranged in alphabetical order) that is intended to provide the reader with additional guidance in understanding the complex concepts that apply to qualified pension and profit sharing plans.

Acceleration Election: An election to increase the rate of recovery of the initial grandfather amount for excess distribution tax purposes from 10 percent to 100 percent if the discretionary method of recovery has been elected.

Accrued Benefit: A benefit that an employee has earned (or accrued) through participation in the plan. In a defined contribution plan (e.g., a profit sharing plan), the accrued benefit of a participant is the balance in his or her individual account at a given time. In a defined benefit plan, the accrued benefit is determined by reference to the benefit that will be provided to a participant when he or she reaches normal retirement age as specified by the plan. The accrued benefit should not be confused, however, with the benefit (or portion thereof) that a participant has a right (nonforfeitable) to receive if he or she leaves prior to retirement. This benefit is determined by reference to the plan's vesting schedule and the years of service credited to a participant.

Actual Contribution Percentage (ACP) Test: A special nondiscrimination test applied to employer matching contributions and employee contributions.

Actual Deferral Percentage (ADP) Test: A special test designed to limit the extent to which elective contributions made on behalf of highly compensated employees may exceed the elective contributions made on behalf of non-highly compensated employees under a 401(k) plan.

Actuarial Assumptions: Contributions to a defined benefit plan depend upon certain assumptions made by the plan's actuary, which may include mortality, investment return, employee turnover, retirement age, and salary scale.

Actuarial Equivalence: Two different sets of values are in an actuarial equivalence when they have an equal present value under a given set of actuarial assumptions.

Administrative Policy Regarding Sanctions: IRS policy designed to allow plan sponsors to correct minor, isolated, operational plan defects without plan disqualification.

Affiliated Service Group: Generally, an affiliated service group consists of two or more related service or management organizations, whether or not incorporated. Employees of the members of an affiliated service group are treated as employed by a single employer for plan qualification purposes.

Age-Based Profit Sharing Plan: A profit sharing plan that uses both age and compensation as a basis for allocating employer contributions among plan participants.

Alternate Payee: A spouse, former spouse, child, or other dependent of a participant who is recognized by a domestic relations order as having a right to receive all or a portion of the benefits payable under the qualified retirement plan with respect to the participant.

Annual Addition: Term used in connection with the limitation on the contributions that may be made for a participant under a defined contribution plan.

Annuity: A series of periodic payments, usually level in amount or adjusted according to some index (e.g., cost-of-living), that typically continue for the lifetime of the recipient. In contrast, an installment payment is one of a specific number of payments that will be paid whether or not the recipient lives to receive them. *See also* "Joint and Survivor Annuity."

Annuity Starting Date: The first day of the first period for which a benefit is payable as an annuity. For benefits payable in any other form, it is the first day on which all events have occurred that entitle the participant to the benefit.

Attained Age Method: The rate of recovery of the initial grandfather amount is calculated based on a formula that takes into account the individual's age both on August 1, 1986 and at the end of the year in which the retirement distributions are received.

Beneficiary: A person designated by a participant or one who, by the terms of the plan, is or may be eligible for benefits under the plan if the participant dies.

C Corporation: *See* "S Corporation."

CAP: *See* "Employee Plans Closing Agreements Pilot Program."

Cash-or-Deferred Plan: A qualified profit sharing or stock bonus plan that gives a participant an option to take cash or to have the employer contribute the money to a qualified profit sharing plan as an "employer" contribution to the plan (i.e., an "elective deferral"). These arrangements are often called "401(k) plans." *See* chapter 22.

CB: Cumulative Bulletin. This is a government publication in which revenue rulings and other pertinent IRS pronouncements are published. The Cumulative Bulletin is published semiannually and incorporates the materials that were published weekly by IRS in its Internal Revenue Bulletins (IRBs).

Closely Held Corporation: A nonpublic corporation that is owned by a small number of shareholders.

Code: The Internal Revenue Code of 1986 (26 USC 1 *et seq.*), as adopted by TRA '86 (Pub L No 99-514). ("Former Code" refers to repealed provisions, including those in the previous Internal Revenue Code of 1954.)

Collectively Bargained Plans: Plans that provide retirement benefits under a collective bargaining agreement. Generally speaking, if more than one employer is required to contribute to the collectively bargained plan, the plan is treated as a multiemployer plan, subject to special rules. If only one employer (including affiliates) is required to contribute to the plan, however, the plan is treated in the same way that other plans that do not cover union employees are treated.

Combination Plans: The use of two or more plans in combination to provide retirement benefits for employees and their beneficiaries. A defined contribution plan (e.g., a money purchase plan) may be combined with a defined benefit pension plan or with another defined contribution plan (e.g., a profit sharing plan). Limitations on contributions or benefits depend on the type of combination used.

Common-Law Employee: A person who performs service(s) for an employer, if the employer has the right to direct both the objective of the services and the manner in which they are performed.

Commonly Controlled Businesses: All employees of corporations that are members of a "controlled group of corporations" are treated as employed by a single employer for purposes of plan qualification. A comparable requirement applies to partnerships, sole proprietorships, and other businesses under common control. *See also* "Controlled Group of Corporations."

Conduit IRA: *See* "Rollover IRA Account."

Contributory Plan: A pension plan under which employee contributions are required as a condition of participation.

Controlled Group of Corporations: There are three types of controlled groups: (1) the parent-subsidiary controlled group, (2) the brother-sister controlled group, and (3) the combined group. Two tests must be met to have a "parent-subsidiary" controlled group: (1) stock equal to 80 percent of the combined voting power of each corporation, or at least 80 percent of the value of all outstanding stock of each corporation, is owned by one or more of the corporations of the group; and (2) the common parent corporation owns at least 80 percent of the voting power or value of at least one of the corporations in the group. Two tests must be met to have a "brother-sister" controlled group: (1) five or fewer persons (individuals, estates, or trusts) own at least 80 percent of the combined voting power or value of two or more corporations; and (2) taking into account the ownership of each stockholder only to the extent that it is identical in each of the corporations involved, the five or fewer persons own more than 50 percent of the combined voting power or value of the corporations involved. A "combined group" is a group of two or more corporations if: (1) each corporation is a member of either a parent-subsidiary group or a brother-sister group; and (2) at least one of the corporations is the common parent of a parent-subsidiary group and also is a member of a brother-sister controlled group. All employees of corporations that are members of a controlled group of corporations are treated as employed by a single employer for plan qualification purposes.

Curtailments: The reduction of benefits or the augmenting of eligibility requirements so as to amount to a partial or a complete termination of the plan.

Death Benefits: Payments to a beneficiary of a deceased participant that may be provided under a qualified plan, but they must be incidental to the retirement benefits, which are the major purpose of the plan.

Defined Benefit Plan: A plan that is designed to provide participants with a definite benefit at retirement (e.g., a monthly benefit of 20 percent of compensation upon reaching age 65). Contributions under the plan are determined by reference to the benefits provided, not on the basis of a percentage of compensation.

Defined Contribution Plan: A plan that provides an individual account for each participant and in which benefits are based solely upon the amount contributed to the account (plus or minus any income, expenses, gain, and losses allocated to the account).

DEFRA: Deficit Reduction Act of 1984. Measure passed by Congress to reduce the budget deficit. One portion of the Act was the Tax Reform Act of 1984. *See also* "Tax Reform Act of 1984."

Delinquent Filer Voluntary Compliance Program; DFVC: A program established by DOL to encourage, through the assessment of reduced civil penalties, delinquent plan administrators to comply with the annual reporting requirements.

Determination Letter: Letter issued by the IRS District Director's office determining that a plan submitted to it meets the requirements for qualification (or does not meet those requirements).

DFVC: See "Delinquent Filer Voluntary Compliance Program."

Direct Rollover: A distribution to an employee made in the form of a direct trustee-to-trustee transfer from a qualified retirement plan to an eligible retirement plan.

Discretionary Formula Plan: A profit sharing plan that provides that the amount of each year's contribution will be determined by the board of directors (or the responsible official(s)) of the sponsoring employer, in its discretion. (Contributions must be "recurring and substantial" to keep the plan in a qualified status.)

Discretionary Method: Under the discretionary method, 10 percent of the total retirement distributions received by an individual during a calendar year will be treated as a recovery of the initial grandfather amount. This method also allows an individual to elect to accelerate the rate of recovery to 100 percent of the distributions received.

Discrimination: A situation in which a plan, through its provisions or through its operations, favors officers, shareholders, or highly compensated employees to the detriment of other employees.

Disqualification: Loss of qualified (tax-favored) status by a plan, generally resulting from operation of the plan in a manner that is contrary to the provisions of the plan or that discriminates against rank-and-file employees. *See also* "Discrimination."

Disqualified Persons: *See* "Party in Interest."

Distress Termination: The termination of a single-employer defined benefit plan covered by PBGC that is unable to pay all its benefit liabilities.

DOL: Department of Labor. The nontax (regulatory and administrative) provisions of ERISA are administered by the Department of Labor. The Department issues opinion letters and other pronouncements, and requires certain information forms to be filed.

Domestic Relations Order; DRO: A judgment, decree or order (including approval of a property settlement agreement) made pursuant to a state domestic relations law (including a community property law) that relates to the provision of child support, alimony payments, or marital property rights to an alternate payee.

Earmarking: Allowing a participant in a defined contribution plan to direct the investment of the amount in his or her account.

Elective Contribution: A contribution made to a 401(k) plan by the employer on an employee's behalf pursuant to the employee's cash-or-deferred election.

Elective Deferral: *See* "Elective Contribution."

Eligible Retirement Plan: An IRA and/or a qualified retirement plan.

Eligible Rollover Distribution: A distribution from a qualified retirement plan that may be rolled over to an eligible retirement plan.

Employee: An individual who provides services for compensation to an employer and whose duties are under the control of the employer.

Employee Contributions: *See* "Mandatory Employee Contributions" and "Voluntary Contributions."

Employee Plans Closing Agreements Pilot Program; CAP: A program that provides a mechanism for resolution of issues in dispute between IRS and plan sponsors where the issues would normally result in plan disqualification.

Employee Stock Ownership Plan; ESOP: A profit sharing, stock bonus, or money purchase pension plan, the funds of which must be invested primarily in employer company stock. Unlike other plans, an ESOP may borrow from the employer or use the employer's credit to acquire company stock. *See also* "Stock Bonus Plan."

Employer Securities: For an ESOP, common stock issued by the employer that is readily tradable on an established securities market. If the employer has no readily tradable common stock, employer securities include employer-issued common stock that has a combination of voting power and dividend rights at least the equal of the class of common stock with the greatest voting power and the class of common stock with the greatest dividend rights. Noncallable preferred stock that is convertible into common stock that meets the requirements of employer securities also qualifies if the conversion price is reasonable.

Employer-Sponsored IRA: An IRA that is sponsored by the employer for purposes of helping its employees make a tax-deductible contribution to an IRA and to invest the funds in a particular type of investment. The employer-sponsored IRA should be distinguished from a simplified employee pension plan (SEP), which requires employer contributions and must meet certain requirements with respect to participation, discrimination, withdrawals, and contributions.

Enrolled Actuary: A person who performs actuarial services for a defined benefit plan. His or her services include making a determination of how much has to be contributed to the plan each year to provide the stated benefits at retirement, and the preparation of a statement that has to be filed with the plan's annual return to IRS. Actuaries who perform these services are enrolled with the Joint Board for the Enrollment of Actuaries.

ERISA: Employee Retirement Income Security Act of 1974. This is the basic law covering qualified plans and incorporates both the pertinent Internal Revenue Code provisions and labor law provisions. ERISA is the basic law designed to protect the rights of beneficiaries of employee benefit plans offered by employers, unions, and the like. ERISA imposes various qualification standards and fiduciary responsibilities on both welfare benefit and retirement plans, and provides enforcement procedures as well. In the retirement area, it also provides standards for tax qualification.

ERTA: Economic Recovery Tax Act of 1981.

Excess Aggregate Contributions: The excess of the aggregate amount of employee contributions and matching contributions made on behalf of highly compensated employees for a plan year over the maximum amount of such contributions permitted under the ACP test.

Excess Contribution: The excess of the elective contributions (including qualified nonelective and matching contributions that are treated as elective contributions) made to a 401(k) plan on behalf of highly compensated employees for the plan year over the maximum amount of such contributions permitted under the ADP test for such plan year.

Excess Deferral: An employee's elective contributions for the taxable year in excess of $7,000 (increased for inflation).

Excess Distributions: A 15 percent excise tax is imposed on excess distributions. Excess distributions mean the aggregate amount of retirement plan distributions made with respect to an individual during a calendar year to the extent that such amount exceeds a threshold amount.

Excess Plan: A plan under which contributions or benefits are based on compensation in excess of the Social Security integration level.

Exclusion Allowance: One of the limitations applicable to the amount of contributions to a tax-sheltered annuity that an employee may exclude from gross income for the taxable year.

Exclusive Benefit Rule: Plan fiduciaries must discharge their duties solely in the interest of participants and beneficiaries for the exclusive purpose of providing benefits to participants and beneficiaries and paying administration expenses. *See also* "Fiduciary."

FASB: Financial Accounting Standards Board; the body that sets uniform standards for treatment of accounting items. In the employee benefits context, FASB has prepared an exposure draft concerning disclosure of unfunded benefit liabilities.

FASB 87: The statement issued by FASB regarding employers' accounting for pensions.

Fiduciary: Any person who exercises discretionary authority or control over the management or disposition of plan assets or who gives investment advice to the plan for a fee or other compensation.

Fiscal year: A 12-month period used for accounting purposes.

5 Percent Owner: Any person who owns, directly or indirectly, more than 5 percent of the stock of the employer. If the employer is not a corporation, the ownership test is applied to the person's capital or profits interest in the employer. *See also* "Key Employee" and "Top-Heavy Plan."

Forfeitures: The benefits that a participant loses if he or she terminates employment before becoming eligible for full retirement benefits under the plan. For example, a participant who leaves the service of an employer at a time when he or she will receive only 60 percent of benefits forfeits the remaining 40 percent.

401(k) Plan: An arrangement (defined by Section 401(k)) under which a covered employee can elect to defer income by making pretax contributions to a profit sharing or stock bonus plan. A cafeteria plan may provide a 401(k) plan as a qualified benefit option. *See* chapter 22.

402(f) Notice: A written examination of the tax effects of a distribution from a qualified retirement plan that must be provided to a distribution recipient.

Frozen Plan: A qualified pension or profit sharing plan that continues to exist even though employer contributions have been discontinued and benefits are no longer accrued by participants. The plan is "frozen" for purposes of distribution of benefits under the terms of the plan.

Funding Deficiency: The excess of total liabilities under a defined benefit, money purchase, or target benefit pension plan over total credits for all plan years. This amount is subject to an excise tax, unless IRS waives the tax. The technical term is "accumulated funding deficiency."

Grandfather Rule: An individual whose total benefits in all retirement plans on August 1, 1986 (initial grandfather amount) had a value in excess of $562,500 was eligible to elect the special grandfather rule. The special grandfather rule permits an individual to offset distributions by the portion of the initial grandfather amount recovered during the year of distribution. The election had to be made no later than the due date of the individual's timely filed 1988 income tax return.

Highly Compensated Employee: An employee who, during the year or the preceding year, is (or was): (1) a 5 percent owner, (2) receiving compensation in excess of $75,000 (adjusted for cost-of-living increases), (3) in the top-paid group of employees and receiving compensation in excess of $50,000 (adjusted for cost-of-living increases), or (4) an officer and receiving compensation greater than $45,000 (adjusted for cost-of-living increases).

H.R. 10 Plan: *See* "Keogh Plan."

Includible Compensation: For the purpose of calculating the employee's exclusion allowance for the taxable year, the amount of compensation received that is includible in gross income for the most recent period that may be counted as one year of service.

Individual Account Plan: A plan that provides for an individual account for each participant and in which benefits are based solely on the amount contributed to an account and any income, expenses, gains, losses, and forfeitures allocated to the account.

Insured Plan: A plan funded exclusively by insurance contracts.

Integrated Plan: *See* "Permitted Disparity."

Interested Parties: Generally means all employees at the time the employer applies for a determination letter. IRS requires that interested parties be notified when the application is made.

IRA: An individual retirement account or an individual retirement annuity. Any working person and certain divorced spouses receiving alimony may establish IRAs and gain deductions for contributions to the IRAs and tax deferrals on the earnings.

IRB: Internal Revenue Bulletin. A weekly collection of materials published by IRS. *See also* "CB."

IRC: Internal Revenue Code of 1986. This is the basic federal tax law.

IRS: Internal Revenue Service: This is an agency of the Treasury Department, headed by the Commissioner of Internal Revenue, charged with primary responsibility for administering, interpreting, and enforcing the Code. (Note, however, that the Secretary of the Treasury—and not IRS—issues regulations under the Code.)

Keogh Plan: A qualified retirement plan, either a defined contribution plan or a defined benefit plan, that covers a self-employed person. (Other employees might also be covered.)

Key Employee: A participant who, at any time during the plan year or any of the four preceding years, is (or was) (1) an officer who earns at least $45,000 a year, (2) one of the ten employees owning the largest interest in the employer and receiving annual compensation of more than $30,000, (3) a more-than-5 percent owner of the employer, or (4) a more-than-1 percent owner earning more than $150,000. *See also* "5 Percent Owner," "Officer," "1 Percent Owner," and "Top-Heavy Plan."

Letter Ruling: A private ruling issued by IRS in response to a request from a taxpayer as to the tax consequences of a proposed or completed transaction. Private letter rulings are published informally by several publishers. They are not considered as precedents for use by taxpayers other than the one that requested the ruling, but they do give an indication of IRS's current attitude as to a particular type of transaction.

Leveraged ESOP: An employee stock ownership plan that borrows to acquire employer company stock. *See also* "Employee Stock Ownership Plan."

Lump-Sum Distribution: A type of distribution that is required for purposes of using the forward averaging method in computing the income tax that is due. The basic requirements to qualify as a lump-sum distribution are (1) the distribution must be made within one taxable year of the recipient; (2) it must include the entire balance credited to an employee's account; and (3) it must be made on account of an employee's death, separation from service (except in the case of a self-employed person), or attainment of age 59 (or, in the case of a self-employed person only, on account of disability).

Mandatory Employee Contributions: Contributions made by an employee in order to become eligible to participate under a plan.

Master Plan: A retirement plan that is sponsored by a financial institution such as an insurance company, bank, mutual fund, or stock brokerage firm, and that may be adopted by an employer merely by executing a participation agreement.

Minimum Funding: The minimum amount that must be contributed by an employer that has a defined benefit, money purchase, or target benefit pension plan. The minimum is made up of amounts that go to cover "normal costs" (for the benefits earned by employees for the current year) plus other plan liabilities such as "past service costs"—liabilities for benefits that have been earned for services performed prior to the adoption of the plan. If the employer fails to meet these minimum standards, in the absence of a waiver from IRS, an excise tax will be imposed on the amount of the deficiency.

Minimum Funding Standard Account: An account that is maintained for a defined benefit, money purchase, or target benefit pension plan for purposes of keeping track of the plan's liabilities and credits. If the account shows a deficiency (excess of liabilities over credits), an excise tax is imposed on that amount.

Money Purchase Pension Plan: A defined contribution plan under which the employer's contributions are mandatory and are usually based on each participant's compensation. Retirement benefits under the plan are based on the amount in the participant's individual account at retirement.

Multiemployer Plan: A pension plan, maintained under a collective bargaining agreement, that covers the employees of more than one employer. Generally, the various employers are not financially related but rather are engaged in the same industry.

Named Fiduciary: A fiduciary who is named in the plan instrument or identified through a procedure set forth in the plan. One of the distinguishing features of the named fiduciary is that he or she has the authority to designate others to carry out fiduciary responsibilities (e.g., invest the plan funds).

New Comparability Plan: Generally a profit sharing plan or a money purchase pension plan in which the contribution percentage formula for one category of participants is greater than the contribution percentage formula for other categories of participants. To satisfy the nondiscrimination requirements, a new comparability plan is tested under the cross-testing rules.

Noncontributory Plan: A pension plan under which employees are eligible to participate and receive accrued benefits without contributing to the plan.

Nonelective Contribution: A contribution to a cash-or-deferred arrangement other than an elective deferral. (An elective deferral is a participant-elected contribution that the participant could have chosen to receive instead as cash.) If the amount of the nonelective contribution depends on the amount of a participant's elective deferral, it is an "employer matching contribution."

Nonforfeitable Benefits: Benefits that cannot be lost by a participant even if he or she terminates service with the employer before qualifying for full retirement benefits. The nonforfeitable benefits are determined by applying the years of credited service to the vesting schedule used by the plan. *See also* "Vested Benefits."

Notice of Intent to Terminate; NOIT: The 60-day advance notice to affected parties advising them of a proposed standard termination of a defined benefit plan covered by PBGC.

Notice of Plan Benefits: The notice to participants and beneficiaries to advise them of their benefits under a terminated defined benefit plan covered by PBGC.

OBRA '87: The Omnibus Budget Reconciliation Act of 1987 contained provisions affecting the minimum funding standards, including the Pension Protection Act of 1987. *See* "Pension Protection Act of 1987."

Officer: An administrative executive of a corporate employer who is in regular and continued service. One employed for a special and single transaction or one who has only nominal administrative duties is excluded.

Offset Plan: A plan that reduces the participant's benefit by an amount specified (i.e., by formula) in the plan.

Old Age, Survivors, and Disability Insurance; OASDI: Payroll tax imposed on employers that is equal to a set percentage of the wages paid to employees. The OASDI tax rate is used for purposes of providing for permitted disparity in a defined contribution plan and a simplified employee pension (SEP). Social Security payroll taxes also include Medicare taxes. *See also* "Permitted Disparity."

1 Percent Owner: Any person who owns, directly or indirectly, more than 1 percent of the stock of the employer. If the employer is not a corporation, the ownership test is applied to the person's capital or profits interest in the employer. A 1 percent owner is a key employee only if his or her annual compensation from the employer is more than $150,000. *See also* "Key Employee" and "Top-Heavy Plan."

Owner-Employee: A sole proprietor or a partner who owns more than 10 percent of either the capital interest or the profits interest in a partnership.

Partial Termination: Reducing benefits or making participation requirements less liberal, although not amounting to a complete termination of the plan, may be considered a partial termination, resulting in the vesting of accrued benefits for at least part of the plan. The typical types of partial terminations include: the employer closing a plant and thereby substantially reducing the percentage of employees participating under the plan, the reduction of benefits for participating employees, the substantial reduction of contributions to the plan, and the exclusion of a group of employees from participation after they were included in the plan.

Party in Interest: A party which, because of his or her or its relationship with the plan (e.g., as a fiduciary, provider of services, or the plan sponsor), is prohibited from entering into certain transactions with the plan. *See also* "Prohibited Transactions."

Pension Annuitants Protection Act (PPA '94): Signed into law on October 22, 1994. Permits a participant, beneficiary, or fiduciary to bring an action if the purchase of an insurance or annuity contract in connection with the termination of a person's status as a plan participant would violate fiduciary standards.

Pension Benefit Guaranty Corporation; PBGC: A nonprofit corporation, functioning under the jurisdiction of the Department of Labor, that is responsible for insuring pension benefits.

Pension Protection Act of 1987 (PPA): Enacted as part of OBRA '87, legislation designed to protect the integrity of the federal pension system by, for example, raising PBGC premiums and tightening the plan termination requirements.

Permitted Disparity: The use of Social Security to determine contributions in a defined contribution plan and benefits in a defined benefit plan. Prior to TRA '86, this was referred to as integration.

Plan Year: Any 12-consecutive-month period that has been chosen by the plan for keeping its records. The 12-month period may be the calendar year, a fiscal year, or a policy year (if insurance is used to fund all plan benefits). The plan year does not have to coincide with the employer's taxable year or begin on the first day of the month. Change of a plan year usually requires the consent of IRS.

Profit Sharing Plan: A defined contribution plan under which the employer agrees to make discretionary contributions (usually out of profits). A participant's retirement benefits are based on the amount in his or her individual account at retirement.

Prohibited Transactions: Specified transactions that may not be entered into (directly or indirectly) by a party in interest with the plan. Those include, for example, sales or exchanges, leases, and loans between the parties. The

Department of Labor may exempt a specific transaction from the prohibited transactions restriction. *See also* "Party in Interest."

Prototype Plans: *See* "Master Plan."

Prudent-Man Rule: The standard under which a fiduciary must act. The fiduciary is required to act "with the care, skill, prudence, and diligence under the circumstances then prevailing that a prudent man acting in a like capacity and familiar with such matters would use in the conduct of an enterprise of a like character and with like aims."

P.S. 58 Costs: Costs applied to current life insurance protection provided under the plan for purposes of determining the amount of the participant's tax liability for the coverage.

Qualified Cash-or-Deferred Arrangement: *See* "401(k) Plan."

Qualified Domestic Relations Order; QDRO: A court order issued under state domestic relations law that relates to the payment of child support or alimony or to marital property rights. A QDRO creates or recognizes an alternate payee's right, or assigns to an alternate payee the right, to receive plan benefits payable to a participant. The alternate payee may be the participant's spouse, former spouse, or dependent.

Qualified Election Period: The six-plan-year period beginning with the plan year after the first plan year beginning after 1986 in which the employee is a qualified participant and during which the employee can make a diversification election.

Qualified Joint and Survivor Annuity; QJSA: An immediate annuity for the life of the participant, with a survivor annuity for the life of the participant's spouse. The amount of the survivor annuity may not be less than 50 percent, nor more than 100 percent, of the amount of the annuity payable during the time that the participant and spouse are both alive.

Qualified Participant: An employee who has completed at least ten years of participation in an ESOP and has attained age 55.

Qualified Preretirement Survivor Annuity; QPSA: An immediate annuity for the life of the surviving spouse of a participant who dies before the annuity starting date.

Qualified Retirement Plan (Qualified Plan): A plan that meets the requirements of the Internal Revenue Code (generally Section 401(a)). The advantage of qualification is that the plan is eligible for special tax considerations. For example, employers are permitted to deduct contributions to the plan even though the benefits provided under the plan are deferred to a later date.

Qualified Replacement Plan: A plan into which 25 percent of the reversion from a terminated defined benefit plan is transferred in order to reduce the excise tax on reversions from 50 percent to 20 percent.

Qualified Replacement Property: Any security issued by a domestic operating corporation that did not have passive investment income (e.g., rents, royalties, dividends, or interest) that exceeded 25 percent of its gross receipts in its taxable year preceding the purchase.

Qualified Securities: Employer securities that (1) are issued by a domestic corporation that for one year before and immediately after the sale has no readily tradable stock outstanding, and (2) have not been received by the seller as a distribution from a qualified retirement plan or pursuant to an option or other right to acquire stock granted by the employer.

REA: Retirement Equity Act of 1984. Among major changes made by the Retirement Equity Act: reduced the age requirement for participation in a plan; increased the period of service considered for vesting purposes; broadened the survivor-benefit requirements; allowed the assignment or alienation of benefits in divorce proceedings.

Replacement Period: The period beginning three months before the date of sale of employer securities to an ESOP and ending 12 months after the sale. The qualified replacement property must be purchased during this period.

Reportable Event: An event that may indicate that the plan is in danger of being terminated. ERISA requires plan administrators and sponsors of certain defined benefit plans to notify the PBGC of the occurrence of such event so as to give the PBGC enough time to protect the benefits of participants and beneficiaries. The notice must usually be given within 30 days of the occurrence of the reportable event unless the PBGC waives notice.

Retirement Protection Act of 1994 (RPA '94): Part of GATT signed into law on December 8, 1994. Primary purposes was to strengthen PBGC. Among its provisions: removed impediments to funding certain plans; phased out the PBGC variable-rate premium cap; rounded down cost-of-living adjustments; extended IRS user fee program.

Rev Proc: A revenue procedure issued by IRS. It is somewhat similar to a revenue ruling, but deals with procedural matters or details the requirements to be followed in connection with various dealings with IRS. Rev Procs also set forth (at times) guidelines that IRS follows in handling certain tax matters.

Rev Rul: A public revenue ruling issued by IRS. These rulings express IRS's views as to the tax results that apply to a specific problem.

Revenue Reconciliation Act of 1993 (RRA '93): Clinton Administration proposals sent to Congress on April 30, 1993 and enacted into law on August 10, 1993. RRA '93 increases income tax rates, repeals the Medicare base dollar limitation, and reduces the annual compensation limit affecting contributions, benefits, and tax deductions.

Reversion of Employer Contributions: A qualified plan (or trust) is prohibited from diverting corpus or income for purposes other than the exclusive benefit of employees. However, this prohibition does not preclude the return of a contribution made by an employer if the contribution was made, for example, by reason of a mistake of fact or conditioned on the qualification of the plan or the deductibility of the contribution.

Rollover: A tax-free transfer of cash or other assets from one retirement plan to another. An IRA account owner may shift assets from his or her present IRA to another. Certain payouts from a pension plan may also be rolled over to an IRA or to another employer's plan.

Rollover IRA Account: An individual retirement account that is established for the sole purpose of receiving a distribution from a qualified plan so that the assets can subsequently be rolled over into another qualified plan.

S Corporation: A corporation whose shareholders have elected not to be taxed as a regular (or "C") corporation, but like a partnership, with profits and losses passing through directly to the shareholders, rather than at the corporate level.

Salary-Reduction Arrangement: Under this type of cash-or-deferred arrangement, each eligible employee may elect to reduce his or her current compensation or to forgo a salary increase and have these amounts instead contributed to the plan on his or her behalf on a pretax basis. *See also* "Cash-or-Deferred Plan."

Savings Plan: *See* "Thrift Plan."

Self-Employed Person: A sole proprietor or a partner in a partnership.

Shareholder-Employee: A more-than-5 percent shareholder of an S corporation.

Simplified Employee Pension Plan; SEP: A retirement program that takes the form of individual retirement accounts for all eligible employees (subject to special rules on contributions and eligibility).

Single Employer Pension Plan Amendments Act (SEPPAA): The Act that changed the single-employer defined benefit plan termination rules of Title IV of ERISA.

Social Security Retirement Age; SSRA: For purposes of calculating adjustments to the dollar limitation on benefits payable under a defined benefit plan, the age used as the retirement age under the Social Security Act (rounded to the next lower whole number) that depends on the calendar year of birth.

Split-Funded Plan: A plan that is funded in part by insurance contracts and in part by funds accumulated in a separate trusteed fund.

Spousal IRA: An IRA that is established for the nonworking spouse of an employee who qualifies for an IRA. A contribution of $2,250, instead of $2,000, is permitted, but the maximum contribution for either spouse is $2,000.

SSRA: *See* "Social Security Retirement Age."

Standard Termination: The termination of a single-employer defined benefit plan covered by PBGC that is able to pay all its benefit liabilities.

Standardized Voluntary Compliance Resolution Program; SVP: A program that permits plan sponsors to voluntarily correct certain operational plan defects using a permitted correction method and to obtain a compliance statement that provides that IRS will not pursue disqualification of the plan.

State Income Taxation of Pension Income Act of 1995: Signed into law on January 6, 1996. Prohibits states from taxing the retirement income payments of their former residents, effective for retirement income payments received after December 31, 1995.

Stock Bonus Plan: A defined contribution plan that is similar to a profit sharing plan except that the employer's contributions do not have to be made out of profits and benefit payments generally must be made in employer company stock. *See also* "Profit Sharing Plan" and "Employee Stock Ownership Plan."

Subchapter S Corporation: *See* "S Corporation."

Summary Plan Description; SPD: A detailed, but easily understood, summary describing a pension plan's provisions that must be provided to participants and beneficiaries.

SVP: See "Standardized Voluntary Compliance Resolution Program."

Table 1: A table, found in the Treasury regulations under Section 79, that gives the monthly cost of providing $1,000 of insurance coverage, based on the employee's age. Table 1 is used to value coverage in excess of $50,000 that is provided to (and generates tax liability for) employees under a group term life insurance policy that qualifies under Section 79.

TAMRA: Technical and Miscellaneous Revenue Act of 1988. Contained many corrections to and clarification of OBRA '87 and TRA '86.

Target Benefit Plan: A cross between a defined benefit plan and a money purchase plan. Similar to a defined benefit plan, the annual contribution is determined by the amount needed each year to accumulate a fund sufficient to pay a targeted retirement benefit to each participant on reaching retirement. Similar to a money purchase plan, contributions are allocated to separate accounts maintained for each participant.

Tax Reform Act of 1984 (TRA '84): Tax measure signed into law on July 18, 1984. Among major changes made by the Tax Reform Act: delayed until 1988 cost-of-living increases in contributions and benefits; repealed the estate tax exclusion for death benefits from a pension plan or an IRA; allowed partial distributions from a pension plan to be rolled over to an IRA; applied restrictive distribution rules to 5 percent owners only.

Tax Reform Act of 1986 (TRA '86): The act that made such major changes to the Code that it renamed the Code as the "Internal Revenue Code of 1986." It was signed on October 22, 1986.

Tax-Sheltered Annuity: A special type of deferred compensation arrangement that is available only to employees of tax-exempt organizations described in Code Section 501(c)(3) or employees of public educational systems.

Tax-Sheltered Annuity Voluntary Correction Program; TVC: A program that permits an employer that offers a tax-sheltered annuity program to voluntarily identify and correct defects. Employers that request consideration under the program, agree to correct the identified defects, and pay the negotiated sanction, will receive written assurance that the corrections are acceptable and that IRS will not pursue revocation of the income tax exclusion with respect to the violations identified and corrected.

Taxable Year: The 12-month period used by an employer to report income for income tax purposes. The employer's taxable year does not have to coincide with the year used by the plan to keep its records.

TEFRA: Tax Equity and Fiscal Responsibility Act of 1982. Lowered limits on contributions and benefits for corporate plans; certain loans from plan to be treated as distributions; reduced estate tax exclusion for retirement plan death benefits to maximum of $100,000; repealed special Keogh plan and S corporation restrictions; added "top-heavy" plan requirements.

Threshold Amount: For excess distribution tax purposes, the threshold amount is either $112,500 (as adjusted for inflation), or $150,000. The $112,500 adjusted threshold amount is used by individuals who elected the special grandfather rule, and the $150,000 unadjusted threshold amount is used by individuals who did not elect or were ineligible to elect the special grandfather rule.

Thrift Plan: A defined contribution plan that is contributory in the sense that employer contributions are geared to mandatory contributions by the employee. Employer contributions are made on a matching basis—for example, 50 percent of the total contribution made by the employee.

Top-Heavy Plan: Beginning in 1984, a plan that primarily benefits key employees is considered top-heavy and qualifies for favorable tax treatment only if, in addition to the regular qualification requirements, it meets several special requirements. *See also* "Key Employee."

Treasury Regulations: Regulations promulgated by the U.S. Department of the Treasury. IRS is a part of the Treasury Department, and regulations interpreting the Internal Revenue Code are technically Treasury regulations.

Trust: A fund established under local trust law to hold and administer the assets of a plan.

Trustees: The parties named in the trust instrument or plan that are authorized to hold the assets of the plan for the benefit of the participants. The trustees may function merely in the capacity of a custodian of the assets or may also be given authority over the investment of the assets. Their function is determined by the trust instrument or, if no separate trust agreement is executed, under the trust provisions of the plan.

TSA: *See* "Tax-Sheltered Annuity."

TVC: *See* "Tax Sheltered Annuity Voluntary Correction Program.".

Unemployment Compensation Amendments of 1992 (UC '92): Tax measure signed into law on July 3, 1992. Expanded rollover rules and introduced mandatory income tax withholding on certain plan distributions.

Unit Benefit Plan: A type of defined benefit pension plan that calculates benefits on the basis of units earned by the employee during his or her employment, taking into consideration length of service as well as compensation.

USERRA: Signed into law on October 13, 1994. Prohibits discrimination against employees because of membership in the uniformed services.

VCRP: *See* "Voluntary Compliance Resolution Program."

Vested Benefits: Accrued benefits of a participant that have become nonforfeitable under the vesting schedule adopted by the plan. Thus, for example, if the schedule provides for vesting at the rate of 10 percent per year, a participant who has been credited with six years of service has a right to 60 percent of the accrued benefit. If he or she terminates service without being credited with any additional years of service, he or she is entitled to receive 60 percent of the accrued benefit.

Voluntary Compliance Resolution Program; VCRP: A program that permits plan sponsors to voluntarily correct operational plan defects and to obtain a compliance statement that provides that the corrections are acceptable and that IRS will not pursue disqualification of the plan.

Voluntary Contributions: Amounts that a participant voluntarily contributes to a plan in addition to the contributions made by the employer. Up to 10 percent of the employee's compensation is generally considered reasonable. Voluntary contributions, unlike employer contributions, are not deductible on the employee's tax return.

Year of Service: A 12-month period during which an employee is credited with at least 1,000 hours of service. For purposes of determining an employee's exclusion allowance, a different calculation is made.

Index

[References are to question numbers.]

[References are to question numbers.]

Index

[References are to question numbers.]

[References are to question numbers.]

Index

[References are to question numbers.]

E

Index

[References are to question numbers.]

G

H

[References are to question numbers.]

[References are to question numbers.]

[References are to question numbers.]

[References are to question numbers.]

[References are to question numbers.]

[References are to question numbers.]

Y